St. John Brebeuf Regional Secondary
2747 Townline Road
Abbotsford, B.C. V2T 5E1
Phone: 855-0571 Fax: 855-0572

NAME	YEAR	RM.
Kate Lahmann	2008	204
Derek Andrews	2009	204
Kirsten vender Buhs	2010	204
Cody Beach	2012	204
Uncle Boby B Baby		420

St. John Brebeuf Regional Secondary
2747 Townline Road
Abbotsford, B.C. V2T 5E1
Phone: 855-0571 Fax: 855-0572

NAME	YEAR	RM.

The History of The Church

A Complete Course

The Didache

[DID-uh-kay]

The *Didache* is the first known Christian catechesis. Written in the first century, the *Didache* is the earliest known Christian writing outside of Scripture. The name of the work, *"Didache,"* is indeed appropriate for such a catechesis because it comes from the Greek word for "teaching," and indicates that this writing contains the teaching of the Apostles.

The *Didache* is a catechetical summary of Christian sacraments, practices, and morality. Though written in the first century, its teaching is timeless. The *Didache* was probably written by the disciples of the Twelve Apostles, and it presents the Apostolic Faith as taught by those closest to Jesus Christ. This series of books takes the name of this early catechesis because it shares in the Church's mission of passing on that same Faith, in its rich entirety, to new generations.

Below is an excerpt from the *Didache* in which we see a clear example of its lasting message, a message that speaks to Christians of today as much as it did to the first generations of the Church. The world is different, but the struggle for holiness is the same. In the *Didache*, we are instructed to embrace virtue, to avoid sin, and to live the Beatitudes of our Lord.

My child, flee from everything that is evil and everything that is like it. Do not be wrathful, for wrath leads to murder, nor jealous nor contentious nor quarrelsome, for from all these murder ensues.

My child, do not be lustful, for lust leads to fornication, nor a filthy-talker nor a lewd-looker, for from all these adulteries ensue.

My child, do not be an interpreter of omens, since it leads to idolatry, nor an enchanter nor an astrologer nor a magical purifier, nor wish to see them, for from all these idolatry arises.

My child, do not be a liar, for lying leads to theft, nor avaricious nor conceited, for from all these thefts are produced.

My child, do not be a complainer, since it leads to blasphemy, nor self-willed nor evil-minded, for from all these blasphemies are produced.

Be meek, for the meek will inherit the earth.

Be long-suffering and merciful and guileless and peaceable and good, and revere always the words you have heard.[1]

The *Didache* is the teaching of the Apostles and, as such, it is the teaching of the Church. Accordingly, this book series makes extensive use of the most recent comprehensive catechesis provided to us, *The Catechism of the Catholic Church*. The *Didache* series also relies heavily on Sacred Scripture, the lives of the saints, the Fathers of the Church, and the teaching of Vatican II as witnessed by the pontificate of John Paul II.

---

1. Swett, Ben H. "The Didache (The Teaching)." © January 30, 1998. http://bswett.com/1998-01Didache.html

The History of
The Church

A Complete Course

Author: Very Rev. Peter V. Armenio
General Editor: Rev. James Socias

MIDWEST THEOLOGICAL FORUM
Woodridge, Illinois

Published in the United States of America by

Midwest Theological Forum
1420 Davey Road, Woodridge, IL 60517
www.theologicalforum.org

Copyright © 2005, 2006, 2007 Rev. James Socias
ISBN 978-1-890177-46-1 (ISBN-10 1-890177-46-6)
Revised First Edition

Jesus the Alpha and Omega. Fourth-century wall painting from the Catacombs of Commodilla, Rome, Italy.

Nihil obstat
Reverend Martin A. Zielinski, Ph.D.
Censor Deputatus
June 6, 2005

Imprimatur
Reverend George J. Rassas
Vicar General
Archdiocese of Chicago
June 7, 2005

The Nihil obstat *and* Imprimatur *are official declarations that a book is free of doctrinal and moral error. No implication is contained therein that those who have granted the* Nihil obstat *and* Imprimatur *agree with the content, opinions, or statements expressed. Nor do they assume any legal responsibility associated with the publication.*

Author: Very Rev. Peter V. Armenio
General and Managing Editor: Rev. James Socias
Editorial Board: Rev. James Socias, Dr. Scott Hahn, Very Rev. Peter V. Armenio, Mike Aquilina, Emmet Flood
Other Contributors: Dan Cheely, Joseph Lechner, Joseph Linn, Russell Shaw, John Shine, Peter Simek
Design and Production: Marlene Burrell, Jane Heineman of April Graphics, Highland Park, Illinois

Acknowledgements

English translation of the *Catechism of the Catholic Church* for the United States of America copyright ©1994, United States Catholic Conference, Inc.–Libreria Editrice Vaticana. English translation of the *Catechism of the Catholic Church: Modifications from the Editio Typica* copyright ©1997, United States Catholic Conference, Inc.–Libreria Editrice Vaticana.

Scripture quotations contained herein are adapted from the Revised Standard Version of the Bible, copyright ©1946, 1952, 1971, and the New Revised Standard Version of the Bible, copyright ©1989, by the Division of Christian Education of the National Council of the Churches of Christ in the United States of America, and are used by permission. All rights reserved.

Excerpts from the Code of Canon Law, Latin/English Edition, are used with permission, copyright ©1983 Canon Law Society of America, Washington, D.C.

Citations of official Church documents from Neuner, Josef, SJ, and Dupuis, Jacques, SJ, eds., *The Christian Faith: Doctrinal Documents of the Catholic Church*, 5th ed. (New York: Alba House, 1992). Used with permission.

Excerpts from *Vatican Council II: The Conciliar and Post Conciliar Documents*, New Revised Edition edited by Austin Flannery, O.P., copyright ©1992, Costello Publishing Company, Inc., Northport, NY, are used by permission of the publisher, all rights reserved. No part of these excerpts may be reproduced, stored in a retrieval system, or transmitted in any form or by any means—electronic, mechanical, photocopying, recording or otherwise, without express permission of Costello Publishing Company.

All maps used with permission. All rights reserved.

Disclaimer: The editor of this book has attempted to give proper credit to all sources used in the text and illustrations. Any miscredit or lack of credit is unintended and will be corrected in the next edition.

Library of Congress Cataloging-in-Publication Data

The History of The Church: a complete course / general editor, James Socias.—1st ed.
    p. cm.— (The Didache Series)
Includes index.
ISBN 1-890177-46-6 (alk. paper)
1. Church history.   I. Socias, James.   II. Series.
BR145.H597 2005
270—dc22   2005025271

The Ad Hoc Committee to Oversee the Use of the Catechism, United States Conference of Catholic Bishops,
has found this catechetical text, copyright 2005, to be in conformity with the *Catechism of the Catholic Church.*

Printed in Canada

CONTENTS

CONTENTS

CONTENTS

CONTENTS

CONTENTS

CONTENTS

CONTENTS

CONTENTS

CONTENTS

ABBREVIATIONS USED FOR THE BOOKS OF THE BIBLE

OLD TESTAMENT

Genesis	Gen	Tobit	Tb	Hosea	Hos
Exodus	Ex	Judith	Jdt	Joel	Jl
Leviticus	Lv	Esther	Est	Amos	Am
Numbers	Nm	Job	Jb	Obadiah	Ob
Deuteronomy	Dt	Psalms	Ps(s)	Jonah	Jon
Joshua	Jos	Proverbs	Prv	Micah	Mi
Judges	Jgs	Ecclesiastes	Eccl	Nahum	Na
Ruth	Ru	Song of Songs	Sg	Habakkuk	Hab
1 Samuel	1 Sm	Wisdom	Wis	Zephaniah	Zep
2 Samuel	2 Sm	Sirach	Sir	Haggai	Hg
1 Kings	1 Kgs	Isaiah	Is	Zechariah	Zec
2 Kings	2 Kgs	Jeremiah	Jer	Malachi	Mal
1 Chronicles	1 Chr	Lamentations	Lam	1 Maccabees	1 Mc
2 Chronicles	2 Chr	Baruch	Bar	2 Maccabees	2 Mc
Ezra	Ezr	Ezekiel	Ez		
Nehemiah	Neh	Daniel	Dn		

NEW TESTAMENT

Matthew	Mt	Ephesians	Eph	Hebrews	Heb
Mark	Mk	Philippians	Phil	James	Jas
Luke	Lk	Colossians	Col	1 Peter	1 Pt
John	Jn	1 Thessalonians	1 Thes	2 Peter	2 Pt
Acts of the Apostles	Acts	2 Thessalonians	2 Thes	1 John	1 Jn
Romans	Rom	1 Timothy	1 Tm	2 John	2 Jn
1 Corinthians	1 Cor	2 Timothy	2 Tm	3 John	3 Jn
2 Corinthians	2 Cor	Titus	Ti	Jude	Jud
Galatians	Gal	Philemon	Phlm	Revelation	Rv

ABBREVIATIONS USED FOR DOCUMENTS OF THE MAGISTERIUM

AA	Apostolicam actuositatem	GS	Gaudium et spes
AAS	Acta Apostolica Sedis	HV	Humanae vitæ
AG	Ad gentes	IOE	Instruction on Euthanasia
CA	Centesimus annus	LE	Laborem exercens
CCC	The Catechism of the Catholic Church	LG	Lumen gentium
CCEO	Corpus Canonum Ecclesiarum Orientalium	LH	Liturgy of the Hours
CDF	Congregation for the Doctrine of the Faith	MF	Mysterium fidei
CHCW	Charter for Health Care Workers	MM	Mater et magistra
CIC	Codex Iuris Canonici (The Code of Canon Law)	ND	Neuner-Dupuis, The Christian Faith in the Doctrinal Documents of the Catholic Church
CL	Christifideles laici	OC	Ordo confirmationis
CPG	Solemn Profession of Faith: Credo of the People of God	OCM	Ordo celebrandi Matrimonium
		OP	Ordo paenitentiæ
DD	Dies Domini	PG	J. P. Migne, ed., Patrologia Græca (Paris, 1857-1866)
DRF	Declaration on Religious Freedom		
DH	Dignitatis humanæ	PH	Persona humanæ
DIM	Decree Inter mirifici	PL	J. P. Migne, ed., Patrologia Latina (Paris, 1841-1855)
DoV	Donum vitæ		
DPA	Declaration on Procured Abortion	PP	Populorum progressio
DS	Denzinger-Schönmetzer, Enchiridion Symbolorum, definitionum et declarationum de rebus fidei et morum (1965)	PT	Pacem in terris
		RH	Redemptor hominis
		RP	Reconciliatio et pænitentia
DV	Dei verbum	SC	Sacrosanctum concilium
EN	Evangeli nuntiadi	SD	Salvifici doloris
EV	Evangelium vitæ	SRS	Solicitudo rei socialis
FC	Familiaris consortio	STh	Summa Theologiæ
GCD	General Catechetical Directory	VS	Veritatis splendor

FOREWORD

"Jesus Christ is the key."

It has been said that to try to do without history is to cease to be Catholic. Faith in Jesus Christ is based on events that have happened and have been witnessed in written records. The truth embodied in the Christian faith came to us from outside ourselves as a revelation. Much more than a reflection or personal experience, the truths of our faith are objective and are reliably handed on.

Much of this Christian story is therefore found in written documents—the Bible, the writings of the Church Fathers, the decisions of early Church councils. Christian history comes down to us in Tradition—in the oral teaching, especially that of the Apostles and their successors, in the liturgy, in spirituality, in culture.

Christian history is the record of God's intervention in the human situation, an account of God's love for his human creatures. Its focus is the Son of God taking on human nature in the Incarnation. Not only are the effects of that divine event traceable in cultures and civilizations, the events that make it up and surround it are documented.

Because Jesus was truly God as well as truly man, human history can take us only so far; faith goes beyond that point to tell us the meaning of the Christ event. The Christ of history is the ground for the Christ of faith; the Christ of faith brings ultimate meaning to the Christ of history. There is only one Christ of God. "Jesus Christ is the key, the center and the purpose of the whole of human history" (Vatican II: Gaudium et spes 10), because in him the boundless mystery of God is manifested in the world.

The Incarnation happened in history as a divine-human event and it continues and is extended in the form of the Church, in her sacraments, in the Eucharist, in her mission. It is a deeply human story of the best and the worst in the human situation; in the end, it is always the story of the victory of grace and of the destiny of humanity.

The Didache Series is remarkably complete and, with this volume, it integrates divine revelation and the story of the Church in light of sound human scholarship. I recommend it warmly for use in the high schools and colleges of the Archdiocese of Chicago.

✠Francis Cardinal George, O.M.I.
Archbishop of Chicago

INTRODUCTION

"Be not afraid!"

The world is waiting for a new era of holiness among the laity. When John Paul II came on to the balcony of St. Peter's Basilica in Rome and spoke about his acceptance of a heavy burden, he declared that no one should be afraid to open the doors of our hearts to the Redeemer. These words became a rallying cry throughout his pontificate. In the midst of an all-pervading moral relativism and dissent within the Church, expressed in a culture of death, the Holy Spirit, through his pope, has tapped into hidden desires for holiness and spiritual renewal especially among the laity.

The twenty-first century is calling for a type of Christianity that was practiced during the first few centuries of the Church's history. This means that the signs of the times call for new age of holiness and martyrdom. In a sense the Holy Spirit is moving the laity to put on a repeat performance of what the earliest Christians accomplished almost seventeen centuries ago when they brought the pagan Roman world literally to its knees.

In order to properly understand the fundamental nature of this new evangelization, however, one must be firmly grounded in the history of the Church. For example, if the people of God are being called to a new age of holiness and martyrdom closer to that of the early Church, one must understand what the early Church was. *The History of The Church* is an account of Christian History based solidly on historical fact viewed through the eyes of Faith, by which students will see both her visible and spiritual reality as bearer of divine life. The book delves deeply into the heroic lives of the saints and the tremendous achievements of the Church, and will bring those who read it to a deeper understanding of Christ and his calling for a new evangelization.

Two thousand years ago, Jesus invited a handful of followers to bring the Gospel message to a world diametrically opposed to everything it stood for. Reading the first chapter of St. Paul's letter of the Romans gives an idea of the challenges faced by the early Christians. The task would seem impossible, if not sheer madness, given the moral corruption, the dislike for matters spiritual and the deification of the emperor and the state if it were not for Christ's assurance of victory. They indeed believed in Jesus' word and accomplished a feat that defies any possible human explanation.

We are now in a new springtime of Christianity, perhaps the same springtime experienced by our first brothers and sisters in the Faith, who generously laid down their lives for Christ. As Pope John Paul II habitually recommended, let us resolve to go to the Mother of God so that we all meet the challenge of extending Christ's kingdom and shoulder the burden of the Church's mission to bring salvation to all.

The Roman World

The Roman Empire, with the unifying forces of its laws and organization, would greatly facilitate the actual spread of the Gospel.

BACKGROUND TO CHURCH HISTORY
The Roman World

Christ was born into a Roman World.

Alexander the Great in the Temple of Jerusalem depicts an event as told by the Jewish historian Flavius Josephus in his *Jewish Antiquities*, written in A.D. 93. "And when he [Alexander] went up into the temple, he offered sacrifice to God, according to the high-priest's direction, . . . And when the Book of Daniel was showed him wherein Daniel declared that one of the Greeks should destroy the empire of the Persians, he supposed that himself was the person intended." (translation by William Whiston)

Since the first century B.C., Rome had occupied Palestine, and like most provinces in the Roman Empire, Palestine featured its own local customs together with an international flavor brought on by many centuries of foreign rule. Jesus was born into a vibrant mix of cultures and languages. Jesus would most likely have spoken Aramaic and Hebrew, but not the two classical languages that dominated the world around him: Latin and Greek. Latin was the language of the Roman Empire, but Greek, the written word of the New Testament, was the language of learning, culture, and commerce in the eastern Mediterranean. Indeed, in many ways, the world at the time of Jesus was still largely Hellenistic. This was due to the lingering legacy left by the great empire built by the Macedonian king Alexander the Great.

Alexander the Great (356-323 B.C.)

PART I

The Hellenistic Worldview

After the death of his father Philip II of Macedon in 336 B.C., Alexander the Great (356-323 B.C.) set out to build a huge empire. He conquered lands along the shores of the eastern Mediterranean Sea, defeating the Persians and establishing control over Palestine, Egypt, and the Middle East by 332 B.C. In 326 B.C., he led his army further into India, establishing the frontiers of his empire, and finally settling in the city of Babylon, located about fifty-five miles south of modern day Baghdad, Iraq. By the age of thirty, Alexander's empire covered almost the entire known world. Only three years later, Alexander suddenly died of a fever in 323 B.C.

Alexander had hoped to build a truly united empire, despite the multiplicity of peoples he conquered. He and his military officers married Persian wives, and Alexander founded many new cities with native Greeks in an effort to introduce Greek language, dress, and learning into his empire. Through this network of cities, Greek ideas, culture, philosophy, and religion all made themselves present in the East. This began the process called Hellenization by which Greek cultural attributes were transplanted to the East.

Strictly speaking, Hellenism was not a purely Greek culture. Alexander himself was a Macedonian, and the culture he brought to his empire was a mixture of Greek and other cultural influences. It was Greek-based culture ripe for absorption into local histories and customs. Alexander's conquered cities would share a strong Greek presence with a native identity. Greek, although the dominant language of communication, was used alongside other native tongues. Put simply, Hellenism was the common thread that held diverse cultures together. This could be compared with the way American language and customs are widely known throughout the world in the commercial sphere today. Rather than an imposition, this coexistence led to an intermingling of cultures and ideas.

Among the most profound and lasting effects of Hellenization was the effect it had on religion. Greek religion was seen widely as simplistic compared to the sophisticated theologies of the Persians and Jews. At the same time, Greek thought supplied these Eastern theologies with new language and philosophies that helped further their development. Hellenism occasioned religious debates over the connection between religion and morality and the existence of a life after death. The introduction of Aristotle into Palestine established a tradition of Jewish commentaries on Aristotle's texts that would help preserve the philosopher's ideas after they were eventually lost in the West.

Plato and Aristotle. A detail from Raphael's *School of Athens.* Aristotle (384-322 B.C.) was born in Macedon and studied in Athens under Plato. Aristotle was summoned back to his homeland by King Philip II of Macedon to become the tutor of his son Alexander, who was then 13. Plutarch wrote that Aristotle imparted to Alexander a knowledge of ethics, politics and the most profound secrets of philosophy.

In many ways the proliferation of Greek thought laid a foundation for the introduction of Christianity in the world. Greek language and philosophy were a very suitable medium through which the teachings of Christ could be transmitted. Most notably, St. Paul's letters and St. John's Gospel show how the richness of the Greek language allowed for the articulation of the intricacies of the Christian religion. Later on, the philosophies of Plato and Aristotle would provide invaluable ideas for the development of Catholic theology and magisterial pronouncements.

ALEXANDER'S EMPIRE

©1997 Lion Hudson plc/Three's Company

A page from St. Thomas Aquinas' *Commentary on the Ethics of Aristotle*.

St. Thomas, along with St. Augustine, held that whatever there was of truth in the writings of pagan philosophers should be taken from them, as from "unjust possessors," and adapted to the teaching of the true religion (*Summa* I: 84: 5). In the *Summa* he quotes from the writings of forty-six philosophers and poets, his favorite authors were Aristotle, Plato, and Boethius. From Aristotle he learned love of order and accuracy of expression. From Boethius, a Christian writer, he learned that Aristotle's works could be used without detriment to Christianity.

Aristotle's works were held in such esteem that he was known as *The Philosopher*. Dante calls Aristotle the "master knower" and places him in Limbo with the "Good Pagans" such as Socrates and Plato in the *Divine Comedy* (Canto IV).

PART II

The Romans

The founding of Rome is surrounded by myths, many of dubious reliability. The most popular myth claims that a she-wolf in the Tiber River found Romulus and Remus, two abandoned sons of the Alba Longa kings. Nursed by the wolf, the foundlings were eventually taken in by a shepherd. The two boys lived with the shepherd and his wife (whom some legends attribute to the nursing of the boys rather than the she wolf), and once they were grown, they established a city on top of one of the seven hills overlooking the section of the Tiber where they were found. During a petty argument, Romulus killed his brother Remus and set himself up as king of the city, naming it Rome, after himself. According to legend this happened on April 21, 753 B.C., which is considered the date of Rome's founding. During the first centuries, the city was ruled as a monarchy.

By 509 B.C., after a string of bad monarchs, the Romans replaced the monarchy with a Republic. The Republic divided the power formerly held by the single king among the Senate, two consuls, and a group of Assemblies. During an emergency, the Romans could appoint someone "dictator" who could rule the city absolutely. His power was, however, limited to six months.

Romulus and Remus nursed by the she-wolf. According to legend, on April 21, 753 B.C., after killing his brother Remus, Romulus set himself up as king of the city and named it after himself. That date is considered the date of Rome's founding.

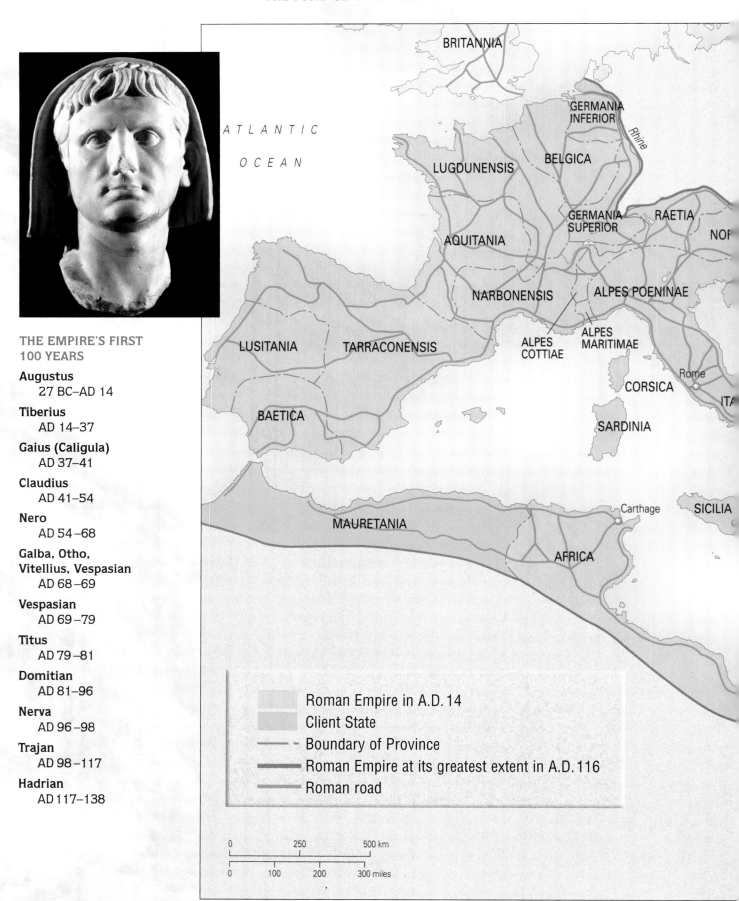

ATLANTIC OCEAN

BRITANNIA

GERMANIA INFERIOR

Rhine

LUGDUNENSIS

BELGICA

AQUITANIA

GERMANIA SUPERIOR

RAETIA

NOR

NARBONENSIS

ALPES POENINAE

LUSITANIA

TARRACONENSIS

ALPES COTTIAE

ALPES MARITIMAE

Rome

CORSICA

ITA

BAETICA

SARDINIA

Carthage

SICILIA

MAURETANIA

AFRICA

THE EMPIRE'S FIRST 100 YEARS

Augustus
27 BC–AD 14

Tiberius
AD 14–37

Gaius (Caligula)
AD 37–41

Claudius
AD 41–54

Nero
AD 54–68

Galba, Otho, Vitellius, Vespasian
AD 68–69

Vespasian
AD 69–79

Titus
AD 79–81

Domitian
AD 81–96

Nerva
AD 96–98

Trajan
AD 98–117

Hadrian
AD 117–138

Roman Empire in A.D. 14
Client State
Boundary of Province
Roman Empire at its greatest extent in A.D. 116
Roman road

0   250   500 km

0   100   200   300 miles

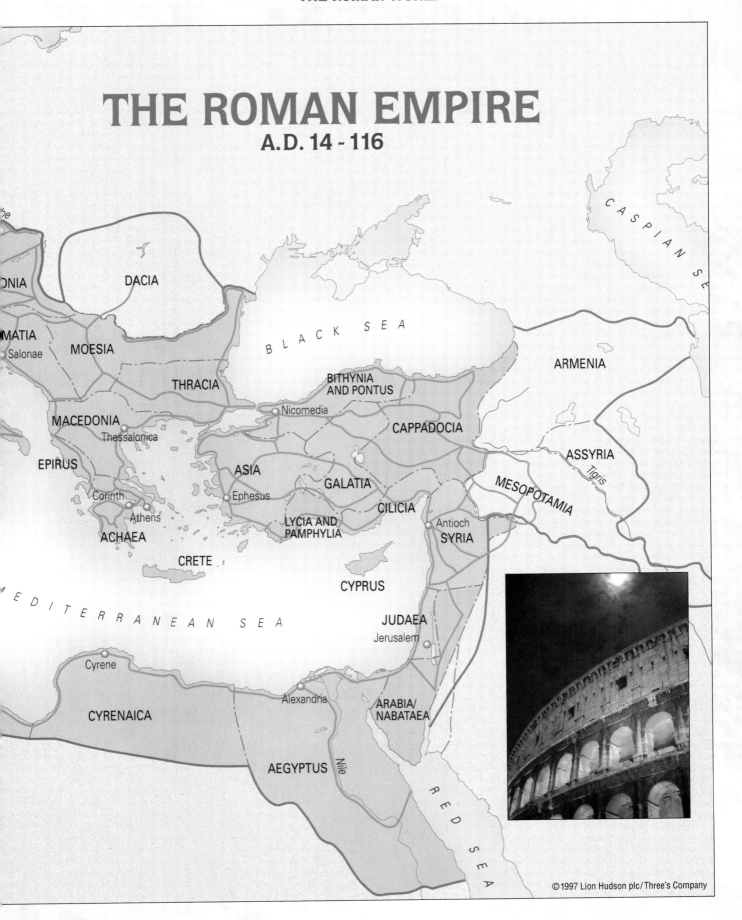

THE ROMAN EMPIRE
A.D. 14 - 116

CASPIAN SE

DACIA

ONIA

MATIA

MOESIA

Salonae

BLACK SEA

THRACIA

ARMENIA

BITHYNIA
AND PONTUS

Nicomedia

MACEDONIA

Thessalonica

CAPPADOCIA

ASSYRIA

EPIRUS

Tigris

ASIA

GALATIA

MESOPOTAMIA

Corinth

Ephesus

Athens

LYCIA AND
PAMPHYLIA

CILICIA

ACHAEA

Antioch

SYRIA

CRETE

M E D I T E R R A N E A N   S E A

CYPRUS

JUDAEA

Jerusalem

Cyrene

Alexandria

ARABIA/
NABATAEA

CYRENAICA

AEGYPTUS

Nile

RED

SEA

©1997 Lion Hudson plc / Three's Company

ROMAN EXPANSION AND THE RISE OF THE EMPIRE

As Rome grew in size, the city took advantage of quarrels it had with neighboring cities and provinces using "defensive" attacks to spread the city's influence and control throughout the Italian peninsula. By 264 BC, Rome controlled the whole of Italy and began to challenge the other great Mediterranean power at the time: Carthage. After three wars, known as the Punic Wars, with the northern African city, the Romans acquired Sicily, Spain and North Africa. Frontier wars with hostile neighbors soon brought Greece, Macedon, and other lands to the East under Rome's control. Eventually, through these opportunistic military ventures, Rome brought much of the Mediterranean world under her control.

Marcus Atilius Regulus departs Rome to return to his captors in Carthage. A Roman general in the First Punic War (264-241 BC), Regulus had been taken prisoner in 255 BC by the Spartan mercenary general Xanthippus along with 500 of his men. In 250 BC, he was sent to Rome on parole to negotiate a peace and exchange of prisoners. On his arrival he strongly urged the Roman Senate to refuse both proposals, but honored his parole by returning to Carthage where he was tortured to death. This legend of courage gave Regulus heroic stature to later Romans.

By 133 BC, Rome was outgrowing her ability to be organized as an effective republic. A long series of civil wars broke out between Republicans (Senate, Optimate) and Democrats (Populares). Three people—the First Triumvirate—finally agreed to share power. One of these men, Julius Caesar, tried to increase his popularity by becoming an ambitious general; he conquered Gaul in 58-51 BC and then invaded Italy itself in 49 BC. Julius soon consolidated his power, overstepping his limits as a consul and pressuring the senate to elect him dictator. The senate obliged, and in 44 BC, Julius Caesar pushed things even further by naming himself dictator for life.

This bold move angered many of the Senate leaders and led to his assassination by a group of conspirators. Marcus Antonius (Marc Antony), a follower of Julius Caesar, succeeded the former dictator as consul. The Senate still feared the consolidation of power around Antony, and they sent Julius' nineteen-year-old stepson to put down Antony. Much to the Senate's surprise, Julius' stepson, Octavian, allied himself with Antony and set up the Second Triumvirate of Roman rulers composed of Octavian, Antony, and a third man by the name of Marcus Lepidus. Immediately after coming to power in 43 BC, Antony ordered the execution of the Senate leader and statesman, Cicero. These three shared dictatorship for ten years (43-33 BC), ruthlessly eliminating their political opponents.

SPARTACUS, LEADER OF A SLAVE REVOLT

Spartacus was a Thracian (from the city Thrace on the southeast portion of the Balkan Peninsula). He was born a freeman, but after serving in the Roman army, he was sold into slavery and trained to become a gladiator. Some accounts claim that Spartacus deserted the army and was enslaved as punishment.

In 73 B.C., at Capua in southern Italy, Spartacus instigated a slave revolt along with one hundred other gladiators. Spartacus, quickly proving himself to be a brave and competent military leader, led an army composed of from seventy thousand to one hundred twenty thousand slaves and impoverished working-class freemen. Harnessing a popular dissatisfaction among these lower-class citizens, Spartacus led the army against the Roman forces, defeating the professional soldiers repeatedly. They fought their way to northern Italy where Spartacus hoped to lead his followers across the Alps to freedom and new lives outside of Italy. His army, however, abandoned their leader's utopian dream, instead continuing to wander Italy waging war.

With the army, Spartacus made his way back to southern Italy where he planned to invade Sicily. There they were betrayed by the pirates they hired to cross to the island. The Roman army attacked and defeated the revolt in 71 B.C. In order to create an example of the revolutionaries and incite fear in any slaves who sought to rebel as well, the Roman leader Crassus ordered the crucifixion of six thousand members of Spartacus' army. These men, hung along the Appian Way from Capua to Rome, were left on the crosses until they rotted away—a powerful warning about the consequences of challenging Roman power.

After crushing Spartacus, Marcus Licinius Crassus soon ruled the Empire with Pompey and Julius Caesar as the first Triumvirate of Rome.

A Roman amphitheater in Pompeii. After their escape from Capua, Spartacus and his followers hid from the Roman Legions on Mt. Vesuvius which overlooks the city of Pompeii. Before Vesuvius became an active volcano, it was covered with forests and vegetation.

After ten years, Lepidus retired, leaving Octavian and Antony with power over two halves of the Roman Empire. Antony concentrated on the East where he lived and made an alliance with his lover, Cleopatra of Egypt. Octavian ruled the West and wisely remained in the city of Rome. Naturally, these two leaders began to contest each other's growing influence. In Rome, Octavian was able to ally himself with the Senate by strengthening dissent against Antony and Cleopatra.

In 31 B.C., Octavian sent his loyal and brilliant naval general Marcus Agrippa against Antony's forces at Actium in Greece and overran Antony's armies. Demoralized by the defeat and accepting the inevitability of Octavian's total victory, Antony and Cleopatra both committed suicide. With the second member of the triumvirate out of the way, Octavian was left singularly in power—completing the transformation of the Roman Republic into the Roman Empire.

THE ROMAN EMPIRE: THE REIGN OF AUGUSTUS

Octavian never formally declared an end to the Roman Republic. Rather, he skillfully maintained the appearance of republican institutions, while he amassed power from the Senate. In 27 B.C. Octavian received the imperial title "Augustus" from the Senate, marking the founding of the Empire of Rome. Octavian also convinced the Senate to give him exclusive control over Spain, Gaul, and Syria, the provinces that held most of the Roman legions. With the army in his full command, Octavian ruled Egypt as his own private possession.

Throughout his reign, Augustus took many other titles of authority. As his empire grew to include other provinces beyond Spain, Gaul, and Syria, he took on the power of a tribune. A title that dated from the early days of the Republic, the tribune was meant to represent the plebeian class (the commoners) in the government. Although Augustus, as a patrician, was technically ineligible to be a tribune, this title helped consolidate the majority of the population under his control, giving him legitimacy on behalf of the common people in Rome. Augustus was also called *princeps*, "first citizen," and finally took the title and office of *Pontifex Maximus* or "high priest" of the pagan religion. Together, all of these titles, names, and offices established Augustus as the preeminent authority in the Roman Empire.

After the long years of civil war, the reign of Augustus brought much appreciated peace and prosperity to the Roman world. Augustus centralized the bureaucratic republican administration, dramatically improving communication in the empire. This reign of peace and prosperity was known as the *Pax Romana*, "the Roman peace." During the *Pax Romana*, the empire enjoyed two hundred years of peace, and Roman civilization flourished. The *Pax Romana* made safe and efficient travel and communication over vast distances possible, and the spread of Christianity was facilitated in no small measure by these peaceful conditions.

The Ara Pacis Augustae (Altar to the Peace of Augustus) was an altar dedicated to "Peace" by the Roman Emperor Augustus Caesar in A.D. 8. This altar sought to portray the peace and prosperity enjoyed as a result of the *Pax Romana* ("the Roman peace") brought about by the military supremacy of the Roman empire. It is elaborately and finely sculpted, depicting scenes of traditional Roman piety. Various figures bring forth cattle to be sacrificed to the gods. Some have their togas drawn over their heads, like a hood, a traditional gesture of respect for the gods before an animal sacrifice. Others wear laurel crowns, traditional symbols of victory.

ALL ROADS LEAD TO ROME

The first section of the Appian Way ("*Via Appia*" in Latin) between Rome and Capua was built by Appius Claudius Caecus (ca. 340-273 B.C.) during his term as censor. He also built the first aqueduct in Rome, the *Aqua Appia*.

As Rome expanded, the empire began to absorb many diverse peoples. Providing for unity and administrative control was difficult, to say the least. In order to establish an effective means of communication between all these various regions, Romans developed a massive system of roads. These roads allowed for people and information to travel to the farthest reaches of the empire in a matter of days.

Public highways radiated from the Roman Forum across Italy and as far away as Britain and Africa (including Egypt). These roads, paved with stone and cement, were marked with mile-stones and ran in a direct line from one city to the next. They crossed every kind of rough terrain from mountains to rivers, enabling soldiers to travel far distances at quick speeds. In addition, every fifty or sixty miles there was a house where a stable of horses and public attendants were stationed to help relay information and decrees. With the help of these relays, it was possible to travel a hundred miles in a day along the Roman roads. The most distant provinces could share information that was only a few days old, a service which aided both public officials and private citizens.

In addition to the Roman roads, effective sea travel aided the free flow of information, and the Mediterranean Sea became a major trade and travel route. From Ostia, an artificial port situated at the mouth of the Tiber River, ships could sail from Rome to Alexandria in only nine or ten days.

CULTURAL IMPACT OF THE ROMANS

Whereas the ancient Greeks excelled in literary expressions of the human spirit—particularly in the areas of philosophy and the arts—the Romans flourished in more practical disciplines like organization, administration, government, and law. The Romans were warriors, builders, and administrators. Never before had such a vast empire been guarded and protected by meticulously organized legions of warriors. The success of Roman unity and organization was achieved not just through the skill of the emperor, but also by the great body of Roman law. Through this sophisticated understanding of jurisprudence, the Roman Empire became the *orbis terrarum*, the "circle of lands" comprising the entire known world in the West in which justice emanated outward from the city of Rome. Within its borders lay stability and the possibility of advancement; beyond its borders, chaos and darkness.

The impact Roman civilization had on the lands it ruled differed slightly between the East and West. Latin culture deeply influenced the western portion of the empire, particularly North Africa, England, Gaul, Iberia, Helvetia (Switzerland) and lands occupied by Germanic tribes. Latin was the root language of the lands of the western provinces. Latin was also the main language of North Africa before Arabic, following the rise of Islam, supplanted it. Latin also heavily influenced the Germanic languages including English.

The eastern portion of the Roman Empire was older and its traditions more deeply rooted. The lands continued to be politically subservient to Rome, and both Greek and Latin were linguistic necessities. Although administrative and civil laws were respected, other cultural attributes of Roman life did not hold fast in the East.

Federico Barrocci's *Aeneas' Flight from Troy.* A scene from Virgil's *Aeneid* depicts the hero Aeneas, ancestor of Romulus and Remus, fleeing from the burning city of Troy. He carries his infirm father, Anchises. At his side are his son Ascanius (covering his ears from the roar of the fire) and his wife Creusa (who would be lost). The *Aeneid* is an epic poem of twelve books. The poetry is polished and complex. Legend has it that Virgil wrote only a single line of the poem each day. The *Aeneid* is one of a small group of writings from Latin literature that traditionally has been required for students of Latin. After reading the works of Julius Caesar, Cicero, Ovid and Catullus, students would then read the *Aeneid.*

Although Roman morality would infamously disintegrate throughout the history of the empire, during the reign of Augustus, legislation did support public moral conduct. For example, Augustus passed legislation that supported the family. In order to increase the population of Italy after the devastating civil wars, laws were made to restrict the rights of both men and women who did not marry, as well as those couples that remained childless. Besides supporting a practical means for population growth, Augustus' laws demonstrated that for the Romans the family was the place to effectively cultivate moral values.

Roman culture was heavily influenced by the Hellenistic world that flourished before Rome became a great city. In fact, Roman understanding of virtue developed out of the Hellenist tradition. This heritage is especially apparent in the Roman literature produced during the Golden Age (30 B.C.-A.D. 18) of Augustus' reign. The greatest writers of that era such as Virgil, Horace, and Livy forged in their works both mythic and historical roots for the empire. Virgil's patriotic epic, the *Aeneid,* related the journey of Aeneas from Troy to Italy, where, according to legend, his descendants eventually founded Rome. In his *Odes, Epodes, and Satires,* the satirist Horace examined the emotions of everyday life. Livy's *Roman History* reaches back to the Republic's conquest of the Mediterranean. All three of these authors worked during the transformation of the Republic into the Empire under Augustus.

During the Silver Age (A.D. 14-96), authors like Tacitus continued the development of Rome's most important literary form: satire. His *Histories* critiques the Empire's governing class from A.D. 69-96, and his *Annals* offers a similar moral judgment on the emperors from Tiberius through Nero. Tacitus' writings detail the first century's desire to return to the moral uprightness of the early Republic.

RELIGION IN THE ROMAN REPUBLIC AND ROMAN EMPIRE

Much of Rome's pagan religion was directly imported from Greece. Indeed many of the myths, stories, and names of their gods were inherited. As the Romans were a practical people, religion also took on a practical end. By the time of Augustus, Roman pagan beliefs were widely enforced to ensure political unity throughout the empire. Romans were generally tolerant of local customs and beliefs, and would even sacrifice to local gods, just as long as they also offered homage to the gods of Rome. There were few exceptions made for the duty to sacrifice to the Roman gods. One exception was made in regards to Judaism. The Jews' monotheistic beliefs forbade them to worship any other gods beside the God of Abraham, and they refused to show deference to Roman paganism. Eventually the Romans exempted the Jews from pagan worship, but not without reservation.

As Rome became more culturally developed, the gods were increasingly seen merely as literary inventions that expressed certain aspects of human behavior. The worship of pagan gods served as a practical means to bring ideological unity to a vast empire. Roman pagan cult worship was much less a personal belief as it was a collective ritual act committed at various times of the year.

The early cults were meant to placate the gods through sacrifice as a means to protect the Roman state. This kind of worship was called *pietas.* The chief manifestations of these rituals were public festivals, offerings of food and wine, and animal sacrifices. Pagan temples housed statues of the gods and provided materials needed for the annual observance of the festivals connected to the deity. Unlike modern churches, they did not hold communal worship activities inside, as sacrifices were usually held outside the temple.

The chief Roman god was the sky-god Jupiter Optimus Maximus (literally "the Best and Greatest"). This cult developed very early in the Republic, and the temple dedicated to Jupiter

The Jupiter Temple located in Baalbek, Lebanon is one of the world's best preserved Roman sites. The monumental temple was started by Augustus (ca. 15 B.C.), and work continued on the complex for a century and a half. The city was known in Hellenistic and Roman times as Heliopolis, the city of the sun. It was one of the largest sanctuaries in the Roman Empire with temples for the gods Jupiter, Venus and Bacchus. Today, only six of the fifty-four giant Corinthian columns that surrounded the sanctuary remain standing. Eight were disassembled and shipped to Constantinople under Justinian's orders for his basilica of Hagia Sophia. The Jupiter Temple was the largest religious building in the entire Roman empire and was shown on many Roman coins. The Roman coin shown here was minted in A.D. 244-249 by Emperor Philip I and shows the Jupiter Temple in Heliopolis with its fifty-four columns.

on the Capitoline Hill was built by 509 B.C. Juno and Minerva were associated with Jupiter's temple, and many cities throughout the empire erected temples dedicated to this Capitoline Triad.

As the emperor rose in prominence, he associated himself more and more with Jupiter, placing himself at the center of the pagan cult. This practice gave a semi-divine stature to the living emperor and insured that he be worshiped after death as a god. Local peoples from around the empire offered sacrifices to the emperor, showing their allegiance.

FOREIGN CULTS

A number of foreign cults also crept into practice. These were brought back primarily by soldiers who had served in various corners of the empire. Unlike the public Roman cults, these foreign cults usually invited the individual to personal religious belief. One prominent example of these cults was the worship of the eastern god Mithras. The Mithraic cult was a fraternal organization open only to men that cultivated virtues important in the life of a soldier. Incidentally, some of their ritual practices were similar to Christianity. They shared a communal meal in which they ate flesh that symbolized their god and believed in personal salvation. Mithraism became firmly established in the Roman Empire. Although a significant body of archeological evidence exists regarding Mithraic structures, very few records of the actual beliefs have survived.

STOICISM

Stoicism was a very influential philosophical school in both Greece and Rome, and over time it became one of the dominant moral philosophies among the intellectuals in Rome. Borrowing much from the Greek philosophers, especially the Athenian Zeno of Citium (335-263 B.C.), stoicism appealed to the Roman sense of law, order, and virtue. Stoics honored the natural law and one's duty to it, as well as encouraging the practice of controlling the passions as a pathway to true freedom. Pain, grief, and joy were not permitted to affect the outward or inward state of the balanced Stoic, who should always be guided by reason alone. Stoics held that the highest good that man can accomplish is to live a life of virtue in accordance with right reason.

Several influential thinkers and emperors in Roman society adhered to Stoicism during the first centuries of the Church's history. Even some of the ancient Christian writers like Tertullian were influenced by this philosophical tradition.

ECONOMIC AND SOCIAL STRATIFICATION OF ROMAN SOCIETY

By the time the republic transitioned into an empire, the population had become increasingly stratified. The governing class enjoyed the wealth of the Empire, and a large class of slaves comprised the majority of the workforce at the bottom of the social ladder. The dwelling masses and the poor freemen of the countryside found themselves significantly below the wealthy clan but at a level above the slaves.

Free people of the countryside faced difficult circumstances including an ever-increasing tax burden. After the rise of the great agricultural estates where slaves provided the labor, many people were forced into the cities. The free people in the city faced economic uncertainty as money and employment were scarce. When conditions grew more severe in the later empire, the emperors began providing food and entertainment to placate their people—hence, the popular phrase "bread and circuses." This free distribution of food was a financial drain, and it would eventually hurt the empire significantly.

In general, women had little opportunity, if any, to rise above their lot of second-class citizens. In many instances they were seen as nothing more than a mere commodity to be bought and sold. Although during the era of the Roman Republic the role of the woman as wife and mother was respected, during the era of the empire, many women were bought and sold to serve as concubines. The relatively stable family structure of the Republic and early empire crumbled during Rome's later imperial era as concubinage became a substitute for marriage on a grand scale.

SLAVERY

As in most societies of antiquity, slavery was an institution vital to the economic structure of both the Roman Republic and Roman Empire. Slaves worked as farm hands, manual laborers, and domestic servants, as well as teachers and tutors for the aristocracy. They formed the backbone of the Roman workforce and were called upon to perform any job, except that of public office. There were even instances where slaves and freemen worked side by side.

Prisoners of war provided the largest source of slaves for the empire. One military campaign alone could result in the capturing and enslaving up to as many as one hundred fifty thousand people. As the empire expanded, the number of slaves grew immensely. It has been estimated that two million people were enslaved at the close of the Roman Republic (roughly one in four people), and that number grew during the time of the empire.

The Romans, like the Greeks, viewed their slaves as "chattel," meaning that the master held power of life and death over the slave. It would therefore follow that this supreme authority over the life of a slave included the possibility for slaves to be set free by their owners. Sometimes it was even possible for the slave to pay his master for his own freedom. Once freed, former slaves could even receive citizenship in Roman society.

The advent of Christianity did not initially affect the institution of slavery, although it found many converts among the Roman slaves. Christianity was perhaps more appealing to slaves because it recognized their individual dignity and encouraged them to share in the cross of Christ through their own suffering. In Ephesians 6:5-9, St. Paul asks slaves to give good service to their masters by placing the rewards of heaven before them, and he instructed masters to disavow violence toward slaves and to recognize Jesus Christ as the universal master. Indeed many of the early leaders of the Church, including popes, were former slaves.

CATEGORIES OF ROMAN SLAVES

Titus Maccius Plautus was a comic playwright of the Roman Republic. The years of his life are uncertain, but his plays were produced between ca. 205 and 184 B.C. Twenty-one plays survive.

Plautus' comedies, which are the earliest surviving intact works in Latin literature, are all adaptations of Greek models for a Roman audience. His most typical character is the clever slave who manipulates his master.

As portrayed by Plautus in his comedies, the categories of Roman slaves included:

agaso - groom
atriensis - steward
auceps - fowler
auri custos - jewelry attendant
bubulcus - plowman
calator - footman
cantrix - singer
cellarius - storekeeper
cistellatrix - wardrobe keeper
coquus - cook
cursor - messenger
factor - poultry and game fattener
genus ferratile - chain gang
holitor - market gardener
ianitrix - doorkeeper
messor - reaper
nuntius renuntius - messengers
nutrix - nurse
obstetrix - obstetrician
opilio - head shepherd
paedogogus - children's chaperon
pastores - shepherds
pedisequa - attendant
salutigeruli pueri - pages
sartor - hoer
sator - planter
tonstrix - hairdresser
unctor - masseur
vestiplica - clothing folder

PART III

The Jews

The history of the Jewish people is particular to the ancient world. Besides being monotheistic, the Jewish people believed that they had a special role in God's providential plans to serve as his chosen people. One of the unique characteristics of the chosen people was their realization of a personal God. A long history of suffering and oppression molded a people whose faith stimulated their expectation for a messiah. Being cognizant of their obligation to worship the one true God and keep his commandments, they shunned the religions and immoral ways of the Gentiles, typified especially by the Greeks and Romans.

The Jewish world of Jesus was a crossroads of cultures, under Hellenist, Latin, and traditional Jewish influences. This Jewish culture was different than the one depicted in the Old Testament. Influenced by Greek thought and ideas, many new groups of scholars, priests, and ascetics developed schools of Jewish theology. Roman, not Mosaic Law governed society, and despite some special concessions for worship, Jews were held as second class to the Roman citizens. Palestine during the life of Christ was rife with tension and expectations as many Jewish groups were looking for the messiah to free Israel from the Roman yoke. In A.D. 70, the temple would be destroyed and the Jews would be cast out of Jerusalem.

A page from *The Sarajevo Haggadah* (fourteenth century) illustrates the Jewish Passover Seder, a ritual which reenacts and celebrates the Jewish Exodus from Egypt. The guiding text for this ritual, the *Haggadah,* has directed Jews through the Passover ritual from the tenth century to the present day.

A BRIEF OVERVIEW OF JEWISH HISTORY

This history of the Jews began with the covenant God made with Abraham. The descendants of Abraham began to worship the one true God in obedience to the covenant made with Abraham. After being enslaved during their exile in Egypt, a new prophet, Moses, led the Jews out of captivity. Through Moses, the whole Jewish community became more united through the gift of God's Law given to Moses on Mount Sinai. This Law transmitted God's explicit will to the chosen people. The central practice of the Jewish faith rested on fidelity to this Law. Reading the Torah (the first five books of the Old Testament), sacrificial worship conducted at the Temple, and, later on, rabbi-led worship at the synagogue, became staples of Jewish life.

Led back into Palestine by Moses' successor Joshua, the Jews eventually established a kingdom. Under kings David and Solomon, the Jewish kingdom reached its zenith and saw the completion of the First Temple during Solomon's reign. A feat of supreme architectural mastery, the Temple was massive and ornate, and its inner sanctum contained the tablets upon which God gave the Law to Moses. After Solomon's death, the kingdom was divided into two parts: Israel and Judah. Eventually, both these Jewish kingdoms were conquered, culminating in the utter desolation and destruction of the Temple by the Babylonians and the exile of the Jews to Babylon. After this second captivity, the Jews were permitted to return to Jerusalem in 458 B.C. Upon their return, they reconstructed the Temple. This Second Temple was very modest in comparison to the grandeur of the first one, but the Jews nonetheless enjoyed the recovery of their freedom to worship in their "new" temple. This freedom would soon be dashed with the arrival of the Romans in 63 B.C. In just over a hundred years, in A.D. 70, the Temple would again be destroyed.

THE SADDUCEES AND THE PHARISEES

There were two main groups of Jewish religious leaders during the time of Jesus. The Sadducees were comprised of many wealthy elite, especially in Jerusalem. Although they were never large in number, they did exercise considerable religious and political influence, dominating the Sanhedrin (a ruling body among the Jews) at the time of Christ. Furthermore, the Sadducees were Hellenized to a greater extent than other Jews, which helped them act as mediators with the Romans in difficult situations. They were generally on good terms with the Romans, which made them very unpopular with the Jewish people.

Unfortunately, no literature has survived from the Sadducees themselves. They are mentioned by Josephus (ca. A.D. 37- ca. 100), a Jewish historian, but his accounts fail to paint a complete picture. The Sadducees considered only the Pentateuch a legitimate authority on the Jewish faith, and they interpreted these first five books of the Hebrew Scriptures along literalist lines. They rejected the idea that there was an afterlife, as well as the belief that there was an individual judgment after death. These beliefs brought them into contention not only with the teachings of Jesus, but also with some of the ideas of the Pharisees.

In contrast to the politically and religiously conservative Sadducees, the Pharisees were a progressive reforming group. The name Pharisee comes from the Aramaic *perishaya,* which means "the separated (ones)." Unlike the Sadducees, the Pharisees were not a group of priests, but rather lay scholars. As scholars, the Pharisees tried to interpret the Law and make it applicable to everyday life.

The New Testament relates how Jesus reprimanded the Pharisees for keeping the letter of the Law to the detriment of its spirit. Christ chastised them, as he did the Sadducees, for their legalism as well as their self-righteousness (cf. Lk 18: 9-14). However, at the Lord's Passion and death, the

THE SEPTUAGINT

Hellenistic culture had a tremendous influence on almost every culture it encountered. Many of the Diaspora Jews, for example, spoke Greek, and as a result, the Hebrew Scriptures were translated from Hebrew into Greek at Alexandria, a major center of Diaspora Jews. This Greek translation of the Old Testament is called the Septuagint because, tradition holds, seventy-two scholars were said to have worked on the project. It is now believed that more than seventy-two scholars worked on the translation and that at least some of the work was completed outside Alexandria.

The Greek translation of the Old Testament took decades to complete. Ptolemy Philadelphus (285-246 B.C.), the king of Egypt, requested a translation of the Pentateuch for his renowned Library of Alexandria. The process began around the year 250 B.C., and by 132 B.C., the entire Hebrew Scriptures were translated.

The Greek translation of the Scriptures would be tremendously influential. The authors of the New Testament, also writing in Greek, used the Septuagint for quotations from the Old Testament. The translation also allowed for non-Jews to read and become acquainted with the Old Testament. As Christianity spread in the first centuries A.D., this Greek translation would become very important to Gentile converts who otherwise would not have been able to read the Hebrew text.

Above: A papyrus fragment with Daniel 1:1-8 from the Greek *Septuagint*.

Left: A reconstruction of the Museum of Alexandria, with doors leading to the rooms of the Library.

Pharisees faded into the background and the religiously and politically established Sadducees took the leading role in putting Christ to death.

Even though the Pharisees were depicted as the main opponents of Jesus, they shared a number of beliefs with him. These included the resurrection of the body, divine punishment and reward in the afterlife, angels, and human freedom.

The Sadducees more or less disappeared after the destruction of the Temple in A.D. 70. The Pharisees, on the other hand, had some influence in training rabbis for the synagogue, and this, together with their *Mishnah* writings, assured the Pharisees a place of importance in Judaism. After the fall of the Holy City, a strong Pharisaical presence was developed at Yavneh (Jamnia) in Palestine where an academy was established for the training of rabbis.

THE ESSENES

The Essenes were a group of Jews that withdrew from the world into the desert in order to live a life of prayer and asceticism. Their name means either "the pious ones" or "the healers," and it has been suggested that the Essenes incorporated a form of baptism and a communal meal into their community. There is some speculation that John the Baptist may have had some connection with the Essenes, but there is no conclusive evidence. Today, the Essenes are best known for their relationship to the Dead Sea scrolls discovered in 1947.

Pages from the *Beatus Apocalypses* (10th Century).

The Arch of Titus in Rome depicts Roman soldiers carrying away looted treasures from the Temple in Jerusalem.

THE DIASPORA

The word "Diaspora" is Greek for "dispersion," and it refers to the emigration of the Jews into areas outside the boundaries of Palestine. Though the term Diaspora has been used many times throughout Jewish history, it began with the Assyrian exile (ca. 721 B.C.), followed by the Babylonian exile (ca. 587 B.C.).

During the time of Christ, the Jews were spread throughout the Roman Empire, and the population of the Diaspora was greater than the Jewish population in Palestine. Alexandria in Egypt, for example, became the most important center of learning for the Jews of the Diaspora. Some records list a population of one million Jews in Alexandria alone.

Throughout the Roman Empire, the Jews enjoyed special concessions and exemptions. In general, Jews of the Diaspora were also exempted from emperor worship and enjoyed special privileges in conjunction with the Sabbath and religious feasts. These same Jews also paid the Temple tax faithfully before its destruction in the first century.

There was a considerable increase in emigration after the revolts against the Romans in 63 B.C., and from A.D. 115-117. After the destruction of Jerusalem, the Jews were forbidden to enter Jerusalem except for only one day each year, the Day of Atonement, in order to weep before the ruins of the Temple. With their temple destroyed and city visitation forbidden, Jews spread to many parts of Europe and North Africa.

CONCLUSION

This background to the history of the Church shows how God through his Providence set the stage for the advancement of his kingdom of truth and justice. Hellenism provided a cultural *milieu* that fostered a disposition to the acceptance of Christianity especially through Greek Philosophy. The Roman Empire, with the unifying forces of its laws and organization, together with the *Pax Romana*, would greatly facilitate the actual spread of the Gospel. God's chosen people would prepare the way for history's protagonist of salvation, Jesus Christ, the Lord of History.

SUPPLEMENTARY READING

Virgil, *Aeneid*, Book 1, 1.359-401
Virgil Links Aeneas with Julius Caesar

And, ripe for heav'n, when fate Aeneas calls,
Then shalt thou bear him up, sublime, to me:
No councils have revers'd my firm decree.
And, lest new fears disturb thy happy state,
Know, I have search'd the mystic rolls of Fate:
Thy son (nor is th' appointed season far)
In Italy shall wage successful war,
Shall tame fierce nations in the bloody field,
And sov'reign laws impose, and cities build,
Till, after ev'ry foe subdued, the sun
Thrice thro' the signs his annual race shall run:
This is his time prefix'd. Ascanius then,
Now call'd Iulus, shall begin his reign.
He thirty rolling years the crown shall wear,
Then from Lavinium shall the seat transfer,
And, with hard labor, Alba Longa build.
The throne with his succession shall be fill'd
Three hundred circuits more: then shall be seen
Ilia the fair, a priestess and a queen,
Who, full of Mars, in time, with kindly throes,
Shall at a birth two goodly boys disclose.
The royal babes a tawny wolf shall drain:
Then Romulus his grandsire's throne shall gain,
Of martial tow'rs the founder shall become,
The people Romans call, the city Rome.
To them no bounds of empire I assign,
Nor term of years to their immortal line.
Ev'n haughty Juno, who, with endless broils,
Earth, seas, and heav'n, and Jove himself turmoils;
At length aton'd, her friendly pow'r shall join,
To cherish and advance the Trojan line.
The subject world shall Rome's dominion own,
And, prostrate, shall adore the nation of the
gown.An age is ripening in revolving fate
When Troy shall overturn the Grecian state,
And sweet revenge her conqu'ring sons shall call,
To crush the people that conspir'd her fall.
Then Caesar from the Julian stock shall rise,
Whose empire ocean, and whose fame the skies
Alone shall bound; whom, fraught with
   eastern spoils,
Our heav'n, the just reward of human toils,
Securely shall repay with rites divine;
And incense shall ascend before his sacred shrine.

Tacitus, *The Annals*, beginning of Book I: Rome becomes an Empire

Rome at the beginning was ruled by kings. Freedom and the consulship were established by Lucius Brutus. Dictatorships were held for a temporary crisis.... the rule of Pompeius and of Crassus soon yielded before Caesar; the arms of Lepidus and Antonius before Augustus; who, when the world was wearied by civil strife, subjected it to empire under the title of "Prince."...

When after the destruction of Brutus and Cassius there was no longer any army of the Commonwealth, when Pompeius was crushed in Sicily, and when, with Lepidus pushed aside and Antonius slain, even the Julian faction had only Caesar left to lead it, then, dropping the title of triumvir, and giving out that he was a Consul, and was satisfied with a tribune's authority for the protection of the people, Augustus won over the soldiers with gifts, the populace with cheap corn, and all men with the sweets of repose, and so grew greater by degrees, while he concentrated in himself the functions of the Senate, the magistrates, and the laws. He was wholly unopposed, for the boldest spirits had fallen in battle, or in the proscription, while the remaining nobles, the readier they were to be slaves, were raised the higher by wealth and promotion, so that, aggrandized by revolution, they preferred the safety of the present to the dangerous past. Nor did the provinces dislike that condition of affairs, for they distrusted the government of the Senate and the people, because of the rivalries between the leading men and the rapacity of the officials, while the protection of the laws was unavailing, as they were continually deranged by violence, intrigue, and finally by corruption.

Thus the State had been revolutionized, and there was not a vestige left of the old sound morality. Stript of equality, all looked up to the commands of a sovereign....

VOCABULARY

AUGUSTUS
Imperial title given to Octavian from the Senate marking the founding of the Empire of Rome.

CHATTEL
Form of slavery in which the master holds power of life and death over the slave.

DIASPORA
Greek for "dispersion," it refers to the emigration of the Jews into areas outside the geophysical boundaries of Palestine.

ESSENES
A group of Jews that withdrew from the world into the desert in order to live a life of prayer and asceticism. Their name means "the pious ones" or "the healers."

HELLENIZATION
Process by which Greek cultural attributes were transplanted to the East.

MITHRAICISM
A pagan cult that was a fraternal organization open only to men that cultivated virtues important to the life of a soldier. Some of their ritual practices, such as the idea of personal salvation and a communal meal in which flesh that symbolized their god was consumed, were similar to Christianity.

PAX ROMANA
Literally "the Roman peace," it refers to the period of peace and prosperity during which the empire enjoyed two hundred years of peace and Roman civilization flourished.

PHARISEES
A progressive, reforming group of Jewish lay scholars. Their name comes from the Aramaic *perishaya*, which means "the separated ones."

PIETAS
Practice of pagan worship which sought the placation of the gods through sacrifice in an effort to secure protection for the Roman state.

PONTIFEX MAXIMUS
Title meaning "high priest" of the Roman pagan religion that was taken by Emperor Augustus.

PUNIC WARS
Three wars fought by Rome against Carthage, after which the Romans vastly expanded their empire, acquiring Sicily, Spain, and North Africa.

SADDUCEES
Comprised of many wealthy elite, especially in Jerusalem, they exercised considerable religious and political influence among Jews at the time of Christ.

SANHEDRIN
A ruling body among the Jews dominated by the Sadducees.

STOICISM
Borrowing much from the Greek philosophers, this ethical code appealed to the Roman sense of law, order, and virtue. Stoics honored the natural law and one's duty to it, as well as encouraging the practical by perfecting moderation of the passions as a pathway to true freedom.

Ptolemy Philadelphus (285-246 B.C.), king of Egypt is credited with having the Old Testament translated into Greek. which allowed non-Jews to study the Old Testament scriptures.

STUDY QUESTIONS

1. Who helped expand Hellenism to the East?

2. According to legend, who founded Rome?

3. When was Rome founded?

4. How did Rome benefit from the Punic Wars?

5. How did Julius Caesar become dictator for life?

6. Who was "Augustus"? How did he receive that title?

7. How did Augustus retain the appearances of a Republic?

8. In what different areas did Greek and Roman civilizations excel?

9. How did early cults placate their gods and secure protection for their state?

10. How did the fundamentals of Stoicism appeal to the Romans?

11. How did the change from republic to empire hurt the Romans?

12. Who led the Jews from captivity?

13. Who were the Sadducees?

14. Who were the Pharisees?

15. What happened to the Jews in A.D. 70?

16. What term describes Jews who do not live in the Holy Land?

PRACTICAL EXERCISES

1. Both Hellenism and the Roman Empire provided cultural and political unity in the world at the time of Christ. How might this have helped the spread of Christianity? Can you identify any attributes of Hellenism or the Roman Empire that are still reflected in Christianity today?

2. How was Jewish culture at the time of Christ different from that described in the Old Testament? How was it the same? The Sadducees and Pharisees played a major role in condemning Christ. Why do you think Jesus frightened them? What do the Sadducees and Pharisees demonstrate about tradition and authority?

3. The history of the Jewish people is filled with incidents concerning God's promises and providence, sometimes unfolding in an unexpected way. How would a Jew explain the fall of Jerusalem and the Great Diaspora? How would a Christian explain these events?

Ruins of the Roman Forum. The Forum was the center of politics and commerce for the Empire.

FROM THE CATECHISM

63 Israel is the priestly people of God, "called by the name of the LORD," and "the first to hear the word of God" (Dt 28:10; *Roman Missal*, Good Friday, General Intercessions VI; see also Ex 19:6), the people of "elder brethren" in the faith of Abraham.

285 Since the beginning the Christian faith has been challenged by responses to the question of origins that differ from its own. Ancient religions and cultures produced many myths concerning origins. Some philosophers have said that everything is God, that the world is God, or that the development of the world is the development of God (Pantheism). Others have said that the world is a necessary emanation arising from God and returning to him. Still others have affirmed the existence of two eternal principles, Good and Evil, Light and Darkness, locked, in permanent conflict (Dualism, Manichaeism). According to some of these conceptions, the world (at least the physical world) is evil, the product of a fall, and is thus to be rejected or left behind (Gnosticism). Some admit that the world was made by God, but as by a watchmaker who, once he has made a watch, abandons it to itself (Deism). Finally, others reject any transcendent origin for the world, but see it as merely the interplay of matter that has always existed (Materialism). All these attempts bear witness to the permanence and universality of the question of origins. This inquiry is distinctively human.

402 All men are implicated in Adam's sin, as St. Paul affirms: "By one man's disobedience many [that is, all men] were made sinners": "sin came into the world through one man and death through sin, and so death spread to all men because all men sinned" (Rom 5:12, 19). The Apostle contrasts the universality of sin and death with the universality of salvation in Christ. "Then as one man's trespass led to condemnation for all men, so one man's act of righteousness leads to acquittal and life for all men" (Rom 5:18).

436 The word "Christ" comes from the Greek translation of the Hebrew *Messiah*, which means "anointed." It became the name proper to Jesus only because he accomplished perfectly the divine mission that "Christ" signifies. In effect, in Israel those consecrated to God for a mission that he gave were anointed in his name. This was the case for kings, for priests and, in rare instances, for prophets (cf. Ex 29:7; Lv 8:12; 1 Sm 9:16; 10:1; 16:1, 12-13; 1 Kgs 1:39; 19:16). This had to be the case all the more so for the Messiah whom God would send to inaugurate his kingdom definitively (cf. Ps 2:2; Acts 4:26-27). It was necessary that the Messiah be anointed by the Spirit of the Lord at once as king and priest, and also as prophet (cf. Is 11:2; 61:1; Zech 4:14; 6:13; Lk 4:16-21). Jesus fulfilled the messianic hope of Israel in his threefold office of priest, prophet, and king.

579 This principle of integral observance of the Law not only in letter but in spirit was dear to the Pharisees. By giving Israel this principle they had led many Jews of Jesus' time to an extreme religious zeal (cf. Rom 10:2). This zeal, were it not to lapse into "hypocritical" casuistry (cf. Mt 15:3-7; Lk 11:39-54), could only prepare the People for the unprecedented intervention of God through the perfect fulfillment of the Law by the only Righteous One in place of all sinners (cf. Is 53:11; Heb 9:15).

781 "At all times and in every race, anyone who fears God and does what is right has been acceptable to him. He has, however, willed to make men holy and save them, not as individuals without any bond or link between them, but rather to make them into a people who might acknowledge him and serve him in holiness. He therefore chose the Israelite race to be his own people and established a covenant with it. He gradually instructed this people.... All these things, however, happened as a preparation for and figure of that new and perfect covenant which was to be ratified in Christ...the New Covenant in his blood; he

FROM THE CATECHISM Continued

called together a race made up of Jews and Gentiles which would be one, not according to the flesh, but in the Spirit" (LG 9; cf. Acts 10:35; 1 Cor 11:25).

839 "Those who have not yet received the Gospel are related to the People of God in various ways" (LG 16).

The relationship of the Church with the Jewish People. When she delves into her own mystery, the Church, the People of God in the New Covenant, discovers her link with the Jewish People (cf. NA 4), "the first to hear the Word of God" (*Roman Missal,* Good Friday 13; General Intercessions, VI). The Jewish faith, unlike other non-Christian religions, is already a response to God's revelation in the Old Covenant. To the Jews "belong the sonship, the glory, the covenants, the giving of the law, the worship, and the promises; to them belong the patriarchs, and of their race, according to the flesh, is the Christ" (Rom 9:4-5), "for the gifts and the call of God are irrevocable" (Rom 11:29).

1537 The word *order* in Roman antiquity designated an established civil body, especially a governing body. *Ordinatio* means incorporation into an *ordo.* In the Church there are established bodies which Tradition, not without a basis in Sacred Scripture (cf. Heb 5:6; 7:11; Ps 110:4), has since ancient times called *taxeis* (Greek) or *ordines.* And so the liturgy speaks of the *ordo episcoporum,* the *ordo presbyterorum,* the *ordo diaconorum.* Other groups also receive this name of *ordo:* catechumens, virgins, spouses, widows,...

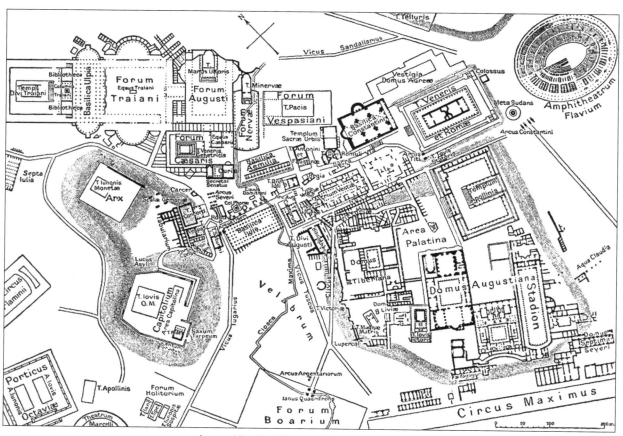

A map of the city of Rome at the height of the Empire.

CHAPTER 1

Jesus Christ And The Founding Of The Church

"Christ is the Spouse and Savior of the Church...
The more we come to know and love the Church,
the nearer we shall be to Christ."

CHAPTER 1

Jesus Christ And The Founding Of The Church

Loving Christ means loving the Church. The Church exists for Christ,
so as to continue his presence and witness in the world.
Christ is the Spouse and Savior of the Church. He is her Founder and her Head.
The more we come to know and love the Church,
the nearer we shall be to Christ.

— John Paul II, Homily, Brisbane, Australia, November 25, 1986

In the days directly following the crucifixion of Jesus, his disciples were afraid. The Sanhedrin had condemned their Master to death, and the disciples believed that they would be the next targets of persecution. They feared for their safety and were uncertain of the future, being for the first time without their leader. At first the Resurrection appearances only increased doubt and fear among the disciples. Though their Master had returned to them, He remained among them for only a short time. After the Ascension, the Apostles, Mary, and other followers of Jesus were again suddenly alone.

But God did not leave His infant Church alone and unguided. Before departing, Christ declared to his disciples that they would soon receive the Holy Spirit. Ten days later, on the Jewish feast of Pentecost, the Holy Spirit descended upon the disciples, and subsequently resolved all their doubts, fears, and worries. The Apostles, through the power of the Holy Spirit, were certain that the Church of Christ would stand throughout all time as a living sacrament of His love, truth, and power. Christ is the cornerstone of His Church, and St. Peter is "the rock," Christ's vicar, upon whom the Church would be built. In the years following the Resurrection, the Apostles, filled with

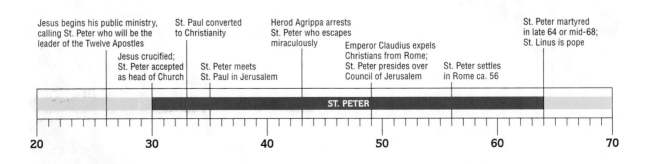

Jesus begins his public ministry, calling St. Peter who will be the leader of the Twelve Apostles

St. Paul converted to Christianity

Herod Agrippa arrests St. Peter who escapes miraculously

St. Peter martyred in late 64 or mid-68; St. Linus is pope

Jesus crucified; St. Peter accepted as head of Church

St. Peter meets St. Paul in Jerusalem

Emperor Claudius expels Christians from Rome; St. Peter presides over Council of Jerusalem

St. Peter settles in Rome ca. 56

ST. PETER

20   30   40   50   60   70

Christ is the cornerstone of His Church, and St. Peter is "the rock," Christ's vicar, upon whom the Church would be built.

the grace of the Holy Spirit, boldly set about the great task of building the Church. They proclaimed the Good News that the long-awaited messiah had come and that he had paid in full the terrible price required for the redemption of all mankind. Christianity began to spread quickly through the ardent and intrepid preaching of the disciples. They carried the message of salvation proclaimed by Jesus all over the known world. Thus began the history of Christianity—a unique history that, simply stated, reflects Christ's constant presence in the Church that at all times interfaces with human history. The history of the Church is a record of the life and actions of men and women under the guiding light of the Holy Spirit acting in the Church. This narrative about the development of Christ's kingdom on earth is forged as the Church interacts and responds to every culture and historical situation.

This chapter will explore the saving work of Christ, the meaning and significance of Pentecost, the nature of the Church, and the unique status and missionary lives of the Apostles.

PART I
The Life of Jesus Christ

*If any man would come after me, let him deny himself and take up his cross
and follow me. (Mt 16: 24)*

Jesus of Nazareth was born in Bethlehem in Judea around the year 4 B.C. In the humblest of surroundings, the Word of God became Incarnate; love and mercy found perfect expression, and the vessel of God's salvation was born into human history. The foundational principles of Christianity were present there in the quiet little stable in Bethlehem with Jesus, Mary, and Joseph. Peace, simplicity, material poverty, spiritual abundance, God's love, and sacrifice are the chief message of Christ's birth.

The Bible only records a few key events concerning Jesus' childhood. One of them is the Presentation in the Temple. After the birth of Christ, in accordance with the Jewish Law, Joseph and Mary took Jesus to the Temple in Jerusalem to be consecrated to God. Through the power of the Holy Spirit, an old man named Simeon, to whom it had been revealed that he should not die until he had seen the messiah, recognized the Infant, blessed His parents, and spoke of Jesus' destiny. Anna, an elderly prophetess, was also present and, recognizing the messiah, began to speak about the child to all who were waiting for Him (Lk 2: 22-39).

Shortly after the birth of Jesus, Joseph was warned in a dream by an angel that Herod, the King of Judea, had learned of the birth of the messiah and planned to murder the baby. The angel instructed Joseph to flee to Egypt with Mary and Jesus immediately, so that the Holy Child would escape Herod's wrath. When Herod failed to discover the precise location of Jesus, he sent his soldiers to kill every male child in Bethlehem aged two and under. Known as the "Slaughter of the Innocents," this dreadful massacre was the first shedding of blood among countless unnamed martyrs for the Christian Faith (Mt 2: 16-18). After some time in Egypt, an angel appeared to Joseph in a second dream, telling him that it was safe for the Holy Family to return to Israel. Ever obedient, Joseph began the journey back to Israel with Jesus and Mary. Upon hearing that Herod's son Archelaus was now king of Judea, Joseph did not return there, but went to Galilee instead, and settled his family in Nazareth (Mt 2: 19-23).

After the Holy Family returned to Nazareth, the Gospels record very little of their lives. One can assume that their lives were very ordinary, consisting of work, observance of the Jewish Law, finding joy in the company of one another and of their friends. Joseph was a carpenter, and Jesus most likely trained in the trade of his father, learning to work with wood and build with his hands. Until the beginning of His public ministry, the only event the Gospels describe is the finding of the twelve-year-old Jesus speaking with the elders in the Temple in Jerusalem. The Holy Family traveled to Jerusalem for the feast of the Passover, and when they set out to return home, Jesus was lost for three days. After frantically looking for their son, his parents finally discovered the child Jesus in the temple, which the boy called his "Father's house." The young Jesus was confidently conversing with the elders, whom he astounded with his wisdom and understanding (Lk 2: 41-52).

PALESTINE IN THE TIME OF CHRIST

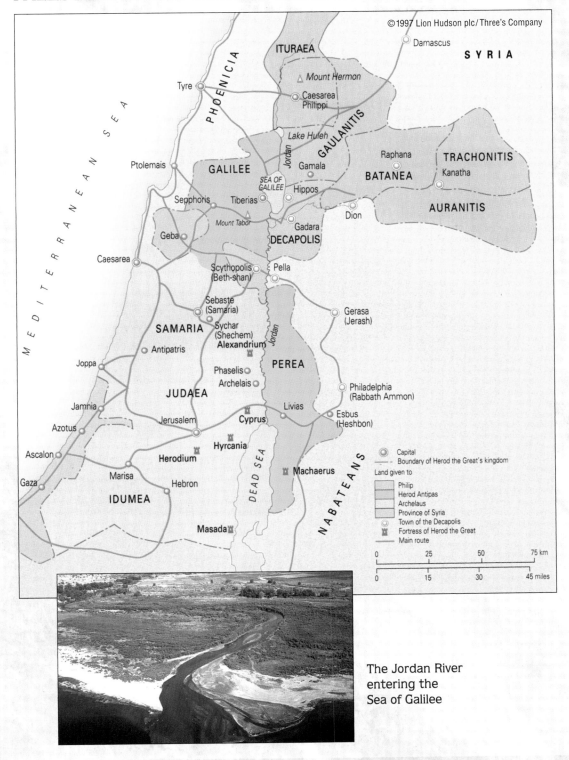

© 1997 Lion Hudson plc / Three's Company

ITURAEA

Damascus

SYRIA

PHOENICIA

Mount Hermon

Tyre

Caesarea
Philippi

Lake Huleh

GAULANITIS

Jordan

Ptolemais

GALILEE

Gamala

Raphana

TRACHONITIS

BATANEA

Kanatha

SEA OF
GALILEE

Hippos

Sepphoris

Tiberias

AURANITIS

MEDITERRANEAN SEA

Mount Tabor

Geba

Gadara

Dion

DECAPOLIS

Caesarea

Scythopolis
(Beth-shan)

Pella

Sebaste
(Samaria)

Gerasa
(Jerash)

SAMARIA

Sychar
(Shechem)

Antipatris

Jordan

Joppa

Phaselis

Archelais

Alexandrium

PEREA

Philadelphia
(Rabbath Ammon)

JUDAEA

Jamnia

Livias

Azotus

Jerusalem

Cyprus

Esbus
(Heshbon)

Ascalon

Hyrcania

Gaza

Marisa

Herodium

Hebron

Machaerus

DEAD SEA

IDUMEA

NABATEANS

Masada

⊚	Capital
—	Boundary of Herod the Great's kingdom

Land given to

Philip

Herod Antipas

Archelaus

Province of Syria

⊚ Town of the Decapolis

🏰 Fortress of Herod the Great

— Main route

0   25   50   75 km

0   15   30   45 miles

The Jordan River
entering the
Sea of Galilee

Jesus' New Law taught his followers to love their enemies and to avoid violence.

Following this event, there is a period of eighteen years before the inaugural event of his public ministry: Jesus' Baptism at the hands of St. John the Baptist. During this time it is recorded that Jesus spent time in the desert fasting, praying, and preparing for his public ministry.

Jesus' teaching constitutes part of the Deposit of Faith, that is the heritage of Faith contained in Sacred Scripture and Tradition, handed down by the Church from the time of the Apostles (cf. CCC 84, 1202). The most succinct and direct collection of Jesus' teaching is given at the Sermon on the Mount (Mt 5-7). Fulfilling the traditional Law found in the Ten Commandments, Jesus taught the Beatitudes and the Lord's Prayer. He transformed the Old Testament notion of justice, fulfilling and perfecting it with the call to charity, which includes compassion and mercy. In contrast to the Old Law, expressed by the rule of "an eye for an eye," Jesus' New Law taught his followers to love their enemies and to avoid all forms of violence, drowning evil in an abundance of good. The institution of mercy to the point of loving one's enemies was radically new. Jesus redirected the spirit of worship, instructing his followers to serve the Father and each other in "spirit and in truth," thereby rejecting a legalistic interpretation of the Law. The New Covenant founded by Christ would perfect the Old Law through the New Law based on love and grace. His teaching and his many miracles — from the wedding feast at Cana to the raising of Lazarus — laid the groundwork for the contents of the Catholic Faith that would develop in response to the circumstances of every time period.

Jesus' teachings were brought to their fulfillment through the example of Christ's suffering, death, and Resurrection. Around the year A.D. 33, Jesus and his followers went to Jerusalem to participate in the celebration of the Jewish Passover. Despite his initial warm welcome on Palm Sunday, the Jewish leaders mounted a major opposition against Jesus. They charged him with heresy and blasphemy, but finally they accused Jesus of being insubordinate to caesar to lay the burden of execution on the civil authorities. Under tremendous pressure and risk of widespread civil descent (not to mention his own blindness to the truth of Christ; cf. Jn 18:38), Pontius Pilate condemned Jesus to death by crucifixion. Jesus, according to the plan of the Father, willingly submitted himself to his passion and death on the cross, the perfect sacrifice for the salvation of all mankind. By his Resurrection three days later, he showed his victory over death, thereby calling every person to repentance and the fullness of filiation with the Father.

THE FOUR GOSPELS

Most of what is known about Christ's life comes from the four canonical gospels: Matthew, Mark, Luke, and John. The word "gospel," which means "good news," is applied to these four books that describe the life and teachings of Jesus.

Although all four gospels share the same subject, each has its own point of view and emphasis, depending on the source of the account and the audience for whom it was written. Matthew, Mark and Luke are known as the "synoptic" gospels (from Greek words meaning "seeing together") because their accounts are so similar. The gospel of St. John stands apart because of its more abstract, theological scope.

Both Sts. John and Matthew were themselves Apostles. Both gospels seem to be directed toward a Jewish Christian audience. St. John's was the last gospel to be written. St. Mark's is thought to be the first gospel written. St. Mark, though not an Apostle, traveled with St. Peter, who is very likely the primary source for this gospel intended for the Christians of Rome. St. Luke, who accompanied St. Paul, wrote mainly for gentile Christians and his main source is thought to be Mary the mother of Christ because this gospel includes stories about Christ's origins and early life.

The four authors, known as the Evangelists, are often identified with four symbols. St. Matthew's symbol is a man because his gospel emphasizes Christ's humanity and opens with his genealogy. St. Mark's symbol is a lion because it opens with the command "Prepare the way of the Lord." St. Luke's symbol is a bull because early on it speaks of priestly duties and temple sacrifices. St. John's gospel is symbolized by an eagle because of the lofty language of its opening verses.

These four gospels have always been held as authentic and canonical (officially declared as such at a synod in Rome in A.D. 382) by the Sacred Tradition of the Church, though there exist several "unofficial" gospels, known as the apocryphal gospels, which appeared in the first centuries of the Church. These gospels were discredited early in the Church's history because of their dubious origins and because many are tainted by errant beliefs.

The Book of Kells
"The work not of men but of angels..."
(Giraldus Cambrensis, ca. A.D.1150)

One of the most famous books in the history of the world completed in A.D. 800 contains the Four Gospels. It was created by Columban monks who lived on the remote island of Iona, off the west coast of Scotland. The Book is on display at the Trinity College Library in Dublin.

PART II

Pentecost, the Birth of the Church

When the day of Pentecost had come, they [the Apostles and Mary] were all together in one place. And suddenly a sound came from heaven like the rush of a mighty wind, and it filled all the house where they were sitting. And there appeared to them tongues as of fire, distributed and resting on each one of them. And they were all filled with the Holy Spirit and began to speak in other tongues, as the Spirit gave them utterance. (Acts 2:1-4)

On the Jewish feast of Pentecost, fifty days after the Resurrection of Christ, Jerusalem was filled with pilgrims from nearly every nation—from Persia, Rome, Arabia, North Africa, and all around the Mediterranean. The Apostles were all gathered in one place, most likely still fearing persecution. Just as Christ promised before he ascended to Heaven, the Holy Spirit descended upon them, anointing the Church for her mission of evangelization of the world.

On Pentecost, the Father and the Son sent the Holy Spirit, the Third Person of the Blessed Trinity, to complete and perfect that which Jesus Christ had begun:

By his coming, which never ceases, the Holy Spirit causes the world to enter into the "last days," the time of the Church, the Kingdom already inherited though not yet consummated. (CCC 732)

Immediately following the Holy Spirit's descent, the Apostles began to preach the crucified and risen Christ with great power and authority (Acts 2:5-47). They were given the gift of tongues and found themselves miraculously speaking to the multitude, each hearing in his own tongue from among the languages spoken by the many pilgrims present in Jerusalem for Pentecost (Acts 2:8-11). St. Peter, responding to skepticism that the disciples were "filled with new wine" (Acts 2:13), addressed all who were present. He proclaimed the special calling of the Jews in God's plan of salvation for the world, used the Old Testament writings as proof of Christ's fulfillment of the prophets and the Law, and, like St. John the Baptist, called his hearers to repentance. St. Peter invited Jesus' new followers to be forgiven of their sins through the reception of Baptism.

Peter said to them, "Repent, and be baptized every one of you in the name of Jesus Christ for the forgiveness of your sins; and you shall receive the gift of the Holy Spirit." (Acts 2:38)

Many converts came to the Faith through this first proclamation at Pentecost:

So those who received his word were baptized, and there were added that day about three thousand souls. And they devoted themselves to the apostles' teaching and fellowship, to the breaking of bread and the prayers. (Acts 2:41-42)

The annual celebration of this feast is an opportunity to recall all that took place at the first Pentecost, whereby the Apostles were empowered with the strength of the Holy Spirit to preach Christ in word and in the heroic witness of martyrdom. Pentecost marks the enduring presence of the Holy Spirit in the Church that enables Christians to announce the truth of Christ's Gospel. It also shows that Christ will live in his Church throughout all ages.

Pentecost marks the enduring presence of the Holy Spirit in the Church.

THE EARLY SPREAD OF CHRISTIANITY

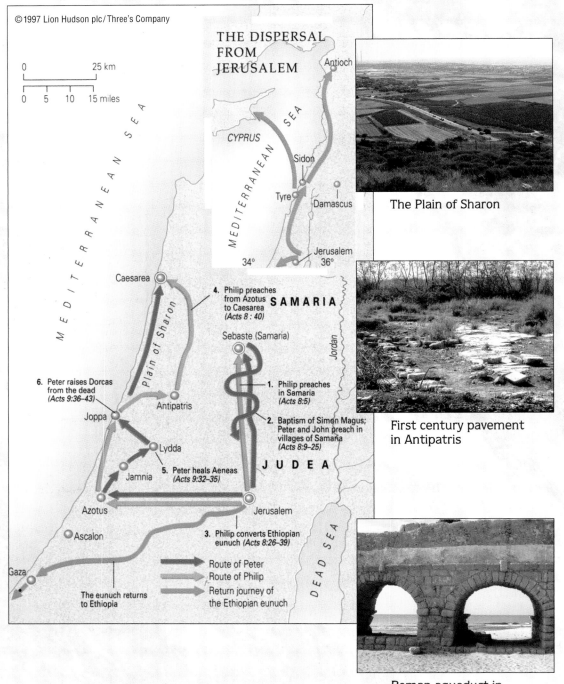

©1997 Lion Hudson plc/Three's Company

THE DISPERSAL FROM JERUSALEM

0 — 25 km
0 5 10 15 miles

MEDITERRANEAN SEA

CYPRUS

Sidon
Tyre
Damascus
Jerusalem
34°
36°

Caesarea

Plain of Sharon

SAMARIA

Jordan

4. Philip preaches from Azotus to Caesarea (Acts 8 : 40)

Sebaste (Samaria)

1. Philip preaches in Samaria (Acts 8:5)

2. Baptism of Simon Magus; Peter and John preach in villages of Samaria (Acts 8:9–25)

6. Peter raises Dorcas from the dead (Acts 9:36–43)

Antipatris

Joppa

Lydda

Jamnia

5. Peter heals Aeneas (Acts 9:32–35)

JUDEA

Azotus

Ascalon

Jerusalem

3. Philip converts Ethiopian eunuch (Acts 8:26–39)

Gaza

The eunuch returns to Ethiopia

DEAD SEA

Route of Peter
Route of Philip
Return journey of the Ethiopian eunuch

The Plain of Sharon

First century pavement in Antipatris

Roman aqueduct in Caesarea

PART III

The Church

What is the Church exactly? The Scriptures teach that the Church is the Body of Christ and the Temple of the Holy Spirit (cf. Eph 1: 22-23). The English word "church" etymologically comes from a Greek word meaning "thing belonging to the Lord," which applied originally to the church building. The Latin word *ecclesia* derives from another Greek word that means "assembly" or "congregation" The origins of these two words help to illustrate the many meanings the word "church" evokes for followers of Christ. This section will briefly look at the meaning of the Church, her aim, nature, names that have been employed to better understand her, and, finally, her four marks.

The *Catechism of the Catholic Church* states that, "The Church is both the means and the goal of God's plan: prefigured in creation, prepared for in the Old Covenant, founded by the words and actions of Jesus Christ, fulfilled by his redeeming cross and his Resurrection, the Church has been manifested as the mystery of salvation by the outpouring of the Holy Spirit. She will be perfected in the glory of heaven as the assembly of all the redeemed of the earth (cf. Rv 14: 4)" (CCC 778).

The Church forms the Mystical Body of Christ.

Willed by the Father, the Church founded by Jesus Christ enjoys the presence and guidance of the Holy Spirit. It is through the Church that God carries out his plan of salvation for all people. The teaching authority and sanctifying power of the Church serve as a means to bring all men and women to greater union with God, and with each other as well.

The groundwork for the Church was already being laid down when God made a covenant with the Jewish people. After this time of preparation in the Old Testament was completed, Jesus instituted the Church. The Church's foundation, goal, and fulfillment is in Jesus Christ. Through the Church, Jesus Christ unites himself with all men and women.

The Church has two dimensions: visible and spiritual. The Church is a visible, hierarchical society that is present in the world, just like any other organization or society. Unlike other societies, the Church has a spiritual dimension. The governing and teaching authority of the Church enjoys perennial guidance from the Holy Spirit. Moreover, she is the Mystical Body of Christ, a spiritual community, imbued with the healing and sanctifying power of God's grace.

The Church is made up of God's people, a people "born" into his family through faith in Christ and Baptism. The term "People of God" is taken from the Old Testament, in which God chose Israel to be his chosen people. Christ instituted the new and eternal covenant by which a new priestly, prophetic, and royal People of God, the Church, participates in the mission and service of Christ (cf. CCC 761, 783 at the end of this chapter). The Head of this people is Jesus Christ, and they enjoy the dignity and freedom of being sons and daughters of God, who dwells within their hearts. This people is governed by the Christ's new commandment: to love each other as Christ loves them. By living this commandment, the People of God bring the hope of salvation to the world until the Kingdom of God is fully established and perfected at the end of time.

The Church is built upon the foundation of the Apostles. The hierarchy of the Church can be traced back to the Apostles.

The Founder of the Church spoke of an intimate communion between himself and his people: "He who eats my flesh and drinks my blood abides in me, and I in him" (Jn 6: 56). The Church, through the work of the Holy Spirit, forms the Mystical Body of Christ. This phrase likens the Church to the human body. The Church is united to Christ as a body is attached to a head. Analogous to a spousal relationship, the people of God are joined to Christ as a bride to her spouse.

The human soul is that which animates the human body; indeed, it is what makes it a living body and not a corpse. In a similar way, the Holy Spirit gives life to the Mystical Body of Christ, the Church. Thus the Holy Spirit, as the soul of the Church, is its source of unity and life.

The Church reflects both a human and divine reality. As Christ's Spouse, she enjoys a divine component in her teaching and sanctifying power. Further expressions of her divine aspect are the Church's charism of infallibility and her durability until the end of time. Nothing will prevail over the divinely instituted Church. At the same time, her members are in constant need of purification in order to achieve holiness.

The Nicene Creed includes four marks that correspond to the Catholic Church founded by Christ. Throughout the course of history, these four marks have always served as the litmus test for the authenticity of the one, true Church.

THE CHURCH IS ONE

The Church acknowledges one God in Whom she professes one Faith. All Catholics adhere to the same teachings regarding the creed, sacraments, and morals. Lastly, they all recognize the authority of the pope as Supreme Pastor of the universal Church.

THE CHURCH IS HOLY

The Founder is holy, the means to salvation is holy, and the aim of the Church's teaching and sacraments is the holiness of its members. Those who live by the Church's teachings in their entirety become holy. Heroic sanctity even to the point of martyrdom has marked the life of some of the faithful throughout the centuries.

THE CHURCH IS CATHOLIC

The word "catholic" means "universal." The universality of the Church includes all ages, all races and nationalities, and every time period. Moreover, all the good traits of every culture are reflected in the teachings of the Catholic Church.

THE CHURCH IS APOSTOLIC

The Church is built upon the foundation of the Apostles. The hierarchy of the Church can be traced back to the Apostles. For this reason, the bishops are known as the successors of the Apostles, and the teaching of the Church finds its source in the very teachings of the Twelve Apostles governed by St. Peter.

PART IV

The Apostles

The word "apostle" comes from the Greek *apostolos,* a form of *apostellein,* meaning "to send away." Thus, an apostle is literally "one who is sent." The designation traditionally refers to the twelve men chosen by Jesus during the course of his public ministry to be his closest followers. They were the pillars of his Church and were to be sent to preach the Good News to all the nations. Matthias, the Apostle chosen after the Resurrection to replace Judas Iscariot, as well as Sts. Paul of Tarsus and Barnabas, also enjoyed the status of Apostles, even though they did not hold that title during Christ's public ministry.

THE CALL OF THE TWELVE

The Twelve Apostles included fishermen, a tax collector, and friends and relatives of Jesus. Upon hearing Christ's call, these men left their former lives and dedicated themselves to following him. Matthew's Gospel relates the story of the call of the first four Apostles:

> As he [Jesus] walked by the Sea of Galilee, he saw two brothers, Simon who is called Peter and Andrew his brother, casting a net into the sea; for they were fishermen. And he said to them, "Follow me, and I will make you fishers of men." Immediately they left their nets and followed him. And going on from there he saw two other brothers, James the son of Zebedee and John his brother, in the boat with Zebedee their father, mending their nets, and he called them. Immediately they left the boat and their father, and followed him. (Mt 4:18-22)

St. Luke's Gospel relates that Jesus selected the Twelve from among his disciples after a whole night of prayer during his public ministry:

> In these days he [Jesus] went out into the hills to pray; and all night he continued in prayer to God. And when it was day, he called his disciples, and chose from them twelve, whom he named apostles; Simon, whom he named Peter, and Andrew his brother, and James and John, and Philip, and Bartholomew, and Matthew, and Thomas, and James the son of Alphaeus, and Simon who was called the Zealot, and Judas the son of James, and Judas Iscariot, who became a traitor. (Lk 6:12-16)

Mark 3:13-19 and Matthew 10:1-4 also contain similar passages. It is worth noting that all three accounts begin by naming St. Peter as the first Apostle, and they end by identifying Judas Iscariot as the traitor. The selection of the Twelve Apostles coincides with the twelve tribes of Israel, over which they would sit in judgment (cf. Mt 19:28; Lk 22:30).

Besides being the first ones sent directly by Christ to all the world, the Apostles were characterized by another singular quality. They were the first witnesses of Christ's life, message, and Resurrection. Before Pentecost, the Apostles wished to restore their number to twelve, because Judas Iscariot had committed suicide. In the book of Acts, St. Peter says:

> So one of the men who have accompanied us during all the time that the Lord Jesus went in and out among us, beginning from the baptism of John until the day when he was taken up from us—*one of these men must become with us a witness to his resurrection.* (Acts 1:21-22) [emphasis added]

"Follow me, and I will make you fishers of men." (Mt 4:19)

The mission of the Apostles therefore consisted in introducing to the world Jesus' message of salvation through their teaching and witness of Christ's love. It was through the profound influence of the Holy Spirit that the Apostles could build and extend Christ's Church throughout the world.

THE APOSTOLIC TRADITION AND THE OFFICE OF BISHOP

The title "Apostle" is preeminent among all others because the Apostles, with St. Peter as their head, received teachings and instructions directly from Christ. They were personally chosen by Christ during his earthly life and empowered by the Holy Spirit to launch the first evangelization with faith and courage.

> "In order that the full and living Gospel might always be preserved in the Church the apostles left bishops as their successors. They gave them 'their own position of teaching authority'" (DV 7 § 2; St. Irenaeus, *Adv. haeres.* 3, 3, 1: PG 7, 848; Harvey, 2, 9). Indeed, "the apostolic preaching, which is expressed in a special way in the inspired books, was to be preserved in a continuous line of succession until the end of time" (DV 8 § 1). (CCC 77)

The Apostles continued Christ's ministry of preaching, healing, and exorcising demons. After his Resurrection, Jesus commanded the Apostles to spread the Gospel to every corner of the world (cf. Mt 28:16-20). They had received instruction with respect to the meaning of the Scriptures directly from Jesus and were the ultimate authority on the meaning of Christ's message. Upon the completion of their own earthly journeys, they passed on their priestly powers and mission to their successors through the office of bishop. A bishop is a successor of the Apostles who has received the fullness of Christ's priesthood. The Church has successfully transmitted the Apostolic Tradition down through the line of bishops, and she will continue to do so until Christ returns.

The killing of St. Stephen, the first Christian martyr, marked the beginning of a severe persecution of the early Church in Jerusalem.

ST. STEPHEN: THE FIRST MARTYR FOR CHRIST

Now when they [certain Jews in Jerusalem] heard these things they were enraged, and they ground their teeth against him. But he [St. Stephen], full of the Holy Spirit, gazed into heaven and saw the glory of God, and Jesus standing at the right hand of God; and he said, "Behold, I see the heavens opened, and the Son of man standing at the right hand of God." But they cried out with a loud voice and stopped their ears and rushed together upon him. Then they cast him out of the city and stoned him; and the witnesses laid down their garments at the feet of a young man named Saul. And as they were stoning Stephen, he prayed, "Lord Jesus, receive my spirit." And he knelt down and cried with a loud voice, "Lord, do not hold this sin against them." And when he had said this, he fell asleep. And Saul was consenting to his death.

And on that day a great persecution arose against the church in Jerusalem; and they were all scattered throughout the region of Judea and Samaria, except the apostles. Devout men buried Stephen, and made great lamentation over him. But Saul laid waste the church, and entering house after house, he dragged off men and women and committed them to prison. (Acts 7:54-8:3)

The early Church grew rapidly, and it soon became clear that certain organizational steps had to be taken in order to better care for the material needs of its members. The Twelve were specifically called to attend to the ministry of the Word, so they asked the community to choose seven holy men from among them to attend to its material needs (cf. Acts 6:2-4). St. Stephen and six others were chosen by the people, blessed, and commissioned by the Apostles. These seven men were called deacons, or ministers of the Church's pastoral mission.

As recorded in the *Acts of the Apostles*, St. Stephen began then to work among the people, evangelizing and working "great wonders and signs" (Acts 6:8). Soon, however, an angry mob seized St. Stephen, dragged him before the Sanhedrin, and accused him of "speak[ing] words

THE SANHEDRIN

The Sanhedrin was the highest judicial court and the primary legislative body of the Jews during the Roman occupation. The word Sanhedrin comes from the Greek word *sunedrion* meaning council. It was made up of seventy-one members, one of whom was president and governed over the council. The Sanhedrin was made up of chief priests, scribes, and elders. The members would sit in a semicircle and preside over all religious matters as well as any civil matters that did not fall under Roman jurisdiction.

They traced their origins to the council of seventy elders that God instructed Moses to institute in order to "bear the burden of the people" with him (cf. Nm 11:17).

In order to be a member of the Sanhedrin, a person was required to receive *semicha*, which was a type of laying on of hands that effected the transmission of rabbinic authority in the Law. According to Jewish tradition, *semicha* had been passed on in unbroken succession since the time of Moses.

The Sanhedrin was entrusted with the authority to judge the Jewish kings and high priests, as well as to set the boundaries of the temple. They also reserved the right to preside over cases of blasphemy, a charge punishable by death. Blasphemy was the charge leveled against Jesus Christ as well as St. Stephen the martyr.

against this holy place and the law" (Acts 6:13). St. Stephen responded to the accusations with a long discourse recounting the history of Israel and God's continuous mercy despite generations of ingratitude. The people and members of the Sanhedrin were enraged, and "they cast him out of the city and stoned him" (Acts 7:58). With his last words, he petitioned the Lord to show mercy to his executioners.

The execution of St. Stephen, the first Christian martyr, marked the beginning of a severe persecution of the early Church in Jerusalem causing many of its members to flee throughout Judea and Samaria. Others remained and faced the constant threat of imprisonment or death. St. Stephen, who loved Christ even unto death and who forgave his attackers, provided an example for all Christians during that perilous time. It is an example that has endured throughout history and has no less relevance today. As the Catechism says:

> *Martyrdom* is the supreme witness given to the truth of the faith: it means bearing witnesses even unto death. The martyr bears witnesses to Christ who died and rose, to whom he is united by charity. He bears witness to the truth of the faith and of Christian doctrine. He endures death through an act of fortitude. "Let me become the food of the beasts, through whom it will be given me to reach God" (St. Ignatius of Antioch, *Ad Rom.* 4, 1: SCh 10, 110). (CCC 2473)

St. Stephen's example quickly seized the imagination of the early Church as a most admirable way to imitate Christ. St. Stephen's feast day is celebrated on December 26, the day after Christmas, highlighting how highly the Church regards St. Stephen's heroic witness.

ST. PAUL

The account of the stoning of St. Stephen includes a few lines about a young man named Saul who consented to the execution and at whose feet the executioners laid down their cloaks. Soon after St. Stephen's death, Saul "laid waste the church, and entering house after house, he dragged off men and women and committed them to prison" (Acts 8:3).

Saul was a pious Jew, well educated in the Law under the tutelage of a Pharisee and renowned doctor of the Law by the name of Gamaliel. Saul firmly believed, as a righteous and devout Jew, that the Law was the sacred covenant between God and his people and that the early Church posed an acute threat to that covenant. The idea that Jesus Christ was the messiah professed by the early Church deviated from what was so long expected in Jewish tradition. Therefore, Saul would certainly see the early Church as dangerous to the integrity of the Jewish faith. He dutifully set out to persecute this Way.

THE CONVERSION OF ST. PAUL

After threatening the early Church throughout Jerusalem, Saul set out on a journey to Damascus to continue suppressing the Church. The Acts of the Apostles tells in detail what happened to Saul during his journey:

> Now as he journeyed he approached Damascus, and suddenly a light from heaven flashed about him. And he fell to the ground and heard a voice saying to him, "Saul, Saul, why do you persecute me?" And he said, "Who are you, Lord?" And he said, "I am Jesus, whom you are persecuting; but rise and enter the city, and you will be told what you are to do." The men who were traveling with him stood speechless, hearing the voice but seeing no one. Saul arose from the ground; and when his eyes were opened, he could see nothing; so they led him by the hand and brought him into Damascus. And for three days he was without sight, and neither ate nor drank. (Acts 9:3-9)

St. Paul's conversion, one of the Church's great ironies, shows how Christ even calls sinners to lead his Church.

As he waited in Damascus, blind and troubled by the event that had befallen him, Saul was visited by a disciple of Christ named Ananias, who, through a vision, was instructed by the Lord to seek out Saul and restore his sight. The Lord told Ananias that this man, who had done great evils to the early Church, "is a chosen instrument of mine to carry my name before the Gentiles and kings and the sons of Israel" (Acts 9:15). Ananias listened to the Lord, sought out Saul, and laid his hands on him and spoke: "Brother Saul, the Lord Jesus who appeared to you on the road by which you came, has sent me that you may regain your sight and be filled with the Holy Spirit" (Acts 9:17). Immediately Saul miraculously recovered his sight and was baptized. Filled with the Holy Spirit, "in the synagogues immediately he proclaimed Jesus, saying, 'He is the Son of God'" (Acts 9:20). St. Paul's conversion, one of the Church's great ironies, shows how Christ even calls sinners to lead his Church. St. Paul (his Roman name, as he was known soon after his conversion) became one of Christianity's greatest evangelizers, traveling and spreading the Gospel throughout the Roman world. The Feast of the Converstion of St. Paul is commemorated January 25.

AN INTERLUDE: THE CONVERSION OF CORNELIUS AND THE COMMENCEMENT OF THE MISSION TO THE GENTILES

The early Jewish Christians, though persecuted by the Jewish community, still considered Christianity a part of the Jewish tradition. They still followed Jewish laws and customs, though they had begun to incorporate many of Christ's teachings into their religious worship and practice. Acceptance of Christ as the awaited messiah did not, in their minds, sever them from their Jewish heritage. One particular Jewish law created a major problem in the formation of the early Church.

Jewish Law forbade Jews "to associate with or to visit [Gentiles]" (Acts 10:28). However, the Apostles remembered how Christ reached out to all people during his life. They understood that Christ's message and salvation are universal. How, if bound by Jewish laws, were the members of the early Church to spread the Word of God to non-Jews? How could a Gentile be baptized into a Church whose traditional law forbids any interaction with people foreign to that tradition?

The Acts of the Apostles relates the story of the Roman centurion Cornelius, a "devout and God-fearing" Gentile in Caesarea. An angel of God came to him in a vision and told him to send for Simon Peter in Joppa. St. Peter at this time also had a vision:

> he saw the heaven opened, and something descending, like a great sheet, let down by four corners upon the earth. In it were all kinds of animals and reptiles and birds of the air. And there came a voice to him, "Rise, Peter; kill and eat." But Peter said, "No, Lord; for I have never eaten anything that is common or unclean." And the voice came to him again a second time, "What God has cleansed, you must not call common." This happened three times, and the thing was taken up at once to heaven. (Acts 10:11-16)

As the vision faded, the men sent by Cornelius arrived to where St. Peter was staying. The meaning of the vision was clear to St. Peter: he must open the Church to the Gentiles, who were, by Jewish standards, considered unclean. He accepted the emissaries, and the next day traveled with them to Caesarea to visit Cornelius.

Upon meeting St. Peter, Cornelius explained to him that he had been told in a vision to send for him, and he told St. Peter that he would listen to all that the Lord had commanded him. Guided by the Holy Spirit, St. Peter took up the task of bringing the Gentiles into the Church. He said to Cornelius:

> Truly I perceive that God shows no partiality, but in every nation any one who fears him and does what is right is acceptable to him. You know the word which he sent to Israel, preaching good news of peace by Jesus Christ (he is Lord of all).... He commanded us to preach to the people, and to testify that he is the one ordained by God to be judge of the living and the dead. To him all the prophets bear witness that every one who believes in him receives forgiveness of sins through his name. (Acts 10:34-36, 42-43)

Then St. Peter and the Jewish Christians with him witnessed the outpouring of the Holy Spirit upon Cornelius and those Gentiles with him. They were amazed to see the Gentiles receive the Holy Spirit as they had, and St. Peter agreed to have them baptized. Recognizing the severe implications of the event, St. Peter went to Jerusalem to explain to the Jewish Christians this recent episode. At first, they were outraged and objected to such dealings with the Gentiles. However, when they had heard the full story, including the descent of the Holy Spirit upon the Gentiles, "they were silenced. And they glorified God, saying, 'Then to the Gentiles also God has granted repentance unto life'" (Acts 11:18). Through the power and guidance of the Holy Spirit, the Church was now ready to include the entire world in her mission.

ST. PAUL, "APOSTLE OF THE GENTILES"

Unlike most of the other Apostles, St. Paul was well educated in the Jewish Law, and enjoyed an intelligent command of Sacred Scripture. His unique gifts and background were well suited to God's plan for his role as the "Apostle of the Gentiles."

St. Paul was a brilliant writer and theologian. Scripture contains thirteen of his epistles (Romans, 1 and 2 Corinthians, Galatians, Philippians, Colossians, 1 and 2 Thessalonians, 1 and 2 Timothy, Titus, Ephesians, and Philemon). In his writings, St. Paul refers to his missionary work, mostly in the cities of Asia Minor, and lays out the first written and highly developed theology of the Church. Most of his letters are believed to have been written in the 50s, prior to the writing of the earliest Gospel. They are thus the oldest writings in the New Testament.

St. Paul's profound writings would become central in the development of the Church's teaching up to this very day as he formed a theology out of the Gospel message. St. Paul particularly delved into the doctrines of the Cross, the Mystical Body of Christ, the power of grace, and the value of charity. The letters to the Romans and 1 and 2 Corinthians are central texts that especially reveal St. Paul's theological thought. His writings serve not only as sound theological sources, but also as invaluable historical references to the early Church. Reading his epistles, one cannot help but marvel at St. Paul's profound insights into Christ's Gospel and his indomitable determination to spread that Gospel to others.

THE TRAVELS OF ST. PAUL

St. Paul's tireless and intrepid missionary work spread the Christian Faith far beyond the borders of Palestine and across most of the Roman Empire, founding some of the earliest and most prominent early Christian communities along the way. By some estimates, St. Paul's travels totaled well over 10,000 miles and brought him to Jerusalem, to every corner of Asia Minor, into Arabia, across Macedonia and Greece, to Eastern Europe, Rome, and many scholars believe he may have traveled as far as Spain.

Along the way, he found many eager disciples, but he also found many enemies among both the Jews and Gentiles. He endured many dangers and sufferings along the course of his travels. He describes some of his experiences in 2 Corinthians 11:24-25: "Five times I have received at the hands of the Jews the forty lashes less one. Three times I have been beaten with rods: once I was stoned. Three times I have been shipwrecked; a night and a day I have been adrift at sea." St. Paul was driven out of many cities by mobs. He narrowly escaped death several times, as when he sneaked out of Damascus in a basket to avoid the guards at the gate (cf. Acts 9:23-25). Other times, he did not escape, as in Lystra where a mob caught him, stoned him until they thought he was dead and dragged him out of the city (cf. Acts 14:19).

St. Paul was fearless in his apostolate despite his physical shortcomings. There are several accounts of what St. Paul looked like. Even in his own words, he writes that his "bodily presence is weak" (2 Cor 10:10). Other early Christian accounts coincide in saying that he was short, broad-shouldered, bow-legged, and balding. He also had big eyes, a rather long nose, a thick, grayish beard and closely-knit eyebrows.

St. Paul also spent a good deal of time in prison. He was arrested in Philippi, and again later in Jerusalem, after which he spent a two-year stint in Caesarea, and two more years on house arrest in Rome. He was finally martyred in Rome around the year A.D. 64 by beheading. Tradition holds that when he was beheaded, his head bounced three times, and each time it hit the ground a fountain miraculously sprang up.

ST. PAUL'S FIRST JOURNEY, ca. A.D. 46-48

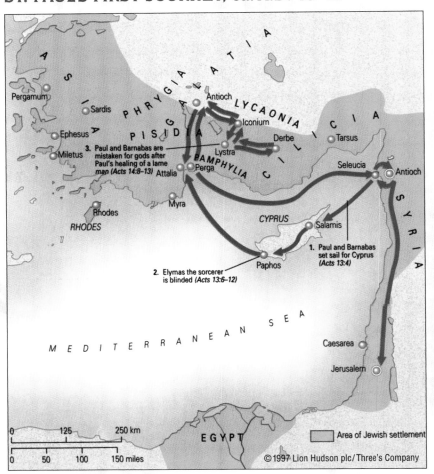

ST. PAUL'S SECOND JOURNEY, ca. A.D. 49-52

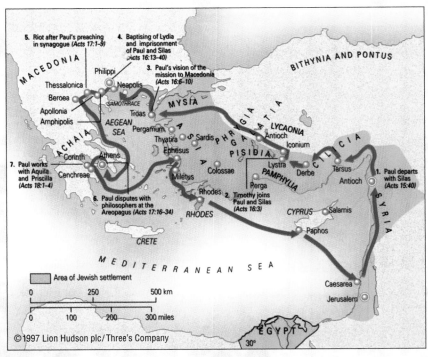

ST. PAUL'S THIRD JOURNEY, ca. A.D. 53-57

In Ephesus, St. Paul performed miracle after miracle, and conversions were many. The new converts brought their books of magic and burned them in public. (Acts 19:1-20)

ST. PAUL'S VOYAGE TO ROME, ca. A.D. 61-62

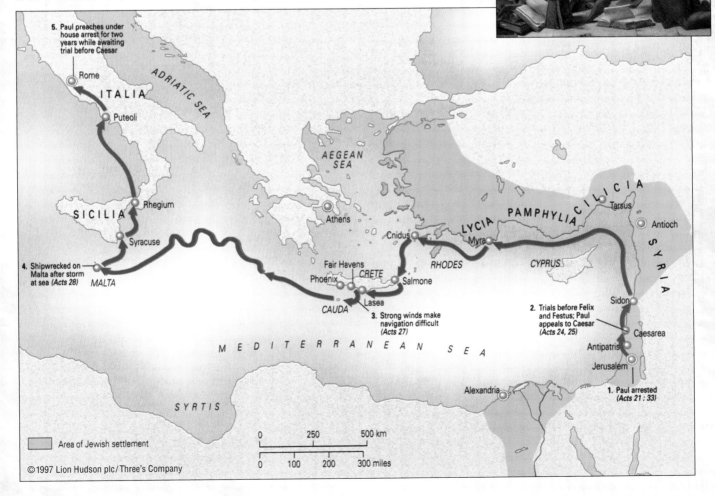

THE COUNCIL OF JERUSALEM (A.D. 49/50)

St. Peter's experience with Cornelius unfortunately did not completely resolve all the issues involved in extending the apostolic mission to the Gentiles. Questions remained whether the Gentiles who converted to Christianity also had to observe the Mosaic Law, including dietary laws and the law requiring circumcision. Jewish Christians understood that Christ was the fulfillment of the Jewish law and therefore wanted to recognize both traditions.

St. Paul had established Christian communities in Asia Minor on the premise that faith in Jesus Christ implied freedom from the Jewish Law. In his epistle to the Galatians, St. Paul defended the New Law of grace against other early Christians who advocated the necessity of observing the Old Law. St. Paul knew that the authority of the Church lay in Jerusalem, and so St. Paul and his pupil Barnabas journeyed back to the holy city to reconcile the matter with the other Apostles and Church leaders.

In Jerusalem, some Pharisees who had converted argued that Gentiles must observe the Mosaic Law. There was much debate, and finally St. Peter addressed the council:

> You know that in the early days God made choice among you, that by my mouth the Gentiles should hear the word of the gospel and believe. And God who knows the heart bore witness to them, giving them the Holy Spirit just as he did to us; and he made no distinction between us and them, but cleansed their hearts by faith. Now therefore why do you make trial of God by putting a yoke upon the neck of the disciples which neither our fathers nor we have been able to bear? But we believe that we shall be saved through the grace of the Lord Jesus, just as they will. (Acts 15: 7-11)

St. Peter, speaking with his authority as head of the Church—supported by St. James, the leader of the Church in Jerusalem—made the definitive statement on this issue. The Gentiles were to adhere to the following guidelines: to avoid eating the meat and blood of animals sacrificed to idols or from animals that had been strangled, and to refrain from unlawful marriage (cf. Acts 15: 29). The dietary laws, circumcision, and other aspects of the Law would not be imposed upon the Gentiles.

The Council of Jerusalem, the first council among many more in the Church's long history, settled the question between the Jewish Christians and the Gentile converts regarding the observance of the Law. Councils would become an important means in understanding the position of the Church.

A council is an authorized gathering of bishops, guided by the Holy Spirit, to discuss ecclesiastical matters with the aim of passing decrees on the themes under discussion. In Jerusalem, St. Paul sought and won permission to preach Jesus Christ crucified and resurrected without forcing circumcision and the formal observance of the Law on the new Gentile converts. St. Paul's teachings on the New Law and Faith, coupled with the conclusions of the Council of Jerusalem, further distanced the early Church from its Jewish foundations.

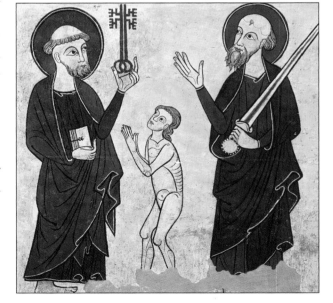

At the first Council of Jerusalem, St. Peter made the definitive statement on the issue of whether Gentiles must observe Mosaic Laws.

The martyrdom of St. Peter

MISSIONARY ACTIVITIES OF THE APOSTLES

The Apostles were witnesses to the Resurrection of Jesus Christ and sent by him to preach the Gospel to all the world. These Jewish men, most of them uneducated — St. Paul being the notable exception — soon came to be regarded by the Roman authorities as a menace to the state.

According to tradition, all the Apostles except St. John, who was miraculously spared, died as martyrs for the Faith. Around the year 64, **St. Peter** was crucified in Rome, upside down at his request, saying that he was not worthy to die right side up as Jesus did. The details of St. Peter's death in Rome have long been attributed to the "*Quo vadis?*" tradition. During persecutions, all groups seek to protect their leadership. As St. Peter was leaving Rome during Nero's persecution in A.D. 64, he is said to have met Christ along the road, asking Him: "*Domine quo vadis?*" ("Where are you going, Lord?") Christ replied, "I am coming to be crucified again." By this St. Peter understood that he should return to the city and suffer martyrdom.

St. Paul also spent his last days in Rome. After working for many years in Palestine and Asia Minor, St. Paul was arrested in Jerusalem and eventually sent to the imperial city for trial. It is unclear whether his dream of evangelizing Spain was ever realized. It is believed that St. Paul, like St. Peter, died in Rome between the years A.D. 62-65. Crucifixion, the cruelest form of execution, was reserved only for non-citizens and criminals; St. Paul, who was a Roman citizen, was beheaded outside the walls of Rome. Sts. Peter and Paul, the two Apostolic cornerstones of the Church — the first pope and the Church's greatest missionary — share June 29 as their feast day.

St. Andrew, the brother of St. Peter, is mentioned twice in the Gospels (cf. Mt 4:18-20; Jn 1:35-42), and the bishop and Church historian Eusebius (A.D. 260-340) recorded that Andrew's missionary activities took him to Scythia (modern day Ukraine and Russia). His last journeys took him through Byzantium and Greece to Patros, where the governor of Patros crucified Andrew on an X-shaped cross. According to tradition, his last words were, "Accept me, O Christ Jesus, whom I saw, whom I love, and in whom I am; accept my spirit in peace in your eternal realm." His feast is celebrated November 30, and he is the patron of Scotland, Greece, and Russia.

Sts. James and **John**, the sons of Zebedee, were, like Sts. Peter and Andrew, simple fishermen. Jesus exhorted them to place the highest impor-

The martyrdom of St. Andrew

St. James "the Greater"

tance in serving others, as they both sought to rank first in his kingdom (cf. Mt 20:20-28; Mk 10:35-45). St. James "the Greater," along with Sts. Peter and John, formed the inner circle among the Twelve, and they witnessed the raising of the daughter of Jairus (cf. Mk 5:35-43; Lk 8:41-56), the Transfiguration (cf. Mt 17:1-13; Mk 9:2-13; Lk 9:28-36), and the agony in the garden of Gethsemane (cf. Mt 26:36-46; Mk 14:32-42). Herod Agrippa had St. James beheaded in A.D. 44, and he thereby became the first of the Twelve to give his life for the Master (cf. Acts 12:2). St. James' feast day is celebrated on July 25.

St. John, according to tradition, authored the fourth Gospel, the Book of Revelation, and three of the Catholic Epistles. He is mentioned numerous times in the New Testament: willing to drink with Christ and his brother St. James the cup of suffering (cf. Mt 20:20-28), imprisoned with St. Peter and summoned before the Sanhedrin (cf. Acts 3:1, 11, and 4:1-21), and going with St. Peter to Samaria (cf. 8:14-25). St. John appears numerous times in the fourth Gospel under the title of the "Beloved Disciple," which tradition supports (cf. Jn 1:35-40, 13:23, 19:26, 20:2-8, and 21:7). During the reign of the Roman Emperor Domitian, St. John was exiled to the island of Patmos off the Turkish coast, where he wrote the book of Revelation. A Latin legend held that Domitian attempted to kill St. John by placing him in a cauldron of boiling oil *ante portam Latinam* ("before the Latin Gate") leading out of Rome to the Roman province of Latium. St. John walked away unharmed. His feast day is celebrated on December 27.

St. Bartholomew is mentioned only in the Synoptic Gospels (cf. Mk 3:18, Lk 6:14, and Mt 10:3) and in Acts 1:13. Some have suggested that Bartholomew may have been Nathanael, the one whom St. Philip brought to Jesus (cf. Jn 1:43-51). The name "Bartholomew" means simply "son of Tomai," and it is quite possible that this Apostle had another, personal name. St. Bartholomew made the journey to preach the Gospel in and around

The martrydom of St. Bartholomew

Persia—an arduous expedition from Palestine in the first century A.D. According to tradition, St. Bartholomew was martyred in Armenia where he was flayed alive. His feast day is on August 24.

According to ancient tradition, **St. Matthew**, one of the Twelve, is also the author of the Gospel with the same name. According to the early Church historian Eusebius, St. Matthew's apostolic mission was directed to the Jews. His Gospel is the only one written in Aramaic, and tradition holds that it was written thus in order to accommodate the Jewish people. It is interesting to note that he corroborates many details of Christ's life and words with Old Testament quotations. Before Christ called him to be his Apostle, St. Matthew was a tax collector who, according to the Gospels of Sts. Mark and Luke, went by the name of Levi. Jesus told St. Matthew to follow him, and then sat and ate with St. Matthew and other tax collectors and sinners that St. Matthew had invited. Some Pharisees criticized Jesus for his association such people, and Christ responded, "Those who are well have no need of a physician, but those who are sick. Go and learn what this means, 'I desire

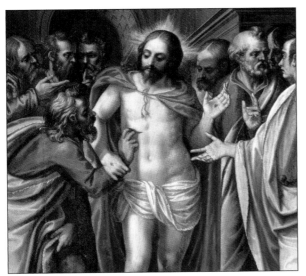

St. Thomas is also known as "Doubting Thomas."

mercy, and not sacrifice.' For I came not to call the righteous, but sinners" (Mt 9:12-13). The same story appears in Sts. Mark and Luke. St. Matthew's name, *Mattai*, means "gift of God" in Aramaic. The feast day for St. Matthew is celebrated on September 21.

St. Thomas, also known as "Doubting Thomas," is listed as one of the Twelve in all four of the Gospels. He also appears in three prominent places in St. John's Gospel. A doubtful but zealous man, St. Thomas urged the other disciples to follow Jesus and die with him upon hearing that he was going to visit the dead Lazarus (cf. Jn 11:16). An eager but apprehensive St. Thomas asked Jesus how the disciples should know the way to the Father's kingdom, to which Jesus replied, "I am the way, and the truth, and the life; no one comes to the Father, but by me" (Jn 14:6); and, finally, a doubtful St. Thomas appears in the account of Christ's Resurrection appearances to the disciples in the locked room (cf. Jn 20:19-28). Sources such as Eusebius (cf. *Church History* 3.1) claim that St. Thomas evangelized the Parthians in present day Iran and Turkmenistan, while others, derived from the apocryphal, Gnostic book, *Acts of Thomas*, suggest that he established the Church in India and was martyred there. The Malabar Christians of India claim St. Thomas as their evangelizer. When the Portuguese explorers arrived in India in the fifteenth century they found, to their amazement, a very old Christian community, traditionally tracing its founding back to St. Thomas. His feast day is on July 3.

Very little is known about **St. James**, the son of Alphaeus, often referred to as "James the Less" in order to distinguish him from St. James, the son of Zebedee. After Pentecost, St. James became the head of the Church in Jerusalem and presided over the Council of Jerusalem. He shares his feast day with St. Philip on May 3. **St. Philip** is listed in the Synoptic Gospels and in the Acts of the Apostles, but only the Gospel of St. John provides any details. Christ called St. Philip, who in turn brought Nathanael to Christ (cf. Jn 1:43-51). St. Philip was present at the miracle of the multiplication of the bread and fish (cf. Jn 6:5-7), and he presented a group of Greeks to Jesus in John 12:20-26. Finally, St. Philip also asked Jesus to show the Father to the Twelve (cf. Jn 14:8-11).

St. Judas, brother of "James the Less," is listed as an Apostle in Lk 6:16 and Acts 1:13; he is referred to as "Judas (not Iscariot)" in Jn 14:22. St. Judas is also referred to as Thaddeus in Mk 3:18 and Mt 10:3, and it is believed that this was meant to further distinguish him from Judas Iscariot. He is sometimes called Judas Thaddeus, and in English speaking countries, St. Judas is typically known by the name of Jude. St. Judas is the patron of lost causes, and he authored the Epistle of St. Jude. St. Simon the Cananean, also known as "the Less" and "the Zealot," shares a feast day with St. Judas on October 28. An apocryphal source, *The Passion of Simon and Jude*, describes the martyrdom of both of these men in Persia.

St. Judas Thaddeus

MAGICIANS AND IMPOSTER APOSTLES

The Apostles left quite an impression wherever they went as they traversed the countryside preaching, baptizing, and performing miracles. They healed the sick and crippled, escaped miraculously from jails, and on one occasion, they even raised a woman from the dead.

All this especially caught the attention of local magicians, sorcerers, and healers who envied what they thought was the Apostles' "magical powers."

The book of Acts recounts that in Samaria, there was a man named Simon Magus, who was a local magician who had been using sorcery to amaze the people of Samaria into believing he had great powers. When the Apostles Sts. Peter and John came to town, Simon saw that people received the power of the Holy Spirit when the Apostles laid their hands on them. Simon wanted a share in this "magic" and offered them silver so that he too might have the power to impart the Holy Spirit magic. Outraged, St. Peter rebuked him saying, "Your silver perish with you, because you thought you could obtain the gift of God with money!" (Acts 8: 20). Upon hearing this, Simon repented and asked them to pray for him.

On another occasion, when St. Paul paid a visit to the proconsul of the island of Paphos, the court magician, a sorcerer named Bar-Jesus, or El'ymas, confronted him. El'ymas withstood the Apostles and tried to turn the proconsul away from the Faith. St. Paul responded by calling him a "son of the devil" and the "enemy of all righteousness" (Acts 13: 10) then announced that by the power of God the magician would be struck blind. Sure enough, Bar-Jesus was blinded and stumbled off to find someone to help him. When the proconsul saw this, he believed.

Later, in Ephesus, some imposters were going around trying to exorcise evil spirits by using Jesus' name. Seven sons of the Jewish high priest Sceva were going around doing this until on one occasion an evil spirit lashed out at them saying, "Jesus I know and Paul I know; but who are you?"(Acts 19: 15). Suddenly, the man in whom the evil spirit resided attacked them and overwhelmed them. The seven sons of Sceva were seen running out of the house naked and wounded. The whole town heard about this and believed.

Even in modern times, the New Age cult relies heavily on ascribing supernatural powers to material objects.

Judas Iscariot betrayed Christ to the Jewish authorities as recorded in Mk 14: 10-11 and 14: 43-44. His motive is unclear; financial gain may have played a role, as it did when Judas criticized the woman who anointed Jesus with ointment (cf. Mt 26: 6-13). Jesus spoke harshly of the man who betrayed him: "Woe to that man by whom the Son of man is betrayed! It would have been better for that man if he had not been born" (cf. Mt 26: 24). Judas' fall serves as a warning that even the graces given to Christ's Apostles—and the familiar friendship of Jesus himself—may be of no avail if one is unfaithful and does not believe.

CONCLUSION

St. John was the last of the Apostles to die, and with his death public revelation ended. Since Christ is the culmination of God's direct revelation to his people, possession of the Deposit of Faith and its interpretation corresponds to the Apostles who were the Lord's closest followers and witnesses to his life. The teachings of the Apostles initiated the body of living truths called the Tradition of the Church, which began with their preaching and instruction. During their lifetimes, the Apostles transmitted their episcopal power and authority to their first successors. The generation succeeding that of Jesus Christ's contemporaries already had a keen notion of this Tradition and of its bishops' direct link to the Apostles. From the earliest times, the successors of the Apostles have been given the duty to protect and transmit Christ's teaching as it was taught and interpreted by the first Apostles.

SUPPLEMENTARY READING

Josephus, *The Antiquities of the Jews*, 18.3.3

Now, there was about this time Jesus, a wise man, if it be lawful to call him a man, for he was a doer of wonderful works—a teacher of such men as receive truth with pleasure. He drew over to him both many of the Jews, and many of the Gentiles. He was [the] Christ; and when Pilate, at the suggestion of the principal men amongst us, had condemned him to the cross, those that loved him at the first did not forsake him, for he appeared to them alive again the third day, as the divine prophets had foretold these and ten thousand other wonderful things concerning him; and the tribe of Christians, so named from him, are not extinct at this day.

John Paul II, *Redemptoris Missio*, 24.1-2

The mission of the Church, like that of Jesus, is God's work, or, as Luke often puts it, the work of the Spirit. After the Resurrection and the Ascension of Jesus, the apostles have a powerful experience which completely transforms them: the experience of Pentecost. The coming of the Holy Spirit makes them *witnesses* and *prophets* (cf. Acts 1: 8, 2: 17-18). It fills them with a serene courage which impels them to pass on to others their experience of Jesus and the hope which motivates them. The Spirit gives them the ability to bear witness to Jesus with "boldness."

When the first evangelizers go down from Jerusalem, the Spirit becomes more of a "guide," helping them to choose both those to whom they are to go and the places to which their missionary journey is to take them. The working of the Spirit is manifested particularly in the impetus given to the mission which, in accordance with Christ's words, spreads out from Jerusalem to all of Judea and Samaria, and to the farthest ends of the world.

The Navarre Bible, *Gospels and Acts*, Acts 9: 6

The calling of Saul was exceptional as regards the manner in which God called him; but the effect it had on him was the same as what happens when God gives a specific calling to the apostolate to certain individual Christians, inviting them to follow him more closely. Paul's immediate response is a model of how those who receive these specific callings should act (all Christians, of course, have a common calling to holiness and apostolate that comes with Baptism).

Paul VI describes in this way the effects of this specific kind of vocation in a person's soul: "The apostolate is…an inner voice…It speaks prophetically and almost in a tone of victory, which eventually dispels all uncertainty, all timidity and all fear, and which facilitates—making it easy, desirable and pleasant—the response of our whole personality, when we pronounce that word which reveals the supreme secret of love: Yes, Yes Lord, tell me what I must do and I will try to do it, I will do it. Like St. Paul, thrown to the ground at the gates of Damascus: What would you have me do?"

VOCABULARY

APOSTLE

The word "apostle" comes from the Greek *apostolos*, a form of *apostellein*, meaning "to send away." An apostle is literally "one who is sent." Refers to the twelve men chosen by Jesus during the course of his public ministry to be his closest followers, as well as Sts. Matthias, Paul of Tarsus, and Barnabas, who were chosen after Jesus' Resurrection.

BISHOP

A bishop is a successor of the Apostles who has received the fullness of Christ's priesthood.

CHURCH

In the Scriptures, the Church is described as the Body of Christ and the Temple of the Holy Spirit (cf. Eph 1: 22-23). The English word "church" etymologically comes from a Greek word meaning "thing belonging to the Lord," which was applied originally to the church building. The Latin word *ecclesia* derives from another Greek word that means "assembly" or "congregation." Willed by the Father, the Church was founded by Jesus Christ and enjoys the presence and guidance of the Holy Spirit. It is through the Church that God carries out his plan of salvation for all people. The teaching authority and sanctifying power of the Church serve as a means to bring all men and women to greater union with God and with each other as well.

CHURCH HISTORY

The history of the Church is the record of the life of Jesus, the actions of men, and the guiding light of the Holy Spirit acting in the Church. This history began with the initial evangelization of the Apostles, and the narrative about Christ's kingdom on earth is forged as the Church interacts and responds to every culture and historical situation.

COUNCIL

An authorized gathering of bishops, guided in a unique way by the Holy Spirit, to discuss ecclesiastical matters with the aim of passing decrees on the themes under discussion.

DEPOSIT OF FAITH

Deposit of Faith, that is the heritage of Faith contained in Sacred Scripture and Tradition, handed on in the Church from the time of the Apostles.

MARTYRDOM

The supreme witness given to the truth of the Faith by bearing witness even unto death.

PENTECOST

Pentecost celebrates the descent of the Holy Spirit upon Mary and the Apostles fifty days after the Resurrection.

PEOPLE OF GOD

Those "born" into the Church through faith in Christ and Baptism. The term "People of God" is taken from the Old Testament in which God chose Israel to be his chosen people. Christ instituted the new and eternal covenant by which a new priestly, prophetic, and royal People of God, the Church, participates in the mission and service of Christ.

The Roman grain ship that St. Paul traveled on carried 276 men. Midships was a high mast, usually of cedar wood, and near the prow was a smaller one for hoisting a small sail. Two large oars were used to steer. On the deck was a wooden hut for the helmsman which was also used as a temple of worship containing an idol.

STUDY QUESTIONS

1. When did Jesus send the Holy Spirit to guide the Church?

2. Who is the cornerstone of the Church?

3. Who is Christ's vicar on earth?

4. What is Church history?

5. What are two basic components of the history of the Church?

6. Who were Simeon and Anna?

7. What was the "Slaughter of the Innocents"?

8. What is the inaugural event of Jesus' public ministry?

9. What was the teaching of the New Law?

10. What effects did the Holy Spirit have upon the Apostles at Pentecost?

11. What laid the groundwork for the Church?

12. What are the four marks of the Church?

13. What sets the Apostles apart from other early members of the Church?

14. What does the Greek root of the word "apostle" mean?

15. Who are the successors to the Apostles?

16. How was St. Stephen killed?

17. What was the role of the first deacons?

18. What occurred after St. Stephen's martyrdom?

19. Who was the famous Jewish teacher under whom St. Paul studied?

20. To which city was Saul going when he met Jesus Christ?

21. How was Saul physically impaired after his encounter with Jesus?

22. Who healed Saul?

23. What is the significance of Cornelius' conversion?

24. Why was it important that St. Peter received this message from God first?

25. Who was the author of the oldest texts in the New Testament and when were they written?

26. Why did Jewish Christians criticize St. Peter?

27. When and why was the Council of Jerusalem called?

28. What was the outcome of the Council of Jerusalem?

29. Why was St. Paul beheaded instead of being crucified like Sts. Peter and Andrew?

30. Which Apostle was exiled to the island of Patmos after allegedly having survived being put into a vat of boiling oil?

31. Who was St. Jude?

PRACTICAL EXERCISES

1. How was Jesus' life authentically human? How was it divine? Cite specific examples from the Gospel.

2. Why is Pentecost one of the most important feast days in the liturgical year? What does it mean that the Holy Spirit "dwells" in the Church?

3. The Gospel is an account of Jesus' calling of the Apostles. How did Jesus convince these total strangers to give up everything and go follow him after meeting him only for the first time? In small groups, write a brief skit in which you try to use Jesus' words to convince someone in today's society to come and follow him.

4. What kind of men were the Apostles? What does their social status, education, and personality demonstrate about how Jesus calls people to live a Christian life?

FROM THE CATECHISM

750 To believe that the Church is "holy" and "catholic," and that she is "one" and "apostolic" (as the Nicene Creed adds), is inseparable from belief in God, the Father, the Son, and the Holy Spirit. In the Apostles' Creed we profess "one Holy Church" (*"Credo...Ecclesiam"*), and not to believe in the Church, so as not to confuse God with his works and to attribute clearly to God's goodness *all* the gifts he has bestowed on his Church (*Roman Catechism* I, 10, 22).

761 The gathering together of the People of God began at the moment when sin destroyed the communion of men with God, and that of men among themselves. The gathering together of the Church is, as it were, God's reaction to the chaos provoked by sin. This reunification is achieved secretly in the heart of all peoples: "In every nation anyone who fears him and does what is right is acceptable" to God (Acts 10:35; cf. *LG* 9; 13; 16).

763 It was the Son's task to accomplish the Father's plan of salvation in the fullness of time. Its accomplishment was the reason for his being sent (cf. *LG* 3; *AG* 3). "The Lord Jesus inaugurated his Church by preaching the Good News, that is, the coming of the Reign of God, promised over the ages in the scriptures" (*LG* 5). To fulfill the Father's will, Christ ushered in the Kingdom of heaven on earth. The Church "is the Reign of Christ already present in mystery" (*LG* 3).

766 The Church is born primarily of Christ's total self-giving for our salvation, anticipated in the institution of the Eucharist and fulfilled on the cross. "The origin and growth of the Church are symbolized by the blood and water which flowed from the open side of the crucified Jesus" (*LG* 3; cf. Jn 19:34). "For it was from the side of Christ as he slept the sleep of death upon the cross that there came forth the 'wondrous sacrament of the whole Church'" (*SC* 5). As Eve was formed from the sleeping Adam's side, so the Church was born from the pierced heart of Christ hanging dead on the cross (cf. St. Ambrose, *In Luc.* 2, 85-89: PL 15, 1666-1668).

783 Jesus Christ is the one whom the Father anointed with the Holy Spirit and established as priest, prophet, and king. The whole People of God participates in these three offices of Christ and bears the responsibilities for mission and service that flow from them (cf. John Paul II, *RH* 1821).

889 In order to preserve the Church in the purity of the faith handed on by the apostles, Christ who is the Truth willed to confer on her a share in his own infallibility. By a "supernatural sense of faith" the People of God, under the guidance of the Church's living Magisterium, "unfailingly adheres to this faith" (*LG* 12; cf. *DV* 10).

890 The mission of the Magisterium is linked to the definitive nature of the covenant established by God with his people in Christ. It is this Magisterium's task to preserve God's people from deviations and defections and to guarantee them the objective possibility of professing the true faith without error. Thus, the pastoral duty of the Magisterium is aimed at seeing to it that the People of God abides in the truth that liberates. To fulfill this service, Christ endowed the Church's shepherds with the charism of infallibility in matters of faith and morals. The exercise of this charism takes several forms:

891 "The Roman Pontiff, head of the college of bishops, enjoys this infallibility in virtue of his office, when, as supreme pastor and teacher of all the faithful—who confirms his brethren in the faith—he proclaims by a definitive act a doctrine pertaining to faith or morals....The infallibility promised to the Church is also present in the body of bishops when, together with Peter's successor, they exercise the supreme Magisterium," above all in an Ecumenical Council (*LG* 25; cf. Vatican Council I: DS 3074). When the Church through its supreme Magisterium proposes a doctrine "for belief as being divinely revealed" (*DV* 10 § 2), and as the teaching of Christ, the definitions "must be adhered to with the obedience of faith" (*LG* 25 § 2). This infallibility extends as far as the deposit of divine Revelation itself (cf. *LG* 25).

CHAPTER 2
The
Early Christians

The early Christians, by their tremendous faith in Jesus and imitation of his life, transformed the Roman world and its values.

CHAPTER 2

The Early Christians

From the Eucharist we all receive the grace and strength for everyday life,
for living a truly Christian existence, in the joy of knowing that God loves us,
that Christ has died for us and that the Holy Spirit lives in us.

— John Paul II, Homily, Dublin, September 29, 1979

"Christians are indistinguishable from other men either by nationality, language or customs. They do not inhabit separate cities of their own, or speak a strange dialect, or follow some outlandish way of life. Their teaching is not based upon reveries inspired by the curiosity of men. Unlike some other people, they champion no purely human doctrine....

"And yet there is something extraordinary about their lives. They live in their own countries as though they were only passing through. They play their full role as citizens, but labor under all the disabilities of aliens. Any country can be their homeland, but for them their homeland, wherever it may be, is a foreign country. Like others, they marry and have children, but they do not expose them. They share their meals, but not their wives. They live in the flesh, but they are not governed by the desires of the flesh. They pass their days upon earth, but they are citizens of heaven. Obedient to the laws, they yet live on a level that transcends the law....

"To speak in general terms, we may say that the Christian is to the world what the soul is to the body....The body hates the soul and wars against it, not because of any injury the soul has done it, but because of the restriction the soul places on its pleasures. Similarly, the world hates the Christians, not because they have done it any wrong, but because they are opposed to its enjoyments.

"Christians love those who hate them just as the soul loves the body and all its members despite the body's hatred. It is by the soul, enclosed within the body, that the body is held together, and similarly, it is by the Christians, detained in the world as in a prison, that the world is held together. The soul, though immortal, has a mortal dwelling place; and Christians also live for a time amidst perishable things, while awaiting the freedom from change and decay that will be theirs in heaven. As the soul benefits from the deprivation of food and drink, so Christians flourish under persecution" (from *Epistle to Diognetus*).

The early Christians enjoyed the special circumstance of historical proximity to Jesus and the Apostles.

The preceding eloquent descriptions of what it means to live one's life as a follower of Christ might have very well been written about the Christians of the third millennium. The source of these excerpts, however, is the *Epistle to Diognetus,* a letter composed by an unknown apologist sometime in the second century. Like that of the author, the identity of the recipient, Diognetus, also remains concealed within the depths of history. Still, its words endure through the centuries for anyone who wishes to understand who the early Christian was. Both the Christian of the second century and the Christian of today should fit the description given by that ancient, unknown author.

The early Christians enjoyed the special circumstance of historical proximity to Jesus and the Apostles. Some of the harshest conditions that the followers of Christ have ever endured came at the beginning, yet these Christians persisted in their faith. They offered their suffering in union with Christ's at those first celebrations of the Mass in their homes and in the catacombs, shared material aid in times of need with neighbors and strangers alike, strove to live morally upright lives amid an often depraved society. They set about the great task of building a new civilization of love in this first period of evangelization. The lives of the early followers of Christ were assuredly far from easy. Some Christians abandoned the Faith when the challenges became overwhelming, while some others openly apostatized. However, there were many faithful Christians in the Church, fortified and guided by the Holy Spirit, who endured and provided spiritual shelter and strength for all who would believe.

Without the strengthening graces of God, these early Christians would have found their many trials insurmountable. They had been born from an ancient and holy, but often persecuted tradition, from which they made an essential departure into a world dominated by pagan cultures. In the face of a hostile world, Christianity proposed a radically new vision of human life. Its morality demanded that the believer make difficult choices both concerning his witness to Jesus Christ and on vital issues that affected daily life—marriage and family, public life, work, and relation to both one's neighbors and all the peoples of the world. Guiding them at all times were the words and life of Christ, transmitted by his Apostles.

It is worth noting that many efforts at reform throughout the history of the Church have looked back to this first period as a model for holiness, simplicity, and fraternity. The Second Vatican Council enacted various reforms to bring modern Christians closer to the spirit of the early Christians.

This chapter will explore the life of the early Christians, their beliefs, practices, traditions, and values. It will also investigate the development of the Church as an institution, especially the development of the hierarchy and the sacraments. Finally, it will chronicle the early theological developments of the Apostolic Fathers and Apologists before briefly looking at a final and often too common aspect of early Christian life, martyrdom.

PART I

Beliefs and Practices: The Spiritual Life of the Early Christians

The beliefs and practices of the early community of Christians took some time to develop—Christ did not leave his Church with a fully developed theology and disciplinary practice. Rather, these emerged through centuries of theological, philosophical, cultural, and historical development under the guidance of the Holy Spirit in and through the institution of the Church. From the Church's inception, the eternal truths present in Christ's teaching were passed on and unfolded within a living and changing body of practicing believers. As the early Christians reflected on the Gospel message and integrated it into their daily lives, the early tradition of Church teaching began to take shape and express itself especially in the liturgy.

As mentioned in the previous chapter, during the earliest years, Christians remained closely associated with the Jewish faith, the tradition from which many early Christians converted. They retained many traditional Jewish practices in the same way that Christ and the Apostles had. This changed, however, after the Council of Jerusalem and the destruction of the Temple—events that brought a huge influx of Gentiles to Christianity and altered the ethnic make-up of the Christian community.

In the first years after the Resurrection, adults who wanted to convert to the Faith were baptized freely.

BAPTISM

Go therefore and make disciples of all nations, baptizing them in the name of the Father and of the Son and of the Holy Spirit. (Mt 28:19)

Truly, truly, I say to you, unless one is born of water and the Spirit, he cannot enter the kingdom of God. (Jn 3:5)

Jesus was baptized by St. John the Baptist with a baptism of repentance (cf. Mt 3:13-17). But it was Jesus who instituted the Sacrament of Baptism in the Holy Spirit (cf. Jn 3:22; Mk 1:8), instructing his disciples to do the same (cf. Jn 4:2; Mt 28:19). By this sacrament, a believer is forgiven of original and personal sin, begins a new life in Christ and the Holy Spirit, and is incorporated into the Church, the Body of Christ (CCC 977, 1213).

In the first years after the Resurrection, adults who wanted to convert to the Faith were baptized freely. As Christianity grew, a more structured program of instruction preceding Baptism evolved. Catechumens ("the instructed," from the Greek *katēkhein*, "to instruct"), those adults seeking admission to the Church, met over a long period of time, normally two to three years, for instruction before being baptized. The lengthy process provided time for the catechumen to learn the message of the Gospels and to develop a strong foundation in the faith. Though one might imagine that there existed a high level of enthusiasm and zeal among prospective believers at a time so soon after Christ had walked the earth, one must keep in mind that these were often times of great persecution, which could easily overwhelm a believer with a burgeoning but poorly grounded faith. The catechumens waited to be baptized at the Easter Vigil on the night of Holy Saturday or on the Saturday before Pentecost.

During the Medieval period, the catechumenate fell into disuse. Adult converts normally received ten weeks of instruction from a priest and then received Baptism during various times of the liturgical year. In 1965, the Second Vatican Council reinstituted the catechumenate to bring back the beautiful custom of preparation for solemn reception into the Church that had been practiced by the early Christians. As in the earliest times, adult converts once again study and pray together for a time before being admitted to the Church at Easter.

The practice of baptizing infants became more common during the third century, and by the early Medieval period, the practice of infant Baptism was universal. There is also evidence that it may have started prior to the third century, in the time of the Apostolic Fathers. St. Justin Martyr refers to Christians who had "from childhood been made disciples" (cf. *Apologies* 1.15). In the third century document written by Hippolytus (A.D. 170-236), *Apostolic Tradition* (21), the Baptism of children is discussed. Tertullian (A.D. 160-225) disagreed with the practice of infant Baptism (though he did not deny its validity). In order to avoid the danger of anyone profaning his Baptism during his youth, Tertullian argued that the baptized ought to be old enough to understand the sacrament. Origen (A.D. 185-254) claimed that the practice of infant Baptism was clearly recommended, and supported it since original sin ought to be wiped away as soon as possible. St. Augustine, son of a pagan father and a Christian mother, in his *Confessions* gives an argument along similar lines, based very much on his own experience:

I ask you, O my God—for I would very much like to know, if it is your will—to what purpose my baptism was postponed at that time? Was it indeed for my good that I was given more free reign to sin? Or, was I not given more free reign? How is it that even now one hears it said of one person or another, "Let him alone, let him do as he pleases, for he is not yet baptized?" In the matter of bodily health, no one says, "Let him alone; let him have a few more wounds; for he is not yet cured!" How much better, then, would it have been for me to have been cured at once—and if thereafter, through the diligent care of friends and myself, my soul's restored health had been kept safe in thy keeping, who gave it in the first place! This would have been far better, in truth. But how many and great the waves of temptation which appeared to hang over me as I grew out of childhood! These were foreseen by my mother, and she preferred that the unformed clay should be risked to them rather than the clay molded after Christ's image. (St. Augustine, *Confessions* I.XI)

The beauty and value of baptizing infants is that original sin is forgiven and the child is incorporated into the Mystical Body of Christ. Baptismal character imprinted on the soul renders the infant a child of God who now shares in the priesthood of Christ called the common priesthood. Lastly, this sacrament confers upon the child a special grace through which he may grow more fully in Christ. Prior to the twentieth century, even in the industrialized nations, many babies and women died during childbirth, and many children died afterwards from diseases that had no known cure. Infant Baptism secures the great gift of forgiveness and salvation from God and commits the family to raising the child in a Christian way.

Baptism has always been administered immediately when the recipient is in danger of death. In such a case, any baptized or non-baptized person can administer the sacrament. During the persecutions there were cases of non-believers administering Baptism to converts as they made their way to the place of torture and execution. These baptisms were valid because they utilized the Trinitarian formula and intended to follow the mind of the Church. There were also cases of catechumens who were martyred before receiving the Sacrament of Baptism. From the earliest times, the Church taught that those who died for the Faith received the graces of Baptism through their martyrdom, which is called Baptism of Blood.

> The Church has always held the firm conviction that those who suffer death for the sake of the faith without having received Baptism are baptized by their death for and with Christ. This *Baptism of blood*, like the *desire for Baptism*, brings about the fruits of Baptism without being a sacrament. (CCC 1258)

Though infants were baptized, it was common for adult converts in the early days of the Church to wait until they were on their deathbeds before they received Baptism. Since Baptism remits all traces of sin, it was believed that waiting until the very last moment would allow a person to commit as many sins as he pleased and then bypass Hell and Purgatory by dying immediately after receiving the sacrament. Not only does this contradict the spirit of Christianity, but also it is very dangerous, and could possibly doom a person in the case of sudden death. It also severely limits the ability of people who could be fully immersed in God's love through the sacraments and his graces to help others and themselves. This practice continued into the fourth or fifth century, when infant Baptism was commonly established, and was taken up again for a while during the Middle Ages.

AGAPE AND THE EUCHARIST

> I received from the Lord what I also delivered to you, that the Lord Jesus on the night when he was betrayed took bread, and when he had given thanks, he broke it, and said, "This is my body which is for you. Do this in remembrance of me." In the same way also the cup, after supper, saying, "This cup is the new covenant in my blood. Do this, as often as you drink it, in remembrance of me." For as often as you eat this bread and drink the cup, you proclaim the Lord's death until he comes. (1 Cor 11: 23-26)

The *Agape* ("love" in Greek) refers to an early Christian religious meal that was at first closely related to the celebration of the Eucharist and often preceded this celebration. The close connection did not last long, however, because of the Eucharistic abuses that arose from its proximity to the *Agape*. St. Paul criticizes these abuses in his first letter to the Corinthians:

> When you meet together, it is not the Lord's supper that you eat. For in eating, each one goes ahead with his own meal, and one is hungry and another is drunk. What! Do you not have houses to eat and drink in? Or do you despise the church of God and humiliate those who have nothing? (1 Cor 11: 20-22)

In order to avoid impiety and denigration of the Eucharistic celebration, the *Agape* was soon celebrated in the evenings. Records of the *Agape*, however, are few, and the practice generally did not last long, except in some smaller and more isolated churches.

The ritual of the Mass developed gradually over time. The beginning of the ceremony included readings from the Bible, singing of the psalms and hymns, common prayers, and a collection for the poor. (Keep in mind, though, that even if the official Canon of Sacred Scripture was not set until the fourth century, many, including Tertullian, St. Irenaeus, and St. Clement of Alexandria held the four Gospels as inspired.) Finally came the Liturgy of the Eucharist, which formed the high point of the liturgical celebration. In the earliest years, fixed prayers did not exist. Rather, the celebrant gave thanks in his own words before praying the Institution Narrative and Consecration. The Consecration, which comprises the actual words of Christ, was already written down in the earliest letters of St. Paul (cf. 1 Cor 11: 23-26) in the A.D. 50s.

The Eucharist, literally meaning "thanksgiving," was, and is, the central act of Christian worship, and it consisted in consuming the Sacrament of Holy Communion, the Body and Blood of Christ. All of the early documents from this period indicate that the early Christians considered Christ truly present in the Eucharist under the appearance of bread and wine, attested by many of the Fathers of the Church, including Sts. Cyril of Jerusalem, John Chrysostom, Gregory of Nyssa, Cyril of Alexandria, Ambrose, Augustine, Justin Martyr, and John of Damascus. This corresponds to the teaching of the Church based on the New Testament accounts. For instance, St. John Chrysostom teaches, "It is not man that causes the things offered to become the Body and Blood of Christ, but he who was crucified for us, Christ himself. The priest, in the role of Christ, pronounces these words, but their power and grace are God's. This is my body, he says. This word transforms the thing offered" (*Prod. Jud.* 1: 6: PG 49, 380). Likewise St. Ambrose says, "Be convinced that this is not what nature has formed, but what the blessing has consecrated. The power of the blessing prevails over that of nature, because by the blessing nature itself is changed....Could not Christ's word, which can make from nothing what did not exist, change existing things into what they were not before? It is no less a feat to give things their original nature than to change their nature" (*De myst.* 9, 50; 52: PL 16, 405-407).

CHURCHES

For the earliest celebrations of the Mass, people gathered together in private homes and in the catacombs, especially during periods of persecution. Some of the Roman emperors permitted Christians to build churches, especially at the beginning of the second century. Renewed persecutions, however, left most of these structures destroyed. It was not until the Edict of Milan (A.D. 313), when Emperor Constantine began a building program favorable to the Christians, that Roman architectural designs like the basilica were transformed into Christian churches.

Basilica of St. Nereus, Domitilla Catacombs, Rome, Italy

THE CATACOMBS

Catacombs were an important gathering place for early Christians in certain areas. A catacomb is an underground series of tunnels, chambers, and tombs that were dug by Christians and served as burial places, shrines, and places of worship during the first few centuries after Christ. The most famous Christian catacombs are those found outside of Rome, but catacombs have also been discovered throughout Italy, France, and Northern Africa.

There are over sixty different catacombs scattered along the outskirts of Rome, and together they account for hundreds of miles of underground tunnels, and they are estimated to have held almost two million graves. The catacombs of St. Callixtus are among the most impressive. These catacombs are four stories deep, include about 12 miles of tunnels and galleries, and in them were buried 16 popes and dozens of martyrs!

The catacombs are made up of long narrow tunnels with several rows of rectangular niches on each side, called "*loculi*." Corpses would usually be wrapped in a shroud and laid in the *loculi*. Then, the *loculi* would be sealed with a marble slab or with tiles. The tombs would often be adorned with inscriptions of the person's name or a short prayer, as well as religious symbols. There were also small rooms called *cubicula* that served as family tombs, and larger rooms called crypts where the tombs of prominent figures, such as popes or martyrs, were converted into small churches.

Most of the catacombs were begun in the second century and initially were merely burial places. Christians shunned the Roman practice of cremation and preferred burial because of their belief in the resurrection of the body. This desire to be buried together showed the strong sense of community in the early Church. Although they were never actually used as hiding places during times of persecution, the catacombs did serve as places of refuge for baptisms and the celebration of the Eucharist. In the privacy of the catacombs, Christians could worship openly, and express themselves in prayer and religious art.

As the persecutions continued, martyrs were given places of honor in the catacombs. The tombs of the martyrs became popular places of prayer where Christians would ask for the martyrs' intercession. The catacombs were continually expanded and used for burial through the fifth century A.D. Eventually, they were abandoned and forgotten, only to be rediscovered in the sixteenth century. Ever since that time, they have remained popular pilgrimage sites for Christians to find inspiration and learn about the early Church.

THE EARLY GROWTH OF CHRISTIANITY

CHRISTIAN CHURCHES IN ASIA MINOR

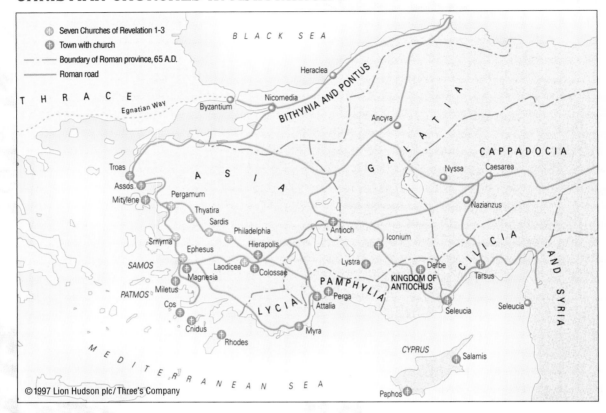

© 1997 Lion Hudson plc / Three's Company

CHRISTIAN COMMUNITIES BY A.D. 100

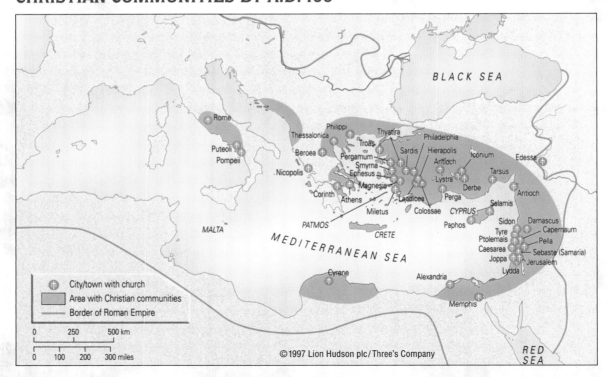

© 1997 Lion Hudson plc / Three's Company

CHRISTIAN COMMUNITIES BY A.D. 300

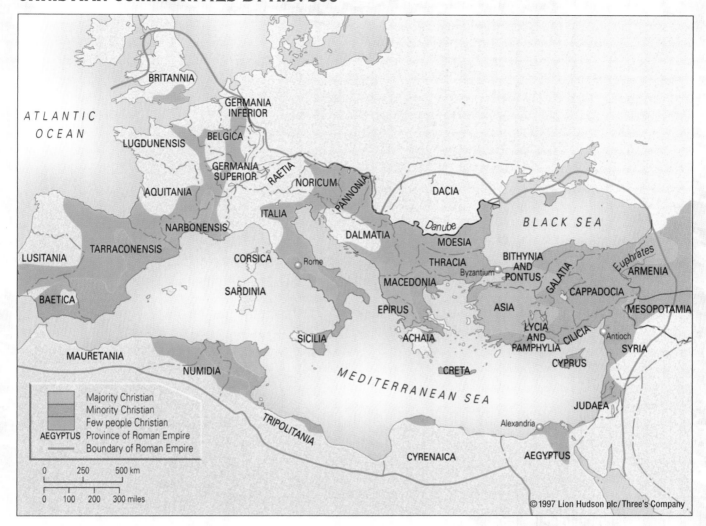

Map legend:
- Majority Christian
- Minority Christian
- Few people Christian
- AEGYPTUS Province of Roman Empire
- Boundary of Roman Empire

0   250   500 km
0 100 200 300 miles

©1997 Lion Hudson plc/Three's Company

With its large population of Hellenized Jews, Asia Minor became the first area of growth for the Church. Many Jews converted to Christianity through the works of Paul and the Apostles. St. John received his apocalyptic visions on the island of Patmos off the west coast of Asia Minor. In his "revelations," seven Asia Minor churches received messages of encouragement and condemnation (Rev 1-3).

By the end of the first century, Christianity was still confined to the Eastern Roman Empire. except for communities in Rome, Puteoli and around the Bay of Naples. Edessa was the only possible church known outside the empire.

By the end of the third century, the Christian world had changed drastically. Christianity and Judaism had gone their separate ways, and Christianity had become largely a religion of the Gentiles. Its informal center had shifted from Jerusalem to Rome. The scene was set for the epiphany of Emperor Constantine in A.D. 312 and the world-changing embrace of Christianity as the official religion of the Roman Empire.

St. Peter's Grotto, first century church in Antioch on the Orontes.

HOLY DAYS

For the early Christians, Wednesdays and Fridays were days of fasting and penance. Though Friday was chosen because it was the day that Christ suffered and accomplished his redemptive sacrifice, it is not clear why Wednesday was also reserved for fasting and penance. Some traditions hold that this was the day that Judas conspired with the chief priests to betray Jesus.

The Jewish Sabbath lasted from sundown on Friday until sundown on Saturday. Christians at first kept the Jewish Sabbath (day of rest), but Sunday quickly replaced Saturday as the holiest day of the week because it represented both the day on which Jesus rose from the dead and the day on which Pentecost occurred. Sunday was reputed to be the first day of creation and it followed that the first day of "re-creation" would be recognized as well. Celebrating the Lord's Day on Sunday also provided convenient cover for Christians during the persecutions because it was observed by pagans as their holy day as well. By the end of the first three centuries, the practice of celebrating Mass on Sundays had taken root.

Feast days also developed throughout the years. The Feast of Epiphany, for example, was celebrated in many separate places in the West before the fourth century. St. John Chrysostom introduced this feast in the East.

CHRISTIAN SYMBOLS

The cross was the most widespread and enduring of all Christian symbols, since it expresses the entirety of the Christian Faith. By the early third century, the practice of making the Sign of the Cross was deeply rooted in the Christian world; Tertullian refers to Christians as "devotees of the cross." The Sign of the Cross took various forms over the centuries, from tracing the cross over the forehead, mouth, and heart to the common sign used to today. In the Eastern Church, people touch their first three fingers together while blessing themselves to symbolize the Trinity.

Another widespread and ancient Christian symbol is the fish. Among the earliest Christians, the fish for a time may have held even greater significance than the cross. It is an ancient symbol, long predating Christianity, and it became a universal Christian symbol for Christ. It recalls the multiplication of loaves and fishes, as well as Christ's appearance to the seven disciples after the Resurrection at the end of St. John's Gospel. The principal reason for its widespread popularity was that the Greek for fish, *ichthys*, can also be an acrostic for the Greek phrase, *Iesous CHristos THeou Yios Soter*, which, as a declaration of the central tenet of the Christian Faith means, "Jesus Christ, Son of God, Savior."

Often appearing with the fish was the symbol of the anchor. Like the fish, it is an ancient symbol of pre-Christian origins, and it long symbolized safety. The early Christians adopted the anchor and developed its significance from safety to hope. It was often paired with the ship—as a ship is kept from drifting by its anchor, so is faith kept from drifting by hope. The anchor also served the role of an esoteric depiction of the cross— easily recognized by Christians, but not by non-believers.

A carving on a tombstone in the early fourth century catacomb of St. Domatilla depicts the fish symbol combined with the cross-like anchor symbol.

THE PAPACY

Pope Benedict XVI was elected the 265th "Vicar of Christ" on April 19, 2005.

As mentioned in the previous chapter, Christ made St. Peter the head of his Church (cf. Mt 16:13-23, Jn 21:15-17), the first pope, the Vicar of Christ, conferring upon him the responsibility and supreme authority of guiding the Church after Christ's departure. There are clear historical sources that indicate that the authority of the Bishop of Rome was recognized and regarded as the supreme authority in all Church matters from the very beginning. The *First Epistle* of Pope St. Clement I (A.D. 88-97) demonstrates the recognized authority of the papacy as he settled controversies that were disrupting the Church in Corinth. The *Epistle to the Romans* written by St. Ignatius of Antioch (ca. A.D. 35-ca. 107), who was appointed Bishop of Antioch by St. Peter himself, affirms the deferential obedience to the authority of the Bishop of Rome. Similarly, St. Irenaeus' writings stressed the importance of the traditional structures in the Church, such as the papacy.

Two popes during the first five centuries of Christendom were especially instrumental in the development of the papacy's ecclesiastical and jurisdictional powers. Pope St. Leo I (d. A.D. 461) explicitly tried to centralize Church governance based on the Bishop of Rome's preeminence. The city of Rome at the time of Pope St. Leo I was dwindling in size and importance. Political power had shifted east to Byzantium. But even as Rome's political significance and temporal power diminished and nearly vanished while at the same time the patriarchs of Constantinople and Alexandria were growing in political importance, the Church Councils still deferred to the pope in Rome before acting on a decision.

Pope St. Gelasius I (d. 496) also actively asserted the primacy of the Roman pontiff and seems to have been the first to have used the title "Vicar of Christ" to denote his divine authority, especially as he battled against a number of heresies in the East. From the eighth century, the title "Vicar of Christ" began to be employed by the popes in addition to being used by bishops, kings, judges, and priests. Many of the early popes used the title "Vicar of St. Peter"; nevertheless, at the time of Pope Innocent III in the thirteenth century, "Vicar of Christ" became used by the pope exclusively.

The Gospel reading at the Inauguration Mass for Pope Benedict XVI on April 25, 2005 was John 21:15-19. "...'Simon [Peter], son of John, do you love me?'...'Lord, you know everything; you know that I love you.' Jesus said to him, 'Feed my sheep.'...And after this he said to him, 'Follow me.'"

"Wherever the bishop shall appear, there let the multitude also be; . . ."

THE EPISCOPACY

As with the papacy, from the beginning the Church held the office of bishop to be of great importance. The bishops, as successors to the Apostles, were responsible for shepherding and guiding the flock in the various—and often dangerous—cities and situations in which Christians found themselves. The bishops baptized, offered up the Holy Sacrifice of the Mass, celebrated weddings, ordained priests, and engaged themselves in all of the sacramental work of the Church.

St. Ignatius of Antioch, of whom more will be said in the following chapter, wrote in his *Epistle to the Smyrnaeans* the following with regard to the importance of the bishop: "Wherever the bishop shall appear, there let the multitude [of the people] also be; even as, wherever Jesus Christ is, there is the Catholic Church" (*Epistle to the Smyrnaeans*, VIII). St. Ignatius was the first to use the term "Catholic Church."

PRIESTHOOD

The word "priest" is a contraction of the Greek word *presbyteros* that is normally translated as "presbyter." In the early Church, the presbyters were the church elders. The full understanding of the priesthood, as minister of Divine worship and of the Eucharistic sacrifice subordinate to the bishop to whom he has sworn canonical allegiance, developed over the centuries. However, there is evidence that as early as the second century there were already many priests being ordained to offer up the Sacrifice of the Mass.

The earliest extant ordination rites come from St. Hippolytus' (ca. A.D. 170 - ca. 236) *Apostolic Tradition*, as well as the fourth century *Apostolic Constitutions*.

MONOTHEISM

Christians believe that there is only one God (monotheism) and cannot compromise this belief in any way. Christianity, like Judaism had since its inception, found itself surrounded by polytheistic, pagan worship. Even if these pagan beliefs and the Roman cult of worship of the emperor did not amount to much of a personal faith, the early Christians rejected all acts of sacrifice and public ritual that acknowledged pagan belief. They also often had to make great changes in their daily lives. For example, sculptors and painters who became Christian could no longer work in pagan temples. Teachers could not teach Roman mythology, nor could they serve as judges or magistrates (because they would be forced, by laws such as the Edict of Nero, to condemn anyone discovered to be a Christian). Many Christians were killed as martyrs for Christ during the persecutions because they refused to adore the images of the emperors, who proclaimed themselves gods.

At the Council of Trent in 1546 the Church made its final definitive statement concerning the Canon of Scripture.

THE SCRIPTURES

During the earliest centuries of the Church, the Canon of the Bible was certainly not intact as one integral whole as it is in its present form. Many of the books that would later come to comprise much of the Canon of the Old Testament, such as the five books of the Pentateuch, were long held to be canonical by the Jewish tradition. Other books, such as Tobit and Wisdom, would be accepted through the course of the formation of the Catholic Canon. Many books of the New Testament, such as St. Matthew's gospel and most of St. Paul's epistles, were from the earliest times universally accepted; others, such as Revelation, required more time.

By the early third century, the universally accepted books of the New Testament canon were the following: the four Gospels, thirteen of St. Paul's Epistles, Acts, Revelation, 1 and 2 Peter, and 1, 2, and 3 John. After much discussion among various Church authorities including Origen, Eusebius, St. Athanasius, and St. Jerome, a definitive Canon was declared at a large synod in A.D. 382 in Rome. Though it took a few more years for churches in Africa and Gaul to accept the canon, by the end of the first decade of the fifth century, the Western Church possessed the complete Canon of the New Testament. The Church in the East, though it had not made nor recognized any formal statement concerning the Canon of the New Testament, generally accepted what the West had affirmed, except for some lingering disputes over the legitimacy of the book of Revelation. The Canon of the Old Testament took longer to be officially determined, though for many centuries St. Jerome's Vulgate was taken as standard for ecclesiastical usage. Finally, in 1546 at the Council of Trent, the Church made its final definitive statement concerning the Canon of Scripture.

The issue of the Scriptures and the establishment of the Canon are very important. In contrast to what the Reformation would falsely teach, the early Church never considered the Scriptures as authoritative apart from their interpretation by the Church through her hierarchy. Indeed, without this perennial guidance by the Holy Spirit, the Church's leadership would not have the wisdom to judge whether a particular book was divinely inspired or apocryphal (a work of literature with scriptural pretensions that is not divinely inspired), there would be no Bible as it exists. The Church, under the guiding grace of the Holy Spirit, over many centuries of careful deliberation and prayer, authoritatively determined those inspired texts that would form the Bible.

A quick example will illuminate this point. *The Infancy Gospel of Thomas* is an apocryphal book that was claimed to be divinely inspired. Though it was never widely recognized, the Church had declared that book lacked divine inspiration. Perhaps one reason for the Church's decision concerns one of the stories contained in this work. The story relates that the Child Jesus, at about eight years of age, became angry with a playmate and turned him into a frog. In her wisdom, the Church declined to add this book to the Canon. Many other books like this one, riddled with various heresies, were rejected.

The Old Testament writings played a significant role in the early Christian community. Though the Church lifted the burden of the Old Law's requirements, the books of the Old Testament were understood to be still authoritative. Christ fulfilled the Old Testament prophecies regarding the messiah. The Old Testament told the important story of how God established his covenant with the chosen people. The early Christians often sang the Psalms, especially in the liturgy and when they were being led to martyrdom.

The Scriptures, though obviously very important, were never seen as a record and interpretation of everything that Jesus and the Apostles did. It is the Tradition of the Church expressed in early Christian literature, liturgical practices, and statements of the Church that clarify and interpret Scripture. Sacred Scripture is a vital and central part of a broader tradition.

SLAVERY AND CHRISTIANITY

There is neither Jew nor Greek, there is neither slave or free, there is neither male nor female; for you are all one in Christ Jesus. (Gal 3:28)

The institution of slavery was, at the time of the birth of Christianity, an ancient and widespread institution. Roman slaves were multitudinous—indeed, no earlier civilization had yet employed slave labor so extensively. By the time of Augustus' death, it is estimated that two million of the seven and a half million inhabitants of the Italian peninsula were slaves. Though slaves in the cities often had a better life than those enslaved for agricultural work, the cruelties and hardships Roman slaves often endured are well known. Dread of punishment drove the slave through his miserable life. Slavery also existed in the Jewish culture, but it existed in a much different form. Mosaic Law demanded a merciful relationship between the master and slave that recognized the dignity of both labor and the laborer, and slaves often gained their freedom after a comparatively short period of service (cf. Ex 21:1-11, Dt 15:12-18).

Jesus never spoke directly concerning the topic of slavery, but it is clear that the Gospel implicitly condemns slavery as a grave offense against humanity and Christ's call to love as he loved. Slavery undermines the essential dignity of the human person, reducing the human being to the status of a machine that can be bought, sold, and exploited until it breaks down. Such treatment of other human beings is entirely inconsistent with Christ's teachings and the two greatest commandments (cf. Lk 10:25-28). Slaves in the early Christian community were welcomed, not as slaves, not as inferior beings, but as equally dignified members of the Christian community in Christ.

It was not early Christianity's place to bring about a sudden and sweeping revolution or emancipation. Indeed, the Mosaic Law itself permitted slavery. Christianity at this time did not have the moral authority capable of social reform on a grand scale. Rather, through the spread of Christianity from individual to individual and the growth of the Church, the institution of slavery was slowly undermined. Christ made clear the essential dignity of every human being and each person's unique call to a holy life.

St. Paul provides an excellent example of the manner in which the early Church dealt with slavery and writes concerning the topic in several letters (cf. the brief letter to Philemon, Col 3:11 and 3:22-25, 1 Cor 12:13, and in Eph 6:5-9). St. Paul sought to bring the spirit of charity and of dignified labor to the master-slave relationship. St. Paul writes:

Slaves, be obedient to those who are your earthly masters, with fear and trembling, in singleness of heart, as to Christ; not in the way of eye-service, as men-pleasers, but as servants of Christ, doing the will of God from the heart, rendering service with a good will as to the Lord and not men, knowing that whatever good any one does, he will receive the same again from the lord, whether he is a slave or free. Masters, do the same to them, and forbear threatening, knowing that he is both their Master and yours is in heaven, and that there is no partiality with him. (Eph. 6:5-9)

Labor and the laborer were not things to be scorned—Christ himself was a carpenter. Nor were service and the servant—Christ came to serve (cf. Lk 22:27). Nor were obedience and the obedient—Christ was obedient to the Father even unto death. The only slavery ever encouraged by St. Paul was slavery to Christ: freely serving him as a beloved master, working not out of fear or to gain favor, but "from the heart," out of love, for the greater glory of God.

Slaves were accepted into the Church as equals and even rose to the highest position of governance in the Church. Two former slaves immediately succeeded St. Peter as pope, Popes Sts. Linus and Anacletus. Pope St. Clement I, the fourth pope, was also a former slave. St. Felicity was the slave of St. Perpetua in Carthage before they both died as martyrs.

Beginning with the Emperor Constantine, the state instituted various reforms of slavery to improve the situation of society, as did Emperor Justinian. By the time Northern and Eastern Europe were converted to Christianity during the early Medieval period, slavery had ended as an institution.

NON-VIOLENCE

You have heard that it was said, "An eye for an eye and a tooth for a tooth." But I say to you, Do not resist one who is evil. But if any one strikes you on the right cheek, turn to him the other also; and if any one would sue you and take your coat, let him have your cloak as well; and if any one forces you to go one mile, go with him two miles. Give to him who begs from you, and do not refuse him who would borrow from you.

You have heard that it was said, "You shall love your neighbor and hate your enemy." But I say to you, Love your enemies and pray for those who persecute you. (Mt 5:38-44; cf. Lk 6:27-31)

Non-violence naturally flows from Jesus Christ's command to love everyone unconditionally. Jesus taught non-violence and prayer in the face of persecution. A heavy burden of responsibility lies upon those who undertake the use of weapons and who can wage war.

At the same time, the ethic of Jesus represents a worthy goal that is not yet realized here on earth where secular powers reign. Some early Christian documents seem to forbid participation in the army (cf. Hippolytus' *Apostolic Tradition* 17-19 and Canon 12 from the Council of Nicaea), while some early Christian writers outright rejected service in the Roman legions (cf. Tertullian's *De Corona Militis* and Lactantius' *Div. Inst.* 6.20.16). Tertullian emphasized clear separation from the pagan Roman society of his day in order to remain faithful to Christ's teaching in such works as *De spectaculis, De corona militis, De idololatria,* and *De paenitentia.* Tertullian taught that martyrdom was preferable to compromising the Faith.

On the other hand, Christians did serve in the Roman army beginning in the second century. The Theban Legion was a Christian legion in the Roman army martyred under Emperor Maximian at St. Maurice-en-Valais. A soldier, St. Maurice, was the leader of this legion. According to legend (chronicled by Krusch, de Montmélian, Besson, Dupraz, *et al.*), when the Christians refused to sacrifice to a pagan god, the entire legion (almost 6,000 men) was murdered. St. Maurice's feast day is on September 22.

Over the course of time, the Church has developed a just war theory. St. Augustine, one of the earliest writers on the topic, permitted war in the case of self-defense. St. Thomas Aquinas refined the guiding principles for a just war almost a thousand years later: war must be initiated on the authority of the sovereign (*auctoritas principis*); the cause must be just (*justa causa*); and those waging the war must have good and right intentions, meaning that the war will not bring about more harm than that perpetrated by the enemy (*recta intentio*). In addition to Aquinas' guidelines, the Spaniard Francisco de Vitoria (1483-1546) added that war must be waged by the proper means (*debito modo*), which finds special pertinence in contemporary warfare.

St. Thomas Aquinas refined the guiding principles for a just war almost a thousand years ago. "...those waging the war must have good and right intentions, ..."

THE STATE

Render therefore to Caesar the things that are Caesar's, and to God the things that are God's. (Mt 22:21)

The Roman state demanded that its people participate in pagan cults, worship the emperor, serve in the legions, and give Rome undivided loyalty. Polytheism and emperor worship were certainly inconsistent with the Gospels. On the issue of absolute loyalty to the state, the Christians would not compromise in what would go against their commitments to Christ. The Romans found commitment to Christianity somewhat incompatible with loyalty to the state, though they had experienced a similar situation with the Jews. The Christians did not fulfill the laws against the teachings of the Church; nevertheless, they obeyed all the just laws issued by the Romans.

MONEY MATTERS

> Now the company of those who believed were of one heart and soul, and no one said that any of the things which he possessed was his own, but they had everything in common....There was not a needy person among them, for as many as were possessors of lands or houses sold them, and brought the proceeds of what was sold and laid it at the apostles' feet; and distribution was made to each as any had need. (Acts 4:32; 34)

As early as apostolic times, there was a clear imperative to tend to the material needs of the whole Christian community. The early Church engaged in education, medical care, and the distribution of alms to the poor. She expected her members to engage in honest commerce, and not to practice usury, which was explicitly condemned by Church councils in the fourth century.

SEXUAL ETHICS: ABORTION AND CONTRACEPTION

The Church Fathers and early Christian thinkers universally rejected the practices of abortion and infanticide, which were both prevalent in Roman society. They also rejected the use of contraception. Such writers and thinkers included the author of the *Didache*, Clement of Alexandria, Tertullian, St. Ambrose, St. John Chrysostom, St. Jerome, and St. Augustine.

Abortion and infanticide violently reject the dignity of the human person and violate the fifth commandment: "You shall not kill" (Ex 20:13). The Church has always held this to be the case. Jesus never spoke directly about either of these topics, but Jewish law and Jesus' teaching concerning the sacredness of human life and the love of neighbor led the early Church to embrace this teaching. Christ "gives [his Apostles and their successors] a share in his own mission. From him they receive the power to act in his person" (CCC 935).

The Church Fathers taught that procreation within Matrimony is good and blessed, and that it is one of the intrinsic purposes of sexual intercourse. Artificial prevention of this possibility denigrates both the act and the subjects of the act. Even ancient Greek philosophy saw contraception as an unnatural violation since it destroys the possibility of one of the natural ends of sexual relations.

Abortion and infanticide violently reject the dignity of the human person.

PURE STRENGTH: WOMEN IN THE EARLY CHURCH

Women in the early Church faced persecution not only for their faith but also for their purity, and many showed heroic bravery in defending both with their lives. They understood the spiritual value of holy purity, and they were willing to give their lives rather than face defilement. Their unflinching heroism and both inner and outer beauty fueled innumerable conversions throughout the persecuted Church.

One such woman was St. Seraphia. She was born to Christian parents in Antioch early in the second century. Her family later fled to Italy to escape persecution. Seraphia led a holy life and consecrated her virginity to Christ. When her parents died, though, many men tried to pressure her into marriage. Young Seraphia chose instead to give her possessions to the poor and sell herself into slavery rather than to submit. She became the slave of a wealthy Roman widow named Sabina, and over time, Seraphia's Christian example convinced Sabina to convert to Christianity. Seraphia was eventually condemned to death for being a Christian; she was to be burned alive, but when the flames did not burn her, the prefect ordered her head cut off. Sabina buried Seraphia in her family's tomb, and later she too was martyred for the Faith.

Another example is St. Cecilia, who lived in the late second century. According to legend, she was the beautiful daughter of a noble Roman family and she too offered her virginity to God, praying always that he help her to remain pure, but her family forced her to marry a rich pagan young man named Valerian. On their wedding night, she told him in secret that there was an angel who guarded her body's purity. When he asked to see it, she responded that first he must be purified through Baptism. He was baptized, and upon returning, he saw St. Cecilia in prayer accompanied by an angel. The angel held two crowns, one of lilies and one of roses; he crowned them and asked them to keep the crowns undefiled, then rewarded Valerian's faith by offering him one favor. Valerian asked that his brother Tiburtius be converted. When Tiburtius visited them, he was overwhelmed by the smell of flowers that he could not see. St. Cecilia and Valerian told him about Christ, and Tiburtius too was baptized. The two brothers dedicated themselves to burying martyred Christians until they were captured and killed. St. Cecilia gathered their bodies and buried them, but later she too was arrested and condemned to be suffocated in a heated bath. When she was miraculously unharmed, a soldier was sent in to behead her. Three times he tried to do so but could not, and fled. St. Cecilia survived for three days before dying from her wounds.

The many women martyrs of the early Church portray well the role that women played in fortifying the early Church as examples of purity, bravery, and heroic fidelity, an example that is no less relevant today.

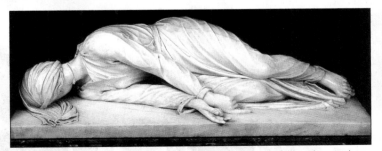

This sculpture of St. Cecilia makes us all eternal witnesses to her faith and martyrdom. It was commissioned by Cardinal Sfondrato, who had opened her tomb in 1599. Tradition holds that this incredible figure represents the position in which St. Cecilia's body was found. On her neck can be seen the three marks of the axe blows that ended her life in the name of Christ.

St. Monica with her son, St. Augustine. As a young man, Augustine was an intellectual and a professor of rhetoric in Milan. He regarded Christianity as a simple faith for good, uneducated people such as his beloved mother Monica. He was called by God and compelled to read St. Paul's *Epistles.* He soon became one of the most influential theological philosophers and writers in Church history. He was considered to be sympathetic to women, especially mothers. One of his most famous sayings is, "Love the sinner, hate the sin!"

WOMEN

While the role of women in early Christianity is a topic of much debate, several points are clear. First, the Roman and Greek cultures regarded women as inferior to men in all areas: physically, mentally, and spiritually. Second, Christianity, by its teachings of equality and charity, greatly improved the position of women, both individually and as a group in society. As with the issue of slavery, Christianity could not effect an immediate or radical alteration of the general position on the rights of women. It did, however, change the perception of women by recognizing and honoring women's spiritual equality and importance. Indeed, after Jesus Christ, the most revered and honored person is a woman, the Queen of All Saints, the Blessed Virgin Mary who was the only human person so privileged and honored by God as to be born into the world free from the stain of original sin. It is through a woman that the Savior of the human race entered the world.

Many women converted to Christianity, and they played an important role in the early Church's evangelization and, as will be seen in later chapters, in the conversion of the European continent. Women spread the Gospel by ordinary and sometimes extraordinary means, through their roles as wives, mothers, and workers. Mothers, such as St. Helena (mother of Constantine the Great) and St. Monica (mother of St. Augustine), played vital roles in the conversions of some of the most influential figures in the history of the Church. Just as women found an equal position in the Christian community, they suffered equally severe persecutions in the first centuries after Christ. St. Perpetua, St. Felicity, and St. Agnes are just a few of the renowned female martyrs, of whom more will be told in the following chapter.

FAMILY LIFE

Christianity raised the status of the family to a "domestic church." It was in and through the family that the ideal of Christian charity found its roots, and it was through the family that the dignity of every person was recognized. Love and service became the hallmark of the Christian family. There is no doubt that Christianity's expectations regarding the family at times clashed with the pagan family structure, which could be brutal to women and children. Christianity imbued an ethic of charity into all human societal relationships, with the family as the model.

CHURCH FATHERS ON CONTRACEPTION

Because the immorality of contraception is such a hotly debated issue, it may seem surprising that this moral question was just as relevant in the times of the Church fathers. The truth is, most major forms of contraception were around in Roman times and the Church fathers were able to see with amazing clarity the moral implications and social ramifications of this practice. St. Epiphanius (ca. 315-403) criticized the Gnostics saying: "They exercise genital acts, yet prevent the conceiving of children. Not in order to produce offspring, but to satisfy lust, are they eager for corruption" (St. Epiphanius, *Panarion* 26.5.2 [GCS 25: 281]). Later, St. Jerome wrote:

> Others drink for sterility and commit murder on the human not yet sown. Some when they sense that they have conceived by sin, consider the poisons for abortion, and frequently die themselves along with it, and go to hell guilty of three crimes: murdering themselves, committing adultery against Christ, and murder against their unborn child. (St. Jerome, *Epistle* 22.13: PL 22.401)

Perhaps the most complete treatment on the matter is St. John Chrysostom's letter to the Romans in the fourth century:

> Why do you sow where the field is eager to destroy the fruit? Where there are medicines of sterility? Where there is murder before birth? You do not even let a harlot remain a harlot, but you make her a murderess as well. Do you see that from drunkenness comes fornication, from fornication adultery, from adultery murder? Indeed, it is something worse than murder and I do not know what to call it; for she does not kill what is formed but prevents its formation. What then? Do you condemn the gift of God, and fight with His laws? What is a curse, do you seek as though it were a blessing? Do you make the anteroom of birth the anteroom of slaughter? Do you teach the woman who is given to you for the procreation of offspring to perpetrate killing? That she may always be beautiful and lovable to her lovers, and that she may rake in more money, she does not refuse to do this, heaping fire on your head; and even if the crime is hers, you are the cause. Hence also arise idolatries. To look pretty many of these women use incantations, libations, philtres, potions, and innumerable other things. Yet after such turpitude, after murder, after idolatry, the matter still seems indifferent to many men—even to many men having wives. In this indifference of the married men there is greater evil filth; for then poisons are prepared, not against the womb of a prostitute, but against your injured wife. Against her are these innumerable tricks, invocations of demons, incantations of the dead, daily wars, ceaseless battles, and unremitting contentions. (St. John Chrysostom, *Homily 24 on the Epistle to the Romans*: PG 60: 626-27)

The issues of the modern day were not only relevant, but also gravely important for the early Christians. The Church Fathers argued against contraceptives for the very same reasons the Church continues to condemn them today.

A mosaic of St. John Chrysostom in the magnificent Byzantine church Hagia Sophia in Istanbul, Turkey.

PART II

Important Writings of the Early Christian Period

"THE APOSTOLIC FATHERS"

"The Apostolic Fathers" is a term given to a number of the earliest Christian writers, some of whom have been mentioned. These men came immediately after the Apostles, and some had direct links to the Apostles or to the communities established by them. They wrote about religious and moral themes, mainly through epistles addressed to individuals or small communities, rather than to the whole Church. Although they do not, for the most part, contain any systematic doctrinal exposition, these writings do record some of the most beautiful and passionate accounts of Christian doctrine and spirituality ever written. These saintly writers of the early Church are recognized by the Church as special witnesses of Faith.

The Apostolic Fathers, of whom more will be told in the following chapter, include among others: St. Clement of Rome, St. Ignatius of Antioch, Herman, St. Polycarp of Smyrna, and St. Papias, as well as the unknown authors of the *Epistle of Barnabas* and the *Epistle to Diogentus*.

APOLOGISTS

Always be prepared to make a defense to any one who calls you to account for the hope that is in you. (1 Pt 3:15)

Apologetics (from the Greek *apologia*, meaning "defense") is a branch of theology that purports to defend and explain the Christian religion. The history of apologetics is as old as the history of the Church and can be divided into four historical periods, each with its particular struggle. The first, which concerns this section, dates from the dawn of Christianity to the collapse of the Roman Empire in A.D. 476. The three great opponents facing Christianity at this time were Judaism, Gnostic heresies, and the various pagan religions throughout the Roman Empire.

Though the title "apologist" refers to anyone who writes an apologetic work, there was a group of early Church Fathers collectively known as Apologists. Writing mainly during the second and third centuries, these men composed some of the greatest Christian literature. The Apologists include St. Aristides, St. Justin Martyr, Tatian, Athenagoras, St. Theophilus, Minucius Felix, and Tertullian. Due in significant part to their work, Christianity had begun to gain more converts from among the educated and elite classes. Most of the writers were not trained theologians, but rather writers with an audience consisting of the public and the emperor with his immediate subordinates.

As previously mentioned, early Christianity found itself attacked by both the Jewish and pagan traditions. For the majority of the Jews at this time, the burgeoning Christian religion, which claimed its roots in the ancient and holy tradition of Israel, denigrated and desecrated Judaism, the Law, and the God of Abraham. In claiming fulfillment of the Mosaic Law, Christianity rejected the need for circumcision and other practices. Christ, the poor, common, humble teacher who was brutally executed beside two thieves, was far from the concept of a messiah so long expected by the Jews. The apologetic writings to the Jews focused on these issues. St. Justin Martyr's "Dialogue with Trypho" is perhaps the most important of these writings. The following excerpt, words spoken by Trypho, a Jew, summarize Judaism's critique of the early Christians:

Christ, the poor, common, humble teacher who was brutally executed beside two thieves, was far from the concept of a messiah so long expected by the Jews.

> But this is what we are most at a loss about: that you, professing to be pious, and supposing yourselves better than others, are not in any particular separated from them, and do not alter your mode of living from the nations, in that you observe no festivals or sabbaths, and do not have the rite of circumcision; and further, resting your hopes on a man that was crucified, you yet expect to obtain some good thing from God, while you do not obey His commandments. (*Dialogue with Trypho, X*)

St. Justin's response includes a defense of the Christian teaching about Christ and his laws as the fulfillment of the Jewish Law and the prophets. The apology also incorporates a condemnation of the Jewish failure to understand and accept Christ as the messiah, the Son of God who came to redeem all sinners and fulfill the Mosaic Law.

The most important aim of apologetic work at this time was to address the pagan culture of the Roman Empire. Roman culture—from its literature and philosophy to its commercial and agricultural activities, from the political sphere to mundane, everyday habits—was imbued with paganism. Pomp, power, and glory of the Empire and its gods dominated the popular mind, and Christianity did not at all fit into this framework. The Christians worshiped in secret, rejected the gods of the land, and refused to follow imperial mandates concerning required sacrifices and venerations. Christians were met first with suspicion and superstition, which soon degenerated into fear and mistrust. The *Agape* and the celebration of the Eucharist soon were rumored to be orgies and obscure cannibalistic rites, and the Christians became known as enemies of the state. Thus, there was a great need for apologetic writings that explained the practices and beliefs of Christianity to the Roman pagan culture, as well as writings that made a case for the benign and even benevolent presence of Christians in the Empire. Particular attention was given to how Christianity forms exemplary citizens, and how it was a bulwark of the state rather than a cancerous tumor of disloyalty. Even as these writings addressed those issues, they also made clear and persuasive arguments concerning both the spiritual dearth of paganism and the promise of eternal life and happiness in Christ.

THE *DIDACHE*

The *Didache* (Greek meaning "teaching"), variously known as *The Doctrine of the Twelve Apostles* and *The Lord's Teaching through the Twelve Apostles to the Nations*, is a short exposition concerning Christian morals, doctrine, and customs that was most likely composed in the first century. Its sixteen chapters cover Christian moral life, Baptism, fasting, prayer, the Eucharist, and the developing Church hierarchy.

The author, exact date, and location are unknown, but many of the early Church Fathers, such as St. Clement of Alexandria, Eusebius of Caesarea, and St. Athanasius, used this text as a reference, and some even sought its admittance to the Canon of Scripture. Lost to scholars for centuries, it was finally rediscovered in 1873 by Philotheos Bryennios, a Greek Orthodox bishop.

TERTULLIAN

Tertullian (ca. A.D. 160 - ca. 225) was born in Carthage around A.D. 160. He was the son of a Roman centurion and received a sound education through his studies of Roman law. He eventually wrote numerous works, mostly apologetic, in both Latin and Greek (though the Greek works have been lost). He converted from Roman paganism to Christianity sometime in the middle of his life, and from that point on, Tertullian worked to demonstrate with compelling argumentation and rhetoric that the Christians posed no threat to the Roman Empire, but rather were a great asset to it. His writings were highly polemical and brilliantly witty—he did not take any pains to avoid vexing his Roman audience in his defense of the Faith. Tertullian's versatility in explaining and defending the Catholic Faith won for him the title "Father of Latin Theology."

At the beginning of the third century, Tertullian joined the heretical Montanist sect and definitively broke from the Church a few years later. Although his writing then turned against certain doctrines of the Church, he was never a consistent Montanist. The sect supported a rigorous form of Christianity that refused forgiveness for certain "irremissible" sins, especially those of a sexual nature. This particular sect also believed in periodic overwhelming outpourings of the Holy Spirit through Montanist prophets and prophetesses. Tertullian, picking and choosing which tenets of Montanism he thought important, eventually formed his own small following before he died.

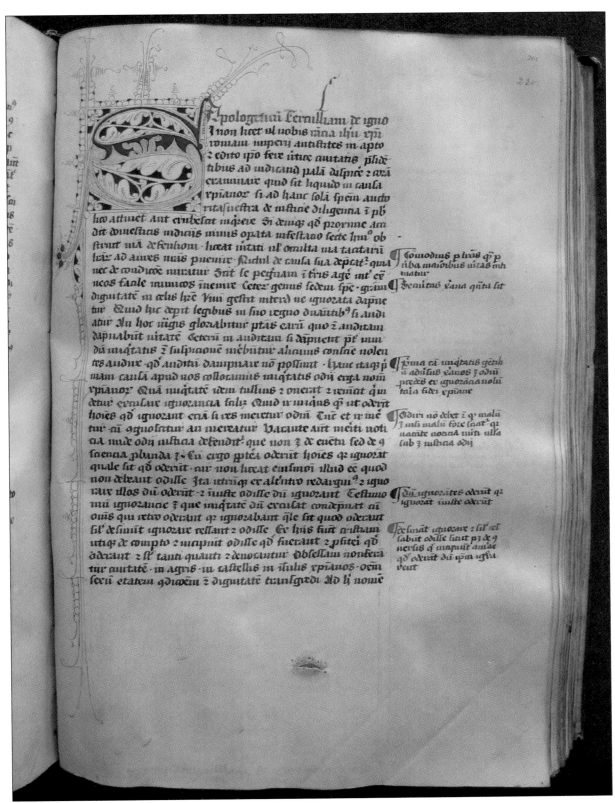

Folio 201 from Tertullian's *Apologeticum*

The Eucharistic Prayer found in *The Apostolic Tradition* became the basis for the second Eucharistic Prayer in the 1970 Roman Missal, which was published as part of the intended reforms for the Second Vatican Council, 1962-1965.

ST. HIPPOLYTUS AND *THE APOSTOLIC TRADITION*

St. Hippolytus (ca. A.D. 170 - ca. 236) was an important writer and Father of the Church of the late second and early third centuries. Even though he was probably the most important theologian in the Roman Church during the third century, his importance was forgotten in the West for some time, perhaps because of his extensive use of Greek.

Hippolytus wrote and spoke against many heresies, but he himself, perhaps because of his vigorous opposition to certain Christological heresies like Modalism, soon began promoting his own extreme position on the nature of the relationship between the Father and Son. He quarreled with Pope St. Zephyrinus (A.D. 198-217), and when Pope St. Callistus I (A.D. 217-222) was elected, St. Hippolytus broke from the Church, and his small group of followers elected him antipope. He persisted in this schism until the persecution under Emperor Maximin (A.D. 235-238), when he and Pope St. Pontian (A.D. 230-235) were exiled together in Sardinia, most likely to a grueling life in the mines. Before dying a martyr's death, St. Hippolytus was reconciled with Pope St. Pontian and the Church.

Though most of Hippolytus' voluminous corpus has been lost, his two most important works, *The Refutation of all Heresies* and *The Apostolic Tradition*, have survived, in part. The latter work describes the passing down of the Faith of the Apostles from generation to generation and provides insight into the rites of ordination, Baptism, and the Eucharist during the third century. The Eucharistic Prayer found in *The Apostolic Tradition* became the basis for the second Eucharistic Prayer in the 1970 Roman Missal, which was published as part of the intended reforms of the Second Vatican Council.

PART III
Martyrdom as the Greatest Testimony to Christianity

Behold, I send you out as sheep in the midst of wolves; so be wise as serpents and innocent as doves. (Mt 10:16)

From as early as the first century, Christians, in the face of both Jewish and Roman opposition, found that they had to be prepared to die for Christ. Those who did actually lose their lives quickly became the most venerated of all saints. An entire theology developed around the martyrs that recognized their importance in the history of the Church.

The vast majority of martyrs were average, everyday people who naturally worried about the pain and suffering that they would endure; this worry was often mitigated by the solidarity of fellow Christians. Before being martyred the early Christians would exchange the kiss of peace, and were often described as dying with a tremendous bearing of peace and joy.

The word "martyr" comes from the Greek word *martyros*, meaning "witness." A martyr bears witness to Christ as the Way, the Truth, and the Life. In the early Church, as today, the actions and words of the martyrs strengthened and edified other Christians. Even in the last moments of their lives, in which the crowds often took sadistic pleasure, martyrs often led the assembled crowds along the path of conversion by giving the supreme witness of loving fidelity to Christ. The serenity, joy, and faithfulness with which the martyrs accepted their deaths deeply affected some of the people, such as the magistrates and the executioners, who witnessed their deaths.

Christians understood martyrdom as an honor and a privilege since it was a direct participation in the sufferings of Christ. The victims were sustained by Christ in their dreadful suffering and they saw martyrdom as the surest means to sanctity and entrance into Heaven. The entire Christian community viewed martyrdom as a grace and a gift, though Christians were not supposed to seek out martyrdom because of the obligation to practice and preserve one's life. Through martyrdom the three theological virtues of faith, hope, and charity would reach unparalleled dimensions. The next chapter will explore many of the early persecutions and their causes, as well as the stories of some of the most renowned martyrs.

CONCLUSION

The early Christians, by their tremendous faith in Jesus and imitation of his life, transformed the Roman world and its values. The decadent Roman culture, with its basis in the law of power, was supplanted by a culture based on Christ's new commandment: "Love one another; even as I have loved you" (Jn 13:34). Guided by the Holy Spirit, the Church grew as an institution and a community of believers united as the Mystical Body of Christ. Ordinary people from all walks of life carried out a peaceful revolution that spread from person to person through the simple living witness to the richness of Christ's kingdom, even in the face of terrible persecution and horrific death.

The Martyrdom of St. Catherine depicts the awesome power of divine intervention which smashed the torture wheel St. Catherine was about to endure. She was ultimately beheaded. St. Catherine was a fourth century scholar who converted many pagans and was one of the voices heard by St. Joan of Arc along with St. Barbara and St. Margaret of Antioch. She is listed as one of the fourteen most helpful saints. One of several legends about her is that angels carried her body to Mt. Sinai, where Emperor Justinian established Saint Catherine's Monastery in A.D. 548-565, which has survived to this day.

SUPPLEMENTARY READING

Tertullian, *To His Wife* II, 8, 6-8

Where can I find words to describe adequately the happiness of that marriage which the church cements, which the oblation confirms and the blessing seals? The angels proclaim it and the heavenly father ratifies it.…What kind of yoke is that of two Christians, united in one hope, one desire, one discipline and one service? Both are children of the same father, servants of the same master; nothing separates them, either in spirit or in the flesh; on the contrary, they are truly two in one flesh. Where the flesh is one, so is the spirit. Together they pray, together they prostrate themselves, together they observe the fasts; they teach each other, exhort each other, encourage each other. They are both equal in the church of God, equal at the banquet of God, equal in trials, persecution, consolations.…

The Didache, Ch. 1
The Lord's Teaching Through the Twelve Apostles to the Nations

The Two Ways and the First Commandment. There are two ways, one of life and one of death, but a great difference between the two ways. The way of life, then, is this: First, you shall love God who made you; second, love your neighbor as yourself, and do not do to another what you would not want done to you. And of these sayings the teaching is this: Bless those who curse you, and pray for your enemies, and fast for those who persecute you. For what reward is there for loving those who love you? Do not the Gentiles do the same? But love those who hate you, and you shall not have an enemy.

Abstain from fleshly and worldly lusts. If someone strikes your right cheek, turn to him the other also, and you shall be perfect.

If someone impresses you for one mile, go with him two. If someone takes your cloak, give him also your coat. If someone takes from you what is yours, ask it not back, for indeed you are not able. Give to every one who asks you, and ask it not back; for the Father wills that to all should be given of our own blessings (free gifts).

Happy is he who gives according to the commandment, for he is guiltless. Woe to him who receives; for if one receives who has need, he is guiltless; but he who receives not having need shall pay the penalty, why he received and for what. And coming into confinement, he shall be examined concerning the things which he has done, and he shall not escape from there until he pays back the last penny. And also concerning this, it has been said, Let your alms sweat in your hands, until you know to whom you should give.

John Paul II, *Crossing the Threshold of Hope*, p. 129-30

The Church itself is first and foremost a "movement," a mission. It is the mission that begins in God the Father and that, through the Son in the Holy Spirit, continually reaches humanity and shapes it in a new way. Yes, Christianity is a great action of God. The action of the word becomes the action of the sacraments. What else are the sacraments (all of them!), if not the action of Christ in the Holy Spirit?

When the Church baptizes, it is Christ who baptizes; when the Church absolves, it is Christ who absolves; when the Church celebrates the Eucharist, it is Christ who celebrates it: "This is my body."

VOCABULARY

AGAPE
Literally "love." The *Agape* was an early Christian religious meal that was at first closely related to the celebration of the Eucharist and often preceded this celebration.

APOCRYPHAL
A work of literature with scriptural or quasi-scriptural pretensions which is not genuine, canonical, or inspired by God.

APOLOGIST
Generally, one who writes a work in order to defend and explain the Christian religion. The title also refers specifically to a group of Church Fathers who wrote during the second and third centuries in the Roman Empire.

APOSTOLIC FATHER
Saintly writers of the early Church whom the Church recognizes as her special witnesses of Faith.

APOSTOLIC TRADITION
Refers to the passing of the Faith of the Apostles from generation to generation. Hippolytus' work of the same name illustrated the principle by preserving the rites of ordination, Baptism, and the Eucharist used during the third century. The Eucharistic Prayer found in *The Apostolic Tradition* became the basis for the second Eucharistic Prayer in the 1970 Roman Missal, which was published as part of the intended reforms for the Second Vatican Council.

BAPTISM
This first Sacrament of Initiation, instituted by Jesus, unites the believer to Christ. In this sacrament, a believer is forgiven of original and personal sin, and thus begins a new life in Christ and the Holy Spirit, and is incorporated into the Church, the Body of Christ (cf. CCC 977, 1213).

CATECHUMENS
Literally "the instructed." Those adults seeking admission to the Church after having met over a long period of time for instruction before being baptized.

THE *DIDACHE*
From the Greek meaning "teaching," a first century treatise concerning Christian morals, practices, and ministry. Its sixteen chapters cover Baptism, fasting, prayers, the Eucharist, and the developing Church hierarchy among the early Christians.

EUCHARIST
Literally meaning "thanksgiving," was, and is, the central act of Christian worship. It consists in consuming the Sacrament of Holy Communion, the Body and Blood of Christ.

ICHTHYS
An acrostic for the Greek phrase *Iesous Christos Theou Yios Soter*, which is a declaration of the central tenet of the Christian Faith meaning "Jesus Christ, Son of God, Savior." The acrostic itself spells the word "fish" in Greek.

INFANT BAPTISM
The practice of baptizing infants that became more common during the third century and became universal by the early Medieval period. It remained the common practice for all western Christians until the Reformation in the sixteenth century.

MARTYRDOM
Being killed for one's Faith. Christians understand martyrdom as an honor and a privilege since it is a direct participation in the sufferings of Christ.

MONOTHEISM
The belief there is only one true God.

PAPACY
The Vicar of Christ as instituted by Jesus who holds the responsibility and supreme authority for guiding the Church.

PRESBYTER
From the Greek word *presbyteros* for "priest," which is a contraction of the Greek. In the early Church, the presbyters were the church elders.

SIGN OF THE CROSS
The act of tracing the cross down from the forehead with the finger to the breast and then from left to right across the breast. By the early third century, the practice of making the Sign of the Cross was deeply rooted in the Christian world.

SYNOD
An assembly of ecclesiastics gathered together under Church authority to discuss and decide on matters pertaining to doctrine, liturgy, or discipline.

STUDY QUESTIONS

1. What are some of the advantages of infant Baptism?

2. Where were the earliest Masses celebrated?

3. Which two days of the week did the earliest Christians keep holy as days of fasting and penance? (Hint: It was not Sunday.)

4. Why did Christians come to observe Sunday as the holiest day of the week?

5. What does the term "Vicar of Christ" mean?

6. What is the value of the episcopacy?

7. From what word does the word "priest" derive?

8. How did Christianity, as a monotheistic religion, cause tension in Roman society?

9. When was the canon of the New Testament declared in the West?

10. Who is the authentic interpreter of Sacred Scripture?

11. What did Popes Sts. Linus and Anacletus have in common?

12. What was the Theban Legion?

13. What is the just war theory?

14. How was money held in the early Christian community?

15. What did the early Christians think about abortion and infanticide?

16. What kind of quality did Christianity initially introduce into the gender relations of the Greco-Roman world?

17. What is so special about the historical position of the "Apostolic Fathers"?

18. What was the goal of the Apologists?

19. How has St. Hippolytus influenced the liturgical reform of the Second Vatican Council?

20. The word "martyr" means "witness." To whom do martyrs bear witness?

PRACTICAL EXERCISES

1. Protestants accept the principle of *sola scriptura*, Scripture alone, as the primary basis for authority. The Catholic position is that the Church alone interprets the Scriptures. Discuss why the Catholic position makes more sense historically.

2. Slavery has existed in almost all places and times throughout history. There have been many Christian defenders of slavery, claiming God supported slavery using such Scriptural passages as Exodus 21:1-11, Leviticus 25:44-55, and Ephesians 6:5-9. After reading these passages, how would you argue against a Christian who supports slavery?

3. Jesus taught, "turn the other cheek," and yet many Christian thinkers developed theories for the just waging of war. Are these two ideas compatible? With both Jesus' words and the writings of St. Augustine in mind, describe Christian justice, both on a personal and political scale.

FROM THE CATECHISM

1231 Where infant Baptism has become the form in which this sacrament is usually celebrated, it has become a single act encapsulating the preparatory stages of Christian initiation in a very abridged way. By its very nature infant Baptism requires a *post-baptismal catechumenate.* Not only is there a need for instruction after Baptism, but also for the necessary flowering of baptismal grace in personal growth. The *Catechism* has its proper place here.

1233 Today in all the rites, Latin and Eastern, the Christian initiation of adults begins with their entry into the catechumenate and reaches its culmination in a single celebration of the three sacraments of initiation: Baptism, Confirmation, and the Eucharist (cf. *AG* 14; CIC, cann. 851; 865; 866). In the Eastern rites the Christian initiation of infants also begins with Baptism followed immediately by Confirmation and the Eucharist, while in the Roman rite it is followed by years of catechesis before being completed later by Confirmation and the Eucharist, the summit of their Christian initiation (cf. CIC, cann. 851, 2°; 868).

1324 The Eucharist is "the source and summit of the Christian life" (*LG* 11). "The other sacraments, and indeed all ecclesiastical ministries and works of the apostolate, are bound up with the Eucharist and are oriented toward it. For in the blessed Eucharist is contained the whole spiritual good of the Church, namely Christ himself, our Pasch" (*PO* 5).

1327 In brief, the Eucharist is the sum and summary of our faith: "Our way of thinking is attuned to the Eucharist, and the Eucharist in turn confirms our way of thinking" (St. Irenaeus, *Adv. haeres.* 4, 18, 5: PG 7/1, 1028).

2270 Human life must be respected and protected absolutely from the moment of conception. From the first moment of his existence, a human being must be recognized as having the rights of a person—among which is the inviolable right of every innocent being to life (cf. CDF, *Donum vitæ* I, 1).

Before I formed you in the womb I knew you, and before you were born I consecrated you (Jer 1: 5; cf. Job 10: 8-12; Ps 22: 10-11).

My frame was not hidden from you, when I was being made in secret, intricately wrought in the depths of the earth (Ps 139: 15).

2271 Since the first century the Church has affirmed the moral evil of every procured abortion. This teaching has not changed and remains unchangeable. Direct abortion, that is to say, abortion willed either as an end or a means, is gravely contrary to the moral law:

You shall not kill the embryo by abortion and shall not cause the newborn to perish (*Didache* 2, 2: SCh 248, 148; cf. *Ep. Barnabae* 19, 5: PG 2, 777; *Ad Diognetum* 5, 6: PG 2, 1173; Tertullian, *Apol.* 9: PL 1, 319-320).

God, the Lord of life, has entrusted to men the noble mission of safeguarding life, and men must carry it out in a manner worthy of themselves. Life must be protected with the utmost care from the moment of conception: abortion and infanticide are abominable crimes (*GS* 51 § 3).

2334 "In creating men 'male and female,' God gives man and woman an equal personal dignity" (*FC* 22; cf. *GS* 49 § 2). "Man is a person, man and woman equally so, since both were created in the image and likeness of the personal God" (*MD* 6).

CHAPTER 3

Persecution Of "The Way"

The complex and often troubling relationship between the Church and the state is one that began in the Roman Empire, and still remains with us today.

CHAPTER 3

Persecution Of "The Way"

We Christians...being instructed in the Faith, know that suffering can be transformed— if we offer it to God—into an instrument of salvation, and into a sacred way which helps us get to heaven. For a Christian, pain is no reason for gloominess but for joy: the joy of knowing that on the Cross of Christ all suffering has a redemptive value.

— John Paul II, Address to the Sick, Cordoba Cathedral, April 8, 1987

In the times of the early Church, the Romans carried fear and mistrust of Christianity to an extreme. In the first three centuries, rulers and mobs alike delighted in finding new and creative ways to torture and kill the followers of Christ in public spectacles. Christians who refused to renounce their Faith were martyred in many different places, including the Circus of Hadrian, the Circus Flaminius, and Nero's Circus. Because some of the circuses in Rome had been the site of so many martyrs' deaths, they were held as sacred by the early Church. When these circuses were dismantled, their material was used in the construction of churches. The Coliseum, also known as Flavian's amphitheater, which is the last and greatest of these arenas still standing, has become associated with the many cruelties and injustices endured by the early martyrs of the Faith, even though it is unclear how many were martyred within its walls.

In the earliest years, the Christians referred to the Faith as "the Way" (cf. Acts 9: 2 and 19: 9). Living the Way required a life of integrity according to the commandments and counsels of the Gospels and a strong commitment to become a disciple of Christ. Although living the Way is always difficult and requires much sacrifice, the early Christians especially suffered in the pursuit of its ideals.

Many thousands of early Christians lost their lives during three hundred years of persecutions in the Roman Empire. There are numerous accounts of martyrs from this period, many of whom were priests and bishops of the early Church. Scores of lay men and women from all walks of life comprised the majority of the martyrs. When reading the accounts of the martyrs, it is hard not to

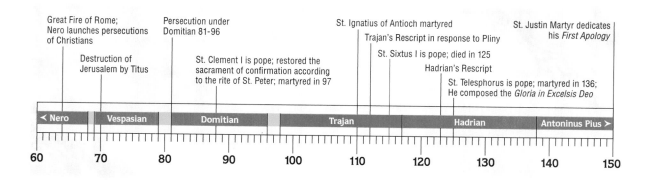

Great Fire of Rome; Nero launches persecutions of Christians

Destruction of Jerusalem by Titus

Persecution under Domitian 81-96

St. Clement I is pope; restored the sacrament of confirmation according to the rite of St. Peter; martyred in 97

St. Ignatius of Antioch martyred

Trajan's Rescript in response to Pliny

St. Sixtus I is pope; died in 125

Hadrian's Rescript

St. Justin Martyr dedicates his *First Apology*

St. Telesphorus is pope; martyred in 136; He composed the *Gloria in Excelsis Deo*

◄ Nero | Vespasian | Domitian | Trajan | Hadrian | Antoninus Pius ►

60 70 80 90 100 110 120 130 140 150

Last Prayers of the Christian Martyrs by Jean-Léon Gérôme

be shaken by the brutality with which they were killed. It is important, however, to understand the reasons behind their persecution and to focus upon the courage shown by so many otherwise ordinary men and women. These martyrs lived with their families, had normal occupations in life, and were simply devoted to Christ. Despite the tremendous pressure put on them by the emperors to renounce their Faith, the early Christians remained faithful to the teachings of Jesus.

Christianity is a religion born in the suffering and death of its founder, Jesus Christ. In like manner, many of his first followers also suffered and died for their belief in him. The Acts of the Apostles describe a number of localized attacks on the Apostles and disciples in Palestine. But the greatest persecutions began under the watchful eye of Rome. Beginning with limited persecution under the Emperor Nero in A.D. 64, the intensity of the persecutions in Rome increased until they reached their climax under the Emperor Diocletian in A.D. 303. For the first three centuries of the Church's existence, Christians were a minority and were considered criminals in the eyes of the state. In short, becoming a Christian meant putting one's life at high risk. In spite of harsh persecution, however, the Church continued to spread the teaching of Jesus at any cost.

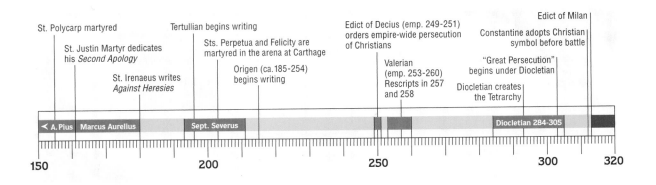

St. Polycarp martyred

St. Justin Martyr dedicates his *Second Apology*

St. Irenaeus writes *Against Heresies*

Tertullian begins writing

Sts. Perpetua and Felicity are martyred in the arena at Carthage

Origen (ca.185-254) begins writing

Edict of Decius (emp. 249-251) orders empire-wide persecution of Christians

Valerian (emp. 253-260) Rescripts in 257 and 258

Diocletian creates the Tetrarchy

"Great Persecution" begins under Diocletian

Edict of Milan

Constantine adopts Christian symbol before battle

A. Pius   Marcus Aurelius   Sept. Severus   Diocletian 284-305

150   200   250   300   320

PART I

The First Roman Persecutions

The earliest Christians had suffered persecution at the hands of the Jews, but the Roman Empire for a time did not trouble itself with what appeared to be merely a small group of schismatic Jews. As the early Church grew and distanced itself from the Jewish tradition, the Roman Empire began to view these early Christians as enemies of the empire who, through their disregard for some imperial institutions and traditions, were seen as a breeding ground for corruption and discord within the empire. Soon, periodic imperial persecutions, many of which were incredibly brutal, became a normal part of the life of an early Christian.

THE FIRST PERSECUTION UNDER EMPEROR NERO (A.D. 64)

The Emperor Nero (A.D. 37-68, emperor A.D. 54-68) was a figure of immense cruelty, psychological sickness, and paranoia. Even the Roman historical tradition portrays him as a tyrant. The stepson of Emperor Claudius and the nephew of Emperor Caligula (infamous for his depravity and psychosis), Nero was the last of the Augustinian line. His rule began in A.D. 54 at the age of seventeen, and for a time, things ran smoothly. The noble Stoic Seneca was an advisor to Nero and had been his tutor when Nero was young. By the year A.D. 59, however, Nero's evil character had clearly emerged. He murdered his mother, and then renounced and slandered his own wife, Octavia, before having her beheaded. In A.D. 65, Nero forced Seneca to commit suicide.

Emperor Nero with his noble advisor, Seneca.

Early on the night of July 19, A.D. 64, fire broke out near the Circus Maximus and engulfed the city of Rome for nine straight days. The city was divided into fourteen administrative districts. Of these, four districts were reduced to rubble, six were heavily damaged, and only four escaped unharmed. The absence of a modern fire department made it virtually impossible to stop urban fires once they had begun. Rome was a dense, compact city of people and buildings, which only increased the damage caused by the fire.

The middle and lower classes were packed into tenements, known as *insulæ*. These buildings had wooden walls, which were filled with a wide variety of rubble for insulation, hence their name. Even prior to the great fire, many died in these poorly constructed buildings due to structural collapses. The homes of the wealthy and members of the upper class, such as the senators and the *equites* ("horsemen/knights"), were filled with combustible wood furnishings and many textiles. Lush gardens filled with trees, arbors, and wooden seating helped feed the fire among these residences. The fire raged throughout the city, and consumed the lives and the property of members of every Roman class.

The fire raged throughout the city, and consumed the lives and the property of members of every Roman class.

Immediately, the rumor began to circulate that Nero had started the fire. The reason behind this rumor was Nero's announced intention to seize private property in the center of Rome in order to build an expansive new palace, later called the *Domus Aurea* (House of Gold). The rumor told of Nero taking delight in watching Rome burn while he read his own poetry. The famous saying, "Nero fiddled while Rome burned," originates from this rumor.

Nero provided emergency shelter to victims, and quickly sought to remove suspicion from himself by falsely accusing the Christians of starting the fire. He tortured several Christians, elicited from them forced confessions, and then ordered large numbers of other Christians to be arrested. The Roman historian Tacitus writes that when it became clear to everyone that Nero's accusations against the Christians were wildly implausible, he charged them with "hating the human race" (*Annals*, XV, 44).

Although Nero's first persecution of Christians was limited to the city of Rome proper, its egregious brutality remains unquestioned. St. Clement of Rome, the third pope, relates that Christians were first taken across the Tiber to an arena on Vatican hill called Nero's Circus, where St. Peter's Basilica now stands. They were then sewn into animal skins and distributed throughout the gardens. Next Nero released hungry mastiff dogs into the gardens, which hunted down and ate the trapped Christians. Other Christians were martyred in an assortment of awful ways in the Circus Maximus. Finally, in perhaps the greatest example of the emperor's cruelty, Nero coated hundreds of live Christians with pitch and resin and then set them on fire to provide light for him as he passed through his gardens and along the city streets at night.

MAD CALIGULA

Despite the grandeur of their office and domain, many of Rome's emperors were insatiable egomaniacs with no regard for human life. This was often seasoned with authentic, clinical insanity. An infamously insane emperor was Caligula, the nephew of Emperor Tiberius, who rose to the throne at the age of twenty-five.

After Tiberius became ill and fell into a coma in A.D. 37, Caligula succeeded him. Some say Tiberius actually emerged from the coma, and Caligula ordered the emperor smothered to death. This sort of violence was commonplace within the imperial family. When Caligula was still in his teens, his mother, along with all of his brothers, were arrested and butchered. Caligula himself committed incest with three of his sisters. When one of them conceived a child, the emperor was so eager to see how their god-like child would turn out that he had the baby prematurely cut out of her womb.

Caligula considered himself a god, but reveled in perversity and depravity. He abused men, women, children, and babies indiscriminately. He would force himself upon married women in public. Once he attended a wedding and ran off with the bride. He even opened a brothel in a wing of the imperial palace.

Caligula particularly enjoyed watching torture and executions. He condemned people to death for no reason and then made sure their deaths were as long and painful as possible. Once when he was watching executions in the arena and the criminals had all been killed, he ordered people from the audience be thrown to the beasts.

Caligula's cruelty was matched only by his deranged imagination. On one occasion, the emperor had a pontoon bridge built across the bay of Naples, and he charged back and forth on it for two days straight for no apparent reason. Afterwards, he had his army celebrate what he called "his victory over the sea" by collecting shells on the beach. Caligula especially loved his horse, Incitatus, and he would send out dinner invitations to people from Incitatus and make the horse the guest of honor. He even wanted to appoint the horse consul of Rome.

Caligula's eccentricities made him unstable and unpopular, to say the least. After thwarting several attempts on his life, he was finally stabbed to death in A.D. 41 by two of his guards who then stormed the palace and brutally exterminated the rest of his family.

Caligula enjoyed watching torture and executions.

Nero's principle of *Christiani non sint!*

Nero was the first to declare Christianity unlawful, and sought to punish all believers with death under his principle *Christiani non sint* (Let the Christians be exterminated).

According to the Roman historian Tacitus, the Church historian Eusebius, and other early Christian writers, Nero's persecution of the early Christians, which included the martyrdom of the first pope, St. Peter himself, helped set the Roman Empire along a path of increased, though irregular, persecution in the coming decades.

Because of his petulance, however, Nero had alienated the established aristocracy. His murder of his mother and wife horrified the elite, and his suspected burning of the city along with his seizure of land essentially sealed his fate. In A.D. 66, Judea revolted against his rule, and by A.D. 68 there were further revolts in Gaul, Africa, and Spain. The army turned against him in A.D. 68 and Nero committed suicide. Before doing so he is said to have lamented, "What an artist dies with me!" (Suetonius, *Nero*, 48-9).

PERSECUTION UNDER EMPEROR DOMITIAN, "LORD AND GOD"

Domitian (A.D. 51-96) served as emperor beginning in A.D. 81. An effective and hard-working ruler, Domitian took particular interest in directing military campaigns and securing the patronage of the army. He had good cause to curry the favor of the army, for his relationship with the Roman Senate was less than ideal. He is reported to have opened his letters to the Senate with the words, "Our lord god orders that this be done." He also habitually referred to himself in the third person as *Dominus et Deus* ("Lord and God"). As the years passed, Domitian became pathologically suspicious of conspirators and once quipped, "No one believes in a conspiracy against an emperor until it has succeeded."

Domitian was particularly intent on stopping the spread of Christianity from the lower classes to the aristocracy, which included members of his own family. When the Emperor murdered his cousin, an office-holding Christian, he set in motion a conspiracy against him (his wife Domitia possibly being one of the conspirators) that culminated in his assassination.

Despite the fact that growing numbers of patricians began to convert to Christianity, all believers remained subject to heavy impositions placed upon them by the empire. Domitian levied a special tax only on Christians and Jews to pay for a new temple dedicated to Jupiter, and Pope St. Clement I speaks of "misfortunes and catastrophes" in the Roman community because of persecution.

THE VOICE OF THE PEOPLE (*Vox populi*)

As Christianity expanded, the greatest threat to Christians often came not from the Roman emperors themselves but from the empire's local populations. The people's misunderstanding of Christian doctrine and practice often evolved into violent hatred and fear. Sometimes Christians were denounced as atheists for refusing to believe in the Roman gods. In addition to such misunderstandings of actual Christian worship, the people falsely accused Christians of engaging in truly outrageous practices, such as sacrificing babies and drinking their blood, and casting evil spells. Hence, the Roman historian Tacitus could write that the Christians held to "pernicious superstition," even though it is evident that such practices were largely a fig-ment of the people's imagination. (cf. Livingstone, *The Oxford Dictionary of the Christian Church*, 1997, p. 1574)

The people also blamed Christians for causing natural calamities such as floods, earthquakes, and famines. Tertullian wrote: "If the Tiber floods the city or the Nile does not inundate the fields, if there is an eclipse, or earthquake, or famine, or plague, men cry, 'Christians to the lions'" (*Apologeticum*, 40).

Angry crowds often looted and destroyed churches, Christian cemeteries, and the homes of those they believed to be Christians. Christians served as scapegoats for the Roman community, and were collectively tortured and killed to provide an outlet for the people's anger.

Death by wild beasts in the Amphitheater is shown in this mosaic from a villa near Leptis Magna, North Africa. The crowd would roar *"Salvum lotum"* (well washed) at the blood-bath.

PART II
"The Five Good Emperors"
(A.D. 96-180)

The five emperors that followed Domitian have been called "The Five Good Emperors" because of their skill in leading the Empire. They are Nerva, Trajan, Hadrian, Antoninus Pius, and Marcus Aurelius. These emperors generally enjoyed the support of the army, senate, and the people, and were certainly much more stable than either Caligula or Nero. They worked to secure the existing borders of the Roman Empire and even expanded them.

While these five emperors were good for the Empire's interests, they were not necessarily supportive of Christianity. Although the first four of these emperors were more moderate than Nero, they by no means halted the persecution of Christians.

TRAJAN'S RESCRIPT (A.D. 112)

Trajan (ca. A.D. 53-117) began to rule in A.D. 98. His nearly twenty year reign is considered to be one of the most excellent in the empire's history, both because of his humane treatment of abandoned children and the poor, and for his military conquests in Dacia (modern Romania) and Parthia (much of modern Iraq). Trajan, who took for himself the title Optimus (Best), was an able military leader who actively sought military glory for himself and Rome. The Roman Senate used the ritual acclamation, "May you be even luckier than Augustus and even better than Trajan."

The Dacians proved worthy opponents of Rome, but they were defeated nonetheless. The great treasure of the Dacian ruler Decebalus financed many of Trajan's public works. With some of the booty, Trajan's Column (A.D. 113) was constructed to commemorate his great victory and serve as his mausoleum. In defeating the Parthians, Trajan extended the Empire to the Persian Gulf, but this gain in territory was short-lived. Trajan's health failed and he died while leading his army against a Jewish revolt in A.D. 117.

Trajan's Eastern expedition was the last major conquest of the Roman Empire. After A.D. 117 the borders of the Empire remained stable and secure for one hundred fifty years. Only a campaign led by Emperor Septimus Severus from A.D. 195-198 brought a small, northern portion of Mesopotamia into Roman hands.

With respect to Christianity, Trajan took what he deemed to be an enlightened and balanced approach. A letter from one of his governors, Pliny the Younger (ca. A.D. 61-ca. 112), asked for Trajan's advice con-

Trajan's Column is made from a series of 18 colossal Luna marble drums, each weighing about 40 tons, and is exactly 100 Roman feet (30 meters) high. The frieze winds around the shaft 23 times and contains over 2,500 figures. Inside the column, a spiral staircase of 185 stairs provides access to a viewing platform at the top. Originally, a gilded bronze statue of Trajan crowned the top of the column. In 1588, Pope Sixtus V replaced it with a statue of St. Peter.

cerning the persecution and punishment of Christians. According to both Nero and Domitian, Christians were to be summarily executed, and Pliny had executed Christians out of a sense of responsibility. Pliny made it clear to Trajan that Christians by this time existed across all strata of society, and lived in rural as well as urban areas. Pliny posed four questions to Trajan: whether anonymous denunciations of Christians were to be pursued; whether the age of Christians should be taken into consideration in determining their punishment; whether Christians who denied their faith publicly should be allowed to live; and whether the profession of Christianity itself, apart from the crimes associated with the practice of the Faith, was sufficient to warrant execution.

Trajan's response to Pliny offered a nuanced, though definite, policy for handling Christianity. Trajan decreed that if Christians renounced their faith and offered sacrifice to the Roman gods, they would be allowed to live in spite of their past Christian life. Furthermore, Trajan declared that anonymous denunciations were not to be pursued. Nevertheless, anyone denounced openly who admitted his status as a Christian was to suffer death. Trajan's decision thus confirmed that the profession of Christianity was itself a crime, but clarified under what conditions it could be prosecuted.

Trajan's Rescript still left Christians with an awful choice: death or apostasy. While Trajan did seek to remedy the gross abuses of the legal system that were often used in the persecution of Christians, in the end, he upheld the principle first attributed to Nero: *Christiani non sint.*

ST. IGNATIUS, BISHOP OF ANTIOCH

St. Ignatius (ca. A.D. 50-ca. 107) was likely the third Bishop of Antioch, after Sts. Peter and Evodius, and he is thought to have listened at the feet of St. John the Evangelist. Because of his close association with Sts. Peter and John, St. Ignatius is an Apostolic Father, i.e., one of those saintly figures who had direct contact with the Apostles, and consequently his writings are considered especially authoritative. In fact, St. Ignatius' letters are considered the most important documents which link the Twelve Apostles with the early Church.

Little is known of St. Ignatius' life up to his arrest during the reign of Trajan for being a renowned Christian bishop. Under a guard of ten soldiers, he traveled to Rome to meet a martyr's death. Along the way he was happily received by the Christian communities of the day, and it was during this time that St. Ignatius carried on a correspondence with the various churches of Asia Minor and the bishop of Smyrna, St. Polycarp.

In these letters, known as the Seven Epistles, St. Ignatius makes clear his ardent desire for martyrdom, going so far as to ask the Christians not to intervene with the pagan officials to save his life. Instead, he wrote, "I am God's wheat, and I am ground by the teeth of wild beasts, that I may be found Christ's pure bread" (*Epistle to the Romans*, IV.1).

St. Ignatius denounced all heresy and schism, and he singled out the episcopacy in the Church as a bulwark against false belief and

THE COLISEUM

The Coliseum's "Door of Death" and the skeleton of cages and cells which were located under the stadium floor.

The Coliseum of Rome remains both a tribute to the brilliant engineering of the ancient Romans and a witness of their gruesome entertainments and disregard for human life. The construction began around A.D. 72 under Emperor Vespasian and was completed by the Emperor Domitian. The Coliseum was originally known as the Flavian Amphitheater.

In its heyday, the building boasted a number of technological wonders. It featured a cooling system made from a large canopy suspended by ropes over the audience that provided shade and created a breeze. Underneath the stadium floor, there were cells to house wild beasts, condemned criminals, and trained gladiators. These "entertainers" could enter the arena through dozens of elevators or trap doors.

Although the standard forms of entertainment were executions, fights between various animals, between men and animals, and, of course, the famous gladiatorial combats fascinated the Romans. During the emperor Titus' hundred-day festival celebrating the Coliseum's inauguration, contests pitted bears, buffalo, elephants, rhinoceri, lions and other wild animals against each other and against armed or unarmed men.

It is possible that some Christians were condemned *ad bestias* in the Coliseum, but it is more likely that they were killed in the circus Flaminius, the Gaianum, the Circus of Hadrian, the *Amphitheatrum Castrense*, or the Stadium of Domitian.

Gladiatorial combats were finally outlawed in 404, largely due to the influence of Christianity, and the Coliseum quickly became a site of pilgrimage. Indeed, it remains standing today, preserved as a testament to those great sacrifices made by Christians during the dark days of persecution.

as a means of unity with Christ. Without bishops, St. Ignatius asserted, neither Matrimony nor celebration of the Eucharist were possible. Indeed, St. Ignatius counseled the early Christians to remain "aloof" from the heretics who "confess not the Eucharist to be the flesh of our Saviour Jesus Christ, which suffered for our sins, and which the Father, of His goodness, raised up again" (*Epistle to the Smyrnaeans*, VII). The Eucharist, St. Ignatius wrote, is "the bread that is the flesh of Jesus Christ, this flesh which has suffered for our sins." St. Ignatius elaborated on the Incarnation, Passion, death, and Resurrection of Christ.

As mentioned in the previous chapter, St. Ignatius was also the first person to use the term "Catholic Church," which he again linked to the episcopacy. Finally, St. Ignatius supported the primacy of the papacy, and advocated deference to the Bishop of Rome.

Upon his arrival in Rome, St. Ignatius was martyred in the Coliseum. St. Ignatius was led out in front of a great crowd and was fed to lions. His feast day is celebrated on October 17.

HADRIAN'S RESCRIPT (A.D. 123/124)

The Emperor Hadrian succeeded Trajan in A.D. 117 and served until his death in A.D. 138. When Hadrian's biological father died, Trajan, who was his second cousin, adopted him. Hadrian later married a great-niece of Trajan. He traveled extensively and strengthened the frontiers of the empire, building many defensive lines such as Hadrian's Wall in England.

Hadrian was an ardent advocate of Hellenism. He was interested in science, art, and philosophy and enjoyed debating the sophists. It was said that Favorinus, a philosopher, yielded the debate to Hadrian saying, "Who could contradict the Lord of Thirty Legions?"

In religion, Hadrian promoted the cult of the gods and designed a special temple built for Venus and Roma in the Roman Forum. Hadrian banned circumcision among the Jews, and planned to turn Jerusalem into a Roman colony called *Aelia Capitolina*. The Jews responded by revolting under their leader Bar Kokhba in A.D. 132. After this revolt was suppressed in A.D. 135, the Jews were forbidden to enter Jerusalem.

In A.D. 123/124 Hadrian answered the request of Serenus Granianus, Proconsul of the Province of Asia, who wanted the emperor's advice on how to handle the often violent crowds intent on murdering Christians and inquired whether they should be prosecuted for simply being Christian.

In his official response, or rescript, Hadrian emphasized the primacy of the rule of law over mob action. Furthermore, he ordered that Christians could only be prosecuted for actual violations of the common law, not just for professing Christian belief. If an accuser made false accusations, then the accuser himself was to be punished. Accordingly, under Hadrian, Christians enjoyed a relative amount of toleration, although there was no official codification of such toleration.

The Hadrian Arch in Athens was built by Hadrian in A.D. 131 as part of a wall separating the old and new cities. On the side facing the Acropolis is the inscription, "This is Athens the former city of Theseus." The side facing the new city reads, "This is the city of Hadrian and not of Theseus."

ST. POLYCARP, BISHOP OF SMYRNA

Lord, I bless you for judging me worthy on this day, this hour, so that in the company of the martyrs I may share the cup of Christ. (St. Polycarp, as quoted in *Martyrium Polycarpi*)

St. Polycarp (ca. A.D. 69 - ca. 155) suffered martyrdom during the long and peaceful reign of Roman Emperor Antoninus Pius (A.D. 86-161, emperor A.D. 138-161). St. Polycarp spent much of his life defending orthodox Catholic belief against various heresies. He is an important link to the Apostles and a great number of Christian writers who lived toward the end of the second century. Along with St. Ignatius and Pope St. Clement I, St. Polycarp is one of the most important Apostolic Fathers. He was a friend and correspondent of St. Ignatius. Only one of St. Ignatius' letters to St. Polycarp has survived.

After traveling to Rome to discuss the date of Easter with Pope St. Anacletus, St. Polycarp returned to Smyrna (modern Izmir, Turkey). Shortly thereafter he was arrested during a pagan festival and charged with being a Christian. The letter "*Martyrium Polycarpi*" (The Martyrdom of Polycarp) was written by someone of the church in Smyrna to the church in Philomelium, and relates the details of St. Polycarp's martyrdom.

The governor wished to save St. Polycarp, and asked him to curse Christ in public so that his life could be spared. St. Polycarp refused to renounce Christ and was sentenced to be burned alive. The executioners, impressed by St. Polycarp's courage, honored his request to be tied to the stake, rather than fastened with spikes. Once the fire began, St. Polycarp remained unharmed from the flames. Finally, an executioner killed St. Polycarp with a sword. The Church celebrates his feast day on February 23.

Excavations of ancient Smyrna and the modern-day city of Izmir, Turkey which is located on Mt. Pagus, the acropolis of ancient Smyrna. This location was selected by Alexander the Great in 334 B.C. Smyrna, whose name is derived from "myrrh," a small tree which grows abundantly in the area, is by far the oldest city on the Aegean coast. The earliest levels date to 3000 B.C. After coming under the rule of Rome, Smyrna never wavered in its loyalty to the Empire. It became a center for the cult of emperor worship.

EMPEROR MARCUS AURELIUS, THE PHILOSOPHER-KING

A page from Marcus Aurelius' *Meditations*

Marcus Aurelius (A.D. 121-180) was a favorite adopted son of Emperor Hadrian. Upon the death of Emperor Antoninus Pius, Marcus Aurelius ascended the throne in A.D. 161. Marcus Aurelius was an ardent Stoic, and philosophy was the central focus of his life. When he died, Marcus Aurelius' book *Meditations* was found on his person. Marcus Aurelius' *Meditations* is a thoughtful and moving work that reflects the profound discipline of a Stoic's life. He exemplified Stoicism's ideal of living free from passion, unmoved by joy or grief, and submitting without complaint to unavoidable fate.

Marcus Aurelius adhered to Trajan's Rescript, outlawing Christianity and persecuting the Christians. He reinstituted the practice of anonymous denouncements, and did not hesitate to kill Christians when it served the empire's interests. Many of the persecutions undertaken during Marcus Aurelius' reign, however, originated not directly from the emperor, but from angry provincial mobs and the governors who were meant to hold them in check. Allowing mobs to kill Christians was an effective way of diffusing their anger, which otherwise might turn against the empire itself. Marcus Aurelius' attitude towards any new religion was generally disdainful. If the new sect excited the people, the emperor was willing to respond with strong punishments.

Emperor Marcus Aurelius

Marcus Aurelius was the first emperor who had to deal aggressively with the *Volkerwanderung* ("people wanderings"), the Germanic invasions on the Empire's northern borders. Emperor Marcus Aurelius was successful in his campaigns, but ultimately these migrations and attacks would overcome the empire in later centuries.

ST. JUSTIN MARTYR

St. Justin Martyr (ca. A.D. 100 - ca. 165) was one of the most famous martyrs to die under the persecution of Marcus Aurelius. Born of pagan parents in Shechem in Samaria in Palestine, Justin studied philosophy from his early youth, and converted to Christianity in his thirtieth year. Tradition has it that Justin was walking along the sea one day and met a mysterious old man whom he had never seen before. The old man began talking to Justin and convinced him that true knowledge of God could not come only from philosophy, but must be supplemented by reading the revealed word of the prophets. After his conversion, Justin continued studying philosophy and became an excellent apologist for the Faith.

Justin worked tirelessly during the Roman persecutions to defend the Church against those pagans who falsely accused her. Justin respected philosophy, but saw that its truths were mere shadows compared to Christ's teachings.

In his *First Apology,* which he addressed to Emperor Antoninus Pius and his two adopted sons, Marcus Aurelius and Lucius Verus, Justin provides important descriptions of the rituals for the celebration of Baptism and the Eucharist. The *Second Apology* was addressed to the Roman Senate just after Marcus Aurelius became emperor in A.D. 161. Shortly thereafter Justin and six others were denounced as Christians. When they refused to sacrifice to the gods, they were beheaded. The official account of their martyrdom is worth quoting in full:

> The Prefect Rusticus says: Approach and sacrifice, all of you, to the gods. Justin says: No one in his right mind gives up piety for impiety. The Prefect Rusticus says: If you do not obey, you will be tortured without mercy. Justin replies: That is our desire, to be tortured for Our Lord, Jesus Christ, and so to be saved, for that will give us salvation and firm confidence at the more terrible universal tribunal of Our Lord and Saviour. And all the martyrs said: Do as you wish; for we are Christians, and we do not sacrifice to idols. The Prefect Rusticus read the sentence: Those who do not wish to sacrifice to the gods and to obey the emperor will be scourged and beheaded according to the laws. The holy martyrs glorifying God betook themselves to the customary place, where they were beheaded and consummated their martyrdom confessing their Savior. (*The Martyrdom of the Holy Martyrs Justin, Chariton, Charites, Pæon, and Liberianus, Who Suffered at Rome,* IV-V)

St. Justin Martyr's feast day is celebrated on June 1.

AD METALLA

During the Roman persecutions, one of the most dreadful sentences a Christian prisoner could receive was *"Ad metalla"* (to the metal mines). Being sentenced to work in a mine meant facing unsanitary and extremely dangerous conditions, inadequate and contaminated food, brutal guards, lack of air, and overcrowded living quarters.

A sentence to the mines meant eventual death. Free men and women, slaves, and criminals were mixed in with one another and led to the mines in long processions after having been branded on the face with red-hot irons. They were chained in twos and were never able to stand erect in the tight confines of the mining shafts. Eventually, prisoners died of exhaustion, prison labor, or the conditions of their captivity.

A stairway down into the bowels of the Rosia Montana Gold Mine in Romania's Apuseni mountains. The mountain is honeycombed with Roman mine-galleries from the first and second centuries. The town was then known as Alburnus Major. Trajan's conquest of Dacia (Romania) brought to Rome the great treasure from these mines.

PART III

Later Persecutions and the Edict of Milan

The reign of Emperor Septimus Severus (emperor A.D. 193-211) was characterized by warfare in Britain and Mesopotamia. By this time the military played an ever-increasing role in the selection of the emperor and the elimination of his enemies. Severus issued a decree in A.D. 202 declaring that circumcision and Baptism were to be forbidden. This threatened not only Christians, but Jews as well. Another round of persecutions followed, which were concentrated mainly in Syria and Africa.

STS. PERPETUA AND FELICITY

Stand firm in faith, love one another and do not be tempted to do anything wrong because of our sufferings. (St. Perpetua to her brother during her death at the games, quoted in *Account of the Martyrdom of the Holy Martyrs of Carthage*, ch. 18.)

Two victims of the harsh persecutions of Septimus Severus were Sts. Perpetua and Felicity. St. Perpetua was a noblewoman who sought instruction in Christianity for herself and her household, and St. Felicity was a slave in that household. When these two women and their fellow catechumens were discovered by Roman officials, both women were jailed and forced to raise their children in prison. St. Perpetua's family, especially her father, a governor in Carthage, begged her to reject Christianity for her own sake and for that of her family, but she refused.

While in prison, St. Felicity gave birth, and as she cried out because of her labor pains, the guards mocked her and told her that she would soon undergo something much more painful. In a great spirit of faith, St. Felicity responded to her tormentors that at the present moment she was bearing her discomfort on her own, but Christ would bear her suffering during her execution.

Above: Her elaborate headdress and gown reveal St. Perpetua as a wealthy noblewoman in this mosaic from Ravenna, Italy.

Emperor Septimus Severus

In A.D. 203, Sts. Perpetua and Felicity were martyred together with the catechumens in the main arena at Carthage. Sts. Perpetua and Felicity suffered a particularly gruesome martyrdom. St. Perpetua's entire household was first scourged, and then attacked by various wild animals including leopards, bears, and wild boars. Finally, some of the Christians, including St. Perpetua, had to be stabbed to death because they were not yet dead. Both Sts. Perpetua and Felicity are honored in the Roman canon; their feast day is celebrated on March 7.

ST. IRENAEUS, BISHOP OF LYONS

St. Irenaeus (ca. A.D. 130 - ca. 200) was a disciple of St. Polycarp, and is believed to have come from Smyrna. Although a native of Asia Minor, St. Irenaeus served as Bishop of Lyons, and is regarded as the preeminent figure of the early Church in Gaul. Irenaeus devoted much of his energy to combating heresies, especially Gnosticism. In his defense of orthodoxy, St. Irenaeus emphasized key elements of the Church: the episcopacy, Sacred Scripture, and Tradition. He spoke explicitly of the importance of recourse to the Church's tradition, even though Christianity was still very much in its infancy. He argued, "If the revelation of God through creation gives life to all who live upon the earth, much more does the manifestation of the Father through the Word give life to those who see God" (St. Irenaeus, *Adversus hæreses*, IV.20.7).

St. Irenaeus' writings are of special interest given the way they systematically describe the origin and history of each heresy before contrasting its false claims with Catholic teaching. St. Irenaeus' work is still necessary and helpful to scholars seeking an in-depth look at early theological disputes. The most famous of these works is the *Adversus haereses,* also known as the Refutation of Gnosticism.

St. Irenaeus subsequently became the Bishop of Lyons in 178, and held the office for approximately twenty-five years. According to tradition, St. Irenaeus was martyred during the reign of Emperor Septimus Severus. His feast day is celebrated on June 28.

THE EDICT OF DECIUS (A.D. 250)

After the reign of Septimus Severus, Christians enjoyed relative peace for about fifty years. Emperor Alexander Severus (emperor A.D. 222-235) even permitted Christians to own property and build churches. However, in the second half of the third century the empire entered into a troubling political period. In a short span of just forty-six years (A.D. 238-284), there were eighteen legitimate emperors, and many others who sought illegitimate ascendance. Most of these emperors ruled for a brief time before meeting with a violent end.

Emperor Decius (emperor A.D. 249-251) reigned for only three years, but he inaugurated the first empire-wide persecution of Christians. Other emperors had limited their directives, horrible as they may have been, to the city of Rome or to specific provincial communities. Decius, however, who believed that the survival of the empire depended upon the restoration of the old pagan cults, sought to extirpate Christianity from the empire.

Decius assumed control of the Roman Empire at a precarious point in its history. The empire was threatened both by the army, which essentially controlled the emperor, and by external enemies, specifically Germanic hordes who constantly attacked along the eastern frontier. Faced with such a bleak political situation, Decius sought to reinvigorate the empire's strength and unity through a return to the ancient religious practices of the state.

Since Christianity called for ultimate allegiance to Christ and not to the state, Decius saw this as incompatible with his plan. In his view, Christianity, which by that time was the religion of roughly one-third of the Roman Empire, was in part the cause of the divided empire.

Emperor Decius promulgated an edict of extermination against the Christians. Anyone suspected of being Christian had to present him or herself before the local magistrate and offer a simple sacrifice to prove he or she had given up the Faith. Those Christians who offered sacrifice to the pagan gods were known as *sacrificanti;* those who burned incense to the pagan gods were called *thurificati.* Certificates, purchased at a price from officials, stating that the bearer had already offered sacrifice to the gods were also available. Christians who purchased these certificates were called *libellatici.*

Decius ordered the arrest of all known Christians who failed to appear before the magistrate or who could not produce a certificate. Christians who refused to renounce their faith were sent into exile or put to death, and all of their property was confiscated.

The Church's loss was two-fold in these times: she lost those faithful Christians who were martyred during the persecutions, and she lost those unfaithful Christians who committed apostasy. Apostasy is the willful denunciation of the Faith in its entirety.

Apostasy denotes a backsliding from God. This may happen in various ways according to the different kinds of union between man and God. For, in the first place, man is united to

CERTIFICATE OF SACRIFICE TO THE OLD GODS

This certificate of sacrifice reads:

"It has never been my practice to sacrifice to the gods; now in your presence, in accordance with the Command, I have sacrificed, poured libation, and tasted the offering.

"I beg you to certify my statement...

"I Aurelia Demos have presented this declaration. I Aurelius Ireneus (her husband) wrote for her as she is illiterate. I Aurelius Sabinus the commissioner saw you sacrificing."

God by faith; secondly, by having his will duly submissive in obeying His commandments; thirdly, by certain special things pertaining to supererogation such as the religious life, the clerical state, or the opulence Holy Orders. Now if that which follows be removed, that which precedes, remains, but the converse does not hold. Accordingly a man may apostatize from God, by withdrawing from the religious life to which he was bound by profession, or from the Holy Order which he had received: and this is called "apostasy from religious life" or "Orders." A man may also apostatize from God, by rebelling in his mind against the Divine commandments: and though man may apostatize in both the above ways, he may still remain united to God by faith.

But if he gives up the Faith, then he seems to turn away from God altogether: and consequently, apostasy simply and absolutely is that whereby a man withdraws from the Faith, and is called "apostasy of perfidy." On this way apostasy, simply so called, pertains to unbelief. (St. Thomas Aquinas, *Summa Theologica*, II-II, Q. xii a. 1)

Emperor Decius

Thus, of the three types of apostasy mentioned, the third, "apostasy of perfidy," which is the general understanding of someone accused of apostasy, is the most grave, and it is a sin that incurs excommunication. Note, however, that the apostate and the heretic differ — the heretic denies one or more doctrines of the Faith; the apostate denies the Faith altogether.

The persecutions of Decius unfortunately resulted in many apostates, and the leaders of the Church at this time had difficult decisions to make regarding the status of apostates and their possible re-entry into the community of believers. The most rigorous factions of the Church denied that the *lapsi*—Christians who formally renounced their faith, offering sacrifices to pagan gods—could be readmitted. The popes decided that with long penances, the *lapsi* would be allowed to return. The controversy surrounding these *lapsi* gave rise to the Novatianist schism. The Roman presbyter Novatian led a "rigorist" faction, declaring that those who had renounced the Faith (the *lapsi*) could never be re-admitted into the Church.

Decius was afraid of the Christians because of their fidelity to Christ and his Church. He felt that the practice of Christianity would detract from allegiance to the state. This bias has reappeared in different forms throughout the history of the Church. It first appeared among the Romans, but has been used as a pretext for persecution and discrimination against Catholics in Elizabethan England, Bismarck's *Kulturkampf* in Germany in the nineteenth century, and in many places today.

ORIGEN: THEOLOGIAN AND BIBLICAL EXEGETE

Origen (ca. A.D. 185-ca. 254) was the most prolific writer and important theologian and biblical exegete in the eastern part of the Empire. Origen was an Egyptian who spent much of his life working and teaching in Alexandria. His father was martyred during a persecution in A.D. 202, and Origen later became the head of the first Catechetical School in Alexandria. This institution combined instruction in Catholic doctrine with an investigation into the sciences and philosophy, and in some ways might be considered the first Catholic university.

Origen came into conflict with his bishop in Alexandria after he visited Palestine at the invitation of the bishops of Caesarea and Aelia. On his first visit to Palestine in A.D. 215, the two bishops there invited him to preach, breaking the ecclesiastical practice of allowing only priests and bishops to give the homily. During a second visit to Palestine in A.D. 230, again at the invitation of the bishops, Origen was ordained to the priesthood. Origen's bishop in Alexandria then stripped him of his teaching position, as well as his faculties for the exercise of his priesthood, claiming that his ordination was not valid. Because of these actions, Origen moved permanently to Caesarea in A.D. 231, where he founded a new school, similar to the one in Alexandria.

During the persecution of the Emperor Decius, Origen was taken into custody in A.D. 250. For approximately two years, he was brutally tortured. Origen, however, held fast to his faith, inspiring many with his zeal. He was eventually released and lived for several more years, but his broken body quickly gave out.

It is estimated that Origen wrote between two and five thousand different tracts, nearly all of which are lost. However, one of his chief works, "*De principiis*," survives. In addition to his many scholarly writings, Origen is considered to have initiated the concept of the homily.

Origen always professed allegiance to the Church in his writings. Nevertheless, his writings on the Trinity in which he tended to subordinate the Son to the Father and his ideas on final salvation of the damned prompted Church officials to reject some of Origen's teachings. In spite of some of his erroneous ideas, he is rightly regarded as one of the greatest and most brilliant theologians of the early Church.

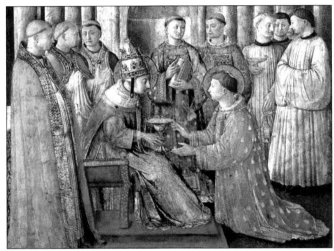

Pope St. Sixtus II ordains St. Lawrence

POPE ST. SIXTUS II AND DEACON ST. LAWRENCE

Emperor Valerian ruled from A.D. 253 to 260, and during this time issued two rescripts, one in A.D. 257 and one in A.D. 258. The rescript of A.D. 257 forbade Christians from meeting in public places and from celebrating the Eucharist in the catacombs. The rescript of A.D. 258, however, was harsher. Under this rescript, issued because of political pressure, bishops, priests, and deacons were immediately executed, and Christians of rank were removed from their offices and often sold into slavery.

Valerian's persecutions subsided toward the end of his reign, largely because the Gothic invasions and the rise of Persia demanded greater imperial attention. Eventually the Persian leader Sapor I captured Valerian and held him as a prisoner of war for five years. Humiliated and tortured, Valerian nonetheless showed courage before dying in captivity. Valerian was the first Roman emperor to be captured by a foreign enemy. After his death, the Persians stuffed Valerian's body and hung it inside a temple.

In the days of Valerian's second rescript, Pope St. Sixtus II was apprehended while celebrating Mass with seven deacons, one of whom was St. Lawrence. Pope St. Sixtus and six of the deacons

The Martyrdom of St. Lawrence. "I am roasted enough on this side; turn me around."

were beheaded on the spot, but Lawrence was spared for the time. The authorities demanded that he bring the Church's treasure to them, and sent him to get it. When he returned a short time later, Lawrence brought with him a group of poor people—the Church's treasure. In response, the Roman authorities sentenced Lawrence to be roasted alive on a gridiron. Tradition holds that as he burned, Lawrence told the judge, "I am roasted enough on this side; turn me around."

PERSECUTIONS UNDER DIOCLETIAN

Born in Dalmatia (modern-day Croatia), Diocletian rose through the ranks of the Roman army to serve with the emperor's guards during the Persian campaign. When Numerian was murdered in A.D. 284 the army made Diocletian the new emperor. Like his predecessors Decius and Valerian, Diocletian desired to unify the empire. He used his organizational prowess to this end, eventually crushing the Persian Empire and ending the crisis of the third century.

Diocletian spent much of his first ten years as emperor battling the barbarians on the German and Persian frontiers. This diversion initially inclined the early Church historian Eusebius to praise Diocletian's clemency toward Christians. But in A.D. 303, with the barbarians defeated, Diocletian turned his attention to the Church. On February 23 a new edict was issued at Nicomedia and The Great Persecution began. Christian Churches were destroyed; books were burned. The palace at Nicomedia was set ablaze prompting additional edicts. For the next ten years, until Constantine's defeat of Maxentius at the Milvian Bridge on A.D. October 28, 312, and the "Edict of Milan" in 313, the Christians throughout the Empire were imprisoned, tortured, forced to offer sacrifices to pagan gods, and martyerd according to the changing fortunes of the Imperial rulers.

THE TETRARCHY (A.D. 293)

Due to the enormous size of the Roman Empire, Diocletian decided to divide it into four administrative districts, each with its own Caesar, or regional ruler. Diocletian himself ruled Thrace, Egypt and Asia Minor; Maximian ruled Italy and Africa; Constantius presided over Gaul, Spain, and Britain; and Galerius ruled along the Danube River. Diocletian himself retained full leadership over the entire empire, but found it expedient to grant his appointed Caesars considerable governing power within their separate spheres. Diocletian effectively split the empire in two; he and Galerius ruled the eastern half, and Maximian and Constantius governed the western half.

Not one of the Tetrarchs lived in Rome, causing this great imperial city to begin to lose its preeminent status as the capital of the empire. (Diocletian visited it only once during his reign.) Diocletian further weakened the senate by removing its effective political influence. He wanted to make the lines of succession clearer, and thus avoid needless conflict; and second, he hoped to fortify the borders of the empire, which in the past decades had been under aggressive foreign attack. Later,

Diocletian and Maximian, senior members of the Tetrarchy.

Diocletian's reforms resulted in some of the most heinous persecutions of Christians during the first centuries of the early Church.

divided the provinces into even smaller units called "dioceses" in an attempt to achieve a higher degree of administrative efficiency.

Military reforms increased the size of the Roman army, and Diocletian developed a set of defensive works along the empire's borders. The cost of the new administration and increasing the army placed a heavy burden on the treasury, but secured for the Roman people almost twenty years of peaceful prosperity.

During Diocletian's reign, his reforms helped spare the empire the crisis of succession that it had known all too well during the previous half-century. However, after Diocletian's abdication in A.D. 305, the tetrarchy failed to function effectively. The four positions of power competed with one another for absolute supremacy.

FOUR EDICTS

Though he was superstitious, Diocletian was initially tolerant of Christianity, and even admired some of its adherents. Maximian and Galerius, on the other hand, were wary of the religion and pressed Diocletian to eradicate it for the good of the empire. At their request, Diocletian issued four edicts. These edicts resulted in the worst of all the persecutions the Christians suffered under the Romans. Diocletian's first edict commanded the destruction of churches and the burning of the Scriptures, as well as banning all Christian gatherings. Those who opposed this law faced execution or enslavement.

The succeeding edicts were applied only in the east by Galerius and Diocletian. The second edict sanctioned the imprisonment of the clergy. The third edict demanded pagan sacrifice from the clergy. Finally, the fourth edict demanded sacrifice from every Christian, not just the clergy. This last edict resulted in the deaths of many thousands of Christians who refused to offer pagan sacrifice. Constantine the Great later commented that if the Romans had slain as many barbarians as they had slaughtered Christians during the reign of Diocletian, there would be no barbarians left to threaten the safety of the Empire.

DIOCLETIAN'S TETRARCHY ca. A.D. 295

THE EMPIRE RULED BY FOUR

Constantius ruled the Prefecture of Gaul.

Maximian ruled the Prefecture of Italia.

Galerius ruled the Prefecture of Illyricum.

Diocletian ruled the Prefecture of the East and retained full leadership over the entire empire as "lord and god."

This gold coin, minted in Antioch in A.D. 293-295 shows the laureate head of Constantius I as Caesar: CONSTANTIVS NOB CAES (Constantine is Caesar for us)

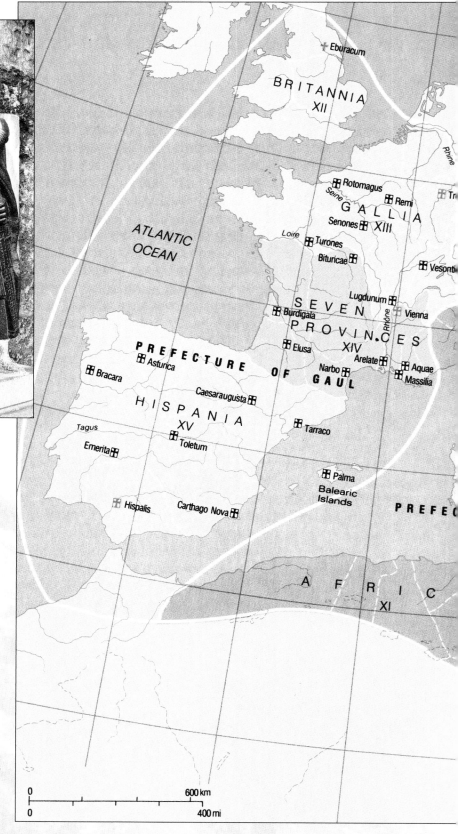

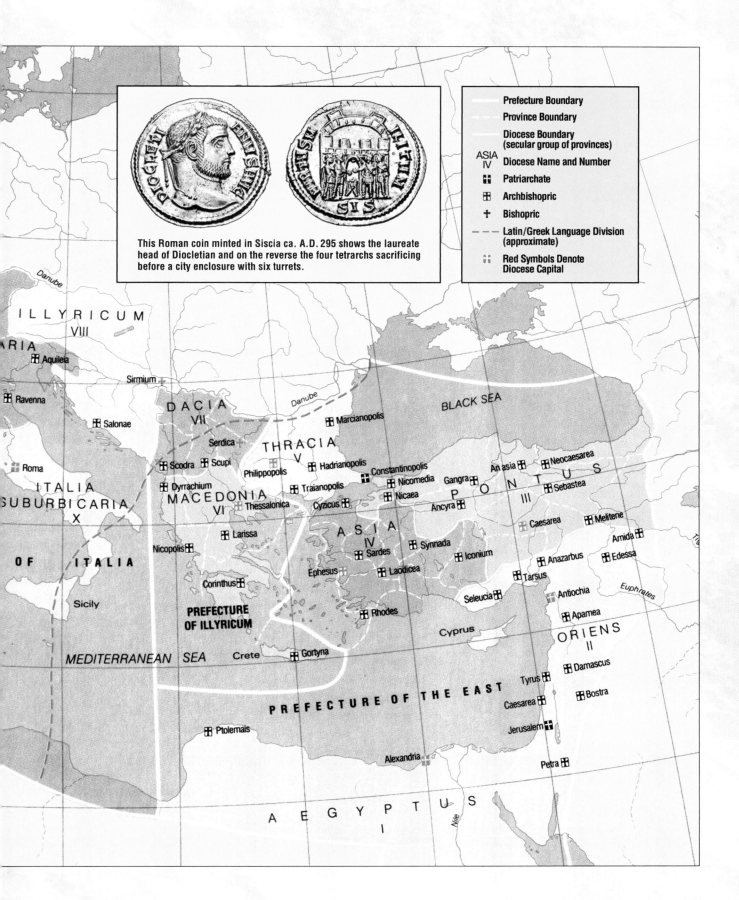

This Roman coin minted in Siscia ca. A.D. 295 shows the laureate head of Diocletian and on the reverse the four tetrarchs sacrificing before a city enclosure with six turrets.

Legend:

Prefecture Boundary	
Province Boundary	
Diocese Boundary (secular group of provinces)	
ASIA IV	Diocese Name and Number
⊞	Patriarchate
⊞	Archbishopric
✝	Bishopric
- - -	Latin/Greek Language Division (approximate)
⊞	Red Symbols Denote Diocese Capital

ILLYRICUM
VIII

Danube

ARIA

✝ Aquileia

✝ Ravenna

✝ Salonae

Sirmium ✝

DACIA
VII

Danube

BLACK SEA

✝ Marcianopolis

Serdica ✝

THRACIA
V

✝ Hadrianopolis

✝ Scodra   ✝ Scupi

Philippopolis

Constantinopolis ⊞

An asia ⊞   ✝ Neocaesarea

✝ Roma

✝ Dyrrachium

MACEDONIA
VI

✝ Traianopolis

✝ Nicomedia

✝ Nicaea

Gangra ✝

P O N T U S
III

✝ Sebastea

ITALIA
SUBURBICARIA
X

✝ Thessalonica

Cyzicus ⊞

Ancyra ✝

✝ Caesarea   ✝ Melitene

✝ Larissa

A S I A
IV

✝ Sardes   ✝ Synnada

✝ Iconium

Amida ⊞

OF   ITALIA

Nicopolis ⊞

Ephesus ⊞

✝ Laodicea

✝ Anazarbus   ✝ Edessa

Sicily

Corinthus ✝

✝ Tarsus

✝ Antiochia   Euphrates

PREFECTURE
OF ILLYRICUM

✝ Rhodes

Seleucia ✝

✝ Apamea

Cyprus

ORIENS
II

MEDITERRANEAN   SEA   Crete   ✝ Gortyna

✝ Damascus

P R E F E C T U R E   O F   T H E   E A S T

Tyrus ⊞

✝ Bostra

Caesarea ⊞

✝ Ptolemais

Jerusalem ⊞

Alexandria

Petra ⊞

A   E   G   Y   P   T   U   S
I

Nile

ST. AGNES: A CHILD MARTYR FOR CHRIST

A new kind of martyrdom! Too young to be punished, yet old enough for a martyr's crown. (St. Ambrose on the martyrdom of St. Agnes, On Virgins, I.8)

St. Agnes is one of the most highly revered of the virgin martyrs. She is believed to have died during Diocletian's persecution sometime during the fourth century, possibly in A.D. 304 or A.D. 305, when she was only twelve or thirteen years old. St. Ambrose, Pope St. Damasus I, and Prudentius, an early Christian poet, all sing her praises, although it is difficult to pin down a single picture of her from their different accounts. Her story existed as an oral tradition before it was set down in writing.

This oral tradition states that St. Agnes was a beautiful young woman, and that many of the leading young men of Rome desired her hand in marriage. However, she decided at a young age to consecrate herself to Christ and to live as a virgin. Her purity so enraged the young men that they denounced her before the magistrate as a Christian.

When taken before the magistrate, St. Agnes refused to renounce her faith in and commitment to Christ. She confessed her faith even while being tortured by fire. Her courage so angered the judge that he sentenced her to forced prostitution at the public brothel. St. Agnes however remained firm in her loyalty to Christ, believing that her purity would be protected even at the brothel. As the story goes, the first young man who looked at her with eyes of lust was immediately struck blind. Amazed and scared, the crowd backed away from her.

The judge, hearing of this, sentenced St. Agnes to be beheaded. When the feast of St. Agnes is celebrated on January 21, the Church also remembers the many women who suffered similar violence during the persecutions under Diocletian.

THE CHURCH TRIUMPHS

Due to his failing health, Diocletian abdicated on May 1, A.D. 305, and he convinced Maximian to step down as well. Galerius remained in power in the East, and Constantius took over control of the West. Constantius was succeeded by his son Constantine in A.D. 307.

Constantine was friendly with the Christians, although he was not one himself, but Galerius continued the persecution in the East until just before his death. In A.D. 311, however, Galerius was stricken with an eastern form of leprosy that left his body crippled and decrepit. He confessed and whimpered in utter terror that his sickness was the divine retribution of the Christian God. On April 30, A.D. 311, Galerius issued an edict admitting the failure of his policy with regard to the Christians. He then instituted the free exercise of the Christian religion as long as Christians obeyed the law and promised to pray for the emperor and the empire. Galerius' edict was also adopted in the West. Thus the last and greatest persecution begun under Diocletian gave way to a tentative peace.

Upon the death of Galerius, a complex struggle for power ensued. Maxentius, who was Maximian's son and who now controlled Italy, sought to defeat the army of Constantine and gain control of the Western empire. Constantine, who was well aware of Maxentius' intentions, decided to attack Rome. At the Milvian Bridge, just outside the city, the two armies met.

Before engaging in battle, Constantine claimed that he had looked above the sun and saw the symbol of the cross inscribed with the words *in hoc signo vinces* ("in this sign you will conquer"). After this vision, Constantine instructed his soldiers to put this sign on their shields. With crosses etched into Roman shields, Constantine's army met Maxentius in battle. Though Maxentius' forces were said to have been four times greater, Constantine won the Battle of Saxa Rubra, securing his rule over the West. Maxentius drowned near the Milvian Bridge.

After his victory against Maxentius, Constantine declared that the Christian God had favored him, and that he intended to stay in this God's good graces. He immediately restored the property of the Church, and began aiding in the construction of churches. In Rome the Arch of Constantine commemorated his victory, and his statue was placed in the city. In one hand the statue held the *Labarum*, the standard of the cross, with the inscription, "Through this saving sign have I freed your city from the tyrant's yoke."

Constantine sought unity in his empire, and he saw that Christianity was a religion likely to provide such unity.

THE EDICT OF MILAN (A.D. 313)

Constantine met with the only other living caesar, Licinius, in Milan in A.D. 313. Together they issued the Edict of Milan. This edict restored all property taken from the Church by the empire, and it granted Christians the freedom to practice their religion. The Edict of Milan represented a milestone for the early Christians and the Catholic Faith. It legitimized a religion that had been outlawed since Nero's decree in A.D. 64, and solidified the presence of Christianity in the public square.

It would be remiss not to mention the clear political motives that were at least partly responsible for the Edict of Milan. Like many Roman rulers before him, Constantine sought unity in his empire, and he saw that Christianity was a religion likely to provide such unity. In this, Constantine followed the regular practice of using religion to support political ends. However, it would be ridiculous to suppose that for Constantine, Christianity was nothing but a tool for the state. He is known to have prayed daily, and to have received instruction in the Faith until he was formally received into the Church, penitent and hopeful, receiving the Sacrament of Baptism on his deathbed.

The Baptism of Constantine
by Giovan Francesco Penni

Constantine received instruction in the faith and was formally received into the Church.

ST. HELEN IN JERUSALEM

St. Helen played an essential role in turning the Roman Empire toward Christianity. Born in Asia Minor and from humble beginnings (some accounts say she was the daughter of an innkeeper), she married the Roman General Constantius Chlorus around A.D. 270. Four years later she gave birth to Constantine, the future emperor of Rome.

Although she converted to Christianity late in life (most likely in her sixties), St. Helen was deeply devout and inspired many Romans by her fervent faith and piety. After her son became emperor in A.D. 324, St. Helen made a pilgrimage to the holy land at the age of 80. She traveled throughout Palestine, following in Christ's footsteps, and making great contributions to the poor along the way. She also had two famous churches constructed on the sites of Jesus' Nativity and Ascension.

By the time of St. Helen's visit, most of old Jerusalem had been destroyed and built over by the Romans. Nonetheless, St. Helen was determined to find artifacts from Jesus' life, so with the help of Macarius, the bishop of Jerusalem, she consulted with local inhabitants regarding legends and traditions concerning sites relating to Christ. Excavations began, and hidden near a Roman temple to Venus she uncovered Mount Calvary and Jesus' sepulcher. Nearby she found three wooden crosses as well as a sign that read "King of the Jews."

They knew they had made a major discovery, but they were unable to determine which of the three crosses had been Christ's. Then, Macarius had an idea. They brought the three crosses to a woman who had been very sick and asked her to touch each cross. When she touched the third one, she was miraculously cured.

Helen wished to share this grace with other Christians throughout the empire, so she sent a piece of the cross to Constantinople and brought a piece of it back to Rome with her where it became the source of renewed zeal for the Christian faith among the Romans. St. Helen died around the year 328 with her son, the emperor Constantine, at her side.

The Titulus Crucis, a piece of ancient walnut wood, is thought by some believers to be part of the headboard which was nailed to Christ's cross. It has been kept for centuries in Santa Croce in Gerusalemme near Rome. St. Helen is said to have brought the Titulus to Rome, leaving another fragment (which has disappeared) in Jerusalem.

In Rome, the Arch of Constantine commemorated his victory over Maxentius. His statue was placed in the city. In one hand, his statue held the Labarum, the standard of the cross, with the inscription, "Through this saving sign have I freed your city from the tyrant's yoke."

CONCLUSION

The early Church was often perceived as a small segment of Judaism, beginning after the Resurrection of Jesus. She then suffered through a long period of intermittent, though intense, persecution, and, finally (and quite remarkably), she emerged as an imperially sanctioned religion in A.D. 313. The first three hundred years of the Church's history were tumultuous, although they contain many lessons that remain perennially applicable. The martyrs of the early Church are emulated today by many Christians who live in cultures that are as hostile to Christianity now as was Rome two-thousand years ago. The lives of martyrs such as Sts. Ignatius of Antioch and Agnes remain quite relevant to Christians then as well as today, who share in the communion of saints. The complex and often troubling relationship between the Church and the state is one that began in the Roman Empire, and still remains today. Lastly, the structure of the episcopacy and the importance of Tradition for resolving theological disputes both found expression in the many writings of Apostolic Fathers like Sts. Ignatius of Antioch and Irenaeus. An understanding of the early Church is therefore essential for an adequately informed conception of the origins of both the structure and the doctrines of Christianity.

SUPPLEMENTARY READING

Pope John Paul II, *Veritatis Splendor*, 92

Martyrdom…*is a violation of man's "humanity,"* in the one perpetrating it even before the one enduring it. Hence martyrdom is also the exaltation of a person's perfect "humanity" and of true "life," as is attested by St. Ignatius of Antioch, addressing the Christians of Rome, the place of his own martyrdom: "Have mercy on me, brethren: do not hold me back from living; do not wish that I die….Let me arrive at the pure light; once there *I will be truly a man.* Let me imitate the passion of my God."

Justin Martyr, *The First Apology*, Ch. 66

And this food is called among us *Eukaristia* [the Eucharist], of which no one is allowed to partake but the man who believes that the things which we teach are true, and who has been washed with the washing that is for the remission of sins, and unto regeneration, and who is so living as Christ has enjoined. For not as common bread and common drink do we receive these; but in like manner as Jesus Christ our Saviour, having been made flesh by the Word of God, had both flesh and blood for our salvation, so likewise have we been taught that the food which is blessed by the prayer of His word, and from which our blood and flesh by transmutation are nourished, is the flesh and blood of that Jesus who was made flesh.

For the apostles, in the memoirs composed by them, which are called Gospels, have thus delivered unto us what was enjoined upon them; that Jesus took bread, and when He had given thanks, said, "This do ye in remembrance of Me, this is My body;" and that, after the same manner, having taken the cup and given thanks, He said, "This is My blood;" and gave it to them alone. Which the wicked devils have imitated in the mysteries of Mithras, commanding the same thing to be done. For, that bread and a cup of water are placed with certain incantations in the mystic rites of one who is being initiated, you either know or can learn.

Constantine Augustus and Licinius Augustus, "The Edict of Milan"

When I, Constantine Augustus, as well as I, Licinius Augustus, fortunately met near Mediolanurn (Milan), and were considering everything that pertained to the public welfare and security, we thought, among other things which we saw would be for the good of many, those regulations pertaining to the reverence of the Divinity ought certainly to be made first, so that we might grant to the Christians and others full authority to observe that religion which each preferred; whence any Divinity whatsoever in the seat of the heavens may be propitious and kindly disposed to us and all who are placed under our rule. And thus by this wholesome counsel and most upright provision we thought to arrange that no one whatsoever should be denied the opportunity to give his heart to the observance of the Christian religion, of that religion which he should think best for himself, so that the Supreme Deity, to whose worship we freely yield our hearts may show in all things His usual favor and benevolence.

Constantine Augustus: "…no one whatsoever should be denied the opportunity to give his heart to the observance of the Christian religion, …"

VOCABULARY

AD METALLA

Literally means "to the mines." It refers to the punishment and death given to many Christians during the Roman persecutions.

APOSTASY

Apostasy is the willful renunciation of the Faith in its entirety.

APOSTATE

A person who denies the Faith altogether.

DOMUS AUREA

Latin for "House of Gold." It refers to the palace that was built at the center of Rome after the fire during Nero's reign. Some have suggested the desire to build this palace was Nero's reason for starting the fire.

HERETIC

A person who denies one or more doctrines of the Faith.

INSULÆ

Tenements for middle and lower class Romans constructed of wood and rubble

TETRARCHY

Emperor Diocletian's division of the Roman Empire into four separate administrative districts, each with its own Caesar.

TRAJAN'S RESCRIPT

Policy for handling Christians in the Roman Empire which stated that Christians who renounced their faith and offered sacrifice would be allowed to live. Those who did not renounce their faith would suffer death.

VOX POPULI

Latin for "voice of the people." The early Church was often more threatened by the unconverted commoners in any given area than by the Roman state.

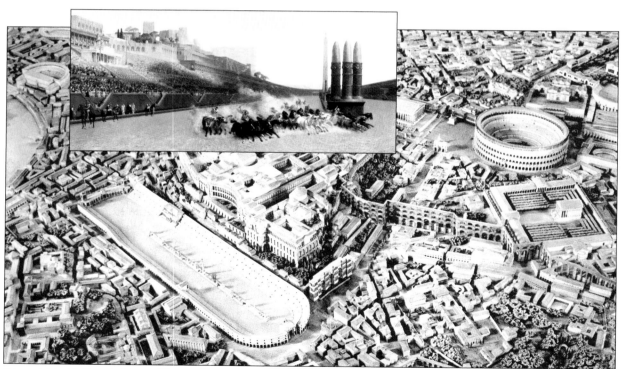

This model depicts Rome in the era of Emperor Diocletian. It shows the size comparison of Circus Maximus (the long oval arena on the left) and the Coliseum (the circular stadium in the upper right). Most Christian executions were held in the Circus Maximus because it held more spectators. Julius Caesar expanded the Circus around 50 B.C., after which the track measured approximately 600 meters in length, 225 meters in width and could accommodate an estimated 150,000 seated spectators. Trajan later added 5,000 more seats and expanded the emperor's viewing section.

STUDY QUESTIONS

1. Where in the ~~Bible~~ is Christianity referred to as "the Way"?

2. If it is true that Nero set the fire in Rome on July 19, what was his ultimate motivation? How did the Christians prove to be expedient political tools?

3. What were some of the accusations against Christians during the first persecutions?

4. Summarize Trajan's Rescript. How does it differ from the previous law of Nero?

5. What does St. Ignatius have to say about the importance of the episcopacy?

6. How did Hadrian's Rescript (A.D. 123/124) improve the situation for Christians?

7. How did the Roman emperor Septimus Severus threaten both Judaism and Christianity?

8. What do the words *ad metalla* mean?

9. Who are probably the two most famous women victims of Septimus Severus' persecution?

10. St. Irenaeus was an important leader in which region of the empire? (This is of particular interest because he came from the Greek-speaking east.)

11. How did the Emperor Decius' systematic persecution of Christianity involve the bureaucracy of the state?

12. What was the name and significance of the institution that Origen led in Alexandria?

13. Emperor Valerian was no friend to Christians. What was his fate at the hands of the Persians?

14. What was Emperor Diocletian's background and how did his Tetrarchy only lead to a weakened Roman state?

15. Summarize Diocletian's Four Edicts.

16. What attempted violence against St. Agnes was the fate of many young women who refused to renounce their faith during Diocletian's persecution?

17. What is the famous story about how Constantine won the Battle at Saxa Rubra?

18. Discuss the importance of the Edict of Milan (A.D. 313).

PRACTICAL EXERCISES

1. During the Columbine school massacre in 1999, one of the shooters asked a young female student if she was a Christian. When she answered "Yes, I believe in God," he executed her. Can you imagine a situation where your faith could be so dramatically tested?

2. Many of the greatest persecutors of the Church in the Roman Empire were educated, intelligent people. How does this demonstrate the nature of evil?

3. How do the presence of martyrs in a culture lead to conversions to the Faith? Which of the early Christian values listed as headings in Chapter 2 do you think were most important for the early Christian martyrs to emulate?

4. How could effective apologists like St. Justin Martyr be of great help to the Catholic Church today? What issues would a modern apologist tackle? To whom would the defense be addressed?

FROM THE CATECHISM

975 "We believe that the Holy Mother of God, the new Eve, Mother of the Church, continues in heaven to exercise her maternal role on behalf of the members of Christ" (Paul VI, *CPG* § 15).

1173 When the Church keeps the memorials of martyrs and other saints during the annual cycle, she proclaims the Paschal mystery in those "who have suffered and have been glorified with Christ. She proposes them to the faithful as examples who draw all men to the Father through Christ, and through their merits she begs for God's favors" (*SC* 104; cf. *SC* 108, 111).

2113 Idolatry not only refers to false pagan worship. It remains a constant temptation to faith. Idolatry consists in divinizing what is not God. Man commits idolatry whenever he honors and reveres a creature in place of God, whether this be gods or demons (for example, satanism), power, pleasure, race, ancestors, the state, money, etc. Jesus says, "You cannot serve God and mammon" (Mt 6:24). Many martyrs died for not adoring "the Beast" (cf. Rev 13-14) refusing even to simulate such worship. Idolatry rejects the unique Lordship of God; it is therefore incompatible with communion with God (cf. Gal 5:20; Eph 5:5).

2473 *Martyrdom* is the supreme witness given to the truth of the faith: it means bearing witness even unto death. The martyr bears witness to Christ who died and rose, to whom he is united by charity. He bears witness to the truth of the faith and of Christian doctrine. He endures death through an act of fortitude. "Let me become the food of the beasts, through whom it will be given me to reach God" (St. Ignatius of Antioch, *Ad Rom.* 4, 1: SCh 10, 110).

2474 The Church has painstakingly collected the records of those who persevered to the end in witnessing to their faith. These are the acts of the Martyrs. They form the archives of truth written in letters of blood:

> Neither the pleasures of the world nor the kingdoms of this age will be of any use to me. It is better for me to die [in order to unite myself] to Christ Jesus than to reign over the ends of the earth. I seek him who died for us; I desire him who rose for us. My birth is approaching... (St. Ignatius of Antioch, *Ad Rom.* 6, 1-2: SCh 10, 114).

> I bless you for having judged me worthy from this day and this hour to be counted among your martyrs....You have kept your promise, God of faithfulness and truth. For this reason and for everything, I praise you, I bless you, I glorify you through the eternal and heavenly High Priest, Jesus Christ, your beloved Son. Through him, who is with you and the Holy Spirit, may glory be given to you, now and in the ages to come. Amen (*Martyrium Polycarpi* 14, 2-3: PG 5, 1040; SCh 10, 228).

Through their supreme witness to the truths of the Faith, St. Catherine and St. Agnes stand forever victorious over their Roman persecutors.

The Church Fathers And Heresies

The popes, the Church Fathers, and the ecumenical councils, lead by the Holy Spirit, guided the Church through the treacherous waters of heresy.

CHAPTER 4

The Church Fathers And Heresies

Dear young people, let us seek the truth about Christ and about his Church!
But we must be consistent: let us love the Truth, live in the Truth, proclaim the Truth!
O Christ, show us the Truth. Be the only Truth for us!
— John Paul II, Address to Young People, Santiago de Compostela, Spain, August 19, 1989

The persecution of Christians in the fourth and fifth centuries was followed by a series of heresies that rocked the emerging Church down to her foundations. Given the gravity and widespread effect of these early heresies, it would seem that nothing less than divine intervention guided the growing Church through these trials, along her road of survival and growth. This segment from the Athanasian Creed, though it now reads in such a sober and clear manner, conceals four centuries charged with painful theological deliberations and debates.

> Whoever wishes to be saved must, / above all, keep the Catholic faith. / For unless a person keeps this faith whole and entire, / he will undoubtedly be lost forever. / *This is what the Catholic faith teaches: we worship one God in the Trinity / and the Trinity in unity.* / We distinguish among the Persons, / but we do not divide the substance. / For the Father is a distinct Person; the Son is a distinct Person; / and the Holy Spirit is a distinct Person. / Still, the Father and the Son and the Holy Spirit / have one divinity, / equal glory, and coeternal majesty. (Introductory lines of the Athanasian Creed) [emphasis added]

The Athanasian Creed, often known by the name of the opening Latin words *Quicumque vult* ("Whoever wishes [to be saved]"), is an excellent example of what was at stake during the time of the great heresies during the third, fourth, and fifth centuries. Like the two other creeds, the Nicene Creed and the Apostles' Creed, the Athanasian Creed is a profession of Faith that the Church still strongly affirms. Though attributed to the Greek Church Father, St. Athanasius of Alexandria, the authorship of this creed is not certain. It was written in the fourth or fifth century (probably 381 - ca. 428) to combat heresies present at the time in both the East and the West.

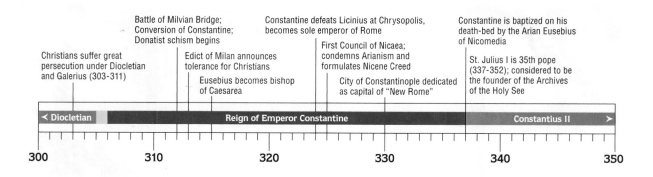

Battle of Milvian Bridge;
Conversion of Constantine;
Donatist schism begins

Constantine defeats Licinius at Chrysopolis,
becomes sole emperor of Rome

Constantine is baptized on his
death-bed by the Arian Eusebius
of Nicomedia

Christians suffer great
persecution under Diocletian
and Galerius (303-311)

Edict of Milan announces
tolerance for Christians

First Council of Nicaea;
condemns Arianism and
formulates Nicene Creed

St. Julius I is 35th pope
(337-352); considered to be
the founder of the Archives
of the Holy See

Eusebius becomes bishop
of Caesarea

City of Constantinople dedicated
as capital of "New Rome"

< Diocletian	Reign of Emperor Constantine	Constantius II >

300   310   320   330   340   350

The Athanasian Creed principally expresses faith in the three Divine Persons of the Blessed Trinity and the Incarnation of God the Son, the Second Person of the Trinity. This creed carefully emphasizes the equality of the three different Persons of the Trinity and their exact relationship with each another. The other remarkable aspect of the creed, which sets it apart from the Nicene and Apostles' Creeds, are the *anathemas* at the beginning and the end. (An *anathema* is a condemnation solemnly pronounced by ecclesiastical authority and at times accompanied by excommunication.) Every sentence, every word of this creed was carefully selected in order to express adequately the Catholic position, as well as to bring back into the fold those who had fallen into heresy. Although words like "substance," "Person," and "nature" may often appear at first glance to have little meaning in the twenty-first century, members of the Church in the third and fourth centuries suffered torture, exile, and even death in order to preserve and transmit the unadulterated Deposit of Faith, with a very precise theological and philosophical vocabulary, to articulate Catholic belief with total accuracy.

Almost from the beginning, Christian thinkers used the tools of Greek philosophy to help explain Christian truths.

From almost the very beginning, many Christian thinkers welcomed the Greek philosophical tradition, and used the tools of Greek philosophy to help explain Christian truths. St. Paul preached at the Areopagus in Athens—though with limited success—and the Apologists utilized philosophy in explaining Christianity to intellectuals and the ruling classes of the Empire.

A dizzying array of heresies and schismatic leaders confronted the Church following the Edict of Milan (313). Over the course of the third to fifth centuries, popes and bishops led the Church through a number of ecumenical councils, addressing each new controversy, and consequently developing a rich theological tradition. This would become the greatest age of heresy until the advent of Protestantism in the sixteenth century, and these heresies were not restricted to a circle of academics but rather affected the entire populace. The random observer may see here confusion and arbitrary decisions; the believer sees the Holy Spirit guiding and directing the Church to protect, define, and promulgate the truths about the Person of Jesus Christ and God's plan for the Church.

This chapter will explore the issues surrounding the various heresies, the ecumenical councils, and the Church Fathers, who rose to the occasion to teach, explain, and herald Catholic beliefs.

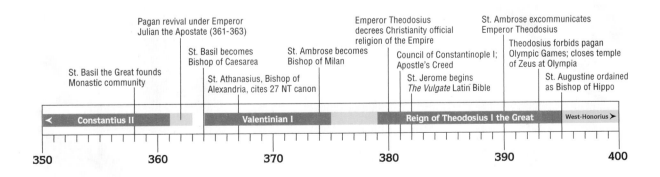

St. Basil the Great founds Monastic community

Pagan revival under Emperor Julian the Apostate (361-363)

St. Basil becomes Bishop of Caesarea

St. Athanasius, Bishop of Alexandria, cites 27 NT canon

St. Ambrose becomes Bishop of Milan

Emperor Theodosius decrees Christianity official religion of the Empire

Council of Constantinople I; Apostle's Creed

St. Jerome begins *The Vulgate* Latin Bible

St. Ambrose excommunicates Emperor Theodosius

Theodosius forbids pagan Olympic Games; closes temple of Zeus at Olympia

St. Augustine ordained as Bishop of Hippo

| Constantius II | Valentinian I | Reign of Theodosius I the Great | West-Honorius > |

350   360   370   380   390   400

PART I
Early Heresies

What exactly is heresy? St. Thomas Aquinas defined heresy as "a species of unbelief, belonging to those who profess the Christian faith, but corrupt its dogmas" (STh II-II, 11, 1, r.). Heresy must be distinguished from other forms of unbelief, namely, the unbelief of other religious traditions such as Judaism or any of the various pagan religions. Orthodox (meaning "right teaching" in Greek) Catholicism derives from the Deposit of Faith (the sum of all truths revealed in Scripture and through Tradition, and entrusted to the care of the Church). Heresy, on the other hand, derives from this same source, i.e., from belief, but denies or alters some part or parts of the Deposit of Faith.

One may enter into heresy in one of two ways:

1. **Material heresy.** It is possible to enter into heresy through ignorance of the truth, mis-understanding, or non-comprehension of particular aspects of the Faith, erroneous judgment, or the like. This type of heresy is not willed by the subject, and thus, lacking one of the necessary conditions of sin (that the action has to be freely willed). This species of heresy is merely a mistake, albeit a grave mistake that needs correction.

2. **Formal heresy.** It is also possible to freely choose, with full understanding of the teaching of the Church, to hold to tenets or doctrines that are clearly contradictory to those of the Church and even doctrines that have been condemned by the Church as false. This species of heresy, depending on all the mitigating circumstances, carries with it a degree of culpability.

The first heresies that afflicted the early Church were especially dangerous since they struck at the heart of Christianity: the figure of Christ. As mentioned above, Greek philosophy, especially Platonic and neo-Platonic thought, was welcomed by early Christian thinkers who found surprising insights and similarities to Christianity. Neo-Platonic thought discusses a Supreme Being, the One, who creates through an emanation of lesser beings, one of which is the *logos*. (*Logos* is a truly ambiguous Greek word with a multitude of meanings including word, account, meaning, reason, argument, saying, speech, and story.) Today, as was the case during the time of the early heresies, the word *logos* is most familiar to Christians since it is recorded in the opening lines of the Gospel of St. John. He uses *logos* to refer to God the Son; in Christian teaching, God the Son, the *Logos,* is the Second Person of the Blessed Trinity, equal to God the Father. However, in neo-Platonic thought the *logos,* albeit an elevated being, is created by and inferior to a Supreme Being, and thus is a separate being. Early heresies, connecting the *Logos* from the Gospel of St. John with the philosophical *logos* of the Greeks, often denied the true divinity of Christ. Instead, they held that He was a most exalted creature of the Father who only enjoyed by analogy the title "the Son of God." Neo-Platonic thought was so ingrained in the minds of the early eastern Christian thinkers that even someone of the stature of the illustrious third century theologian, Origen, tended to subordinate the Divine *Logos* to the Father.

Plato

Platonic philosophies also viewed the material world as inferior to the world of ideas. Material entitied were thought to be merely images of the world of ideas. Matter was viewed as an obstacle to contemplation and personal perfection. Thus, besides denying Christ's true divinity, many of the early heresies greatly de-emphasized—if not completely denied—Christ's humanity.

Striking at the heart of Christianity, early heresies made Jesus Christ inferior to the Father. In Christian teaching, God the Son, the Logos, is the Second Person of the Blessed Trinity, a person in the Divine Nature, and therefore equal to God the Father.

These early heresies that make Jesus Christ inferior to the Father and, at the same time, deny his divinity, set the stage for the advent of the Arian heresy, which occasioned one of the worst crises the Church would ever face. In fact, a few difficult centuries of painful struggle would have to pass before the Church could put these early heresies behind her.

GNOSTICISM

The word "Gnosticism" is derived from the Greek word *gnosis* (knowledge). The name refers to one of the principle tenets of this multifaceted heresy, namely, that salvation may be achieved through knowledge. There were many forms of Gnosticism (many whose origins predate Christianity), and therefore it is difficult (if not impossible) to encapsulate them into one coherent system. In the second century, Gnosticism, which had eastern origins and influences from Persia and India, very successfully perverted the meaning of Christianity and its symbols. Gnosticism co-opted the Old and New Testaments for some of the contents of the Gnostic religions and to give some particular Gnostic teachings a certain authority.

As mentioned above, Gnosticism is a blanket term for a very broad and complex group of beliefs. Despite these complexities, it is possible to delineate some of Gnosticism's fundamental points. Gnostic beliefs held that a secret knowledge regarding God and the origin and destiny of man had been given to a select few. Its cosmology pitted the Demiurge, the creator god of the material and visible world, against the remote and unknowable Divine Being. The Demiurge was of lesser stature than the Divine Being, from whom the Demiurge had originated through a series of emanations. The Gnostics claimed that the Demiurge was the author and ruler of the created world. Being material and imperfect, the created world would naturally have an antagonistic and inferior relationship to the spiritual, perfect world of the Divine Being. Thus, the spiritual Divine Being is the agent of goodness, and the Demiurge, the author of the material world, propagates evil in the world.

A divine spark, belonging to the Divine Being, could, however, be found among some people in the created order. The redeemer, sent from the Divine Being, came in order to release the sparks trapped in the bodies so they might return to the Divine Being. This was only possible if the individuals understood the secret knowledge of the redeemer's teaching and practiced the appropriate Gnostic rituals.

A contemporary New Age medicine wheel in Arizona.

The principle involved here of finding the light within oneself through a pagan ceremony is the essence of the New Age movement in contemporary times. As will be seen in this chapter, the Church has witnessed a staggering range of heresies and schisms in her two-thousand year history. Many of the false teachings that appeared in the Medieval period, during the Reformation, and even in the contemporary world are not new, but, rather, the reemergence of ancient heresies under fresh guises.

Gnostics divided people mainly into two classes. Those who understood this cosmic struggle between the material and the spiritual were known by the Greek word *pneumatikoi* ("spiritual"). Most of the unfortunate masses fell into the *sarkikou* ("material" group), unaware of the great struggle going on around them. Some branches of Gnosticism incorporated a third group, known as the *psychikoi*, in between these two.

In Gnosticism's view, Judaism was a false religion that worshiped the wrong god, the Demiurge, who is evil. Instead of trying to free the divine spark from its evil material confines, Judaism mistakenly affirmed the material world as good.

A Coptic image of Pisces.

Gnosticism rejected the Church's teaching regarding both Christ's human and divine nature. According to Gnostic thought, Jesus did not have a human nature; for a human nature, being materially bound, is naturally evil. Instead, he was a good divine being whose purpose, as the Gnostic redeemer, was to bring the secret knowledge (*gnosis*) and make it known to man. They believed that Jesus came as the representative of the supreme Divine Being. This Jesus did not inhabit a human body, nor did he die on the cross. Instead, the spirit of the divine being was present in Jesus temporarily, Jesus' body was only an apparition, and his spirit left his "body" before he was put to death on Calvary. In Gnosticism's cosmological view, a divine being could never have suffered the humiliation of death, let alone death on a cross.

Gnosticism existed prior to Christianity in pagan religions, and there is evidence of the existence of early Gnostic Jewish sects. A number of early Christian thinkers and apologists combated Gnostic

ROOTS OF GNOSTICISM

The early Christians considered Simon Magus (Acts 8: 9-24) the founder of Gnosticism. Magus claimed to have secret knowledge of the mysteries of God and hoped to gain magical powers through his conversion to Christianity. Despite the similarities between Magus' claims and Gnostic beliefs, the origin of Gnosticism has long been a matter of controversy and is still the subject of much scholarly research.

Recent scholarship has attempted to show that traces of Gnostic beliefs can be found in religions that existed before the coming of Christ. Some scholars, for example, have tried to establish links between Gnosticism and the Babylonian religion that arose after the conquest of Cyrus. Other scholars have noted similarities between Gnosticism and Greek thought. Attempts have even been made to associate Gnosticism with certain schools of pre-Christian Judaism, but this theory has not met with widespread acceptance.

The seeming appearance of Gnostic thought in many ancient religious systems owes to philosophical and religious pessimism, which is both a central feature of Gnosticism and a common perversion of intemperate religious fervor. While the precise emergence of Gnosticism is difficult to pinpoint, magical powers, secret knowledge of the divine, and the belief that present existence is essentially evil are misconceptions that have long corrupted religious belief.

Gnostic systems combined magic and astrology with the Bible. The Hebrew name of God, IAO, fascinated sorcerers. IAO was often represented as a demon spirit with a cock's head.

influences in Christianity. Chief among them were St. Irenaeus, Tertullian, and St. Hippolytus. In their arguments they emphasized the goodness of the created world, the supremacy of the Christian God, the clear meaning of the Scriptures, and Christ's human experiences — especially his passion and death.

Many of the later heresies are derivatives of Gnosticism. Generally, a Gnostic religion holds the following beliefs:

1. Matter is a corruption of spirit, and thus the world is corrupt;

2. Man must seek through knowledge to overcome this fallen state and return to God; and

3. God has made this possible by sending a savior (usually held to be Jesus).

MARCIONISM (144 - 400s)

Marcion recognized only St. Paul (above) as a legitimate Christian authority.

Marcion (d. ca. A.D. 160) founded his heretical movement very early in the life of the Church, and it lingered well into the fifth century in the West and for centuries longer in the East. Marcion came from the Black Sea port of Sinope in the Roman province of Pontus (what is today Turkey), where he was most likely involved in shipping. He was the son of a bishop, and as the story goes, his father excommunicated him on the grounds of immorality. He went to Rome ca. 140. He started his own community and was formally excommunicated in 144. It was not long before his heresy grew into the one of the greatest threats to orthodox belief in the second half of the second century.

Marcion adapted important ideas from Gnostic beliefs to form his own theology. From Gnosticism he took the idea of the Demiurge, whom he identified as the jealous, revengeful God of the Old Testament. The Jewish God, the Demiurge, is the God of the Law. In opposition to this cruel God of the Law, Marcion heralded the God of Jesus Christ, the true God, sent to bring about the demise of the Demiurge. The God of Jesus Christ is the God of Love who has no connection with the Law. Jesus' teaching was taken from the true God. His Passion and death came about through the machinations of the evil Creator God of the Old Testament. This dualism of Law and Love is the main thesis of Marcion's system.

Marcion recognized only St. Paul as a legitimate Christian authority because of his teaching regarding freedom from the Law. The Apostles, in Marcion's view, did not fully understand the mission of Christ being blinded by Judaism and its Creator God. Therefore, only ten of St. Paul's Epistles and a modified version of the Gospel of St. Luke (any Jewish influence was removed) were given canonical status in Marcionism. Marcion was either not aware of the Pastorals — other epistles of the New Testament — or rejected them outright. This canon reflected Marcion's attempt to free the New Testament from Jewish influence.

Unwittingly, Marcion helped the development of the Catholic Church's canon of Sacred Scripture. Partially in reaction to Marcion's flawed and incomplete group of inspired texts, the Church gradually determined the canon: the official, inspired writings of the New Testament.

Marcion had established his own church before being excommunicated in 144. He admitted people from all backgrounds, just as the Church did, but by the third century, most of Marcion's followers were incorporated into Manichæism. His followers had to practice a most rigorous asceticism, fasts were multiplied, and eating meat was forbidden. Many orthodox writers of the period fought Marcionism, including St. Irenaeus, Tertullian, St. Hippolytus, Pope St. Clement I, and Origen.

Marcion was not the only person to reject Judaism and the Old Testament as incompatible with Christianity. Down through the ages other groups have done the same. The Lutheran theologian Alfred von Harnack (1851-1930) similarly proposed a canon free of Jewish influence early in the twentieth century. Later, National Socialism (Nazism) in Germany proposed "German Christianity," a Christianity cut off from its Jewish roots. Christianity cannot exist without its Jewish heritage, and hence Pope John Paul II continually singled out the Jews as "the elder brothers in faith."

MANICHÆISM (250s -1000s)

Manichæism was probably the most elaborate and polished branch of Gnosticism. Its founder, Mani (ca. 216-276), was born in Persia. He developed this particular brand of Gnosticism in Persia and India during the third century until he was eventually condemned to death by the Persian emperor Bahram I. Accounts of his death conflict—some report that he died in prison, others that he was crucified, flayed, and his skin stuffed with straw and hung upon the gates of the city. Despite his condemnation, by the fourth century Manichæism had spread to Rome and was already deeply rooted in North Africa.

Manichæism continued the age-old dualist cosmology involving the conflict between darkness and light. This heresy stated that Satan had managed to steal light particles and place them in the brains of humans. The goal of Manichæism was to share the secret knowledge which liberates this light so it could return to its original source. Mani understood himself as just another spiritual leader in a long line of leaders that included the Jewish prophets, Jesus, and Buddha, all of whom showed the path to true freedom. The ritual acts of Manichæism also incorporated the movements of the cosmic bodies—the Sun, the Moon, and stars—also points of light. The "hearers" and the "elect" comprised the two groups in the sect. The latter group was comprised of the authentic followers of Mani.

Manichæism borrowed heavily from the Scriptures, especially from the writings of St. Paul. Mani incorporated many of St. Paul's arguments and imagery to support his own teaching concerning the struggle between darkness and light.

Followers of Manichæism adhered to a strict form of asceticism, and it is here that one understands part of the appeal of Gnostic and other heretical teachings. In the Roman world of lax morals, Christianity required faithfulness to a demanding moral life as inspired by Jesus. Manichæism and other movements attempted to out-perform Christianity in terms of their moral rigor. If Christianity required fasting, Gnostic groups would require tougher and longer fasts. Manichæism also drew adherents by its intellectual appeal. St. Augustine, for instance, drawn by the philosophical bases of the heresy, was a fervent adherent of Manichæism for nine years.

Teachings similar to Manichæism reappeared in the Medieval Albigensians of the twelfth through fourteenth centuries, who are also known by the name "Cathars." Though unlikely to have a direct, historical link to Manichæism, the Albigensians used much of the same imagery and beliefs. Manichæism periodically re-emerged in isolated areas for many centuries and did not completely die out until sometime during the beginning of the second millennium.

MONTANISM (156 - 200s)

Montanism was an apocalyptic movement founded by Montanus in Phrygia (Asia Minor, modern day Turkey) following what he said were private revelations made to him. Montanus worked closely with two female prophets, Prisca and Maximilla. Montanus' central principle was that the new, heavenly kingdom was about to begin in Pepuza, a small town in Phrygia (the exact location of this town is lost to history); he knew this because of the outpouring of the Holy Spirit upon him. Montanism also held that Christians who had fallen from grace could never be redeemed. Because Montanus and his followers believed they were directly inspired by the Holy Spirit, they rejected the authority of the Church.

The movement also appeared in North Africa, where its most famous adherent was the Christian thinker Tertullian, who rejected Catholic Christianity after having been one of its greatest apologists for many years. In its African form, Montanism placed a high value on the ascetical life. It forbade second marriages, enacted stricter fasting disciplines than the Church, and rejected flight from persecutions.

Montanism is rightly understood as one of the first apocalyptic movements in Christianity that claimed to supersede the Church because of its direct inspiration by the Holy Spirit. Its expectation of the New Jerusalem on earth in Pepuza is also unique.

Montanists believed that the "New Jerusalem" foretold by St. John in Revelations would descend to earth on a hill in Pepuza, Phrygia. The Montanist prophets required everyone to acknowledge their utterances as the true work of the Holy Spirit.

DOCETISM (30s - 100s)

Docetism, yet another Gnostic heresy rising from the presupposition of the corrupt nature of matter, maintained that Jesus was not truly human and did not actually suffer the pain of crucifixion and death. The name of the heresy derives from the Greek word *dokesis*, meaning appearance or semblance. It often taught that someone else (e.g., Judas Iscariot or Simon of Cyrene) miraculously switched places with Christ just before the crucifixion and suffered death in Christ's place. Many of the Apologists, including St. Ignatius of Antioch, wrote at length against this belief.

Docetism held that the human form of Jesus as well as his crucifixion was an illusion.

First Vatican Council 1869-1870

PART II
The Ecumenical Councils

In order to meet the challenges posed by the various heresies, the Church convened several ecumenical councils, the first being the First Council of Nicaea, in 325. Altogether, there have been twenty-one ecumenical councils throughout the history of the Church (the Second Vatican Council, 1962-1965, being the most recent). The first six councils addressed the various Christological heresies that have been examined in this chapter in an effort to provide a true theological answer to the question, "Who is Jesus Christ?" The word "ecumenical" comes from the Greek word *oikoumene*, meaning "the whole inhabited world." Ecumenical councils bring bishops under the leadership of the pope together from all over the world to discuss central issues of the Church.

Current canon law in the Church grants the power to convene a council only to the papacy. The pope governs the council and he alone has the power to accept or reject the decrees passed by it. If the pope should die during a council, as happened during the Second Vatican Council in the 1960s, the council is halted until the election of a new pope, who then decides whether to continue the council as well as the selection of the topics it considers.

Besides ecumenical councils, members of the Church hold a number of other types of councils. A **diocesan council** is often called a synod, and it is a meeting of a bishop, representatives of the clergy, religious and laity in which matters of diocesan Church discipline and procedure are discussed. A **provincial council** is an assembly of the metropolitan archbishop with his suffragan bishops, while a **plenary council** summons all the bishops of a nation. What distinguishes an ecumenical council is that it convenes all the bishops of the world, and its teachings are regarded as having the highest authority. An ecumenical council's definitions regarding tenets of faith and morals are held to be infallible, if infallible pronouncements are the intentions of the pope and the bishops. Furthermore, the resolutions and conclusions of an ecumenical council must always be approved by the Supreme Pontiff.

The first seven councils are recognized by both East and West. However, Eastern Orthodox Christians do not recognize the ecumenical nature of any of the councils held in the West after 787 because they did not participate. At the time of the Reformation, the mainline Protestant bodies recognized at least the special status of those first seven councils, though later Protestant churches often gave no special recognition to them.

ECUMENICAL COUNCILS

COUNCIL NAME	YEAR	CONCERN OF COUNCIL
1 Nicaea	325	Arianism and the Nicene Creed
2 Constantinople I	381	Divinity of the Holy Spirit
3 Ephesus	431	Nestorianism and Mary as Mother of God
4 Chalcedon	451	Monophysitism (specifically the Eutychian form)
5 Constantinople II	553	The Three Chapters Controversy: Nestorianism, Monophysitism, and imperial-papal relations
6 Constantinople III	680 - 681	Monothelitism; admonished Pope Honorius I
7 Nicaea II	787	Iconoclasm
8 Constantinople IV	869 - 870	Photian Controversy: potential East-West schism; deposed Patriarch Photius
9 Lateran I	1123	Investiture Controversy; simony; clerical celibacy
10 Lateran II	1139	Arnold of Brescia's (twelfth century heretic who condemned all clerical material possession) teaching and criticism of the Church; put an end to papal schism
11 Lateran III	1179	Process for papal elections (only cardinals); condemned Albigensianism and Waldensianism
12 Lateran IV	1215	Transubstantiation of the Eucharist; annual Penance; suppression of Albigenses; crusades
13 Lyons I	1245	Deposition and excommunication of Emperor Frederick II; crusades
14 Lyons II	1274	Healing of the Great Schism with Constantinople
15 Vienne	1311-1312	Suppression of the Knights Templar
16 Constance	1414-1418	Great Schism of the papacy; condemnation of Jan Hus
17 Basel-Ferrara-Florence	1431-1445	Reform and union with the East
18 Lateran V	1512-1517	Reform of the Church, especially discipline (failed)
19 Trent	1545-1563	Protestantism and reform
20 Vatican I	1869-1870	Papal infallibility; condemnation of various errors
21 Vatican II	1962-1965	Renewal of the Church in the modern world

There were other councils convened in Rome, Carthage, Alexandria, and other cities. These councils were of a local, governing nature only. Their decisions did not carry the same weight as ecumenical councils and therefore are not included as solemnly defined tenets of faith.

PART III
The Church Fathers

Anumber of great and holy leaders arose to lead the Church, explain the Faith, and meet the unique challenges posed by the different heresies. They are known as the Church Fathers. This title and some of their names have already appeared in previous chapters. This chapter will focus on several of them. The Church Fathers shared the following characteristics: orthodoxy in doctrine, holiness, notoriety, and antiquity. The title "Church Father" is not conferred by the Church; it is simply a traditionally held title. While no definitive list exists, the Church Fathers are typically divided into two groups: Latin (West) and Greek (East) Fathers. The Golden Age of the Church Fathers was from 320 to 461. St. Isidore of Seville (ca. 560-636) in the West and St. John of Damascus (ca. 655-ca. 750) in the East are generally regarded as the last significant Church Fathers.

The study of the Church Fathers and their many writings is known as patristics. The writings of the Fathers provide a unique opportunity to learn and appreciate the wealth of the earliest Christian tradition. Because of their proximity to the teachings of the Apostles, the Fathers' clarification and interpretation on Scripture will always serve as a standard reference point for Church teaching.

The following is a list of ten important Church Fathers:

CHURCH FATHERS	
LATIN	**GREEK**
St. Ambrose of Milan*	St. Athanasius*
St. Augustine of Hippo*	ST. BASIL THE GREAT*
Pope St. Gregory the Great*	ST. GREGORY OF NYSSA
St. Jerome*	ST. GREGORY OF NAZIANZUS*
St. Hilary of Poitiers*	St. John Chrysostom*

*Denotes a Doctor of the Church
(Names in all capitals indicate the Three Cappadocian Fathers.)

A Doctor of the Church (*Doctor Ecclesiæ*) is a specific title granted by the pope to those whose development of theology and personal sanctity are exemplary. This tradition began in the Medieval period and continues into the present. Currently, there are over thirty Doctors of the Church. The last three Doctors proclaimed in the twentieth century were St. Teresa of Avila and St. Catherine of Siena by Pope Paul VI in 1970, and St. Thérèse of Lisieux by Pope John Paul II in 1997. A complete list of Doctors may be found on page 789.

The study of the Church Fathers and their many writings is known as "patristics."

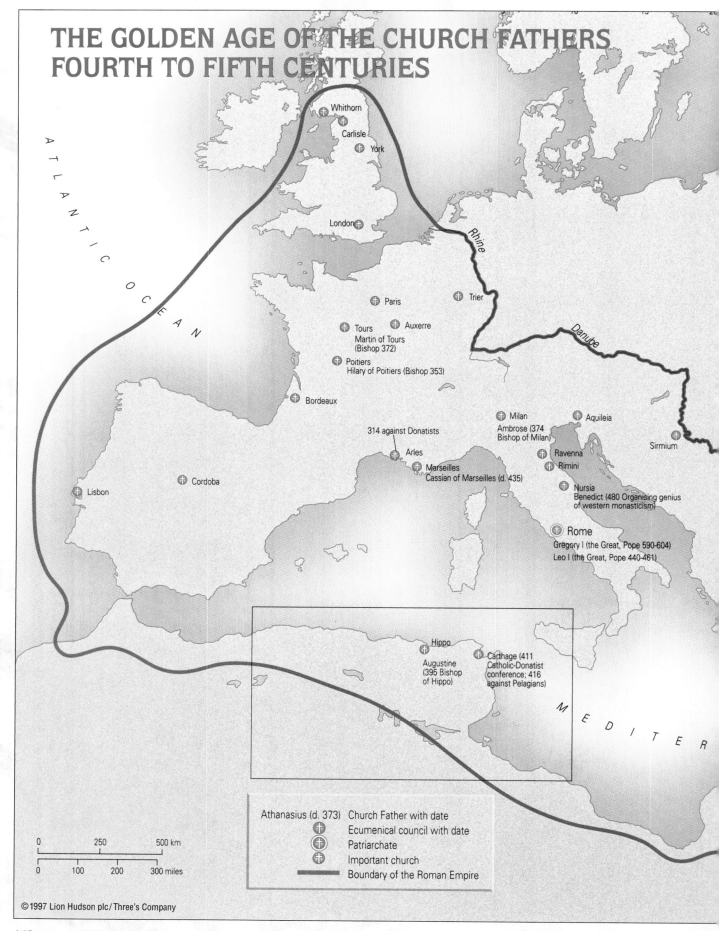

THE GOLDEN AGE OF THE CHURCH FATHERS FOURTH TO FIFTH CENTURIES

ATLANTIC OCEAN

Whithorn

Carlisle

York

London

Rhine

Paris

Trier

Tours
Martin of Tours
(Bishop 372)

Auxerre

Danube

Poitiers
Hilary of Poitiers (Bishop 353)

Bordeaux

Milan
Ambrose (374
Bishop of Milan)

Aquileia

314 against Donatists

Sirmium

Arles

Ravenna

Marseilles
Cassian of Marseilles (d. 435)

Rimini

Cordoba

Nursia
Benedict (480 Organising genius
of western monasticism)

Lisbon

Rome
Gregory I (the Great, Pope 590-604)
Leo I (the Great, Pope 440-461)

Hippo
Augustine
(395 Bishop
of Hippo)

Carthage (411
Catholic-Donatist
conference; 416
against Pelagians)

MEDITER
R

Athanasius (d. 373) Church Father with date
Ecumenical council with date
Patriarchate
Important church
Boundary of the Roman Empire

0   250   500 km
0   100   200   300 miles

©1997 Lion Hudson plc/Three's Company

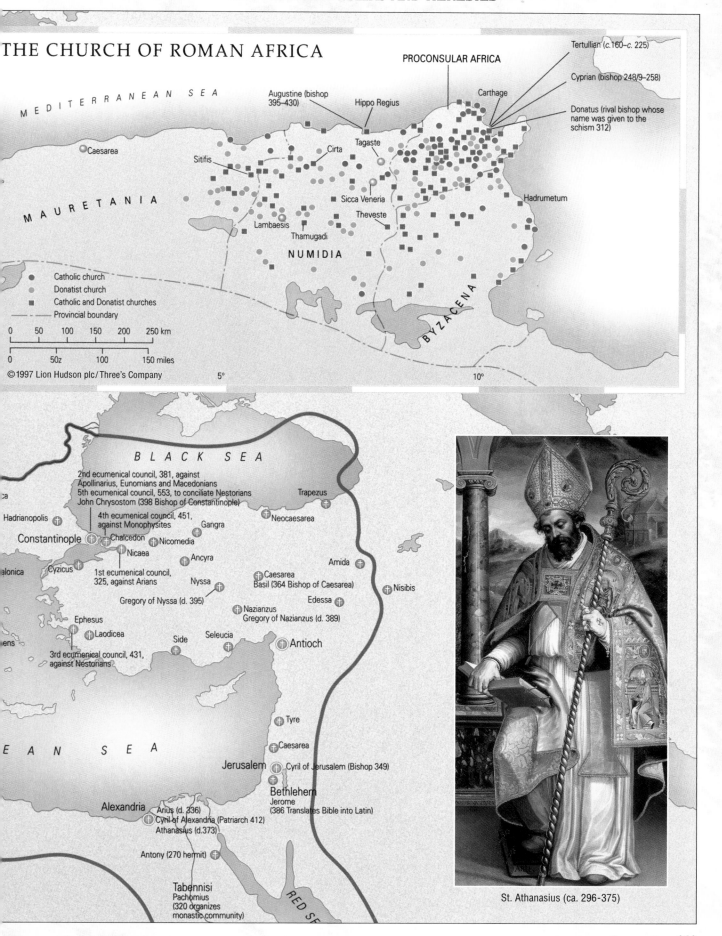

THE CHURCH OF ROMAN AFRICA

MEDITERRANEAN SEA

PROCONSULAR AFRICA

Tertullian (c.160–c. 225)

Cyprian (bishop 248/9–258)

Donatus (rival bishop whose name was given to the schism 312)

Carthage

Augustine (bishop 395–430)

Hippo Regius

Caesarea

Sitifis

Cirta

Tagaste

MAURETANIA

Sicca Veneria

Hadrumetum

Lambaesis

Theveste

Thamugadi

NUMIDIA

BYZACENA

● Catholic church
● Donatist church
■ Catholic and Donatist churches
—·— Provincial boundary

0 50 100 150 200 250 km

0 50z 100 150 miles

©1997 Lion Hudson plc/Three's Company

5°   10°

BLACK SEA

2nd ecumenical council, 381, against Apollinarius, Eunomians and Macedonians
5th ecumenical council, 553, to conciliate Nestorians
John Chrysostom (398 Bishop of Constantinople)

Trapezus

Neocaesarea

Hadrianopolis

4th ecumenical council, 451, against Monophysites

Gangra

Constantinople

Chalcedon

Nicomedia

Nicaea

Ancyra

Amida

Cyzicus

1st ecumenical council, 325, against Arians

Nyssa

Caesarea
Basil (364 Bishop of Caesarea)

Nisibis

alonica

Nyssa

Gregory of Nyssa (d. 395)

Edessa

Nazianzus
Gregory of Nazianzus (d. 389)

Ephesus

Laodicea

Side

Seleucia

Antioch

ens

3rd ecumenical council, 431, against Nestorians

EAN SEA

Tyre

Caesarea

Jerusalem

Cyril of Jerusalem (Bishop 349)

Bethlehem
Jerome
(386 Translates Bible into Latin)

Alexandria
Arius (d. 336)
Cyril of Alexandria (Patriarch 412)
Athanasius (d.373)

Antony (270 hermit)

Tabennisi
Pachomius
(320 organizes monastic community)

RED SEA

St. Athanasius (ca. 296-375)

ST. AMBROSE OF MILAN

Although the elements of this world constantly beat upon the Church with crashing sounds, the Church possesses the safest harbor of salvation for all in distress. (from a letter by St. Ambrose, "Ambrose of Milan")

St. Ambrose of Milan (ca. 339-97) was born in Trier, Germany, close to the frontier with the barbarians. He was the son of the Praetorian Prefect for Gaul. St. Ambrose studied law, became a lawyer, and eventually governor, based in Milan. Upon the death of Milan's Arian bishop around 373, the people clamored for St. Ambrose to succeed him. Though from a Christian family, St. Ambrose was only a catechumen, and he initially resisted accepting the office. Eventually, he acceded and was soon baptized, ordained, and installed as bishop.

St. Ambrose was a zealous defender of the Church's independence from the state. He both counseled and, at times, condemned decisions of the emperors. St. Ambrose supported Emperor Gratian's decision to remove the Altar of Victory, a powerful symbol of pagan influence on the Republic and Empire, from the Senate house in Rome. Later, he threatened Emperor Valentinian II with ecclesiastical sanction if he restored it. In 388 St. Ambrose forbade Theodosius from rebuilding a synagogue that had been destroyed in a riot in Callinicum.

St. Ambrose took a courageous stand against Emperor Theodosius in 390, excommunicating and forcing him the emperor to make public penance for slaughtering 700 village people in Thessalonika that year. (The people of Thessalonika had assassinated one of Theodosius' generals after he imprisoned their favorite charioteer.) Having been barred from even entering the Church by St. Ambrose, let alone receiving Holy Communion, the emperor prostrated himself in the form of a cross in normal clothes in the vestibule just like any other penitent of the time. After eight months of penance and public prayer, St. Ambrose finally pardoned the emperor.

As Bishop of Milan, St. Ambrose became an ardent opponent of the Arian heresy, as well as a renowned preacher. St. Ambrose encouraged monasticism, facilitated theological exchanges with the East due to his knowledge of Greek, and incorporated hymns into the liturgy, a number of which he composed in Latin. His feast day is celebrated on December 7.

THE CHURCH FATHERS AND HERESIES

THE APOSTLES' CREED

I believe in God, the Father almighty, / creator of heaven and earth. / I believe in Jesus Christ, his only Son our Lord. / He was conceived by the power of the Holy Spirit / and born of the Virgin Mary. / He suffered under Pontius Pilate, / was crucified, died and was buried. / He descended into hell. / On the third day he rose again. / He ascended into heaven, / and is seated at the right hand of the Father. / He will come again to judge the living and the dead. / I believe in the Holy Spirit, / the holy Catholic Church, / the communion of saints, / the forgiveness of sins, / the resurrection of the body, / and the life everlasting. Amen.

Though bearing their name, the creed was not written by the Apostles. However, the contents of the creed are based upon the New Testament and may be rightly judged as a profession of faith in the Apostles' teaching. Exact authorship and date do not exist, but its first reference comes from St. Ambrose around 390. The Apostles' Creed was only recognized in the West, where it has been traditionally associated with the baptismal rite. It is also sometimes used at Sunday Masses for children.

The Apostles' Creed is based upon a baptismal creed used especially in Rome, known as the Old Roman Creed. Thus, the Apostles' Creed has a particular association with the Church of Rome, which facilitated its adoption in the West. It follows the baptismal command of Jesus in Matthew 28:19 ("baptizing them in the name of the Father and of the Son and of the Holy Spirit"). This is why the creed is divided into three sections: Father, Son, and Holy Spirit. Besides the Roman Catholic Church, many of the Reformation era churches also accept the Apostles' Creed as a profession of faith.

ST. JEROME

For if, as Paul says, Christ is the power of God and the wisdom of God, and if the man who does not know Scripture does not know the power and wisdom of God, then *ignorance of Scripture is ignorance of Christ.* (St. Jerome, from the Prologue to *Commentary on Isaiah*) [emphasis added]

St. Jerome (ca. 345-420) led a very interesting life. Born in Strido in Dalmatia, near Aquileia, St. Jerome traveled and lived throughout Italy, Gaul, northern Africa, the Holy Land, and Constantinople. His two enduring passions were the ascetical life and scholarship.

St. Jerome spent four to five years in the Syrian desert leading an ascetical life with companions, and while there he learned Hebrew, which would prove vital for his future work of translating Scripture into Latin. St. Jerome never stopped advocating or living a penitential life even when he lived in cities. From 382 to 385 St. Jerome served as a secretary to Pope St. Damasus I. After 386 he spent the last years of his long life in Bethlehem as the head of a new monastery where he continued his scholarship.

Being of a cantankerous and passionate character, St. Jerome, with righteous indignation, was known to insert himself and his sharp pen into the important issues and heresies of his day. Nevertheless, his most important work was undoubtedly the translation of the Bible from the original sources into Latin, known as the Vulgate, which is still the normative text in the Church today. With the Vulgate, the Scriptures were for the first time brought into a uniform translation for the people of the Western Empire. The name Vulgate comes from the Latin *vulgus*, "common," as it was written in the common language of the people of the day. St. Jerome translated the Old Testament from Hebrew, the Psalms from the Greek Septuagint (the Greek version of the Old Testament). He translated the New Testament from Greek and revised what had been already translated into Latin. His feast day is celebrated on September 30.

With St. Jerome's Vulgate, the Scriptures were for the first time brought into a uniform translation for the people of the Western Empire.

TRANSLATIONS OF THE BIBLE

It is widely believed that St. Jerome's Vulgate translation is most faithful because he had access to manuscripts of the original languages that no longer exist. The Douay-Rheims (1582-1609) translation into English was based upon the Vulgate.

The issues involved in translating are manifold, and deeply affect the text that is produced. A high school student who reaches a certain proficiency in a foreign language understands that the different ways ideas and issues are understood in one language are not necessarily the same as in another. Obviously, the process becomes even more crucial in translating a text, such as the Bible, on which people will ground their religious faith. The Church teaches that the books of the Bible are divinely inspired, and that even those books written in different ages by different authors in several languages enjoy the status of God's Word. This issue would become particularly important at the time of the Reformation, but St. Jerome had already set the standard for translation of the Bible with his Vulgate.

Other approved Catholic translations into English use the original sources, including the Jerusalem Bible and the New American Bible (NAB), the latter of which has become the standard translation for American liturgies today, except for the Gospels.

The Revised Standard Version (RSV) translation, which was compiled from 1946-1952, is based upon the King James Bible, otherwise known as the Authorized Version (1611). Though based on the Protestant King James Bible, the RSV was given Church approval when it also included the deuterocanonical texts, those books of the Old Testament that the Orthodox and Catholic

Churches recognize, but which the Protestants do not. (Protestants refer to these books as the Apocrypha.) The RSV was the first ecumenical Bible produced with Catholic, Protestant, Orthodox, and Jewish scholars. The RSV has been lauded for the beauty of its English usage and idiom, and has been used as the source for biblical quotations in this text. There is a Catholic edition with all the deuterocanonical books as well.

The New Revised Standard Version (NRSV) appeared in 1989. Though remarkable because it translates all the poetry of the original texts into English poetry as well, it was not approved for Church liturgy. This translation uses gender neutral language as often as possible in the text (some scholars have argued perhaps more often than appropriate), and it also updated the language of the RSV by eliminating archaic forms ("Thee," "Thou" and verb forms like "wast"). This translation, as well as the RSV, NAB, and the Jerusalem Bibles, bears the *Imprimatur*, Latin for "let it be printed." The *Imprimatur* is granted by a Catholic bishop to assure the reader that nothing therein is contrary to Catholic Faith or morals.

THE CANON OF SCRIPTURE

The word "canon" comes from the Greek *kanon*, which means "reed" or "measuring rod." As it applies to the Scriptures, the canon is the authoritative list of writings included in the Bible and proclaimed by the Church to be divinely inspired. During the first few centuries of the Church's existence, all the books of the Bible were not universally accepted as being divinely inspired.

The Church knew that an authoritative canon of Scripture would have to be established, and so she convened a series of synods and councils in the latter part of the fourth century in order to settle the issue. The Synod of Rome in 382 collected twenty-seven books into the New Testament and forty-six into the Old Testament.

However, after the Synod of Rome, the Scriptural character of the Old Testament deuterocanonical texts (from Greek *deuteros* meaning "second") was still contested. These consist of seven books: Tobias, Judith, Baruch, Sirach, Wisdom, and 1 and 2 Maccabees, as well as certain parts of Esther and Daniel. Three later councils, at Hippo (393) and Carthage (397 and 419),

established finally that the deutero-canonical texts were divinely inspired writings and were to be included in the Old Testament.

While the councils listed above were not ecumenical councils, the Second Council of Nicaea (787), itself an ecumenical council, formally ratified the same canon of Scripture established at Rome, Hippo and Carthage. This canon, which consisted of the twenty-seven books of the New Testament and forty-six books of the Old Testament, was reaffirmed again at the Council of Florence (1335) and the Council of Trent (1545). Protestants, however, do not currently recognize the "deuterocanonical" books of the Old Testament as being part of Scripture.

Pope St. Damasus I (37th Pope; 366-384). In 377, St. Jerome became Pope St. Damasus' secretary. St. Damasus ordered St. Jerome to correct and translate into Latin the Septuagint (a Greek version of the Old Testament) and the New Testament, thus providing the Western Church with its authoritative edition of the Scriptures, the Vulgate. This event also helped to establish Latin as the principal liturgical language at Rome.

ST. PAULA

St. Jerome with St. Paula and her daughter St. Eustochium

St. Paula, the patroness of widows, was born in Rome to a noble family in 347. At the age of thirty-two she lost her husband, Toxotius, and shortly thereafter the eldest of her five children. She suffered greatly from these losses, and was led to consecrate herself entirely to God. After meeting St. Jerome in 382, who had come to Rome along with St. Epiphanius and St. Paulinus of Antioch, she became inspired by the desire to leave Rome and live a monastic life in the East.

Three years later, St. Paula divided her fortune among her family and in September 385 left for the East along with St. Eustochium, one of her daughters. She met up with St. Jerome in Antioch, and the hermit began to offer St. Paula spiritual guidance. Leaving Antioch, they crossed Syria and remained a while in Palestine. St. Paula visited all of the famous places in the Holy Land, and even spent time with the Anchorites

in Egypt. Finally settling in Bethlehem, near the birthplace of Christ, she helped found two monasteries, one for men and one for women.

St. Paula passed the last twenty years of her life in Bethlehem, continuing and developing the intellectual and spiritual discourse she began in Rome with St. Jerome. She studied Scripture, worked with her hands, gave alms, and practiced the most severe austerities, going to church six times a day, singing the psalms she taught her nuns to memorize. St. Jerome, who remained St. Paula's mentor throughout her life, best explained the monastic life the two saints led: "[A]ll is simple and rustic: and except for the chanting of psalms there is complete silence. Wherever one turns the laborer at his plow sings alleluia, the toiling mower cheers himself with psalms, and the vine-dresser while he prunes his vine sings one of the lays of David."

ST. JOHN CHRYSOSTOM, THE GOLDEN MOUTHED

What are we to fear? Death? Life to me means Christ and death is gain....The confiscation of our goods? We brought nothing into this world, and we shall surely take nothing from it. (St. John Chrysostom, *Ante exsilium*, nn. 1-3: PG 52, 427-430)

St. John Chrysostom (ca. 347-407) was an outstanding preacher and commentator on the Bible. He studied law in Antioch, as well as theology under Diodorus, the future bishop of Tarsus. Thus, Chrysostom studied in the influential Antiochene school and became well versed in Greek scholarship and classical culture.

St. John Chrysostom decided to become a monk, and, following the Pachomian Rule (the first cenobitical monastic rule, founded by St. Pachomius — see Chapter 5) for around eight years from ca. 373-ca. 381. The last two years of his monastic life were spent as an anchorite. (An anchorite, from the Greek *anachôrein*, "to withdraw," is sometimes called a hermit.) Severe fasting and other forms of self-denial during those two years greatly damaged his health and forced him to return to Antioch to recuperate.

In 386 he was ordained a priest in Antioch, where he became such a renowned preacher that he earned the name "Chrysostom," meaning "golden-mouthed." His many sermons capture the deep spiritual meaning of biblical texts, without excluding their literal sense. In addition, St. John Chrysostom combined this biblical meaning with a real-world, practical application to the Christian life. He also wrote the celebrated treatise *On the Priesthood*, a work that discusses the importance and duties of a priest.

Against his wishes, the emperor named him Patriarch of Constantinople in 398. St. John Chrysostom recognized the overwhelming task of leading the imperial city's faithful along paths of virtue and holiness. St. John Chrysostom criticized the prevailing moral laxity in Constantinople, including that of the imperial family. Very forthright and direct in his declaration of the truth, he repeatedly clashed with the Empress Euodoxia, who twice had St. John Chrysostom removed from his position as patriarch and banished. He quickly returned from his first period of exile, and the Empress feared some great punishment from Heaven. Shortly thereafter, in 404, even though he enjoyed the firm support of the people of Constantinople, Pope St. Innocent I, and the western Church, St. John Chrysostom was banished again by Euodoxia. This time, he was exiled to the area around Antioch, and then the Roman province of Pontus. While there, he was forced into a death march despite his already failing health, and died in 407. His feast day is celebrated on September 13.

PART IV

Heresies of the Fourth and Fifth Centuries

The fourth and fifth centuries saw a golden age in the history of the Church. Persecutions had ceased, and it was during this time that there emerged some of the greatest leaders the Church had ever seen. The newfound freedom from the fear of persecution allowed for a greater outward expression of ideas in the Church. This not only paved the way for great theological and doctrinal developments, but it also opened the door for new heresies and for one of the most serious crises in the history of the Church. Moreover, this same freedom of Christian expression and practice made it possible for the entire hierarchy of the universal Church to meet in ecumenical councils in response to these heresies. The pronouncements of these councils over the course of the fourth and fifth centuries comprised the Church's teaching on Trinitarian and Christological belief. These first councils owe their success in significant part to many of the Church Fathers, who displayed an imposing intellectual acumen, exceptional leadership qualities, and extraordinary sanctity.

This section will examine some of the heresies faced by the early Church and how they were addressed and resolved by the Church. The roles played by various Church Fathers in resolving these heresies will also be discussed. The statements and teachings of these Fathers of the Church would strongly contribute to the first dogmatic pronouncements of the early Church.

Among the many causes of these heresies, inaccurate interpretations of the Gospels coupled with imprecise philosophical explanations played a significant role. The intervention of the Church led to the development of a theology that was firmly rooted in the true meaning of the Gospel. The principle Christian teaching about the Incarnation—the belief that God the Son became man—raised essential questions regarding the Person of Christ. The Church Fathers made an effort to explain the mysteries of Faith with an accurate terminology. After the Church gave an authoritative answer, those groups who nevertheless adhered to false teaching were known definitively as heretics. A heretic is a baptized person who deliberately and obstinately disavows a revealed truth of established Church dogma.

During this time, two competing cities, Alexandria and Antioch, were the sites of theological study and debate. The prestige, honor, history, and orthodoxy of these centers of learning were on the line. Both cities appealed to their apostolic founding and traditions in their attempts to delineate the theology of the Incarnation and the Trinity. The Alexandrian school was based in Alexandria, Egypt. Hellenistic Alexandria was the second largest city in the Empire, and had the largest Jewish population. In terms of its educational opportunities, it was the best. The Alexandrian school was committed to allegorical exegesis of the Scriptures, and produced luminaries of the likes of Origen and St. Cyril of Alexandria. Employing the language of St. Cyril, this school gave special status to the divinity of Christ and the unity of his person. This did not, however, keep some members of the Alexandrian school from sliding into the heresies of Monophysitism and Monothelitism, which compromised Christ's human nature. On the other hand, in defense of Christ's human nature, Nestorianism appeared in the Antiochene School. This heresy disrupted the unity of Christ's divine and human natures in the one Divine Person of the Son.

The Antiochene School was based in Antioch, Syria, and it was in this city that Jesus' followers were first called "Christians." St. Peter was its first bishop before moving on to Rome. Though still spiritual in its exposition of Scripture, this school tended to focus more on the literal and historical

St. Cyril of Alexandria. Employing the language of Cyril, the Alexandrian school gave special status to the divinity of Christ and the unity of his person.

meanings of the Scriptures. In its theological language and discipline, some people within the Antiochene School tended to isolate Christ's human and divine natures to the detriment of the unity of the two natures in the Person of Christ. St. John Chrysostom and Nestorius are the most famous figures of this school, the former being one of the great Church Fathers; the latter, a condemned heretic.

The following pages will examine a number of Christological heresies, as well as dogmatic and sacramental heresies, and the Church's response to these troubles. The first of these heresies is the most pervasive and perhaps most infamous: Arianism.

CHRISTOLOGICAL HERESIES
ARIANISM (Fourth Century)

The whole world groaned and marveled to find itself Arian. (St. Jerome, *The Dialogue Against the Luciferians*, quoted in "A meditation for Pentecost," *America*, vol. 186 no. 16, May 13, 2002)

Arius (ca. 250-336) was a priest in Alexandria who studied in Antioch. He was an extremely charismatic individual and attracted huge crowds of listeners and devotees on account of his intellectual and rhetorical gifts. He was ordained a priest in 310 and became a pastor of a parish in Alexandria. His study of Origen and Neo-Platonism together with his familiarity with Gnosticism prepared the way for his erroneous interpretation of Christ's relation to the Father.

Using Neo-Platonism and scriptural passages, Arius claimed that Jesus Christ is neither God nor equal to the Father. For example, certain passages of the Gospel of St. John clearly maintain that Christ was sent by the Father and only did the will of the Father. Arius erroneously interpreted passages such as these to mean that Christ was not equal to the Father.

Nevertheless, Arius argued that Christ was an exceptional creature and was raised to the level of "Son of God" because of his heroic fidelity to the Father's will and his sublime holiness. Neo-Platonic thought held that God is a radically transcendent supreme "being" whose nature is incommunicable. This belief is certainly consistent with Christianity. However, the neo-Platonic God was absolutely One, and neo-Platonists could not conceive that anything emanating from the One could be equal to the One. This is at the root of the Arian heresy and its denial of Christ's divinity. This issue of the relationship between God the Father and God the Son was resolved by the Church, as is well addressed in the Athanasian Creed: "He is equal to the Father in his divinity, / but inferior to the Father in his humanity" (n. 31). Christ, according to his divine nature, is equal to the Father, and, according to his human nature, he is inferior to the father. It would take a few centuries to surmount all the theological difficulties connected to Arianism.

~ Arius reduced Jesus Christ to the status of a creature of the Father, although above every creature in dignity and perfection. The Son of God, the *logos*, was created before the world began and served as a vehicle to bring the rest of creation into existence. This heresy was an extremely serious threat to Christianity because the rejection of Christ's divinity invariably leads to a rejection of virtually all of the Church's central tenets, especially her doctrine on the Trinity and the Redemption. For this reason, Arius was responsible for ushering in the greatest doctrinal crisis that the Church would experience until the sixteenth century.

~ As Arius' theology stirred up the suspicions of certain Catholic faithful, the bishop of Alexandria—along with one hundred other North African bishops—asked for a detailed explanation of his thoughts on Christ's divinity. A synod of African bishops condemned Arianism in the year 320 and urged Arius to recant his teachings, but he refused, leaving Egypt to settle in Caesarea. Eventually his ideas spread throughout the East to such an extent that the Church's unity was in great peril. It was vital for the Church to give clarity on the issue of Christ's divinity since the whole deposit of Faith depended on Christ being divine.

After a long career advocating the heresy identified with him, Arius died suddenly in 336 in the streets of Constantinople, just before being named the city's new patriarch and taking possession of that see. As will be seen throughout the Church's history, disobedience to the teaching authority of the Church will often mushroom into a crisis for the entire Church. Had Arius remained obedient to his bishop in 320, one of the worst theological firestorms in history could have been avoided.

The Church as a whole was to become intimately involved in the matter. Arianism found a wide following, and eventually spread to the entire Eastern Church, part of the Western church, and the Germanic tribes. Its impact was large and lasting.

THE COUNCIL OF NICAEA

The whole world has gone Arian; then it is Athanasius against the world.
(St. Athanasius on the pervasiveness of the Arian heresy)

St. Athanasius marshaled the necessary orthodox forces to defeat the Arian heresy in the Church.

St. Athanasius (ca. 296-373) marshaled the necessary orthodox forces to defeat the Arian heresy in the Church. His task was not easy, but St. Athanasius was a persistent and fearless man who would not be silenced. When almost the entire Eastern Church had fallen to the Arians, St. Athanasius still raised his voice to testify to the truth. Even after at least five forced exiles, he was not deterred. The process by which the Church determined her own teaching regarding the divinity of Christ took time, and it was a road with many twists and turns. This was not just an academic dispute. Rather, it was a fight for the heart and soul of Christianity. The Arians used all the tools at their disposal—threats, beatings, exile, even murder—to gain the upper hand.

The Emperor Constantine pushed for a General Council at Nicaea in 325. He was anxious to promote unity in the Empire through a general adherence to Christianity, which was then divided over Arianism. Constantine even paid for the traveling expenses of the western Bishops to secure their involvement and resolve the problem promptly. At the Council of Nicaea, Constantine opened the first session and played the important role of peacemaker between the two factions, Arian and Catholic, though it is doubtful that he understood all the subtleties involved in the discussions on the divinity of Christ.

This was the first of the great ecumenical councils that would be convened over the next few centuries to deliberate, pray, and make pronouncements about the beliefs of the Church in light of contemporary heresies. The ecumenical councils of the first eight centuries are held in the greatest esteem because they brought together bishops from the entire Christian world, East and West. The Council of Nicaea opened with 250 bishops present and ended with 318.

This First Ecumenical Council of Nicaea (325) was especially meaningful since only twelve years prior, the Roman Empire had granted toleration to Christianity after nearly 300 years of persecutions. There were many bishops in attendance who bore physical scars that they had suffered for their Faith during the persecutions under Diocletian, the worst of all the persecutions.

All but two Bishops signed the Nicene Creed, and these two were exiled by the emperor.

The discussions and proceedings at Nicaea were held primarily in Greek, as Nicaea was just outside Constantinople in the East, and the Greek language was considered the language of learning of that period. It was also the language of the New Testament.

At the beginning of the council, the pope led and guided the councils in their deliberations through his legates. In the case of the Council of Nicaea, Pope St. Sylvester I was too old and infirm to travel. Bishop Hosius of Cordova, Spain, represented Pope St. Sylvester I, who happened to be a close friend of the emperor.

St. Athanasius proposed a statement of Catholic belief regarding the divinity of Christ that included the Greek term *homoousios* (Latin, *consubstantialis*), which means "of the same essence or substance." The outcome was the Nicene Creed, the first solemn declaration of Catholic teaching which proclaimed more fully the central truths of Christianity.

The Church utilized Greek philosophy as a tool to better explain the mystery of Jesus Christ and his mission in the world. Specific Greek terms carried very important meanings in terms of explaining Christian belief. For example, Greek thought supplied valuable terms for "person," *hypostasis* (literally "responds to whom") and "substance," *ousia* ("responds to what"). These philosophical words provided a language that distinguished substance from person and nature from person. Although a philosophical analysis of person and substance is beyond the scope of this book, suffice it to say that a person responds to the individuality (the "who") of a natural being, whereas substance and nature define essentially what the being is. For example, what am I? I am a man (my nature and substance). Who am I? I am Joe (my person).

The Church, through her teaching and interpretative role under the guidance of the Holy Spirit, is the final arbiter of all such matters regarding the terminology used for her statements. Two camps emerged from the Council of Nicaea: the *homoousians* (meaning "identical *ousia*" and representing the orthodox position), and the *homoiousians* (meaning "similar *ousia*" and representing the Arian position). Though the council concluded with the Nicene Creed, Arianism still lingered in various forms of Semi-Arianism, and later on re-emerged.

All but two Bishops signed the Nicene Creed, and these two were exiled by the emperor, who supported the creed. The Arian camp included Eusebius of Nicomedia (not to be confused with the Eusebius of Caesarea who wrote the first history of the Church, *Ecclesiastical History*), an important bishop who was favored by Constantine's sister Constantia. Though Eusebius of Nicomedia signed the Nicene Creed, he had only signed under pressure from the emperor, and he was exiled within months for giving aid and support to the Arians.

Emperor Constantine, however, reversed course in 328 and permitted Eusebius of Nicomedia and Arius to return. Leaders of the Nicene party who supported the orthodox position were then forced into exile. This included St. Athanasius, who fled in 336 from his diocese in Alexandria to Trier. In 336 the emperor decided that Arius would be recognized as the bearer of the orthodox position, when Arius suddenly died in Constantinople.

A dizzying array of councils was convened in the East and West over the next twenty-five years. When the councils functioned freely, they chose the Nicene Creed. However, when they operated under duress (the bishops were at times threatened with exile or torture), the bishops—even Bishop Hosius, and St. Hilary of Poitiers—sometimes signed Arian statements (Hosius was beaten and whipped when he was one hundred years old, and Pope Liberius, also in old age, was forced into exile). When these bishops returned to their dioceses from the forced councils, they would renounce the heresy and profess the Nicene Creed.

When Emperor Constantine died in 337, the Arian Eusebius of Nicomedia, who had become the patriarch of Constantinople, baptized him on his deathbed. Of Constantine's three sons, one was Arian and the other two were orthodox Catholic.

The image of the Arian Emperor Constantius II is shown on this gold coin minted in Nicomedia in 337-361.

The East succumbed to Arianism under Constantius, and after Constans I, who controlled the West, was murdered in 350, Constantius eventually became the sole emperor. The West soon also fell into heresy. Many forms of Arianism were found around this time including: (1) an extreme party called the Anomoeans (from the Greek *anhomoios*, meaning "dissimilar") who stressed the essential difference between the Father and the Son; (2) a Scriptural purist party known as the Homoeans (Greek *homoios*, meaning "similar") who rejected any use of the word *homoousius* because it does not appear in the Bible; and, (3) a variety of Semi-Arian groups who stressed the differences and similarities between the Father and the Son with the Greek term *homoiousios* ("similar substance").

Joint synods, one in the West and one in the East, were convoked in 359 at Seleucia and Ariminum under the emperor's influence, and they approved an Arian statement. It was at this time that St. Jerome made his famous statement at the apparent triumph of Arianism: "The whole world groaned and marveled to find itself Arian."

This heretical triumph was short-lived. Emperor Constantius died in 361, and the Council of Paris affirmed the Nicene Creed. The Semi-Arians returned to the Catholic fold after seeing the threat that Arianism posed. After a short term of exile imposed upon him by Emperor Julian the Apostate, St. Athanasius returned to Alexandria, where he labored for the remaining six years of his life among his people. During his lifetime St. Athanasius wrote many books and tracts in defense of the Nicene Creed and against Arianism. The Council of Constantinople (381) reaffirmed the Nicene Creed, which was St. Athanasius' life-long work. His feast day is celebrated on May 2.

THE NICENE-CONSTANTINOPOLITAN CREED

I believe in one God, / the Father, the Almighty, / maker of heaven and earth, / of all that is seen and unseen. / I believe in one Lord, Jesus Christ, / the only Son of God, / eternally begotten of the Father, / God from God, Light from Light, / true God from true God, / begotten, not made, one in Being with the Father. / Through him all things were made. / For us men and for our salvation / he came down from heaven: / by the power of the Holy Spirit / he was born of the Virgin Mary, and became man. / For our sake he was crucified under Pontius Pilate; / he suffered, died, and was buried. / On the third day he rose again / in fulfillment of the Scriptures; / he ascended into heaven / and is seated at the right hand of the Father. / He will come again in glory / to judge the living and the dead, / and his kingdom will have no end. / I believe in the Holy Spirit, / the Lord, the giver of life, / who proceeds from the Father and the Son. / With the Father and the Son he is worshiped and glorified. / He has spoken through the Prophets. / I believe in one, holy, catholic, / and apostolic Church. / I acknowledge one Baptism for the forgiveness of sins. / I look for the resurrection of the dead, / and the life of the world to come. Amen.

The Nicene-Constantinopolitan Creed has its origins in the similar, though shorter, Nicene Creed which was the decisive document of the first ecumenical Council of Nicaea (325) in support of the orthodox Faith of the Church against Arianism. This longer form of the Nicene Creed came out of the Second Ecumenical Council of Constantinople (381). Though the creed was probably not written at the council, it gained support in opposition to heresy. The Nicene-Constantinopolitan Creed appears to have been the baptismal creed in use in Constantinople at the time.

The chief differences between the Nicene and the Nicene-Constantinopolitan Creeds are that the latter is longer in three distinct places: (1) the second section concerning the Son; (2) the third section concerning the Holy Spirit; and (3) the last section, regarding the Church, Baptism, the forgiveness of sins, and the Resurrection. Also, the phrase from the Nicene Creed "from the substance of the Father," a key part of the discussion regarding the *homoousios*, is absent in the later creed.

The Nicene-Constantinopolitan Creed is recited as the Profession of Faith on most Sundays immediately following the homily in the Mass. Bear in mind that the exact wording of the creed is important because of its theological complexity, opposition to heresy, historical continuity, and the unity that it provides throughout the Church.

The Nicene and Nicene-Constantinopolitan Creeds represent an area of agreement and unity for both East and West as the summation of the work of the first two ecumenical councils. A number of the Reformation era churches also recognize its authority, particularly the Lutheran and Anglican churches.

ST. HILARY OF POITIERS: "THE ATHANASIUS OF THE WEST"

Impart to us, then, the meaning of the words of Scripture and the light to understand it, with reverence for the doctrine and confidence in its truth....May we have the grace, in the face of heretics who deny you, to honor you as God, who is not alone, and to proclaim this as truth. (St. Hilary of Poitiers, De Trinitate, Lib. 1, 37-38: PL 10, 48-49)

St. Hilary of Poitiers (d. ca. 375-367/8) was a Latin Church Father during the period of the Arian heresy, and the leading Latin theologian of his day. St. Hilary ardently defended orthodox teaching against the Arians, and for this he is often called the "Athanasius of the West." Rather than merely condemning all heretics without exception, St. Hilary tried to explain to some (especially many of the Semi-Arians who were moving toward reconciliation with the Catholic Church) that often many of their disagreements were merely semantic and that the ideas were actually the same. The author of many brilliant theological texts, St. Hilary was named a Doctor of the Church by Pope Bl. Pius IX in 1851; his feast day is celebrated on January 13.

THE THREE CAPPADOCIANS

The following three Greek Fathers were central figures in the defeat of Arianism in the East: St. Basil the Great, St. Gregory of Nazianzus, and St. Gregory of Nyssa. Cappadocia lies on the Anatolian Plateau on the eastern edge of Asia Minor. Today most of Cappadocia is part of Turkey.

St. Basil became Bishop of Caesarea in Cappadocia, and his brother St. Gregory became Bishop of Nyssa. (A sister was also a saint, St. Macrina, and another brother became a bishop.) St. Gregory of Nazianzus was the son of a bishop. The fruit of their life-long work against Arianism came at the Council of Constantinople (381) where it was decisively defeated. All three appear to have been uniquely influenced by Origen, and all of them focused their studies and reflections on the Holy Spirit.

ST. BASIL THE GREAT

St. Basil the Great (ca. 330-379) looms over Eastern Christianity as St. Augustine does in the West. St. Basil was one of ten children whose parents had suffered under the persecutions of Galerius. He received an excellent education, which he put into the service of the Church. St. Basil is marked by his strong intellect combined with a deep personal holiness and keen administrative abilities.

He settled at Neocaesarea in 358, where he lived as a hermit while working with St. Gregory of Nazianzus in spreading the Faith. St. Basil's ascetical life set the example for the structure and spirit of Eastern monasticism. Unlike in the West, monasticism in the East never fractured into new orders and rules but has remained together as an organic whole under St. Basil's Rule.

As the Bishop of Caesarea, St. Basil encountered opposition from the emperors and other churchmen regarding Arianism. He remained a staunch defender of orthodoxy against the heresies of his time. His work as Bishop of Caesarea extended beyond the intellectual realm of theological debate. St. Basil worked tirelessly for clerical rights, and he saw to it that his priests were rigorously and properly trained. As leader of a great diocese, he strove to care for the material and spiritual needs of the Christian laity. In one of his most important acts as Bishop, a system of hospitals and social service institutions was built up to serve the poor.

Finally, the Divine Liturgy of St. Basil was authored by him. It was the chief liturgy of the Eastern Churches, though in successive centuries the Divine Liturgy of St. John Chrysostom became more widely celebrated outside Lent. The Divine Liturgy of St. Basil has also greatly influenced the composition of Eucharistic Prayer IV as in use in the Roman Missal of the Catholic Church. His feast day is celebrated on January 2.

ST. GREGORY OF NAZIANZUS, "THE THEOLOGIAN"

Different men have different names, which they owe to their parents or to themselves, that is, to their own pursuits and achievements. But our [Sts. Basil and Gregory of Nazianzus] great pursuit, the great name we wanted, was to be Christian, to be called Christians. (St. Gregory of Nazianzus, *Oratio* 43, *in laudem Basilii Magni*)

St. Gregory of Nazianzus (329/30-389/90), like St. Basil, enjoyed the benefits of a philosophical education at Athens. He has often been given the title "The Theologian" because of his writings and teachings. Like St. Basil, he led a rigorous ascetical life and was elevated to the episcopacy at Sasima around 372.

Also like St. Basil, St. Gregory devoted much of his theological writing to the topic of the Holy Spirit. His Five Theological Orations expound upon the third Person of the Trinity.

St. Gregory played an important role at the Council of Constantinople in 381. Through his preaching in the city, he helped to bring the Arians back to the Nicene Faith. The emperor even appointed him Patriarch of Constantinople, but St. Gregory served less than a year before returning to his native Cappadocia. He shares his feast day with his life-long friend St. Basil on January 2.

ST. GREGORY OF NYSSA

St. Gregory of Nyssa (ca. 330 - ca. 395), the younger brother of St. Basil, planned an ecclesiastical career after a short time as a rhetorician. Deeply opposed to the Arian beliefs, St. Gregory was forced into exile by the Arian Emperor Valens, a fate common to many of his brother bishops who espoused the Nicene Creed.

St. Gregory utilized neo-Platonic philosophy in his theological work, which served as an important tool for his teaching. He also defended the popular title *Theotokos* for Mary. *Theotokos* is Greek for "Mother of God" (literally, "the one who gave birth to God"). His feast day is celebrated on March 9.

APOLLINARIANISM (ca. 360-381)

Apollinaris (ca. 310-390) is an example of how even a thoughtful and conscientious Christian thinker, loyal to the Church, could easily develop an erroneous theology by refusing to accept the Church's authority. Apollinaris ardently supported orthodox positions, especially against the Arians, but his unguided fervor led him into heresy. Originally from Beirut and raised to the episcopacy around 360, he was a close friend of St. Athanasius.

Though he affirmed that Christ had a human body, Apollinaris denied the existence of a human mind and will in Christ as a misguided defensive measure against Arianism. Therefore, it would follow that Christ did not live a complete human life as a man. This is incompatible with the Church's teaching that Christ is true God and true man. Beginning with councils in Rome from 374-380,

This 16th century fresco in a Cyprus church shows Emperor Theodosius II exiling Nestorius and another heretic during the Third Ecumenical Council at Ephesus in 431.

Apollinarianism was declared erroneous. The Second Ecumenical Council of Constantinople (381) specifically condemned this heresy, and the state prohibited adherence to it as well.

NESTORIANISM (ca. 351 - ca. 451)

Nestorius became the Patriarch of Constantinople through the intervention of Emperor Theodosius II in 428. In an attempt to escape Apollinarianism, Nestorius maintained that Christ was the unity of a divine Person and a human person in an effort to emphasize his full divinity and full humanity. He attempted to eliminate the title *Theotokos* (bearer of God) to avoid falling into Apollinarianism. The term *Theotokos* had always before been used in orthodox circles, and it was gaining acceptance in popular culture as a devotion to Mary. (In 1969 Pope Paul VI declared the feast of *Theotokos* (*Mary, Mother of God*) to be observed in the West on January 1, a holy day of obligation.) Nestorius professed that though Mary was the Mother of Christ, she was not the Mother of God. Nestorius defended his rejection of this Marian title by his doctrine that Jesus Christ is the result of the union of two separate persons, one man and one God.

The orthodox position taught that Jesus Christ is one Person with two natures, human and divine. St. Cyril of Alexandria described the relationship of the two natures as the Hypostatic Union, a doctrine that was formally accepted by the Church at the Fourth Ecumenical Council of Chalcedon (451). The Definition of Chalcedon was a declaration of Catholic teaching that reaffirmed the Nicene and Nicene-Constantinople Creeds and rejected Nestorianism.

St. Cyril and Pope St. Celestine rejected as heretical the teachings of Nestorius in August 430 at a council in Rome. Pope St. Celestine also charged St. Cyril with the task of dealing with the Nestorian heresy. Legates delivered to Nestorius, the Patriarch of Constantinople, a set of twelve anathemas on December 7, 430. Nestorius was asked to repudiate his teachings within ten days.

Since Nestorius did not recant, Emperor Theodosius II called the Third Ecumenical Council at Ephesus (431) the following summer, where the council condemned Nestorius' teachings and declared Mary as the true Mother of God (*Theotokos*). The emperor accepted its decision, and Nestorius was removed as patriarch and sent to a monastery. So overjoyed were the people over this pronouncement that they carried the council fathers on their shoulders in great jubilation. In 435, the emperor ordered Nestorius' books to be burned, and in 436 Nestorius was banished to Egypt where he died.

MONOPHYSITISM (400s - 600s)

Monophysitism claimed that there is only one nature in Christ, and not two, as the definition of the Council of Chalcedon (451) would state. The name is derived from the Greek *monos* (alone, single) and *physis* (nature) that together mean "only one nature." This concept was developed in the Alexandrian school, and may be understood in part to be a reaction to Nestorianism. It was a way of preserving the theological teaching of Christ's Divinity—the human nature of Christ would be "incorporated" into the Divine Nature. This particular heresy took on a various number of forms and attracted those who rejected the two-nature definition given at Chalcedon.

One of these erroneous doctrines was Eutychianism, initiated by Eutyches. Eutyches (ca. 378-454) was the head of an important monastery in Constantinople. He held that there was only one nature in Christ after the Incarnation, and he denied that Christ's humanity was identical with that of a man. For Eutyches, Christ's nature had the unique quality of being joined to the Divine Nature. He claimed that the human nature of Christ was, as it were, absorbed into the Divine Nature as a drop of water is absorbed into an ocean. His friendship with the influential eunuch Chrysaphius at the court of the emperor seems to have offered him some protection, as well as a hearing before Pope St. Leo the Great, before his teaching was finally condemned at the Fourth Ecumenical Council of Chalcedon (451).

Pope St. Leo was steeped in the heretical challenges threatening the Church. His support was sought by all sides involved in the Monophysite controversy. At the Council of Chalcedon (451), whose primary task was handling Monophysitism, St. Leo's legates spoke first, and his *Tome* (449) was accepted as the orthodox position by the ecumenical council. It declared that Jesus Christ was the God-man, one Person with two natures. Thereafter it was said, "Peter has spoken through Leo."

The cumulative effect of Arianism, Apollinarianism, Nestorianism, and Monophysitism was a tremendous weakening of the unity of the Empire in the East. Many Christians resented the power of the emperor and his attempts to force theological unity. A number of Christians broke away from the Church and became known as members of the Oriental Orthodox Church. For centuries several groups adhered to the one nature heresy of Monophysitism: the Coptic/Egyptian Orthodox, the Abyssinians (Ethiopian Orthodox), and the Syrian Orthodox. Recent officially approved common declarations of faith between the Roman Catholic Church and these churches have concluded that they no longer hold to the Monophysite heresy.

GREGORY THE ILLUMINATOR: "APOSTLE OF ARMENIA"

Most of the faithful of the Church in Armenia also broke away over this issue of Monophysitism, but it is not in full communion with the other Oriental Orthodox churches. (There is, however, a segment of Armenians that is still in communion with Rome with its own eastern Catholic rite of the Chaldean tradition.) Armenia has the distinction of being the first nation to officially become Christian in 314. Bishop Gregory the Illuminator (ca. 257-337) brought Christianity to the Armenian king Tiridates III (king 228?-330), which initiated the Christianization of the Armenian people. This model of baptizing the king followed by the general population was a model often emulated in the decades and centuries following.

POPE ST. LEO THE GREAT

Pope St. Leo I (d. 461) consolidated papal power through a variety of means based upon Jesus Christ's strong endorsement of the papacy transmitted through the New Testament. (Mt 16:18: "You are Peter, and on this rock I will build my church.") With the firm conviction of God's will and authority behind the Chair of St. Peter, he secured a rescript from Emperor Valentinian III that acknowledged papal jurisdiction in the West.

St. Leo also took very bold positions *vis-à-vis* the barbarian invaders, which will be discussed in more detail in the following chapter. His leadership regarding the heresies of the time and dealings with the barbarians, as well as his administration in the Church earned St. Leo the title "the Great." His pontificate gave great moral authority and prestige to the papacy.

St. Leo's writings in Latin have been lauded for their clarity and precision, particularly at a time when the response to heresies required the use of precise language. St. Leo did not speak Greek and had to rely on translations to communicate with the East. This absence of a common language contributed to a strained relationship between the West and the East. In addition to being considered a Father of the Church, St. Leo has also been given the title Doctor of the Church, and his feast day is celebrated on November 10.

MONOTHELITISM (600s)

Monothelitism is the doctrine that professes the existence of only one will in Christ but still maintains that he has two natures. The name is derived from the Greek *monos* (alone, single) and *thelos* (one who wills). This heresy originated not with a churchman, but with the emperor. The tenets of Monothelitism were proposed in 624 as part of a conciliatory document to reconcile the Monophysites with the Church. Emperor Heraclius supported the document. Heraclius' predecessor, Emperor Justinian I, had deeply wounded the unity of the Empire by persecuting the Monophysites, and Heraclius sought to repair that damage. At that time the Empire was facing a growing Persian threat, and Heraclius wanted the Empire to be united religiously to face the Persians. Asia Minor and Palestine, which bordered Persia, were at odds with each other because of these religious controversies, and the emperor needed to know that the entire Empire would work together to defeat the Persians. He thought that Monothelitism would help to maintain unity.

Patriarch Sergius of Constantinople approved the formula, though Sophronius (ca. 560-638), the Patriarch of Jerusalem, opposed it. Patriarch Sergius then wrote to Pope Honorius to clarify the matter. The pope approved of Sergius' handling of the matter and used the term "one will" in his reply, which the patriarch and emperor then quoted in the official document of Monothelitism known as the *Ecthesis* in 638. Two subsequent councils at Constantinople in 638 and 639, though not ecumenical, accepted the *Ecthesis* for the Eastern Church. The local councils confirmed that Patriarch Sergius had successfully won over a number of the Monophysites.

However, the next three papal successors to Honorious—Severinus, John IV, and Theodore I— all condemned Monothelitism and the *Ecthesis*. The Sixth Ecumenical Council of the Church (680-681)—the third at Constantinople—condemned the heresy and even anathematized Pope Honorius.

Pope Honorius' use of the term "one will" in an unguarded letter has often been cited as an example of papal fallibility. However, his private reply to a concern of only the Eastern Church does not meet the conditions for infallibility. In this case the pope did not define a doctrine for the entire, universal Church, nor was it the pope's intention to descend into theological details on the "wills" in Christ. He could very well have meant simply that Christ's will was in faithful conformity with the will of His Father. The incident does indicate, once again, that the other churches, even the patriarch in Constantinople, would appeal to the papacy to settle theological questions.

In essence, Monothelitism appealed to the Monophysites because it substituted the word "will" for "nature." The Church developed precise terminology when referring to will and nature made clear by Greek philosophical language. The official teaching stood with Jesus being a divine Person but with a human and divine nature, as well as having two wills—one divine and the other human. As was the case in the previous Christological heresies, Christ's humanity, as well as his divinity, was theologically called into question.

DOGMATIC AND SACRAMENTAL HERESIES
DONATISM (311-411)

Donatism rejected the validity of sacraments celebrated by priests and bishops who had formerly betrayed their faith. This schism in the Church in Africa began around 311 when Bishop Caecilian of Carthage was ordained by Bishop Felix of Aptunga, who had been a *traditor* during Diocletian's persecution. (A *traditor* was any early Christian who renounced the Christian Faith during the Roman persecutions.) The Donatists rejected the validity of Bishop Caecilian's ordination because of the sin of being a *traditor*. The heresy gets its name from Donatus, who was a bishop elected in opposition to the legitimate one.

Moreover, the Donatists claimed that the Church of the saints must remain holy and free from sin and even from those who have sinned. Sinful priests and bishops, the Donatists maintained, were incapable of validly celebrating the Sacraments. Indeed, the Donatists re-baptized persons who joined them because they did not consider the Sacrament valid except in their own circle. The Donatists went so far as to identify the true Church with only themselves.

St. Augustine was their chief opponent. He developed the Catholic position that Christ is the true minister of every Sacrament, even if the person celebrating the Sacrament is in a state of sin. St. Augustine separated the issue of worthiness on the part of the priest from the validity and efficacy of the Sacrament.

The Donatists were finally suppressed by the state in 411, though they were never fully defeated until Islam destroyed the Church in Africa in the seventh and eighth centuries.

PELAGIANISM (late 300s - 431)

Pelagianism advocated a theological position in which man can be redeemed and sanctified without grace. Specifically, it denied the existence of original sin as well as its transmission into the human family. According to this opinion, the sacraments are superfluous since salvation and holiness could be solely achieved through mere human endeavor.

This heresy was started by Pelagius, an English monk, who attracted several other defenders of these positions. They included Celestius and Julian of Eclanum; the latter engaged St. Augustine in a bitter and protracted debate that ended only with the death of St. Augustine in 430.

Pelagius and Celestius were repeatedly condemned at two councils in Carthage and Milevis in 416, and they were eventually excommunicated by Pope St. Innocent I (410-17). The Council of Carthage of May 1, 418 issued a teaching that adopted St. Augustine's positions on the Fall and original sin, which subsequently became the teaching of the Church. Emperor Honorius denounced the Pelagians on April 30, 418.

Nothing is known of what became of Pelagius, but Celestius appealed to Nestorius for support in 429 with the hope of gaining favor with Pope St. Celestine I. The Council of Ephesus (431) condemned Pelagianism yet again. Though this heresy still had some following in Britain, it eventually died out. However, the issues surrounding the Fall, original sin, and grace reappeared during the Middle Ages and again at the time of the Reformation (sixteenth century).

ST. AUGUSTINE OF HIPPO

I sought a way to gain the strength which I needed to enjoy you [God]. But I did not find it until I embraced the mediator between God and men, the man Christ Jesus, who is above all, God blessed for ever. (St. Augustine, *Confessions*, Book VII)

St. Augustine (354-430) was perhaps the greatest Father of the Church. He fulfilled many roles: pastor, penitent, monk, preacher, bishop, teacher, and theologian. He is one of the greatest theologians of the Catholic Church. For almost a thousand years, he was the dominant figure in Catholic thought. No other theologian rivaled St. Augustine's importance until the thirteenth century when St. Thomas Aquinas would make his mark.

Born in Thagaste in Northern Africa (modern Souk-Ahras, Algeria) to a pagan father and a Christian mother, St. Monica, St. Augustine lived a dissolute life for many years before coming to the Faith. St. Augustine received a good education in the Latin classics and in rhetoric, though his Northern African accent was often mocked in Rome.

The intense attractions of both lust and heresy proved to be very powerful for St. Augustine. For this reason, even after more than a thousand years, his conversion story has not lost its appeal. He once prayed, "Lord, give me chastity and continence, but not yet" (*Confessions*, Book VIII.VIII). At 17 he cohabitated with a woman, and they later had a son, Adeodatus, who died in 389. Around the age of 20, St. Augustine also became deeply involved with the heresy of Manichæism.

ST. AUGUSTINE AND THE PEAR TREE

St. Augustine sought to understand the reason he committed this sin, having "no inducement to evil but the evil itself."

One reason that St. Augustine's work *Confessions* is such an engaging and insightful book is the way he weaves events from his life together with reflections on human nature. One such incident comes from a retelling of a childhood event. St. Augustine recalls how as a child he and a group of friends, hanging out in the street late one night, decided to steal the fruit of a neighbor's pear tree. St. Augustine remembers that he did not steal the fruit because he was hungry, but because "it was not permitted." The satisfaction of stealing the fruit, the "theft and sin itself," was what he and his friends really desired, and so, after barely tasting the stolen fruit themselves, he and his friends threw the remaining pears to some hogs.

St. Augustine sought to understand the reason he committed this sin, having "no inducement to evil but the evil itself." In this incident, he recognizes something fundamentally wrong with the deep impulses of human nature: "It was foul, and I loved it. I loved to perish. I loved my own error—not that for which I erred, but the error itself."

The event shows that any act of sin, no matter how small, reflects a person's rebellious nature against God, turning away from Him. Because of fallen human nature, St. Augustine concluded, people are naturally inclined to sin and are all in need of the grace of Christ in order to overcome this weakness and turn ourselves back towards God.

Around the year 375, St. Augustine taught rhetoric in Thagaste. In 383 he moved to Rome and eventually Milan, where he continued his teaching career. St. Augustine was under tremendous stress not long after arriving in Italy: he lost his belief in Manichæism, and he separated from his mistress after many years of being together. It was at this same time, however, that he found great intellectual stimulation through a deeper introduction to neo-Platonic philosophy and the moving and edifying preaching of St. Ambrose.

In July 386, St. Augustine had a conversion experience while in a garden in Milan. He heard a voice from a young boy singing, "*Tolle et lege,*" ("Take and read"). St. Augustine obeyed, picked up the Scriptures, and turned to a passage without looking. In Romans 13:13 he found in St. Paul's words comfort and direction for his life: "Let us conduct ourselves becomingly as in the day, not in reveling and drunkenness, not in debauchery and licentiousness, not in quarreling and jealousy." St. Augustine resolved at this time to convert to the Catholic Faith and to abandon his sinful life and embark upon the road to holiness. From this point on, St. Augustine lived a life that is summarized by his constant affirmation: "Our hearts are restless until they rest in Thee, O Lord" (*Confessions,* Book I.I).

At the Easter Vigil on Holy Saturday of 387, St. Augustine and his son Adeodatus were baptized by St. Ambrose, but misfortune followed swiftly. In 388 his mother St. Monica, who had prayed for her son's conversion her entire life, died, and Adeodatus died the next year.

Then St. Augustine returned to Thagaste, where he established a monastic community dedicated to prayer and penance. In 391 he was seized by the people on a visit to Hippo Regius and ordained a priest by Bishop Valerius. By 395 he had been ordained to the episcopacy and became coadjutor for Valerius, and subsequently succeeded Valerius as Bishop of Hippo. St. Augustine's ordination and elevation to the office of bishop were very controversial, especially in view of his former life.

St. Augustine's ordination and elevation to the office of bishop were very controversial.

St. Augustine's writings are voluminous. They include a wide range of themes that delve into almost every conceivable issue of the time. Not only does he address the heresies of his day—the Manicheans, Donatists, Pelagians, and Arians—he also defends Christianity from pagan attackers who blamed the religion for Rome's enfeeblement and collapse. St. Augustine's two most important works are the *Confessions* and *City of God,* the latter of which was his answer to the pagan charges and the barbarian invasions. *Confessions* is St. Augustine's autobiography of his life and conversion.

In *City of God* St. Augustine identifies two cities, one earthly and the other heavenly. The earthly city reflects the world, and St. Augustine focuses on the failures of the old Republic before turning to the Empire's situation under a Christian emperor. St. Augustine bemoans the violence and evils present in the world. The Church, though made up of sinful members, represents the forgiveness and hope that the heavenly city offers. Much of this text, in addition to St. Augustine's other contributions, helped to usher in the Medieval spirit toward religion, the world, and the Church.

St. Augustine's theology included works that dealt with the Trinity, grace, the Fall and original sin, repentance, the sacraments, predestination, and atonement. St. Augustine's theology and writings came to be adopted as the official teaching of the Church. For instance, his discussion on the relationship of the Father, Son, and Holy Spirit laid the essential groundwork for the addition of

While in a garden in Milan. St. Augustine heard a voice from a young boy singing, *"Tolle et lege,"* ("Take and read"). In St. Paul's words he found comfort and direction for his life.

the *Filioque* clause expressing the double procession of the Holy Spirit from the Father and the Son (cf. Chapter 7) to the Nicene Creed during the Medieval period.

St. Augustine's spirit for the ascetical life is found throughout his rule. A number of monastic orders adopted his rule beginning in the eleventh century. They include the Augustinian Canons, the Augustinian Hermits and Friars, the Dominicans, and the Servites, as well as the Visitation and Ursuline nuns.

Though St. Augustine was born shortly after the Edict of Milan (313), he lived in a tumultuous age for the Church and for Roman society. Intransigent heresies tore at the unity of the Church, and the Empire was well along the path to oblivion in the temporal order. As St. Augustine lay dying in Hippo, the Vandals were destroying the city, and other Germanic tribes were invading throughout the Roman Empire. The entire temporal, social, and economic order that St. Augustine knew was abruptly ending. St. Augustine set the theological tone in the West, and his philosophy and theology dominated Christian thought for some eight hundred years, until the thirteenth century, when Scholasticism and St. Thomas Aquinas would emerge, enriching the philosophy and theology of St. Augustine. St. Augustine's feast day is celebrated on August 28.

PART V

Christianity: Official Religion of the Roman Empire

The purpose of this section is not to discuss the reign of the Roman emperors, but rather to understand the ways in which the Church-State relationship developed and shaped the Church. The dominant theme in this relationship is the union of the throne of the Empire and the altar of the Church. For political reasons, the State wanted religious unity and uniformity. The Church in the East, influenced by the growing power of the patriarch of Constantinople under the strong influence of the emperor, tended to accept a role for the Church which was subservient to the interests of the State. This dual role of head of State and leader of the Church on the part of the emperor was called caesaropapism. The emperor played a major role in selecting the patriarch of Constantinople, who in turn was beholden to the emperor.

The papacy wanted a good, working relationship with the State, as it asserted its divine jurisdiction over spiritual matters. As St. Ambrose demonstrated, the Church in the West did not allow anyone, not even emperors, to be above the Law of Christ.

Yet Constantine's abandonment of Rome left the papacy with temporal power in the West. If the papacy had not taken up the reigns of temporal power in Rome and in the West, the barbarians would have found absolutely no one to stop their attacks. When the State collapsed in the West, the papacy was there to defend and preserve the Faith and culture of the people.

The Christogram symbol (Chi-Rho), which Constantine carried into his battle with Maxentius, appeared on Roman coins after the Edict of Milan (313).

CONSTANTINE'S ASCENDANCY

Constantine and Licinius ruled the Empire after the Edict of Milan (313), though Licinius was not faithful to his promised religious toleration. Around 321 Licinius began a persecution directed at the bishops and clergy, and in 324 he openly declared war against Constantine. Licinius was defeated, thus making possible religious toleration throughout the Empire.

Constantine increasingly supported Christianity as the years passed. Through law and his own actions, he set the tone: priests and churches were freed from taxation, individual churches were permitted to receive donations, work on Sunday was forbidden, and crucifixion as a state form of execution was ended. Constantine himself withdrew from participation in the pagan rites and ceremonies to which the emperors had always been connected.

Constantine's other great influence was to found the city of Constantinople on the site of the Greek city of Byzantium in 330. On May 11, 330 the city was officially dedicated under Christian and pagan rites. Constantinople was dedicated to the protection of Mary under the title of *Theotokos*. The city's natural defenses protected it for over a thousand years until it fell to the Ottoman Turks in 1453.

After Constantine moved the capital of the Empire to Byzantium along the Bosporus Straits in 330, economic, cultural, and linguistic power shifted. The ruling city of the Roman Empire did not speak Latin but Greek. Byzantium, as the new Eastern Empire came to be known, was wealthier and more heavily populated and looked upon Italy and the West as backward and poor. During that period, knowledge of the Greek language was becoming less common in the West, adding to the cultural breach between East and West. Not until the Renaissance did the West take a renewed interest in Greek and the access to the great body of ancient knowledge it provided.

On his deathbed on May 22, 337, Constantine was baptized by an Arian bishop. The Church in the East proclaimed him a saint; the Church in the West had not concurred. Constantine did not embody the totality of the Christian principles necessary for such an important position as emperor, though Constantine does carry the title "the Great" in the West. Constantine convicted and executed his oldest son and probably also his wife after she, having been influenced by another woman, had made false charges against the eldest son. Despite his negative aspects, Constantine freed the Church from the persecutions she had known for three hundred years through his persuasive enactment of the Edict of Milan in 313.

Constantine was proclaimed a saint by the Eastern Church, and is known as "the Great" in the Western Church.

JULIAN THE APOSTATE

Julian (332-363, emperor 361-363) was the nephew of Constantine the Great and the cousin of Constantius II (emperor 337-361). When Julian was only five years old, his father, brothers (except for his half-brother Gallus), and male cousins were all executed as the Flavian dynastic line of Constantine the Great was purged. Julian was subsequently entrusted to the pagan eunuch Mardonius and Eusebius of Nicomedia, the Arian bishop who baptized Constantine the Great. As Julian increased in years, he became attached to the pagan school in Athens, the city where he and St. Gregory of Nazianzus were classmates.

Julian became a Caesar in 355. In 361 he came into conflict with Emperor Constantius II when Julian's army refused to join the emperor for the Persian campaign. Civil war was averted only because Constantius died of natural causes. Julian was then immediately promoted by the military to the imperial throne.

The title "Apostate" (one who willingly renounces his faith) has been given to Julian because, though he was baptized a Christian, as emperor he tried to de-emphasize Christianity. Julian did not persecute the Christians, but he sought to re-establish paganism on equal footing with Christianity and to strip Christianity of the special benefits that Constantine the Great and his successor had granted.

Julian took several steps to achieve these ends. He pushed to re-establish pagan worship throughout the Empire, and this included the development of an elaborate pagan liturgy and organized his pagan religion in imitation of the Church's ecclesiastical and sacramental structures. Julian himself lived a very ethical life, to which he was committed in order to raise the moral tone of pagans in the Empire. The curriculum in the Empire's schools was paganized (there was probably no system of general education for the society; these schools were for a select few of the privileged classes for the perpetuation of the bureaucracy). Julian revoked the financial exemption and benefits that had been given to the Church by his predecessors. He wrote many tracts in support of paganism and in opposition to Christianity and imposed harsh sentences on his subjects because of their faith. Finally, Julian generated great confusion in the Church when he permitted exiled heretical bishops to return.

The Altar of Victory, a replica of the Greek "Winged Victory of Samothrace," was the ultimate symbol of Roman supremacy. The Altar was a "majestic female standing on a globe, with expanded wings, and a crown of laurel in her outstretched hand."

Julian also had to deal with the Persian threat. On June 26, 363, he was struck by an arrow while on a campaign in Mesopotamia, and he died the same day. A story has it that Julian's last words were "*Vincisti Galilæe*" ("Thou hast conquered, Galilean!" referring to Jesus Christ, who was from Galilee). But this story has been discredited as fiction written by Theodoret, the Bishop of Cyrrhus (ca. 393 - ca. 457).

Julian had been viewed in a negative way in much of the Empire, especially in the East where the largest numbers of Christians dwelt. Succeeding emperors moved to progressively reduce paganism to oblivion, and to re-grant the special status of Christianity. Jovian (emperor 363-364), the immediate successor to Julian, returned to Christianity the rights Julian had stripped from it. Gratian (Western emperor 375-383) gave up the insignia of the Pontifex Maximus because it was pagan and he considered it unbecoming for a Christian ruler. (The title was later Christianized in the fifteenth century and taken over by the papacy as a title of honor.) He also removed the Altar of Victory from the Senate house, and stripped the pagan priests and the Vestal Virgins of their property.

The Second Vatican Council (1962-1965) set aside the union of throne and altar.

THEODOSIUS I THE GREAT (379-395)

Theodosius I cemented the union between the Church and State with his 391 decree declaring Christianity the official religion of the Empire. Heresy became a legal offense before the state, pagan sacrifice was outlawed, and, essentially, all other forms of paganism as well. Clearly, this was a watershed moment in the history of the Church. Within eighty years Christianity emerged from the worst persecution it had ever known to official toleration under the Edict of Milan and finally to the status of official religion of the Empire.

While this was a moment of triumph for the Church, it has also been a topic greatly contested by scholars. The phrase "union of throne and altar" refers to everyone within a given state (usually a monarchy) — even the rulers — having the same religion. This union of throne and altar became the standard relationship between the Church and State until it was officially set aside at the Second Vatican Council (1962-1965). The union of throne and altar posed many challenges and occasioned many crises for the Church over the centuries.

Being a persecuted minority forced Christians to rely authentically on their faith and to forge deep bonds of solidarity. Now these same values of sacrifice and love were officially being taken up by the State. If carried out correctly, the situation provided the Church with an extraordinary possibility to evangelize the Empire and others outside of it. However, an established religion can also find its voice and values co-opted. In any case, given the historical circumstances of that era, it seems that a close connection between Church and State was necessary.

THRONE AND ALTAR

It seems worthwhile to frame the discussion of throne and altar in order to see the ways in which the emperors made use of their power to influence the Church. The involvement of the temporal power in spiritual matters of the Church was a defining aspect of Byzantium, and the tug of war between kings and popes in the West especially during the Medieval period.

Constantine and his three sons, as well as subsequent emperors, set a pattern of imperial intrusion into the affairs of the Church. The Eastern emperors carried the greatest power even when they did not rule the entire Empire, for it was divided permanently between East and West after Emperor Jovian's death in 364.

In this chapter alone, there have been many examples of the emperor interacting with and directing the Church:

1. Constantine the Great took an interest in and influenced the convening of the Council of Nicaea (325) and the suppression of dissident bishops;

2. Julian the Apostate (emperor 361-363) reasserted paganism and suppressed the Church;

3. The Western Emperor Honorius suppressed the Pelagians in 418;

4. Theodosius II called for the Council of Ephesus (431); and

5. Heraclius (emperor 610/611-641) instigated Monothelitism and authorized the *Ecthesis* in 624.

CONCLUSION

Emperor Theodosius I the Great declared Christianity the official religion of the Empire in 391. *Above:* The image of Theodosius I the Great embossed on a 4th century silver plate.

The Church experienced a moment of freedom and hope with the Edict of Milan in 313, but this by no means meant that the situation in the Church was relaxed over the next two centuries. The Church was convulsed by one theological controversy after another, any number of which threatened to destroy the Faith. Only the providential leadership of the popes, the Church Fathers, and the ecumenical councils under the influence of the Holy Spirit guided the Church through the treacherous waters of heresy that threatened to sink her at any time. The proclamation of Christianity as the official religion of the Empire in 391 by Theodosius I the Great inaugurated a new era in Christianity, one filled with the promise of evangelization, as well as with the dangers of temporal meddling in the affairs of the Church.

SUPPLEMENTARY READING

St. Gregory of Nazianzus, *Letters on the Appolinarian Controversy*

Do not let the men deceive themselves and others with the assertion that the "Man of the Lord" as they [Appolinarians] call him, who is rather, Lord and God, is without human mind. For we do not sever the man from the Godhead, but we lay down as a dogma the unity and identity [of persons], who of old was not man but God, and the only Son before all ages, unmingled with body or anything corporeal; but who in these last days has assumed manhood also for our salvation; passable in his flesh, impassible in his Godhead; circumscript in his body, uncircumscript in the Spirit; at once earthly and heavenly, tangible and intangible, comprehensible and incomprehensible; that by one and the same [Person], who was perfect man and also God, the entire humanity fallen through sin might be created anew.

If anyone does not believe that holy Mary is the Mother of God, he is severed from the Godhead. If anyone should assert that he passed through the Virgin as through a channel, and was not at once divinely and humanly formed in her (divinely, because without the intervention of man; humanly, because in accordance with the laws of gestation), he is in like manner godless. If any assert that the manhood was formed and afterwards was clothed with the Godhead, he too is to be condemned.

The Council of Ephesus, *The Formula of Union*, 431

We will state briefly what we are convinced of and profess about the God-bearing virgin and the manner of the incarnation of the only begotten Son of God—not by way of addition but in the manner of a full statement, even as we have received and possess it from the holy scriptures and the tradition of the holy fathers, adding nothing at all to the creed put forward by the holy fathers at Nicaea. For, as we have just said, that creed is sufficient both for the knowledge of godliness and for the repudiation of all heretical false teaching. We shall speak not presuming to approach the unapproachable; but we confess our own weakness and so shut out those who would reproach us for investigating things beyond the human mind.

We confess then, then, our Lord Jesus Christ, the only begotten Son of God, perfect God and perfect man of a rational soul and body, begotten before all ages from the Father in his Godhead, the same in the last days, for us and for our salvation, born of Mary the virgin, according to his humanity, one and the same consubstantial with the Father in godhead and consubstantial with us in humanity, for a union of two natures took place. Therefore we confess one Christ, one Son, one Lord. According to this understanding of of the unconfused union, we confess the Holy Virgin to be the mother of God because God the Word took flesh and became man and from his very conception united to himself the temple he took from her.

John Paul II, *Redemptoris Mater*, 42.2-3

Mary believed in the fulfillment of what had been said to her by the Lord. As Virgin, she believed that she would conceive and bear a son: the "Holy One," who bears the name of "Son of God," the name "Jesus"("God who saves"). As handmaid of the lord, she remained in perfect fidelity to the person and mission of this Son. As Mother, *"believing and obeying…"* she brought forth on earth the *Father's Son.* This she did, knowing not man but overshadowed by the Holy Spirit.

For these reasons Mary is honored in the Church "with special reverence. Indeed, from most ancient times the Blessed Virgin Mary has been venerated under the title of 'God-Bearer.' In all perils and needs the faithful have fled to her protection."

VOCABULARY

ANATHEMA

A ban solemnly pronounced by ecclesiastical authority and accompanied by excommunication

ANOMOEANS

From the Greek *anhomoios,* meaning "dissimilar," this sect of Arianism stressed an essential difference between the Father and Son in the Trinity.

APOCRYPHA

Old Testament books recognized by the Catholic and Orthodox Churches, but not by Protestants.

APOLLINARIANISM

Founded by Apollinarius in the fourth century, this heresy denied the existence of a human mind and will in Christ.

APOSTLES' CREED

A statement of belief of the Apostles based upon the New Testament. It is derived from a baptismal creed used especially in Rome known as the Old Roman, and it is therefore associated particularly with the Church of Rome.

ARIANISM

Third and fourth century heresy founded by the Alexandrian priest Arius. It denied Jesus' divinity, claiming that Jesus is neither God nor equal to the Father, but rather an exceptional creature raised to the level of "Son of God" because of his heroic fidelity to the Father's will and his sublime holiness.

ATHANASIAN CREED

A statement of Faith that the Church still affirms whose author is not known.

CAESAROPAPISM

Refers to the dual role of head of State and leader of the Church in which the temporal ruler extends his own powers to ecclesiastical and theological matters. The Church in the East, influenced by the growing power of the patriarch of Constantinople at the hands of the emperor, tended to accept a role for the Church in which it was subservient to the interests of the State.

CHRYSOSTOM

Moniker of St. John Chrysostom meaning "golden mouthed," it refers to the saint's extraordinary preaching skills.

CHURCH FATHERS

Great, holy leaders who have come forward to lead the Church, explain the Faith, and meet the unique challenges posed by different heresies.

DEMIURGE

Gnostic creator god of the material world.

DOCETISM

Derived from the Greek word *dokesis,* meaning appearance, this Gnostic heresy maintained that Jesus did not die on the cross but was spared by someone else who took his place.

DOCTOR OF THE CHURCH

Doctores Ecclesiae, a specific title given by the pope to those whose development of theology and personal sanctity are exemplary.

DONATISM

Heresy that rejected the sacraments celebrated by clergy who had formerly betrayed their faith.

DOKESIS

Greek word for appearance. Referred to heresy which claimed Jesus only appeared to die on the Cross.

VOCABULARY Continued

ECUMENICAL COUNCIL

Derived from the Greek word *oikoumene,* meaning "the whole inhabited world," Ecumenical councils bring bishops and others entitled to vote from all over the world to discuss central issues of the Church. They are presided over by the pope and issues decrees which, with the approval of the pope, bind all Christians.

FILIOQUE

Latin word meaning "and the Son," it is used to express the double procession of the Holy Spirit from the Father and the Son. St. Augustine's discussion on the relationship of the Father, Son, and Holy Spirit laid the essential groundwork for the addition of the *Filioque* clause to the Nicene Creed in the Medieval period.

GNOSTICISM

Derived from the Greek word *gnosis* ("knowledge"), the name refers to one of the principle tenets of this multifaceted heresy, namely, that salvation may be achieved through knowledge. In the second century, Gnosticism, which had eastern origins and influences from Persia and India, very successfully perverted the meaning of Christianity and its symbols. To prove its authenticity, Gnosticism co-opted the Scriptures, the Old and New Testaments, and erected an entirely new cosmological structure that challenged the intent of Christianity.

HERESY

The refusal to accept one or more truths of the Faith which are required for Catholic belief. It is a species of unbelief belonging to those who profess the Christian Faith, but corrupt its dogmas.

HOMOEANS (SABELLIANS)

From Greek *homoios,* meaning "similar," this Scriptural purist party rejected the use of the word *homoousios* at the Council of Nicaea because it was not used in the Bible.

HOMOOUSIOS

Greek word meaning "of the same substance."

INFALLIBLE

Free from error. Ecumenical councils' definitions on Faith and morals are considered free from error, or infallible, if that is the intention of the pope and bishops in union.

LOGOS

An ambiguous Greek word with a multitude of meanings that include: word, account, meaning, reason, argument, saying, speech, story and many more. The Gospel of St. John utilizes the word's complex meaning, referring to the Person of Jesus, the Son of God and a member of the Blessed Trinity, as the *logos.*

MANICHÆISM

Heresy founded by Mani in the 3rd century. An elaborate form of Gnosticism, it involved the relationship between light and darkness, believing that through rituals and sharing their knowledge believers could regain the light stolen by Satan and hidden in the brains of men, thus freeing the light to return to its original source. Manichæism heavily borrowed from the Scriptures, especially from the writings of St. Paul. Mani incorporated many of St. Paul's arguments and imagery to support his own teaching concerning the struggle between darkness and light.

MARCIONISM

Founded by Marcion in the second century, he borrowed the Gnostic idea of a Demiurge, calling this force the jealous and vengeful God of Law. According to Marcionism, the God of Jesus Christ, the true God, has no law and is sent to bring about the demise of the Demiurge. He renounced all Jewish influence on the Church, believing that the God of the Old Testament was the evil Demiurge.

VOCABULARY Continued

MONTANISM

Founded by Montanus in the second century, he believed that due to an outpouring of the Holy Spirit upon him, he knew that a new, heavenly kingdom was imminent. One of the first apocalyptic heresies, his followers lived a very austere life rejecting second marriages and flight from persecution.

MONOPHYSITISM

From the Greek *monos*, meaning "alone," and *physis*, meaning "nature," this heresy claimed that there is only one nature in Christ and that His human nature is "incorporated" into the Divine Nature.

MONOTHELITISM

Heresy claiming that Christ has two natures but only one will.

NEO-PLATONISM

School of philosophy which held that the *logos* was a created being, not the Supreme Being. Platonic philosophies, in general, viewed the material world as less perfect than the world of ideas. Thus, besides denying Christ's true divinity, many early Platonic heresies greatly deemphasized Christ's humanity, if not openly denying it.

NESTORIANISM

Founded in the fourth century by Nestorius, the Patriarch of Constantinople, this heresy maintained that Christ was both human and divine but was not himself fully human or fully divine. Instead, he believed that Christ was a union of two men, one human the other divine.

PELAGIANISM

Heresy denying original sin and the need for grace in man's salvation. According to this heresy, the sacraments are superfluous since salvation and holiness can only be achieved through human endeavor.

QUICUMQUE VULT

"Whoever wishes [to be saved]," opening of the Athanasian Creed.

THEOTOKOS

Literally "bearer of God," often translated "mother of God." Used since the early centuries of the Church, this title of Mary was defended by the Council of Ephesus in 431.

VULGATE

First translation of the Bible from its original languages into Latin by St. Jerome.

St. Jerome never stopped advocating or living a penitential life.

STUDY QUESTIONS

1. A creed is an official statement of belief. What two points of belief does the Athanasian Creed emphasize?

2. What were the guiding premises of Gnosticism?

3. What role did asceticism play in Manichaeism and other Gnostic heresies?

4. Who has the power to start, change, and end an ecumenical council?

5. Who is a "Church Father" and what are the five characteristics of a Church Father?

6. How and why did St. Ambrose stand up to the very powerful emperor Theodosius in 390?

7. List two translations of the Bible discussed in this chapter and specific information about them.

8. For what is St. John Chrysostom best known?

9. What was Arianism, and why was Arianism such a threat to Christianity?

10. Who convened the Council of Nicaea in 325 and what was the council's outcome?

11. What is the Hypostatic Union and when was it adopted?

12. Under what circumstances was it said of Pope St. Leo I that "Peter has spoken through Leo"? What does this statement really mean?

13. Which regional churches form the Oriental Orthodox Church, and why did they separate from the Catholic Church?

14. How did Pope St. Leo I increase papal power?

15. What is dogma?

16. How did St. Augustine answer the challenges posed by Donatism?

17. Describe St. Augustine's background. Why would his ordination as bishop have been particularly controversial with the Donatists?

18. What do the words "*tolle et lege*" mean, and what is their significance in St. Augustine's life?

19. What topics did St. Augustine address in two of his best-known works, *Confessions* and *City of God*?

20. When and by whom was Christianity declared the official religion of the empire?

St. Augustine is one of the greatest theologians of the Catholic Church. For almost a thousand years, he was the dominant figure in Catholic philosophical and theological thought.

PRACTICAL EXERCISES

1. Check out a local bookstore's religion and philosophy sections. How many books on "finding the light inside yourself" or other New Age movement texts did you find? Why do you think so many people have turned to the New Age movement? What is the difference between these "self-help" solutions and the way of life offered in the example of Christ?

2. Conduct research on one of the over thirty Doctors of the Church, and prepare a three minute oral report after conducting the research.

3. What might be some reasons why the pope has authority over the ecumenical councils? If another ecumenical council were called today, what do you think would be the topics for discussion?

4. Think of reasons and examples of how the union of the throne and altar might cause conflict between the Church and the state.

FROM THE CATECHISM

465 The first heresies denied not so much Christ's divinity as his true humanity (Gnostic Docetism). From apostolic times the Christian faith has insisted on the true incarnation of God's Son "come in the flesh" (cf. 1 Jn 4: 2-3; 2 Jn 7). But already in the third century, the Church in a council at Antioch had to affirm against Paul of Samosata that Jesus Christ is Son of God by nature and not by adoption. The first ecumenical council of Nicaea in 325 confessed in its Creed that the Son of God is "begotten, not made, of the same substance (*homoousios*) as the Father", and condemned Arius, who had affirmed that the Son of God "came to be from things that were not" and that he was "from another substance" than that of the Father (Council of Nicaea I (325): DS 130, 126).

688 The Church, a communion living in the faith of the apostles which she transmits, is the place where we know the Holy Spirit:

— in the Scriptures he inspired;
— in the Tradition, to which the Church Fathers are always timely witnesses;
— in the Church's Magisterium, which he assists;
— in the sacramental liturgy, through its words and symbols, in which the Holy Spirit puts us into communion with Christ;
— in prayer, wherein he intercedes for us;
— in the charisms and ministries by which the Church is built up;
— in the signs of apostolic and missionary life;
— in the witness of saints through whom he manifests his holiness and continues the work of salvation.

FROM THE CATECHISM Continued

817 In fact, "in this one and only Church of God from its very beginnings there arose certain rifts, which the Apostle strongly censures as damnable. But in subsequent centuries much more serious dissensions appeared and large communities became separated from full communion with the Catholic Church—for which, often enough, men of both sides were to blame" (*UR* 3 § 1). The ruptures that wound the unity of Christ's Body—here we must distinguish heresy, apostasy, and schism (cf. CIC, can. 751)—do not occur without human sin:

> Where there are sins, there are also divisions, schisms, heresies, and disputes. Where there is virtue, however, there also are harmony and unity, from which arise the one heart and one soul of all believers (Origen, *Hom. in Ezech.* 9,1: PG 13,732).

2089 *Incredulity* is the neglect of revealed truth or the willful refusal to assent to it. "*Heresy* is the obstinate post-baptismal denial of some truth which must be believed with divine and catholic faith, or it is likewise an obstinate doubt concerning the same; *apostasy* is the total repudiation of the Christian faith; *schism* is the refusal of submission to the Roman Pontiff or of communion with the members of the Church subject to him" (CIC, can. 751: emphasis added).

2419 "Christian revelation…promotes deeper understanding of the laws of social living" (*GS* 23 § 1). The Church receives from the Gospel the full revelation of the truth about man. When she fulfills her mission of proclaiming the Gospel, she bears witness to man, in the name of Christ, to his dignity and his vocation to the communion of persons. She teaches him the demands of justice and peace in conformity with divine wisdom.

2420 The Church makes a moral judgment about economic and social matters, "when the fundamental rights of the person or the salvation of souls requires it" (*GS* 76 § 5). In the moral order she bears a mission distinct from that of political authorities: the Church is concerned with the temporal aspects of the common good because they are ordered to the sovereign Good, our ultimate end. She strives to inspire right attitudes with respect to earthly goods and in socio-economic relationships.

"The glorious city of God is my theme in this work, which you, my dearest son Marcellinus, suggested, and which is due to you by my promise. I have undertaken its defense against those who prefer their own gods to the Founder of this city—a city surpassingly glorious, whether we view it as it still lives by faith in this fleeting course of time, and sojourns as a stranger in the midst of the ungodly, or as it shall dwell in the fixed stability of its eternal seat, which it now with patience waits for, expecting until 'righteousness shall return unto judgment,' and it obtain, by virtue of its excellence, final victory and perfect peace."

Opening text from *City of God*, Book I by St. Augustine.
(In Latin *De Civitate Dei*).

CHAPTER 5
Light In The Dark Ages

Throughout all of the insecurity, one institution remained firm: the Church. Amid the darkness, the Church held up the powerful light of Christ.

CHAPTER 5

Light In The Dark Ages

To the Church and the human race of every age, the Divine Master has left his everlasting testament of love: "Love one another as I have loved you!" A sense of great sadness invades the mind at the thought of God's infinite goodness on the one hand and on the other hand, human indifference, hatred and wars that obscure Divine Providence's plan on earth. You, with your prayers and your testimony of goodness, can offer a daily contribution to the cause of pacifying hearts and establishing peace on earth.

— John Paul II, Meeting with handicapped children, Assisi, Italy, January 9, 1993

As St. Augustine waited for death in Hippo, Vandals beset the city. The collapse of the Roman Empire during the fifth century inaugurated a period of decline in the West as the old world passed away, and confusion reigned as the basis for a new order had yet to coalesce. Throughout all of the insecurity, one institution remained firm: the Church. She continued to spread the Gospel message while providing continuity in an uncertain time. Regardless of the transitoriness of any age, the Church proclaims a message of trust in the life and light of Christ amid trials and tribulations and promises eternal life after death. Amid the darkness, the Church holds up the powerful light of Christ.

This chapter will look at the repercussions of the fall of Rome, the rise and importance of monasticism, and the rise of Islam.

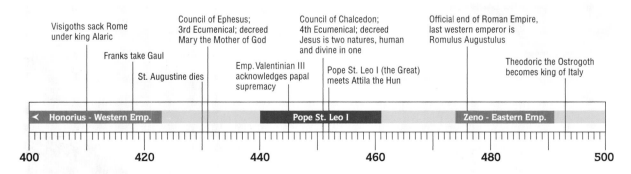

Visigoths sack Rome under king Alaric

Franks take Gaul

St. Augustine dies

Council of Ephesus; 3rd Ecumenical; decreed Mary the Mother of God

Emp. Valentinian III acknowledges papal supremacy

Council of Chalcedon; 4th Ecumenical; decreed Jesus is two natures, human and divine in one

Pope St. Leo I (the Great) meets Attila the Hun

Official end of Roman Empire, last western emperor is Romulus Augustulus

Theodoric the Ostrogoth becomes king of Italy

Honorius - Western Emp. | Pope St. Leo I | Zeno - Eastern Emp.

400   420   440   460   480   500

PART I

The Collapse of the Roman Empire

The collapse of the Roman Empire resulted in a crisis that took the early Church by surprise. The Church now had to dissociate herself from the fallen Empire, which was assumed would last forever. Throughout the decline of the Roman Empire and the rise of monasticism, the Holy Spirit inspired and strengthened the Church for the next great wave of evangelizing activity among the German tribes. By the time the different groups in Europe had converted in the eleventh century, Christianity had spread to virtually the entire European continent.

THE FALL OF ROME (476)

The City which had taken the whole world was itself taken!
(St. Jerome on the Fall of Rome, *Letter CXXVII [To Principia]*, no. 12)

Historians do not have an official date for the fall of Rome, but sometime during the fifth century, the West collapsed. In 410, Alaric, king of the Visigoths, sacked Rome. Odoacer (sometimes Odovacar), chieftain of the Heruli, who served as a mercenary in Rome, led a revolt and overthrew the last western emperor in 476. Soon after, the Ostrogoths, united under Theodoric, invaded Italy in 489 and overthrew Odoacer by 493. The last ten western emperors rarely sat for more than a few years on the throne before they were deposed by invading barbarians.

The moral situation from the fifth through eighth centuries was grim as the former Roman order crumbled. The Roman Empire was not yet completely Christianized when the barbarian invasions injected a foreign and often violent character into the culture. The concept of human rights was unfamiliar to many Romans as well as to the invading barbarian tribes. The brutality of the Romans has already been discussed. The barbarians brought their own variations of tribal law with them — law that was based on very primitive understandings of justice. For instance, in some tribes, in order to determine guilt or innocence, the accused would be forced to immerse his hand in a pot of boiling hot water. If the burned hand healed, then the accused was understood to be innocent. Two people who sought justice would fight to the death to determine who was right. Adulterous wives were handed over to their husbands, who punished them by whatever means they deemed fit. Barbarian kings had harems, and it was common for a teenage king to have many children with his servants. Their religious practices were both primitive and brutal. The Franks, for example, sacrificed women and children to placate battle spirits.

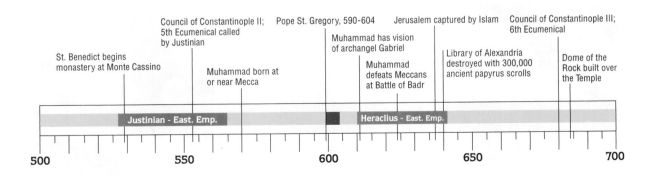

Council of Constantinople II;
5th Ecumenical called
by Justinian

Pope St. Gregory, 590-604

Muhammad has vision
of archangel Gabriel

Jerusalem captured by Islam

Council of Constantinople III;
6th Ecumenical

St. Benedict begins
monastery at Monte Cassino

Muhammad born at
or near Mecca

Muhammad
defeats Meccans
at Battle of Badr

Library of Alexandria
destroyed with 300,000
ancient papyrus scrolls

Dome of the
Rock built over
the Temple

Justinian - East. Emp.

Heraclius - East. Emp.

500   550   600   650   700

The absence of academic pursuits among the Germanic Franks quickly undermined the great Greco-Roman tradition of learning and culture. Thus, the fall of Rome brought about a dramatic and immediate collapse in intellectual activity throughout the former empire of the West. Classical literature was lost, Latin deteriorated, and illiteracy became the norm. The loss of literacy particularly affected the Church because most people could no longer read the Scriptures. The Church remained the only locus of intellectual activity. Academic training was limited to priests and religious studying the Scriptures and theology. The long GrecoRoman tradition of philosophical inquiry came to a halt.

In addition to the collapse of education, the vibrant economy of the empire entered a period of decline as well. Roads became unsafe. People lived in fear and distress, and crime increased. As production and commercial activity declined, the cities and towns began to shrink. Consequentially, the former empire dissipated into a rural society of isolated towns and villages.

The influence of the Church was not yet sufficiently profound to impact on the daily life of the whole population. Some Christians acted like pagans: they participated in eating and drinking orgies, often on a saint's feast day. If games were held on Sundays, the churches would be empty. Idol worship was still found among Christians, as well as among the invading tribes.

With the disappearance of the Roman Empire, the Church had the important task to adapt herself to a deamatic cultural change. The Church's organization reflected the ways and customs of the Empire. The governing structure of the Church was modeled after the rule and territorial division of the Empire. Christians had assumed, as had the Roman emperors, that the destiny of Christianity was permanently intertwined with the Empire, especially after Theodosius I made Christianity the official religion in 379. The Barbarian invasions helped the Church realize that she was not wedded to the Roman Empire and had to adapt to a significant cultural shift.

Historians do not have an official date for the fall of Rome, but sometime during the fifth century, the West collapsed.

The baptism of the leader of the Franks, Clovis. Under his leadership, the Franks were the first Germanic tribe to convert to Christianity.

THE GERMANIC TRIBES

The mission of the Church is to bring the Good News to all peoples. This effort invariably involves Christianizing cultures and at the same time adapting insofar as possible to these cultures. With the advent of the barbarian invasions, the Church was now called to extend her messages to the Germanic tribes who were different in many ways from the citizens of the previous Roman civilization.

The Germanic tribes began pressing on the Roman frontier in the early fourth century as the Huns steadily pushed west from Mongolia and China (China had built its Great Wall to keep the Huns out). The Germanic tribes came from the area around the Vistula River in Poland down to the Black Sea, and may have originally come from Scandinavia. The culture of the Germanic tribes is complicated and multi-faceted, by no means unified, although they shared the same family of languages. They were the second largest Northern European group after the Celts, who had been such powerful warriors that they had settled as far south as Austria and even managed to sack Rome in 390. After settling down, they developed into a peaceful people engaged in agrarian life. By the time of the Germanic invasions, the Celts had been long conquered by the Romans or were being taken over by the advancing Germanic tribes.

Ever occupied with the difficult task of defending the vast borders of the Empire, the Roman legions had battled the barbarians for some time but were never able to conquer them in their own territory. For three centuries the barbarians pushed to enter into the Empire, but the Romans used whatever advantage they could to stop them. They did, however, invite many of the tribes to settle along the frontier in Roman territory. The Romans intermittently battled the barbarians to keep them out and settled them along the frontier in exchange for conscripts for the Roman legions. The peaceful settlement of some tribes also helped to bolster the Empire's lagging population.

Over time, the Roman legions were Germanized to such an extent that the army remained Roman in name only. This influx of Germanic soldiers afforded a great opportunity given the obvious vulnerability of the Roman Empire. That the Roman army no longer consisted primarily of Romans—as the Germanic tribes eagerly desired the conquest of new territory—partially explains the fall of Rome.

German Barbarian Chief

It was only a matter of time before the Germanic barbarians would score a number of military victories against the Romans which would lead to their ultimate defeat. It was common for the tribes to arrive in waves, only to be supplanted by succeeding tribes. In 378, the Visigoths defeated the Byzantine army at the Battle of Adrianople, and by December 406, many tribes had crossed the Rhine to settle in Gaul. With the border of the Empire penetrated, Gaul soon fell to the Visigoths, led by Alaric. Soon thereafter Rome fell on August 24, 410, and was pillaged for four days.

Of the different tribes that merit mention here, the two branches of Goths—Visigoths and Ostrogoths—were first to invade the empire. Alaric, as mentioned above, was the Visigoth leader who led the invasion of the Italian Peninsula. Later, the Visigoths were pushed into the Iberian Peninsula by the Franks, where they remained until Spain fell to the Muslims in the eighth century. Theodoric led the Ostrogoths who occupied the Italian Peninsula, replacing the Visigoths. Ostrogoth rule would end with their defeat in 536 by Byzantine forces.

The Franks—a name meaning "fierce" or "bold"—were a Germanic people who settled in Gaul late in the third century. They are the ancestors of modern France and, under the leadership of the great chieftain Clovis, were the first Germanic tribe to convert to Christianity (497). A more detailed account of the conversion of the Franks appears in the following chapter.

The Alemanni (meaning "All Men") were another Germanic people. They settled south of the Main River in central Germany around 260 before moving later to Alsace and Switzerland.

The Burgundians arrived on the Main River around 250. They established a capital at Worms before being defeated by the Romans in 436.

The Lombards lived along the Elbe and began advancing toward the Danube by the middle of the second century. Eventually they settled in the Roman province of Pannonia (eastern Austria and western Hungary, bounded on the north and east by the Danube River) before finally migrating to Italy in the sixth century.

The Vandals were the most ruthless of the Germanic tribes. Beginning in 406 they attacked Gaul before moving to Spain and then to North Africa. The Vandals were so fierce and committed such atrocities that the word "vandal" is still used in English today. They were also relentless persecutors of the Church.

ULPHILAS: APOSTLE OF THE GOTHS

Ulphilas (ca. 311-388) was born in Cappadocia but was captured by the Goths. Under the influence of the Arian bishop Eusebius of Nicomedia, Ulphilas translated the Bible into Gothic, and he was made a bishop around 341. His translation is the oldest Germanic document. Because of Ulphilas' missionary efforts, the Goths, Burgundians, Lombards, and Vandals were converted to Arian Christianity.

THE BARBARIAN INVASIONS, 4TH AND 5TH CENTURIES

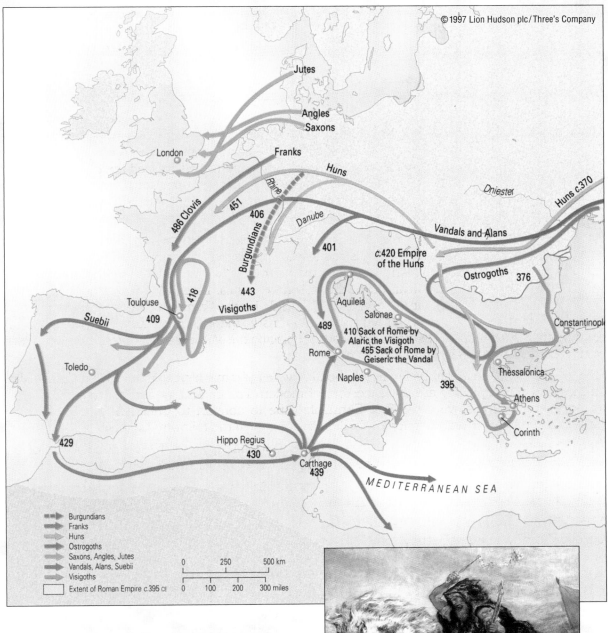

© 1997 Lion Hudson plc / Three's Company

Map labels:
Jutes
Angles
Saxons
Franks
Huns
London
Rhine
Dniester
Huns c.370
486 Clovis
451
406
Burgundians
Danube
Vandals and Alans
401
c.420 Empire of the Huns
Ostrogoths 376
418
443
Toulouse
409
Visigoths
Aquileia
Salonae
489
410 Sack of Rome by Alaric the Visigoth
455 Sack of Rome by Geiseric the Vandal
Constantinople
Suebii
Toledo
Rome
Thessalonica
Naples
395
Athens
Corinth
429
Hippo Regius
430
Carthage
439
MEDITERRANEAN SEA

Legend:
Burgundians
Franks
Huns
Ostrogoths
Saxons, Angles, Jutes
Vandals, Alans, Suebii
Visigoths
Extent of Roman Empire c.395 CE

0   250   500 km
0   100   200   300 miles

The Germanic tribes began pressing on the Roman frontier in the early fourth century as the Huns steadily pushed west from Mongolia and China.

It is reported that the Huns' imposing physical appearance shocked the people of the Roman Empire.

With relentless swiftness, Attila's Huns devastated Gaul, and Attila continually augmented his army by assimilating conquered Germanic tribes.

THE HUNS

As the Empire was struggling to control the invading Germanic tribes, a new unforeseen threat to both the Romans and the barbarians emerged from the Far East in the first half of the fifth century. The Huns, a powerful nomadic people of unknown ethnic origins, swept west from northern China and had crossed into the Volga valley by the end of the fourth century. They were ferocious and ruthless fighters, and by 432 they had established themselves in the Eastern Empire, forcing tribute from Emperor Theodosius II. By 451, the Huns had invaded Gaul and threatened the heart of the Western Empire.

These were a people foreign to the West. Many of the ancient reports were no doubt exaggerated, but through their embellishment they present a picture of the meeting of two alien cultures. It is reported that the Huns' imposing physical appearance shocked the people of the Roman Empire. Their physical attributes were distinctive: squat bodies with enormous arms and shoulders and huge heads covered with thick facial scarring. Many of the Huns slashed their own faces so much that they became disfigured. Roman reports relate that many Romans were not sure if the Huns were people or beasts. It was believed that they always remained on horseback, whether at meetings or while selling and buying goods—even when they ate and slept. Women and children lived in wagons; the Huns did not settle down to live in homes on farms as other groups did. The Huns rarely, if ever, cooked. Instead, they ate raw meat, which they kept with themselves, and as a consequence, was usually rotten and rancid. During battle the stench coming from the Huns was said to be so powerful that the Roman soldiers could not bear to get close to them. Though these reports cannot be taken as one hundred percent accurate, it is clear that these were a powerful and frightening people who devastated much of the Empire.

ATTILA THE HUN
MEETS POPE ST. LEO THE GREAT (452)

Attila (d. 453), "the Scourge of God," succeeded to joint kingship over the Huns with his brother in 433. Not long after, his brother died (perhaps murdered by Attila), and Attila for the first time successfully united the Hunnish hordes under one rule. He was a tremendously brave warrior, a skilled diplomat, and a keen military strategist. He was also ruthless—if he discovered that a Hun had served the Romans as a mercenary soldier, he ordered his crucifixion. Earlier in his life, he had been held as a hostage in Rome where he learned Latin and discovered Rome's weaknesses. His ambition was to establish an Asiatic empire with himself as emperor. He did succeed, but the empire collapsed after his death.

After having successfully united the hordes, Attila moved west, began engaging the Romans in the 440s, and invaded Gaul. With relentless swiftness, Attila's Huns devastated Gaul and continually augmented their army with each military victory. Finally, in 451, an allied army of Romans and Visigoths defeated Attila on the Plains of Chalons, forcing Attila back across the Rhine.

Defeated in Gaul, Attila turned his sights south to Italy. Beginning in 452, his Huns ravaged northern Italian cities and towns. As they drew closer to Rome, Pope St. Leo the Great went to meet him. In one of the great mysteries of history, it remains unknown exactly what words Pope St. Leo used to dissuade Attila from attacking Rome. Attila is said to have come upon a procession of priests, deacons, and acolytes singing hymns and psalms. At the end of the procession there was an old man sitting on a horse praying intensely. Attila asked him, "What is your name?" The old man replied, "Leo the Pope." In an unprecedented move, Attila did not attack Rome, and he withdrew entirely from Italy. Attila died shortly thereafter, and his empire, divided among his sons, soon disintegrated. This confrontation with Pope St. Leo in a certain sense changed the course of

In one of the great mysteries of history, it remains unknown exactly what words Pope St. Leo used to dissuade Attila from attacking Rome.

history. The pope was able to repeat the same success in 455 when he convinced the leader of the Vandals, Genseric, not to burn Rome, and spare the lives of the people.

HISTORICAL INTERPRETATION OF THE GERMANIC INVASIONS

It took some time for the Church to digest the historical significance of the Germanic invasions, and what they meant for her mission of evangelization. Over time, several concrete ideas emerged.

Primarily, the Church recognized that Christianity was universal. The Faith needed to be communicated as much to the Germanic tribes as it was in previous centuries to the Greco-Roman world. Christianity was meant to incorporate everyone, and this would be emphatically reinforced in the future when the Church was presented with opportunities to evangelize the Americas, Africa, Asia, and Australia.

Though the Church was identified with the Roman Empire for four centuries and adopted its governmental structures (dioceses), customs, language, and laws, the Church now began a monumental shift, civilizing and evangelizing the Germanic peoples.

The effort to reach out to the Germanic tribes was no small task. The German character was very different from the Greco-Roman one: the Germans were less philosophically and theologically inclined, placed less emphasis on order, culture, organization, and law. In effect, most of what the Church learned and developed within the context of Roman culture had to be radically altered in order to work with the Germanic populace without changing the essential doctrines of the Catholic

Faith. Through monasticism the Church found access to these people. Monasticism had established itself firmly by the end of the fifth century, by which time the Roman Empire had been reduced to a mosaic of kingdoms ruled by Germanic chieftains.

THE CHRISTIAN ATTITUDE TOWARD THE INVASIONS

Initially Christians experienced profound discouragement as the Greco-Roman world passed away. Many thought the disintegration of the Roman Empire meant that the Second Coming of Christ was at hand. Indeed, the predictions, signs, and lessons from the parables in the Gospels in significant part seemed to have been fulfilled by the state of the world of that time.

Some Christians also understood the fall of the Roman Empire as the just punishment for the sins of the Romans and of all humanity. Leading politicians, philosophers, and cultural thinkers pointed to the moral degradation of the Roman Empire—not to mention the infidelity of some Christians—as a sign of impending doom for their civilization.

The moral deterioration of the cities, coupled with the desire to pursue a heroic imitation of Jesus Christ, prompted some men and women to depart from the hustle and bustle of the world in order to dedicate themselves to a demanding life of asceticism, expressed in a faithful commitment to the evangelical counsels of poverty, chastity, and obedience. This radical separation from the world for the sake of Christ's kingdom through prayer, penance, and the evangelical counsels characterized monasticism. Monasticism offered a path for some Christians to make reparation for the sins of the world in general, and of the Roman world in particular.

ATTILA'S LOVE: WHY HE INVADED THE WEST

The events that led to Attila the Hun's great defeat on the Plains of Chalon began by a very strange request. Valentinian III was the emperor of the Western Roman Empire during the time Attila the Hun was attacking Europe. His sister, Honoria, had been sent into exile after having a scandalous affair. In an attempt to escape, Honoria purportedly sent Attila the Hun a ring along with a letter asking him to rescue her from exile. The Hun, however, treated the letter and ring as a marriage proposal, which he accepted. He then felt justified in asking Valentinian III for half of the Western Empire as a dowry. Naturally, Valentinian III refused, but when Attila the Hun finally crossed the Rhine and invaded the West, he felt that he was merely taking by force what he was rightfully owed.

PART II

The Rise of Monasticism

THE FIRST APPEARANCE OF MONASTICISM

Monasticism is a way of life characterized by prayer and self-denial lived in seclusion from the world and under a fixed rule with professed vows. Monastic communities withdraw from the affairs of the world in order to seek God through asceticism and silence. Though monasticism is common to many of the world's religions, Christian monasticism is unique. Men and women who enter the monastic life seek to model themselves on Christ by dedicating themselves to a life of prayer and penance. Once the call from God has been recognized, the person makes a life-long commitment to the monastic life.

There are two types of monastic life. The eremitical, or hermit life, involves individuals withdrawing into loosely organized groups to live an isolated ascetical life. The word hermit comes from Greek word *erēmia*, meaning "desert," which comes from *erēmos*, "lonely." The second, and more common form, is known as the cenobitical, or common life. Cenobitical monastic life is lived in community.

Monasticism started very early with St. Paul of Thebes (d. ca. 340) and St. Anthony (251?-356), both of whom lived eremitical lives of prayer and seclusion in Egypt. St. Paul of Thebes is held by tradition to be the first hermit; he had fled a persecution under the Roman Emperor Decius (A.D. 249-51). St. Anthony indirectly influenced Western monasticism through his impact on St. Athanasius, who, during one of his exiles, wrote a celebrated biography of St. Anthony. St. Athanasius brought this book to Rome, and it would later serve as a handbook for Western monasticism. In the beginning, hermits like St. Paul and St. Anthony generally withdrew to desert areas in order to lead a contemplative life. Though hermits in principle do not follow a rule by which they organize themselves, two monastic orders have taken much inspiration from the eremitical life: the Carthusians and Carmelites. In the West the eremitical life almost died out after the Catholic Reformation, possibly because those attracted to such a life joined the Carthusians and Carmelites.

Monasticism started very early with St. Paul of Thebes and St. Anthony, both of whom lived eremitical lives of prayer and seclusion in Egypt.

St. Pachomius (ca. 290-346) founded cenobitical monasticism in Egypt. Born to pagan parents in Egypt, he converted and was baptized after serving in the army until 313. Pachomius found himself in a situation similar to many of the holy men and women in Egypt. He desired to withdraw from the world in order to be more united with God, but as word of his holiness grew, ordinary people sought him out in the desert to ask for intercessory prayers and guidance. His eremitical solitude disrupted, Pachomius instead allowed many to join him in his way of life, and he wrote an early form of monastic rule for his followers. His *Rule* influenced St. Basil the Great, St. John Cassian, and St. Benedict in their establishment of monastic orders. At the time of his death, St. Pachomius ruled over nine monasteries and convents in Egypt. His feast day is celebrated on May 9.

THE FIRST MONKS, 4TH TO 8TH CENTURIES

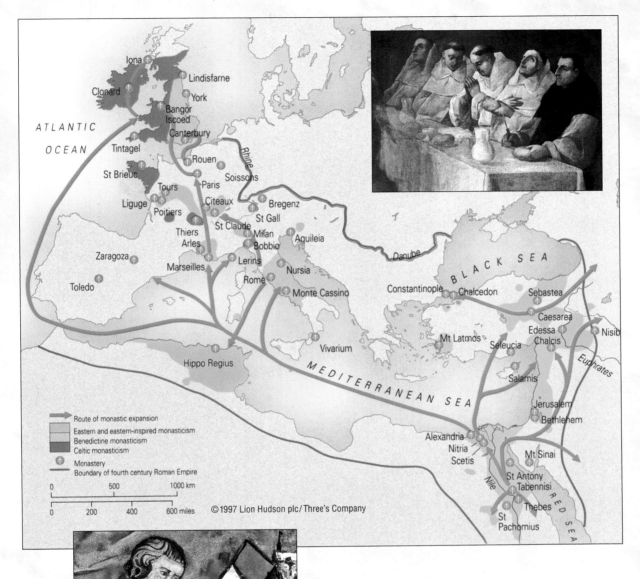

After the barbarian invasions, academic matters fell into neglect except among the monks who copied and retained literary works. Monks meticulously copied manuscripts of texts in an age when it took months and years to copy a book by hand. Benedictine monasteries quickly established *scriptoria* (singular, *scriptorium*), large rooms in the monasteries set aside for the purpose of copying and maintaining texts.

MONASTICISM AND THE EMERGENCE OF A NEW CHRISTIAN CULTURE

The rise of monasticism in the early Church proved vital for the spread of Christianity, the preservation of Greco-Roman writings, and the formation of a new Christian culture. For the Church, monasteries served a triple purpose: (1) they were a source of great spiritual strength; (2) they served as seminaries for priests and bishops; and (3) they functioned as centers of evangelization of the barbarian tribes through various forms of education.

The monasteries also had three major effects on Europe. The first effect was the recovery and evangelization of rural society. Up until the barbarian domination, a significant part of the population was concentrated in cities. However, as the cities began to depopulate and disintegrate, people scattered and clustered around landowners. As the former empire became more rural, forming pockets of isolated agricultural towns and villages, a new evangelizing force was called into play. Communities of monks and nuns spread into these farming areas to meet the spiritual needs of the people. This movement had a powerful impact on European agriculture, which was suffering due to the slow depopulation of the Roman Empire and attacks of the barbarians. The invasions caused so much havoc that many farmlands had reverted into forests. The monks established monasteries deep in the woods, in rugged mountains, and in swampy areas, which were drained, and in the process established new farmlands and farming communities.

The second great effect of the monasteries on Europe was intellectual. Monasteries became the chief centers of learning until the rise of the great universities beginning in the thirteenth century. The barbarian invasions had dismantled the empire and with it intellectual and cultural centers of learning. Academic matters fell into neglect except among the monks who copied and retained the literary works of the Greco-Roman civilization. Monks meticulously copied manuscripts of texts in an age when it took months and years to copy a book by hand. Benedictine monasteries quickly established *scriptoria* (singular, *scriptorium*), large rooms in the monasteries set aside for the purpose of copying and maintaining texts. It could be said that the monasteries single-handedly saved Western culture during this dangerous period. If monasteries had not been established and become depositories for the great patrimony of Greek and Roman learning, it would have been lost. The oldest manuscripts of ancient Greece and Rome owe their survival to the Benedictine *scriptoria*.

The third effect was one of civilization. As a consequence of their work of evangelization, the monasteries had a great civilizing effect on these Germanic peoples. Attracted by the holiness and goodness of the monks and nuns, the tribes proved to be willing pupils in many practical disciplines. Through their agricultural work, the monks taught the barbarians, who were nomads, how to farm. Monks trained them in the skilled trades of carpentry, stone masonry, and ironwork as the monasteries were being erected. The monks infused a spiritual meaning into the act of work itself and thus taught the dignity of work as a form of adoration and emulation of Jesus Christ, who was also a worker.

Through its educational work, the monastery also taught the surrounding population how to read and write. The monks elevated them intellectually, which facilitated the development of a new culture expressed in a fusion of the old Greco-Roman tradition and a Germanic culture. Once a student at the monastery learned Latin, he was taught Sacred Scriptures, the writings of the Church Fathers, geometry, and music for the singing of the Divine Office. This emphasis on the Bible and the Church Fathers would plant deep Christian roots into this new people.

ST. BENEDICT:
THE "PATRIARCH OF WESTERN MONASTICISM"

Ora et labora. (motto of the Benedictines, "Pray and work.")

Little is known about the early life of St. Benedict (ca. 480-ca. 547). He was born at Nursia, Italy, and educated in Rome, but eventually the moral decay of the city impelled him to withdraw to a cave in Subiaco to live the life of a hermit. As time passed, others joined him, and his reputation for sanctity spread. At one point, the abbot of a local monastery died, and the monks invited St. Benedict to join them. He at first refused, seeing that discipline and life at the monastery was different from what he wanted, but eventually, in the face of their constant supplications, he agreed. As he had expected, the other monks disagreed with his brand of monasticism to such an extent that some tried to poison him. He blessed the pitcher of poisoned wine, and it broke into pieces. Thereafter, he left the undisciplined monks.

St. Benedict intended that the monastery would be a family and a self-sustaining community.

A short time later, St. Benedict gained a reputation as a miracle worker, which led people to seek him out for guidance. Finally, he founded twelve monasteries and placed a superior to head each one. He then began a thirteenth monastery at Monte Cassino around 529. It was there that he died some years later, and was buried in the same grave as his sister St. Scholastica. St. Benedict's feast day is celebrated on July 11 (formerly March 21), and St. Scholastica's feast day is celebrated on February 10.

St. Benedict composed his *Rule* at Monte Cassino, which, though destroyed during World War II, was subsequently rebuilt. The *Rule of St. Benedict* was adopted by virtually all monastic communities throughout the Medieval period. The *Rule* has been lauded for its spirit of peace and love, as well as its moderation in the ascetical life. For example, monks were to sleep between six to eight hours a night (with a siesta in the summer following lunch) and were to have a bed, pillow, and sufficient food. This was in stark contrast to the austerity of the Egyptian hermits, who prided themselves on a strict ascetical life that included sleep deprivation and little food as a means of furthering the quality of their spirituality.

The *Rule* essentially divides the schedule of the monk into four parts: chanting the Psalms and reciting prayers in community (four hours), private prayer and Scriptural reading (four hours), physical labor (six hours), and meals and sleep (ten hours).

According to the Benedictine model, the monastic life is lived in common. No one is allowed to own personal property, though the monastery itself may. The *Rule* made provision for an abbot, who holds virtually all power to govern the monastery. St. Benedict intended that the monastery would be a family and a self-sustaining community. Different monks had different tasks and functions, which were organized and distributed in such a way as to ensure self-sufficiency. Not all monks were literate or expected to study theology diligently; not all monks were expected to work in the garden; not all monks were expected to be able to rebuild damaged monastery walls. Working together for the good of the whole and the glory of God, the monastery was a place

MONTE CASSINO: CAUGHT IN THE STORMS OF HISTORY

The strategic position of Monte Cassino made it the repeated scene of battles and sieges. In World War II, the Battle of Monte Cassino (also known as the Battle for Rome) was a costly series of four battles fought by the Allies from January 4 - May 19, 1944 with the intention of breaking through the Nazi Gustav Line. The Allies won the fourth battle. The four battles cost 54,000 Allied lives and 20,000 Nazi lives.

Above: The pulverized skeleton of St. Benedict's Monte Cassino on May 19, 1944. Its irreplaceable library had been removed for safekeeping to Rome and survived the war.
Right: The rebuilt Monte Cassino today.

where the noble man and commoner labored, each in his own and separate way, but always for the common good.

The *Rule* divides the day into two parts: prayer and work, in that order. The chief aim of the monk or nun following the Benedictine *Rule* is to give praise and glory to God. The habitual prayer in common is called the *opus Dei* ("work of God") or *laus Dei* ("praise of God"). Prayer in common was divided among eight periods of the day: *Vigils/Matins* (12 midnight), *Lauds* (6 a.m.), *Prime* (7 a.m.), *Terce* (9 a.m.), *Sext* (12 noon), *None* (3 p.m.), *Vespers* (6 p.m.), and *Compline* (9 p.m.). As explained by St. Benedict in Chapter 16 of his *Rule*, this division of the hours has its root in Scripture: "At midnight I rise to praise thee," and "Seven times a day I praise thee" (Ps 119 [118]: 62, 164). This practice would comprise what is now called the Divine Office or Liturgy of the Hours. The continual focus on God throughout the day and the use of the Scriptures, especially the Psalms of the Divine Office, brings the monastic community into contact with God as the members habitually contemplate the life of Christ. The *Rule* instructs, "let nothing be preferred" to the Divine Office (chapter xliii). Reading and meditating on Scripture, called *lectio divina*, forms an important facet of monastic life.

St. Benedict did not specify a particular area or type of work for those adhering to the *Rule*, thus many types of labor were permitted. However, the first monasteries focused on the manual labor associated with agriculture and, later, education of the young was entrusted to the care of the Benedictines. Work was given spiritual meaning by the monks, and it became for them a form of prayer and penance offered for the praise and glory of God.

Even in the earliest years, Benedictine monks made vows of poverty, chastity, and obedience after undergoing a year-long novitiate. These vows are binding for life. A vow is a solemn promise made voluntarily by a person of reason, to practice a virtue or perform some specific good deed in order to accomplish a future good, viz., the individual's growth in the spiritual life.

ST. SCHOLASTICA

St. Scholastica (ca. 480 - ca. 543) was St. Benedict's twin sister. Most of what is known of her is told in the *Dialogues* of St. Gregory the Great. St. Scholastica, as St. Gregory reports, was consecrated to God from her infancy, and after St. Benedict founded the monastery at Monte Cassino, she established and governed a convent at Plombariola, only five miles from her brother. The nuns at Plombariola followed the Benedictine *Rule*. Although these siblings were very close, they were not allowed to visit each other at their respective homes. Once a year, however, St. Benedict and St. Scholastica would meet for the day in another house, some distance from Plombariola and Monte Cassino. There they would spend the day discussing spiritual issues and praying.

St. Gregory tells the story of the last of these annual visits. They spent the day as usual, but as night approached, St. Scholastica, having had a presentiment that this would be the last time they would see each other in this life, entreated her brother to stay the night. Not wishing to break his own *Rule* by spending the night outside his monastery, St. Benedict refused. St. Scholastica, desperate to spend a little more time with her brother, decided to petition God that her brother might stay. She bowed her head in concentrated prayer, and immediately, the skies opened in a tremendous storm. St. Benedict was unable to return to Monte Cassino, and the two spent the rest of the night in deep spiritual discussion. St. Benedict returned home the next morning, and three days later beheld a vision of St. Scholastica's soul in the form of a dove rising to Heaven. He sent for her corpse, and St. Benedict buried his sister's body in the grave he had prepared for himself. Some years after, St. Benedict's soul joined his beloved sister in Heaven, and their bodies were reunited in the same grave.

POPE ST. GREGORY THE GREAT

I am forced to consider the affairs of the Church and of the monasteries. I must weigh the lives and acts of individuals. I am responsible for the concerns of our citizens. I must worry about the invasions of roving bands of barbarians, and beware of the wolves who lie in wait for my flock. I must become an administrator lest the religious go in want. I must put up with certain robbers without losing patience and at times I must deal with them in all charity. (St. Gregory the Great, from a homily on Ezekiel, *Lib.* 1, 11, 4-6: CCL 142, 170-172)

St. Gregory (ca. 540-604) became pope in 590. A Church Father, he is considered the last of the traditional Latin Doctors. St. Gregory's papacy is often used as a marker for the beginning of the Medieval age, and certainly his papacy illustrates the noblest ideals of Medieval Christianity, as well as some of the tensions of his day.

St. Gregory was the son of a senator, a nobleman, and he played an important role in the civic affairs of the city of Rome. In 573 he became prefect for the police and a judge for criminal cases. After the death of his father (his mother Silvia and two aunts Tarsilla and Æmiliana were eventually canonized as saints), St. Gregory sold his properties and gave away his wealth in order to found seven monasteries and alleviate the plight of the poor. This was a common cultural phenomenon of the time among some of the nobility, a practice that was subsequently extolled as model Christian behavior in the Medieval Church. One of the monasteries was in Rome. Here St. Gregory became a regular monk, and he placed an abbot in charge, to whom he pledged obedience.

After several years of living the holy, austere life of a monk, the pope made St. Gregory one of the seven deacons of Rome. Around 579 Pope Pelagius II appointed him as the *nuncio*, the pope's personal ambassador, to the court in Constantinople. Though St. Gregory preferred to remain a simple monk, he deferred to the pope and went to Byzantium. Later St. Gregory returned to Rome and worked directly for Pelagius II, who died in 590.

Upon Pelagius' death, the Roman populace universally acclaimed St. Gregory as the new pope. Initially St. Gregory fled the city to avoid taking the office of St. Peter, but after intense soul searching, he relented to God's will.

Given the precarious situation of Italy, a man of his talents and gifts for leadership was greatly needed. Violent Lombard invaders pillaged towns and cities. The population of the cities decreased, the roads became extremely dangerous, and prisoners were reduced to slavery. Rome's population, for example, was reduced by seventy-five percent, and the entire area surrounding Rome was racked by famine, plagues, and floods.

Though in weak health from the physical austerities he had imposed on himself as a monk, St. Gregory was a tireless worker, and he enjoyed the support of the people. He wrote many treatises and commentaries on Sacred Scripture, many of which have survived, as have over eight hundred of his letters. St. Gregory's greatest strength was his combination of humility and skillful administrative ability. He took the title *Servus servorum Dei* ("Servant of the servants of God"), which highlights the humble view of his position. He also helped to establish plainsong chant in the liturgical life of the Church, more commonly known as Gregorian Chant.

St. Gregory was also very active in the temporal sphere. Papal relations with Byzantium and with the Eastern Church were not very good. St. Gregory adamantly refused to acknowledge the title "Ecumenical Patriarch," which the Patriarch of Constantinople adopted by canon 28 at the First Council of Constantinople (381). The council was not recognized at first as ecumenical because it was not convened under the pope's authority, and no western bishops were present. By the sixth century, however, it was recognized as an ecumenical council. However, as for the legitimacy of the

St. Gregory's missionary success, along with his continual support of the poor through the administration of the Church's estates, won for St. Gregory the title "the Great."

title of "Ecumenical Patriarch," St. Gregory had recognized it for what it was: an attempt to usurp the Petrine primacy.

The Lombards began threatening Rome shortly after St. Gregory became pope. The Eastern emperor's *exarch* (an imperial representative) displayed no intention of preventing or averting a Lombard invasion; he simply remained idle in Ravenna. When St. Gregory received a threatening letter from the Lombard king Agiluf and then found him just outside the walls of Rome, he took action himself—without the consent or counsel of the exarch or emperor—and succeeded in achieving a separate peace in 592-593. This only lasted a short time, however, due to hostile actions of the hitherto idle exarch. Again working without the consent of exarch or emperor, St. Gregory finally made peace with the Lombards in 599. This peace was short-lived, but the brief warring eventually gave way to a peace that lasted throughout the remainder of St. Gregory's life. St. Gregory's actions demonstrate the growing temporal power of the popes and their care for Rome. It also marked the beginning of a rejection of the Eastern emperor's political power in the West. This instance only highlighted the fact that the Eastern emperors and the popes increasingly viewed each other as competitors.

St. Gregory's missionary initiatives included some of his most successful endeavors, more of which will be covered in the following chapter. For now, it is sufficient to recall the account of the conversion of St. Ethelbert and the Saxons in England. St. Gregory also influenced the Lombard princess Theodelinda, a Catholic, to marry the Lombard king Agiluf. Their children were raised Catholic and Theodelinda worked to build many churches. By the seventh century, the Lombards had converted to Christianity. St. Gregory's missionary success, along with his continual support of the poor through the administration of the Church's estates, won for St. Gregory the title "the Great." His feast day is celebrated on September 3.

GREGORIAN CHANT: THE DEVELOPMENT OF MUSICAL NOTATION

Monasticism in the Middle Ages played a pivotal role in developing Western music, especially with regard to musical notation. Gregorian Chant, attributed to Pope St. Gregory the Great, was a Roman form of plainchant sung without harmony that was eventually embellished by the Carolingians living north of the Alps. It was used extensively for the Mass and the Divine Office throughout Europe and the Middle East. Although St. Gregory the Great probably did not write any of the melodies, he did encourage the orderly use of music in church, which led to the eventual cataloging of the melodies in an early form of musical notation.

Gregorian Chant was written, preserved, and distributed to numerous lands by writing down its melodies in a series of marks and dashes. The signs—*neumes*—

used in the earliest type of notation are small marks placed above each syllable in order to indicate how high or low it be sung. The shape of a *neume* reminds the chanter how the pitch varies up or down within a syllable. *Neumes* also indicate the grouping of pitches within a melody. They did not, however, indicate a precise relation of pitches within a syllable or from one syllable to the next.

During the tenth and eleventh centuries, marks arranged above and below a fixed-pitch line—*heightened neumes*—were used to make the intervals of a melody more discernible. In the first half of the eleventh century, an Italian Benedictine monk, Guido d'Arezzo, developed the system of four-line staff notation in which Gregorian Chant is still notated today. The modern five line staff is developed from this system of notation.

Gregorian Chant had fallen out of use, especially at the Mass, to more fashionable forms of music by the eighteenth and nineteenth centuries. During the latter half of the nineteenth century, some groups of Benedictine monks began to revive the use of Gregorian Chant, making it available worldwide for use at the Mass. The revival became popular, prompting Pope St. Pius X in 1903 to declare Gregorian Chant "proper to the Roman Church." He added, "[Holiness and universality] are to be found, in the highest degree, in Gregorian Chant." The fathers of the Second Vatican Council reiterated these statements: "Gregorian chant [is] specially suited to the Roman liturgy: therefore . . . it should be given pride of place in liturgical services" (*Sacrosanctum concilium* [Constitution on the Sacred Liturgy], no. 116).

PART III

The Rise of Islam

There is no god but Allah, and Muhammad is his prophet.
(The *Shahada*, the creedal belief statement of Islam)

The rise of Islam is important for a number of reasons. It joined Judaism and Christianity as the third great monotheistic religion. Its history is intimately linked to the Arab peoples and, later, the peoples conquered by Islamic invaders in Asia, Africa, and Europe. Islam grew rapidly, and became a threat to the existence of Christianity. This particular religion relates to the history of the Church insofar as wars between Christians and Muslims have unfortunately persisted throughout the centuries. These religious wars have had a profound impact on Christian history.

ARABIA

The Arabian Peninsula is mostly barren desert and in the sixth century was sparsely populated by Bedouin tribes. These nomadic tribes controlled the few caravan trade routes that crossed the peninsula. A strong and proud people, the Arabs were also fierce warriors. The time at which Islam appeared was a tenuous period in the history of the peninsula: the various tribes were in a state of constant warfare with one another and the economic situation was dire.

The Arabs were pagans who worshiped various local objects of nature. One object in particular commanded a striking following, the *Kaaba*, a large black stone, in Mecca. Folklore dates the *Kaaba* to the time of Abraham, and is supposed to occupy the spot where he worshiped the one true God. The *Kaaba* is an *axus mundi* (turning-point of the world), a connection between Heaven and earth; hence, it is the focal point of prayers in the individual Muslim's life. Christianity and Judaism both had a very small presence among the Arabs. The Arabs were searching for a religion that would give them certainty about this life and the next. In the person of Muhammad, the Jewish, Christian, and pagan traditions were woven into a uniquely new Arabic religious tradition called Islam.

MUHAMMAD (ca. 570-632) AND THE *KORAN*

In the Name of God, The Compassionate, the Merciful / All praise belongs to God, / Lord of all worlds, / the Compassionate, the Merciful, / Ruler of Judgment Day.
(*Koran*, opening lines of *The Essential Koran*, 1)

Muhammad was born near Mecca around 570. By the age of six he was an orphan, and an uncle took over his upbringing. He worked as a camel driver until he married a wealthy, widowed woman, Khadeejah, when he was twenty-five years old. He had six children, all of whom died except his daughter Fatima. Shortly thereafter, Muhammad decided to withdraw from the world to pursue a life of mystical prayer.

By the age of 30, Muhammad had become despondent. Pagan worship gave him no spiritual peace. He retired to a cave and around the year 612, he announced to his acquaintances that he had had a vision of the archangel Gabriel that called him to be the herald of Allah, the Jewish God. He said that over a period of time he wrote exactly the words that Gabriel told him, resulting in the *Koran*. Thus, Muslims believe that the *Koran* (Arabic for "recitation") is not Muhammad's work but God's. The *Koran* is comprised of 114 chapters of sayings that Muhammad recorded.

THE EXTENT OF ISLAM BY A.D. 661

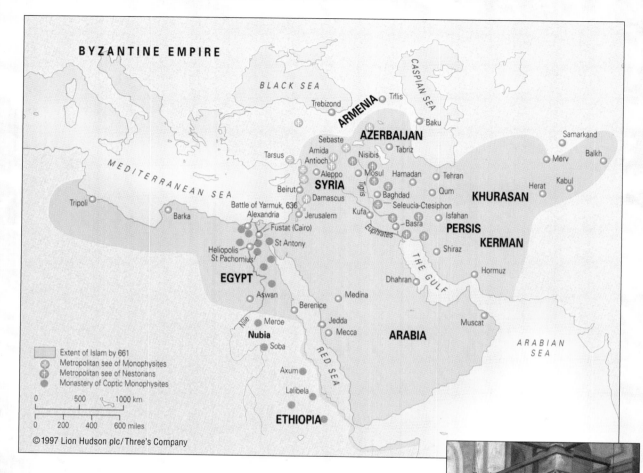

BYZANTINE EMPIRE

BLACK SEA

Trebizond

Tiflis

ARMENIA

Baku

CASPIAN SEA

Sebaste

AZERBAIJAN

Samarkand

Tarsus

Amida

Nisibis

Tabriz

Merv

Balkh

Antioch

Mosul

Hamadan

Tehran

Herat

Kabul

MEDITERRANEAN SEA

Aleppo

Beirut

SYRIA

Damascus

Baghdad

Qum

KHURASAN

Tripoli

Battle of Yarmuk, 636

Jerusalem

Seleucia-Ctesiphon

Isfahan

PERSIS

Barka

Alexandria

Kufa

Basra

KERMAN

Fustat (Cairo)

Euphrates

Shiraz

Heliopolis

St Antony

St Pachomius

Dhahran

Hormuz

EGYPT

Aswan

Medina

Berenice

Nile

Meroe

Jedda

Muscat

Nubia

Mecca

ARABIA

ARABIAN SEA

Soba

Axum

RED SEA

Lalibela

ETHIOPIA

Extent of Islam by 661
Metropolitan see of Monophysites
Metropolitan see of Nestorians
Monastery of Coptic Monophysites

0   500   1000 km

0   200   400   600 miles

©1997 Lion Hudson plc/Three's Company

Above: Muslims worship in a mosque.

Left: Muslim pilgrims making their way to Mecca.

Muhammad continued to suffer a great deal of spiritual anxiety throughout his life. He questioned, at times, whether he was being divinely inspired or if he was suffering delusions. His wife and his cousin gave him constant encouragement, the latter saying that the revelations of the *Koran* were part of the truths of Judaism and Christianity.

The *Koran's* language and revelation have special status in Islam. Because Arabic was the language of revelation, it is considered the only true language in which to read the *Koran*. Though translations are made, Muslims are encouraged to learn Arabic in order to grasp the full nature and power of the *Koran's* revelation. The *Koran* is also written in the form of poetry, and is meant to be read aloud, which aids the goal of memorization. Finally, the *Koran* is considered technically to be "God's Word," perfect and eternal.

Ishmael and his father Abraham pray after building the Kaaba

Ishmael and his mother Hagar moved to Mecca where Ishmael and his father Abraham established the sanctuary and rebuilt the Kaaba. After this, God sent Ishmael as a prophet to the Amalekites and the tribes of Yemen. When the time of Ishmael's death was at hand, he bequeathed to his brother Isaac that he should marry his daughter to Esau, son of Isaac. Ishmael lived for 137 years and was buried in al-Hijr in the tomb of his mother Hagar.

—The Teaching of Islam

ISLAM'S BIBLICAL REINTERPRETATION

So she [Sarah] said to Abraham, "Cast out this slave woman with her son."...And the thing was very displeasing to Abraham on account of his son. But God said to Abraham, "Be not displeased because of the lad and because of your slave woman....I will make a nation of the son of the slave woman also, because he is your offspring." So Abraham rose the early in the morning, and took bread and a skin of water, and gave it to Hagar, putting it on her shoulder, along with the child, and sent her away. And she departed, and wandered in the wilderness of Beer-sheba. (Gen 21:10-14)

Islam reinterpreted the Jewish and Christian narratives for its own purposes. Islam traces itself back to Abraham, Hagar, and Ishmael in the story from Genesis quoted above. Ishmael is the father of the Arabic people, and Islam became the means for transforming them into a great nation.

Muhammad eventually proclaimed his worship of the one true God a national religion. Islam (Arabic for "submission") borrows from Judaism and Christianity in that it recognizes the Jewish prophets and Christian writings, but it contends that both Jews and Christians have misunderstood the intentions of God. Jesus and Mary are both respected in Islam, but only as a prophet and his holy mother. Islam holds that God's revelation culminated not in the birth, death, and Resurrection of Jesus Christ, but in Muhammad's visions recorded in the *Koran*. Muhammad was God's last prophet who brought to the world the perfect religion.

"PEOPLE OF THE BOOK"

Be they Muslims, Jews, / Christians, or Sabians, / those who believe in God and the Last Day / and who do good / have their reward with their Lord. / They have nothing to fear, / and they will not sorrow. (*Koran*, verse 62).

The *Koran* teaches that Jews and Christians are "People of the Book," that is, they share with Muslims the great monotheistic tradition and a common religious history. The *Koran* recognizes Jesus saying that Allah "strengthened him with the holy spirit" (*Koran*, verse 87), but Jesus to the *Koran* was only a prophet. According to Muhammad, Christianity failed as a religion by misinterpreting God's intentions as they were communicated through Jesus. Most of the unique mysteries of Faith in Christianity are denied by Islam: the Incarnation, redemption and atonement of the cross, the Resurrection, and the Trinity.

At first Christians were generally tolerated by Muslims. But as the religion became increasingly militant and nationalized in the seventh and eighth centuries, tensions dramatically mounted. Jews and Christians were forced to pay a special tax called the *jizya* in order to retain the right to practice their own religion. This financial burden and the difficulties of trying to live in a Muslim state eventually coerced many Jews and Christians to convert to Islam.

MUHAMMAD'S PREACHING

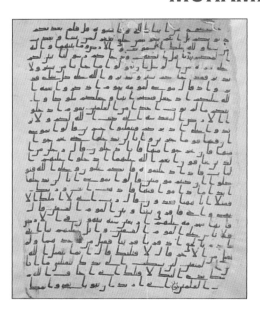

Muhammad preached monotheism, the immortality of the soul, the resurrection of the body, justice to the poor, and a sensual paradise in the next life. When he began his preaching, his critique of the pagan religion in Mecca and call for moral reform among the ruling elite upset many in the city, and Muhammad was forced to flee for his life to Medina (which means "the city of the prophet" in Arabic) with his followers on Friday, July 16, 622. This emigration is known as the *hejira* (Arabic for "flight" or "emigration"), and it marks the year 1 in the Islamic calendar. In the West, the Muslim year is represented by the abbreviation "A.H.," which stands for the Latin *anno hegiræ* ("in the year of the *hejira*"). Thus, the Jubilee Year 2000 was the year 1478 A.H. in the Muslim world.

Dated to the seventh century A.D., this *Koran* manuscript is thought to be the earliest style of *Koran* writing. It is located in the Tareq Rajab Museum in Kuwait.

IN MEDINA ISLAM MATURES

In Medina, Muhammad was hailed as a religious leader. The leaders of the city invited Muhammad to be the new ruler as a means to avoid further bloodshed among contending parties. Muhammad immediately set about the task of building up Islam. From the beginning of Islam, there was never any separation between the civil powers and religious authority. Islam functions in unity between the temporal and spiritual powers in one organic whole. With Islam rooted in Medina, Muhammad also became the head of the military force, which was used to expand Islam.

There was also a small Jewish population in Medina that numbered at least five hundred men. Upon his arrival Muhammad demanded that this community recognize him as a prophet in line

Muslims circle the Kaaba in Mecca.

with the Old Testament prophets Moses, Ezekiel, Jeremiah, and Isaiah. The Jews refused because they held that the prophetic line had ended over a thousand years before. During a later confrontation with Mecca, the Jewish community appeared to have supported the Meccans against Muhammad, who in turn slaughtered the Jewish men and sold the women and children into slavery.

The year 624 proved to be a key turning point in the development of Islam. After a new inspiration, Muhammad changed the direction of Muslim prayer (*qibla*) one hundred eighty degrees from Jerusalem to Mecca. In 624 Muhammad also led his forces in a *jihad* (holy war) against the Meccans, and he defeated them at Badr. With only three hundred men, Muhammad was able to defeat a much larger Meccan force of about 900, as well as capture an entire caravan as booty. The Battle of Badr (624) has often been interpreted by Muslims as their Exodus story.

This paved the way for Muhammad to take control of Mecca as well, which he purged of all the pagan religions. The *Kaaba* (Arabic for "square building") alone was spared destruction, though its meaning was transformed. Under Islam, the *Kaaba* became the focus of pilgrimage, which every Muslim is required to visit at least once in his lifetime, means permitting. The *Kaaba* itself is housed inside a square building that Muslims believe Abraham built. Only Muslims are permitted to see the *Kaaba*, and shoes are removed before entering.

THE FIVE PILLARS OF ISLAM

The Five Pillars of Islam are the requirements of all Muslims. They are the following:

- The *Shahada:* the creedal statement of Islam
- Prayer
- The *Hajj:* pilgrimage to Mecca
- *Ramadan:* the holy month (ninth month of the Islamic calendar)
- *Zakah:* (alms) for purification

Prayer is required five times daily in the direction of the *Kaaba* in Mecca, and includes a ritualistic format of prayers and prostration. (Hotel rooms in the Muslim world normally have a marker in the corner that points toward Mecca.) In Muslim lands, the *muezzin,* a man who calls the community to prayer, stands atop a minaret and calls Muslims to pray with the sound of the human voice. The holy day for Muslims is Friday, taken from the Jewish Sabbath, which begins at sundown on Friday. Typically, the Muslim community gathers for prayers on Friday at the *mosque* (Arabic for "place of prostration") where the Muslim cleric will also speak.

The *Hajj* is the pilgrimage to Mecca. It is required at least once in the adult life of every Muslim if the monetary means exist. It normally takes place on the eighth through twelfth days of the last month of the lunar year, which places it after the holy month of *Ramadan.* Through a number of ritualistic ceremonies and prayers that include three laps on foot around the *Kaaba,* Muslims share in the history of the *Kaaba* and the *heijra*, and express unity with all Muslims. Through the ritualistic re-enactment around the *Kaaba*, Muslims symbolically share in Muhammad's flight to Medina from Mecca. The entire Hajj is a profound expression of unity with Muslims throughout the world.

The *Shahada* contains the beliefs of Islam. In order for one to be a Muslim, the following statement must be made in freedom and with belief: "There is no god but God ('*Allah*' in Arabic), and Muhammad is his prophet." There are no sacraments.

Ramadan is the holy month, celebrated during the ninth lunar month. A strict fast from sunrise to sunset is enforced that encompasses eating, drinking, smoking, and sexual relations. This challenging fast increases one's spiritual dependence on God and openness to the material plight of the poor, who normally go without food. In the evenings families and friends come together for a meal. *Ramadan* is a sacred, joyful time that carries a great deal of historical significance: the *Koran* was given during this time to Muhammad, the Battle of Badr took place in this month, Khadeejah died on the tenth, Mecca was occupied on the nineteenth, and Ali, the grandson of Muhammad who is especially important to Shiite Muslims, died on the twenty-first.

In support of the poor, Muslims are also asked to give alms in the form of a special tax, given yearly based on a percentage of one's wealth. In some countries the government collects the alms; in others, individuals freely give it. This is separate from charitable giving, which Muslims are also encouraged to do on a regular basis.

THE MORAL CODE OF ISLAM

In addition to the Five Pillars (requirements), Islam also holds its followers to a strict moral code. From Judaism, Islam borrowed dietary prohibitions including pork, and it accepts the Jewish practice of kosher in the preparation of meat products. Thus, in many places Jews and Muslims share butchers and stores in order to meet the obligations of their religions. For example, in order for meat to be properly prepared for human consumption, all the blood must first be drained from the animal.

Idolatry is strictly forbidden. Islamic art does not depict the image of Allah or the human person because it is considered a form of idolatry. Rather, Islamic art has developed complex and beautiful geometric shapes and architecture as the central focus of artistic output. It is also quite likely that Islam's strict prohibition against depictions of the divine affected Christianity during the iconoclastic controversy, about which more will be said in Chapter 7.

Apostasy and adultery are also strictly forbidden. Polygamy was permitted, though with strict conditions: a man may have no more than four wives, and he must treat them with perfect equality, financial support, and equal love. Otherwise, he must remain monogamous. Hence, though polygamy is technically permitted by the *Koran*, it is generally impossible to show complete impartiality and meet the necessary conditions for the maintenance of multiple wives. Thus polygamy has been generally outlawed.

JIHAD

Jihad is a Muslim holy war waged in the name of religion against "infidels." Those who die fighting in a *jihad*—according to Muslim belief—go straight to Heaven where swords provide shade and the man is met with a limitless number of virgins.

The use of religious feeling to promote war has prompted the labeling of *jihad* as the "sixth pillar" of Islam because it was so intricately linked to Muhammad and Islam's expansion. When Muhammad died in 632, he had already expertly utilized *jihad* to defeat his foes in Mecca. In 634 his suc-

THE SPLIT IN ISLAM: SUNNI VERSUS SHIITE

After Muhammad's death in 632, his followers disagreed over questions of succession and political leadership in the Muslim community. These disagreements led to the early split of Islam into two factions, Sunni and Shiite.

Shiite (or Shi'a) is short for "Shi'at Ali"—Arabic for "the party of Ali," and constitutes Islam's largest non-Sunni sect. Shiites claimed that Ali, the son-in-law and cousin of Muhammad, was the only rightful successor. This claim was based on Muhammad's alleged designation of Ali as his successor and the tribal custom of preserving leader-ship through bloodline. The community leaders, however, did not agree, and instead chose a close companion of Muhammad, Abu Bakr, to become the first Caliph (Arabic for "successor"). After the third Caliph, Uthman, was murdered in 656, Ali was named the fourth Caliph. Ali himself was assassinated in 661. Today, Shiites constitute ten to fifteen percent of all followers of Islam.

Unlike the followers of Ali, the Sunni Muslims accept the order of succession of the first four Caliphs (including Ali as the fourth Caliph) and oppose political succession based on bloodline. "Sunni" comes from the Arabic "Sunna" meaning "tradition." Sunni Muslims adhere to doctrines and practices based on the traditions of Muhammad as understood and interpreted by Muslim scholars all through history. Because the Sunnis have no centralized authority, the tra-dition is better understood as a general identity that includes many smaller, local offshoots. Today Sunni Muslims constitute almost eighty-five percent of the world's Muslim population.

Many differences in emphasis and style may be found between Shiites and Sunnis. While the Sunnis emphasize following Muhammad's Sunna (traditions) and recognize the authority of religious scholars, Shiites believe that the Imam, the successor of Ali, is a spiritual and temporal leader—a descendant of Muhammad divinely appointed to guide humans. The spirituality of Shiites is also very mystical. Shiites emphasize suffering, martyrdom, veneration of Ali, and praying at the tombs of Muslim prophets and saints. The rivalry between these two sects is evident even today throughout the Muslim world.

The Prayer at the Tomb in the Blue Mosque in Cairo.

cessors began to wage *jihad* along the caravan trade routes. Syria and Mesopotamia quickly fell, and soon it became clear that Christian lands were the main target. The use of war also served to unite the Arabs, which had been nearly impossible to do before Islam's rise.

THE SPREAD OF ISLAM

Islam's success in spreading and establishing a strong and long-lasting empire remains one of the most remarkable stories in history. Beginning in 634, the Muslims remained unstoppable for the next one hundred years. Within eighty years of Muhammad's death, Muslim territory already spread from the Indus River in India to parts of North Africa and southern Spain. Asia Minor and Europe, for the most part, were as yet unthreatened by Muslim expansion.

The spread of Islamic territory and faith went hand in hand. Believers were obligated by their religion to seek converts and wage a holy war to destroy unbelievers. With an excellent cavalry and light archery (learned from the Persians and Byzantines), the Muslim army became the best in the world. As the army expanded, Islam did as well.

Muslim forces began by defeating the Persians and sacking Jerusalem in 638. The fall of the city sent a shockwave throughout the East and West and would eventually prompt Christians to launch a counterattack to try to retake the Holy Land during the Crusades. Having taken Jerusalem, Muslims spread westwards sacking Christian Alexandria, also a great repository of one thousand years of Greek culture, in 643. With Alexandria taken, Muslims quickly spread throughout North Africa. Nestorians and Monophysites in North Africa for the most part welcomed the Muslim invaders since they were at odds with the Byzantine emperor. By 698, all of North Africa was under Muslim rule. Six hundred years of North African Christianity, with its apologists, early Doctors of the Church, and martyrs, were destroyed. The Old Roman (Byzantine) Empire was reduced to an area not much larger than Greece.

In 684 the Dome of the Rock was erected on the site of the Temple Mount in Jerusalem as a Muslim shrine to commemorate "the Night Journey" of Muhammad.

In 711, Spain fell to the Muslims as well. The Muslims then crossed the Pyrenees and entered France where they were met in 732 by the Frankish chieftain Charles Martel, known as Charles "the Hammer." The subsequent battle, the Battle of Tours, marked the high water mark of the Muslim expansion into Europe. The Franks dressed in armor and stood firm before the hail of arrows. When the Muslims charged, their general was killed and the defeated army slinked back towards Spain. After their retreat to Spain, the Muslims never attempted any further advance into Europe through Spain. But the Muslims did remain in Spain for over 700 years, and it would not be until the *Reconquista* under the reign of Queen Isabella in 1492 that Spain would be completely liberated from Muslim domination.

In 717, the Muslim army laid siege to Christian Constantinople, but Emperor Leo III defeated them. The Muslims would attempt to breach the city again in 740 but would suffer a second defeat against Leo III. The emperor's successful defense against the Muslim forces established Byzantium's position as an eastern bulwark to the Muslim empire.

JERUSALEM, THE HOLY CITY

The capture of Jerusalem in 638 by the Muslims has had historical consequences felt even today. The Muslim caliph Umar cleared the Temple Mount, the site of the two Jewish temples, and built a temporary mosque. In 684 the Dome of the Rock was erected, on the site of the former Temple, as a Muslim shrine to commemorate "the Night Journey" of Muhammad. The Dome of the Rock was intended to surpass the beauty and size of the Church of the Holy Sepulchre in Jerusalem, the church built on the site where Jesus was buried.

According to Muslim beliefs, while sleeping one night near the Kaaba, Muhammad was taken by the angel Gabriel to Jerusalem, where he met the other prophets Abraham, Moses, and Jesus, among others, before ascending through seven heavens before he stood in the presence of God. After this direct experience of God, Gabriel returned Muhammad to Mecca. Whether Muhammad's experience was an actual event, a dream, or a result of a hallucination is not clear, but the seventeenth verse of the *Koran* describes Muhammad's "Night Journey." For this reason, Jerusalem is reckoned as the third holiest city in Islam after Mecca and Medina.

The "temporary" mosque was eventually replaced by the magnificent Al-Aqsa Mosque (Arabic for "farthest mosque," a reference to the *Koran*) also on the Temple Mount. It was completed around 710, and quickly became an important center of learning. At Friday prayers, the mosque and the area surrounding it often hold four to five thousand people.

The appropriation of the site of the former Temple by the Muslims has caused great tensions through the centuries. Jews were not able to rebuild a third Temple because of the Diaspora after 70, and they have today only the Wailing Wall, an outer wall of the Temple Mount, remaining from the Temple.

Prophet Muhammad returns from his Night Journey and Ascension

The Prophet Muhammad is the seal of the prophets, sent to all humanity. He was born in Mecca and sent first to the Arabs to revive the religion of Abraham. Early in his mission he is taken on a special Night Journey to the ends of the Earth, and to visit locations of former prophetic activity such as Mount Sinai, Bethlehem, and Jerusalem. From Jerusalem, the Prophet Muhammad ascends into the seven heavens where he meets the prophets who came before him, and eventually comes into the presence of God.—*The Teaching of Islam*

A PAPAL PERSPECTIVE ON ISLAM

Despite aggressive and expansionistic tendencies, westerners have since learned to see some of the positive characteristics of the Islamic religion. Pope John Paul II in particular said much regarding Islam and had hoped to enter into positive dialogue with members of that religion. In his book *Crossing the Threshold of Hope*, Pope John Paul II wrote the following about the nature of Islam as a religion:

> Some of the most beautiful names in the human language are given to the God of the *Koran*, but He is ultimately a God outside of the world, a God who is *only Majesty, never Emmanuel*, God-with us. *Islam is not a religion of redemption.* There is no room for the Cross and the Resurrection. Jesus is mentioned, but only as a prophet who prepares for the last prophet, Muhammad. There is also mention of Mary, His Virgin Mother, but the tragedy of redemption is completely absent. For this reason not only the theology but also the anthropology of Islam is very distant from Christianity. Nevertheless, *the religiosity of Muslims deserves respect.*

CONCLUSION

In this tumultuous period, the Church made the transition from existing within the Roman Empire to surviving amidst the Germanic invasions. However, the Church did not merely survive. Rather, she set about a proactive mission of the evangelization of Germanic tribes, facilitated largely by the rise of monasticism. The next chapter relates the stories of the men and women who brought the Gospel message to all corners of Europe. Though beset by great challenges, the steadfast labors of these holy monks, nuns, kings, queens, and soldiers under the guidance of the Holy Spirit brought a new unity to the West after the fall of the Empire. The rising specter of Islam, however, would soon pose a severe challenge of its own to the entire Christian world.

SUPPLEMENTARY READING

St. Benedict, *The Rule of St. Benedict,* Ch. 33, "Whether Monks Ought to Have Anything of Their Own"

The vice of private ownership is above all to be cut off from the monastery by the roots. Let none presume to give or receive anything without leave of the Abbot, nor to keep anything as their own, either book, or writing tablet, or pen, or anything whatsoever; since they are permitted to have neither body nor will in their power. But all that is necessary they may hope to receive from the father of the monastery; nor are they allowed to keep anything which the Abbot has not given, or at least permitted them to have. Let all things be in common to all, as it is written: "Neither did anyone say that aught which he possessed was his own." But if anyone shall be found to indulge in this most baneful vice, and after one or two admonitions does not amend, let him be subject to correction.

John Paul II, *Crossing the Threshold of Hope,* On the Question: "Muhammad?"

Whoever knows and reads the Old and New Testaments, and then reads the *Koran,* clearly sees the *process by which it completely reduces Divine Revelation.* It is impossible not to note the movement away from what God said about himself, first in the Old testament though the prophets, and then finally in the new Testament through his Son. In Islam all the richness of God's self-revelation, which constitutes the heritage of the Old and New Testaments, has definitely been set aside.

Josef Cardinal Ratzinger (future Pope Benedict XVI), quoted in "Ratzinger on Europe," *Homiletic and Pastoral Review,* January 2005.

The rebirth of Islam is not only bound up with the new material riches of the Muslim lands, but also it is fed by the knowledge that Islam is in a position to offer a spiritual base that is valid for the life of a people. The traditional Christian basis that made Europe seems to be fleeing from the land of the old Europe, which, notwithstanding the perdurance of its political and spiritual power, has come to be seen ever more as condemned to decline and crumble.

St. Gregory the Great, *The Book of Pastoral Rule,* I.VI To John, Bishop of the city of Ravenna

That those who fly from the burden of rule through humility are then truly humble when they resist not the Divine decrees. There are some also who fly by reason only of their humility, lest they should be preferred to others to whom they esteem themselves unequal. And theirs, indeed, if it be surrounded by other virtues, is then true humility before the eyes of God, when it is not pertinacious in rejecting what it is enjoined to undertake with profit. For neither is he truly humble, who understands how the good pleasure of the Supernal Will ought to bear sway, and yet contemns its sway. But, submitting himself to the divine disposals, and averse from the vice of obstinacy, it be be already prevented with gifts whereby he may profit others also, he ought, when enjoined to undertake supreme rule, in his heart to flee from it, but against his will to obey.

St. Benedict's Rule has been lauded for its spirit of peace and love, as well as its moderation in the ascetical life.

VOCABULARY

ALLAH
Arabic word for God.

CENOBITICAL LIFE
More common form of monasticism, called the common life, that is monastic life lived in community.

DIOCESE
A territorial division of the Church, adapted from the Roman Empire.

ECUMENICAL PATRIARCH
Title adopted by the Patriarch of Constantinople.

THE *HAJJ*
The pilgrimage to Mecca required of all Muslim faithful once during their lifetime.

THE *HEJIRA*
Arabic for "flight." The flight of Muhammad and his followers from Mecca to Medina on Friday, July 16, 622. Marks year 1 in the Islamic (A.H.) calendar.

HERMIT
One who, for religious motives, has retired into solitary life, especially one of the early Christian recluses. Derived from the Greek word *erēmia,* meaning "desert," it is also known as eremitical life.

HUNS
A powerful nomadic people of unknown ethnic origin who invaded Europe ca. 375.

ISLAM
Arabic for "submission," the faith of the prophet Muhammad, it traces its roots back to Abraham, Hagar and Ishmael.

JIHAD
Holy war waged by Muslims in the name of religion. Muslim men who die in a jihad are believed to go straight to Heaven.

JIZYA
Tax placed upon Jews and Christians under Muslim rule. It allowed them to keep their religious laws, and retain the right to practice their own religion.

KAABA
Arabic for "square building," this large black stone is the main focus of the pilgrimage to Mecca, which every Muslim is required to take at least once in his lifetime. Housed inside a square building that Muslims believe Abraham built, Muslims gather around the stone to re-enact Muhammad's flight to Medina from Mecca.

KORAN
Arabic for "recitation," this is the holy book of the Muslim faith, written by Muhammad, and containing all of the writings that Muhammad claimed he was told by the archangel Gabriel under God's direction.

LAUS DEI
Latin for "praise of God," in Benedictince life it referred to the four hours of the day spent in communal prayer. Alternatively called *opus Dei* (work of God).

LECTIO DIVINA
Reading and meditation on Scripture.

MONASTICISM
A way of life characterized by asceticism and self-denial lived more or less in seclusion from the world and under fixed rule and vows. Monastic communities withdraw from the affairs of the world in order to seek God through asceticism and prayer.

NUNCIO
Personal ambassador of the pope.

OPUS DEI
See *laus Dei.*

ORA ET LABORA
Benedictine motto meaning "pray and work."

VOCABULARY Continued

RAMADAN

The holy month of Islam believed to be the time when the *Koran* was given to Muhammad. Celebrated in the ninth lunar month of each year, a strict fast is observed from sunrise to sunset.

SCRIPTORIUM

Large room in a monastery dedicated to the copying and maintaining of texts.

SERVUS SERVORUM DEI

Latin for "servant of the servants of God," this title was adopted by Pope St. Gregory the Great.

THE SHAHADA

The first pillar and creedal statement of Islam: "There is no God but Allah, and Muhammad is his prophet."

VOW

A solemn promise made voluntarily by a person of reason, to practice a virtue or perform a specific good deed in order to accomplish a future good which is better than its contrary.

Once a student at the monastery learned Latin, he was taught Sacred Scriptures, the writings of the Church Fathers, geometry, and music for the singing of the Divine Office.

STUDY QUESTIONS

1. Describe conditions in the Roman Empire during the fifth century when the empire collapsed.

2. How did Ulphilas influence the Germanic tribes and Christianity?

3. What was the key for the Church in converting the Germanic tribes?

4. How did the Germanic invasions change the Christian attitude in the fifth century?

5. How is Christian monasticism unique?

6. How is the eremitical life structured, and which two orders have taken much of their inspiration from eremitical monasticism?

7. What was a common problem of the early hermits in Egypt?

8. What were the three major effects of the monasteries on Europe?

9. What are the chief qualities that lend the *Rule of St. Benedict* to harmonious religious life?

10. What three vows were accepted by the Benedictines?

11. Who was St. Scholastica, and what was her chief accomplishment?

12. In what ways was Pope St. Gregory I (the Great) an historical marker?

13. What was Pope St. Gregory I's background?

14. What title did Pope St. Gregory I use during his papacy, and what title did he reject for the Patriarch of Constantinople. What did these titles imply?

15. What is unique about the use of Arabic as the original language in the *Koran*?

16. Who is the common ancestor for Judaism, Christianity, and Islam. To whom do Muslims trace the origin of their people?

17. What does the *Koran* have to say about Mary and Jesus?

18. List the Five Pillars of Islam, and give a brief description of each.

19. Islam's expansion came at whose expense?

20. At the famous Battle of Tours in France in 732, who defeated the Muslim forces from Spain?

21. What religious significance does Jerusalem hold in Islam?

22. How did Pope John Paul II analyze Islam?

St. Paul of Thebes is held by tradition to be the first hermit. He had fled a persecution under the Roman Emperor Decius.

PRACTICAL EXERCISES

1. Why is it easy to understand why many Christians thought that the Second Coming was close at hand when the Roman Empire collapsed? Can you think of other times in history when conditions also seemed to be right for the Second Coming?

2. The "Dome of the Rock" was built in 684 over the site of the former Jewish temple in Jerusalem. What psychological impact might this have had upon Jews?

3. What arguments would you use to try and convince a Muslim that the Christian teaching on the Trinity does not violate monotheism nor commit idolatry?

4. What did Pope John Paul II mean when he stated that Islam is not a religion of redemption? How does Christianity differ?

5. The largest mosque in Europe was built in 1995 in Rome. What reasons might there be for choosing Rome for this mosque?

6. The *Rule of St. Benedict,* written in the sixth century, is still used by Benedictines and a number of other monastic communities today. Its focus on a simple life of prayer and work and its adaptability to different circumstances have been credited with the *Rule's* enduring to the present day. Find a copy of the *Rule* and comment on any two of its chapters. What is contained within each of your two chosen chapters? Why are these topics important to cenobitical life? How might following these chapters of the *Rule* help a monk get to Heaven?

Jesus speaks immediately after his birth

God revealed to the Jesus' mother Mary to set out with him for Syria. She did what she was commanded. The revelation came to him when he was thirty years old. His prophethood lasted three years, then God raised him up to heaven. Some of the early Muslims said that Jesus used to wear hair and ate the leaves of trees. He had no house, no family, and no property. Jesus is the seal of the Israelite prophets. After his rejection by the Israelites, Jerusalem was destroyed.

—*The Teaching of Islam*

FROM THE CATECHISM

916 The state of consecrated life is thus one way of experiencing a "more intimate" consecration, rooted in Baptism and dedicated totally to God (cf. *PC* 5). In the consecrated life, Christ's faithful, moved by the Holy Spirit, propose to follow Christ more nearly, to give themselves to God who is loved above all and, pursuing the perfection of charity in the service of the Kingdom, to signify and proclaim in the Church the glory of the world to come (cf. CIC, can. 573).

922 From apostolic times Christian virgins (cf. 1 Cor 7:34-36) and widows (cf. John Paul II, *Vita consecrata* 7), called by the Lord to cling only to him with greater freedom of heart, body, and spirit, have decided with the Church's approval to live in the respective status of virginity or perpetual chastity "for the sake of the Kingdom of heaven" (Mt 19:12).

923 "Virgins who, committed to the holy plan of following Christ more closely, are consecrated to God by the diocesan bishop according to the approved liturgical rite, are betrothed mystically to Christ, the Son of God, and are dedicated to the service of the Church" (CIC, can. 604 § 1). By this solemn rite (*Consecratio virginum*), the virgin is "constituted...a sacred person, a transcendent sign of the Church's love for Christ, and an eschatological image of this heavenly Bride of Christ and of the life to come" (*Ordo Consecrationis Virginum, Praenotanda* 1).

924 "As with other forms of consecrated life," the order of virgins establishes the woman living in the world (or the nun) in prayer, penance, service of her brethren, and apostolic activity, according to the state of life and spiritual gifts given to her (cf. CIC, can. 604 § 1; *OCV Praenotanda* 2). Consecrated virgins can form themselves into associations to observe their commitment more faithfully (cf. CIC, can. 604 § 2).

925 Religious life was born in the East during the first centuries of Christianity. Lived within institutes canonically erected by the Church, it is distinguished from other forms of consecrated life by its liturgical character, public profession of the evangelical counsels, fraternal life led in common, and witness given to the union of Christ with the Church (cf. CIC, cann. 607; 573; *UR* 15).

926 Religious life derives from the mystery of the Church. It is a gift she has received from her Lord, a gift she offers as a stable way of life to the faithful called by God to profess the counsels. Thus, the Church can both show forth Christ and acknowledge herself to be the Savior's bride. Religious life in its various forms is called to signify the very charity of God in the language of our time.

St. Gregory took the title "servus servorum Dei"...the servant of the servants of God.

The Conversion Of The Barbarian Tribes

The great evangelizers of this period were fervent in their faith in Jesus and his Church and hoped for everyone to share in the spiritual and moral treasure of Christianity.

CHAPTER 6

The Conversion Of The Barbarian Tribes

God desires the salvation of everyone. In a mysterious but real way,
he is present in all. Humanity forms one single family, since all human beings have
been created by God in his own image. All have a common destiny,
since they are called to find fullness of life in God.

— John Paul II, Homily, Parakou, Benin, February 4, 1993

The invasion and conquest of the Roman Empire opened a new chapter in both the history of the Church and Western civilization. The Church, recognizing her mission to spread the Gospel to all people, set about the task of converting both the Germanic invaders and the different tribes populating the surrounding areas of the former Roman frontier. The process was long and arduous with many advances and setbacks — a period of evangelization that stretched from the first Germanic invasions in the fourth century through the eleventh century, when the last European peoples, the Slavs, converted.

In today's cultural climate it is often heard that Christian missionaries have no business in trying to convert those peoples following pagan religions or other religious traditions, a charge that itself often belies an anti-Christian prejudice. According to this logic, Christianity is no better or worse than any other religion or philosophy. To deny Christians the right to evangelize would strip them of their right to express their religious beliefs freely, and it would deprive unbelievers of the freedom to embrace the liberating and saving Truth of the Gospel of Jesus Christ.

The missionary task implies a *respectful dialogue* with those who do not yet accept the Gospel (cf. John Paul II, *Redemptoris missio* 55). Believers can profit from this dialogue by learning to appreciate better "those elements of truth and grace which are found among peoples, and which are, as it were, a secret presence of God" (*Ad gentes* 9). They proclaim the Good News to those who do not know it, in order to consolidate, complete, and raise

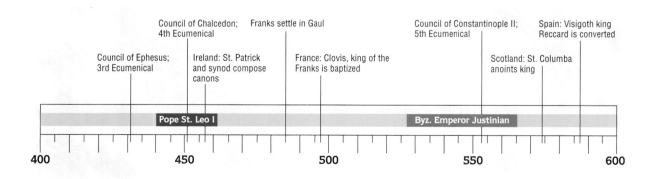

Council of Chalcedon;
4th Ecumenical

Franks settle in Gaul

Council of Constantinople II;
5th Ecumenical

Spain: Visigoth king
Reccard is converted

Council of Ephesus;
3rd Ecumenical

Ireland: St. Patrick
and synod compose
canons

France: Clovis, king of the
Franks is baptized

Scotland: St. Columba
anoints king

Pope St. Leo I

Byz. Emperor Justinian

400   450   500   550   600

up the truth and the goodness that God has distributed among men and nations, and to purify them from error and evil "for the glory of God, the confusion of the demon, and the happiness of man" (*Ad gentes* 9). (CCC 856)

The great evangelizers of this period were fervent in their faith in Jesus and his Church, and hoped for everyone, including the different pagan peoples, to share in this spiritual and moral treasure of Christianity. These heralds of Christ not only wanted to prepare their people for everlasting life, but also wanted to spread the benefits of a more civilized society and higher human culture.

In exploring the issue of converting the barbarians, this chapter will highlight a number of the men and women who brought the Gospel to these pagan tribes. This section will also examine the unique role monasticism played in creating a Christian culture through their witness and teachings. Lastly, this chapter will explore the crucial work of the papacy in promoting and supporting evangelization.

The Church's Work of Conversion

Most of the German tribes were Arians. Though these Arian tribes did not understand the subtleties of theology, they were fanatical promoters of that heresy. Many, in fact, attempted to destroy Catholicism.

The work of conversion and assimilation into a Christian mindset would take many generations since the barbarians were generally uncivilized, bellicose peoples with little developed culture. Over the succeeding centuries, the Germanic tribes mixed with the Romans and adopted some aspects of the Greco-Roman culture. The great work of conversion and evangelization was the fruit of patient and dedicated labor of the monks.

During the fifth century, the bishops were gifted leaders who guided and educated their people not only with good preaching, but also through their pastoral example. The bishops exhibited many roles, such as that of father, teacher, preacher, leader, administrator, liturgist, and sometimes even military leader. Because of the chaos of the age, the bishops took on leadership positions, and they worked to preserve the safety of the people, whom they often protected through their dialogue with the invaders. This dialogue with the Germanic tribes, who formed a minority of the population and were the occupying military power, also paved the way for their conversion. Due primarily to the power vacuum created by the fall of the Roman Empire, these bishops gained influence in the political as well as in the spiritual sector.

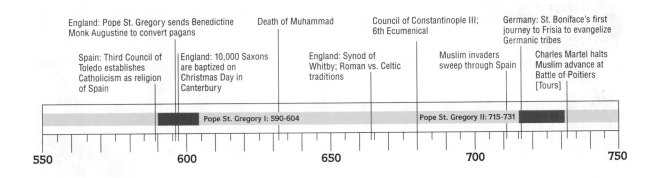

England: Pope St. Gregory sends Benedictine Monk Augustine to convert pagans

Death of Muhammad

Council of Constantinople III; 6th Ecumenical

Germany: St. Boniface's first journey to Frisia to evangelize Germanic tribes

Spain: Third Council of Toledo establishes Catholicism as religion of Spain

England: 10,000 Saxons are baptized on Christmas Day in Canterbury

England: Synod of Whitby; Roman vs. Celtic traditions

Muslim invaders sweep through Spain

Charles Martel halts Muslim advance at Battle of Poitiers [Tours]

Pope St. Gregory I: 590-604

Pope St. Gregory II: 715-731

550   600   650   700   750

The task before the Church was truly immense. The monks and bishops not only had to build the churches, monasteries, and institutions of the Church from scratch, but also had to raise the moral and cultural level of the tribes so they could be fully disposed to internalize the Gospel.

As previously mentioned, the Germanic tribes were exceedingly violent and terribly cruel even within their own families. For example, St. Clotilda's daughter was punished by her Alemanni husband for trying to attend Mass. One of Clovis' sons murdered a nephew with his bare hands in a rage. In Spain, the Visigoth prince St. Hermengild converted under the influence of his wife Ingund. Ingund's mother-in-law punished her in response, and eventually St. Hermengild's entire family betrayed him and had him beheaded. St. Hermengild's brother Recared's conversion initiated the conversion of Spain. Through their conversions, these peoples began to rise to a humanity purified and elevated by grace.

There were two forces at work during this period. First, missionaries emerged from those lands that were most recently evangelized—especially Ireland, England, and Germany. Secondly, Christian queens influenced their pagan husbands to convert to Christianity. The general population usually soon followed the conversion of their king.

St. Benedict blesses one of his pupils, St. Maurus, before the monk leaves on a mission to teach in France. In the background is an event from St. Maurus' life when he saved a drowning boy named Placid by walking on the water.

PART I

Conversion of France, the "Church's Eldest Daughter"

Over time the Franks would become the Church's greatest defender. In fact, this special relationship between the papacy and the Franks would result in the formation of the Papal States. The conversion of the Franks was a huge victory in the Church's effort to bring the message of the Gospels to the Germanic tribes, as the Franks were the first of the Germanic tribes to convert to the Faith.

CONVERSION OF THE FRANKS

The Franks, unlike most of the other invaders, were not Christians (Arian, orthodox, or otherwise) when they settled Gaul (modern-day France) in 485. A bishop introduced the beautiful Burgundian princess St. Clotilda, a Christian, to the Frankish chief Clovis. Since Clovis was a pagan, St. Clotilda worked ceaselessly to obtain his conversion. Yet, the death of their first child and the near death of their second child strengthened Clovis' view that the Christian God was ineffective. Over the course of 496 and 497, Clovis and his troops battled the barbarian Alemanni. With defeat staring him in the face, Clovis promised the Christian God that if he won he would convert and be baptized. At Tolbiac the Franks were triumphant, and in 497, Clovis was faithful to his promise.

Clovis presented himself to the church in Rheims to be baptized with three thousand of his troops. They were dressed in fur coats, wore long hair, and held their battle-axes in hand. Clovis disrobed and entered a pond, followed by his soldiers. Bishop Remigius pronounced the

After his baptism, Clovis united Gaul.

words of Baptism. By this act of Baptism, the Franks were the first of the Germanic tribes to embrace the Catholic Faith, thereby making France "the Church's eldest daughter."

After his Baptism, Clovis united Gaul by conquering neighboring Germanic tribes. Burgundy, an eastern province of France, was annexed. Part of this unity involved a fusion of the Greco-Roman culture with the German warrior culture. The descendants of Clovis were known as the Merovingian Dynasty, named after Meroveus, an ancestor of Clovis.

By the middle of the sixth century, all of Gaul—from the English Channel to the Pyrenees—was Christianized. Other than Gaul, only Italy, Ireland, and a small part of England made up the Church's faithful in the West. The rest of central and northern Europe remained to be evangelized.

ST. GREGORY OF TOURS

St. Gregory of Tours (ca. 538-ca. 594) was elected Bishop of Tours in France in 573. Born of a Gallo-Roman senatorial family with relational ties to most of the aristocratic houses in Gaul, St. Gregory became one of the leading churchmen in the period following the collapse of the Roman Empire. He also wrote the *Historia Francorum* (History of the Franks). Beginning with creation in the Bible, St. Gregory told the history of the Franks through the year 591. Any study of this period of French history would be virtually impossible without referring to St. Gregory's work.

PART II

Spain

Christianity arrived in Spain while still part of the Roman Empire. According to tradition, Spain received Christianity directly from the Apostles St. James the Greater and St. Paul, and from that time until the eighth century, Christianity flourished, despite much suffering under Roman persecution. By the middle of the fourth century, Spain enjoyed a stable hierarchy of bishops who periodically held councils to combat the heresies of that time.

With the invasion of the Visigoths, the Church in Spain suffered greatly until 589. Spain collapsed with the invasion of the Visigoths who conquered most of the Iberian Peninsula. Though nominally Arian, the Visigoths demonstrated great intolerance toward the Church in Spain. In the middle of

According to tradition, Spain received Christianity directly from the Apostles St. James the Greater and St. Paul.

The Council of Toledo in 589 condemned Arianism and established Catholicism as the religion of Spain.

the sixth century, however, St. Hermengild, son of the Visigoth king Leovigild, married the Catholic Merovingian princess, Ingund. Leovigild sent his son to rule in Seville, and there Ingund and Leander, the Bishop of Seville, worked together for the conversion of the future St. Hermengild.

With St. Hermengild's conversion came a very tense and fragile standoff between himself and his Arian father, each one hoping that the other would relent peacefully. The situation escalated into civil war in 582, and Leovigild finally captured his son in 584. St. Hermengild spent a year in captivity before being killed in 585. His wife died at around the same time en route to Constantinople. Leovigild died soon after, and his other son, Reccard, ascended the throne. After executing his brother's murderer, Reccard converted to Catholicism in 587. In 589, the Third Council of Toledo condemned Arianism, and Catholicism thus became the religion of Spain. But this political and religious unity, achieved after so much hardship, would not last long. Subsequent monarchies gradually weakened, and the former unity began to dissolve — thus opening the door for the Muslim invasion at the beginning of the eighth century.

In 711, the Muslim invaders began to sweep through Spain. Within three years, they had conquered the entire Iberian peninsula — a task which had taken the Roman legions nearly a century to accomplish. The Spanish peoples chose either to live under Muslim rule or to retreat to the most northerly provinces of Spain, mainly in Asturias, protected by the *Picos de Europa,* a mountain range in northern Spain. Those who chose to live under Muslim rule called themselves Mozarabs. Mozarabic Christians did not fare poorly at first; but, in the early ninth century, persecutions began. Years of struggle and slow re-conquest followed. Not until 1492, when the *Reconquista* (Spanish for "re-conquest") was complete, did Christians again rule all of Spain.

BRITISH AND IRISH/CELTIC MISSIONS TO EUROPE
6TH TO 8TH CENTURIES

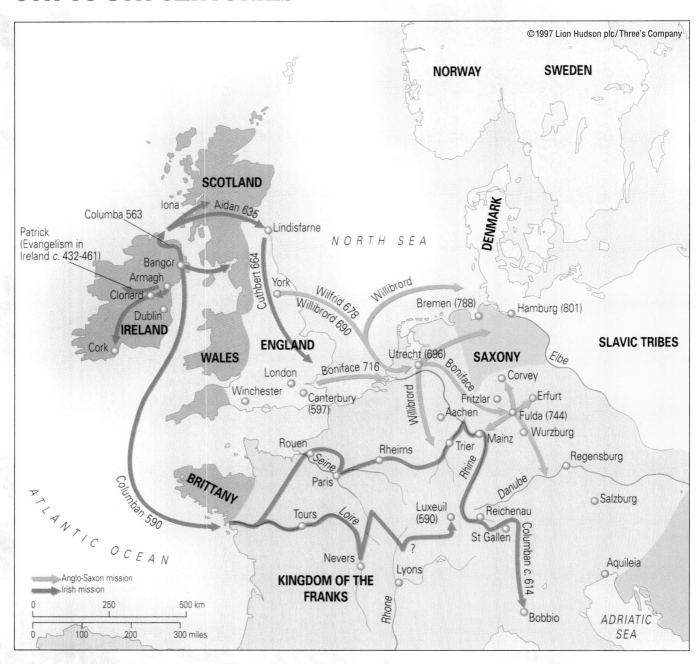

© 1997 Lion Hudson plc/ Three's Company

CHRISTIANITY IN RUSSIA
10TH TO 11TH CENTURIES

VOLGA
BULGARS

BALTIC SEA

Lake
Ladoga

Jurev
(Dorpat)

✠ Novgorod

● Pskov

Volga

Volga

✠ Pereyaslavl   ● Rostov

✠ Nizhniy Novgorod

Dvina

✠ Vladimir

LITHUANIANS

● Moscow

✠ Polotsk

✠ Ryazan

✠ Smolensk

✠ Minsk

**KIEVAN
RUSSIA**

POLES

✠ Pinsk
● Ugrovsk   ✠ Turov

✠ Krakow

✠ Chernigov

✠ Vladimir-Volynsk

Don

Kiev
✠ Przemysl   Belgorod ✠

✠ Pereyaslavl

✠ Galich   ✠ Yurev

Dnieper

PECHENEGS

Dniester

MAGYARS

KHAZARS

✠ Tmutarakan

Danube

©1997 Lion Hudson plc/Three's Company

| 0 | 250 | 500 km |

Extent of Kievan Russia, c.1050
✠ Archbishopric
● Bishopric

BLACK SEA

| 0 | 100 | 200 | 300 miles |

PART III
The Conversion of the Celts

Christianity in Ireland adapted itself to the Celtic culture, given its geographic distance from the Roman provinces. By the fifth century, Christianity had reached the island, though Druidic paganism was by far the dominant religion. Through extraordinary efforts inspired by the faith of ordinary individuals, Christianity spread quickly throughout the island. Ireland soon developed a strong monastic tradition that would serve the Church as a source of great missionaries.

ST. PATRICK: THE "APOSTLE OF IRELAND"

> I came to the Irish peoples to preach the Gospel and endure the taunts of unbelievers, putting up with reproaches about my earthly pilgrimage, suffering many persecutions, even bondage, and losing my birthright of freedom for the benefit of others. (St. Patrick, *Confessions*, Cap. 14-16: PL 53, 808-809)

A boy named Patricius (d. 493) was born sometime around the end of the fourth century. He was a Roman Briton and the son of a former Roman city official who had become a deacon in order to avoid taxation. When he was about sixteen, Irish pirates kidnapped him off the southwest coast of Britain and took him to the northwest of Ireland. There he lived the life of a slave in that foreign land, working as a herdsman. Prayer gave him strength (St. Patrick wrote that he prayed one hundred prayers in a given day), and after six years, St. Patrick escaped back to Britain and his family. Soon after his return, he wrote of a vision which called him back to Ireland to walk among its people again. This supernatural experience prompted him to begin his studies for the priesthood.

Sometime in the early 430s, St. Patrick, now a priest, was on the road back to Ireland with several clerics. He had been commissioned by Pope St. Celestine I to aid the Bishop of Ireland, Palladius; but somewhere on the road in Gaul they received the news of Palladius' death. As a consequence St. Patrick was consecrated as the new bishop immediately, and sailed to the north of Ireland. He was familiar with this area, which had not yet been evangelized by Palladius, who had confined his work to the southern regions. Within fifteen years, despite resistance from many of the Druid chieftains, the entire northern half of the island heard the Word of God, thousands were baptized, and consecrated religious communities were started. St. Patrick governed this new Christian community from his episcopal headquarters in Ultster. Humility, eloquence, and many miracles were St. Patrick's tools. He began working with bishops who arrived in the south in 439; and in 457, they met in a synod to establish laws and directives for the newborn Church in Ireland.

Within a generation of St. Patrick's work, the island had converted to the Faith. St. Patrick, being such a strong advocate of monasticism, promoted the foundation of many monasteries in Ireland. St. Patrick's most important written work is his *Confessions*, which he wrote in Latin in the period around 461 and 462. In it, he humbly describes his spiritual journey of conversion and faith. St. Patrick lived to an old age, and was fortunate enough to see the fruits of his labor. His feast day is celebrated on March 17.

IRISH MONKS: PROTECTORS AND PROMOTERS OF WESTERN CIVILIZATION

Irish monasticism was inspired not by the Rule of St. Benedict, but by the austere Eastern monastic tradition. It is not certain, but it is believed that the Eastern form of monasticism was brought to Ireland through commercial contacts with the East during the earliest days of Christianity's presence in Ireland.

Following the Eastern spirit, Irish monks slept on cold flagstones, prayed in icy water, and slept in wet blankets. Anything that could be done to deny the body comfort was employed as a means to bring the soul closer to God. It is, therefore, easy to understand why St. Benedict's Italian model, which took into consideration the health and needs of the body, lasted and became the norm in the West.

During the sixth and seventh centuries, the Irish monks enjoyed the height of their influence on Christian culture and the work of evangelization. In the early sixth century, the Irish monasteries were the most important centers of learning in all of Europe. The scriptoria and libraries in the Irish monasteries saved a great deal of the Greco-Roman literary tradition, even though Ireland was never colonized by the Romans. Through trade and the influx of some Greek monks, the Irish even gained a certain proficiency in the Greek language, which had virtually disappeared in the West.

Christianity among the Celtic peoples, which had developed separately from Roman Christianity, also had some unique features. For example, in Ireland there were no diocesan priests, but the only priests were from the ranks of the monks. In addition, the abbots exercised most of the governing power in the church in Ireland.

By the 800s, the importance of the Irish church on the growing European culture rapidly declined. Due to tensions with the Church in mainland Europe, the Irish monks played less a role in evangelizing England and the continent overall. Another cause of decline was a series of attacks by the Vikings on Irish monasteries. Around the ninth century, the evangelizing mission was firmly being led by the papacy, as Christian roots deepened among the Germanic peoples and would soon extend to Slavic populations.

ST. COLUMBA: THE "APOSTLE OF SCOTLAND"

Alone with none but Thee, my God, / I journey on my way; / What need I fear when Thou are near, / Oh King of night and day? / More safe am I within Thy hand / Than if a host did round me stand. (A prayer attributed to St. Columba)

St. Columba (521-597) was an important evangelizer of northern Britain and Scotland, as well as the founder of a number of important monasteries in the Irish tradition. Of royal lineage from the O'Donnells and the O'Neills, his name *Columba* is Latin for "dove." To the Irish he is best known as Columcille, the "Dove of the Churches."

St. Columba had been preparing for the monastic life from an early age, and even before he left Ireland he is reputed to have founded monasteries in Durrow and Derry. St. Columba was a fervent

Christian all his life, even to the point of quarrel with High King Diarmait. To cite some examples, Diarmait would not allow St. Columba to grant sanctuary to a murderer and severely criticized St. Columba for copying parts of St. Finian's Vulgate without permission. A small war, at St. Columba's prompting, exploded between Diarmait's forces and the combined forces of the O'Neills and the O'Donnells. During the fighting, St. Columba would be seen praying for the O'Neills and O'Donnells, and St. Finian could be seen praying for Diarmait's men. Diarmait was defeated, but scandal followed. There are conflicting accounts of what happened next. Some say St. Columba was briefly excommunicated for starting a war, and that the excommunication was lifted on condition of a lifetime of penance in missionary exile. Other accounts mention nothing of excommunication and report that this penance was given to St. Columba by his confessor. By either account, St. Columba left Ireland and went to Scotland in 563.

St. Columba

On the isle of Iona, St. Columba built a monastery and set about evangelizing the Picts, a Celtic tribe with deep pagan roots. Successful in this, he continued his work throughout Scotland. A man of constant study and prayer, St. Columba is said to have written some 300 books, only two of which have survived. The Latin poem "*Altus Prosator,*" a description of the Last Judgment in all its fury, is believed to have been written by him. In 574, St. Columba anointed the new Scottish king, which led to the eventual conversion of the Scottish population. His feast day is celebrated on June 9.

ST. COLUMBANUS AND THE IRISH ON THE CONTINENT

Let us not imprint on ourselves the image of a despot, but let Christ paint his image in us with his words: My peace I give you, my peace I leave with you. But the knowledge that peace is good is of no benefit to us if we do not practice it. (St. Columbanus, *Instr.* 11, 1-2. quoted in *Opera,* 1957, pp. 106-107)

St. Columbanus (d. 615) is the most famous among a band of Irish monks who helped to evangelize the northern coast of France as well as Switzerland. He helped renew the spiritual life and discipline in areas where Christian practice was waning. He was a huge man, capable of killing a bear with his own bare hands. When leaving by boat for his missionary undertaking, he would just travel wherever the boat took him. In his last years, Columbanus worked in Switzerland and founded a monastery in the Italian Alps in a small town called Bobbio, near Genoa, in 612. In later years Bobbio became an important center of learning. He died there in 615. St. Columbanus' feast day is celebrated on November 23.

The Celtic spirituality that St. Columbanus helped to spread around Europe bore many lasting fruits. One such fruit of this spirituality was promotion of frequent sacramental Penance, which has become one of its greatest contributions to the Christian Faith. The practice of frequent Penance—at first limited to the Irish monks and those under their care—quickly became incorporated into the universal Church.

In the Roman tradition by the third century, a system of austere public penance had developed. Under it, the penitent was enrolled publicly with other penitents, with whom he committed himself to a rigorous and lengthy period (the length varied depending on the seriousness of the sin) of prayer, almsgiving, and severe fasting. Besides the strict spiritual regimen, there were two other

ST. PATRICK ON THE HILL OF TARA

From ancient times until the sixth century, the Hill of Tara was known as the seat of the high kings of Ireland, and it may have been used in prehistoric religious ceremonies. In the time of St. Patrick, Christianity had not yet gained complete acceptance in Ireland, and Easter was not yet celebrated. Every spring, the Druids marked the Beltaine festival by lighting a great bonfire on the Hill of Tara. Adding to the significance of the bonfire, no other fires in the vicinity were to be lit during the festival. This rule was not to be taken lightly; those who lit another fire in violation of Beltaine rules could be punished by death.

Because he wanted to celebrate Easter, however, St. Patrick and his followers went to the nearby Slane Hill and boldly lit a small Paschal Fire. Seeing the fire from the Hill of Tara, the King ordered that St. Patrick and his followers be taken before him to answer for their crime. Using his deep knowledge of Irish custom and language, St. Patrick preached to the King about Christianity. St. Patrick used the clover, an ancient symbol in Ireland, to explain the Holy Trinity.

St. Patrick's boldness in lighting the Paschal Fire brought him attention and respect from the Irish King and he was given the freedom to preach Christianity across the country. Thus, the small, but defiant act of lighting a fire proved central in the conversion of the Irish people. If you were to visit the Hill of Tara today, you would find a great statue of St. Patrick, which marks the location of the Lia Fail, the Coronation Stone of the ancient high kings.

St. Patrick keeps vigil at his church on the Hill of Tara.

unique aspects of this system that eventually led to this system's decline. The public penitential practice was understood as a second Baptism, and Baptism can be received only once. In addition, the individual was bound to life-long continence. For these reasons, many people delayed Penance until the approach of death given the obvious challenges connected to this sacrament during those first centuries.

For the Irish, Penance remained lengthy, severe, and public, but penitents were not officially enrolled with others, nor was reception of the sacrament limited to a single time, as with Baptism. Thus the promise of lifelong continence—a difficult task, even for the saints—was no longer a necessity. Hence, the nearly exclusively "deathbed" recourse to the Sacrament of Penance fell into decline. Eventually, absolution, which had previously been withheld until the completion of the public penance, was granted upon confession of sins, and Penance became a matter of private responsibility. To determine specific penances, the Irish monks made use of Penitential Books, books that listed various sins with the corresponding penance.

The Irish had a tremendous influence in bringing about the custom of frequent Penance. Not until 1215, at the Fourth Lateran Council, did the Church officially teach that every individual Christian was bound to make at least one private Penance each year if one were conscious of having committed mortal sin.

PART IV
The Conversion of England

It is not known exactly how the Celts in England were first evangelized during the era of the Roman Empire, but English bishops were already present at the Council of Arles (314) in France. The spread of Christianity suffered a tremendous setback as invading Angles, Jutes, and Saxons pushed the burgeoning Christian communities to the farthest western reaches of England. It was into this situation that St. Augustine of Canterbury and his brother monks were thrown in the late sixth century.

ST. AUGUSTINE OF CANTERBURY: THE "APOSTLE OF ENGLAND"

> Who, dear brother, is capable of describing the great joy of believers when they have learned what the grace of Almighty God and your own cooperation achieved among the Angles? They abandoned the errors of darkness and were bathed with the light of holy faith. With full awareness they trampled on the idols which they had previously adored with savage fear. (Pope St. Gregory the Great to the missionaries of England, *Lib.* 9; 36: MGH *Epistolæ*, 2, 305-306)

St. Augustine of Canterbury (d. ca. 604-609) is often overshadowed by another saint bearing the same name, the great St. Augustine of Hippo. St. Augustine of Canterbury, a giant in the Church's history of evangelization, brought the Catholic Faith to the pagan and violent Anglo-Saxons. The date of his birth and details of his early life are unknown. St. Augustine was a Benedictine monk and prior of St. Andrew's monastery in Rome, one of the monasteries founded by Pope St. Gregory the Great, when he was asked by Pope St. Gregory himself to bring the Gospel message to England.

Perhaps the most salient aspect of Pope St. Gregory the Great's pontificate was his strong support for the conversion of the Anglo-Saxons, especially in England. During his service to his monastery

Perhaps the most salient aspect of Pope St. Gregory the Great's pontificate was his support for the conversion of the barbarians, especially of the mission to England.

as abbot in 585, before becoming pope, St. Gregory saw a group of blond, blue-eyed foreigners in the streets of Rome. He asked who they were, and an assistant told St. Gregory that the men were slaves, Angles from England. St. Gregory replied, "*Non Angli, sed angeli*" ("Not Angles, but angels"). St. Gregory never forgot the Angles, and he selected St. Augustine as his personal emissary and missionary to England when he became pope.

Christianity had already made its way to England by this time, but only to certain limited areas. The Celts in Britain had already converted due to the efforts of the Irish monks. St. Columba had already visited the Picts in Scotland. However, the invading Saxons, Angles, and Jutes nearly annihilated the Celts in Britain—and with them, the Christian Faith. Even though the Celts had attempted to convert the new tribes to the Faith, they failed. Outside help was needed, and it came from Rome.

In 596 Pope St. Gregory sent St. Augustine with a group of forty other monks to travel by land through Italy and France to reach England. In France the band of monks halted, and St. Augustine wrote a frantic letter to Pope St. Gregory that the monks were frightened by the frontier and heard appalling stories of the brutality of the barbarians in England. St. Augustine asked for permission to return to Rome, but Pope St. Gregory declined the request, and told the group to continue its mission. Before departing from France, St. Augustine was made abbot of the missionaries. Upon arriving in England, they had discovered that the rumors were most likely exaggerated.

Learning from historically tested experiences, St. Augustine tried to gain the favor of a king with a Christian wife. Ethelbert, the king of Kent had married Bertha, a Frankish princess, and the great-granddaughter of King Clovis. Bertha had remained Christian after her marriage to Ethelbert, but she had not attempted to influence her husband in the manner that her ancestors St. Clotilda and Ingund had influenced theirs. When St. Augustine and his monks arrived, Ethelbert, though he had heard of Christianity, was still pagan. He received the monks quite openly, but he did not convert immediately. He gave them freedom to preach the Catholic Faith and to win over as many willing converts as possible. Ethelbert also gave them a dwelling in Canterbury, his capital. Nevertheless, Ethelbert for some time remained set in his ways.

On Christmas Day in 597, more than ten thousand Saxons were baptized in Canterbury. Accounts conflict on precisely when Ethelbert was baptized—some say before that Christmas, some say four years later. Soon Christianity was rapidly spreading throughout England. St. Augustine was presented with a palace in Canterbury, which became the most important episcopal see in England. Monasteries quickly spread over the land, and St. Augustine ordered that all pagan temples be converted into Christian churches. Though the Celts and the Saxons now shared the same religion, their mutual antagonism unfortunately persisted.

Pope St. Gregory named St. Augustine the Primate Bishop of England in 601 and sent him the pallium, a sign of authority and papal favor. In its current form the pallium is a circular band of white woolen material with two hanging strips and six black crosses, and is worn around the neck on the shoulders. The wool for the pallium comes from wool blessed by the pope on the feast of St. Agnes in Rome. Before it is placed on an archbishop on the Feast of Sts. Peter and Paul, the pallium rests for one night on the tomb of St. Peter in St. Peter's Basilica.

St. Augustine consecrated others to the episcopacy and sent them to other centers in England, including Rochester and London. Upon his death in the first decade of the seventh century, St. Augustine had secured such a strong foundation of Christianity that England would serve as a venue for a Christian renaissance in the early middle ages. His feast day is celebrated on May 27.

THE MISSION IN ENGLAND CONTINUES

An unrivaled string of missionaries and scholars emerged from England because of the vision, faith, and dedicated labor of Pope St. Gregory the Great and St. Augustine of Canterbury.

After many trials and setbacks, Christianity eventually spread to the rest of the six other kingdoms in England. Paganism would not disappear so easily. Even if one king did convert, his successor could, and sometimes did, revert to paganism. By 633 there had been a steady regression to old pagan ways, except in Kent. At this critical juncture, the Irish supplemented a deeper and more widespread work of evangelization among the English.

St. Augustine wearing his pallium.

Through the missionary work of the Irish over the next several decades, the Catholic Faith became firmly established in England by 655, the year that the first native Englishman became Archbishop of Canterbury, St. Deusdedit.

South of the Thames River, Christianity of a more Roman tradition predominated due to the mission of St. Augustine. However, the Roman and Celtic traditions clashed, especially over the question of when to celebrate Easter. The Synod of Whitby (664), held in the kingdom of Northumbria in England, sought to reconcile the two divergent traditions. At the synod, St. Wilfrid (634-709), later Bishop of York, led the party that was pushing in favor of the Roman tradition. With this finally accomplished, the English accepted the Roman tradition's practice of the observance of Easter and the Benedictine form of monasticism. The Irish monks eventually withdrew to a Celtic monastery on the island of Iona and to other monasteries in Ireland proper.

Over time, the Church in England became especially united to the papacy. Of all the areas of Europe that had so far converted, England identified most closely with the Church of Rome. This set the stage for English missionary activity in Germany and the Low Countries, as well as for the development of scholarship in England through the emergence of many Benedictine monasteries. England became the strongest supporter of Benedictine monasticism.

ST. BEDE: THE "FATHER OF ENGLISH HISTORY"

They [St. Willibrord and his companions] arrived there, twelve in number, and turning aside to Pepin, duke of the Franks, were graciously received by him; and as he had lately subdued the Hither Frisland, and expelled King Rathbed, he sent them thither to preach, supporting them at the same time with his authority, that none might molest them in their preaching, and bestowing many favors on those who consented to embrace the faith. Thus it came to pass, that with the assistance of the Divine grace, they in a short time converted many from idolatry to the faith of Christ. (St. Bede, *Ecclesiastical History of the English People*, V.X)

St. Bede (ca. 673-735) was the most important Anglo-Saxon scholar of his time, and much of his scholarly work became standard subject matter in the Medieval curriculum. St. Bede represents the finest example of the role played by the English monasteries as centers of learning in the seventh and eighth centuries. This is especially remarkable when one considers that in 590, upon the ascension of Pope St. Gregory the Great to the throne of St. Peter, England was a pagan and unconverted land.

Little is known of the life of St. Bede other than what he records at the end of his great *Ecclesiastical History of the English People*. He writes:

Thus much of the Ecclesiastical History of Britain, and more especially of the English nation, as far as I could learn either from the writings of the ancients, or the tradition of our ancestors, or of my own knowledge, has, with the help of God, been digested by me, Bede, the servant of God, and priest of the monastery of the blessed apostles, Peter and Paul, which is at Wearmouth and Jarrow; who being born in the territory of that same monastery, was given, at seven years of age, to be educated by the most reverend Abbot Benedict, and afterwards by Ceolfrid; and spending all the remaining time of my life in that monastery, I wholly applied myself to the study of Scripture, and amidst the observance of regular discipline, and the daily care of singing in the church, I always took delight in learning, teaching, and writing. In the nineteenth year of my age, I received deacon's orders; in the thirtieth, those of the priesthood, both of them by the ministry of the most reverend Bishop John, and by the order of the Abbot Ceolfrid. From which time, till the fifty-ninth year of my age, I have made it my business, for the use of me and mine, to compile out of the works of the venerable Fathers, and to interpret and explain according to their meaning these following pieces. (*Ecclesiastical History of the English People*, V.XXIV)

Following the last lines of this excerpt is an extensive list of works covering a wide variety of topics. St. Bede was a dedicated and prolific scholar. St. Bede's guiding principle for all his scholarly works is expressed in the perennial question: How can one clearly communicate a particular body of knowledge to students? His works covered topics that included Latin grammar and poetry, astronomy and the tides, chronology, a biography of St. Cuthbert, commentaries on many books of the Bible, and history. His *Ecclesiastical History of the English People* places the Roman Catholic Church at the foundation of the development of English culture.

St. Bede's *Ecclesiastical History of the English People* places the Roman Catholic Church at the foundation of the development of English culture. The manuscript shown above is the front cover of this masterpiece completed in 731 which is the primary source of historical reference for this period.

In his commentaries on the Bible, St. Bede preferred clear exposition and found no use for philosophical speculation. He based his spirituality and scholarship on the biblical-patristic tradition. Through the Scythian monk Dionysius Exiguus (fifth-sixth centuries), St. Bede did the mathematical computations for the B.C./A.D. distinction, and his work utilized the Christian measurement of time and made it popular throughout Europe.

Within a century of his death, St. Bede was given the title "Venerable," and in 1899 Pope Leo XIII declared him a "Doctor of the Church." The title "Venerable" generally denotes a particular stage in the canonization process, but it can also simply refer to a person's holy life, as was the case with St. Bede. His feast day is celebrated on May 25.

Unfortunately, one of St. Bede's fears that he recorded at the end of his *Ecclesiastical History of the English People* came to pass. After 800 the Church in England suffered a great decline. Again, the Vikings were a factor—they destroyed the important monastery at Jarrow at the end of the eighth century. In addition, the English kings failed to achieve a strong unity among their people. Finally, England contributed some of its greatest evangelizers, like St. Boniface, for the evangelization of the Germanic peoples of Freisland. Despite such a flourishing of sanctity and Christian culture in the seventh and eighth centuries, England would suffer great spiritual decline during the years from 800 to 1000. By 1000 England was considered backward, thereby losing her momentum in deepening and spreading Catholic culture.

PART V

The Conversion of Germany and the Low Countries

The conversion of the lands that have become Germany was a long and arduous task. Some of the small Roman cities, such as Cologne, were evangelized during the time of the Roman Empire. Beginning in the seventh century, English missionaries played a pivotal role in carrying on missionary activities, especially in northwest and central Germany, north of the Mainz River. Groups of Germanic tribes were still being converted along the Baltic Sea long after the beginning of the second millennium, even as the German church focused much of its energies on converting the Slavs.

ST. WILLIBRORD: THE "APOSTLE OF FRISIA"

St. Willibrord (658-739) was one of the earliest Anglo-Saxon missionaries to evangelize in the Germanic lands. His work is notable for two reasons. First, he was successful in converting the peoples of western Frisia (the northwest corner of Germany along the North Sea and part of the Netherlands). Secondly, he secured papal approval and support for his mission, demonstrating the important connection between the expansion of Christianity and the papacy.

St. Willibrord successfully converted many of the Frisians; but in 714, his entire evangelizing project was compromised when the Carolingian (modern-day French) emperor Pepin died and a pagan Frisian king reconquered the territory. St. Willibrord and his companions then fled to a secure monastery in Luxemburg. St. Willibrord then continued his work in Denmark, Heligoland (an island in the North Sea), and Thuringia (central Germany). In 693, St. Willibrord made his first visit to Rome, where he obtained papal support for his mission. During a second trip to Rome in 695, Pope St. Sergius I made him Archbishop of the Frisians. His feast day is celebrated on November 7.

ST. BONIFACE: THE "APOSTLE OF GERMANY"

> In her voyage across the ocean of this world, the Church is like a great ship being pounded by the waves of life's different stresses. Our duty is not to abandon ship but to keep her on her course. (St. Boniface, *Ep.* 78: MGH, *Epistolæ*, 3, 352. 354)

St. Boniface (ca. 675-754) set the stage for a radical reshaping of the heart of Europe. Before his arrival on the continent, conversion efforts among the Germans had failed. Not only did St. Boniface succeed in converting the Germans, he also laid the foundation of a church based on a monastic model that would continue to flower for the next three centuries. He also revitalized the deteriorating practice of the Faith among the Franks.

St. Boniface was born with the name Winfrid, most likely somewhere in Wessex, England. Like St. Bede, he also entered a Benedictine monastery at the age of seven. By temperament he was unsteady, timid, and tended to discouragement and despair. However, St. Boniface matured into a brilliant pupil and eventually became a teacher and the head of the monastic school.

St. Boniface loved his homeland tremendously, but he discerned a call from God to leave England and evangelize the German people. Therefore, in 716 he left for Frisia to begin his work of evangelizing the Germanic tribes. Since the Frisians had received Catholic teachings of St. Willibrord with mixed results, St. Boniface hoped to bring the Frisians fully into the Church.

St. Boniface's tendency to discouragement seemed to have reappeared when he met formidable obstacles in Frisia over the next couple years. He researched the lives of the early Christians to see if any of the saints were exempt from suffering, and to his dismay he found no exceptions. St. Boniface struggled to be courageous and thus looked upon the most ferocious barbarians as his brothers.

His temptations towards despair were so great that St. Boniface felt compelled to consult with the reigning pope, St. Gregory II (715-32). St. Boniface believed that he had failed in his missionary efforts in Frisia, and he sought the pope's counsel: Should he return to England or persevere in Frisia? Pope St. Gregory II was so impressed with Winfrid's sanctity that he gave Winfrid a new Latin name, Boniface—from the Latin words *Bona Facere*, meaning "doer of good"—which symbolized his favor with the pope. By this action Pope St. Gregory II also made St. Boniface his personal papal legate to Germany.

The pagan god Thor

Upon his return to Germany, St. Boniface turned his attention south of Frisia to Hesse and the conversion of the Hessians. On a second trip to Rome in 722, the pope consecrated St. Boniface to the episcopacy. Around 732 Pope St. Gregory III (731-741) sent the pallium to St. Boniface.

After he felled the Oak of Thor (Wata), the sacred tree of the pagans of Hesse, St. Boniface gained so much moral authority that he enjoyed a new-found freedom to establish a string of monasteries. Cutting down the tree brought many converts into the Church when the pagan people saw that Thor did not strike St. Boniface down with a thunderbolt. Out of the wood of the tree St. Boniface made a small chapel dedicated to St. Peter.

Much of St. Boniface's work was accomplished during the reign of Charles Martel, whose renown blossomed after he defeated the Muslims at Tours in 732. In a letter, St. Boniface wrote about his special relationship with the temporal ruler who proved so vital and necessary for his missionary work:

> Without the protection of the prince of the Franks [Charles Martel], I can neither rule the people of the church nor defend the priests and clerks, monks and nuns; nor can I prevent the practice of pagan rites and sacrilegious worship of idols without his mandate and awe inspired by his name.

During a third trip to Rome in 736, St. Boniface was made Archbishop of Mainz. When he returned to Germany, St. Boniface founded many more monasteries, the most important of which was located in the city of Fulda (744). St. Boniface planned that the monastery at Fulda would serve as a center for conversion and spiritual renewal and a training facility for priests and missionaries.

At this time, St. Boniface spent much energy building the ecclesiastical structure of the Church in Germany by establishing dioceses in a number of cities. Moreover, he initiated an extensive reform in those lands ruled by the Franks. The practice of the Faith had weakened there, and the clergy and bishops had become notoriously corrupt. In cooperation with the sovereign, Karlmann, the successor to Charles Martel in Austrasia (the eastern portion of the kingdom of the Franks), St. Boniface convened a German synod in 742 which resulted in an effective plan for the reform of the Frankish church.

It was St. Boniface's great dream to return to the mission land of his youth, Frisia. Though seventy-six years old, he set out from Mainz with fifty other monks and sailed down the Rhine to Frisia.

TREES IN GERMAN MYTHOLOGY

After St. Boniface felled the Oak of Thor, he was respected everywhere among the German peoples, and his new authority allowed him the freedom to begin the work of the Church in the region that had previously seemed so difficult to Christianize. Why was this simple act—chopping down a tree—such a monumental event in the conversion of the Germans?

For the Germans, some of the oldest sanctuaries were the natural woods. These sacred spaces were places for tree-worship, and as Sir James George Frazer says in his study in mythology: "How serious that worship was in former times may be gathered from the ferocious penalty appointed by the old German laws for such as dared to peel the bark of a standing tree. The culprit's navel was to be cut out and nailed to the part of the tree which he had peeled, and he was to be driven round and round the tree till all his guts were wound about the trunk. The intention of the punishment clearly was to replace the dead bark by a living substitute taken from the culprit; it was a life for a life, the life of a man for the life of a tree." (Frazer, *The Golden Bough*, 1922, Ch. 9, Section 1, Paragraph 2)

The severity of this punishment seems ridiculous, but for German pagans, the tree was central to their understanding of mankind. According to some legends, two gods, one from the land of ice and mist and one from the land of fire, created the first man and woman from two trees. The universe was also supported by a great tree, whose roots and branches extended into the heavens, the earth, and the underworld. Near the roots of this tree, a fountain produced sacred waters to which all the wisdom of the world was attributed. Fate lived near another root and was associated with the importance of the tree. Fate was a very important concept in Germanic religion because both gods and humans were subject to it.

The tree was the center of the Germanic pagan world. When St. Boniface chopped down the tree and survived, he seemed to possess a power greater than that of the German gods. When the saint preached about Christ, who was both true God and true man, and who died for the remission of sins by being nailed to a tree, many Germans began to believe. Despite converting from paganism to Christianity, the tree (in the form of a devotion to Christ's passion and the crucifix) remained central to the German sense of the sacred.

St. Boniface felled the Oak of Thor.

There at Dorkum he and his comrades were martyred by the pagans. His body was returned to Fulda for burial.

St. Boniface converted German pagans, founded monasteries, established the ecclesiastical structure of the Church in Germany, and reformed the Church in the lands under Frankish rule. The religious fervor of the German monasteries that he founded in the eighth century was still robust in the tenth and eleventh centuries. Like their Irish and English counterparts before them, the German monasteries became important centers of learning with their libraries and scriptoria. They were aided, in part, by the *privilegium* that St. Boniface won for them from the papacy. With this papal privilege (*privilegium*) the monasteries were exempted from local diocesan control and answered directly to the papacy. In succeeding decades, Benedictine monasteries took an active part in imbuing the Carolingian dynasty with a strong Catholic culture that reached a high point under Charlemagne. St. Boniface's feast day is celebrated on June 5.

The Battle of Poitiers. Charles Martel (Martel means "the Hammer") is best remembered for winning the Battle of Poitiers (also known as the Battle of Tours) in 732, has been characterized as the salvation of Europe, stopping the spread of the Arab (Islam) empire further than the Iberian Peninsula (Spain and Portugal). Martel's Frankish army defeated a skilled Arab army, which had swept through southern Asia and North Africa, before conquering most of the Iberian Peninsula and much of southern France. It was this battle that earned Charles the surname "Martel" for the harsh way he conquered his enemy. Most historians believe that had he failed at Tours, Islam would probably have overrun Europe. Although it took another two generations for the Franks to drive all the Arab garrisons out of what is now France and across the Pyrenees, Charles Martel's halt of the invasion of French soil turned the tide of Islamic advance, and unified the Frankish kingdom under Charles Martel. His son Pepin the Short, and his grandson Charlemagne also fought to prevent the Muslim kingdom from expanding over the Pyrenees to the rest of Europe.

PART VI
Conversion of Scandinavia

Just as England supplied the missionaries for the conversion of German peoples, they in turn provided missionaries for the evangelization of Scandinavia and the Slavs—though Anglo-Saxon missionaries were also active in Scandinavia for some time.

ST. ANSGAR: THE "APOSTLE OF THE NORTH"

Every disciple of Christ is responsible in his own measure for the spread of the faith, but Christ the Lord is always calling from among his followers those whom he will, so that they may be with him and be sent by him to preach to the nations. (St. Ansgar, *Ad gentes*, IV.23)

St. Ansgar (801-865) was born in the part of the Carolingian empire that would include modern France. When he was of age, he became a monk and spent time in northwest Germany before moving on to his missionary work in Denmark and Sweden, where he built the first Christian church.

Pope Gregory IV made St. Ansgar Bishop of Hamburg, and later he was named the Archbishop of Bremen. In 854 he successfully converted Erik, king of Jutland. He worked with Erik to improve the conditions of the slave trade. Unfortunately, upon his death, all of his work crumbled as the converted Scandinavians returned to paganism. St. Ansgar's feast day is celebrated on February 3, and he is amicably known among the Scandinavians as St. Oscar.

DENMARK

St. Ansgar was invited to Denmark by a defeated Danish chieftain, Harold. Harold sought the aid of Louis the Pious, the son of Charlemagne, in order to regain his position in Denmark. Louis the Pious agreed, on condition that Harold be baptized and start to promote Christianity. Harold complied, was baptized, and set off for Denmark with St. Ansgar to recover it by force. Harold was decisively defeated, and St. Ansgar moved on to other missionary fields.

A century after St. Ansgar's death, another Danish king, Harold Bluetooth accepted Baptism in 965, upon the influence of his wife Gunheld. A short time later the Danish ruler Cnut the Great (1014-1035) declared Christianity the established religion in Denmark.

SWEDEN

Christianity's progress in Sweden was difficult at first, as it had been in Denmark. St. Ansgar's initial efforts failed, as did later attempts until the English Bishop Siegfried baptized King Olaf III around the year 1000. In 1078, the pagan temple at Uppsala was destroyed after the Christian chieftain Inge defeated the pagan chieftain Svend. Not until the early twelfth century was the Christianization of Sweden completed.

ST. OLAF: PATRON SAINT OF NORWAY

The evangelization of Norway began around the middle of the tenth century. In those years, a series of kings favorable to Christianity and hard-working Anglo-Saxon monks brought Christianity to Norway.

The first of those Christian kings, Haakan the Good (938-961), received his education in England before ascending the throne. At his request, English monks went to Norway to teach the Catholic Faith to the population. Pagan successors to Haakan, however, left the emerging Norwegian Christianity vulnerable. During the brief reign of St. Olaf Tryggvason (995-999), the establishment of the Church seemed to have solidified. Unfortunately, Tryggvason purportedly employed a variety of grossly inhumane methods of coercion in establishing Christianity as the official religion of Norway.

The reign of St. Olaf (995?-1030, king 1016-1028), who was baptized in Rouen, France, marks the end of pagan opposition in Norway. In sharp contrast to Tryggvason's barbaric enforcement of Christianity, St. Olaf ruled his people and spread Christianity with a civil but stern hand. He invited English and German missionaries to come during his reign, and he destroyed many of the old pagan temples and erected churches over their sites. Together with pagan beliefs, traditional political institutions and practices began to disappear. Consequently, the old clans began losing power as St. Olaf guided Norway away from a conglomeration of independent clans toward a more unified kingdom. The growing resentment of the clans exploded in 1028, and St. Olaf was deposed and exiled. When he attempted to regain his throne in 1030, nobles from various clans aligned themselves with Canute the Great of Denmark. St. Olaf perished in the battle, and within a year he was proclaimed a saint. His shrine at Trondheim was a significant pilgrimage site during the Medieval period. St. Olaf's feast day is celebrated on July 29.

ICELAND

Missionaries reached Iceland from Norway around 980. Twenty years later the ruling tribal council, known as the Althing (the Icelanders lived in a kingless society), accepted Christianity. Christianity was not foreign to them when the missionaries arrived since Irish Christian slaves had been brought to the island, and some of the native aristocracy had already converted to Christianity. The missionary work proceeded slowly at first until 996, when Stefnir Thorgilsson, a missionary commissioned by St. Olaf Tryggvason, arrived on the island. Though they were deeply troubled by the high-handed measures that St. Olaf Tryggvason had imposed on the independent farmers in the Trondelag, many of the Icelanders soon converted.

In the year 1000, the Althing authorized the Law Speaker, Thorgeir of Ljosvatn, to decide for the island whether it would become Christian. After an entire night spent in prayer, Thorgeir, who was a pagan, declared himself for Christ. Thus, Iceland maintained its unity by becoming Christian. Paganism was suppressed, and over the next fifty years, through much labor and teaching, Christianity spread throughout the island. In 1056, Iceland received its own bishop.

FINLAND AND ST. HENRY OF UPPSALA

The origin of Christianity in Finland is not as clear as in the other Scandinavian countries. It appears to have arrived later than in other Scandinavian countries—probably in the twelfth century. Again, the English missionaries led the way.

St. Henry of Uppsala, a bishop and Englishman, was a major evangelizer of Finland. By 1220 the Church was established under the guidance of Bishop Thomas, probably another Englishman. Finland, unlike Frisia in Germany or Denmark, is a considerable distance from the British Isles. The presence of English missionaries in Finland attests to their continuing, deep religious convictions, courage, and missionary zeal. St. Henry is the patron saint of Finland.

PART VII

The Conversion of the Slavs

Central and Eastern Europe were the scenes of competing missionary tensions and interests. German missionaries converted the rest of Germany and Poland, while Greek missionaries evangelized much of Eastern Europe. The conversion of the Bohemians (Czechs), Moravians (Slovaks), Slovenes, Croats, and Poles was directed from Rome; the Serbs, Bulgarians, Ruthenians (Ukrainians), and Russians received Christianity from Constantinople.

STS. CYRIL AND METHODIUS: THE "APOSTLES OF THE SLAVS"

Inspire the hearts of your people with your word and your teaching. You called us to preach the Gospel of your Christ and to encourage them to lives and works pleasing to you. (A prayer of St. Cyril, just before his death, Cap. 18: *Denkschriften der kaiserl. Akademie der Wissenschaften*, 19 [*Wien* 1870], p. 246)

Two brothers, Sts. Cyril (827-869) and Methodius (826-885), were the first missionaries among the Slavs. They were from a senatorial Greek family in Thessalonica. Rather than continuing with their family's secular activities, St. Cyril (who originally bore the name Constantine) and St. Methodius entered the priesthood. St. Cyril, a man of great intellectual ability, joined the philosophy faculty at the university in Constantinople. St. Cyril then gave up a promising career in scholarship, and undertook a mission to the Khazars in south Russia. Then, in 863, Emperor Michael III commissioned the brothers as missionaries to Moravia (Slovakia).

The brothers knew the difficult Slavic language quite well—Thessalonica was surrounded by Slavic settlements and was itself populated by a fair number of Slavs. Before their departure, St. Cyril developed the Glagolithic script for use with the Slavs. (The Cyrillic alphabet, which bears St. Cyril's name, is a later development of his original Glagolithic alphabet. Both alphabets are rooted in Greek.) Use of the Glagolithic script ceased and gave way to Cyrillic after the 1100s, except in Croatia, where it was used until around 1900.

During their missionary work, Sts. Cyril and Methodius used the vernacular Slavonic language for the celebration of the liturgy and translated the Bible into Slavonic, using the new Glagolithic alphabet. Though their innovative use of the vernacular proved a vital tool in reaching many people with Christ's message, German missionaries were offended by Sts. Cyril and Methodius' use of Slavonic instead of Latin in the liturgy, and denounced them to the pope as heretics.

In order to clarify the situation, Sts. Cyril and Methodius went to Rome for guidance from Pope St. Nicholas I (858-867). St. Nicholas died before their arrival, but Pope Adrian II (867-872), his successor, received them warmly in 868 and granted them permission to use Slavonic in the liturgy. St. Cyril made his final vows as a monk, but died in Rome before being able to return to Moravia. Pope Adrian II made St. Methodius Bishop of the Moravians, and St. Methodius continued his evangelizing mission.

The Glagolithic Alphabet							
✝	Ⰱ	ⰞⰞ	℀	ⱇ	Ⲫ	ⰽ	⚓
a	b	v	g	d	ε	ž	dz
ⰑⰒ	Ⰽ	ⰞⰞ	Ⰹ	ⱀ	ⰔⰔ	ⰞⰞ	Ⱂ
z	i	i	ǵ	k	l	m	n
Ⱁ	Ⱂ	Ƅ	Ⱎ	⫟	ⰔⰔⱀ	φ	ⱈ
ɔ	p	r	s	t	u	f	x (kh)
Ⱁ	Ⰲ	Ⱈ	Ш	Ⱋ	Ⱅ	ⰕⰞⰞ	Ⱅ
ɔ	ts	č	š	št	w/ə	ɨ	y
⚠	ⰳ	ⰼ€	ⰴ€	ⰺ€	ⰶ€	⚓	ⱁ
æ/e	yu	ε̃	yε̃	ɔ̃	yɔ̃	f	i/v

In spite of papal support, St. Methodius was arrested by German missionaries and held in captivity for three years upon his return to Moravia. The Germans, who were harsh and forceful with the Slavs, scourged and denounced St. Methodius yet again. Pope John VIII eventually secured St. Methodius' release. The Holy Father reaffirmed the use of the Slavonic language, though he later distanced himself from St. Methodius' work, as did later popes because of miscommunication and political intrigue. Because later popes refused to recognize the use of Slavonic, many Slavs turned away from Rome to Constantinople.

By the time St. Methodius died in 885, all of Moravia was converted. In 1980 Pope John Paul II named the brothers "Patrons of Europe." The feast day of Sts. Cyril and Methodius is February 14.

STS. LUDMILLA AND WENCESLAUS: PATRON SAINTS OF THE CZECH REPUBLIC

St. Methodius' work extended indirectly to Bohemia. In 871, St. Methodius baptized St. Ludmilla (d. 927) and her husband, Duke Borzwoi (who thus became the first Christian duke of Bohemia). The holy St. Ludmilla worked to spread the Faith among the Bohemian people. Borzwoi soon passed his power on to his son Wratislaw, who had married a pagan woman named Drahomira who had feigned conversion. Drahomira bore twin sons, Wenceslaus and Boleslaus. St. Wenceslaus lived with his grandmother St. Ludmilla, and when his father passed away, the duchy passed to him. Drahomira, jealous and frightened of her Christian mother-in-law's influence over her son, had St. Ludmilla murdered by two noblemen. Before her murder, St. Ludmilla had replicated a model often used in the conversion of the different ethnic groups of Europe: conversion of the ruling family through the influence of a Christian woman, and the subsequent conversion of the subjects. St. Ludmilla's feast day is celebrated on September 16.

Drahomira took control of the duchy and attempted a reversion to paganism. The people of Bohemia opposed Drahomira's violence and her attempted revival of paganism, and they managed

THE CHURCH OF SAN CLEMENTE IN ROME

When St. Cyril died in Rome, he was buried in the Basilica of San Clemente, and his tomb became a place of pilgrimage for many Slavic Catholics. In additional to being buried there, St. Cyril made another great contribution to San Clemente during his life. Around 861 the Emperor Michael III sent both Sts. Cyril and Methodius to work with the Khazars northeast of the Black Sea into an area now a part of Russia. While there, they are believed to have found the relics of St. Clement I, the fourth pope, in the Crimean Sea. St. Cyril brought these remains back to Rome to be interred in San Clemente, the Church bearing his name.

The present San Clemente was built in the twelfth century upon the remains of a similar basilica erected in the fourth century and is one of only a handful of Medieval Churches remaining in Rome. Besides some exceptional mosaics which have been recently restored, San Clemente also contains a fresco depicting both St. Cyril and his brother St. Methodius. Both Sts. Cyril and Methodius are buried in San Clemente.

to have her overthrown. St. Wenceslaus, though only about fourteen years old at the time, became duke. The young duke moved quickly to suppress the near feudal anarchy that plagued Bohemia. He turned to Germany for protection, and both political and religious support. The lingering pagan populace and many of the Bohemians in general resented this relationship with Germany and movements toward internal unification. These tensions and the insidious promptings of his deposed mother inspired his brother Boleslaus to commit fratricide in 935, killing St. Wenceslaus on his way to Mass. Boleslaus later repented and converted to Christianity, and he transferred the relics of his brother St. Wenceslaus to Prague. Quickly, the Bohemians recognized the sanctity of St. Wenceslaus, and throughout Bohemia he became an object of veneration and popular piety. Otto the Great of the Holy Roman Empire compelled Boleslaus to reinstate Christianity, and Boleslaus' son, Boleslaus II made Christianity the religion of the Bohemians. The feast day of St. Wenceslaus is celebrated on September 28.

ST. ADALBERT OF PRAGUE: THE "APOSTLE OF THE PRUSSIANS"

St. Adalbert (939-997), born Vojtiekh, is another key figure in the conversion of the Slavs. He worked among the Bohemians, the Hungarians, and the Poles, and faced difficult opposition from pagans and even from members of the Church. He was born of a noble Bohemian family and studied in Magdeburg under a German archbishop of the same name. Eventually he was named Bishop of Prague. (The German city Magdeburg was given the status of an archdiocese specifically for missionary activity among the Slavs.)

Twice St. Adalbert fled Prague because of the hostility he engendered on account of his clerical reforms. In both instances, St. Adalbert went to Rome to seek counsel from the pope. It was during his time away from Prague (ca. 996) that St. Adalbert became the confessor of the teenage Holy Roman Emperor Otto III. St. Adalbert made a deep impact on the young Otto III through his Christian example and teaching.

After he fled a second time from Prague, St. Adalbert went to Hungary as a missionary, where he most likely baptized the Hungarian leader Geysa and his son, Stephen. Subsequent missionary journeys took him to Poland and to Prussia. The pagan Prussians martyred him in 997. Boeleslav I (the Brave) of Poland, who had worked with St. Adalbert during his missionary work, had such high regard for St. Adalbert that it has been said that he purchased St. Adalbert's remains for an equivalent weight of gold. Later, when Otto III visited St. Adalbert's grave at Gniezno, he granted ecclesiastical independence to the Polish church from the Germans. The Holy See also recognized this independence. St. Adalbert's feast day is celebrated on April 23. He is revered by the Slavs and the Germans.

POLAND

Christianity most likely arrived in Poland in the tenth century through Moravian refugees who fled north to Poland during the Hungarian invasion. German monks were also intent on converting Poland. Though there was no organized Church, the presence of Christianity among the pagan

Otto III Enthroned. St. Adalbert became the confessor of the teenage Holy Roman Emperor Otto III. St. Adalbert made a deep impact on the young Otto III through his Christian example and teaching.

Poles made the official transition smooth and peaceful. A Polish noble, Duke Mieszko (962-992) was the first Polish ruler to encourage his subjects to become Christian. He had married St. Dubravka, the daughter of Boleslaus I of Bohemia, and, consistent with the familiar model, it was under her Christian influence that Mieszko converted.

In 973 Duke Mieszko and St. Dubravka placed their seven-year-old son, Boleslav Chrobry the Brave, in the care of Otto II for his education. Duke Mieszko sent a locket of his son's hair to the pope to show that he considered his son to be under the special protection of the papacy. In 992 Mieszko placed all of Poland at the service of the Holy See, thus making Poland a vassal land of the popes. Thus began a unique relationship between the Polish people and the papacy—one that proved essential for the survival of the Polish people in the many difficult centuries ahead.

ST. STEPHEN THE GREAT, KING OF HUNGARY

> Be merciful to all who are suffering violence, keeping always in your heart the example of the Lord who said: I desire mercy and not sacrifice. Be patient with everyone, not only with the powerful but also with the weak. (St. Stephen to his son, St. Emeric, on the exercise of royal power, Cap. 1. 2. 10: PL 151, 1236-1237, 1242-1244)

The Hungarians were an Asian nomadic tribe who were decisively defeated by Otto I (the Great) in 995 at the Battle of Lech. Afterwards they were a sedentary and peasant people who became open to the Gospel. Hungarian prisoners in Germany drew the interest and attention of German missionaries, who succeeded in obtaining permission to evangelize Hungary. St. Adalbert of Prague was instrumental in leading Hungary along the path of conversion.

St. Stephen (975-1038) became the ruler of Hungary in 997, and later its first king. In 985 he had become a Christian with his father, Duke Geza, when they had been baptized by St. Adalbert of Prague. Geza's wife, Sarolta, was already a Christian of the Byzantine rite, though she pointedly welcomed Latin rite missionaries into Hungary.

St. Stephen faced a difficult revolt from pagan opposition within one year of ascending to the throne. He successfully put down the rebellion, and immediately set about building up the Church in Hungary, establishing dioceses and monasteries. Like Duke Mieszko, St. Stephen placed Hungary into the hands of the papacy. In 1001 he received a royal crown from the pope, which was also recognized by the Holy Roman Emperor, Otto III. St. Stephen's feast day is celebrated on August 16.

ST. VLADIMIR: THE "APOSTLE OF THE RUSSIANS AND UKRAINIANS"

Russia's introduction to Christianity begins with St. Olga (ca. 980-969), the wife of the pagan Prince Igor of Russia. She had embraced Christianity in Constantinople in 945. However, there were many obstacles for missionaries in Russia, a land dominated by ancient Viking traditions and practices. Paganism was widespread, and many of the practices included polygamy and human sacrifice (e.g., slave girls were brutally murdered so as to join their dead masters during the pagan funeral rites).

The story of the conversion of Russia is inseparable from the story of St. Vladimir (d. 1015). The life of the man responsible for the Christianization of Russia itself parallels the country's miraculous movement from barbaric paganism to Christianity. St. Vladimir was the grandson of St. Olga, but her Christianity had not passed down to her descendants. She had been unable to convert her son Sviatoslav (St. Vladimir's father), and Sviatoslav raised his son St. Vladimir to be a pagan chieftain in the tradition of the Viking culture from which Sviatoslav was descended. St. Vladimir had two brothers, Yaropolk and Oleg, who, upon their father's death, controlled Kiev and Drevlani, respectively, and St. Vladimir was the leader of Novgorod. Yaropolk turned on Oleg and defeated him, seizing control of most of Russia. He then marched on Novgorod and St. Vladimir, who fled to Scandinavia. For a short while, Yaropolk controlled all of Russia. St. Vladimir soon returned with a great force and not only retook Novgorod, but also pushed all the way to Kiev, where he defeated and killed his brother. St. Vladimir then ruled all Russia (980) and lived a very typical pagan life — he had five wives and twelve children, he erected many idols and shrines to pagan gods, and he was a ruthless ruler.

He eventually set his sights on the Greco-Roman empire, and as he was planning his campaign, he began to take a slight interest in Christianity. St. Vladimir never stopped looking for ways to strengthen his rule, so much so that he even began to survey, compare, and contrast Islam, Judaism, and both Latin and Byzantine Christianity to see if any of these foreign religions would solidify his rule. St. Vladimir sent emissaries to investigate the three monotheistic faiths. The emissaries are said to have found both Islam and Judaism rather unedifying, though the Latin rite they thought suitable. During the Byzantine Divine Liturgy at Hagia Sophia in Constantinople, the emissaries "knew not whether they were in Heaven or on earth." They reported their findings to St. Vladimir, who was aware that his grandmother Olga had accepted this same Byzantine Christianity. Christianity had faintly entered his mind, though for purely utilitarian purposes.

The Byzantine emperor, Basil II, found himself in need of aid in the late 980s. He faced two internal rebellions, and St. Vladimir had suddenly appeared, dangerously close to Constantinople. The

Vladimir and Rogneda by Anton Losenko. As a pagan chieftain, Vladimir took the royal Norsewoman Rogneda by force to be his wife after he learned she was betrothed to his brother Yaropolk. To eliminate witnesses, he had her parents and brothers killed. She bore Vladimir several children.

emperor finally made a military deal with St. Vladimir (St. Vladimir proposed the terms): the Russian would take Basil's sister Anna in marriage (or else he would march on Constantinople), and in return St. Vladimir would provide the hard-pressed emperor with 6,000 Viking warriors to put down the rebellions. The Byzantines were shocked that a pagan and virtual barbarian would dare to ask for the hand of a Byzantine princess in marriage. Basil had very few other options, and therefore agreed, but only on the condition that his sister would be marrying a Christian. As St. Vladimir was familiar with Christianity and had been considering Baptism, this condition proved to be no problem. Around 989 St. Vladimir was baptized, and he and Anna were married.

The conditions under which St. Vladimir came to be baptized and the situation of his entire life prior to that point certainly suggest that he merely assented to Basil's request, treating Baptism as a formality rather than as the sacrament of Faith. But the radical changes that followed upon St. Vladimir's Baptism instead suggest the powerful work of Grace moving in a man who truly understood Baptism and desired faith. No influential priest aided in his conversion, and his new bride was yet terrified of her new Viking husband, his lands, and his people. With the same deliberate and pragmatic will that had been previously aimed at building up a pagan kingdom, St. Vladimir then focused on living as a serious follower of Christ. He dismissed his five wives for Anna. He tore down the same idols and shrines he himself had erected years before, and he built churches in their places. He also established a number of monasteries and Christian schools. Zealously wishing to follow the examples in the Gospels, he threw huge banquets for the poor and even sent wagonloads of food to the sick who could not get to the banquets. St. Vladimir focused relentlessly on converting his people. The Christian Viking was still a Viking, and he made Baptism compulsory—though many were quite willing to be baptized. By the time of his death in 1015, St. Vladimir had firmly established the Christian Faith throughout Russia. His feast day is celebrated on July 15.

BULGARIA: A DIFFERENT PATH

Christianity developed differently and separately in Bulgaria. The Faith reached the Bulgarians when King Boris was baptized in 864/5; he had feared that Bulgaria would be the last pagan land. At this time the Bulgarians also ruled what is today Romania. Boris was at first oriented toward Constantinople, but it is clear that he feared political and religious domination from the Byzantine emperors. For some time Byzantine and German missionaries worked among the people of Bulgaria.

The baptism of King Boris of Bulgaria.

In 866 Boris turned to Rome. He wrote Pope St. Nicholas I a letter containing 106 questions about how to handle Bulgaria's transition from paganism to Christianity. Pope St. Nicholas I answered all of the questions, clearly delineating those pagan customs that conflicted with Christianity. Pagan traditions that contradicted doctrinal and moral teaching of the Church would be abolished. Pagan practices that did not endanger or contradict the Catholic Faith would be kept as part of the Bulgarian culture. Along with these directives, the pope also sent a bishop to Boris. In the end, Boris wanted a separate patriarchate, but the pope would not grant him this, and Bulgaria thus turned to Constantinople. This proved to be a tenuous relationship, and in subsequent centuries, Bulgaria asserted its own religious and political independence from Constantinople. This independence was finally recognized by the Patriarchate of Constantinople in the twentieth century.

Pope St. Nicholas I (858-867)
To help Bulgaria's transition from paganism to Christianity, Pope Nicholas answered all of King Boris' 106 questions, clearly delineating those pagan customs that conflicted with Christianity. The pope also sent a bishop to Boris.

St. Benedict and his monks. Benedict's "Holy Rule" has been the fundamental monastic code in Europe and was a potent factor in the development of Western civilization.

CONCLUSION

At the core of her mission in the world, the preaching and spreading of the Gospel is one of the Church's chief responsibilities. Through the many challenges that this period of evangelization posed, the Church remained focused on expanding the message of Christ to all who would listen. Not until the Spaniards and the Portuguese arrived in the Americas late in the fifteenth century would Christianity again experience such growth among new peoples. At the same time that the West was the beneficiary of this great work of evangelization, tensions began to mount between Christianity in the West and Christianity in the East. Seemingly irreconcilable differences drove the two traditions farther apart, despite great efforts to improve the situation. The next chapter will look at these differences and their sources, which would unfortunately lead to the Great Schism.

SUPPLEMENTARY READING

St. Patrick, *Confessions*, Ch. 1

I am Patrick, a sinner, most unlearned, the least of all the faithful, and utterly despised by many. My father was Calpornius, a deacon, son of Potitus, a priest, of the village Bannavem Taburniæ; he had a country seat nearby, and there I was taken captive.

I was then about sixteen years of age. I did not know the true God. I was taken into captivity to Ireland with many thousands of people and deservedly so, because we turned away from God, and did not keep His commandments, and did not obey our priests, who used to remind us of our salvation. And the Lord brought over us the wrath of his anger and scattered us among many nations, even unto the utmost part of the earth, where now my littleness is placed among strangers.

And there the Lord opened the sense of my unbelief that I might at last remember my sins and be converted with all my heart to the Lord my God, who had regard for my abjection, and mercy on my youth and ignorance, and watched over me before I knew Him, and before I was able to distinguish between good and evil, and guarded me, and comforted me as would a father his son.

Hence I cannot be silent, nor, indeed, is it expedient—about the great benefits and the great grace which the lord has deigned to bestow upon me in the land of my captivity; for this we can give to God in return after having been chastened by Him, to exalt and praise His wonders before every nation that is anywhere under the heaven.

St. Bede, *Conversion of England,* "The Arrival in Kent of the missionaries sent by St. Gregory the Great"

In this island [England] landed the servant of our Lord, Augustine, and his companions, being, as is reported, nearly forty men. They had, by order of the blessed Pope Gregory, brought interpreters of the nation of the Franks, and sending to Ethelbert, signified that they were come from Rome, and brought a joyful message, which most undoubtedly assured to all that took advantage of it everlasting joys in heaven, and a kingdom that would never end with the living and true God....

...As soon as they entered the dwelling place assigned them, they began to imitate the course of life practiced in the primitive church: applying themselves to frequent prayer, watching, and fasting; preaching the word of life to as many as they could; despising all worldly things, as not belonging to them; receiving only their necessary food from those they taught; living in all respects conformably to what they prescribed to others, and being always disposed to suffer any adversity, and even to die for that truth which they preached. In short, several believed and were baptized, admiring the simplicity of their innocent life and the sweetness of their heavenly doctrine....

...In this they first began to meet, to sing, to pray, to say Mass, to preach and to baptize, till the king, being converted to the faith, allowed them to preach openly and to build or repair churches in all places.

SUPPLEMENTARY READING Continued

John Paul II, *Slavorum Apostoli*, (Apostles of the Slavs), 14, 1-2

It seems in no way anachronistic to see Sts. Cyril and Methodius as the authentic precursors of ecumenism, in as much as they wished to eliminate effectively or to reduce any divisions, real or only apparent, between the individual communities belonging to the same Church, (but) provides a stumbling block to the world, and inflicts damage on the most holy cause of proclaiming the gospel to every creature.

The fervent solicitude shown by both brothers and especially by Methodius by reason of his Episcopal responsibility, to preserve unity of faith and love between the Churches of which they were members, namely, between the Church of Constantinople and the Church of Rome on the one hand, and the Churches which arose in the land of the Slavs on the other, was and always will remain their great merit. This merit was all the greater if one takes into account the fact that their mission was exercised in the years 863-885, thus in the critical years when there emerged a more serious and fatal discord and bitter controversy between the Churches of the East and West.

VOCABULARY

BONIFACE (*BONA FACERE*)
Latin for "doer of good" and the name given to St. Boniface, the missionary to Germany who set the stage for a radical reshaping of the heart of Europe.

CANTERBURY
The most important episcopal see in England in the sixth century and the site of St. Augustine's mission to England.

GLAGOLITHIC SCRIPT
Based on the Greek alphabet, it was developed by St. Cyril to aid his mission to the Slavic peoples.

MOZÁRABES
Spanish people who chose to live under Arab rule after the Muslim invasion of Spain in 711.

PALLIUM
A sacred vestment symbolic of the fullness of Episcopal authority, worn by popes and archbishops. It is circular, one inch in width with six small crosses.

PATRONS OF EUROPE
Title given by Pope John Paul II in 1980 to Sts. Cyril and Methodius were responsible for the conversions of all of Moravia and other Slavic territories. They used Slavic in the liturgy and translated the Bible into Slavic to reach more people.

VENERABLE
This title refers either to a particular state in the process of canonization or to a person's holy life, as in the case of St. Bede.

WATA
"Oak of Thor," the sacred tree of the pagans of Hesse cut down by St. Boniface.

STUDY QUESTIONS

1. Discuss the role of the bishop in the work of conversion in Europe.

2. Why is France known as the "Church's eldest daughter"?

3. Who is known as the "Apostle of Ireland," and what is his background?

4. How did Irish monasteries protect and promote Western civilization?

5. Why did Celtic Christianity enter into a period of decline by the 800s?

6. Who was the "Apostle of Scotland"?

7. What are two ways in which Celtic Christianity differed from Roman Christianity?

8. When did the Church finally implement the Sacrament of Penance in the form recognized today? How often are Catholics required to go to Penance?

9. How is it known that English Christianity existed at least before 314?

10. Who was the "Apostle of England"?

11. What was the most important episcopal see in England?

12. What is the significance of the Synod of Whitby (664)?

13. Who is the "Father of English History" and what important contribution did he make with regard to the calendar?

14. What precipitated the decline of the Church in England from 800-1000?

15. Who is the "Apostle of Frisia"?

16. Who is the "Apostle of Germany," and how did he shape the heart of Europe?

17. The monastery of which city became the most important in all of Germany?

18. From where did the missionaries for Scandinavia come?

19. Who is the "Apostle of the North"?

20. Which saintly king's grave was a major pilgrimage site of Northern Europe until the Reformation?

21. How was Christianity's acceptance in Iceland different from the usual model of the king converting first?

22. What does the presence of English churchmen like Bishop Henry of Uppsala in Finland demonstrate about the English church?

23. How did the conversion of the Slavs cause tension?

24. Who were the "Apostles of the Slavs," and what were their backgrounds?

25. Why did many Slavs later turn against the Catholic Church in favor of Constantinople?

26. What title did Pope John Paul II give Sts. Cyril and Methodius in 1980?

27. What do the martyr deaths of St. Ludmilla and St. Wenceslaus indicate about the role of martyrs?

28. What German city was made an archdiocese specifically for the formation of missionaries for the Slavs?

29. Which Polish ruler made Poland a vassal land of the popes, thus beginning a long and important relationship between Poland and the papacy?

30. Much of Russia was inhabited by the descendants of what tribe?

PRACTICAL EXERCISES

1. The introduction mentions bias against missionaries. Respond to someone who said the following: "Missionaries cause destruction. They find native peoples, and then force western conceptions of God on them. Christian missionaries destroy the families and culture of natives, who have been living just fine without Christianity."

2. What are three ways that every Christian today can evangelize?

3. Discuss Sts. Cyril and Methodius and the trials which they faced. How did their methods exemplify the Church's respect for different cultures?

4. By the end of the twentieth century, practically every nation discussed in this chapter has suffered in its practice of Christianity after the effects of materialism, communism, and war. For example, in the states within the former East Germany, more than seventy percent of the people are not baptized. What do you think might be the effects of the loss of faith in these European cultures? How might things be changed?

FROM THE CATECHISM

830 The word "catholic" means "universal," in the sense of "according to the totality" or "in keeping with the whole." The Church is catholic in a double sense:

First, the Church is catholic because Christ is present in her. "Where there is Christ Jesus, there is the Catholic Church" (St. Ignatius of Antioch, *Ad Smyrn.* 8,2: *Apostolic Fathers,* II/2, 311). In her subsists the fullness of Christ's body united with its head; this implies that she receives from him "the fullness of the means of salvation" (*UR* 3; *AG* 6; Eph 1: 22-23) which he has willed: correct and complete confession of faith, full sacramental life, and ordained ministry in apostolic succession. The Church was, in this fundamental sense, catholic on the day of Pentecost (cf. *AG* 4) and will always be so until the day of the Parousia.

831 Secondly, the Church is catholic because she has been sent out by Christ on a mission to the whole of the human race (cf. Mt 28: 19).

All men are called to belong to the new People of God. This People, therefore, while remaining one and only one, is to be spread throughout the whole world and to all ages in order that the design of God's will may be fulfilled: he made human nature one in the beginning and has decreed that all his children who were scattered should be finally gathered together as one....The character of universality which adorns the People of God is a gift from the Lord himself whereby the Catholic Church ceaselessly and efficaciously seeks for the return of all humanity and all its goods, under Christ the Head in the unity of his Spirit (*LG* 13 § 1-2; cf. Jn 11: 52).

832 "The Church of Christ is really present in all legitimately organized local groups of the faithful, which, in so far as they are united to their pastors, are also quite appropriately called Churches in the New Testament....
In them the faithful are gathered together through the preaching of the Gospel of Christ, and the mystery of the Lord's Supper is celebrated....In these communities, though they may often be small and poor, or existing in the diaspora, Christ is present, through whose power and influence the One, Holy, Catholic, and Apostolic Church is constituted" (*LG* 26).

833 The phrase "particular Church," which is first of all the diocese (or eparchy), refers to a community of the Christian faithful in communion of faith and sacraments with their bishop ordained in apostolic succession (cf. *CD* 11; CIC, cann. 368-369; CCEO, cann. 171,1; 178; 311,1; 312). These particular Churches "are constituted after the model of the universal Church; it is in these and formed out of them that the one and unique Catholic Church exists" (*LG* 23).

834 Particular Churches are fully catholic through their communion with one of them, the Church of Rome "which presides in charity" (St. Ignatius Of Antioch, *Ad Rom.* 1, 1: *Apostolic Fathers*, II/2, 192; cf. LG 13). "For with this church, by reason of its pre-eminence, the whole Church, that is the faithful everywhere, must necessarily be in accord" (St. Irenaeus, *Adv. haeres.* 3, 3, 2: PG 7/1, 849; cf. Vatican Council I: DS 3057). Indeed, "from the incarnate Word's descent to us, all Christian churches everywhere have held and hold the great Church that is here [at Rome] to be their only basis and foundation since, according to the Savior's promise, the gates of hell have never prevailed against her" (St. Maximus the Confessor, *Opuscula theo.*: PG 91: 137-140).

849 *The missionary mandate.* "Having been divinely sent to the nations that she might be 'the universal sacrament of salvation,' the Church, in obedience to the command of her founder and because it is demanded by her own essential universality, strives to preach the Gospel to all men" (*AG* 1; cf. Mt 16: 15):

"Go therefore and make disciples of all nations, baptizing them in the name of the Father and of the Son and of the Holy Spirit, teaching them to observe all that I have commanded you; and Lo, I am with you always, until the close of the age" (Mt 28: 19-20).

850 *The origin and purpose of mission.* The Lord's missionary mandate is ultimately grounded in the eternal love of the Most Holy Trinity: "The Church on earth is by her nature missionary since, according to the plan of the Father, she has as her origin the mission of the Son and the Holy Spirit" (*AG* 2). The ultimate purpose of mission is none other than to make men share in the communion between the Father and the Son in their Spirit of love (cf. John Paul II, *RMiss* 23).

851 *Missionary motivation.* It is from God's love for all men that the Church in every age receives both the obligation and the vigor of her missionary dynamism, "for the love of Christ urges us on" (2 Cor 5: 14; cf. *AA* 6; *RMiss* 11). Indeed, God "desires all men to be saved and to come to the knowledge of the truth" (1 Tm 2: 4); that is, God wills the salvation of everyone through the knowledge of the truth. Salvation is found in the truth. Those who obey the prompting of the Spirit of truth are already on the way of salvation. But the Church, to whom this truth has been entrusted, must go out to meet their desire, so as to bring them the truth. Because she believes in God's universal plan of salvation, the Church must be missionary.

Iconoclasm, The Carolingian Renaissance, And The Great Schism

The communion between East and West was shattered in the Great Schism that separated two traditions with the same sacraments.

CHAPTER 7

Iconoclasm, The Carolingian Renaissance, And The Great Schism

As I celebrate among you and wish you the Eucharist of our Lord Jesus Christ,
I wish us to find in it peace with our fellow man. Peace: the fruit of justice.
Peace: the fruit of love. How easily this peace is broken! How often people are divided
among themselves, even though they are physically close, even in the same family!
May Christ give us the ability to remain at peace with others. May there be realized in us
the words of His Sermon on the Mount: "Blessed are the peacemakers."

— John Paul II, Prayer during his Pastoral visit to the Roman parish of
St. Giovanni Battista dei Fiorentini (March 8, 1981)

From the fourth century into the eleventh century, the Church channeled her energies into the conversion of peoples on the European continent. However, this was only one aspect of the many challenges facing the Church. In the eighth and ninth centuries, a number of political and religious factors coalesced that proved to have important ramifications for Christianity. During these two centuries, the deep-rooted, growing divergence between East and West began to surface clearly as the different languages, cultures, geography, and conceptions of political and religious power that had long divided the East and West became more acute. These two diverse cultures, born from the same sources but now separated by deep cultural heterogeneity, were yet united by the same sacramental Christianity. It proved, however, a fragile unity. The rise of the patriarchs and the question of papal supremacy, liturgical and disciplinal differences, the Iconoclastic Controversy, and other disagreements all pushed East and West towards a final confrontation.

This chapter will explore the development of Christianity in the Byzantine Empire, with special emphasis on the religious and political questions raised in Byzantium over the issues of papal supremacy and icons. The chapter will also look at the concurrent development of the Church in the West, specifically focusing on the relationship of the Church and the Carolingian kings.

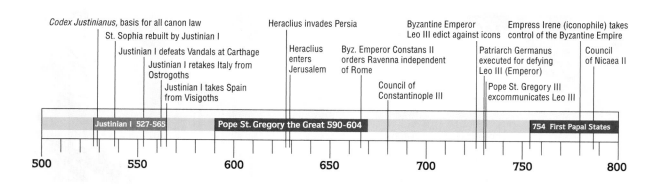

Codex Justinianus, basis for all canon law
St. Sophia rebuilt by Justinian I
Justinian I defeats Vandals at Carthage
Justinian I retakes Italy from Ostrogoths
Justinian I takes Spain from Visigoths

Heraclius invades Persia
Heraclius enters Jerusalem
Byz. Emperor Constans II orders Ravenna independent of Rome
Council of Constantinople III

Byzantine Emperor Leo III edict against icons
Patriarch Germanus executed for defying Leo III (Emperor)
Pope St. Gregory III excommunicates Leo III

Empress Irene (iconophile) takes control of the Byzantine Empire
Council of Nicaea II

Justinian I 527-565   Pope St. Gregory the Great 590-604   754 First Papal States

500   550   600   650   700   750   800

PART I
Byzantium

BYZANTIUM: THE LONG VIEW

Byzantium was at one time the most important center of political, religious, cultural, and economic activity in the world of the former Roman Empire. During the periods of its greatest geographical breadth, the Byzantine Empire encompassed the entire Mediterranean world: North Africa, Palestine, the Anatolian Plateau, Greece, the Balkans, and Italy. Much of the Black Sea was controlled by Byzantium, which extended as far east as modern Syria and Iraq. Byzantium was a mighty maritime power and a key trading center for commerce with East Asia.

Constantine the Great founded the Byzantine Empire when he moved his capital to Byzantium, renaming it Constantinople and formally dedicating it on May 11, 330. The Empire lasted until May 29, 1453, when it fell to the Ottoman Turks. Byzantium lasted for more than eleven hundred years—longer than the combined duration of the Roman Republic and the Roman Empire which together lasted some nine hundred eighty-five years (taking 509 B.C. as the beginning of the Republic and A.D. 476 as the collapse of the Empire). Unlike the Republic and the Empire, Byzantium enjoyed the blessing of a wholly Christian orientation and development from its inception. Even though the capital was dedicated under both pagan and Christian rites, Constantine always heavily favored the Church, and, as mentioned previously, Emperor Theodosius I made Christianity the official religion of Byzantium in 379. The intricate theological disputes of the fourth and fifth centuries demonstrated a deeply Christian culture that marked the Empire even until its decline and fall.

The rise of Islam, however, proved to be a mortal enemy to the Eastern Empire. As Islamic expansion constantly loomed on the horizon in the Middle East, Africa, and Asia Minor as a powerful threat to the Empire's territorial integrity. Certain tenets of the Muslim faith prompted the Arabic people to raise a strong military force that had already conquered Byzantine lands by the seventh century, including three of the four great Eastern Christian patriarchates (Jerusalem, Antioch, and Alexandria). Islam remained a constant threat to the empire until finally, in the fifteenth century, Constantinople, and with it the remnants of the decaying Byzantine Empire, fell to the Muslim Ottoman Turks on May 29, 1453.

Constantinople was located on the tip of the Balkan Peninsula just across from Asia Minor along the narrow Bosporus Strait, which connects the Black Sea to the Mediterranean. The city was built

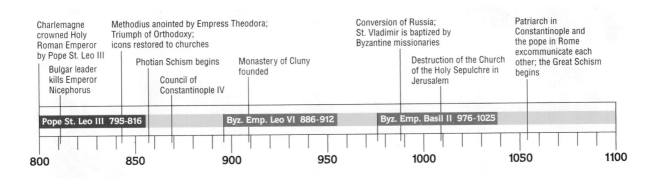

Charlemagne crowned Holy Roman Emperor by Pope St. Leo III

Bulgar leader kills Emperor Nicephorus

Methodius anointed by Empress Theodora; Triumph of Orthodoxy; icons restored to churches

Photian Schism begins

Council of Constantinople IV

Monastery of Cluny founded

Conversion of Russia; St. Vladimir is baptized by Byzantine missionaries

Destruction of the Church of the Holy Sepulchre in Jerusalem

Patriarch in Constantinople and the pope in Rome excommunicate each other; the Great Schism begins

Pope St. Leo III 795-816   Byz. Emp. Leo VI 886-912   Byz. Emp. Basil II 976-1025

800   850   900   950   1000   1050   1100

The Bosporus is a strait that separates the European part of Turkey from the Asian part and connects the Sea of Marmara with the Black Sea. Two bridges cross the Bosporus Strait. Due to the importance of the strait for the defense of Istanbul, the Ottoman sultans constructed a fortification on each side, the Anadoluhisari (1393) and the Rumelihisari (1451) shown above.

on this triangular rocky promontory, surrounded by the sea on the northern, southern, and eastern borders. Emperor Constantine, Emperor Theodosius II, and later Emperor Anastasius I soon erected a series of formidable walls (Anastasius' walls were some forty miles long) along its western edge to complete the boundaries of the triangular city—an impressively secure military site that British warships were not capable of taking during the First World War, even with heavy bombardment.

The Byzantines were Roman in their laws, Greek in their culture, and oriental in their habits. All of these traditions came together in Constantinople, which rose as a center of learning, art, and architecture. Hagia (or Saint) Sophia (the Church of "Holy Wisdom," dedicated to Christ), the cathedral of the patriarch of Constantinople, is still regarded as a wonder of Byzantine art and architecture. The riches of Byzantium likewise converged in Constantinople. The docks were crowded with exotic goods from all over the world—wood, grains, silks from Asia, spices, luxuriant clothing, and precious jewelry filled the markets.

BYZANTINE CHRISTIANITY

The numbers of Christians in Byzantium far exceeded those in Rome and the West. It must be remembered that all of the areas to which Christianity first took hold, such as Palestine and the cities of Asia Minor, were located within the boundaries of the Byzantine Empire; and Greek, the language of the East, was the original language of almost the entire New Testament.

Although Rome remained the location of St. Peter's successors, it no longer enjoyed the influence that it once had during the era of the Roman Empire. The pope continued to serve as the ultimate authority in the Church, but the intimate relationship between the emperor and the patriarchs of Constantinople would come to overshadow the authority of the papacy. Furthermore, the Church in the East developed along very different lines than the Church in the West. In the West, as the political structures of the Empire collapsed and missionary activity surged across Europe, the notion of the Church as universal began to take an even stronger form. This universal conception of the Church took root in the absence of any strong political communities to which Christians could attach themselves. Hence the Church came to be viewed as something that transcended all national boundaries or allegiances.

In the East, however, missionary activity, though equally successful, regularly culminated in the creation of national churches attached to specific political communities. Hence various eastern churches arose in partial concert and conflict with the imperial church of the Byzantine Empire. The burgeoning nationalism of some of these minor churches was strong enough to cause several schisms within the Eastern Church. The Eastern Church soon found itself ministering solely to its Greek subjects.

The political environment of the Eastern Empire also gave rise to a manner of rule called caesaropapism, in which the sovereign temporal ruler extends his authority to ecclesiastical and theological matters. To be sure, strains of caesaropapism could be detected as early as Constantine the Great, but the emperors who succeeded him only intensified their desire to have a hand in the governance of the Church. Such emperors appointed bishops and the Eastern Patriarch, directed the development of liturgical practices, and even aided in the recruitment of monks. In time, the increasing power of Eastern emperors put them into direct conflict with the authority of the papacy, paving the way for many contentious disputes and schisms.

EMPEROR JUSTINIAN I

The eastern Emperor Justinian I (ca. 482-565, emperor 527) may be considered the last, great ruler in the Roman tradition before the political transformation that shook Byzantium in the eighth century. Justinian I succeeded in resurrecting the glory of imperial Rome in the Eastern Empire, and is responsible for many advances in architecture, the fine arts, and civil law. Justinian I's view of himself as head of both the state and the Church, however, led him into conflict with the papacy over the question of the heresy of Monophysitism.

In a mosaic panel in the Church of San Vitale, Ravenna, northeast of Florence, Italy, ca. 540, Emperor Justinian I holds the paten for the bread of the Eucharist. Bishop Maximian holds a cross. Others hold the Gospel book and incense. The group is walking in a procession as part of the ceremony of the Little Entrance, when the congregation entered the church following the Gospel book.

MILITARY CAMPAIGNS

In 553/4 Justinian I led a campaign against the Vandals in northern Africa. The Vandals were disorganized and ill-equipped, but had, during the collapse of the West, overrun the northern shores of Africa. In addition to his desire to restore the empire, Justinian I was moved by the African bishops' pleas for help, as the Vandals were particularly harsh on Christians. Justinian I sailed five hundred ships carrying ten thousand infantry and five thousand cavalry against the Vandals and marched on Carthage, the Vandal stronghold. Justinian I took Carthage and captured the Vandal king Gelimer, bringing him as a prisoner to Constantinople, thus temporarily resuscitating the empire's presence in Africa.

Apart from his African campaign, Justinian I retook Italy (562) from the Ostrogoths after a long and expensive war, and secured most of Spain (555), capturing this land from the Visigoths. In all, by the time of Justinian I's death he had reconquered half of Europe as well as northern Africa. His campaigns toward the west and the south came at a price. The Persians, who had threatened the empire from the beginning of Justinian I's reign, never ceased harassing the eastern frontiers. Furthermore, the Bulgars and Slavs threatened the empire in the Balkans and even Constantinople itself.

Justinian I's rekindling of the empire, however brilliant and amazing, was also brief. Italy fell into the hands of the Lombards just three years after his death in 565, and was never recovered. Northern Africa was lost within a century thereafter to the Muslims.

The Barberini Ivory from the early sixth century, Constantinople, portrays a triumphant Christian emperor.

Although he resembles Constantine, historians date the style of the ivory to the reign of Justinian I. One interpretation is that the ivory celebrates Justinian I's victory over the Persians.

CODEX JUSTINIANUS (529)

As part of his ambitious quest to restore the empire, Justinian I undertook the collection and systemization of all Roman law as it had developed from his earliest predecessors. Justinian I wanted to ensure a uniform rule of law throughout his growing empire, and sought to provide an ultimate reference for any legal question that might arise. The result, the *Codex Justinianus,* represents the highest achievement in classical legal scholarship. Justinian I's Codex is an important basis for the development of Canon Law—the law of the Church—as well as for civil law in all the countries of Europe.

Hagia Sophia. The minarets belong to the Ottoman conversion of the church into a mosque. Hagia Sophia remains one of the great achievements of world architecture. In it, every Byzantine saw the perfect church. "The church is an earthly heaven in which the super-celestial God dwells and walks about." Germanos, Patriarch of Constantinople (715-730).

HAGIA SOPHIA (538)

As wondrous and long-lasting as Justinian I's advancements in the arena of legal scholarship proved to be, his innovations in architecture were perhaps even more impressive. From Justinian I's patronage grew a unique style of architectural design, which is now called "Byzantine," and virtually all building in the West and East owes much to his influence. The most famous work built under his reign, the magnificent church of Hagia Sophia (Holy Wisdom) at Constantinople, is widely thought to be one of the most perfect buildings in the world.

MONOPHYSITISM AND JUSTINIAN I

Monophysitism, or the belief that Christ possesses only one nature and that his human nature is "incorporated" into the divine nature, remained a prevalent and troubling heresy in Justinian I's time. His own wife, Theodora, had definite Monophysite sympathies, and her influence over Justinian I was not always for the best. Theodora had been a popular actress known for both her beauty and antics, many of which fell well short of propriety. At some time in her adult life, however, she converted to Christianity, and by the time Justinian I married her she was living a respectable and reformed life in relative seclusion.

Theodora's conversion was probably aided by many of the East's famous spiritual athletes, monks who were known for their asceticism and zeal. Unfortunately, many of these same monks, if they were not Monophysites, were very close to being so. The notion of Christ's two natures present in one Divine Person was supposedly resolved at the Council of Chalcedon (451). There, it was to have been shown that the West—in the person of Pope St. Leo I—and the East—in the person of St. Cyril—were united in their understanding of Christ's Person. Unfortunately, controversy still remained. Many Eastern Christians felt that St. Leo's formulation of Christ's two natures did not truly square with St. Cyril's teaching on the same subject matter and represented a kind of creeping Nestorianism. This was the first council not recognized by any of the Churches of the Eastern Christian tradition (called "Old Oriental Churches").

JUSTINIAN'S EMPIRE ca. 560

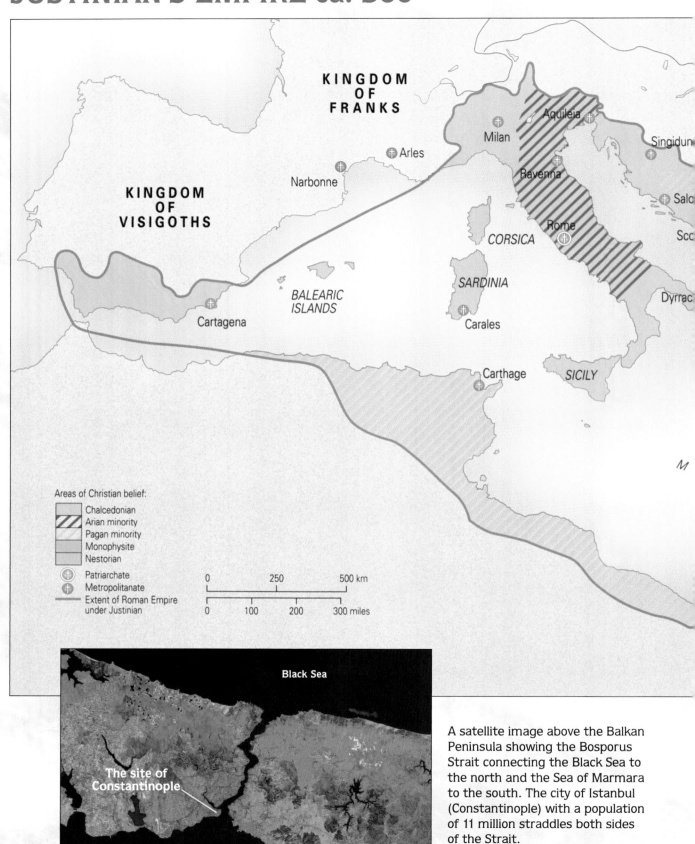

KINGDOM OF FRANKS

Aquileia

Milan

Arles

Singidun

Ravenna

Narbonne

Salo

KINGDOM OF VISIGOTHS

CORSICA

Rome

Scc

SARDINIA

Dyrrac

Cartagena

BALEARIC ISLANDS

Carales

Carthage

SICILY

M

Areas of Christian belief:

Chalcedonian
Arian minority
Pagan minority
Monophysite
Nestorian

⊕ Patriarchate
⊕ Metropolitanate
—— Extent of Roman Empire under Justinian

0	250	500 km

0	100	200	300 miles

Black Sea

The site of Constantinople

Sea of Marmara

A satellite image above the Balkan Peninsula showing the Bosporus Strait connecting the Black Sea to the north and the Sea of Marmara to the south. The city of Istanbul (Constantinople) with a population of 11 million straddles both sides of the Strait.

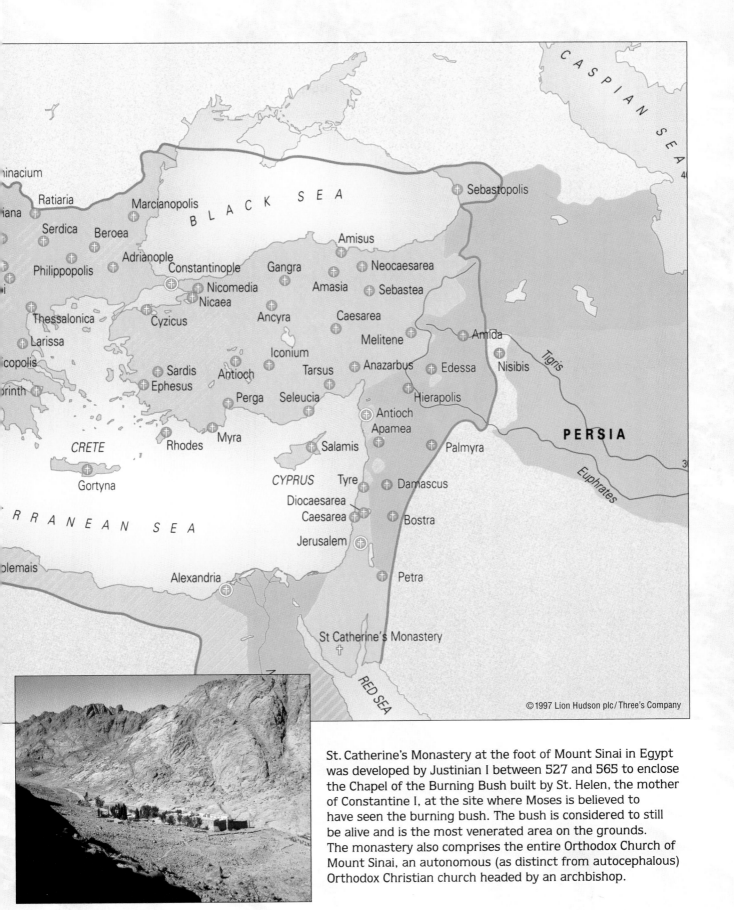

St. Catherine's Monastery at the foot of Mount Sinai in Egypt was developed by Justinian I between 527 and 565 to enclose the Chapel of the Burning Bush built by St. Helen, the mother of Constantine I, at the site where Moses is believed to have seen the burning bush. The bush is considered to still be alive and is the most venerated area on the grounds. The monastery also comprises the entire Orthodox Church of Mount Sinai, an autonomous (as distinct from autocephalous) Orthodox Christian church headed by an archbishop.

Justinian I's desire was to reconcile the remaining Monophysites in the East with the Church. This in itself was laudable. Often, however, Justinian I's desire for such reconciliation, combined with his great love for his wife—who privately held Monophysite tendencies—proved disastrous for the Church. The case of Pope St. Silverius provides an apt example.

Pope St. Silverius was elected in 536 to succeed Pope St. Agapitus. However, Theodora wished that Vigilius, a Monophysite who had risen to great power in the Church, be made pope instead. Theodora and Vigilius conspired against Pope St. Silverius and forged documents proving his betrayal of the empire. Pope St. Silverius was deposed and sent into exile. Justinian I, largely because of his wife's influence, was unable to investigate fully the accusations leveled against St. Silverius. Hence the emperor's deference to his wife in this instance led to St. Silverius' continued exile and eventual death.

Justinian I's activity in ecclesiastical activities led to other abuses in the same vein, and constitutes the main flaw of his otherwise admirable reign.

At the Battle of Nineveh in 627, Byzantine forces led by Flavius Heraclius Augustus, Byzantine emperor from 610 to 641, defeated the Persian forces of King Chosroe. Heraclius took for himself the title of *Basileus,* the Greek word for "emperor," and that title was used by the eastern Roman emperors for the next 800 years. Heraclius also discontinued the use of Latin as the empire's official language, replacing it with Greek. Although the empire called itself Roman throughout the rest of its history, it was in reality a Hellenic empire from Heraclius onward.

EMPEROR HERACLIUS: A PILGRIM IN JERUSALEM

After Justinian I's death in 565, the empire fell into disarray. The lands he had reclaimed were soon lost again, and none of his immediate successors approached his level of charisma or focus. Further, Justinian I's many civic projects had drained the empire's treasury, and there was little wealth coming into Constantinople because of the raids abroad. The overextension of the empire, the lack of any singular leader, and even diminishing revenues crippled a once-magnificent empire.

At the same time, the Persians were garnering strength. The Persians had first warred against the old Roman Empire under Valerius, and had even taken this emperor prisoner. Ever since then, they had continually raided the eastern-most stretches of Byzantium, but were unable to make any substantive incursions for a very long while. After Justinian I's death, however, the Persian King Chosroes prepared to realize the Persians' long-awaited hopes.

In 611, King Chosroes, after a series of lesser engagements, marched against Byzantium with the largest invading force yet mustered in Christian times. In 614 his son-in-law Shaharbarz took

Jerusalem. He held the city siege for twenty days, and finally overran it with the help of 26,000 Jews who were eager to destroy Christian sovereignty in their city. Historians estimate that in the plundering of Jerusalem between sixty and one-hundred thousand Christians lost their lives. Churches, Christian shrines, and monasteries were destroyed, and the True Cross was carted off as a trophy of war. Jews, as a reward for their help, were allowed to retain the city.

By this point in time, Emperor Heraclius had acceded to rule the Byzantine Empire. When the Persians invaded Jerusalem, Heraclius had neither the men nor the funds to resist them. His existing forces were occupied elsewhere, warring against the Slavs, and his economic reforms had not yet generated enough revenue to equip another army. After much negotiation, Heraclius worked out an agreement with the Patriarch of Constantinople in order to fund his campaign against the Persians. He would be allotted all the wealth of the churches so long as he would repay these loans after defeating the Persians and liberating Jerusalem. His funding secure, Heraclius built up his army for two more years and in 622 began a counter-offensive against the Persians.

Heraclius' campaign, sometimes called the Byzantine Crusade, culminated in his invasion of Persia in 627. King Chosroes fled, and in 629 Heraclius, victorious, entered Jerusalem to venerate the relic of the True Cross, which had been restored to the holy city.

PART II

The Iconoclastic Controversy
(ca. 725-843)

I am the LORD your God, who brought you out of the land of Egypt, out of the house of bondage. You shall have no other gods before me. You shall not make for yourself a graven image, or any likeness of anything that is in heaven above, or that is on the earth beneath, or that is in the water under the earth; you shall not bow down to them or serve them; for I the LORD your God am a jealous God, visiting the iniquity of the fathers upon the children to the third and fourth generation of those who hate me, but showing steadfast love to thousands of those who love me and keep my commandments. (Ex 20: 2-6; Dt 5: 6-10)

The first section of this chapter set the stage for the Iconoclastic Controversy. The Iconoclastic Controversy and its attendant heresy, iconoclasm, served as the breaking point between the Eastern emperors and the popes. Though religious communion was maintained between the Eastern and Western Church for several centuries more, the emperors and popes assumed permanent, adversarial positions regarding the status and use of icons. This impasse eventually led the papacy to seek the protection of the Western Franks to protect against the sometimes oppressive measures of dissenting emperors.

The Iconoclastic Controversy may be broken down into several periods:

- First Iconoclasm under the reigns of Emperors Leo III and Constantine V, ca. 725-775;
- Iconophile recovery under the Empress-regent Irene, the mother of Constantine VI, and the Seventh Ecumenical Council of Nicaea (787), 775-815;
- Second Iconoclasm under the reigns of Emperors Leo V, Michael II, and Theophilus, 815-842;
- Triumph of Iconophiles, celebrated on the first Sunday of Lent as the "Feast of Orthodoxy," 843.

ICONS

An icon is a flat, two-dimensional picture of Christ, the Virgin Mary, or one of the saints. Icons became numerous in the East beginning in the fifth century, and were used as aids for Christian acts of piety. Highly ritualized prayer before icons involving bowing and the lighting of incense became the norm among the Christian faithful. These practices, to a greater or lesser extent, remain in both the Western and Eastern Rites of the Church today. The general artistic style of icons reflects a certain mystical beauty of Christ the Savior and the saints. When rightly understood, the icon, by virtue of what is represented, is seen as an invitation to prayer and not as an object to be worshiped.

There are various explanations as to the rise of iconoclasm. The word "iconoclast" is the translation of the Greek word *eikonoklastēs,* which, as the compound of *eikôn* (image) and *klan* (to break), literally means "image breaker." Some scholars point to the influence of Judaism and Islam, which both proscribed the use of images in worship, to explain the rise of iconoclasm. Others argue that from the beginning of the Church, a latent strain of iconoclasm lay hidden below the surface, clouded over for a time by other, more pressing theological disputes.

In any case, many scholars agree that by the beginning of the eighth century, abuses of icons had sprung up among the faithful. Many people came to believe that icons held special powers. This devolved quickly into a kind of superstition, and worshipers often fixed their attention on the icon itself, rather than at the spiritual mysteries the icon was intended to represent. A kind of idolatry, forbidden by the First Commandment, emerged from this incorrect use of the icons. As a guard against such idolatry, the iconoclasts sought to destroy the icons, and, in their view, purify the practice of the Christian religion.

Our Lady of Vladimir (also known as *Eleousa,* Greek meaning "Mother of tenderness") is one of the most venerated Orthodox icons. Regarded as the holy protectress of Russia, the icon is displayed in the Tretyakov Gallery, Moscow. Patriarch Luke Chrysoberges of Constantinople sent the newly written icon as a gift to Grand Duke Yury Dolgoruky of Kiev ca.1131. The beautiful image was loved by Yury's son, Andrei the Pious, who brought it to his favorite city Vladimir in 1155.

When the horses that transported the icon stopped near Vladimir and refused to go further, it was interpreted as a sign that the Blessed Virgin wanted to stay in Vladimir. To house the icon, the great Assumption Cathedral was built there, followed by other churches dedicated to the Virgin throughout northwestern Russia.

One of the most exquisite icons ever written, Our Lady of Vladimir is imbued with universal feelings of motherly love and anxiety for her child known as the *Eleousa* type. By the 16th century the Vladimirskaya (as the Russians call it) was a thing of legend. One legend is that the image was painted by St. Luke on the table of the Last Supper.

The venerated image was considered to be miraculous and used in coronations of czars, elections of patriarchs, and other important ceremonies of state.

THEOPHANES THE GREEK—A WRITER OF ICONS

The Transfiguration by Theophanes the Greek, early 15th century, from the Cathedral of Transfiguration of the Savior in Pereslavl. Now it hangs in the Tretyakov Gallery, Moscow

An *iconographer* (literally "icon-writer") is a writer—called a "writer" because he paints a story—in icons. Theophanes the Greek is considered one of the greatest iconographers of all time. He was born in Crete around 1330 and moved to Novgorod, Russia, in 1378. Theophanes went to Russia with a deep knowledge of religious literature and art. While in Novgorod he wrote many famous icons in churches across the city.

Theophanes moved to Moscow in 1395, where he worked on the *Book of Gospels* of Boyar Koshka. In 1405 he wrote icons for the Deesis tier in Moscow's Cathedral of the Annunciation, inviting Andrei Rublev to help him on this project. In doing so, he helped develop the artistic talents of Rublev, who went on to become one of the greatest Russian iconographers of all time.

In all, Theophanes the Greek wrote icons for over forty churches in Russia and Constantinople. Unlike most iconographers of his time, he never used models when making his icons. He was also instrumental in developing the iconostasis (the screen of icons dividing the sanctuary from the nave) as it is still used today in an Eastern Church.

FIRST ICONOCLASM

EMPEROR LEO III, THE ISAURIAN (717-741)

Leo III's distrust of icons must be viewed in the context of the preceding centuries. Two or three centuries earlier, the Monophysite heresy had minimized or denied the humanity of Christ, and Manicheanism denied that Christ possessed corporeality. Although both heresies had already been condemned by the Church, remnants of heterodox belief had survived here and there. These specific heresies were aided by Islamic and Jewish influences upon Christian thought. In these other monotheistic religions, representations of God are definitively forbidden. The icons, which were representations of Christ in his full corporeality, thus came under fire from both sides. The Monophysites objected to the icons' portrayals of Christ as human; and those Christians allied with Muslims and Jews objected to the representation of any Person of the Godhead.

Aside from these theological pressures, political ones played a role as well. Leo III, like his Roman predecessors, desired a unified state, and one way of obtaining such unification was to secure a unity of religious belief. Hence it was in Leo's interest to persuade Muslims and Jews to convert to Christianity. He soon became convinced, however, that the chief impediment to their conversion was the Christian use of icons in liturgical practice. By discouraging the use of icons, Leo III thought to appease certain influential factions of Christians (those tending toward Monophysitism) and at the same time win over countless Jews and Muslims, thus consolidating his state.

Leo III's desire to placate the Muslims was somewhat understandable. Byzantium at the beginning of the eighth century was teetering on collapse. Between 634 and 644, the Muslims had captured the entire Holy Land, and had continued their march into the Anatolian Plateau. The Muslims laid siege to Constantinople for five years from 673 to 678, and again in 717. Were it not for the city's walled defenses, Byzantium would have fallen in the eighth century instead of the fifteenth. Upon his accession, Emperor Leo III managed to end the siege of 717, but he remained all too aware of the dangers his empire still faced.

Thus, in 726 Leo issued an edict declaring that all icons were occasions for idolatry and ordered their destruction. Pope St. Gregory II, Patriarch St. Germanus I of Constantinople, most bishops, and nearly all monks, immediately condemned Leo's edict. Leo wasted no time in combating his opponents, and forcibly deposed Patriarch St. Germanus I. Meanwhile, Pope St. Gregory II, after corresponding with Leo III regarding the icons, suddenly died in 731. Consequently, Leo's proscription of iconography remained in force, and when the Eastern monks refused to surrender their icons to the emperor, he unleashed a brutal persecution upon them. Many of the oldest Byzantine icons were destroyed, and hundreds of monks and nuns lost their lives in the icons' defense. Finally, Pope St. Gregory III, who succeeded Pope St. Gregory II, convened two councils in Rome in 731 that condemned Leo's actions, and then excommunicated him.

Nevertheless, Leo III remained obstinate. At his death in 741, iconoclasm was still in force in the East, and the Eastern Church was no longer in communion with Rome regarding this matter.

Above: Emperor Leo III on a gold coin from the Constantinople mint, 720-725

ST. JOHN OF DAMASCUS

Greek icon of St. John of Damascus,
early 14th century

A great defender of icons and their veneration was St. John of Damascus (ca. 655 - ca. 750), also known as St. John Damascene. At a young age, St. John renounced his family wealth and became a monk near Jerusalem. During the years 726 to 730, St. John wrote the iconophile works in defense of Pope St. Gregory II against Leo III. (*Iconophile* — Greek for "lover of icons" — refers to support of the proper use of icons in Christian worship.) Aside from criticizing iconoclasm itself, St. John also decried imperial interference in ecclesiastical matters.

St. John's crowning work is the *Fount of Wisdom*, especially the section titled "*De Fide Orthodoxa*." In it, St. John explicates the teaching of the Greek Fathers on all the important doctrines of Christianity. Here St. John defends the use of icons by reference to the mystery of the Incarnation. In coming to the world as the God-man, Jesus Christ, God gave implicit permission for the depiction of Christ's human form in art. It would therefore follow that dignified and respectful representations of God would be praiseworthy.

Considered the last of the Eastern Church Fathers, St. John of Damascus was made a Doctor of the Church by Pope Leo XIII in 1890. He enjoys the same feast day in both the East and West, celebrated on December 4.

CONSTANTINE V (741-775)

When Constantine V succeeded Leo III as emperor he moved to strengthen the theological basis against the icons by gaining the support of the Greek church. To this end he convened the Council of Hiereia (754), a non-ecumenical council which was a carefully orchestrated to deliver the results Constantine V sought. Not only did Constantine V exclude Rome and the rest of the West from the council, he did not even invite the ancient patriarchies of Jerusalem, Antioch, and Alexandria. The bishops of all these patriarchies, obviously, were iconophiles.

Constantine V encountered an unexpected and powerful adversary: the monks. These same monks had opposed Leo III, and their continued opposition to Constantine V's policy earned them several hardships: exile, imprisonment, and death. One of these monks who died under Constantine V's persecutions was St. Stephen the Younger (d. 765). A street mob, incited by iconoclasts, stoned him to death. Three hundred additional monks were put to death for the Faith.

ICONOPHILE RECOVERY: THE SEVENTH ECUMENICAL COUNCIL: THE SECOND COUNCIL OF NICAEA (787)

Constantine V was succeeded in 775 by his son, Leo IV. Leo IV eased the persecutions of the monks, and did not enforce, though he did not repeal, his predecessors' iconoclast measures. Leo IV ruled only for a short while, and died in 780. Upon Leo IV's death, his wife, the Empress Irene, who was mother to the child heir, Constantine VI, took control of the empire. The Empress Irene had Catholic sympathies, and was secretly an iconophile. In a move to restore the icons, she persuaded Pope Adrian I to convene the Seventh Ecumenical Council, the second council at

Nicaea (787). The chosen location was no accident. Empress Irene and the iconophiles hoped that those in attendance would be reminded of the First Ecumenical Council at Nicaea called by Constantine the Great, and would restore orthodoxy in the East.

Pope Adrian I was represented by two legates who arrived with written condemnations of the Council of Hiereia, which, because it was convened in opposition to the papacy, could not be valid. The important patriarchs of Alexandria, Antioch, and Jerusalem were not permitted to attend the council by their Muslim ruler, the caliph. Instead, each sent two monks. In all, more than three hundred bishops attended the Seventh Ecumenical Council, Nicaea II. The Eastern Churches celebrate the feast of the Fathers of the Seventh Ecumenical Council every October.

The Council, just one month after convening, declared its acceptance of the veneration of icons in line with the papal position regarding their legitimacy. It then went on to distinguish between two types of adoration. An icon may be venerated through acts of respect and honor (Greek, *dulia*), since bowing, lighting lamps, or burning incense before the picture of a saint is honor paid for the person it represents, and not for the image itself. God alone is worthy of absolute adoration (Greek, *latria*). The Scholastic tradition in the West later solidified this distinction when it used the terms *dulia* to indicate the reverence due to creatures such as saints, and the term *latria* to indicate the absolute adoration due to God alone.

SECOND ICONOCLASM (815-843)

Although the Ecumenical Council of Nicaea officially denounced iconoclasm as a heresy and restored communion between East and West, a political crisis inaugurated by events in the Balkans led to a second period of iconoclasm beginning in 815.

The Bulgar Slavs had proved resistant to Christianity and had constantly pressed upon Byzantium for some time. Finally, in 811 the Bulgar leader Khan Krum (ruled 811-814) killed the Byzantine emperor Nicephorus. Not since the Roman emperor Valens was slain in 378 at Adrianople by a Germanic tribe had such a thing happened. In a gesture of contempt for weakening Byzantium, Krum drank wine from Nicephorus' skull.

Two years later, the Byzantine military staged a successful coup against the defunct Byzantine leadership under Michael I. The new emperor Leo V (775-820) sought to rehabilitate iconoclasm in Byzantium as a way of strengthening the influence and power of the military. For even though the recent Second Council of Nicaea had officially ended iconoclasm's status as a viable theological view, the heresy retained many adherents in the military and upper echelons of Byzantine society. Leo V, in propagating iconoclasm, hoped to solidify this base. As a result, both he and his two successors Michael II (emperor 820-829) and Theophilus (emperor 829-842) continued the iconoclast policy.

Leo V deposed the Patriarch of Constantinople, who clung to orthodoxy despite the emperor's threats, and in his stead appointed Theophilus, a patriarch friendly to him. This patriarch soon called a council with the aim of returning to the Council of Hiereia's (753) conclusions. When in the course of the council Leo V encountered a surprisingly strong resistance from the episcopacy, he revived the persecutions, which continued unabated until Theophilus' death in 842.

Above: Empress Irene on a gold coin from the Constantinople mint, 797-802.

ICON: MICROCOSM OF CREATION

Icons are stylistic paintings on wood that are both symbolic of the spiritual world and "written" in accordance with sacred rules. One such rule requires that an icon uses elements from all of creation: vegetable, animal, mineral, and human.

Vegetable. An icon is written on wood, often birch or linden. (Usually a recessed area is carved from the face of the wood to represent the separation of the earthly and spiritual worlds.) Linseed oil protects the surface of the icon after painting; it also brightens the color, making the icon appear more transparent.

Animal. Egg yolk is mixed with vinegar and water; this is then mixed with dry colors to make egg tempera, the paint used for icons. Gelatin, dissolved into water, is heated and applied to the raw wood to seal it. Rabbit skin or fish glue binds powdered stone to form *gesso*. Brushes of animal fur apply the egg tempera.

Mineral. Gold leaf is used for halos and thin rays on clothing. Marble or chalk is crushed to powder, mixed with glue (*gesso*), and heated; this forms a base for the painting. Colors are added to the egg solution to create egg tempera. Clay is used as a base for gold leaf.

Human. The iconographer writes an icon (see *Theophanes the Greek* on page 263). He prepares the other elements from creation in an ordered way to produce an icon. He utilizes his status as created in the image of God to re-form creation into new elements for the worship of God and honor of the saints.

Writing an icon

Icon of the Triumph of Orthodoxy, Constantinople, late 14th century. This icon depicts those who fought for Orthodoxy during the period of iconoclasm.

In the top row, Empress Theodora and her son Michael III stand on the left and Patriarch Methodius on the right. In the center is the *Hodigitria* icon, attributed to St. Luke. (*Hodigitria* means "She who shows the way.")

Two icons of Christ are held by iconophiles in the bottom row.

THE FEAST OF THE TRIUMPH OF ORTHODOXY (843)

It required another empress and regent, Empress Theodora, to reverse the new wave of iconoclasm and restore orthodoxy in the East. Theodora deposed the iconoclast Patriarch Theophilus of Constantinople, and in 843, put in his place Bl. Methodius, who had been tortured and imprisoned by Theophilus. Under Bl. Methodius, iconoclast bishops were deposed and replaced by orthodox iconophiles, and the first Sunday of Lent was named the Feast of the Triumph of Orthodoxy in order to celebrate the triumph of the icons. The Eastern Churches still celebrate this feast today.

Hence, in 843—after more than one hundred years of controversy and schism—the barren walls of churches were again decorated with beautiful icons, and the orthodox practice of venerating icons was finally secure.

PART III

The Rise of the Carolingians and an Independent Papacy

During the iconoclast controversies, the popes had regularly turned to the Western Franks for protection against the Byzantine emperors. The Franks' conversion and rise to power came to provide the West with a semblance of political unity and a relatively stable support for the Church. This alliance between the papacy and the Franks would culminate in the crowning of Charlemagne as Emperor in 800. To understand the alliance and its importance it is necessary to look back some sixty years earlier, to the transfer of power from the Merovingian line of Frankish inheritance to the Carolingian one.

THE ORIGIN OF THE CAROLINGIAN LINE

Dating back to Clovis, the Merovingian Dynasty (named for Meroveus, an ancestor of Clovis) ruled the Franks. Due to the corruption and incompetence of the Merovingian kings and nobles, they had only nominal control over their kingdom. Since the end of the seventh century, the real power over the Franks had been in the hands of the Carolingians (named for Charles Martel, who established the dynasty), whose official title was "Mayors of the Palace."

Pepin the Short (741-767) was a Carolingian and the son of the famed Charles Martel, who had defeated the Muslims at Tours in 732. Pepin appeared to be a brute in his physical characteristics: short, broad-shouldered, and strong. However, he also had a keen intelligence and understanding of others. He combined these qualities with an extraordinary ambition for power.

Pepin solidified his position as the only heir to the Carolingian dynasty when his other brother became a monk. Pepin wrote to Pope St. Zachary requesting that he and his progeny be given kingship over the Franks, since it was they who retained actual power among the Franks. St. Boniface, who was the papal legate in the Germanic territories, successfully acquired Pope St. Zachary's permission to recognize the new Carolingian dynasty as the rightful rulers in central Europe, officially transferring power from the Merovingian Dynasty.

St. Boniface anointed Pepin king in 751, marking the beginning of a long and complicated allegiance between the Carolingians and the papacy in the West.

ESTABLISHMENT OF THE PAPAL STATES

Pope Stephen II (752-757), who succeeded St. Zachary, expected protection from Pepin the Short in exchange for the official papal support of the Carolingians. To reiterate the papacy's expectations, Pope Stephen traveled across the Alps into France to meet with Pepin. The Lombards were presently threatening Rome, and the Byzantines did not intend to protect Italy. Pope Stephen, aware that the Byzantines would not hesitate to abandon the papacy, sought to recruit Pepin's aid in the defense of Rome. On July 28, 754, the pope publicly anointed Pepin and his two sons—repeating with more pomp the consecration already performed by St. Boniface— and threatened to condemn anyone who disobeyed them. This consecration was designed to show that the Church could bestow secular authority to kings. Pepin in turn agreed to intervene on behalf of the pope before the Lombard ruler.

Later that same year, Pepin and his army marched into northern Italy and asked the Lombard leader Aistulf to refrain from taking Rome. As a show of force, Pepin laid siege to an outlying Lombard stronghold just over the Alps. Aistulf initially accepted Pepin's conditions, but when Pepin withdrew back across the Alps, Aistulf reneged on the agreement and marched on Rome. Consequently, Pepin again moved his troops over the Alps and launched an attack on the Lombards, soundly defeating them. This time, Pepin left behind a contingent of his army to ensure that Aistulf followed through on the terms of peace.

In the end, Pepin won Rome for the papacy, as well as securing Ravenna and Perugia. These lands would become known as the Papal States. For the first time in the history of the Church, the pope, who had always been a spiritual leader, became a sovereign one as well. This direct administration of temporal lands by the papacy would last until 1870, when Italy would unify itself as a nation-state.

The direct involvement of the papacy in the administration of a state was both advantageous and troublesome for the Church. On the one hand, it ensured that the papacy would enjoy independence from Byzantine emperors who wished to exert influence over the Church's ecclesiastical affairs. Hence, it made the ongoing missionary work and ecclesiastical organization more manageable for the Church hierarchy. Furthermore, the defined territory of the Papal States would also serve as a means of protection against the Lombards and other bellicose peoples. On the other hand, the kinds of temptations that always beset those in political power became suddenly relevant for those in authority. Because of this, some abuses arose in the Church which otherwise might have been avoided. It is pointless to deny that there were such abuses—they are well documented—but it is also wrongheaded to place an undue importance upon them. The ministers of the Church, who are human, are as capable of sin and error as any secular leader. This is evidenced in St. Peter's early denial of Jesus. But the Church herself, insofar as she is the spiritual Bride of Christ, continued (and continues) to teach the truth and sanctify her people despite human failings. It bears repeating that it is the Holy Spirit who holds in existence and guides the Catholic Church.

CHARLEMAGNE (REIGNED 769-814)

Charlemagne's simple throne in the Palace Chapel in the Aachen Cathedral chapel.

Charles, the son of Pepin, became after the death of his brother Carolman the inheritor of his father's kingdom. Charles ruled for a long period, many years of which were devoted to securing and expanding his kingdom. Although economically draining, his frantic military activity—he led at least fifty military campaigns—was not in vain. By the time of his death in 814, Charles had unified most of Western Europe under one Christian ruler.

Charles, known as "the Great" (in English, the French title "Charlemagne" is used; in Latin, *Carolus Magnus*), was the most powerful and charismatic ruler to emerge in the West since the days of the great Caesars. He was a powerful and ruthless warrior, as was his grandfather; but unlike his grandfather, he combined his military excellence with extraordinary political ability. No common warlord, Charlemagne knew both Latin and Greek, and had committed large parts of St. Augustine's *City of God* to memory. His interest in ecclesiastical and civil reforms did much for the growth of European culture. Centuries after his death European leaders and kings sought to emulate his reign.

Charlemagne's public policy was explicitly Christian. He drew from the laws of the Church (Canon Law) for his own civic legislation, and he considered the decrees of synods and councils to be lawfully binding for his subjects. Moreover, officials of the Church also served in Charlemagne's civil posts, and often acted as his diplomats. Charlemagne himself, in an effort to model his rule on the Person of Christ, built himself a throne without precious stones to signify the simplicity of Christ's Incarnation.

Providentially, Charlemagne acted in the best interests of the Church. He tried to reform the clergy, established new dioceses, and raised the necessary funds to support worship and the priests. In order to maintain control over his empire, Charlemagne appointed *missi dominici*, civil servants who were investigators. Their responsibility was to enter all the different parts of the empire and provide reports on the civil and religious life of particular areas.

A devout Catholic, Charlemagne rigorously observed his times for prayer and fasting, and attended many liturgical ceremonies. In addition, he sang in the choir and read the Bible daily.

Despite Charlemagne's sincere religiosity, it would be wrong to idealize him excessively. He was all too willing to interfere in ecclesiastical governance—for instance, he appointed his own bishops—and treated cruelly the people of Saxony. Nonetheless, his very real faults were often the result of a misapplied or ill-informed zeal, rather than manifestations of any truly evil intent, and he died in the arms of the Church, which he loved so much and defended so often.

This portrait of Emperor Charlemagne by Albrecht Dürer portrays him with a divine, iconic countenance. He is shown with the robe, crown, sword and orb used in the actual coronation, which were sketched from the originals by Dürer.

CHARLEMAGNE'S RELATIONSHIP TO THE PAPACY

The Lombards, who had been defeated under Pepin, again threatened Rome in July of 773. Pope Adrian I (772-795) sought Charlemagne's aid, and in response Charlemagne and his troops routed the invading Lombards. As Charlemagne marched into Rome on Easter the following year, he received a hero's welcome. Three doors of St. Peter's were opened wide to receive Charlemagne, and upon entering, he prostrated himself before the pope. Adrian granted the title "Patrician of Rome" to Charlemagne and renewed the papacy's alliance with the Franks. Charlemagne subsequently made himself king of the Lombards, and thus became the first ruler to unite all the Germanic kingdoms.

Charlemagne marched into Rome again in 800, this time to investigate charges of corruption that had been brought against Pope St. Leo III, Adrian's successor. The Roman nobility, who for at least a hundred years had been a source of pain for the Church, had accused St. Leo III of conspiracy and corruption and locked him in a monastery to await trial. Pope St. Leo III escaped his imprisonment and begged Charlemagne to restore him to power. Charlemagne wept over the injustices committed against the successor to St. Peter and made plans to rectify the situation.

Under oath and before Charlemagne, Pope St. Leo III swore that he was innocent of the crimes charged him. Fortunately, with the help of Charlemagne, St. Leo III was able to escape the Romans' machinations.

CHARLEMAGNE CROWNED EMPEROR (800)

Only a couple days after the completion of his trial, Pope St. Leo III crowned Charlemagne emperor during the Christmas day Mass at St. Peter's Basilica in 800. This crowning, which sources say took Charlemagne by surprise, was not just a reaffirmation of Charlemagne's title as "King of the Franks and Lombards" which he had held for some years, it now made him a Roman Emperor. The new imperial title given by the pope placed Charlemagne's Carolingian empire in a direct line of descent from the old Roman Empire. Charlemagne's crowning by the pope meant that the Germans were finally incorporated into Roman civilization.

The actions of Pope St. Leo III and Charlemagne infuriated the Byzantine emperors. Since the Byzantine emperors still considered themselves the rightful imperial rulers of Western Europe, they viewed the papacy's actions with contempt. In place of Byzantine rule, which they traced to Constantine the Great, the West was now ruled by a person whom they considered a barbarian. At first Byzantium refused to recognize the legitimacy of this newly formed empire, but because of Charlemagne's power and influence, they eventually recognized him, referring to him as the *Basileus* (king) of the West.

CHARLEMAGNE AND THE SAXONS

The Saxons were a band of pagan tribes that lived along the northeastern frontiers of Germany. Charlemagne engaged in war against them over the course of a number of years, 772 to 803. The Saxons were well known for their resistance to the Christian Faith. They would initially convert and be subdued, only to rebel and kill Christians. Therefore, Charlemagne believed that he had no other choice than to force their conversion by the sword. To this end, he treated them with excessive harshness, at one point ordering the beheading of four thousand of them.

The Saxons perhaps best exemplify Charlemagne's weaknesses as a ruler, but the wrath that led to their ill-treatment found other expressions as well. Charlemagne sometimes forced the conversion of peoples through terror. He also made liberal use of capital punishment. Under Charlemagne's law, any of the following merited the supreme penalty: killing a priest, belonging to a heathen group that resisted Christianity, stealing, eating meat on Friday, refusing to fast, refusing Baptism, or cremating a body. Charlemagne considered infractions against Christ's teachings as crimes, without recognizing that his disproportionate punishments egregiously contradicted the true message of the Gospel.

THE CAROLINGIAN RENAISSANCE

The years before Charlemagne's rule had decidedly been years of decline in the West. Political instability and corruption led quickly to an intellectual collapse, and when Charlemagne assumed office, the study of theology and literature — so rich in the East — was absent in large part in the continental West. Further, Latin had so deteriorated that it was rendered almost unintelligible to a listener from Classical Rome. One of Charlemagne's most enduring legacies was to combat this cultural decay by emphasizing the importance of education and artistic excellence in his political vision. He commanded that every monastery and parish had to have a school.

Charlemagne receives the scholar Alcuin at his palace in Aachen, Germany.

Because of Charlemagne's insistence, the clergy of the Church were better instructed in classical and biblical texts than they had been for several hundred years. This improved literacy led to a renewed enthusiasm for the Catholic Faith and the rich, profound literature connected with it, thus paving the way for a new wave of missionary activity.

ALCUIN, CAROLINGIAN SCHOLAR

Alcuin (ca. 740-804) was the best and most influential scholar of the Carolingian Renaissance. Born an Englishman in Northumberland and educated at York, Alcuin had spent some time in Italy before being asked to join Charlemagne's court at Aachen in 782 and to participate in the new spirit of learning along with other scholars of the Carolingian Renaissance. He retired in France as the abbot of St. Martin's monastery in Tours.

Alcuin's scholarly output included a wide variety of texts covering the Bible and the theological tradition, as well as a Latin grammar and several mathematical tracts. During his time in France, he oversaw the production of a new edition of the Tours Bible (four were prepared by him). Alcuin also took a keen interest in the liturgy of the Church; he revised the Roman Lectionary and the Gregorian Sacramentary.

THE EMPIRE OF CHARLEMAGNE, 768-814

NORTH SEA

York

BRITAIN

Hamburg

SAXONY

Corvey

THURINGIA

Cologne · Mainz · Fulda

St Wandrille · St Riquier · Laon · Echternach · Aachen
Corbie · Soissons · Rheims · Prum
Rouen · Chartres · Trier · Metz
BRITTANY
Paris · Lorsch
Le Mans · Orleans · Auxerre · Hirsau
Angers · Tours · Sens · Strasbourg · Kremsmunster
Noirmoutier · Luxeuil · Reichenau · Salzburg
ATLANTIC OCEAN · Bourges · Besançon · St Gallen
Poitiers · **ALAMANNIA**
AQUITANIA · Ferrières · **BURGUNDY** · Aquileia
Limoges · Lyons · **LOMBARDY** · Venice
Bordeaux · Vienne · Tarentaise · Milan · Brescia · Pavia
Embrun · Bobbio
GASCONY · Toulouse · Arles · **PROVENCE** · Ravenna
Narbonne · Aix-en-Provence
Marseilles

BOHEMIA

BAVARIA

CARINTHIA

UMAYYAD CALIPHATE
Barcelona

CORSICA

Rome
Monte Cassino

MEDITERRANEAN SEA

Frankish Empire at accession of Charlemagne, 768
Conquests of Charlemagne to 814
Marches
△ Archbishopric
✠ Important monastery
✠ Notable Carolingian school (and monastery)

© 1997 Lion Hudson plc / Three's Company

| 0 | 250 | 500 km |
| 0 | 100 | 200 | 300 miles |

Above right: The Imperial Crown of the Holy Roman Empire, the "Crown of Charlemagne," is crafted of gold, cloisonné enamel, precious stones, and pearls. Eight hinged plates form the octagonal body of the imperial crown. Four plates bear pictorial representations from the Old Testament in cloisonné enamel, and four plates have precious stones and pearls. The twelve precious stones on the brow plate correspond to the number of the Apostles. The twelve stones on the neck plate refer to the breast-plate of the Jewish high priest and are engraved with the names of the twelve tribes of Israel.

THE GREAT SCHISM, 1054

ATLANTIC
OCEAN

Trondheim

Uppsala

Don

NORMANS

Kiev

Vistula

Prague   Krakow

Danube   Halicz

ROME   CONSTANTINOPLE   CASPIAN

BLACK SEA

Ravenna   Trnovo

Belgrade

Rome   Sardica

Constantinople   Chalcedon

Bari   Thessalonica   Nicaea

Naples   Melitene

SARDINIA   Salerno

SICILY   Antioch

CRETE   RHODES

CYPRUS

MEDITERRANEAN SEA

MUSLIM

Boundary of communion with Rome, c. 1050
Boundary of communion with Constantinople, c. 1050
Overlapping area of churches with allegiance to Rome or Constantinople
Norman invasions, 1057–85
Northern limit of Islamic rule, c. 1050

0   500   1000 km

0   200   400   600 miles

©1997 Lion Hudson plc / Three's Company

PART IV
The Great Schism

The final shattering of communion between East and West in 1054 is one of the saddest chapters in the history of the Church. Though the seed of division had already been planted with the founding of Constantinople in the fourth century, alienation intensified during the ninth century because of both the Iconoclast controversy and Charlemagne's rise in power. By the eleventh century, the East and West were held together by only the most tenuous of relationships, and the slightest event was likely to separate them.

THE EMERGENCE OF DIFFERENCES

Aside from the subtleties of theological disputes and the many misunderstandings that arose, the growing distance between East and West also owed much to their different conceptions of Church government and hierarchy. It may be helpful to present a brief account of this difference.

The Bishop of Rome, the pope, had a dual jurisdiction in the Church: the Latin West, centered in Rome, as well as the universal Church. As Constantinople grew in power over successive centuries, it tightened its grip around the other ancient eastern centers of Christianity at Antioch, Alexandria, and Jerusalem. After the doctrinal statements at the Ecumenical Council of Chalcedon in 451, these were recognized along with Rome as especially ancient and important centers of Christianity.

For both political and theological reasons, however, the Christians of the East tended to minimize the pope's status as chief shepherd of the Church. Eastern Christians seldom referred to him except in extreme cases, often during a difficult dispute in the Church, at which point he was often sought out to settle the dispute. From very early on—for varying reasons covered in this chapter—Eastern believers allied themselves more closely with their own national patriarchs than with the successor of St. Peter.

In addition to this, caesaropapism, expressed in the symbiotic relationship between the patriarch of Constantinople and the eastern emperor, was also a cause of tension. The patriarch crowned the emperor, and in turn the emperor made an oath to protect the Church and preserve the Faith. Thus, the patriarch of Constantinople often acted as a very important government official in the bureaucracy of imperial administration in the East, and the emperor, in turn, often acted as a very high-ranking member of the Church's body.

It will be noted that this was similar to the relationship the popes later sought with the Carolingians. However, as has already been seen, the eastern emperors were often at the heart of heresy in the East, which was not the case with Charlemagne, and they played a major role in each of the five schisms that occurred between 325 and 825.

Finally, the relationship of the religious to the laity in the East was very different from that in the West. In the West the monasteries and convents worked together with the surrounding pop-

Above: An artist's concept of Justinian I's Church of Holy Wisdom in ca. 538.

LITURGICAL PRACTICES OF THE EASTERN CHURCHES

There are two basic kinds of Eastern Churches: Orthodox and Catholic. Whereas the Eastern Orthodox Churches are not in communion with Rome, a number of Orthodox Churches have reunited with Rome at various times during the last millennium. These are called Eastern Uniate (from *union*) Churches or Eastern Catholic Churches. Though some theological differences divide them, the Orthodox and Uniate Churches share the same liturgical and devotional practices.

His Holiness Patriarch Alexy II of Moscow and Russia celebrating the Divine Liturgy, 2003.

The liturgy practiced in both the Eastern and Western (Roman) Churches is ultimately based on the liturgical practices of the Apostles and Fathers of the Church. Because Greek was the common language and culture of the Roman Empire in the first century, it was no surprise that liturgical practices in the early Church were essentially Greek. The liturgy of the Eastern Churches has always been conducted in the vernacular; a good example of this may be found in the story of Sts. Cyril and Methodius, who translated the Bible and liturgical texts into the native language of the Slavs (see chapter 6). Over time, however, the liturgy of the West incorporated more Latin (Roman) customs, whereas in the lands east of the Mediterranean Sea, the liturgy remained Greek.

Music in the Eastern Churches is divided into two main traditions: Byzantine and Russian. Byzantine music—generally sung *a cappella*—is based on modes developed by the Greeks before the time of Christ. Mixed with elements of Jewish chant and psalmody, this music sounds foreign and unfamiliar to westerners. Russian music is based on Byzantine but developed in the seventeenth century under Polish influence. Most Russian liturgical music employs western scales, making it incorporable with German, French and Italian musical traditions.

One of the basic differences between West and East is the sign of the cross. In the Eastern Churches, the tradition is retained of bringing together the thumb, forefinger, and middle finger whereas the other two are pressed against the palm. This is a symbolic reminder of the three Persons of the Triune God and the two natures of Christ. In addition, the horizontal "beam" of the cross is traced from right to left. For blessing, a bishop or priest joins his thumb, ring, and little fingers while forming a cross with the other two.

His All-Holiness Bartholomew I, Patriarch of Constantinople, blessing the congregation.

In the Eastern Church's blessing the fingers form the shape of the Greek letters "IC XC," the abbreviation in Greek for Jesus Christ.

ulations to teach them the rudiments of agrarian life along with the fundamentals of Christianity. In the East the monks were more secluded, if not more learned, and had little contact with the outside world whatsoever, thus limiting their influence.

THE *FILIOQUE* CONTROVERSY

Beginning at a local council, the Third Council of Toledo in 589, the words "and the Son" (Latin, *Filioque*) were added to the Nicene-Constantinopolitan Creed. By 800 this formulation of the creed was standard throughout the Frankish empire of Charlemagne.

This addition was meant to clarify a theological point. The Nicene-Constantinopolitan Creed could be read to attribute the procession of the Holy Spirit from the Father but only through the Son, though this was not what that creed intended. The Nicene-Constantinopolitan Creed was developed in opposition to those who denied that the Holy Spirit proceeded from the Father. The Nicene-Constantinopolitan Creed, then, did not deny that the Holy Spirit proceeded from the Son as well as the Father; it just failed to mention it explicitly. So the new Toledo creed merely clarified what was already an ancient belief in both East and West, namely, that the Holy Spirit proceeded from the Father and the Son.

The Patriarch of Constantinople steadfastly refused the addition to the creed, even though historical evidence suggests that most of the Greek Fathers believed in the Holy Spirit's double-procession from the Father and the Son. Eastern scholars argue that the Catholic Church violated the Council of Chalcedon's (449) injunction not to change the creed, but it is accepted all around that the addition of *Filioque* amounts to a clarification rather than an alteration intended to improve or change belief. Nonetheless, the Greeks did not accept *Filioque* even when it was imposed upon them during two councils aimed at healing the Great Schism (Councils of Lyons [1274] and of Florence [1439]), and have not accepted it to this day.

THE PHOTIAN SCHISM (857-867)

In 857, Patriarch Ignatius of Constantinople refused a high government official, by the name of Bardas, Holy Communion on the Feast of the Epiphany because of rumors regarding an adulterous affair. Bardas' reaction, and Ignatius' determination interpreted as insolence, convinced emperor Michael III to depose Ignatius in 858.

In Ignatius' place, Emperor Michael III elevated Photius (ca. 810-895) to Patriarch of Constantinople. Photius, though a layman, was a brilliant and ambitious scholar. He was quickly ordained and ushered into the patriarchate.

When Ignatius refused to step aside, Michael III and Photius wrote obsequious letters to the pope, requesting that he send legates to Constantinople to handle the situation. Pope St. Nicholas I (858-867) sent two legates who were promptly bought off by Michael and Photius. The legates settled the dispute in favor of Photius and returned to Rome with the intention of convincing the pope of their decision. When the pope discovered their treachery, he excommunicated them. He, then in 862, wrote letters to both the emperor and Photius claiming that his legates had exceeded their authority and that Ignatius was to be reinvested as Patriarch. In 863 another council in Rome voided the settlement in Constantinople. Photius and all his appointments in the Church were denied recognition.

This infuriated the emperor. He wrote the pope demanding that the matter be reexamined. The pope agreed in 865 to look at the case again. During this time Photius remained silent, but carried out the duties of his office. In 867, however, Photius rejected the presence of Latin missionaries in Bulgaria, which he considered the missionary territory of Constantinople. In addition, Photius charged the papacy with tampering with the Nicene Creed through its use of the *Filioque* clause, and tried to stir a popular uprising against Rome.

The year 867 marked a turning point in the dispute. Pope St. Nicholas I died, and Michael III and Bardas were assassinated during a revolution in Constantinople. The new emperor Basil I desired reconciliation with the new pope, Adrian II, and at the Eighth Ecumenical Council, Constantinople IV (869-870), Photius was removed. Ignatius was reinstated but continuing tension over Bulgaria and the *Filioque* kept hard feelings of the schism alive. When Pope Adrian II denied the institution of a patriarchate in Bulgaria, King Boris of Bulgaria chose Constantinople as the spiritual center for his people. In 870 Ignatius began consecrating bishops for Bulgaria in disobedience to the pope, and this renewed hostilities between Rome and the East.

Ignatius died in 877, and Photius, who had spent the intervening years building a strong base of support, once again became patriarch. The Holy See could not but recognize his appointment, for even though he was an unqualified candidate for the patriarchy, the position was, this time, legitimately open. Once reinstated, Photius renewed his campaign against Rome, excommunicating the entire Latin Church for their liturgical irregularities and their alteration of the creed of 451. Although many Eastern bishops realized the error of Photius' ways, he possessed so much power among the people, whom he had turned against Rome, that it was impossible to resist him. Photius finally was forced into a second, and final, resignation upon the ascension of the new emperor Leo VI in 886. The East remained in communion with Rome for the next two hundred years, but Photius' dissension had struck deep roots among the Greek people and would resurface later, during the Great Schism.

Interior and dome of Hagia Sophia, Istanbul (formerly Constantinople). In this magnificent location Cardinal Humbert, on July 16, 1054, laid down upon its altar a bull of excommunication from Pope Leo IX, which would have a negative impact on the Christian world that has lasted for centuries.

THE GREAT SCHISM (1054)

The final split between the eastern and western Churches came in the year 1054. In the Great Schism all of the tension that had developed over the previous centuries came to a head. The doctrinal dispute over the *Filioque,* the crowning of Charlemagne as emperor of the West in 800, the issues of authority raised in the Photian schism, and the reforming tendencies under the leadership of the papacy in the West all came into focus. In addition, Byzantium had increased its military strength, and wanted to achieve a greater degree of independence from the West. These circumstances combined to shatter the thousand-year communion between East and West.

PATRIARCH MICHAEL CERULARIUS

Before being appointed patriarch, Michael Cerularius (1043-1058) had lived in seclusion in a monastery in the East. Many, though not all, Eastern monasteries had been decidedly influenced by Photius' dissent. When Cerularius became patriarch, his anti-Latin sentiments came out into the open, and the target of his attack was the papacy, which he regarded with disgust.

Patriarch Michael Cerularius objected to many Western practices that differed from the East. In particular he objected to a celibate priesthood, the Saturday fast, the use of unleavened bread in the Mass, beardless priests, eating meat with blood, and omitting the alleluia during Lent.

The patriarch was so disenchanted with the West that he closed Latin parishes in Constantinople. When consecrated hosts from Latin churches were trampled upon, Cardinal Humbert in the West translated this as a Greek attack on the Latin Church and Pope Leo IX (1049-1054). Cardinal Humbert was entrusted with the papal reply that would prove disastrous.

Cardinal Humbert made it plain to the patriarch that it is impossible to excommunicate the pope, and that the pope holds primacy in the Church, even over patriarchs. Patriarch Cerularius is said to have replied: "If you venerate my name in a single church in Rome, I will venerate your name in all the churches in the East." The papal response came in the form of an ultimatum: "Either be in communion with Peter or become a synagogue of Satan." Henceforth the patriarch deleted the pope's name from all liturgies.

Two papal legates, Cardinal Humbert and Frederick of Lorraine, the latter of whom would later become pope, were sent to Constantinople. Neither possessed much diplomatic skill, and because of their arrogance, Patriarch Cerularius was able to turn the population of Constantinople against them.

Pope Stephen X (IX) was pope for only eight months, 1057-1058. His original name was Frederick of Lorraine, one of the two papal legates sent to Constantinople by Pope Leo IX to confront Patriarch Cerularius. The results from that journey in 1054 precipitated the final split between the eastern and western churches. He continued his position as abbot of Monte Cassino during his short reign as pope. An ardent reformer, he was advised by Peter (St.) Damian, Cardinal Humbert and Hildebrand who would become Pope St. Gregory VII.

CONTEMPORARY EFFORTS TO HEAL THE SCHISM

While schisms are easily made, they can be very difficult to heal. Unfortunately, misunderstandings and disputes have caused seemingly permanent damage and weakened the Church to this very day. Pope John Paul II realized this, and made great efforts to reach out to the Eastern Orthodox Church by opening dialogue that may, someday, ultimately heal this ancient schism. In an unprecedented visit to Greece in May 2001, the pope addressed the Orthodox Archbishop and Holy Synod in Athens. An excerpt of the pope's address sheds light on his mission and goal to heal the Schism:

"Finally, Your Beatitude, I wish to express the hope that we may walk together in the ways of the kingdom of God. In 1965, the Ecumenical Patriarch Athenagoras and Pope Paul VI by a mutual act removed and cancelled from the Church's memory and life the sentence of excommunication between Rome and Constantinople. This historic gesture stands as *a summons for us to work ever more fervently for the unity which is Christ's will.* Division between Christians is a sin before God and a scandal before the world. It is a hindrance to the spread of the Gospel, because it makes our proclamation less credible. The Catholic Church is convinced that she must do all in her power to 'prepare the way of the Lord' and to 'make straight his paths' (Mt 3:3); and she understands that this must be done in company with other Christians—in fraternal dialogue, in cooperation, and in prayer. If certain models of reunion of the past no longer correspond to the impulse towards unity which the Holy Spirit has awakened in Christians everywhere in recent times, we must be all the more open and attentive to what the Spirit is now saying to the Churches (cf. Rv 2:11)"

(John Paul II, "Holy Father Asks Pardon for Past Sins," *L'Osservatore Romano,* Weekly Edition in English, no.19, May 9, 2001, p. 5).

Pope John Paul II in Athens in 2001.

Pope John Paul II in Syria in 2001.

Patriarch of Constantinople Athenagoras meets with Pope Paul VI in 1964.

THE ACTUAL SCHISM

On July 16, 1054, Cardinal Humbert attended the Divine Liturgy at Hagia Sophia in Constantinople. There he denounced the patriarch for refusing papal authority. Upon the high altar in Hagia Sophia, Cardinal Humbert laid a document excommunicating Patriarch Cerularius. Humbert and Frederick then left the cathedral and shook the dust from their shoes outside.

Technically, however, the two legates did not have the authority to excommunicate in the pope's name because Pope Leo IX had just died.

The Eastern Emperor Constantine IX wanted to heal the rift, especially since he needed military help from the West against the Normans. In response to his call for reconciliation the patriarch incited riots; the emperor, not wanting to face a civil war, backed down from his position. The documents of excommunication were burned by the patriarch, and a council in Constantinople declared on July 24, 1054 that the Latins had perverted the Faith. Patriarch Michael Cerularius had returned excommunication for excommunication.

Since that time, the Patriarch of Constantinople has been known as the "Ecumenical Patriarch" of the East, and in Eastern tradition is regarded as the "first among equals" among the eastern patriarchs. On December 7, 1965, before the closing Mass of the Second Vatican Council, Pope Paul VI and Patriarch Athenagoras of Constantinople participated in a show of reconciliation. In a joint declaration they expressed regret over the mutual excommunication of Patriarch Cerularius and the papal legate Cardinal Humbert in 1054.

CONCLUSION

During this period two distinct forms of Christianity came into being. While the East turned violently onto itself in the Iconoclastic Controversy, the West developed its first unity under the leadership of the Franks and the popes. However, the communion between East and West was shattered in the Great Schism that has separated, to this day, the two traditions with the same sacraments. From the perspective of the Catholic Church, the major difference between Eastern and Western Christianity primarily involves the teaching authority and jurisdiction of the papacy established by Christ through his Apostle St. Peter.

Mosaic in the apse of Hagia Sophia in Istanbul (Constantinople), dedicated by Photius on March 29, 867 as the first new mosaic after the period of iconoclasm.

Photius' celebratory oration, Homily XVII, is one of the key documents in Byzantine art history.

"For though the time is short since the pride of the iconoclastic heresy has been reduced to ashes, and true religion has spread its lights to the ends of the world, . . . this too is our ornament."

SUPPLEMENTARY READING

Codex Justinianus, II, 1-2, 9, 11

Natural, Common, and Civil Law. The law of nature is that law which nature teaches to all animals. For this law does not belong exclusively to the human race, but belongs to all animals, whether of the earth, the air, or the water. Hence comes the union of the male and female, which we term matrimony; hence the procreation and bringing up of children. We see, indeed, that all the other animals besides men are considered as having knowledge of this law.

1. Civil law is thus distinguished from the law of nations. Every community governed by laws and customs uses partly its own law, partly laws common to all mankind. The law which a people makes for its own government belongs exclusively to that state and is called the civil law, as being the law of the particular state.

2. Civil law takes its name from the state which it governs, as, for instance, from Athens....But whenever we speak of civil law, without adding the name of any state, we mean our own law.

9. The unwritten law is that which usage has established; for ancient customs, being sanctioned by the consent of those who adopt them, are like laws.

11. The laws of nature, which all nations observe alike, being established by a divine providence, remain ever fixed and immutable.

Joint Declaration made by Pope Paul VI and the Patriarch Athenagoras, December 7, 1965

Among the obstacles in the way of the development of these brotherly relationships of trust and esteem (between the Roman Catholic Church and the Orthodox Church) is the memory of painful decisions, acts and incidents which in 1054 came to a climax with the sentence of excommunication pronounced against the Patriarch Michael Cerularius and two other figures by the legates of the Holy See, led by cardinal Humbert, legates who were themselves then the object of a similar sentence passed by the Patriarch and Synod of Constantinople....

...Pope Paul VI and Patriarch Athenagoras I, in this synod, confident of expressing the common desire for justice and the unanimous feeling of love among their faithful, and recalling the precept of the Lord, "When you present your offerings at the altar..." Mt 5: 23-24, declare with one accord that they:

a) Regret the offensive words, the unfounded accusations and the despicable act which, form one side or the other, marked or accompanied the sad events of this period;

b) Equally regret and blot out from memory and form the realm of the church the sentences of excommunication which ensued, the memory of which, even on our day acts as an obstacle to reconciliation in love, and consign them to oblivion;

c) Finally, deplore the disturbing precedents and the subsequent events which, under the influence of various factors, including a failure to understand and a mutual distrust, finally led to the effective schism in communion.

John Paul II, *Ut Unum Sint*, 54.2, 55.1

The Church must breathe with her two lungs! In the first millennium of the history of Christianity, this expression refers primarily of the relationship between Byzantium and Rome. From the time of the Baptism of Rus' it comes to have an even wider application: evangelization spread to a much vaster area, so that it now includes the entire Church....

In its historical survey the Council decree *Unitatis redintegratio* has in mind the unity which, in spite of everything, was experienced in the first millennium and in a certain sense now serves as a kind of model....The Church's journey began in Jerusalem on the day of Pentecost and its original expansion in the *oikoumene* of that time was centered around Peter and the Eleven. The structures of the Church in the East and in the West evolved in reference to that apostolic heritage.

VOCABULARY

CAESAROPAPISM

System in which the temporal ruler extends his own powers to ecclesiastical and theological matters. Such emperors appointed bishops and the Eastern Patriarch, directed the development of liturgical practices, and even aided the recruitment of monks.

CODEX JUSTINIANUS

Compiled under Emperor Justinian I, the codex was the collection and systemization of all Roman law as it had developed from his predecessors put together for the purpose of legal uniformity throughout the empire. It is the basis for canon law as well as the civil law throughout Europe.

COUNCIL OF HIEREIA

A local (non-ecumenical) council convened by Constantine V to condemn the use of icons.

DULIA AND LATRIA

Two types of adoration whose distinction was drawn at the seventh Council of Nicaea. An icon may be venerated through acts of respect an honor, called *dulia*, but God alone is worth of absolute adoration, known in Greek as *latria*.

FILIOQUE

Latin meaning "and the Son," this was first added at the Third Council of Toledo (589) to the Nicene-Constatinopolitan Creed to clarify that the Holy Spirit proceeded from both the Father and the Son. Later, the Patriarch of Constantinople and the bishops of the East refused the addition, thus contributing to the Great Schism.

GREAT SCHISM

The final split between the eastern and western Churches in the year 1054.

HAGIA SOPHIA

Most famous example of Byzantine architecture, it was built under Justinian I and is considered one of the most perfect buildings in the world.

ICON

A flat, two-dimensional picture of Christ, the Virgin Mary, or one of the saints which is used as an aid for Christian acts of piety. The general artistic style of icons reflects a certain mystical beauty of Christ the Savior and the saints. When rightly understood, the icon, by virtue of what is represented, is seen as an invitation to prayer.

ICONOCLASM

Thoughts or deeds of an iconoclast. Refers to periods in history when a large number of iconoclasts were present.

ICONOCLAST

From the Greek word *eikonoklastēs* meaning "image breaker," iconoclasts saw icons as occasions of idolatry and sought to destroy them and purify the practice of the Christian religion. They were condemned at the second council of Nicaea in 787.

ICONOPHILE

Greek for "lover of icons," this term refers to those who defend and promote the proper use of icons in Christian worship.

LATRIA

See *dulia*.

MONOPHYSITISM

Heresy claiming that there is only one nature in Christ and that His human nature is "incorporated" into the Divine Nature.

PAPAL STATES

Lands around Rome, Italy, won by Pepin on behalf and given to the papacy, making the pope a sovereign as well as spiritual leader. The Papal States were ruled by the pope from 754 to 1870.

STUDY QUESTIONS

1. Describe the geography of the location for Constantinople.

2. What was Emperor Justinian I's great ambition?

3. How did monophysitism cause problems for Justinian I?

4. How is an icon not a violation of the first commandment?

5. What were the results of Emperor Leo III's forbiddance of icons?

6. Why did the Council of Hiereia not meet the conditions for an ecumenical council?

7. What was St. John of Damascus' basic argument in support of icons?

8. What happened to Emperor Nicephorus, and how did this help to inaugurate the Second Iconoclasm?

9. What role did the papacy and St. Boniface play in raising the Carolingian line to that of king of the Franks and deposing the Merovingians?

10. What was the significance of the relationship between the papacy and the Frankish king?

11. How did the Papal States come into existence?

12. Who was Charlemagne, and how did he help the Church?

13. When was Charlemagne crowned emperor by Pope St. Leo III?

14. Define the Carolingian Renaissance.

15. How does Alcuin symbolize the unity of western Europe in general and of Charlemagne's empire in particular?

16. What was the Photian Schism?

17. What were some practices that Cerularius disliked in the Latin Church?

18. What did the Eastern emperor think about the schism?

PRACTICAL EXERCISES

1. Bible churches and even some of the Reformation era churches claim that by the presence of statues and icons, the Catholic Church violates the First Commandment. What arguments would you give, for example, that veneration of a statue of Mary is not idol worship?

2. What would you say to someone who said that creeds and arguments over creeds are irrelevant because all that one needs is faith in Jesus? "Creeds are not in the Bible, so they don't count," someone might say. Are the creeds important?

3. Describe the situation between the Roman Catholic Church and Eastern Orthodox Churches. Why is unity desirable? How is unity among the bishops of the Church invaluable? Why should bishops be men of great conviction, humility, and understanding?

FROM THE CATECHISM

817 In fact, "in this one and only Church of God from its very beginnings there arose certain rifts, which the Apostle strongly censures as damnable. But in subsequent centuries much more serious dissensions appeared and large communities became separated from full communion with the Catholic Church—for which, often enough, men of both sides were to blame" (*UR* 3 § 1). The ruptures that wound the unity of Christ's Body—here we must distinguish heresy, apostasy, and schism (cf. CIC, can. 751)—do not occur without human sin:

> Where there are sins, there are also divisions, schisms, heresies, and disputes. Where there is virtue, however, there also are harmony and unity, from which arise the one heart and one soul of all believers (Origen, *Hom. in Ezech.* 9, 1: PG 13, 732).

818 "However, one cannot charge with the sin of the separation those who at present are born into these communities [that resulted from such separation] and in them are brought up in the faith of Christ, and the Catholic Church accepts them with respect and affection as brothers....All who have been justified by faith in Baptism are incorporated into Christ; they therefore have a right to be called Christians, and with good reason are accepted as brothers in the Lord by the children of the Catholic Church" (*UR* 3 § 1).

819 "Furthermore, many elements of sanctification and of truth" (*LG* 8 § 2) are found outside the visible confines of the Catholic Church: "the written Word of God; the life of grace; faith, hope, and charity, with the other interior gifts of the Holy Spirit, as well as visible elements" (*UR* 3 § 2; cf. *LG* 15). Christ's Spirit uses these Churches and ecclesial communities as means of salvation, whose power derives from the fullness of grace and truth that Christ has entrusted to the Catholic Church. All these blessings come from Christ and lead to him (cf. *UR* 3), and are in themselves calls to "Catholic unity" (cf. *LG* 8).

2502 *Sacred art* is true and beautiful when its form corresponds to its particular vocation: evoking and glorifying, in faith and adoration, the transcendent mystery of God—the surpassing invisible beauty of truth and love visible in Christ, who "reflects the glory of God and bears the very stamp of his nature," in whom "the whole fullness of deity dwells bodily" (Heb 1: 3; Col 2: 9). This spiritual beauty of God is reflected in the most holy Virgin Mother of God, the angels, and saints. Genuine sacred art draws man to adoration, to prayer, and to the love of God, Creator and Savior, the Holy One and Sanctifier.

2503 For this reason bishops, personally or through delegates, should see to the promotion of sacred art, old and new, in all its forms and, with the same religious care, remove from the liturgy and from places of worship everything which is not in conformity with the truth of faith and the authentic beauty of *sacred* art (cf. *SC* 122-127).

2513 The fine arts, but above all sacred art, "of their nature are directed toward expressing in some way the infinite beauty of God in works made by human hands. Their dedication to the increase of God's praise and of his glory is more complete, the more exclusively they are devoted to turning men's minds devoutly toward God" (*SC* 122).

Collapse, Corruption, And Reform In Europe And The Church

This period contained some of the worst scandals in the history of the Church. In response, saintly priests, monks and nuns brought about some of the most important reforms in Christian history.

CHAPTER 8

Collapse, Corruption, And Reform In Europe And The Church

The face and function of the Church cannot be understood unless we go right to the depths of her nature: in conferring Baptism on us, she is our Mother, she gives us life in Christ, she makes us holy and transmits the gift of the Holy Spirit to us. In the Eucharist, a thank-offering to the Father and a bond of fellowship among us, we are privileged to share in Christ's redemptive sacrifice. Outside of this sacramental dimension, we cannot but have a superficial and totally perverted vision of the Church.

— John Paul II, To the Bishops of the Apostolic Region, Provence Mediterranée, France, December 22, 1992

The end of Charlemagne's reign in 814 marked the end of a tenuous, but nonetheless satisfactory, balance of power in Western Europe between the Papal States on the one hand and their Frankish protectors on the other. Although Charlemagne involved himself excessively in ecclesiastical affairs, he never lost his respect for the proper autonomy of the Church, and even when he interfered, he retained a pious and respectful attitude toward her spiritual mission. Further, Charlemagne's steel will and heavy hand proved more than a match for the Roman nobility who, well before the emperor's reign, had pestered the Church with intrigue and conspiracies. But upon Charlemagne's death these different Roman factions returned more powerfully than ever. The papacy was, by this time, a very lucrative and strategic state office to hold. Sadly, the Holy See was often viewed as a political pawn to be seized and used by anyone with the power to do so. Thus three parties, as it were, struggled for the control of the papacy: leaders within the Church herself, the Roman nobles, and the Holy Roman Emperors (successors of Charlemagne). This period, lasting roughly from 814 to 1046, contains some of the worst scandals that have ever visited the Church. At the same time, this period also contains the most important ecclesiastical reformations since the earliest days of Christianity. These reforms were launched and imple-

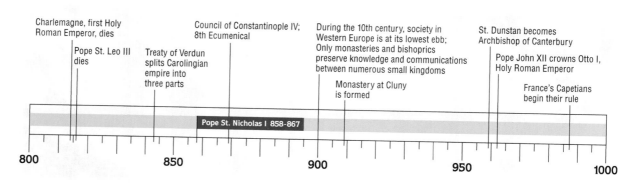

Charlemagne, first Holy Roman Emperor, dies

Pope St. Leo III dies

Treaty of Verdun splits Carolingian empire into three parts

Council of Constantinople IV; 8th Ecumenical

During the 10th century, society in Western Europe is at its lowest ebb; Only monasteries and bishoprics preserve knowledge and communications between numerous small kingdoms

Monastery at Cluny is formed

St. Dunstan becomes Archbishop of Canterbury

Pope John XII crowns Otto I, Holy Roman Emperor

France's Capetians begin their rule

Pope St. Nicholas I 858-867

800   850   900   950   1000

mented by many saintly priests, monks, and nuns. Where sin and corruption abounded among corrupt bishops and abbots, grace abounded all the more in such saints as Pope Nicholas I, Cyril and Methodius (cf. chapter 6), Pope Gregory VII, and the many anonymous holy monks of Cluny, France.

PART I

The Carolingian World Collapses

Charlemagne died in 814 and was succeeded by his son, Louis the Pious (814-830). Louis, though well-intentioned, lacked the political talent and strength of his father. Upon his death, he would make one of his worst mistakes by dividing the kingdom among his three sons: Lothar, who would become emperor, Charles, and Louis the German.

For a time, his sons jockeyed for power before signing the Treaty of Verdun in 843. This treaty divided the Carolingian empire into a western kingdom including France (Charles), a middle kingdom that stretched from the Low Countries to northern Italy (Lothar), and an eastern kingdom comprised of Germany (Louis). The middle kingdom, lacking true geographical or ethnic borders, collapsed immediately. Parts of it were brought into the German kingdom later in the tenth and eleventh centuries. Other parts, such as Alsace-Lorraine, became the objects of centuries-long conflict between France and Germany.

Simultaneous with the destruction of Carolingian unity was the influx of a new breed of invaders. Christian Europe, which under Charlemagne had defended and expanded its existing borders, came under attack from three different fronts after his death. The Saracens (Muslims) pressed from the south and advanced as far as Rome, the Vikings pressed from the north, attacking Paris, and the Slavs and Magyars advanced from the east.

The Treaty of Verdun in 843 divided the Carolingian empire among Charlemagne's three grandsons: Charles, Lothar, and Louis.

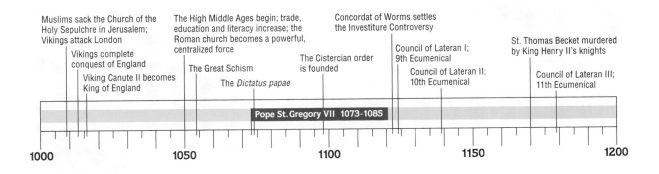

CORRUPTION OF THE PAPAL OFFICE

From the death of Stephen IV in 817 to the accession of Hildebrand as Pope Gregory VII in 1073, the course of the papacy ran a long and tortuous route, some of whose details, according to one historian, "are so grotesque that they lose all relation to reality." (Hughes, A History of the Church to the Eve of the Reformation, 1976, p. 192)

Nearly all the difficulties and corruption that the papacy faced in this period were due to the unhappy combination of domestic strife — due to political intrigue and jealous greed among the emperors, popes, and Roman nobility — and foreign invasions, especially of the Saracens in the south. While all three factions vied for power at home, all three were equally fearful of defeat from abroad. This combination of stresses cast the political world into chaos and the religious one into a litany of ecclesiastical abuse.

Aside from Pope St. Nicholas I, who served from 858 to 867, the popes of this period were either too weak to resist the emperor and Roman nobility or too corrupt even to try. This led to a convoluted series of short papacies, punctuated by occasional murders. John VIII, who was poisoned and then beaten in 882, was the first pope to suffer this end, but several of his successors soon followed suit. Many of these popes — in bizarre imitation of late Roman emperors — served for only a handful of days or months before being assassinated, usually by rival factions seeking control of the papacy.

Although a creeping mediocre corruption was the norm in this period, a few excessive abuses stand before the rest. For example, after Pope Formosus (891-896) died, his successor Pope Stephen VI exhumed his corpse and placed it on trial. A terrorized priest was forced to testify against the corpse. After a verdict of guilty, Stephen VI cut the three fingers used in blessing from his corpse, stripped it of papal garb, and threw the naked body to the mob, who, in a frenzy, tossed it into the Tiber River. Immediately after, Rome was hit by an earthquake that wrecked the Lateran Basilica. Many Romans understood this as a sign from God.

Pope John XII (955-964) was elected pope at the age of eighteen. Moreover, Pope John was already in a position of great temporal power in Rome. Having crowned Otto I as Roman emperor, Pope John's papacy was unimpeded by any imperial restraint. Unfortunately, the young pope used this freedom to cultivate his vices, and his papacy was marked by "hunting and banqueting." To pay for his wantonness, Pope John engaged in blatant simony, i.e., the selling of spiritual benefits, granting dispensations and ecclesiastical positions for temporal gain. Under Pope John XII's direction, boys were consecrated bishops as favors to their wealthy fathers, dissenting clergy were tortured or exiled, and the treasury of the Church was pilfered by the pope and his entourage. Emperor Otto I deposed Pope John XII in 963, replacing him with a layman, who would become Pope Leo VIII.

As lurid as the details are of many of the popes of this period, it would be wrong to think that the office of the papacy itself, or the Church, had completely disintegrated. Already mentioned is Pope St. Nicholas I, who in his all too brief reign of nine years, beat back imperial meddling, squelched ecclesiastical disobedience, and developed a reputation of strength and holiness that even his most depraved contemporaries respected and feared. Other popes of this period no doubt had holy intentions, but lacked the means to see them through. Apart from the popes, there remained heroic monks and priests who fought and suffered for attempted reform. A case in point is Erluin, a Benedictine monk in Belgium, who for the sake of monastic reform suffered beatings and bodily mutilation. In short, although in this dark moment in the life of the Church when there was real abuse at the highest levels, the Church provided her own best remedy through the spiritual strength of her sons and daughters.

INVASIONS OF EUROPE, 7TH TO 10TH CENTURIES

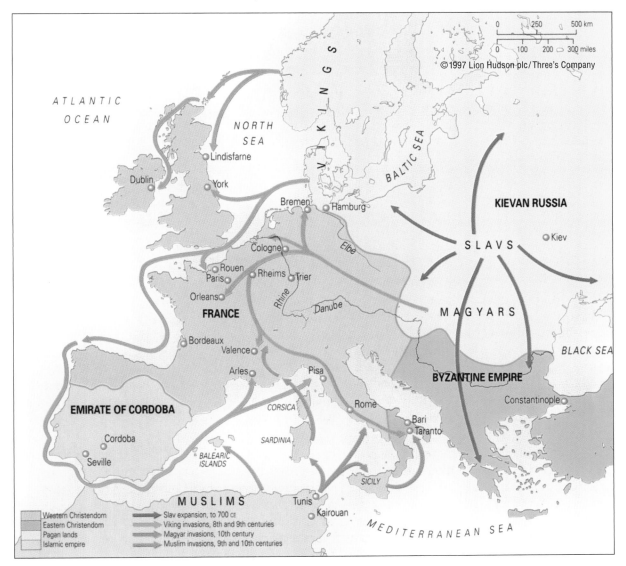

THE RISE OF FEUDALISM

As the Carolingian authority collapsed, a new system of organization emerged throughout western society. First, the Carolingian empire broke down into about fifty duchies, which spread across France and Italy and throughout Germany. Because few of these duchies were strong enough to protect all those living under their domain, eventually even smaller communities formed themselves around towns or monasteries. These communities built castles or fortifications and usually allied themselves around one lord.

This emergent system, known as feudalism, is most simply understood as a contractual system between the king and his vassals (wealthy, landowning lords) and the remainder of the population, which included common villagers, farm-workers, and even religious. Though a relatively simple arrangement, feudalism came to organize the politics, economy, and social life throughout Medieval Europe. Ownership of land accorded one rights, but it also accorded one duties, and this held both for secular and religious landholders. Therefore, in return for the lord's military protection against foreign or domestic foes, his vassals (those who were under his rule) would pay him in labor or services. Some of his vassals would have to serve in his army. There were, of course, different levels of vassals. Some were landowners themselves, who chose to ally themselves around a more powerful lord. Others, by far the majority, were serfs, who barely enjoyed any freedom since they were completely tied to the land and lord they were serving. A feudal kingdom was a vast pyramid of such arrangements, with many levels of lord and vassals at the apex of which stood the king and his attendant dukes.

FEUDALISM AND THE CHURCH

During the period of civil unrest following the collapse of the Carolingians, many of the Church's lands and possessions were confiscated. Paradoxically, the Church retained its status as a major landowner in most parts of Europe. Even though in theory the Church lost much of its land after the Carolingian demise, much of it remained, either because the Church was able to muster the money and resources to defend it, or because the lord or duke in the area happened to be on friendly terms with the episcopacy. In any event, feudalism increased the interaction between ecclesiastical and secular leaders in rural parts of Europe. As this close interaction between rulers of the Church and rulers of the realm increased, so grew instances of abuse on the part of secular authorities toward the Church.

In exchange for protecting the Church, some secular rulers demanded control over episcopal appointments. This was nothing new. Both Charlemagne and the Eastern emperors claimed the right to appoint bishops, but this right was always held in check by a strong, central Church. Now, with the papacy under the thumb of the emperor and Roman nobility, and the precarious political situation of the region, some of these rulers took it upon themselves to become the ultimate authorities of the Church. This exaggerated secular interference in ecclesiastical affairs spawned two terrible abuses in the Church: nepotism and simony. Nepotism is the appointment of family members to important positions of authority; and simony, in this context, is the selling of ecclesiastical offices by either secular or spiritual rulers. Many lords believed they could distribute ecclesiastical offices just as they would secular ones. For instance, it was not uncommon for a powerful lord either to sell a bishopric to the highest bidder or to install his own son as bishop.

A feudal kingdom had many levels of vassals serving under a lord. Some feudal lords believed they could distribute ecclesiastical offices.

On the ecclesiastical side, bishops and abbots often received extra income from royal benefices that was distinct from the income of their community. Even more scandalously, several bishops and abbots were known to have married and had children. Many of these bishops and abbots then bequeathed to their eldest son their own ecclesiastical title! These abuses were more destructive to the work of the Church than the violence hurled at the people of God during the time of the Roman persecutions. Hence, when reform came to the Church (as it soon would), monastic and episcopal abuse, in the form of nepotism and simony, was one of the first issues to be addressed.

THE VIKING INVASIONS

Besides the internal decay of monastic life in these centuries, a very real external threat helped thwart for some time any effective monastic reform. This threat materialized in the figures of the Norsemen, or Vikings, who originated in Scandinavia and, beginning in the late eighth century, wreaked havoc on Europe for nearly three hundred years. The Vikings were not a centrally governed empire, like Persia or Byzantium; rather, they were small bands organized and led by local chieftains. The Norsemen, originating in Norway, concentrated their attacks upon England, Ireland, and Scotland. Those from present day Denmark hit nearly every major European city.

Carolingian Europe was poorly equipped to handle the Viking invasions. The factions that took hold after the death of Charlemagne were too busy fighting among themselves to mount a reliable defense against these foreign invaders. The Vikings instilled overwhelming dread in the Christians of Medieval Europe as they were warriors of unparalleled skill on both sea and land, and they were guilty of unimagined cruelty and mercilessness in their plunder and slaughter.

With their great mobility and swift ships, it did not take long for the Norsemen to discover that the monasteries, particularly of Ireland, England, and along the major rivers in Germany and France, were the repository of Carolingian society's wealth. The Vikings began to occupy the mouth of major rivers in northern Europe as bases from which they might raid every Church and monastery they could find. Because of the Vikings, many of the most important Irish and Anglo-Saxon monasteries involved in the conversion of England and Germany—including Jarrow, the monastery where St. Bede died in 735—were destroyed in this period.

The combination of the Norse threat and internal decay of monastic life led to a weakening of monasteries' civilizing influence upon society. Much of their learning, both secular and religious, was forgotten, their discipline fell by the wayside, and some abbots were no better than brigands, who, in order to protect their own monasteries from the Vikings, would lead raids upon other monasteries for food and money.

A VIKING INVASION

"From the fury of the Northmen deliver us, O Lord"

This prayer was purportedly said by the ninth-century Europeans living in dread of Viking attacks. For nearly three hundred years, coastal towns and monasteries were at the mercy of the feared Norsemen, who attacked and plundered at will. Typical Viking raids used the element of surprise. Approaching in ships, Vikings would appear suddenly, attack and plunder, abduct people and disappear before any defense could be made.

One of the first recorded attacks took place in 793 when the monastery on Lindisfarne, an island off the east coast of England, was raided. Simeon of Durham later wrote about this terrible event:

> In the same year the pagans from the northern regions came with a naval force to Britain like stinging hornets and spread on all sides like fearful wolves, robbed, tore and slaughtered not only beasts of burden, sheep and oxen, but even priests and deacons, and companies of monks and nuns. And they came to the church of Lindisfarne, laid everything waste with grievous plundering, trampled the holy places with polluted steps, dug up the altars and seized all the treasures of the holy church. They killed some of the brothers, took some away with them in fetters, many they drove out, naked and loaded with insults, some they drowned in the sea. (*Historia Regum*, Sken, i. 303)

Another account of the Viking raids was written by the Anglo-Saxon monk Alcuin of York in a letter to Ethelred, king of Northumbria around the year 800, and it too captures the fear and terror felt by the people of Europe.

> Never before has such terror appeared in Britain as we have now suffered from a pagan race, nor was it thought that such an inroad from the sea could be made. Behold the church of St. Cuthbert, spattered with blood of the priests of God, despoiled of all its ornaments; a place more venerable than all in Britain is given as prey to pagan peoples. (quoted in Loyn, *The Vikings in Britain*, 1977, pp. 55-56)

After years of raids, monks learned how to frustrate the Vikings by building tall stone towers known as Round Towers. The door was placed one floor up, accessible only by a ladder. Inside the tower, each floor was accessed by further ladders. If Vikings were sighted, the monks would grab as much food and valuables as they could carry, climb into the tower and pull up the ladder. The Vikings would then raid the empty monastery while the monks watched from the safety of the tower. Even if the Vikings did get into the tower, the monks retreated further up the tower by pulling up more ladders. Such a strategy did not save the monastery itself, but did save the monk's lives and some of their belongings.

Another feature to appear at this time was the High Cross. It was customary for monasteries to display a wooden cross, but from the 700's, it became common to carve them from stone. Some scholars have theorized that they were made so large and heavy to prevent the Vikings from carrying them away.

PART II
Cluny and Monastic Reform

In this sea of corrupt churchmen and invading Norsemen, of simony and war, of debauchery and religious collapse, there suddenly sprung up in the Church a reform movement, led by saintly men and women of great courage, which would not only stem the decay in the Church, but also prompt regeneration. The monastic reform begun in Cluny emphasized both the ideal of a universal Church within a political framework and the inherent dignity of the human person. Both ideals had fallen into shambles, with nobles vying for increasing ecclesiastical power, and with corrupt monks and popes often indulging in cruelty and sensuality. Though these abuses were widespread, more widespread still was the desire for real reform in the hearts and minds of the majority of the laity and those clergy who had remained faithful to the Gospel. Cluny gave voice to this majority, and the reform began.

THE FOUNDING

In 909/10 William the Pious, Duke of Aquitaine and a strong supporter of reform, generously and without thought of recompense, donated land in the little town of Cluny in Burgundy, France for the founding of a new monastery.

St. Berno, the first abbot (909/10-927) of the monastery, settled at Cluny with twelve companions. Together they instituted a renewed commitment to the rule of St. Benedict. The monks imposed demanding austerities on themselves, and put all of their energies into giving glory to God. Soon St. Berno's reputation grew, and Cluny began to be recognized as a center of saintliness in troubled times. The trend would continue. Before Berno's death, the Cluniac model was adopted by five or six neighboring monasteries for the purpose of reform; and, even more impressively, over the next two centuries four saints assumed the abbotship of Cluny.

Pope Bl. Urban II consecrated the high altar of the Cluny Church in 1095.

Berno's first successor, St. Odo (927-942), greatly extended the influence of Cluny. Many monasteries in southern France and even some in Italy reformed themselves using the renewed Benedictine rule. One important difference between Cluny and other monastic communities was the role played by the abbot. The Cluny monks—in all their various incorporated monasteries—had only one abbot, that of Cluny. Other monasteries followed the tradition of placing an abbot over each individual monastery. Hence the abbot of Cluny was responsible not only for his own monastery at Cluny, but also for all those monasteries that had joined his rule. This helped curb abuse, since it kept wayward abbots from assuming control of monasteries for their own advantage.

The prestige of the monastery spread, and in 1088 Cluny built a new church. Pope Bl. Urban II, a Cluniac monk and one of the period's most upright popes, consecrated the high altar in 1095, and Pope Innocent II consecrated the entire church upon its completion in 1132. At its time of construction the church at Cluny was Europe's largest at 555 feet long.

CLUNIAC SPIRITUALITY

How did the Cluniac monks live out their vocation differently from the regular Benedictine monks? First, as has been noted, the monks at Cluny reinstituted a strict adherence to Benedictine rule. Second, they placed greater emphasis upon the spiritual life of the individual monk. The idea was that a community of holy men was built on the holiness of each member. To this end they reinstated the divine office, which in some monasteries had fallen out of fashion, and decreased manual labor so as to allot more time for spiritual reflection. As an aid to this spiritual reflection, Cluny also lengthened the divine office and the liturgy. The goal was active, continuous, prayer, whether liturgical or meditative, and a close emulation of the life of Christ.

Many anonymous treatises were written at Cluny on the spiritual life. These spiritual tracts were a vital help in removing obstacles to the development and perfection of the interior life. A renewed commitment to chastity and celibacy served as an indespensible means to habitual contemplation. It was precisely this burgeoning monastic mysticism that would deliver the Church from the dangers confronting her.

Cluniac spirituality brought forward the old idea that the monk's role in the world was to keep fresh the mystery of Pentecost by living in silence and peace. This tranquil lifestyle was meant to present a foretaste of the eternal peace of God's reign, and ultimately the beatific vision.

Through asceticism the monk aimed to dwell in the depths of the heart of Christ. Through mastering the body the monks were not only able to free their hearts to love Christ, they were also better equipped to unite themselves to his cross. Through their hidden lives dedicated to prayer and penance, the monks would obtain the grace of conversion of so many individuals alienated from God and the grace to live their faith as well. It was precisely the prayer and self-denial of these monks that revitalized and energized the Church. Such is the efficacy of a life of contemplation, that it bears its fruits across all time and space.

The rise of a powerful monastic spirituality was vital for the reform of the Church at this time in history. However, this emphasis on the monastic life as a powerful means to holiness was a shift from the implicit awareness of the universal call to holiness among the early Christian communities. This was now the era of monasticism, which associated the call to holiness primarily with a departure from the world. During that period, ordinary people usually assumed no more than a passive role of being guided and spiritually nourished by the monks. This was a necessary development in the face of the historical circumstances of the ninth, tenth, and eleventh centuries; the recognition of the lay person's call to sanctity and evangelization would have to wait for another thousand years.

THE INFLUENCE OF THE CLUNIAC MONKS

Within just one hundred years, the monks of Cluny were a force to be reckoned with in the Church. As more and more monasteries signed on to the Cluniac reform, their ranks swelled, and by the year 1100, one thousand four hundred fifty houses inhabited by over ten thousand monks were all under the rule of Cluny.

Neither was Cluny's success confined to monastic communities. As word of the sanctity of Cluny spread, more and more bishops and secular rulers supported their reforms. In 1016 Pope Benedict VIII granted a special *privilegium* to Cluny: the monastery was to be absolutely free from the authority of kings, bishops, and nobles. Cluny answered directly to the papacy as its final authority. This freed Cluny from the troublesome accompaniments of feudalism already discussed, such as nepotism and simony.

LIFE AS A MONK AT CLUNY

The daily schedule by which monks at Cluny lived their lives stood in sharp contrast to some other monasteries of the time. The *horarium* (daily schedule) followed by the monks of Cluny allocated a great portion of time to religious ceremony, and often the observances of Mass and other rites would require that the monks spend almost the entire day in prayer. Psalms and votive offerings were added to the Divine Office, and following the custom introduced into monasteries in France by St. Benedict of Aniane, other devotional exercises were added as well, increasing the hours of the Divine Office. Apart from the increase in the hours of the Divine Office, however, Cluniac observances were similar to that of the Benedictines.

When possible, Cluniac monks would perform as little manual labor as possible to dedicate more time to prayer. Thus, most tasks were delegated to lay servants. In the poorer monasteries further removed from Cluny, however, the monks would have to perform more work in order to survive. While this situation may not have been ideal, it should be noted that every monk was required to spend some years at Cluny itself.

The monks at Cluny placed much emphasis on the observance of the rule of silence in their houses. Conversation was only allowed at certain times and in certain areas. Whenever communication became absolutely necessary, hand gesturing was used. These gestures may have become quite sophisticated over time.

The third church (above) built at the Benedictine Abbey of Cluny was, at the time, the largest church in Christendom. It was designed by the monk Gunzo. Begun in 1088 and consecrated by Pope Innocent II in 1132, the "great church" or Cluny III was a structure of overwhelming magnificence. The five-aisled nave echoed that of Old St. Peter's in Rome, and unusual for the architectural period, Cluny III had two sets of transepts (the shorter length of the "crossing" of a cruciform church). Only one transept with a bell tower survives today (shown at right). By the time of the French Revolution in 1790 the monks were persecuted by the "enlightened" leaders of the Revolution. As a result, they were suppressed in France, and the Abbey at Cluny was almost completely demolished.

CLUNIAC AND CISTERCIAN MONASTIC REFORMS

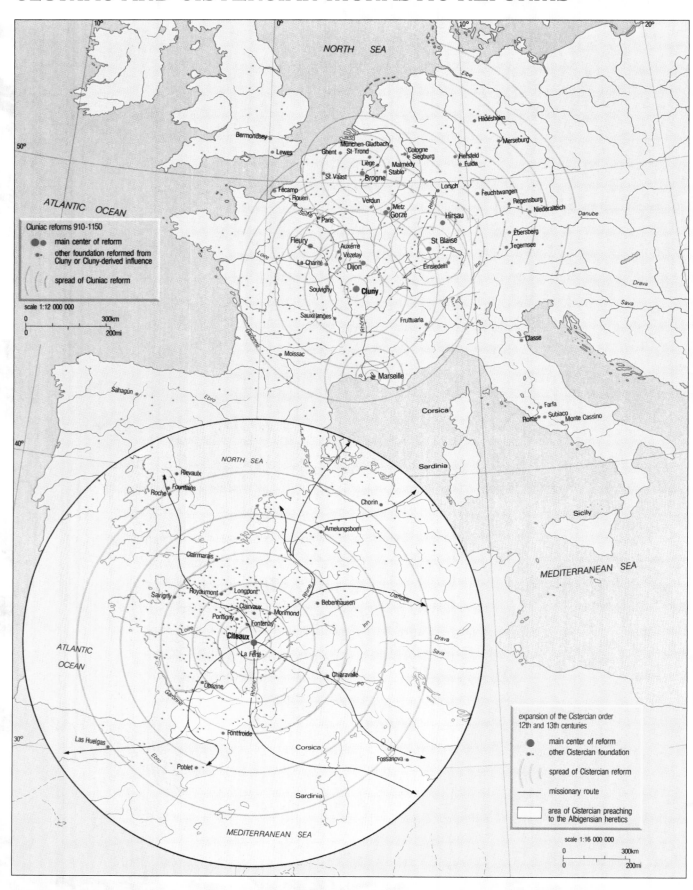

CHURCH AND STATE IN THE MIDDLE AGES

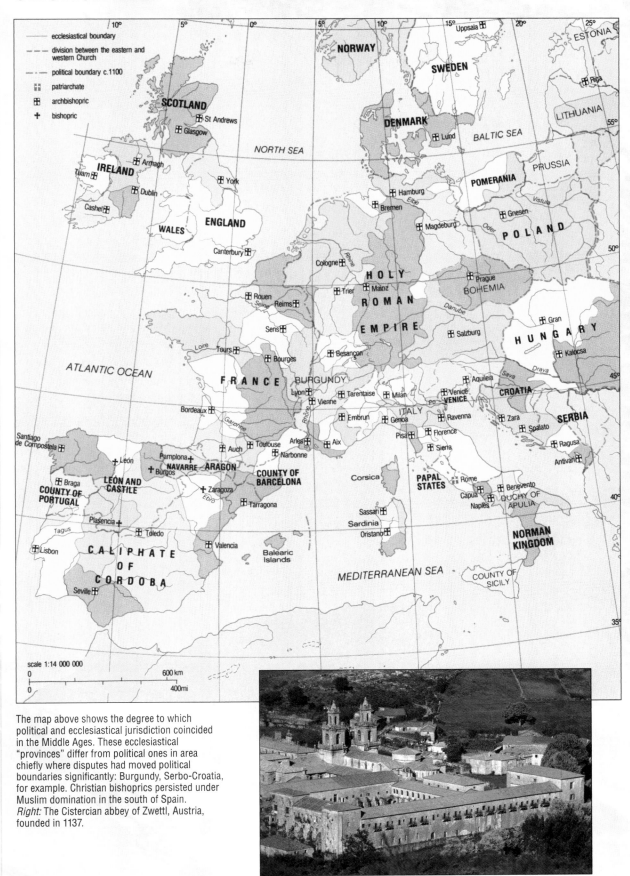

The map above shows the degree to which political and ecclesiastical jurisdiction coincided in the Middle Ages. These ecclesiastical "provinces" differ from political ones in area chiefly where disputes had moved political boundaries significantly: Burgundy, Serbo-Croatia, for example. Christian bishoprics persisted under Muslim domination in the south of Spain.
Right: The Cistercian abbey of Zwettl, Austria, founded in 1137.

Several of Cluny's monks became the leading churchmen of their day. Abbot Hugh the Great (1049-1109) was the most important churchman of his time and played a pivotal role in the lay investiture controversy. Cardinal Humbert and Frederick of Lorraine, the papal legates to Constantinople, excommunicated the patriarch of Constantinople as part of the Great Schism of 1054. Otto of Lagery became Pope Bl. Urban II, the first pope to preach the Crusades. St. Peter Damian (1007-1072) became the most respected contemporary theologian in Europe.

Cluny exercised considerable influence well into the twelfth century. In the thirteenth century, it reformed itself under the Cistercian model, which by this time had surpassed Cluny in influence and prestige. The later Medieval period saw a precipitous decline in Cluny's influence, which ended in its physical destruction during the French Revolution in 1790.

PART III
The New Temporal Orders
THE OTTONIAN EMPIRE (HOLY ROMAN EMPIRE)

Though in steady decline from the death of Charlemagne onwards, the Carolingian line officially ended in the East in 911 when Conrad I was chosen as king. No real central authority existed until Otto I (936-973, emperor 962), the Saxon ruler who formed the Holy Roman Empire. The Ottonian line came to fill the role that the Carolingian line had provided in the previous century: offering the Church temporal protection in exchange for its support and recognition of its emperors. Not surprisingly, the protection came at a price, for the Ottonian line became entangled with the Church in what came to be known as the lay investiture controversy.

OTTO I, THE GREAT (936-973)

Otto's intention was to secure his own royal power through a mutually beneficial alliance with the Church. Thus, his crowning in Aachen (Germany) by the archbishop of Mainz served the double purpose of invoking the memory of Charlemagne's authority and wedding the Church to the Ottonian dynasty.

The Ottonian line exercised its influence over the Church in Germany in three different ways: first, through lay investiture, i.e., the appointment of bishops and abbots by secular rulers; second, through the assertion of royal power over proprietary churches, which gave the landowner on which a church stood power to make ecclesiastical appointments; and third, through appropriation of ecclesiastical funds for the royal coffers. In addition, many German ecclesiastical office-holders were vested with secular powers by the royal house in exchange for their allegiance.

By 950 the wealth and power of Germany was unrivaled. And in 955 Otto I decisively defeated the Magyars at the Battle of Lechfeld, winning the support of Western Europe. In 962 Otto I traveled to Rome, where Pope John XII crowned him emperor.

There were a number or reasons why Otto desired the imperial title. Primarily, it raised him to the level of Charlemagne, whom he wished to emulate. Second, the pope's allegiance was a powerful support against Otto's rivals in France. Finally, the imperial title provided the Ottonian dynasty with the legal basis for attempts to bring part of the old middle kingdom, specifically Lorraine and parts of Italy, into the empire.

Otto the Great's son, Otto II, squandered his time and energy trying to bring southern Italy under his firm control. In the meantime, the still barbaric Slavs destroyed German settlements east of the Elbe River (central Europe, in the modern-day Czech Republic).

OTTO I, THE GREAT

In 962 Otto the Great traveled to Rome, where Pope John XII crowned him Holy Roman Emperor. The Ottonian Empire provided the Church with the temporal protection that the Carolingian Empire had provided in the previous century, but the Ottonian line ultimately entangled the Church in the lay investiture controversy and similar abuses of authority.

OTTO III AND POPE SYLVESTER II

It was Otto III's Byzantine mother and his grandmother who ruled during his regency. Otto III (983-1002) spent the majority of his reign in Rome with Gerbert of Aurillac, the greatest Latin scholar of his day. Gerbert had studied in Spain under the Muslims, and this gave him the opportunity to study philosophy and mathematics at Cordoba in an age when the Muslim thinkers were making remarkable headway in both subjects. (Not only had the Muslims preserved ancient Greek writings by conquering Hellenistic cultures, but also they were the sole possessors of most of Aristotle's works.)

Through his power over ecclesiastical affairs, Otto III raised Gerbert to the See of St. Peter as Pope Sylvester II. Together Otto and Sylvester II hoped to build a new empire based in Rome that would incorporate all of Europe. Otto III helped to bring the Poles into the empire in the hopes that a German-Slav contest for eastern hegemony could be averted. Finally, Sylvester II thought that an empire under Otto would eventually secure a lasting peace, which would assist the Church in concentrating on her spiritual mission.

Though Otto III died prematurely in 1002 and Pope Sylvester the following year, their cooperation caused serious difficulties for the Church. Their joint efforts accentuated the problem of temporal interference with ecclesiastical affairs, which gave rise to the lay investiture crisis.

ST. DUNSTAN AND SCOTTISH MONASTICISM

St. Dunstan was born to an upper-class family near Glastonbury in the early part of the tenth century. Viking raids had a devastating affect on monasteries, and by the time St. Dunstan was born, English monasticism had been virtually destroyed.

When St. Dunstan was a child, his father committed him to the care of the Irish monastic scholars who frequented the abandoned and desolate monastery at Glastonbury. St. Dunstan was an exceptional student and he soon received minor orders (the first preparations for ordination) before being summoned to Canterbury at the request of his uncle Athelm, the Archbishop of Canterbury. At Canterbury, St. Dunstan was respected for his scholarly intellect and soon became a favorite of King Aethelstan. However, after some time, those envious of St. Dunstan's success convinced the King to force him to leave the court.

Returning to Glastonbury, St. Dunstan became a monk, built a tiny cell close to the ruins of the old monastery, and lived as a hermit. He devoted himself to study, music (he played the harp), and metalworkings (in particular casting church bells). Upon the death of King Aethelstan in 940, the new King Eadmund asked St. Dunstan to return to his court and serve him. Just as before, members of the court became jealous and convinced the new King to send him away. King Eadmund soon regretted exiling

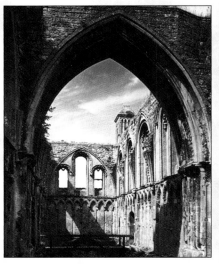
The ruins of Glastonbury Abbey

St. Dunstan, and to show his gratitude for the monk's service, the king commissioned St. Dunstan to reestablish the monastery at Glastonbury.

St. Dunstan set about this task with exceptional success. Not having personal contact with the new monasteries being founded on the continent (Cluny, for example), St. Dunstan strictly followed Benedictine rule, and under his guidance, Glastonbury again became a center for study and the monastic life. His success was recognized by the king who appointed St. Dunstan as the Archbishop of Canterbury in 960. St. Dunstan used his influential position to further the monastic revival in Britain and reestablished monasteries at Malmesbury, Westminister, Bath, Exeter, and other places. In 970, St. Dunstan convened a monastic conference for the entire British Isles. The conference drafted a national code for monastic observance, called the "*Regularis concordia*," helping to establish and regulate monastic revival in Britain. After these successes as Archbishop, St. Dunstan spent the last years of his life running the Canterbury Cathedral School for boys and died in 988.

St. Dunstan of Canterbury

SAINTLY RULERS: EMPEROR ST. HENRY II AND QUEEN ST. CUNEGOND

St. Henry II (1002-1024), who was cousin to Otto III, succeeded him as emperor. St. Henry II abandoned Otto's grandiose plans of reinstituting a Holy Roman Empire, and was content to maintain his rule over the Italian peninsula. Though a weak and sickly man, St. Henry II traveled throughout his kingdom to maintain peace and ensure that justice was being served.

He was an ardent Catholic and a true reformer and did much to support the Cluny monks. He did, however, involve himself excessively in ecclesiastical governance — and this was true of virtually all leaders of his day — but he did so with grace and humility.

Emperor St. Henry II and Queen St. Cunegond lived a blessed married life. Rumors of their virgin marriage are apocryphal and should not be taken seriously. After their deaths, they were both canonized by the Church. Both Sts. Henry II and Cunegond are buried in the cathedral at Bamberg, Germany. In fact, one can view their heads encased in glass with golden crowns.

Moreover, Henry III in 1046 greatly influenced the Synod of Sutri (a small town near Rome) by resolving the crisis involving the three claimants to the papacy. During that synod and with the full authority of the synod fathers, Henry chose Suidger, bishop of Bamburg and a man of spotless character, to be the next pope, Clement II.

CAPETIAN FRANCE

In the west, the Carolingian line ended in 987, whereupon Hugh Capet, with the blessing of the Church, became the king of France. The Capetian line would rule France for many centuries, but initially lacked the power to rule the entire area under one centralized government.

NORMANDY: THE VIKINGS, WILLIAM THE CONQUEROR, AND LANFRANC

One part of France that resisted Capetian rule was Normandy. Normandy first took shape as a duchy in 911 under a band of Norsemen led by the warrior-king Rollo. Rollo planned to establish Normandy as a viable kingdom, and by 980 — chiefly through intermarriage and adaptation — Rollo's band of Vikings transformed this once-backward part of Europe into a formidable power.

The Normans imposed the status of vassalage upon the existing nobility and developed allegiances with the monasteries in the area. Monks, besides providing some amount of credibility to Norman rule, helped raise the cultural bar through their education and writings.

The French Capetian king, Henry I, made the final attempt to bring the Norman duke, William the Conqueror (reigned 1035-1087), under his control in the 1040s. William I had the effective support of the nobility and the local church, and Normandy maintained its autonomy in feudal France. Later, in 1066, William headed the last successful invasion of England.

LANFRANC, THE NORMAN ARCHBISHOP OF CANTERBURY

The most important monk brought to Normandy by the Viking dukes was Lanfranc (ca. 1010-1089). He entered the chief monastery founded by the Normans at Bec, located between Rouen and Lisieux, France. At Bec he was a famed educator and prior (his most famous student was St. Anselm) and under William the Conqueror, Lanfranc became the first Archbishop of Canterbury.

Lanfranc was a strong administrator who transformed Bec from an impoverished monastery into one of the leading centers of learning of its day. Equally impressive, he managed to negotiate his allegiance to Church and State in a truly remarkable way. He served at first as counselor to King William I, and later even served as a skilled regent during the king's travels to the continent. But his chief allegiance as Archbishop of Canterbury was to Rome, and though his dual responsibilities seemed at times to be a source of conflict, Lanfranc adroitly walked through the two worlds. Lanfranc supported the reforms of his day, specifically those enforcing clerical celibacy and curbing simony. On the issue of lay investiture, however, he tended to side with secular rulers against the Church. Nonetheless, Lanfranc continually supported the popes even at their weakest moments. Although he supported the secular lords, he refused to recognize any of their anti-popes, even going so far as to send financial aid to the legitimate popes in need.

William I of England likewise remained on good terms with the pope even though he continued to appoint bishops. Because William appointed such good and holy men to these offices, he avoided any direct conflict with Rome.

William I (ca. 1027- September 9, 1087), was King of England from 1066 to 1087. William was the only son of Robert the Magnificent, Duke of Normandy, and Herleva, the daughter of a tanner. Born in Falaise, Normandy, now in France, William succeeded to the throne of England by right of conquest by winning the Battle of Hastings in October of 1066 in what has become known as the Norman Conquest.

William was crowned King of England on December 25, 1066 in Westminster Abbey.

Below: The Bayeux Tapestry, (embroidery on wool), dates from 1077. It was created in England, after the Norman Conquest of 1066, and commemorates the victory at the Battle of Hastings.The tapestry is almost 230 feet long and only 18 inches wide. It has 58 scenes. The scene in this section depicts the death of King Harold II who had been crowned King of England on January of 1066 by an assembly of England's leading nobles known as the Witenagemot.

PART IV

The Lay Investiture Controversies

On the surface, the issue of the lay investiture conflict was relatively clear and could be formulated in a simple question: Who should appoint bishops, secular or religious leaders? But in reality, the depths of this controversy were far more complex. Due to the lack of any clear delineation between the powers of Church and State, those who hoped to rule the State in more than a nominal sense were almost forced to have a hand in ecclesiastical affairs as well. It was common at that time that bishops and abbots of powerful dioceses and monasteries wield considerable political influence. While in principle it was wrong for secular leaders to have any hand in Church matters, given the current state of affairs, it was quite difficult to avoid this secular interference. The crisscrossing of secular and religious authority left little room on either side of the dispute. Moreover, it needs to be pointed out that lay investiture had been going on since the reign of Charlemagne, and in certain cases it worked to the Church's advantage. However, in many instances it proved disastrous. Due to the negative effect lay investiture had on the Church, the reforming popes realized that they needed to retain control over appointments of bishops, thereby reducing the chance of out-and-out political corruption in the episcopacy.

THE GREGORIAN REVOLUTION

The lay investiture controversy reached its height during the latter part of the eleventh century. As the controversy had reached such a universal scale by this time, a series of reforms, which were outgrowths of the Cluniac Reforms, was instituted by the papacy itself. The pope at the center of the reform addressing this problem head-on was Pope St. Gregory VII, born Hildebrand. Pope St. Gregory was aided by several remarkable men under the guiding light of Cluny, among them Humbert of Moyenmoutier of Cluny; St. Peter Damian; Duke Frederick of Lorraine; and Otto of Lagery, the future Pope Bl. Urban II.

POPE ST. GREGORY VII

Hildebrand, a Cluniac monk and native Roman, became Pope St. Gregory VII in 1073 and served until 1085. Hildebrand entered the Church as a young man, and was for some time an influential leader in the College of Cardinals. In addition, he carried out important tasks for his papal predecessors, particularly for Pope Alexander II (1061-1073). At Alexander II's funeral, the crowd is said to have shouted enthusiastically for Hildebrand as pope. He initially resisted, but understood their call to reflect God's will. And so at fifty-three years of age, Hildebrand took the name Gregory VII. Hildebrand was blessed with a penetrating mind, an iron will, much energy, and relentless perseverance in the face of adversity.

THE *DICTATUS PAPÆ*

Pope St. Gregory VII wasted little time in making his intentions of reform known. Within a year of becoming pope, he issued a decree called *Dictatus papæ*. Pope St. Gregory asserted in his decree that the pope possessed specific powers bestowed by God that rested on him alone. These powers most notably included the power to convene and ratify a council, to define tenets of the faith, and to appoint, transfer, and remove bishops from office. But St. Gregory went further with this, and claimed that the papacy had the power to depose temporal rulers. Furthermore, subjects of any temporal ruler had the right to appeal to the papacy in order to bring charges against their sovereign.

Pope St. Gregory levied stiff penalties for the practice of simony. Anyone who obtained ordination or spiritual benefice through the practice of simony was excluded from the Church hierarchy and lost his authority of governance. In addition, any priest guilty of fornication was barred from saying the Mass, which in effect stripped the priest of his most important function in the Church and the means for his financial support. All church clerics were to avoid and shun any cleric who failed to abide by the pope's decrees.

In addition to Pope St. Gregory's punitive measures, he sought to codify the law of the Church, called canon law, as an effective measure to avoid future abuse. While this project was not completed in his lifetime, he is considered to be the "father of canon law."

There was little, if anything, new in Pope St. Gregory VII's decrees. Much of what he laid out had already been stated earlier by other popes or was theologically based in the Scriptures. But St. Gregory's re-formulation of and intent to enforce these measures greatly angered the Holy Roman Emperor and the nobility. Not surprisingly, the temporal powers—most notably Emperor Henry IV—angrily rebelled against these papal directives.

"TO GO TO CANOSSA": THE HUMILIATION OF EMPEROR HENRY IV

Pope St. Gregory VII had taken advantage of the papacy's practice of crowning the emperor in order to claim that the papacy held final say on matters of temporal rule. This perceived usurpation of temporal rule placed the Holy Roman Emperor, Henry IV, on a collision course with the pope.

In defiance of the papal decree, Henry on his own appointed the bishop of Milan. Pope St. Gregory VII asked Henry to refrain from carrying out the appointment. Henry declined the pope's request. St. Gregory acted quickly and severely in response, declaring Henry deposed as emperor, and releasing his subjects from his rule. This proved decisive since Henry did not enjoy popular support at home and many of his subjects were opposed to his strong, autocratic rule.

Pope St. Gregory VII not only deposed Henry IV, but he also excommunicated him. (Excommunication is a censure from a bishop stating a person is cut off from communion with the Church because he is in a persistent state of mortal sin.) The act of excommunication had rarely been used, and caused many of the bishops and important abbots in Germany who had previously supported Henry's cause to withdraw. Since two-thirds of Germany was under the immediate authority of bishops who owned most of the land, it followed that two-thirds of Henry's potential and taxing military power disappeared overnight.

Henry for a time was thus strategically outflanked by the pope. His only recourse was to obtain the pope's forgiveness, thereby being accepted back into the Church, and regaining his office—all before the pope could appoint a new emperor to take his place.

Pope St. Gregory's decree known as *Dictatus Papæ* (Dictate of the Pope), 1075

After observing Henry IV's contrition for three days, Pope St. Gregory VII heard Henry's confession, granted him absolution, and restored his royal status.

On January 25, 1077, Henry IV set out for Canossa, Italy, with a small party. Pope St. Gregory VII and his entourage were staying there with the Countess Mathilda of Tuscany. Mathilda, who happened to be a relative of Henry, was the first of a group of influential Medieval women who demonstrated great influence at key political and spiritual moments on account of their holiness and wisdom.

Henry arrived at Canossa and stood barefoot in the snow outside the gates of Mathilda's villa for three days. He was dressed in sackcloth. Still, the pope refused to meet with him. St. Gregory doubted Henry's true contrition, and rightfully so. By repenting of his crime, Henry would be reinstituted in the Church and would thereby gain the military support of the bishops he had lost. For some time St. Gregory held back.

Hugh of Cluny, the revered abbot of the famed monastery, appeared on the scene. More than anyone else, he forced St. Gregory's hand. According to long-standing tradition and the rules of the Church, a penitent who requests forgiveness cannot be turned away. St. Gregory knew that he could not dismiss the advice of Hugh, who was the most respected churchman of the day.

Thus after three days St. Gregory relented and agreed to meet with Henry. Pope St. Gregory heard the emperor's confession, granted him absolution, restored his royal status, and admonished him to observe all of the papal decrees.

For a time it appeared that St. Gregory had achieved a tremendous victory: the most important temporal ruler in Christendom had bent to the pope's will. This victory did not last long. Within a year Henry had again rejected St. Gregory's authority and installed Clement III as anti-pope, (i.e., someone who is not — but claims to be — the legitimate successor of St. Peter). St. Gregory and his successors turned to the Normans for protection.

In the end, St. Gregory fled from Henry's army to southern Italy where he died in exile. Henry IV's fate was not much better since he had to fight the nobility and his own son to maintain power.

CONCORDAT OF WORMS

Canossa did not end the struggle between the papacy and the Holy Roman Emperors. Similar, though less dramatic, struggles took place in England and France. After many such battles, the Concordat of Worms (1122) officially ended the investiture matter with a new understanding between the Church and the Holy Roman Empire.

The Concordat of Worms had two parts. First, it left spiritual investiture to the Church alone, and temporal investiture to civil authorities. The emperor renounced all claims to invest churchmen with ring and crosier—symbols of spiritual authority—and had to permit the free election of bishops. The practice of simony was again condemned. The emperor, however, retained veto power over the electoral process since he had the right to invest churchmen with signs of temporal authority. Thus, if an emperor did not like a candidate for the episcopacy, he could withhold the temporal power accompanying the post, and indirectly force the Church to pick another candidate.

INVESTITURE CONFLICT AND THE ENGLISH CHURCH (1154-1189)

Henry II was the most powerful of all Medieval English monarchs. The Church in England had developed its own set of courts and laws independent of the secular administration, but Henry II desired to consolidate the legal structures of England and to place all authority under the crown. Moreover, the English Church, it seemed to him, was growing too powerful and independent. To accomplish this task he chose as Archbishop of Canterbury his trusted friend and advisor St. Thomas à Becket.

St. Thomas à Becket had been Henry II's Chancellor and had worked with him to strengthen the powers of the state. Aware of Henry II's designs for changes within the governance of the English Church—changes that, as archbishop, St. Thomas à Becket knew he could not support or allow—he warned Henry II not to make him archbishop. Henry II and Cardinal Henry of Posa pressured St. Thomas à Becket to accept the position, and he ultimately accepted. With his elevation, he resigned his position as Chancellor and undertook a life of prayer and penance. He resisted the king's effort to overstep his boundaries in violating canon law.

CONSTITUTIONS OF CLARENDON

Henry II asserted his royal authority in the Constitutions of Clarendon in 1164. The king attempted to gain control over the revenues of episcopal sees and abbeys and sought to control the election of all abbots and bishops. All clerics were to be tried in civil courts. Any appeal to Rome first required the consent of the king. The king's court was to be the last resort for ecclesiastical appeals.

St. Thomas à Becket stood almost alone in England in his absolute opposition to the Constitutions of Clarendon, but Pope Alexander III also refused to recognize them. St. Thomas à Becket was forced to flee to France to escape the king's wrath, and he spent time with some Cistercians before Henry II threatened the entire order if they did not give him up. At the same time,

The murder of St. Thomas à Becket would haunt Henry II for the rest of his life.

fearing excommunication, Henry II feigned reconciliation with St. Thomas à Becket. He returned to England and continued to fight against the king's programs. Out of desperation, Henry II asked if anyone could rid him of this priest. St. Thomas à Becket was murdered in the cathedral by a band of knights in 1170. To what extent Henry II was involved with the murder is unknown. St. Thomas à Becket's martyrdom sparked an almost immediate devotion all across Europe, and it would be the undoing of many of Henry II's programs.

For the remaining 19 years of his rule, Henry II was a haunted man. Betrayed by his wife and children, guilt-ridden by the death of his friend, perhaps a result of a moment of anger, Henry did public penance for his crime—he was violently scourged at the tomb of his old friend, who was canonized only two years after his martyrdom. Disgraced, the king gave up his program of control over the Church.

THE CHURCH AND THE EMPIRE
(1152-1254)

During the late twelfth century through the thirteenth century, the Church produced some of keenest legal minds of Europe. These men led the Church to some of its greatest achievements during the Medieval period. At this time, the German Hohenstaufen emperors desired to reclaim the glory of the Carolingian era by expanding their control from Germany to the Italian Peninsula. The Church feared that if such unification occurred, she would lose her independent status and would become a pawn of the German Emperors. Thus emerged the greatest struggle of the investiture conflict to date.

FREDERICK I, BARBAROSSA (1152-90)

Emperor Frederick I attacks Milan, Italy (1158).

Frederick I, Barbarossa, was the ablest and most powerful ruler of the Holy Roman Empire. He thought his vocation as emperor was to revive the Roman Empire. He believed that absolute power was bestowed upon him directly from God and therefore this power extended over the Church. Since Rome was the first city of the ancient empire, Frederick I believed he should have the authority to appoint the Bishop of Rome.

Pope Adrian IV saw immediately that Frederick I was overstepping his boundaries and threatened him with excommunication if he continued to infringe on the rights of the Church. The Italian city-states also greatly resented the interference of the German emperor. Frederick I, however, continued to appoint bishops in violation of the 1122 Concordat of Worms, and he imprisoned the papal legate sent to stop him.

Frederick I attempted to conquer Italy with five military expeditions into the peninsula. During one of his invasions of Rome, plague claimed 25,000 of his soldiers and he had to retreat. Eventually, the fierce resistance of the Italian city-states, the loyalty of many German princes and bishops to the Church, and the steadfastness of popes Adrian IV and Alexander III (who at one point was driven into exile) thwarted Frederick I, Barbarossa's exploits. Frederick I would reconcile with the Church before departing for the Crusade that would end his life.

INNOCENT III (ca. 1160-1216)
AND FREDERICK II (1194-1250)

At age 37, Lothar Segni Conti became Pope Innocent III. His pontificate brought the Church to the height of its power during the Middle Ages. Historians have often disputed whether the papacy of Innocent III was that of a pious man or virtual tyrant. Nevertheless, Innocent III had a very specific understanding of the papacy. Rather than choosing the title Vicar of St. Peter, as previous popes had done, Innocent III immediately showed his intentions and his understanding of the role of the pope by naming himself the Vicar of Christ.

> [T]he Pope was the judge of the world, set in the midst between God and man, below God and above Man; he is the representative of Him to whom the earth belongs with all that it contains and all its inhabitants; he is a priest after the order of Melchizedek; at once priest and king who unites in his person the fullness of all power and authority. (Dawson, *Medieval Essays*, p. 85)

Innocent III used the metaphor that the pope was like the sun and the king like the moon. As the moon derives its light from the sun, so the king derives his power from the Vicar of Christ. Nevertheless, in all matters in which he intervened, he never declared supreme right over temporal affairs, but he did exercise absolute authority over spiritual matters

Innocent III's primary interest throughout his pontificate was to maintain a balance of power throughout Europe with himself as arbitrator. To achieve this, he found it necessary to keep European sovereigns from assuming independent power. He intervened in the affairs of all the

Innocent III and his successors of the thirteenth century saw the papacy as the guardian of Christendom.

feudal kingdoms of Europe and took to task any king who had fallen from the state of grace. Philip II of France had divorced his wife and then attempted to marry another; subsequently, Innocent III placed the entire kingdom of France under interdict until Philip returned to his lawful wife. King John of England tried to control the election of the Archbishop of Canterbury and refused to accept the pope's choice of Stephen Langdon. John was excommunicated and England was placed under interdict (denial of liturgy, the sacraments, and even Christian burial). Innocent III then called upon Philip II of France to invade England in a crusade if John did not capitulate. John eventually was forced to make England a vassal of Innocent III in order to avoid punishment. Eventually King John's poor conduct led him to sign the *Magna Charta* in 1215.

Conflict soon had erupted over the successor to Frederick I, Barbarossa, after his death. For fourteen years Germany was in a state of civil turmoil. Innocent III was made the guardian of the young Frederick II of Germany, who was only three years old when his father died. Innocent III used his influence to gain the acceptance of the German princes for Frederick II's rule. Frederick II, now 17, promised to respect the sovereignty of the Papal States and not to attempt a unification of Germany and Italy. He also assured the pope that he would lead a crusade.

Frederick II meets with Muslim leaders in Jerusalem (1229).

Frederick II, however, would renege on his promise and attempt to crush the Papal States after the death of Innocent III. Because of his evil ways, his agnosticism and cruelty, Frederick II was viewed by many as "the antichrist." He became friendly with the Muslims and even maintained a harem. Frederick II broke his oath ten times and delayed going on a crusade for ten years. He invaded Italy and drove Pope Gregory IX from Rome. Gregory excommunicated the emperor and declared that Frederick II's subjects no longer owed him obedience. Frederick II began to execute clergy and desecrate churches until the new pope, Innocent IV, declared Frederick II deposed. He imposed excommunication on anyone who recognized him as emperor and he anathematized the entire Hohenstaufen family. Frederick II was finally forced to capitulate. Abandoned by his nobles, Frederick II repented and went to Penance. He died clothed in a Cistercian habit.

Innocent III and his successors of the thirteenth century saw the papacy as the guardian of Christendom. They treated the kings as vassals and penalized monarchs for violations of chastity and matrimonial fidelity. They provided strong leadership to the Church and brought Medieval society to its greatest heights. This leadership unfortunately immersed the Church in secular affairs, which would especially exacerbate tensions between Church and state with the advent of nationalism.

PART V

The Cistercians and Carthusians

THE CISTERCIANS

In addition to Cluny, two other monastic reform movements began later in the eleventh century, the Cistercians and the Carthusians.

The Cistercians, or the White Monks, were first founded by St. Robert of Molesme, a Cluniac monk, in 1098. Like Cluny, the Cistercians used the Benedictine rule, though with a special emphasis on austerities, farming, and simplicity of lifestyle. The white habits of the Cistercians were meant to imply their poverty and simplicity; most other monks wore black habits at the time.

The Cistercians were particularly important in the conversion of the Slavic tribes of Poland, Bohemia, and eastern Germany.

ST. BERNARD OF CLAIRVAUX

St. Bernard of Fontaine (1091-1153) joined the Cistercians in 1113 at Citeaux. Known as St. Bernard of Clairvaux, he is often considered the second founder of the order. It was under his leadership that the Cistercians grew dramatically and their influence spread. When he entered the monastery, he brought along thirty friends, four of whom were his brothers. St. Bernard became the first abbot of the new monastery founded at Clairvaux. At Clairvaux the monastery was austere: the walls were barren with small windows, and beds consisting of planks of wood. The monks ate nothing but bread and boiled leaves and roots with some salt and oil.

St. Bernard came from a noble background, as did practically all of the founders of orders in the Medieval period. He enjoyed the benefits of a classical education, and was a model student, though he was reserved.

ST. BERNARD: THE POWER OF A SINGLE MONK

The life of St. Bernard of Clairvaux is filled with countless fascinating stories. Despite longing to simply remain in his monastery in prayer, St. Bernard healed schisms, advised popes, led councils, wrote many influential books, and helped launch a crusade.

When Pope Hororius II died in 1130, a schism broke out in the Church over the alleged election of two popes: Innocent II and Anacletus II. A national council of the French bishops was called at Etampes, and St. Bernard, summoned there by consent of the bishops, was asked to judge between the two rival popes. He chose Innocent II, and by this act all the great Catholic powers of the time recognized Innocent II as the true pope. St. Bernard then accompanied Innocent II back to Italy and calmed the troubles brewing in that country.

A few years later, in 1134, St. Bernard was called to Aquitaine to help persuade William, the Duke of Aquitaine (who had lapsed into schism), to stop persecuting the supporters of Pope Innocent II.

William, a prince of great wealth and stature, was invited to attend a Mass celebrated by St. Bernard. During the Mass, however, William and those loyal to him stood at a door of the Church. After the consecration and before distributing communion, St. Bernard placed the Host on the paten and approached William holding the Host over his head. St. Bernard implored the duke to end the schism:

> "Into His hands your obstinate soul will one day fall. Will you despise Him? Will you scorn Him as you have done His servants?" ("Saint Bernard of Clairvaux, Abbot, Doctor of the Church," taken from Crawley, *Lives of the Saints,* 1954).

William immediately abandoned his schism and restored the bishops he had expelled. The duke afterwards founded a new Cistercian monastery and went on pilgrimage to Compostella, Spain, along the course of which he died.

St. Bernard displayed a nobility of nature, a wise charity and tenderness in his dealings with others, and a genuine humility, that made him one of the most perfect exponents of the Christian life.

When he became a monk, St. Bernard focused his studies on the Scriptures and the Fathers of the Church. Profoundly humble, St. Bernard refused all promotions, including the episcopacy and papacy. A major part of his service to the Church was his extraordinary writing to encourage and strengthen others in the Faith. His central theme, in conjunction with extensive quotation of Scriptures, was the divine life communicated to the world in the Person of Jesus Christ.

The middle of the twelfth century was called the "Age of St. Bernard." St. Bernard counseled rulers, bishops, and popes, including Pope Bl. Eugene III, the first pope who was a Cistercian. He carried out a legendary debate with Peter Abelard, the most renowned thinker of the time other than St. Bernard. Abelard had advocated certain theological errors, but St. Bernard, so logically forceful and clear in his condemnation of Abelard's teachings, left the master logician with no response but silence.

With the desire to live a simple and disciplined life, St. Bruno declined the office of bishop of Rheims.

THE CARTHUSIANS

The Carthusians were founded by St. Bruno at Chartreuse, near Grenoble in France. Like many churchmen of the day, St. Bruno also served the civil state in France. He was a brilliant scholar and he counted among his pupils Eudes of Châtillon, who would become Pope Bl. Urban II. Despite his prestigious position as chancellor at Rheims, St. Bruno remained a model priest, resisting political pressures. When offered the chance in 1080 to become the bishop of Rheims, he declined.

Instead, inspired by a burning love for God and a desire to live a more spiritually disciplined and simple life, St. Bruno left his position and went off with two friends to live as hermits in the mountains. Like the Egyptian monks centuries before, St. Bruno and his companions lived in isolation, practiced severe mortifications, and observed perpetual silence.

St. Bruno and his two friends settled at Chartreuse in the French Alps where they established a unique monastery for their day. The monks at Chartreuse did not live together like other monks; instead, each had his own cell around the cloister. St. Bruno wanted to bring the ascetic life of the

The Carthusians were founded by St. Bruno at Chartreuse, near Grenoble in France.

desert hermit into the context of the monastery, establishing an oasis of peace and prayer outside the busy developing cities of the Medieval world.

The Carthusians did not become as numerous as some of the other monastic orders of the day, but their positive example had its own influence. Rumors of their ascetic life spread throughout important centers in Europe, helping to revive Christian devotion to simplicity and prayer.

CONCLUSION

The period from Charlemagne's death in the ninth century to the Concordat of Worms in the early twelfth century represents an unstable time in the history of the Church and Europe. The splintering of European political order, external threats of invasion, and conflicts between civil and spiritual authority challenged not only the Church's stability, but its identity as a temporal institution. Regrettably, monastic and diocesan landholdings tied the Church to the developing feudal world in a way that made corruption almost inevitable. Abuses such as simony and nepotism, as well as the weakening of fidelity, celibacy, and piety among the clergy posed a strong threat to the Church. Ironically, at a time when segments of the Church seemed to drift further from the example of the early church, monastic reformers and popes like St. Gregory VII and Innocent III helped transform this period into a time of renewed piety and spiritual devotion. These reformers would begin a rehabilitation that would eventually develop into the golden age of the High Middle Ages.

SUPPLEMENTARY READING

St. Gregory VII, *Dictatus papæ*
(The Dictate of the Pope)

1. That the Roman church was founded by God alone.

2. That the Roman pontiff alone can with right be called universal.

3. That he alone can depose or reinstate bishops.

4. That, in a council his legate, even if a lower grade, is above all bishops, and can pass sentence of deposition against them.

5. That the pope may depose the absent.

6. That, among other things, we ought not to remain in the same house with those excommunicated by him.

7. That for him alone is it lawful, according to the needs of the time, to make new laws, to assemble together new congregations, to make an abbey of a canonry; and, on the other hand, to divide a rich bishopric and unite the poor ones.

8. That he alone may use the imperial insignia.

9. That of the pope alone all princes shall kiss the feet.

10. That his name alone shall be spoken in the churches.

11. That this is the only name in the world.

12. That it may be permitted to him to depose emperors.

13. That he may be permitted to transfer bishops if need be.

14. That he has power to ordain a clerk of any church he may wish.

15. That he who is ordained by him may preside over another church, but may not hold a subordinate position; and that such a one may not receive a higher grade from any bishop.

16. That no synod shall be called a general one without his order.

17. That no chapter and no book shall be considered canonical without his authority.

18. That a sentence passed by him may be retracted by no one; and that he himself, alone of all, may retract it.

19. That he himself may be judged by no one.

20. That no one shall dare to condemn one who appeals to the apostolic chair.

21. That to the latter should be referred the more important cases of every church.

22. That the Roman church has never erred; nor will it err to all eternity, the Scripture bearing witness.

23. That the Roman pontiff, if he have been canonically ordained, is undoubtedly made a saint by the merits of St. Peter; St. Ennodius, bishop of Pavia, bearing witness, and many holy fathers agreeing with him. As is contained in the decrees of St. Symmachus the pope.

24. That, by his command and consent, it may be lawful for subordinates to bring accusations.

25. That he may depose and reinstate bishops without assembling a synod.

26. That he who is not at peace with the Roman church shall not be considered catholic.

27. That he may absolve subjects from their fealty to wicked men.

St. Bernard of Clairvaux, *On Loving God*, Ch. 5

Admit that God deserves to be loved very much, yea, boundlessly, because He loved us first, He infinite and we nothing, loved us, miserable sinners, with a love so great and so free. This is why I said at the beginning that the measure of our love to God is to love immeasurably. For since our love is toward God, who is infinite and immeasurable, how can we bound or limit the love we owe Him? Besides, our love is not a gift but a debt.

And since it is the Godhead who loves us, Himself boundless, eternal, supreme love, of whose greatness there is no end, yea, and His wisdom is infinite, whose peace passeth all understanding; since it is He who loves us, I say, can we think of repaying Him grudgingly? "I will love Thee, O Lord, my strength. The Lord is my rock and my fortress and my deliverer, my God, my strength, in whom I will trust" (Ps 18:1 ff.). He is all that I need, all that I long for.

My God and my help, I will love Thee for Thy great goodness; not so much as I might, surely, but as much as I can. I cannot love Thee as Thou deservest to be loved, for I cannot love Thee more than my own feebleness permits. I will love Thee more when Thou deemest me worthy to receive greater capacity for loving; yet never so perfectly as Thou hast deserved of me. "Thine eyes did see my substance, yet being unperfect; and in Thy book all my members were written" (Ps 139:16). Yet Thou recordest in that book all who do what they can, even though they cannot do what they ought. Surely I have said enough to show how God should be loved and why. But who has felt, who can know, who express, how much we should love him.

"For since our love is toward God, who is infinite and immeasurable, how can we bound or limit the love we owe Him?"

– St. Bernard of Clairvaux

VOCABULARY

AGE OF ST. BERNARD
Refers to the middle of the twelfth century during which St. Bernard of Clairvaux exhibited enormous influence through his counseling of rulers, bishops and popes.

CAROLINGIAN
The French dynasty of rulers descended from Charlemagne.

CISTERCIANS
So called "White Monks," after the color of their habits, this order was founded by the Cluniac monk St. Robert of Molesme in 1098. They adopted the Benedictine rule and placed a special emphasis on austerities, farming, simplicity, and strictness in daily life.

CLUNY
City in east-central France which gave birth to monastic reform in 910. The first abbey began with twelve monks committed to renewing the rule of St. Benedict.

DICTATUS PAPÆ
Decree given by Pope St. Gregory VII asserting that the pope possesses specific powers given by God that rested on him alone. These powers included the power to convene and ratify a council, to propound doctrine, and to appoint, transfer, and remove bishops from office. He also claimed that the papacy had the power to depose temporal rulers and subjects of any temporal ruler had the right to appeal to the papacy in order to bring charges against their sovereign.

FEUDALISM
System that came to organize the politics, economy, and social life of Medieval Europe after the split of the Carolingian empire. Based on the relationship between wealthy, landowning lords and the common villagers, farm-workers, it was a relatively simple arrangement in which the commoners would pay the landowner in labor or services in return for the lord's military protection against foreign or domestic foes.

LAY INVESTITURE
The appointment of bishops and abbots by secular rulers, often in exchange for temporal protection.

NEPOTISM
From the Italian *nepote,* "nephew" and Latin *nepos,* "grandson." The appointment of family members to important positions of authority.

SERF
The majority of people within feudalism. They barely enjoyed any freedom since they were completely tied to the land and lord they were serving.

SIMONY
The selling of ecclesiastical offices, pardons, or emoluments by either secular or spiritual leaders.

TREATY OF VERDUN
Signed in 843, the treaty divided the Carolingian empire into three sections, which led to the eventual destruction of Charlemagne's empire.

VASSAL
In feudalism, those under the rule of the lord who paid him in labor or services.

VICAR OF CHRIST
Title used by Pope Innocent III rather than the earlier title, Vicar of St. Peter. "Vicar of Christ" emphasized Innocent III's understanding of the pope as a representative of Christ himself.

The magnificent church of Cluny.

STUDY QUESTIONS

1. What three groups coming from which three directions threatened western Europe during the ninth century?

2. Why were monasteries often the targets of the Viking invasions?

3. When and by whom was Cluny founded?

4. What did the monastic reform at Cluny emphasize?

5. What were two things that separated Cluniac monks from other monks?

6. What did Pope Benedict VIII grant to Cluny in 1016? How did this help Cluny not to become involved in the problems of feudalism?

7. Name at least four important Cluniac monks who rose to positions of importance.

8. Otto I's (the Great) coronation at Aachen as Holy Roman emperor served what two purposes?

9. List the three ways in which the Ottonian line exercised influence over the Church.

10. How did Lanfranc negotiate his responsibilities to the Church and his relationship to the state?

11. Why did the Church want to regain control over the ecclesiastical appointments?

12. What act by Henry IV initiated his struggle with Pope St. Gregory VII?

13. What does excommunication mean? Why would Henry IV not ignore the act of excommunication?

14. What was the Concordat of Worms (1122)?

15. What were King Henry II's aims with the Constitutions of Clarendon?

16. How did the contest between St. Thomas à Becket and King Henry II end?

17. What was Pope Innocent III's goal during his papacy?

18. How did Pope Innocent III and his immediate successors view kings? For what kinds of behavior were kings penalized?

19. Which rule do the Cistercians follow and what do they emphasize along with it?

20. What did the color white signify for the Cistercian habit, and what color did most religious orders wear?

21. What were the two areas of focus for St. Bernard's studies, and what was the central theme of his spirituality?

22. Who founded the Carthusians, and how did he live with the earliest Carthusians?

23. What kind of spirituality did the Carthusians create in their order?

PRACTICAL EXERCISES

1. Cluny monks lived in isolation. Explain how their isolation did not hinder the beneficial role they served in western European society.

2. One of the criticisms of the Catholic Church is that it was too often involved in a struggle with secular rulers during the Medieval period, and that this involvement led to such corruptions as simony and lay investiture. Is this a fair charge, historically speaking? In what way did the political organization of this era help to ensure justice and moral righteousness on the part of the sovereign? How did it fail to achieve those ends?

3. Explain why the pope was both a temporal ruler and a spiritual ruler. To which aspect of the papacy does infallibility apply? How is the papacy different today than it was in the Middle Ages? How is it the same?

4. What are your thoughts on Pope Innocent III's letter to the prefect Acerbius that opened this chapter? How do you think people would view Pope Innocent III's ideas about the relationship of the state to the Church today?

Feudalism was a relatively simple arrangement in which the commoners would pay the landowner in labor or services in return for the lord's military protection against foreign or domestic foes.

FROM THE CATECHISM

889 In order to preserve the Church in the purity of the faith handed on by the apostles, Christ who is the Truth willed to confer on her a share in his own infallibility. By a "supernatural sense of faith" the People of God, under the guidance of the Church's living Magisterium, "unfailingly adheres to this faith" (*LG* 12; cf. *DV* 10).

890 The mission of the Magisterium is linked to the definitive nature of the covenant established by God with his people in Christ. It is this Magisterium's task to preserve God's people from deviations and defections and to guarantee them the objective possibility of professing the true faith without error. Thus, the pastoral duty of the Magisterium is aimed at seeing to it that the People of God abides in the truth that liberates. To fulfill this service, Christ endowed the Church's shepherds with the charism of infallibility in matters of faith and morals. The exercise of this charism takes several forms:

891 "The Roman Pontiff, head of the college of bishops, enjoys this infallibility in virtue of his office, when, as supreme pastor and teacher of all the faithful—who confirms his brethren in the faith—he proclaims by a definitive act a doctrine pertaining to faith or morals….The infallibility promised to the Church is also present in the body of bishops when, together with Peter's successor, they exercise the supreme Magisterium," above all in an Ecumenical Council (*LG* 25; cf. Vatican Council I: DS 3074). When the Church through its supreme Magisterium proposes a doctrine "for belief as being divinely revealed" (*DV* 10 § 2), and as the teaching of Christ, the definitions "must be adhered to with the obedience of faith" (*LG* 25 § 2). This infallibility extends as far as the deposit of divine Revelation itself (cf. *LG* 25).

2051 The infallibility of the Magisterium of the Pastors extends to all the elements of doctrine, including moral doctrine, without which the saving truths of the faith cannot be preserved, expounded, or observed.

In order to pursue his claim to the throne of England, William of Normandy obtained the Pope's support for his cause. He assembled an invasion fleet of 600 ships and an army of 7,000 men. He landed at Pevensey in Sussex on September 28, 1066 and assembled a prefabricated wooden castle near Hastings as a base.

CHAPTER 9
The Crusades, Military Orders, And The Inquisition

*By 1071, Muslims had conquered two-thirds of the Christian world.
Christian Europe was on the brink of annihilation.
Church unity was also threatened by growing heretical groups.*

CHAPTER 9

The Crusades, Military Orders, And The Inquisition

In no way is the Church to be confused with the political community...and it would be deplorable if individuals and institutions...were tempted to make use of her for their own particular advantage....But, this said, we should not conclude that the message of salvation entrusted to the Church has nothing to say to the body politic in order to enlighten it with the Gospel....It is not a question of undue interference in a field to which she is a stranger, but of a service offered, for love of Jesus Christ, to the whole community, and prompted by a desire to contribute to the common good, encouraged by the Lord's words: "The truth will make you free" (John 8:32).

— John Paul II, *Address to the Bishops*, Santiago, Chile, April 2, 1987

After Charlemagne's death, the Carolingian empire fragmented into thousands of principalities, counties, and fiefs (landed estates), and an economic system called feudalism arose. Broadly speaking, because of this economic organization all of Europe's population fell into three class distinctions: clergy, nobility, and peasantry. Every member of society was beholden to someone else: serfs served small landholders, small landholders served lords, and lords served kings.

At first, this system was very effective for the prosperity of the continent, and the population expanded. As the population grew, those class distinctions widened and land became scarce. Landholders competed for land, superiority, and lordship. Many landholders at the time believed that they had no other means of deciding who would be lord over the other except by going to war.

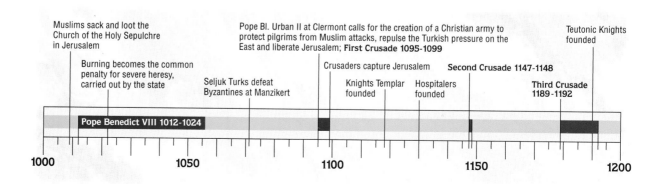

Muslims sack and loot the Church of the Holy Sepulchre in Jerusalem

Burning becomes the common penalty for severe heresy, carried out by the state

Seljuk Turks defeat Byzantines at Manzikert

Pope Bl. Urban II at Clermont calls for the creation of a Christian army to protect pilgrims from Muslim attacks, repulse the Turkish pressure on the East and liberate Jerusalem; **First Crusade 1095-1099**

Crusaders capture Jerusalem

Knights Templar founded

Hospitalers founded

Second Crusade 1147-1148

Third Crusade 1189-1192

Teutonic Knights founded

Pope Benedict VIII 1012-1024

1000   1050   1100   1150   1200

The feudal wars of the tenth and eleventh centuries were characterized by ferocity, cruelty, and injustice. The Church understood that in order to maintain peace in the Christian lands and thereby create a Christian culture, this violence would have to be reduced. The Church also saw that a warrior class imbued with Christian principles would not only put the breaks on such incessant feuds but also provide protection for the feudal kingdoms.

The rise of the Seljuk Turks during the eleventh century resumed expansion of Islamic forces in the East. At first, this caused Christian pilgrims to be persecuted in the Holy Land, but with the defeat of the Byzantine army at the Battle of Manzikert in 1071, it became clear that the Turks could launch full-scale expansion of Islam into the remainder of the Christian world. Christian Europe was on the brink of possible annihilation.

This chapter covering the Crusades, Military Orders, and the Inquisition shows the different ways that the Church sought to unify the Christian world and defend it against internal and external threats. Some of these methods may seem cruel and uncompromising today, and indeed there were many abuses. Nonetheless, the problems these Medieval people were responding to were real and dangerous. Any infighting, whether civil or theological, threatened to split the Christian world and possibly destroy both Medieval society and Christ's Church. It bears mentioning that heresy in the Medieval mindset was ranked as a crime worse than murder since heresy risks the death of the soul and eternal damnation. The gross excesses of the era and the way in which some of these matters were mishandled reflect the severity of the dangers confronting the Church at that time, as well as the failure of some members of Christ's Church to live up to the full message of the Gospel.

Toward the end of his pontificate, Pope John Paul II addressed some of the sins and excesses made during this period. During the Jubilee Year, he presided over what he called a "Service Requesting Pardon." Cardinal Ratzinger—the future Pope Benedict XVI—invited everyone to pray with the pope:

> Let us pray that each one of us, looking to the Lord Jesus, meek and humble of heart, will recognize that even men of the Church, in the name of faith and morals, have sometimes used methods not in keeping with the Gospel in the solemn duty of defending the truth. ("Confession of Sins Committed in the Service of Truth," March 12, 2000)

There were some atrocities committed by Christians in the name of Christ. These methods of protection correspond to an eleventh-century worldview that differs greatly from the present day, but it must be remembered that the end never justifies the means in any age.

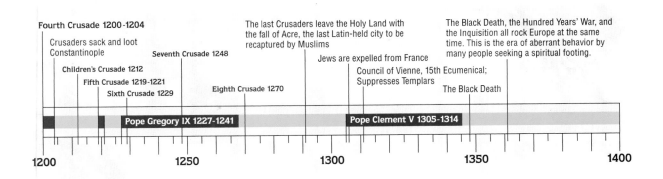

Fourth Crusade 1200-1204

Crusaders sack and loot Constantinople

Children's Crusade 1212

Fifth Crusade 1219-1221

Sixth Crusade 1229

Seventh Crusade 1248

Eighth Crusade 1270

The last Crusaders leave the Holy Land with the fall of Acre, the last Latin-held city to be recaptured by Muslims

Jews are expelled from France

Council of Vienne, 15th Ecumenical; Suppresses Templars

The Black Death

The Black Death, the Hundred Years' War, and the Inquisition all rock Europe at the same time. This is the era of aberrant behavior by many people seeking a spiritual footing.

Pope Gregory IX 1227-1241

Pope Clement V 1305-1314

1200   1250   1300   1350   1400

PART I

The Crusades

Modern literature has applied the word *crusade* to all wars of a religious character. However, in the Middle Ages, the word *crusade* referred specifically to a series of eight expansive military expeditions that the Christian people undertook roughly between the years of 1096 and 1270 as a action in the Holy Land and against continued Muslim expansion. These efforts were not only directed against the Turks in the Holy Land and the Muslims in Spain, but also against heretics, like the Albigensians, whose teachings violated the most fundamental principles of Christianity. The word *crusade* itself may be traced to the cross, or *crux*, made of cloth and worn as a badge on the crusading knight's outer garments. After pronouncing a solemn vow, each warrior received a cross from the hands of the pope or his legates. He was thenceforth considered a soldier of the Church.

Uniting themselves under the popes and the Christian rulers, the Crusaders fought these wars against Muslim expansion, which in part avoided infighting among European rulers, and offered a chance to embark upon an authentic religious pilgrimage.

THE FALL OF THE HOLY LAND

Within one hundred years of the death of Muhammad, Islam spread throughout much of the Christian world. As discussed previously, this had as much to do with the success of militant Muslim expansion as it did with authentic religious conversion. Quickly after the birth of the religion, Islamic forces seized most of the Christian world. Palestine, the Holy Land and home of Jesus; Egypt, the birthplace of monasticism; Asia Minor, where St. Paul preached and planted the seeds of early Christian communities; and North Africa had all fallen to Muslim forces. Muslim expansion was finally brought to a halt by Charles Martel's defense of Western Europe in France and the Byzantine Empire's defense in the East. With these new borders established, Muslim and Christian lands remained more or less stable.

Christians being executed by their Muslim captors. At some point, Christianity would have to defend itself or be taken over by Islam.

After a long period of tolerance, the rise of the Fatimite Muslims in Egypt during the first decades of the eleventh century led to a renewed Christian persecution. In the second half of the century, a new militant Islamic nation, the Seljuk Turks, persecuted Christians, especially in Palestine and Syria, and expanded westwards into lands previously protected by Byzantium. In 1071, in the Battle of Manzikert, the Turks annihilated the Byzantine army and were on the verge of taking Constantinople. By this time, two-thirds of the Christian world had been taken by Muslim forces, and now the last vestiges of the Roman Empire were threatened. The Eastern emperor looked West for assistance, in desperation, asking them to aid their brothers and sisters in the East.

The Western Christians were concerned with their Eastern brethren. Despite the schism of 1054, many (including both Pope Bl. Urban II and the Eastern emperor) hoped that the split could be

In the summer of 1095, Pope Bl. Urban II preached a momentous sermon in Clermont, France that would launch the First Crusade. "A great commotion arose through all the regions of France, so that if anyone earnestly wished to follow God with pure heart and mind, and wanted to bear the cross faithfully after him, he would hasten to take the road to the Holy Sepulchre" (extract from the *Gesta Francorum*).

healed. In 1095, Bl. Urban II held a council in Clermont in central France to try to rouse support from Westerners to aid the Eastern Christians. At Clermont, Bl. Urban II appealed for help:

> For your brethren who live in the east are in urgent need of your help, and you must hasten to give them the aid which has often been promised them. For, as most of you have heard, the Turks and Arabs have attacked them and conquered the territory of Romania [the Greek empire] as far west as the shore of the Mediterranean and the Hellespont. They have occupied more and more lands of those Christians and have overcome them in seven battles.... On this account I, or rather the Lord, beseech you as Christ's heralds to publish this everywhere and to persuade all people of whatever rank, foot-soldiers and knights, poor and rich, to carry aid promptly to those Christians. (quoted in Thatcher and McNeal, *A Source Book for Medieval History*, 1905, p. 514)

Pope Bl. Urban II began the crusades by proclaiming an organized assault in defense of Christian Europe. Rather than a Christian offensive, the crusades were a desperate attempt to fend off Islamic expansion. Islam was the strongest power of the Medieval world, and it now threatened to overrun the entire West. At some point, Christianity had to defend itself or be taken over by Islam. Islam was born in war and grew the same way. Muslim thought at this time divided the world into two spheres: the abode of Islam and the abode of war. Christianity or any other non-Muslim religion has no abode. Pope Bl. Urban II's crusade was the first of a series of military expeditions meant to ward off the very probable fall of the Christian world to the Muslims.

For Christians, the Muslim threat was no better realized than through the plight of pilgrims in the Holy Land. Pilgrims faced an increasingly hard journey to the Holy Land. They were often robbed, beaten, or killed. Pope St. Gregory VII (1073-1085) was ready to invade the Holy Land with 50,000 crusaders nearly two decades before Bl. Urban II's call to arms, but the lay investiture controversy made his crusade impossible. By 1095 Muslim expansion meant, above all, the hostile occupation of the Holy Land, the very ground upon which Jesus walked. As Crusaders set out to the east, they had two objectives: to fend off Turkish (Muslim) expansion into Byzantium and to free the Holy Land for safe pilgrimage and worship of sacred sites. Both objectives had as an end the avoidance of the further killing of Christians.

Pope Bl. Urban II toured France and Italy with his public appeal for Christian warriors to take back Jerusalem from the Muslims. "For Pope Bl. Urban II began to deliver eloquent sermons and to preach, saying that if anyone wished to save his soul, he should not hesitate to undertake with humble spirit the way of the Lord, . . . For the lord pope said, 'Brothers, you must suffer many things in the name of Christ, wretchedness, poverty, nakedness, persecution, need, sickness, hunger, thirst and other things of this kind, just as the Lord says to his disciples: "You must suffer many things in my name" ' " (extract from the *Gesta Francorum*, an anonymous Crusader's chronicle).

MOTIVATION FOR THE CRUSADERS

There is no doubt that religion was a major motivation for soldiers who went on a crusade. The crusades combined the concept of a defensive war with religious pilgrimage and were primarily viewed as acts of religious devotion by the Christians who participated in them. Even before the First Crusade, the concept was understood in the West that God would reward those who fought for the good cause of defending Christendom. In addition, many of the popes, clerics, and bishops who preached the crusades offered religious indulgences to the soldiers. An indulgence is a remission before God of temporal punishment due to sins, the guilt of which has already been forgiven through the sacrament of Penance. Volunteering for a crusade became a way of earning an indulgence and a prolonged time of penance to make reparation for personal sins.

In addition to spiritual motivations, the Church offered other incentives including the reduction of taxes, dissolving of debt payments, and the protection of the crusaders' families. Crusaders took the vow of the Cross, expressing sentiments of piety, self-sacrifice, and love for God. The Christian world was a prime target for the earliest caliphs, and it would remain so for Muslim leaders for the next thousand years.

THE UNKNOWN'S MANUSCRIPT

Although many of the soldiers who marched on the Crusades were illiterate, there was one soldier in the army of Bohemund of Antioch who did keep a journal of the harsh life crusaders experienced on the road to Jerusalem. This writer never mentions his name in the journal, and so he has been dubbed by historians as "the Unknown." Without his narrative, the *Gesta Francorum et aliorum Hierosolymytanorum* (The Deeds of the Franks and the Other Pilgrims to Jerusalem), knowledge of many of the details, events, and battles of the First Crusade would have been lost.

The Unknown's manuscript provides a candid view into the fear and excitement of the Crusades. An excerpt from his account of the battle of Dorylaeum captures the mood of the front lines:

> Turks made a violent assault on Bohemund and his companions. The Turks began unceasingly to shout, babble, and cry in a loud voice, making some devilish sound, I know not how, in their own tongue. . . . By the time all this had been done, the Turks had already surrounded us on all sides. They attacked us, slashing, hurling, and shooting arrows far and wide, in a manner strange to behold. Although we could scarcely hold them back or even bear up under the weight of such a host, nevertheless we all managed to hold our ranks.

Elsewhere, the Unknown talks about the fall of Antioch, another city taken back by the crusaders on the march to Jerusalem:

> Moreover, when at earliest dawn those in the tents outside heard the most violent outcry sounding through the city, they rushed out hurriedly and saw the standard of Bohemund up on the mount, and with rapid pace all ran hastily and entered the city. They killed the Turks and Saracens whom they found there, except those who had fled into the citadel. Others of the Turks went out through the gates, and by fleeing escaped alive.

PREACHING THE CRUSADES

Pope Bl. Urban II's call to arms found enormous appeal among the lower classes. The pope specifically appealed to sinners to join the crusade as a means of reconciliation with God:

> You, oppressors of orphans and widows; you, murderers and violators of churches; you, robbers of the property of others; you, who, like vultures are drawn to the scent of the battlefield, hasten, as you love your souls, under your Captain Christ to the rescue of Jerusalem. All you who are guilty of such sins as exclude you from the kingdom of God, ransom yourselves at this price, for such is the will of God. (quoted in Laux, *Church History: A Complete History of the Catholic Church to the Present Day*, 1992, p. 314)

Although the popes were primarily instrumental in unifying the armies bound for the Holy Land, other clerics preached the Crusades as well.

Bl. Peter the Hermit of Amiens traveled from city to city preaching for a crusade. According to the chronicler Alber of Aix-la-Chapelle, Bl. Peter led the rigorous life of a hermit for a number of years before undertaking a pilgrimage to Jerusalem. During his journey, the hermit was harassed and beaten by the Turks. One day when he was asleep in the Basilica of the Holy Sepulchre, Jesus appeared to him and ordered him to go to Europe proclaiming the miseries that had befallen the Christians in Palestine. Though many scholars now discount the magnitude of the effect Bl. Peter the Hermit's experience had on inciting the First Crusade, his story is typical of the dangers that befell pilgrims of that time.

The spellbinding preaching of St. Bernard of Clairvaux inspired thousands to join the Second Crusade in the twelfth century. St. Bernard traveled all across Europe, sometimes convincing entire parishes to set out to the east the next day. St. Bernard later frankly affirmed that all but a few of the knights on the crusades were "criminals and sinners, ravishers and the sacrilegious, murderers, perjures, and adulterers" (quoted in Chambers, *et al., The Western Experience,* 2002, p. 267). St. Bernard observed the double benefit of having the crusaders out of Europe: "Their departure makes their own people happy, and their arrival cheers those whom they are hastening to help. They aid both groups, not only by protecting the one but also by not oppressing the other." The

The spellbinding preaching of St. Bernard of Clairvaux inspired thousands to join the Second Crusade.

crusades were, in one respect, an effective means of draining so much of the violence from Medieval life. In reality, the ranks of Muslim soldiers were filled with the same sorts of individuals from their society (conscripts).

Kings in Western Europe often participated in leading the Crusades or offering financial support at the request of the papacy. Most famously, Richard the Lionheart of England led an army to Jerusalem along with Philip II of France in the Third Crusade.

The Taking of Jerusalem by the Crusaders, July 15, 1099

THE FIRST CRUSADE (1095-1099)

The First Crusade was a popular movement that took place without any direct support or leadership from the kings of Europe, since many of the rulers were either excommunicated or in opposition to the papacy at the time. In northern France and the Rhineland, a number of preachers took Pope Bl. Urban II's message to the people, motivating and organizing armies to set out for the Holy Land. The message was met with enthusiasm throughout all of Europe, and armies from every corner of the continent set out on various routes towards the east. Regretfully with the occasion of the crusades, some crusaders attacked Jewish communities on their way to the Holy Land.

The First Crusade was considered the best organized. The armies were divided into four groups all set to meet in Constantinople. Godfrey of Bouillon, Duke of Lower Lorraine, led the people of Lorraine, the Germans, and the northern French. They followed the valley of the Danube, crossed Hungary, and arrived in Constantinople in late 1096. Hugh of Vermandois, brother of King Philip I of France and Robert Courte-Heuse, the Duke of Normandy and the son of William the Conqueror, led bands of French and Normans across the Alps and set sail from Apulia, on the boot heel of Italy, to Dyrrachium, which is in modern day Albania. From there the army continued overland to Constantinople where they arrived in May of 1097.

The southern French, under the lead of Raymond of Saint-Filles and the bishop of Puy, Adhemar of Moneil, set out overland through the eastern Alps where they met tough resistance from the Slavs, delaying their arrival in Constantinople until the end of April 1097. The fourth army consisted of Normans from Southern Italy led by Bohemund and Tancred, who were both related to the founder of Norman Sicily, Robert Guiscard. On their way across Italy and on through the Byzantine

Empire, the army picked up many enthusiastic bands of local crusaders, who joined ranks, and eventually arrived in Constantinople with the Normans in April of 1097. The crusaders came from every corner of Europe, and when they arrived in Constantinople they were a mismatched group and everything but a unified army.

In the spring of 1097 the campaign began, and the four armies proved very successful. First, they staged a successful siege of Nicaea, and after that, moved on to Antioch, which they took in 1098. Jerusalem fell in 1099. Pope Bl. Urban II, whose dream was to recover the Holy Land, died before receiving news of the sacking of Jerusalem. The reconquest of Jerusalem unfortunately resulted in a brutal massacre of the mostly Muslim population.

The First Crusade came at a time when Muslims were politically divided. Seljuk Turks had recently risen to power in the Holy Land and they did not yet have firm control over the area. The crusaders took advantage of their disunity and established authority over Palestine. After the reconquest of Jerusalem, the crusaders organized the lands into a number of counties, fiefs, and principalities based on the Medieval feudal system to build a Christian state in Palestine.

As is still evident today, the organization of a government for a population which included Muslims, Jews, Eastern and Western Christians was no easy task. The job fell to Godfrey of Bouillon, and after his death in 1100, his younger brother Baldwin. Baldwin kept direct control of Jerusalem and its surrounding areas. To the north, three fiefs — the County of Tripoli, the Principality of Antioch, and the County of Edessa were established. Muslims who lived in crusader-won territories were generally allowed to retain their property and livelihood and, as always, their religion.

However, the kingdom of Jerusalem was difficult to maintain, as it shrunk continuously until 1291 when the last acres were overrun. A big problem was that not many Europeans stayed in the Holy Land as settlers, and despite a steady influx of traveling pilgrims and soldiers, the kings found themselves trying to maintain control over a people of largely different faiths, cultures, and sympathies. It is indeed remarkable they were able to maintain control for nearly 200 years.

SUCCESSIVE CRUSADES

The popularity and success of the First Crusade inspired a string of crusades that lasted for nearly five centuries. None of these crusades was ever as well organized or effective as the first. In fact, the wars more often resembled a steady stream of people heading east rather than an organized military campaign.

Shortly after the end of the First Crusade, the Christian kingdom in Palestine was under attack. In 1144, the Turks recaptured the city of Edessa in the north. King Louis VII of France and Emperor Conrad II of Germany set out to capture the city of Damascus and establish a defensive front for the Kingdom of Jerusalem. They failed and were forced to retreat. Convinced that God was punishing the West for its sins, lay piety movements arose throughout Europe to purify Christian society in order to be worthy of future victory in the East.

The Third Crusade (1189-1192) is perhaps the most famous due to its role in providing the background of the Robin Hood stories. Richard the Lionheart of England set out with Emperor Frederick I, Barba-

On July 22, 1099, Godfrey of Bouillon was chosen as ruler of Jerusalem with the title "Advocate of the Holy Sepulchre." It was agreed to by the leaders that no one should be called "king" and wear a crown in the land where Christ had worn the crown of thorns. After the majority of pilgrims returned home, Godfrey had only 300 knights and 2,000 foot-soldiers to protect Jerusalem. His one year reign was a struggle to ensure the survival of the infant Christian state.

Legendary military rivals of the Third Crusade. *Above:* A monumental statue of Saladin stands in Damascus, the capital of Syria and the site of Saladin's tomb. *Left:* A statue of Richard the Lionheart in London. King Richard was a natural leader with great skill as a military strategist and an ability to inspire his warriors to follow him into battle. His Muslim contemporaries considered him their greatest enemy.

rossa and King Philip of France to defend the Christian kingdoms against the Turks, who had now unified under their great military leader Saladin. Saladin, the great unifier, had forged the Muslim Near East into a single entity while preaching *jihad* against the Christians. In 1187 at the Battle of Hattin, his forces wiped out the combined armies of the Christian kingdom of Jerusalem, and they captured the relic of the True Cross. The response was the Third Crusade.

Later crusades failed, abounding with mistakes and accidents. The Fourth Crusade (1201-1204) resulted in the sack of Constantinople, the great Christian city, in 1203. Various conditions led the crusaders to sack the city. The crusaders were significantly in debt to the city of Venice, so they favored a Byzantine emperor who would repay the debt for them. The preachers of the crusade thought the Constantinopolitans had sided with Saladin and the Muslims during the Third Crusade and had not assisted in the Second.

In 1212, children, caught up in the popular crusader movements, set off to mount a "Children's Crusade" against the Turks. Before they even arrived in the Holy Land, many of the children either starved to death or were killed by disease during the perilously rugged journey east. Those who did not die along the way were captured and sold into slavery.

These two Crusades, as well as a number of unofficial expeditions, diminished enthusiasm and religious fervor for the Holy Wars. Eventually Christians lost possession of the Holy Land when the last of the Latin Kingdoms fell in 1291. Muslim forces succeeded in killing or ejecting the last of the crusaders, thus erasing the crusader kingdoms from the map. Christian forces were unable to gain another foothold in the region until the nineteenth century.

This late medieval illustration depicts Richard the Lionheart and Saladin in a symbolic joust. In a real battle, the crusaders fought with heavy horses and swords wielded with two hands. The Saracens had smaller, quick horses and short, curved scimitars which were slashed at the crusaders from horseback at a full gallop.

THE FIRST CRUSADE, 1095-1099

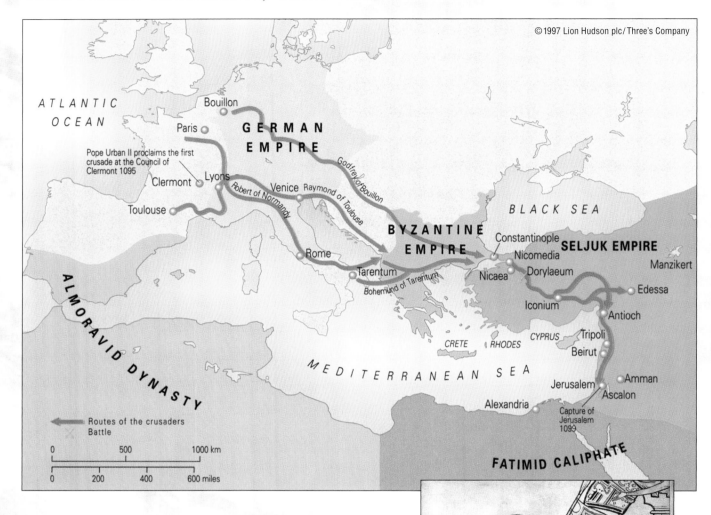

©1997 Lion Hudson plc / Three's Company

Krak des Chevaliers was the headquarters of the Knights Hospitaler in Syria during the Crusades. It was the largest Crusader fortress in the Holy Land. The castle is located east of Tripoli atop a high cliff along the only route from Antioch to Beirut and the Mediterranean Sea. The original fortress had been built in 1031 for the emir of Aleppo. It was captured by Raymond IV of Toulouse early in 1099, during the First Crusade. The Hospitalers expanded it in 1144. It fell to Sultan Baybars in 1271. The fortress is one of the few sites where Crusader frescoes have been preserved.

THE CRUSADER STATES, 1081-1375

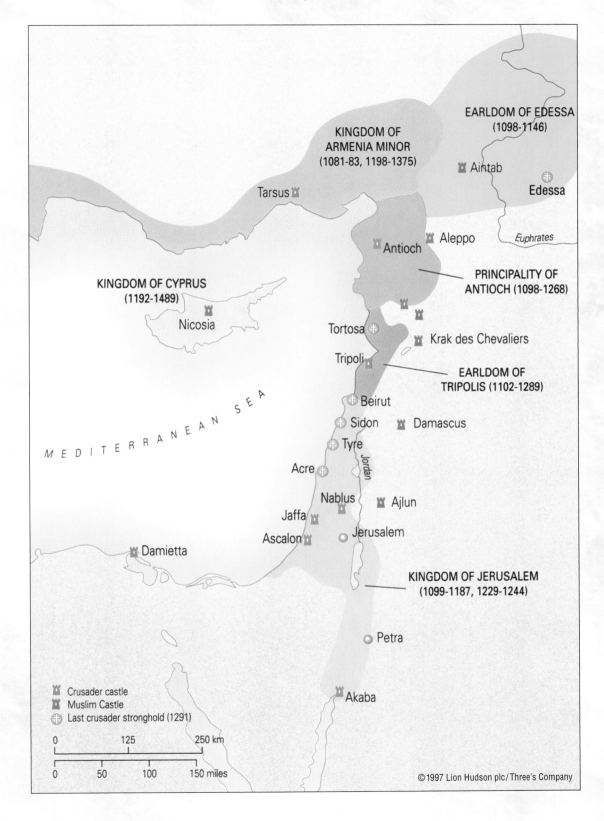

KINGDOM OF ARMENIA MINOR
(1081-83, 1198-1375)

EARLDOM OF EDESSA
(1098-1146)

Aintab

Edessa

Tarsus

Euphrates

Aleppo

Antioch

PRINCIPALITY OF ANTIOCH (1098-1268)

KINGDOM OF CYPRUS
(1192-1489)

Nicosia

Tortosa

Krak des Chevaliers

Tripoli

EARLDOM OF TRIPOLIS (1102-1289)

M E D I T E R R A N E A N   S E A

Beirut

Sidon

Damascus

Tyre

Jordan

Acre

Nablus

Ajlun

Jaffa

Ascalon

Jerusalem

Damietta

KINGDOM OF JERUSALEM
(1099-1187, 1229-1244)

Petra

Crusader castle
Muslim Castle
Last crusader stronghold (1291)

Akaba

0   125   250 km

0   50   100   150 miles

©1997 Lion Hudson plc/Three's Company

On April 12, 1204 the men of the Fourth Crusade spent three days sacking and looting Constantinople, a city so filled with treasures and holy relics that it was one of the most destructive and profitable conquests in history. Many of the looted treasures remain in Venice including the Four Golden Horses of San Marco and a piece of the True Cross. The feelings of betrayal would create a great rift between the Western and Eastern Churches which still exists today.

BYZANTIUM'S RESPONSE

At first, many westerners (especially Pope Innocent III) were optimistic about the positive effect the Crusades might have on the relationship between the western and eastern churches. Politically speaking, the Byzantines needed the help of the western Crusaders to contain the Turks and protect the Byzantine Empire. In addition, the Crusades also allowed for a positive exchange of ideas and culture between the more educated Byzantines and the Western Christians. Many hoped that the constant communication between the west and east would help heal the Great Schism of 1054.

The Eastern Empire, for its part, feared the Crusaders and saw the western armies as a threat against their own territory. Emperor Alexius usually tried to transport the Crusaders as quickly as possible across the Bosporus Straits and out of Byzantine territory given the high intensity of suspicion and hostility many Eastern Christians had for the Latin Church. After the sacking of Constantinople during the fourth Crusade, the relationship between the east and west was ruined.

The Byzantines regained control over their own capital in 1261, but would be eventually defeated by the Turks in 1453. The Crusades became a turning point in the life of the eastern empire, and the rift created between the Eastern and Western Churches was so great that after eight centuries it still remains open.

CRITICISM

After these initial expeditions, soldiers and princes alike lost the religious passion that fueled the excitement and desires of the First Crusade. As St. Bernard of Clairvaux said, many of the soldiers were far from pious and from having sensitive consciences. During this time, regretfully, Jews and

St. Francis of Assisi met with Sultan Malik-al-Kamil and impressed him by agreeing to walk barefoot through fire to prove the strength of his faith and the power of his God.

Muslims living in Europe also became the subjects of increased violence. Religious men of the Church soon turned their backs on the idea of the Crusade and looked for other ways to secure safety and holiness in the Holy Land.

In 1219, a young St. Francis of Assisi asked the cardinal overseeing the Fifth Crusade for permission to travel to Palestine and meet with the Muslim leader Sultan Malik-al-Kamil in order to convert him. The Cardinal refused at first, but eventually gave in to St. Francis' persistence. When he arrived in the Holy Land with his friend, Brother Illuminato, the two were captured, beaten, and tortured. Their appearance — unarmed, unafraid, and dressed in beggar's robes — piqued the sultan's curiosity. St. Francis met with the sultan daily for a month discussing religion. Though the sultan never converted, the

two became friends, and the sultan granted St. Francis safe travel to and from the Holy Land. St. Francis' example suggested that there were peaceful and more effective means of establishing safety and friendly dialogue in the Holy Land.

OUTCOME OF THE CRUSADES

The main objectives of the Crusades — the deliverance of the Holy Land and the rescue of the Christians in the East — were ultimately frustrated. Nonetheless, the sacrifice of so many lives was not entirely in vain. The Crusades held back Turkish expansion into Europe for four hundred years and gave Christians a more acute consciousness of their Christian unity, which transcended nationality and race. Contact with Eastern Christian culture through the exchange of people, goods, and ideas had an enormous influence on the intellectual life of Europe. The Crusades made pilgrimages to the Holy Land easier, and the Muslims eventually entrusted Christian Holy Places in Palestine to the Franciscans due to St. Francis of Assisi's friendship with Muslim leaders.

The Crusades also had a powerful influence on military technology. After initial invasions, Crusaders largely waged a defensive war, becoming skilled in constructing castles. Along with castles, there were improvements in siege engines to break down walls and gates including battering rams, towers, and catapults.

The Crusades encouraged travel and fostered a new curiosity for foreign culture among the Latin Christians. Missionaries and merchants set out deep into central Asia, and by the thirteenth century had reached China. The reports from those expeditions (from explorers such as Marco Polo) gave Western Europe abundant information about Asia and fed the desire to explore and evangelize new territories. As a result, the world in many ways became more open for Westerners, and consequently the technological and academic achievements of the Arabic world and the Greek writings on medicine and mathematics facilitated a flowering of Western culture.

PART II

The Military Orders: The Knights Templar, the Hospitalers, and the Teutonic Knights

With the recovery of the Holy Places in Palestine during the Crusades, Military Orders sprang up out of the necessity to defend the holy sites as well as the pilgrims who traveled there. These orders combined both military and religious life, emphasizing dedication, discipline, and monastic organization. These soldier-monks were bound by vows of poverty, chastity, and obedience and were devoted to the care and defense of pilgrims. Although historians of the military orders have enumerated as many as a hundred different types of orders (stressing the eagerness with which the Middle Ages welcomed an institution so thoroughly corresponding to the two occupations of that period, war and religion), the three oldest and most respected were the Knights Templar, the Knights Hospitalers, and the Teutonic Knights.

The kings and the nobility availed themselves of military orders to strengthen their own position and to protect their kingdoms and fiefdoms. Since this mode of protection, self-defense through warfare, squared so well with Medieval culture, virtually every king and prince had a military order at his disposal.

THE KNIGHTS TEMPLAR

In 1118, a group of nine French knights founded the oldest of these three orders, the Knights Templar, specifically to protect pilgrims traveling to Jerusalem. The order derived their name, "The Poor Brothers of the Temple of Jerusalem," or Templars, from the Palace of King Baldwin of Jerusalem, which was built on the site of the ancient Temple of Solomon.

The Pope approved the order at the Council of Troyes in 1128, and St. Bernard of Clairvaux, who was present at the council, wrote a rule for them based on the Cistercian Rule. In his treatise *In Praise of the New Knighthood,* St. Bernard wrote:

> In this Order, knighthood blossomed forth into new life: warriors, whose sole aim in life it once was to rob, to plunder, and to kill, have now bound themselves by solemn vow to defend the poor of the Church.

WARRIOR MONKS

St. Bernard of Clairvaux

The monastic rule drafted by St. Bernard of Clairvaux and followed by the Knights Templar established a strict ascetic way of life that fostered their dedication to physical warfare. According to the rule, the Templars had to wear white monastic garments, distinguishing them on the battlefield where their fierce reputation preceded them. However, off the battlefield the Templars lived the quiet lives of pious monks, exemplifying a seemingly paradoxical existence of war and peace. Their lives of prayer, however, sustained them in war. The prospect of death in battle did not frighten the Templars; they had already given up all worldly pleasures.

Never numerous, at their height there were only four hundred knights in Jerusalem. Nevertheless, these dedicated warrior monks inspired other Christian forces. Never fearing death, if the knights were captured in battle they could not offer a ransom. In addition, those captured would always refuse their freedom if it meant denying their faith. At the siege of Safed in 1264, for example, eighty Templars were taken prisoner. After refusing to yield to their captor's wishes to deny Christ, they all were martyred. Over the course of the first two centuries of their existence, it is estimated that almost twenty thousand Knights Templars were killed.

St. Bernard saw the military order as an effective way of tempering the knights' bad habits and explicitly tying the mission of the crusading armies to the mission of Christ's Church. These monks made the three traditional vows of poverty, chastity, and obedience and lived lives of monastic warriors.

The Knights Templar were organized in a three rank division with aristocratic soldiers, clergy, and lay brothers from the lower ranks of society who acted as helpers of the aristocratic soldiers. They assumed a major role in the maintenance of safe routes between Europe and the crusader states and the defense of the Kingdom of Jerusalem. This often included safeguarding western money that was flowing to the east in support of the western kingdoms there. As a result, the Templars became one of the most important banking institutions of the age.

After the Holy Land fell again to Muslim forces, the Templars returned to their landholdings in Europe, becoming even wealthier and expanding their banking organization even more. Now based out of Paris, the Templars were excellent transferors and loaners of capital. Their clients included the popes and the French kings.

Feeling threatened by their wealth and influence, the French king Philip the Fair maliciously sought to destroy the order. He falsely charged the Templars with heresy and pressured Pope Clement V to suppress it in 1312. These charges, along with other trumped-up accusations of sacrilege, sodomy, and idolatry, made the order increasingly unpopular in France. The French King extracted "confessions" from the members of the Templars through torture, suppressed the order, and seized most of its property. The Templar Grand Master Jacques de Molay was burned at the stake in 1314. He died courageously, publicly condemning the actions of Philip.

"On Friday 13 October 1307, at precisely the same time, the first glimmer of dawn, all the Templars throughout the kingdom of France were arrested and delivered to various prisons at the command of the king, Philip IV. Among those detained was the master of the whole Order, Jacques of Molay, who was seized at the Templar's Paris house." (from the chronicle of William of Nangis)

Jacques of Molay was burnt at the stake on the Ile-des-Javiaux, an island in the Seine in the center of Paris, on March 18, 1314. He was said to have cursed Philip and Pope Clement V, calling them to join him before God's tribunal. They both died soon after.

THE KNIGHTS HOSPITALERS

Never as numerous or as wealthy as the Templars, The Knights of the Hospital of St. John of Jerusalem, or Hospitalers, founded in about 1130, grew out of an already existing work of charity consisting of the care of sick pilgrims. The knights, typically dressed in a black cloak adorned with a white cloak, made a major contribution in the defense of Jerusalem, and served as a medical corps to the Crusaders. After the fall of the last Christian stronghold in Palestine in 1291, the Hospitalers retreated to the island of Rhodes.

They held Rhodes for two centuries against the Turks. After the capture of Rhodes in 1523 by the Turks, Emperor Charles V bestowed upon them the island of Malta. Although they were expelled from the island in 1798 by Napoleon, the order still exists today. Known as the Knights of Malta, the order has long since put down the sword and exists only as a philanthropic confraternity.

The Hospitalers held Rhodes for two centuries.

THE TEUTONIC KNIGHTS

Around 1190, a number of crusaders from Bremen and Lübeck in Germany joined with the members of the German Hospital in Jerusalem to form the Order of the Teutonic Knights. Officially known as the Brothers of the Hospital of Saint Mary of Jerusalem, the Teutonic Knights were modeled largely after the Hospitalers and maintained a headquarters in Jerusalem. As early as 1226 they turned their attention away from the Holy Land. The King of Prussia and the Bishop Primate of Prussia invited the Teutonic Knights to aid in battles against the heathen Slavs and Tartars. In 1229 the Knights moved their headquarters to Prussia and helped aid the German expansion eastward, conquering lands along the Baltic Sea. The Teutonic Knights took Prussia and other lands of Estonia, Lithuania, and Russia until it finally stopped advancing around 1400. The knights remained a cohesive and efficient group until the sixteenth century, when then grand master, Albert of Hohenzollern, abandoned Catholicism (1525) and became a Lutheran Grand Duke of secularized Prussia.

LEGACY OF THE MILITARY ORDERS

Besides these three orders, there were a great number of lesser military orders. The culture of the Middle Ages offered the right setting for military orders. After the Crusades stopped in the thirteenth century, most of the military orders died out, but their effects on the development of Europe were long lasting.

The Templars were important forerunners in banking, developing an early system of capitalism in Europe. Their immediate successors were the Fugger and Medici families that played important banking roles in the fourteenth and fifteenth centuries. The Teutonic Knights were key in making possible the great German expansion into the East known as the *Drang nach Osten* (Urge to the East).

Royalty afterwards utilized the model of military orders to form a legion of knights who were ceremoniously invested into the order of knighthood. Some countries today, most notably England, still bestow these titles as a sign of honor or gratitude.

PART III

The Inquisition

In 1231, Pope Gregory IX established the Inquisition as a means of finding and judging heretics.

The first Christian emperors believed that one of the chief duties of an imperial ruler was to use his political and military power to protect the orthodoxy of the Church. The titles they used, like "Pontifex Maximus" and "Bishop of the Exterior," implied their understanding of their office as a divinely appointed agent of Heaven, a civil authority whose duty was bound up with their service of the Church.

Nevertheless, for centuries, Church leaders were reticent to embrace this explicit connection between the interests of the Church and civil society. The Catholic hierarchy was not in favor of stern measures against heresy, which they deemed inconsistent with the spirit of Christianity.

In the Middle Ages, as the Catholic Faith became dominant in Europe, the Church became tied socially, politically, and economically to European life. Christianity provided the moral foundation for law and civil authority. As a major landholder, the Church's well-being had a major economic influence on Europe. Civil authorities, despite their impiety or any dishonest intention, regarded themselves as the political arm of the Church, divinely appointed to assist and preserve the Christian world.

King Peter of Aragon emphasized the connection between the safety of Europe and of the Church when he said: "The enemies of the Cross of Christ and violators of the Christian law are likewise our enemies and the enemies of our kingdom, and ought therefore to be dealt with as such" (quoted in Blötzer, "Inquisition," *The Catholic Encyclopedia,* vol. VIII, 1910).

Catholic doctrine and practice was no longer a matter of private belief. Its stability and validity allowed for and protected the stability of Europe. Heretical attacks on the Church were treated as serious threats against the Christian world, and in the thirteenth century, some of these heresies became increasingly more violent.

THE ORIGINS OF THE INQUISITION

The Inquisition began largely in reaction to the Albigensian heresy, which was growing strong and fast during the early part of the thirteenth century in Southern France. Like the Manichean heresy during the time of St. Augustine, Albigensianism appealed to a misunderstood sense of Christian piety and self-sacrifice, as it saw the soul as good and the body evil. Many were attracted to its emphasis on its ostensible fidelity to the Gospel, expressed in austerity regarding poverty and fasting. Their radical asceticism was driven by their belief in the evil of war, physical pleasure, and even matter itself.

The teachings of Albigensianism posed a dangerous threat to the Christian world since their teachings struck at the core of the Catholic Faith. A form of Gnosticism, Albigensianism believed in two gods that governed the universe: one spiritual and good, the other physical and evil. As a result, all things of the temporal world were considered evil and dangerous. The Albigensians were hostile to Christianity, and rejected the Mass, the sacraments, and the ecclesiastical hierarchy and organization. In addition to hating anything that had to do with the world, Albigensians rejected feudal government and refused to abide by oaths or allegiances. They were unaccountable to any authority, religious or civil. Often leaders instructed them to burn down churches and destroy their property. They also forbade marriage and the propagation of the human race, and thus they allowed for homosexual relations as an alternative to heterosexual relations, since producing offspring was considered evil. The Albigensians preached suicide as a way to obtain spiritual purity. By shedding themselves of their bodies through suicide, Albigensians believed they would be pure enough to obtain eternal life.

Both civil and religious authorities in Europe saw this heresy as more than a theological disagreement, but as a destructive illness that would have devastating effects on both the Church and Christian societies.

In 1208, an Albigensian follower killed the Papal Legate Pierre de Castelnau, and Pope Innocent III reacted by calling a crusade to suppress the Albigensians in France and rid the heresy from Christendom. He justified his actions by saying:

> If a crusade were holy which aimed at delivering the Lord's Sepulcher from the infidels, was it not as holy when it took up arms in defense of the priesthood, Sacraments, the Commandments themselves, and the social order?

The purging dragged on for more than twenty years, and although thousands died and Albigensian lands in southern France were seized, many adherents to the heresy were still scattered throughout Europe.

French kings Louis VIII and Louis IX, as well as Emperor Frederick II, took strong measures against the Albigensians by applying capital punishment. Consequently, burning heretics at the stake became a common practice. Civil rulers were becoming increasingly more involved with the prosecution and punishment of heretics to maintain civil order.

Pope Gregory IX became anxious over this extension of civil authority into matters of Faith and doctrine. He wanted to protect the ecclesiastical authority of the Church from being usurped by the secular rulers. Although the pope sought to reserve authority over faith, he also wanted to remain on good terms with the emperor and kings.

In 1231, Pope Gregory IX established the Inquisition as a means of detection and purgation of heresy. He appointed a number of Papal Inquisitors, mostly Dominicans and Franciscans, who could serve as independent judges free from any secular interest and influence.

The Spanish friar and papal Inquisitor Dominic Guzman believed in peaceful methods of persuasion such as debating the Albigensians in public.

THE INQUISITORS

The pope did not establish the Inquisition as a distinct tribunal. Rather, he appointed special judges who examined and judged the doctrinal opinions and moral conduct of suspicious individuals. They often worked within the context of the civil system, but with papal authority. The judge, or Inquisitor, had to adhere to the established rules of canonical procedure. Gregory IX also provided that the inquisitional tribunal could only work with the diocesan bishop's co-operation.

The Dominicans and Franciscans were two new orders that enjoyed rigorous and solid theological training and spiritual formation. This education prompted the hierarchy to employ them as inquisitors. Given their spirituality and lifestyle, the Dominicans and Franciscans would be less likely to be swayed by worldly motives or pressure from the secular authorities. It was safe to assume that they were not merely endowed with the requisite knowledge, but that they would also, quite unselfishly fulfill their duty for the good of the Church. In addition, there was reason to hope that, because of their great popularity and moral authority, they would not encounter too much opposition.

It was a heavy burden of responsibility that fell upon the shoulders of an inquisitor, who was obliged, at least indirectly, to decide between life and death. The Church insisted that he possess the qualities of a good judge expressed in an ardent zeal for protecting and promoting the Faith, the salvation of souls, and the extirpation of heresy. Amid all difficulties, pressures, and dangers of the task, he should never yield to anger or passion. Nevertheless, he should meet hostility fearlessly, but should not encourage it.

This painting depicts an event that occurred in 1207, in Albi, France, when St. Dominic proved to the Albigensians that their books containing heretic ideas burn in the fire while the Catholic books fly up away from the fire undamaged.

He should yield to no inducement or threat and yet not be heartless. When circumstances permitted, he should observe mercy in allotting penalties. Finally, he should listen to the counsel of others, and not trust too much in his own opinion or first impressions.

Inquisitors tried to answer to this ideal. Far from being inhuman, the Church tried to find men with spotless character, and sometimes they were of truly admirable sanctity. A number of them have even been canonized by the Church.

PROCESS FOR INQUISITION

The procedure for inquisition began with a month long "term of grace" proclaimed by the inquisitor when he came into a heresy-ridden district, which allowed the inhabitants to appear before the inquisitor, confess their sins, and perform penance. Of those who confessed heresy of their own accord, a suitable penance (such as a pilgrimage, fasting, or wearing crosses on their clothes) was imposed, but never a severe punishment like incarceration or surrender to the civil power.

If the accused did not confess, the trial began. The accused would be asked to swear his innocence on the four Gospels. If he or she still claimed innocence, there were a number of methods used to extract a confession. First judges would remind the accused the punishment that awaited if he or she were convicted without a confession, hoping that the fear of punishment may convince a guilty man to admit to the truth, in hopes of a more lenient sentence. If the accused still did not confess, he or she was subject to close confinement (possibly emphasized by curtailment of food), visits of an already tried man (who would attempt to induce free confession through friendly persuasion), and confinement to an inquisition prison for serious offenders. When no voluntary admission was made, evidence was still necessary for conviction. Legally, there had to be at least two witnesses, and conscientious judges often required even more witnesses to convict someone of heresy.

Witnesses for the defense hardly ever appeared, as they would almost inevitably be suspected of being heretics or at least favorable to heresy. For the same reason those impeached rarely secured legal advisers, and therefore made a personal response to the main points of a charge. False witnesses were punished without mercy. If caught, they risked life imprisonment or worse punishment. It must be noted that secret examination of witnesses during the Inquisition was not a peculiarity of the time. This procedure was common to all civil courts as well throughout Europe.

The accused was not given the right to know the names of his accusers. However, the accused was given the right to submit a list of names of his alleged enemies, which often facilitated a just verdict. Furthermore, the accused could appeal to higher authority, including the pope (cf. Shannon, *Medieval Inquisition*, 1983, pp. 139-140).

In addition to the inquisitor, *boni viri* (good men) were frequently called upon. Thirty, fifty, eighty, or more persons—laymen and priests; secular and regular—would be summoned, all highly respected and independent men, and sworn to give verdict on the cases before them to the best of their knowledge and belief. They were always called upon to decide two questions: culpability (and the reason for it) and the punishment to be imparted. Although the *boni viri* were entitled only to an advisory vote, the final ruling was usually in accordance with their views.

The judges were also assisted by a *concilium permanens*, or standing council, composed of other sworn judges.

SIMON DE MONTFORT AND THE BATTLE OF MURET

One of the most important battles against the Albigensians took place at Muret, a small town south of Toulouse in southern France, on September 12, 1213. With the support of Pope Innocent III, Simon de Montfort led a small army of Catholics against the Albigensians, led by Count Raymond VI and Peter II of Aragon. The Albigensian army was far larger than that of Simon de Montfort, and so the Catholic general waited for reinforcements to arrive from the North. Help never came.

With about eight hundred cavalry, Simon was facing a heavily reinforced enemy of over two thousand cavalry and fifteen thousand infantry. This massive force marched towards the Catholic position at Muret from Toulouse, intent on crushing the small Catholic resistance. Faced with a seemingly helpless situation, Simon and his army turned to St. Dominic (the founder of Mendicant order that will be studied in the next chapter) for spiritual guidance. At his suggestion the Catholic forces began praying the Rosary, and the night before battle, Simon heard Mass at midnight, and prayed to God for a victory. His enemy Peter II spent the night with his mistress and could barely stand straight the next morning.

That morning Simon's tiny army charged across a mile of open country and attacked the stunned Raymond and Peter. During the course of the battle, St. Dominic knelt before the altar of Saint-Jacque in Muret asking God for a miraculous victory. God answered his prayers, and in a surprisingly short time Peter II was killed and the heretics were defeated. It is believed that Simon erected a chapel dedicated to Our Lady of the Rosary in thanks to St. Dominic and his prayers.

THE FINAL VERDICT IN THE INQUISITION

The ultimate decision was usually pronounced with a solemn ceremony. One or two days prior to this ceremony, everyone concerned had the charges read to him again, briefly. The ceremony began very early in the morning. Secular officials were sworn in and made to vow obedience to the inquisitor in all things pertaining to the suppression of heresy. Then the offenses were announced and punishments were assigned to the guilty party. This announcement began with the minor punishments, and went on to the most severe, such as perpetual imprisonment or death. Those found guilty were then turned over to the civil power, whose duty it was to carry out the punishments.

Most of the punishments that were inflicted were largely humane. Most frequently, certain good works were ordered like the building of a church, the visitation to a church, a pilgrimage, the offering of a candle or a chalice, or participation in a crusade. Other stiffer penalties included fines, whose proceeds were devoted to such public purposes as church-building or road-making; whipping with rods during religious service; the pillory; or wearing colored crosses (Livingstone, *The Oxford Dictionary of the Christian Church,* 1997, p. 836).

The hardest penalties were imprisonment and various degrees of exclusion from the communion of the Church, as well as consequent surrender to the civil power for harsher sentencing.

Imprisonment was not always seen as punishment in the proper sense: it was rather looked on as an opportunity for repentance, a preventive measure against backsliding or infecting others. It was known as *immuration* (from the Latin *murus,* a wall), or incarceration, and was inflicted for a definite time or for life. *Immuration* for life was the lot of those who had perhaps recanted only from fear of death or had once before abjured heresy.

Our twenty-first century minds consider Medieval punishments abhorrent and barbaric, but the punishments inflicted in those times were normal for Medieval cultures.

Although it is hard to know exactly how many victims were handed over to civil power, there are some historical approximations. At the height of the Inquisition in southern France in the thirteenth century, three people were burned for heresy per year (Livingstone, *The Oxford Dictionary of the Christian Church,* 1997, p. 836).

A more terrible fate awaited the heretic when judged by a secular court. In 1249 Count Raymond VII of Toulouse ordered many confessed heretics to be burned in his presence without permitting them to recant. It is impossible to imagine any such procedures before the Inquisition courts.

The punishments inflicted were considered, at the time, the normal expression not only of the legislative power, but also of the popular hatred for heresy in an age that dealt both vigorously and roughly with criminals of every type. Civil authorities dealt much more severely with heretics than did the papal inquisitors, and in many ways the Inquisition helped curtail what could have become a brutal and widespread popular reaction to Medieval heresy. The heretic, in a word, was an outlaw whose offense, in the popular mind, deserved severe punishment. But this does not excuse the abuses of those who failed to witness Christ's mercy and forgiveness when acting as a representative of Christ's Church. Even if the Inquisition helped lessen an evil of the time, it still

The greatest battle of the Reconquista was fought on July 12, 1212 at Las Navas de Tolosa in southern Spain, when the Muslim forces were defeated by a great Christian army which included kings of Aragon, Castile, Navarre, the military orders and 70,000 French crusaders. This battle was decisive, pushing Muslims back to Granada in the far south.

allowed for a certain amount of injustice to remain. Nonetheless, every historic age must be evaluated in light of its own value system, not ours. Incidents taken out of context can lead to misunderstanding. To Christians during the Inquisition, threats to one's immortal soul (eternal damnation) were much more feared than most people can appreciate today.

THE INQUISITION IN SPAIN

Religious conditions similar to those in Southern France led to the establishment of the Inquisition in Spain, where it lasted until the eighteenth century. However, motives for the Inquisition developed differently in Spain. The Spanish Inquisition coincided with the *Reconquista*, the reconquering of Spain by the Christians against the Muslims and the Jews. National unification was not completed until 1492, and before and after that date, the Inquisition was used to promote and retain Spanish unity under a common Christian religion.

The Spanish Inquisition formally began after the establishment of the Papal Inquisition around the time of the reign of Ferdinand and Isabella. Beginning in 1480, Spanish civil authorities took over the Inquisition in Spain.

Though the Spanish Inquisition developed into mostly a civil tribunal, theologians never questioned its ecclesiastical nature. The Holy See sanctioned the Spanish Inquisition and granted to the grand inquisitor judicial authority concerning matters of Faith. The grand inquisitor—technically appointed by the pope, though the Spanish Inquisition operated quite independently of the Holy See—could also pass down jurisdiction to subsidiary tribunals under his control. An understanding of Spanish history—uniquely its own—reveals both the perceived and actual threats from Muslim and Jewish militancy against Spain.

The Spanish Inquisition was significantly crueler than the earlier papal inquisition against the Albigensians. Certainly, many reports of the atrocities committed have been the product of fable. Especially with today's much more refined appreciation of human dignity, it is especially clear that many of the methods employed by the Inquisition flagrantly violated the dignity of the person. Nevertheless, disedifying practices of the Medieval churchmen, by modern standards, intended to preserve the purity of Church teaching and protect her children from the corrupting effects of heresy as displayed by the Albigensians. Although some of the disedifying practices of individuals and groups within the Medieval Church have no justification, it is always important to view them in their proper historical context. It bears repeating that heresy was viewed as a serious crime during the Middle Ages, and the usual punishment was excommunication.

A Spanish Court of Inquisition in Madrid in 1680. It is especially clear to Christians today that many of the methods employed by the Inquisitions throughout medieval Europe flagrantly contradict Christ's message of compassion and mercy. The methods, however, must be viewed in context with the cultural norms of medieval times and real threats to the survival of the Church.

CONCLUSION

Like virtually all the periods of the Church's history, the era of the Crusades shows both lights and shadows. Although the guiding light of Divine Providence continually helps the people of God to push the kingdom of God forward, amid the Church's efforts to spread and protect the Faith, sins and shortcomings of her children will always be present. However, without compromising objective moral truth, judgment must take into careful consideration the zeal and uncompromising faith in Christ's Church exemplified by the era of the Crusades. Muslim expansionism "by the sword" posed serious threats to Christian Europe and engulfed and eradicated all the major Christian cities and shrines of the East. Hence, the rigorous response of a people with defects and weaknesses who at the same time see the Catholic tradition as a treasure of inestimable value.

THE SPANISH INQUISITION (1480-1834)

King Ferdinand and Queen Isabella, Crown Heads of Aragon and Castille, instituted the Spanish Inquisition in 1480 to investigate Jewish and Muslim converts (*conversos*) to Christianity suspected of secretly practicing their former religions. These rulers believed their authority was derived from God and that lasting civil unity would be achieved through a united national faith. They feared that Jewish and Islamic elements might seep into the national religion, as they had in art, architecture, and language, and cause religious confusion and possibly lead to civil unrest.

Pope Sixtus IV believed that the situation in Spain posed a legitimate threat to Catholicism and issued a papal bull in November of 1478 approving the Inquisition. Sixtus IV mandated that judges of the Inquisition be at least forty years old, of excellent reputation, renowned for their virtue and wisdom, and that they possess specific degrees in theology and canon law. The Inquisition had authority over baptized Christians only. Civil authorities were responsible for the persecution of non-Christian Jews and Muslims.

In 1480 Ferdinand and Isabella appointed two Dominicans, Miguel Morillo and Juan de San Martin, as the first inquisitors in Seville. By 1482 Sixtus IV received reports of torture, unjustifiable imprisonment, and seizure of executed prisoners' property. He censured the inquisitors and would have deposed them, but Ferdinand and Isabella intervened.

In 1487 Fray Tomas Torquemada was named Grand Inquisitor. He developed the Inquisition as it lasted until its abolition in1834. Courts of the Inquisition were commissioned throughout Spain and centralized under the *Consejo Supremo* (High Council). Local courts required the approval of the *Consejo Supremo* prior to actions like imprisoning accused priests.

According to procedure, an accused person had forty days to renounce the accusation against him. This period was often extended. False accusers could be punished severely or executed. Lawyers defended the accused, who could be imprisoned if the accusation against them was proven or if the court unanimously deemed it necessary. Accused persons denying proven accusations could be tortured. Those charged with heresy were offered a public reconciliation called an *auto de fe* (act of faith), which gradually evolved to include Mass, reconciliation of the accused, and in some cases the pronouncement of punishment. Those professing heretical beliefs who did not recant were burned at the stake. Contrary to misleading reports, executions did not take place at the *auto de fe* ceremony.

After the Jews and Moors were expelled from Spain in 1492, the Inquisition focused on Protestant heresies. Although it was active until 1820 and abolished 14 years later, discussions of the Inquisition typically reference the time before 1700.

Historical accounts of the Spanish Inquisition are often naively defensive or wildly exaggerated. Some ignore the Inquisition's blatant disregard for human dignity; others use it as a vehicle for contemporary anti-Catholic sentiments. Many accounts originated from the "Black Legend," an anti-Spanish smear campaign conducted by enemies of the Spanish crown. No one knows how many people were executed during the Inquisition, but recent studies of court records suggest that less than two percent of those accused of heresy were condemned to death. This rate of execution was far less than that of the European civil courts of that time.

From Bl. Humbert of Romans' preaching in defense of the Crusades, ca. 1272

Some of these critics say it is not in accordance with the Christian religion to shed blood in this way, even that of wicked infidels. For Christ did not act thus; rather, "When he suffered, he threatened not, but delivered himself to him that judged him unjustly," as Peter says. The saints of old did not teach this either. One should conclude, therefore, that the Christian religion, which ought to adhere to the example and teaching of Christ and the saints, ought not to initiate wars of any kind whatsoever.

[But] Who is so stupid as to dare say that, were infidels or evil men to desire to kill every Christian and to wipe out the worship of Christ from the world, one ought not to resist them? It is clear in the teaching of Christ himself, who says, "He that hath no sword, let him sell his coat and buy a sword." What the Lord said to Peter, "Put up again thy sword," etc., applied to Peter on that particular occasion. It must be held without doubt that it is not inconsistent with the Christian religion to wage war according to circumstances against Saracens, extremely wicked men and particular enemies of Christendom.

A battle-weary Teutonic knight heads his horse toward home.

Pope Innocent III, On the Jews
Decree of 1199

We decree that no Christian shall use violence to compel the Jews to accept baptism. But if a Jew, of his own accord, because of a change in his faith, shall have taken refuge with Christians, after his wish has been made known, he may be made a Christian without any opposition. For anyone who has not of his own will sought Christian baptism cannot have the true Christian faith. No Christian shall do the Jews any personal injury, except in executing the judgements of a judge, or deprive them of their possessions, or change the rights and privileges which they have been accustomed to have. During the celebration of their festivals, no one shall disturb them by beating them with clubs or by throwing stones at them. No one shall compel them to render any services except those which they have been accustomed to render. And to prevent the baseness and avarice of wicked men we forbid anyone to deface or damage their cemeteries or to extort money from them by threatening to exhume the bodies of their dead....

John Paul II, Apostolic Exhortation
Ecclesia in Asia

Because Jesus was born, lived, died and rose from the dead in the Holy Land, that small portion of Western Asia became a land of promise and hope for all mankind. Jesus knew and loved this land. He made his own the history, the sufferings and the hopes of its people. He loved its people and embraced their Jewish traditions and heritage. God in fact had long before chosen this people and revealed himself to them in preparation for the Savior's coming. And from this land, through the preaching of the Gospel in the power of the Holy Spirit, the Church went forth to make "disciples of all nations" (Mt 28:19).

VOCABULARY

BONI VIRI
Latin meaning "good men," these groups of thirty or more highly respected and independent men, both laymen and priests, were summoned during the Inquisition to give verdict on cases and decide punishment.

CONCILIUM PERMANENS
Standing council of sworn judges who assisted the judge during an inquisition.

CRUSADE
From the Latin word *crux* (cross) it refers to wars of a religious character, or specifically to a series of eight defensive military expeditions between 1096 and 1270 undertaken by Christians to liberate the Holy Land and stop the expansion of Islam.

DRANG NACH OSTEN (URGE TO THE EAST)
German expansion into the East.

IMMURATION
Imprisonment for those who recanted their heresy because of fear of punishment or death.

INDULGENCE
A remission before God of temporal punishment due to sins, the guilt of which has already been forgiven through the sacrament of Penance.

INQUISITOR
Special judges appointed by the pope during the Inquisition who examined and judged the doctrinal opinions and moral conduct of suspicious individuals.

MILITARY ORDER
Arising out of the necessity of defending the Holy Places in Palestine as well as the pilgrims who traveled there, these orders combined both military and religious life, emphasizing dedication, discipline and monastic organization.

RECONQUISTA
The Christian reconquering of part of the Iberian Peninsula (modern-day Spain) following 700 years of Muslim and Jewish control.

TERM OF GRACE
The procedure for inquisition began with this month long period which allowed for the inhabitants of a heresy-ridden district to appear before the inquisitor, confess their sins, and perform penance.

Discovery of the Holy Lance at Antioch during the First Crusade.

During the hardships of the siege of Antioch in 1097-98, the Crusaders were encouraged by miraculous visions which assured them of their continued support from God. One such vision came to a priest named Peter Bartholomew who was repeatedly urged by St. Andrew to dig up the Lance which had pierced Christ's side on the cross. Peter's subsequent unearthing of the Lance was hailed as a miracle by the battered troops.

STUDY QUESTIONS

1. What were the crusades?

2. What new Muslim people appeared on the scene in the Middle East as a new threat to Byzantium?

3. When and where did Pope Bl. Urban II preach the First Crusade and why?

4. What were the temporal and spiritual motivations for participation in the Crusades?

5. When was the First Crusade?

6. How was the timing of the First Crusade particularly fortuitous with regard to the Seljuk Turks and other Muslims?

7. How long did the Europeans control Jerusalem?

8. What Seljuk Turkish leader was an excellent military commander and essentially forced the Europeans into a retreat?

9. What was the result of the "Children's Crusade"?

10. How did the Byzantines view the crusaders?

11. What minority groups within Europe sometimes became victims of violence and murder during the crusades?

12. Describe the relationship between St. Francis of Assisi and Sultan Malik-al-Kamil.

13. What were some of the effects of the crusades?

14. What was a military order?

15. What was the Knights Templar's specific mission?

16. Who wrote the rule for the Knights Templar?

17. How were the Knights Templar organized?

18. How did the Knights Templar become wealthy?

19. When were the Knights Hospitalers founded and what was their vocation?

20. Where did the Knights Hospitalers go after the fall of Palestine?

21. What other island were the Knights Hospitalers given in 1523 by Holy Roman emperor Charles V?

22. The Teutonic Knights did not keep Jerusalem and hospitals for very long before turning their attention to which lands?

23. Who secularized the Teutonic Knights?

24. What was the Inquisition?

25. What two orders were placed in charge of the Inquisition?

26. What group was the initial target of the Inquisition?

27. What were the five methods of extracting a confession from an accused person?

28. Who actually carried out the sentences of the guilty?

29. How was the Spanish Inquisition different from Inquisitions in other parts of Europe?

PRACTICAL EXERCISES

1. Many people believe that the Crusades were aggressive excursions with only negative outcomes. Is this true? Cite reasons for your answers.

2. Is there a conflict of interest with the papacy preaching a crusade in a religion that professes peace? Do you think the papacy would call for a crusade today? Do you think the papacy would call for the establishment of a military order today?

3. Why was the Inquisition instituted? What modern ideas make the Inquisition seem absurd by today's standards?

FROM THE CATECHISM

841 *The Church's relationship with the Muslims.* "The plan of salvation also includes those who acknowledge the Creator, in the first place amongst whom are the Muslims; these profess to hold the faith of Abraham, and together with us they adore the one, merciful God, mankind's judge on the last day" (*LG* 16; cf. *NA* 3).

2244 Every institution is inspired, at least implicitly, by a vision of man and his destiny, from which it derives the point of reference for its judgment, its hierarchy of values, its line of conduct. Most societies have formed their institutions in the recognition of a certain preeminence of man over things. Only the divinely revealed religion has clearly recognized man's origin and destiny in God, the Creator and Redeemer. The Church invites political authorities to measure their judgments and decisions against this inspired truth about God and man:

> Societies not recognizing this vision or rejecting it in the name of their independence from God are brought to seek their criteria and goal in themselves or to borrow them from some ideology. Since they do not admit that one can defend an objective criterion of good and evil, they arrogate to themselves an explicit or implicit totalitarian power over man and his destiny, as history shows (cf. *CA* 45; 46).

2245 The Church, because of her commission and competence, is not to be confused in any way with the political community. She is both the sign and the safeguard of the transcendent character of the human person. "The Church respects and encourages the political freedom and responsibility of the citizen" (*GS* 76 § 3).

2266 The efforts of the state to curb the spread of behavior harmful to people's rights and to the basic rules of civil society correspond to the requirement of safeguarding the common good. Legitimate public authority has the right and the duty to inflict punishment proportionate to the gravity of the offense. Punishment has the primary aim of redressing the disorder introduced by the offense. When it is willingly accepted by the guilty party, it assumes the value of expiation. Punishment then, in addition to defending public order and protecting people's safety, has a medicinal purpose: as far as possible, it must contribute to the correction of the guilty party (cf. Lk 23: 4-43).

FROM THE CATECHISM Continued

2297 *Kidnapping* and *hostage taking* bring on a reign of terror; by means of threats they subject their victims to intolerable pressures. They are morally wrong. *Terrorism* threatens, wounds, and kills indiscriminately is gravely against justice and charity. *Torture* which uses physical or moral violence to extract confessions, punish the guilty, frighten opponents, or satisfy hatred is contrary to respect for the person and for human dignity. Except when performed for strictly therapeutic medical reasons, directly intended *amputations, mutilations,* and *sterilizations* performed on innocent persons are against the moral law (cf. DS 3722).

2298 In times past, cruel practices were commonly used by legitimate governments to maintain law and order, often without protest from the Pastors of the Church, who themselves adopted in their own tribunals the prescriptions of Roman law concerning torture. Regrettable as these facts are, the Church always taught the duty of clemency and mercy. She forbade clerics to shed blood. In recent times it has become evident that these cruel practices were neither necessary for public order, nor in conformity with the legitimate rights of the human person. On the contrary, these practices led to ones even more degrading. It is necessary to work for their abolition. We must pray for the victims and their tormentors.

2309 The strict conditions for *legitimate defense by military force* require rigorous consideration. The gravity of such a decision makes it subject to rigorous conditions of moral legitimacy. At one and the same time:

— the damage inflicted by the aggressor on the nation or community of nations must be lasting, grave, and certain;

— all other means of putting an end to it must have been shown to be impractical or ineffective;

— there must be serious prospects of success;

— the use of arms must not produce evils and disorders graver than the evil to be eliminated. The power of modern means of destruction weighs very heavily in evaluating this condition.

These are the traditional elements enumerated in what is called the "just war" doctrine.

The evaluation of these conditions for moral legitimacy belongs to the prudential judgment of those who have responsibility for the common good.

2312 The Church and human reason both assert the permanent *validity of the moral law during armed conflict.* "The mere fact that war has regrettably broken out does not mean that everything becomes licit between the warring parties" (*GS* 79 § 4).

2328 The Church and human reason assert the permanent validity of the moral law during armed conflicts. Practices deliberately contrary to the law of nations and to its universal principles are crimes.

The High Middle Ages:
Scholastic Development
And The Flowering Of Culture

*Christian philosophy, piety, and art boldly ventured into new depths,
and the saints of the period showed how sanctity can pervade
all of our human endeavors.*

CHAPTER 10

The High Middle Ages: Scholastic Development And The Flowering Of Culture

Training and spiritual life! These two things are inseparable for anyone who aspires to lead a Christian life which is truly committed to forming and building a more just and more brotherly society. If you wish to be faithful in your daily lives to the demands of God and to the expectations of humanity and history, you must constantly nourish yourselves on the word of God and the sacraments, "so that Christ's word may dwell in you abundantly" (Col 3:16).

— John Paul II, *Homily*, Viedma, Argentina, April 6, 1987

Before the twelfth and thirteenth centuries, most educational activity in Europe took place in monasteries and cathedral schools. Over time, as the demand for education among monks and nobles increased, these schools began to develop expanded areas of study for their student bodies. The schools added philosophy, astronomy, civil and canon law, and medicine to their curricula and reorganized to meet administrative demands. Modeling themselves after feudal trade guilds, schools began to develop into university systems that provided the proper environment for unprecedented educational and intellectual advancement.

One result of the Medieval university system was Scholasticism. Led by thinkers like St. Thomas Aquinas, St. Bonaventure, and the English Franciscan Bl. John Duns Scotus, Scholasticism grew out of the style of Medieval teaching, combining theological and philosophical methods in their efforts to understand the highest truths of philosophy and theology and man's relationship to God and his Church. These Scholastics produced some of the most lasting and valuable works in the Western Tradition.

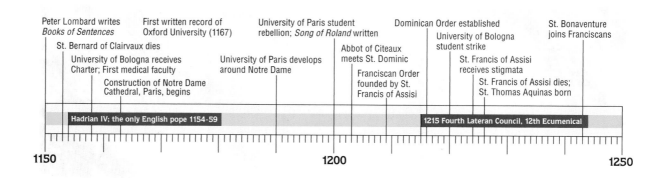

Peter Lombard writes *Books of Sentences*

St. Bernard of Clairvaux dies

University of Bologna receives Charter; First medical faculty

Construction of Notre Dame Cathedral, Paris, begins

First written record of Oxford University (1167)

University of Paris develops around Notre Dame

University of Paris student rebellion; *Song of Roland* written

Abbot of Citeaux meets St. Dominic

Franciscan Order founded by St. Francis of Assisi

Dominican Order established

University of Bologna student strike

St. Francis of Assisi receives stigmata

St. Francis of Assisi dies; St. Thomas Aquinas born

St. Bonaventure joins Franciscans

Hadrian IV; the only English pope 1154-59

1215 Fourth Lateran Council, 12th Ecumenical

1150   1200   1250

It is training and spiritual life, faith and love of God that leads us closer to knowing Christ.

In the midst of this flourishing of Medieval thought there came another movement led by two extraordinary saints. St. Francis of Assisi and St. Dominic founded the first two mendicant orders whose devotion to simple piety and poverty helped rejuvenate religious zeal in the late Medieval age. These orders remained a constant reminder that, despite the potential glory of the human capacity to understand, ultimately, as John Paul II reminded, it is "training and spiritual life," faith and love of God that leads to greater knowledge and understanding of Christ.

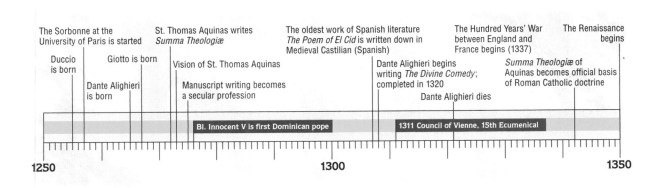

PART I
The Universities

Beginning in the mid-eleventh century, the demand for education among both clergy and nobles increased dramatically. More and more students flocked to schools, and as the student bodies began to outgrow the cathedral and monastic schools, teachers and students alike recognized the need to reorganize the established educational systems. Following Feudal organizations, schools began to restructure into guilds. Rather than training as a knight or a craftsman, many people began to study at the universities, apprenticing to expert teachers and eventually mastering their disciplines. Degrees awarded to students reflected the same type of recognition bestowed upon members of other trades.

In the North, masters united to form a *universitas,* a type of corporation that protected the educational and administrative interests of its members. In Southern Europe, students formed similar organizations that helped ensure their safety and the quality of their education. As it were, the students at those universities held authority over their teachers, hiring and firing them as they saw fit. In the North, teachers determined the curriculum and the nature of the student body.

ORIGIN OF UNIVERSITIES

The development of the University of Paris in 1175 typified the growth of most northern universities. In Paris, there existed three cathedral schools that became especially famous during the early part of the Medieval period: the Palatine or palace school, the school of Notre-Dame, and Sainte-Geneviève. Over time these schools began producing renowned professors, and as their reputations grew, more pupils enrolled in schools where these celebrated lecturers taught. As schools expanded, more lodging was provided, and the numbers of courses increased. Eventually the three schools formed a corporation that protected the professors and combined each individual school's discipline. Although each school continued to teach its specialty, students could now receive a broader education from the unified schools that made up the University of Paris.

In the South, the Italian city of Bologna succeeded Ravenna as the home of jurisprudence in Europe. As the Lombard cities grew together with the demand for legal instruction, the school at Bologna in 1088 became a center for legal study. The University of Bologna began teaching the *Dictamen,* or Art of Composition, which included rules for drawing up briefs and other legal documents. This specialized training attracted many students, and there soon developed another intense program specializing in grammar and rhetoric, which were both closely connected with the study of law. As the number of disciplines increased, students organized to help ensure their educational security. Bologna became the undisputed center of legal training in Europe, and almost all of the important scholars of canon and Roman law studied, at least for some time, at that school.

The school at Salerno had more singular origins. The Benedictine monastery of Salerno, established in 794, devoted much of its work to the study of ancient works on botanical and medical sciences. The fame of the monastery's expertise in these areas grew after Constantino Africano, a Christian who studied in the Arabic schools in Babylon, Baghdad, and in Egypt, took up residence at the monastery around the year 1070. Under the influence of Africano, the monastery school added philosophical and Arabic works to the medical studies, helping the school advance its reputation as an institution with a superior understanding of medicine. As the school grew, it became the first university in Europe to offer degrees and licenses for its studies.

STUDENT REBELLION IN EARLY UNIVERSITIES

The formation of the university was often not a peaceful or pleasant process. Many universities emerged following violent student rebellions.

In Paris, France, in 1200, for example, a collective of students demanded legal and economic concessions from the city. Their demands were a result of a recent altercation between local townspeople and students at the university. A student insulted a local tavern's wine and was thrown out of the tavern. In response, a number of students stormed the tavern and attacked the owner and some of the patrons. Locals retaliated further. They tracked down the students and beat them severely, killing a number of the students. Afterwards, students protested and demanded justice. As a result, the city government freed the students from local taxes and prosecution.

A similar altercation led to the solidifying of student independence at the University of Bologna, Italy, in 1220. Protesting the city's economic practices, students withdrew from Bologna and refused to return until the city made concessions. Officials granted students special privileges and agreed to prosecute teachers who skipped or were late for classes. Thus, by rebelling, the students achieved some level of power over their teachers and independence from local jurisdiction.

Left: University of Paris in Medieval school days
Below: University of Paris today

The university is often referred to as the Sorbonne which was originally created for the use of 20 theology students in 1257 as Collège de Sorbonne by Robert de Sorbon (1201-1274), a chaplain and confessor to King St. Louis IX of France. However, the university itself was started years earlier.

The Sorbonne (now organized as University of Paris I-XIII) remains one of the most famous and prestigious universities in the world, having produced Nobel Prize winners from its faculty and student body, as well as a number of the greatest intellectuals, political theorists, scientists, engineers, doctors, theologians, and artists of the Western tradition and canon.

Because of their gradual and undocumented origins, myths concerning their true beginnings surrounded all of the Medieval universities. The University of Oxford claimed the most extraordinary beginnings. Fanciful popular myths allege that its foundation dates as far back to when Samuel was judge over Judea or by the Trojans having escaped from their conquered city. The most popular myth attributed Oxford to the patronage of the Saxon King Alfred the Great (849-899), who was known as a supporter of education. Like the other universities, the exact date of the establishment of Oxford is hard to pinpoint since it grew gradually out of schools which in Saxon times were grouped around the monastic foundation of St. Frideswide (eighth century). Over time, well-known scholars lecturing on theology and canon law attracted students from all of Europe to Oxford.

ORGANIZATION OF THE UNIVERSITY

Although the organization of Northern and Southern European universities differed, normally both were collections of different schools that taught their respective disciplines. It was not until 1230 that several branches of learning were taught at one university.

At Bologna, Italy, which became the template for most of the Southern European universities, students from all over Europe came to the city to study. For protection and housing, foreign students formed groups called "nations." They elected a rector who led the nation and helped administer the affairs of the university.

Paris is the center that typified the structure of the northern European universities; the chancellor had full authority over issuing licenses to teach and awarding degrees. Naturally, this led to friction between teachers and the chancellor. To protect their own interests and authority, teachers bound together to form a guild, or *universitates*. The students also organized into nations, but they never had the same authority as those in Southern Europe. By the middle of the thirteenth century, the teachers' guilds had separated into faculties according to the corresponding discipline that was being taught. A dean headed each faculty, and those same deans voted for a rector who was the head of all the faculties and the university (similar to the modern-day president).

This Medieval illustration depicts a professor and students at the University of Paris.

The guild organizations allowed these universities to remain independent, and they were theoretically exempt from arrest or punishment by the secular authorities. Each university eventually secured independence from both lay and local ecclesiastical authorities. This fostered an environment of free inquiry and unobstructed explorations into all aspects of learning.

ACADEMIC COURSEWORK

By unifying various schools and disciplines, the universities were able to offer a program called *studium generale*, which included the study of theology (including philosophy), law (both civil and canon law), medicine, which was called physics, and the arts. The arts were also divided into two main sections: the *trivium* (Latin for "three ways"), in which Latin grammar, rhetoric, and logic were studied, and the *quadrivium* (four ways), which included arithmetic, geometry, astronomy, and music.

THE CHURCH AND LEARNING, 1100-1700

Paris   Law school

✝   Centre of monastic reform

★   Important cathedral school

★   Important monastic school

University founded

■   before 1300

■   1300–1500

■   1500–1700

©1997 Lion Hudson plc/Three's Company

A student needed to be able to read and write in Latin before being admitted into the university. Once admitted, he began his studies with the *trivium*, mastering writing and reading and studying Classical and Christian works on the subjects. The teacher, or master, would read the text of a work on a topic along with his predecessors' comments on the text before adding his own ideas. This method of teaching was called "hearing" a book, i.e., lecture (from the Latin *lectio*, the act of reading). After completing the *trivium*, the student became a "bachelor of arts," and was considered qualified to instruct others in those subjects. He then moved on to study the *quadrivium*, during which he spent five or six years studying before earning a "master of arts" degree. All students who finished university studies received both degrees, and they could then leave the school or continue on to study more intensively for a doctorate degree in law, medicine, or theology. To earn these higher degrees, students not only "heard" books, but also debated their professors on the subjects and prepared formal responses to tough questions posed by their superiors.

A student needed to be able to read and write in Latin before being admitted into the university.

THE EFFECTS OF THE UNIVERSITY

The cultural exchange brought about by the Crusades ushered in a flood of previously unknown books and ideas into Western Europe. The universities were able to maintain significant academic liveliness through the continued introduction of these new books to their curriculum. As works in mathematics, philosophy, and theology were discovered or written, they would be adopted into various university studies. Legal studies at Bologna advanced the understanding of canon law and produced skilled and scholarly clergy who became experts in both Roman and Church law. These hubs of expert academic learning helped lead Europe into a period of exceptional intellectual growth.

The universities grew immensely, and many of the foremost rulers and church leaders passed through their doors. The University of Paris, for example, educated the most distinguished youths of the kingdom, and the courses at Paris were considered so necessary that many foreigners flocked to them. Popes Celestine II, Innocent III, and Adrian IV studied at Paris, and Pope Alexander II sent his nephews there. St. Thomas of Canterbury; St. Stanislaus, the Archbishop of Krakow; and St. Bernard of Clairvaux all studied in Paris. At one time there were as many students in the city of Paris as residents. Bologna's student body also expanded, and at one time it numbered as many as ten thousand students. Oxford is said to have had even more. Art, philosophy, and science all flourished because of these universities, and the work of many of the academics would shed new light on the many mysteries of the Faith.

PART II
Scholasticism

New philosophical texts entered into Europe as the crusaders returned, and scholars set about the task of reconciling these "new" ideas with over a thousand years of Christian belief and doctrine. Previously, European scholars only had access to neo-Platonic philosophy and Aristotle's logic to use as a tool for their theology. Until the latter part of the twelfth century and the beginning of the thirteenth, most of Aristotle's words were unknown in the West. By contrast, in the East there existed both Arab and Jewish commentaries on Aristotle's works, espeially his *Metaphysics*. This new discovery of Aristotle's thought would revolutionize theology and subsequently elicit debate and controversy.

With access to Aristotle's works, universities fostered a new style of inquiry in philosophy, known as Scholasticism, or "science of the schools." This method led to a rebirth of interest in Classical philosophy and the relationship between Faith and reason.

METHODS AND MYSTERY

The methods of Scholasticism came largely out of a teaching technique that developed in the universities. When a scholar read an ancient or authoritative text, he drew up lists of contradictory statements. Then, by means of logical reasoning, the scholar tried to reveal the underlying agreement between these points of contradiction, hoping to attain the central and underlying truths of the work. Over time this system of philosophical and theological inquiry developed in the Medieval schools of Christian Europe, creating its own technical language and methodology. This method became known as Scholasticism.

Anselm of Laon was a student of St. Anselm, who is known as the "father of Scholasticism" because he first studied and analyzed the beliefs of Christian Faith resorting to logic and discursive reasoning while lecturing on Scripture at Paris. He achieved it mainly by following the methods of Boethius, Charlemagne, and Alcuin that were available to him, Anselm collected authoritative statements from the Church Fathers and attached them to matching texts in the Bible. When two Fathers differed in their interpretation, their contradictory statements were compared in Anselm's classroom. Students would argue, debate, and hope to find the underlying truths behind the contradictions.

Peter Lombard further refined this method of questioning. He set forth two requirements for the Scholastic method. First he proposed that questioning is the key to perceiving truth.

A 13th century manuscript of Peter Lombard's *Books of Sentences*, IV. Written ca.1150, this work became a standard university textbook.

Scholasticism, in this way, did not grow as an independent school of thought, but rather out of a continual questioning of the contradictions that arose in already formulated schools of thought. Secondly, he proposed that the differences that will arise in questioning could usually be resolved by determining the meaning of terms used by different authors in varying ways. Thus, out of comparatively studying the works and the language of the great thinkers, truth and clarity can be drawn between them. In his four *Books of Sentences*, Peter Lombard collected and discussed the opinions of the Church Fathers and earlier theologians on all questions pertaining to Revelation. His thorough and comprehensive work on the rational understanding of God's revealed truth; this opus became the handbook of theologians and part of every professor's curriculum.

ST. THOMAS AQUINAS

Utilizing Aristotle's philosophy, St. Thomas Aquinas was able to discuss in a cogent way Christ's dual nature as God and man and his presence in the Eucharist.

Many insightful commentaries came out of this approach to learning, but perhaps none can match the work of the Dominican friar St. Thomas Aquinas during the thirteenth century. St. Thomas Aquinas studied theology at the University of Paris and then returned to hold a chair of theology at the university. St. Thomas systematically approached virtually all the questions that confronted Christianity, eventually creating his encyclopedic work, the *Summa Theologiæ*. The *Summa* sets about understanding the most fundamental tenets of Christianity, including, among other things, the existence of God, the divinity of Christ, and Christian morality.

Much of St. Thomas' work was directed toward rectifying a philosophical problem that arose from the rediscovery of the Greek philosopher Aristotle. Many feared that Aristotle's works would undermine the truth of Christianity. St. Thomas showed by his integration of Aristotelian philosophy with Christian belief that Aristotle's thought was an added tool for Catholic theology.

During the Middle Ages, some of Aristotle's work was known in the West through Boethius, but many of Aristotle's books, most notably the *Metaphysics*, were not. In the East, both Muslims and Jews had a tradition of thought included Aristotelian philosophy. During the time of the Crusades, both Aristotle's works and the commentaries began circulating in Europe.

Until Aristotle's works were made known again to the West, most Christian thinkers since the time of the Church Fathers looked to Plato and Plotinus for a philosophical tool to explain the theological truths of Christianity. Neo-Platonism appeared as the ideal philosophy for a deeper understanding of Christian teaching. Plato's ideas about God and contemplation appeared to reinforce Christian teaching. Plato deduced a world of ideas, or "forms" emanating from the highest form, called the *Logos*. Some Christian thinkers equated the *Logos* with the Second Person of the Trinity. Aristotle broke ranks with his former teacher and contended that the universe was infinite and that the individual soul was mortal. This directly contradicted Christian teachings of creation and the immortality of the soul. Aristotle and Plato disagreed with each other concerning the reality of material existence. Whereas Plato held that matter was a pale shadow of the eternal form (idea) of a material object, Aristotle argued that the reality of each material being pertains to both its form and its material component. For example, all trees are not simply shadows of a greater perfect form of a tree, the philosopher would contend. Rather, each tree is a unity of form and matter, which makes it an individual tree.

Averroes (1126-1198) was an Andalusian philosopher and physician. Born in Cordoba, Spain, he was a master of philosophy and Islamic law, mathematics and medicine. It was through the Latin translations of Averroes' work beginning in the 12th century that the legacy of Aristotle was recovered in the West.

Aristotle's works were first introduced into Spain through Arab thinkers, the most familiar being Averroes and Avicenna. The form in which Aristotle was initially introduced to the West would be a source of consternation and confusion. Not only did Aristotelian philosophy pose a problem to traditional Christian theology, but the interpretations and commentaries of the Arab philosophers disturbed Franciscans Scholastics who espoused a more Augustinian and therefore Neo-Platonic approach to theology. The most problematic position, held by Averroes, was the double truth theory.

The double truth theory compares the value of theological tenets against philosophical truths. Averroes claimed that philosophical truth was superior to theological truth since philosophical conclusions are drawn through demonstration whereas theology is formed by opinion. He goes on to say that an individual can accept two contradictory truths, one coming from theology and the other philosophy. In short, Averroes stated that a philosophical truth can be at odds with theological truth, but ultimately philosophical conclusions will enjoy pride of place over theological statements.

St. Thomas confronted this apparent problem and intellectual dichotomy by first saying that theology is superior to philosophy because of the absolute veracity of divine revelation. Philosophy is the servant (*ancilla*) of theology if it is purified from falsehood. The role of theology is to guide, correct, and modify philosophical principles so that they reflect eternal truths. If there is ever a contradiction between a theological position based on divine revelation and philosophical speculations, philosophy must submit to the guiding light of theology. According to St. Thomas, there is never a real dichotomy between philosophy and theology because truth is one and absolute.

In addition to the double truth theory, the consequences of Aristotle's thinking for traditional Christian thinkers were drastic since they implied a materialistic view of the world with little emphasis on the divine or transcendent. Aristotle reasoned that there was a "prime mover" that was the initial and perfect cause of all being, and played a small role, if any, in maintaining the world in existence. While most Christians held to the Platonic camp, St. Thomas Aquinas was convinced of Aristotle's superior logic and sought to reconcile the compatibility between reason and revelation. He set out to systematically employ the philosophy of Aristotle to expound on the Christian Faith. Rather than dismiss the problems that arose between Aristotle's logic and Christian doctrine, the dutiful

Rembrandt's portrait of Aristotle. St. Thomas Aquinas was convinced of Aristotle's superior logic and sought to reconcile Aristotelian logic and Christian Faith.

Scholastic thinker set out to ask questions and arrive at a fundamental conclusion in their mutual applicability. Faith and reason, St. Thomas contended, did not need to be opposed to one another.

St. Thomas Aquinas was able to use this reasoned approach with respect to Faith and reason in updating Catholic theology. For instance, utilizing Aristotle's philosophy, he was able to discuss in a cogent way Christ's dual nature as God and man and his presence in the Eucharist. St. Thomas used philosophy to shed light on the mysteries of Christian doctrine, explaining theology in a philosophical context. The saint never subjugated reason to revelation. He said that even some truths that are available to man through reason would be very hard, if not nearly impossible to understand were it not for God's revelation. This wise thinker, together with his brilliant mind, retained a childlike faith throughout his life. Towards the end of his life, he had a mystical vision while offering Mass in Naples in 1273. After that vision, he stopped his philosophical work, saying that "Everything I have written seems like straw by comparison to what I have seen and what has been revealed to me" (quoted in Livingstone, *The Oxford Dictionary of the Christian Church*, 1997, pp. 1614-15.). Despite his incredible philosophical output, the Angelic Doctor saw himself as a teacher of theology in service of the Church. St. Thomas Aquinas' books and treatises remain unsurpassed in offering a comprehensive and thorough theological and philosophical understanding of God, his works, and his laws.

EARLY CHALLENGES TO THOMISTIC THOUGHT

The work of St. Thomas Aquinas was not immediately accepted as orthodox and reliable Christian theology since various thinkers were apprehensive concerning his use of Aristotle. The Franciscan Bl. John Duns Scotus tried to find a medium between the thought of St. Thomas and the neo-Platonic Christians of the Augustinian school. He argued that there are limits to reason and logic when it came to understanding the nature of God. Bl. John Duns Scotus held that St. Thomas was relying too much on Aristotle's conception that intellectual ideals are strictly dependent on sensible experience and data. Like the Augustinians, Bl. John Duns Scotus argued that there could be intuitive knowledge of things independent of the external senses. He also rejected a leading Augustinian idea that certitude can only come from divine illumination. He found a middle ground by showing how far reason can take human understanding, while respecting its limitations and the necessity of Faith.

The Franciscan Order erected this memorial to Bl. John Duns Scotus in Duns, Scotland in 1966, the 700th anniversary of his birth.

Bl. John Duns Scotus, like Scholasticism in general, would become an object of derision as the humanism of the Renaissance shifted the focus from God to man and his gifts. Students today who joke about the dunce cap do not realize their jokes are at the expense of this progressive Franciscan thinker. However, Bl. John Duns Scotus and his school of thought did not die out without first leaving behind priceless contributions to the areas of theology and philosophy. For example, the theological reasoning behind the dogma of the Immaculate Conception is due in significant part to Bl. John Duns Scotus' theology. Both St. Thomas and Bl. John Duns Scotus, despite their differences, furthered the development of philosophy in the West, and their contributions to Christian thought remain one of the Church's great intellectual treasures. In 1993, Pope John Paul II recognized the importance of these philosophic contributions when he beatified John Duns Scotus. More importantly, the beatification honors a man, who like many of his Scholastic counterparts, lived and studied the Catholic Faith with a devotion and love that facilitate a deeper understanding of the Gospel and Church teaching down through the ages

THE DUMB OX

While the importance of St. Thomas Aquinas' philosophical and theological works cannot be overstated, much can also be learned from his deep humility and saintly life. Born to a noble family in Belcastro, Italy, in 1226, he was placed under the care of the Benedictines of Monte Cassino at the age of five. While there he exhibited signs of great brilliance and holiness, and at the age of ten was sent to study at the University of Naples. It is said that after a lesson St. Thomas would repeat what he just learned with more depth and clarity than could his teachers. In spite of his worldly surroundings at the university, St. Thomas grew in humility and holiness.

Despite vehement opposition from his family, by the time St. Thomas reached the age of seventeen he had resolved to become a Dominican. In an effort to stop St. Thomas from answering his vocation, his two brothers locked him in castle for over a year. While St. Thomas was locked in the castle, his brothers sent a woman into his room to try to seduce him. St. Thomas responded by snatching a firebrand from the fireplace and driving her away. He finally escaped imprisonment with the aid of his sisters, who helped lower him over the castle walls in a basket.

After escaping, St. Thomas began to study under St. Albert the Great, a brilliant Dominican father who taught in Cologne, Germany. At first, St. Thomas' quiet nature and extreme humility prevented him from speaking up during class or participating in debates. Because of this, many of St. Thomas' fellow students at Cologne thought the young scholar simple-minded. These false impressions, combined with St. Thomas' hefty size, prompted a number of these students to nickname St. Thomas the "Dumb Ox." St. Albert the Great, who already recognized St. Thomas' incredible intellect, responded to these students by saying "you call him the Dumb Ox; I tell you this Dumb Ox shall bellow so loud that his bellowings will fill the world." These words proved prophetic.

"I tell you this Dumb Ox shall bellow so loud that his bellowings will fill the world."

PART III
The Mendicant Orders

Both St. Thomas Aquinas and Bl. John Duns Scotus belonged to a new type of religious order: the Mendicant Friars. The name mendicant, which is taken from the Latin word *mendicare* meaning to beg, describes the strict life of poverty lived by the mendicant orders. Unlike the monks of prior generations, this new form of religious life did not include a cloistered existence of prayer and work. These Mendicant Friars were forbidden to own property; they lived off alms. Through their public witness of poverty, chastity and obedience, and preaching, they brought the Gospel message into towns and cities. Although other orders were added to the list of Mendicant Friars as time went on, the original two were the Franciscans and the Dominicans. Both were started by great saints, and each order took to the cities with its own particular spirituality and charism. Following the example of their great founder, St. Francis of Assisi, the Franciscans were dedicated to preaching to the poor and lived lives of radical poverty as a way of reflecting more faithfully the love of Christ. Based upon their founder, St. Dominic, the Dominicans focused on teaching and education and eventually produced some of the greatest intellectuals in Europe, among them St. Thomas Aquinas. Together, these orders would initiate a powerful Christian renewal among the Catholic population of Europe. At the same time scores of people joined these orders making their presence felt throughout the Christian world.

ST. FRANCIS OF ASSISI

On a small hilltop town in the Italian region of Umbria, a wealthy merchant returning from France found that his wife had given birth to a son. He named his son John, but inspired by his love for the country he had just visited, he changed his son's name to Francesco or "the Frenchman." From birth this boy was marked as a stranger in his own land, and he would eventually lead the life of a stranger throughout the entire world. The Church's history has seen very few men and women who can rival St. Francis of Assisi in his display of the heart of Christ.

As a youth, St. Francis was no different from most boys in the town of Assisi. He reveled in good times and jubilant festivals. He loved to feast and enjoy the finer things in life. Although it is said that he always had sympathy for the poor, as a young man St. Francis' heart lay more with the romantic dream of a crusader than as a servant to the poor. When he was sixteen, St. Francis got his chance to live out his dream, and he participated in one of the frequent skirmishes his townsmen waged against the Perugians who held the castle at Assisi. In the battle St. Francis was wounded and captured. During his many long months in captivity, St. Francis was stricken with a lingering illness.

This experience proved traumatic to the young St. Francis, and after his brush with death, he began to turn his thoughts towards more serious matters. St. Francis began to pray and meditate on the life of Christ. His companions continued with their celebratory lives, but St. Francis became increasingly distant and detached. As the years went on St. Francis grew more and more diligent in prayer. He began to lose interest in the pastimes of his friends and started to despise the things of this world.

St. Francis claimed that his conversion did not occur until he was twenty-two. He underwent a spiritual crisis at twenty-two that led him to devote himself entirely to prayer and penitential practices. During these intense sessions of prayer, St. Francis had a mystical experience. While praying in the little church of St. Damian, St. Francis heard a voice saying, "Francis, go and build up

my house again!" The young and eager St. Francis took the message literally and immediately set out to renovate the church. He took his father's horse and an armful of linens and cloth and sold them at the market. He brought the money to the poor priest at the church who refused the gift. Finding no need of wealth for himself and frustrated with this obstacle to God's command, St. Francis flung the money aside.

St. Francis' father was a practical and economical man who did not appreciate the generosity of St. Francis' actions, to say the least. He was infuriated when he heard what his son had done and beat St. Francis. St. Francis ran away and hid in a cave for a month, and when he emerged, he was emaciated and sickly. The people of the town tormented him, threw stones, and called him a madman. His father grew more unhappy with his son. Not only did he disown St. Francis from his inheritance (which St. Francis gladly accepted), he also wanted his son to suffer further civil punishment. When the young St. Francis heard of his father's desire, he claimed that he was on a mission from God and was outside civil jurisdiction. This of course only further aggravated his father who then dragged his son to the city center in order to have the bishop resolve the matter. There, in front of the bishop and the gathered villagers of Assisi, St. Francis stripped nearly naked and professed "Hitherto I have called you my father, henceforth I desire to say only 'Our Father who art in Heaven.'" (quoted in Robinson, "St. Francis of Assisi," *The Catholic Encyclopedia*, vol. VI, 1909). The bishop, moved by this straggly man's conviction to serve God, covered St. Francis in his ecclesiastical robes and accepted him as a servant of God.

Under the protection of the bishop, St. Francis retreated to the hills surrounding Assisi and began fasting and praying. He composed songs to God and professed his marriage to "Lady Poverty." St. Francis would climb down into the valley only to camp out next to the Church and attend Mass. One day, while attending Mass, St. Francis heard the gospel reading in which Christ instructs his Apostles to go and preach taking no shoes, cloak, staff, or money. When St. Francis heard these words, he knew that it was to be his vocation. He wrapped himself in a brown peasant's tunic and began walking the Spoleto Valley, preaching to and begging with the poor.

ST. FRANCIS AND THE WOLF

There are many stories and legends about St. Francis' love for nature and his ability to communicate with animals. In one famous story, first recorded by Thomas of Celano in the thirteenth century, a ravenous wolf had been eating animals and people near the town of Gubbio. The beast's ferocious teeth caught every villager brave enough to face it, and so the entire village was too afraid to venture outside the city walls. Hearing about the terror brought about by the wolf, St. Francis, who was staying in Gubbio at the time, decided simply to find the wolf and ask it to stop attacking the poor villagers. Accompanied by a friar and some local peasants, St. Francis left the city to seek out the dreaded creature. Outside the city walls, the villagers quickly became afraid and returned to Gubbio. St. Francis and his friar went on.

While they were passing the woods rumored to be the home of the wolf, the animal appeared and charged the two friars. Standing his ground, St. Francis made the Sign of the Cross toward the wolf. The wolf immediately slowed down and closed its mouth. St. Francis spoke to the creature, calling it "brother wolf," and ordering it in the name of Christ to stop attacking the villagers. The wolf put its head down and meekly approached St. Francis, who explained to it that humans are made in the image of God and should not be harmed. He asked the wolf to promise not to eat any more villagers, and said he would make sure that the villagers in turn did not kill him. The wolf indicated its assent by moving its body and nodding in agreement, and St. Francis and the wolf returned together to the village.

When they arrived, St. Francis astonished the crowd of villagers by walking straight to the town square with the wolf and giving a sermon, asking them to repent from their sins. After St. Francis explained the agreement he had made with the wolf, the villagers agreed to feed the wolf and let it live in peace. After that, the wolf became a village pet, and when it finally died years later, everyone in the town mourned.

THE PRAYER OF SAINT FRANCIS
Lord, make me an instrument
of Thy peace;
where there is hatred,
let me sow love;
where there is injury, pardon;
where there is doubt, faith;
where there is despair, hope;
where there is darkness, light;
and where there is sadness, joy.
O Divine Master,
grant that I may not so much
seek to be consoled as to console;
to be understood, as to understand;
to be loved, as to love;
for it is in giving that we receive,
it is in pardoning that we are
pardoned,
and it is in dying that we are born
to eternal life.
Amen.

"'My brothers, you have a great obligation to praise your Creator. He clothed you with feathers and gave you wings to fly, appointing the clear air as your home, and he looks after you without any effort on your part.'...the birds showed their pleasure in a wonderful fashion; they stretched out their necks and flapped their wings, gazing at him with their beaks open."
—Bonaventure, *Major Life*

St. Francis became known in the surrounding countryside, and in 1209 two men were inspired by his example and joined the saint in his travels. Their arrival marks the founding of the Franciscan Order. More and more men began flocking to St. Francis, and when his following grew to eleven, he decided to make a rule. Rather than carefully noting the rules for day-to-day life in a monastic community, St. Francis simply told his followers to live like Christ. For his rule, St. Francis listed the passages in the gospels where Jesus asks his followers to give away all they own and live a life of poverty, and his followers obliged.

In 1210, St. Francis went to Rome with a few companions to obtain approval from the pope for his pastoral work. Although the cardinals were initially suspect of this wayward beggar knocking on their door, Pope Innocent III saw differently. The pope had a dream of a poor and despised man holding up St. John Lateran, the cathedral of Rome. The next day St. Francis came before the pope, and Innocent was amazed that the man from his dream now stood before him. The pope verbally approved St. Francis' mission. Some years later, St. Francis would compose a more detailed rule that would be formally accepted by Pope Honorius III in 1223.

St. Francis and his followers set out to the principal centers of Europe. Preach peace to all, St. Francis told his followers, but have it in your hearts still more than on your lips. St. Francis dedicated his life especially to the Eucharist and drew strength from Jesus' presence in Holy Communion. He begged the clergy to show more reverence and respect to everything concerning the Sacrifice of the Mass and even swept out and cleaned chapels and churches. St. Francis asked bishops to provide even the most rural of chapels with beautiful sacred vessels for the Blessed Sacrament. The traveling saint also baked bread for the Eucharist, which he gave the Churches.

In 1219, St. Francis traveled to Syria during the Fifth Crusade. When St. Francis arrived in the Holy Land, he had no weapons or armor and was quickly seized and beaten by Muslim troops. The Sultan was so impressed by St. Francis' poverty and humility that he took in the saint and the two became friends. Through their friendship, St. Francis secured future safe passage for himself and his followers, and he ensured that Franciscans be the caretakers for the shrines of the Holy Land, a duty they perform to this day.

Humility was St. Francis' driving virtue. He was never ordained a priest because he felt himself unworthy of the honor, and stepped down as head of the order before his death.

By the end of his life, St. Francis' order had already grown to nearly five thousand friars. After his resignation from the headship of the order, he lived in retreat on Mount Alverna. During his last years on the mountain, St. Francis prayed to participate more fully in the Passion of Christ, and on September 14, 1224, on the Feast of the Exaltation of the Cross, St. Francis received the mark of the stigmata. The stigmata is a phenomenon in which a person bears all or some of the wounds of Christ's Passion on his or her own body. Two years later, on October 4, 1226, St. Francis died at Assisi. He was canonized in 1228 by Pope Gregory IX. His feast day is celebrated on October 4.

St. Bonaventure wrote the definitive biography of St. Francis.

ST. BONAVENTURE AND THE GROWTH OF THE FRANCISCANS

Inspired by their founder's example, the Franciscans grew rapidly. They strove to live lives like St. Francis, but as the order grew, things became more difficult. One difficulty was that St. Francis prohibited anyone in his order to own property. When the order included only St. Francis and a few followers, this never proved a problem. As they traveled throughout their home country, the poor preachers found shelter in the barns and houses of their neighboring countrymen. By now there were many Franciscans living as strangers in all of the major European cities. The friars had to find a practical means of surviving, while keeping up with the spirit of St. Francis.

St. Bonaventure (1221-1274), the great organizer of the order, is often called its second founder. St. Bonaventure joined the Franciscans in 1243, and was Minister-General of the order for 17 years. St. Bonaventure was an important churchman of the day. He was a gifted theologian and spiritual writer who, among his many philosophical works, wrote the definitive biography of St. Francis. He was also instrumental in helping elect Pope Bl. Gregory X. As minister general, St. Bonaventure was confronted with a difficult problem that threatened to destroy the order: How could St. Bonaventure keep the order poor, yet also provide for its existence?

St. Bonaventure made a new provision that allowed individual Franciscans to receive donations meant for the well-being of the order. The money would not be held by the Franciscans in common, as it was with other monastic orders—keeping the individual poor but the order sustainable. Rather, St. Bonaventure made it so that everything received by the Franciscans would be given to the Holy See, which would then see to the preservation of the order according to its

own good will. The Pope would own houses and permit the Franciscans to stay in them. Thanks to St. Bonaventure's system, the friars never handled nor decided how to use any money. There were no abbots charged with the administration of funds or securing a financially sound future. As every friar relied on the good will of the pope to sustain the order, there was no financial temptation for the friars, who were free to travel between the papal safe houses. St. Bonaventure's rule allowed the friars to prosper in numbers and vocations, while retaining the poverty so loved and cherished by the order's founder.

ST. DOMINIC

As discussed in the previous chapter, southern France in the twelfth and thirteenth centuries was struggling with the proliferation of heresy, most notably, Albigensianism. One reason that the Albigensian heresy appealed so widely was that it preached extreme poverty that seemed to honor more faithfully the example of Christ. For the common people of the Middle Ages, this heresy seemed preferable to the lax moral behavior exhibited by

The meeting of St. Francis and St. Dominic at the Fourth Lateran Council in Rome in 1215 may be a legend. However the images painted of this meeting, symbolically represent the shared piety, beauty, and simplicity of the orders founded by these two mendicant friars.

wayward clergymen. The Albigensians were essentially Gnostics, and their understanding of God and the world were not merely false, but detrimental to the human person. The goodness of life in this temporary world was not only denied, it was considered evil. Suicide as a form of purification proliferated, and physical attacks against those who did not abide to their extreme self-mortification were common. Since marital union and conception were seen as sinful, they encouraged abortion and allowed for immoral activities as an alternative to marriage. In addition to practices that were egregiously injurious to the individual and in flagrant violation of human dignity, they rejected the priesthood and the entire sacramental system of the Catholic Church.

Nonetheless, many Catholic preachers found it difficult, if not impossible, to win back these wayward heretics to the Church. In 1203, the Abbot of Citeaux in southern France was lamenting

THE SPREAD OF FRANCISCAN MONASTERIES BY 1300

Dublin
Cambridge
Cologne
Oxford
ATLANTIC
OCEAN
Angers
Paris
Prague
Padua
Bologna
Genoa
Florence
Salamanca
Montpellier
Perugia
Toulouse
Lerida
Naples

MEDITERRANEAN SEA

©1997 Lion Hudson plc/Three's Company

The two mendicant orders, Franciscans and Dominicans, helped rejuvenate the spiritual life of the Church by combining a simple Christian life with strong devotion to the Eucharist and education.

THE SPREAD OF DOMINICAN MONASTERIES BY 1300

© 1997 Lion Hudson plc / Three's Company

Skanninge

Visby

Edinburgh

Lund

Ribe

Roskilde

Stralsund

York

Lübeck

Cambridge

Bremen

Norwich

Magdeburg

Oxford

London

Krakow

Canterbury

Cologne

Mainz

Beauvais

Trier

Paris

Strasbourg

Vienna

Basel

Limoges

Bern

A T L A N T I C

O C E A N

Bologna

Rome

Naples

Toledo

M E D I T E R R A N E A N   S E A

In a vision, Mary, the Mother of God, appeared to St. Dominic. She urged St. Dominic to pray the Rosary for his work of evangelization. This miraculous Marian intervention served as a springboard in popularizing the devotion of the Rosary.

his difficulties with these heretics to two Spaniards who were passing through on their way back from Rome. These two men, the Spanish bishop Diego of Osma and his canon Domingo de Guzman, reminded the Abbot that the Lord's disciples were sent to preach barefoot, without a staff and with no money. That example, they said, was just as important for spreading the Faith as the words used to preach.

They stayed in the region for two years in order to help the Abbot in his efforts. Both were well trained and educated in the Spanish Universities, and they found winning public discussions with the heretics to be easy. However, they still did not succeed in converting them. After some time, Diego was obliged to return to his diocese, but Domingo (St. Dominic) stayed on. He lived in a monastery with a few other zealous priests and took on the Rule of St. Augustine. St. Dominic set out to follow more closely his own words addressed to the Abbot of Citeaux and began to live a life of poverty. He wore a simple white habit and scapular covered by a black mantel. He heard about the preacher St. Francis and began to follow in his footsteps of absolute poverty. Furthermore, St. Dominic saw that sound intellectual training was necessary in dialoguing effectively with the Albigensians. St. Dominic began sending his followers to the University of Paris, and those who had training, he sent out in pairs throughout the region to live and preach like Christ's Apostles. Hence, they are called the Order of Preachers (O.P.).

St. Dominic died on his way to preach to the pagans of Hungary. By then, the Dominicans were nicknamed *Domini canes* or "hounds of the Lord."

Eventually St. Dominic's efforts in living an ascetical life modeled after the life of Christ, coupled with his powerful preaching, began to pay off. Nonetheless, it would be a serious oversight to leave out the recitation and promotion of the Rosary as a ritual means of converting the Albigensians. Tradition has it that Mary, the Mother of God, appeared to St. Dominic who was crushed with disappointment and discouragement for his failure in converting them back to the Catholic Faith. She urged St. Dominic to be hopeful and optimistic and pray the Rosary for his work of evangelization as he entrusted his work to Mary and promoted the Faith. This miraculous Marian intervention served as a springboard in popularizing the devotion of the Rosary.

St. Dominic's order did not enjoy the same popularity as that of St. Francis. At the time of St. Dominic's death in 1221, the order numbered sixty. Eventually the Dominicans spread far and wide and became famous for their preaching and intellectual expertise. Over time, the University of Paris became filled with these simple and humble teachers who became their strongest professors. The Dominicans traveled all over Europe as far East as Poland, Greece, and into the Holy Land, preaching, founding schools, and bringing many to the Catholic Faith.

THE LEGACY OF THE MENDICANT FRIARS

Around the time that the Franciscan and Dominican orders began, many priests were distracted by worldly affairs, and some were even losing their moral and spiritual fervor. Heresies like Albigensianism became popular because of people's desire for a more complete and wholehearted dedication to Christ, even if their teaching was erroneous in some aspects. The two mendicant orders appealed to that popular desire and helped rejuvenate the spiritual life of the Church by combining a simple Christian life with strong devotion to the Eucharist and serious education. Spiritually and intellectually prepared, many Franciscans and Dominicans rose to positions of prominence in the Church. Priests, Bishops, and eventually popes came from these two orders, helping to keep the Church connected with its founding principles and purpose. It is no coincidence that the proliferation of the mendicant friars underscored the flourishing of Medieval culture in the arts and in learning. This period illustrated that the strengths of the Church still lay in holiness, expressed in her piety, beauty, and simplicity.

PART IV

The Flowering of Culture

It is often the case that when one mentions the Middle Ages, images spring to mind of knights in armor, spired castles, and tall, ominous gothic steeples hovering over poor towns riddled with plague. It is a picture of a hard life filled with contraries: rich and poor, holy and barbaric. It is a picture that is not entirely true. Certainly the Medieval period was characterized by a hard existence where disease and injustice proliferated. Punishments were more brutal and religious conviction, in the case of the Albigensians, more extreme. Nevertheless, it is useful to look more closely at the Medieval culture to appreciate and discover its mindset and spirit. Along with these grim images, there is also the radiant beauty of stain glass, the brilliant intricacy of learning and philosophy, the humor and joyous insight of Chaucer's *Canterbury Tales*, and the majestic beauty of Dante's *Divine Comedy*. The period's saints were also not dark, foreboding characters. St. Bernard of Clairvaux wrote endlessly on love and Solomon's *Song of Songs*, and St. Francis' joy and charisma, his humble spirit as much as his poor life, inspired popular devotion. Troubadour minstrels traveled the countryside singing the first romantic poems, and love of life and as romantic themes blossomed in art as well as literature. Indeed, the Medieval period saw a moment in which all aspects of life and culture were identified with Faith. The Christian spirit of that period permeated every facet of human life from trade guilds to universities and ultimately to religious art and architecture, and every phase of human existence, from infancy, childhood, youth, middle and old age. The individual was in harmony with the world, the Faith, and God in the journey through life.

MEDIEVAL ARCHITECTURE

There is no doubt that of all the artistic and cultural advances of the Medieval period, architecture was among the most extraordinary and long-lasting. From the time of Constantine, Christian architecture centered around the form of the Roman Basilica. Modeled after the large meeting halls in the Roman forum, basilicas were heavy structures that combined a long nave with a perpendicular transept that divided the Church in a way that resembled a cross. The wooden roof was raised above the aisles on two interior walls running the whole length of the building. The walls were supported by round arches joining columns that ran down each side of the nave. Side aisles had small windows cut in order to let in light.

The Cathedral of Notre Dame in Paris is among the most famous buildings designed with flying buttresses.

The Romanesque style, which succeeded the basilica, resembled the ancient basilicas in their basic shape, but rather than a flat roof, Romanesque churches added round stone vaults. A more permanent structure, the heavy stone Romanesque churches were durable and resistant to fire. The buildings also provided a space that alluded to the eternal God, a permanent structure heavy with a sense of the power and infinitude of God. Various types of vaulting were developed to support these heavy structures as architects grew in their understanding of the displacement of weight in the buildings.

As the Medieval period began, the Christian liturgy, complete with developments in liturgical song, began to take new shape. Polyphonic musical styles layered, blended, and harmonized complex and intricate melodies in extraordinary unity. The Church year became centered around the idea of Christ as the "light" coming into the world at Christmas, and this offered a new look into the mysteries of the Faith. With the emphasis on Christ, the Light of the World, Christians began to look for a new style of architecture that could provide a space that held light, music, and air in a suitable way. These Medieval architects built Churches according to a gothic structure that would clearly reflect God's transcendence, power, and beauty. Medieval architects began building stone vaulted churches that were higher than ever before, at the same time creating larger transepts and rounded apses. Medieval architects sought to build still higher, allow more light into the building, and provide as much space for music to echo throughout as possible.

Architects developed ribbed vaulting and the pointed arch, which crisscrossed arches and allowed them to displace the weight of the roof more effectively. Roofs resembled a series of triangles that

The Chartres Cathedral

held light slabs of stone effortlessly, a welcome change from the heavy Romanesque masonry. The arches were also more vertical and could be raised higher and rested on lighter pillars. Pointed arches displaced all of the weight onto the pillars instead of the walls. Flying buttresses, external supports that arched towards the roof added extra support, and this new building technique was held together by a series of columns and vaults that made walls virtually unnecessary for structural support. This allowed architects to install huge stained glass windows that stretched nearly from floor to ceiling, allowing in light and creating a huge and open internal space.

This style of building became known as gothic architecture, and the most important innovation was the freedom it gave masons, artists, and architects to dress the building with works of art. The new windows were filled with stained glass depicting scenes and stories from the Bible and the lives of saints. Statues were carved into the structures of the doorway and pillars. Arches and columns were decorated with ornate carvings and designs. As the style progressed, cathedrals like those of Paris, Rheims, Cologne, and Chartres gave the visual impression of soaring grace, delicate poise, and perfect balance flooded with light and seemingly held up by the figures carved into the stone. Gothic architecture developed a space for the liturgy brimming with warmth and joy.

Gothic architecture (shown left) allows non-loadbearing areas for stained glass and carvings. Gothic cathedrals are celebrations of light and color compared to heavy Romanesque architecture (shown below).

Allegory of The Divine Comedy by Domenico Michelino. Dante is shown holding a copy of *The Divine Comedy,* on the left, the entrance to Hell. Behind Dante is Mount Purgatory with seven terraces leading to Paradise with Adam and Eve at the summit. Dante's city of Florence is on the right. In *The Divine Comedy,* Dante recounts his travels through the three realms of the dead during Holy Week in the spring of 1300. His guide through Hell and Purgatory is the Latin poet Virgil, author of *The Aeneid.* His guide through Paradise is Beatrice, Dante's ideal of a perfect woman. Originally titled *Comedia,* it was later christened *Divina* by Giovanni Boccaccio. Poems in Medieval times were classified as High (Tragic) or Low (Comedy). Low poems had happy endings and were stories of everyday subjects and common people.

THE BIRTH OF VERNACULAR LITERATURE

Despite the increased importance that universities placed on Classical texts, the Medieval Period saw for the first time the composition of vernacular literature. Vernacular literature in Europe grew largely out of folk stories handed down orally for generations. The earliest example of these recorded stories is *Beowulf*. Written in Old English about A.D. 1100, *Beowulf* is about a Scandinavian warrior of the sixth century A.D. This story had been transcribed by monks for generations, taking on distinctively Christian elements from its adaptation from the original Anglo-Saxon tale. Other early manuscripts of Germanic lore began to appear in the eleventh-century. These works mixed heroism and magic, a special brew that became an important part of Western Europe's literary heritage.

In France, towards the end of the eleventh century, poetry became popular due in part to the influence of Arab love poetry, flooding in from Muslim Spain. These works helped form a long tradition of vernacular French love poetry. Duke William of Aquitaine was won over by this new style, and he began writing his own work as well as patronizing other poets. His support helped influence the emergence of troubadour poets, traveling minstrel lyricists who sang of love and romance. Love took on new meanings in the Medieval world. Poets sang of romantic love and composed stories about knights courting women. The French writer Chrétien de Troyes utilized some of the English tales of King Arthur and his knights and wrote works that foreshadowed the emergence of the literary device known as the novel. These poetic serenades enhanced a greater appreciation of the dignity of women through an exaltation of their virtue and feminine qualities.

In Italy, the impact that this poetic genre had on the local dialect can be seen in St. Francis of Assisi's *Canticle of the Sun.* Troubadours traveled throughout Italy and their ideas of love influenced, among others, a Florentine named Dante Alighieri. One warm summer day, Dante (1265-1321) was crossing a bridge over the river Arno in Florence. He passed a young girl, Beatrice, and fell completely in love with her. Although they both married other people (Dante scarcely ever said a single word to her), Beatrice would become the love and inspiration that fueled all of Dante's writings. She was to him the end of all desire and the inspiration of love through which he learned to love God. In his writings, romantic and divine love became intertwining images.

Written in the last years of his life, the *Divine Comedy* recounts how the poet, guided by his love of Beatrice, travels through the entire Christian universe, from Hell to Heaven, blending theology, philosophy, and literature into a complex and beautiful poem. Dante draws together Classical and Christian elements and produces an unparalleled work that extracts virtue and vice from the complexity of human action and approaches the deepest, most profound mysteries of Christianity. Certainly some of his characters are the most memorable in literature, both for their poignant humanity and their depiction through the eyes of moral clarity. His work reveals a synergy between all the elements of Medieval life: philosophy, poetry, beauty, love, and God and is one of the most wonderful pieces of literature ever written.

Yet in th' abyss,
That Lucifer with Judas low ingulfs,
Lightly he plac'd us; . . .

Left: *Descent To The Last Circle* by Gustave Dore. The giant Antæus lowers Dante and Virgil into the abyss. *The Inferno,* Canto 31

Above: Illustration from a Medieval manuscript of *The Divine Comedy* in the Madrid National Library collection.

THE VERNACULAR IN POETRY

Geoffrey Chaucer as a Canterbury pilgrim in a page from the Ellesmere manuscript, an early copy of *The Canterbury Tales*. Written in Middle English, this work popularized the literary use of vernacular English.

The High Middle Ages saw a great flowering of works of literature written in the vernacular throughout Europe. In England, for example, Geoffrey Chaucer wrote the *Canterbury Tales* during the thirteenth century, a massive poem of over seventeen thousand lines that follows a group of pilgrims who, traveling from London to Canterbury, pass the time telling stories to each other. A masterful exposition of human character and motive as well as a candid look into Medieval life, Chaucer's *Canterbury Tales* is often credited as one of the first works to prove the artistic legitimacy of the English language.

El Cid (also known as *El Cid Campeador* or "My Lord, the Champion"), is a twelfth century epic poem written by an anonymous author. The poetry of *El Cid* is written in the language of the day, a version of Spanish that was slowly developing out of Latin, and is thus considered the oldest work of Spanish literature. Though based on historical facts, the poem tells the legendary story of the adventurous Castilian knight Rodrigo Díaz de Vivar, called Cid, and the mythical marriage of his two daughters to the Counts of Carrion.

The oldest surviving French poem, *The Song of Roland*, was also written around the year 1200 somewhere in the north of France. *The Song* is based on the Battle of Roncevaux Pass in which Roland fought for the Franks against the Basques. While the poem takes many historical liberties, such as changing the Basques to Muslims, it is regarded as a classic illustration of the value of chivalry.

A detail from *The Lamentation Over The Dead Christ* by Giotto (1267-1337) from the Scrovegni Chapel in Padua, Italy painted in 1303-1305. This detail illustrates the concentrated dramatic force of Giotto's frescoes and the influence he would have on Renaissance painters like Michelangelo who studied this cycle of 100 scenes when planning his Sistine Chapel. The chapel recently went through major restoration and repair after a severe earthquake in 1997 literally brought the ceiling down, and Giotto's brushstrokes became a jigsaw puzzle. Centuries of damage from neglect, air pollution and water damage were also repaired. The restored chapel was reopened in the year 2000.

PAINTING AND THE FINE ARTS

Medieval painting usually holds a lower place of counterpoint to the developments of the Renaissance. Compared with the works of Michelangelo and Raphael, Medieval paintings usually seem oversimplified and one dimensional—lacking in any real human emotion. However, this subtle art, one that is indeed as imitative as it is symbolic, requires a careful eye to appreciate its rare beauty.

The paintings of the Middle Ages often come from altarpieces that were set behind the tabernacle in the sanctuary of the church. They were largely meant as objects of devotion and reflection. Figures set on a flat golden background represented scenes from the life of Christ, the saints, and Mary (often depicted holding the Christ child). Painters focused primarily on two aspects of the painting. First, they were concerned with the symbolic relationship between the elements of the painting. Juxtaposition of figures, angels, or saints, as well as Mary and the Christ child related Christian truths, ideas about God and the Trinity, and conveyed stories from the Gospels. Besides this symbolic meaning in the work, artists paid particular attention to the facial expressions of the subjects, trying to reveal the inner souls of the saints through subtle artistic representation. The faces of Mary and others reflect the agony and ecstasy of the Christian religious experience.

Giotto di Bondone, a Florentine painter, is known for his series of 38 frescoes in the Arena Chapel in Padua and *The Scenes from the Life of Saint Francis* in the Upper Basilica in Assisi. His paintings embody sweetness and an ordinary eloquence that typified Medieval art. The simplicity of his forms combined with a subtle complexity of emotional content was widely imitated, and Giotto is considered the founder of the Italian school of painting in Italy. This painter was a friend of Dante (whom he painted often), and these two artists shared ideas and inspirations. Though his work was a bridge between the Medieval and renaissance periods of art, from his content, style, and purpose, it is clear that this Italian painter represents the pinnacle of the Medieval style.

The Maestà by Duccio di Buoninsegna (1255-1319) was painted for the High Altar of the Siena Cathedral. This two-sided masterpiece was carried through the streets of Siena on June 9, 1311 in a great procession from Duccio's studio to the Cathedral. In its original form, the huge altarpiece measured over 16 feet high and 16 feet long. When installed behind the altar, the *Enthroned Madonna and Child surrounded by Saints* faced the congregation, and the back of the panel with twenty-six scenes from *The Passion* faced the sanctuary for scripture study. Sadly, this magnificent piece was sawn into pieces in 1771. Several pieces were sold to foreign museums and private collectors. The restoration seen here was completed in 1956 and is in the Cathedral's museum.

Santa María de León Cathedral, also called "The House of Light," is located in the city of León, Spain. Designed by the master architect Enrique in the thirteenth century, the León Cathedral is considered a masterpiece of the gothic style.

CONCLUSION

The High Middle Ages saw a significant flourishing in Christ's Church, and in many ways, this period of time was a golden age in the history of the Church. Christian philosophy, piety, and art boldly ventured into new heights, and the saints of the period showed how holiness redounds to the benefit of all of society. This does not mean, of course, that the Medieval period was bereft of dark shadows in its reflection of Christ's Gospel. Nonetheless, Medieval culture, expressed in its breakthroughs in philosophy, theology, architecture, art, and literature, offers a glimmer of the magnificent ramifications of the Christian ideal.

SUPPLEMENTARY READING

St. Francis of Assisi, *Canticle of Brother Sun*

Most High, all-powerful, all-good Lord,
All praise is Yours, all glory, all honour and all blessings.
To you alone, Most High, do they belong,
    and no mortal lips are worthy to pronounce Your Name.
Praised be You my Lord with all Your creatures,
    especially Sir Brother Sun,
Who is the day through whom You give us light.
And he is beautiful and radiant with great splendour,
Of You Most High, he bears the likeness.
Praised be You, my Lord, through Sister Moon and the stars,
In the heavens you have made them bright, precious and fair.
Praised be You, my Lord, through Brothers Wind and Air,
And fair and stormy, all weather's moods,
    by which You cherish all that You have made.
Praised be You my Lord through Sister Water,
So useful, humble, precious and pure.
Praised be You my Lord through Brother Fire,
    through whom You light the night
    and he is beautiful and playful and
    robust and strong.
Praised be You my Lord through our Sister,
Mother Earth who sustains and governs us,
    producing varied fruits with coloured
    flowers and herbs.
Praise be You my Lord through those
    who grant pardon
    for love of You and bear sickness and trial.
Blessed are those who endure in peace,
By You Most High, they will be crowned.
Praised be You, my Lord through Sister Death,
    from whom no-one living can escape.
Woe to those who die in mortal sin!
Blessed are they She finds doing Your Will.
No second death can do them harm.
Praise and bless my Lord and give Him thanks,
And serve Him with great humility.

St. Francis' Mystical Marriage with Poverty

SUPPLEMENTARY READING Continued

St. Thomas Aquinas, *Summa Theologiæ*, I. 2. 3

Whether God exists?

Objection 1. It seems that God does not exist; because if one of two contraries be infinite, the other would be altogether destroyed. But the word "God" means that He is infinite goodness. If, therefore, God existed, there would be no evil discoverable; but there is evil in the world. Therefore God does not exist.

Objection 2. Further, it is superfluous to suppose that what can be accounted for by a few principles has been produced by many. But it seems that everything we see in the world can be accounted for by other principles, supposing God did not exist. For all natural things can be reduced to one principle which is nature; and all voluntary things can be reduced to one principle which is human reason, or will. Therefore there is no need to suppose God's existence....

Reply to Objection 1. As Augustine says (*Enchiridion*, XI): "Since God is the highest good, He would not allow any evil to exist in His works, unless His omnipotence and goodness were such as to bring good even out of evil." This is part of the infinite goodness of God, that He should allow evil to exist, and out of it produce good.

Reply to Objection 2. Since nature works for a determinate end under the direction of a higher agent, whatever is done by nature must needs be traced back to God, as to its first cause. So also whatever is done voluntarily must also be traced back to some higher cause other than human reason or will, since these can change or fail; for all things that are changeable and capable of defect must be traced back to an immovable and self-necessary first principle, as was shown in the body of the Article.

John Paul II, *Fides et ratio*, 85

I believe that those philosophers who wish to respond today to the demands which the word of God makes on human thinking should develop their thought on the basis of these postulates and in organic continuity with the great tradition which, beginning with the ancients, passes through the Fathers of the Church and the masters of Scholasticism and includes the fundamental achievements of modern and contemporary thought. If philosophers can take their place within this tradition and draw their inspiration from it, they will certainly not fail to respect philosophy's demand for autonomy.

In the present situation, therefore, it is most significant that some philosophers are promoting a recovery of the determining role of this tradition for a right approach to knowledge. The appeal to tradition is not a mere remembrance of the past; it involves rather the recognition of a cultural heritage which belongs to all of humanity.

From the commentaries of St. Thomas Aquinas.

VOCABULARY

DICTAMEN

The "Art of Composition" taught at Bologna, which included rules for drawing up briefs and other legal documents. This training attracted many students and soon developed into another intense program specializing in grammar and rhetoric.

DOUBLE TRUTH THEORY

Compares the value of theological tenets against philosophical truths. According to the Muslim philosopher Averroes, one can hold contradictory truths coming from theological and philosophical speculation, but ideas gathered from philosophical thought are superior to theological tenets.

GOTHIC

Style of Medieval building that flourished from 1200-1500. By using pointed arches, ribbed vaulting and flying buttresses, this style created an airy and well-lit space and gave masons, artists, and architects the freedom to adorn buildings with works of art.

"HEARING A BOOK"

Method of teaching in the university. A teacher would read the text of a book along with his predecessors' comments on the text before adding his own commentary to the lecture.

MENDICANT FRIARS

From the Latin word *mendicare,* meaning "to beg," this new type of religious order was not bound to a place or community and subsisted entirely on alms. The Franciscans and Dominicans are the largest orders of mendicant friars.

PLATONIC FORMS

Philosophical construct developed by the fifth century Greek philosopher Plato that held that all things that exist emanate from the primal unity of the unseen idea, at the very core of which is the Form of the Good.

QUADRIVIUM

Latin for "four ways." More advanced program in the Medieval liberal arts program, it included the study of arithmetic, geometry, astronomy, and music.

SCHOLASTICISM

The system of philosophical and theological inquiry first developed in the Medieval schools of Christian Europe, creating its own technical language and methodology.

STIGMATA

Phenomenon in which a person bears all or some of the wounds of Christ in his or her own body.

STUDIUM GENERALE

Unified program of study offered by Medieval universities which included theology, law, medicine and the arts.

TRIVIUM

Latin for "three ways," this was one of two sections into which the arts were divided in Medieval universities. It referred to the three primary branches of Medieval education: grammar, rhetoric and dialectic.

TROUBADOUR

Traveling minstrel lyricists who sang of love and romance, assisting the development of the European vernacular literatures.

UNIVERSITAS

A type of corporation that protected the educational and administrative needs of masters and students in schools of the mid-eleventh century.

STUDY QUESTIONS

1. What is Scholasticism?

2. Which university became the most famous during the Medieval period because of the talent that it attracted?

3. Which university became known for its study of jurisprudence?

4. Which university became an important center for the sciences and later added philosophy and Arabic related texts to its curriculum?

5. What did the guild system and the independence from lay and ecclesiastical authorities create on the university campus that is still highly regarded on today's college campus?

6. What was the *studium generale* at the universities?

7. What was St. Thomas Aquinas' largest work, and what are two of the topics that this work addresses?

8. Until St. Thomas Aquinas, what ancient Greek philosopher had given the philosophical framework within which Christianity usually operated?

9. Why did Aristotle need to be "re-discovered"?

10. What was the main task of St. Thomas Aquinas?

11. Who were the two best known philosophers in the Muslim world?

12. In Aristotle's philosophical system, who created everything?

13. What is St. Thomas Aquinas reported to have said after his mystical experience in Naples?

14. Why is St. Thomas' work so valuable to the Christian tradition?

15. How did Bl. John Duns Scotus negotiate St. Augustine's neo-Platonism and St. Thomas Aquinas' Scholasticism?

16. What are the two mendicant orders and who founded them?

17. How were the mendicants different than the monks of previous centuries?

18. What was St. Francis' dream as a young man? How did he live?

19. How did St. Francis organize the common life of his followers?

20. Pope Innocent III and the Vatican were initially suspect of St. Francis. What reportedly happened that changed Pope Innocent's mind?

21. What order oversees many of the holy shrines in the Holy Land?

22. Who is often called the "second founder" of the Franciscans, and when did he live?

23. How did St. Bonaventure negotiate the problem of keeping the Franciscans faithful to their vow of poverty while at the same time providing for the order's needs?

24. What rule of life did St. Dominic take for his order?

25. What color habit did the Dominicans take?

26. What heresy did the Dominicans set out to correct?

27. What devotion did the Dominicans advocate as a means of evangelization?

28. What was the legacy of the mendicant friars?

29. What architectural innovations were developed for gothic churches?

30. What contribution to literature first appeared in the Medieval period?

31. What was Dante's major work?

32. What was the purpose of Medieval Church art?

PRACTICAL EXERCISES

1. The Scholastic method answered questions by first stating objections to a statement, then giving an answer, and finally offering replies to each of the initial objections. Following the method of inquiry used in St. Thomas Aquinas' *Summa Theologiæ*, answer the following questions by using the Scholastic method:

a) Is the Scholastic method an effective way of reaching philosophic conclusions?

b) Were the Mendicant Orders really following the words of Christ?

c) Did the High Middle Ages experience a true flowering of culture?

FROM THE CATECHISM

35 Man's faculties make him capable of coming to a knowledge of the existence of a personal God. But for man to be able to enter into real intimacy with him, God willed both to reveal himself to man, and to give him the grace of being able to welcome this revelation in faith. The proofs of God's existence, however, can predispose one to faith and help one to see that faith is not opposed to reason.

36 "Our holy mother, the Church, holds and teaches that God, the first principle and last end of all things, can be known with certainty from the created world by the natural light of human reason" (Vatican Council I, *Dei Filius* 2: DS 3004 cf. 3026; Vatican Council II, *Dei Verbum* 6). Without this capacity, man would not be able to welcome God's revelation. Man has this capacity because he is created "in the image of God" (cf. Gen 1: 27).

159 *Faith and science:* "Though faith is above reason, there can never be any real discrepancy between faith and reason. Since the same God who reveals mysteries and infuses faith has bestowed the light of reason on the human mind, God cannot deny himself, nor can truth ever contradict truth" (*Dei Filius* 4: DS 3017). "Consequently, methodical research in all branches of knowledge, provided it is carried out in a truly scientific manner and does not override moral laws, can never conflict with the faith, because the things of the world and the things of faith derive from the same God. The humble and persevering investigator of the secrets of nature is being led, as it were, by the hand of God in spite of himself, for it is God, the conserver of all things, who made them what they are" (*GS* 36 § 1).

2293 Basic scientific research, as well as applied research, is a significant expression of man's dominion over creation. Science and technology are precious resources when placed at the service of man and promote his integral development for the benefit of all. By themselves however they cannot disclose the meaning of existence and of human progress. Science and technology are ordered to man, from whom they take their origin and development; hence they find in the person and in his moral values both evidence of their purpose and awareness of their limits.

2462 Giving alms to the poor is a witness to fraternal charity: it is also a work of justice pleasing to God.

2463 How can we not recognize Lazarus, the hungry beggar in the parable (cf. Lk 17:19-31), in the multitude of human beings without bread, a roof or a place to stay? How can we fail to hear Jesus: "As you did it not to one of the least of these, you did it not to me" (Mt 25: 45)?

FROM THE CATECHISM Continued

2500 The practice of goodness is accompanied by spontaneous spiritual joy and moral beauty. Likewise, truth carries with it the joy and splendor of spiritual beauty. Truth is beautiful in itself. Truth in words, the rational expression of the knowledge of created and uncreated reality, is necessary to man, who is endowed with intellect. But truth can also find other complementary forms of human expression, above all when it is a matter of evoking what is beyond words: the depths of the human heart, the exaltations of the soul, the mystery of God. Even before revealing himself to man in words of truth, God reveals himself to him through the universal language of creation, the work of his Word, of his wisdom: the order and harmony of the cosmos—which both the child and the scientist discover—"from the greatness and beauty of created things comes a corresponding perception of their Creator," "for the author of beauty created them" (Wis 13: 3, 5).

> [Wisdom] is a breath of the power of God, and a pure emanation of the glory of the Almighty; therefore nothing defiled gains entrance into her. For she is a reflection of eternal light, a spotless mirror of the working of God, and an image of his goodness (Wis 7: 25-26). For [wisdom] is more beautiful than the sun, and excels every constellation of the stars. Compared with the light she is found to be superior, for it is succeeded by the night, but against wisdom evil does not prevail (Wis 7: 29-30). I became enamored of her beauty (Wis 8: 2).

2502 *Sacred art* is true and beautiful when its form corresponds to its particular vocation: evoking and glorifying, in faith and adoration, the transcendent mystery of God—the surpassing invisible beauty of truth and love visible in Christ, who "reflects the glory of God and bears the very stamp of his nature," in whom "the whole fullness of deity dwells bodily" (Heb 1: 3; Col 2: 9). This spiritual beauty of God is reflected in the most holy Virgin Mother of God, the angels, and saints. Genuine sacred art draws man to adoration, to prayer, and to the love of God, Creator and Savior, the Holy One and *Sanctifier.*

2544 Jesus enjoins his disciples to prefer him to everything and everyone, and bids them "renounce all that [they have]" for his sake and that of the Gospel (Lk 14: 33; cf. Mk 8: 35). Shortly before his passion he gave them the example of the poor widow of Jerusalem who, out of her poverty, gave all that she had to live on (cf. Lk 21: 4). The precept of detachment from riches is obligatory for entrance into the Kingdom of heaven.

St. Francis simply told his followers to live like Christ. For his rule, St. Francis listed the passages in the gospels where Jesus asks his followers to give away all they own and live the life of poverty dedicated to God. His followers obliged.

A Century Of Suffering: Plague, War, And Schism

The survival of Europe would be threatened by both internal and external forces. Plague and famine would shake Medieval society to its very foundations.

CHAPTER 11

A Century Of Suffering: Plague, War, And Schism

The first thing I want to offer you is an invitation to optimism, hope and trust.
Certainly, the human race is going through a difficult patch, and we often have a
painful impression that the forces of evil...have got the upper hand....And yet,
we are called to overcome the world by our faith, since we belong to him who by his
death and resurrection obtained for every one of us the victory over sin and death,
and so has made us able to affirm humbly, serenely but certainly,
that good will triumph over evil.

— John Paul II, *Address to Salesian Youth*, Rome, May 5, 1979

With the pontificates of Innocent III, Gregory IX, and Boniface VIII, Church authority together with a united Western Christendom reached its zenith. During the thirteenth century, the Church established the legal foundation of the Medieval state, combated heresy and contested with emperors and kings for its legitimate role in regulating society. During this period, the Church finally achieved a balance between its temporal responsibilities and its spiritual authority.

The fourteenth century, however, would witness a dramatic change sweep across the face of Europe, and the accomplishments of the thirteenth century would begin to unravel. The rising kingdoms of France, Germany, and England would no longer be willing to submit themselves to the leadership of the pope. Furthermore Church authority would be almost fatally eroded by its long tenure under the influence of the French Kings at Avignon and by forty years of schism. The survival of Europe would be threatened by both internal and external forces. Plague and famine would shake Medieval society to its very foundations; war within Christendom (between England and France) would destroy the flower of feudal aristocracy; and the Turks would ravage Constantinople and threaten further expansion into Christendom. Indeed, it was a dark time, but as John Paul II's encouraging words reminded, like Christians throughout history, "we are called to overcome the world by our faith."

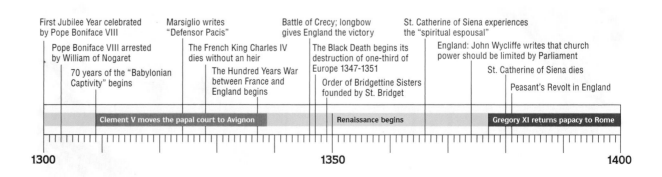

First Jubilee Year celebrated by Pope Boniface VIII

Marsiglio writes "Defensor Pacis"

Battle of Crecy; longbow gives England the victory

St. Catherine of Siena experiences the "spiritual espousal"

Pope Boniface VIII arrested by William of Nogaret

The French King Charles IV dies without an heir

The Black Death begins its destruction of one-third of Europe 1347-1351

England: John Wycliffe writes that church power should be limited by Parliament

70 years of the "Babylonian Captivity" begins

The Hundred Years War between France and England begins

Order of Bridgettine Sisters founded by St. Bridget

St. Catherine of Siena dies

Peasant's Revolt in England

Clement V moves the papal court to Avignon

Renaissance begins

Gregory XI returns papacy to Rome

1300   1350   1400

In southern France, the *Palais des Papes* (Palace of the Popes), now a museum, towers over the city of Avignon and the Rhône River. Beginning with Clement V, seven popes resided in Avignon from 1309-1377. It remained a papal possession until the French Revolution incorporated Avignon into France in 1791. Avignon is 400 miles southeast of Paris.

PART I

The Road to Avignon

POPE ST. CELESTINE V

After Pope Nicolas IV died in 1294, the papal throne remained vacant for more than two years while rival Italian parties vied for their own papal candidate. In order to break the deadlock, three cardinals sought a compromise candidate. In the hills of Abruzzi there lived an 80-year-old saintly hermit by the name of Peter Murrone. He spent much of his life in a small cave, living a rigorously ascetic existence of prayer, labor, and fasting. In 1294, the three dignitaries, accompanied by a huge gathering of monks, priests, and laymen, begged Peter to accept the papacy. Though he did not wish to leave his simple life of prayer and solitude, Peter accepted, choosing the name Celestine V. As pope, this simple, holy, old man was beloved by the people, but before the year was out, the immense task of shepherding the Church proved too much for him. Without training or experience, especially in dealing with the various political machinations of certain cardinals, nobles,

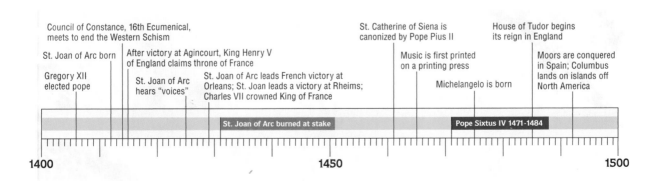

Council of Constance, 16th Ecumenical,
meets to end the Western Schism

St. Catherine of Siena is
canonized by Pope Pius II

House of Tudor begins
its reign in England

St. Joan of Arc born

After victory at Agincourt, King Henry V
of England claims throne of France

Music is first printed
on a printing press

Moors are conquered
in Spain; Columbus
lands on islands off
North America

Gregory XII
elected pope

St. Joan of Arc
hears "voices"

St. Joan of Arc leads French victory at
Orleans; St. Joan leads a victory at Rheims;
Charles VII crowned King of France

Michelangelo is born

St. Joan of Arc burned at stake

Pope Sixtus IV 1471-1484

1400   1450   1500

and emperors, the task of directing all of Christendom was humanly overwhelming and certainly beyond this hermit's abilities. After making many imprudent and ill-informed political decisions, he, without precedent and in the face of much opposition, chose to resign his office and return to his private life of prayer and penance. Most of his decisions and official acts not affecting Faith and morals were annulled by the succeeding pope, Boniface VIII (Benedetto Gaetani). While pope, St. Celestine split the College of Cardinals, appointing twelve new cardinals in his short, five month pontificate—seven of them French, the rest, Neapolitan.

Free of the burden of the papacy, St. Celestine sought to return to his beloved eremitic life. Boniface VIII feared that the previous pope might be used by certain oppositional groups who wished to advance schism in the Church. The new pope attempted to apprehend St. Celestine in order to keep him in confinement. St. Celestine avoided capture for some time, but was eventually imprisoned quite uncomfortably for the remaining ten months of his life. While prudence dictated to Boniface VIII to protect St. Celestine, and with him the integrity of the Church, the unfortunate treatment of this simple, saintly man remains a regrettable chapter in Boniface's pontificate.

BONIFACE VIII AND PHILIP IV

Pope Boniface VIII (1294-1303) was in certain ways like a Renaissance pope. He was a patron of artists, Giotto in particular, and of sculptors; he founded the University of Rome; he reorganized the Vatican archives and had the Vatican library catalogued.

Though a courageous man of action, with political experience and knowledge of the current situation of the Church, Boniface VIII also lacked the necessary diplomacy required to deal with the difficult and changing political landscape. Before Pope St. Celestine V, his predecessors had used the office of the papacy to direct the actions of kings and emperors, bending them to the will of the Church. In the same way, Pope Boniface tried to force the lords and princes of the Christian kingdoms to accept his temporal authority. He issued a number of decrees and attempted to over-awe the princes of Europe with excessive displays of pomp and pageantry—always with little success. When Pope Boniface instituted the first jubilee year for the forgiveness of sins in 1300, he marched in the opening procession holding two swords: one representing his spiritual authority, the other his temporal authority. Tension would soon mount between pope and king over the temporal authority of the Church, and Pope Boniface VIII found that wielding these two swords would be nearly impossible in the changing European political climate.

The grandson of the late King St. Louis IX of France shared none of his predecessor's saintly admiration for the Church. Philip, called the Fair, assumed the throne in 1285, and, intent on extending the boundaries of France, he undertook a series of wars, particularly against England. These wars depleted Philip's funds, and he turned to Church lands to supplement his royal treasury. Except in times of a crusade, the Church had always been exempt from the taxation policies of the royal government, but the king ignored this precedent, collecting revenue from Church estates and confiscating properties to suit his desires.

In 1296, to chastise Philip, Boniface wrote *Clericis laicos* in which he asserted that kings did not have the right to tax clergy without the permission of the pope. Philip responded by cutting off all French shipments of gold, silver, and jewels to Italy. The loss of Church revenue from this action forced Boniface to compromise on this issue.

Philip the Fair was King of France from 1285 until his death in 1314.

In 1301, a more serious dispute broke out between Philip and Pope Boniface. Philip, in order to assert his authority over the Church in France, arrested Pope Boniface's papal legate on a series of secular charges. Pope Boniface condemned Philip's actions and ordered the prelate released. In the letter *Unam Sanctam*, Boniface declared that in order to save his or her soul, every human being—including the king—must be subject to the pope. Philip responded by calling his own national council, the Estates General, to condemn and depose the pope. Boniface was falsely charged with a ridiculous list of crimes ranging from idolatry and magic, to the death of Pope St. Celestine V and the loss of the Holy Land. In 1303 with some six hundred men, William of Nogaret, advisor to King Philip, and Sciarra Colonna, head of a powerful Roman family, marched through Italy to the small town of Anagni. There they stormed the papal palace to find Boniface dressed in full papal regalia, waiting calmly and righteously, resolute in the authority and integrity of his exalted position as the Vicar of Christ. He was captured, slapped, and held prisoner at Anagni for three days. Though he was soon released, the affair and the abuse he suffered during his short captivity ruined his health. He soon died of a raging fever.

THE AVIGNON PAPACY

In the aftermath of the death of Pope Boniface VIII, Italy fell into a state of turmoil. Rome was subjected to the semi-anarchy of the masses and powerful Italian families, and the Italian peninsula began breaking up into a series of independent city-states. Pope Boniface VIII was succeeded by Pope Bl. Benedict XI, who attempted to work out some sort of peace with King Philip. The king clamored for the formal condemnation of Boniface VIII, but Pope Bl. Benedict XI resisted, taking steps to redress the scandalous events surrounding the last days of Boniface's pontificate by excommunicating William of Nogaret, Sciarra Colonna, and their accomplices. The pope's bold move was not met lightly, and within eight months of ascending the papal throne, Pope Bl. Benedict XI was found dead. Though the cause of his death is listed as acute dysentery, many suspect the cause of his death to be a fatal combination of an angry William of Nogaret and poison.

For nearly a year, the chair of St. Peter remained vacant. Under pressure from King Philip IV, the eleven-month conclave finally appointed Bertrand de Got, the Archbishop of Bordeaux and personal friend of the French king, who took the name Clement V. In order to avoid the political chaos of Rome, Clement chose to establish his papal court elsewhere, eventually settling in the town of Avignon (at that time beholden to Naples), near the French border. In Avignon, the pope surrounded himself with French cardinals, a move that exposed Pope Clement, and the Church, to the pressures and whims of the French crown. A far cry from Pope Boniface VIII's exposé of symbolic temporal power, Pope Clement V never left French soil, and for the next 70 years (1305-1377), the popes (all French) would reside in Avignon under the watchful eye of the French king in what would be called "The Babylonian Captivity."

Pope Clement and King Philip were boyhood friends. The king hoped that this new pope would vindicate his recent actions by declaring Pope Boniface VIII a heretic and revoking all of Boniface's anti-regal acts. Pope Clement V refused to give in to this demand. Wishing to placate the powerful French king, nonetheless, Pope Clement allowed the inquisition in France to investigate the military order of the Knights Templar; this affair would end in a terrible disaster. The inquisition spun away from papal control as Clement was too weak and indecisive to keep it under his charge. Though accused of heresy and worldliness, the Templars' real "crime" was possessing property and wealth coveted by the king. Those knights captured by King Philip were brutally tortured until they admitted to all of the various crimes with which they were falsely charged. Many knights were eventually burned as heretics, and when the order was permanently dissolved, King Philip seized half of their possessions.

The Church at Avignon tried to stem the threats posed by the rising tide of secular governments by strengthening its own administrative system. Though not completely under the influence of the French king, the papacy at Avignon seemed to have lost its independent position in Christendom. The Medieval popes had fought German Imperial designs on Italy to secure the independence of the Church, but by staying at Avignon, they lost this same independence to the French King. The growth of nationalism at this time made it imperative that the pope remain above particular national interests. Since this was not the case with the Avignon popes, the prestige and authority of the papacy quickly declined. England and Germany began to view the pope more as a puppet of the French king than the supreme pastor of the universal Church.

King Philip IV and his children. Three of Philip's sons became kings of France: Louis X, Philip V and Charles IV. His daughter Isabella became Queen Consort of England.

To make matters more difficult for the popes, the idea that the kings' power extended into ecclesiastical affairs favored the nationalization of the Church in each European kingdom. This phenomenon became especially more widespread as the papacy took up residence at Avignon. Gallicanism (the idea that the French Roman Catholic clergy favored the restriction of papal control and the achievement by each nation of individual autonomy) has its origins in this period of history, emerging in France when King Philip IV called for his Estates General to move against Pope Boniface VIII. English laws of 1351-1393 helped to establish the foundations for an Anglican Church years before the Reformation and King Henry VIII. The German Emperor Louis IV of Bavaria, fearing French influence over the pope at Avignon, harbored a large number of anti-papal agitators at his court, including the Englishman William of Ockham who strongly supported the democratization of Church government. Pope Clement V only exacerbated the situation when, in order to please King Philip IV, he retracted Pope Boniface VIII's *Clericis laicos* and reinterpreted *Unam Sanctam*, stripping the document of any claims to temporal authority.

In 1324, the most damaging attack from the proponents of Gallicanism came from a former rector of the University of Paris by the name of Marsiglio of Padua. In the book *Defensor Pacis* (Defender of Peace), Marsiglio made the first clear assertion of the supremacy of secular rulers over the Church. He declared that the faithful were the true authority of the Church. This book held that the pope derived his authority not from Christ, but from the General Council, a body made up of clergymen and laymen and directed by the state. It further maintained that the emperor, as the representative of the people, had the right to depose and punish Church officials and dispose of ecclesiastical property as he saw fit.

As long as the pope remained in Avignon, the independence of the papacy was severely compromised. Writers such as William of Ockham and Marsiglio of Padua paved the way for anti-clerical attacks on the authority of the pope and sowed the seeds of religious rebellion. As if the situation was not grim enough, in the midst of these troubles came a series of events that would by themselves shake the very foundation of Medieval society.

PART II
The Black Plague

T he thirteenth century brought Medieval society to its peak of prosperity. The structures of feudalism had produced a growing population and strong economic expansion. In principle, the lord held his property from the king; the knight held his manor from his lord; the small landlord from the knight, and the local peasant from the small landlord. It could be said that everything ultimately belonged to someone else. By the beginning of the fourteenth century, cracks in this system were becoming evident. As prosperity brought in surplus goods, money began to replace the service of labor. An agricultural boom brought a higher standard of living and a greater life expectancy, and maintenance of the large, growing population required continued good harvests. However, with no other source of food, harvest failures would result in widespread starvation and susceptibility to contagious diseases.

FAMINE AND BLACK DEATH

From 1315-1317, large-scale famines struck Europe for the first time in two hundred years. By 1300, the population had grown so quickly that only the cultivation of marginal lands could feed the ever-growing populace. A series of bad harvests and cool, wet weather made lands virtually unusable and widespread famine broke out. Peasants resorted to eating their seed grain to feed their families, trade declined, business fell, and there was widespread economic depression. The Hundred Years War greatly contributed to this economic and social dislocation, forcing peasants from the countryside into the perceived safety of overcrowded and unsanitary walled cities. By the middle of the fourteenth century, large sectors of the population had grown very susceptible to contagious disease.

The Black Death tore into the weakened population of Europe from 1347-1351. (Subsequent epidemics would occur regularly every ten years until the eighteenth century.) The Black Death would be the greatest demographic catastrophe to hit Western Europe. Since immunity could not be transmitted from one generation to the next, the plague acted as a continuous check on population growth. It is estimated that during these years, approximately twenty-five million people—a third of the population of Europe—perished.

The Black Death first broke out in the small, Genoese Black Sea trading post of Kaffa on the Crimean Peninsula. Tartar invaders, attacking the Genoese settlement, brought the disease from Asia. It is reported that the Tartars helped spread the disease by casting plague-ridden corpses into the Genoese settlement after they were forced to abandon the siege. Genoese sailors, returning from their settlements, brought the plague with them back to Italy.

The Black Death, also known as the bubonic plague, actually took three different forms. Bubonic plague is characterized by a swellings of the lymph glands to nearly the size of eggs in the groin, neck, and armpit areas. Black patches would appear all over the body as blood pooled below the surface of the skin, thus the name "Black Death." The common carrier of plague bacteria was small black rats, which were quite common throughout Europe, infesting unsanitary villages and towns. Plague was passed from rat to rat by fleas. The rats carried the fleas throughout Europe, and the fleas eventually spread the plague to humans. Bubonic plague was extremely lethal with a death rate of over fifty percent. Still, this was not the most common, nor the deadliest form of the plague, which became pandemic when it took on its pneumonic form. Even more deadly (a ninety-five percent mortality rate), the pneumonic form of plague spread directly from person to person without blood transmission through flea bites. Coughs, sneezes, and the sputum of the plague victim spread the bacilli far and wide to any bystander who inhaled them. This form of plague spread rapidly in the overcrowded cities of Medieval Europe. The third, least common form, septicemic, infected the blood. With a more than ninety-five percent mortality rate, this form of plague killed its victims rapidly, before any evident symptoms could develop. Whatever its form, the Black Death killed more people than any war had ever done. The highest percentage of the population was struck with plague between 1347 and 1351, and recurrent waves of plague would continue to decimate those who survived the first spate.

It is not hard to understand the devastating impact that such a pandemic can have on a society. Since the cause of the plague was unknown at the time, proper treatment and prevention was unavailable. Remote regions remained untouched while huge segments of concentrated, urban population were being decimated. The plague knew no cultural, social, racial, or political boundaries—rich and poor, learned and common, priest and layman, everyone was vulnerable to the plague.

The plague laid waste to the political, intellectual, and economic leadership of Europe. Sometimes entire towns or monasteries would be destroyed by plague. Interpersonal relationships were tested—mothers would flee from their children and husbands from their wives to avoid contamination. Priests and bishops, who aided plague victims, died in great numbers. The situation became so bad that many people could not receive the last rites because there was no priest to administer them. The huge numbers of infected corpses also posed a huge sanitation problem. At one point, the pope consecrated the river Rhone at Avignon, so that corpses flung into the river might be considered to have received Christian burial.

Besides suffering the plague along with every one else, Jews were accused of poisoning wells and causing the plague. Popular outrage against Jews became so fierce that Pope Clement VI issued two Bulls declaring Jews innocent in order to stem mob violence.

Petrarch, an author and historian living in Avignon during the outbreak of the plague, wrote vivid descriptions of what occurred. He wrote that future generations would be incredulous and be unable to imagine the empty houses and the abandoned towns. They would not believe the fields littered with dead and the dreadful silence that hung over the entire world (cf. *Epistolo Metrica I,* 14). Indeed, the sights and sounds of Europe were as bleak and black as the disease that caused them.

BOCCACCIO AND THE PLAGUE

Giovanni Boccaccio (cf. chapter twelve) was a fourteenth century poet who survived the plague and lived to write about it. Boccaccio's vivid descriptions provide a deep appreciation of the horror and devastation experienced by Europe.

It was the common practice of most of the neighbors, moved no less by fear of contamination by the putrefying bodies than by charity towards the deceased, to drag the corpses out of the houses with their own hands, aided, perhaps, by a porter, if a porter was to be had, and to lay them in front of the doors, where any one who made the round might have seen, especially in the morning, more of them than he could count; afterwards they would have biers brought up or in default, planks, whereon they laid them. Nor was it once or twice only that one and the same bier carried two or three corpses at once; but quite a considerable number of such cases occurred, one bier sufficing for husband and wife, two or three brothers, father and son, and so forth. And times without number it happened, that as two priests, bearing the cross, were on their way to perform the last office for some one, three or four biers were brought up by the porters in rear of

them, so that, whereas the priests supposed that they had but one corpse to bury, they discovered that there were six or eight, or sometimes more. Nor, for all their number, were their obsequies honored by either tears or lights or crowds of mourners rather, it was come to this, that a dead man was then of no more account than a dead goat would be to-day. (Rigg, trans., *The Decameron*, 1921, vol. 1, p. 11)

Giovanni Boccaccio (1313-1375) was an Italian author and poet. He was the greatest of Petrarch's disciples and an important Renaissance humanist. Boccaccio authored a number of notable works including *On Famous Women* and *The Decameron*.

THE SPREAD OF THE BLACK DEATH IN EUROPE, 1347-1352

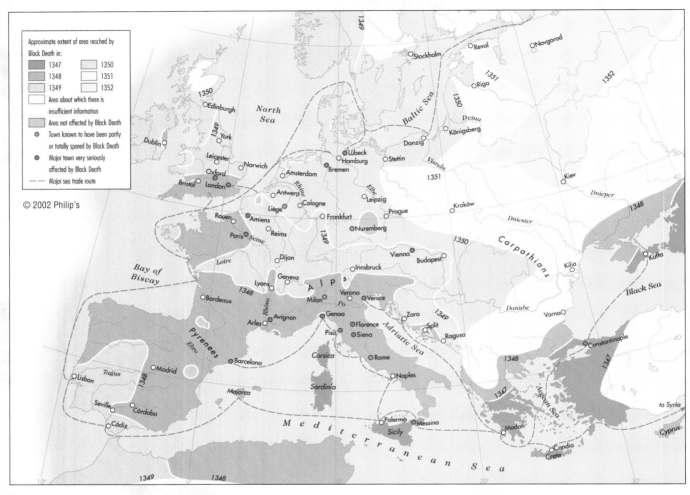

Petrarch wrote that future generations would be incredulous at the toll taken by the Black Death and be unable to imagine the empty houses and the abandoned towns.

THE WESTERN CHURCH SCHISM, 1309-1417

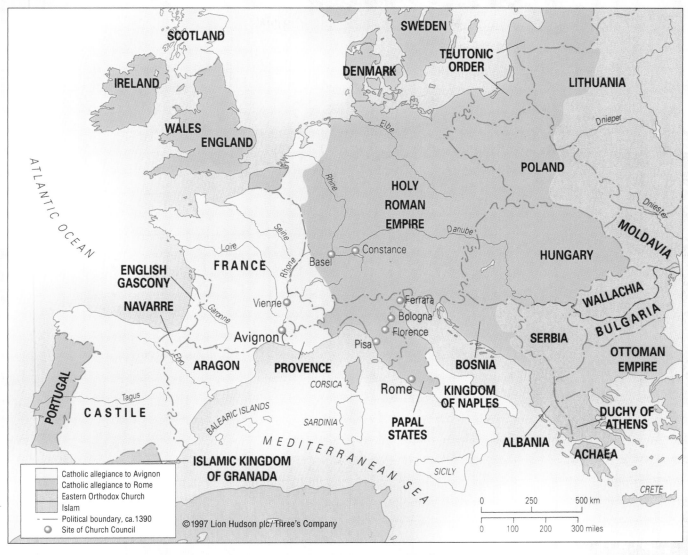

Catholic allegiance to Avignon
Catholic allegiance to Rome
Eastern Orthodox Church
Islam
- - - Political boundary, ca.1390
◯ Site of Church Council

©1997 Lion Hudson plc/Three's Company

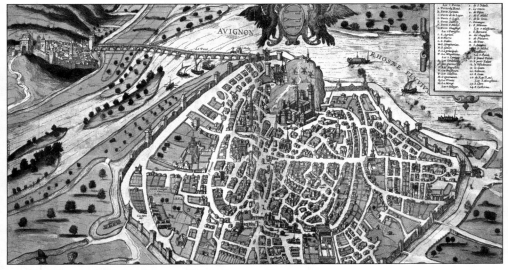

An antique map of Avignon shows the *Palais des Papes*, the Rhone river and the Saint Bénezet bridge (with its original 22 arches of which only 4 remain) and the surrounding city.

The lofty gothic palace, walls 17-18 feet thick, was a cross between a monastery and a fortress. It was built on a natural spur of rock by Pope Benedict XII and enlarged by Clement VI to match the grandeur and opulence of the French court.

PART III

The Hundred Years War (1337-1453)

Another major crisis struck Medieval Europe while the popes took up residence in Avignon. For much of the Middle Ages, the Church had managed to prevent and avoid major confrontations between the various kings of Christendom through what was known as the Peace and Truce of God. According to this principle, European kings recognized a common unity of Faith, keeping peace between European peoples who otherwise did not share nationality or custom. Those religious bonds were no longer held sacred, and the problems of inheritance and conflicting economic interest that arose out of the feudal system put many kings at odds against each other. Ultimately, the conflict that arose between England and France during the fourteenth century would change the nature of knightly warfare and transform not only the kingdoms of England and France, but also the entire political makeup of Europe. Out of the ashes of more than one hundred years of warring rose a new sense of national identity—the first steps towards the formation of the European nation-states.

THE ENGLISH IN FRANCE

Since the time of William the Conqueror in the eleventh century, the English and French thrones were linked through a number of matrimonial alliances. Through those marriages, England had inherited large portions of French land. The largest portion came from Henry II's marriage to Eleanor of Aquitaine, through which the king acquired the huge Duchy of Aquitaine in southwestern France. Although officially Henry held this land as a vassal of the French king, the English kings never really considered their possessions subject to the foreign ruler. Hostile to the foreign occupiers, the French kings long aspired to drive the English from their feudal estates in France.

Relations between England and France were further agitated by France's continued support of the rebellious nobles of Scotland and encouragement of piracy on the English Channel, England's chief trade route with Europe. On the continent, disputes over the Flanders region (modern day Belgium) also put the two countries at odds. The feudal lords of Flanders had been French vassals, and France had long sought to regain control of this region, which was a very wealthy and important trading center for both France and England. King Edward III of England enraged the French monarchy when, in the interest of retaining trade between England and Flemish textile manufacturers, he proclaimed Flanders under the protection of the English crown. English wool was vital to the Flemish textile trade, and Edward used this economic necessity to sway Flemish loyalty away from the French.

All these hostilities exploded when the French king Charles IV (Charles the Fair), the last son of the French king Philip IV, died without an heir in 1328. The Capetian line was broken and no one was left with a clear claim on the throne of France. Both King Philip IV's nephew (the grandson of King Philip III) and King Edward II of England (whose mother was the sister of King Charles IV of France) claimed the right of succession. This dispute began the long series of armed conflicts between England and France, known as the Hundred Years War.

THE BATTLE OF CASTILLON

The Hundred Years War was significant in military history because of its technological and tactical advancements. Most notably, during the closing years of the war, gunpowder weaponry was used effectively for the first time in European warfare. By the final conflict of the war, the Battle of Castillon in 1453, gunpowder had offered a deadly advantage.

At the Battle of Castillon, the French army laid siege to the small town located east of Bordeaux. The English force, commanded by John Talbot, marched from Bordeaux to meet the French and fight off the siege. The English first engaged an outpost of French archers encamped some distance from the main French camp, and then rested for the night. The next morning, Talbot led his army against the main French camp. Ignorant of what he was marching into, Talbot led the English directly into a line of French gunners. The French, possessing more muskets and canons than was expected at that time, tore apart the English army, killing Talbot and soundly defeating the English.

THE HUNDRED YEARS WAR

The Hundred Years War was in fact a series of short battles interrupted by long periods of relative peace. The English gained the upper hand early in the conflict. Though outnumbered, English forces destroyed the French knights at Crecy in 1346, thanks in part to the introduction of the long bow. This new weapon could shoot a yard-long arrow as far as 400 yards at the rate of five to six arrows a minute. It was one of the many deadly military innovations that would change the style of combat during the Hundred Years War.

The English defeated the French at Crecy in 1346 with the help of the deadly long bow which could shoot an arrow 400 yards.

Shortly after Crecy, plague broke out in France. Ten years of war forced many peasants into the safe confines of walled cities where the plague spread rapidly. Conditions in France were dreadful, and the coming years saw no changes.

In 1356, King Edward III's eldest son Edward (the Black Prince) led an English offensive at Poitiers. Both sides exhausted each other through a long battle of attrition, and eventually a truce was signed. However, peace lasted only four years before war broke out again in 1360. Learning from Crecy and Poitiers, the French knights avoided meeting the English in full-scale battles; instead, they skirmished with the English, scattering the troops. This style of warfare proved slow and deadly, never allowing either side to gain a clear upper hand. Twenty years of grueling fighting passed.

By 1380 both King Edward III and the Black Prince were dead, and England held only the coastal towns of Bordeaux, Bayonne, and Calais. England was on her heels, and an end to the war was in sight. But a civil war between the major noble houses of France broke out, helping to prolong the military conflict. The new French king, Charles VI, took the throne at the age of twelve, and besides being too young to rule in his own right, he was exceedingly mad. (Among his many fits and eccentricities, he believed himself to be made of glass and about to break.) The Dukes of Burgundy and Orléans took advantage of Charles' handicap and fought for control of France. The infighting left France vulnerable to an invasion, and England's King Henry V did not miss his opportunity.

King Henry V destroyed the elite of the French aristocracy and overwhelmed the king of France at Agincourt in 1415. The aftermath of Henry's victory at Agincourt demonstrated the failing legacy of the Medieval feudal system. French cavalry butchered young pages waiting at the wagons off the field of battle and French prisoners were executed rather than ransomed, as was the custom. Henry V claimed the throne of France and married the French king's daughter, Catherine. Henry only ruled for two years before his death, after which he left his infant son Henry VI on the throne.

A succession of young, incompetent, and partially mad kings left France demoralized and subject to the English crown. As the Hundred Years War dragged on, the future of France looked bleak. The ominous fate of the kingdom was radically changed by the appearance of a young peasant girl named Joan.

ST. JOAN OF ARC

St. Joan was born at Domremy in Champagne, probably on January 6, 1412. At the age of 13, she began to hear voices and had a vision of light in which St. Michael the Archangel, St. Margaret, and St. Catherine of Alexandria appeared to her. These guiding councilors elected her as liberator of France and, in particular, the city of Orléans. St. Joan was instructed by the saints to inform Charles VII that she would make possible his coronation.

Dressed in men's clothes, St. Joan succeeded in convincing the king of the sincerity of her mission, and in May 1429, she led a small army against the captured city of Orléans. Under her leadership, French soldiers overwhelmed English fortifications and drove them from the city, liberating the regions of Loire, Troyes, and Châlons. During the battle, St. Joan was wounded by an arrow, but desired to move on to Rheims. Rheims was finally captured in July 1429, and there Charles was formally crowned king Charles VII.

With the crowning of King Charles VII, St. Joan's principal aim was complete, and after a failed attack on Paris, she did not lead any assaults until the following year. During the winter, Charles and his advisors grew increasingly apathetic to her mission. The following May, St. Joan led a small army of five hundred soldiers against a far stronger force. During the attack she was captured by the English.

Charles did not attempt to bargain for St. Joan's life, and with no support from the French, St. Joan was put on trial for heresy and witchcraft by Pierre Cauchon, the Bishop of Beauvais. The Bishop was an unscrupulous, ambitious man and a puppet of the English rulers in Burgundy. St. Joan was convicted of heresy, largely because she was allowed no defense of her supernatural premonitions. Before leading her first strike with French forces, King Charles had St. Joan examined by a number of doctors and bishops. They found nothing sick or heretical in St. Joan's message, but neither those officials nor their documents proving St. Joan's innocence were allowed to be used in St. Joan's defense during her English trial. St. Joan was burned at the stake on May 30, 1431.

Twenty-five years later, in 1456, the sentence was lifted after a re-examination by Pope Callistus III. St. Joan was eventually beatified in 1909 and canonized by Pope Benedict XV in 1920.

Through the services of St. Joan of Arc, the tide of battle turned against the English. Although St. Joan was captured and killed, her efforts enabled the French army to begin a counter-offensive against the English. Now fighting a divided enemy, the French retook Paris in 1436. One by one, English posts fell rapidly, and by 1453 the English only controlled Calais. The memory of St. Joan was vindicated, and popular devotion to her grew. The people of France rallied around St. Joan of Arc, and by the end of the Hundred Years War, St. Joan became a symbol of French unity and national spirit.

ST. JOAN OF ARC'S IMPOSSIBLE MISSION

This tapestry depicts the meeting of St. Joan of Arc and King Charles VII at Chinon in March 1429.

God made it clear to St. Joan that she was to lead an army against the English. Despite the certainty of God's will for her life, her mission was no easy task. Nevertheless, through St. Joan's strong faith and committed persistence, God enabled her to carry out this nearly impossible mission.

The first obstacle to St. Joan's mission was the king. Securing an audience with the French monarch was difficult enough, let alone persuading him to let a poor peasant girl lead one of the French armies in battle. Initially, she could not get into the king's court. St. Joan continued to hear mystical voices that instructed her on how to proceed. In May 1428, these voices told her to seek out Robert Baudricourt, a commander of the king's army in the nearby town of Vaucouleurs.

Accompanied by her cousin, St. Joan traveled to Vaucouleurs and spoke with Baudricourt about her instructions to lead an army. The commander remained skeptical, to the say the least, and rather then helping St. Joan, he told St. Joan's cousin to bring the girl home and have her whipped. Despite Baudricourt's indignation, the voices persisted in urging St. Joan to seek the commander's help. St. Joan returned to Vaucouleurs, this time with a prophetic message. Although it was too soon for anyone in Vaucouleurs to have known about a recent French defeat at the Battle of Herrings, she told Baudricourt about the details of the battle. Baudricourt, struck by St. Joan's prophetic insight, sent the young girl to see the king at Chinon in March 1429.

St. Joan finally had her chance to speak with the king, but convincing the king to allow her to lead an army still did not seem likely. St. Joan would be aided, ironically, by the king's own trickery. Seeking to test her, the king disguised an aid as king. Upon entering the court, however, St. Joan saluted the real king, who disguised himself as a simple attendant. She then revealed to the king a secret sign that the Lord disclosed to St. Joan before her arrival. While no one knows what the secret was, many believe it had to do with the king's doubts about the legitimacy of his birth. After these revelations, the king was convinced and proceeded to help St. Joan carry out her mission.

PART IV

Return to Rome and Schism

Plague and war had devastating effects on the institutions and leadership of Medieval Europe, and the continuing presence of the popes at Avignon undermined the ability of the Holy See to reform itself and restore order to Christendom. The long-awaited return of the pope to Rome finally came in 1378 during the pontificate of Gregory XI. Avignon itself was no longer safe as French and English armies fought for domination of the French mainland. Ongoing civil war in Italy, including war between Florence and the papacy (1375), made it clear to Pope Gregory XI that the Holy See needed to return to the City of St. Peter in order to recover its absent leadership. Gregory hesitated to take the fateful step. Nevertheless, the pope would receive the strength and confidence to return to Rome through the work of another extraordinary woman of the fourteenth century, the Dominican Tertiary mystic St. Catherine of Siena.

ST. CATHERINE OF SIENA

St. Catherine (1347-1380) was the youngest of twenty-five children. As a young girl, St. Catherine had a precocious understanding of her own vocation and by age seven had consecrated her virginity to Christ. St. Catherine began to receive visions and wasted no time in committing herself to God's mission for her. At sixteen years of age, she joined the Dominican Tertiaries.

For a time she lived a secluded and demanding ascetical life during which she had visions and strong mystical experiences, including conversations with Christ. In 1366, St. Catherine underwent a mystical experience common to a number of saints known as a "spiritual espousal." In this "mystical marriage," Christ tells a soul that he takes it for his bride. The apparition is accompanied by a ceremony in which the Blessed Virgin, saints, and angels are present, after which the soul receives a sudden surge of charity and an increased familiarity with God.

After her spiritual espousal and years of seclusion, St. Catherine returned to the world to dedicate herself to the service of the poor and the sick—especially those suffering from the plague.

St. Catherine underwent a mystical experience common to many saints known as the "spiritual espousal."

St. Catherine lived extreme poverty amongst the sick and constantly suffered physical pain. She went for long periods with practically no food, save Holy Communion. Despite these physical deprivations, she was radiantly happy and full of practical wisdom and spiritual insight. Even members of her own order who saw her extraordinary personal charm, despite her physical sufferings, teased and tormented her. Nonetheless, her spiritual purity and charisma drew followers, both men and women, who flocked to her, united by the bonds of mystical love. She continued to experience all types of visions, including a series of special manifestations of the Divine mysteries and a prolonged ecstasy in which she had a vision of Hell, Purgatory, and Heaven. During that vision,

St. Catherine heard God ask her to enter public life and help "heal the wounds of the Church."

St. Catherine began to send letters to men and women of every walk of life. She entered into correspondence with many princes and leaders of Italy and began imploring Pope Gregory XI to return to Rome. Upon meeting with Pope Gregory, God miraculously revealed to St. Catherine Gregory's secret desire to return the papacy to Rome, a personal vow he had never disclosed to any human being. "Fulfill what you have promised," she told him, and the pope knew that she was indeed sent from God (quoted in "Saint Catherine of Siena, Virgin," taken from Crawley, *Lives of the Saints,* 1954).

Amid storms and frightening intrigues, Pope Gregory XI returned to Rome on January 17, 1377, with the hope of bringing reform and peace to the Church in Italy. He sent St. Catherine to Florence hoping that she could negotiate peace between some of the Italian princes, but her efforts proved fruitless against the

Upon meeting with Pope Gregory XI, St. Catherine reminded him of a personal vow he had made to himself.

chaotic politics of the Italian city-states. She narrowly escaped an attempt on her life. St. Catherine went from Florence to Siena where she rested for some time and dictated her *Dialogue,* the book containing her meditations and revelations.

In November 1378, St. Catherine was summoned back to Rome by Pope Urban VI. In her absence, the Great Western Schism had broken out, and the pope sought St. Catherine's help. In Rome, she

In her prayers, St. Catherine asked Christ to allow her to bear the punishment for all the sins of the world and to sacrifice her body for the unity of the Church. During her intense ecstasies, St. Catherine received the wounds of Christ, the stigmata.

spent the remainder of her life working to reform the Church, serving the destitute and afflicted, and writing eloquent letters in support of Pope Urban's legitimacy. She continued to suffer immense physical pain, and in her prayers, asked Christ to allow her to bear the punishment for all the sins of the world and to sacrifice her body for the unity of the Church. She received the stigmata, but prayed that it would not show on the surface of her skin. The marks only became visible after her death.

After a prolonged and mysterious agony, which she bore with happiness for three months, St. Catherine of Siena died on the Sunday before the Ascension in 1380 at the age of thirty-three. The Stigmata was revealed, and in 1430 her body was discovered incorruptible. St. Catherine was canonized in 1461, and her relics are the object of pilgrimages and venerated to this day. Her feast day is celebrated on April 29. She is a Doctor of the Church.

ST. BRIDGET OF SWEDEN

Before St. Catherine of Siena, another mystic visionary, St. Bridget of Sweden played an important role in urging the pope to return to Rome. St. Bridget was born in 1303, and after her husband's death, she founded the Order of the Most Holy Savior, also called the Brigettines. In 1349 she traveled from her home in Sweden to Rome where she founded hospices for the poor and needy.

While St. Bridget was in Rome, Pope Bl. Urban V returned to the city from Avignon, and many hoped his stay would be permanent. However, in 1370, he returned to Avignon in order to help intervene in the ongoing negotiations that sought an end to the Hundred Years War. After the pope's departure from Rome,

St. Bridget received a message from Mary. Unless the pope returned to Rome, she said, "he will be struck such a blow...that his teeth will shake in his mouth. His sight will be darkened and all his limbs will tremble." St. Bridget sent word to Bl. Urban, warning him of the message and telling him to return to Rome. The pope, however, did not comply. When Pope Bl. Urban reached Avignon, he was stricken with an illness and died within the year. The prophecy was fulfilled.

Soon after Gregory XI was elected the next pope, St. Bridget received another vision. This time Mary clearly told her that "it is the will of God that [the pope] humbly bring back the Chair of St. Peter to Rome." St. Bridget told the pope of this command, but he remained hesitant to return. Finally, in 1373, St. Bridget sent her last letter to Gregory XI in which she warned him sternly. "You must go to Rome as quickly as you can," she wrote, "the sooner you come the more will the virtues and gifts of the Holy Spirit inflame your soul." St. Bridget died that same year, but St. Catherine continued her efforts to bring the pope back to the Eternal City, and in 1377, Pope Gregory XI finally left Avignon and restored the papacy to Rome.

This miniature depicts St. Bridget witnessing the Transubstantiation of the Eucharist bread and wine into the body and blood of Christ. The saint is seated at her writing desk. In front of her the Eucharist is being celebrated. Her head is lit by a divine ray which descends from an open heaven in which the angels and saints have gathered. The Virgin and Christ impart the rays which reveal the miracle of the Eucharist. Only Bridget is able to see the body of Christ rising from the wafer.

THE WESTERN SCHISM

The jubilation over the pope's return to Rome did not last after the death of Pope Gregory XI. After seventy years of French domination, the people of Italy desired an Italian pope. A mob of Romans, tired of the Avignon papacy, had invaded the conclave, violently demanding an Italian pope. The cardinals elected the Italian archbishop of Bari, Bartolomeo Prignano, who chose the name Urban VI. After the crowd had calmed, these same cardinals confirmed their choice, gave a sign of obedience to Urban, sent letters throughout Christendom announcing the election of the new pope. They reported to their colleagues at Avignon that they had voted "freely and unanimously."

The Avignon cardinals had thought they had found a docile and malleable candidate for the papacy, but Urban VI turned out to be an inflexible and aggressive reformer. Urban clearly stated that there would be no return to Avignon; he declared war on every moral abuse, harshly criticizing the materialistic lifestyle of the worldly cardinals. His overzealous and violent character soured the previously favorable opinions of many of his electors. Even St. Catherine, who supported the new pope for the remainder of her life, attempted to intervene. She pleaded with Urban: "For the love of Christ, moderate a little the violent actions to which your nature drives you!" (St. Catherine, *Letter to Urban VI,* January 29, 1380). Six months after his election, the French cardinals returned to Avignon and declared that they had invalidly elected Urban out of fear and under duress. The French Cardinals then voted for the antipope Clement VII in place of Urban VI. The Western Schism, which would open gaping wounds in the Church, had begun.

Each country of Europe rallied around its own choice for pope. Western Christendom was split into two camps. Even many saints were confused as to who was the real pope. At a time when the Church needed to bring together the faithful, division and chaos became the order of the day. Bishops and abbots contested for the same benefices and monasteries. Church authorities conceded large control of ecclesiastical affairs to secular rulers to gain political support. The absence of strong papal leadership allowed new antipapal heresies, which especially included Conciliarism, Gallicanism, Wycliffeism and Hussitism (the last two of which will be discussed near the end of this chapter), to gain followers. This schism, which lasted for forty years, would result in untold confusion and a weaker Church and would pave the way for mass defections in the sixteenth century.

RESOLUTION OF THE SCHISM: COUNCIL OF CONSTANCE

By 1400, the situation of the Church seemed hopeless. The schism had lasted twenty-two years and no end was in sight; efforts to resolve the schism had failed. Many within the Church began to believe that only a general church council could solve the dilemma. This belief resulted in the Conciliar Movement and its attendant heresy, Conciliarism. Taking its authority from such works as *Defensor Pacis,* the Conciliarists tried to maintain that a Council could depose the rival claimants to the papacy and choose a compromise candidate. The first attempt to end the schism in this way occurred at Pisa, Italy, in 1409. However, neither Gregory XII, the legitimate pope, nor Benedict XIII, the antipope, would abdicate, so the Pisan Council deposed them both and chose a second antipope, Alexander V, to replace both of them. The authority of Pisa was rejected by Gregory, Benedict, and key European kings, and rather than having solved the problem, the predicament was merely compounded. There were now three claimants to the papacy.

It would take another five years to find a more lasting solution. The Holy Roman emperor Sigismund, then in the imperial city of Constance, dedicated great efforts to achieve Church unity. He forced the Pisan antipope John XXIII to call a council at Constance and to resign his position. Peace between France and England as well as the protection of Sigismund were key to the success of the Council of Constance. Pope Gregory XII sent a representative to the Council of Constance

The Council of Constance was the sixteenth Ecumenical Council. Called by Holy Roman Emperor Sigismund, the council was held from November 1414 to April 1418 in the Cathedral of Constance. Its main purpose was to end the papal schism. Antipopes John XXIII and Benedict XIII were deposed, the resignation of Pope Gregory XII was accepted, and Pope Martin V was elected in 1417. Martin V remained pope until his death in 1431. He resided in Mantua and Florence before entering Rome in 1420.

The Council also dealt with the heresies of John Wycliffe and Jan Hus.

Sigismund was Holy Roman Emperor from 1433 to 1437. He was the third and last German emperor.

(1414-1418) with the offer that he would recognize the authority of Constance and would abdicate if the Council would recognize him as pope. Benedict XIII refused to cooperate with the council, and as a result, he lost most of his support. Gregory's abdication cleared the way for the election of Pope Martin V and an end to the Western Schism.

Conciliarism would continue in the aftermath of Constance, and regular councils were held to direct the leadership of the Church. The Council of Constance had only succeeded due to the support of Pope Gregory XII, and many of the later councils failed through lack of participation or quarrels between rival groups. Finally, in 1439 at Ferrara-Florence, the pope's superiority over a general council was established. It was decided that three essential characteristics must be maintained for a council to be valid. First, it must be called by the pope; second, it must be presided over by the pope or his legate; finally, its dogmatic decrees are considered valid only if they are accepted and approved by the pope.

The authority of the papacy was shaken by its long tenure at Avignon, further still, with more than forty years of schism. The unity of Christendom had been broken, and secular rulers continued to dominate the Church within thier borders. Though the pope had weathered a great wave of Conciliarism, the heresy continued to plague much of Europe. At the same time, new threat to the security of Europe had arrived: the Turks. The Turkish advance in the East would do much to change the relations of Church and State in the fifteenth century.

PART V

Decline of Scholastic Philosophy and Theology and the Rise of Heresy

As the disasters of the fourteenth century unfolded, the social stability of the Medieval Period began to break down. Plague, war, and Church divisions created a moral instability that affected all elements of society. There were major swings between religious idealism and brutal, skeptical realism.

Many who were disenchanted with the Church hierarchy became more introverted in their faith and increasingly anti-clerical. Some swung to religious extremes, joining groups such as the Flagellants, who thought they could escape divine punishment by scourging themselves. Others sought support through superstition and personal mystical experiences. Still others lost their faith completely and turned to Satanic cults and witchcraft, or to orgies of gluttonous sensuality.

Economic breakdown followed war and pestilence. The Black Death helped destroy the traditional relationship between lord and peasant. The century following 1350 was a time of extraordinary mobility. Peasants could leave their manor seeking out better land and better opportunity, and laborers could demand higher wages in a labor-strapped market. In 1351, the English aristocracy attempted to freeze wages and limit peasant mobility by passing the *Statute of Laborers*. In 1381, to recover their loss of revenue, the English nobility passed a head tax which resulted in the Watt Tyler rebellion. In France, during the Hundred Years War, French peasants rebelled against a tax they had to pay their lords. This rebellion, called *the Jacquerie* (Jacques being a common name of a French peasant), ravaged the countryside with war as peasants attacked castles and towns out of desperation.

WILLIAM OF OCKHAM

Intellectual life of the fourteenth century was undergoing subtle changes. Scholastic theology and its handmaiden, philosophy, which had reached their pinnacle in the works of St. Thomas Aquinas and Bl. John Duns Scotus, were now in decline. Scholasticism became increasingly technical, to the point of quibbling over insignificancies, and it had lost the rich content and understanding of purpose it once held. Challenges to Scholastic thought arose, and a new debate began over the relationship of reason to revelation. The Franciscan friar William of Ockham was one of the early critics of the old Scholastic tradition. He attempted to "simplify" the excessive formalism of the Scholastic method by separating what he claimed could truly be known by reason and what must be accepted only on faith. Ockham was an intensely religious individual, but he made the mistake of confusing philosophy and theology. His guiding philosophical principle was a theological tenet: "I believe in God, the Father Almighty."

With this statement of faith as his philosophical foundation, Ockham concluded that God, if he is almighty, must be the only and direct reason why things are true or false. Ockham's "nominalism" taught that the human mind can only know individual, sensible objects, such as "this textbook right here." Universal concepts (such as "what it means to be a textbook in general") are not concepts but merely general names — in Latin, *nomina.* Only God guarantees that knowledge of particular things consistently correspond to the *nomina,* which people have falsely assumed to be self-generated concepts. From this way of thinking, it follows that moral and religious truths are inaccessible through mere human reason, and can only be known through revelation. This is problematic since actions can no longer be said to be good or bad by nature. Instead, it is only because God determines an action to be good or bad that it is morally right or wrong. Religion, he argued, is a mystery of faith with no room for philosophical discourse. Ockham's philosophy is one of the roots of the skeptical crisis in metaphysics that finally erupted in the seventeenth century with René Descartes and has continued for hundreds of years in modern philosophy.

Ockham was an early critic of Church authority and, with his companion Marsiglio of Padua, advocated the supreme authority of the state. Since the Church deals with mysteries of Faith and the state works with empirical and therefore sure facts, according to Ockham, the Church should be subordinate to the authority of the state. As the unity of Christendom faded and nationalistic movements spread, similar heretical ideas began to appear throughout Europe. Writers such as the Englishman John Wycliffe and the Bohemian Jan Hus began to attack the authority of the Holy See and traditional beliefs of the Catholic Church.

JOHN WYCLIFFE

John Wycliffe's popularity in England arose in conjunction with some of the difficulties posed by the Hundred Years War. The Avignon popes were seen as allies of the enemies of England, and the need for new revenues directed the English crown's attention to the wealth of Church lands. John Wycliffe, a professor at the University of Oxford, had long been a critic of the temporal practices and material possessions of the Church. He had advocated that the Church should rid itself of all political power and practice strict poverty. "Dominion is founded in grace" he claimed, believing that no monks or clergy, not even the righteous, could hold temporal possessions without sin. Through this principle he advocated that it was lawful for the king to seize Church lands.

Wycliffe was one of the first pre-Protestant thinkers. In addition to attacking the authority of the pope, he rejected Scholastic theology and claimed that religious knowledge was derived from the Bible only, and not from Tradition. He advocated predestination and concluded that the Church did not need the clergy or the Sacraments. Together with the renunciation of the priesthood, he attacked the validity of indulgences, and denied man's free will, claiming that man was completely subjected to the will of God. Like many critics of the twelfth and thirteenth centuries, Wycliffe began with an attack on clerical wealth; but he then went on to dispute the authority of the Church and, finally, he attacked its sacramental system.

Popular support among the upper classes for Wycliffe's ideas began to wane after the Peasants' Revolt of 1381. Many nobles feared that Wycliffe's attack on the authority of the Church would find a parallel in the relationship between the peasants and the aristocracy or king. The Lollards, those who embraced Wycliffe's ideas in the late fourteenth and fifteenth centuries, helped pave the way for Protestantism in England during the sixteenth century.

JAN HUS

Wycliffe's ideas had even more popularity in the kingdom of Bohemia. The Czechs were dominated by the Holy Roman Empire, and they found in Wycliffe's anti-clerical principles a vehicle through which to separate themselves from their German overlords. As nationalism grew in Bohemia, the population tended towards heresy. Jan Hus, rector of the University of Prague, adopted many of Wycliffe's ideas in his attempts to reform the Church in Bohemia. The ecclesiastical authorities of Bohemia owned about half the land, and the peasantry resented the heavy tax burden and corruption among the established clergy. At first, Hus was supported by the king and the clergy as a reformer, but he lost that support as he moved from reform into heresy.

This monument to Jan Hus stands in the city of Prague, Czechoslovakia.

Like Wycliffe, Hus attacked the abuses of the clergy and the authority of the Church. He proclaimed the supremacy of private judgment over Church pronouncements and advocated the free interpretation of the Bible. He denied the authority of tradition, attacked the veneration of relics and rejected the existence of Purgatory. While rejecting many of the Sacraments, he advocated Communion under both species, but denied Transubstantiation. He was the spiritual precursor to Martin Luther, arguing that Faith alone, apart from good works, is the means of salvation.

Holy Roman Emperor Sigismund had pushed the Council of Constance to resolve the crisis of the Western Schism. Hus, being excommunicated, was granted a pass of safe conduct by Sigismund to plead his case in Constance. There Hus was imprisoned and brought to trial for heresy. The council was not anxious to execute Hus, and they encouraged him to admit his errors and recant. With full knowledge of the consequences, Hus refused to accept the judgment of the Council and was tragically burned at the stake on July 6, 1415. National strife continued in Bohemia after the death of Hus, who came to be revered as a martyr for the Czech national cause. Churches were burned and priests killed during the Husite wars, and the conflict would not be resolved until the Thirty Years War of the seventeenth century.

CONCLUSION

The tragedies of the fourteenth century make a powerful case for the need of an authentic papacy as an indispensable means of unity and spiritual and moral health in the Church. Without the clear supernatural leadership of the pope, the people of God become like sheep without a shepherd. A firmly established papacy devoid of temporal concerns would likely have effected a different outcome of this sad chapter in the history of the Church's history. The ultimate consequence to this papal crisis was the defection of millions to the Protestant cause in the sixteenth century. Still, as the fourteenth century — along with the Middle Ages — ended, the fifteenth century ushered a new era into the Western world. The Church and Europe were in the midst of great transition with the emergence of new ideas, the growth of powerful new nation-states, and the discovery of a new world. It was an explosive time of great intellectual, scientific, and artistic achievement. The new learning and intellectual framework confronted the Church with new challenges, but it also opened the door for wonderful, much needed growth. It was the time of the Renaissance.

SUPPLEMENTARY READING

From a letter by Petrarch to his brother about the Plague

Alas! My beloved brother, what shall I say? How shall I begin? Whither shall I turn? On all sides is sorrow, everywhere is fear. Would, my brother, that I had never been born, or, at least, had died before these times. How will posterity believe that there has been a time when, without the lightnings of heaven or the fires of earth, without wars or other visible slaughter, not this or that part of the earth, but well nigh the whole globe, has remained without inhabitants.

When has any such thing ever been heard or seen? In what annals has it ever been read that houses were left vacant, cities deserted, the countryside neglected, the fields too small for the dead, and a fearful and universal solitude spread over the whole earth? Consult your historians, they are silent; question your doctors, they are dumb; seek an answer from your philosophers, they shrug their shoulders and frown, and with their fingers on their lips bid you to be silent.

Will posterity ever believe these things when we, who see, can scarcely credit them? We should think we were dreaming if we did not see with our eyes, when walking abroad, the city in mourning with funerals, and returning to our home, find it empty, and thus know that what we lament is real.

Oh, happy people of the future, who have not known these miseries and perchance will class our testimony with the fables. We have, indeed, deserved these and even greater punishments; but our forefathers also have deserved them, and may our posterity also not merit the same.

Boniface VIII, *Unam Sanctam*, November 18, 1302, "The Doctrine of the Two Swords"

There being one faith and one Baptism, and the Church constituting but one body, there can necessarily be but one head. The invisible head is Jesus Christ; the visible head, His representatives, the successors of St. Peter. Christ has established two swords or powers in the Church—the one temporal the other spiritual. The latter he has committed to the priesthood, the former to the kings; and both being in the Church, have the same end. The temporal power, being inferior, is subject to the spiritual, which is the higher and more noble, and governs the former as the soul does the body. Should the temporal power turn away from its prescribed course, it becomes the duty of the spiritual to recall it to its true duty. It is of faith that all men, even kings, are subject to the pope; for if kings were not subject to the censures of the Church whenever they sin in the exercise of the power committed to them, they would, as a consequence, be out of the Church, and the two powers would be essentially distinct, having, in that case, their origins in two different and opposite principles—an error not far removed from the heresy of the Manicheans.

John Paul II, *Ut Unum Sint*, 6

The unity of all divided humanity is the will of God. For this reason he sent his Son, so that by dying and rising for us he might bestow on us the Spirit of love. On the eve of his sacrifice on the Cross, Jesus himself prayed to the Father for his disciples and for all those who believe in him, that they *might be one*, a living communion. This is the basis not only of the duty, but also the responsibility before God and his plan, which falls to those, who through Baptism become members of the Body of Christ, a body in which the fullness of reconciliation and communion must be made present.

VOCABULARY

BABYLONIAN CAPTIVITY
The seventy years (1305-1377) the papacy spent in Avignon under the watchful eye of the French kings.

BLACK PLAGUE
Known commonly as "The Black Death," this deadly epidemic broke out in Europe around the year 1347, decimating the population. The disease took on three forms: The bubonic plague, carried by fleas which had bitten infested rats, was characterized by swelling lymph glands and black patches on the skin; the pneumonic plague spread quickly through coughing and sneezing and was more deadly than the bubonic; the septicemic plague was the deadliest form, infecting the blood stream and killing its victims the most quickly.

CLERICIS LAICOS
Written by Pope Boniface VIII to King Philip the Fair in 1296, this letter asserted that kings did not have the right to tax clergy without permission from the pope. Philip responded by cutting off all French shipments of gold, silver, and jewels to Italy. The loss of Church revenues from this action forced Boniface to back down.

CONCILIARISM
Movement which supported the power of a council to appoint a candidate for the papacy, thus placing a council's authority over that of the pope.

DEFENSOR PACIS (DEFENDER OF PEACE)
Written by Marsiglio of Padua, a former rector of the University of Paris, this book made the first clear assertion of the supremacy of secular powers over the Church. He declared that the faithful were the true authority of the Church.

GALLICANISM
The idea that the French Roman Catholic clergy favored the restriction of papal control and the achievement by each nation of individual administrative autonomy.

HUSITISM
Movement started by Jan Hus which denied the authority of tradition, the existence of Purgatory, transubstantiation, and the necessity of good works in salvation. It was especially popular in Bohemia.

JACQUERIE
Rebellion of French peasants who opposed the taxes forced upon them during the Hundred Years War. The name comes from the traditional name of a French peasant.

NOMINALISM
Put forth by William of Ockham, this theory taught that the human mind can only know individual, sensible objects, and that universal ideas, like truth, goodness, and humanity are only names—*nomina*. Only God guarantees that individual experiences properly and consistently correspond to the *nomina*, which people have falsely assumed to be self-generated concepts. From this way of thinking it follows that moral and religious truths are inaccessible through mere human reason, and can only be known through revelation.

PEACE AND TRUCE OF GOD
Principle which, for much of the Middle Ages, kept European kings at peace by recognizing a common unity in Faith between European peoples who otherwise did not share common nationalities or customs.

SPIRITUAL ESPOUSAL
These "Mystical Marriages" were experienced by a number of great saints, most notably St. Catherine of Siena. They occur when Christ takes a soul as his bride, leading it to an increase of charity and familiarity with Christ.

UNAM SANCTAM
Letter written by Pope Boniface claiming that in order to save his or her soul, every human being—including the king—must be subject to the pope. King Philip responded by calling his own national council, the Estates General, to condemn and depose the pope.

WYCLIFFEISM
Heretical movement founded by John Wycliffe which held that authority to rule depends on moral virtue; the Bible alone contains all divine revelation, preaching is more important than the sacraments or the Mass, and the pope has no primacy of jurisdiction.

STUDY QUESTIONS

1. How did Pope St. Celestine V contribute to the problems of the Avignon papacy and the Western Schism?

2. Pope Boniface VIII declared the first Jubilee Year in 1300. At the procession he carried two swords. What did they represent?

3. What did Philip the Fair want that instigated a struggle with the papacy?

4. What did *Clericis laicos* by Pope Boniface VIII state?

5. What did Pope Boniface assert in *Unam Sanctam?*

6. How did the Babylonian Captivity compromise the papacy and the Church?

7. Define Gallicanism.

8. What changed the demographic and economic outlook of the thirteenth and fourteenth centuries?

9. How many people died in Europe from the Black Death?

10. How did the Black Death affect society?

11. How did the Black Plague affect anti-Semitism?

12. How did the English king come to govern a large section of western France?

13. How did the English convince Flanders (modern day Belgium) to align itself with England and not France?

14. What were the three main battles of the Hundred Years War?

15. How did St. Joan of Arc give new hope to the French?

16. Describe St. Catherine's spirituality.

17. What is the Western Schism?

18. How did the co-existence of three "popes" prove to be a scandal to the faithful?

19. How did the Council of Constance handle the situation of three popes?

20. When was conciliarism definitively defeated?

21. Who were the Flagellants, and how did people respond to them?

22. What did the *Statute of Laborers* do?

23. What was the Watt Tyler rebellion?

24. Of what was William of Ockham critical?

25. What was John Wycliffe's profession?

26. What did Wycliffe criticize?

27. What English movement used Wycliffe as a basis for their criticism of the Church?

28. In what empire did John Hus live?

29. What did Hus criticize?

PRACTICAL EXERCISES

1. St. Joan of Arc and St. Catherine of Siena are too very different saints. Explain how the lives of these two great women reflect the multifaceted role of women in fourteenth century society. What were each saints' great accomplishments? How did they serve God? How did they serve society?

2. The Black Plague killed nearly a third of the population of Europe. In your town or city, how would life change if a third of its citizens, from every section of society, disappeared

tomorrow? In a few paragraphs, describe a day in which, upon waking, a third of your town or city vanished.

3. How did both the Avignon papacy and the Hundred Years War reflect a changing sense of social identity in western Europeans?

4. Throughout the history of the Church, many heresies have threatened the Faith. Why were the writings of the three heretics described in this chapter so influential?

FROM THE CATECHISM

815 What are these bonds of unity? Above all, charity "binds everything together in perfect harmony" (Col 3: 14). But the unity of the pilgrim Church is also assured by visible bonds of communion:

—profession of one faith received from the Apostles;

—common celebration of divine worship, especially of the sacraments;

—apostolic succession through the sacrament of Holy Orders, maintaining the fraternal concord of God's family (cf. *UR* 2; *LG* 14; CIC, can. 205).

817 In fact, "in this one and only Church of God from its very beginnings there arose certain rifts, which the Apostle strongly censures as damnable. But in subsequent centuries much more serious dissensions appeared and large communities became separated from full communion with the Catholic Church—for which, often enough, men of both sides were to blame" (*UR* 3 § 1). The ruptures that wound the unity of Christ's Body—here we must distinguish heresy, apostasy, and schism (cf. CIC, can. 751)— do not occur without human sin:

Where there are sins, there are also divisions, schisms, heresies, and disputes. Where there is virtue, however, there also are harmony and unity, from which arise the one heart and one soul of all believers (Origen, *Hom. in Ezech.* 9, 1: PG 13, 732).

820 "Christ bestowed unity on his Church from the beginning. This unity, we believe, subsists in the Catholic Church as something she can never lose, and we hope that it will continue to increase until the end of time" (*UR* 4 § 3). Christ always gives his Church the gift of unity, but the Church must always pray and work to maintain, reinforce, and perfect the unity that Christ wills for her. This is why Jesus himself prayed at the hour of his Passion, and does not cease praying to his Father, for the unity of his disciples: "That they may all be one. As you, Father, are in me and I am in you, may they also be one in us,… so that the world may know that you have sent me" (Jn 17: 21; cf. Heb 7: 25). The desire to recover the unity of all Christians is a gift of Christ and a call of the Holy Spirit (cf. *UR* 1).

FROM THE CATECHISM Continued

821 Certain things are required in order to respond adequately to this call:

—a permanent *renewal* of the Church in greater fidelity to her vocation; such renewal is the driving-force of the movement toward unity (cf. *UR* 6);

—*conversion of heart* as the faithful "try to live holier lives according to the Gospel" (*UR* 7 § 3); for it is the unfaithfulness of the members to Christ's gift which causes divisions;

—*prayer in common,* because "change of heart and holiness of life, along with public and private prayer for the unity of Christians, should be regarded as the soul of the whole ecumenical movement, and merits the name 'spiritual ecumenism'" (*UR* 8 § 1);

—*fraternal knowledge of each other* (cf. *UR* 9);

—*ecumenical formation* of the faithful and especially of priests (cf. *UR* 10);

—*dialogue* among theologians and meetings among Christians of the different churches and communities (cf. *UR* 4; 9; 11);

—*collaboration* among Christians in various areas of service to mankind (cf. *UR* 12). "Human service" is the idiomatic phrase.

822 Concern for achieving unity "involves the whole Church, faithful and clergy alike" (*UR* 5). But we must realize "that this holy objective—the reconciliation of all Christians in the unity of the one and only Church of Christ—transcends human powers and gifts." That is why we place all our hope "in the prayer of Christ for the Church, in the love of the Father for us, and in the power of the Holy Spirit" (*UR* 24 § 2).

1900 The duty of obedience requires all to give due honor to authority and to treat those who are charged to exercise it with respect, and, insofar as it is deserved, with gratitude and good-will.

> Pope St. Clement of Rome provides the Church's most ancient prayer for political authorities (cf. as early as 1 Tm 2:1-2): "Grant to them, Lord, health, peace, concord, and stability, so that they may exercise without offense the sovereignty that you have given them. Master, heavenly King of the ages, you give glory, honor, and power over the things of earth to the sons of men. Direct, Lord, their counsel, following what is pleasing and acceptable in your sight, so that by exercising with devotion and in peace and gentleness the power that you have given to them, they may find favor with you" (St. Clement of Rome, *Ad Cor.* 61: SCh 167, 198-200).

2089 *Incredulity* is the neglect of revealed truth or the willful refusal to assent to it. "*Heresy* is the obstinate post-baptismal denial of some truth which must be believed with divine and catholic faith, or it is likewise an obstinate doubt concerning the same; *apostasy* is the total repudiation of the Christian faith; *schism* is the refusal of submission to the Roman Pontiff or of communion with the members of the Church subject to him" (CIC, can. 751: emphasis added).

2238 Those subject to authority should regard those in authority as representatives of God, who has made them stewards of his gifts (cf. Rom 13:1-2): "Be subject for the Lord's sake to every human institution.... Live as free men, yet without using your freedom as a pretext for evil; but live as servants of God" (1 Pt 2:13, 16). Their loyal collaboration includes the right, and at times the duty, to voice their just criticisms of that which seems harmful to the dignity of persons and to the good of the community.

FROM THE CATECHISM Continued

2244 Every institution is inspired, at least implicitly, by a vision of man and his destiny, from which it derives the point of reference for its judgment, its hierarchy of values, its line of conduct. Most societies have formed their institutions in the recognition of a certain preeminence of man over things. Only the divinely revealed religion has clearly recognized man's origin and destiny in God, the Creator and Redeemer. The Church invites political authorities to measure their judgments and decisions against this inspired truth about God and man:

> Societies not recognizing this vision or rejecting it in the name of their independence from God are brought to seek their criteria and goal in themselves or to borrow them from some ideology. Since they do not admit that one can defend an objective criterion of good and evil, they arrogate to themselves an explicit or implicit totalitarian power over man and his destiny, as history shows (cf. *CA* 45; 46).

2245 The Church, because of her commission and competence, is not to be confused in any way with the political community. She is both the sign and the safeguard of the transcendent character of the human person. "The Church respects and encourages the political freedom and responsibility of the citizen" (*GS* 76 § 3).

A teenage girl, St. Joan of Arc, witnesses the coronation of Charles VII as King of France. She had fulfilled the command of her voices.

CHAPTER 12

The Renaissance

*This movement of intellectual "re-birth" created
new challenges for the Church.
It also initiated needed growth and reform
"imbued with Jesus' strength."*

CHAPTER 12

The Renaissance

In knowledge of Christ not only will you discover and understand
the limitations of human wisdom and of human solutions to human needs,
but you will also experience Jesus' power and the importance of human reason
and human strength when these are imbued with Jesus' strength,
when these are redeemed in Christ.

— John Paul II, *Address to Seminarians*, Philadelphia, October 3, 1979

As the fourteenth century ended, the Church and Europe were changing. In the wake of war, plague, and schism, feudalism was crumbling as new political and social entities were emerging. All the achievements of the Middle Ages—the creation of the Western monarchies, the development of English law and Parliament, the foundation of universities, the beginning of great vernacular works of literature, and the revival of commerce—pushed Western civilization in a new direction. The nation-state began to rise from the collections of kingdoms and fiefs, and universal access to commerce and capital began to erode the feudal system's vassal-lord relationship.

Along with these social-political changes, there were changes in people's intellectual pursuits. As education became more widely available, people looked away from the theological Scholasticism that flourished in the days of St. Thomas Aquinas and instead turned to the ancient Latin and Greek classics. Familiarity with these texts gave rise to a popular desire to return to the civilization of the Greco-Roman world, to re-awaken a sense of human beauty and appreciate man's achievements. The name given to this movement by its contemporaries was the "Renaissance," a French word meaning "rebirth," and it was a period of rebirth in almost every area of study. With this phenomenon came new challenges for the Church, but in many ways, it also opened the door for much needed humanistic growth and reform as exemplified by John Paul II's words, "the importance of human reason and human strength when these are imbued with Jesus' strength."

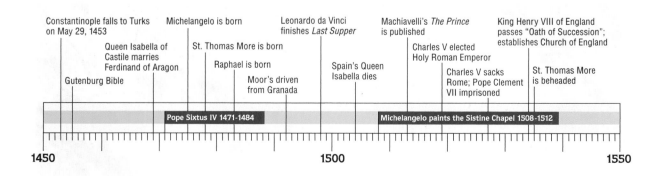

Constantinople falls to Turks on May 29, 1453
Michelangelo is born
Leonardo da Vinci finishes *Last Supper*
Machiavelli's *The Prince* is published
King Henry VIII of England passes "Oath of Succession"; establishes Church of England

Queen Isabella of Castile marries Ferdinand of Aragon
St. Thomas More is born
Charles V elected Holy Roman Emperor

Raphael is born
Spain's Queen Isabella dies
Charles V sacks Rome; Pope Clement VII imprisoned
St. Thomas More is beheaded

Gutenburg Bible
Moor's driven from Granada

Pope Sixtus IV 1471-1484
Michelangelo paints the Sistine Chapel 1508-1512

1450 — 1500 — 1550

PART I

The Fall of Constantinople and the Rise of the Italian Free Cities

The economic growth of the Italian cities was a key contribution to the Renaissance. Throughout the thirteenth and fourteenth centuries, as the rest of Europe warred with each other, the Italian cities became centers of commerce—trading ports of diverse peoples who exchanged goods and ideas. Cities like Florence, Venice, and Genoa were ruled by noble families whose interest in trade, wealth, and power helped form a society based on merchants and commerce. These merchants enjoyed the freedom to buy and sell as they pleased. The economic growth of these Italian "free cities" was also aided by the seventy-year papal absence from Rome. As Italy decentralized, noble families set up their own means of governing. This rise in independence among the nobility occasioned petty wars as these ruling families expanded their sphere of influence into new lands.

As the Byzantine Empire declined in the East, the center of trade shifted to the Italian cities, bringing a burgeoning business economy with a dramatic increase of goods and merchants. Along with the growth in trade, there was a significant increase of scholarship due to the influx of Greek intellectuals. Fleeing the instability of Constantinople and the surrounding lands, Greek scholars sought after safer employment in the Italian cities. This greatly enhanced a rich exchange of ideas already enjoyed by the Italian cities.

THE COUNCIL OF BASEL-FERRARA-FLORENCE (1431-1445) AND THE END OF THE BYZANTINE EMPIRE

The Byzantine Empire never really recovered from the aftermath of the Fourth Crusade, which involved the sacking of Constantinople together with the establishment of a Latin empire on Byzantine soil. During the fourteenth century there arose a new threat to the Byzantine Empire and the whole of Europe: the Ottoman Turks. The Turks, an Islamic people with ties to the nomadic central Asians, were emigrating into the Baltic Peninsula. They conquered Gallipoli (northwest Turkey) in 1354, and moved as far west as Kosovo, Serbia, by 1389, and then north to Bucharest, Hungary, in 1393. The weakened Byzantine Empire was no match for the Turkish

Basel is located in northwest Switzerland on the Rhine river and borders both Germany and France. In 1431 Basel became the focal point of Western Christendom hosting the first session of the Seventeenth Ecumenical Council.

armies who, in addition to massive numbers, used cannons to breach city walls. In 1391, the Turks put Constantinople under siege, but due to Mongol attacks on the eastern Ottoman Empire, the siege was abandoned.

At first, the serious threat posed by the Turks on the Byzantine Empire seemed to strengthen relations between the Latin and Greek churches. Recognizing a common enemy and a mutual danger to their safety, Greeks and Latins were drawn together in a common cause, which helped heal some of the wounds that divided the Church. Venetians, fearful that any further Turkish advance would severely threaten their trade and territory, were particularly concerned with reestablishing favorable relations with the Greeks. Taking advantage of his Venetian background, Eugene IV, who became pope in 1431, sought reunification of the East and West and dreamed of launching a unified crusade against the Turks.

The Council of Basel-Ferrara-Florence was convoked just before Pope Martin V's death in 1431, and it initially dealt with problems of heresy arising in central Europe; however, Pope Eugene IV later decided to use the council as an opportunity to reunite the Western and Eastern Churches. He worked busily, sending delegates to every corner of the Christian world for support. Finally, in 1437, Greek churchmen sailed from Constantinople to Ferrara, where the council resumed. The council had a rocky start. Since the Eastern Emperor John VIII sought a firm military alliance against the Turks, he tried to avoid theological debates that might cause friction between the East and West. The Latin Bishops carefully steered the discussions towards the objections the Greek bishops had with the Latin Church.

There were four major points of disagreement between the two churches were anything but easy to resolve. First, the Greeks objected to the Latin Church's teaching about the relation of the Holy Spirit to the other two Persons of the Blessed Trinity. They rejected the *Filioque* clause, which stated that the Holy Spirit proceeded from both the Father *and* the Son, whereas the Greeks professed that the Holy Spirit proceeded from the Father *through* the Son. The Greeks also used leavened bread for the celebration of the Eucharist and disagreed with the Latin insistence on using only unleavened bread. Two old disagreements with the Latin Church—the existence of Purgatory and the primacy of the Roman See over the whole Church of Christ—were also debated during the council. In order to discuss these issues, the pope formed commissions consisting of both Greeks and Latins that could argue out and draft clear conclusions to these theological questions.

Much to the disappointment of the Eastern Emperor, these theological discussions, which lasted for more than a year, totally absorbed the attention of the Council Fathers to the detriment of addressing the issue of military defense. In any case, the emperor did manage to pressure the bishops to come to an agreement, which was finally reached in 1439 and recorded in Pope Eugene IV's bull *Lætentur cœli* (Let the Heavens Rejoice). Much to the joy of the Latin Church, the Greeks accepted the question of *Filioque*, the existence of Purgatory, and the primacy of the pope, and there was a temporary reunification between the two churches.

Unfortunately, the reunification existed more on paper than in reality. With the Turks threatening Constantinople, popular Greek sentiment against the Latin Church was extremely acute. Many Greeks blamed the Latin Church and the Crusades for weakening the Byzantine Empire. Moreover, once they were away from the pressures of the council, many Greek bishops who accepted the agreements reversed their positions and campaigned against the Latin Church. Indeed, popular hatred of the West was so fierce that the emperors withheld the documents of reunification for fifteen years.

Emperor John VIII was dissatisfied with the council since it was limited to theological matters and that none of the Western princes attended. His hopes for an effective military alliance were dashed since it was already too late. Furthermore, much of the fear and negative sentiment that preceded

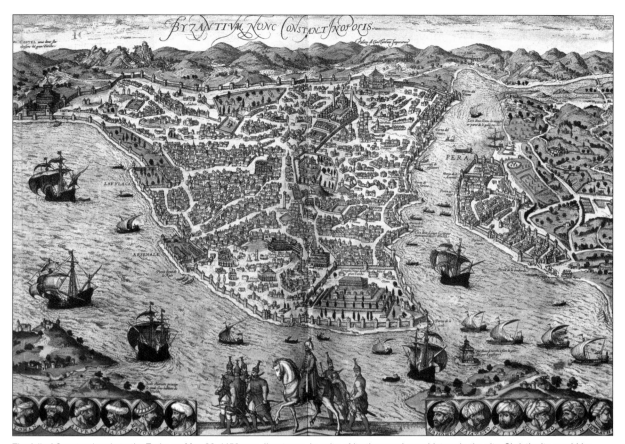

The fall of Constantinople to the Turks on May 29, 1453 was disastrous. In spite of its thousand-year history in the city, Christianity would be immediately replaced by the Muslim culture of the Ottoman Turks. The magnificent Saint Sophia's mosaics would be plastered over, the High Altar destroyed and what was once the center of Byzantine Christianity would become a mosque.

the city's fall was directed towards the West. A popular line was heard in the city: "Better the turban of the Prophet than the Pope's tiara" (quoted in Hughes, *A History of the Church to the Eve of the Reformation*, 1976, p. 351). In December 1452, the reunion of the two Churches was finally proclaimed by the bishops in a ceremony at Hagia Sophia. The people vehemently refused to accept the proclamation and it only fueled their deep resentment toward the West.

Five months later, papal ships arrived to aid the city in the ensuing battle with the Turks, but it was too late. The population of Constantinople watched as 160,000 Turkish troops surrounded the city. After two months of siege, on May 29, 1453, Constantinople fell to Turkish Muslim forces, bringing down a thousand-year-old Christian empire.

The fall of Constantinople solidified the split between the Western and Eastern Churches and created an animosity and historical sense of injustice that has yet to be overcome. It seems probable that if the Latin kingdoms had defeated the Ottomans, it would only have meant years of occupation by Western princes. It can only be speculated that this hypothetical scenario would have further inflamed hatred of the West by the Greeks. Nonetheless, the fall of Constantinople was disastrous. In spite of its thousand-year history and tradition in the city, Christianity would be immediately replaced by the Muslim culture of the Ottoman Turks, subjugating the Greeks to foreign rule. After the siege, the Ottomans pillaged Constantinople for three days and three nights. They stripped Hagia Sophia, turning it into a mosque.

Despite their efforts in defending Constantinople, the Italian city-states benefited greatly from its fall because trade shifted from the "Golden Horn" of Constantinople to Venice, Genoa, and

Florence. Italian ports became even greater centers of ideas from areas outside of Christendom with their cosmopolitan bazaars bustling with people from all over the world. Christians, Jews, and Muslims bought and sold side by side, experiencing a level of toleration unseen elsewhere in Europe.

THE ITALIAN WORLD OF THE FIFTEENTH CENTURY

Because most of Italy's economic activity was bound up in trading and commerce, the Italian peninsula experienced increasing urbanization. Peasants moved into the cities from the countryside to trade and sell goods. For this reason, feudalism never took as strong of a hold in Italy as it did in Northern Europe. The urbanized population remained relatively independent, resulting in the acquisition of great wealth among the business class.

As the city-states prospered, a middle class arose. Ordinary citizens became more interested and involved in the political life of the small Italian republics. Education also became more vital. There arose a new demand for a less theological and more humanistic curriculum, known as *studia humanitatis*. This program placed great emphasis on Classical texts and literature, as well as occasioned a great revival in the mastery of classical Latin and Greek. Although the populace was not free and democratic in the modern sense of the word, each citizen, relatively speaking, had

THE FALL OF CONSTANTINOPLE IN 1918

After the fall of Constantinople in 1453, the Ottoman Empire occupied the city until 1918, when, at the end of World War I, British-led allied forces defeated the Turks and entered the ancient city. After the defeat of the Ottomans, some Allies considered turning Constantinople over to Greece as part of a plan to dismember the Ottoman Empire. A series of events prevented this from ever being carried out.

Internal bickering among the Allied Powers, including Great Britain, France, Italy, and Greece, stalled the division of the Ottoman Empire. Meanwhile, the Turkish leader Mustafa Kemal began organizing the Ottoman forces into a Turkish army. Kemal exploited the disunity of the Allied Powers and mobilized a successful Turkish nationalist movement. By 1923 Kemal and his Turkish forces defeated the Allies and established the new Turkish Republic. The new government occupied Constantinople and renamed the city Istanbul in 1930.

Mustafa Kemal Atatürk (1881-1938) was the founder and first President of the Republic of Turkey. The Grand National Assembly gave him the deferential name Atatürk, meaning "father of Turks." Usage of that name by any other man is still forbidden by law.

great control over his own life. With this greater independence and individuality came a wider demand and possibility for education.

It is important to remember that the Italian city-states were not nationalistic. Many attempts to consolidate the Italian states during this time were unsuccessful. This was largely because, unlike France and England, Italy had never had a strong sense of national unity. Local dialects, customs, cuisine, and family ties kept Italy a collection of smaller, independent regions having little in common with each other. Any efforts towards unification were driven by local patriotism or a desire for personal enrichment rather than national identity.

Upon returning to Rome after the Western Schism, the popes tried to consolidate their power. As sovereigns over the Papal States, many of the Renaissance popes came into conflict with the various princes fighting for temporal power in Italy. Among the benefits of the Church's wealth and influence was her ability to finance huge productions of exquisite Renaissance art and architecture, whose breathtaking beauty dazzles the viewer even to the present day. The Church continued to play an active role in university life, chartering dozens of new schools and guiding the new spirit of learning with a Christian spirit. Between the years 1400 and 1506, about twenty-eight charters were granted by the popes to establish new universities. Among these universities were the schools of St. Andrews in Scotland, Alcala in Spain, Caen and Poitiers in France, and Wittenberg and Frankfurt-on-the-Oder in Germany.

PART II

The Birth of Humanism and the Flourishing of Arts and Letters

As the new schools of the fifteenth century opened, the academic emphasis significantly changed. Universities placed greater stress on rhetoric, grammar, and history rather than theological studies; moreover, students studied the classical works of Greco-Roman civilization. This intellectual shift created a more secular education than what was offered by the Scholastic tradition. This new focus led students to the exciting rediscovery of the glories of the classical world. Greco-Roman literature, art, and architecture elicited a newfound enthusiasm and depth, inspiring many to seek to revive Rome's unsurpassed culture and civilization. They looked back to antiquity for lessons that could help bring European society out of the wars and disease of the fourteenth century and into a new era modeled after the memory of the great civilization of Rome. These men of the Renaissance wanted to apply their newly acquired knowledge to the societal challenges of the day, believing that solutions to problems were linked to the classical culture of ancient Greece and Rome.

This return to the humanism of antiquity led to an increased emphasis on the individual: his form, beauty, and usefulness in society. Especially in the ancient Roman world, there was a certain fascination with human achievement and the individual's ability to shape his own destiny. In similar fashion, the Renaissance world concentrated on the wonders of man's abilities rather than God's omnipotence in controlling their destiny. Man was no longer at the mercy of chance since he could now protect himself through his own skill and craft. The Medieval man sought his fortune mostly in the next world, whereas the Renaissance man focused more of his energies on the here and now. The Renaissance man wanted to enjoy life and at the same time serve his community actively with his gifts and talents.

Renaissance art especially reflects the new mindset of the fifteenth and sixteenth centuries. Art was considered to be the pinnacle of human achievement since the human person could display skill and ability in crafting beautiful productions exhibited in perfect form, balance, and composition. The aristocracy were responsible in great part in promoting the arts as portrait painting came into fashion.

The new appreciation for the richness of human nature prompted by a renewed enthusiasm for classical thought distinguished the Renaissance world from the religiously-centered Medieval period. However, in itself this new perspective is not detrimental to spiritual fervor and Christian living as long as God's hand is recognized in all human progress.

HUMANISM

Faith and reason are like two wings on which the human spirit rises to the contemplation of truth; and God has placed in the human heart a desire to know the truth—in a word, to know himself—so that, by knowing and loving God, men and women may also come to the fullness of truth about themselves. (John Paul II, opening words of *Fides et ratio*, [Faith and Reason], 1998)

Scholastic thought reached its zenith in the High Middle Ages and then underwent a steady decline in the fourteenth and fifteenth centuries. Scholasticism is a philosophical movement combining Christian doctrine with patristic philosophy, especially St. Augustine and later Aristotle. This movement was severely attacked and questioned by the celebrated nominalist William of Ockham and his disciples. There was a growing discontent among intellectually gifted people over the corruption of Thomism by the generation of thinkers following St. Thomas Aquinas. An excessively formalistic Scholasticism, which began to obscure the original beauty and brilliance of Thomistic thought, created the right setting for the rise of nominalism. In short, nominalism argues that true knowledge pertains to empirical knowledge only, and not to metaphysical or formal concepts. Many new scholars viewed Medieval philosophy as old, monkish, and stagnant, being lost in intricate subtleties, distinctions, and technicalities. Some of the Renaissance thinkers accused Scholasticism of ignoring the most important questions concerning the human subject: What am I, and what is my final purpose? What ought I do? What should I love? What follows death?

Like the word "Renaissance," "humanism" also carries with it a certain ambiguity. Humanism denotes a certain general mood and intellectual climate which focuses on the richness of the human spirit over the almost exclusive theological focus of the Medieval era. Nevertheless, the writers and thinkers who fall under its broad umbrella are often so diverse in their aims and beliefs that the term loses much precision without the clarifying prefixes of "theistic," "atheistic," "secular," "aesthetic," "Christian," "pagan," and the like. Humanism was a literary genre that would elaborate on different facets of human life. This fascination with humanity spilled over into the fine arts as well, beginning in the Italian city-states during the late fourteenth century. Medieval Scholastic education was a very specialized, practical aim; for example, one studied medicine to become a doctor; logic, philosophy, and theology to become a theologian; law to become a lawyer. The humanists reacted against this functional specialization of education since it did not include the exciting subject matter of the human condition. Education not only should offer training, but must have the moral purpose of making the individual wiser and more virtuous.

The humanists revived the study of the many texts of the great authors of ancient Rome: Virgil, Cicero, Ovid, Seneca, Tacitus, and Catullus. Eventually, as knowledge of Greek culture was acquired in the West, mostly through Byzantine refugees after 1453, they retrieved the works of

The humanist philosophers, though giving priority to the works and virtues of the classical world over the Medieval era, never sought to replace Christian teaching with pagan philosophy. Their education still included study of the Scriptures and the Church Fathers.

ancient Greek thinkers: Homer, Aristotle, Plato, and Thucydides. The humanists called their works the *bonae litterae* (good letters) or *litterae humaniores* (more humane letters), as these texts focused on man's relation to the world rather than man's relation to God and eternal salvation.

Certainly this opened the door to a worldly outlook devoid of a true Catholic sentiment as many humanists displayed an inordinate reverence for pagan thinkers and writers. The Catholic Church developed a Christian humanism to the already rich storehouse of theological and philosophical thought. The Renaissance, from a Christian perspective, underscored the revealed truth that the human person is made in the image and likeness of God.

Fourteenth and fifteenth century humanism walked a fine line between fascination with the grandeur of the human person and the fact that every person is a fruit of God's creative power.

Petrarch, Boccaccio and Dante—Petrarch succeeded Dante as the great sage of Florence. He was crowned "poet laureate" by a Roman senator when he was only thirty.

DANTE ALIGHIERI (1265-1321)

Dante Alighieri had been the premier Florentine writer at the close of the Medieval Era. He had suffered amid the political turmoil of the Italian citystates and had been a victim of the many power struggles and political intrigues. His writings struck a balance between the person's earthly condition and life after death. His epic poem, *The Divine Comedy*, is a poetic reflection in many ways reflective of the Scholastic tradition. At the same time, he had a great admiration for the classical writers in their dedication to the pursuit of natural truth. In *The Divine Comedy*, the poet assigns the souls of pagan writers and thinkers to limbo, a place where they are not condemned by God, but do not share the Beatific Vision since they are not baptized in the Catholic Church and therefore do not have the fullness of truth. Christian revelation provides the necessary divine light that would have guided them to knowledge of God.

PETRARCH (1304-1374)

Petrarch succeeded Dante as the great sage of Florence. His fame and renown as a writer was such that, in keeping with an ancient tradition, a Roman senator crowned Petrarch "poet laureate" (a reference to the custom of crowning heroes with laurel leaves) when he was only thirty years old. Born Francesco di Petracco in 1304, he was sent by his father to study law. Francesco, however, disliked this chosen career path, and spent as much time as he could reading classical literature instead of law. Virgil and Cicero became his teachers, and his command of Latin was impeccable. Much of his fame, however, is derived from his poetry, especially from his sonnets to Laura, written in his vernacular Italian. He had soon changed his name from Petracco—its sharp, flat quality did not ring well enough in the ear of such a poet—to Petrarch.

Unlike Dante, however, Petrarch could not detach himself from the world of Florence. Though his love of learning and study of Latin would win him the title "Father of Humanism," this deeply religious Christian was constantly torn between his love of the present life and hope for eternity. He intensely wanted to resolve his inner turmoil as demonstrated in his *Secretum*, a series of personal meditative dialogues between himself and St. Augustine under the watchful eye of Lady Truth, earning him the title "Man of Letters." The following excerpts from one of his letters give a sample of Petrarch's lifelong struggle:

> O bounteous, O saving Jesus, true God and true Giver of all learning and all intelligence, true "King of Glory" and "Lord of all powers of virtue," I now pray to Thee on the knees of my soul: If Thou dost not wish to grant me more, let it be my portion at least to be a good man. This I cannot be if I do not love Thee dearly and do not adore Thee piously. For this purpose I am born, not for learning.

> I want to be good, to love Thee, and to deserve to be loved by Thee—for no one repays his lovers like Thee—to think of Thee, to be obedient to Thee, to set my hope in Thee, and to speak of Thee. "Let all that is obsolete, shrink back from my mouth; let all my thoughts be prepared unto Thee." For it is true: "The bow of the mighty man has been overcome and the weak have been girded with strength." Happier by far is one of these feeble ones who believe in Thee, than Plato, Aristotle, Varro, and Cicero, who with all their knowledge did not know Thee. (*On His Own Ignorance and That of Many Others II*)

A 15th Century manuscript from Petrarch's *Trionfi* (*Triumphs*), an allegorical poem that Petrarch wrote over a period of eighteen or more years. The poem consists of a procession of six figures: Love, Chastity, Death, Fame, Time, and Divinity. Each "triumphs" over its predecessor. Chastity triumphs over Love, Death over Chastity, etc., and finally Divinity triumphs over all as the symbol of peace, eternal life, and the everlasting union of the poet with his beloved Laura.

Laura was the artistic love of Petrarch's life for whom he perfected the sonnet and wrote his masterpiece the *Canzoniere*. Laura was possibly Laure de Noves from Avignon who died from the Black Death at the age of 38. She was already married when Petrarch first saw her and fell in love at first sight. It is unknown if she ever knew of his feelings for her.

Several years after Laura's death, Maurice Sceve, a humanist, visiting Avignon had her tomb opened and discovered a lead box. Inside the box was a medal representing a woman ripping at her heart, and under that, a sonnet by Petrarch.

This illustration shows *The Triumph of Chastity*.

PETRARCH AND DANTE

Dante Alighieri

An unlucky generation of poets faced the daunting task of writing soon after the death of Dante (1265-1321). For Petrarch (1304-1374), who met Dante only once as a child, living in the shadow of the great poet haunted his entire career. Petrarch seemed obsessive about ignoring Dante. Of the four hundred letters written by Petrarch, he never once mentions Dante's name. Petrarch did not even own a copy of the *Comedia* until he was forty-five years old. Many attributed Petrarch's attitude toward the great poet to envy. However, one of Petrarch's letters to his friend and fellow poet Boccaccio indicates it was another reason that led Petrarch to disregard the work of perhaps the greatest Italian poet.

In the letter, rather than referring to Dante by name, Petrarch refers to the elder poet as "a certain poet, a fellow-citizen of ours, who in point of style is very popular, and who has certainly chosen a noble theme." Petrarch was responding to a letter written by Boccaccio in which his friend had praised Dante in an almost apologetic tone, believing that Petrarch may be offended by any fondness of Dante's work. In his response, Petrarch acknowledges Dante's genius and supported his friend's praise. "Continue, then," Petrarch writes, "not by my sufferance simply, but with my approbation, to extol and cherish this poet, the guiding star of your intellect."

It was not Dante, Petrarch goes on to say, nor Dante's work to which he took particular offense. Instead, Petrarch's main problem is with those who sing Dante's praises without truly appreciating the depth of the great poet's work. Moreover, he hated that these sycophants accused him of jealousy. "They lie," Petrarch writes, "then, who assert that I carp at his renown; I, who probably understand better than the majority of these foolish and immoderate admirers of his what it is that merely tickles their ears, without their knowing why, but cannot penetrate their thick heads, because the avenues of intelligence are obstructed." Petrarch explains in his letter that the reason he lived so many years without reading Dante was that he wanted to develop his own style of poetry. Petrarch was afraid of being so influenced by Dante that he "might perhaps unconsciously and against [his] will come to be an imitator."

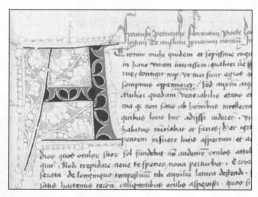

A page from Petrarch's *Secretum* handwritten by scribes in Northern France in 1450.

The *Decameron* is a collection of one hundred novellas finished by Giovanni Boccaccio in 1353. Boccaccio begins his work with a description of the Plague which hit Florence in 1348 and leads into an introduction of a group of seven young women and three young men who flee the plague-ridden Florence to a villa outside of Naples. To pass the time, each member of the party tells one story for each one of the ten nights spent at the villa. In this manner, one hundred stories are told by the end of the ten days. The themes range from "stories of bad luck unexpectedly changed to happiness" (day two, under Filomena) to the "stories of deceptions women have played on their husbands" (day seven, under Dioneo).

BOCCACCIO (1313-1375)

Giovanni Boccaccio was born in 1313. He was sent to study canon law and, like Petrarch, opted for the study of the "good letters." He, along with most Italians, soon encountered the poetry of Petrarch, and in 1350 Boccaccio had the pleasure of meeting him in Florence. This encounter initiated a friendship that would last throughout his life. Unlike Petrarch, Boccaccio never completely mastered Latin, though he did write several Latin texts. The majority of his works were written in his vernacular Italian. His masterpiece, the *Decameron*, is a collection of one hundred stories told by ten travelers who fled the Black Plague to Naples (each tells one story a day for ten days). This work provides a resource for understanding life in the Italian city-states. Nevertheless, it is not a work whose main purpose is edification of the reader. The tales in the *Decameron* are witty, bawdy, satirical, and adept at providing a realistic picture of that period of history. It is argued that Boccaccio opened the door to a new, secular era of literature and culture with the publication of the *Decameron*. Contempt for stupidity and ignorance, rather than vice, echoes in many of his works. Boccaccio, like Petrarch, hardly rejected Christianity, but rather concentrated his writing skills on themes that touch on the foibles and weaknesses inherent in human nature. Indeed, later in life he grew more devout, even expressing regret for the looseness of some of his writings. Not long after his friend and colleague died, Boccaccio passed away as well.

NICOLÒ MACHIAVELLI (1469-1527)

Not all pursuits of classical thought resulted in the total acceptance of classical principles. Nicolò Machiavelli (1469-1527), the renowned Florentine ambassador and statesman, was one of the founders of modern political thought. His name has become synonymous with ruthless, underhanded conduct, which is especially reflected in his most famous work, *The Prince* (1513). After spending many years in the political arena of warring Italian city-states and at the same time having the bitter experience of exile and betrayal, Machiavelli became disgusted by that state of affairs. In reaction to the precarious political situation, he composed a treatise presenting a radical development of the classical political ideals of justice, clemency, and magnanimity. Machiavelli always dreamed of a united Italy, but given the rampant chaos and injustice, he despaired of ever achieving unity through classical and Christian methods. He disliked the papacy, which he saw as an obstacle to Italian unity. He eventually viewed virtues like mercy, humility, and pity as obstacles to political effectiveness. The gentle sheep of Christianity, he thought, would simply not survive in the political world of the Renaissance:

> A prince, therefore, being compelled knowingly to adopt the beast, ought to choose the fox and the lion; because the lion cannot defend himself against snares and the fox cannot defend himself against wolves. Therefore, it is necessary to be a fox to discover the snares and a lion to terrify the wolves. (*The Prince*, XVIII)

Machiavelli's political theories do not completely reject classical and Christian virtues, but they do cast them down from their preeminent positions. The concept that "the ends justify the means" as an absolute finds its origins somewhat in Machiavelli's thought. "Machiavellianism" (using any means necessary to get ahead) has evolved into a common, however crude, political principle in the modern world.

Machiavelli is representative of a major element of humanist Renaissance writers who focused on the secular world to the exclusion of anything religious. The growing split between religious life and secular life was a rather significant historical development. The early Christians lived Christianity in every aspect of daily life, and the rise of monasticism during the Middle Ages made the religious life the only life for many people. In many pagan cultures, gods and spirits are everywhere and play an integral part in human existence. Even in the classical civilizations of Greece and Rome, political, social, and economic life was in part dictated by an objective moral law. Nevertheless, as the Renaissance unfolded, Christianity began to lose a foothold in the political as well as the academic sphere.

Tribute Money by Masaccio (1401-1427?), the first great Italian Renaissance painter. Masaccio's innovations in the use of scientific perspective (knowledge of mathematical proportion acquired from Brunelleschi) inaugurated the modern era in painting. Masaccio's work exerted a strong influence on later Florentine art and particularly on the work of Michelangelo. This painting depicts the arrival in Capernaum of Jesus and the Apostles, based on Matthew 17: 24-27. Masaccio has included the three different moments of the story: the tax collector's request, with Jesus indicating to Peter how to find the money, in the center; Peter catching the fish in Lake Genezaret and extracting the coin, on the left; and Peter handing the tribute money to the tax collector in front of his house, on the right.

HUMANISM IN PAINTING AND SCULPTURE

The rebirth of art in Italy during the fifteenth century expressed similar cultural changes, as was the case regarding philosophy and literature. Increased interest in classical literature and art prompted a new resolve for observation of the individual and study of the natural world. Subjects from Greek and Roman mythology found their way into the art of the day in response to the renewed interest in the classical era. The study of ancient architecture also inspired new techniques in building involving spatial perspective, elegance of form, and symmetry.

The first generation of Renaissance artists (most notably Donatello, Brunelleschi and Masaccio) applied rational inquiry to discover laws of proportion, formal balance, and symmetry. They remained keenly observant of natural phenomena, but also sought to render spiritual ideals through their art forms of painting and architecture. In his *Letter to Artists,* John Paul II described this blending of religious themes with earthly beauty thusly:

> The favorable cultural climate that produced the extraordinary artistic flowering of Humanism and the Renaissance also had a significant impact on the way in which the artists of the period approached the religious theme....Writing from this Apostolic Palace, which is a mine of masterpieces perhaps unique in the world, I would rather give voice to the supreme artists who in this place lavished the wealth of their genius, often charged with great spiritual depth. From here can be heard the voice of Michelangelo who in the Sistine Chapel has presented the drama and mystery of the world from the Creation to the Last Judgement, giving a face to God the Father, to Christ the Judge, and to man on his arduous journey from the dawn to the consummation of history. Here speaks the delicate and profound genius of Raphael, highlighting in the array of his paintings, and especially in the "Dispute" in the Room of the Signatura, the mystery of the revelation of the Triune God, who in the Eucharist befriends man and sheds light on the questions and expectations of human intelligence. From this place, from the majestic Basilica dedicated to the

Prince of the Apostles, from the Colonnade which spreads out from it like two arms open to welcome the whole human family, we still hear Bramante, Bernini, Borromini, Maderno, to name only the more important artists, all rendering visible the perception of the mystery which makes of the Church a universally hospitable community, mother and traveling companion to all men and women in their search for God. (John Paul II, *Letter to Artists*, 1999, no. 9)

The late fifteenth century, the period known as the High Renaissance, produced some of the most magnificent works of art ever seen. Commissioned by wealthy families, kings, and popes alike, artists such as Leonardo da Vinci, Michelangelo, and Raphael filled Italian churches and palaces with breathtaking paintings and sculptures which alternated between religious and secular themes. More than just thematic content, these artists presented unified balance and color composition with a talent that combined the dramatic force of a physical representation with sublime harmonic and lyric beauty.

MICHELANGELO

Michelangelo Buonarroti, born in 1475, played an unparalleled role in the development of Western art. He embodies the Renaissance man who excels in many disciplines in a way that is larger than life. Michelangelo was a sculptor, painter, and architect of almost superhuman capacity, whose works hold the viewer of every age in utter amazement.

An unmistakable quality of Michelangelo's art was his depiction of the contours of the human body in such a manner that the grandeur of man comes out with overwhelming force. His sculpture "David" typifies the artist's use of scale and exaggeration along with detailed studies of the human anatomy to create this massive figure that exudes power and strength.

Like many artists of the time, Michelangelo was supported financially by the popes. His relationship with these men was not always cordial. Commissioned to paint the Sistine Chapel as well as to design the dome of St. Peter's Basilica, the popes needed to coerce Michelangelo to complete the task. Painted from 1508 until 1512, the ceiling of the Sistine Chapel was a painstaking and torturous endeavor for the artist who was left nearly blind by the time of its completion. The chapel ceiling remains an incredible achievement in Renaissance art that perfectly displays dazzling beauty through an idealized human form.

Michelangelo in his Studio by Delacroix

Michelangelo had an unparalleled influence on Western art. He is the foremost Renaissance man, one who excelled in many disciplines.

MICHELANGELO AND THE POPES

Interior of the dome of St. Peter's Basilica designed by Michelangelo. The shape is a parabola which gives it more strength. The dome was completed by the architect Giacomo della Porta after Michelangelo's death.

The sculptor and painter Michelangelo lived for ninety years and received commissions from four different popes. Unfortunately, as he lived during a time when corruption and intrigue dominated the papacy, relations with these popes were often strained.

Born in Florence, Michelangelo was thirty years old when he was first called to Rome by Pope Julius II. Michelangelo was commissioned by Pope Julius II to design and erect a stately tomb for himself, a four-sided marble structure decorated with forty massive figures. The planning went on for a year, but Julius suddenly changed his mind and began to focus exclusively on the rebuilding of St. Peter's Basilica. Losing his commission and abandoning the mausoleum, Michelangelo left Rome for Florence in despair and even considered moving to Constantinople. At Julius' insistence, Michelangelo eventually returned to Rome in order to paint the ceiling of the Sistine Chapel. When Julius II died in 1513, Michelangelo labored for two years on a scaled-down version of the original mausoleum, adorning it with the famous "Moses" found today in the church of St. Peter in Chains, located in Rome.

Before he could complete the mausoleum, the sculptor was again interrupted by the new pope, Leo X, who asked Michelangelo to construct a new facade for a church at San Lorenzo. After four years, that contract was rescinded, and this project was also left incomplete. In 1523 a new pope, Clement VII, was elected after the short reign of Adrian VI. Pope Clement commissioned Michelangelo to build a mortuary chapel for the Medici family. Surprisingly, this commission was not revoked, and Michelangelo completed the chapel in 1524. After Clement VII died, Pope Paul III appointed Michelangelo as chief architect for the reconstruction of St. Peter's Basilica in 1546. Before he died, Michelangelo almost completed the dome of the church and four columns for its base.

"From here can be heard the voice of Michelangelo who in the Sistine Chapel has presented the drama and mystery of the world from the Creation to the Last Judgement, giving a face to God

the *Father, to Christ the Judge, and to man on his arduous journey from the dawn to the consummation of history."*

—John Paul II, *Letter to Artists*, 1999

Portrait of Pope Julius II by Raphael. Julius II was a great patron of the arts. Michelangelo, Bramante and Raphael all benefited from his commissions.

RAPHAEL

Another painter commissioned by the pope and a contemporary of Michelangelo was Raphael Sanzio (1483-1520), admired for his clarity of form and ease of composition. Whereas Michelangelo preferred sculpture, Raphael was primarily a painter best known for his Madonnas (Italian for "my Lady"; paintings of the Blessed Virgin Mary) as well as his large paintings in the Vatican apartments.

Like most artists of the day, Raphael spent much of his life in Florence. There he immersed himself in the artistic milieu of the day which helped shape his own ideas and methods. In Florence, Raphael's principal teachers were Leonardo da Vinci and Michelangelo. During his early years in Florence, Raphael worked to perfect his painting of the Madonna, concentrating on creating intimate and simple paintings that masterfully balanced the use of light, composition, and a sense of depth.

During the last twelve years of his life, Raphael worked in Rome and was commissioned by popes and wealthy families alike. Pope Julius II hired this artist to paint a series of rooms in the papal apartments, and these murals are still considered some of Raphael's greatest works. Demonstrating the humanistic trends of his period, these paintings also deal with philosophical themes.

Like many of the artists of the Renaissance, Raphael was well known and admired during his life. The artist died on his thirty-seventh birthday and was given a funeral in St. Peter's in Rome. Since many held him in very high esteem, Pope Leo X had him buried in the Pantheon in Rome.

Self-Portrait by Raphael

HUMANISM IN THE NORTH

The circumstances surrounding humanism in Northern Europe were different from those in Italy. The North (Flanders, the Hanseatic League, the Rhineland cities) did not see a significant change of economy, social life, and education. During the Renaissance in Italy, these northern regions remained remarkably the same. Most of the North was rural; life was hard, and the majority of the population was poor. Northern Europe did not experience the same rise in prosperity along with the appearance of a middle class that so marked the Italian Renaissance.

The Renaissance in the North was more of a blend between the Christian-centered Medieval world and the new mindset exhibited by the Renaissance. Rather than wholeheartedly embracing the traditions of antiquity, they integrated and elaborated on the human person in relation to Christianity. It would take longer for a Christian orientation to be lost in the humanistic literature of the North. Moreover, that region would see some of the greatest Christian humanists.

ST. THOMAS MORE (1478-1535)

The life and martyrdom of Saint Thomas More have been the source of a message which spans the centuries and which speaks to people everywhere of the inalienable dignity of the human conscience, which, as the Second Vatican Council reminds us, is "the most secret core and sanctuary of a man. There he is alone with God, Whose voice echoes in his depths" (*Gaudium et spes*, 16).

Whenever men or women heed the call of truth, their conscience then guides their actions reliably towards good. Precisely because of the witness which he bore, even at the price of his life, to the primacy of truth over power, Saint Thomas More is venerated as an imperishable example of moral integrity. (John Paul II, *On Saint Thomas More*, 2000, no. 1)

St. Thomas More by Peter Paul Rubens

On the opposite end of the political spectrum from Machiavelli, there appears another renowned humanist, a certain lawyer, knight, Lord Chancellor, saint, martyr, and one of the greatest minds of the Renaissance: St. Thomas More (1478-1535). He mastered Greek, French, and Latin; studied mathematics, history, music, law, and philosophy; and wrote numerous works, among them his famous *Utopia*. The word "utopia," first coined by St. Thomas More himself, is Greek meaning "no place." In this modern parallel to Plato's *Republic*, More described a religious society, heavily influenced by divine revelation, in which goods were held in common and the state regulated business. More meant exactly what the etymology implied by the name of his island — Utopia is no place, and can never be, but it offers a remarkable humanist critique of the socio-political state of sixteenth century England.

Besides his work *Utopia*, St. Thomas More is best remembered for his heroic Christian witness during the tumultuous events surrounding Henry VIII's defection from the Catholic Church. More served as Lord Chancellor for Henry VIII until 1532. When Henry, whom the pope once named *Defensor Fidei* (Defender of the Faith) because of his work against Lutheran heresies, passed the *Act of*

Succession and Oath of Supremacy in 1534, thereby establishing the Church of England. St. Thomas More refused to swear allegiance to these schismatic decrees. He was accused of high treason and imprisoned in the Tower of London, where he remained until his beheading on July 6, 1535. Pope Pius XI canonized St. Thomas More in 1935. His feast day is celebrated on June 22.

ERASMUS OF ROTTERDAM (ca. 1466-1536)

Perhaps the most renowned of all Renaissance humanists is Desiderius Erasmus of Rotterdam (ca. 1466-1536), who was a close friend and correspondent of St. Thomas More. This father of Northern humanism was recognized throughout Europe—by King Henry VIII, Holy Roman Emperor Charles V, various popes, St. Thomas More, and Martin Luther—for his brilliance and intellect. A master of Greek and Latin, Erasmus traveled all over Europe, lecturing, counseling, and writing. He epitomized the intellectual character of humanism. He saw the Middle Ages and Scholasticism as unenlightened and stagnant while holding the classical thinkers in highest esteem. He extolled the primacy of human virtues such as prudence, intellectual honesty, zeal for truth, and consideration for others. He had deep desires for reform and progress through education and tolerance. Although he never spoke against its divine origin and fundamental beliefs, Erasmus was highly critical of the way many societies within the

Erasmus of Rotterdam by Hans Holbein

Church functioned. His biting and sarcastic critiques of ecclesiastical and monastic life brought out the need for a profound spiritual renewal of the sixteenth-century Church.

In his *Handbook of a Christian Knight,* Erasmus confronted the difficult question Petrarch and many Christian humanists raised: How does one remain a good Christian while taking part in world affairs? Unhappy with the contemporary structure and practices of the Church from the popes to Christian rulers to everyday people, Erasmus suggested a more personal and subjective spirituality and understanding of the Faith. He called for study and meditation on the writings of the Church Fathers and the Scriptures. He strongly encouraged research into the classical thinkers together with continuous practice of rational virtue and adherence to the "philosophy of Christ." His most famous work, however, is *Moriae encomium* (Praise of Folly), written for his friend St. Thomas More. In this short work, Folly speaks on the state of human society. From ruler to peasant, she says, all favor Folly over Reason, though they are dishonest about their preference and give her disparaging names. The work, a satirical exposition of the Renaissance world, is at once a celebration and a critique that harshly criticizes members of the Church. Erasmus remained a Christian throughout his life, and he never balked at criticizing the Church's many members who did not uphold the dignity and respect of the Church. Because his faith and love of the Church was devoted and deep, Erasmus continually expressed zeal for necessary reform.

RABELAIS (ca. 1490-1553)

Though many of the early humanists neither sought to reject Christianity nor escape its moral demands, the ideological forces driving the humanistic movement—with its new fascination with worldly life—led some humanists to turn disdainfully against the morality and the theological education of the Medieval period. Consequently, the more cynical and critical humanists

Francois Rabelais by Gustave Dore

embraced, both in their writings and in their lives, a wholly secular and worldly existence. The French satirist Rabelais (ca.1490-1553), a brilliant scholar and literary genius who had mastered Greek, Latin, and Hebrew, penned the farcical, chaotic adventures of giants, *La Vie de Gargantua et de Pantagruel,* (The Life of Gargantua and the Heroic Deeds of Pantagruel), which appeared serially from 1533 until shortly after his death. Rabelais was highly reactionary in his writings, and this most likely contributed to his reaction to monastic ideals. Rabelais' giants engage in a ridiculous series of bawdy, obscene, and licentious adventures, and in the process, simultaneously critique and celebrate man. No one is safe — monks, priests, scholars, Protestants, Catholics — but it is ultimately man, who is by nature good, who is elevated. It is, however, a purely secular vision of man for whom contentment (albeit enlightened contentment), rather than God, is the highest good, and for whom honest self-knowledge, rather than faith, is the means to his true fulfillment.

PART III

Popes and Politics

POLITICAL LIFE IN FLORENCE

The history of Florence during the Renaissance was dominated by one family: Medici. By 1429 this banking family completely controlled the political scene of the city thanks to the rise of Cosimo de Medici. Although a Republican government was nominally maintained, the Medici family held the major offices and approved appointments. Cosimo de Medici was a skilled politician who ended the wars that had plagued Florence for a century, bringing peace and increased prosperity to the city. Cosimo de Medici's grip over Florence was so strong that his son Piero and grandson Lorenzo the Magnificent were able to take the reins of power without any opposition. Besides political strength and wealth, the name Medici would go down in history for extraordinary generosity and patronage to the arts.

Cosimo de Medici seems to have been a devout Catholic (especially in his latter years), and at the same time the Medici were close friends with the heads of Franciscan and Dominican convents. Religion, like politics in Renaissance Florence, would often fluctuate between coldness and fervor. Occasionally, the Florentines would loathe their worldly ways and decadent lifestyles and repent with a fervent resolve to

Lorenzo Medici (1449-1492) by Michelango (from the Medici Tomb). Ruler of the Florentine Republic during the height of the Italian Renaissance, Lorenzo the Magnificent (*il Magnifico*) was a glittery individual who loved to enter tournaments, compose poetry and songs, play games, hunt, and indulge in the Florentine love of practical jokes. Lorenzo was an avid patron of the arts, fascinated by technology and a very religious man who deeply loved his country.

THE RISE OF MERCHANT BANKING

It is not surprising that along with the great increase in merchant activity during the fourteenth and fifteenth centuries, especially among the Italians, many merchants began to develop various banking systems in order to deal with credit, finance, and other issues that arose in the merchant community.

Most merchant bankers handled financial issues through remittance, that is, transferring money to distant places. They began using "bills of exchange," and consequently, the buying, selling, and trading of these bills helped establish an international exchange market. Along with the running of this market, some merchants began lending money for investments, one of the principal functions of a bank. When successful, a lending merchant could earn enormous profits, and although most merchants retained their commercial businesses, they began to serve a dual role as banker and merchant.

Merchant banking was mostly an Italian business, and the family name that became synonymous with banking was Medici. When the family's banking business was at its height, the Medicis enjoyed tremendous wealth and power, virtually controlling Florence for much of the sixteenth century. Three popes and two queens of France were members of the Medici family—a clear indicator of their far-reaching influence. Because many members of the Medici family were enthusiastic patrons of the arts, Florence became the most important cultural center in Europe.

Outside of Italy, Germans, Englishmen, Spanish, and other nationalities also took up the business of banking. The Fuggers, a German family of merchant princes, were by far the wealthiest and most successful banking family outside Italy. The Fuggers amassed great wealth from the mining and trading of silver, copper, and mercury, and eventually used this wealth to establish a banking empire. Under Jacob Fugger II ("Jacob the Rich"), the Fuggers became tremendously powerful. In 1519 the influential Jacob even helped ensure the election of Charles V as Holy Roman Emperor through bribes. Like the Medicis, the Fuggers were well-known philanthropists, supporting the arts and learning.

Above: *Cosimo the Great.* The Medici family produced three popes, numerous rulers of Florence, and later members of the French royalty. Left: *The Villa Medici* by Claude Lorrain

wholeheartedly live as good Catholics. When this change of heart occurred, there would be resurgences of faith accompanied by bonfires designed to burn ornaments, fashionable clothes, and secular books. Nonetheless, most of these manifestations of repentance were short-lived.

There was a three-year period, from 1494 to 1497, in which a resurgence of faith forced the Medicis from power. The puritanical Dominican friar Savonarola temporarily drove the family from Florence in an attempt to morally reform the populace and re-establish the Republic. At first there was an enthusiastic outpouring of repentance and faith. As usual, the Florentines became weary of the reforms and longed for their lost worldly lifestyles. Consequently, Savonarola was hanged, then burned at the stake as a heretic (though he was not one); the Medici family returned to power, and Florence returned to her old ways.

THE RENAISSANCE POPES

Much has been said of the worldly lives of the Renaissance popes. Unfortunately, these popes lived more like worldly princes than men called to reflect the holiness of Christ's vicar and successor of St. Peter. It is worth mentioning that the popes of the Renaissance acted as temporal princes who were trying to strengthen the temporal authority of the Church after the long period of schism and establish a stronger security for the Papal States. Some of the popes were men of letters who helped sponsor the artistic works of the Renaissance, whereas others acted more as princes interested in increasing their power.

The Church at the time was in need of strong leadership. Rising discontent in the Holy Roman Empire and political infighting among European Christian states weakened Europe in its ability to defend itself successfully against the Turks. Internal European conflict also seriously hampered the leadership of the Church. The Church was faced on all sides by growing political turmoil as one state vied with another for temporal sovereignty. This tumultuous time of continuing political strife and violence threatened the unity of the Church. Nonetheless, it was also a period of great intellectual growth and an extraordinary period for artistic expression. The Renaissance period also shows that, despite the human limitations of the members of Christ's Church, the Holy Spirit continued to direct the Barque of St. Peter.

NICHOLAS V (1447-1455)

Born Tommaso Parentucelli, Pope Nicholas V ascended to the papacy in 1447 and remains one of the greatest of the Renaissance popes. From an early age he took up the burgeoning humanism of that period, serving for some twenty years under the patronage of Nicolò Albergati, the bishop of Bologna. During that time he began his lifelong hobby of collecting and caring for rare books and at the same time demonstrated a deep capacity for learning and scholarship. At the Council of Basel-Ferrara-Florence (1431-45), Parentucelli's familiarity with Scholastic philosophy and the Church Fathers gave him prominence during the discussions with the Greek bishops who had come to reconcile with Rome. He became a cardinal in 1446 and was elected to the papacy the following year upon the death of Eugene IV. In thankful remembrance of his longtime patron Nicolò, he took the name Nicholas.

As pope, Nicholas V undertook three major tasks: to make Rome once again a city of grand monuments; to make Rome a center of art and literature; and to strengthen, both spiritually and temporally, the capital of Christendom. He set about restoring churches, repairing the Roman infrastructure, cleaning the city, and repairing the ancient aqueducts. He also made many grandiose plans and laid the foundation for the future St. Peter's Basilica. Nicholas, driven by his love of literature and beautiful books, vigorously searched the monasteries and palaces of Europe, and saved thousands of ancient and precious texts from being swallowed by neglect. Perhaps the greatest achievement of his pontificate was founding the Vatican Library, which, by the end of his life, had accumulated more than five thousand works. Nicholas also generously sponsored many humanist writers as well as the translation of Greek classics, thus reintroducing to the West the great works of Thucydides, Herodotus, and Xenophon.

Nicholas V continued to work at restoring the authority of the Church by finalizing the condemnation of the Conciliarist heresy and winning the submission of the antipope Felix V. He sent Cardinal Nicholas of Cusa, one of the greatest theological and philosophical minds of the age, to England and Northern Germany, and sent the Franciscan St. John of Capistrano to southern Germany in the hope of stemming the growing religious dissension among both the clergy and laity. He also made valiant attempts at achieving greater political unity in Europe as a way of counteracting the growing Turkish threat. Unfortunately, the ongoing division among the Italian states and the lack of cooperation among the competing European states made it impossible for Nicholas to organize sufficient resistance to the Turkish threat to Constantinople. The Byzantine Empire fell to the Turks in 1453.

Though often sickly and physically weak, Nicholas was a man of great spiritual and intellectual strength. He was truly a man of his time, a humanist pope who was highly successful in integrating the new learning with the Catholic Faith.

Pope Callistus III as the protector of the city of Siena by Pietro. Pope Callistus III reversed Joan of Arc's sentence and proclaimed her innocent.

CALLISTUS III (1455-58)

The Spanish-born Alfonso Borgia became Pope Callistus III in 1455. Callistus was preoccupied with the looming Turkish threat. He sent missionaries throughout the West to preach a crusade and to recruit volunteers and money. Bells were rung at midday to remind the faithful to pray for the welfare of the Crusades. Unfortunately, the temporal rulers of the West, still embittered and embattled against each other, were slow to respond to the pope's call. France and England were still engaged in the Hundred Years War and the German Empire was at odds with Polish and Hungarian princes who were fighting the Turks. Even though the crusaders won a major victory in July 1456 at Belgrade, the absence of leadership among the Western states, the continuing Hussite conflict in Bohemia, and the general lack of cohesion among European states all prevented any chance of completely driving out the Turks after this victory. Put simply, Christendom was in no condition to wage war in the hopes of a resounding victory.

Though nearly all of his energies throughout his pontificate were focused upon stemming the Turkish threat, Callistus enjoyed a number of accomplishments. He oversaw the reversal of the sentence against St. Joan of Arc and formally proclaimed her innocence. Though he was not a great literary patron, Callistus did spend a good amount of time, money, and effort in securing artistic treasures for the Vatican. Furthermore,

Callistus began to realize, through his futile attempts to unite Europe against the Turks, that responsibility for the military security of the West lay outside the capacity and duty of the papacy. Unfortunately, this understanding would be forgotten by succeeding popes. Nevertheless, the distraction of a Turkish invasion remained an obstacle to Church reform as it would occupy the mind of the popes for years.

PIUS II (1458-64)

Pope Pius II, born Enea Silvio de' Piccolomini, was a man of multiple facets and in his youth was marked by moral laxity. He possessed an extraordinary intellectual acumen and, as a young man before his ordination, had become passionately involved in the humanist movement. Unfortunately, his fervent embrace of the pagan culture of the past led him to indulge in many worldly pursuits, and for a time he lived a dissolute life, though he was known to have inflicted great penances upon himself. He had been politically involved with various Italian and German princes and at one time supported the Conciliar movement against the pope, serving as secretary for the antipope Felix V. In 1445, however, he reconciled with Pope Eugene IV and underwent a spiritual conversion.

Pope Pius II in Ancona trying to raise a crusade against the Turks threatening Constantinople.

Like his predecessor, the central focus of Pius' pontificate was overcoming the Turkish threat. Again like Callistus, Pius could not win the support of the many feuding princes constantly at war with each other. In addition to his abortive attempts at launching a successful crusade, Pius seriously endeavored to restore monastic discipline and canonized St. Catherine of Siena. He continued giving papal support for humanist writing and penned a number of literary works.

SIXTUS IV (1471-84)

Francesco della Rovere was a virtuous Franciscan monk and professor of philosophy and theology at a number of Italian universities before being called to Rome as a cardinal in 1467. As a scholar, he devoted his time to writing a number of theological and philosophical works, taking special interest in the greatest and most notable of Scholastic philosophers, St. Thomas Aquinas and Bl. John Duns Scotus. He was elected Pope in 1471 and took the name Sixtus IV.

Like his predecessors, Sixtus IV continued to fight the advance of the Turks, but with little success. He commenced dialogue with the Russian Orthodox Church in the hopes of reunion, but failed at this as well.

Most of Sixtus IV's efforts as pope were devoted to maintaining Church strength and independence amid continual growth of nationalism in Europe. The Gallican movement continued to erode papal authority in France. Internal fighting among the Italian states also drew Sixtus into the political fray. Sixtus compounded these political difficulties through rampant nepotism, as he mistakenly tried to build up Church unity by filling its administration with friends and relatives. To his credit, other than his political shortcomings, Sixtus IV lived the rest of his days in blamelessness and virtue. He took steps to suppress abuses in the Inquisition and continued the fight against heresy. He was a patron of the arts and letters, improved the sanitary conditions of Rome, and built the famous Sistine (Sixtine) Chapel.

After the papacy of Sixtus IV to the time of the Reformation, secular interests dominated the policies of the popes. The need to maintain and protect papal independence against rival Italian city-states together with an inordinate interest in worldly matters made the leaders of the Church appear more like princes than Vicars of Christ. Nevertheless, it is important to remember that even though the papacy has not been at all immune to weakness, the teaching of the popes on Faith and morals has never changed. Moreover, the Lord's words, "the powers of death shall not prevail against it" (Mt 16:18), assures the Church of her perseverance in spite of the frailty of her children or officeholders. It bears repeating that the Church is not a mere human institution; rather, it is the Mystical Body of Christ guided and enlivened by the Holy Spirit.

INNOCENT VIII, ALEXANDER VI, AND JULIUS II

The most notorious Renaissance pope, Alexander VI.

The end of the fifteenth and beginning of the sixteenth centuries brought the Church three popes who demonstrated poor moral leadership and worldly attitudes unfit for the Vicar of Christ. The first of these, Innocent VIII, the son of a Roman noble, rose to the papal throne in 1484. He lived a worldly life and primarily tried to restore order to the chaotic Italian political scene. Though earnestly interested in unifying Europe against the possible onslaught of Islam, he failed to take any significant action. While he was pope, the Moors and Jews were expelled from Spain in 1492 during the *Reconquista*.

The most notorious of the Renaissance popes was Alexander VI, born Rodrigo Borgia. This ambitious man attempted to unify Italy under his control by placing family members as the heads of various states and by embroiling himself in a variety of political intrigues. Despite his moral shortcomings and religious insincerity, Alexander was a gifted leader and an able administrator. He dispensed justice in an admirable way and put an end to the lawlessness in Rome. He also was able to negotiate a peace settlement between Spain and Portugal, dividing their colonial possessions with the famous Line of Demarcation. Alexander also sent the first missionaries to the New World.

Like most Renaissance popes, Alexander was a generous patron of the arts, particularly embellishing the art and architecture of Rome. Among other improvements he made to the city, Alexander decorated the ceiling of Santa Maria Maggiore with a shipment of gold from Columbus' voyage to America.

Alexander VI's political skill made him a strong secular leader, but his political involvement and his scandalous personal life (fathering nine illegitimate children) tarnished the moral authority of the Church and made many political enemies. Alexander divided the papal lands for his sons and formed many political marriages with his children. Much to the pope's historical shame, Alexander's son Cesare was the model ruler for Machiavelli's famous treatise on political intrigue, *The Prince*.

The successor to Alexander was his powerful rival in the College of Cardinals, Giuliano della Rovere, who took the name Julius II. Julius continued Alexander's attempt to pacify the Italian peninsula and devoted his pontificate to military endeavors and the artistic glorification of Rome. He was a great patron of the arts and sponsored the great works of Michelangelo and Raphael as well as a host of other builders and artists whose works have beautified the Eternal City. Julius, like Alexander, was a strong military and secular leader who firmly established the temporal authority of the Church over the Papal States. Despite his secular interests, Julius did help bring about some minor reforms in the Church. He abolished simony in the papacy, established the first bishoprics in the New World, and authorized Henry VIII to marry Catherine of Aragon.

Although the private lives of the Renaissance popes were quite unbecoming for the successor of St. Peter, remarkably, they still fulfilled their religious duties as popes. In a time of confusion and secularization, they upheld the teachings of the Church. Still, they failed to live good, moral lives and missed opportunities for much-needed reform.

PART IV

The Rise of New Monarchs

In the fifteenth century, a new breed of monarch began to develop out of the old feudal kingdoms of Christendom. The Hundred Years War (1337-1453), which had pitted France against England, was ending, and the two emerging kingdoms took on new forms. Civil war and feudal rebellion had afflicted a good deal of Europe in the later part of the Middle Ages, and a different type of monarch emerged to lay down the foundations for the modern state. These new rulers expanded their domains and instituted a broader, tighter, and more efficient form of government. They initiated policies to encourage trade and economic growth in order to find other sources of income for the royal treasuries. They fought feudal traditions and local customs, thus enhancing their own national power. Manorial (territorial) courts in England were replaced with the reintroduction of Roman law. Due to the on-going wars and rebellions from which these monarchs arose, the kings continued to tax their subjects and have access to a ready source of income. Maintenance and support of local nobles was declared illegal and the monarchs moved to bring down local castles and coats of arms of their opposition. Bureaucratic administration and diminished power of the aristocracy led to increased central authority. These new states would dominate the start of the new modern era.

King Louis XI of France.

FRANCE AND ENGLAND

King Louis XI (1461-1483) and his successors emerged as the new monarchs in France. Because of the Hundred Years War, these Valois kings had developed a professional army to suppress brigands and subdue rebellious nobles. When the Duke of Burgundy died without a male heir, Louis XI was able to absorb the powerful state of Burgundy, which had supported England. The Hundred Years War allowed Louis to institute the *taille*, a perpetual tax that made it possible for him to rule his domain without the need to call upon the Estates General for more funds. Finally, when the French defeated the English, the national spirit of France solidified. Louis XI took advantage of this strong French national spirit and sought to remove all restrictions to the exercise of his authority by promoting a kind of Conciliarism within the Church in France.

England entered into its own civil conflict at the end of the Hundred Years War. Two major feudal houses clashed for the English crown in the War of the Roses. The war lasted for thirty years and left the two noble houses (York and Lancaster) decimated. The Tudors proved victorious, and Henry Tudor became Henry VII, the new king of England. He expanded trade, encouraged private enterprise, ended the practice of maintenance and support of the local nobles, and consolidated his kingdom. By avoiding war and granting monopolies, he enhanced his own financial resources. Perhaps his most shrewd and effective move as king was offering for marriage his son and heir, the future Henry VIII, to the powerful Spanish kingdom (Catherine of Aragon, the daughter of Isabella). England recovered and rallied behind the Tudor family, and over time would become one of the foremost powers in Europe.

SPAIN – ISABELLA, THE CATHOLIC QUEEN

At the beginning of the fifteenth century, Spain as a nation did not exist. The Iberian Peninsula was comprised of five major kingdoms: Portugal (the first to unite), Castile, Leon, Aragon, and the Muslim kingdom of Granada. These kingdoms were made up of a very cosmopolitan population that included Christians, Muslims, and Jews. Various language groups and conflicting nobility dominated the peninsula and made Spanish unification unlikely. The only institution crossing feudal and ethnic boundaries was the Catholic Church. Thus, the Catholic Faith would become the means of unity for the kingdom of Spain. The marriage between the king of Aragon and a pious queen from Castile established the unification of the kingdoms.

Queen Isabella of Castile, *Isabel La Católica*

Queen Isabella of Castile was an extraordinary woman and a devoutly Christian ruler. Because of her efforts, the Catholic Church regained much of the authority it had lost in the preceding centuries. Strengthened by Isabella's Spain, the Church would stave off disaster after the Protestant Reformation. Isabella's role within the Catholic Church had as much to do with her personal faith and piety as with her skillful politics.

Isabella was a devout, loyal wife who ruled Spain with determination and prudence. She came to the throne following a series of weak monarchs and worked hard to restore the authority of the monarch and bring about internal reforms. When she married Ferdinand of Aragon in 1469, the two largest states in Spain (Castile and Aragon) were united, paving the way for the *Reconquista* (Reconquest) of the peninsula.

After their marriage, the largest hinderance to Christian unity in Spain was the Moorish (North African Muslim) kingdom of Granada, which was poised to overwhelm the Peninsula as it had done centuries earlier. In 1492, Spanish forces captured Granada, driving out the Moors and uniting the kingdom of Spain. As in France and England, war allowed the Spanish monarchs to gain the much-needed taxes that could mold an army loyal to the monarch. The success of the *Reconquista* would turn Spain into the most powerful country in Europe for the next 150 years. Also in 1492, Isabella sponsored the young Italian Christopher Columbus on a mission to find a water route to

The Surrender of the Moors at Granada. In 1492, Spanish forces captured Granada, driving out the Moors, and uniting the kingdom of Spain. The success of the *Reconquista* would turn Spain into the most powerful country in Europe for 150 years and neutralize much of the religious tension that led to the wars of religion across Europe (see chapter 14).

India. Little did she know that in his failing, Columbus would stumble upon the American continent and open the way to Euorpean expansion into the New World.

As queen, Isabella took personal charge of her kingdom. She traveled with her husband Ferdinand during the *Reconquista,* bringing medical care to the wounded and administering justice in the field. She opposed the many spoils and excesses of war, and she would punish by hanging any soldier who raped, pillaged, or plundered. Isabella lived a life of prayer and great ascetical virtue, dedicating herself to helping the poor. During her reign, she prohibited slavery of native Africans and sent missionaries for their conversion. She detested the superstitions of her times and worked to protect those accused of witchcraft or sorcery. She believed and showed that the main force needed to unite the cosmopolitan kingdom of Spain was the Catholic Faith.

Despite Spain's unity, many feared that nonChristian populations—especially in the south of Spain—would threaten Spanish unity. Whereas Jews had been expelled from England in 1290 and France in 1306, they had always enjoyed relative security in Spain until the late fourteenth century. After the conquest of Granada, many believed that newly converted Muslims (*Moriscos*) and converted Jews (*Marranos*) were acting as spies for Moors in Africa or putting forward a Catholic façade of having been baptized yet practicing their old religions in the secrecy of their homes. Acting under the principle of "unity of Faith," Isabella felt compelled to expel Muslims and Jews who would not convert. She helped institute the Spanish Inquisition to ensure the patriotism, orthodoxy, and true conversion among the *Moriscos* and *Marranos.* To guarantee unity within Spain, large communities of Jews and Muslims, including craftsmen, merchants, and skilled workers, were forced to leave the country. Some historians credit the *Reconquista* with avoiding the "wars of religion" (cf. chapter 14) that ravaged the rest of the continent, but many agree it also contributed to Spain's eventual economic decline.

Cardinal Ximenes de Cisneros liberates prisoners at Oran, a city on the northwestern tip of Algeria on the Mediterranean coast. Oran was founded in the 10th century by Moorish Andalusian traders. Supported by Ferdinand, a preliminary expedition, equipped at the expense of Ximenes, captured the port of Mers-el-Kebir in 1505. In 1509 a strong force accompanied by the Cardinal set sail for Africa, and in one day the city of Oran was taken from the Moors.

CARDINAL XIMENES DE CISNEROS

Gonzalo Ximenes de Cisneros was appointed bishop and named a cardinal during the political turmoil of the late fifteenth century. He sought to leave the world and devote his life to simplicity and prayer. When he joined the Franciscan order, he modestly dreamed of living his life as an ordinary cleric with the hopes of obtaining a small benefice near his home in Toledo. By the age of fifty, his reputation as a confessor spread throughout the peninsula and eventually to the royal court at Castile. Isabella summoned the friar and asked him to be her personal confessor. Ximenes de Cisneros agreed on the condition that he could still live in his small village community. Isabella agreed but was soon so pleased with the holy priest that she insisted on making him Bishop of Toledo. Ximenes de Cisneros still did not want anything but the simple life of a country friar, but Pope Alexander VI reminded him of his vow of obedience.

When Ximenes de Cisneros became bishop, he helped Spain become the only European country to undergo major reform. He built the University of Alcala and introduced the first humanist school in Spain. He reformed all the clerical orders of Spain, including his own Franciscan order. When he inherited the task of grand inquisitor of Spain, he made great reforms and protected those who had been wrongly accused of heresy. After Isabella's death in 1504, Ximenes de Cisneros acted as regent to Spain and insisted on honoring her commands of protecting African slaves and Native Americans. He diplomatically kept the nobles in line and was able to preserve a united kingdom for Isabella's heir, her grandson Charles V, the future Holy Roman emperor. Ultimately it was Isabella of Castile and Cardinal Ximenes de Cisneros who prepared the way for the Catholic reform of the sixteenth century which would eventually defend the Church against the rising Protestant tide.

THE HAPSBURG EMPIRE OF CHARLES V

Germany in the fifteenth century consisted of a confederation of eighty-nine cities, two hundred principalities, and three major bishoprics. The emperor was elected and his authority over these municipalities was severely limited by centuries of feudal agreements. After 1356 the right of electing an emperor was vested in seven electors—namely, four of the princely lords; the count of Palatine, duke of Saxony, marquis of Brandenburg, and king of Bohemia; and in three ecclesiastical lords; the archbishops of Mainz, Trier, and Cologne. In 1452 the electors chose King Frederick III of Austria, the House of Hapsburg, and this family would dominate the empire from 1452 to 1806.

The greatest of these emperors was the grandson of Isabella, Charles V. Charles united the inheritances of his four grandparents: Austria from Maximilian, the Netherlands from Mary of Burgundy, Castile and Spanish America from Isabella, and Aragon and its Mediterranean and Italian possessions from Ferdinand. Upon his election as Holy Roman Emperor in 1519, Charles would become the most powerful ruler in Europe. Charles V would champion the Catholic cause in Europe against Turkish attacks. Despite this great Catholic ruler's efforts at preserving European unity and strength, the fear of his growing power among German nobles and the French king, the continuing Muslim threat, and the explosive actions of Martin Luther would bring about the great conflicts of the sixteenth century: the Protestant Reformation and peasant wars.

Grandson of the *Catholic Queen*, Isabella, Charles V became Holy Roman Emperor in 1519.

Emperor Charles V and Pope Clement VII ride into Bologna. Pope Clement VII experienced a difficult relationship with the Emperor as Clement shifted his papal allegiance back and forth between Charles V and Francis I, king of France. Both emperor and king sought to dominate Italy, and Clement was trapped between their military power.

THE HAPSBURG EMPIRE, 1556-1618

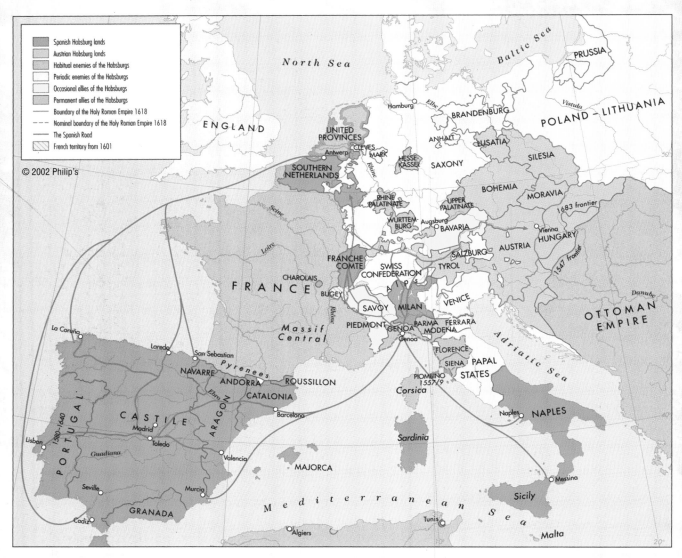

By the 1520s the Habsburgs had accumulated under Emperor Charles V the largest conglomeration of territories and rights since the age of Charlemagne.

Charles V presided over a vast empire of territories and faced formidable enemies—Valois France, the Ottoman Empire and various alliances of German princes.

In 1552 the rebellion of the League of Princes in Germany allied to Henry II of France forced him to the decision that the Empire was too large to be ruled by one man, and that as a family with a dynastic concern, it had to be shared. As a result, Charles V abdicated in 1556.

After Charles' abdication, the Empire was divided in two, with his brother Ferdinand I ruling the Austrian domains and his son Philip II inheriting his father's Spanish lands.

Michelangelo's *Pieta*. The Renaissance offered the social climate perfect for the rise of Christian humanism, a rebirth in Classical principles, and magnificent developments in the fine arts.

CONCLUSION

Though often heralded as one of the pinnacle moments in human history, the Renaissance did not pass without its high and low points. At its best the Renaissance offered the social climate perfect for the rise of Christian humanism, a rebirth in classical principles, and magnificent developments in the fine arts. However, the Renaissance in its excesses exaggerated the understanding of human capacity and encouraged a false sense of self-sufficiency. This period represents a significant crossroads in the history of the West, a time when thinkers and artists grew confident enough to explore human understanding and beauty outside the realm of religion. New developments in art, politics, and economics showed the people of the Renaissance that society could function, and function effectively, outside the traditional restraints of religion and morality. This confidence helped advance the material quality of life, but in many ways it also led to the indulgence and extravagance of the baroque and rococo periods.

The contradictions of the Renaissance are no better exemplified than in the lives of the popes of that period. Certainly much has been said about the gross excesses and hypocritical immorality of these men. At the same time, their artistic and intellectual heritage survives to this day. These men did much to advance the quality of life both in Rome and in the rest of Italy, and they helped to reestablish the papacy as a patron of intellectual and spiritual exploration. It bears mentioning that some of the most pious popes have not always been effective in governing the Church from a political, social, artistic, and economic viewpoint, whereas these "princes of men" helped protect and strengthen the Church according to the ways and means of their time. They represent the ironic reality familiar to the hierarchical Church: often in history, less than worthy men are chosen to carry and sustain the Mystical Body of Christ.

SUPPLEMENTARY READING

Nicolò Machiavelli, *The Prince*, Chapter 14, "That Which Concerns a Prince on the Subject of the Art of War"

A Prince ought to have no other aim or thought, nor select anything else for his study, than war and its rules and discipline; for this is the sole art that belongs to him who rules, and it is of such force that it not only upholds those who are born princes, but it often enables men to rise from a private station to that rank....The first cause of your losing it is to neglect this art; and what enables you to acquire a state is to be master of the art....For among other evils which being unarmed brings you, it causes you to be despised, and this is one of those ignominies against which a prince ought to guard himself...therefore a prince who does not understand the art of war, over and above the other misfortunes already mentioned, cannot be respected by his soldiers, nor can he rely on them. He ought never, therefore, to have out of his thoughts this subject of war, and in peace he should addict himself more to its exercise than in war; this he can do in two ways, the one by action, the other by study.

St. Thomas More, *Utopia*, Book II, "Of the Religions of the Utopians"

There are several sorts of religions, not only in different parts of the island, but even in every town; some worshipping the sun, others the moon or one of the planets: some worship such men as have been eminent in former times for virtue or glory, not only as ordinary deities, but as the supreme God: yet the greater and wiser sort of them worship none of these, but adore one eternal, invisible, infinite, and incomprehensible Deity; as a being that is far above all our apprehensions, that is spread over the whole universe, not by His bulk, but by His power and virtue; Him they call the Father of All, and acknowledge

that the beginnings, the increase, the progress, the vicissitudes, and the end of all things come only from Him; nor do they offer divine honors to any but to Him alone. And indeed, though they differ concerning other things, yet all agree in this, that they think there is one Supreme Being that made and governs the world, whom they call in the language of their country Mithras. They differ in this, that one thinks the god whom he worships is this Supreme Being, and another thinks that his idol is that God; but they all agree in one principle, that whoever is this Supreme Being, He is also that great Essence to whose glory and majesty all honors are ascribed by the consent of all nations.

John Paul II, *Message to the Sixth National Meeting of Catholic University Professors*

Christian humanism is not abstract. The freedom in research that is so precious cannot imply neutral indifference to the truth....*The service of the truth* is the epoch-making mission of universities. It recalls the contemplative dimension of knowledge which heightens the humanistic feature of every discipline in the areas addressed by your convention. The ability to interpret the meaning of events and to appreciate the most daring discoveries stems from this interior attitude. The service of truth is the mark of free and open intelligence.... Christians are called to bear witness to the dignity of human reason, to its requirements and its capacity for seeking out and knowing reality, thereby overcoming epistemological skepticism, the ideological reductions of rationalism and the nihilistic dead ends of weak thought.

VOCABULARY

BONÆ LITTERÆ OR LITTERÆ HUMANIORES

Latin for "good letters" or "more humane letters," these terms were used by humanists to describe works which focused on man's relation to the world rather than man's relation to God and eternal salvation.

FREE CITIES

Italian cities ruled by noble families whose interest in trade, wealth, and power helped form a society based on commerce in which merchants were free to trade with whomever they pleased.

HIGH RENAISSANCE

Period beginning in the late fifteenth century, it produced some of the most well-known religious and secular artwork of the period from such figures as Leonardo, Raphael and Michelangelo.

HUMANISM

An intellectual and literary movement that began in the city-states of Italy during the late fourteenth century. Moving away from the Scholastic education of the Medieval era, the humanists thought that education had a moral purpose, the end of which was to make the individual a better, wiser, and more virtuous human being. To achieve this, they aimed to base every branch of learning on classical Greek and Roman culture.

MACHIAVELLIANISM

A political philosophy that developed from Machiavelli's works, most notably *The Prince*, most simply understood as "the ends justify the means."

MARRANOS

Jews who converted to Catholicism after the *Reconquista* to avoid being exiled.

MORISCOS

Muslims who converted to Catholicism after the conquest of Granada to avoid being exiled.

NORTHERN HUMANISM

Humanism had a different effect in Northern Europe where there were not the same economic and social changes as there were in Italy. Life was much like it was during the Medieval age, and rather than redirecting study to classical, pagan culture, those in the North sought to reconcile humanism with Christianity.

RENAISSANCE

French for "re-birth," this period is characterized by the popular desire to return to the civilization of the Greco-Roman world and re-awaken a sense of human beauty and personal achievement.

STUDIUM HUMANITAS

Study of the humanities which placed a great emphasis on Classical texts and literature, as well as revival of the study of Greek and Latin.

TAILLE

Perpetual tax instituted by the French king Louis VI which made it possible for him to rule his domain without the need to call upon the Estates General for more funds.

UTOPIA

Meaning "no place," this term was coined by St. Thomas More who, in his book by that name, describes a religious society, heavily influenced by divine revelation, in which goods were held in common and the state regulated business.

STUDY QUESTIONS

1. What does the French word *Renaissance* mean in English?

2. Name three important cities involved in trade and commerce in Italy other than Rome.

3. When did Constantinople fall?

4. What was the main topic handled by the Council of Basel-Ferrara-Florence (1431-45)?

5. Was the council's aim successful?

6. To what did the Italian city-states aspire to return in the fifteenth century?

7. What old languages received new attention and generated new interest?

8. What did urbanization bring about?

9. What was another over-arching theme of the Renaissance that stood out in contrast not only to the Medieval period, but also the classical age?

10. What discipline was considered the pinnacle of human achievement during the Renaissance?

11. What opened the door to secularity and worldly morality?

12. Which fourteenth century poet was known as "the man of letters"?

13. This "man of letters" was famous for writing poetry to whom?

14. Who wrote the *Decameron*?

15. How did the *Decameron* exemplify a break with Medieval literature?

16. What text has become the foundational bedrock of Western politics for the past 500 years, and who is its author?

17. Who authored *Utopia*?

18. Name two works written by Erasmus.

19. What qualities led to Erasmus' recognition as a humanist?

20. Who was St. Thomas More?

21. What kind of influence did the Medici family have in Florence? What affect did they have on the cultural blooming of the Renaissance?

22. Who was Savonarola?

23. Characterize the holiness of the Renaissance popes.

24. What is the relationship of the "Rise of New Monarchs" to many of the nation-states in Europe today?

25. What new royal line led France?

26. What domestic turmoil was the outcome of the Hundred Years War in England?

27. Who became the new king in England?

28. Who were the reigning monarchs of Spain?

29. What two events occurred in Spain in 1492?

30. The unification of Spain resulted in the expulsion of which two groups from Catholic Spain?

31. How did Cardinal Ximenes de Cisneros make the development of a Protestant Reformation in Spain virtually impossible?

32. What family line dominated the Holy Roman Empire from 1452-1806?

PRACTICAL EXERCISES

1. What distinguished the Renaissance from the High Middle Ages? Compare and contrast an artist or writer from each period to explain your answer.

2. If one is a person in public life today, is it better to be feared or loved? Do you think the principles embodied in *The Prince*— essentially that "the ends justify the means"— should be the basis of modern political considerations? Are there other texts that provide better alternatives?

3. The Renaissance held art in very high esteem. How does the way that the Renaissance culture understood art help explain the motives for the Renaissance popes? Choose two popes and explain how they might defend their decisions to a contemporary audience.

FROM THE CATECHISM

285 Since the beginning the Christian faith has been challenged by responses to the question of origins that differ from its own. Ancient religions and cultures produced many myths concerning origins. Some philosophers have said that everything is God, that the world is God, or that the development of the world is the development of God (Pantheism). Others have said that the world is a necessary emanation arising from God and returning to him. Still others have affirmed the existence of two eternal principles, Good and Evil, Light and Darkness, locked, in permanent conflict (Dualism, Manichaeism). According to some of these conceptions, the world (at least the physical world) is evil, the product of a fall, and is thus to be rejected or left behind (Gnosticism). Some admit that the world was made by God, but as by a watchmaker who, once he has made a watch, abandons it to itself (Deism). Finally, others reject any transcendent origin for the world, but see it as merely the interplay of matter that has always existed (Materialism). All these attempts bear witness to the permanence and universality of the question of origins. This inquiry is distinctively human.

1676 Pastoral discernment is needed to sustain and support popular piety and, if necessary, to purify and correct the religious sense which underlies these devotions so that the faithful may advance in knowledge of the mystery of Christ (cf. John Paul II, *CT* 54). Their exercise is subject to the care and judgment of the bishops and to the general norms of the Church.

> At its core the piety of the people is a storehouse of values that offers answers of Christian wisdom to the great questions of life. The Catholic wisdom of the people is capable of fashioning a vital synthesis.... It creatively combines the divine and the human, Christ and Mary, spirit and body, communion and institution, person and community, faith and homeland, intelligence and emotion. This wisdom is a Christian humanism that radically affirms the dignity of every person as a child of God, establishes a basic fraternity, teaches people to encounter nature and understand work, provides reasons for joy and humor even in the midst of a very hard life. For the people this wisdom is also a principle of

FROM THE CATECHISM Continued

discernment and an evangelical instinct through which they spontaneously sense when the Gospel is served in the Church and when it is emptied of its content and stifled by other interests (CELAM, Third General Conference (Puebla, 1979), Final Document, § 448 (tr. NCCB, 1979); cf. Paul VI, EN 48).

1732 As long as freedom has not bound itself definitively to its ultimate good which is God, there is the possibility of *choosing between good and evil,* and thus of growing in perfection or of failing and sinning. This freedom characterizes properly human acts. It is the basis of praise or blame, merit or reproach.

1738 Freedom is exercised in relationships between human beings. Every human person, created in the image of God, has the natural right to be recognized as a free and responsible being. All owe to each other this duty of respect. The *right to the exercise of freedom,* especially in moral and religious matters, is an inalienable requirement of the dignity of the human person. This right must be recognized and protected by civil authority within the limits of the common good and public order (cf. *DH* 2 § 7).

1898 Every human community needs an authority to govern it (cf. Leo XIII, *Immortale Dei; Diuturnum illud.*). The foundation of such authority lies in human nature. It is necessary for the unity of the state. Its role is to ensure as far as possible the common good of the society.

1899 The authority required by the moral order derives from God: "Let every person be subject to the governing authorities. For there is no authority except from God, and those that exist have been instituted by God. Therefore he who resists the authorities resists what God has appointed, and those who resist will incur judgment" (Rom 13:1-2; cf. 1 Pt 2:13-17).

1915 As far as possible citizens should take an active part in *public life.* The manner of this participation may vary from one country or culture to another. "One must pay tribute to those nations whose systems permit the largest possible number of the citizens to take part in public life in a climate of genuine freedom" (*GS* 31 § 3).

2255 It is the duty of citizens to work with civil authority for building up society in a spirit of truth, justice, solidarity, and freedom.

A 1630 painting of the Basilica of St. Peter by Viviano Codazzi.

The Reformation: Protestant And Catholic

The political chaos resulting from the Hundred Years War, the breakdown of feudal loyalties, and the tarnished moral authority of the papacy created an environment ripe for rebellion.

NO · ÆTATIS ·   · SVÆ · XLIX ·

CHAPTER 13

The Reformation: Protestant And Catholic

> Disappointments...were bound to arise in the case of individuals or groups that viewed the problem of Christian unity in too casual and superficial a way. Many enthusiastic people, sustained by great optimism, were ready to believe that the Second Vatican Council had already resolved the problem. But the Council only opened the road to unity, committing first of all the Catholic Church; but that road itself is a process, which must gradually overcome many obstacles—whether of a doctrinal or a cultural or a social nature—that have accumulated over the course of centuries. It is necessary, therefore, to rid ourselves of stereotypes, of old habits. And above all, it is necessary to recognize the unity that already exists.
>
> — John Paul II, *Crossing the Threshold of Hope*

In the middle of the sixteenth century, a series of reformers began to question the teaching of the Church, shaking the very foundations of Christendom. Many of these reformers' ideas can be traced to the earlier heresies of Jan Hus and John Wycliffe. With this new movement, heretical ideas took hold in Europe in an unprecedented way. The political chaos caused by the Hundred Years War, the breakdown of feudal loyalties resulting from the plague, and the tarnished moral authority of the papacy after years of schism and political preoccupations, created a situation ripe for rebellion. Worldliness in the hierarchy, clerical abuses, rising nationalism, and unsupervised individual preaching contributed to what would be known as the Protestant Reformation.

The legacy of this time poses one of the greatest challenges for full Christian unity. As evident from history, this challenge can be difficult and disheartening. Nonetheless, John Paul II urged all peoples "to recognize the unity that already exists" and strive for a time when Christ's Church will once again bring together all who call themselves "Christian."

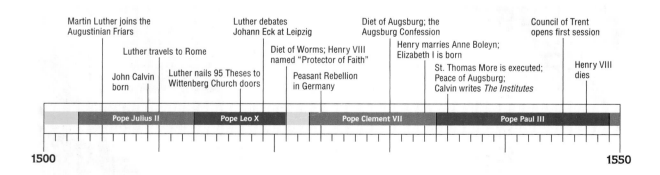

Martin Luther joins the Augustinian Friars

Luther travels to Rome

John Calvin born

Luther nails 95 Theses to Wittenberg Church doors

Luther debates Johann Eck at Leipzig

Diet of Worms; Henry VIII named "Protector of Faith"

Peasant Rebellion in Germany

Diet of Augsburg; the Augsburg Confession

Henry marries Anne Boleyn; Elizabeth I is born

St. Thomas More is executed; Peace of Augsburg; Calvin writes *The Institutes*

Council of Trent opens first session

Henry VIII dies

Pope Julius II | Pope Leo X | Pope Clement VII | Pope Paul III

1500 — 1550

PART I

The Protestant Revolt

Reform was needed in the Church. Simony, nepotism, and the abuse of indulgences and improper veneration of relics had spread throughout Western Europe. Many clerics collected benefices for personal gain, some failed to keep their promises of celibacy and obedience, and others had been corrupted by the lure of wealth and worldliness. Along with moral character, the level of learning among parish priests had also declined. Many could neither read nor write in Latin, and superstition grew in many rural areas where ignorant peasants often resorted to witchcraft or astrology to determine the fate of their lives. Leo X (1425-1521), the reigning pope who excommunicated Luther, typified the worldly lifestyle of Renaissance Rome.

Given the moral crisis in the Church and the different vested interests among ecclesiastics, unity among the hierarchy was seriously compromised. Society was changing. Despite the advancements of the Renaissance on the Italian peninsula, in the sixteenth century, most of Europe was still primarily an agrarian society. Nonetheless, increasing divides between the nobility and the poor contributed to animosity between the classes. New monarchs emerged who undermined older feudal arrangements and consolidated their power with new taxes and centralized law. Impoverished gentry landholders began to fear loss of authority and sought ways to recover their wealth and position. As a result, various princes fought each other for their own personal aggrandizement. While this was occurring in Northern Europe, the papacy was caught up in the political intrigue of the Italian city-states and the cost of rebuilding Rome and patronizing the arts. One sad side effect of the Church's prolific patronage of Renaissance art and architecture was the increasing abuse regarding the sale of offices and indulgences. These transactions served as lucrative means of raising funds needed to pay for dazzling churches and works of art. The now infamous sale of indulgences would also provide an opportunity for a young and gifted monk to voice dissent that would snowball into a crisis of unparalleled gravity.

An indulgence sold by Johann Tetzel, a Dominican priest, in 1517. The text reads: "By the authority of all the saints, and in mercy towards you, I absolve you from all sins and misdeeds and remit all punishments for ten days."

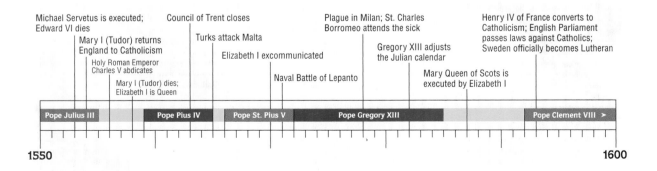

Timeline:

- Michael Servetus is executed; Edward VI dies
- Mary I (Tudor) returns England to Catholicism
- Holy Roman Emperor Charles V abdicates
- Mary I (Tudor) dies; Elizabeth I is Queen
- Council of Trent closes
- Turks attack Malta
- Elizabeth I excommunicated
- Naval Battle of Lepanto
- Plague in Milan; St. Charles Borromeo attends the sick
- Gregory XIII adjusts the Julian calendar
- Mary Queen of Scots is executed by Elizabeth I
- Henry IV of France converts to Catholicism; English Parliament passes laws against Catholics; Sweden officially becomes Lutheran

Pope Julius III | Pope Pius IV | Pope St. Pius V | Pope Gregory XIII | Pope Clement VIII ➤

1550 — 1600

MARTIN LUTHER'S EARLY LIFE

Martin Luther was born in Eisleben, Saxony, in 1483. He was the second of eight children, and he received the customary education of his time. Luther's father had risen slightly in society, starting as a poor peasant and then a copper miner, eventually gaining some wealth and obtaining a minor elected position in his village. As a father, he was a strict disciplinarian, and he had hoped that his son would enter the field of law. However, Martin Luther would choose a very different path.

Rather than study law, Luther joined the Augustinian Friars in 1505. Legend has it that he made the decision to enter the monastery after surviving a violent thunderstorm. After a bolt of lightning crashed near the young Luther, he made a vow, promising that if he survived the storm he would dedicate his life to God. Although the importance of this event may have been exaggerated over time, similar events in Luther's early life all seem to have helped solidify a spirituality that sought comfort in God as a response to great difficulty. A serious illness during adolescence, the sudden death of a friend, a sword wound acquired in a student's duel (which had bled for a long time) — all these brought Luther face to face with the reality of death. The bolt of lightning only helped convince young Luther that his life was fragile and best spent in the monastery at the service of God. As a monk, Luther believed he could better seek perfection and forgiveness from a God who seemed indifferent to the life and death of his people.

IN THE MONASTERY

Luther took his vows and was ordained after only nine months in the monastery. He showed to be a promising scholar and lived an exemplary life as far as his piety and ascetical struggle were concerned. Luther was promoted rapidly as a professor, and after only a year and a half of formal theological studies, he was appointed to lecture at the university. But despite his success, Luther's life in the monastery was far from happy.

It was during his early years in monastic life that he had a problem with scrupulosity, the habit of imagining sin when none exists or grave sin when the matter is not serious. More and more, Luther began to see God exclusively as a righteous lawgiver and administrator of justice. Much of Luther's understanding of God's judgment and his misconception of his love and mercy — through grace — was a consequence of the severe image of God stirred up by the culture of the day, particularly in Germany. The heavy emphasis on damnation, divine justice, and the absolute necessity of contrite repentance fostered the notion of a god who would deal out abundant punishment and whose wrath towards sinners was difficult to appease. Luther wondered how much penance a sinner could possibly do before finally obtaining God's mercy.

This monk would later say that during this time, the thought of God as a righteous judge who passes sentence on the weak made him increasingly angry. During these tough spiritual times, Luther said he was tempted with "evil thoughts, hatred of God, blasphemy, despair and unbelief" (quoted in Daniel-Rops, *Heroes of God: Eleven Heroic Men and Women Who Risked Everything to Spread the Catholic Faith*, 2002, p. 20). Stricken with an acute sense of his own unworthiness, he imagined that God, the all-righteous judge, would most likely withhold forgiveness and salvation from him. In turn, he began to seek comfort through intense prayer, fasting, and penance. Unfortunately for the young monk, no amount of prayer or fasting would give him relief from his internal turmoil. He would ask how weak, sinful humans could ever possibly achieve a state of grace and the necessary righteousness to win God's approval and mercy. For Luther, they obviously could not.

Despite his moral anguish, Luther's life was normal, reputable, and according to many accounts, upstanding. He was an exceptional scholar and preacher, and his efforts in both capacities won him

Martin Luther (1483-1546) painted by his friend Lucas Cranach the Elder in 1529.

popular praise and advancements within his order. His supervisor said of Luther's preaching, "God speaks through your mouth" (quoted in Daniel-Rops, *Heroes of God: Eleven Heroic Men and Women Who Risked Everything to Spread the Catholic Faith*, 2002, p. 19), and his trip to Rome in 1510 reflected the esteem with which other Augustinians had for him. Even though in later years Luther would reflect negatively on this trip to Rome, where his stay as any other pious pilgrim would consist in visiting churches, obtaining the many indulgences available through acts of penance, and climbing the Scala Santa. He would have heard rumors of ecclesiastical corruption, but probably would not have been directly exposed to any of the inner workings of the Church.

Luther's objections to the Church developed over time, and in some sense, they were all rooted in the spiritual struggles of his own soul, and not the politics of ecclesiastical life. Luther's exaggerated understanding of God as judge began to influence his conception of God's love and mercy. His own theological inclinations found a counterpart in a popular, though heretical, theologian that Luther encountered in his studies: William of Ockham. For someone like Luther, the teachings of William of Ockham offered little comfort. Ockham taught that man could not overcome sin alone, and that all meritorious human action must be willed by God. This reduced man's ability to perform good deeds. The teachings of Ockham appealed to Luther, and he began to speculate about similar theological tendencies in the writings of St. Paul and St. Augustine. These misreadings and miscomprehensions of the nature of Divine justice and man's sinfulness laid the foundation for Luther's future heresy, and in 1517, they helped fuel his distaste for the practice of selling indulgences. Outraged with the Church's teaching that indulgences, when obtained within the context of the Sacrament of Penance could help lessen or remit one's temporal punishment due to sin. His inner tensions over personal salvation and the practice of selling indulgences prompted him to write and nail the Ninety-five Theses to the door of the Church at Wittenberg.

THE NINETY-FIVE THESES

By 1517, the practice of selling indulgences was being thoroughly abused, and although indulgences helped bring many people to Penance and inspire repentance, some Church administrators became distracted by the financial benefits of these twisted transactions. At the time, the cost of maintaining the works of charity provided by the Church was becoming increasingly expensive. In addition, the massive artistic and architectural undertakings of the Renaissance were requiring more funds. Running the Church was costly, and to meet those demands, clerics and secular rulers alike started looking for additional ways to raise money.

In 1517, Albrecht of Brandenburg, Archbishop of Magdeburg, sought an appointment to the archepiscopal see of Mainz. Appointment to this position required a tax of thirty-one thousand gold ducats. Neither the bishop nor his diocese could afford the cost and so Albrecht was forced to borrow from the wealthy Fugger family at a high interest rate. In addition to this financial burden, the massive and costly construction of St. Peter's Basilica in Rome put a particular strain on the Church in Germany. Looking for a way to afford all of these costs, Albrecht requested that a special papal indulgence be instituted and preached throughout his realm as a means of raising money. The proceeds from the alms received in payment for the papal indulgence would be split between Rome and the archdiocese of Mainz.

Unfortunately, preaching about this indulgence brought Albrecht into direct conflict with his neighbor, Duke Frederick of Saxony. Frederick had collected a great number of relics that he put on display for the veneration of the faithful, and the duke hoped to lure large numbers of pilgrims to his city for its great feast day on November 1, All Saints Day. However, the promotion of the papal indulgence in nearby Brandenburg would draw people away from Frederick's project. This competition over the hearts and pockets of the German faithful was quite disedifying, to say the least, and was certainly deserving of criticism. On October 31, 1517, the day before the Saxon feast day, Martin Luther, a subject of Frederick, nailed to the Cathedral door ninety-five theses, attacking the sale of indulgences.

None of Luther's theses was explicitly heretical, but implicitly because they directly undermine the teaching authority of the Church. In them, Luther criticizes the use of indulgences for distracting sinners from true repentance. Luther argued that indulgences imply the forgiveness of sin through human as opposed to divine authority, and he saw this as a grave deviation. Luther questioned the validity of indulgences since the Church seemed to be usurping the authority of Christ in his role as mediator of grace and reconciliation with God the Father. Moreover, Luther started to place personal interpretation of Scripture over the teaching authority of the Church. These arguments reveal trends in Luther's thought that, in hindsight, point towards his future break with the Catholic Church.

Martin Luther nailed his ninety-five theses to the door of the Church of All Saints in Wittenberg (the University's customary notice board) as an open invitation to debate his objections.

FROM DEBATE TO DISSENSION

Luther's posting of the Ninety-five Theses to the door of the church at Wittenberg was not, in and of itself, an action provoking scandal. It was the academic custom of the age to offer an argument in this manner and invite public debate on an issue. At first, no one came forward to argue with Luther on the subject of indulgences. In earlier years, this kind of dissent would not have spread,

Gutenberg's invention of the printing press allowed mass circulation of Luther's ideas and criticism of Rome.

but due to the advent of the printing press, copies of Luther's theses were able to be printed and circulated, finding their way to the doorsteps of most of the prominent clerics and scholars in Germany. His ideas met a mixed response. The theses, which now sound unmistakably Protestant, were not immediately condemned. In fact, many students began to rally behind Luther and praise the monk's bold criticism of the abuses that detracted from the Church's spiritual mission.

Luther's criticism did, however, upset the Archbishop of Mainz who forwarded Luther's theses to Rome. At first Pope Leo X considered the critique a minor incident. Luther was summoned before the Dominican Cardinal Cajetan at Augsburg who asked the theologian Sylvester Prierias to study Luther's theses and issue a rebuttal. Applying Prierias' findings, Cajetan objected to Luther's attack on the notion of merit and his questioning of the Church's infallibility. He sent a response to Luther that the pope himself hoped would settle the matter and allow the monk to fade back into obscurity.

Luther did not recant. Instead, while retaining a certain tone of respect and subordination towards the pope, he issued his *Resolution on the Virtue of Indulgences,* which restated his position on the matter. Surprised by Luther's bold reply, the Holy See responded more authoritatively. Pope Leo had the head of the Dominican order draw up an indictment that summoned Luther to Rome in order to explain his position before Cardinal Cajetan. In his efforts to drive home his theological position, the Dominican's letter, which was a strong reprimand of Luther, gave much importance to some of the points of disagreement, including the scope of papal authority. The change in tone and severity on the part of the papal representative angered Luther, who still believed that his arguments were sound. He also reacted to the harsh letter from Rome by becoming firmer in his sense of righteousness.

Rather than having Luther travel to Rome, Duke Frederick of Saxony intervened on behalf of Luther and arranged for a public debate between Cajetan and Luther in Augsburg (Germany). When Luther arrived, Cajetan instructed Luther, scolding him like a father and urging him to return to the teachings of the Church. However correct Cajetan's theology was, his fatherly method did not take into account that Luther, more than a simple wayward monk, was a celebrated theologian and considered an expert in his field. Tired of dismissals and still desiring a debate, Luther felt very much offended and did not recant.

At this point Luther still did not wish to break with the Church. He wrote a letter to Leo X, subordinating himself to the authority of the supreme pontiff and showing his desire for the problem to be resolved. Theologically, Luther was still unconvinced, and the longer his points remained unresolved, the more justified he felt in his position. At the same time, Luther was also winning popular support, which further reassured and justified the monk in his theological position. However, many of his supporters were indifferent to theology and instead wanted to merge their

In a Leipzig debate, Professor Johann Eck forced Luther to reveal the heretical content of his ideas.

own social discontent with the revolutionary spirit of the theologian. As Luther started disobeying his superiors, he became known as the ringleader for a long awaited social upheaval. For Luther, the problems were still exclusively theological, and the longer he waited for a debate, the more radical his ideas became.

Luther was finally invited to debate beginning on June 27, 1519, at Leipzig. There, many of the foremost Catholic theologians of the day met with Luther, hoping to put the matter to rest for good. Among them was Johann Eck, the well-known professor at Ingoldstagt. Eck, a master rhetorician, required Luther to expound on his positions more extensively and concretely than ever before, perhaps in much more depth than Luther had actually considered up until that time. Then Johann Eck revealed the true philosophy behind Martin Luther's thought, which led him to voice direct opposition to the Church. Luther dismissed papal supremacy, the authority of the councils, and at one point, the Epistle of St. James because that portion of Scripture disagreed with Luther's own ideas about the effectiveness of good works. Backed into a corner, Luther further committed himself to the idea of justification by faith alone and the limitations of free will.

By the end of the debate, Luther's ideas were clearly heretical. Even those scholars who had at one time sympathized with Luther's criticisms, such as the renowned humanist Erasmus, began to withdraw their support. Germany was divided into two camps: those who supported Luther and those who recognized his heresy and stood firmly with the Church. Pope Leo X issued a bull, which gave Luther two months to formally retract his opinions under threat of excommunication. He was now forced with the decision to save or split the Church.

Despite Luther's mixed emotions over the matter, he responded to the bull in a proud and aggressive manner, burning it in a bonfire along with the code of canon law. During his lecture on the following day, Luther said that the act was symbolic since it was the pope who should have been burned. Luther then wrote the pamphlet *Against the Bull of the Antichrist,* which called for an all-out rebellion against the Church. His words did not fall on passive ears, and shortly after there were disorders at Leipzig, Erfurt, and Magdeburg.

The matter now fell into the hands of the new Holy Roman Emperor, Charles V, who had risen to the throne in October 1520 at the age of nineteen. Threatened with revolts throughout his realm, Charles called the Diet (Assembly) of Worms in January 1521. There Luther was again questioned on his position, and when asked to retract his writings, the reformer famously retorted, "I cannot submit my faith either to the Pope or the Councils,

If the Reformation began with a single event, it's possible that it was not the posting of the ninety-five theses, but the burning of the papal bull *Exsurge Domine* and the canon law by Martin Luther in 1520.

because it is clear as day that they have frequently erred and contradicted each other. Unless I am convinced by the testimony of Scripture or on plain and clear grounds of reason, so that conscience shall bind me to make acknowledgement of error, I cannot and will not retract, for it is neither safe nor wise to do anything contrary to conscience. Here I stand, I can do no other. May God help me. Amen" (quoted in Oberman, *Luther*, 1992, pp. 39-40). Judgment was passed, and Luther was granted twenty-four hours of safe passage before being subject to execution. Under fear of death, Luther fled to Wittenberg. Along the journey, he was escorted by a band of knights who brought the monk to the Castle of Wartburg where he was kept in hiding under the protection of Duke Frederick of Saxony.

LUTHER DEVELOPS HIS THEOLOGY

Luther remained at the castle in Wartburg for one year. During this time he translated the New Testament into German and continued to develop his theories, writing his three most famous works: *Address to the Christian Nobility of the German Nation, On the Babylonian Captivity of the Church,* and *On the Freedom of a Christian.* In these works, Luther worked out the theological principles that would become the cornerstone of Protestantism.

Many of Luther's ideas were inspired by the writings of John Wycliffe, William of Ockham, and Jan Hus. These writers, who criticized the Church and downplayed man's capacity for theological knowledge and the merit of good works, appealed to Luther's pessimistic view of human nature. Luther believed that sinfulness was impossible to overcome and that man could never fully escape the deceptive attraction to sin. Since any act was essentially sinful, for Luther, good works could not play a role in perfecting the human person or obtaining God's forgiveness. Incapacitated by sin, an individual can simply have faith in God, and it is through this faith that God will grant salvation. For Luther, salvation is not a matter of perfecting oneself for God by taking advantage of his grace, but

Martin Luther stayed at the Wartburg Castle under an alias: the Knight George. Duke Frederick had little personal contact with him and remained a Catholic.

simply believing that God's mercy will ultimately grant salvation. He thought the soul will always remain corrupt, but through faith, the grace of Jesus Christ covers over sin so that one may be saved.

Luther referred to this idea of justification through faith alone as his major theological "discovery." Taking a passage from the letter of St. Paul to the Romans which reads, "For in it the righteousness of God is revealed through faith for faith; as it is written, 'He who through faith is righteous shall live'" (Rom 1:17), Luther began to believe that it is only "through faith" that one becomes righteous. In this passage, Luther thought that he finally found the answer to his scrupulosity and spiritual anguish. Righteousness, that lofty goal towards which Luther's thought rendered man incapable, was now possible through faith. Good deeds, penance, and works of charity do not contribute to righteousness. Faith alone saves a person, he concluded.

From this idea of justification through faith, Luther developed four major theological principles: *sola Scriptura, sola fide, sola gratia,* and *solo Christo* (Scripture alone, faith alone, grace alone, and Christ alone). Each of Luther's four main theological principles was conceived in reaction to what he believed were false teachings of the Church. Scripture alone (which held Sacred Scripture as the

The protection of Duke Frederick of Saxony at the Castle of Wartburg provided Luther with safeharbor to translate the Bible into German and to develop his theological principles.

sole authority on Faith and doctrine) rejected tradition's role in its close link with the Scriptures, the authority of the councils and the pope, and the idea that the Holy Spirit continues to dwell and teach through the Church. Faith alone dismissed the value of corporal and spiritual works of mercy as a means to attaining righteousness. His teaching, "grace alone," held that every good action is a direct result of God's saving grace since it is beyond human capacity to do good. Along with this principle of *sola gratia*, Luther abandoned the idea that people can freely choose to do good (although he would certainly hold that they can choose evil freely and that they sin by their own will). At the center of these three principles was *solo Christo*. Martin Luther held that Christ must be the sole content of the Scriptures, the mediator of grace, and the subject of faith. Luther objected to some books of Scripture, including the Epistle of St. James, which he considered insufficiently centered on the Person of Christ.

Luther's theology brought into question the entirety of Christian worship and practice. He attacked the sacraments, arguing that God did not need material means through which he could impart grace, so one is normally saved not through the sacraments but only by faith. He denied all but the two sacraments explicitly instituted in the Gospels, Eucharist and Baptism, but even with those, he gradually replaced the Church's teaching with his own interpretation. He maintained that after the consecration, both the substance of bread and wine together with Christ's Body and Blood are present. He used the term *consubstantiation*, explaining that Christ is present in the Eucharist in the same way heat is present in a red-hot iron. His ideas about *consubstantiation* contradict the Church's teaching that the substance of the bread and wine completely change into the Body and Blood of Christ, called *transubstantiation*, with only the accidents (or properties) remaining.

In addition to his translation of the Bible and major theological works, Luther wrote *On Monastic Vows* and *The Abolition of Private Masses* while at Wartburg. In these works, Luther virulently attacks celibacy and the monastic life. He claimed that living celibacy was an impossible burden and called for all religious to break their vows and marry. In 1525, Luther himself married an ex-nun, Katherine von Bora.

While Luther was hiding in Wartburg, the Reformation began to gain momentum. In Wittenberg, two friends and followers of Luther, Carlstadt and Melanchthon, brought extreme reforms to the university town. The Augustinian monastery saw forty members leave their order and a Franciscan monastery was attacked, its altars demolished and its windows smashed. In answer to Luther's call to marriage, Carlstadt married, and on Christmas Day 1521, Carlstadt proceeded to say Mass in German without vestments, publicly denying the real presence of Christ in the Eucharist. Luther would condemn Carlstadt and try to bring about more moderate reforms. Carlstadt, and later his successor Zwingli, would continue to push his ideas further, contributing to the eventual growth of Calvinism, as will be explained later.

Martin Luther's German Bible was the first mass produced book on the Gutenberg press. It had great impact on unifying German culture. Its language became the people's language. Regions which previously had multiple dialects now could communicate with each other.

THE EPISTLE OF ST. JAMES

The only place where the expression "faith alone" appears in the Bible is in the Epistle of St. James. Therein he offers a strong argument against Martin Luther's theology of *sola fide* (faith alone):

> What does it profit, my bretheren, if a man says he has faith but has not works? Can his faith save him?... So faith by itself, if it has no works is dead.... Do you want to be shown, you foolish fellow, that faith apart from works is barren? Was not Abraham our father justified by works, when he offered his son Isaac upon the altar? You see that faith was active along with his works, and faith was completed by works, and the scripture was fulfilled which says, "Abraham believed God and it was reckoned to him as righteousness"; and he was called the friend of God. You see that a man is justified by works and not by faith alone.... For as the body apart from the spirit is dead, so faith apart from works is dead. (Jas 2:14, 17-18, 20-24, 26)

This passage contradicts Martin Luther's position on the effectiveness of good works. Needless to say, it was not one of his favorites. In fact, Luther once referred to this letter as "an epistle of straw" and, comparing the work to other parts of the New Testament, Luther considered

St. James: "faith apart from works is dead."

"throwing Jimmy into the fire." Luther also had problems with the Book of Revelation, Hebrews, Jude, and 2 Peter. In addition to these New Testament books, Martin Luther attacked the Old Testament deuterocanonical texts, although he did not take them out of his translation of the Bible, where they remained as an appendix (cf. *The Canon of Scripture* in chapter four).

PART II

The Peasant Rebellion and the Splintering of Protestantism

THE GERMAN PRINCES

Prince Philip I of Hesse. When Luther was asked to condone the bigamy of Prince Philip I of Hesse, he granted him a dispensation to keep his two wives.

Frederick of Saxony and other princes of the realm became concerned with some of Carlstadt's tendencies and called upon Luther to moderate affairs in Wittenberg. The princes of Germany had little in common with Luther's religious sentiments. They did, however, share in his rebelliousness toward the papacy. They saw in Luther's new movement a way to free themselves from the pope and the Catholic emperor and to enrich themselves with expropriated Church lands.

After 1524 other German princes joined Frederick of Saxony in support of Luther. Knights of the Empire, such as Franz von Sickingen and Ulrich von Hutten, used their private armies to press for Lutheran reforms. In 1522, von Sickingen laid siege to Trier whose bishop was a strong opponent of Luther. Albert of Brandenburg, the cousin of the Bishop of Mainz and head of the Teutonic Knights, used the Lutheran cause to declare himself Duke of Prussia. The Teutonic Order was disbanded and Albert, a priest, broke his vows in order to marry. The future kings of Germany would now descend from the House of Brandenburg.

Other relations between Luther and the princes proved embarrassing. Philip of Hesse demanded that Luther support his bigamous marriage, a measure he was hesitant to condone. A compromise was made with Philip. There would be no general law permitting dual marriage, but Philip would be granted a dispensation and he would thus continue to live with both wives. In defending his position, Luther argued that all things are proper for the sake of the Church. Luther said, "What harm would there be, if a man to accomplish better things and for the sake of the Christian Church, does tell a good thumping lie" (Lenz, *Briefwechsel*, I, p. 382; Kolde, *Analecta*, p. 356).

THE PEASANT REBELLION

Luther became a pawn of the German princes. The greatest example of this was his reaction to the great peasant uprising in 1524. Luther's attack on the authority of the Church had wide-ranging consequences. Denying the authority of the Church was a kind of model for denying secular authority. This radical democratization of the Church, which gave everyone the same authority to preach and interpret the Gospel, led to an attempt to overthrow the feudal system of rule by the nobility. Peasants throughout Germany rebelled in social revolution.

Luther was called upon to condemn the uprising. He urged the princes to "Strike, slay front and rear; nothing is more devilish than sedition. There must be no sleep, no patience, no mercy; they are the children of the devil" (quoted in Harney, *The Catholic Church Through the Ages,* 1974, p. 239). Over 100,000 men, women, and children were slain; hundreds of villages were burned and crops destroyed. The civil authorities were willing to usurp the authority of the Church in Germany, but not share that same power with common people below them.

THE AUGSBURG CONFESSION

Between 1522 and 1530 Charles V was beset with problems of even greater magnitude outside of Germany. The Turks had seized parts of Hungary and were besieging the city of Vienna. Italian city-states and the king of France were supporting the Turkish offensive against the Hapsburg dominions of Austria. Charles was divided between civil war in Germany and the problems within the rest of his realm and he therefore could not take the necessary actions to stamp out the Lutheran revolution.

In 1530 a diet (legislative assembly) was to be held in Augsburg to attempt to resolve the conflict between Lutherans and Catholics in the hopes of forming an alliance against Turkish aggression. Melanchthon was sent to draft a list of principles from which a compromise could be made. The draft of these principles became known as the Augsburg Confession, establishing the basic tenets of Lutheranism for the future. The principles understated the basic theological differences between Lutheran theology and the teachings of the Catholic Church. Cardinal Campeggio, the papal legate at Augsburg, noted these divergent views and admitted the need for studying a reform of some of these abuses in the Catholic Church. The diet ended with a call for reform and for the princes of the north to return to the Church.

In response to the Diet of Augsburg, the northern princes met in Schmalkalden, Thuringia (Germany). The Northern princes formed a pact among themselves that insisted on their rights as independent monarchs, refusing to accept the terms of Augsburg in order to increase their control. With the need to gain their support in his wars against the Turks, Charles V authorized a temporary truce with the League of Schmalkalden in 1532, a turning point in the history of the conflict. The truce allowed the rebellious nobles equal rights and was a latent recognition of the existence of a permanent Protestant state. Though future conflict would erupt between Charles V and the League of Schmalkalden, a precedent was created and would be formalized thirty years later at the Peace of Augsburg in 1555. There it would be decided that the religion of the prince would be the religion of the people within his realm.

THE DEATH OF LUTHER

Luther was eventually pushed to the side in the newly constituted Protestant Germany. His marriage to Katherine von Bora gave him six children. In his later life, he would continue to write, but his style became increasingly coarse and crude. He continued attacking the papacy and added anti-Semitic attacks as well. Slowly his irascible nature caused by physical impairments and unchecked disease, along with a vicious temper, would drive his friends and colleagues away. "Hardly one of us," lamented one of his followers, "can escape Luther's anger and his public scourging" (*Corp. Ref.,* V, 314).

Luther died in his sleep on February 18, 1546, without having reconciled with the Church.

JOHN CALVIN

The second major figure of the Protestant reformation was John Calvin. Born in 1509 in Noyon, France, Calvin was the son of a middle-class attorney. In many ways Calvin was a great contrast to Luther. Where Luther was born of peasant stock, uncouth in language and mystical in his religious zeal, Calvin was born into a middle-class family and in his growing years was in contact with intellectuals. His strong intellectual inclinations are especially seen in his rational treatises and humorless sermons. Luther was a monk who had forsaken his vows and left his Church to lead his religious crusade; Calvin was a layman who never took vows, who structured and codified the reform movement and turned it into a militant crusade.

John Calvin held that human nature is totally corrupted, rotten, and vicious.

Early in his life, Calvin studied for an ecclesiastical career at the University of Paris. Because of disagreements between his father and his family's local bishop, Calvin's father had his son study law. For three years Calvin studied philosophy and law and afterwards he became familiar with humanistic writings at the University of Orléans (France). Much of the structure and spirit of his celebrated work *Institutes of the Christian Religion* can be attributed to his study of Roman law and the *Codex Justinianus*. After his father's death, Calvin returned to Paris where he finished his theological studies. While at university, Calvin discovered the teachings of Luther. Shortly after his return to Paris, Calvin was implicated in the "Affair of the Placards," which consisted of scurrilous literature appearing all over Paris attacking the Catholic Church in a degrading way. Because of this, Calvin was forced to flee the city to avoid arrest and punishment. He reached Basel, Switzerland, in January 1535 where he undertook the first draft of his major work, *Institutes of the Christian Religion*. The book began as an apology of Protestantism written to the king of France, Francis I, whom Calvin hoped to convert to the cause.

THE INSTITUTES OF THE CHRISTIAN RELIGION

The Institutes contained four books with a complete presentation by Calvin of his view concerning Protestant theology and church organization. It was a law manual codifying the principles first taught by Luther. After numerous revisions and editions, it became the most widely read book of the sixteenth century.

Ultimate authority, according to Calvin, is contained in the Scriptures. Following the tradition of Wycliffe and Luther, he stated that the Bible is the only source of revelation. Calvin was a great Scripture scholar and used his knowledge of Sacred Scripture to present rationally the teachings of Protestant theology. Like Hus and Luther, Calvin rejected the power of human freedom to elicit good actions and the ability of man to merit through good works. For Calvin, human nature is totally corrupted, rotten and vicious; man is no more than a savage beast. Like Luther, Calvin maintained that man's sinfulness is so great that he can never overcome it. However, Calvin went even further than Luther regarding the Sacraments. Whereas Luther maintained some sacramental elements of Baptism and Eucharist, Calvin denied all sacramental grace. Baptism and the Eucharist became merely memorials, and he rejected all Catholic practices that were not explicitly based in Scripture. He directed iconoclastic actions against all crucifixes, statues, sacred paintings, vestments, altars, confessionals, and stained-glass windows depicting saints. His followers would move through towns leveling destruction against Catholic churches throughout Europe.

PREDESTINATION

Since salvation depended solely on God's free decision, Calvin maintained that some were predestined to Heaven and most others to Hell. Those who were chosen by God—through no effort of their own—were known as the elect. These few elect had some inclination of their salvation by their good moral behavior and their earthly success. This principle was eagerly accepted by the middle classes who began to favor Calvinist doctrine. Just as some were chosen for Heaven, others were chosen by God for damnation. This damnation, according to Calvin, was necessary to show God's great justice. It would follow, therefore, that the sorry lot of the underprivileged and those considered reprobated would be the just chastisement for those doomed to the fires of Hell.

THEOCRACY IN GENEVA

Calvin first came to Geneva in 1536 when he was passing through on his way to Strasbourg. At the time, Geneva was in the midst of religious turmoil. Guillaume Farel, a Lutheran, sought Calvin's aid in persuading the town council to accept the Lutheran position. At first, the town fathers accepted Calvin's reforms, but by 1538 the implementation seemed too severe, and Calvin was forced into exile for four years. He traveled to Strasbourg where he married Idelette de Bure, the widow of an Anabaptist whom he had converted. Idelette gave birth to Calvin's only son who died in infancy. She also died not too long after in 1541. In that same year, Calvin was summoned back to Geneva.

In Geneva, Calvin transformed the city's government into a theocracy dominated by Calvin himself. Although the city council never elected him, through his influence, Calvin would make the state subservient to the Church.

In Geneva no expression of religious freedom was tolerated. The old, Catholic creed was forbidden, no prayer could be said in Latin, and no words of sympathy for or recognition of the pope could ever be uttered. Disagreement with Calvin, or even criticizing his preaching, could easily result in punishment. One unfortunate individual, Jacques Gouet, was imprisoned on charges of impiety in June 1547, and after severe torture, was beheaded in July. It was said that coughing during a sermon or making other such rude noises could bring a prison sentence. Under Calvin, one citizen of Geneva remarked:

> No tyrant of our own times was more terribly the master of men's lives than this long gray beard, old long before his time, whose eyes flashed so terribly when justly angered—and of course when angered it was always justly. (quoted in Hughes, *A History of the Church to the Eve of the Reformation*, 1976, p. 230)

The most famous episode of religious intolerance was with the execution of Michael Servetus in 1553. Servetus, a Spanish Unitarian, had met with Calvin and debated against him in Paris in 1534. (A Unitarian believes in individual freedom of belief from any authority.) In a series of letters, Servetus had criticized Calvin's *Institutes*. Calvin railed against Servetus and was reported to have said, "If he comes here and I have any authority, I will never let him leave the place alive." Calvin's prediction came true when Servetus was passing through Geneva in 1553. The Spaniard was arrested and burned at the stake. Adultery, pregnancy outside of marriage, heresy, striking a parent, and blasphemy all incurred the death penalty. During a five-year period, fifty-five people were executed and another seventy-six were driven into exile.

Calvin's church was organized with pastors, doctors, elders, and deacons with the supreme power given to the magistrate. Divine worship was reduced to prayers, sermons, and singing psalms. Each congregation elected its own pastor, and the congregations were overseen by a local synod. Moral behavior was strictly regulated, and church attendance and conduct were carefully monitored.

There were punishments for dancing, card playing, drinking, braiding hair, or falling asleep during sermons. Twice a year a commission of inquisitors inspected every home to ensure orthodoxy. Any new book or manuscript was censored and had to include the author's initials and the censor's initials on every page. All findings of the commission were listed in a book where each person's name would be followed with the notation of "pious," "lukewarm," or "corrupt."

Calvin justified and maintained this severe environment by his appeal for an impeccable moral life and habitual practice of prayer. The example of his personal virtue and mastery of Scripture called upon everyone to forsake any disposition toward materialism and seek the holiness of the elect. His teachings rapidly spread throughout Europe as other reforms movements adapted his teachings. John Knox would create the Presbyterian Church according to Calvinist teachings, as would the Huguenots in France and the Puritans in England. Thus John Calvin can be credited with the explosive diffusion of Protestantism throughout Europe.

ULRICH ZWINGLI

Ulrich Zwingli (1484-1531) was the third major reformer and founder of the Reformation in Switzerland. His humanistic studies, beginning in the university where he studied for the priesthood, led him to study Greek and read the classics and the Fathers of the Church. He became acquainted with and entered into friendly discussions with the leading humanists of his day: Heinrich Loriti (Glareanus), Erasmus, and Vadian. While serving as a priest in Zurich, he fell into sins against priestly celibacy (like many Renaissance-era clerics), and before long converted many of the faithful to his increasingly anti-Catholic views on Church-state relations, the veneration of the saints, the removal of images, good works, and the Sacraments. With much political power behind him, he used the state to seize Church property, suppress the Mass and Sacraments such as Penance and Anointing of the Sick, destroy images, statues, relics, altars, and organs (regardless of even their artistic value), and melt down chalices and monstrances into coins. As the head of both government and church in Zurich, Zwingli was able to establish and stabilize the Reformation during his lifetime.

Ulrich Zwingli's reformation spread from the Zürich canton (Swiss state) to five other cantons of the Swiss Confederation. The remaining five cantons firmly held onto the Catholic Faith.

Ulrich Zwingli was killed in a military battle between the Zürich canton and the Catholic cantons at Kappel am Albis.

PART III

The English Reformation

The last of the movements to bring about a Protestant revolution occurred in England. The spread of Protestantism in England did not originate from theological or dogmatic issues, but over the issue of papal authority, specifically regarding the issue of the king's marriage and, later, with the English monarch as head of the Church in England.

The Catholic Church in England at the beginning of the sixteenth century was in better condition than in any country in Europe save Spain. Relations between the clergy and the laity were very good; there were relatively few clerical scandals and there was popular support for the religious and the Church in general. A visitor to the British island at the time could admire the universal observation of Catholic practices and the general manifestation of English piety. The king himself had been named "Protector of the Faith" by the pope in 1520 for defending the Church against Lutheran attacks in the work entitled *Defense of the Seven Sacraments* (Livingstone, *The Oxford Dictionary of the Christian Church*, 1997, p. 752).

HENRY VIII

The Tudors had come to the throne at the end of the English civil war (War of the Roses). This forty-year struggle wrought havoc on the island nation and brought it to the brink of destruction. Henry VII ended the conflict and restored calm and prosperity to England. He managed to increase his treasury by avoiding war and allying himself with Spain, the strongest European state. (His eldest son Arthur was betrothed to Catherine of Aragon, the daughter of the king and queen

Henry VIII and Anne Boleyn. Henry was a hunter, a dancer and a womanizer. He wanted Anne and would turn the world upside-down to have her.

of Spain.) Henry's second son, only seventeen at the time, was never supposed to be king. He was a handsome, popular youth who was a renowned wrestler, hunter, dancer, and womanizer. The life of this young man, however, would be forever changed by the death of his older brother. In order to save the Spanish alliance, young Henry was given to the older Catherine in marriage. Legally, a dispensation was needed since, technically, Catherine was Henry's sister through marriage. Pope Julius II granted the dispensation, and the Spanish alliance was preserved through Catherine and Henry's marriage.

The marriage at first was a happy one. Catherine gave Henry a daughter whom they named Mary. Other children soon came, including a number of sons, but all died before their first year. As Catherine grew older, the 35-year-old Henry realized that he would not have a male heir. To complicate the problem, Henry's affections were drawn toward one of his Queen's attendants, Anne Boleyn. Henry began to seek a way to end his marriage with Catherine. Quoting Leviticus, King Henry asserted

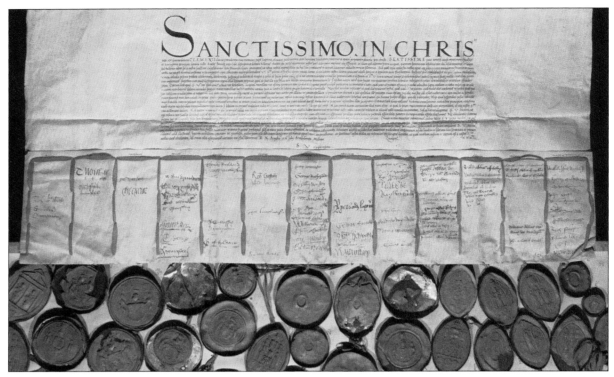

A letter from King Henry VIII to Pope Clement, July 13, 1530. The letter is composed on behalf of the Peers of the realm requesting that the Pope annul the first marriage of their king to Catherine of Aragon. The document bears the personal signatures of the petitioners and 85 red wax seals.

that Julius II had wrongfully granted a dispensation; God was punishing Henry by refusing him an heir for having taken his brother's wife. Henry sent his legates to Rome and asked Pope Clement VII for an annulment.

CARDINAL WOLSEY

The legate in charge of the annulment was Cardinal Wolsey, Chancellor and the most powerful churchman in England. He had accumulated large benefices throughout England and at one time strove for the papacy itself. Wolsey was not a scholar trained in law or theology, but a skillful and pragmatic chancellor. A few years before, he tried to gain Henry the title "Holy Roman Emperor," and although he had failed, Wolsey's efforts clearly showed him to be the most capable advocate for Henry's cause.

Wolsey obtained permission from Rome to begin the trial for the annulment case in England, where he would be able to control the outcome. At first, he was given assurances from Rome that the decision would not be questioned regardless of the outcome. Since Pope Clement VII was a cautious man and realized that England might fall into schism over the issue of the annulment, he insisted on a legitimate trial for Catherine. Clement also had to contend with Catherine's powerful nephew, Emperor Charles V of Spain, and so before judgment was reached, Clement ordered the case to be brought to Rome.

Henry VIII derided the pope's decision and declared Wolsey a traitor to England, claiming that he was attempting to enforce the laws of a foreign ruler. Wolsey was stripped of his power and ordered back to London to answer the charges. On this journey the cardinal died in a monastery at Leicester. When Wolsey's body was prepared for burial, caretakers discovered that he was wearing a hair shirt for penance under his splendid robes.

THE ACT OF SUPREMACY

After Wolsey's death, relations between England and Rome became even more strained. Henry wanted desperately to resolve his problem. He had turned to his friend St. Thomas More in the hopes that the scholar's good reputation would sway the mind of the pope. More became Chancellor and helped Henry reform the Church in England, but he refused to touch the matter of the annulment. Henry would find an answer to his problem in Thomas Cranmer and Thomas Cromwell.

When Archbishop William Warham of Canterbury died, Henry named Thomas Cranmer, the personal confessor of Anne Boleyn and a secret Lutheran, as the new archbishop. Cranmer had officiated over the illicit marriage of Henry and the now pregnant Anne in a secret ceremony on January 25, 1533. In May of that year, Archbishop Cranmer nullified Henry's first marriage to Catherine and recognized the validity of Henry's new marriage to Anne and the legitimacy of her unborn child. On September 7, 1533, Anne gave birth to a girl, Elizabeth.

Henry turned to parliament for an acknowledgement of his supremacy. With the "Act of Supremacy" law, the king was proclaimed the supreme head of the Church in England, and Anne Boleyn was recognized as Queen. Their daughter Elizabeth would become heir to the throne of England. The pope was no longer recognized as having even any religious authority within England, so all matters

Archbishop Cranmer nullified Henry's first marriage and recognized Henry's new marriage to Anne Boleyn.

of faith, ecclesiastical appointment, and maintenance of ecclesiastical properties were in the hands of the king. All subjects of the crown were required to take an oath of allegiance to the king under penalty of imprisonment, and anyone who spoke against the Act of Supremacy would be punished by death.

BISHOP STS. JOHN FISHER AND THOMAS MORE

Henry was determined to enforce his will upon England. A young Benedictine nun, Elizabeth Barton, known as the Holy Maid of Kent, and four parish priests were executed after they had called upon the king to return to the Faith and send Anne away. Only one of England's Bishops refused to go along with Henry's actions: St. John Fisher, the Bishop of Rochester. St. John Fisher refused to sign the allegiance to the royal supremacy, and was imprisoned. With the idea of saving his life, Pope Paul III made St. John Fisher a cardinal while he was imprisoned. This elevation backfired and so enraged Henry that the king had the cardinal beheaded in 1535, less than one month later.

St. Thomas More, Chancellor of England, a renowned humanist writer and lifelong friend of Henry, also refused to take the oath of supremacy. His high standing in England threatened Henry's plans, so St. Thomas More was arrested and sent to the Tower of London. He was a gifted lawyer and writer who struggled heroically to make his Catholic Faith an absolute priority. He had a jovial and cheerful nature and a great sense of humor. He would frequently have the poor and destitute join him and his family for meals. Though a layman, he habitually wore a hair shirt and regularly engaged in other penitential practices. He was a family man, devoted to his wife and daughters. A

ST. JOHN HOUGHTON AND THE BLESSED MARTYRS OF THE CARTHUSIAN ORDER

Some of the earliest martyrs of the English Reformation were members of the Carthusian Charterhouse of London. The Carthusian order, founded by St. Bruno in France during the eleventh century, is unique among western monastic orders for its nearly eremitical life and emphasis on strict austerity. According to the Carthusian rule, each monk lives alone in a cell with a small garden, and the monks come together only for communal worship.

In sixteenth-century England, the Carthusians were held in such high regard that Henry VIII was set on winning them over to Anglicanism or destroying the order. The Prior of the Carthusian Charterhouse in London, St. John Houghton, was the first man who refused Henry VIII's Oath of Supremacy. On May 4, 1535, just weeks before the deaths of Sts. Thomas More and John Fisher, three Carthusians, including St. John Houghton, were hanged, drawn, and quartered at Tyburn for their fidelity to the Church of Rome. During the subsequent five years, fifteen more Carthusians were martyred for the Faith. The eighteen Carthusian martyrs were beatified by Pope Leo XIII

in 1886. Pope Paul VI canonized St. John Houghton in 1970, including him among the Forty Martyrs of England and Wales, a group representative of the English and Welsh martyrs of the Reformation who died at various dates between 1535 and 1679.

leading humanist writer of his time, he undertook the education of his daughters in Latin and classical literature.

St. Thomas More was learned in the law and knew he could be imprisoned but not executed for refusing to sign the Oath of Supremacy. For more than one year, St. Thomas More was kept in the Tower where he refused to speak for or against the Oath. When asked, his only response was:

> I am (quoth I) the king's true faithful subject and daily bedesman, and pray for His Highness, and all his, and all the realm. I do nobody harm, I say none harm, I think none harm, but wish everybody good. And if this be not enough to keep a man alive, in good faith I long not to live. (quoted in Hughes, *A History of the Church to the Eve of the Reformation*, 1976, p. 182)

Henry turned this case over to his new Chancellor, Thomas Cromwell. Using perjured testimony, Cromwell gained a conviction. Originally sentenced to be hanged, drawn, and quartered,

St. Thomas More was beheaded on July 6, 1535, two weeks after St. John Fisher. On the scaffold he said, "I die the King's good servant, but God's first" (quoted in Hughes, *A History of the Church to the Eve of the Reformation*, 1976, p. 183). Both Sts. John Fisher and Thomas More were canonized in 1935, 400 years after they were martyred; they share a feast day celebrated on June 22.

CONFISCATION OF CHURCH PROPERTIES

Thomas Cromwell became the major advocate for Henry's new regime. As an administrator under Cardinal Wolsey, it had been Cromwell's task to administer the confiscation of monastic properties that were declared vacated. Cromwell oversaw the seizure of monastic lands now that the king was the new head of the church. Nearly a third of English property was held by the Church, a gross income of nearly £300,000 a year. The first move by Cromwell was to take over the small monastic lands. In the *Act for the Dissolution of the Lesser Monasteries*, some 318 houses were closed, displacing nearly 1500 religious. The larger monasteries met the same fate shortly after. Lead was stripped from the roofs of the monasteries and melted down; jewels and plate were confiscated and sent to Henry's treasury. This greatest land redistribution in England since the time of William the Conqueror occurred between 1533 and 1536, vastly enriching the nobility loyal to Henry and his new church.

Not all were pleased with Henry's new policies. Many peasants suffered tremendously as towns were ruined by the wholesale redistribution of land. An insurrection broke out in October 1536, known as the Pilgrimage of Grace. Lincolnshire and Yorkshire exploded in open rebellion with over 40,000 well-armed men. The Duke of Norfolk was called upon to quell the uprising. He met with the leaders and agreed to take their terms of reform to the king. The leaders of the uprising believed they could impress the king with their demands by a show of force, but Norfolk undermined the resistance by appeasing the leaders of the uprising. After the mobs subsided, the leadership was arrested and executed.

AFTERMATH OF HENRY VIII: ENGLAND BECOMES PROTESTANT

In spite of his break from Rome, Henry still considered himself a Catholic, and he continued to fight against the introduction of Lutheran ideas into his realm. In 1539 Henry compelled Parliament to adopt his *Six Articles* that determined the main teachings of the English Church. These articles included maintaining the doctrine of transubstantiation, Communion under one species, Masses for the dead, the Sacrament of Penance, vows, and celibacy of the clergy. Tyndale's English translation of the Bible was condemned and heretics were still to be burned at the stake.

Henry soon grew tired of Anne Boleyn. He was angry that she had born him a daughter instead of a son and blamed her for the presence of Lutheranism in England. He had also fallen in love with one of Anne's attendants, Jane

Henry fought any introduction of Lutheran ideas into his realm. Thomas Cromwell tried to unite England with Protestant Germany through Henry's marriage to Anne of Cleves. He paid for this final manipulation with his life.

Seymour. With Catherine of Aragon's death in January 1536 the way was clear for Henry to rid himself of Anne and marry Jane. Thomas Cromwell brought charges of adultery against Anne who was beheaded in 1536. Henry married Jane who gave birth to Henry's heir, Edward VI.

Thomas Cromwell would also lose favor with Henry by trying to unite England with Protestant Germany. After Jane Seymour died during childbirth, Cromwell arranged a marriage between Henry and a German princess, Anne of Cleves. Henry was angered at being drawn into a conflict with Spain because of the union, and he executed Cromwell for treason.

Henry married two more times before his own death. Aged before his time, obese and racked with gout, Henry died on January 28, 1547, at age 55. He left an infant son to deal with the growing Protestant movement in England.

EDWARD VI

The Protestant cause seemed triumphant with the death of Henry VIII. The *Six Articles* of Henry were quickly repealed and the seat of government fell into the hands of Edward VI's two major ministers: the Duke of Sommerset (Edward's uncle) and Thomas Cranmer, the Archbishop of Canterbury. The two would attempt to turn Anglican England into a Lutheran-Calvinist country.

England was flooded with translations of Lutheran writings. Cranmer published a Lutheran catechism and *The Book of Common Prayer.* Altars were destroyed and replaced by simple tables as the essential parts of the Mass were swept away. Bishops who protested the changes were imprisoned, and political opportunists took control of the government. Public outcry to the changes led to a series of local rebellions, but the regency did not last. In 1553, Edward, who had always been sickly, died at age 15. The Duke of Northumberland tried unsuccessfully to place a distant cousin, Lady Jane Grey, on the throne in order to maintain Protestant succession. Support, however, turned to Henry's eldest daughter, Mary Tudor.

This allegorical painting from 1548 shows the dying Henry VIII pointing to the new order of Edward VI. Edward is surrounded by his council, the Duke of Sommerset and Thomas Cranmer. The pope and monks are deposed, while through the window Calvinist iconoclasts are destroying religious images. Under the boy king, there was a dramatic shift to a Swiss-style theology. The Reformation was given free rein, the Mass was essentially abolished, and Cranmer wrote two prayerbooks which introduced English into the church liturgy.

Mary Tudor, an ardent Catholic like her mother Catherine, repealed all of Edward VI's Protestant changes and executed Cranmer and other Reformation proponents.

MARY I

Mary was the daughter of Catherine of Aragon and an ardent Catholic. She acted quickly to restore the Church of England to the old Faith. All of the Edwardian enactments were repealed, and England was reunited with Rome in 1554. She accepted the advice of her cousin Charles V not to press for the return of Church lands confiscated by her father. Mary attempted to strengthen her reforms by marrying Charles' son, Philip II, King of Spain.

Later English writers have vilified Mary's short-lived reign. However, one must keep in mind that Mary's reign was a hard and volatile time. Many of the leaders of Edward VI's reign attempted to keep Mary from the throne and further the Lutheran cause. They continuously fought Mary's Catholic reforms. In response, Mary had Cranmer and other leading opponents tried for heresy and burned at the stake. In all, 277 were executed under Mary's rule, hence, her legendary nickname, Bloody Mary.

Mary had only ruled England for five years upon her death in 1558. These troubled years were too short to bring about permanent reform. After Mary's death, her half sister Elizabeth would undo the positive effects of Mary's reign, and push England even further away from the Catholic Faith.

ELIZABETH I

Elizabeth I was crowned on January 15, 1559. There was no Archbishop of Canterbury at the time. The last Roman Catholic Archbishop had died shortly after Mary I. Senior bishops declined to participate in the coronation since Elizabeth was illegitimate under both canon law and statute and because she was a Protestant. The Communion was celebrated by the Queen's personal chaplain, to avoid the use of the Roman Catholic rites. Elizabeth I's coronation was the last coronation to use a Latin service.

Elizabeth's reign began with many questions of succession. She was the daughter of Anne Boleyn whose marriage to Henry VIII had been annulled, calling into question Elizabeth's legitimacy. Without Elizabeth, the throne would have fallen to the young Mary Stuart of Scotland. Unfortunately for Mary, she was recently married to the King of France and the English Parliament was wary of an alliance between the two countries. Henry's confiscation of Church lands had made Parliament very wealthy, and it was now concerned with retaining the power that resulted from that expropriation. Enmity with Catholic France encouraged Parliament to support Elizabeth's claim to the throne. In short, Elizabeth's forty-year reign reflected the desire of Parliament to hold on to their wealth and property and Elizabeth's uncanny capacity to maintain her royal power. The result of her alliance with Parliament cemented the Protestant cause in England.

Elizabeth surrounded herself with strong advisors, the most important being William Cecil, the Lord Burghley who helped her complete the Protestant revolution in England. Maintaining all the outward appearances of Catholicism, Elizabeth incorporated Protestant doctrine into the Church of England. The majority of England was still Catholic in practice and custom, and so Elizabeth worked on the Anglican Compromise to help make the transition to Protestantism smoother for the English. She issued the Thirty-Nine Articles. In those articles, Elizabeth kept the old organization of the Church with its ceremonies and vestments, but rigorously re-imposed the Oath of Royal Supremacy and decreed a uniformity of prayer following Protestant lines.

In 1563, The Council of Trent closed after accomplishing a monumental effort to reform the Catholic Church. Legates of the pope attempted to meet with Elizabeth and reconcile the differences between the Anglican and Roman Churches, but Elizabeth refused to meet with the Papal representatives. Instead, the Queen threatened to execute any papal representative who set foot in England. In 1569, Elizabeth ruthlessly put down a series of uprisings against her rule. Elizabeth began a campaign of legislation that tore away Catholicism from the English countryside. She forbade any public celebration of Catholic rites and imprisoned her Catholic cousin, Mary of Scotland. After St. Pius V excommunicated the queen in 1570, persecution followed in 1571. Parliament made it treasonable for any papal document to be published in England or any English subject to be reconciled with Rome. Fines and imprisonment were imposed for celebrating or attending Mass; fines were imposed for failing to show up for Anglican services. Elizabeth would eventually execute 189 Catholic priests and imprison hundreds of English gentry and thousands among the lower classes on account of their practice of the Catholic Faith.

PART IV

The Catholic Revival

In the midst of the religious revolution of the sixteenth century, the Catholic Church had its own spiritual revival. Opposition to the Catholic Church during the sixteenth century was both so strong and damaging that its steady progress of reform is an indication that the Church was indeed guided by the Holy Spirit and not merely a human institution. Unfortunately, reform was delayed by war between the major Christian kings and the interference of secular rulers. Many Protestant reformers were afraid that a successful council might undermine their doctrinal changes, and they used their political and military influence to try to thwart Catholic revival. In spite of these difficulties, the Council of Trent would meet the challenge of the Protestant reformers and bring about a renewed spirit of Catholicism.

Despite his doctrinal heresy, Martin Luther pointed out a number of areas that did need to be addressed and improved within the Catholic Church. Uneducated priests, inordinate number of benefices, the abuse of indulgences, and moral and spiritual lethargy all signified a Church in dire need of reform and renewed religious zeal. The Catholic reformation was a period of revival of the Faith and an increase of religious devotion. Although the Protestant revolt intensified the Catholic desire for reform, this nevertheless was already beginning throughout the Church. Christian humanist writers such as Erasmus of Rotterdam and St. Thomas More had called upon the Church to embrace the values of the Gospel. Cardinal Ximenes de Cisneros began a reform of the various religious orders in Spain and built the University of Alcala to help better educate the clergy. New orders such as the Theatines were created to address the need for an improvement in the training of bishops. Soon the Society of Jesus (Jesuits) would emerge to martial support for the pope and the Roman Church.

ADRIAN VI AND CLEMENT VII

The forerunner to the Catholic Reformation was Pope Adrian VI. The Dutch-born Adrian was the last non-Italian to be Pope before John Paul II. As bishop of Tortosa in Spain, Adrian became an associate of Cardinal Ximenes de Cisneros in the Spanish reform. He was a man of impeccable morals with deep piety and a strong penitential asceticism. As pope he attempted to bring the Spanish revival to Rome. He wanted to win back the Lutherans by force of good example and dialogue. He worked tirelessly to reform the Church but tragically died only one year after his election. Though little progress was made towards reform during his short pontificate, Adrian identified the major areas that needed a change for the better, and many of his recommendations would eventually be put into practice.

Adrian's successor was Clement VII, a man of strong intellectual ability, but indecisive in action. Clement wanted to reform the clergy and religious orders, while the Christian kingdoms were looking for a response to Lutheran challenges to Catholic doctrine. In his attempt to call a council for renewal of the Church, Clement found himself stuck between political infighting of Emperor Charles V and Francis I of France. These rulers wanted to dominate any council of the Church and refused to allow bishops to attend in areas out of their control. Wars between Charles and Francis continuously delayed attempts to call an ecumenical council. In addition to the Lutheran challenge, Clement also had to deal with Henry VIII's marital situation.

POPULAR RELIGIONS IN 1560

ICELAND

Roman Catholic
Eastern Orthodox
Lutheran
Zwinglian or Calvinist
Anglican
Muslim
Hussite
Anabaptists
Political Boundary

500 km

300 miles

NORWAY

SCOTLAND
Glasgow
Edinburgh

NORTH SEA

DENMARK
Cop

IRELAND
Dublin

ENGLAND
York
WALES

London
Canterbury

Groningen
Amsterdam
Munster
Antwerp

Bremen Hamburg

Magdeb

Witten

HOLY ROMAN
EMPIRE
Frankfurt

Zv

ATLANTIC
OCEAN

Rouen
Rheims
Paris

Nantes
Tours

Poitiers
Nevers
FRANCE

Lyons
Geneva

Bordeaux

Toulouse
Avignon

Marseilles

Edict of Worms, 1521,
condemns Lutheranism
Worms

Peace of Augsburg, 1555,
recognizes existence of Lutheranism

Regensburg
Augsburg
Munich
Zurich
Salzbu

Milan
Venice

Modena
Ferrara
Florence

PA
STA

CORSICA

PORTUGAL
Oporto

Valladolid
Zaragoza

Madrid

SPAIN
Toledo

Barcelona

BALEARIC ISLANDS

SARDINIA

Valencia

Seville
Granada

MEDITERRANEAN SEA

© 1997 Lion Hudson plc / Three's Company

Holy Roman Emperor Charles V condemned Martin Luther's teachings at the Diet of Worms in 1521. But many German princes supported Luther. The princes were able to force the Peace of Augsburg in 1555 in which a prince was allowed to adopt either Catholicism or Lutheranism for his subjects.

Luther was obliged to turn against radical dissenters in Germany such as the Anabaptists who precipitated the Peasants' Revolt in 1525.

Calvinism took root in France, Poland, Hungary and Scotland. The Calvinist Church of Scotland was formed in 1560.

PAUL III AND CALLING OF THE COUNCIL OF TRENT

Many credit Pope Paul III with the official start of the Catholic revival.

Alessandro Farnese became Pope Paul III in 1534. Before his election he had been a Renaissance Cardinal who loved the arts and raucous parties. Farnese underwent a late spiritual conversion and was ordained to the priesthood at age 51. He immediately began to dedicate his life to reforming the Church. For this reason, many credit Paul III with the official start of the Catholic revival. Paul III appointed exemplary cardinals and bishops to study the problems needing to be addressed, approved the Jesuit order, and launched the Council of Trent.

Paul III took strong action to begin revitalizing the Church. He excommunicated Henry VIII in 1538 for his rebellious actions and placed England under interdict. He urged the Catholic princes of Germany to unite against their Lutheran counterparts and managed to convince Charles V and Francis I to call a ten-year truce. Capitalizing on the truce as an opportunity for a council, in 1537 he appointed *Consilium de emendanda Ecclesia*, a commission to study and report on needed Church reform. He chose for this commission Cardinals Gasparo Contarini as president, Gian Pietro Caraffa (the future Pope Paul IV), Jacopo Sadoleto, and Reginald Pole (almost elected pope in 1549); Archbishops Federigo Fregoso and Jerome Aleander; Bishop Gian Matteo Giberti; Abbot Gregorio Cortese; and Friar Tommaso Badia. (cf. Olin, *Catholic Reform from Cardinal Ximenes to the Council of Trent, 1495-1563*, 1994, p. 79) This commission established a blueprint for the upcoming Council of Trent.

There were many obstacles for Paul III in the calling of a general council. Many of his closest advisers were against a council, fearing an end to patronage and financial benefits of their positions that reform might bring. Lutheran reformers wanted acceptance of their theological positions in advance of a council. They wanted to be on equal footing with the bishops present and demanded that only the gospels be used in the deliberations and pronouncements. When it was clear they would not get their way, the Protestant League of Schmalkalden attempted to disrupt the council.

Secular rulers were also opposed to a council: Henry VIII had started his own church, Francis I did not want the French Church to lose its independence, and Charles V was afraid his subjects would react badly to a condemnation of Lutheranism. The secular princes wanted no dogmatic decrees discussed at the council and argued that only matters of discipline should be addressed. A compromise was established which agreed to have each session of the council deal with both doctrine and reform. Paul III summoned a council to meet in Mantua in 1537, but Francis I refused to allow any French Bishops to attend, and Charles V did not want the location in an Italian city outside his control. Consequently, when the Duke of Mantua could not guarantee the safety of the members, the council disbanded. It was finally agreed that the Italian city of Trent, a city under Charles V's jurisdiction, should host the council. However, war broke out again between Charles V and Francis I, and the council was delayed for another three years. Finally, on December 13, 1545, the Council of Trent opened its first session.

CHURCH'S TEACHING

Luther's theology broke away from the Church's teaching mainly in its deflated view of humanity. The Church teaches that no one can merit the *initial* grace of forgiveness and justification, this grace is granted by God at Baptism and the other sacraments. However, Catholics believe that "moved by the Holy Spirit and by charity, *we can then merit* for ourselves and others the graces needed for our sanctification, for the increase of grace and charity, and for the attainment of eternal life" (CCC 2010). Works are more than mere indicators of one's faith, but free actions inspired by faith through which grace is obtained, flowing from Christ's redemptive sacrifice. As the Catechism of the Catholic Church states:

> The merit of man before God in the Christian life arises from the fact that God has freely chosen to associate man with the work of his grace....This is our right by grace, the full right of love, making us "co-heirs" with Christ and worthy of obtaining "the promised inheritance of eternal life" (Council of Trent (1547): DS 1546). The merits of our good words are gifts of the divine goodness (cf. Council of Trent (1547): DS 1548). "Grace has gone before us; now we are given what is due....Our merits are God's gifts" (St. Augustine, *Sermo* 298, 4-5: PL 38, 1367). (CCC 2009)

Original sin does not leave man totally corrupt, as Luther believed, but rather wounds his nature. Human freedom, aided by grace, makes it possible for man to cooperate with God and to unite his personal good works to the merits of Christ, thereby meriting further grace. By Baptism Christians are incorporated into the Mystical Body of Christ whereby they become children of God the Father. Through this divine filiation, obtained through the goodness and mercy of God, they gain grace through good works, whereby they grow in sanctity and win graces for others as well.

The contents of the Bible is considered divine revelation and therefore the word of God. Nevertheless, it is the work of man in its composition and expression of the divinely inspired teaching. "'God chose certain men who, all the while he employed them in this task, made full use of their own faculties and powers so that, though he acted in them and by them, it was as true authors that they consigned to writing whatever he wanted written, and no more' (DV 11)" (CCC 106). Luther denied the role played by human cooperation in the transmission of divine revelation; this erroneous opinion lines up with his view of fallen humanity. The approval and explanation of Sacred Scripture is also intimately bound up with the early tradition of the Church: without the clarification of Sacred Tradition and the guiding light of the Church there would be confusion and uncertainty regarding the identification of inspired texts and its right interpretation. In summary, the traditions of the Church ultimately come from Christ through his Apostles and their successors (bishops) under the authority of the pope.

The Seven Sacraments were instituted over time by Christ as a means of salvation. Christ, who perfectly knew human nature, instituted the Sacraments to impart all the necessary graces for forgiveness, healing, conversion, and ultimately salvation. Due to Luther's attack on the Sacraments, the Council of Trent would elucidate on each Sacrament with a thorough theological explanation which would cogently and logically counteract all the erroneous ideas in circulation at the time.

Luther's original and chief criticism of the Church regarded the sale of indulgences. Indulgences concern the forgiveness of temporal punishment in Purgatory due to sins. Even after Penance, which forgives the guilt associated with sin, the penitent still needs to make reparation and undergo purification for sins committed. This can take the form of prayer, almsgiving, or corporal works of mercy. Indulgences are granted for certain good acts of piety or charitable actions. The Church teaches that through Christ's merits an individual can make reparation for sin and thereby cooperate with that grace through his willing efforts to please God. Therefore, the efficacy of indulgences comes from Christ's redemption applied to an individual who appeals to God's mercy expressed in devotions and good actions. The abuse of indulgences, which was prevalent during Luther's time, was to preach that a monetary sum could gain such release from temporal punishment without the proper interior dispositions of sorrow for sin and efforts to follow Christ. This abuse was corrected and condemned by the Church.

Modern efforts are underway to clarify and even lessen the divide between the Lutheran and Catholic understandings of justification. In 1998 the Congregation for the Doctrine of the Faith and the Lutheran World Federation issued a joint declaration on justification. This joint declaration documented the similarities of belief between the two churches, and seems to have been a large step toward the mutual understanding of each side's position.

THE COUNCIL OF TRENT (1545-47): SESSIONS 1-10

The Council of Trent was in session at irregular intervals for eighteen years throughout three pontificates. When the first session of Trent convened, three papal cardinal legates directed the affairs of the council: Gian Maria del Monte, Marcello Cervinni, and Reginald Pole. Over sixty bishops and fifty other theologians met to discuss the reform agenda put forward by Paul III's *Consilium* of 1537. The secretary of the council, Angelo Massarelli, later Bishop of Telese, compiled

The Council of Trent turned out to be a detailed response to all the Protestant theological positions. Council sessions were held in the Trent's Romanesque cathedral and in the Church of Santa Maria Maggiore. Many of the reforms and doctrinal formulations worked out over twenty-five sessions remained the framework of Catholicism until the 1960s.

A view of Trento (Trent) from Castello del Buonconsiglio. In the background is the Monte Bondone. Trent, in English, Italian *Trento*, German *Trient*, Latin *Tridentum* (the Latin form is the source of the adjective *Tridentine*) is located in the Adige river valley in the Italian region of Trentino-Alto Adige. It is the capital of the region and of the autonomous province of Trento. Originally a Celtic city, Trent was later conquered by the Romans in the first Century B.C. In 1027, the Holy Roman Emperor Conrad II created the Prince, Bishop of Trent, who wielded both temporal and religious powers.

a detailed diary of the events of the council. The council met in Particular Congregations where theologians and laymen discussed the topic of each session. Decisions of these Congregations would be sent to the General Congregation of Bishops for their review. Final promulgation of each topic occurred at the end of each session. All decisions were then sent to the pope for his final approval.

The first seven sessions of Trent addressed a number of doctrinal issues. The first topic dealt with the question of Sacred Scripture. Two decrees came out of the fourth session, which declared that in matters of Faith and morals, the Tradition of the Church together with the Bible is the source of Catholic belief. This session also indicated that the Latin Vulgate (originally translated into Latin by St. Jerome) was the authoritative text for Sacred Scripture and the books contained therein was the complete canonical list, though nothing was decided concerning translation of the Bible into vernacular languages.

Original sin was the second topic discussed at Trent: its nature, consequences, and its remission through Baptism. The council discredited the notion that original sin destroyed human freedom and man's ability to cooperate with grace. This led the council to begin the discussion brought up by Luther on the topic of justification. Perhaps the most divisive topic among the Germanic princes of the North, the council nevertheless took up this stormy debate with sessions of sixty-one general congregations and forty-four particular congregations. Though it is true that Christ justifies and restores each person's relationship to God the Father by his death on the Cross, the council declared that Baptism makes people "sons of God" who can freely choose to cooperate with God's salvific mission. Although Faith is a gratuitous gift, good works guided by faith are necessary for salvation.

During these sessions the council also took up the topic of the Sacraments in general and identified those seven which were instituted by Christ. They then proceeded to examine each of the Sacraments in turn. Baptism and Confirmation were the first discussed in detail by the council.

In matters of reform, the council candidly addressed abuses of clerical benefices and the need to provide better training for the clergy. Pluralism, i.e., having charge over more than one diocese, was strictly forbidden, and strict laws were devised for the appointment of bishops and the awarding of benefices.

Before the seventh session was complete, war broke out between the Emperor and the Protestant League of Schmalkalden. Plague also killed many in Trent, including the general of the Franciscan order. The cardinal legates proposed in the eighth session of Trent to move the council to Bologna for protection from war and disease. Though Paul III had not ordered the move, both Francis I and Charles V were outraged by the relocation. Due to the political interference of the secular princes, nothing further was accomplished during the ninth and tenth sessions. The council itself was temporarily closed with the death of Paul III on November 10, 1549.

THE COUNCIL OF TRENT (1551-1553): SESSIONS 11-16 UNDER JULIUS III

Paul III's successor was the first cardinal legate of the council, Giovanni del Monte, who took the name Julius III. Though fearful of the growing power of the Emperor Charles V, Julius pushed for the re-opening of the council in Trent in May 1551. The council continued to undertake a detailed discussion of each of the Seven Sacraments. During sessions thirteen and fourteen, the congregations outlined the doctrines of the Eucharist, Penance, and Anointing of the Sick. In addition to these doctrinal issues, the council continued its reform with further discussion on discipline of clergy regarding benefices and jurisdictional questions and supervision of bishops.

A delegation of Protestant theologians arrived in Trent demanding participation in the council. The first demand of this party was to throw out the work of the preceding sessions of the council and begin anew. They again set before the council the demand that their theological arguments be accepted as the starting point of discussion and that the subordination of the pope to the council be defined. The fifteenth session of the council began to honor the requests of the Protestants by postponing the consideration of any further issues. The appearance of the League of Schmalkalden, however, placed Trent and the members of the council in danger. Subsequently, the council was again forced to close temporarily.

PAUL IV

After the death of Julius III in 1555 and the short-lived pontificate of Marcellus II, the papacy fell to the austere reformer Cardinal Carafa who took the name Paul IV. This 80-year-old pope had been a co-founder of the Theatine order and sought to bring about internal reform throughout the Roman Curia rather than continue with the council. Paul IV was an ascetical and pious man who zealously sought to free the Church from imperial control. He recreated the inquisition in Rome to root out heresy and demanded that members of the Roman Curia give up their materialistic lifestyle. Those who refused to give up pluralistic benefices were severely disciplined. He ended the practice of collecting payment for many clerical appointments, cutting papal revenues and making it less financially lucrative to seek such appointment. He tried to stop Spanish political influence in Rome, but was soundly defeated by the armies of the new Spanish king Philip II. Paul IV also refused to recognize the elevation of Elizabeth I as Queen of England due to her illegitimacy. Although many historians have criticized Paul IV's rigid reform, his actions helped to restore the Papacy to its spiritual mission.

THE COUNCIL OF TRENT (1562-1563): SESSIONS 17-25 UNDER PIUS IV

The final stage of the Council of Trent took place with the elevation of Pius IV in 1559. The major adversaries of the council were gone: Charles V had abdicated his throne in 1557, dividing his empire between his son Philip II of Spain and his brother Ferdinand of Germany. Charles then entered a monastery to live out the last years of his life. Francis I of France had died. The council re-convened in 1562, and there were nine sessions in three months. These sessions finished the discussion of the remaining sacraments with declarations on the Sacrifice of the Mass, Holy Orders, and Matrimony. The council also covered the topics of veneration of saints and relics and more clearly defined the true nature of indulgences. Probably the greatest reform was accomplished during these sessions. The council established the seminary system for the education of the clergy, directly attacking the problem of ignorance among parish priests. The seminaries established liturgical guidelines insuring adequate priestly guidance and uniform practice of the Faith among the Christian faithful. A list of forbidden books was established as well as the authorization to publish a new catechism for the faithful. To help curb episcopal abuses, bishops were not permitted to be away from their diocese for more than three months, and they were urged to visit all their Churches and care for the clergy and people.

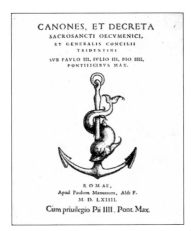

The title page of the *Council of Trent Canons.*

The Council of Trent turned out to be a detailed response to all the Protestant theological positions. Each dogmatic decree included a canon anathematizing (denouncing as accursed) those who deny the doctrine in question. The contents filled fourteen volumes addressing the major concerns brought by the Protestants regarding justification, grace, Sacred Scripture, original sin, and the Seven Sacraments. The reform that began in Rome would work its way down to the laity. All bishops were required to faithfully bind themselves to uphold the conciliar decrees.

APPLICATION OF THE TRIDENTINE REFORM

The conclusion of the Council of Trent did not bring about immediate reforms. Many secular princes refused to accept the council's statements and would not allow the publication of its decrees. It was only through the personal example and dedicated holiness of a number of particular individuals that the fruits of Trent were bought forth.

ST. PIUS V

Michele Ghislieri was elected Pope Pius V in January 1566. A Dominican monk, St. Pius spread the religious reform of Trent throughout Christendom by living in a monastic cell as pope. He fasted, did penance, and passed long hours of the night in meditation and prayer. Despite the heavy labors and anxieties of his office, his piety did not diminish. He abolished lavish feasts and the use of fancy carriages by cardinals. He visited churches barefoot and cared for the poor and sick of Rome. An English nobleman was converted to the Faith upon seeing this holy man kiss the feet of a beggar who was covered in ulcerous sores. In his bull, *In cœna Domini,* Pope St. Pius V strove for the independence of the Church and of churchmen everywhere against dominance by secular

The naval Battle of Lepanto took place on October 7, 1571, at the northern edge of the entrance to the Gulf of Corinth (then the Gulf of Lepanto), off western Greece. A galley fleet of the Holy League, a coalition of Pope St. Pius V, Spain, Venice, Genoa, Savoy, Naples, the Knights of Malta and others, defeated a force of 230 Ottoman galleys and 60 galliots. The Holy League fleet consisted of 206 galleys and 6 galleasses, and was ably commanded by Don Juan of Austria. The League suffered 9,000 casualties and lost 12 ships; the Ottomans suffered 30,000 casualties and lost 240 ships. The famous Spanish author Cervantes was wounded in this battle and lost the use of his left hand.

powers. He fought German Emperor Maximilian II's attempt to abolish celibacy among the clergy, excommunicated Elizabeth I for her imprisonment of Mary Stuart and her attacks upon the Catholic faithful in England, and helped stem the tide of the Turkish threat from the East.

THE TURKISH THREAT AND THE BATTLE OF LEPANTO

By the late 1560s, the Turks were reaching the height of their power. Under the leadership of Suleiman the Magnificent, the Turkish fleet controlled the Mediterranean. In 1521 Belgrade fell, and the following year the Knights Hospitalers were driven from the Island of Rhodes. Hungary fell to Turkish forces in 1526, and Vienna itself was placed under siege in 1529. At sea, Tripoli became the harbor of Corsair raiding ships that struck at Sicily and Southern Italy.

Pope St. Pius V had concerns that Turkish armies could overwhelm the Austrians in Vienna or that a Turkish fleet amassing in Greece could invade any part of Europe. He worked tirelessly to form a league of Christian princes to stop the Turkish menace. In 1565 this threat seemed about to be realized when the Island of Malta, a very strategic center of the Mediterranean, was attacked by 30,000 Turkish soldiers. The Knights Hospitalers with only 600 knights and 8000 men outlasted a summer-long siege and nearly total annihilation before the Turkish force withdrew. Pope St. Pius feared that the Turkish fleet in the Gulf of Patros near Greece would bring Europe to its knees within the year. To offset this imminent danger Pope St. Pius financed a Christian fleet to be led by Don Juan of Austria, the illegitimate son of Charles V, the former Holy Roman emperor.

The Christian League was beset by internal rivalry. The largest fleets of Europe were held by Venice and Spain, but Venice attempted diplomacy with the Turks in the hope of maintaining its large trading empire in the East. They were loath to aid in a war that could bring them financial ruin. The Spanish fleet was expensive to maintain, and Philip II was not eager to risk his entire fleet in a single engagement.

The turning point came when Turkish forces attacked Famagusta on Cyprus where the Venetians had established a diplomatic enclave. The Turks had previously guaranteed security for the Venetians, but during the attack, the entire Venetian delegation was murdered. This drove the Venetians into the Christian League against the Turks, and the Spanish fleet agreed to join the coalition if the young Spaniard Don Juan of Austria would lead it.

With the alliance strengthened and the attack approaching, Pope St. Pius V urged every Christian to prepare for the naval offensive by praying the Rosary. On October 7, 1571, the Christian fleet met the Turkish fleet at Lepanto. Owing to superiority in gun power and a sudden shift in the wind, the Christian fleet defeated the larger Turkish force. The Turkish fleet was broken, and the Christian powers were freed from the fear of the Mediterranean becoming a "Muslim lake." In thanksgiving for this victory in the crucial Battle of Lepanto, St. Pius V added "Help of Christians," to the Litany of Loreto. Mary's assistance is remembered on every October 7, the Feast of Our Lady of the Rosary.

Pope St. Pius V urged every Christian to prepare for the naval battle at Lepanto by reciting the Rosary.

St. Pius V was dedicated to implementing the decisions of the Council of Trent. He was canonized in 1712 by Clement XI.

Left: An original battle plan for The Battle of Lepanto on October 7, 1571.

ST. PETER CANISIUS

For his work in successfully implementing the reforms of the Council of Trent in Germany and defending the Church against the spread of Protestantism, St. Peter Canisius is often called the "Second Apostle of Germany" (St. Boniface being the first— cf. chapter five). Born in 1521, St. Peter began his studies at the University of Cologne at the age of fifteen. In 1543, still only twenty-two, he went on a retreat directed by Bl. Peter Faber, a Jesuit and companion of St. Ignatius of Loyola, where he decided to enter the Society of Jesus. St. Peter founded the first Jesuit house in Germany, and for fourteen years served as the first Jesuit provincial to that country.

Attending a session of the Council of Trent in 1547, St. Peter Canisius became deeply involved in the debates and issues surrounding the reform of the Church. In 1549, at the request of the pope, he was entrusted with the nearly impossible task of stopping defections of Catholics in Germany and bringing back into the Church those who had already left. Realizing that one way to prevent the spread of Protestantism was through the teaching of proper Catholic doctrine, he helped develop or establish colleges at Ingolstadt, Vienna, Prague, Munich, Innsbruck, Dillingen, Tyrnau, Hall-in-Tyrol, and other places in the Protestant North of Germany.

In 1555 St. Peter Canisius introduced what is considered his most lasting contribution. In response to the Reformation, many German Catholics left the Faith out of ignorance of the teachings of their own Church. To respond to the problem, Canisius was asked to write a Catholic Catechism that offered a clear and readable exposition of Catholic doctrine. St. Peter Canisius ended up writing three Catechisms: one for children, one for students, and one for adults. The impact of his work was immediate. These immensely popular Catechisms were translated into fifteen languages and used for centuries. In 1925 Pope Pius XI canonized St. Peter Canisius and named him a Doctor of the Church. His feast day is celebrated on December 21.

In 1925 Pope Pius XI canonized St. Peter Canisius and named him a Doctor of the Church.

ST. CHARLES BORROMEO

St. Charles Borromeo was named a cardinal and made secretary of state under his uncle, Pope Pius IV, where he oversaw the final sessions of the Council of Trent. It was through his efforts that the successful completion of the Council of Trent was accomplished. St. Charles was one of those remarkably able men whose personal example managed to bring about effective reform. After the council, St. Charles was made Archbishop of Milan, one of the most important archdioceses outside of Rome and one that did not have a resident bishop for over eighty years. Milan was beset with all the problems of the contemporary age. Many of its clergy were ignorant or ill-equipped to fulfill their pastoral duties. It naturally followed that due to a weak clergy, the laity were deprived of the guidance and direction to lead good Christian lives. This weakened faith among both priests and laity created an ideal situation for heresy and immorality.

To accomplish this great reform, St. Charles set about reorganizing his archdiocese. During his tenure as archbishop, he held a series of provincial councils and diocesan synods to implement the terms of Trent. He established three seminaries for training clergy and required annual retreats for all clerics. His reforms were published in *Acts of the Church of Milan*, which became a pattern for reform throughout Europe. St. Charles Borromeo regularly made visits to his parishes and brought to his aid the services of other reforming orders such as the Barnabites and Jesuits. St. Charles founded the Confraternity of Christian Doctrine with 2,000 teachers to instruct the children of Milan in over 740 schools.

Resistance to reform in Milan was strong. Agents of the secular powers sought to block his authority, and some religious communities attempted to block his entry. Someone even attempted to assassinate this zealous reformer. In the summer of 1578, plague raged throughout Milan and most of the important dignitaries left the

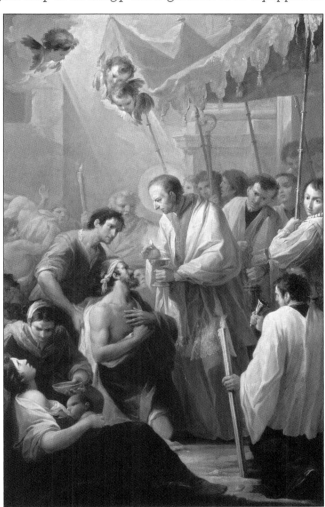

St. Charles Borromeo personally attended to plague victims in Milan in 1578.

city. Throughout the epidemic, St. Charles continued his work in the city and personally helped to provide food for the poor and care for the sick and dying. Personal example and strong determination helped bring about an exemplary archdiocese in Milan, showing that the Tridentine reforms could be put into practice.

The Spanish mystic St. Teresa of Avila is one of only three female Doctors of the Church.

REFORMING THE ORDERS:
STS. PHILIP NERI AND TERESA OF AVILA

Equally important to post-Tridentine reform was the need to revive the old religious orders. The renewed spiritual example of monks and friars would help influence the reform of diocesan clergy and lay faithful. This reform especially prompted monastic orders to return to their original spirit expressed in a serious practice of prayer and penance and a strict observation of the evangelical counsels through vows of poverty, chastity, and obedience. The Council of Trent provided invaluable support for the renewal of the older orders and the establishment of new "regular" orders created to serve the Church in its task of reform.

Sometimes referred to as the "Reformer of Rome," St. Philip of Neri helped to bring back a spirit of piety to the Eternal City. St. Philip founded the Oratorians, a congregation of secular priests who dedicated themselves to the spiritual formation and support of the clergy. For forty years St. Philip helped restore Rome as the central city of Catholicism. In 1559 one of the first Protestant works on the history of the Church appeared. Entitled *The Centuries*, this book attempted to discredit the Church hierarchy and attack the authority of the pope. St. Philip appointed the Venerable Cardinal Baronius to write a suitable response, and Baronius published his *Annales Ecclesiastici* in twelve volumes in response to *The Centuries*. His work became a pioneer in historical criticism and easily eclipsed its Protestant counterpart. His feast day is celebrated on May 26.

A spiritual resurgence took place in the wake of the Tridentine reforms. In place of the pessimistic outlook toward the unworthiness of man, the denial of free will, and the futility of good deeds, there came about an optimistic spirit that placed trust in the goodness of human nature and in the beauty of the human soul. One of the great representatives of this movement was the Spanish mystic St. Teresa of Avila. As a young Carmelite nun, St. Teresa's early life was wracked with serious illnesses and suffered from failed medical treatment that reduced her health to a pitiful state. Through her sufferings, St. Teresa began the practice of mental prayer (meditation) and became immersed in God. She was granted a series of ecstasies from God and gained a great reputation among those around her. Believing God wanted her to found a convent of perpetual prayer, she established the Discalced Carmelites. Within her lifetime she founded sixteen houses for her new order. St. Teresa wrote magnificent treatises on the interior life that have become part of the patrimony of the Church's spirituality, including *The Way of Perfection, Foundations,* and *Life* (her autobiography). Pope Paul VI proclaimed her a Doctor of the Church in 1970; St. Teresa of Avila, along with Sts. Catherine of Siena and Thérèse of Lisieux, is one of only three female Doctors of the Church. St. Teresa of Avila's feast day is celebrated on October 15.

ST. IGNATIUS OF LOYOLA AND THE SOCIETY OF JESUS

Probably the most significant of the new orders brought about to help realize Tridentine reform involved the Society of Jesus founded by St. Ignatius of Loyola. In 1491, St. Ignatius was born in a castle in Loyola, Spain, and he trained from boyhood to be a knight. He served at court where he lived the worldly life of a typical young nobleman. In 1517 he was transferred to Pamplona. When war broke out between Charles V and Francis I in 1521, St. Ignatius led the defense of the fortress at Pamplona where he was seriously injured in both legs. His captors, much impressed by his courage, attempted to dress his wounds and set his bones. During his return to his castle in Loyola, it was apparent that a second operation would be necessary. In order to save his leg, the surgeons attempted to saw off part of the bone that protruded. This operation left St. Ignatius permanently crippled and it ended his military career.

During his convalescence, St. Ignatius read all the romantic books and books of chivalry he could find. After finishing all those, he grudgingly read the remaining two books: one on the life of Christ and the other on the lives of the saints. These last two books had a profound effect on St. Ignatius and led to his conversion. His injuries left him unable to be a soldier for the king, so he sought to be a soldier for Christ.

After spending the night dressed in military regalia praying before an image of Mary, St. Ignatius set out to the shrine of Our Lady of Montserrat. At the shrine he made a general confession, laid his sword and dagger at the feet of Mary, and exchanged clothes with a poor beggar. He proceeded to spend a year in the seclusion of a cave called Manresa, near the town of Cataluña. For an entire year, he knelt everyday for seven hours at a time, completely absorbed in prayer. He hardly ate and eventually became very sick. Despite his physical discomfort, during his year in seclusion, St. Ignatius realized that God had called him for a special task. He was inspired to write *Spiritual Exercises,* a guide for spiritual perfection meant to help the believer learn to emulate Christ.

St. Ignatius left his sanctuary to study at the University of Alcala in Barcelona and eventually went to study at Paris. Already forty, St. Ignatius was unimpressive in appearance. He had a severe limp, was a poor speaker, and was not especially brilliant. He did, however, have a high capacity for work and a serene and self-controlled temperament. His spiritual example alone began to attract a number of followers. On August 15, 1524, St. Ignatius gathered seven companions from the Sorbonne to climb a mountain, on top of which, in a small Benedictine chapel, they made a vow of poverty and selfless service to others. St. Ignatius of Loyola's feast day is celebrated on July 31.

Pope Paul III confirmed the Society of Jesus on September 27, 1540.

Pope Paul III approved this new order founded by St. Ignatius—known as the Society of Jesus or Jesuits—with the bull *Regimini militantis Ecclesiae.* St. Ignatius of Loyola's *Spiritual Exercises* was written for the Jesuits, who were growing in number, as a response to the rising militancy of Protestantism and Calvin's *Institutes.* The new Jesuit order added a vow of obedience to the pope himself to the traditional vows of poverty, chastity, and obedience. The order became characterized by militaristic discipline and total availability to the service of the Church and the poor. Wherever the pope sent them, they would go.

Jesuits soon became involved in every facet of the Church's ministry. They served as nuncios, theologians, professors, and missionaries. They were sent all over the globe—especially to the wilderness of the Americas and Asia—to spread the Gospel. The Jesuits also suffered persecution in England and other Protestant countries. For the next four centuries, Jesuits stood out as exceptional servants to Christ, the Church, and the pope, leading the world as saints, martyrs, intellectuals, advisors and confessors.

CONCLUSION

The unfailing light and strength of the Holy Spirit explains not only the Church's survival amid one of the greatest crises She has ever faced, but also her vigorous renewal. It is indeed remarkable that in the face of the Church's greatest upheaval, renewal and revitalization within the Church reflected in a special way the power of the Holy Spirit to protect and renew the Church. The many and varied examples of saints is a marvelous testimony to the perennial truth that the Church is always young and vibrant in spite of the constant need of purification of her children. The political and religious upheavals of the sixteenth century would challenge the Church's part to play as leaven for society but would never manage to stop her work in extending Christ's kingdom.

SUPPLEMENTARY READING

Martin Luther, from the *Ninety-Five Theses*

4. The penalty [of sin], therefore, continues so long as hatred of self continues; for this is the true inward repentance, and continues until our entrance into the kingdom of heaven.

5. The pope does not intend to remit, and cannot remit any penalties other than those which he has imposed either by his own authority or by that of the Canons.

6. The pope cannot remit any guilt, except by declaring that it has been remitted by God and by assenting to God's remission; though, to be sure, he may grant remission in cases reserved to his judgment. If his right to grant remission in such cases were despised, the guilt would remain entirely unforgiven.

26. The pope does well when he grants remission to souls [in purgatory], not by the power of the keys (which he does not possess), but by way of intercession.

75. To think the papal pardons so great that they could absolve a man even if he had committed an impossible sin and violated the Mother of God — this is madness.

76. We say, on the contrary, that the papal pardons are not able to remove the very least of venial sins, so far as its guilt is concerned.

77. It is said that even St. Peter, if he were now Pope, could not bestow greater graces; this is blasphemy against St. Peter and against the pope.

79. To say that the cross, emblazoned with the papal arms, which is set up [by the preachers of indulgences], is of equal worth with the Cross of Christ, is blasphemy.

Henry VIII, *Act of Supremacy*, 1534

Albeit the King's Majesty justly and rightfully is and ought to be the supreme head of the Church of England, and so is recognized by the clergy of this realm in their Convocations,...Be it enacted by authority of this present Parliament that the King, our sovereign lord, his heirs and successors, kings of this realm, shall be taken, accepted and reputed the only supreme head in earth of the Church of England, called *Anglicana Ecclesia;* and shall have and enjoy, annexed and united to the imperial crown of this realm, as well the title and style thereof, as all honors, dignities, pre-eminences, jurisdictions, privileges, authorities, immunities, profits and commodities to the said dignity of supreme head of the same Church belonging and appertaining; and that our said sovereign lord, his heirs and successors, kings of this realm, shall have full power and authority from time to time to visit, repress, redress, reform, order, correct, restrain and amend all such errors,...

John Paul II, *Apostolic Letter Proclaiming St. Thomas More the Patron of Statesmen and Politicians*

It is helpful to turn to the example of Saint Thomas More, who distinguished himself by his constant fidelity to legitimate authority and institutions precisely in his intention to serve not power but the supreme ideal of justice. His life teaches us that government is above all an exercise of virtue. Unwavering in this rigorous moral stance, this English statesman placed his own public activity at the service of the person, especially if that person was weak or poor; he dealt with social controversies with a superb sense of fairness; he was vigorously committed to favoring and defending the family; he supported the all-round education of the young. His profound detachment from honors and wealth, his serene and joyful humility, his balanced knowledge of human nature and of the vanity of success, his certainty of judgment rooted in faith: these all gave him that confident inner strength that sustained him in adversity and in the face of death. His sanctity shone forth in his martyrdom, but it had been prepared by an entire life of work devoted to God and neighbor.

VOCABULARY

ACT OF SUPREMACY

Proclaimed King Henry VIII the supreme leader of the Church in England, which meant that the pope was no longer recognized as having any authority within the country, and all matters of faith, ecclesiastical appointment, and maintenance of ecclesiastical properties were in the hands of the king.

CONSUBSTANTIATION

A term describing Christ's co-existence in the Eucharist. Luther taught that the Eucharist was not truly Christ, but that He was present in it as heat is in a hot iron. Accordingly, the substance of Christ's body co-exists with the substance of the bread and his blood with the wine.

INSTITUTES OF THE CHRISTIAN RELIGION

Written by John Calvin, it contained four books which codified Protestant theology. Among these beliefs were the ultimate authority of the word of God, the depravity of man, and his belief that the Bible is the only source of Revelation.

PLURALISM

Within the Church, a bishop having control over more than one diocese.

PREDESTINATION

A doctrine of Calvin which taught that salvation depended solely on God's pre-determined decision. According to this principle, those who are saved (the elect) are chosen by God through no effort of their own. God also chooses others to be damned. This damnation is necessary to show God's great justice.

SCRUPULOSITY

The habit of imagining sin when none exists, or grave sin when the matter is not serious.

SOLA SCRIPTURA

"Scripture alone." It is the belief that all man needs for salvation is the Bible. This is a tenet for most Protestants.

SPIRITUAL EXERCISES

During a year of intense prayer, St. Ignatius was inspired to write this guide for spiritual perfection, which is divided into reflections and meditations meant to help the believer emulate Christ.

THIRTY-NINE ARTICLES

Issued by Elizabeth I, these provided for the foundation of the Anglican Church, maintaining all the outward appearances of Catholicism, but implanting Protestant doctrine into the Church of England.

TRANSUBSTANTIATION

The change of the substance of bread and wine into the Body and Blood of Christ with only the accidents (properties) of bread and wine remaining.

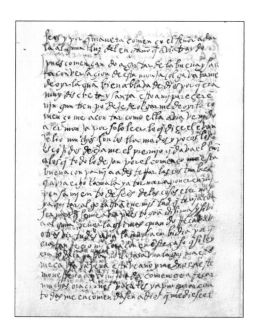

A page in the handwriting of St. Teresa of Avila from the manuscript for her autobiography *Life*, written in 1565-66.

STUDY QUESTIONS

1. What abuses in the Church required reform?

2. What was the name of the document that Martin Luther nailed to the door of the Wittenberg cathedral? On what date did this happen?

3. What abuse initially captured Luther's attention and compelled him to write the document he nailed on the cathedral door?

4. What two sacraments did Luther retain?

5. What is consubstantiation?

6. Where and at what meeting did Luther answer charges before Emperor Charles V?

7. Where did Luther go to escape capture by the emperor?

8. What text did Luther translate from the original Greek into German while at Wartburg?

9. What was the key passage from St. Paul in Romans 1:17 that led Luther to the theological idea of "justification through faith alone"?

10. What book of the New Testament did Luther especially reject?

11. What relationship to secular authority did Luther and Lutheranism develop?

12. What happened in 1524 that caused Luther to rely heavily on the state to restore order against radicals and the Anabaptist movement?

13. What was the Augsburg Confession (1530)?

14. Who developed the Reformed tradition in the Protestant Reformation?

15. What was the name of Calvin's most important work?

16. In what ways did Calvin go beyond Luther's theology?

17. What was Calvin's teaching regarding predestination?

18. In which city did Calvin establish a theocracy?

19. What work did Henry VIII of England write against Luther's ideas?

20. What was the state of the Catholic Church in England at the beginning of Henry VIII's reign?

21. What was Henry VIII's disagreement with the Church?

22. What was the Act of Supremacy? When was it issued?

23. Who were two of the most important martyrs during Henry VIII's reign?

24. What happened to Church lands and religious houses in England?

25. How was the Church of England that Henry VIII started theologically different from the Catholic Church?

26. What book did Thomas Cranmer, Archbishop of Canterbury, publish under King Edward VI's reign?

27. Under whose reign did the Church of England truly accept the ideas of the Protestant reformation?

28. What are the Thirty-nine Articles?

29. What were some of the challenges posed by a Church council being called?

30. When did the Council of Trent occur?

31. What topics did the Council of Trent address?

32. At what important battle were the Turks defeated by European forces?

STUDY QUESTIONS Continued

33. Who was the holy bishop of Milan who implemented the reforms of the Council of Trent?

34. Who helped reform the Carmelite order?

35. What important book did St. Ignatius of Loyola write that is still used for retreats today?

36. What kind of work did the Society of Jesus (Jesuits) do?

PRACTICAL EXERCISES

1. Martin Luther developed four major theological principles: *sola Scriptura, sola fide, sola gratia,* and *solo Christo* (Scripture alone, faith alone, grace alone, and Christ alone). Each of Luther's four main theological principles was conceived in reaction to what he believed were false teachings of the Church. Using the Scholastic method, construct a Catholic rebuttal to Luther's ideas.

2. The lives of John Calvin and St. Thomas More reveal two distinct understandings of how Christ's life and teachings apply to living as a Christian. By comparing these two men, explain how their lives reflect their theological understanding of Christianity. (Use the teachings of the Council of Trent and Calvin's *Institutes of the Christian Religion* as a guide.)

After St. Ignatius of Loyola made a general confession at the shrine of Our Lady of Montserrat, he laid his sword and dagger at the feet of Our Lady, and exchanged clothes with a poor beggar. He then lived a year in the seclusion of a cave near the town of Catalunia, called Manresa. For an entire year, he knelt everyday for seven hours at a time, completely absorbed in prayer.

FROM THE CATECHISM

814 From the beginning, this one Church has been marked by a great *diversity* which comes from both the variety of God's gifts and the diversity of those who receive them. Within the unity of the People of God, a multiplicity of peoples and cultures is gathered together. Among the Church's members, there are different gifts, offices, conditions, and ways of life. "Holding a rightful place in the communion of the Church there are also particular Churches that retain their own traditions" (*LG* 13 § 2). The great richness of such diversity is not opposed to the Church's unity. Yet sin and the burden of its consequences constantly threaten the gift of unity. And so the Apostle has to exhort Christians to "maintain the unity of the Spirit in the bond of peace" (Eph 4: 3).

818 "However, one cannot charge with the sin of the separation those who at present are born into these communities [that resulted from such separation] and in them are brought up in the faith of Christ, and the Catholic Church accepts them with respect and affection as brothers.... All who have been justified by faith in Baptism are incorporated into Christ; they therefore have a right to be called Christians, and with good reason are accepted as brothers in the Lord by the children of the Catholic Church" (*UR* 3 § 1).

819 "Furthermore, many elements of sanctification and of truth" (*LG* 8 § 2) are found outside the visible confines of the Catholic Church: "the written Word of God; the life of grace; faith, hope, and charity, with the other interior gifts of the Holy Spirit, as well as visible elements" (*UR* 3 § 2; cf. *LG* 15). Christ's Spirit uses these Churches and ecclesial communities as means of salvation, whose power derives from the fullness of grace and truth that Christ has entrusted to the Catholic Church. All these blessings come from Christ and lead to him (cf. *UR* 3), and are in themselves calls to "Catholic unity" (cf. *LG* 8).

834 Particular Churches are fully catholic through their communion with one of them, the Church of Rome "which presides in charity" (St. Ignatius of Antioch, *Ad Rom.* 1, 1: *Apostolic Fathers,* II/2, 192; cf. *LG* 13). "For with this church, by reason of its pre-eminence, the whole Church, that is the faithful everywhere, must necessarily be in accord" (St. Irenaeus, *Adv. haeres.* 3, 3, 2: PG 7/1, 849; cf. Vatican Council I DS 3057). Indeed, "from the incarnate Word's descent to us, all Christian churches everywhere have held and hold the great Church that is here [at Rome] to be their only basis and foundation since, according to the Savior's promise, the gates of hell have never prevailed against her" (St. Maximus the Confessor, *Opuscula theo.*: PG 91 137-140).

836 "All men are called to this catholic unity of the People of God.... And to it, in different ways, belong or are ordered: the Catholic faithful, others who believe in Christ, and finally all mankind, called by God's grace to salvation" (*LG* 13).

838 "The Church knows that she is joined in many ways to the baptized who are honored by the name of Christian, but do not profess the Catholic faith in its entirety or have not preserved unity or communion under the successor of Peter" (*LG* 15). Those "who believe in Christ and have been properly baptized are put in a certain, although imperfect, communion with the Catholic Church" (*UR* 3). *With the Orthodox Churches,* this communion is so profound "that it lacks little to attain the fullness that would permit a common celebration of the Lord's Eucharist" (Paul VI, Discourse, December 14, 1975; cf. *UR* 13-18).

FROM THE CATECHISM Continued

1126 Likewise, since the sacraments express and develop the communion of faith in the Church, the *lex orandi* is one of the essential criteria of the dialogue that seeks to restore the unity of Christians (cf. *UR* 2; 15).

1129 The Church affirms that for believers the sacraments of the New Covenant are *necessary for salvation* (cf. Council of Trent (1547): DS 1604). "Sacramental grace" is the grace of the Holy Spirit, given by Christ and proper to each sacrament. The Spirit heals and transforms those who receive him by conforming them to the Son of God. The fruit of the sacramental life is that the Spirit of adoption makes the faithful partakers in the divine nature (cf. 2 Pt 1:4) by uniting them in a living union with the only Son, the Savior.

1325 "The Eucharist is the efficacious sign and sublime cause of that communion in the divine life and that unity of the People of God by which the Church is kept in being. It is the culmination both of God's action sanctifying the world in Christ and of the worship men offer to Christ and through him to the Father in the Holy Spirit" (Congregation of Rites, instruction, *Eucharisticum mysterium*, 6).

2242 The citizen is obliged in conscience not to follow the directives of civil authorities when they are contrary to the demands of the moral order, to the fundamental rights of persons or the teachings of the Gospel. *Refusing obedience* to civil authorities, when their demands are contrary to those of an upright conscience, finds its justification in the distinction between serving God and serving the political community. "Render therefore to Caesar the things that are Caesar's, and to God the things that are God's" (Mt 22:21)."We must obey God rather than men" (Acts 5:29):

> When citizens are under the oppression of a public authority which oversteps its competence, they should still not refuse to give or to do what is objectively demanded of them by the common good; but it is legitimate for them to defend their own rights and those of their fellow citizens against the abuse of this authority within the limits of the natural law and the Law of the Gospel (*GS* 74 § 5).

The All Saints Church in Wittenberg today. The wooden doors from the time of Martin Luther were destroyed in a fire in 1760 and were replaced in 1858 by bronze doors bearing the Latin text of the 95 theses.

CHAPTER 14

Wars Of Religion

The religious wars of the sixteenth century were fought with extreme ferocity. Civil conflict spread throughout Europe as kings, nobles, and peasants clashed. When it was over, Europe remained divided: Catholic and Protestant.

CHAPTER 14

Wars Of Religion

"Deliver us from evil!" Reciting these words of Christ's prayer, it is very difficult
to give them a different content from the one that opposes peace, that destroys it,
that threatens it. Let us pray therefore: Deliver us from war, from hatred, from
the destruction of human lives! Do not allow us to kill! Do not allow the use of those
means which are in the service of death and destruction, and whose power,
range of action, and precision go beyond the limits known hitherto.

— John Paul II, *Prayer during Mass in the Sistine Chapel*, January 7, 1979.

Charles V abdicated his imperial throne in 1557, dividing his holdings between his son Philip and his brother Ferdinand. But Charles' abdication was not the only occasion for division in Europe at the time. The Peace of Augsburg settlement of 1555 and its principle *cuius regio huius religio* ("whose region, his the religion"; this principle was used to try to quell religious tension by mandating that each prince determined the faith of his own region) clearly defined religious and political boundaries on the continent, and each nation sought to push back those boundaries. German, Danish, and Swedish lords each sought to place the Baltic seaway under their control. Spain and the Holy Roman Emperor attempted to unify their domains at the expense of France and other smaller German states. France supported both Lutheran Germany and the Muslim Turks so as to assert her independence from the Spanish Empire and increase her influence over her smaller neighbor states.

To make matters more difficult, the rise of Calvinism brought about even more division. Calvinism arose in Scotland in the form of Presbyterianism and in France with the Huguenots. Germany and the Low Countries also saw an increase in the followers of Calvin as Europe split into Catholic and Protestant zones. Each denomination vied for territory, and bloody wars broke out.

The religious wars of the sixteenth and seventeenth centuries were fought with extreme bitterness and ferocity. Widespread civil conflict spread throughout Europe as kings and nobles clashed. Northern German princes continued to fight the Austrian emperors, and Dutch nobles in the Low Countries sought independence from the Spanish. Protestantism found its roots in smaller noble families in France as the Huguenots attempted to defeat their Catholic rivals who controlled the monarchy. English peasants marched on the heretical Queen Elizabeth I in the Pilgrimage of Grace,

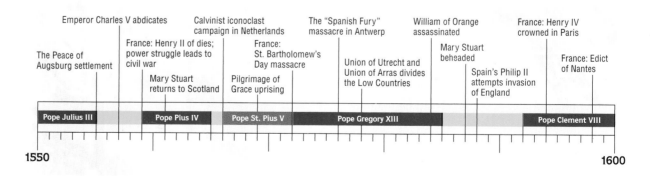

and Bohemian nobles tried to gain independence from their Austrian feudal lords. All these wars of religion that took place in the sixteenth and seventeenth centuries can be grouped into four major conflicts:

- **The Revolt of the Low Countries** (1559-1592)
- **The Huguenot Wars in France** (1562-1593)
- **The Struggle for the British Isles** (1561-1603)
- **The Thirty Years War in Germany** (1618-1648)

Philip II's El Escorial is an immense palace, monastery, museum, and library complex located in Madrid, Spain.

PART I

Spain and the Empire of Philip II

For thirty-five years Emperor Charles V tried in vain to maintain religious unity in his domain. By the time he relinquished his throne and left his empire to his son Philip II, his realm stretched across a wide and religiously divided land. Besides Spain, Philip was given control in the Netherlands and the County of Burgundy adjacent to France. Philip also controlled Milan, Naples, the major Western Mediterranean islands, and the vast Spanish empire in the Americas. For five years, until 1558, Philip was also titular king of England, and in 1589, he was able to claim the kingship of France for his daughter by his third marriage to Elizabeth de Valois. After 1580, the entire Portuguese Empire came under Philip's control, completing the ruler's worldwide empire. At the same time, these lands were fragmented and supported various Protestant sects. Religious zealots and nobles alike were looking to throw off the yoke of Catholic Spain.

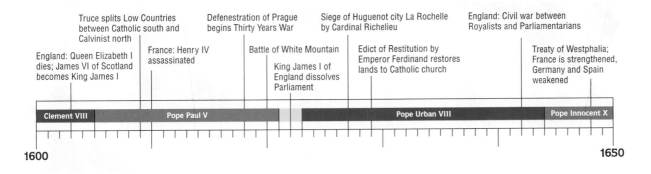

Truce splits Low Countries between Catholic south and Calvinist north

Defenestration of Prague begins Thirty Years War

Siege of Huguenot city La Rochelle by Cardinal Richelieu

England: Civil war between Royalists and Parliamentarians

England: Queen Elizabeth I dies; James VI of Scotland becomes King James I

France: Henry IV assassinated

Battle of White Mountain

King James I of England dissolves Parliament

Edict of Restitution by Emperor Ferdinand restores lands to Catholic church

Treaty of Westphalia; France is strengthened, Germany and Spain weakened

Clement VIII   Pope Paul V   Pope Urban VIII   Pope Innocent X

1600   1650

THE CRUSADE OF CATHOLIC SPAIN

Philip II was an ardent Catholic, and the Catholic Faith permeated every facet of Philip's life. He was a grave and somber man known for working tirelessly for 12 hours at a time. He spent hours in prayer, frequently confessed his sins, had the Blessed Sacrament close to his room, and only read works on spirituality. His palace, the cold and austere El Escorial, was built as a reflection of his personality. His private room in the massive palace complex, for example, was as simple as a monk's cell.

Philip II sought to root out heresy and rebellion throughout his realm and provide a good centralized government to all his provinces. Absolutism seemed to work in Spain, and Philip attempted to impose this same rigorous form of rule in all the territories under his control. Spanish governors were sent out to enforce the will of the king, who issued thousands of orders throughout the world from his small cell.

Early in Philip's reign, the *Moriscos*, descendants of the Islamic conquerors of the Spanish kingdom of Granada, rebelled against his rule. The *Moriscos* were in close communication with Turkish agents who were trying to prepare for a Turkish assault on Spain. The Austrian Don Juan, the half brother of

An ardent Catholic, Philip II worked tirelessly for twelve hours at a time. He spent hours in prayer and frequently confessed his sins. His private room in his palace, El Escorial, was as simple as a monk's cell.

Philip, was sent to remove this danger and transplant all of the *Moriscos* to the interior of Spain where communication with the Turks was near impossible. The Turks would continue to threaten Spain until they were defeated at the great Battle of Lepanto in 1571.

Spanish imperialism offset the balance of power in the rest of Europe. Fearing Spanish control in Italy, Pope Paul IV allied himself with the French in an effort to drive the Spanish from Naples. Philip II responded by sending an army with the Duke of Alba into the Papal States. They defeated French and papal forces in 1559. Philip further instructed the Duke to give good terms to the pope and apologize for his need to invade the papal territories.

THE REVOLT OF THE LOW COUNTRIES

The seventeen provinces making up the Low Countries included some of the richest and most populous regions in Europe. It was a cosmopolitan area made up of Dutch in the north, Flemish in the center, and Walloons (Francophones) in the south. An industrious people, they had a thriving agricultural and commercial economy and were ruggedly independent. Few countries, it was said, were so well governed, and none was richer. The city of Antwerp was a commercial metropolis; everyday a fleet of 500 seafaring vessels would enter and leave its port.

Each province in the Low Countries was a state unto itself, and each had its own legislature and local customs. A central government, or Estates General, was located in Brussels and was led by the traditional local prince known as the "*Stadtholder*" who led the provinces in times of trouble. Otherwise, business and politics were carried out locally and independently.

The House of Burgundy reigned over the territory of the Netherlands since the preceding century, and with Charles V's ascent, it became part of his greater empire. Charles V was, in fact, born in the Low Countries and spoke Flemish from birth. As a ruler, he respected the unwritten constitution of the provinces (known as the *Joyeuse Entrée*), and gave lucrative government positions to the local nobles. Because of his fair and evenhanded treatment of the Low Countries, Charles and Catholic Spain were popular. When Protestantism crept into the area, it took hold of only a minority of the population. But as the region's weaving industry opened itself to trade with England and Bohemia, Calvinism and Anabaptism began to appear. French Calvinists also arrived in the Low Countries fleeing violence in France. Although Charles V had passed certain laws against heresy, he did not largely enforce them, still respecting the tradition of toleration. When Philip ascended the throne, that policy changed. He quickly sent Spanish governors to enforce his own jurisdiction over the Low Countries—a move that pushed the local rulers to revolt.

The revolt against Philip II in the Low Countries had both political and religious dimensions. Politically the nobility of the Low Countries became resentful that Spanish governors were sent to rule their land. At first, when Philip's regent, Margaret of Parma, was sent to the region, she tried to rule with a moderate hand. But her efforts were frustrated by the presence of 3000 Spanish troops sent by the king to protect the southern frontier with France. The arrival of the Spanish dashed the local nobility's hopes for gaining privileged and lucrative positions in Philip's government. Furthermore, the high cost of maintaining these foreigners' lavish lifestyles intensely embittered the Dutch.

Philip also tried to implement religious reforms that were spelled out by the Council of Trent. Prior to Philip's rule, the heavily populated Low Countries had only three dioceses, which were governed by foreign bishops. Pope Paul IV attempted to apply the Tridentine Reforms by restructuring the current dioceses and adding fourteen more. This redistribution of authority from the older system took power away from local nobles and abbots. Adding to the discontent, rumors began to spread that the inquisition was going to be brought into the Low Countries.

Two local princes, William of Orange and the Count of Egmont, protested the presence of Spanish troops in the region and asked Philip to moderate his program for religious reform. At their request, Philip did remove some Spanish soldiers, but the king refused to alter his position on doctrinal uniformity. He was stubborn and insistent on incorporating the Low Countries into his larger empire.

Philip II was seen as despotic, severe, crafty, and desirous of keeping his own hands on all the reins of government—in minor details as well as in matters of greater significance. His style of ruling caused delays in resolving difficulties and occasioned obstacles to needed rapid transaction. Philip II sincerely desired to fulfill his royal office and ardently prayed for the ability to do so.

William I, Prince of Orange, Count of Nassau (1533-1584), was the main leader of the Dutch revolt against the Spanish. In the Netherlands, he is also known as the *Vader des vaderlands*, "Father of the Fatherland." The Dutch national anthem, the *Wilhelmus*, was written in his honor.

Conflict between Spain and the Low Countries erupted when small Calvinist groups launched an iconoclastic campaign across the countryside in late August 1566. Over 1000 churches and monasteries, including the cathedral of Antwerp, were plundered over a two-week period. Manuscripts, paintings, and statues were destroyed; gold chalices were stolen and tabernacles desecrated. At first, public opinion condemned the outrage and sided with the government. Philip mishandled the situation and lost any good will he might have gained. Rather than skillfully capitalizing on this turn of events to win back those who were shocked by the violence of the Calvinists, he looked upon all his subjects in the Low Countries as equally guilty. His regent, Margaret of Parma, was beginning to win favor among the people, but instead of supporting her efforts to handle the rebellion locally, Philip swore by his father's soul to make an example of the rebels. He condemned the people of the Low Countries for the atrocities, and against the advice of the regent and in spite of the pope's exhortation to clemency, he sent a Spanish army led by the Duke of Alba to restore order.

THE COUNCIL OF TROUBLES AND WILLIAM OF ORANGE

Alba was a superior general, but not a gifted statesman. Under his governance, Spanish soldiers began a system of merciless repression; blood flowed freely, and all the traditional rights of the people were discarded. The dissident *Stadtholder* William of Orange fled into exile while the Catholic nobleman, Count of Egmont, remained to deal with the Spanish assault. Without trial, the Duke of Alba executed the Count of Egmont, and sentenced thousands to death. The land of the aristocracy was confiscated, and the Duke of Alba levied heavy taxes to finance his military campaign. His policies consequently brought trade to a virtual standstill throughout the Low Countries, and general public outrage united peasants and nobles alike against the Spanish.

In exile, William of Orange tried to use his position as *Stadtholder* to gain support and muster a military force against the Spanish invasion. To generate strong opposition to Spain, William wielded religion as a political mechanism. He was a Catholic in the court of Philip II, but a Lutheran when dealing with the German princes whom he hoped would aid him against the Spanish. When Calvinism emerged as the prominent religious denomination among the Dutch, he in turn adopted their creed.

Fernando Álvarez de Toledo, the third Duke of Alba (or Alva) (1508-1583), was nicknamed "the Iron Duke" by Protestants of the Low Countries because of his harshness. His cruelty united the Dutch against the Spanish.

Encouraged by local support, William and his brother invaded the Low Countries with an army of German mercenaries, but was quickly driven back by the Spanish soldiers. The Duke of Alba pompously thought he secured victory, and he had a statue of himself erected in the city of Antwerp. News soon reached the general of a rebel fleet attacking the port of Den Briel and rebel forces advancing against a number of other cities. The war was far from over.

The Spanish Fury. On November 4,1576, Spanish troops began the sack of Antwerp, three days of horror among the Flemish population. The Spanish soldiers, tired of fighting the Dutch without rest and without payment from Philip II, decided to take their "salary" from the population of Antwerp. The mutinous troops destroyed six hundred houses and killed over six thousand people.

DIVISION OF THE LOW COUNTRIES

William of Orange strove to unite the Low Countries against the Spanish, and Protestant minorities flocked to him. Because of the Spanish repression, leading Catholic lords also joined William's camp. By 1576, whatever Catholic support remained in the Low Countries was destroyed after the Spanish army mutinied. The army had not received pay, and they rebelled against their commanders and unleashed terrible violence. Known as the "Spanish Fury," soldiers pillaged the country and killed over six thousand people. Any resistance to William dissolved. The Estates General signed the Pacification of Ghent in November of that year, granting toleration of worship and placing authority of the provinces under the Calvinist regions of Holland and Zeeland. Practicing the Catholic religion was no longer allowed in the North, and the southern provinces were becoming Protestant.

Philip II, realizing that the Duke of Alba had failed to subdue the Low Countries, recalled the governor to Spain. In his place, Philip sent the victor of Lepanto, Don Juan of Austria. Don Juan realized that William of Orange was playing upon the fear of the provinces, and so he accepted the Pacification of Ghent and sought to win back the Low Countries to Spain. After a series of military victories, it appeared that Don Juan was on the verge of defeating the Protestant forces and re-uniting the provinces. However, an illness took his life in 1578. Another great general and diplomat replaced Don Juan: the son of Margaret of Parma, Alessandro Farnese. This Prince of Parma broke up the unity of the seventeen provinces by promising a return to their original liberties enjoyed before the fighting. Catholics who had become fearful of William of Orange's growing power were drawn back to the Spanish throne. William, whose ambitions were thwarted by this reversal of Dutch sentiment, united the seven Northern provinces in an alliance called the Union of Utrecht. This union declared their independence from Spain, and re-organized as the United Provinces of the Netherlands or the Dutch Republic. In 1578, the ten southern provinces that remained loyal to the Spanish crown formed the Union of Arras or the Spanish Netherlands (Belgium).

THE REVOLT OF THE LOW COUNTRIES AGAINST SPAIN, 1559-1592

GRONINGEN

FRIESLAND

DRENTHE

Zuider Zee

N O R T H   S E A

OVERIJSSEL

HOLLAND

Haarlem ○ ○ Amsterdam

UNITED PROVINCES
OF THE
NETHERLANDS

○ Leiden UTRECHT

The Hague ○

GELDERN

○ Rotterdam

ZEELAND

H O L Y
R O M A N
E M P I R E

○ Eindhoven

Bruges ○

○ Antwerp

○ Ghent

S P A N I S H   N E T H E R L A N D S

LIEGE

Maastricht

Rhine

○ Brussels

○ Lille

○ Liege

Meuse

○ Mons

○ Arras

Majority denomination:

Roman Catholic
Calvinist

0   20   40   60   80   100 km

0   20   40   60 miles

SPANISH
NETHERLANDS

© 1997 Lion Hudson plc / Three's Company

As one of the most prominent and popular politicians of the Netherlands, William I, Prince of Orange emerged as the leader of an armed resistance. He financed the *Watergeuzen*, refugee Protestants who formed bands of corsairs and raided the coastal cities of the Netherlands. He also raised an army of mercenaries to fight the Spanish Duke of Alba on land.

THE HUGUENOT WARS IN FRANCE, 1562-1593

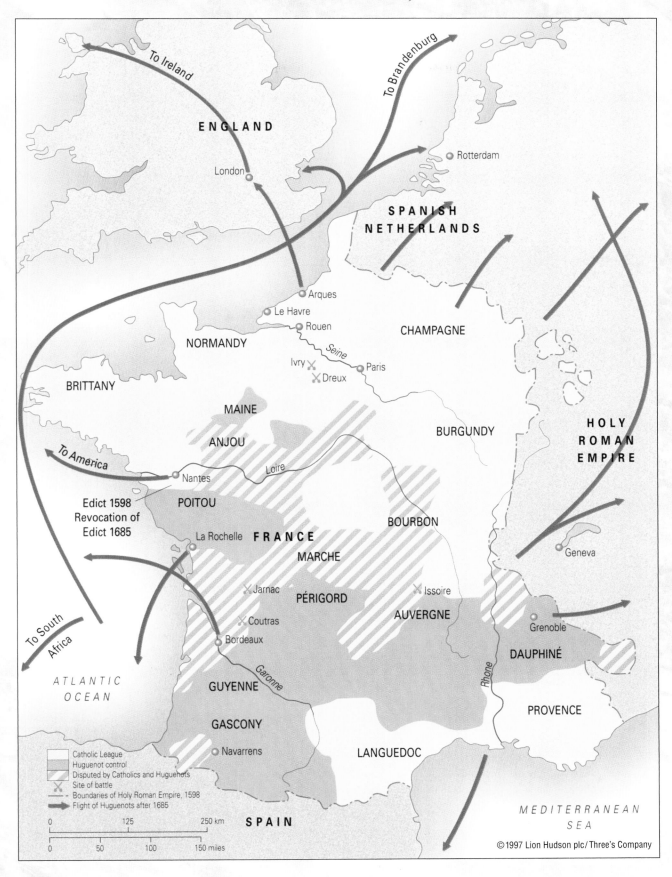

To Ireland

ENGLAND

London

To Brandenburg

Rotterdam

SPANISH
NETHERLANDS

Arques

Le Havre

Rouen

NORMANDY

CHAMPAGNE

Seine

Ivry

Paris

Dreux

BRITTANY

MAINE

BURGUNDY

ANJOU

HOLY
ROMAN
EMPIRE

To America

Loire

Nantes

Edict 1598
Revocation of
Edict 1685

POITOU

BOURBON

La Rochelle

FRANCE

Geneva

MARCHE

Jarnac

Issoire

PÉRIGORD

AUVERGNE

Coutras

Bordeaux

Grenoble

To South
Africa

DAUPHINÉ

Garonne

ATLANTIC
OCEAN

GUYENNE

Rhone

PROVENCE

GASCONY

Navarrens

LANGUEDOC

Catholic League
Huguenot control
Disputed by Catholics and Huguenots
Site of battle
Boundaries of Holy Roman Empire, 1598
Flight of Huguenots after 1685

MEDITERRANEAN
SEA

SPAIN

©1997 Lion Hudson plc/Three's Company

0   125   250 km
0   50   100   150 miles

On July 10, 1584, William of Orange was shot in his home in Delft by Balthasar Gérard, a French supporter of Philip II. In Gérard's opinion, William had betrayed the Spanish king and the Catholic religion. William's last words were in French: *"Mon Dieu, mon Dieu, ayez pitié de moi et de ton pauvre peuple"* (My Lord, My Lord, have pity on me and your poor people). Gérard was tortured before being drawn and quartered by order of the city magistrates of Delft.

ENGLISH SUPPORT
AND THE END OF THE CONFLICT

Unfortunately, neither the newly formed Netherlands nor Belgium accepted the partitions between their countries, and war continued. Philip II declared William of Orange a national outlaw; Balthasar Gérard, a French supporter of Philip II, killed William in 1584. After William's death, his son took up his father's mantel and continued the war effort. The Prince of Parma moved on Antwerp, the leading port of the North Sea, a move that prompted England to enter the war on the side of the Dutch. Already for some time, relations between Spain and England were tense over the economic and political policies of Elizabeth I. Philip II was already planning an eventual invasion of the British Isles, and Antwerp was a perfect location to launch an invasion of England. Elizabeth entered the Dutch conflict, hoping to neutralize Spanish power in that region.

The Prince of Parma died in 1592, leaving the task of reunifying the Low Countries unfinished. The economy of the southern provinces was ruined by endless war, and the English seized the mouth of the Scheldt River cutting off all trade routes to Antwerp and Ghent. On account of that blockade, Amsterdam in the north became the commercial and financial center of northern Europe for the next two centuries. Finally, in 1609, a twelve-year truce, which split the Low Countries between the Catholic south and the Calvinist north, was established.

PART II
The Huguenot Wars

During the middle of the sixteenth century, France was embroiled in its own internal religious conflict. The rising absolutist tendencies of the Valois kings threatened the independence of the landed nobility. Many landed gentry of France who sought to maintain their independence from the crown became French Protestants, called Calvinist Huguenots. Calvin himself, being a Frenchman, managed to spread his ideas rapidly throughout France. Soon, Protestantism in France was too strong to be considered the dissent of a few scattered individuals.

The Western Schism, the progress of Gallican ideas, the Pragmatic Sanction of Bourges, and the war of Louis XII against Pope Julius II all considerably weakened the prestige and authority of the papacy in France. (The French king Charles VII issued the Pragmatic Sanction of Bourges, wrongly enthroning an ecumenical council above the authority of the pope.) The autonomous tendencies of the Church in France made it difficult for the reforms of Trent to make any significant headway.

France was the most populous and powerful of all the European kingdoms. It was three times the size of England and five times as populated. Like Germany, the kingdom of France was made up of some three hundred areas with their own legal systems and specific liberties. Traditionally the nobles of these regions wielded strong influence. As the public began to seek relief from these powerful lords, they supported the rising tide of the French kings. Seeking to defend their power, more than a third, and possibly half of the nobility in France turned to Protestantism in the 1560s and 1570s. Many regions defied the local bishop and adopted Protestant services. Unlike Anglicanism in England and Lutheranism in Germany, Calvinism was a pretext used by the nobles against the monarchy in France, and thus both Francis I and Henry II opposed its spread. After the death of Henry II in 1559, the stage was set for a confrontation among the various nobles over the control of France.

THREE FACTIONS: GUISE, HUGUENOT, AND *POLITIQUE*

After the death of Henry II, France was split between three major groups. The House of Guise was an ardent Catholic faction that was led by the Dukes and Cardinals of Lorraine. The Guise family had aided Francis I in his many wars against Charles V and had become very influential in directing the affairs of France. As descendants of Charlemagne, the Guise family also had a distant claim to the French throne. Adding to their power and prestige, Mary of Guise was Queen of Scotland, and her daughter Mary Stuart was once Queen of France and heir to the English Throne. The Guise family made an aggressive bid for the throne and pressed their political and hereditary advantage during the ensuing conflicts to such an extent that it tarnished their prior reputation as Catholic reformers.

The Huguenot faction was led by the Prince of Conde and the Admiral de Coligny. These nobles sought to undermine the authority of the Guise family and fought for local liberties in religious worship. They were opposed to Spanish influence in France and hoped to convince the kings of France to support the Protestants in the Low Countries against Philip II. Being part of the professional warrior class, the Huguenot nobles aggressively waged war to press their demands. No less than nine civil wars were fought in the concluding four decades of the sixteenth century.

Between the Catholic and Huguenot sectors were the *politiques*. This group had no strong religious ties, but used the political situation to further their own ambitions. The most famous of

Mary Stuart, daughter of Mary of Guise, Queen of Scotland; widow of King Francis II of France; heir to the throne of England.

Huguenot leader Admiral Gaspard de Coligny of France was murdered during the St. Bartholomew's Day massacre.

Catherine de Medici, the Queen mother of France, an influential *politique*, the instigator of the St. Bartholomew's Day massacre.

these *politiques* was the Queen mother of France, Catherine de Medici. Her three young sons, the future Francis II, Charles IX and Henry III, would be little more than puppets of the queen mother. Lacking any real religious conviction, Catherine de Medici tried to play the Catholics and Protestants off each other to maintain her own power. Eventually her intrigues would backfire and the throne would fall to the French Huguenot House of Navarre.

FRANCIS II AND CHARLES IX

Francis II came to the throne at age fifteen after his father Henry II was killed in an accident during a tournament in 1559. Francis' uncles, Francis, Duke of Lorraine, and Charles, Cardinal of Lorraine, dominated the young king's reign, and their policies improved religious unity in France. This effort to maintain Catholicism as the only licit religion in France led to an ongoing persecution of various Huguenot factions, which helped sharply define the divisions between the Huguenot, Guise, and *politique* factions. Catherine de Medici remained powerless against the rise of the Guise family, who continued to strengthen their position in France. After an unsuccessful war against Spain, Catherine sent her daughter Elizabeth to wed the young king of Spain, Francis II, giving France a greater Catholic influence. Francis died of an ear infection after only two short years in power, leaving his ten-year-old brother Charles IX on the throne.

Now Catherine was able to use her regency of Charles to offset the influence of the Guise family over France. She supported further toleration of the Huguenots and named the Protestant Anthony of Bourbon lieutenant general of the kingdom. Catherine also blocked Mary Stuart's attempted marriage to Philip II's son, which she regarded as an excessive consolidation of Catholic power. Instead, Catherine tried to arrange a marriage between her son Charles and Elizabeth I of England. Catherine also worked to arrange another marriage, this one successfully, between her daughter Margaret and the Huguenot prince Henry of Navarre. Strengthening her ties with French Protestants seemed the best way to offset the power of the Catholic Guise Family. But just as she seemed to reach the pinnacle of her power, Catherine's scheming fell apart. In February 1563, Francis, Duke of Guise, was assassinated, and civil war broke out between the Catholics and the Huguenots, thrusting Catherine, Charles, and the crown in the middle of the "French Wars of Religion," a bloody power struggle that would last eighteen years.

THE ST. BARTHOLOMEW'S DAY MASSACRE

During the eighteen years of civil war, many attacks and brutalities were meted out by both Protestants and Catholics. Perhaps the worst atrocity was schemed by Catherine herself. The Huguenot Admiral Coligny was a very close advisor and friend of Catherine's son, King Charles. Fearing the influence Admiral Coligny could have over her son, Catherine looked for a way to assassinate the admiral. At the time, many of the leading Huguenots were in Paris attending the marriage of Henry of Navarre to Catherine's daughter, Margaret. Seizing the opportunity, the queen mother spread rumors of a Protestant insurrection being planned in Paris during the wedding. Catholic supporters were outraged and they responded to the rumors by planning a preemptive counterattack.

On the night of St. Bartholomew's Feast Day (August 24) 1572, Catholics took to the streets, butchering Protestants. Catherine's menacing scheme was successful, as the Admiral Coligny was indeed killed. The admiral was first stabbed to death in his apartment, and then thrown out of the window into the garden, where he was beheaded and his body was burned. The admiral was not the only victim, as the same violent and brutal end met much of the Huguenot nobility that night. The estimated number of victims in Paris exceeded 2000, but violence spread to the surrounding regions, and victims from mob attacks over the next few weeks throughout all of France have been estimated between 2000 and 100,000 people. Huguenots, furious over the attacks, renewed the civil war, and both parties hired companies of mercenary soldiers that slaughtered each other and terrorized civilians. In the wake of the war, more than 20,000 Catholic churches in France were sacked, looted, and destroyed by Huguenot mobs. Thousands of priests and religious were also massacred.

Admiral Coligny was murdered in his apartment on a bloody St. Bartholomew's Feast Day, August 24, 1572. The mob violence against the Protestants lasted for several months. This massacre stiffened Huguenot resistance and was a turning point in the French Wars of Religion.

The reconverted Catholic Henry of Navarre rides triumphantly into Paris for his coronation as King of France. He was crowned King Henry IV at the Cathedral of Chartres on February 27, 1594. He was a popular king showing great care for the welfare of his subjects, as well as displaying an unusual religious tolerance for the time. He was murdered by a disturbed man, Ravaillac, on May 14, 1610. Henry IV is informally nicknamed *le bon roi Henri* ("good king Henry"). He had six children with Marie de Medici.

THE WAR OF THE THREE HENRYS

Catherine's third son Henry became king after Charles died from tuberculosis in May 1574. King Henry III attempted to end the religious conflict by agreeing to concessions of toleration. This move led Henry of Guise to form the Catholic League, which demanded an end to toleration of Protestants. When Catherine's youngest son Francis died, thus making the Protestant Henry of Navarre heir to the French throne, the Catholic League forced Henry III to issue an edict suppressing Protestantism and excluding Henry of Navarre from the throne. Henry of Navarre resisted the measure, and civil war once again erupted between Henry III, Henry of Guise, and Henry of Navarre. Henry III allied himself with Henry of Navarre against the Catholic League and orchestrated the assassination of the head of the Guise family in 1589. Afterwards, Henry III was himself assassinated, which left only Henry of Navarre alive, and therefore victorious and king by default.

At first, the Catholics refused to recognize Henry of Navarre and sought Spanish aid to resist the Protestant king. This pressure, in addition to Henry of Navarre's fear that Philip II might use disunity in France to claim the throne for himself, convinced Henry that it was unwise to place his hopes in the Huguenot minority. Henry, therefore, reconverted to the Catholic Faith, justifying his conversion by saying infamously: "Paris is well worth a Mass." The phrase adequately reflected the less than pious attitude that was typical of the majority of rulers of Europe at that time. The new Catholic king was welcomed into Paris where he was crowned King Henry IV.

THE EDICT OF NANTES

After years of civil war, Henry understood well that religious tensions could destroy his tenuous hold on the throne. The Huguenots demanded positive guarantees protecting their religious liberties, and Henry responded by issuing the Edict of Nantes in 1598. The Edict allowed every noble who was also a landholder the right to hold Protestant services in the privacy of his own household. It also allowed legal practice of Protestantism in towns where the majority of the population was Protestant, excluding diocesan sees and towns in and around Paris. About a hundred towns were also granted the right to fortify themselves with Protestant garrisons under Protestant commanders. The Edict promised Protestants the same civil rights as Catholics and the same chances for public office and admittance into Catholic universities. By granting toleration to the Huguenots, Henry removed the main cause of conflict in France and helped the country recover from the long era of civil war.

The city of La Rochelle (above) was a Huguenot center. The city came into conflict with King Louis XIII when cannon shots were fired on royal troops in September 1627. Cardinal Richelieu blockaded the city in the Siege of La Rochelle until it surrendered (left). Many Huguenots left the city, emigrated to the New World and founded New Rochelle, New York, in 1689.

CARDINAL RICHELIEU

In 1610, Henry IV was assassinated, leaving the throne to his very young son, Louis XIII. Too young to wield full power over France, the affairs of state fell into the hands of his secretary of state, Cardinal Richelieu. Richelieu worked tirelessly to centralize the government and advance the power of the monarchy by fostering religious unity and promoting anti-Hapsburg policies. He helped France recover financially from the civil wars by encouraging a mercantile economic system that included oversees exploration. In an effort to increase the power of the French monarchy, Richelieu ordered the destruction of all fortified castles that were not manned by the king's forces. The Huguenot towns created by the Edict of Nantes acted like virtual states within a state and were hostile to monarchical centralization. Richelieu responded by suppressing these towns and the Protestant nobility that led them.

Backed by the English, a Huguenot rebellion broke out in La Rochelle in 1627, which Richelieu quickly put down. Richelieu used the opportunity to modify the Edict of Nantes. Through the king, he issued "The Peace of Alais" which retracted the right of Huguenots to fortify and garrison towns and forbade Protestants from actively participating in the functions of government. Huguenots were still allowed to practice religion in their own private homes, but Richelieu made Protestantism an obstacle to political advancement in France. He kept Protestants out of government, thus protecting the country against more civil unrest by strengthening and centralizing authority around the king.

RICHELIEU'S INFLUENCE AND POWER

Born in 1585, Cardinal Richelieu originally intended to serve in the military, but when his elder brother resigned the bishopric in 1607, Richelieu's family gave him the preferment, a position which both secured his religious training and jumpstarted his political career. His political career eventually dominated whatever religious intentions Richelieu may have had.

In 1614 Richelieu was a deputy representing the clergy at the Estates General, the French national assembly. During his work at the Estates General, Richelieu gained favor with Louis XIII's mother, Marie de Medici, and was eventually made secretary of state. In 1624, Richelieu was named chief minister, the most powerful governmental position in France.

In spite of all the political instability and intrigue in the king's court, Richelieu proved to be a master politician, managing to retain the King's confidence until his death. He supported the idea of the absolute sovereignty of the king in all domestic affairs and helped break the influence of powerful French families. He once assured the young Louis XIII that it was the clergy's wish for royal power to be "as a firm rock which crushes all that opposes it." Despite his voicing of this "clerical intention," there is little indication that Richelieu ever thought matters of religion to supersede the importance of matters of state. Figures like Richelieu help explain the distrust with which the clergy was later held in France, during and after the period of the French Revolution.

Triple Portrait of Richelieu by the great French painter Philippe de Champaigne, ca. 1640

PART III
The British Isles

Elizabethan England emerged as the major defender of Protestantism in the latter half of the seventeenth century. Both at home and abroad Britain sought to tip the balance of power into the hands of Protestant nobles. On the continent, the British intervened and attempted to influence the religious conflicts in the Low Countries, France, and the German states. Within the British Isles threats of a Spanish invasion led Elizabeth to intensify persecutions of the Catholic faithful within England and in nearby Ireland. The rise of Presbyterian Protestantism (Calvinism) in Scotland also aided the English crown's consolidation of power.

The rise of Presbyterianism in Scotland reflected in many ways the Protestant uprisings in Germany and France. A large party of nobles sought to enrich themselves and gain political power by seizing various Scottish churches and monasteries. These nobles were encouraged by Elizabeth who wanted to over-throw her rival to the throne, Mary Stuart, Queen of Scotland. Mary had returned to Scotland in 1561 after the death of her husband Francis II. Upon her return, she found herself alone in her Catholic beliefs. Her regent mother was dead, and her half brother James Stuart was intent on securing the crown.

THE FIRST COVENANT

The Protestant preacher John Knox founded the Presbyterian Church of Scotland. Knox encouraged violence against Catholics, and his preaching and writing inspired a wave of iconoclastic attacks in Scotland that saw the destruction of many churches and monasteries. Driven by both political and religious motives, Scottish lords resolved to do everything in their power to renounce and destroy the Catholic Church. They signed a document known as the "First Covenant" that adopted a Calvinistic profession of faith and rejected the jurisdiction of the pope. Though Mary, Queen of Scots, tried for more than seven years to save the Church in Scotland, Catholic priests were forced to flee as church lands were confiscated and the practice of the Catholic Faith was suppressed.

When Mary Stuart returned to Scotland from France in 1561, she found herself alone in her Catholic beliefs.

Mary's position in England was continually entangled in controversy. The possibility for her to become heir to the English crown made her a threat to Elizabeth. Even though Mary herself never voiced any desire for the English crown, others wanted her to be queen of England to further their own ends. Rumors of her involvement in plots against Elizabeth circulated, and eventually the queen reacted by leveling false charges against Mary, including marital infidelity and murder. These charges forced Mary to abdicate her claim to the crown in favor of her one-year-old son, James.

Furthermore, Scottish unrest forced Mary to hand over rule of Scotland to her half brother (also named James). In addition, her son, the future James I of England, was raised a Protestant. Mary finally fled Scotland seeking sanctuary in England. Elizabeth answered Mary's pleas for protection by placing her under house arrest for nineteen years.

CONTINUING PERSECUTION IN ENGLAND

With the rise of the Presbyterian Church in Scotland and the dominance of the Church of England, Catholics were quickly losing their place in British society. Many saw Catholics as traitors disloyal to the English Crown. In 1559, Elizabeth took discrimination against Catholics to an extreme by prohibiting the practice of the Catholic Faith. The queen hoped that most Catholics would convert to the Church of England, and those who did not would simply die out quietly. Many Catholics refused to give up their Faith and continued to practice in secret. At first, they were tolerated, but it soon became clear that Catholics in England were not fading out of the population as quickly or as quietly as Elizabeth had hoped. Catholics continued to call for a return to union with Rome, and Elizabeth, angered by the failure to stop allegiance to the Catholic Faith, increased the severity of the penal laws against the Church. Finally, she made the practice of the Catholic Faith or adherence to Rome a treasonable offense.

Now with their religion publicly abolished, a major problem that faced English Catholics was the shortage of priests. Without a seminary to train new priests, the English clergy was in danger of dying out. In 1568, Cardinal William Allen helped found a seminary for the English at Douay in the Spanish Netherlands. This seminary would for generations help keep the Catholic Faith alive in England by sending missionary priests to administer the sacraments and uphold the teachings of the Catholic Church in the British Isles.

During the reign of Elizabeth, there were many martyrs accused of treason on account of their Catholic Faith. One of the greatest examples of the English martyrs under Elizabeth I was St. Edmund Campion. Campion was a young Oxford scholar who, in 1568, became a celebrated leader of the Anglican Church. Wooed by the success and advancement that membership in the Church of England promised for him, St. Edmund Campion took the Oath of Supremacy.

St. Edmund Campion (1540-1581) was an English Jesuit and martyr.

Soon after having taken the oath, St. Edmund Campion had a personal conversion, left his promising teaching position, and fled England in order to study at the seminary at Douay. There he joined the Society of Jesus in 1573 and was ordained in 1578. Upon his return to England in 1581, St. Edmund Campion was arrested and charged with treason. Once convicted, he suffered a cruel and public punishment. Amid violent excitement, he was paraded through the streets of London, bound hand and foot, riding backwards, with a paper stuck in his hat to denote him as a Jesuit. On the scaffold, St. Edmund Campion was taunted by the crowd concerning the bull of Pope St. Pius V excommunicating Queen Elizabeth. Reminiscent of St. Thomas More, St. Edmund Campion simply prayed for her, proclaiming loudly: "your Queen and my Queen." His feast day is celebrated on December 1.

St. Edmund Campion's death encouraged some growth of Catholicism in England. Among those who returned to the Faith was St. Henry Walpole. The young St. Henry was at St. Edmund's execution, and the incident had a powerful effect on him. St. Henry's shirt was splattered with St. Edmund's blood as he was being drawn and quartered. Afterward St. Henry Walpole converted and lived to become a Jesuit martyr as well.

Mary Stuart was executed at Fotheringhay Castle on February 8, 1587, on suspicion of having been involved in a plot to murder Elizabeth I. She chose to wear red, thereby declaring herself a Catholic martyr.

Mary Stuart was initially buried at Peterborough Cathedral, but her body was exhumed in 1612 when her son, King James I of England, ordered she be reinterred in Westminster Abbey. It remains there, only thirty feet from the grave of her cousin Elizabeth I.

THE EXECUTION OF MARY, QUEEN OF SCOTS

The growth of Catholic resistance within England and the imminent threat of foreign invasion made Mary Stuart, Queen of Scots, potentially dangerous to Elizabeth's rule. In 1569, an uprising took place in the north of the country where the Catholic Faith remained strong. The uprising, known as the second "Pilgrimage of Grace," tried to restore the Catholic religion, drive Protestant leadership out of London, and acknowledge Mary Stuart as heir and successor to the English throne because Elizabeth I was illegitimate. This rebellion was crushed, and in turn Elizabeth's vengeance was terrible. The queen declared martial law throughout the North, and English troops conducted house-to-house searches to find and execute Catholic priests. The Duke of Norfolk, who sought to marry Mary Stuart and gain the throne of England, was executed in 1572 after he was caught negotiating with the Spanish. Her crown threatened on so many fronts, Elizabeth looked for a way to rid herself of Mary Stuart.

Elizabeth held Mary under house arrest for 19 years while the queen's chief secretary, Francis Walsingham, tried to find evidence that could lead to Mary's execution. Lacking data of any credible crimes, Walsingham sent a spy named Gilbert Gifford to encourage a young admirer of Mary named Babington to plot an escape. The young accomplice wrote letters to Mary discussing his escape plans and desire to assassinate Elizabeth. Mary never received the letters. Instead, Gifford intercepted the letters and forged responses from Mary that urged Babington to reveal his accomplices. This forgery allowed Walsingham to put together a case accusing Mary Stuart of conspiracy to commit treason. Consequently, Babington and his companions were executed in 1586, and Mary was tried for treason. Mary freely confessed to her attempts at escaping Elizabeth's confinement but insisted on her innocence regarding any designs on Elizabeth's life. Nonetheless, Mary was convicted based on the forged documents and beheaded on February 8, 1587.

The Spanish fleet was scattered by an English fire ship attack sent in by Francis Drake in the Battle of Gravelines.

THE SPANISH ARMADA

The beheading of Mary and the continuing persecution of Catholics in Britain enraged Philip II of Spain, and he planned to lead a crusade against the heretical queen of England. Philip had a claim to the English throne through his marriage to Mary Tudor, and Elizabeth's continuing support of the Protestant cause in Europe further prompted the Spanish king to take up arms against the island nation. Elizabeth aided the Dutch revolution of Utrecht and supported the Huguenot cause in France. Her "Sea-Dogs" led by Francis Drake attacked Spanish treasure ships in the New World and pirated Spanish gold for England. To add to the insult, rather than punish Drake's piracy, Elizabeth knighted him and granted him a new fleet of ships. As a consequence, Philip II set out to invade England and remove Elizabeth from the throne. In 1588 he launched an invasion using his "invincible armada."

The Armada was forced to return to Spain by sailing around the northern coasts of Scotland and Ireland—a dangerous voyage during which the Armada was buffeted by severe currents and September storms that caused enormous damage to the fleet. Many ships were forced onto the rocky coast of Ireland. The final toll of the battle: only 67 of 130 ships and 10,000 of 30,000 men survived in the Spanish fleet. The English lost no ships and had half the casualties of the Spanish, but then lost over 6,000 men to typhus and dysentery.

The *Queen Elizabeth Armada Portrait*. The battle between the English fleet and the Spanish Armada lasted from June 19 to August 12, 1588. On August 8, Elizabeth went to Tilbury to encourage her forces. The next day she gave to them what is considered her most famous speech: "...I am come amongst you as you see, at this time...in the midst and heat of the battle to live or die amongst you all, to lay down for my God and for my kingdom, and for my people, my honour and my blood, even in the dust. I know I have the body of a weak and feeble woman, but I have the heart and stomach of a king."

The planned invasion was unsuccessful. The Spanish admiral was delayed by poor organization, and Spanish troops waiting to invade from the Netherlands were not prepared in time. The smaller and better-equipped English fleet harried the bigger and clumsy Spanish ships for two weeks without sustaining significant damage. An unexpected storm eventually drove the Spanish fleet to the north where many ships were lost while attempting to return to Spain. The defeat of the Spanish Armada shattered the image of an invincible Spain, establishing an English naval supremacy that continued to support the Protestant cause.

WAR IN IRELAND

Ireland did not fare well during the reign of Elizabeth. Elizabeth inherited Ireland from her father Henry VIII, and after declaring the kingdom Protestant, she waged a war of extermination against the Emerald Isle. English troops butchered men, women, and children. The decimated and demoralized Irish fought back, staging three revolts in an effort to hold on to their religion and culture. All three rebellions failed, and Elizabeth responded to the revolts by launching a complete military conquest and legal suppression of the island. The Gaelic language was abolished, and Protestant overlords were sent to control the agricultural estates. Soldiers destroyed all the crops and livestock in areas of rebellion and implemented systematic starvation. The *Annals of the Four Masters* describes the plight of the provinces: "neither the lowing of a cow nor the voices of a

ST. JOHN OGILVIE

The most prominent Scottish martyr of the Reformation was St. John Ogilvie, a Jesuit priest and convert to Catholicism. St. John was born to Calvinist parents in Banfshire, Scotland, around the year 1579. When he was thirteen, St. John was sent abroad by his parents in order to receive a French Calvinist education at Louvain, France. In France it was common for Catholic and Calvinist scholars to debate religion, and while at school, St. John came to know the teachings of the Catholic Church. St. John was deeply impressed by how the Roman Catholic Church was comprised of all types of people. Kings, princes, peasants, and beggars could all renounce the world and devote their lives wholly to God. Furthermore, many of these people had given their lives as martyrs, a reality that had a tremendous influence on St. John Ogilvie.

In 1600 at the age of seventeen, St. John converted to Catholicism at Louvain. Four years later, he joined the Jesuit novitiate at Brünn, and for ten years worked in Austria, mostly at Graz and Vienna, before being sent to the French province. Finally ordained in 1610, St. John expressed a desire to return to his Scottish homeland and minister to the persecuted Catholics who remained there. He received permission, and in 1613, St. John disguised himself as a soldier returning to Scotland

from the wars in Europe. Upon his return, he ministered to many Catholics and even won back some converts to the Church. Unfortunately, St. John was betrayed by someone pretending to be interested in the Faith. St. John was eventually imprisoned and tortured by the authorities for refusing to give the names of other Catholics he knew. On March 10, 1615, St. John Ogilvie, who so admired the martyrs of the Church, was himself martyred for his faith by being hanged for high treason. He was canonized by Pope Paul VI in 1976. His feast day is celebrated on March 10.

ploughman was heard from Cashel to the farthermost parts of Kerry" (Vidmar, *The Catholic Church through the Ages*, 2005, p. 352). According to an English official in the year 1582, over a six-month period more than 30,000 people starved to death. By the end of that ordeal, Elizabeth had little to rule except ashes and carcasses.

Ireland would continue its fight against English Protestantism, while the Faith of the Irish deepened in the face of persecution. Irish seminaries were established in Spain, Portugal, the Low Countries, France, and Rome, where Irish boys were smuggled out of Ireland to be trained for the priesthood. These renegade Irish priests would return to their island to administer the sacraments and preach the word of God to their persecuted flock.

PART IV

The Thirty Years War (1618-1648)

The final great war of religion took place within the Holy Roman Empire between 1618 and 1648. This last religious conflict would permanently divide Germany between Protestant and Catholic camps and undermine the political development of a unified Germany. Whereas the rest of Europe, in the aftermath of the seventeenth-century wars, developed into powerful nation-states, the Thirty Years War crippled the German states and insured that they would remain a collection of small, disunited kingdoms.

Many different factors brought about the war within Germany. A religious war pitted Protestants and Catholics against each other, each vying for domination of the region. The Thirty Years War was waged by independent German princes, both Catholic and Protestant, who resisted the growing imperial designs of the Austrian Hapsburgs. In the end, with the aid of Richelieu's France, the Hapsburgs would be defeated, and as a result, Christendom would be permanently divided.

The Peace of Augsburg (1555) divided Germany roughly between Lutheran Princes in the North and Catholics in the South. The Peace's famous line *"cuius regio huius religio"* (whose region, his the religion), provided that each prince determine the faith of his region. The Peace of Augsburg succeeded in pacifying each individual region from infighting, and the Ecclesiastical Reservation Clause protected Catholic regions from further territorial expansion by Protestant princes. But as weak emperors succeeded Charles V, they proved incapable of protecting Catholic interests, and consequently allowed several violations of the Ecclesiastical Reservation Clause to occur. Quarrels also broke out in Protestant areas between Lutheran princes and the members of the newly-emerging Calvinist faith. Not included in the Augsburg settlement, Calvinist princes made efforts to gain ecclesiastical properties from both Catholics and Lutherans.

These scuffles took on new severity as they soon affected religious change in the seats of the imperial electors. Two out of seven total imperial electorships (the Palatinate and Brandenburg) transferred from Lutheranism to Calvinism. With the loss of these seats, Lutheran princes began to fear a loss of influence in the empire. To add to Lutherans' dismay, one of the new electors, Frederick of the Palatinate, was supported by the Dutch Republic and his father-in-law, James I of England, and he formed a Calvinist league known as the Evangelical Union. The Union backed up Frederick's Calvinist policies with militarily might, and their aggression disrupted peace in Germany.

Catholic reform also changed the political landscape in southern Germany. Since the Augsburg settlement, St. Peter Canisius' Catechism of Trent and the preaching of Capuchin friars and Jesuits helped energize the Catholic reform movement. Thousands returned to the Catholic Faith, and with the aid of the king of Spain and the pope, the Bavarian Duke Maximilian formed the Catholic League in 1620 to oppose Frederick's Evangelical Union. The Austrian Ferdinand of Styria (the future Ferdinand II) restored Catholic unity in Austria and the Hapsburg domains.

In 1621, the twelve-year truce that ended the Dutch conflict lapsed, and the Spanish saw an opportunity to renew the struggle and re-establish a Catholic presence in Europe. Philip II launched a campaign from Spanish-controlled Burgundy, through the Calvinist Palatinate and into the Netherlands. Through this campaign, the Spanish hoped to deliver a resounding defeat to rising Calvinist power with one blow. However, the military campaign did not prove easy, and it eventually sparked the long and arduous Thirty Years War, which played out in four phases: the Bohemian (1618-1625), Danish (1625-1629), Swedish (1630-1635), and French (1635-1648).

BOHEMIAN PHASE: 1618-1625

Since the days of Jan Hus, Bohemia's nobility had been predominantly Protestant. For some time the Holy Roman Emperor Matthias (who was also the King of Bohemia) allowed for toleration of these Protestant nobles. As his reign drew to a close, Protestants became increasingly fearful of what a new Catholic—specifically Hapsburg—domination of their land could mean. As it were, the seven electors of the emperor were split: three Catholic and three Protestant. The tie-breaking vote that would decide the fate of the Protestants in Bohemia was held by the King of Bohemia.

When Matthias named the Hapsburg Catholic Ferdinand of Styria his successor—both as king of Bohemia and Holy Roman emperor—the nobles were outraged. They showed their dissatis-faction by tossing two of the Emperor's emissaries out of the window of the castle in Prague. The event marked the mobilization of a resistance to the Emperor's successor known as the Defenestration of Prague (1618). The Defenestration of Prague commonly marks the beginning of the Thirty Years War.

The Bohemian nobles rejected Ferdinand of Styria and chose the elector Frederick of Palatine as their king. Frederick, using Dutch and English funds and support, raised an army to defend Bohemia. Ferdinand assembled his own army with the support of the papacy and Spain, and marched on Prague. In 1620 the two forces met at White Mountain outside Prague where Frederick and the Protestants were defeated. Nicknamed the "Winter King" for his short reign, Frederick was deposed and Ferdinand regained power over the kingdom. He confiscated the defeated nobles' land and redistributed it as endowments for Catholic churches, orders, and monasteries.

After the Battle of White Mountain, Spanish troops who helped Ferdinand against the Bohemian nobles invaded the Palatinate and gave Frederick's former electorship to Maximilian of Bavaria, a Catholic. Demoralized after having lost two electoral seats, the Protestant Union dissolved in 1621.

DANISH PHASE: 1625-1629

With Protestant fortunes at their lowest, the King of Denmark, Christian IV, took the lead of the Protestant resistance. In addition to being King of Denmark, as the Duke of the Northern German region of Holstein, Christian was a major Protestant prince, and he desired to use his control of Denmark and Holstein to extend a Danish sphere of influence throughout Northern Europe. With this objective in mind, Christian obtained aid from England, the Dutch, and France to put a stop to the Catholic resurgence.

To counter this new Protestant threat, Ferdinand II asked his general Wallenstein, whose skill largely contributed to the success of the Bohemian campaign, to create a new army. Wallenstein raised a private and unruly army, whose soldiers, rather than receive pay, simply pillaged the lands through which they traveled. The army did not have any sense of imperial loyalty, and were loyal only to Wallenstein. The general was driven largely by personal motives, and though his intentions were not entirely clear, many have speculated that he was inspired by a sense of German nationalism or perhaps even a desire to establish his own realm. Nonetheless, armed with his hired marauders, Wallenstein drove back the armies of Christian IV, securing large portions of the northern German states. The general's efforts placed Germany firmly under Ferdinand's control, and in 1629 the emperor issued the Edict of Restitution, which returned to the Church all lands confiscated by the Protestant states in 1555.

With Wallenstein's advance into the North, the successes of the Protestant Reformation were on the verge of being undone. German Lutheran princes, who at one time supported Ferdinand against the Calvinists, now rejected all Catholic opposition. Confronted with a hostile Catholic army and an imperial policy directed at undermining their independence, Lutherans and Calvinists alike united in resisting the Catholic empire, whatever the cost.

Catholic princes also became worried about Ferdinand's consolidation of power. Cardinal Richelieu opposed the prospect of a Hapsburg-dominated Europe, and he threw French support behind the Protestant resistance.

SWEDISH PHASE: 1630-1635

Cardinal Richelieu used his influence to place the King of Sweden, Gustavus Adolfus, at the helm of the Protestant cause. The Swedish king had become concerned with Ferdinand's growing power, and the emperor's drive to the Baltic Sea threatened to cut off trade between Sweden and the Dutch Republic. Adolfus himself wanted to dominate the Baltic region, and he saw Ferdinand's advance as a perfect excuse to seize the divided northern German kingdoms and incorporate them into a larger Swedish empire. At the same time the electors of Germany, both Catholic and Protestant, pressured Ferdinand to disband Wallenstein's wild army and dismiss the powerful general. Ferdinand needed the support of the electors to continue the Hapsburg succession, and so the reluctant emperor relieved the brilliant, yet renegade, Wallenstein.

CAPUCHIN FRANCISCANS

Since its foundation, the Franciscan order has undergone several reform movements, sometimes resulting in the formation of a new branch. One major reform established the Capuchin friars. The Capuchins were Franciscans who wanted to follow closely the spirit and life of St. Francis by returning to small hermitages and living as wandering preachers.

The founder of the Capuchin movement, Matteo di Bassi of Urbino (d. 1552), established this new order of Franciscans in part by an event that evokes the life of St. Francis himself. As the story goes, Matteo was returning to his convent from a funeral when he noticed a beggar along the side of the road. Moved by pity, he gave the beggar part of his own clothing. A short while later, when the friar was at prayer, he heard a voice telling him three times to "observe the Rule to the letter," after which he got up, made a long

pointed hood from his *cappa*, and set out for Rome at once. (Capuchins have always worn long pointed hoods, or capuches, as a symbol of their desire to follow the Rule of St. Francis to the letter.) In Rome, Matteo asked Pope Clement VII for the liberty to follow strictly the Rule of St. Francis in hermitages, preaching the gospel in the world and bringing sinners back into the Church. The Capuchins were formally recognized as a distinct order by the pope on July 3, 1528.

Along with the Jesuits, the Capuchins were by far the most effective preachers and evangelizers of the tumultuous sixteenth century. Since the order's founding, the Church has canonized twenty-two Capuchin friars, including St. Padre Pio in June 2002. Addressing the Capuchins, John Paul II once remarked, "They say that you Capuchins are poor. You are actually very rich . . . in saints!"

THE THIRTY YEARS WAR IN GERMANY, 1618-1648

Philip II launched a campaign from Spanish-controlled Burgundy, through the Calvinist Palatinate and into the Netherlands. Through this campaign, the Spanish hoped to deliver a resounding defeat to rising Calvinist power with one blow. However, the military campaign did not prove easy, and it eventually sparked the long and arduous Thirty Years War, which played out in four phases: the Bohemian (1618-1625), Danish (1625-1629), Swedish (1630-1635), and French (1635-1648).

AFTER THE WARS...THE CATHOLIC RECOVERY, 1650

SCOTLAND

NORTH SEA

DENMARK-NORWAY

SWEDEN

BALTIC SEA

RUSSIA

BALTIC STATES

IRELAND

WALES

ENGLAND

London

UNITED PROVINCES

Antwerp

Mons

Douai

Rouen

Rheims

Paris

La Flèche

Verdun

Pont-à-Mousson

Tours

Bourges

Dôle

Geneva

FRANCE

Lyons

Bordeaux

Toulouse

Avignon

Liège

Trier

Mainz

Molsheim

Nancy

Zurich

Dillingen

SWISS CONFEDERATION

MILAN

Milan

SAVOY

Genoa

GENOA

PARMA

MODENA

CORSICA

TUSCANY

East Prussia

Copenhagen

Danzig

Königsberg

Hamburg

Münster

Elbe

HOLY ROMAN EMPIRE

Rhine

Würzburg

Prague

Ingolstadt

Danube

Vienna

Graz

HUNGARY

REPUBLIC OF VENICE

Venice

Ravenna

Florence

PAPAL STATES

Colonies of Venice

Rome

Vilnius

Warsaw

Vistula

POLAND

Krakow

Budapest

OTTOMAN EMPIRE

ATLANTIC OCEAN

Santiago de Compostela

PORTUGAL

Valladolid

Salamanca

Madrid

Toledo

Ebro

Tagus

Lisbon

SPAIN

Valencia

Seville

BALEARIC ISLANDS

SARDINIA

Sassari

Cagliari

KINGDOM OF TWO SICILIES

Naples

Palermo

Messina

MEDITERRANEAN SEA

Catholic
Protestant
Eastern Orthodox
Muslim
☐ Important Jesuit centre
— Political Boundary

© 1997 Lion Hudson plc/Three's Company

Gustavus Adolfus was a magnificent military leader. His tactical and technical military innovations made his armies the quickest and most advanced on the continent. Without Wallenstein, the Catholic forces had no chance against the Swedish army. Adolfus invaded the mainland and drove Ferdinand's forces out of Germany and south to the Danube. During the campaign, the emperor's army was continually routed and demoralized, and eventually Ferdinand was again forced to call upon Wallenstein's help. Even this extraordinarily gifted general could not stop Adolfus' advance. They met in Lutzen in 1632, and Wallenstein's army was defeated. During that battle Gustavus Adolfus died, and his death marked the turning point in the Swedish campaign.

The Swedish army fought on, but without Adolfus and with diminishing support from the Protestant princes. Due to these factors, they made no further advance. Negotiations began between Ferdinand and the Lutheran princes over returning territory. As an emergence measure to save his empire, Ferdinand agreed to repeal a majority of the Edict of Restitution.

Despite these discussions between Ferdinand and the Protestants, a final resolution could not be reached. As a larger portion of Europe became the battle ground of a powerful Swedish army, Protestant princes were less inclined to concede their independence to a Swedish overlord. Ferdinand also abhorred the occupying Swedes, who found themselves deep within Germany, surrounded by hostile forces.

FRENCH PHASE: 1635-1648

This war would continue for another twelve years. Richelieu, sensing that the German princes were unifying against the Swedes, came out openly for the Swedes. Richelieu's action showed how neither France nor Spain wished peace or reconciliation with Germany. The Thirty Years War thus provided the perfect context for the pursuit of various international interests.

The final phase of the Thirty Years War, the French Phase, was perhaps the most devastating to Germany. The war now became an all out international struggle, and foreign armies crisscrossed indiscriminately throughout Germany, causing economic and political chaos to the entire realm. Saxony, Bohemia, and Bavaria were reduced to deserts, and the whole of Germany was afflicted with horrible atrocities resulting in mass starvation. In the end, over 300,000 soldiers were killed in battle and millions died of malnutrition and disease. Nearly three quarters of the entire peasant population perished, and it is estimated that the population of Germany fell from 21,000,000 to 13,500,000. As the war ended in 1648, Germany was permanently divided into hundreds of tiny principalities, and huge, powerful nation-states grew up around them.

THE TREATY OF WESTPHALIA: 1648

The Treaty of Westphalia, signed in 1648, brought an end to the hopes of a united Germany. France, working to weaken her neighbors and protect her own military advantage, guaranteed that each of the 300 sovereign German states would be recognized as independent. France helped create a provision in the treaty that would prohibit any decree for taxes or military action to occur without the complete consensus of all the independent German states. The diversity and independence of these states made it virtually impossible for them to function as a political unit. The Treaty of Westphalia completed the dissolution of the Holy Roman Empire. German political unity would not be realized for another two hundred years, and Richelieu's France was left as the most powerful political state on the continent.

To deal with religious divisions, the terms of the Peace of Augsburg settlement of 1555 were renewed and rewritten to include the interests of Calvinist rulers. Lutherans and Calvinists permanently retained their independence, and northern Germany remained predominately

The Treaty of Westphalia in 1648 completed the dissolution of the Holy Roman Empire. France became the most powerful state on the continent.

Protestant. The treaty also created independent Dutch and Swiss states, and gave the Swedes control of the Baltic Sea.

The Thirty Years War concluded, the wars of religion essentially divided Europe into two camps: Protestant and Catholic. What had begun as a war to restore religious unity became a war that ended in political compromise. Although the papal nuncio at Westphalia protested the compromise, the secular leaders in attendance ignored his concerns, and the pope refused to sign the terms of the treaty.

CONCLUSION

By the end of the seventeenth century, the pope would no longer play a significant role in the political development of Europe, and religion would no longer be the chief motivating factor in political affairs. Instead, politics and economics would drive the leaders of Europe as they sought to transform their realms into powerful and self-sufficient nations. Exploration in the New World turned the interests of many leaders towards the economic possibilities which overseas expansion offered. Through these wars of religion, the Christian world was reshaped and reorganized as new values and interests began to overshadow their Christian heritage.

In light of the Wars of Religion, the need for dialogue and mutual Christian charity becomes quite obvious. This period of history is a powerful reminder that the heart of the Christian message to love as Christ loved must always be an absolute priority for all Christians, both rulers and citizens. The alternative to Christ's new law of love is tragedy expressed in terrible violations of human dignity.

SUPPLEMENTARY READING

Henry IV, *Edict of Nantes*, 1598

VI. And in order to leave no occasion for troubles or differences between our subjects, we have permitted, and herewith permit, those of the said religion called Reformed to live and abide in all the cities and places of this our kingdom and countries of our sway, without being annoyed, molested, or compelled to do anything in the matter of religion contrary to their consciences,…upon condition that they comport themselves in other respects according to that which is contained in this our present edict.

VII. It is permitted to all lords, gentlemen, and other persons making profession of the said religion called Reformed, holding the right of high justice [or a certain feudal tenure], to exercise the said religion in their houses.

XIII. We very expressly forbid to all those of the said religion its exercise, either in respect to ministry, regulation, discipline, or the public instruction of children, or otherwise, in this our kingdom and lands of our dominion, otherwise than in the places permitted and granted by the present edict.

XIV. It is forbidden as well to perform any function of the said religion in our court or retinue, or in our lands and territories beyond the mountains, or in our city of Paris. or within five leagues of the said city.

Mary Queen of Scots, February 8, 1587, *Letter to her brother Henry III*

To Henri III, the Most Christian King of France,

Royal brother, having by God's will, for my sins I think, thrown myself into the power of the Queen my cousin, at whose hands I have suffered much for almost twenty years, I have finally been condemned to death by her and her Estates.…

Tonight, after dinner, I have been advised of my sentence: I am to be executed like a criminal at eight in the morning…The Catholic faith and the assertion of my God-given right to the English throne are the two issues on which I am condemned, and yet I am not allowed to say that it is for the Catholic religion that I die, but for fear of interference with theirs. The proof of this is that they have taken away my chaplain, and, although he is in the building, I have not been able to get permission for him to come and hear my confession and give me the Last Sacrament, while they have been most insistent that I receive the consolation and instruction of their minister brought here for that purpose.…

Again I commend my servants to you. Give instruction, if it please you, that for my soul's sake part of what you owe me should be paid, and that for the sake of Jesus Christ, to whom I shall pray for you tomorrow as I die, I be left enough to found a memorial Mass and give the customary alms.

Your most loving and most true sister.

— Mary Queen of Scots, February 8, 1587

John Paul II, *Crossing the Threshold of Hope*, 153

More generally we can affirm that for human knowledge and for human action a certain dialectic is present. Didn't the Holy Spirit in his divine "condescendence," take this into consideration? It is necessary for humanity to achieve unity through plurality, to learn to come together in the one Church, even while presenting a plurality of ways of thinking and acting, of cultures and civilizations.… Nevertheless, this cannot be justification for the divisions that continue to deepen! The time must come for the love that unites us to be manifested!

VOCABULARY

EL ESCORIAL

The palace of Philip II which reflected the emperor's cold austerity. His private room in the massive palace complex was as simple as a monk's cell.

FIRST COVENANT

Document drawn up and signed by Scottish lords that adopted a Calvinist profession of faith and abolished the power of the pope, establishing Presbyterianism in Scotland.

JOYEUSE ENTRÉE

Unwritten constitution of the provinces of the Low Countries that was generally respected by the Holy Roman emperors.

PILGRIMAGE OF GRACE

Catholic uprising in England in 1569 that tried to restore the Catholic religion, drive Protestant leadership from London, and acknowledge Mary Stuart as England's rightful heir.

POLITIQUES

French political faction with no strong religious ties that tried to manipulate political divisions in France for its own political gain.

SPANISH ARMADA

Attempting to remove Elizabeth from the throne of England, Philip II sent this "invincible" fleet of ships in 1588. The invasion was unsuccessful.

SPANISH FURY

During the occupation of the Low Countries by Philip II's forces, the Spanish army mutinied after not having received pay. During the subsequent rampage, these Spanish troops pillaged and murdered over six thousand people in Antwerp.

STADTHOLDER

Local prince who led the provinces of the Low Countries during times of trouble. Otherwise business and politics in the region were carried out locally and independently.

WINTER KING

Nickname of Frederick of Palatine who was deposed after only a few months in the winter of 1620, ceding the throne of Bohemia to the Hapsburg emperor-elect Ferdinand of Styria.

Defeat of the Spanish Armada at the Battle of Gravelines. The English attacked the Spanish fleet on July 29, 1588. Eleven Spanish ships were lost or damaged and the Spaniards suffered nearly 2,000 casualties, before both sides ran out of ammunition and hostilities ceased.

STUDY QUESTIONS

1. What lands did Philip II inherit from his father?

2. What was the name given to the Muslims who lived in Spain?

3. How did Philip II deal with these Muslim people in Spain?

4. What was the economic foundation of the Low Countries?

5. What did William of Orange and the Count of Egmont protest? Were they successful?

6. What actions taken by Calvinists in the Low Countries enraged Philip?

7. What was the "Spanish Fury"?

8. Whom did Philip send to replace the Duke of Alba? Was he more effective?

9. How were the Low Countries divided in 1578?

10. What cities were affected when the English aided the Netherlands?

11. What developments weakened the influence of the papacy in France by the sixteenth century?

12. What three factions battled over control of French politics after the death of Henry II?

13. Who was the most influential *politique*?

14. How did Catherine de Medici use marriage to further her political ends?

15. Why did Catherine de Medici instigate the St. Bartholomew's Day Massacre?

16. What famous statement did Henry of Navarre make shortly before being crowned King Henry IV of France?

17. How did the Edict of Nantes help Catholic-Protestant relations in France?

18. During the reign of Louis XIII, who really held power in France?

19. How did Cardinal Richelieu deal with the religious divisions in the country?

20. Who founded Presbyterianism in Scotland?

21. What was the First Covenant?

22. How did Cardinal William Allen help the Catholic Church in England?

23. Why was Mary, Queen of Scots, a threat to Elizabeth I?

24. How did Francis Walsingham acquire evidence to convict Mary?

25. Who were the "Sea Dogs"?

26. How did Elizabeth I set about ridding Ireland of Catholicism?

27. What made the Thirty Years War more than just a religious war?

28. How did the Peace of Augsburg temporarily resolve the political problems of religion in Germany?

29. Why did the Bohemians reject Emperor Matthias' choice of Ferdinand of Styria as his successor?

30. What did the Edict of Restitution provide?

31. Why was Cardinal Richelieu concerned with Ferdinand's success in Germany?

32. How were the last twelve years of the Thirty Years War disastrous?

33. What treaty ended the Thirty Years War?

PRACTICAL EXERCISES

1. What kind of Europe did Philip II inherit from his father Charles V? What were some of the divisions and problems he had to deal with? How did his faith help him? How did it hurt his ability to rule?

2. Cardinal Richelieu and Catherine de Medici had two different approaches to establishing order in France. How did they differ? How were they the same? Was the stability Richelieu established in France worth his use of negative methods?

3. England was particularly harsh in its treatments of Catholics. Why did Elizabeth I see Catholics as a severe threat? What countries today repress religious groups, including Catholics?

In 1590 King Henry IV of France held the south and west, and the Catholic League the north and east. The new king knew that he had to take Paris if he stood any chance of reuniting the kingdom. Paris was besieged, but the siege was lifted with Spanish support. Realizing that there was no prospect of a Protestant king succeeding in fanatically Catholic Paris, Henry with the famous phrase *"Paris vaut bien une messe"* (Paris is worth a mass) announced his conversion to the old faith and was crowned at Chartres in 1594.

FROM THE CATECHISM

1904 "It is preferable that each power be balanced by other powers and by other spheres of responsibility which keep it within proper bounds. This is the principle of the 'rule of law,' in which the law is sovereign and not the arbitrary will of men" (*CA* 44).

1931 Respect for the human person proceeds by way of respect for the principle that "everyone should look upon his neighbor (without any exception) as 'another self,' above all bearing in mind his life and the means necessary for living it with dignity" (*GS* 27 § 1). No legislation could by itself do away with the fears, prejudices, and attitudes of pride and selfishness which obstruct the establishment of truly fraternal societies. Such behavior will cease only through the charity that finds in every man a "neighbor," a brother.

2104 "All men are bound to seek the truth, especially in what concerns God and his Church, and to embrace it and hold on to it as they come to know it" (*DH* 1 § 2). This duty derives from "the very dignity of the human person" (*DH* 2 § 1). It does not contradict a "sincere respect" for different religions which frequently "reflect a ray of that truth which enlightens all men" (*NA* 2 § 2) nor the requirement of charity, which urges Christians "to treat with love, prudence and patience those who are in error or ignorance with regard to the faith" (*DH* 14 § 4).

2105 The duty of offering God genuine worship concerns man both individually and socially. This is "the traditional Catholic teaching on the moral duty of individuals and societies toward the true religion and the one Church of Christ" (*DH* 1 § 3). By constantly evangelizing men, the Church works toward enabling them "to infuse the Christian spirit into the mentality and mores, laws and structures of the communities in which [they] live" (*AA* 13 § 1). The social duty of Christians is to respect and awaken in each man the love of the true and the good. It requires them to make known the worship of the one true religion which subsists in the Catholic and apostolic Church (cf. *DH* 1). Christians are called to be the light of the world. Thus, the Church shows forth the kingship of Christ over all creation and in particular over human societies (cf. *AA* 13; Leo XIII, *Immortale Dei* 3, 17; Pius XI, *Quas primas* 8, 20).

2307 The fifth commandment forbids the intentional destruction of human life. Because of the evils and injustices that accompany all war, the Church insistently urges everyone to prayer and to action so that the divine Goodness may free us from the ancient bondage of war (cf. *GS* 81 § 4).

2308 All citizens and all governments are obliged to work for the avoidance of war.

However, "as long as the danger of war persists and there is no international authority with the necessary competence and power, governments cannot be denied the right of lawful self-defense, once all peace efforts have failed" (*GS* 79 § 4).

2316 *The production and the sale of arms* affect the common good of nations and of the international community. Hence public authorities have the right and duty to regulate them. The short-term pursuit of private or collective interests cannot legitimate undertakings that promote violence and conflict among nations and compromise the international juridical order.

CHAPTER 15

Exploration And
Missionary Movements

*The "opening of the New World" provided a new opportunity
for evangelization, a chance to help people from every corner
of the globe find the "fullness of life in God."*

CHAPTER 15

Exploration And Missionary Movements

God desires the salvation of everyone. In a mysterious but real way, he is present in all. Humanity forms one single family, since all human beings have been created by God in his own image. All have a common destiny, since they are called to find fullness of life in God.

— Pope John Paul II, Homily, Parakou, Benin, February 4, 1993.

While Europe was divided along religious and political lines in the sixteenth century, the Church embarked upon the greatest missionary expansion of her history, reaching out to millions of new faithful around the world. This remarkable period of evangelization came about through the efforts of a relatively small number of holy missionaries who truly believed that "God desires the salvation of everyone." Through their courageous travels, the good news of Christ was being preached in Asia, Africa, and the New World.

These missionary expeditions followed in the wake of new explorations throughout the world. The curiosity for discovery so characteristic of the Renaissance together with new navigational advancements helped to open trade routes to the Orient and lead to monumental achievements in exploration. In 1487, the Portuguese sailor Bartholomew Dias rounded the southern tip of Africa opening a new way to India. Five years later another ambitious explorer set off westwards to find an alternative route to India. That explorer, the Italian Christopher Columbus, discovered a New World in the Western hemisphere. For the Church, the "opening of the New World" would provide a new opportunity for evangelization, a chance to help people from every corner of the globe find, as John Paul II said, "fullness of life in God."

Dias rounded the tip of Africa in 1487.

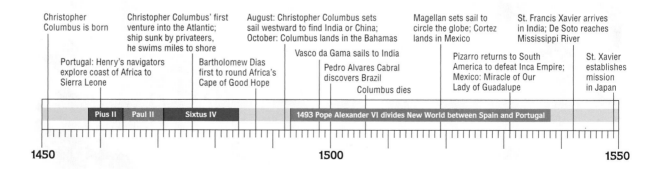

Christopher Columbus is born

Portugal: Henry's navigators explore coast of Africa to Sierra Leone

Christopher Columbus' first venture into the Atlantic; ship sunk by privateers, he swims miles to shore

Bartholomew Dias first to round Africa's Cape of Good Hope

August: Christopher Columbus sets sail westward to find India or China; October: Columbus lands in the Bahamas

Vasco da Gama sails to India

Pedro Alvares Cabral discovers Brazil

Columbus dies

Magellan sets sail to circle the globe; Cortez lands in Mexico

Pizarro returns to South America to defeat Inca Empire; Mexico: Miracle of Our Lady of Guadalupe

St. Francis Xavier arrives in India; De Soto reaches Mississippi River

St. Xavier establishes mission in Japan

Pius II   Paul II   Sixtus IV

1493 Pope Alexander VI divides New World between Spain and Portugal

1450   1500   1550

A 1540 map of the New World, the Americas

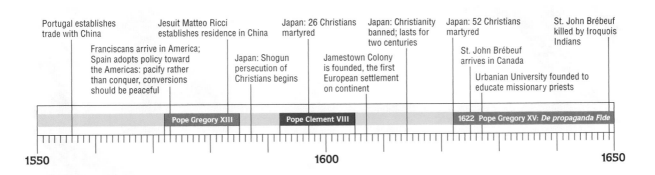

Portugal establishes trade with China

Jesuit Matteo Ricci establishes residence in China

Japan: 26 Christians martyred

Japan: Christianity banned; lasts for two centuries

Japan: 52 Christians martyred

St. John Brébeuf killed by Iroquois Indians

Franciscans arrive in America; Spain adopts policy toward the Americas: pacify rather than conquer, conversions should be peaceful

Japan: Shogun persecution of Christians begins

Jamestown Colony is founded, the first European settlement on continent

St. John Brébeuf arrives in Canada

Urbanian University founded to educate missionary priests

Pope Gregory XIII

Pope Clement VIII

1622 Pope Gregory XV: *De propaganda Fide*

1550

1600

1650

PART I

Opening the Atlantic

Before the sixteenth century, the predominant avenue of trade for Europe was the Mediterranean Sea. Attempts to traverse other seas to the west of the Mediterranean were hindered by disputes about the size of the earth and claims that the ocean southwest of Gibraltar was unnavigable. In addition, stories of sea monsters and boiling waters in the popular mind further deterred the exploration of the western seas. Although no educated man of the Renaissance truly believed these stories, for many, the world was filled with superstition and fairy tales—stories that discouraged venturing beyond one's own feudal village, much less into the wide, open sea.

A number of factors began to change in the late fifteenth century. During the Middle Ages, the Italian city-states dominated trade in the Mediterranean, bringing back exotic goods to Medieval Europe from the Crusader Kingdoms in Palestine. In the fifteenth century, the Ottoman Turks conquered the last of these Crusader Kingdoms, and when Byzantium fell in 1453, trade with the East became increasingly more difficult and costly. Trade continued, but the Ottomans exacted a heavy toll. The cost of silks and spices increased dramatically, and the farther West one went, the higher the prices rose. High prices did not quell the steady demand for these goods, and sea-bound western states such as Portugal and Spain began to look for alternative ways to bypass Turkish and Italian middlemen.

Beginning in the Renaissance, the power of monarchs was becoming centralized, and as modern nation-states slowly took shape, princes began to accumulate the resources necessary to fund new exploratory voyages. Encouraging merchant trade also increased tax revenue, which allowed nations to sponsor even more explorations. All these nations were looking for brave men ready to risk their lives for adventure and the glory of discovery. The Renaissance culture stimulated that spirit and provided new ideas, eagerness for experimentation, and the technology that allowed seafarers to undertake bolder expeditions.

HENRY THE NAVIGATOR

Prince Henry the Navigator (1394-1460), the brother of the king of Portugal, helped advance the technical innovations needed to explore uncharted land. Portugal wanted to open a direct trade route to the Orient, and Henry opened a school for navigation where cosmographers and mathematicians improved the quality of maps, charts, and navigational techniques. Henry's school helped develop an efficient sail ship called the *caravel* which allowed pilots to sail against the wind and through high waves. Other innovations, such as the compass and astrolabe, allowed captains to navigate and plot courses on the open sea. By the mid-fifteenth century, Henry's men were sailing farther along the African coast than any other explorers before, and they were returning with more gold, ivory, spices, and slaves.

Infante Dom Henrique, Duke of Viseu, known in English as Henry the Navigator, (1394-1460). At his *Vila do Infante* (Prince's Town) at Sagres, Henry established a school of navigators and map-makers and became the patron of the Portuguese voyages of discovery.

The port of Lagos (West Africa) was near Henry the Navigator's school at Sagres. It provided a convenient harbor for ship-building. The development of the caravel ship would make exploration of the world possible. Initially the carrack ship was used for exploration by the Spanish and Portuguese who ventured out along the west African coast and into the Atlantic Ocean. But the large, fully-rigged carrack could not be sailed with the precision necessary for inland coastal exploration. The explorers soon came to prefer smaller carracks known as caravels. Because of its smaller size the caravel was able to explore upriver in shallow coastal waters. With its lateen sails (a triangular sail of Arab origin), it was able to go swiftly over shallow water and take deep wind, while with the square rigged sails the caravel was very fast over ocean waters. Its economy, speed, agility, and power made the caravel the best sailing vessel of its time. At the end of the 15th century the caravel was modified by giving it the same rig as a carrack with a foresail, square mainsail and lateen mizzen but did not have a high forecastle or much of a sterncastle, unlike the unweatherly carrack. In this form it was known as the *caravela redonda,* and it was in such ships that Christopher Columbus set out on his expedition in 1492. The *Santa Maria* was a small carrack, which served as the mother ship, and the *Pinta* and *Nina* were caravels.

THE ROUTE TO INDIA

In 1487, the Portuguese sailor Bartholomew Dias sailed down the western coast of Africa, and after being cast out to sea, he mistakenly rounded Africa's Cape of Good Hope, entering the Indian Ocean. His voyage showed that it was possible to reach India by sailing around the tip of Africa, thus bypassing the Muslim-controlled land route, but unfortunately for Dias, dwindling supplies and a mutinous crew forced him to return to Lisbon. Nine years later another Portuguese, Vasco da Gama, set out to sail around Africa with larger, full-rigged vessels that carried more supplies and handled difficult weather better. Storms and wind almost forced da Gama all the way to the coast of Brazil before he found the westerly trade winds that brought him rapidly around Africa. In May 1498, Vasco da Gama reached the Indian coastal city of Calcutta.

Thanks to the explorations of Dias and da Gama, Portugal established a commercial empire in Asia based out of the Indian ports of Goa and Malacca. In 1543, trade was initiated with Japan, and the trading post of Macao in China opened in 1556. Portugal became the first European nation to establish a worldwide trading empire, and this success opened trading waters for the future Dutch and English empires. Portuguese exploration along the coast of Africa would also accidentally bring Pedro Alvares Cabral to the shores of Brazil.

VOYAGES OF DISCOVERY, 15TH AND 16TH CENTURIES

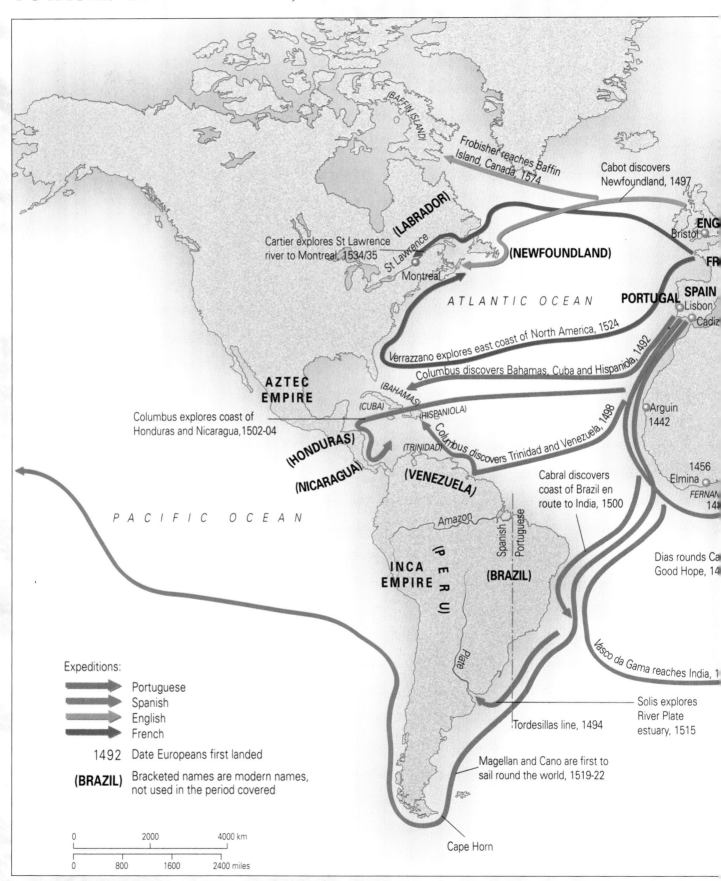

(BAFFIN ISLAND)

Frobisher reaches Baffin Island, Canada, 1574

Cabot discovers Newfoundland, 1497

(LABRADOR)

Cartier explores St Lawrence river to Montreal, 1534/35

St Lawrence

Montreal

(NEWFOUNDLAND)

ENG

Bristol

FR

ATLANTIC OCEAN

PORTUGAL SPAIN

Lisbon

Cadiz

Verrazzano explores east coast of North America, 1524

Columbus discovers Bahamas, Cuba and Hispaniola, 1492

AZTEC EMPIRE

(BAHAMAS)

(CUBA)

(HISPANIOLA)

Arguin 1442

Columbus explores coast of Honduras and Nicaragua, 1502-04

Columbus discovers Trinidad and Venezuela, 1498

(TRINIDAD)

1456

Elmina

(HONDURAS)

(NICARAGUA)

(VENEZUELA)

Cabral discovers coast of Brazil en route to India, 1500

FERNAN 14

PACIFIC OCEAN

Amazon

Spanish

Portuguese

Dias rounds Ca Good Hope, 14

INCA EMPIRE

(P E R U)

(BRAZIL)

Plate

Vasco da Gama reaches India, 1

Expeditions:

Portuguese

Spanish

English

French

1492 Date Europeans first landed

(BRAZIL) Bracketed names are modern names, not used in the period covered

Tordesillas line, 1494

Solis explores River Plate estuary, 1515

Magellan and Cano are first to sail round the world, 1519-22

0   2000   4000 km

0   800   1600   2400 miles

Cape Horn

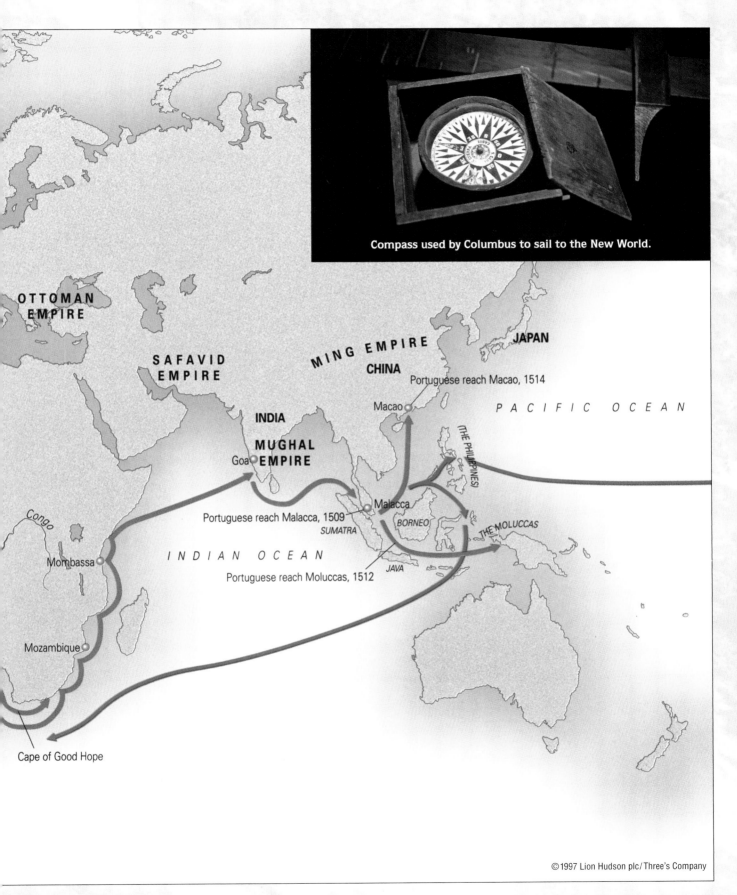

Compass used by Columbus to sail to the New World.

OTTOMAN EMPIRE

SAFAVID EMPIRE

MING EMPIRE

CHINA

JAPAN

Portuguese reach Macao, 1514

Macao

PACIFIC OCEAN

INDIA

MUGHAL EMPIRE

Goa

(THE PHILIPPINES)

Malacca

Portuguese reach Malacca, 1509

SUMATRA

BORNEO

THE MOLUCCAS

Congo

INDIAN OCEAN

Portuguese reach Moluccas, 1512

JAVA

Mombassa

Mozambique

Cape of Good Hope

Before leaving on his historical expedition on August 3, 1492, Columbus received the Sacraments of Penance and Holy Eucharist from Father Juan Perez. It was Juan Perez who persuaded the navigator not to leave Spain without consulting Queen Isabella, when, footsore and disspirited, Columbus and his son arrived at the Franciscan Monastery La Rábida in January 1492 in Huelva, Spain. Father Juan Perez was the prior and also the confessor to Queen Isabella. While resting at the monastery, Father Perez was impressed with Columbus and his ideas and traveled to Santa Fe near Granada to induce the Queen to take an interest in Columbus' proposed voyage. Father Perez joined Columbus on his second voyage.

COLUMBUS AND THE DISCOVERY OF THE NEW WORLD

By the time the young Italian Christopher Columbus arrived in the Spanish court with a proposed venture to sail West across the Atlantic in order to reach the Indies, the Spanish were ready to begin competing with their Portuguese rivals. That same year, 1492, the Muslims were driven out of Granada, and Queen Isabella's Spain wanted to take advantage of her new unified strength. Columbus proposed his voyage to the Portuguese in 1484, but was turned down since the Portuguese were already committed to opening a route to India around Africa. Spain, on the other hand, needed to find a new route in order to compete with Portugal. Isabella accepted Columbus' proposal and funded his voyage.

Columbus was confident that by sailing westward across the ocean, he could reach the opposite side of the world. He had read the second century geographer, Ptolemy, who postulated that the known world was part of one Eurasian land mass that stretched halfway around the Northern hemisphere. Columbus believed that by sailing westward across the ocean, he could arrive at the easternmost reaches of this landmass. After reading Marco Polo's *The Description of the World*, Columbus was convinced that the great cities of China were in fact part of a large archipelago off the far eastern coast of Asia. He calculated that this group of islands could be reached by sailing two thousand four hundred miles west of Spain across the Atlantic.

Columbus tried in vain for fourteen years to find a patron who trusted his theories. Luckily for the explorer, a minister of Isabella and Ferdinand of Spain calculated a way to finance Columbus' mission with little risk to the crown. The project was approved, and on August 3, 1492, Columbus set sail with three ships and a crew of ninety men. He sailed westward, past the Canary Islands, and out into the unknown ocean. Columbus underestimated the size of the Earth by nearly seven thousand miles, and he and his crew spent an unexpected three months at sea. Finally, land was sighted on October 12, 1492. When he landed, Columbus thought he had found a new route to the Indies, but he had in fact stumbled upon the Bahamas.

When Columbus returned to Spain, he received a hero's welcome. The explorer was awarded the title "Admiral of the Ocean Sea" and made governor of all lands in the West. Even though he would make three more voyages before his death in 1506, until the end, Columbus insisted that he had found the passage to Asia.

Columbus' success immediately set off a frenzy of exploration to the New World. Spanish and Portuguese explorers began following Columbus' routes, expanding into the new territory. This quest for new lands put Spain and Portugal in direct competition, but before any blood was shed between the two nations, Pope Alexander VI was called upon in 1493 to negotiate a division of the discovered lands. The pope drew up the "Line of Demarcation" (Tordesillas line, cf. p. 554) which ceded to Spain all newly discovered lands 100 leagues west of the Azores and beyond; it ceded to Portugal all newly discovered lands east of this line. Pope Alexander did not realize that his line would give Spain the vast majority of the Americas.

EXPANSION OF EXPLORATION

The Spanish discovery of the New World created a craze for exploration, which resulted in expansion and trade in the Americas and beyond. Still looking for a route to India, Spain sent Fernando Magellan westwards around South America and across the Pacific Ocean in 1519. Magellan's ship would be the first European vessel to circumnavigate the globe, a voyage that helped to determine the broad outlines of the world. Magellan also claimed the Philippines for the Spanish Empire, and Spanish missionaries were sent there to Christianize the population.

Ferdinand Magellan (1480-1521) was the first to sail from Europe to Asia, the first European to sail the Pacific Ocean, and the first to lead an expedition for the purpose of circumnavigating the globe. Though Magellan was killed in an attack by Philippine natives and never returned to Europe, eighteen members of his crew and one ship of the fleet returned to Spain in 1522, having circled the globe.

Conquistadors were sent to the Americas to help establish and secure Spanish landholdings. Sometimes bold adventurers, other times opportunistic soldiers of fortune, these Conquistadors conquered the Americas and conquered the great Aztec and Inca empires.

France, the Netherlands, and England joined in the exploration of the New World during the sixteenth century, each seeking a sphere of influence and an opportunity to increase trade abroad. French fur trappers sailed from the northern coast of North America to the Great Lakes and down the Mississippi River, carving out a new commercial empire in the forests of North America. Both the Dutch and English established colonies on North America's Atlantic coast.

SOCIAL CONSEQUENCES OF EXPLORATION

The discovery of the New World brought about a commercial revolution in Europe. Known as the Columbian Exchange, traders brought new goods and materials back to Europe that eventually helped secure a better standard of living. New foodstuffs like the potato, squash, and new species of beans increased the available food supply for the common laborer. The increased supply of gold and silver from the Spanish lands would also help Spain become a world power.

Growing trade in America helped the leaders of Europe break local guild monopolies and increase control over vast resources of capital. Countries created national economies, and a middle class made up of bankers and merchants began to replace the older aristocracy. Nations adopted a new economic system called mercantilism to manage the demands of prolific trade. The mercantile system is based on the premise that a nation could best obtain wealth and power by exporting more goods than it imported. Nations tried to produce enough goods to satisfy all of their own needs while leaving a surplus to export abroad. By limiting imports and increasing exports, nations could earn more capital. The discovery of the New World supported this economic system because nations now had access to colonies that could provide necessary raw materials for producing a large surplus of goods. With the advent of mercantilism, European nations began to develop trading empires in the New World.

Economic transition did not happen overnight, and it was anything but smooth. The increased importation of gold from America caused widespread inflation in the sixteenth century. Those countries that did not have access to new trade routes began to lag behind the economies of Spain and Portugal. England resorted to piracy as a way of increasing wealth by seizing Spanish treasure ships in the Atlantic. The rich agricultural states like Germany and Austria could not keep up with the newly established colonies, and they reacted by creating a system of serfdom that dramatically reduced the cost of peasant labor. Serfdom bound peasants to the land on which they worked, reducing generations of peasants to poverty. Serfdom would last until the nineteenth century in lands east of Germany and Austria, and would plant the seeds of discontent that would make the society ripe for the introduction of communism.

Indeed, many suffered from the labor demands of mercantilism. Portugal needed to fill a falling labor supply and introduced slavery into the European economy. Their use of slaves would spread to other European nations as mercantilism became dependent on slave labor, and African slavery lasted as a major industry throughout Europe until the eighteenth century. In the Americas, although they were never widely enslaved, Indians fared little better than their African counterparts. Disease brought by Spanish conquerors wiped out major portions of the indigenous population, and millions of Indians died from epidemics such as small pox and measles.

THE COLUMBIAN EXCHANGE

The Columbian Exchange has been one of the most significant events in the history of world ecology, agriculture, and culture. The term describes the widespread exchange of agricultural goods, animals, plants, and diseases between the Eastern and Western Hemispheres that occurred after 1492.

This exchange of plants and animals transformed European, American, African, and Asian ways of life. Before 1492 no potatoes were grown outside of South America. By the 1800s, Ireland was so dependent on the potato that a disease based crop failure led to the devastating Irish Potato Famine. The first European import, the horse, changed the lives of many Native American tribes on the Great Plains, shifting them to a nomadic lifestyle based on hunting bison on horseback. Tomato sauce, made from New World tomatoes, became an Italian staple, while coffee and sugarcane from Asia became the main crops of Latin American plantations. Before the Columbian Exchange, there were no oranges in Florida, no bananas in Ecuador, no rubber trees in Africa, no cattle in Texas, no burros in Mexico, no chile peppers in Thailand, no tobacco in France and no chocolate in Switzerland. Even the dandelion was brought to America by Europeans for use as an herb. (excerpted from *www.en.wikipedia.org*)

EXAMPLES OF PLANTS AND ANIMALS EXCHANGED BY THE OLD WORLD AND NEW WORLD

FROM THE OLD WORLD		FROM THE NEW WORLD	
Agricultural Plants	**Domesticated Animals**	**Domesticated Animals**	**Agricultural Plants**
Rice	Horse	Turkey	Maize (corn)
Wheat	Donkey	Llama	Potato
Barley	Camel	Alpaca	Sweet Potato
Oats	Pig	Guinea Pig	Manioc
Rye	Cattle		Peanut
Turnip	Goat		Tomato
Onion	Sheep		Squash
Cabbage			Pineapple
Lettuce			Papaya
Peach			Avocado
Pear			Cashew
Sugar			Cocoa
Coffee			Rubber
Black Pepper			Tobacco
			Bell Pepper
			Chile Pepper

The Old World horse changed the culture of the New World Great Plains Indian tribes.

MISSIONARY VOYAGES, 16TH AND 17TH CENTURIES

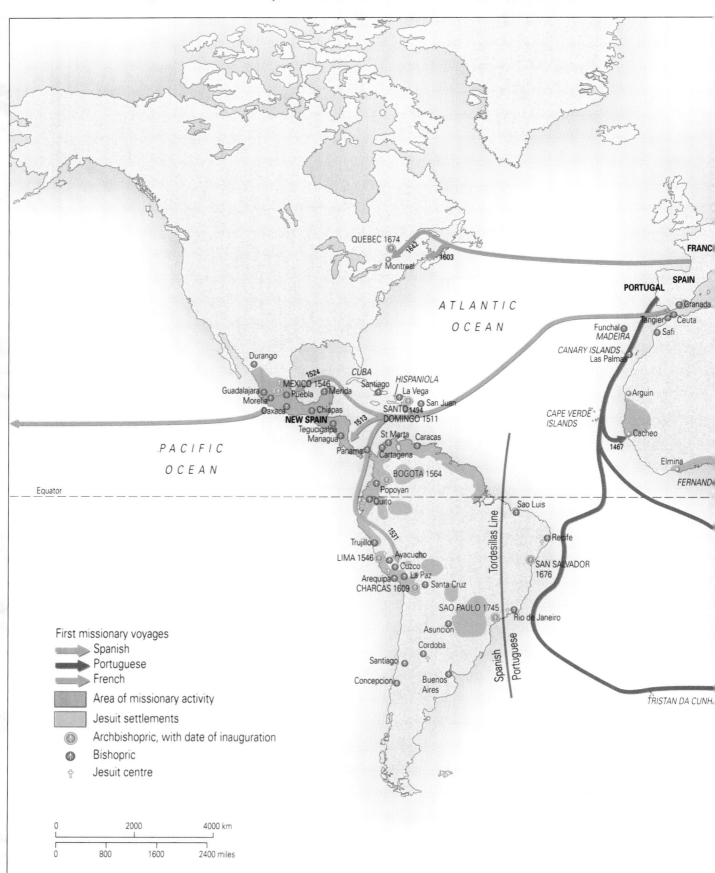

First missionary voyages
- Spanish
- Portuguese
- French
- Area of missionary activity
- Jesuit settlements
- ✛ Archbishopric, with date of inauguration
- ✚ Bishopric
- ✝ Jesuit centre

QUEBEC 1674
Montreal
1642
1603

FRANC
PORTUGAL SPAIN

ATLANTIC OCEAN

Granada
Funchal Ceuta
MADEIRA Tangier Safi
CANARY ISLANDS
Las Palmas
Arguin
CAPE VERDE ISLANDS
Cacheo
1467
Elmina
FERNAND

Durango
1524
CUBA HISPANIOLA
MEXICO 1546 Santiago La Vega
Guadalajara Puebla Merida San Juan
Morelia SANTO 1494
Oaxaca Chiapas DOMINGO 1511
NEW SPAIN 1513
Tegucigalpa St Marta Caracas
Managua Panama Cartagena
BOGOTA 1564
PACIFIC OCEAN Popoyan
Quito

Equator

Sao Luis
Recife
SAN SALVADOR
1676

Trujillo 1531
LIMA 1546 Ayacucho
Cuzco
Arequipa La Paz
CHARCAS 1609 Santa Cruz
SAO PAULO 1745
Asunción Rio de Janeiro
Cordoba
Santiago
Concepcion Buenos Aires

Tordesillas Line

Spanish Portuguese

TRISTAN DA CUNH

| 0 | 2000 | 4000 km |
| 0 | 800 | 1600 | 2400 miles |

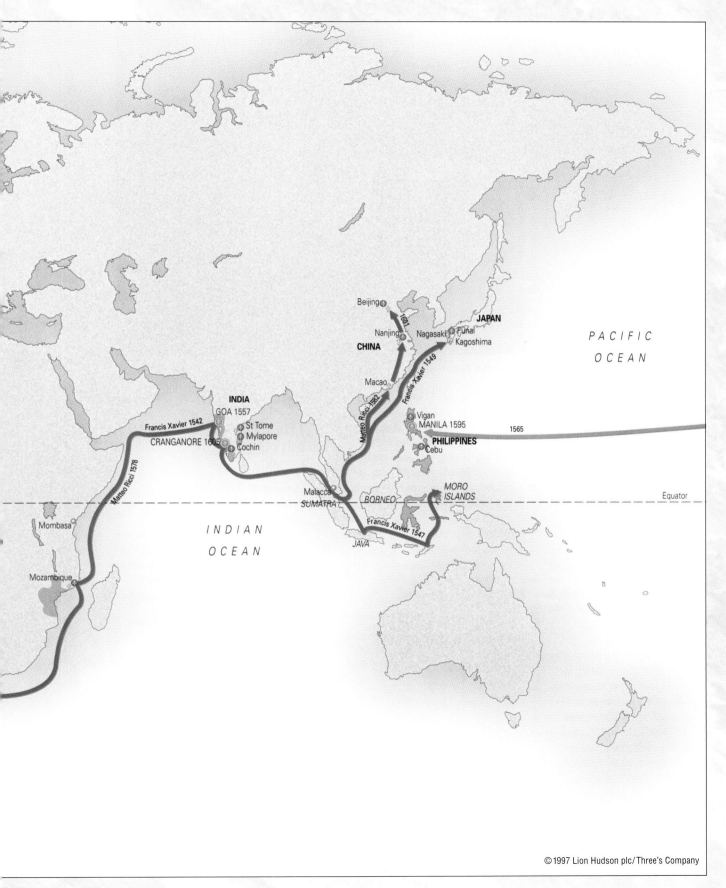

Beijing
Nanjing
1601
CHINA
JAPAN
Nagasaki Funai
Kagoshima
Macao
Francis Xavier 1549
Matteo Ricci 1582
INDIA
GOA 1557
St Tome
CRANGANORE 1605
Mylapore
Cochin
Vigan
MANILA 1595
1565
PHILIPPINES
Cebu
Francis Xavier 1542
Matteo Ricci 1578
Malacca
SUMATRA
BORNEO
MORO
ISLANDS
Equator
Mombasa
INDIAN
OCEAN
Francis Xavier 1547
JAVA
PACIFIC
OCEAN
Mozambique

© 1997 Lion Hudson plc/Three's Company

PART II
Missionary Apostolate

Settlement into the New World opened new apostolic opportunities just as the Church was undergoing a renewal. The Catholic Reformation helped enthuse dedicated missionaries who ardently desired to spread the Good News of Christ into these newly-founded territories. Older orders were refilled with zealous and disciplined monks and friars, and newer religious orders, such as the Jesuits, Capuchins, and Vincentians, turned out many priests eager to evangelize the indigenous peoples of the New World. The popes encouraged these missions and often helped finance these apostolic ventures. In 1622, Pope Gregory XV founded the congregation *De propaganda Fide* to promote and establish apostolic missions, and in 1627, the Urbanian University was established in Rome to help educate missionary priests.

OBSTACLES

There were many difficulties facing the new missionaries. Travel distance alone was staggering. From Europe, it took two years to reach the Portuguese outpost of Goa in western India. From Goa it was another thousand miles to the Far East. It took less time to reach the Americas, but missionaries still had to trek though hundreds of miles of jungles and over mountains to reach the mission settlements.

Climate was also an obstacle. Forests, jungles, and mountain passes had to be traversed in climates never experienced by Europeans. The burning heat of the plateaus, the steaming tropical dampness of the jungle interiors, the icy blasts of the mountains, snow, and bitter cold all took their toll on these selfless missionaries.

Language was also a great barrier. Natives from the Americas, Africa, and Asia all spoke languages that were foreign in structure to European languages. The limited vocabulary (200-500 words) in some of these dialects made explaining the doctrines of Christianity exceedingly difficult. Missionaries had to invent new words and create written alphabet systems to help them in their catechesis. Using translators at the start, the missionaries created new vocabularies and dedicated themselves to learning the grammatical structure of the native tongues they encountered.

Many of these native people did not immediately accept these foreign evangelizers. Missionaries came into conflict with medicine men, witch doctors, and pagan priests who were vehemently opposed to the Christian Faith. Their deeply superstitious practices made it difficult to accept the new Creed, and they often reacted violently, inciting bitter persecutions against missionaries and their converts. Hence, there were numerous Christian martyrs in these foreign lands.

A missionary picture book used to communicate the catechism to native peoples.

Perhaps the greatest challenge for the missionaries was the poor example of many of the settlers. Opportunistic adventurers mistreated and enslaved local people, and greedy politicians and officials resisted measures aimed at protecting the basic human rights of the local citizens. In light of the abuse and mistreatment suffered by the native population, many natives were skeptical of accepting their persecutors' Faith.

The treatment of particular groups of natives in the New World differed slightly according to the country controlling the area. In the Spanish colonies, missionary activities were generously supported, and monarchs passed legislation meant to protect the native populations. Spain prohibited the enslavement of local peoples, and in many of their territories, the indigenous people were granted Spanish citizenship. Colonists inter-married with the native people and helped to assimilate them into their own Spanish culture. The strong Spanish tone still present in the cultures of Central and South America testifies to these policies.

St. Francis Xavier (1506-1552) was a pioneering Christian missionary and co-founder of the Society of Jesus (Jesuit Order). The Xaverian Brothers are named after him. He is considered to have converted more people to Christianity than anyone else since St. Paul.

Unlike the Spanish, some of the North American colonies did not encourage native assimilation. The Dutch and English treated Indians as reprobate, seizing their lands and driving them further to the West. Indians were more warmly received by French missionaries who traversed the midwest region of North America.

In spite of these obstacles, missionary evangelizers established solid Catholic foundations in many regions of the New World. Many came to the Faith, and the heroic sacrifices of a handful of Christian missionaries brought Christianity to the farthest reaches of the globe.

One such missionary, the Spaniard Fr. Bartolome de las Casas, was the first priest in the New World. Having served as chaplain during Christopher Columbus' conquest of Cuba, he received an *encomienda*, or land with native Cuban slaves. Mistreatment of the Cubans prompted him to renounce his *encomienda* and denounce the exploitation. Appealing to the Spanish crown, he suggested using African slave labor because they held no claim to the land, but soon thereafter renounced his proposal and worked to eradicate slavery.

ST. FRANCIS XAVIER

In 1500, missionary friars arrived at the small trading port of Goa in India established by the Portuguese. As they began preaching to the Indians, they discovered a group of Christians who claimed descent from the original missionary activity of the Apostle

ST. THOMAS CHRISTIANS

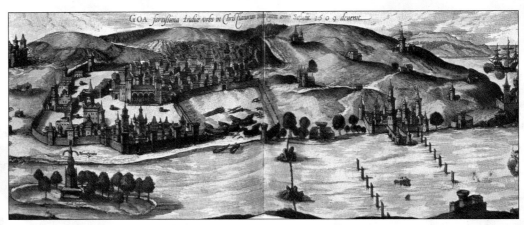

The city of Goa, India in the sixteenth century. Encouraged by the presence of the group called "St. Thomas Christians," a diocese was established in 1533 in Goa with a seminary for training native priests. St. Francis Xavier was sent to Goa to help the struggling mission in 1542.

St. Thomas Christians are Christians from the Malabar Coast (west coast) in southern India whose customs date back to the evangelization of St. Thomas the Apostle. According to their tradition, St. Thomas traveled from the Holy Land to India in A.D. 52 and established seven Churches in Maliankara, Palayur, Kottakavu, Quilon, Niranom, Nilakkal, and Chayal. He was killed in A.D. 72 and buried in Mylapore on the East coast of India (although his relics were later relocated to Edessa). This tradition has been consistently agreed to by many scholars from the third century onwards and seems to be supported by modern developments and advances in archaeology, geography, anthropology and other disciplines.

In the fourth century, a group of Jewish Christians led by Thomas Cana settled in Kerala at the request of the Assyrian Church of the East. Thomas Cana was said to have collected seventy-two Christian families and settled on the southern shore of the Perigar. In the fifth century, the Christians of Malabar were exposed to the Nestorian churches of Iraq, whose theology and doctrine influenced the St. Thomas Christians until the arrival of the Portuguese in the sixteenth century.

Before the arrival of the Portuguese, St. Thomas Christians were able to obtain high social status and were granted privileges within the complex caste system of southern India. The head of the Church was the archdeacon, and "Palliyogams"—Parish Councils—were given charge of temporal matters. The lives of the St. Thomas Christians were centered on a liturgy that included days of fasting and abstinence, and their churches were of a similar style to Hindu Temples and Jewish Synagogues. Unfortunately, no written records of the St. Thomas Christians exist from the time of St. Thomas until the sixteenth century.

Pope Paul III sent St. Francis Xavier to Goa, India, as a special emissary to evangelize the Indian people. For five months Francis worked to remedy the appalling behavior of the Portuguese against the Indians. He worked in the city's three prisons, in the hospital and among the lepers. Moving around the country with only an umbrella and a piece of leather to mend his shoes, he found the language barrier his greatest problem. He had the *Creed, Ten Commandments, Lord's Prayer, Hail Mary, Salve Regina* and the *Rite of Confession* translated into pidgin Tamil and memorized them. He gathered flocks of children by walking with a handbell and taught them to chant the prayers. In one month he had baptized 10,000 people. (Excerpted from *Cultural Atlas of the Christian World,* Graham Speake, Editor, 1987, p.122)

St. Thomas. Encouraged by these "St. Thomas Christians," as they were called, a diocese was established in 1533 in Goa with a seminary for training native priests. Unfortunately, many difficulties limited the success of these first missionary friars. The vast Indian subcontinent, with its densely packed populations, the highly structured caste system of the Hindu culture, and the abysmal example of the many recently arrived colonists made progress for conversion slow and difficult.

In 1542, one of the greatest missionary apostles of the age, St. Francis Xavier, arrived in India to help the struggling mission. St. Francis Xavier was one of the founding members of the Society of Jesus; he helped form the order after he met St. Ignatius Loyola at the University of Paris. After his ordination, St. Francis' exceptional zeal for the Gospel was recognized by Pope Paul III, and the pontiff designated him a special emissary for the evangelization of the Indian people.

The first task confronting St. Francis in India was the scandalous activities of the European settlers in the region. For five months St. Francis worked to remedy their immoral behavior, and he finally managed to improve conduct among the Portuguese. The improved moral character of the settlers helped St. Francis gain the trust of the local Indians and concentrate his efforts on spreading the Christian Faith.

Over the next ten years, St. Francis traveled across the subcontinent, helped strengthen the faith of the nominal St. Thomas Christians, and baptized thousands of local people. He later continued on to the city of Malacca in modern day Sri Lanka, the second most important trading post of the Portuguese empire, where St. Francis established his headquarters. From Malacca, he made many journeys further eastward to the Molucca (Spice Islands), and some accounts say he traveled as far as the Philippines. St. Francis' simple charity and straightforward approach (he always tried to learn the native tongue of the regions he visited) helped convert many people wherever he traveled. St. Francis' missionary work was further strengthened by the strong administrative systems he established for the missions he founded. After St. Francis left a region, he instructed well-trained successors to continue ministering to the newly evangelized peoples.

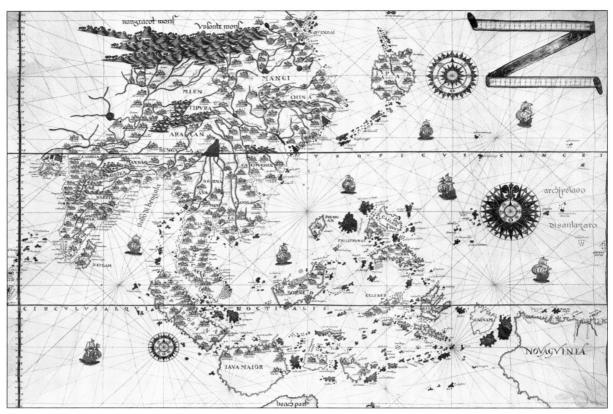

Sixteenth century map of China, Japan, India, Indonesia and the Phillipines.

In 1549, St. Francis traveled to Japan along with Jesuit Father de Torres and three Japanese converts to set up a mission on the island farthest east. He spent his first year in Japan familiarizing himself with the culture, learning the language, and translating the principal articles of the Faith into Japanese. Unfortunately for St. Francis, the political situation in Japan was unlike the countries he had already visited. At the time, Japan had an established feudal structure, and as in Medieval Europe, Japanese priests (*bonzes*) were tied to the political system. They saw St. Francis and his missionaries as a danger to their traditional authority and worked to oust him. Evangelizing in Japan became even more difficult for St. Francis when he petitioned the emperor for protection from the *bonzes* and, to his dismay, found that the ruler was simply a puppet dominated by strong feudal lords. St. Francis understood that the rigid society in Japan would make long-term growth of Christianity difficult. St. Francis left Japan in 1552 after converting two thousand Japanese. He now set his sights on the nearby kingdom of China.

In Japan, St. Francis had heard stories and myths about the "Celestial Empire," as China was known at the time. Hearing of a magnificent culture across the sea in China, St. Francis was eager to bring the Faith to the legendary empire. Just before he set off, the Viceroy of India appointed St. Francis ambassador and the Holy See made him a Papal Nuncio, giving the missionary diplomatic prestige to bolster his efforts in China.

At the time, China was closed to foreigners, and anyone who tried to enter the country was subject to immediate execution. To avoid this peril, St. Francis appealed to some Chinese smugglers who promised to help him enter the mainland. Tragically, on his way to China, St. Francis caught a serious fever. The smugglers abandoned him in a small hut on the island of Sancian, and he died five days later. St. Francis Xavier was only forty-six years of age when he died in 1552, and he was canonized just seventy years later. His feast day is celebrated on December 3.

INDIA

When missionaries landed in a new area of India, they would encounter a complex multiplicity of cultures. Missionaries had to work at winning acceptance from tightly closed communities and adapt the practice of Christianity to the particular cultural traditions of the people. To achieve this, missionaries dedicated a huge part of their efforts to assimilating local customs, learning dialects, and earning the trust of the locals by integrating themselves into the community. By understanding the culture thoroughly, missionaries could tailor the teachings of Christ in a more effective and convincing way.

In India, the missionary Robert de Nobili exemplified the effectiveness of this "inculturation." Catholic missionaries had difficulties reaching India's intellectual class, the Brahmins. The Portuguese missionaries who preceded de Nobili won over many converts among the lower classes. However, the Brahmins rejected Christianity since it was perceived as unfit for the upper class. De Nobili realized that in Indian society divisions were so strong that Christianity had to be presented differently to each caste. He took a year to master Hindi, Sanskrit, and the local dialects. He studied the Brahmin caste and learned about what they held sacred and worthy of reverence. De Nobili then asked permission from his archbishop to present himself as a Christian Brahmin holy man as a way of showing Christian virtue in a form understandable to the Indian Brahmin. He followed the Brahmins' rigorous traditions of fasting and abstaining from foods considered unclean. The leaders of the Brahmin class were also impressed by de Nobili's goodness and kindness. Gradually, de Nobili showed how Christianity could be adapted to their philosophical and religious ideas. Some estimate that around 150,000 Brahmin converted through de Nobili's work.

Maintaining a vibrant and active church in India proved difficult in subsequent centuries. The strong divisions between upper- and lower-class Christians in India was criticized by many Westerners. In 1742, Pope Benedict XIV, insisting that missions publicly admit members of the lower classes into full communion with the Church, condemned some Indian Christian rites. These changes were not welcomed by local Indians, and after the suppression of the Jesuit order during the eighteenth century, the Christian population in India shrank.

CHINA

St. Francis Xavier was not the only missionary who could not penetrate China's closed borders. Despite the flourishing missions in the surrounding lands, China resisted Christian and European visitors for years. In 1583 (thirty years after St. Francis Xavier's death), an Italian Jesuit named Matteo Ricci was finally able to set up a permanent residence in China. Like de Nobili in India, Ricci understood that the best way to reach the Chinese people was to adopt their local customs and traditions. However, China posed particular problems for Catholic missionaries. The Chinese culture prided themselves on adherence to traditions of family worship and philosophical principles of truth and justice. These traditions were old and deep-rooted, and they had produced many centuries of sophisticated and refined civilization. The Chinese were satisfied with their ways and proud of their culture, with no inclination to embrace a new one.

Ricci understood this and recognized the beauty and richness of the Chinese culture. Rather than preach in opposition to these traditions, Ricci blended the Eastern and Western worlds in an attractive and compatible way. He dressed as a Mandarin scholar but filled his residence in Canton with western works of art and scientific instruments. Ricci lived as a public witness to the Christian Faith, and he offered a moving example of charity and patience that won the admiration of the Chinese. Through his exemplary virtue, as well as exposing them to the fruits of Western civilization, he won the respect of the local people. Eventually, the emperor summoned Ricci to his court, and the two developed a friendship. While in the emperor's court, Ricci gave lectures on science and astronomy, translated Christian principles into Chinese, and developed a Chinese liturgical rite that used the Chinese language, not Latin, in the Mass. Ricci wrote a treatise on the Catholic Faith in Chinese called *The True Doctrine of God,* in which he was able to express the complex theological dogmas and concepts of Catholicism in a language that had never before conveyed Christian ideas. By his death in 1610, Ricci had established five residences in China and brought two thousand converts to the Faith.

Father Johann Adam Schall succeeded Ricci in China, and the number of converted Chinese Christians rose to over 237,000 by 1664. Father Schall continued to expose the Chinese to Western culture. He held the presidency of the Mathematical Tribunal in the Imperial City and was made a first class citizen by the emperor. In many ways, the success of his missionary activity depended upon the support and good graces of the emperor. In 1692, the emperor issued an edict giving complete toleration to the Church, and by 1724, the number of Chinese Catholics rose to 800,000.

Matteo Ricci (1552-1610) was an Italian Jesuit priest whose missionary activity in China during the Ming Dynasty marked the beginning of modern Chinese Christianity. The church he built remains the largest Catholic church to survive the Cultural Revolution.

Nonetheless, the Church did not remain in good graces with the emperors of China for long. As western nations expanded their trading empires in the East, the Chinese became wary of Western domination, and Western Christian missionaries began to lose favor. In 1724 persecutions of Christians in China resumed and missionary activity quickly declined. The suppression of the Society of Jesus in 1773 also diminished the number of available missionary priests. By the end of the eighteenth century, China's faithful numbered around 300,000, less than half the number at the beginning the the century.

JAPAN

Persecution posed a difficult obstacle for Christian missionaries in Japan as well. Within thirty years of St. Francis Xavier's work in Japan, Japanese converts numbered over 200,000. However, the success of the Church in Japan was at the mercy of the whims of the strong feudal warlords that dominated Japanese society. As long as the leading warlord, the Shogun, permitted missionary activity, Christianity thrived. In 1587 power shifted, and the Shogun Hideyoshi began a new era of persecution.

This persecution was largely the result of paranoia affecting many Asian countries at that time. Western expansion made many ancient civilizations fearful of invasion and suppression. In Japan, a ship captain suggested that the missionaries were preparing for a larger European invasion, and Japanese authorities responded by arresting the missionaries. Twenty-six of them were martyred by crucifixion in Nagasaki on February 5, 1597 (canonized by Pope Bl. Pius IX in 1862). Persecution intensified in 1614 after the Shogun officially outlawed the practice of Christianity in Japan. In 1622, fifty-two Christians were killed, and the faithful were driven underground.

Japanese martyrs came from all classes of society. Clergy and laity, Europeans and Japanese, men and women, elderly and children were all subject to persecution, and the punishments were especially cruel.

Years later, in 1865, Japan was reopened to the West, and French missionaries returned to the Islands. To their surprise, the French discovered over 50,000 Japanese Christians in hiding. Despite persecutions, these Christians had kept the Faith alive, passing it down from generation to generation for nearly three centuries. Remarkably, these Japanese Christians retained their orthodoxy, finding solidarity with the French missionaries in their mutual obedience to the pope in Rome, veneration of the Blessed Virgin, and practice of celibacy by the clergy.

THE PHILIPPINES AND AFRICA

By far the most successful missionary effort in the East occurred in the Philippines. Various religious, including the Augustinians, Dominicans, and Franciscans, flocked to the Spanish colony, teaching the natives, among other skills, new farming techniques and textile manufacturing. These missionaries also helped build roads and bridges throughout the islands, and in 1611, the University of Santo Tomas was established.

The missionary efforts gave rise to an improved capacity to work efficiently and a higher standard of living. These advances had a positive impact on the general moral character of the people. These long-lasting effects of these missionary achievements in the Philippines is still strongly reflected in the deep faith of the Filipino people.

During this period of great missionary activity, Africa showed the least results. Disease proved to be the harshest opponent to opening the vast interior of the African Continent to the Christian

THE CHURCH IN CHINA TODAY

Christianity in China appeared to be on the rise during the early part of the twentieth century. However, when the communists came to power in 1949, Christian Churches were seized, missionaries forced to leave, and Christians were pressured to follow the strict requirements of the communist party. In 1957 the situation worsened as the Roman Catholics who remained in China were forced to sever relations with Rome, driving those who pledged allegiance to the Holy Pontiff underground. This has resulted in the existence of two Churches in China: the official or government-sanctioned church ("Patriotic Church"), which does not recognize the supremacy of the pope, and the unofficial or "underground" Church, which is still united with Rome.

The underground Church today continues to suffer fierce persecution. Both clergy and laity are regularly detained and beaten, and Churches and shrines destroyed. Nevertheless, as occurred in Eastern Europe, the underground Church is also growing in popularity as those disillusioned with communist ideology join the fold. The underground Church continually asks all Catholics to pray that their government stop persecution and grant the freedom to practice Catholicism.

Faith. Nearly every missionary who entered the Dark Continent before the middle of the nineteenth century would succumb to a variety of lethal tropical diseases. In addition, hostile Muslims, reprisals over the slave trade, and jealous pagan priests took a great toll on the missionaries. During this time, many lost their lives to persecution, and since it was nearly impossible to maintain a steady missionary presence, only a few would convert to the Catholic Faith. But the late nineteenth and twentieth centuries saw new and effective inroads in the evangelization of Africa where now the Church in a number of countries is thriving.

PART III

The New World

Although at first many explorers thought that they had discovered a new route to the Orient, they soon realized that they had come across a new continent. Anything but a disappointment, this New World provided a wealth of opportunity. Land-starved Spanish nobles carved out feudal estates, while others looked for easy access to new sources of gold, silver, and other goods. To achieve these ends, the Conquistadors let nothing stand in their way. They conquered the large Aztec and Inca empires as well as countless other native cultures in order to establish a strong and affluent hold on Central and South America.

For the Catholic kings Charles V and Philip II, the propagation of Christianity was a primary goal in the New World. Since the very first explorations, priests accompanied the various expeditions, seeking to bring native peoples to Christ. The Spanish crown generously supported the missionary clerics and passed legislation that protected the basic human rights of the Indians.

Missionaries did not simply introduce the Christian religion. As in other parts of the world, they learned native traditions and dialects and helped teach and train the Indians in agriculture and technical crafts. Thanks to work of the missionaries, Spanish culture intermingled with the culture of America and eventually the natives intermarried with Spanish settlers. These efforts brought millions to the Church and helped bring a Christian culture the Latin world.

Cortes landed at Veracruz (True Cross) on March 4, 1519, with 11 ships, 500 men and 15 horses. He ordered the fleet to be sunk (after anything usable was salvaged) except for one small ship with which to communicate with Spain. This prevented his men from returning to Cuba with any plundered gold.

HERNANDO CORTES AND THE AZTECS

In the Americas, Spanish settlers first encountered the great civilization of the Aztec Empire. A warrior people, the Aztecs were an ethnic minority that enslaved the majority of the natives that lived in Mexico and Central America. They followed a fierce, pagan religion that held the population in a grip of fear through frequent human sacrifice. The Aztecs believed in a warrior god, Quetzalcoatl, and according to their beliefs, Quetzalcoatl was supposed to return to lead the Aztec Empire to victory. Aztec religious leaders calculated that the warrior god was supposed to return to their empire

When the Spaniards saw the island city of Tenochtitlan for the first time they asked each other if they were dreaming. Surely it was the most magnificent city in the world. The expedition arrived in the Mexica-Aztec capital on November 8, 1519. Montezuma welcomed Cortez to Tenochtitlan on the Great Causeway into the "Venice of the West."

around the year 1519. Seeming to fulfill the Aztec prophecy, Hernando Cortes landed in Mexico that very year with a small force of 500 soldiers.

The governor of Cuba, Diego Velasquez, sent Cortes to open trade with the rich and impressive Aztec Empire. Cortes set off, and on his way into central Mexico, he encountered an Indian girl who agreed to act as an interpreter for the Spaniards. During their travels, this girl, Marina, helped Cortes by providing him with information about Indian politics and culture. Cortes learned about the prophecies surrounding the return of the warrior god, and more importantly, he learned that most of the native population was burning with hatred for the brutal Aztecs and would likely support the Spanish in their conquest. Taking her advice, Cortes allied himself with local Indian tribes throughout the region surrounding the Aztec capital of Tenochtitlan (present-day Mexico City).

When Cortes and his men finally arrived at Tenochtitlan, the emperor of the Aztecs, Montezuma, was convinced that Cortes was the returning Quetzalcoatl and his Spanish soldiers were godmen. The emperor received the Spaniards with great pomp and ceremony. However, the Spaniards feared that Montezuma was plotting further attacks. Distrustful and wary of any possible ambushes, Cortes captured the emperor and brought him to his quarters.

With the emperor under Cortes' control, the Spaniards seemed to control the city. Soon, his influence became so great that the governor of Cuba began to fear Cortes' growing power. The governor sent out an embassy of Spanish soldiers to the Aztec capital to arrest Cortes, but when Cortes met the soldiers, they joined him instead. Upon returning to the Aztec capital with these men, Cortes found the city in rebellion. Enraged by the human sacrifices they witnessed while

"La Noche Triste," the Night of Sorrow, July 1, 1520. After Montezuma II was killed by his own people, Cortes and his men escaped from the palace in a bloody battle. Over 400 Spaniards and 2,000 Indian allies were killed. Cortes managed to escape by riding over the bodies piled up in the causeway.

Cortes was away, the Spaniards in Tenochtitlan had attacked a number of Aztec priests. Cortes swooped into the city to help his men. As they fought their way out of the city, Emperor Montezuma II was killed by his own people and a number of Spaniards were captured.

Cortes reorganized his forces and plotted a return to the Aztec capital. Building a small fleet of ships to control the Aztec lake, Cortes appeared with six hundred men and five thousand allied Indian warriors to retake the capital. Aided by an outbreak of small pox, which decimated the Aztec population, Cortes managed to capture the city and gain control of the Aztec Empire. Shortly after the fall of the Aztec Empire, Cortes obtained from the Spanish crown twelve Franciscans to begin the work of evangelization in Mexico.

PIZARRO AND THE INCAS

The Inca Empire of South America fell to another Spaniard, Francisco Pizarro. For nearly a century, the Inca Empire dominated the South American continent and managed to fend off every attacking force. Organized under an emperor and a strong ruling noble class, the Incas maintained order over a vast territory that included modern day Ecuador, Peru, Bolivia, Chile, and Argentina.

In 1526, Pizarro visited the city of Tumbez in the North of the empire (northern Peruvian coast) accompanied by only few men. Impressed by the rich empire, Pizarro left the city and returned to Spain to plan a future expedition. Since the Inca Empire was at the peak of its power under the leadership of the emperor Huayna Capac, Pizarro would not have been able to defeat a united empire with just a few men. He returned in 1531 with a stronger force. Luckily for Pizarro, the Inca Empire was embroiled in a civil war.

When Pizarro returned, the Inca Empire was politically divided. Pizarro took advantage of the disorder within the Inca Empire, entering the heart of the realm without confrontation. Atahuallpa, the son of Huayna Capac who claimed the right to the throne, welcomed Pizarro and attempted to over-awe him with wealth and majesty. He invited the Spanish soldier to his resort town of Caxamarca in the Andes. Fearing a trap, Pizarro returned the offer by inviting the emperor to dinner at the Spanish camp. Typical of Inca political custom, Atahuallpa arrived amidst great pomp

and ceremony and with thousands of his highest nobles, all unarmed. The power of the Inca emperor was understood by all in the empire as absolute, and it was unthinkable for Atahuallpa to fear any danger

The Ransom Room is a small room located in Caxamarca, Peru. It is considered by some Peruvian historians to be the room that Inca Emperor Atahuallpa filled with gold and silver to ransom his release. It is also thought by some to be the room Atahuallpa was kept prisoner.

or attack from his Spanish hosts. The emperor gravely misjudged the foreigners' ambition. Pizarro surprised the entourage, killing the majority of the noblemen and capturing the Incan emperor.

Pizarro ruled through the captive emperor for nine months. Believing that the Spaniards were after treasure, Atahuallpa offered a room full of gold in ransom for his release. The Spaniards thought that the amount of treasure offered was absurd and unattainable, and so they agreed to the bargain. However, the Spaniards were still too afraid to free the emperor. They feared an ambush by supporters of Atahuallpa, so rather than release the emperor, they had Atahuallpa tried and executed for the slaughter of Quito Indians at Cuzco, where he had obtained his treasure for the Spaniards. Without the leadership of the emperor and his administrative staff of nobles and with allied Indian support, the Incan Empire quickly fell to the Spaniards.

Spanish *conquistador,* Francisco Pizarro (1475-1541)

SPANISH RULE IN AMERICA

For much of the sixteenth century, Spanish Conquistadors crisscrossed the American Continents seeking personal fortune and fame. Ponce de Leon explored Florida in North America looking for the famed "fountain of youth." Hernando de Soto pushed into what is now the southwestern United States and later reached the Mississippi River in 1542. Francisco de Coronado led a group northward from Mexico and reached modern-day Kansas. Though not finding the treasures they sought, these Conquistadors helped to open the continent for further settlement, and in their wake, missionaries came to evangelize.

The native tribes were largely animists, a form of religious belief that attributes human qualities to material objects or nonhuman living creatures, and were steeped in superstition. Many of the tribes participated in wholesale human sacrifice and gruesome rituals led by "priests" or medicine men. These medicine men resisted Christianization and were bitter enemies of the missionaries. In addition to the perversities that marked some of their pagan customs, the missionaries had to contend with the terrible example of some Spanish conquerors who ravaged the native villages and enslaved local peoples. It was the main objective of many priests and bishops to defend the rights of the Indian people and hold the Spanish colonists accountable for their wrongdoing.

Bartolome de Las Casas (1484-1566) was the first Bishop of Chiapas. He vigorously defended the rights of the natives of Peru.

The Church did much to promote native rights. In 1512, Bartolome de Las Casas helped convince the Spanish king to pass the "Laws of Burgos" which protected Indians. Cardinal Ximenes de Cisneros and Pope Adrian VI urged Holy Roman emperor Charles V to treat the Indians of the New World with Christian charity. In 1537, Pope Paul III increased the penalty for abuse of the indigenous people to include anyone who enslaved Indians or plundered their villages. The rulers of Spain also protected natives by making all Indians vassals of the Crown. Bishop Juan de Zumarraga, the first bishop of Mexico, helped found schools for the Indians; universities were built in Mexico (Royal and Pontifical University of Mexico founded by King Philip II) and Peru (University of San Marcos) to promote further educational opportunities.

OUR LADY OF GUADALUPE

The early missionaries had a difficult time eradicating the superstition of the Indian people. Initially the cessation of human sacrifices and the destruction of the pagan temples by the Spanish hindered the missionaries' efforts to win converts to Christ. However, a spectacular intervention of Mary would help remedy this lackluster interest in Christianity by occasioning a staggering number of converts to the Church. Within ten years, nine million Indians would receive Baptism.

On December 9, 1531, ten years after the conquest of Mexico, a new convert to the Faith, St. Juan Diego, was walking his usual six miles to attend Holy Mass, when he heard angelic voices and saw a rainbow of dazzling colors. Mary appeared to St. Juan Diego and asked him to go to the Bishop to ask that a temple be erected in her name. St. Juan Diego obeyed and informed the bishop of the apparition. Bishop Juan de Zumarraga listened patiently to St. Juan Diego's account, but was skeptical. He told St. Juan Diego to return another day.

St. Juan Diego returned to his home feeling he had failed Mary. As the sun set, she appeared again to St. Juan Diego and encouraged him to return the next day to the bishop to again make her request. Upon his return the next day, the bishop asked that she give a sign to prove the veracity of her visitation. St. Juan Diego returned home, once again disappointed.

On December 12, St. Juan Diego's uncle became very ill, and fearing that his uncle might die, he summoned a priest to give his uncle the last rites. Because of the urgency to attend to his uncle, he tried to detour away from the hill where Mary had first appeared to him, but it made no difference. She appeared to St. Juan Diego again, and asked him about her request for the church. When St. Juan Diego spoke about his sick uncle, she reassured him that she had already seen to his uncle's recovery. As for the bishop's request for a sign, she directed St. Juan Diego to a nearby hill to collect the roses he found there and deliver them to the bishop. It was not the season for roses; nonetheless, St. Juan Diego discovered a large patch of roses in full bloom. He filled his *tilma* (cloak) with the flowers and rushed to the bishop's residence. When Bishop Zumarraga received

RECENT INVESTIGATION OF THE IMAGE

Modern science has recently revealed some extraordinary characteristics of the apparition of Our Lady of Guadalupe. The *tilma*, upon which the image of Mary was received, was examined in 1977 with infrared photography and digital enhancement techniques. This study concluded that the method employed to create this image is unknown. The *tilma* shows absolutely no sketching or outline normally used by an artist to create such a painting. The image has retained its original colors despite having no protective covering for the first one hundred years of its existence (a *tilma* usually lasts no more than sixty) and having been exposed to a wide variety of environmental hazards, including floods and smoke. In addition, the scientists could not find any residue of dye or paint on the cloak.

In 1921, a bomb placed by a Freemason factory worker exploded right in front of the *tilma*. While the explosion severely twisted a cast-iron cross directly next to the *tilma* and damaged the marble altar rail, the *tilma* remained miraculously untouched.

Possibly even more miraculous was the discovery of images reflected in both eyes. First identified using photography in the 1920s, the image found in the right eye of the Virgin looks like that of a bearded man. In the 1950s, the same image, from a slightly different angle, was found in the Virgin's left eye. Since this discovery, many ophthalmologists have studied the Virgin's eyes, verifying the presence of the "triple reflection" phenomenon (also called the Samson-Purkinje effect). Discovered in the nineteenth century, the "triple reflection" phenomenon is caused by the reflection of an object on the surface of the cornea and the anterior and posterior surfaces of the eye lens. In addition, ophthalmologists discovered that the distortions of the images reflected in the eyes are consistent with the curvature of the cornea. In 1979 Dr. Jose Aste Tonsmann took high resolution photographs from the original image, and, after filtering and processing the digitized image, not only saw with astonishing clarity the same human image in both eyes, but also a group of Indians and Franciscans.

St. Juan Diego opened his cloak, and dozens of red roses fell to the floor. Appearing on his *tilma* was the image of Mary, a message to all the people of America.

St. Juan Diego, he asked about the sign. He opened his cloak and dozens of red roses fell to the floor. The bishop immediately fell to his knees, and St. Juan Diego eventually realized that Mary's image was imprinted on his *tilma* (cloak made of cactus fibers). This miracle prompted Bishop Zumarraga to build her church.

The image of Our Lady of Guadalupe was a message to all the people of America. In the image, Mary appeared greater than the sun, moon, stars, and all the pagan deities. Yet Mary was bowing in submission. She herself was not a god, the image seemed to say, but she prayed to the one God. The cross around her neck was the same that flew on Cortes' flag, and through this image, Indians began to embrace the Catholic Faith. For over four hundred thirty years, the image that first appeared on St. Juan Diego's cloak has expressed the protection of Our Lady for all the Americas. She is the patroness of the Americas. Her feast day is celebrated on December 12 in the universal Church.

SPANISH MISSIONS

Spanish missionaries wanted to create Indian communities away from the influence of the white settlers so that their efforts at evangelization would be untouched by the bad example and meddling of outsiders. They received permission from the king to found mission settlements. These missions gave Indians complete control over their own affairs. The Indians chose their own civic authorities and judges and were protected by their own warriors. Only the missionaries were able to visit these settlements. Two priests and up to four laymen were assigned to each community. They taught the Faith, established schools, and transcribed the spoken native language into a written language. They also taught natives reading and writing, modern farming techniques, and industrial crafts.

Between 1610 and 1767, thirty-two mission settlements were established within newly-acquired Spanish territories, ministering to over 700,000 neophyte Catholics. Father Bl. Junipero Serra began similar settlements along the coast of California. Bl. Junipero Serra founded nine missions, and his collaborators twelve more after his death, for a total of twenty-one California missions.

SLAVERY AND ST. PETER CLAVER

The Portuguese, like the Arabs in the Middle East and Africa, introduced slavery to Europe in the sixteenth century in an effort to solve its labor shortages. During their expeditions along the coast of Africa, Portuguese sailors enslaved many Africans and helped create a market for slave labor. As their trading empires grew, the Dutch and English would eventually dominate the traffic in African slaves in the West, bringing thousands of Africans to their colonies in North America. This dark period of European and American history lasted through the end of the nineteenth century.

The horrors of the slave trade were numerous and well-documented. Travel was extremely hazardous, and many of the Africans taken from Africa died during the long, disease-ridden voyages to the New World. Families suffered as children were separated from their parents and husbands from their wives.

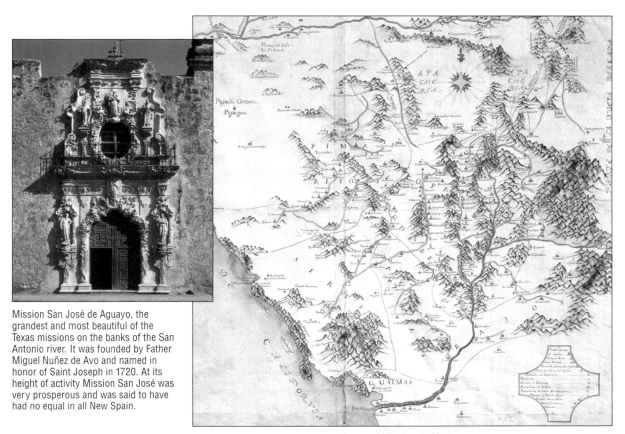

Mission San José de Aguayo, the grandest and most beautiful of the Texas missions on the banks of the San Antonio river. It was founded by Father Miguel Nuñez de Avo and named in honor of Saint Joseph in 1720. At its height of activity Mission San José was very prosperous and was said to have had no equal in all New Spain.

A map of Missions in Mexico.

In the Spanish missions, one missionary in particular did much to alleviate the suffering of the African slaves. In 1610, St. Peter Claver landed in Cartagena (Colombia), the chief slave market in the New World. He was appalled by the harsh, inhumane treatment of the African slaves, and decided to devote himself to their care. Although St. Peter Claver could not single-handedly stop the slave trade, for forty years he attempted to temper its evils. When ships arrived from Africa, St. Peter Claver would meet them on a pilot boat bringing food for the slaves. He helped care for the sick, tended their sores, and offered kind words and support to the wounded victims of the trade. After they arrived, while the slaves were waiting to be traded, St. Peter Claver instructed them in the Catholic Faith. During his tenure in Cartagena, he baptized over 300,000 slaves. He declared himself "the slave of the Negroes forever." St. Peter Claver's feast day is celebrated on September 9.

MISSIONARY ACTIVITY IN NORTH AMERICA

The French first colonized North America in the seventeenth century while searching for fur skins to sell in Europe. French trappers lived among the Indians and established trading posts along the St. Lawrence River Valley and down the Mississippi River to New Orleans. Jesuit missionaries accompanied the French settlers and made heroic efforts to convert the scattered Indian tribes that dominated the interior of the continent. Although their success was limited, the Jesuit missionaries persevered in faith and sanctity, even to the point of martyrdom.

Among these missionaries were the Jesuits St. John de Brébeuf and St. Isaac Jogues. St. John de Brébeuf arrived in Canada in 1625 and established a mission among the Huron Indians. For sixteen

THE POPES AND SLAVERY

Even before Columbus landed in the New World, the popes had already explicitly condemned the institution of slavery. Pope Eugene IV was the first pope to address this issue as it became manifested from the Age of Exploration. On January 13, 1435, Eugene IV sent the bull *Sicut dudum* (Not Long Ago) to Bishop Ferdinand, who had charge over the Canary Islands off northwest Africa. In it, Pope Eugene condemns the enslavement of the Guanches and other native peoples of the newly colonized Canary Islands. He writes in the bull:

> They have deprived the natives of their property or turned it to their own use, and have subjected some of the inhabitants of said islands to perpetual slavery, sold them to other persons and committed other various illicit and evil deeds against them . . . Therefore We . . . exhort, through the sprinkling of the Blood of Jesus Christ shed for their sins, one and all, . . . every kind among the Christian faithful . . . that they themselves desist from the afore-mentioned deeds, cause those subject to them to desist from them, and restrain them rigorously. And no less do We order and command all and each of the faithful of each sex that, . . . they restore to their earlier liberty all and each person of either sex who were once residents of said Canary Islands . . . who have been made subject to slavery.

After the discovery of the New World, and as European colonizers expanded the institution of slavery into the newly discovered lands, Pope Paul III (1534-1549) wrote again about the evils of slavery. In his pontifical decree *Sublimis Deus* (The Sublime God), Pope Paul III condemns those "who, desiring to satisfy their own avarice, are presuming to assert far and wide that the Indians of the West and the South who have come to our notice in these times be reduced to our service like brute animals, under the pretext that they are lacking the Catholic faith." Instead, the pope argues, "the Indians themselves indeed are true men and are not only capable of the Christian faith, but, as has been made known to us, promptly hasten to the faith."

The popes continued to condemn slavery throughout the following centuries. Even when slavery took on new forms, such as the exploitation of workers during the industrial revolution of the nineteenth century, the popes issued teachings that condemned any infringement on the inherent human dignity of all men and women.

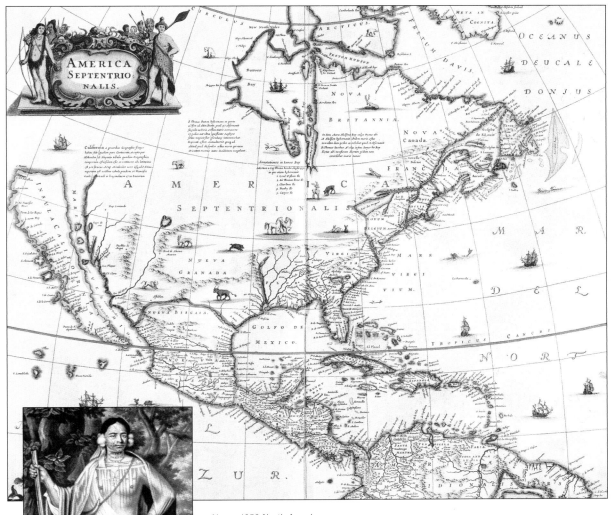

Above: 1653 North American map.
Left: Engraving of an Iroquois Chief from 1710. His linen shirt, wool blanket, beaded moccasins, and musket are the result of contact with European traders.

years St. John de Brébeuf endured grueling poverty as he worked to evangelize the Indian tribes. In 1647, war broke out among the Huron and Iroquois tribes, and although St. John de Brébeuf and his missionaries had the opportunity to leave the area, they chose to stay with their mission. In March 1649, St. John de Brébeuf was seized by Iroquois Indians and tortured mercilessly before being killed in a disgusting and blasphemous fashion. Boiling water was poured over his head in a mockery of Baptism and a red-hot iron was thrust down his throat. Throughout the entire ordeal, St. John de Brébeuf never cried out in pain, suffering his torment in silence.

St. Isaac Jogues also suffered at the hands of the Iroquois tribes. While working on a mission near the Great Lakes, he was taken prisoner in August 1642 and forced into slavery for thirteen months. When St. Isaac Jogues was rescued, he was near death and the fingers of his hands were mutilated from being bitten off. St. Isaac Jogues returned to France, but soon insisted upon returning to Canada to negotiate a peace settlement to the Indian wars. St. Isaac Jogues returned to Canada and was successful with the negotiations at first. Unfortunately, blight struck the crops in the region, and some Indians accused him of sorcery, insisting that the priest had caused the famine. In 1646 Iroquois warriors seized St. Isaac Jogues and beat him to death with a tomahawk. Sts. John de Brébeuf, Isaac Jogues, and their companions, known as the North American martyrs, share a feast day celebrated on October 19.

FOUNDING THE CATHOLIC COLONY OF MARYLAND

Unlike the Spanish and French missionaries, English Catholics came to the New World in order to seek refuge from fierce persecution in their native country and practice the Faith. In 1632, the Lord of Baltimore, George Calvert, used his influence with King Charles I to gain a charter for colonization. The king granted the charter, and Calvert and a group Catholics left England to establish the colony of Maryland.

At first, Catholics and Protestants coexisted peacefully in Maryland thanks to the Act of Toleration (1649). The act was originally passed to pacify conflict between English Protestants and French Canadians, but some Protestants in Maryland soon felt that it did not protect the English Catholic settlers. As Protestant numbers grew in Maryland, Catholics began to suffer restrictions on their religious freedom. In order to protect the Catholic minority in the colony, the colonial representative legislature was split into two parts. This precedent would eventually influence the establishment of a bicameral (two-house) legislature specified by the U.S. Constitution.

Maryland was not the only safe haven for Catholics in America. Pennsylvania also granted religious toleration to Catholics. Set up as a Quaker colony, Pennsylvania allowed the free expression of any Christian religion. The American Revolution solidified freedom for the Catholic faithful in all the colonies by creating a republic which endorsed and promoted religious toleration. Non-establishment of religion would be legally enshrined in the first amendment to the Constitution. After the revolution, the Holy See appointed John Carroll of Baltimore, the brother of one of the signers of the Declaration of Independence, as the first Catholic bishop in the United States.

CONCLUSION

In spite of the tragic divisions between the Protestants and Catholics in sixteenth century Europe, divine providence was at work in the newly-discovered lands. As millions of Christians separated from the Church of Rome, millions of indigenous peoples of the New World of Central and South America embraced the Catholic Faith. The lands of Asia, most notably the Philippines, also produced an extraordinary number of converts to the Faith. This unparalleled period of evangelization is highlighted by the apparition of Our Lady of Guadalupe, whose appearance served as a moving sign and offered hope to the New World, and the rest of the world, that her Son, in words of John Paul II, is the "Lord of history."

SUPPLEMENTARY READING

Fr. Bartolome de las Casas, *History of the Indians*

To erect crosses and to invite the Indians to show them respect is a good thing, provided that one can make them understand the significance of these acts. But if one does not have enough time, or cannot speak their language, it is useless and superfluous, because the Indians can suppose that one is offering them a new idol which represents the God of the Christians. In this way one may be encouraging them to revere a piece of wood as a god, which is idolatry. The safest way to proceed, the only rule which Christians should observe when they are in pagan countries, is to give a good example by virtuous works, in such a way that, according to the words of our redeemer, "seeing your works, they may praise and glorify your father" and may think that a God who has such worshippers can only be good and true.

St. Francis Xavier on his method in India

When the prayers were over, I gave them in their own language an explanation of the articles of faith and the commandments of the law. Then I made all of them ask forgiveness publicly from God our lord for their past life.... After the sermon, I asked them all, men and children, if they really believed the articles of faith. They all told me that they did, so I recited each of the articles in a loud voice.

After each article I asked them if they believed, and crossing their arms in front of me they told me that they did. Then I baptized them, writing down the names of each one for them. The men then returned home and sent their wives and families for me to baptize in the same way as I had baptized them. When I had finished the baptizing, I sent them to tear down the buildings in which they kept their idols, and once they were Christians I made them break the statues of the idols into little pieces.

Pope John Paul II, *Crossing the Threshold of Hope*, 11

A great new wave of evangelization began at the end of the fifteenth century, originating above all in Spain and Portugal. This is all the more extraordinary because it was precisely in that period, after the schism between the Eastern and Western Churches in the eleventh century, that the tragic division in the West was taking place. By now the great splendor of the medieval papacy was past; the Protestant Reformation was spreading rapidly. At the very moment in which the Roman Church was losing the peoples north of the Alps, Providence opened up new prospects. With the discovery of America, the evangelization of that entire hemisphere, from north to south, was set in motion.

VOCABULARY

ANIMISM
Superstitious religious belief that attributes human qualities to material objects or non-human living creatures.

BONZES
Japanese Buddhist monks who saw St. Francis Xavier and his missionaries as a danger to their established influence; they worked to oust him from Japan.

COLUMBIAN EXCHANGE
Commercial revolution brought about by the discovery of the New World in which traders introduced new goods and materials to Europe.

CONQUISTADORS
Sometimes bold adventurers, other times opportunistic soldiers of fortune, they were sent by Spain to the Americas to help establish and secure Spanish landholdings.

DE PROPAGANDA FIDE
Congregation founded by Pope Gregory XV to promote and establish apostolic missions.

LAWS OF BURGOS
Laws passed by the Spanish crown at the request of Bishop Bartolome de las Casas which protected the rights of the Indians.

LINE OF DEMARCATION
Drawn up by Pope Alexander VI, this line split the newly-discovered lands into two areas, ceding to Spain all newly discovered lands 100 leagues west of the Azores and beyond; it ceded to Portugal all newly discovered lands east of this line.

MERCANTILISM
Economic system adopted by European nations that was based on the premise that a nation could best secure wealth and power by exporting more than it imported.

QUETZALCOATL
Warrior god of the Aztec people.

St. THOMAS CHRISTIANS
Group of Christians in India who are descended from the original missionary activity of St. Thomas the Apostle.

TILMA
Cloak worn by Indians in Mexico. It was on his *tilma* that Our Lady of Guadalupe left her image to St. Juan Diego.

STUDY QUESTIONS

1. Before 1500, what was the predominant avenue of trade for Europe?

2. Who dominated trade in the fifteenth century?

3. How did Henry the Navigator advance technical innovation?

4. Which two men enabled Portugal to establish a commercial empire in Asia?

5. Where did Christopher Columbus land on his first trip?

6. What did Pope Alexander VI do to avoid bloodshed between the Spanish and Portuguese?

7. What effect did the discovery of the New World have on Spain?

8. Whose ship was the first to circumnavigate the globe?

9. Who were the Conquistadors?

10. What was the Columbian exchange?

STUDY QUESTIONS Continued

11. What were the social consequences of the discovery of the New World?

12. What was mercantilism?

13. How did England avoid falling behind the mercantile economies?

14. How did Portugal solve its labor shortages?

15. How did the Church respond to new opportunities for conversion?

16. What were some obstacles faced by the missionaries?

17. Where did St. Francis Xavier carry on his missionary work?

18. Who carried on evangelization in India, and how did he do it?

19. Who evangelized in China, and what was his approach?

20. What hindered evangelization in Japan?

21. What delayed the spread of the Faith in Africa?

22. What was the first civilization encountered by the Spanish, and who conquered it?

23. When did the Franciscans begin their work in Mexico?

24. What was the second civilization encountered by the Spanish, and who conquered it?

25. To whom and where did Our Lady of Guadalupe appear?

26. What was the direct result of Mary's appearance?

27. How many missions were established between 1610 and 1767 in Spanish lands?

28. Who founded the California missions, and how many did he found?

PRACTICAL EXERCISES

1. What scientific developments helped bring about the Age of Exploration? Would it be correct to say that exploration resulted from science and technology? What other factors helped bring about this period of discovery and adventure?

2. What were the major obstacles, physical and cultural, to Catholic missionary activity? How did the missionaries overcome these obstacles?

3. Choose a contemporary culture, either in the United States or elsewhere, and explain how a missionary could adapt his or her lifestyle in order to earn that culture's trust. Choose a Gospel story, and retell it in a way suited to that specific culture.

4. How was European exploration and colonization good for natives in the Americas? How was it detrimental? How did northern and southern Europeans differ in their treatment of the natives of the New World?

FROM THE CATECHISM

153 When St. Peter confessed that Jesus is the Christ, the Son of the living God, Jesus declared to him that this revelation did not come "from flesh and blood," but from "my Father who is in heaven" (Mt 16:17; cf. Gal 1:15; Mt 11:25). *Faith is a gift of God, a supernatural virtue infused by him.* "Before this faith can be exercised, man must have the grace of God to move and assist him; he must have the interior helps of the Holy Spirit, who moves the heart and converts it to God, who opens the eyes of the mind and 'makes it easy for all to accept and believe the truth'" (*DV* 5; cf. DS 377; 3010).

160 To be human, "man's response to God by faith must be free, and...therefore nobody is to be forced to embrace the faith against his will. The act of faith is of its very nature a free act" (*DH* 10; cf. CIC, can. 748 § 2). "God calls men to serve him in spirit and in truth. Consequently they are bound to him in conscience, but not coerced...This fact received its fullest manifestation in Christ Jesus" (*DH* 11). Indeed, Christ invited people to faith and conversion, but never coerced them. "For he bore witness to the truth but refused to use force to impose it on those who spoke against it. His kingdom...grows by the love with which Christ, lifted up on the cross, draws men to himself" (*DH* 11; cf. Jn 18:37; 12:32).

836 "All men are called to this catholic unity of the People of God....And to it, in different ways, belong or are ordered: the Catholic faithful, others who believe in Christ, and finally all mankind, called by God's grace to salvation" (*LG* 13).

849 *The missionary mandate.* "Having been divinely sent to the nations that she might be 'the universal sacrament of salvation,' the Church, in obedience to the command of her founder and because it is demanded by her own essential universality, strives to preach the Gospel to all men" (*AG* 1; cf. Mt 16:15): "Go therefore and make disciples of all nations, baptizing them in the name of the Father and of the Son and of the Holy Spirit, teaching them to observe all that I have commanded you; and Lo, I am with you always, until the close of the age" (Mt 28:19-20).

856 The missionary task implies a *respectful dialogue* with those who do not yet accept the Gospel (cf. *RMiss* 55). Believers can profit from this dialogue by learning to appreciate better "those elements of truth and grace which are found among peoples, and which are, as it were, a secret presence of God" (*AG* 9). They proclaim the Good News to those who do not know it, in order to consolidate, complete, and raise up the truth and the goodness that God has distributed among men and nations, and to purify them from error and evil "for the glory of God, the confusion of the demon, and the happiness of man" (*AG* 9).

900 Since, like all the faithful, lay Christians are entrusted by God with the apostolate by virtue of their Baptism and Confirmation, they have the right and duty, individually or grouped in associations, to work so that the divine message of salvation may be known and accepted by all men throughout the earth. This duty is the more pressing when it is only through them that men can hear the Gospel and know Christ. Their activity in ecclesial communities is so necessary that, for the most part, the apostolate of the pastors cannot be fully effective without it (cf. *LG* 33).

905 Lay people also fulfill their prophetic mission by evangelization, "that is, the proclamation of Christ by word and the testimony of life." For lay people, "this evangelization...acquires a specific property and peculiar efficacy because it is accomplished in the ordinary circumstances of the world" (*LG* 35 § 1, § 2).

This witness of life, however, is not the sole element in the apostolate; the true apostle is on the lookout for occasions of announcing Christ by word, either to unbelievers...or to the faithful. (*AA* 6 § 3; cf. *AG* 15)

CHAPTER 16

The Church And The Age Of Enlightenment

Out of the rubble of the religious wars rose strong monarchs who desired absolute control of their realms. Intellectuals focused on the individual and reason, challenging traditional philosophy and the Church.

CHAPTER 16

The Church And The Age Of Enlightenment

We are aware that, unfortunately, much of modern, atheistic, agnostic, secularized thought persistently states and teaches that the supreme question is in fact a human malady, a psychological and emotional exaggeration, from which we need to be cured by bravely facing up to the absurd, to death, to nothingness....Jesus Christ alone is the adequate and final answer to the supreme question about the meaning of life and history!

— John Paul II, *Address to Italian Servicemen*, March 1, 1979.

The Reformation, and the wars that followed, brought to a close an era of a united Western Christendom. Out of the rubble of religious wars rose strong monarchs who looked to solidify control before their realms slipped back into internal turmoil. Typified by Louis XIV of France, monarchs began reorganizing their nations and assuming absolute power over their domains. Their efforts would unleash new tensions between kings and subjects, resulting in the emergence of constitutional monarchies together with various new political philosophies.

These new philosophies in significant part found their origins in the Renaissance and Reformation. They focused on the rights of the individual and the power of reason as a replacement for religious beliefs, which had caused so much tension in the past. Beginning with the scientific revolution in the seventeenth century, which significantly contributed to the eighteenth-century Age of Enlightenment, rulers, scientists, and philosophers throughout Europe challenged political authority, traditional philosophy, and the value of the Church. The proponents of the Enlightenment would conceive philosophies that would dismiss the guiding light of divine revelation and the Church's teaching authority. These new ideas, some of which were divorced from Christian principles, would give rise to revolutions that would do enormous harm to the Catholic Church.

The Church, in the aftermath of Trent, suffered over the wars of religion and the challenges of implementing the conciliar reforms. Throughout Europe, traditional beliefs and authority were being called constantly into question. New discoveries were providing greater confidence in the

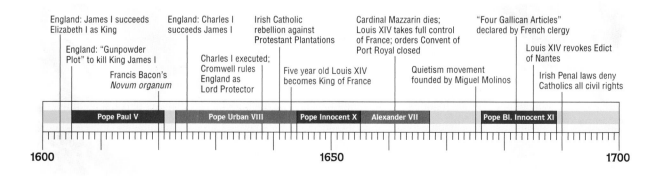

England: James I succeeds Elizabeth I as King

England: "Gunpowder Plot" to kill King James I

Francis Bacon's *Novum organum*

England: Charles I succeeds James I

Charles I executed; Cromwell rules England as Lord Protector

Irish Catholic rebellion against Protestant Plantations

Five year old Louis XIV becomes King of France

Cardinal Mazzarin dies; Louis XIV takes full control of France; orders Convent of Port Royal closed

Quietism movement founded by Miguel Molinos

"Four Gallican Articles" declared by French clergy

Louis XIV revokes Edict of Nantes

Irish Penal laws deny Catholics all civil rights

Pope Paul V | Pope Urban VIII | Pope Innocent X | Alexander VII | Pope Bl. Innocent XI

1600 | 1650 | 1700

role of reason, and as the human mind penetrated the laws and mysteries of the material world, this newfound knowledge led some thinkers to give primacy to human reason over the truths of the Faith and the teachings of the Church. The Church would have to contend with the increasing influence of civil rulers on Church matters and the influence of new ideas that eventually challenged the whole deposit of the Catholic Faith. Amid rising trends of atheism, agnosticism, and secularism, the Church would have to stand by her anchor, so well stated by John Paul II: "Jesus Christ alone is the adequate and final answer to the supreme question about the meaning of life and history!"

PART I

King Louis' France

After the Thirty Years War, the Treaty of Westphalia helped determine the balance of power on the European continent for nearly two centuries. France emerged as the dominant power, while Germany remained divided into some three hundred semi-independent states. Cardinal Richelieu, the regent to Louis XIII, was as much responsible for dividing Germany in the Treaty of Westphalia as he was for uniting France under a strong monarchy.

By the end of the Thirty Years War, France, too, was politically fragmented due to the recent religious conflicts and found herself composed of some three hundred feudal provinces. Against these obstacles, Richelieu worked to unify the country. He broadened the powers of the Bourbon kings and ended the toleration of Protestants. Henry IV's Edict of Nantes, he argued, created a state within a state, and for Richelieu, only strict loyalty to the King of France could provide effective cohesion in the realm. His policies cultivated a political environment ripe for a king to rule with absolute power over the entire country.

Shortly after the Cardinal's death, an Englishman named Thomas Hobbes wrote a celebrated and influential work, which would help verify Richelieu's policies among certain thinkers. Hobbes' book, *Leviathan*, painted a grim vision of man. Hobbes described man as a selfish beast who, if left alone to his own whims, would live a life described as "solitary, poor, nasty, brutish, and short" (cf. *Leviathan*, chapter 13). Without the imposition of a strong political structure, people would destroy each other and society would wither and collapse. He argued that the state must impose unity from above, preferably through an absolute authority which could solve this natural tendency toward mutual hostility. Inspired by Richelieu's efforts and Hobbes' ideas, states throughout Europe strongly asserted the authority of the crown. The king who most epitomized this trend was Louis XIV of France.

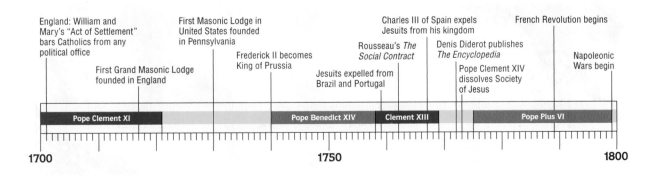

England: William and Mary's "Act of Settlement" bars Catholics from any political office

First Grand Masonic Lodge founded in England

First Masonic Lodge in United States founded in Pennsylvania

Frederick II becomes King of Prussia

Jesuits expelled from Brazil and Portugal

Rousseau's *The Social Contract*

Charles III of Spain expels Jesuits from his kingdom

Denis Diderot publishes *The Encyclopedia*

Pope Clement XIV dissolves Society of Jesus

French Revolution begins

Napoleonic Wars begin

Pope Clement XI   Pope Benedict XIV   Clement XIII   Pope Pius VI

1700   1750   1800

LOUIS XIV, THE SUN KING

Louis XIV ascended the throne in 1643 at the age of five. Too young to rule, power fell to another regent, Richelieu's successor, Cardinal Mazzarin. Mazzarin was so unpopular among the nobility that while Louis was still young, the nobility tried to rally against the king's rising power. The nobles came together to form an opposition group called the *Fronde* (French for "rebellion"). However, the *Fronde* was not a unified body, and Mazzarin was able to use the internal divisions between the nobles to suppress the rebellion. Rather than loosening the control of the king, the *Fronde* proved in the mind of the young king the necessity to control powerful noble factions. When Mazzarin died in 1661, the twenty-three-year-old Louis took tight hold of the reins of power and for the next fifty-four years kept France firmly under his thumb.

To secure his power, Louis first dismissed all the great lords of France and anyone who could claim power through noble birth. The king freed these nobles from taxation in a shrewd move that in effect removed them from any interference in the affairs of his government. Instead, he turned the affairs of government over to persons belonging to minor families. Without any prior hope for such esteemed positions, these lower nobles felt eternally indebted to the king, assuring the king unfailing loyalty. He replaced the traditional feudal power structure with a central bureaucracy centered around himself.

More than imposing absolute power, Louis XIV himself embodied it. He loudly proclaimed, "I am the state," and in many ways he was. In Louis' France, the entire well-being of the country lay in his decisions, moods, and generosity. Law and privilege all flowed from the king, and the guarantee of one's position meant living in the presence of the king and securing his good graces. Nobles of all backgrounds vied with each other at the great palace of Versailles to gain the king's favor, and with it, a better livelihood. As Louis' persona took on divine proportions, he became known as the "Sun King." "To live in the awesome presence of the Sun King," one contemporary remarked, "was like living in the presence of God" (quoted in Blitzer, *Age of Kings*, 1967, p. 61).

GALLICANISM

Since the conflict between Pope Boniface VIII and King Philip IV in 1303, the relationship between the Church and the kings of France became strained. Throughout the Middle Ages, French kings attempted to control the affairs of the Church in France and appoint their own bishops. Philip IV asserted the independence of the French Church from Rome, and his successor Charles VII formally declared this independence with the Pragmatic Sanction of Bourges in 1438. Although in 1516 Pope Leo X persuaded Francis I to abolish the Pragmatic Sanction, the principles of an independent national or "Gallican" Church of France were deeply entrenched in the country. Louis XIV, who was strongly affected by the Gallican tradition, was a strong proponent of an independent Church in France.

Not surprisingly, as Louis XIV moved to control every aspect of French society, he especially tried to exert his influence over the Church in France. As monarch, Louis saw himself as king and high priest, subject only to God. This belief manifested itself in both his policies and his personal life. He was devoted to his faith and attended daily Mass. He felt a particular devotion to the Rosary and often made retreats in monasteries. On Holy Thursdays, Louis would kneel down, wash the feet of the poor in imitation of Christ, and serve them a meal. His actions were not a mere political show, but rather prompted by true religious sentiment. Louis exemplified an authentic spirituality that was rare for a king at the time.

King Louis' difficulties with the Church arose over administration, not from matters of doctrine and spirituality. King Louis believed that everyone in France should be subject to his reign, both lay and

Louis XIV "The Sun King" (1638-1715) reigned as King of France and King of Navarre from May 14, 1643, until his death. As monarch, Louis saw himself as king and high priest, subject only to God. He felt a particular devotion to the Rosary and often made retreats in monasteries. On Holy Thursdays, Louis would kneel down, wash the feet of the poor in imitation of Christ, and serve them a meal. This famous portrait of Louis is by Hyacinthe Rigaud and records for us to see the extremes of power and vanity.

clergy. He believed that his authority extended into matters of Church supervision and even doctrinal issues. In spite of his authoritarian disposition, Louis XIV tried to keep a delicate balance between his directives and those coming from the ecclesiastical authorities in Rome. Nevertheless, his relations with the Church often alternated between submission and schism.

The following examples demonstrate Louis' docility to Church authority. When the Sorbonne University in Paris was censored by the Church for condemning papal teachings on infallibility, Louis did not object. When one of Louis' ministers tried to limit the number of priests in France, the Church condemned his actions, and Louis ordered the minister to abandon the policy.

On the other hand, there are many instances of Louis' resistance to Church rulings and decisions. For example, asserting "Gallican" privileges, Louis collected revenues from vacant ecclesiastical benefices. The pope naturally protested, and Louis formed an assembly of French clergy to draft a declaration asserting the authority of the Gallican Church. In 1682, the assembly issued a declaration known as the "Four Gallican Articles." These articles attempted to resurrect the heresies that claimed that the king of France was independent of the pope in temporal matters and that a general council enjoyed higher authority than that of the pope. Papal authority, they argued, was limited to ecclesiastical law and the pope's dogmatic decisions were not irrevocable until approved by a council.

Establishing himself as head of the Gallican Church, Louis ordered these principles to be taught in all the seminaries in France. Pope Bl. Innocent XI condemned these articles and threatened to excommunicate the king. The pope put further pressure on the king by refusing to appoint new bishops to vacant sees that had participated in the assembly of 1682. The conflict turned into a standoff between the king and the pope and nearly ended in schism.

It was not until 1693 that a compromise was reached. Louis XIV agreed to disavow the declarations of 1682 and end the mandatory teaching of the "Four Gallican Articles." In return, Bl. Innocent XI agreed to appoint all of the bishops Louis had nominated for the vacant sees in France. Despite this compromise, which respected the authority of Rome, the principles of Gallicanism continued to dominate the ecclesiastical community in France until the French Revolution in 1789, and would be resurrected again to a lesser degree within the Organic Articles of the 1801 Concordat.

The army of Louis XIV crosses the Rhine to attack the Netherlands in 1672. In a coalition with Charles II, France and England declared war on the Seven United Provinces (the Netherlands). Louis gained more territory in the Low Countries and regained the Franche-Comté (the former County of Burgundy) which France had lost to Spain in the 1668 Treaty of Aix-la-Chapelle.

THE COURTLY LIFE OF THE SUN KING

Molière at breakfast with King Louis XIV. Molière (1622-1673) whose real name was Jean-Baptiste Poquelin was a great French playwright, director, actor, and master of comic satire. In 1658 his theater troupe, the Illustre Theatre, played before Louis XIV. As a result, the king's brother became Molière's patron and Molière and his colleagues were appointed official providers of entertainment to the Sun King.

Life in the court of Louis XIV was regimented and regular. Each day followed a strict schedule in which the king received officials and dignitaries, attended Mass, enjoyed public meals, and participated in sport.

The king woke each morning at 8:30 and was groomed by a number of attendants who washed him and shaved him in a ceremonial fashion. After he was groomed, the king would eat a breakfast of broth during which he would meet with nearly a hundred important officials to discuss matters of the kingdom.

After breakfast, the king attended Mass at ten o'clock where his private choir sang new compositions for the liturgy. After Mass, Louis held council with his cabinet at eleven o'clock at the royal apartments. On Sundays and Wednesdays they discussed the affairs of the state, and on Tuesdays and Saturdays they dealt with finances. Mondays, Thursdays, and Fridays were spent discussing either domestic or religious issues. During these councils, the king spoke very little as the ministers informed and advised the king.

Lunch was taken at one o'clock in the king's bedchamber. Although the meal was supposed to be private, Louis XIV often met with various dignitaries as he did at breakfast. After lunch, the king then enjoyed an afternoon of hunting or walks during which he could enjoy either in the magnificent gardens of Versailles or the surrounding forests.

The evenings were spent socially, beginning with a six o'clock social gathering followed by supper at ten o'clock, which many members of the royal family attended. After dinner was over, Louis either returned to his bedchamber or spoke with his close acquaintances. Bedtime, called the *couchee*, was similar to Louis' rising. The king was groomed and prepared for a night of sleep.

JANSENISM

Cornelius Jansen

There were a number of heresies that were popular in France during the reign of Louis XIV, but none affected the nobility as profoundly as Jansenism. Jansenism is named after its founder Cornelius Jansen (1585-1638), the Bishop of Ypres (Belgium). Early in his life, Jansen applied for entrance into the Jesuit order, but was rejected. A brilliant scholar, he nonetheless went on to become a priest and devoted himself to studying the works of St. Augustine of Hippo.

During his studies, Jansen became attracted to what he thought was a new way of understanding St. Augustine's understanding of grace. Believing he uncovered an overlooked truth of Catholicism, Jansen dedicated his life to formulating his own theory of grace and recording his ideas in his monumental work *Augustinus.*

The ideas of Jansen seemed to adapt a rigid Calvinist approach to Catholic teaching. According to the five principles of *Augustinus*, man was entirely free in the state of innocence and his will tended to do what was right. But original sin made man a slave to sin and all his actions reflected a sin-ridden soul. His only hope was God's grace, which could save him. But Jansen taught that God only granted salvific grace to a small number of people. According to Jansen, Christ did not die for all men, since most people were predestined to damnation. The austere theology that grew out of these teachings eventually denied the validity of the Sacrament of Penance and taught that only the "just" or predestined should receive Holy Communion.

During his life, Jansen's ideas were unknown and the thinker himself never intended to contradict the Church's teachings. He shared his ideas with his close friend, Jean-Ambroise Duyegier, the Abbot of St. Cyran, and left his book to his friend for publication upon his death with the disclaimer to accept whatever decision the Church made concerning his book. After Jansen died, Jean-Ambroise promoted his friend's work, and it soon became very popular throughout France and Belgium. Antoine Arnauld (1612-1694), a French philosopher who wrote his doctoral thesis on space, was closely associated with the famous convent which housed nuns of Jansenist persuasion, Port Royal, for three years. He effectively promoted the theology and thought of Cornelius Jansen. It is interesting to note that the celebrated

The Jansenist artist Philippe de Champaigne had two daughters educated at the Convent of Port Royal. One daughter, Catherine, remained there as a nun. This painting portrays the healing of his daughter's paralysis in 1661 by the prayers of the prioress, Mère Agnes Arnauld.

French mathematician Blaise Pascal (1623-1662) wrote anonymously in defense of the spirit of Port Royal. In his writings he atacked the casuistry—at least according to his perception—of the Jesuits and advocated a more effective relationship with Christ.

In 1653 Pope Innocent X condemned Jansenism and pointed to the teachings of the Council of Trent on God's grace to support his position. Innocent insisted that the Church teaches that God wills for everyone to be saved. God gives sufficient grace to each person for salvation, and everyone is given a free will which is designed to cooperate with God's grace. Trent taught that the Sacrament of Penance conferred sufficient grace to forgive all sins and that Holy Communion purifies the soul from venial sin and strengthens it against mortal sin.

Despite official condemnation, Jansenism continued to spread in France. After Pope Innocent X condemned Jansenism as heresy, Louis XIV saw the Jansenists as schismatic and threatening to his royal authority. He responded swiftly and strictly at the administrative and intellectual center of Jansenism, the Convent of Port Royal. As an extreme measure to erase the example of Port Royal and prevent the site from becoming a center of Jansenist pilgrimage, Louis ordered the entire convent razed in 1709 and had the bodies of the cemetery of the convent exhumed and placed in unmarked graves.

QUIETISM

Another heresy that developed during the reign of Louis XIV was Quietism. Founded around the year 1675 by a well-known confessor, Miguel Molinos, Quietism advocated absolute passivity during prayers and contemplation. The soul, according to Molinos, should be indifferent to everything, including temptation, and should simply rest perpetually in God. Unlike Jansenism, asceticism was not necessary, since it was sufficient for the soul to humble itself in order for God to accept someone with sins. Some Quietists even taught that God allowed demons to make persons perform sinful acts. One must make no effort to fight sin, they would say, but rather let the demon have his way. By stressing total abandonment in God, without the need for personal effort, the Quietist's spirituality leaned towards excessive comfort. Personal prayer and the Sacraments were unnecessary for the Quietist who believed merely in immersing oneself in God in order to find complete spiritual tranquility. Both King Louis XIV and Pope Bl. Innocent XI condemned Quietism in 1687.

REVOCATION OF THE EDICT OF NANTES

In addition to suppressing the Jansenist and Quietist movements in France, King Louis XIV put a stop to the last vestiges of autonomy held by the Huguenots under the 1598 Edict of Nantes. Although Cardinal Richelieu had reduced the rights held by Protestants in France, Louis XIV demanded the abolition of all heretical movements. In 1681, Louis XIV granted special privileges to those who renounced Calvinism, and he deprived the Huguenots of many rights and privileges. Many insurrections broke out over Louis' actions, and although Bl. Innocent XI tried to encourage the king to be tolerant to Protestants living within France, Louis XIV saw the Huguenots as disloyal subjects and attempted to force conversion to the Catholic Faith. He revoked the Edict of Nantes in 1685 and prohibited the Huguenots from practicing their religion. Huguenot churches

In October 1685, King Louis XIV issued the Edict of Fontainebleau, which revoked the 1598 Edict of Nantes.

and schools were destroyed and congregations were banished from France. Many Huguenots fled to Prussia, England, and the Low Countries to escape Louis' persecution. Louis' actions resulted in retaliation against Catholics in countries like Ireland, England, and Holland, which were dominated by Protestant rulers.

Charles I was king of England, Scotland and Ireland from March 27, 1625, until his execution on January 30, 1649. He engaged in a struggle for power with Parliament. He was an advocate of the divine right of kings. His struggles with ecclesiastical affairs—denying episcopal rights to the Scots and the victorious English parliamentarians—brought about his execution.

PART II

The Stuart Kings of England

Monarchs throughout Europe sought to replicate the ruling style of Louis XIV. In England, after the death of Elizabeth I, the Stuart kings rose to the throne and began efforts to solidify an absolutist monarchy. Their efforts set in motion conflicts that would lead to the development of a constitutional democracy based on a parliamentary form of government. Despite England's political democratic leanings, Catholics living in the British Isles continued to be persecuted, and that persecution only intensified under the Puritan dictator Oliver Cromwell who seized power in 1649. The Stuart Kings eventually regained power, and the Catholic Faith was once again tolerated. However, the "Glorious Revolution" in 1688 guaranteed the permanent succession of a Protestant on the throne and the status of Catholics as second-class citizens.

JAMES I AND CHARLES I

The death of Elizabeth I ended the Tudor line, and the son of Mary Queen of Scots, James I (a Stuart), succeeded Elizabeth to the throne in 1603. Despite his mother's fervent Catholic faith, James was raised a Protestant by Mary's half brother, and any question of James' affection for the Catholic Church was soon dispelled after the famed "Gunpowder Plot" of 1605. In the Gunpowder Plot, Guy Fawkes, a Catholic, plotted to blow up the king and Parliament. He failed, and in retribution, James renewed persecution of Catholics throughout England. Like Louis XIV, religion was very important to the English king as a means to solidify his authority. Under James I, Catholic education at home and abroad was totally prohibited. It was against the law to serve as a priest, and heavy fines were imposed on anyone who missed Anglican Sunday services.

Equally threatening to the king's power was the growing influence of Calvinism in England. James tolerated Puritan churches, but tithes had to be paid to the Anglican Church (to show loyalty to the English crown). Disgruntled by this taxation, a small band of Puritan separatists, called Pilgrims, left

Oliver Cromwell (1599-1658). After leading the overthrow of the British monarchy and executing King Charles I, Cromwell ruled England, Scotland, and Ireland as Lord Protector until his death. During his ten year reign, a genocide was attempted against the Catholics of Ireland.

England during the reign of James I and set up a colony in the New World in September 1620. Catholics would also take advantage of the religious toleration that the New World offered, and in 1634 George Calvert received royal permission to create a colony in the New World as a refuge for Catholics. That colony, Maryland, was populated by more Catholics than any other English colony in the New World.

Charles I succeeded his father James in 1625. Unlike James, who was considered a foreigner from Scotland, Charles had been born in England, and he thought he could use the advantage of his English heredity to expand the limits of royal authority. Charles tried to increase royal revenues and centralize the English bureaucracy around the crown. However, without guarantees of religious toleration, the Calvinist-dominated Parliament refused to grant Charles enough money to carry out his policies. Charles responded by ruling on his own without Parliament for twelve years. When a war with Scotland broke out, Charles was forced to convene Parliament to help raise much-needed troops. The war did not go well for the king, and after attempting to force Anglican uniformity on his Scottish and Puritan subjects, the English Civil War of 1642-

1649 broke out. Out of the war rose the Calvinist dictator Oliver Cromwell who seized power, established a harsh puritanical regime, and beheaded King Charles I.

Cromwell ruled England as "Lord Protector" from 1648 to 1658. His inability to come to terms with both the King and Parliament forced him to establish his own rule in the form of a military dictatorship based on Puritan principles. During his decade-long reign, Catholic faithful throughout the British Isles were persecuted with great vigor, and especially the people of Ireland suffered terribly.

PERSECUTION OF THE IRISH

Catholics in Ireland had suffered persecution ever since the time of Henry VIII. As English Protestant rulers worked to secure their power, they promoted successive policies designed to eradicate the Catholic population from the Emerald Isle. Irish bishops and priests were executed and exiled, access to even the most elementary of educations denied, lands seized, famine frequent, Masses and the sacraments illegal, and the Irish language (Gaelic) forbidden.

The situation in Ireland grew even worse under James I who established the first "Plantations" on the island. Plantations were large areas in the northeastern part of the island that were cleared of Catholics (without compensation for the lands) and resettled by Scottish Protestants. The idea was that the Protestants would eventually "breed-out" the Catholics. The effects of this policy are still felt today as both Catholic and Protestant Irish feel that they have a hereditary right to the land in Northern Ireland, thus making peace in the region terribly difficult. In 1641, rebellion broke throughout Ireland in retaliation to the Protestant "Planters," and about three thousand Protestants were killed.

After Oliver Cromwell defeated Charles I in 1648, he led a military campaign throughout Ireland. Cromwell entered Ireland with ten thousand troops, and at Drogheda and Wexford, his forces massacred every defender. Entire towns were destroyed, and properties were confiscated and given to the Protestants. Cromwell planned to create a huge plantation that covered most of Ireland. He sought to kill one-third of all Catholics in Ireland and enslave another third, forcibly raising their children Protestant. The remainder of Ireland, the most destitute portion, was to become a penal colony. Although Cromwell failed to destroy the Catholic Faith in Ireland, his invasion turned the country into a wasteland.

The Effect of Cromwell's Persecutions on Catholic Landowners

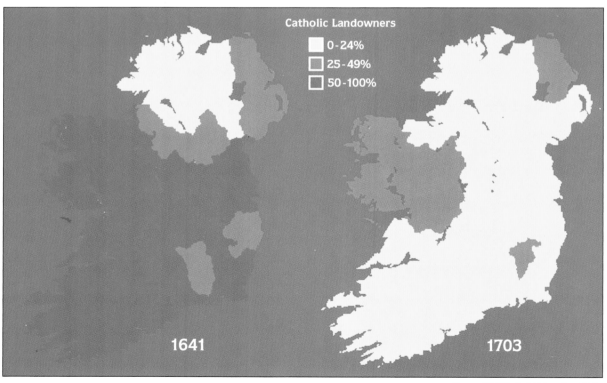

Source: CAIN Project, University of Ulster

LEGACY OF THE PLANTATIONS: IRISH PROBLEMS TODAY

Not surprisingly, the British policy of resettling English and Scottish Protestants in Ireland has had long-lasting effects in that region. There were three major plantation movements in the seventeenth century, and as a result, eighty-one percent of all the productive land in Ireland was confiscated from the native Irish and transferred to immigrants from the English Isle. These immigrants introduced a new community that differed from the Irish in culture, ethnicity, national identity, and religion. Furthermore, the socio-economic system in place in Ireland at the time did not yet use money as a means of commerce. Land was wealth for the Irish, and rent was paid in foodstuffs. Confiscating land meant taking the only wealth the Irish possessed, instantly creating an impoverished population. The new immigrants introduced a monetary system and began charging the native Irish exorbitant rents. For these and similar reasons, the social, political, and economic effects of the Plantations created long-lasting rifts that are still apparent today.

Of the three Plantations, the most successful was the first Ulster Plantation in 1609. This plantation saw the confiscation of three million acres (thirty percent of Ireland) in six counties in west and central Ulster, the northern most region of Ireland. One reason that the Ulster Plantation was so successful was that it was, before the settlement, the most fiercely Gaelic region of Ireland. The British feared revolution from this region of the Island and decided to "reduce" Gaelic strength by encouraging thousands of immigrants to settle the region. Ironically, because of the plantations, this once strongly Gaelic region is today the most British in culture and style.

In 1921, after Ireland won its independence from Great Britain, the island was partitioned, and the six northern counties that still contained a strong Protestant population since the time of the plantations became "Northern Ireland," remaining under the jurisdiction of the British crown. As they had since the time of the plantations, the Protestant population still identified themselves as British and wished to remain a part of that country. The tensions in those northern counties between these descendants of plantation immigrants and the native Irish has led to violence and reciprocal hostilities that, despite many efforts to secure peace, remain today.

A plan for the Londonderry Plantation, 1622 (Thomas Raven)

In 1691, the Irish Penal Laws attempted to destroy the Catholic Faith by enslaving the Irish population. Catholics were denied education, land ownership, and medical practice and treatment. Catholics were not allowed to enter the legal profession nor could they hold government offices. These harsh and oppressive regimes brought about a greater unity among the Irish and increased their loyalty to the Church of Rome. The Irish continued to suffer official persecution until the nineteenth century.

RISE OF PARLIAMENTARY DEMOCRACY IN ENGLAND

After the death of Oliver Cromwell in 1658, Parliament returned power to the sons of Charles I. Learning from his father's failed attempts to impose absolutist rule, Charles II ruled England with tact and care. He was sympathetic to Catholics because he spent most of his exile in France, under the protection of Louis XIV. As king he tolerated the Catholic religion, but kept his measures discreet so as not to agitate the still prevalent anti-Catholic sentiment. Charles II allowed Catholics to practice their Faith in the privacy of their own homes and let some prominent Catholics become his advisors.

In 1678, a group of Protestants led by Titus Oates accused the Catholic minority of plotting a French invasion of England and with it the massacre of all prominent Protestants. Although completely fabricated, the imagined "Popish Plot" brought pressure on Charles to renew persecution of Catholics in England, and a wave of anti-Catholic witch-hunts spread through England.

In 1685, Catholics became hopeful when Charles II died without an heir. His brother, James II, had converted to the Catholic Faith while in exile in France, and many Catholics hoped his rise to the throne might reestablish Catholicism in England. The Protestant-dominated Parliament was wary of Catholic succession, and they only allowed the elderly James to claim the crown because his daughter and successor, Mary, was Protestant.

In 1688 James II's young, Catholic wife gave birth to a son who was baptized Catholic. This new successor, a threat to the Protestant claim to the crown, provoked Parliament to take direct measures to protect England against Catholic succession. They responded by claiming the "right to revolution" put forth in John Locke's *Two Treatises on Government.* According to this principle,

Locke argued that whenever a monarch violated the social contract with his subjects, the people had the right to replace the ruler with someone of their own choosing. Claiming that James II had violated the social contract, the English launched the bloodless "Glorious Revolution" of 1688, in which James II was forced to abdicate the throne and place power in the hands of William of Orange, his son-in-law, and Mary, his Protestant daughter. To help strengthen the new monarchy, the English Parliament allowed itself to be taxed and then used the funds to help centralize the government around the new rulers. In the English Bill of Rights of 1689, Parliament

William III of England (1650-1702), also known as William III of Orange-Nassau, was a Dutch aristocrat and the Holy Roman Empire's Prince of Orange from birth. Born a member of the House of Orange-Nassau, William III won the English, Scottish and Irish Crowns following the Glorious Revolution, during which his uncle and father-in-law, James II, was deposed. He ruled jointly with his wife, Mary II, until her death in 1694. He is affectionately known as "King Billy" among Protestants in Scotland and Northern Ireland.

agreed to share power with the king, creating a governmental system called a "Constitutional Monarchy" that blended the monarchical and republican (parliamentary) systems.

William and Mary worked to ensure that the crown remained free from Catholic possession. In 1701, they passed the "Act of Settlement" which barred Catholics from politics and prohibited Catholics from sitting on the throne. Later "Test Acts" would add that no Catholic could practice a profession or even attend university within the British Isles. Over time, these laws would virtually remove any Catholic presence in England.

PART III

The Scientific Revolution and the Age of Enlightenment

The great scientific discoveries of the seventeenth century laid the foundation for what is known as the Age of Enlightenment. This intellectual movement in significant part sprang up from a wholehearted enthusiasm for, and faith in, scientific progress. As scientific discoveries began to prove the effectiveness of human reason and show that scientific knowledge could be useful in many areas of human life, many began to believe that the study of science and nature could help correct all the problems of society, including poverty, disease, and war.

But with this deep-rooted belief in the potential of scientific thought came a new skepticism. Soon, everything that did not fall under the umbrella of scientific explanation was dismissed or regarded with disdain. For the thinkers of the Enlightenment, what could not be proved could not be called true. Rationalism took precedence over faith, and reason became the guiding principle of this new philosophy.

As mentioned previously, the Enlightenment was closely linked to the Renaissance and the Reformation since both helped shape man's new understanding of himself and the world. The Renaissance opened up new fields of research which focused on the richness and grandeur of the human spirit. The Reformation challenged traditional religious authority and gave priority to the individual's subjective interpretation of Scripture and fulfillment of God's will. Between the heavy emphasis on humanism and the view that religious practice was governed by subjective inspiration, the value and power of the human person began to take center stage. Man became fascinated with his newly discovered power to reason, and thereby probe, the mysteries of the universe.

As these new ideas became popular and spread throughout Europe, statesmen and rulers adopted the new philosophical attitudes and based their political agendas on rationalistic principles derived from the Enlightenment. Many sought to divorce themselves and their countries from any guidance from the Church. During the Age of Enlightenment, the Church was increasingly disregarded as an enemy of scientific progress and a promoter of "superstition."

Some good did come out of these new intellectual trends. Rationalist philosophers began to speak of the need for religious toleration and respect for the opinions of others. They began to see religious, social, and racial prejudice as unbefitting the dignity of the person. These attitudes led to a much greater appreciation for political freedom and individual human rights. However, at least in academic circles, there was a negative reaction against religious doctrine based on authority and tradition. Previous moral and ethical codes were also regarded as outdated and superstitious, and contempt grew for things of the past. Many attacked the moral authority of the Church, and proponents of the Enlightenment looked to create a world devoid of supernatural meaning by totally ignoring the reality of divine revelation. As human reason made moral conduct dependent upon subjective interpretation, it would soon follow that secularism and agnosticism would take hold as popular new "religions." This rejection of God would first tragically manifest itself in the disasters of the French Revolution, whose effects permeate cultures even today.

DESCARTES AND BACON

The Frenchman René Descartes was a brilliant mathematician whose achievements include, among others, the invention of coordinate geometry (called "Cartesian geometry" in his honor). He had a superb mathematical mind, which ultimately led him to consider the universe in mechanistic terms. In his writings, Descartes would describe the world mathematically, hoping to attain for philosophy the same kind of absolute certainty provided by the clarity of mathematical demonstration. He proposed to sweep away traditional learning and replace it with a new system based on logical reasoning and certain proof.

In 1637, Descartes published his celebrated treatise called *Discourse on Method* in which he advanced his principle of "systematic doubt." Given the subjective knowledge of every individual, Descartes questioned the possibility of achieving knowledge with absolute certainty. Human knowledge was flawed, Descartes argued, since it was never assured of clear certainty. Only the awareness of one's own existence was certain because even if one doubts his existence, he knows that he exists in order to

René Descartes (1596-1650). Considered by many as the founder of modern philosophy and the father of modern mathematics, he influenced generations of philosophers

be able to doubt. *"Cogito ergo sum,"* he famously posited, "I think, therefore I am" (cf. *Discourse on Method,* chapter 4). St. Augustine of Hippo used similar logic to refute Skeptic philosophy. However, Descartes applied this line of thought to a doubting mind instead of a rational mind. "On none of these points do I fear the arguments of the Skeptics of the Academy who say: what if you are deceived? For if I am deceived, I am. For he who does not exist cannot be deceived. And if I am deceived, by this same token I am" (*City of God,* 11:26). The widespread acceptance of Descartes' deceptively simple and logical statement turned the world of philosophy upside down, as it rooted all philosophic inquiry from the reality of the outside world to the thought process of a person's subjectivity.

Although a very brief summary does not do justice to this father of modern philosophy, suffice it to say Cartesian philosophy opened a Pandora's Box to an inordinately rationalistic view of reality. Knowledge of truth, according to many thinkers beginning in the Enlightenment and influenced by Descartes, would be governed by subjective intellectual musings. Descartes believed that man is incapable of knowing truth that is metaphysical, i.e., what transcends empirical data. By dismissing the validity of any understanding that was not based on empirical, provable data, Descartes unwittingly placed a huge wedge between Faith and reason.

Another thinker who contributed to the growth of scientific inquiry was the Englishman Sir Francis Bacon. Like Descartes, Bacon held that reason provided a true and reliable method of knowledge. Bacon advocated that this knowledge would help man control nature, and contribute to the wealth and comfort of civilization. Bacon described his new method of acquiring knowledge in his *Novum organum,* published in 1620. Moving away from the Aristotelian view of knowledge through logical

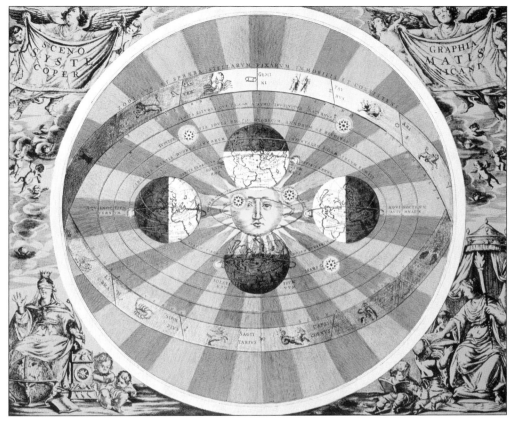

In his book *On the Revolutions of the Heavenly Bodies* published in 1543, Nicolas Copernicus postulated a heliocentric (sun-centered) system of the universe. His theory inaugurated the scientific revolution.

deduction proceeding from general principles, Bacon posited that knowledge must originate from specific observations to a more general theory. This new "inductive" method involved the collection of vast quantities of empirical data from which general principles could be derived. Known as empiricism, this new philosophy gathered knowledge through observation and experience as a way of understanding how things worked. Bacon's methods showed how knowledge could produce many practical advancements to improve the quality of life.

A NEW UNDERSTANDING OF THE UNIVERSE

All the way through the Medieval Era, people had been satisfied with the Greek Ptolemaic (earth-centered) view of the universe that believed that all the heavenly bodies revolved around the earth. This model of the universe, with the earth at its center, squares well with observations from earth and a Scriptural-Christian understanding of Heaven and earth. It also accurately explains the movement of the stars, sun, and planets of the cosmos. As thinkers challenged traditional explanations and based knowledge on observation, small errors began to be discovered which made the Ptolemaic model untenable. The Polish priest and astronomer Nicolas Copernicus suspected that the Ptolemaic model was erroneous after having made mathematical analyses and calculations of the rotation of the earth. In his book *On the Revolutions of the Heavenly Bodies* published in 1543, he postulated that the sun, rather than the earth, was the center of the universe. Although he believed the earth to be the actual, physical center of the universe, Copernicus argued that a sun-centered model made it much easier because it was easier to calculate planetary

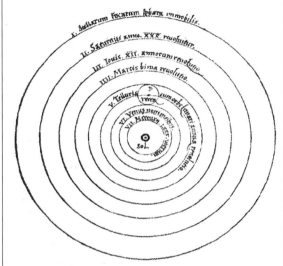

The diagram that shook the world, in chapter 10 of Book I of Copernicus' "On the Revolutions of the Heavenly Bodies" (*De revolutionibus orbium coelestium*). In the Copernican system the Earth is given three distinct motions: a daily axial rotation, an annual rotation about the Sun, and a third motion related to precession.

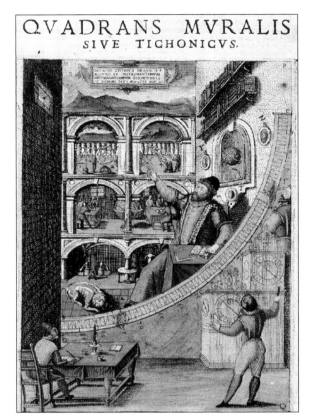

A tinted engraving from Tycho Brahe's 1598 publication *Astronomiae instaurata mechanica*. The illustration shows Tycho and his Great Quadrant at Uraniborg. The accuracy of this instrument, based on comparison with eight reference stars, has been estimated to 34.6 seconds of arc.

motions than in the Ptolemaic model. A seemingly small matter, the Copernican model would elicit a debate that would change the way man perceived the universe.

In the spirit of Bacon and Descartes (observation and mathematical demonstration), two scientists' work seemed to theoretically prove the Copernican model. From 1576 until his death in 1601, Danish astronomer Tycho Brahe devoted his life to plotting the movements of the stars, modifying the Ptolemaic (earth-centered) model along the way. Through his meticulous observations, Brahe discovered that the planets moved in elliptical, not circular, orbits. Following Brahe's death in 1601, his assistant, German astronomer and mathematician Johannes Kepler, devised a mathematical formula that described planetary motion, thereby verified the Copernican model. Kepler's theories translated the concrete world of matter into mathematical form; thus, Brahe's observations and Kepler's interpretations gave birth to modern scientific observation and experimentation (the "scientific method").

GALILEO GALILEI AND THE SCIENTIFIC METHOD

The future of scientific development was reinforced by the work of the Italian scientist Galileo Galilei. Prior to Galileo, theorists simply made observations to form general principles. Galileo, however, seeing science as a useful tool for solving practical matters, applied the principle of experimentation to reach verifiable conclusions. Through his experiments, Galileo began to offer hard evidence for the theories of other scientists. He combined observation, experimentation, and application into a new "scientific method" that standardized the study of the different areas of natural science.

Galileo's use of the scientific method allowed him to draw many verifiable conclusions about the workings of the natural world. Through his use of the telescope (developed by Dutch lens grinders in 1604), Galileo observed that the planets were constructed from the same material as earth. Galileo also proved the validity of the Copernican system that claims identical conclusions for both the earth and heavenly bodies. He was increasingly popular among the people since he could explain complex scientific breakthroughs in a simple manner. Galileo's new methodology and his findings would pave the way for Newton's laws of motion.

Galileo Galilei

Unfortunately, Galileo's new discoveries came at a time when many churchmen were growing increasingly defensive and wary of science. During the Protestant Reformation, the Church had come under attack for advocating human reason and Scholastic education to the neglect of the study of Sacred Scripture. The great patron and supporter of education in all intellectual pursuits, the Church, was now trying to give greater emphasis to using Scripture to explain her origins. Balancing the pressure to remain faithful to the gospel with new and challenging scientific advancements would prove to be a difficult task, resulting in some unfortunate decisions by several churchmen.

Some of Galileo's observations contradicted prevalent interpretations of Scripture, and his theories brought him into conflict with ecclesiastical authority. Attempting to demonstrate faithful adherence to Sacred Scripture, ecclesiastical authorities condemned the theories of Galileo and required him to abandon his ideas. Galileo agreed to the condemnation under protest and continued to pursue his studies in astronomy. Despite the scientist's defiance, Pope Paul V and his successor Gregory X continued to support Galileo.

In 1632, Galileo presented his greatest work: *Dialogue on the Two Chief Systems of the World*. In it he defended the Copernican theory of the universe and ridiculed the geocentric (earth-centered) position. (Pope Urban VIII understood the geocentric fool "Simplicio" to be himself.) Ecclesiastical authorities again objected to Galileo's writings, and they asked that he present his findings as a hypothesis rather than a declaration. Galileo refused, and he was arrested and held in confinement at palaces in Siena and Florence. During this confinement, Galileo pursued his work and research. Most people in later centuries have viewed the incident as a source of embarrassment for the Church.

In 1979 Pope John Paul II felt it necessary to reopen the case against Galileo and publicly pardon the scientist, not because his refined theory (a "fact not yet definitively proven") was vindicated, but for the treatment he had received. At a papal audience in 1992, the commission that reexamined the case affirmed the possibility that

> certain theologians, Galileo's contemporaries...failed to grasp the profound, nonliteral meaning of the Scriptures when they described the physical structure of the created universe....It is in that historical and cultural framework, far removed from our own times, that Galileo's judges...believed quite wrongly that the adoption of the Copernican revolution, in fact not yet definitively proven, was such as to undermine Catholic tradition....These mistakes must be frankly recognized, as you, Holy Father, have requested. ("Faith Can Never Conflict with Reason," *L'Osservatore Romano*, November 1, 1992, pp. 1-2).

SOME OF GALILEO'S OTHER CONTRIBUTIONS

Galileo is famous for his use of the telescope and his astronomical discoveries. However, the Italian scientist, like many of his day, also made a number of significant mathematical discoveries. His experiments with falling bodies concluded that gravity is a force that acts equally on all bodies despite their weight. He recorded observations about the oscillation of pendulums, which contributed to the invention of the pendulum clock—an improvement over sand and water clocks. Galileo also proved that the path of an object through space is a parabola, helping to predict the path of travel for, among other things, a cannonball.

In addition to these more famous mathematical discoveries, Galileo's inquisitive undertakings uncovered the mathematical principles of a number of more whimsical daily events. Galileo created an early water pump powered by a horse; he created a table to figure out the probabilities of gambling with three dice; and he came up with the principle of flotation. In 1595 Galileo also worked out a mechanical explanation of the tides based on the Copernican motions of the earth. Like many of the early scientists, Galileo's accomplishments were not limited to a single field. Instead, his untiring mind sought explanations for countless daily phenomena.

THE NEW ORDER IN SCIENCE AND POLITICS

Sir Isaac Newton (1643-1727)

The famous physicist Sir Isaac Newton's great achievement was to bring together the theories of Kepler and the observations of Galileo. By showing that Kepler's laws of planetary motion and Galileo's laws of terrestrial motion were two aspects of the same laws, Newton formulated laws governing falling bodies. In his *Mathematical Principles of Natural Philosophy,* published in 1687, Newton presented a systematic interpretation of how the universe worked. For many, Newton's explanation of the laws of nature gave an assurance that the entire universe could be understood by the human mind. Man was no longer seen as a small creature in an alien world, but rather as a superior being who could unlock the secrets of the universe.

In the political sphere, these same attitudes of discovery and intellectual self-confidence pervaded academic circles throughout Europe. In England, the failure of absolutism under the Stuart kings led to a new theory of government, which was John Locke's idea of the "social contract." In contrast to Thomas Hobbes' view that society needed an absolute monarch to safeguard the rights of the propertied interests of England, Locke advocated natural rights given to all men and the legislation of laws that promoted those inalienable rights. According to Locke, society was a contract between the ruled and the ruler. The ruled agreed to give up their right to pillage and plunder for the security of good rule. The ruler, however, was required to safeguard the life, liberty, and property of the ruled. If any king violated this prime objective, the ruled had the right to throw off the tyrant and choose another king. This right to revolution justified the removal of James II of England, and it set the stage for the political liberalism of the eighteenth century. Parliament's "Glorious Revolution" marked the beginning of the revolutionary fervor that would dominate the next century.

PART IV

The Protagonists of the Enlightenment and its Effects

The Enlightenment would dominate the intellectual culture of Europe throughout the eighteenth century as thinkers and rulers alike would endeavor to implement ideas derived from the Enlightenment. The proponents of this new philosophy, called the *philosophes*, would become authorities on virtually all issues. Their work and influence would lay the foundation for the cultural, social, and political revolutions that would blossom in the late eighteenth and nineteenth centuries.

Given the powerful impact the Enlightenment would have, the Church would be forced to play an increasingly defensive role in protecting the deposit of Faith. Rulers tried to secure control of the Church in their respective countries, and *philosophes* hoped to rid the continent of what they saw as superstitious religion. The Church would have to rethink her methods and means of articulating Christ's salvific teachings to meet the challenges of the overly confident rulers and thinkers of the Enlightenment.

DEISM AND MASONRY

The greatest setback to the Church during the Enlightenment was the *philosophes'* rejection of Divine revelation and supernatural religion. The *philosophes* believed that all knowledge ought to be based on demonstration by the light of human reason. In keeping with the rationalistic position, the *philosophes* came up with a notion of God and his relationship to the world called Deism. Deism is a rationalist philosophy that accepted the principle of a first cause (similar to a creator) but denied divine intervention or providence in the world. These Deists saw God as a kind of great watchmaker who created the universe with laws and guiding principles that were "wound up," and then left to man's discovery and domination.

Deists believed that God did not demand faith, nor require prayers. God does not intervene in the world, and graces and blessings seen as expressions of God's loving providence should be considered absurd and impossible. Only reason—not divine assistance—is necessary to guide an individual through a life of decency, generosity, and honesty.

This painting depicts the initiation of Mozart into a lodge of the Freemasons. Mozart's last opera, *The Magic Flute*, includes Masonic themes and allegory. He was in the same Masonic Lodge as Joseph Haydn.

By 1717, many Deists had organized into a secret fraternal organization known as the Freemasons. Freemasonry quickly became an efficient vehicle for spreading rationalistic ideas, and many eighteenth-century leaders were members (including Americans George Washington and Benjamin Franklin, Britain's Edmund Burke, the Frenchman Voltaire, and Italian nationalists Giuseppe Mazzini and Giuseppe Garibaldi). Masonry is a Deistic sect that sees God as the grand architect of the universe and bases its practices, rules, and organization on Enlightenment philosophy and reason. More than simply dismissing Christian beliefs, Freemasons secretly have worked to destroy the Catholic Church and undermine her influence. Especially in the past, they have directly opposed the Church in many areas and are overtly antagonistic to organized religion. For example, Masons cremate their dead as a way of flouting the Christian concept of the resurrection of the body, daring God to put back together what they have destroyed. Pope Clement XII in 1738 and Pope Benedict XIV in 1751 condemned Masonry, as well as has seven popes since; in 1884 Pope Leo XIII wrote the lengthy encyclical *Humanum genus* (The Race of Man) in condemnation of Freemasonry.

THE ENCYCLOPEDIA

Denis Diderot (1713-1784) was the Editor-in-Chief of the influential Encyclopedia.

One of the most monumental achievements of the Enlightenment was the creation of the Encyclopedia. This massive, seventeen-volume work sought to catalogue general principles of description for virtually every known subject. Conceived and supervised by Denis Diderot in 1772, the Encyclopedia was a way to spread his rationalistic ideas. In this particular work, the authors presented the world in materialistic terms and dismissed anything supernatural. The great majority of the contributors were atheists or Deists who, without openly attacking Catholicism, attempted to discredit the Faith and sow doubt among the Christian faithful. The work became so popular that, despite being formally condemned by the political authorities of France, even King Louis XV ordered the Encyclopedia for Versailles.

By the eighteenth century, the number of literate people had greatly increased. As a result, the Encyclopedia was read in all parts of Europe and among the most influential members of society. About twenty-five thousand sets were sold before the French Revolution (cf. Palmer, *A History of the Modern World*, 2002, p. 318). Aided by the success of the Encyclopedia, the ideas of the Enlightenment quickly spread throughout Europe and were immensely influential in Prussia, Austria, and Russia.

VOLTAIRE

France emerged as the intellectual center of the Enlightenment, and it produced the most influential thinkers of the time. Francois-Marie Arouet, better known as Voltaire, was one of the most renowned writers of the Encyclopedia, and became one of the period's most prominent thinkers associated with the Enlightenment.

Voltaire had a genius for expressing the Enlightenment's sentiments. Through his use of satire, Voltaire's wit won him an entourage of followers, and he used humor as a tool for expressing his ideas about philosophy, politics, and religion. Voltaire was sharply critical of institutions,

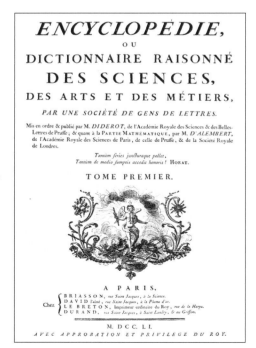

Francois-Marie Arouet (1694-1778), known by the pen name Voltaire, was an influential French Enlightenment writer, satirist, Deist and philosopher.

exemplified by his infamous slogan, "*Ecrasez l'infame!* Crush the infamous thing!" which has become especially associated with the philosopher's disdain for the Catholic Church. Indeed the philosopher thought so little of the Church that he once famously exclaimed that twelve philosophers could surely destroy a religion started by twelve fishermen.

Voltaire was Jesuit-educated, but as he grew older, his writing grew increasingly more anti-religious, and his hatred for Christianity became one of the main driving forces in his works. He habitually attacked Catholic dogma, the priesthood, Sacred Scripture, and even Christ himself. In his writings, Voltaire wrongly attributed to Christianity some of the greatest historical atrocities. Above all, his hatred of intolerance fueled Voltaire's attacks against the Church, and his fierce reaction to Catholicism was propelled by what he saw as the intolerance of the Church in France. He loved England, on the other hand, where he saw many different religions co-existing side by side.

Voltaire thought that belief in God and the discernment between good and evil arose from reason alone, and he argued for natural religion and natural morality. For Voltaire, Christianity was a foolish and absurd religion that developed only to keep the masses quiet. He was the first to present a purely secular view of world history, presenting Christianity and other religions of the world as merely human invention and opinion.

Although one might expect this lover of absolute freedom to advocate revolution, politically speaking Voltaire was a royalist who supported the power of the monarchy as long as it followed what he considered enlightened thought. If a government were enlightened, Voltaire did not object to the extent of its power. Powerful governments could implement the great reforms needed to end bigotry and intolerance and advance the cause of material and technological progress. In fact, the development of the idea of enlightened despotism, in which an educated and autocratic ruler would strive to govern justly and effectively through the practical application of reason, owed its development in many ways to Voltaire's ideas.

As far as personal religious beliefs were concerned, Voltaire remained an enigmatic character throughout his life. He criticized Catholicism severely in his works, but built a Catholic chapel on his property, attended Mass, and had sermons read to him during solitary meals. Voltaire even belonged to a Catholic lay order and requested a Catholic burial after his death. Even though he could boast as one of Christianity's most bitter opponents, Voltaire allegedly repented at the end of his life. In spite of everything, his love for toleration did not exclude those good works and ideas of members of the Church, and he was partially won over by the intellectual and pious Pope Benedict XIV. Voltaire even dedicated one of his works to Benedict with the epitaph, "To the vicar of the God of Truth and meekness."

Voltaire's *Elements of the Philosophy of Newton* (1738) was the most important conduit for Newton's new system of natural philosophy in France. Voltaire's admiration for Newton is also evident in his letters on Newton in *Letters Concerning the English Nation.*

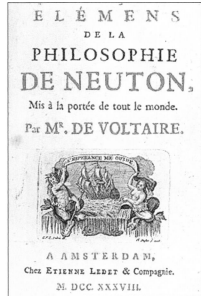

ROUSSEAU

Jean-Jacques Rousseau was born in 1712 to a lower-class Swiss family. Rousseau complained throughout his life that he was misunderstood and neglected as a child. As an adult, Rousseau was quite resigned to having no social status and no money. Instead of marrying, he had a mistress who bore him five children whom he deposited into an orphanage. By the age of forty, Rousseau was still poor and unknown. Only after his work was discovered did he skyrocket into popular acclaim and thereby considered as one of the most profound writers of his age.

Rousseau drew much of his work from his own life experiences. He blamed society for all of man's difficulties. "Man was born free," said Rousseau, "but everywhere he is in chains" (cf. *Social Contract*, I.1). Rousseau believed society created rules to subjugate individual freedom. He saw man as naturally good, but society forced him to be a creature of violence and falsehood. If man were restored to his original liberty and equality, he believed, every human being would flourish. Rousseau imagined a primitive state of nature in which man was happy and innocent.

Rousseau's chief work, *The Social Contract*, espoused his principles of liberty and equality. He argued that individuals should not be subject to anyone, and any subjection to authority was contrary to man's nature. However, for the sake of protection, people agreed to form societies. Since the people allowed themselves to be governed, Rousseau reasoned that political authority came from the people, not from God. Free individuals living in a society created a "social contract" through which the people would choose an authority whose task was to rule and legislate.

Rousseau in many ways was the antithesis of Voltaire. Whereas human reason and rationalist philosophy were the center of Voltaire's writings, Rousseau began to call into question the trustworthiness of human reason, preferring to rely more heavily upon personal conscience or emotive feeling. Voltaire justified absolute authority meant to bring about progressive reform, but Rousseau advocated the total subjugation of the state to the "general will." It is unclear what Rousseau meant by his term "general will." Over time it has come to mean both the democratic voice of the people, and the willingness of a society to be ruled by a dictator. Both interpretations have led, in their extremes, to revolutionary movements and totalitarian regimes of the eighteenth, nineteenth, and twentieth centuries. In many ways, Rousseau laid the philosophical groundwork for the French Revolution and, indirectly, the Bolshevik Revolution and the emergence of fascism.

ENLIGHTENED DESPOTISM

The philosophical principles of the Enlightenment were not stagnant ideas. The ideas of the Enlightenment expressed in politics, law, and orderly administration quickly spread throughout the developing nation-states in Europe. Many of the leading ministers of Europe, such as Pombal of Portugal, Kaunitz of Austria, and Struensee of Denmark, adopted secularist, *philosophe* attitudes towards governing. Monarchs also began distancing themselves from the traditional belief that authority was based on "divine right." The age in which Louis XIV was able to declare "I am the state" was passing away. Instead, monarchs placed new emphasis on what was most reasonable and useful to society. This attitude is perhaps best exemplified by Frederick the Great of Prussia's famous quote: "I am the state's first servant."

These "enlightened" rulers were motivated to prove the effectiveness of their reasonable rule. They attempted to impose national uniformity over their domains by establishing a bureaucracy of salaried officials loyal to the crown. They drained swamps and built roads and bridges to allow for more trade within their realms. They also codified law in order to limit the autonomy of local towns and undermine the independence of the nobility. Any groups that claimed independence from the state, be it minority language groups, religious denominations, or international organizations, were suppressed.

France's attempts at forming an enlightened despot proved ineffective. The reign of Louis XIV had already brought about civil uniformity. Louis' policies of civil organization and court life kept the French nobility from retaining too much individual authority. He aggressively stopped any attempt in questioning his authority. His control of the Church of France also helped to assure the loyalty and cooperation of the French hierarchy. Nevertheless, since these policies were centralized around the king, they would also hinder Louis' successor's ability to resolve the severe political and economic problems that would beset France at the end of the century.

In Germany, the Enlightenment (*Aufklärung*) was slower in finding an audience. The Thirty Years War divided Germany into over 300 competing sovereignties, leaving Germany without a principal patron to embrace these new ideas. Eventually two states would emerge to lead the fragmented Germany: Prussia and Austria.

Prussia was an agricultural region dominated by a military caste and a large Lutheran landed aristocracy known as the *Junker* class. After the Peace of Westphalia, Prussian princes had long dominated the Lutheran Church. Because the treaty guaranteed their independence from the Roman Church, skepticism easily flared up among the Protestant intellectuals. They were intent on bringing religious belief into harmony with the scientific attitudes of the age, and religion began to be associated more with duty than with dogmatic definitions. As the *Aufklärung* became popular in Germany (thanks to a flood of books and pamphlets from France and England), the ideas of Voltaire and Rousseau took root among small intellectual circles of Germany.

The greatest adherent to Enlightenment philosophy was Frederick the Great of Prussia. A friend of Voltaire, Frederick spoke multiple languages, but preferred French. He wrote poetry and essays and saw himself as the intellectual head of state — the best to lead the nation. Frederick personally attended to all matters of business and made all of the important decisions that affected Prussia. He codified the laws and brought about civil service reform.

Voltaire, Frederick II (the Great) of Prussia and guests in a lively philosophical conversation during dinner at the beautiful rococo Palace Sanssouci in Potsdam. Frederick preferred to speak French rather than German and surrounded himself with a French-speaking court.

FREDERICK THE GREAT AND THE EMERGENCE OF PRUSSIA

Perhaps the best example of political success possible under the tyranny of an enlightened despot was that of Frederick Wilhelm II, also known as Frederick the Great. During his reign, Frederick the Great turned Prussia from a large German state into a major European power. In the nineteenth century, Prussia's strength would help unify the many German states and principalities into a single German nation.

Frederick the Great, son of Frederick Wilhelm I, was groomed to lead. He spent most of his childhood engaged in rigorous military training and education, and as a commander, he earned a reputation as ambitious and aggressive. Once king, Frederick devoted himself to building Prussia into a strong state. Both in the War of Austrian Succession (1740-1748) and in the Seven Years War (1756-1763), he annexed territory and helped double the size of Prussia. His successes, as well as his taste for enlightened thinking in culture, won him the reputation as a military genius. What made Frederick so effective, however, was that his genius was combined with a willingness to engage in strategic warfare. "Diplomacy without arms is like music without instruments," he famously said.

In addition to building Prussia in size and strength, Frederick the Great issued a series of domestic reforms that modernized Prussia and strengthened her within. He consolidated power by giving territorial princes positions in his government's bureaucracy. He established programs of religious toleration and ensured freedom of the press. Frederick also reformed the judicial system, abolished torture, placed restrictions on capital punishment, and established individual protections by passing the first German law code. Prussian judges became known throughout Europe as the most honest in Europe. In addition, Frederick built thousands of miles of roads, financed the rebuilding of towns, and instituted agricultural reforms that greatly improved the standard of living in Prussia. Within a lifetime, Frederick the Great created a major modern power that would soon emerge as one of the most sophisticated and prosperous in the world.

He expanded the territory of Prussia through a series of wars with neighboring states and began the process of modernizing the Prussian state. Although he attempted to end intolerance, the powerful influence of the landed *Junker* class resisted the end of serfdom. In the end, Frederick managed to bring about one of the first modernized political states. Unfortunately for Frederick, he did not leave a worthy successor, and his reforms had little permanent success.

FEBRONIANISM AND JOSEPHINISM

Protestantism offered European princes an ideological foundation for their expansive ambitions. Having neither legal nor religious ties to the Catholic Church, Protestant princes could now control and influence all aspects of society. It was much more difficult for Catholic leaders to have absolute domination within their territory since the ecclesiastical hierarchy wielded significant moral authority. To achieve greater independence from Rome, both secular and Church leaders embraced a Gallican view of the Church. Long condemned by the Church, these Gallican ideas spread throughout Catholic states in part because they seemed to offer a viable way for Catholic rulers to compete with their Protestant neighbors. Furthermore, in an age of burgeoning nationalism, Gallicanism offered the possibilities of greater independence on both the secular and ecclesiastical fronts.

Gallican influence entered Germany through the writings of Johann Nikolaus von Hontheim, the auxiliary bishop of Trier, who wrote under the pen name of Febronius. Febronius argued that the pope was merely an administrative head of the Church who did not have the power to legislate laws. He denied both the primacy of the pope over other bishops and his authority to speak definitively on matters of Faith and morals. Febronius rehashed arguments from conciliarism that stated that the ultimate authority of the Church rests on ecumenical councils and not the bishop of Rome. He urged the German bishops to assert their independence from Rome and called upon the secular authorities to abandon their allegiance to the pope and seize jurisdictional authority of their churches and ecclesiastical landholdings.

Pope Clement XIII was quick to condemn the writings of Febronius, and in 1764, he urged the German bishops to reject his teachings and suppress their diffusion. Febronius made a halfhearted retraction in 1778, but his writings continued to be quite influential, especially in inspiring German nationalism within the Church. A few of the German bishops employed arguments taken from Febronius' work to assert their independence from Rome, but their dissention did not take a strong hold among the majority of the German bishops. Eventually, all but one bishop pledged their fidelity and allegiance to Rome. Febronius reconciled himself with the Church before his death in 1790.

Joseph II's mother, Maria-Theresa, was responsible for many reforms in Austria. Maria-Theresa was a devout Catholic, and her court is widely viewed as the most moral in Europe. Just, efficient, and patient, she unified the loose-knit Austrian territories through a well-maintained bureaucracy that abolished internal tariffs and created the largest free trade zone in Europe. She improved the situation of the serfs in her country by passing laws to protect them against abuses of their rights and limited their service. Her good rule and sensible reforms helped maintain stability in Austria after a series of conflicts with neighboring German princes.

Joseph II of Austria regrettably espoused the ideas of Febronius, and the state of Austria would eventually suffer for it. Contrary to Maria-Theresa's prudence and good sense, her son, Joseph II, was impulsive and impatient and resented the slow pace of reform. He thought his mother was unnecessarily cautious and believed that he could change the Austrian state much more quickly. Much of Joseph's headstrong behavior was a result of an education imbued by principles of the Enlightenment. Seeing himself as a *philosophe* and encourages by the success of Frederick the

Maria Theresa (1717-1780), Holy Roman Empress. A Habsburg by birth and one of the most powerful women of her time, she ruled over most of central Europe. Maria Theresa was married to Francis Stephen of Lorraine with whom she had sixteen children, six daughters (all named "Marie" including the future Queen of France, Marie Antoinette) and five sons surviving to adulthood (including the future emperors Joseph II and Leopold II). She recognized Joseph II, her eldest son, as co-regent and emperor, but allowed him only limited power because she felt he was rash and arrogant.

Great of Prussia, Joseph embraced the principles of Febronianism and set out to establish progressive policies in Austria.

Joseph II launched massive reforms to bring uniformity into the Austrian empire. He abolished local governments, removed privileges from nobles and free cities, and created one of the first secret police forces. Moreover, he mandated that the German language be spoken by all his subjects, a policy that alienated the Hungarians under his rule. Irritated with the slow progress of his mother's reforms regarding serfs, Joseph II attempted to free them with a single stroke of the pen. This quick remedy to the problem of serfdom in fact brought economic disaster to Austria. Although there was a certain wisdom in Joseph's reforms, the lack of prudence and sensitivity with which he instituted them alienated the nobility and angered his subjects.

Joseph's desire to exercise absolute, enlightened authority prompted him to dominate the Church in almost every area of its competence and jurisdiction. He insisted that all papal documents be approved by his office before publication and forbade the bishops of Austria to communicate directly with Rome, forcing them to take an oath of allegiance to the king. Joseph was especially influential in the seminary system of his country. He required all prospective priests to study in Austrian seminaries under his control. The seminarians were required to use a watered-down catechism that Joseph authorized, and the seminary professors were restricted to preaching on moral subjects and barred from teaching Catholic doctrine. Monasteries that Joseph thought served no practical purpose were suppressed, and religious communities were cut off from their superiors in Rome. Joseph micro-managed the Austrian Church to the extreme extent of determining the number of candles used for Mass.

Unfortunately for Joseph II and Austria, the emperor's reforms began to unravel before his death. The emperor recognized his mistakes and tried to rectify the situation, but in many cases it was too late. In one instance, much to his embarrassment, when the Austrian Netherlands rose in rebellion, Joseph II was forced to turn to the pope in the hopes that he could persuade the Belgians to return to their original allegiance with Joseph. Despite Joseph's promises to withdraw his restrictions on the Church, it was too late to save Austrian control of the Netherlands. Joseph II recognized his incompetent leadership, and tragically wrote his own epitaph: "Here lies a prince whose intentions were pure, but who had the misfortune to see all his projects fail" (quoted in Harney, *The Catholic Church through the Ages*, 1974, p. 452). He died alone, after a ten-year reign, in 1790, the same year as Febronius.

SUPPRESSION OF THE JESUITS

As secular rulers rose to power, they sought to suppress all opposition that could seriously hinder the exercise of their authority. Any groups associated with the old order of European rule were seen as a danger to progress and prosperity. The Jesuit order had long been influential in Europe. They served as advisors to all the Catholic rulers and noble houses throughout Europe and held a large number of key positions at the major universities. Founded to help counteract the Protestant Reformation, the Jesuits were well educated, well connected, and well established. The order was dedicated to the service of the pope, and their missionary success brought millions to the Church of Rome. In short, there was no other Catholic order or group that could seriously counteract the rationalist ideology Enlightenment as the Jesuits. As the *philosophes* grew increasingly dominant, the Jesuits became more and more the object of severe hatred for their intellectual prowess and loyalty to the pope.

Typically, the Jesuits were accused of all types of criminal intrigue. All of the major ministers of Europe at the time were disciples of the Enlightenment and had at their disposal the military and police power of the state. They controlled the press and helped shape public opinion against the Church and the Jesuit Order. By 1767, through the actions of these powerful secular authorities, the Jesuit Order was banished from Portugal, France, Spain, and the Kingdom of Naples. French and Italian princes threatened Pope Clement XIII, but he did not support them in their general antagonism against the Jesuits, remaining firm in his support of the order until his death.

Prime Minister Pombal of Portugal was the first to attack and banish the Society of Jesus. Educated in London and trained in the philosophy of the Enlightenment, Pombal was avidly anti-Christian and believed the Church was a threat and hinderance to his secular leadership in Portugal. He was not entirely misled. The Jesuits had strongly opposed Pombal's foreign policy and for a long time attacked Portugal's leading role in the slave trade. However, the lucrative reward of suppressing the order was far more enticing than the moral counsel the Jesuits offered. Portugal had gained territory from Spain in 1754 near the Jesuit missions in Paraguay and Brazil, and the Portuguese now desired to extend their territory and wealth by annexing lands protected by the Jesuit missionaries. When the Guarani tribes of Paraguay launched fierce resistance against the Portuguese, burning their lands rather than turning them over, Pombal blamed the Jesuits for inciting the Guarani rebellion. This was only one of the many national tragedies that were pawned off on the Jesuits. After an attempted assassination of the King of Portugal, Pombal accused prominent Jesuits of plotting the assassination. Without trial, many Jesuits were condemned to life imprisonment, many dying of illness and neglect. Although the pope protested, Pombal banished the papal nuncio and had an eighty-year-old Jesuit who protested that action strangled and then burned alive.

Charles III (1716-1788), King of Spain, was an "enlightened despot." He expelled the Jesuits from Spain and South America in 1767.

France and Spain were quick to follow the lead of Portugal. By 1754, Gallicans, Jansenists, self-proclaimed *philosophes*, and even the mistress of Louis XV worked to suppress the Jesuits in France. In 1767, D'Aranda, the president of the council of Castile and a close friend of Voltaire, convinced King Charles III of Spain that the Jesuits were inciting riots and were spreading rumors of the King's illegitimacy. Using evidence planted by agents of D'Aranda, Charles III condemned and banished all the Jesuits from his kingdom. He confiscated all Jesuit properties throughout Spain and South America, leaving more than five hundred thousand faithful in the missions without priests. Nearly six thousand Jesuits were forced to leave Spain.

After the suppression of the Jesuits in Spain, a campaign spread against the entire order. In 1768, French troops took over Avignon, and Neapolitan troops took over papal duchies in central Italy. With mounting military and political pressure at his doorstep, the pope was being threatened with deposition if he did not take actions against the Jesuits. Clement XIII refused to give-in to the Bourbon demands, but the resistant pontiff died in February 1769. The new pope, Clement XIV, was faced with new ultimatums from Spain to destroy all religious orders throughout its realm and cut off the Church in Spain entirely from the Holy See. The pope delayed action for two years, hoping that he could restore peace and security within the Church. Finally, in 1773, under heavy pressure, Clement XIV issued his brief *Dominus ac Redemptor* that dissolved the Society of Jesus. The pope, and others in the Church, saw the action as merely an administrative measure meant to restore peace and tranquility to the Church. No blame was placed on the Jesuits and it did not impugn the orthodoxy of their doctrines. Jesuit priests simply became part of the diocesan clergy and were allowed in some places to continue as professors of universities. However, the execution of the dissolution was left to the local bishops, resulting in widely varied treatment of the Jesuits (Livingstone, *The Oxford Dictionary of the Christian Church*, 1997, p. 498).

Unfortunately for Clement, the suppression of the Society of Jesus did not restore tranquility to the Church. Confident of their success against the Jesuits, secular rulers continued to make demands upon the papacy. Although Clement's successor, Pius VI, tried to restore order, the ensuing revolution in France made that impossible. During the French Revolution, forty-four Jesuits were martyred, and of those, twenty-three are now beatified. Former Jesuit priests continued their work despite the suppression, and in 1814, forty years after their suppression, Pope Pius VII solemnly restored the Society of Jesus throughout the world.

CONCLUSION

The seventeenth and eighteenth centuries were difficult and tumultuous times for the Church. Faced with both political and philosophical opposition, it seemed as if the whole world was turning against the Catholic Church. In any case, some of the reforms of the Enlightenment would eventually fall in line with the Church's social doctrine. Reacting against the previous centuries of religious war, secular states in Europe and America tried to institute tolerance and religious equality. While the rulers and thinkers of Europe turned away from religion, the Church still found ways to minister to the faithful in the midst of persecution. As the new dominant ideologies of the modern world arose, the Church stood fast in proclaiming Jesus Christ as the ultimate embodiment of truth and meaning of human life.

SUPPLEMENTARY READING

Rousseau, *The Social Contract*, Book I

The most ancient of all societies, and the only one that is natural, is the family: and even so the children remain attached to the father only so long as they need him for their preservation. As soon as this need ceases, the natural bond is dissolved. The children, released from the obedience they owed to the father, and the father, released from the care he owed his children, return equally to independence. If they remain united, they continue so no longer naturally, but voluntarily; and the family itself is then maintained only by convention.

This common liberty results from the nature of man. His first law is to provide for his own preservation, his first cares are those which he owes to himself; and, as soon as he reaches years of discretion, he is the sole judge of the proper means of preserving himself, and consequently becomes his own master.

Renè Descartes, *Rules for the Direction of the Mind*

RULE I. The aim of our studies must be the direction of our mind so that it may form solid and true judgments on whatever matters arise.

RULE II. We must occupy ourselves only with those objects that our intellectual powers appear competent to know certainly and indubitably.

RULE III. As regards any subject we propose to investigate, we must inquire not what other people have thought, or what we ourselves conjecture, but what we can clearly and manifestly perceive by intuition or deduce with certainty. For there is no other way of acquiring knowledge.

RULE IX. We ought to turn our entire attention upon the smallest and easiest points, and dwell on them a long time, until we get accustomed to behold the truth by distinct and clear intuition.

RULE XII. Finally, we must make use of all the aids of understanding, imagination, sense, and memory; and our aims in doing this must be, first, to gain distinct intuitive knowledge of simple propositions; secondly, to relate what we are looking for to what we already know so that we may discern the former; thirdly, to discover those truths which should be correlated with each other, so that nothing is left out that lies within the scope of human endeavor.

John Paul II, *Fides et ratio*, 5

Modern philosophy clearly has the great merit of focusing attention upon man. From this starting-point, human reason with its many questions has developed further its yearning to know more and to know it ever more deeply. Complex systems of thought have thus been built, yielding results in the different fields of knowledge and fostering the development of culture and history. Anthropology, logic, the natural sciences, history, linguistics and so forth—the whole universe of knowledge has been involved in one way or another. Yet the positive results achieved must not obscure the fact that reason, in its one-sided concern to investigate human subjectivity, seems to have forgotten that men and women are always called to direct their steps towards a truth which transcends them. Sundered from that truth, individuals are at the mercy of caprice, and their state as person ends up being judged by pragmatic criteria based essentially upon experimental data, in the mistaken belief that technology must dominate all...Abandoning the investigation of being, modern philosophical research has concentrated instead upon human knowing. Rather than make use of the human capacity to know the truth, modern philosophy has preferred to accentuate the ways in which this capacity is limited and conditioned.

VOCABULARY

AGE OF ENLIGHTENMENT
Intellectual movement which sprang up from a whole-hearted enthusiasm for, and faith in, man's use of reason and scientific progress. Enlightened man believed that the study of science and nature could help correct all the problems of society, including poverty, disease, and war.

CONSTITUTIONAL MONARCHY
System of government established in England in 1689 which blended the monarchical and parliamentary systems.

DEISM
Rationalist philosophy which accepted the principle of a first cause, but denied Divine intervention or Providence in the world. Deism understood God as a great watchmaker who created the universe with laws and guiding principles, but then left the world to man's discovery and domination.

ENCYCLOPEDIA
Seventeen-volume work which sought to offer general principles of description for virtually every known subject. Conceived and supervised by Diderot in 1772, the authors of this popular publication presented the world in materialistic terms and dismissed anything supernatural. The majority of its contributors were atheists or Deists.

ENLIGHTENED DESPOTISM
Monarchical government in which an educated, autocratic ruler tries to govern justly through the practical application of reason.

FEBRONIANISM
"Gallican" movement that influenced the Church in Germany. It argued that the pope was merely an administrative head of the Church who did not have the power to legislate. According to this, ultimate authority of the Church is found in the national leader. It further denied the primacy of the pope with over bishops and the pope's authority to speak definitely on matters of Faith and morals.

FOUR GALLICAN ARTICLES
Declaration that asserted the authority of the Gallican Church under Louis XIV. It attempted to resurrect the heresies that claimed the King of France was independent of the pope in temporal matters and that a general council enjoyed higher authority than that of the pope.

FREEMASONRY
A major vehicle in the spreading of rationalist ideas, this secret, fraternal organization bases all its practices, rules, and organization on Enlightenment philosophy and reason. Many eighteenth-century European and American leaders were members of this organization that sought (and still seeks) to destroy the influence of the Church.

FRONDE
French for rebellion. Body of French nobles who came together to rebel against the monarchy and Cardinal Mazzarin, regent to Louis XIV.

GLORIOUS REVOLUTION
Bloodless revolution in England in which James II was forced to abdicate the throne and power was placed in the hands of his children, William and Mary.

JANSENISM
Developed by Cornelius Jansen, erroneous belief that man was entirely free in the state of innocence and his will tended to do what was right. According to him, original sin made man a slave to sin and all his actions corrupted him. His only hope was God's grace, which could save him. Jansen taught that God only granted salvific grace to a small number of "predestined" people.

VOCABULARY Continued

PHILOSOPHES

French word describing the proponents of Enlightenment philosophy who arose as the new authorities on virtually all matters. They rejected divine revelation and supernatural religion, rather believing that all knowledge ought to be based on demonstration through human reason.

PLANTATIONS

Large areas in the northeast of Ireland that were cleared of Catholics by James I and resettled by Scottish Protestants in an effort to "breed out" the Catholics.

PRAGMATIC SANCTION OF BOURGES

Charles VII's formal declaration of the independence of the French church from Rome.

QUIETISM

Movement founded by Miguel Molinos which advocated absolute passivity during prayers and contemplation. The soul, according to Molinos, should be indifferent to everything, including temptation, and should simply rest perpetually in God. Asceticism was not necessary, since it was sufficient for the soul to humble itself in order for God to accept someone with sins. Quietists taught people to make no effort to avoid sin nor cooperate with God's grace for his salvation.

SCIENTIFIC METHOD

Method that combined observation, experimentation, and application in order to standardize the discovery of scientific principles and theories.

SUN KING

Nickname for Louis XIV whose persona took on divine proportions as he expanded control over the French state.

SYSTEMATIC DOUBT

Principle developed by Descartes that asked whether, if people have a subjective existence, it was possible to have absolute certainty about anything. This principle implicitly denies divine revelation and ultimate truth (God).

Cromwell at Dunbar. Oliver Cromwell invaded Scotland in 1650-1651 after the Scots had crowned Charles I's son as Charles II and tried to re-impose the monarchy on England. He acted with ruthlessness in Scotland. Despite being outnumbered, his veteran troops smashed Scottish armies at the battles of Dunbar and Worcester and occupied the country. Cromwell treated the thousands of prisoners of war he took in this campaign with great cruelty, allowing thousands of them to die of disease and deporting others to penal colonies in Barbados. In both Scotland and Ireland, Cromwell is remembered as a remorseless and ruthless enemy.

STUDY QUESTIONS

1. Who was Thomas Hobbes and what was the name of his primary work?

2. Who was the Sun King?

3. What was the *Fronde*?

4. What was significant about the Four Gallican Articles?

5. What belief of Jansenism made it heretical?

6. Why did the Church condemn Quietism?

7. Who was Guy Fawkes?

8. Who was the "Lord Protector"?

9. Who founded the colony of Maryland and why?

10. How does a decree of James I still affect Ireland today?

11. How did the teachings of John Locke further the cause of Protestants in England?

12. William and Mary passed which laws against Catholics?

13. What movement in the seventeenth century helped lead to the Age of Enlightenment?

14. How did Enlightenment philosophy affect the religious convictions of Europeans?

15. What supposition did René Descartes and Sir Francis Bacon make regarding human reason?

16. Why did Galileo Galilei find himself in conflict with the Church?

17. What was Sir Isaac Newton's greatest accomplishment?

18. How did the Enlightenment threaten the Church?

19. What is Deism?

20. Who were/are the Freemasons?

21. Who was Denis Diderot?

22. Why was the Encyclopedia created?

23. Who was Voltaire? What did he think about the Catholic Church?

24. How did Jean-Jacques Rousseau differ from other Enlightenment thinkers?

25. How did "enlightened despots" differ from previous monarchs and ministers?

26. Who was Febronius? On what matters did he disagree with the Church?

27. What were some differences between Maria-Theresa and her son Joseph II?

28. Why were the Jesuits persecuted and dissolved in the eighteenth century?

Conspirators of the "Gunpowder Plot" of 1605. Guy Fawkes, a gunpowder expert, and a group of English Catholics, plotted to kill King James I of England, his family and most of the Protestant aristocracy by blowing up the House of Parliament during the State Opening. The plot failed because of a tip-off to authorities who found Fawkes and his barrels of gunpowder in the basement of Parliament. All the conspirators were cruelly tortured and executed. On November 5th each year, Protestant Britons celebrate the failure of the plot on what is known as Bonfire Night (Fireworks Night or Guy Fawkes Night).

PRACTICAL EXERCISES

1. Jansenism and Quietism are two heresies with almost opposite understandings of piety and faith. They offered opposing exaggerations of aspects of Christianity. Why did these heresies appear at around the same time? What was appealing to believers about each of these heresies?

2. The First Amendment to the United States Constitution (1789) states in part: "Congress shall make no law respecting an establishment of religion." In light of the political developments in France and England during the seventeenth and eighteenth centuries, why were the founders concerned with drafting this provision?

3. How did scientific rationalism employed in the work of thinkers like Descartes, Bacon, and Galileo differ from St. Thomas Aquinas and other Scholastics? How were they similar? Why should Christians be wary of the claim that human reason can provide absolute certainty?

4. The Enlightenment was a philosophical reaction to the Reformation and the Wars of Religion of the preceding centuries. In what way is this statement true? In what way is it false? Why did Enlightenment thinkers voice so much opposition to religion?

FROM THE CATECHISM

50 By natural reason man can know God with certainty, on the basis of his works. But there is another order of knowledge, which man cannot possibly arrive at by his own powers: the order of divine Revelation (cf. *Dei Filius*: DS 3015). Through an utterly free decision, God has revealed himself and given himself to man. This he does by revealing the mystery, his plan of loving goodness, formed from all eternity in Christ, for the benefit of all men. God has fully revealed this plan by sending us his beloved Son, our Lord Jesus Christ, and the Holy Spirit.

88 The Church's Magisterium exercises the authority it holds from Christ to the fullest extent when it defines dogmas, that is, when it proposes, in a form obliging the Christian people to an irrevocable adherence of faith, truths contained in divine Revelation or also when it proposes, in a definitive way, truths having a necessary connection with these.

371 God created man and woman *together* and willed each *for* the other. The Word of God gives us to understand this through various features of the sacred text. "It is not good that the man should be alone. I will make him a helper fit for him" (Gen 2:18). None of the animals can be man's partner (Gen 2:19-20). The woman God "fashions" from the man's rib and brings to him elicits on the man's part a cry of wonder, an exclamation of love and communion: "This at last is bone of my bones and flesh of my flesh" (Gen 2:23). Man discovers woman as another "I," sharing the same humanity.

1952 There are different expressions of the moral law, all of them interrelated: eternal law—the source, in God, of all law; natural law; revealed law, comprising the Old Law and the New Law, or Law of the Gospel; finally, civil and ecclesiastical laws.

FROM THE CATECHISM Continued

1953 The moral law finds its fullness and its unity in Christ. Jesus Christ is in person the way of perfection. He is the end of the law, for only he teaches and bestows the justice of God: "For Christ is the end of the law, that every one who has faith may be justified" (Rom 10:4).

1954 Man participates in the wisdom and goodness of the Creator who gives him mastery over his acts and the ability to govern himself with a view to the true and the good. The natural law expresses the original moral sense which enables man to discern by reason the good and the evil, the truth and the lie:

> The natural law is written and engraved in the soul of each and every man, because it is human reason ordaining him to do good and forbidding him to sin...But this command of human reason would not have the force of law if it were not the voice and interpreter of a higher reason to which our spirit and our freedom must be submitted. (Leo XIII, *Libertas praestantissimum*, 597)

2036 The authority of the Magisterium extends also to the specific precepts of the *natural law*, because their observance, demanded by the Creator, is necessary for salvation. In recalling the prescriptions of the natural law, the Magisterium of the Church exercises an essential part of its prophetic office of proclaiming to men what they truly are and reminding them of what they should be before God (cf. *DH* 14).

2088 The first commandment requires us to nourish and protect our faith with prudence and vigilance, and to reject everything that is opposed to it. There are various ways of sinning against faith:

Voluntary doubt about the faith disregards or refuses to hold as true what God has revealed and the Church proposes for belief. *Involuntary doubt* refers to hesitation in believing, difficulty in overcoming objections connected with the faith, or also anxiety aroused by its obscurity. If deliberately cultivated doubt can lead to spiritual blindness.

The army of Louis XIV prepares to attack Tournai in 1667. The Treaty of Aachen in 1668 marked its attachment to France. In the background, the city of Tournai spreads out behind its medieval walls. The artist, Adam Frans van der Meulen, traveled with the French army and made preparatory drawings. Van der Meulen was commissioned with drawing the views of the cities conquered by the king. The Brussels painting belongs to the first series of the King's Conquests painted for the Royal Pavilion.

The French Revolution And Napoleon

*In France, discontent would give rise to a massive
social revolution that would change and influence the entire world.
Much of today's religious cynicism has its roots in this revolution.*

CHAPTER 17

The French Revolution And Napoleon

The condemnation of God by man is not based on the truth, but on arrogance, on an underhanded conspiracy. Isn't this the truth about the history of humanity, the truth of our century? In our time the same condemnation has been repeated in many courts of oppressive totalitarian regimes...God is always on the side of suffering. His omnipotence is manifested precisely in the fact that He freely accepted suffering.

— John Paul II, *Crossing the Threshold of Hope.* pp. 65-66

The French Revolution, which began in 1789, was in many ways a culmination of centuries of political and social erosion. The wars of religion, the growing power of the nation-state, and new intellectual movements, such as the Enlightenment and the scientific revolution, all changed the way traditional authority was understood and helped to spark new political and social unrest.

The causes that ignited the revolution in France were not particular to that country. The transition into the modern age put massive strains on the economies of many European nations. With these social and economic changes came inflation, job shortages, and social inequality, which all contributed to disenchantment among the wider population. In France, resentment gave rise to a massive social revolution that would in turn change and influence the entire world.

As well as being the largest and wealthiest country in Europe, France was considered the continent's cultural and intellectual center. France was seen as a modern and fashionable state, and it influenced everything from style and dress to art and language. France also gave birth to philosophical ideas expressed in rationalism, secularism, and agnosticism. Since France was such a cultural model, the French Revolution there would fall under the scrutiny of nearly every nation-state.

Unfortunately, one effect of the French Revolution would involve a widespread rejection of the Church as a teacher and guide for society. By the time the revolution unfolded, Gallican-style independence was a common trend in many European governments, and control of the Church fell under the rule of the eighteenth century monarchs. This usurpation of Church authority greatly slowed down the pace of reform and violated the basic rights of the Church to govern herself and

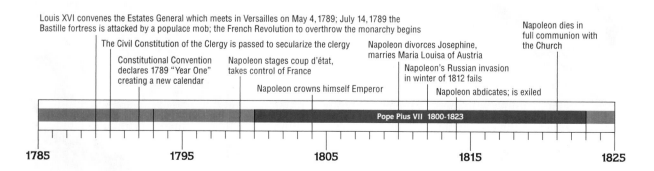

Louis XVI convenes the Estates General which meets in Versailles on May 4, 1789; July 14, 1789 the Bastille fortress is attacked by a populace mob; the French Revolution to overthrow the monarchy begins

The Civil Constitution of the Clergy is passed to secularize the clergy

Constitutional Convention declares 1789 "Year One" creating a new calendar

Napoleon stages coup d'état, takes control of France

Napoleon crowns himself Emperor

Napoleon divorces Josephine, marries Maria Louisa of Austria

Napoleon's Russian invasion in winter of 1812 fails

Napoleon abdicates; is exiled

Napoleon dies in full communion with the Church

Pope Pius VII 1800-1823

1785　　1795　　1805　　1815　　1825

serve as a basic moral voice for society. This sad state of affairs led some to believe that the Church ceased to be a beacon of truth and guide for every person due to the pervasive rationalism, Deism, and atheistic Enlightenment philosophies.

Much of the modern era's religious cynicism has its roots in this period. The French Revolution would bring to the Church painful persecution. Thousands of bishops, priests, monactics, and laymen went to their death by the guillotine because of their loyalty to the Gospel. Throughout this ordeal, the Church not only remained firm in her mission, but also enjoyed growth through new religious orders, missionary work in new lands, and the appearance of great saints. Even powerful dictators such as Napoleon were stymied by the spiritual and moral strength of the Church exhibited through the likes of Popes Pius VI and Pius VII.

PART I

From Revolution to Republic

The French Revolution of 1789 was the culmination of various political currents coupled with popular demands for greater equality and justice. Ever since the death of Louis XIV, divisions between the aristocratic nobility, the growing upper middle class (called the *bourgeoisie* in France), and the underprivileged masses contributed to economic and social unrest. Nobles blocked tax reform, the *bourgeoisie* paid their way out of economic responsibilities, and the poor bore the brunt of an ever-increasing national debt caused by the monarchy's lavish lifestyle and costly wars.

Both agrarian and urban poor grew increasingly hostile during the late eighteenth century. Squabbles between the king, nobles, and *bourgeoisie* left their the peasantry impoverished and desperate. Rural farmers intensely resented the last vestiges of feudal influence and saw in the revolution their chance to clamor for both political and economic reform. Urban workers, on the other hand, protested inflation, low wages, and a tremendous tax burden. Together, protests from these two poor segments of society snowballed into a fierce social upheaval that precipitated the revolution and ultimately brought down France's *Old Régime*.

Marie Antoinette's Petit hameau (hamlet) on the grounds of Versailles. After Louis XIV, several smaller buildings were added to Versailles by Louis XV and Louis XVI including the Grand Trianon, the Petit Trianon, and the Hamlet of Marie Antoinette known as Petit hameau.

THE *OLD RÉGIME:* THREE ESTATES

Before the revolution, French society was legally divided into three "estates" or classes. These three main social divisions included the clergy, nobility, and the commoners (everybody else). Clearly, these class distinctions were a remnant of the Medieval age and were no longer compatible with the political and economic changes of the time.

By 1789, there were about 100,000 clerics in France out of a total population of 24,000,000. Nonetheless, the Church played a significant role as both guardian and guide for society. For instance, the Catholic Church was connected to virtually every charitable institution, from orphanages and hospitals to schools and universities. The Church also took responsibility for unemployment compensation and distribution of food to the destitute. All these services were a costly endeavor, and understandably required tithes from the people. In addition to the tithe, landholdings provided a vast source of wealth for the ecclesiastical hierarchy charged with Church administration. By 1789, the Church of France was the largest landholder in the kingdom, owning approximately one-fifth of the total lands available.

In addition to serving the many who were in need, some of the clergy served as regents to the kings and advisors to the nobility, making themselves available for spiritual guidance and political advice. Although the special services given to the king and the aristocracy gave those particular clerics special honor and prestige, it tended to shift their loyalties more to the state than to the Church.

This **First Estate**, comprised of clergy, was itself divided between wealthy and influential clerics and the great majority of poor parish priests. Most of the priests lived simple and impoverished lives no different from the people to whom they ministered. This great disparity within the Church in France showed the urgent need for reform. Unfortunately, the excessive resistance of kings, nobles, and wealthy clerics to the mandates of the papacy severely compromised the implementation of the Tridentine Reforms.

The **Second Estate** consisted of about 400,000 nobles. Since the death of Louis XIV, these noble aristocrats enjoyed a resurgence of power, and again they began to exercise some of their traditional feudal privileges. They exempted themselves from taxation and blocked every attempt at modernizing France's economic structure. Because of those self-serving exemptions, France's tax coffers remained empty, despite being the wealthiest country of eighteenth-century Europe.

The **Third Estate** (the remaining ninety-seven percent of the population) consisted of an absurdly disparate portion of society. Wealthy bankers, lawyers, merchants, and other elite members of society who could not claim nobility from birth composed the *bourgeoisie*. The *bourgeoisie* held great political and economic power and were constantly in conflict with the nobility. They resented the nobility's parasitic drain on the society's economy and their unwarranted legal privileges. At the same time, the *bourgeoisie,* who could have easily paid taxes, exempted themselves as well. It logically followed that the poor masses were left to shoulder the burden of the taxes, fueling a dark future for France.

Along with the wealthy *bourgeoisie,* the Third Estate included the poorest of the poor, both urban workers and rural peasants. Economic differences in France were so dramatic at this time that those who were not extremely wealthy, like the nobility or the *bourgeoisie,* were dreadfully poor. Inflation devastated these lower classes. Since the 1730s, the price of consumer goods had risen sixty-five percent even though wages rose a meager twenty-two percent. In addition to coping with higher prices, the lion's share of the tax burden of the country fell on this lower class. A series of poor harvests in the 1780s exacerbated the situation of the poor and drove many starving farmers into Paris seeking charitable aid. The French economy could no longer provide for its people as a political crisis loomed over the country.

Louis XVI (1754-1793) was King of France until his arrest and execution during the French Revolution. King Louis XVI was guillotined in front of a cheering crowd on January 21, 1793. His wife, Marie Antoinette, followed him to the guillotine on October 16, 1793. Beloved by the people at first, Louis' indecisiveness and conservatism led the people to reject and hate him and associate him with the tyranny of former kings of France. Today, some historians see him as an honest man with good intentions but who was unfit for the huge task of reforming the monarchy. He was tragically used as a scapegoat by the Revolutionaries.

THE FINANCIAL CRISIS

France's financial crisis, which led to the political turmoil of 1789, was the result of nearly a century of economic mismanagement and abuse typified by Louis XIV's lavish lifestyle and careless wars. Obviously, irresponsible expenditures had produced a severe strain on the economy. In 1739, France spent thirty-six percent of her annual income on paying off the debt incurred by Louis XIV's wars. In addition, the cost of Versailles and the monarchy's lifestyle cost ten percent of the entire national budget. Compared to the eight percent delegated to social programs and pensions, it was clear that economic priority was inordinately given to the kings' whims and caprices. By 1763, the debt reached sixty-two percent of the annual income, and after France supported the American Revolution, debt consumed one hundred percent of the entire national income.

Surprisingly, France's monumental debt was not much larger than most European countries in the late eighteenth century. What made France's situation worse were the severe inequities heaped on the meager financial resources of the poor. The nobility and *bourgeoisie* did not pay taxes; therefore, the entire sum fell on the lowest classes of society. These poor farmers and city workers simply had nothing with which to pay the debt.

Both Louis XV and Louis XVI realized that their country was in a dire economic situation and tried to reform the system of taxation. Unfortunately, the nobility opposed whatever reforms the kings tried to pass. The nobility's motives were twofold: they wanted to remain free from taxation, but more importantly, they hoped economic constraints on the kings would insure their own political power. They pressured Louis XVI to call the Estates General in order to fix the debt problem. The nobles hoped to use that legislative body to force concessions from the king on their behalf and establish for themselves long-term influence in the affairs of France. Backed into a corner, Louis XVI agreed, and convened the Estates General in 1788.

THE ESTATES GENERAL

The Estates General had not been convened since 1614, and reconvening it was not a simple task. Each Estate hoped that through the Estates General they could further their own cause and influence. The nobility hoped the body would organize as it was in 1614 with each of the three Estates having one vote and sitting in separate chambers. However, both the First and Third Estate rejected this organization, claiming that it was out of date and inadequately represented the French people. Clearly, the nobility had worn out its welcome, and the French people were quite eager for a dramatic change.

In response to the convocation of the Estates General, the clergyman Abbé Sieyès wrote a pamphlet called "What is the Third Estate?" In it the clergyman argued that the Third Estate by itself represented the people of France. Sieyès believed that since the Third Estate best represented the majority of France, its interests were in fact the interests of France. He saw no need to include any other minorities in the future government of the country. Sieyès' pamphlet became immensely popular and roused the general population to support the aboli-

Emmanuel Joseph Sieyès (1748-1836) was a French abbé (abbot) and one of the chief theorists of the revolutionary era. He renounced his faith during the Cult of Reason, voted for the death of King Louis XVI, and defended his conduct with the ironical words "I lived."

The Tennis Court Oath (*serment du jeu de paume*) was a pledge signed by 577 members of France's Third Estate on June 20, 1789. King Louis XVI had locked the deputies of the Third Estate out of their meeting hall so they met instead in a nearby tennis court. The Tennis Court Oath is often considered the moment of the birth of the French Revolution.

tion of the First and Second Estates. Amid growing public pressure, the king responded by allowing the Third Estate to bring twice as many representatives to the Estates General. This enraged the nobility, but delighted the French public who found new hope. When the Estates General finally met on May 4, 1789 at Versailles, popular unrest and social tensions were high.

In Versailles, the Third Estate immediately tried to exert its popular demand. They requested that the three-chamber distinction between the Estates be abolished and that the legislature meet as a single body. A number of clerics and bishops from the First Estate who sympathized with the plight of the poor masses supported this motion and joined the Third Estate in their chamber. The Third Estate understood itself as the only true representative body in France, and so on June 17, the Third Estate proclaimed itself the "National Assembly," assuming sovereign power and free jurisdiction over France.

Predictably, the nobility rejected the National Assembly and pressured the king to suppress the new legislature. On June 20, King Louis XVI acceded to the nobility's wishes and had the National Assembly locked out of the meeting hall. Rather than discouraging the new legislature from further action, the Assembly simply moved to a nearby tennis court where they promised to stay in session until a new constitution was drafted.

The king was fearful of the popular power held by the National Assembly. He tried to reach a compromise and agreed to limit his authority if the three Estates continued to sit separately in the Estates General. However, his provisions came too late. The National Assembly rejected his proposal and continued to meet. With the situation out of his hands and revolution immanent, the king ordered 20,000 troops to Versailles and Paris.

THE BASTILLE

In the streets of Paris, rumors of reform were met with both hope and skepticism. The lower classes suffered from an awful food shortage, and many began to believe that the nobles were purposefully creating the food shortage in order to starve the common people into submission. When news of the lockout of the National Assembly reached the streets, many feared the end of reform and the prolongation of their hard, miserable existence. The arrival of troops helped tip popular anxiety towards hysteria.

On July 12, riots broke out in Paris over the food shortages. Mobs of poor, hungry commoners took to the streets demanding food, and French troops, wary of firing on their fellow countrymen and starting a full-scale revolt in Paris, withdrew to the outskirts of the city. Mobs began looting stores and warehouses. They burned tariff houses and sacked the convent of Saint-Lazare in hopes of finding food.

On July 14, 1789, a mob attacked the Bastille, a Medieval fortress used as an arsenal and a prison, and seized 40,000 muskets and a dozen pieces of artillery. A skirmish ensued between the mob and the Bastille guards that left a hundred rioters and a half-dozen soldiers dead. Violence spilled into other parts of Paris, and the governor and a number of officials were killed or maimed. Still unsure about marching against their fellow countrymen, the troops on the outskirts of Paris did not intervene.

This day, July 14, 1789, is remembered as Bastille Day, the beginning of the French Revolution, because it marks the beginning of the common people's role in the overthrow of the French monarchy. The attack tipped the balance of power and frightened both the king and the nobility into making concessions to the people. The king recognized a citizens' committee that had been formed in Paris as the new municipal government. He disbanded the armies at Paris and urged the First and Second Estates to join the National Assembly. To restore order in Paris and other cities, the *bourgeoisie* in the National Assembly set up a force called the "National Guard." The tri-color flag that these forces adopted would become the symbol of the revolution.

Rural districts fared worse than the cities. Rumors of the nobles' plans to use foreign forces as a measure of suppression spread panic and paranoia throughout the countryside. This "Great Fear," as it became known, quickly degenerated as hungry mobs of peasants stormed aristocratic manors seeking food and destroying feudal records. The Great Fear turned into an all-out agrarian revolution, in which peasants eventually organized to destroy the last vestiges of the feudal regime by force.

THE DECLARATION OF
THE RIGHTS OF MAN AND CITIZEN

The proliferation of agrarian revolts throughout France complicated the political situation in Versailles. The National Assembly, which was largely made up of *bourgeois* leaders, was forced to deal with these riots and promote peace by meeting the demands of the peasants. In order to respond quickly, the Assembly convened a meeting with a small group of liberal nobles during the night of August 4, 1789, hoping the odd hour would discourage high attendance and consequently simplify the passage of legislation. Their plan worked, and the Assembly was able to pass radical legislation that ended the feudal obligations of peasant serfs and eliminated most of the special rights and privileges of the nobility. The Assembly issued a decree that summarized the resolutions of the "night of August 4" that read simply: "feudalism is abolished" (quoted in Palmer, et al., *History of the Modern World*, 2002, p. 371).

With these far-reaching provisions in place, the National Assembly set out to construct a new order in France. On August 26, 1789, the Assembly issued *The Declaration of the Rights of Man and Citizen*, declaring the following principles of the revolution: all men were born equal and held rights to liberty, property, security, and resistance. Influenced by Rousseau's "social contract,"

The Declaration embodied the major philosophical principles of the Enlightenment. Law was understood as the expression of the General Will of the people, and all public officials and armed forces were subject to the authority of the nation founded on the will of its people. The publication of *The Declaration* officially ended the *Old Régime.*

The Declaration was particularly vague on matters of religion. The only article relating to religion alluded to religious tolerance as long as religious beliefs did not "disturb the public order established by law" (translated by Robinson, *Declaration*, art. 10). Although this clause seemed to secure toleration for all religions, it would soon serve as a pretext to squelch the Church's freedom. Since the Catholic Church was associated with the *Old Régime* that robbed the people of their rights and welfare, the article opened the road to persecution of the Church.

Given the negative effect it would have on the *Old Régime*, King Louis XVI and the nobility did not accept *The Declarations of the Rights of Man and Citizen.* For this reason, many aristocrats fled the country. Despite the document's resolutions, economic conditions kept on deteriorating and political instability continued to incite unrest. On October 3, it was rumored that King Louis XVI held a banquet with a number of aristocrats during which they scorned the National Assembly and the tri-colored flag, the new symbol of French liberty, equality, and fraternity. Several thousand women, along with a large contingency of the Paris National Guard, marched to Versailles from Paris to protest. On October 6, the mob stormed the palace grounds, captured the king, and forced him and his queen, Marie Antoinette, to accompany them back to Paris. After that episode, the National Assembly established a single chamber for the governing body called the Legislative Assembly that met in Paris together with the king.

Assault on Versailles, October 6, 1789

THE CIVIL CONSTITUTION OF THE CLERGY

With the king in Paris, the Legislative Assembly set about reorganizing the country's governing body as it tried to solve the ever-growing problems of debt, poverty, and widespread famine. Seen as a relic of the *Old Régime*, the Church was the first to fall victim to these new measures of financial reform. The Assembly hoped to balance the budget by seizing the Church's wealth and landholdings. They passed laws to confiscate all Church lands, disband monasteries and convents, and redistribute the land among the French people. The Church was the largest landowner in France, and within ten years, nearly ten percent of all the lands and buildings in France were passed to the French citizens in the form of paper bonds called *Assignats.* These paper bonds became so numerous that in some circles they circulated like paper currency. Unfortunately, rather than resolving the debt crises, this largest transfer of property in European history largely benefited the upper middle class *bourgeoisie* who dominated the Legislative Assembly. In addition, the massive confiscation of the Church's possessions put the incipient revolution in opposition to the very Church that was working to improve the situation of the country.

THE FRENCH UNDERGROUND: BL. WILLIAM JOSEPH CHAMINADE

Many priests refused to take the oath of *The Civil Constitution of the Clergy*, and as a result, were forced to take their priestly ministry underground. One of these priests was Bl. William Joseph Chaminade, a native of Périgueux, France who was ordained a priest in 1785. Just fours years after his ordination, the French Revolution broke out, and Chaminade moved to Bordeaux, where he would spend most of his life. In 1791, Chaminade refused to take the oath of *The Civil Constitution of the Clergy*, instead practicing his priestly ministry in secret, putting his life in constant danger.

Many recognized Chaminade's extraordinary Faith during this time of persecution in France, and in 1795, he was given the task of receiving back into the diocese those priests who had taken the oath. During this time he reconciled some fifty priests with the Church. Two years later, in 1797, The Directory came to power. A price was put on his head, and Chaminade was forced to flee France to Saragossa, Spain, where he lived for three years. While in Spain, Chaminade was inspired to found a family of religious and laity: the Society of Mary. He wished to return to France and begin to re-evangelize the country that had suffered so much under the tyrannies of the revolution.

After returning to Bordeaux in 1800, Chaminade asked for and received the title of "Missionary Apostolic" from Rome. He was going to be a new kind of missionary, one that reconverted those who had fallen away from the Church. On December 8, 1800, the Feast of the Immaculate Conception, Chaminade gathered twelve young Catholics to form the Marian Sodality, which would become the basis of his new evangelization. "You are all missionaries" he told them, called to "multiply Christians."

Chaminade strove to provide a solid religious formation to the members of his Sodality, hoping to make these groups the basis of the re-Christianization of France. Soon the Sodality of Bordeaux spread to other cities. Chaminade encouraged groups of young men and women who, desiring greater dedication, made private vows and dedicated themselves to the apostolate of the Sodality without leaving their secular work. His followers, called Marianists, dedicated themselves to teaching and opened primary and secondary schools throughout France. They also established a network of teachers' schools for Christian education. Continuous revolution, however, made long-term growth difficult. In the mid-nineteenth century the Marianists spread to Switzerland and the United States where they continued to establish schools and educate young people in the Faith.

The last years of Chaminade's life were difficult. Health problems, financial difficulties, the departure of some of his disciples, misunderstandings and distrust, and obstacles to the exercise of his mission as founder all tested Chaminade's Faith. Nonetheless, he faced these difficulties with great confidence in Mary, faithful to his conscience and to the Church, filled with faith and charity. He died peacefully in Bordeaux on January 22, 1850, and he was beatified by Pope John Paul II on September 3, 2000.

Underlying the motives of this grand-scale seizure of Church lands was the Legislative Assembly's desire to bring the Church in line with the principles of the revolution and establish a Gallican Church that would merely serve as a social arm of the secular government. In July 1790, the Legislative Assembly passed *The Civil Constitution of the Clergy*, a piece of legislation designed to secularize the clergy, govern the Church in France, and separate all its administrative decisions from the papacy. Divided into four parts, *The Civil Constitution* dealt with everything from the number of bishops to the length of travel allowed to priests. In an effort to "democratize" the Church, priests would be chosen by local assemblies, and all citizens, including non-Catholics, would choose the hierarchy of the Church. The Assembly also reorganized the clergy's salary structure, reducing their status to state officials and their authority to that of simple civil servants. In order to separate the French Church from Rome, *The Civil Constitution of the Clergy* prohibited clergy from leaving their parishes for more than two weeks and outlawed the publication of any papal documents. This legislation placed the Catholic Church in France under the jurisdiction of the civil authorities. Diplomatic ties with the Holy See were severed in 1791.

At first Pope Pius VI only privately condemned this legislation in the hopes that the French bishops themselves would be more vocal and reject its provisions. The Archbishop of Aix formally rejected *The Civil Constitution* and called upon the faithful to do the same. Although the Assembly forced the French clergy to comply with *The Civil Constitution*, "only four of one hundred thirty-four bishops…and only 30,000 of 70,000 priests" recognized the document (cf. MacDonough, "French Revolution and the Napoleonic Era," Massachusetts Council for the Social Studies, 2005).

The Legislative Assembly responded to the clergy's defiance by threatening to revoke clerical offices. Those who did not agree to the document were labeled disturbers of the peace and were threatened with legal action. The strong-arm tactics scared a number of priests into accepting *The Civil Constitution*, but others went underground and continued to reject it. *The Civil Constitution* created a schism within the Church in France, dividing it between "constitutionalist" clerics who submitted and "non-jurors" who continued to reject the legislation. In 1791 Pope Pius VI came out publicly in support of the non-jurors and formally condemned *The Civil Constitution of the Clergy*. The Legislative Assembly reacted by accusing the pope of being an enemy of the state. The revolutionaries seized Avignon and urged all Catholics to separate themselves from Rome. Large regions of France, such as Vendee, Normandy, and Brittany, rejected the Legislative Assembly's treatment of the Church and formally supported the pope's rejection of *The Civil Constitution*. Frustrated by the resistance, the revolutionaries of the Legislative Assembly became more and more radical in implementing their programs.

THE FRENCH REPUBLIC

In addition to the suppression of the Church in France, certain revolutionary members of the Legislative Assembly known as "Jacobins" worked to uproot all the traditional institutions of the *Old Régime*. Internal tariffs were abolished throughout France and royal lands were nationalized. Networks of nobles who blocked attempts at tax reform were replaced by elected legislative assemblies.

On June 20, 1791, Louis XVI, fearing the extremist tendencies of the Legislative Assembly, attempted to flee France with the aim of securing foreign aid against the Jacobin leaders. The king was caught and brought back to Paris a prisoner, thereby dashing any hope for an English-style constitutional monarchy. Other European monarchs began to worry about the rapid collapse of the French monarchy. In order to prevent further expansion of revolutionary fervor into their own lands, Austria formed an alliance with Prussia to invade France so as to restore the king.

The infamous Jean-Paul Marat (1743-1793), was a member of the radical Jacobin faction during the Revolution. He helped launch the Reign of Terror. Marat composed the death lists from which the innocent and the guilty alike were executed. He was assassinated by Charlotte Corday, an aristocrat who supported the Girondists. She was sent to the guillotine four days later. Marat became a martyr for the Revolution, and busts of Marat replaced religious statues in the French churches.

Within the Legislative Assembly, *bourgeois* Jacobin leaders became increasingly fanatical. They believed that the French Revolution could not succeed unless it spread to every nation of the world, creating a federation of republics. For this reason, they endeavored to sow unrest in the Netherlands, Switzerland, Poland, and elsewhere. Realizing the intense opposition of the Austrian monarchy to the French Revolution, the Legislative Assembly declared war on Austria.

Prussian and Austrian troops quickly mobilized against France, and early Prussian victories slowed down momentum of the revolution. Internal unrest also hampered the work of the Legislative Assembly as commoners became angry with the *bourgeoisie* Jacobin domination of the Assembly. Riots soon broke out in many French cities. In Paris, on August 10, 1792, a mob of working-class people stormed the Tuileries, where King Louis XVI was being held, and seized the king. These rebels set up a revolutionary government, or "Commune" in the city. The Commune assumed the power of the Legislative Assembly and immediately clamored for a more democratic constitution. As the group organized a Constitutional Convention in order to draft a new constitution, violence continued in many cities throughout the month of September causing the death of over 1100 people of all classes and occupations.

The Constitutional Convention met in September 1792. These popular, working class revolutionaries threw out the constitution drafted by the National Assembly and completely reorganized France's political structure. They created a strictly republican model of government, abolished the monarchy, and emphasized the jurisdiction of neighborhood clubs and assemblies in order to open the democratic process up to the ordinary citizen. Believing they had finally established a government with real equality with the lower classes, the Convention declared 1789 "Year One" of the new political age. The founding of the republic became known as the "second" French Revolution.

In that same month, French armies won their first victory over Prussian forces. The new government harnessed popular jubilation and called upon the people of France to join the army and help establish the new republic. The French army quickly swelled from 180,000 to 650,000 troops, and the massive army seemed unstoppable. French troops entered Belgium, the German Rhineland, and northern Italy. Established by the Constitutional Convention, the National Convention would serve as the main legislative body for the next three years.

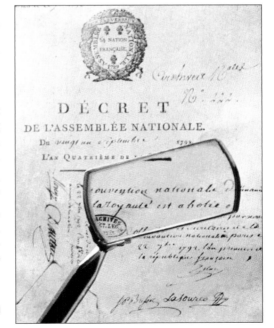

The National Assembly Decree abolishing the monarchy, September 22, 1789

The French Republican Calendar was adopted by the Jacobin-controlled National Convention on October 24, 1793. Years were counted from the beginning of the "Republican Era," September 22, 1792, the day the French First Republic was proclaimed, and one day after the Convention abolished the monarchy. There were twelve months, each divided into three ten-day weeks called décades. Each day was divided into ten hours, each hour into 100 decimal minutes and each decimal minute had 100 decimal seconds. Clocks were manufactured to display decimal time. The Republican calendar year began at the autumn equinox. The twelve months were given new names based on nature such as "harvest" and "windy." Instead of most days having a saint associated with it as in the Catholic Church's calendar, each day had a plant, a tool or an animal association such as "horse" and "turnip." Napoléon abolished the Republican calendar effective January 1, 1806.

MAD MOB VIOLENCE OF THE FRENCH REVOLUTION

The following is an excerpt from the London Times printed on Monday, September 10, 1792. The writer is reporting on the September Massacres that broke out the week prior to this article's printing. The events, the reporter says, are all based on eyewitness accounts.

The number of Clergy found in the Carmelite Convent was about 220. They were handed out of the prison door two by two into the Rue Vaugerard, where their throats were cut. Their bodies were fixed on pikes and exhibited to the wretched victims who were next to suffer. The mangled bodies of others are piled against the houses in the streets; and in the quarters of Paris near to which the prisons are, the carcases [sic] lie scattered in hundreds, diffusing pestilence all around.

The streets of Paris, strewed with the carcases of the mangled victims, are become so familiar to the sight, that they are passed by and trod on without any particular notice. The mob think no more of killing a fellow-creature, who is not even an object of suspicion, than wanton boys would of killing a cat or a dog. We have it from a Gentleman who has been but too often an eye witness to the fact. In the massacre last week, every person who had the appearance of a gentleman, whether stranger or not, was run through the body with a pike. He was of course an Aristocrate, and that was a sufficient crime. A ring, a watch chain, a handsome pair of buckles, a new coat, or a good pair of boots in a word, every thing which marked the appearance of a gentleman, and which the mob fancied, was sure to cost the owner his life. EQUALITY was the pistol, and PLUNDER the object.

As every body the mob assassinates, is called an Aristocrate, it is highly dangerous for any one to express himself compassionately at what passes. He would then become himself an object of suspicion.

The army marching from Paris exhibits a very motley group. There are almost as many women as men, many without arms, and very little provision. A principal object with them is to destroy the corn and lay waste the country, so that the confederates may be cramped for want of supplies.

"...every person who had the appearance of a gentleman, whether stranger or not, was run through the body with a pike."

PART II

The Death of Louis XVI and the Age of the Revolutionary Republic

The new French Republic never achieved a stable government. Rather, as power shifted between various political factions and committees, France remained in a perpetual state of unrest and fear. Along with the establishment of the National Convention, came the power shift from the *bourgeois* party, called the *Girondins,* to the poor urban "*sans-culottes,*" named after their working class pants. These "*sans-culottes*" represented the commoners of the cities and drew strength from both radical and popular elements. They worked to institute republican reforms and continued the policies of revolutionary expansion. These popularists never balked at using violence and brutality to better enforce and promote the principles of the revolution.

In December 1792, the National Convention, under the heavy influence of the *san-culottes*, put King Louis XVI on trial for treason. The king was condemned to death by a slim majority (361-360) and was guillotined on January 16, 1793. The execution of the king marked a new era of prolonged violence in France. Old problems, such as civil disorder, food shortages, and rising prices, continued to frustrate the lower classes. The poor began to doubt the principles of the revolution, which seemed only to bring about anarchy. Wishing to protect the revolution, the *sans-culottes* pressured the Convention to take more radical measures against dissent. They declared France to be in a state of emergency and formed the Committee of Public Safety to suppress all "counterrevolutionary" factions. This Committee began instituting a systematic policy of curbing violence through more frequent and persistent accusations and mass executions. Their rule during this period became known as "The Reign of Terror."

THE REIGN OF TERROR AND THE "DE-CHRISTIANIZATION" OF FRANCE

The Reign of Terror promoted by The Committee of Public Safety was meant to suppress counterrevolutionary tendencies and utilize all of France's resources to support the wars abroad. Control of the Committee was dominated by Maximilian Robespierre, a firm believer in the principles of the revolution. Out of a desire to promote civic virtue and create a society of good and honest citizens, Robespierre did not hesitate to use brutal and unjust means to achieve his ends.

The Reign of Terror severely harmed people of all classes. A vast machinery of merciless committees and tribunals was assembled to send thousands to the guillotine. No political faction was immune from the horrors of this dark chapter in the history of France. For instance, Queen Marie Antoinette was infamously executed in 1793 as a supporter of the royalist faction, while many members of the lower classes were killed for supporting revolutionary activities in opposition to the National Convention. Rebellions were suppressed most violently; citizens merely accused of petty crimes were brutally punished. As the Reign of Terror spread throughout the country, mob violence soon followed. Gangs of marauders, who believed they were acting in the best interest of the Committee, destroyed farms, houses, and churches. Mutinies broke out in the army and navy, and many nobles and political monarchists were forced into exile. During the Reign

Robespierre and his colleagues decided to replace both Catholicism and the rival, atheistic Cult of Reason (promoted by the Hébertists) with the Cult of the Supreme Being. On May 7, 1794 he secured a decree from the Convention recognizing the existence of the Supreme Being. This worship of the Supreme Being or Godhead (a kind of Deistic God, rejecting a personal God) was based upon the ideas of Rousseau in *The Social Contract*. On June 8, 1794, the then still powerful Robespierre personally led a vast procession through Paris to the Tuileries garden in a ceremony to inaugurate the new religion. It was not a popular concept. Robespierre was guillotined with Saint-Just and other supporters on July 28, 1794.

of Terror, no suspect was left unharmed, and many innocent were punished unjustly. The Committee's desire to comprehensively purge French society of anyone who did not support the revolution was perhaps best voiced by the twenty-six-year-old revolutionary and Committee member, Louis Saint-Just, who demanded that "punishment be handed out not only to traitors, but even to the indifferent" (quoted in Hause and Maltby, *Western Civilization: A History of European Society*, 2004, p. 588).

The Church in France was hit particularly hard by the Reign of Terror. Considering any religion counterrevolutionary, the Committee launched a program of "de-Christianization" in November 1793. "Missionary Representatives" were sent out into the countryside to close down churches, hunt down priests, and punish anyone accused of harboring clergy. The Cathedral of Notre-Dame de Paris was dedicated as a temple to the Goddess of Reason.

Maximilien Robespierre, (1758-1794) was a fanatical disciple of Rousseau and architect of the Cult of the Supreme Being.

Church buildings were vandalized; Gospel books and crucifixes burned; statues and relics of the Saints destroyed; and church bells and sacred vessels melted down for artillery pieces. Citizens were offered bounties for turning over priests who refused to take an oath of loyalty to the revolution. Furthermore, any priest found resisting the policies of the National Convention was ordered to be executed within twenty-four hours. Under the pretext of enforcing the Committee's policies, Catholics were killed publicly in cruel and gruesome ways. Mobs massacred entire monastic communities and Christian women and children were murdered in an effort to stop the spread of Christianity to future generations.

The Goddess of Reason procession. The Cult of Reason was a religion based on Deism devised by Jacques Hébert and Pierre Gaspard Chaumette in opposition to Robespierre's Cult of the Supreme Being. They considered Robespierre's cult a return to theism and in response advocated worship of Reason, personified as a goddess. Statues of the goddess were placed in the Cathedral of Notre Dame after the destruction of all Christian statues. She is considered by some to be the forerunner of "Marianne," the national emblem of France, personifying the triumph of Liberty and Reason. Her profile is on the official seal of the country, engraved on French Euro coins, and appears on French postage stamps.

In place of Christianity, the Committee of Public Safety set up a state-sponsored Deistic religion. The Mass was replaced with a civil ceremony celebrating the Goddess of Reason, and Paris' Notre Dame Cathedral was renamed the "Temple of Reason and Liberty." In the cathedral, wives and daughters of the revolutionaries took turns acting out the part of the Goddess of Reason on the altar. In addition to establishing new pagan cults, the Committee completely changed the calendar in an effort to suppress Christian worship. They eliminated the Lord's Day by instituting a ten-day week and exchanged saint and feast days for yearly celebrations of reason, liberty, and the republic. During the Reign of Terror all talk, practice, and promotion of religion was strictly and brutally repressed. The tomb of Genevieve, patroness of Paris, was replaced with a pantheon of France's great revolutionary men.

Despite their efforts to retain a tight grip on French society, revolts and rebellions continued throughout the Reign of Terror. Frequent attacks and executions by the Committee angered the working masses, turning the Committee's largest group of supporters against them. Robespierre upset members within the National Convention by trying to pass legislation that allowed his Committee to convict political opponents in the Convention without trial. In the end, Robespierre and his policies proved too much. The National Convention executed Robespierre and a number of his fellow Committee members in July 1794. Power shifted again, and the lower class revolutionary spirit typified by Robespierre was replaced with *bourgeois* leadership. The *bourgeoisie* threw out the constitution drafted in 1793 and set up a new French Republic governed by a *bourgeois*-dominated ruling party known as The Directory.

THE DIRECTORY

In many ways, The Directory was a weak party formed in reaction to the extremists who had dominated the previous government. The Directory primarily consisted of *bourgeoisie* who had not only retained their influence during the volatile instability and anarchy of the revolution, but in fact profited from the chaos. Among the French people, loyalties were still scattered. Some hoped for the return of the monarchy with certain reforms of the old system. Others longed for the return to the revolutionary activism of Robespierre. Still others thought that Robespierre had been too moderate and formed a radical group known as the "Conspiracy of Equals." Although The Directory was active in suppressing all these factions, while in power, it did little to solve the ongoing, pervasive problems of hunger and inflation.

The Directory's policies were particularly hard on the Church. Although it claimed to promote republican liberalism, freedom, and toleration, oppressive laws were restored regarding priests who refused to take the Oath of the Republic. Hunting parties were organized throughout France to arrest recalcitrant priests. Consequently, thousands of priests were killed or deported to the penal colony in Guiana (northeast South America). Hoping that the Church might simply die out due to a lack of leadership, The Directory also refused to fill vacancies in dioceses where bishops died. Throughout the years of revolution, the Church was considered an obstacle to the revolution, and therefore outlawed aggressively.

In 1797, The Directory held France's first free election to choose permanent members of the legislature. Some traditionally-minded candidates were tired of revolution and war, and promised to work for peace and promote a constitutional monarchy in France. Louis XVIII (one of Louis XVI's sons; Louis XVII dies in 1795) was in exile and was waiting for a chance to reestablish the monarchy. These advocates for a constitutional monarchy successfully won support, and in March 1797, a large number of royalists were elected to the legislature. *Bourgeois* leaders in The Directory were outraged over their loss of power.

Faced with a possible halt to the pursuit of the core objectives of the revolution, The Directory looked to a young and successful general to remedy the conflict between the monarchists and the *bourgeoisie.* Napoleon Bonaparte had led the French army in northern Italy, and more than simply winning control over the region, he had become a self-sufficient and independent administrator. Napoleon ruled so effectively that the civilian government in Paris had become dependent on him for administrating France's military acquisitions. Because they allowed for his freedom of movement and independent diplomacy, Napoleon supported The Directory and their expansionist policies. Since he was beholden to The Directory, Napoleon was upset with the elections of 1797. Now The Directory turned to Napoleon to help preserve the republic. Napoleon sent his general, Augereau, who organized the *coup d'état* of Fructidor on September 4, 1797. The coup annulled the elections, threw out the constitution, and restored the previous *bourgeoisie* leadership.

The coup of Fructidor was a turning point in the revolution. After the coup, the idea of maintaining a free, democratic republic was

Young General Bonaparte carries the French tri-color at the Battle of the Bridge of Arcole, November 17, 1796. In this battle, the French army was victorious over the Austrians. Arcole is a small village in Italy on the Alpine River.

In March 1798, Napoleon proposed an expedition to colonize Egypt, then a province of the Ottoman Empire. Although Napoleon had a massive success in the Battle of the Pyramids on July 21, 1798 (his 25,000 men defeated 75,000 native Mamluks), ten days later his naval fleet was destroyed by Britain's Rear Admiral Horatio Nelson at the Battle of the Nile. As a result, Napoleon became land-bound and cutoff from French supply ships.

A unique aspect of the Egyptian expedition was the inclusion of a large group of scientists, surveyors and technical artists with the invading force. Among many discoveries by this expedition was the Rosetta Stone (left). The Stone was found at a French construction site in the Egyptian port city of Rosetta (present-day Rashid) on July 15, 1799. The Stone contained an ancient decree of 196 B.C. by Ptolemy V in three scripts: Egyptian demotic script, Greek, and Egyptian hieroglyphs. (The Stone was translated in 1822 by Jean-François Champollion.) When the French surrendered Egypt to Britain in 1801, Britain took possession of the Stone (after much resistance by French scientists). It has been in the British Museum since 1802. Today, Egyptian officials continue to demand its return.

given up. The legislature became more dependent on the military, and semi-independent generals spread throughout Europe. Napoleon took foreign policy into his own hands and helped negotiate peace with Austria. The 1797 Treaty of Campo Formio established peace between the two countries at the expense of the German States, which were divided between the two nations. Church lands in Germany were confiscated and redistributed to compensate and appease the leaders involved.

Much of Italy fell under Napoleon's military might, and the peninsula became dominated by France. French troops attacked the Papal States, and Napoleon forced Pope Pius VI, who was by this time very old and ill, to relinquish his lands. The pope was arrested and taken on a long, arduous journey to the town of Valence. Along the way large crowds came to see the dying pope and, dropping to their knees, cried out for his blessing. On August 29, 1799, Pius VI died. One revolutionary commented, "The late pope has just died. We have seen the last of them and the end of superstition" (quoted in Harney, *The Catholic Church through the Ages*, 1974, p. 469).

Napoleon returned from Italy a popular hero and was assigned to lead an invasion of England. Deciding against a direct assault, he invaded Egypt in the hope of marching on India and destroying the English trade network. Successfully occupying Egypt, Napoleon left his armies and returned to France in late 1799. In Paris, the general joined some civilian leaders in The Directory who had totally given up on the republican model of government and were planning a change. Napoleon, still only thirty years old, seized the opportunity, and on November 9, 1799, staged the *coup d'état* of Brumaire. Troops stormed the legislature and proclaimed the formation of a new republic headed by three consuls. Napoleon became the First Consul, the leader of a new France.

THE ELECTION OF PIUS VII

Despite the sack of Rome and the eagerness of many French leaders to proclaim the Church extinct after the death of Pius VI, the cardinals assembled to elect a new pope. Before he died, Pius VI gave orders to elect the new pope in the city with the most cardinals. On November 30, 1799, the cardinals met in Venice, which enjoyed complete independence from French influence.

The conclave at Venice was divided. Some cardinals supported the wishes of the late Pius VI to elect a successor who would espouse moderate political views. Others, influenced by the Austrian monarchy, hoped for a pope who would favor the monarchical rule of the past. The debate continued for three months, and in the end, the supporters of Pius VI helped lead the College of Cardinals to a unanimous decision. They elected Barnaba Chiaramonti who took the name Pius VII.

Cardinal Chiaramonti, who had a strong personality, wanted to see the life of the Church restored in France as well as the rest of Europe. He understood how deeply the Faith was still rooted in the French people and for this reason believed in the possibility of a Christian revival. However, far from siding with old monarchical regimes, Chiaramonti was a progressive thinker who sympathized with the plights of the masses in France and their desire to establish liberty and equality in their country. He never condemned the principles of democracy outright, but rather the unjust means through which some of the revolutionaries sought them. Throughout the revolution, Chiaramonti had insisted that God preferred no particular form of government and that Democracy was not contrary to the Gospel. Nevertheless, he distinguished himself from the revolutionaries in France by arguing that liberty and equality were ideals that could only be achieved in Christ. Therefore, a Democracy required people of virtue and upright character that could only be made possible with the help of divine grace. Pope Pius VII clearly showed that the Church was open to a changing political climate but would always resist ideas or laws that would compromise her mission and violate her freedom. On July 3, 1800, Pius VII arrived in Rome with courage and faith to push Christ's kingdom forward amid cheering crowds.

Pope Pius VII was born Giorgio Barnaba Luigi Chiaramonti on August 14, 1740. He was Pope from March 14, 1800 until August 20, 1823.

PART III
Napoleon Bonaparte

Napoleon Bonaparte was born in Corsica in 1769 to a family of minor nobility. During the days of the monarchy, he attended French military schools and proved to be an outstanding student. Despite his extraordinary gifts, there would have been little hope for advancement up the military chain of command during the *Old Régime;* the revolution changed that. Napoleon was already an officer before the revolution, but after 1789 he quickly rose through the ranks of the army. He was made a brigadier general during the Reign of Terror and, in 1796, received command of an army in which he proved his superior military skill. Crossing the Alps, Napoleon drove the Austrians from Northern Italy and began governing the region on his own. Like many of the French generals of the time, Napoleon acted independently of the government in Paris.

The civilian government on their own never had firm enough control to implement both their domestic and foreign policies, and therefore became increasingly more reliant on their generals to enforce their policies. Napoleon set up a republic in northern Italy and counseled the government in Paris. When the 1797 election ushered in a more conservative government, the weak, expansionist government in Paris gladly accommodated the wishes of the French victor. Given his proven abilities as a leader, Napoleon was chosen to serve as the First Consul (1799) in the new government. Napoleon's ascent to power managed to stabilize the country, thereby ending the revolution in France. Out of the chaos of the preceding years, Napoleon would set up a new French Empire that blended the revolutionary idealism of 1789 with the power and control of an absolute monarch.

THE CONSULATE AND THE CONCORDAT OF 1801

The French diplomat Charles Maurice de Talleyrand (1754-1838) is regarded by many historians as one of the most versatile and influential diplomats in European history.

As Napoleon began his term as First Consul (a term that was supposed to last for ten years), he set about reorganizing the French Republic and began to restore peace and order. A vital part of stabilizing France after ten years of near anarchy was to restore religious freedom to the French people and rebuild a severely persecuted Church. Napoleon understood how deeply rooted the Catholic Faith was in the hearts of most French people and also realized that the revolution's violent suppression of religion was a key factor in fostering strong desires for a return to the *Old Régime.* Part of restoring the Catholic Church would involve re-establishing favorable relations with the pope.

Napoleon began normalizing relations between the government and the Church by securing a commitment of fidelity to the laws of France among priests who had refused to take the Oath to the French Republic. Once the priests assured patriotic loyalties to France, they were again able to carry out their priestly ministry publicly. He reopened the churches in France and released any imprisoned priests. Napoleon discarded the ten-day week and reestablished a nationwide day of rest. His policies immediately won the confidence of the French people, and most especially, the trust of French Catholics.

Napoleon Crossing the Great St. Bernard Pass. The Great St. Bernard Pass is the most ancient pass through the Western Alps, bordering Switzerland and Italy. Travel through the pass dates back to the Bronze Age. Hannibal crossed with elephants in 217 B.C.; Julius Caesar crossed in 57 B.C.; Emperor Augustus built a road across the pass and built a temple to Jupiter at the top; Charlemagne crossed in A.D. 800 following his coronation in Milan. In May 1800, Napoleon led 40,000 troops over the pass into Italy.

In 1049, St. Bernard of Menthon founded a hospice on the pass for weary and harassed travelers. The hospice, which still functions today, became famous for its St. Bernard dogs. The rescue dogs were bred by the monks to be large enough to handle the deep snow and to scent out lost persons.

Napoleon sent his secretary of state, the famous revolutionary and former bishop Charles Maurice de Talleyrand, to meet with the illustrious Vatican diplomat, Cardinal Ercole Conslavi. In 1801, the two worked on drawing up a concordat that would create a new legal framework between the Church in France and the papacy. This concordat occasioned a repeal of revolutionary laws that were harmful to the Church. After a series of rejected proposals that attempted to create a Gallican national French church under the authority of Napoleon, Pius VII agreed to a final version of the Concordat on August 15, 1801.

Outlining the new policies in seventeen articles, the Concordat guaranteed the free and public practice of Catholicism in France. Civil authorities could only intervene in Church matters in instances of "public safety." In return, the Church agreed to the realignment of the French dioceses according to the new geographical breakdown of the country. This territorial reconfiguration occasioned a reduction in the number of French bishops from one hundred thirty six to sixty. The Pope also agreed to ask bishops who had lost their sees because of this realignment to resign from their offices. As for the appointment of new bishops, the pope agreed to allow Napoleon to nominate candidates, but it was ultimately up to the pope to give his final word. The Concordat rejuvenated Christian life throughout France. All the cathedrals and churches were reopened, and the government of France agreed to compensate for the loss of Church property by providing suitable salaries to the clergy. The dark days of religious suppression seemed to be over.

THE ORGANIC ARTICLES

The renewal of relations between France and the pope in Rome brought about great rejoicing for Catholics in France and around the world. But the joy did not last long. Soon after the signing of the Concordat, the French government passed a series of legislative restrictions limiting the Church's independence. Appealing to the provision in the Concordat regarding intervention in the Church's affairs in the interest of "public safety," the legislature passed the Organic Articles. These articles are best summed up as a combination of the Gallicanism prevalent during the reign of Louis XIV and the restrictions of *The Civil Constitution of the Clergy*. The worst of both worlds, the Organic Articles forbade the publication of all papal documents, decrees of the councils, or the convocation of any synod without the consent of the government. The new French government introduced a Gallican Catechism to be taught in all French seminaries, limited the administrative powers of the bishops in France; promoted civil marriages; and suppressed religious orders.

The Articles nullified whatever apparent liberty was granted to the Church by the Concordat of 1801, and they re-asserted the authority of Napoleon over the Church of France. It was clear that there was still strong animosity toward the Church, and these articles sought to appease the anti-Catholic forces by imposing damaging restrictions on the Catholic Church.

THE CORONATION OF NAPOLEON I

By 1802, thanks to the successful establishment of the Consulate, the Revolution was over. The French political scene had been finally pacified with the emergence of the strong Consulate, and Napoleon's power over Europe continued to grow. As First Consul, Napoleon soon made peace with the pope, Britain, and all the continental powers. This period of peace, which lasted from 1802 until 1803, was called the "Peace of Amiens" (Amiens being the city in which the treaty was signed), and it made Napoleon very popular. During the peace, Napoleon quietly advanced his interests, reorganized France's possessions, and annexed a number of small German principalities. In August 1802, Napoleon's popularity was so great that he named himself consul for life. Two years later in 1804, Napoleon had himself named emperor.

NAPOLEON'S ROMAN ASPIRATIONS

In the aftermath of the bloody and unstable French Revolution, security and unity were hard to come by. Napoleon, for personal and public reasons, fostered Roman ideology and nostalgia of Classical antiquity in order to unite France in the desire to establish a new Roman Empire. Napoleon introduced Roman architecture, art, and sculpture all over France to create associations between his imperial ambitions and that of the ancient empire.

At Napoleon's coronation, he carefully organized the ceremony to reflect the glorious façade of the Roman Empire. The ceremony combined aspects of the Bourbon coronations with those of Charlemagne, the great Holy Roman Emperor, and made use of a number of imperial symbols, including a laurel wreath made of gold for his crown. On a medal commemorating his coronation, Napoleon is depicted on one side with the laurel wreath and being hoisted on a shield on the other by both a soldier and a Roman senator.

Napoleon crowned himself Emperor on December 2, 1804 at Notre-Dame Cathedral. Napoleon then crowned his wife Joséphine as Empress. On May 26, 1805, in Milan's Cathedral, Napoleon was crowned King of Italy, with the Iron Crown of Lombardy.

As soon as Napoleon was named emperor, despite his revolutionary pretenses, he surrounded himself with a lavish court and took on all the pomp of nobility. He desired to have himself crowned in a dazzling ceremony and exquisite pageantry. In keeping with the long tradition of the French monarchy dating back to Charlemagne, Napoleon wanted the pope to crown him. Napoleon sent word to the pope, requesting that Pius VII crown him in the cathedral at Notre Dame in Paris on December 2, 1804.

The pope was cautioned that a rejection of Napoleon's request might prove detrimental to the recent friendly relations between Rome and France since the Concordat of 1801. Since those relations, although much improved, were far from ideal, Pius VII still hoped to convince the emperor to revoke some of the provisions of the Organic Articles. The pope therefore felt that his involvement in the coronation of Napoleon might work to further the freedom of the Church in France. Pope Pius VII graciously assented to the invitation. However, before leaving for Paris, he signed a conditional act of abdication that provided for the election of a new pope in the event that Napoleon prevented his return to Rome.

In Paris, the pope tried to use his visit to influence Napoleon's policies and retain some authority over the French church that now was controlled by the new emperor. Pope Pius VII established a moral advantage over Napoleon by objecting to the emperor's marriage to Josephine, which was not celebrated according to the Church's specifications. The pope refused to attend the coronation until the marriage was preformed validly. Napoleon reluctantly conceded and was married in private on December 1, the night before the coronation.

The next day Napoleon would be crowned emperor. However, before the pope could crown Napoleon, he snatched the crown from the pope's hands and placed it on his own head. Napoleon wanted to acknowledge publicly that his authority did not come from the pope, but rather from himself. After crowning himself emperor, Napoleon crowned his wife empress.

Pius VII was never able to secure from Napoleon needed concessions for the Catholic Church in France. Napoleon ignored most of the pope's requests, in part to show that his authority would not be influenced by the Roman pontiff. To prevent relations from completely souring, Napoleon did agree to replace the calendar of the revolution (with 1789 recognized as year one) with the traditional, Gregorian calendar. With only this small concession in place, Pius VII left Paris very displeased with the emperor.

EMPEROR NAPOLEON AGAINST PIUS VII

In the years that followed his coronation, Napoleon extended his interests throughout Europe. Through an unprecedented series of military victories, the French empire expanded across the continent. With each new area he conquered, Napoleon enforced his legal code, called the "Napoleonic Code," which introduced the emperor's typical mix of revolutionary and traditional ideas. The Code provided for equality among religious denominations and freedom of religious practice, but it also introduced civil marriage and divorce and placed heavy restrictions on the Church. In the region of Italy under his control, Napoleon and the pope came into conflict once again, this time over the marriage of Napoleon's brother Jerome.

In 1805, Napoleon asked Pius VII to annul his brother's marriage. The emperor wished his brother to remarry for political reasons, and the pope refused to grant the dispensation. Pius VII also refused to go along with Napoleon in joining the Continental System. Angered by the pope's rejection, Napoleon threatened to abolish priestly celibacy throughout Europe, suppress more religious orders, and establish a French patriarch to oppose the pope's authority over the Church in France. Pius VII still refused to compromise the position of the Church on marriage. Frustrated with the pope's resistance, Napoleon ordered his troops to march on Rome.

Napoleon Meets With Pope Pius VII. Napoleon seized huge portions of the Papal States and assumed jurisdiction over the power of the pope. After Pius VII excommunicated Napoleon, Napoleon had the pope arrested on July 5, 1805 and taken to Savona, in France, where he was imprisoned for six years.

As emperor, Napoleon claimed succession from Charlemagne, and with that, he claimed the right to revoke the "donation of Pepin," which established the Papal States in 756. Napoleon then seized huge portions of the Papal States in 1808 and assumed jurisdiction over the pope. These moves involved a rejection of the pope's temporal authority and transferal of the Papal States to French rule. Rome was made the second city of the Empire, and the pope was issued a salary. The pope's authority was restricted to the supervision of the papal palaces. Although not totally clear, it is generally agreed that Pius VII responded by excommunicating the responsible parties with the bull *Quum memoranda* and possibly Napoleon himself. Napoleon in turn had the pope arrested on July 5 and taken to Savona (France) where he was imprisoned for six years.

In 1809 Napoleon divorced his wife Josephine, hoping to build an alliance with Austria and secure an heir by marrying Maria Louisa, the daughter of the Hapsburg emperor. Although Napoleon had his marriage to Josephine dissolved by the French Senate, the Austrian court would not accept the senate's authority over such matters. They insisted that the emperor have his marriage annulled by the Church. Knowing that Pius VII would refuse to annul the marriage, Napoleon turned to the Gallican Church Court of Paris which gladly granted a dispensation. Despite vehement protests of Pius VII from his prison, Napoleon married Maria Louisa on April 1, 1810.

Many rejected the authority of the Gallican Church Court and its decision to annul Napoleon's marriage. In protest, thirteen cardinals refused to attend the wedding ceremony. Napoleon reacted by having these cardinals arrested and their properties confiscated. They were forbidden to wear their red cardinalatial robes, and forced to wear the plain garb of ordinary clerics. These dissenting cardinals, as a result, became known as the "black" cardinals.

THE FRENCH COUNCIL OF 1811 AND THE CONCORDAT OF FONTAINEBLEAU

Despite his imprisonment, the pope continued to issue Papal Bulls that rejected many of Napoleon's policies. The emperor wanted a remedy to the situation, and in 1811 called for a national council of French bishops in an effort to gain authority over all ecclesiastical affairs.

Despite Napoleon's intentions, the council remained loyal to the pope and refused to grant Napoleon's requests. Rather than grant authority to the emperor to make ecclesiastical appointments in the pope's absence, at the advice of Pius VII, the council agreed to allow the archbishop of a province to appoint new bishops in the event of a papal absence lasting more than six months. As an assertion and endorsement of the pope's authority, the installation was to be performed in the name of the absent pope. Napoleon was outraged at the decision of the council. He closed the council and arrested three bishops involved with the decisions. Failing to gain the support of "his council," as he called it, Napoleon tried to pressure the pope into submission.

Before leaving for his Russian military campaign in 1812, Napoleon moved Pius VII from Savona to the palace of Fontainebleau. Cut off from the contact of his supporters, sick and alone, the pope was pressured to comply with the emperor's wishes. After Napoleon's return from Russia and under tremendous pressure, Pius VII agreed to preliminary discussions over the issue of Napoleon's authority in making ecclesiastical appointments. Before the pope gave any formal agreement to the measures under study, Napoleon had these discussions published. This forced "agreement" in 1813 was called the Concordat of Fontainebleau, and if it had been allowed to stand, it would have placed all French and Italian bishops under the control of the Emperor.

One benefit of the Concordat of Fontainebleau was that it allowed the "black" cardinals to visit with the pope. As soon as these loyal servants met with Pius VII, the "black" cardinals suggested that the pope publish his rejection of the Concordat of Fontainebleau. Pius formally rejected the Concordat of Fontainebleau two months after its publication and sent letters disavowing the signature he had given and voiding all of the recent episcopal appointments. Although Napoleon ordered this letter kept secret, news of the pope's retraction spread throughout Europe.

THE FALL OF NAPOLEON

Napoleon's empire began to collapse with the loss of his army in his failed invasion of Russia in the winter of 1812. Encouraged by Napoleon's defeat, a renewed coalition between Austria, Prussia, Russia, and England marched towards Paris and forced the emperor's abdication. With Napoleon's defeat in 1814, Pius VII was free to return to Rome. The people cheered as Napoleon's great adversary returned to the Eternal City.

Despite the difficulties between Napoleon and the Church, after his downfall, Pope Pius VII took measures to protect the former emperor's family from any harsh retribution. Pius also interceded on Napoleon's behalf when he learned that the former emperor sought the services of a Catholic priest while in captivity on the Island of St. Helena. Pius VII continued to show charity to Napoleon and his family, and he did not abandon the former emperor during his captivity. During the end of his life, Napoleon spoke of Pius VII as "an old man full of tolerance and light". "Fatal circumstances," he added, "embroiled our cabinets. I regret it exceedingly" (quoted in Goyau, "Napoleon I [Bonaparte]," *The Catholic Encyclopedia*, vol. X, 1911). Napoleon was eventually restored to full communion with the Church before he died in his confinement on May 5, 1821.

Napoleon I on His Imperial Throne by Jean Auguste Dominique Ingres

CONCLUSION

Although his rise to power ended the revolution, Napoleon's death marked the close of the revolutionary era. The storm of revolutionism, the ideas of secularism, and the passions that fueled the upheaval of the old European regimes had crisscrossed the continent for over thirty years. Nations had fallen and new ideologies had taken root in the popular imagination of almost every nation. Although the nations that toppled Napoleon would attempt to restore the old order, the principles of revolution had already begun to erode the old political order.

In 1814, members of all the European nations met in Vienna to determine the aftermath of the Napoleonic era. Napoleon's France had restructured most of Europe, and representatives at the Congress of Vienna, as the meeting was called, sought to reorganize the continent. There was an immense amount of reconstruction to be done, especially for the Church. All over Europe dioceses had been redrawn and Church properties redistributed. Religious orders had been decimated, seminaries were closed, and communication with Rome was, in many regions, destroyed. The Church would dedicate much of its work throughout the nineteenth century to recovering the losses from the period of Napoleonic conquest. The example of Pius VII had impressed many nations and would help the Church as it negotiated with European powers. Nonetheless, in the face of new ideologies and emerging nationalism and industrialization, the road ahead for the Church would not prove easier than the road it left behind.

THE FRENCH REVOLUTION'S PAINTER

Self Portrait by Jacques-Louis David

Jacques-Louis David (1748-1825) was the strongest influence in French art of the nineteenth century because of his vast number of pupils. David was an active supporter of the French Revolution, friend of Maximilien de Robespierre, and a Jacobin. David was imprisoned after Robespierre's fall from power, and upon his release, aligned himself with Napoleon. It was at this time that he developed his "Empire style," notable for its use of warm Venetian colors.

Napoleon visited his studio in 1797. David recorded his face, which later became his famous painting Napoleon Crossing the St. Bernard Pass. Napoleon had high esteem for David, and asked him to Egypt, but David declined. After the proclamation of the Empire, David became the official court painter. One of his more important commissions was The Coronation of Napoleon in Notre Dame. David was permitted to watch the event. He had plans of Notre Dame delivered to his studio, and participants in the coronation came to his studio to pose individually. The pope came to sit for the painting, and blessed David. Napoleon came to see the painting, stared at the canvas for an hour and said "David, I salute you."

SUPPLEMENTARY READING

John Paul II, *Crossing the Threshold of Hope*, 52

In fact, about 150 years after Descartes all that was fundamentally Christian in the tradition of European thought had already been pushed aside. This was the time of the Enlightenment in France, when pure rationalism held sway. The French Revolution, during the Reign of Terror, knocked down the altars dedicated to Christ, tossed crucifixes in the streets, introduced the cult of the goddess Reason. On the basis of this there was the proclamation of liberty, equality, and fraternity. The spiritual patrimony and, in particular, the moral patrimony of Christianity were thus torn from their evangelical foundation. In order to restore Christianity to its full vitality, it is essential that these return to that foundation.

Declaration of the Rights of Man and Citizen, August 26, 1789

Consequently, the National Assembly recognizes and declares, in presence and under the auspices of the Supreme Being, the following rights of the man and the citizen.

Article the First: Men are born and remain free and equal in rights. The social distinctions can be founded only on the common utility.

Article Two: The goal of any political association is the conservation of the natural and imprescriptible rights of the man. These rights are personal freedom, liberty, the ownership of property, personal safety and resistance, the ability to resist oppression.

Article Three: The principle of any sovereignty lies primarily in the nation as a whole. No body nor individual can exert authority which does not emanate from the nation expressly.

Article Four: Freedom consists in being able to do all that does not harm others. Thus, the exercise of the natural rights of each man has limits only to the extent of those which ensure that the other members of society obtain the pleasure of these same rights. Such limitations can be determined only by the law.

Article Five: The law has the right to proscribe the actions harmful of society. All that is not forbidden by the law cannot be prevented, and no one can be constrained to do what the law does not specifically order.

Article Six: The law is the overt expression of the general will. All the citizens have the right to contribute personally, or by their representatives, to the formation of law. The law must be the same one for all, either that it protects, or that it punishes.

The Civil Constitution of the Clergy, July 12, 1790

Article I. Beginning with the day of publication of the present decree, there shall be but one mode of choosing bishops and parish priests, namely that of election.

Article II. All elections shall be by ballot and shall be decided by the absolute majority of the votes.

Article VII. In order to be eligible to a bishopric, one must have fulfilled for fifteen years at least the duties of the church ministry in the diocese, as a parish priest, officiating minister, or curate, or as superior, or as directing vicar of the seminary.

Article XIX. The new bishop may not apply to the pope for any form of confirmation, but shall write to him, as to the visible head of the universal Church, as a testimony to the unity of faith and communion maintained with him.

Article XXI. Before the ceremony of consecration begins, the bishop elect shall take a solemn oath, in the presence of the municipal officers, of the people, and of the clergy, to guard with care the faithful of his diocese who are confided to him, to be loyal to the nation, the law, and the king, and to support with all his power the constitution decreed by the National Assembly and accepted by the king.

VOCABULARY

ASSIGNATS
Paper bonds. After the Legislative Assembly passed laws to confiscate all church property, the lands were redistributed to the people in the form of *Assignats.*

BLACK CARDINALS
Cardinals who were forced to wear the same black vestments as priests instead of their usual red as a punishment by Napoleon for refusing to recognize his marriage to Maria Louisa.

BOURGEOISIE
French upper middle class composed of mostly wealthy bankers, merchants, and lawyers.

ESTATES GENERAL
Legislative body of the *Old Régime* in France. Although it had not been called since 1614 and was widely held as misrepresentative, Louis XIV convened it in 1788 to respond to the growing financial crisis in France.

GREAT FEAR
Widespread panic in the French countryside due to rumors that the nobility were employing foreign forces to suppress the peasants.

JACOBINS
Revolutionary members of the Legislative Assembly who worked to uproot the traditional institutions of the *Old Régime.*

NAPOLEONIC CODE
Napoleon's code of law which blended revolutionary and traditional ideas. It provided for equality and freedom of religion, but it also introduced civil marriage and divorce and placed heavy restrictions on the Church.

NON-JURORS
French clerics who rejected *The Civil Constitution of the Clergy* and were forced to go underground.

PEACE OF AMIENS
Period of peace lasting from 1802 to 1803 during which Napoleon quietly advanced his interests, reorganized France's possessions, and annexed a number of small German principalities.

REIGN OF TERROR
Describes rule under the Committee of Public Safety in which the committee instituted a systematic policy of curbing violence through frequent and persistent accusations and mass execution in the interest of suppressing counterrevolutionary tendencies.

Marie Antoinette on the Way to the Guillotine sketched by Jacques-Louis David

STUDY QUESTIONS

1. What caused extreme divisions in France during the eighteenth century?

2. How were the classes structured within the "*Old Régime*"?

3. Why was the Estates General reconvened?

4. What is the significance of the Bastille?

5. What were the major principles held by *The Declaration of the Rights of Man and Citizen*?

6. What was *The Civil Constitution of the Clergy,* and why was it passed?

7. Who were the "non-jurors"?

8. Who were the Jacobins?

9. Why did Louis XVI try to flee France?

10. Why did Jabobins try to cause unrest elsewhere in Europe?

11. What was "the Commune"?

12. What is the "second" French Revolution?

13. Who were the "sans-culottes"?

14. What was the Reign of Terror? Who were its main supporters?

15. Who was Robespierre?

16. What happened to the Church during the Reign of Terror?

17. Who belonged to The Directory, and who was its most famous leader?

18. What was Pope Pius VII's attitude towards democracy?

19. What were the Organic Articles?

20. Who crowned Napoleon emperor?

21. Who were the black cardinals?

22. Which event led to the collapse of Napoleon's empire?

23. How did Napoleon's reign affect the rest of Europe?

24. How did Napoleon's reign affect the power of the Church?

PRACTICAL EXERCISES

1. From a Christian perspective, was the French Revolution justified? (Consider the situation of each social class before, during, and after the revolution.)

2. Why did the revolution work to "de-Christianize" France? What were the political motives? What were the ideological motives?

3. How was Napoleon Bonaparte like a monarch? How was he a proponent of the revolution? How did the way Napoleon combine these two roles make recovering from Napoleonic rule so difficult?

FROM THE CATECHISM

309 If God the Father almighty, the Creator of the ordered and good world, cares for all his creatures, why does evil exist? To this question, as pressing as it is unavoidable and as painful as it is mysterious, no quick answer will suffice. Only Christian faith as a whole constitutes the answer to this question: the goodness of creation, the drama of sin and the patient love of God who comes to meet man by his covenants, the redemptive Incarnation of his Son, his gift of the Spirit, his gathering of the Church, the power of the sacraments and his call to a blessed life to which free creatures are invited to consent in advance, but from which, by a terrible mystery, they can also turn away in advance. *There is not a single aspect of the Christian message that is not in part an answer to the question of evil.*

401 After that first sin, the world is virtually inundated by sin There is Cain's murder of his brother Abel and the universal corruption which follows in the wake of sin. Likewise, sin frequently manifests itself in the history of Israel, especially as infidelity to the God of the Covenant and as transgression of the Law of Moses. And even after Christ's atonement, sin raises its head in countless ways among Christians (cf. Gen 4: 3-15; 6: 5, 12; Rom 1: 18-32; 1 Cor 1-6; Rv 2-3). Scripture and the Church's Tradition continually recall the presence and *universality of sin in man's history:*

> What Revelation makes known to us is confirmed by our own experience. For when man looks into his own heart he finds that he is drawn towards what is wrong and sunk in many evils which cannot come from his good creator. Often refusing to acknowledge God as his source, man has also upset the relationship which should link him to his last end, and at the same time he has broken the right order that should reign within himself as well as between himself and other men and all creatures. (*GS* 13 § 1)

2125 Since it rejects or denies the existence of God, atheism is a sin against the virtue of religion (cf. Rom 1: 18). The imputability of this offense can be significantly diminished in virtue of the intentions and the circumstances. "Believers can have more than a little to do with the rise of atheism. To the extent that they are careless about their instruction in the faith, or present its teaching falsely, or even fail in their religious, moral, or social life, they must be said to conceal rather than to reveal the true nature of God and of religion" (*GS* 19 § 3).

2155 The holiness of the divine name demands that we neither use it for trivial matters, nor take an oath which on the basis of the circumstances could be interpreted as approval of an authority unjustly requiring it. When an oath is required by illegitimate civil authorities, it may be refused. It must be refused when it is required for purposes contrary to the dignity of persons or to ecclesial communion.

2577 From this intimacy with the faithful God, slow to anger and abounding in steadfast love (cf. Ex 34: 6), Moses drew strength and determination for his intercession. He does not pray for himself but for the people whom God made his own. Moses already intercedes for them during the battle with the Amalekites and prays to obtain healing for Miriam (cf. Ex 17: 8-12; Nm 12: 13-14). But it is chiefly after their apostasy that Moses "stands in the breach" before God in order to save the people (Ps 106: 23; cf. Ex 32: 1-34: 9). The arguments of his prayer—for intercession is also a mysterious battle—will inspire the boldness of the great intercessors among the Jewish people and in the Church: God is love; he is therefore righteous and faithful; he cannot contradict himself; he must remember his marvelous deeds, since his glory is at stake, and he cannot forsake this people that bears his name.

The Nineteenth Century:
The Age Of Revolution And The Emergence Of Nationalism

During this century of rapid political and cultural change, the Church began to speak on behalf of the working class and would be strengthened by the leadership of two celebrated popes.

CHAPTER 18

The Nineteenth Century: The Age Of Revolution And The Emergence Of Nationalism

The Church's social doctrine is not a "third way" between liberal capitalism and Marxist collectivism, nor even a possible alternative to other solutions less radically opposed to one another: rather, it constitutes a category of its own. Nor is it an ideology, but rather the accurate formulation of the results of a careful reflection on the complex realities of human existence, in society and in the international order, in the light of faith and of the Church's tradition. Its main aim is to interpret these realities, determining their conformity with or divergence from the lines of the Gospel teaching on man and his vocation, a vocation which is at once earthly and transcendent; its aim is thus to guide Christian behavior. It therefore belongs to the field, not of ideology, but of theology and particularly of moral theology.

— John Paul II, *Sollicitudo rei socialis*, 41.

After the fall of Napoleon, the victorious nations met in Vienna to restore the balance of power in Europe. European leaders hoped to restore peace by reestablishing the monarchy in France and conservative governments throughout Europe. However, the events of the previous decades proved irreversible. Although the diplomats who gathered in Vienna drew new political boundaries and supported traditional regimes, the inertia of radical social and economic developments already left a permanent mark on the cultural landscape of Europe.

Despite the Congress of Vienna's efforts to reinstate the regimes of the past, widespread Liberalism would effectively counteract any endeavor to turn back the political clock. Widely embraced by the professional and business class who had risen to prominence during the age of the revolution, Liberalism was a political philosophy that strove to create an enlightened society marked by freedom and equality. As these self-made men tried to improve the organization of

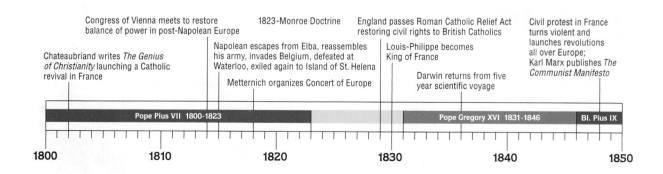

Congress of Vienna meets to restore balance of power in post-Napolean Europe

1823-Monroe Doctrine

England passes Roman Catholic Relief Act restoring civil rights to British Catholics

Civil protest in France turns violent and launches revolutions all over Europe; Karl Marx publishes *The Communist Manifesto*

Chateaubriand writes *The Genius of Christianity* launching a Catholic revival in France

Napolean escapes from Elba, reassembles his army, invades Belgium, defeated at Waterloo, exiled again to Island of St. Helena

Louis-Philippe becomes King of France

Metternich organizes Concert of Europe

Darwin returns from five year scientific voyage

Pope Pius VII 1800-1823

Pope Gregory XVI 1831-1846

Bl. Pius IX

1800   1810   1820   1830   1840   1850

society and its relationship to its governing body, economic and technological innovations would powerfully weigh in as a new social order was formed. Liberalization of government, accompanied by the emergence of industrialization, in significant part defined the nineteenth century.

During nineteenth century, the economies of Europe and the United States rapidly moved from agricultural commerce towards mechanized manufacturing and industry. This rapid industrialization had tremendous social and economic effects on the world, transforming centuries-old ways nations operated and people lived within the course of a few years. The economic changes caused by industrialization occasioned the birth of a number of new ideologies and philosophies. Economic ideologies such as capitalism and Marxism, and political orientations such as nationalism, and imperialism all enjoyed a strong connection with the Industrial Revolution. These monumental changes prompted the Church to expand her doctrinal base and develop her social teachings. Popes responded to the different philosophies spawned by both the Enlightenment and Industrialization. The Church worked to assist those who were victims of the rapid social changes brought about by the Industrial Revolution. The popes spoke of the dangers of a materialistic view of work and the human person. As the industrialization of society gave rise to abuses of human rights, the Church began to speak on behalf of the working class. During this century of political, economic, and cultural change, the Church became vulnerable to virulent attacks and persecutions, which would violate her own rights of free expression. Lastly, the nineteenth century would see the long pontificates of two celebrated popes, Bl. Pius IX and Leo XIII, whose leadership and authority would make the Church stronger through the First Vatican Council and well-crafted social doctrine at the service of human rights.

PART I
The Post-Napoleonic Era

The Congress of Vienna met in 1814 to restore the balance of power in Europe offset by fifteen years of Napoleonic domination. Representatives of the four nations that made up the victorious alliance — Britain, Prussia, Austria, and Russia — wanted to make sure that their countries remained strong and prepared to defend themselves against any future aggression.

The mastermind of the Congress was the Austrian diplomat, Clement von Metternich. Metternich began directing Austria's foreign affairs in 1809 (at the height of Napoleon's power) and would retain control for nearly forty years. In Vienna, he worked to extend Austria's domains into northern Italy and block Prussia and Russia from gaining too much power during the new division

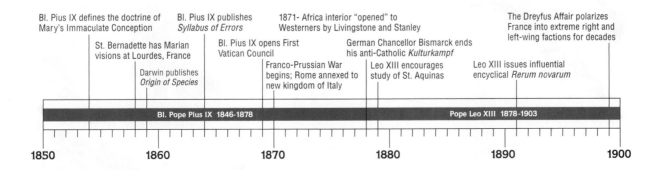

of Europe. With Napoleon defeated, Russia's increasing military strength under Czar Alexander I posed a new threat. After months of debate, new boundaries were drawn, and the three major European powers, Austria, Prussia, and Russia, all came out strong.

LIBERALISM

The participants of the Congress of Vienna were particularly wary of the new ideology, Liberalism, originated from the Enlightenment, featured a democratic form of government based on liberty and equality rather than a monarchy. Metternich and the other leaders of Old Europe realized that the restoration of the old regimes not only depended on defeating Napoleon, but would also include the vigorous suppression of the many movements to establish liberal governments.

John Locke (1632-1704) was an English philosopher concerned with society and the limits of human knowledge. He is best known as the popularizer of natural rights and the right of revolution. His ideas of a "government with the consent of the governed" and man's natural rights—life, liberty, and estate (property)—formed the basis for American law and government and influenced the written works of Thomas Jefferson and other Founding Fathers of the United States.

Liberalism, like many political ideologies, is an ambiguous term since it refers to an *ethos* or disposition rather than a definite set of principles or ideas. For the most part, Liberalism bases society and its rules on the General Will of the people. Moreover, many of its principles regarding human rights do actually reflect natural law. The first proponents of liberal philosophy, John Locke and Jean-Jacques Rousseau, firmly believed that monarchies were out-of-date and unjust since the will of the people was rendered superfluous. Constitutional governments and free societies that emphasized man's ability to solve social problems, such as poverty, ignorance, and superstition, reflected liberal principles. Liberalism glorified absolute individual freedom and supported the overthrow of any government or institution that limited that freedom. Many liberal thinkers believed that freedom of religion, conscience, speech, and press was incompatible with Catholic teaching since the Church was associated with the monarchy. There was a strong tendency to view the Church as a hindrance to political and social progress because of its past connection with the old Regimes.

It bears mentioning that liberal ideas were not necessarily anti-Christian. In the United States, liberal democracy helped secure freedom of worship and put an end to Catholic persecution that had existed there during English rule. In France, a number of nineteenth-century clerics attempted to adopt liberal principles by pushing for a broader interpretation of Christian dogmas and limit the authority of the bishops and the pope. Other Catholic thinkers argued that the Church should work to find common ground with the liberal governments as a way of maintaining her freedom and independence. Some of the encyclicals of Leo XIII would eventually outline those beliefs that the Church held in common with liberal democracy, but unfortunately, throughout most of the nineteenth century, many liberals would seek to destroy the Church.

METTERNICH'S EUROPE: 1815-1830

The arrangements made at the Congress of Vienna beginning in 1814 were briefly interrupted by Emperor Napoleon I's remarkable escape from the island of Elba in March 1815. Returning to France and retaking power, the emperor made one last attempt to restore his rule. Napoleon invaded Belgium and was met there by the British commander, the Duke of Wellington, who

ESCAPE FROM ELBA

On April 20, 1814, the defeated Emperor Napoleon was sent to the island of Elba, the largest island in the Tuscan archipelago, which lay a little over six miles from the continental mainland. There, Napoleon was supposed to live in retirement with his mother and sister.

On Elba, Napoleon maintained his good spirits, and rather than sinking into complacency, he set about enacting reforms on the island. The dethroned emperor worked to improve the island's infrastructure, ordered hospitals built, and tried to increase the availability of drinking water. He also spent time drilling some four hundred loyal soldiers who had followed the emperor to his exile.

Napoleon was kept abreast of the world's events on Elba through newspapers and the thousands of letters that were sent to him. Although he was under the constant watch of Austrian and French guards, the forty-five-year-old general kept in contact with sympathizers on the mainland, all the while plotting an escape. Finally, on February 16, 1815, Napoleon somehow managed to sneak past his guards, slip past a British vessel patrolling the island, and escape from Elba. Once he arrived in France, people and troops immediately flocked to the returning emperor, pledging their loyalty. On March 20, 1815, Napoleon triumphantly returned to Paris amidst celebration and jubilation. The Bourbon king Louis XVIII fled to Belgium, and Napoleon once again seized power, marking the beginning of his second, short-lived reign known as the "Hundred Days."

The Congress of Vienna soon heard of Napoleon's return. They declared the emperor to be an outlaw and disbanded their meeting once again to engage in Napoleonic war.

Napoleon in exile at Elba

soundly defeated the emperor at Waterloo aided by the arrival of 30,000 Russian troops. This second threat thwarted, the nations of Europe reconvened to make certain that peace would not again be disturbed.

Late in 1815, Russian Czar Alexander I proposed the creation of a "Holy Alliance" which promised to uphold Christian principles of charity and peace. Russia, Prussia, and Austria joined the Holy Alliance, but Pope Pius VII and Great Britain refused to join. Despite Alexander's pious intentions, the Holy Alliance did not outline an effective program to ensure peace and was thus not taken seriously by its members.

Metternich, who remained suspect of Alexander's intentions, sought to balance Russian power by warming Austria's relations with the other European powers. Disregarding the Holy Alliance as a reliable treaty or a binding coalition, Metternich tried to forge a more stable alliance. He helped restore the Bourbon family to the throne of France and included them in a conservative coalition of European powers that included France. Through a series of Congresses at Aix-la-Chapelle in 1818, Troppau in 1820, and Verona

Clement von Metternich (1773-1858) was an Austrian statesman and perhaps the most influential diplomat of his era. He was the mastermind at the Congress of Vienna and established the anti-liberal, anti-revolution "Concert of Europe."

in 1822, Metternich established the "Concert of Europe" which aimed at dismantling the reforms institutionalized by Napoleon and crush any liberal revolution. The arrangement left Austria—and Metternich—as the main arbiter of European affairs.

Metternich's conservative Concert soon provoked sharp reaction. Secret societies were founded in Spain, Italy, and Germany to overturn the monarchies. In Greece and Poland, patriots fought to restore their independence. During the time of the French Revolution, Latin American states had won their independence from Spain, and they now wanted to keep that independence. Metternich, fearing any successful defiance, worked with his conservative coalition to put down all threats.

In 1820, members of the Italian secret political society, the *Carbonari* (charcoal burners) led a successful revolution against the King of Naples, the Bourbon monarch Ferdinand I. During that same year, the Spanish government also fell to revolutionaries who forced King Ferdinand VII to adopt a liberal constitution. Metternich considered these revolutions the beginnings of a larger

movement, and at Troppau, Austria, on December 8, 1820, he convinced the Concert to take strong and immediate action against the revolutionaries. An army entered Naples and suppressed the Italian revolutionaries, restoring Ferdinand I to the throne. In 1822, Metternich convinced the Concert of Europe to intervene in Spain and restore the government of Ferdinand VII.

James Monroe (1758-1831) was the fifth President of the United States (1817-1825). Monroe is best known for the Monroe Doctrine devised by his Secretary of State, John Quincy Adams. Monroe delivered the Doctrine in a message to Congress on December 2, 1823. Not only must Latin America be left alone, he warned, but also Russia must not encroach southward on the Pacific coast. "...the American continents, by the free and independent condition which they have assumed and maintain, are henceforth not to be considered as subjects for future colonization by any European Power."

The next step for the Concert was to stop the revolutions in Latin America. Before that happened, United States president James Monroe interceded by issuing the Monroe Doctrine in 1823. The Monroe Doctrine announced that the Western Hemisphere was closed to further European colonization and that any attempt by European states to intervene in the affairs of Latin America would be considered an act of war against the United States. Britain had already established economic interests in the Western Hemisphere during Napoleon's reign and to maintain them supported the United States' isolationist policy. As a result, the Americas would remain independent of European political developments during the nineteenth century.

Czar Alexander I of Russia (1777-1825), Emperor of Russia (1801-1825), King of Poland (1815-1825). Alexander was one of the most important figures in the 19th century. His relationships with European rulers fluctuated back and forth between cooperation and hostility. His complex nature was a result of his early environment and education. Raised in the free-thinking atmosphere of the court of Catherine the Great, he was immersed in the principles of Rousseau by his Swiss tutor. From his military training, he acquired the traditions of Russian autocracy. His father, Emperor Paul I, taught him to combine a theoretical love of mankind with a practical contempt and distrust of men.

THE BREAKDOWN OF THE CONCERT OF EUROPE: 1830-1848

Metternich's coalition began to break down after the death of Czar Alexander I in 1825. Alexander was succeeded by Nicholas I who, while maintaining his predecessor's desire to expand Russian influence, did not share Alexander's policy of unanimously supporting traditional regimes. In 1821, Alexander I had refused to support the Greek revolution against the Ottoman Empire. However in 1830, Nicholas I assisted the Greeks to victory, thus extending Russia's influence further west. The Greek revolution marked a turning point for the Concert of Europe.

The fatal blow to the Concert came from France after the Bourbon king, Louis XVIII, died in 1824. Louis' successor, Charles X, introduced a number of counterrevolutionary policies, including an indemnity to be paid to those who lost their land during the revolution and the death penalty for those who committed sacrilege in church buildings. Opposition against the king immediately broke out and newspapers and political leaders criticized his actions. Finally, in July 1830, revolution broke out. Charles X fled to England, and the revolutionaries set up a constitutional monarchy, choosing Louis-Philippe of Orléans as their new king. He would rule France for the next eighteen years.

The successful revolution in France encouraged similar uprisings in Poland and Belgium. Poland had been restored by the Congress of Vienna in 1814 but was under the direct rule of the Russian Czar. In 1830 Polish nationals rebelled, but Russia moved in and crushed the resistance. At the Congress of Vienna, Belgium was united with Holland, and now Belgian nationals hoped to win independence. Thanks to the support of Louis-Philippe and the new regime in France, the Belgian revolution was successful. After Greece and Belgium won independence, the counterrevolution launched by Metternich and the Concert of Europe seemed destined to fail.

PART II

The Church in the Post-Napoleonic Era

After the fall of Napoleon, the Church was widely seen as an ally of the anti-liberal counter-revolution. In reality, the Church faced opposition on both sides. The conservative regimes tried to assert control over the national churches in their respective countries and reestablish Gallican or Febronian-style Church-state relations. Liberal reformers, on the other hand, followed the precedent set by the revolution in France and were intent on secularizing their countries and minimizing the Church's influence — especially in the area of education.

Despite aggressive political opposition, the Church experienced some revitalization during this period as many holy men and women worked to remedy the new problems of these times. In 1814 Pope Pius VII restored the Society of Jesus, and new charitable organizations were founded. In 1833 Frederick Ozanam founded the Society of St Vincent de Paul to provide material support to the thousands of poor and destitute. By 1848 over five hundred St. Vincent de Paul societies were working in England, Ireland, France, Belgium, Spain, and the United States.

GERMANY AND FRANCE

After 1815, Germany was dominated by the northern, predominately Protestant state of Prussia. Seeking to impose rigid unity over the other German states, Prussia began to introduce policies designed to undermine Catholic influence in Germany. In 1825, Prussia passed a law requiring children to be raised in the father's religion. Prussian executives were then sent into Catholic German states with the purpose of marrying young Catholic girls. They hoped to establish a Protestant leadership in these Catholic states through effective breeding.

In response to the Prussian law, Pius VIII required that all Catholics who married outside of the Faith instruct their children in the Catholic Faith, thus directly opposing the Prussian law. Catholics throughout Germany responded to the pope's request by condemning the Prussian law and refusing to follow the anti-Catholic guidelines. In 1837, the Archbishop of Cologne, Clement Droste von Vischering, was arrested by Prussian authorities for supporting the Papal directive. As persecution continued, Catholics in Germany began to unify behind the pope.

In the years following Napoleon's defeat, a Catholic intellectual revival took place in France, which generated enthusiasm toward their Catholic identity. In part, this renewal was prompted by the French writer

François-René de Chateaubriand (1768-1848), a French writer and diplomat, is considered the father of Romanticism in French literature. He began a post-revolution Catholic revival in France with *The Genius of Christianity*, written in 1802. His refusal in 1830 to swear allegiance to King Louis-Philippe put an end to his political career.

François-René de Chateaubriand whose *The Genius of Christianity*, written in 1802, defended Catholic dogma against liberal and atheistic attacks. After that publication, a number of Catholic French intellectuals worked to counteract anti-Catholic sentiment arising from both liberal and conservative sectors of society.

In 1830, the journalistic trio of Fr. Felicité Robert de Lamennais, Fr. Henri-Dominique Lacordaire, and the layman Charles René Montalembert founded the paper *L'Avenir* (the Future), which attacked both radical Liberalism and conservative Gallicanism. In their writings, they demanded social justice for the working classes and called for the Church to reform her historical attitude toward liberal politics. Sharp criticism of papal views in *L'Avenir* caught the attention of Rome, and consequently Pope Gregory XVI issued his encyclical *Mirari vos* in August 1832, which was meant to help moderate the views of *L'Avenir*. All the authors accepted Rome's directives, but disillusioned Lamennais eventually left the priesthood, and sadly the Church, over the issue. Lacordaire and Montalembert remained faithful and continued to champion the Catholic cause in France.

THE UNITED STATES

Shortly after the independence of the United States was recognized in the Treaty of Paris (1783), Baltimore became the first diocese within the thirteen original states in 1789. Immigrants began to flock to the United States, and this immigration created the need for a well-structured Church in America. In 1808, Pope Pius VII erected the Dioceses of Boston, New York, Philadelphia, and Bardstown (which eventually moved to Louisville), and named Baltimore a metropolitan see. In 1820 the Dioceses of Charleston and Richmond were added, and in 1821, the Diocese of Cincinnati.

The first immigrants from Ireland and Germany began to flood into the United States in 1820, and immigration continued throughout the century. By 1850 immigrants from Germany, Italy and Eastern Europe made Catholicism one of the largest Christian denominations in the country. This massive influx of Catholic immigrants frightened the Protestant-American public and led to a fierce anti-Catholic backlash. Books and pamphlets were distributed that attacked the morals and uprightness of priests and nuns; Churches were burned down; and some Catholics were lynched. Political cartoons depicted the Irish as monkeys or wild-eyed terrorists, and the Catholic Church was accused of sending papal spies to America. Political parties, such as the infamous Know-Nothing Party, became popular on nativist, anti-Catholic, and anti-immigrant platforms.

To protect each other, Catholics developed support networks that centered on parish life and parochial schools. Immigrants also built Catholic orphanages, hospitals, and nursing homes as a way of living out their Christian vocation and preservering their Catholic Faith.

THE BRITISH ISLES

Catholic persecution persisted in Britain since the time of the Reformation. Catholics could not vote, sit in Parliament, nor hold civil offices. In 1778 and 1791, the British passed reform bills that helped bring about the revocation of many anti-Catholic laws in Great Britain and Ireland. In 1801, British parliament was considering freedom of Catholic worship in Ireland but unfortunately dropped the idea. Moreover, the British government dissolved the Dublin parliament and declared Anglicanism as the official religion of Ireland. Consequently, Irish Catholics were forbidden to hold public office and denied a right to vote. Nonetheless, the support of England by Pope Pius VII during the Napoleonic wars helped ease ill feelings towards Catholics in Britain, and to avert an Irish uprising, Parliament passed the Catholic Relief Act in 1829, thereby granting emancipation to Catholics. Lastly, the life of the Church in the British Isles would be largely affected by industrialization, since many of the laborers employed in many of the new factories would be Catholic.

A nineteenth century textile factory. By 1823, there were ten thousand of these "mills" throughout Britain.

PART III
The Industrial Revolution

As political revolution was changing the ruling structures of continental Europe, at the same time an economic revolution was occurring all over Europe, but especially in Great Britain, whose effects would be felt throughout the world. Toward the end of the eighteenth century, some key social changes and technological innovations would turn Britain to change rapidly from an agricultural to an industrial economy. This change—traditionally called the Industrial Revolution—would dramatically affect the culture and life style of British society.

The Industrial Revolution in Great Britain was closely linked to its agricultural developments. During the late seventeenth and eighteenth centuries, farmers and landowners in Britain began experimenting with various technological and scientific improvements in farming, including new breeding techniques and methods of cultivation. In order to implement these new agricultural improvements, the landowners began to accumulate farming plantations by buying up many small farms. Unlike other parts of Europe, which were still ruled by powerful monarchs, these wealthy British landowners were extremely influential in the English Parliament and used this influence to obtain a number of land reforms. Landowners acquired new farmlands formally held in common by towns or villages and worked to bring all of the farming in England under private ownership. As a result, peasant farmers who used to work on common lands or small farms were now displaced from their lands and needed to look for other ways to make a living. These farmers were hired by the wealthy landowners for a daily wage. This created a large, mobile workforce that was dependent on wages.

As these agricultural changes were occurring, those involved with Britain's already prosperous textile trade were also looking for new ways to increase their profits. New technologies, such as the fly shuttle, spinning jenny, and water frame, led to the development of a power loom, which could produce more cloth and material than ever before. Other explorations into ways of powering these new machines produced the steam engine, and with it, a greater reliance on burning coal for energy. Factories, or "mills," were built in towns and cities to house the new machines and the volume of production immediately grew. The first steam loom factory opened in Manchester in 1806, and by 1823 there were more than 10,000 throughout Britain. As jobs proliferated in the factories, many farm workers headed to cities to find work in the mills.

SOCIAL CONSEQUENCES OF INDUSTRIALIZATION

As cities grew, so did the population. Between 1750 and 1850, the population of England tripled to over thirty million. Nonetheless, the population explosion in no way signified a rising standard of living among the masses. Life for the common worker became increasingly difficult.

During industrialization, cities became densely packed and overcrowded industrial centers where poor workers earned very meager wages in the factories. Skilled workers lost their jobs to new, more efficient technologies. Out of desperation to support themselves and their families, people were forced to work in factories or mines under dangerous conditions, sometimes for fourteen or more hours a day. Women and children, sometimes better suited for jobs because of size or famil-iarity with looms, worked similar hours for even lesser wages.

In the mid-nineteenth century, more than twenty percent of all employees in textile mills and coal mines were under the age of ten years old.

City life also changed familial relationships. On the farm, family members worked and lived together, complementing each other's roles and skills. But in urban centers, families were apart for long hours, and employment was often necessary for every member of the family. Large families became beneficial to bring home extra wages as children as young as six worked along side grown men, enduring the same conditions and long hours. Mine owners employed children to pull coal carts in the small recesses of the mineshaft, and mill owners used children to crawl into tight spaces. Child wages were the lowest and loss of life was frequent. In the mid-nineteenth century, more than twenty percent of all employees in textile mills and coal mines were under the age of ten years old.

Urban life was typically squalid and destitute. For a great number of people in most cities, services were poor due to a lack of city planning. Families crammed together in poorly-built tenement houses, sometimes sharing just a single room. Sanitary conditions were awful, and fresh water was rare. At the time, most buildings and factories burned coal for heat and fuel, producing black soot that clouded the air and stained buildings. Diseases such as tuberculosis, cholera, and dysentery were rampant in working-class districts. Life expectancy was low among the working class. A study conducted by the British Parliament in 1842 found that in Manchester the average age of death was thirty-eight for professional classes, twenty for shopkeepers, and seventeen for the working class.

The birthplace of the Industrial Revolution in England was Coalbrookdale, in Shropshire, England. It was here, in 1709, that an English Quaker, Abraham Darby, developed a blast furnace fired by coke (a clean-burning fuel derived from coal) to smelt iron. Before Darby's invention, the iron industry chopped down entire forests to obtain enough charcoal for smelting. The iron industry as a whole was continually moving to new forested locations to maintain access to charcoal. Deforestation in Europe had progressed to the point that fuel-wood had become scarce and expensive, as a result, iron was expensive. The use of coke to smelt iron instead of charcoal led to inexpensive iron. The availability of inexpensive iron led to the European Industrial Revolution. Darby combined technologies of casting iron with casting brass, producing metals of greater detail, thinness, and smoothness, making the production of steam engines possible. Darby's son Abraham Darby II produced the iron for Thomas Newcomen's steam engines, replacing the more expensive brass cylinders. Darby's grandson Abraham Darby III constructed the world's first cast-iron bridge, over the Severn river at Coalbrookdale, Shropshire in 1779.

LAISSEZ-FAIRE CAPITALISM AND THE MANCHESTER SCHOOL OF ECONOMICS

The development of the Industrial Revolution was driven largely by the profits earned by wealthy English landholders during the preceding centuries. Landowners used their profits to earn more money, by investing in technological developments, building factories, or investing in companies. Money used to generate more money through investment, rather than for simply buying a product, is called capital. The proliferation of available capital helped create a new economic system, aptly called capitalism, which replaced mercantilism and helped give birth to the industrial age.

Although capitalism gradually emerged out of the old British economy, the writer Adam Smith first described its principles and characteristics in his monumental work *The Wealth of Nations,* published in 1776. Smith argued that economies exist according to their own "natural laws" that dictated economic behavior independently of governmental regulation. These laws, such as the law of supply and demand, determine how people, all acting according to their own self-interests, work together to produce a prosperous economy. The best economy, therefore, is one that is free from external (especially governmental) regulation and is allowed to function solely according to these natural principles. This theory, which became known as *laissez-faire* (leave alone) capitalism, argued that state regulation of the economy, as found in mercantilism, only deterred the development of a healthy economy. A free market, on the other hand, would create a robust economic order where self-interest and voluntary charity would provide for all the needs of society.

Another economist named Thomas Malthus wrote about other economic "laws" which he believed governed modern economies. Malthus described the "iron law of wages," which stated that workers should not expect to receive a wage higher than the bare minimum needed to survive. If workers received more, he argued, they would simply produce more children, thus requiring an even higher wage. Malthus' bleak conclusions led many contemporaries to refer to economics as the "dismal science." Some of his theories inspired the novelist Charles Dickens' infamous character Ebenezer Scrooge of *The Christmas Carol*, who says of the poor in that book, "If they would rather die, they had better do it, and decrease the surplus population."

These economic theories, referred to as the Manchester School of economics, expected little more than a dreadful existence for the majority of people. Manchester economics had little regard for individual human dignity or the foundation of the family. Instead, it treated people like machines—tools for securing capital. This dehumanizing vision of man would find fierce opposition in the Church's social teaching, which would respond to the exploitation of the working class.

FROM ECONOMIC TO POLITICAL REVOLUTION

At the end of the eighteenth century, political power in Britain rested in the hands of about five hundred wealthy landed gentry. This gentry class pushed for many of the land reforms that helped bring about the Industrial Revolution. However, rapid economic and social developments quickly caused the country's political organization to become obsolete. As cities grew, new industrial leaders gained wealth and influence, and they pressed for political reform.

The Duke of Wellington with Sir Robert Peel. As British statesmen they both supported reforms to end oppression.

Representation in British Parliament had not been altered since 1688. At that time, large cities like Manchester and Birmingham did not exist, and so despite their growth, they lacked real political representation. Adding to the discontent of the powerful, city-based industrialists, the landed gentry continued to pass laws that taxed imports, thus restricting free economic exchange. These laws, known as the Corn Laws, angered industrialists who sought to minimize their expenses and maximize their profits by following *laissez-faire* economic principles. Political unrest began to build, and fearing similar civil disorder that plagued continental Europe, Parliament passed the Great Reform Bill of 1832. This re-apportioned representation in England and brought about a shift in power that would eventually help "free-trade" legislation pass through Parliament. The Corn Laws would be overturned in the 1840s.

These new reforms also helped end centuries of government-sanctioned Catholic oppression. In 1829, thanks to the support of the British Home Secretary Robert Peel, the Roman Catholic Relief Act was passed which granted Catholic emancipation and enabled Catholics to hold Parliamentary seats. The Irish activist Daniel O'Connell became the first Irishman to represent his people in London. Daniel O'Connell had worked to organize Irish Catholics for political representation since 1800. He had instituted "Catholic Rent," gathering as little as a penny a month from poor Irish Catholic families to help finance his political organization and unite Catholics behind a common cause. O'Connell went on to become a major figure in the House of Commons, prominent in the struggles for prison and law reform, free trade, the abolition of slavery, and universal suffrage.

PART IV

Bl. *Pio Nono* and the Rise of Nationalism

In June 1846, a conclave met to choose Gregory XVI's successor. The cardinals picked the fifty-five-year-old Cardinal Giovanni Maria Mastai-Ferretti, who took the name Pius IX, or *Pio Nono* as he would be affectionately called throughout the world. Bl. *Pio Nono* was young, popular among Italians, poor (he borrowed money to afford the trip to the conclave), and sympathetic to the liberal cause. His election gave new hope to revolutionaries throughout Europe, especially in Italy, while worrying Metternich and other conservatives who feared a liberal pope could tip the balance of the continent towards revolution.

Metternich was right to worry. One of the earliest acts by the new pope was to threaten the Austrian leader with excommunication unless Austrian troops withdrew from Ferrara in northern Italy. Metternich complied, and this tough diplomacy made Bl. *Pio Nono* immensely popular in Italy. Some even hoped the pope might become president of a new Italian republic.

In Rome, the new pope took his pastoral mission very seriously. He visited hospitals and schools, made improvements to the city, and allowed for greater toleration of Roman Jews. As ruler of the Papal States, he created an assembly with lay representatives to help govern, granted amnesty to revolutionaries in the Papal States, helped to introduce tax reform, and established an agricultural institute to provide advice and assistance to farmers. Bl. *Pio Nono's* generous reforms won support from Catholics, Protestants, and secular liberals alike. Nevertheless, in 1848, Bl. *Pio Nono's* popularity dwindled. Revolution once again erupted all over Europe, and Bl. *Pio Nono* found himself pulled from every side to join in the violence.

THE REVOLUTIONS OF 1848

By 1848, Metternich's Europe — the tight conservative grip that kept unhappy peasants and unruly revolutionaries at bay — was slowly weakening. After thirty years of mounting unrest, revolution erupted throughout the continent. Once again, revolution started in France. In February 1848, an accidental shot fired into a protesting mob sparked violence and turned the protest into a full-scale insurrection. Barricades were set up in the streets and King Louis-Philippe, fearing for his life, fled to Great Britain.

In Paris, France, February 1848, a shot fired into a mob of protestors set off a year of anti-conservative revolutions across Europe.

In France a group of *bourgeois* liberals set up a provisional government. The new government harnessed the support of poor urban workers by employing them in communal workgroups. But the Parisian *bourgeoisie* underestimated the rural French who used the elections held in April of that year to swing support behind candidates who would establish a conservative republic. The newly elected government dissolved the workgroups, and the urban workers once again took to the streets in protest. During

CENTERS OF REVOLUTION, 1848-1849

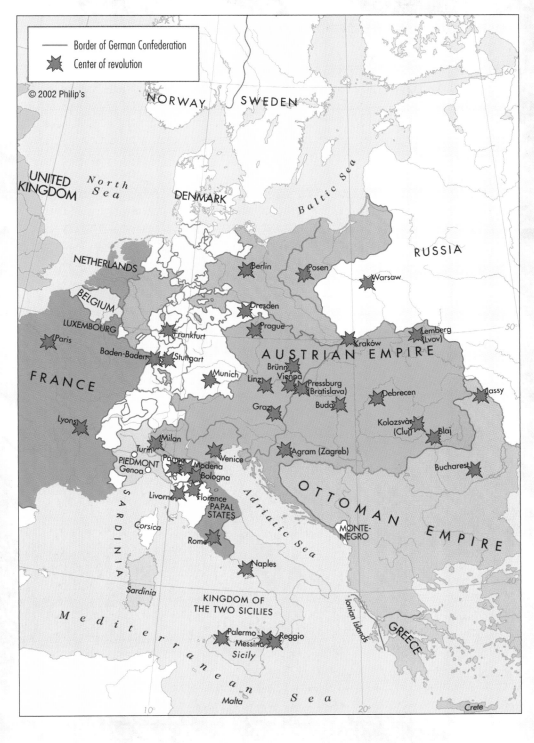

the month of June 1848, hundreds of people were killed and hundreds more sent overseas to French colonial prisons. Civil unrest continued throughout the year, and in December, elections were held again. This time Louis-Napoleon Bonaparte, the nephew of Napoleon, won an overwhelming majority. It would take this new Bonaparte only three years to seize total control of France in a *coup d'état* and proclaim himself Napoleon III. Tragically, the 1848 revolution only helped widen an ever-growing cultural divide between rural and urban French.

News of the Parisian insurrections reached the German-speaking world in early March 1848. Liberal students immediately took to the streets, demanding an end of Metternich's undemocratic system. The uprising gained momentum, and Metternich was forced to flee for his life.

Unlike France, the spirit of revolution in central Europe was linked to a latent desire for national unity. Protests quickly spread to the capitals of Hungary and Bohemia where nationalists met to discuss the establishment of new, independent states. In May, over eight hundred delegates from all over the Germanophone world met in Frankfurt in order to draft a constitution that could consolidate the Hapsburg and Prussian empires into a new German state. Debates between Protestant Prussia and the Catholic South prolonged the meeting for eleven months. During a delay in the congress, the reigning Austrian government managed to suppress the rebellion in Vienna and regain an authoritative hold on the country. After Czar Nicholas I mobilized his army to win Hungary back for the Austrians, Prussia also backed out of the convention in Frankfurt. The liberals' effort to unify Germany had failed.

Napoleon III, (1808-1873), Emperor of France, sent French troops to drive out Italian revolutionaries and restored control of the Holy City and the Papal States to Bl. Pope Pius IX.

In Italy, Pope Bl. Pius IX faced growing pressure to declare war on Austria on behalf of Italy. Italians wanted to win back the regions of Lombardy and Venice that Austria seized during the Congress of Vienna. Because of the pope's popular liberal policies, many had hoped that the pope would actually lead in the initiative to fight Austria. Not surprisingly, the pope refused to involve the papacy in a war against another Catholic nation. He condemned the idea of a federal Italy led by the pope and urged the Italian people to stay faithful to their respective princes.

In the eyes of the people, Bl. *Pio Nono's* opposition to the revolution made him an enemy. On November 15, 1848, Bl. Pius IX's prime minister was murdered as he attempted to open the Parliament, and mobs over-ran the assembly. The endangered pope was forced to flee the city. Insurrections sprang up throughout the peninsula as the nationalist movements led by Giuseppe Manzzini (a Freemason) and his "Young Italians" and the liberal Freemason and revolutionary Giuseppe Garibaldi gained momentum.

With the pope out of Rome, Manzzini and Garibaldi proclaimed a new Roman Republic, and for nearly a year, revolutionaries had control over the Holy City. Finally, Pope Bl. Pius IX called on the Catholic powers of Europe to restore his temporal rule over the papal states. French troops sent by the new Emperor Napoleon III retook the city and the Papal States, and on April 12, 1850, Bl. Pius IX returned to Rome. He was no longer the beloved pope of the people, and having protested the excesses of the revolution in Italy, Bl. Pius IX was no longer seen as a friend to the liberal cause.

Pope Blessed Pius IX or affectionately, *Pio Nono,* born Giovanni Maria Mastai-Ferretti (1792-1878), was pope for a record pontificate of over 31 years, from June 16, 1846 until his death. Pope Pius IX was the last pope to hold temporal powers.

The revolutions of 1848 and his exile from Rome not only changed Bl. Pius IX's political position, but also the focus of his papacy. As liberalism was spreading throughout Europe, Italian unification, which was spreading across most of the peninsula, now threatened the independence of the Papal States. If those lands were lost, the pope thought, so would be the freedom of the Church. To defend his sovereign territory, Bl. Pius IX raised an international army of volunteers.

Leadership of the newly unified Italy now passed to the Piedmont king Vittorio Emmanuelle and his Freemason premier Count Camillo Cavour. Bl. Pius IX privately admired Emmanuelle as a champion of Italy, but was very apprehensive over Cavour's revolutionary tendencies and his policies. In 1854, Cavour had all the monasteries and convents in Piedmont closed, a move that made Pope Bl. Pius IX increasingly suspicious and fearful of the unification movement's effect on the life of the Church.

ULTRAMONTANISM

The ongoing liberal revolutions of the nineteenth century divided Catholics. Some believed that anti-clericalism was implicit in Liberalism and that revolutions would threaten to unleash a new period of prolonged religious persecution. Others hoped that Catholicism and Liberalism could find common ground. After the exile of Bl. Pius IX, Catholics were uneasy and divided as to what should be the Church's next step.

During the nineteenth century, two schools of Catholic thought developed over the idea of Liberalism, and two German universities became the centers of these ideological discussions and deliberations. In Mainz, thinkers believed that liberal ideas were too secular, rational, and anti-clerical. They began to look to the pope as the last defender of the Catholic cause, the final bulwark against a liberal world. These Catholics became known as the ultramontanists (over the mountains) because as they looked to the pope for support and leadership, emphasizing his centrality and authority more than ever before.

In Munich, another Catholic school recognized an inevitable trend of European governments towards liberal democracy and sought to build bridges of mutual understanding between the Church and democratic regimes. These thinkers were optimistic about modern culture and believed that Church leaders could co-exist with liberal ideas and that dialogue with the modern world was beneficial for the future of the Church. The German theologian Johann Mohler proposed a number of reforms, like the use of the vernacular in the liturgy, some of which would eventually be adopted following the Second Vatican Council.

In response to the ultramontanists, the famous Anglican convert John Henry Cardinal Newman worried that by bypassing the diocesan ordinaries, the ultramontanists were creating a "Church within a Church" subservient exclusively to Rome. He criticized their immoderate dismissal of liberal ideas, saying, "we are shrinking into ourselves, narrowing the lines of communication, trembling at freedom of thought, and using the language of dismay and despair at the prospect before us" (quoted in Gilly, *Newman and His Age*, 1990, p. 344). As the gap between these two Catholic opinions widened, some Catholics seemed to have experienced a growing identity crisis.

THE IMMACULATE CONCEPTION

Ironically, it was a religious proclamation, not a political one, that would bring the questions of Liberalism and papal authority to the forefront of debate within the Church. In 1854, four years after his return to Rome, Bl. Pius IX solemnly defined the doctrine of Mary's Immaculate Conception.

Throughout the history of the Church, Mary had been venerated as the Immaculate Conception, and the theological foundations of this title go back to the early centuries. Many of the Church Fathers referred to Mary as the "new Eve" (Eve was also created without original sin), and St. John of Damascus argued that the sinlessness of Mary was implicit in her title "*Theotokos*" (literally, "bearer of God"). Although the feast of her Immaculate Conception had been celebrated since the seventh century, debate over the issue continued during the twelfth century. St. Bernard of Clairvaux and St. Thomas Aquinas were not sure concerning the doctrine of the Immaculate Conception, but Bl. John Duns Scotus defended it. In 1439, the Council of Basel ruled that the Immaculate Conception was a pious opinion in accordance with Faith, reason, and Scripture. Over one hundred years later, the Council of Trent declared that the Blessed Virgin Mary did not suffer being born with the stain of original sin. After these conciliar decisions, the issue was generally defended, but the exact nature of the Immaculate Conception was never officially defined as a dogmatic statement of the Church.

VENERABLE JOHN HENRY CARDINAL NEWMAN

Catholics in England had been disliked and persecuted ever since the Reformation, and were considered second-class citizens within English society. The Penal Laws that tried to wipe out Catholicism in England were quite successful. While the nineteenth century also saw the development of rights for Catholics in England, society at large was still suspect of all so-called "papists." After such a long period of oppression, by this century the Catholic minority in England was scorned and hated by the Protestant majority.

It was under these conditions that the unthinkable happened. The Reverend Ven. John Henry Newman, the most famous and influential Anglican preacher in all of England, a writer of incomparable ability, converted to Catholicism. His life was then dedicated to leading thousands of other English Protestants down the same path, and to this day, his writings still bring many back into the Church.

Born in 1801 to Anglican parents, Ven. John Henry Newman grew up holding the traditional English ideas towards Roman Catholicism—that the Catholic Church taught superstitious doctrine contrary to the gospels. From an early age he exhibited great potential. A highly gifted student, at the age of fifteen he went to Oxford University, and was later ordained in the Anglican Church, establishing himself as a great preacher. He began to study the teachings of the Church Fathers, and to his surprise discovered that many doctrines taught in the early Church—apostolic succession and the Sacraments, for example—were still found in the Catholic Church but had been long abandoned by his own Anglican Church. He soon joined the "Oxford Movement," a group of Anglicans who attempted to reestablish these lost doctrines back into the Anglican Church.

Ven. John Henry Newman, the leader of the Oxford Movement in the Church of England, was received into the Catholic Church in 1845. He is considered a sensitive Christian thinker, and his influence brought many converts to the English Roman Catholic Church. He was appointed cardinal in 1879 and proclaimed "venerable" in 1991.

While Ven. John Henry Newman's extraordinary gifts established him as the leading spokesman for this cause, he eventually came to the realization that what he was defending could be found in its entirety in the Catholic Church. This realization led to his conversion to Catholicism, after which he was ordained a priest, later in life being named a cardinal by Pope Leo XIII. Ven. John Henry Cardinal Newman died on August 11, 1890. Some of his greatest works published during his Catholic years include *The Idea of University* (1852), *An Essay in Aid of a Grammar of Assent* (1870), and *Apologia pro vita sua* (1864).

The lady in St. Bernadette's vision proclaimed
herself as "the Immaculate Conception."

Although the dogma of the Immaculate Conception was not a surprising proclamation, the way in which Bl. Pius IX proclaimed it certainly was. The Immaculate Conception was no longer debated theologically, and Bl. Pius IX had consulted with bishops before his definition, but ultimately he defined this tenet of Faith on his authority as pope. Furthermore, he spoke as the voice of the Church and certainly not as the first among bishops or within the context of an ecumenical council. This bold move implied that the authority of the Church on doctrinal and moral matters lay within the competence of the papal office. Ultramontanists rejoiced at this victory for papal centrality, but others feared the implications of Bl. Pius' pronouncement.

Four years later, in 1858, at the grotto of Massabielle, in Lourdes, France, a young girl named Bernadette Soubirous had a vision. Mary appeared to the girl, proclaiming in the ninth vision, "I am the Immaculate Conception." It seems that she was pleased with Bl. Pius' solemn declaration.

OUR LADY OF LOURDES

The appearance of Our Lady of Lourdes to St. Bernadette is one of the most famous of all Marian apparitions. The story began on Thursday, February 11, 1858, when Bernadette, 14, a poor, uneducated peasant girl in Southern France, went to a nearby river with her sister Marie and a friend to gather firewood. After these two crossed the river, leaving St. Bernadette alone, she heard what sounded like a storm coming from a nearby grotto called Massabielle. Looking inside the grotto she saw a golden cloud, and shortly thereafter a beautiful lady with a rosary draped over her right arm. St. Bernadette fell to her knees and began to pray the rosary with the lady (although the lady only recited the Our Father and the Gloria). After completing the rosary, the lady disappeared into the grotto without telling St. Bernadette who she was. St. Bernadette herself later wrote of this first apparition:

St. Bernadette kneeling at the grotto in Lourdes taken in 1862, three years after the Marian apparitions.

> While I was saying the Rosary, I was watching as hard as I could. She was wearing a white dress reaching down to her feet, of which only the toes appeared. The dress was gathered very high at the neck by a hem from which hung a white cord. A white veil covered her head and came down over her shoulders and arms almost to the bottom of her dress. On each foot I saw a yellow rose. The sash of the dress was blue, and hung down below her knees. The chain of the rosary was yellow; the beads white, big and widely spaced.

This was the first of many apparitions. As word spread, many people would accompany St. Bernadette to the grotto, but only St. Bernadette was able to see the lady. During these apparitions the lady would tell St. Bernadette to pray for sinners and on one occasion asked her to dig and scratch the ground and drink from the spring that flowed forth. This spring was later discovered to contain miraculous healing powers. At the request of the village Curé, St. Bernadette asked the lady who she was. On the Feast of the Annunciation, March 25, the lady told St. Bernadette, "I am the Immaculate Conception." St. Bernadette repeated these words, which she probably did not even understand, to the astounded Curé. (The dogma of the Immaculate Conception had been solemnly defined only four years prior to this apparition.)

In all, St. Bernadette received eighteen visitations from Mary over a six month period. The Church declared the apparitions authentic in 1862, and today Lourdes is one of the world's most popular pilgrimage sites. The miraculous spring has healed thousands of people from all over the world.

On December 8, 1869, the Feast of the Immaculate Conception, Pope Pius IX opened the first Vatican Council. The decrees issued from the council condemned modern-day materialism, atheism, and declared papal infallibility.

THE FIRST VATICAN COUNCIL

Pope Bl. Pius IX continued to assert his opposition to the liberal world. In 1864, Bl. Pius issued the encyclical *Quanta Cura* with its *Syllabus of Errors*. In this encyclical, the pope attacked many ideologies and opinions that challenged Church authority, which included socialism, Gallicanism, rationalism, and the separation of Church and state. Many ultramontanists were calling for an all out denouncement of liberal thought, and they urged the pope to reprimand those Catholics sympathetic to liberal democracy. This desire was fulfilled by the publication of Bl. Pius' encyclical, which would widen the rift between the liberals and ultramontanists.

The *Syllabus* condemned many errors prevalent in nineteenth-century Europe, including pantheism; naturalism; rationalism, whether absolute or moderate; false tolerance in religious matters; socialism; communism; secret societies; errors regarding the Church and her rights, especially in relation to the state; and errors regarding Christian Matrimony. Many of the faithful received the *Syllabus* well. It was essentially a compilation of errors which Bl. Pius IX had been addressing for almost two decades. The enemies of the Church nevertheless received it as an affront to the modern state and a rejection of modern culture.

For centuries popes had written encyclicals for the express purpose of counseling and instructing members of the Church on certain aspects of her teaching. However, in the wake of the declaration of the Immaculate Conception, many ultramontanists erroneously believed that every papal pronouncement stood as official Church doctrine. Specifically, they declared that all the contents of Bl. Pius' *Syllabus* must be followed unquestioningly since "all papal declarations were infallible."

At the time, all Catholics generally agreed that the pope taught infallibly. Like the Immaculate Conception, this belief had never been solemnly defined, and as a result, Catholics held diverse opinions on the subject. Some argued that the pope spoke as the first among all bishops and that his role as leader did not mean that Church authority lay exclusively in the pope himself. Others argued that as the Vicar of Christ, the pope himself was infallible and that all his letters, encyclicals, and teachings stood as official Church doctrine.

On December 8, 1869, the Feast of the Immaculate Conception, Bl. Pius IX opened the First Vatican Council to help reconcile these growing divisions between members of the Church. The council met over eleven months in three sessions approving just two constitutions: the "Dogmatic Constitution on the Catholic Faith" and the "First Dogmatic Constitution on the Church of Christ." The "Faith" constitution spoke about proof for the existence of God, revelation, Faith, and the role of Faith and reason while at the same time condemning contemporary errors on those topics. The second constitution dealt with the main issue of the council: papal infallibility.

The chief arguments against *papal* infallibility—as specific and distinct from the Church's infallibility—involve instances wherein popes stand accused of teaching heresy. The most common among these arguments pertains to Popes Liberius, Honorius, and Vigilius in the early centuries of the Church and the Galileo affair in the seventeenth century. Pope Liberius, however, whether an Arian or semi-Arian as critics claim, at worst acted under duress and coercion. This lack of freedom certainly does not allow a pope to teach *ex cathedra* (from the chair [of St. Peter]). Pope Honorius is accused of both teaching the Monothelite heresy and being condemned by the Third Ecumenical Council of Constantinople. Based on his letters to the heretic Sergius, he was most likely imprecise in his theological terminology about the question as to whether Christ had two wills or one. As for the condemnation of the Third Council of Constantinople, Pope St. Leo II, who ratified the decrees, noted that Honorius was condemned for his lack of papal zeal in combating heresy, not for teaching heresy himself. Pope Vigilius simply wavered in the face of a controversy about whether to condemn three contentious letters as containing heresy. As for the Galileo affair, the Holy Office—the Roman congregation that advises the pope on doctrinal questions—handled the inquiry and

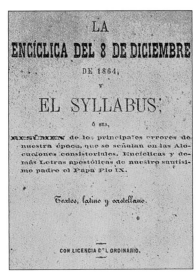

The title page of Bl. Pius IX's *El Syllabus*, December 1864

meted out the punishment. Although, from a modern perspective, this matter should have been handled better, the silencing of Galileo was a disciplinary measure and not a doctrinal one. It bears repeating: disciplinary actions do not fall within the context of infallibility.

Proof in favor of papal infallibility can be found in both Scripture and Tradition. Sacred Scripture includes three specific proofs. Matthew 16:18 records Christ's words to St. Peter: "You are Peter, and on this rock I will build my church, and the powers of death shall not prevail against it." This text contains the promise that St. Peter was to be the rock-foundation of the Church, and it follows that his successors are heirs to this promise. Luke 22:31-32 records Christ saying to St. Peter: "Simon, Simon, behold, Satan demanded to have you, that he might sift you like wheat, but I have prayed for you, that your faith may not fail; and when you have turned again, strengthen your brethren." This prayer of Christ was specifically for St. Peter as head of the Church. John 21:15-17 recounts the post-Resurrection triple command of Christ to St. Peter, culminating with: "'Simon, son of John, do you love me?'... And he said to him, 'Lord, you know everything; you know that I love you.' Jesus said to him, 'Feed my sheep.'" The whole of Christ's flock is thus entrusted to St. Peter and his successors.

Sacred Tradition offers several proofs. The letter of Pope St. Clement I in the first century—even while St. John, one of the Twelve, was still alive—was written to correct the Corinthians' behavior. St. Irenaeus claimed that conformity with the Roman bishop was proof of Apostolicity of doctrine (cf. *Adv. hær.*, III, iii). History has recorded many statements in almost every century to the effect of "Peter has spoken through _ _ _" (whoever was the reigning pope at the time). St. Augustine famously denounced the Pelagian heresy in a sermon after the receipt of Pope St. Innocent I's letter: "Rome's reply has come: the case is closed" (*Serm.* 131, c. x). Specific or indirect reference to papal infallibility is even found in many councils before Vatican I, including the Councils of Ephesus (431), Chalcedon (451), Constantinople III (680-681), Constantinople IV (869-870), and Florence (1438-1445).

The bishops debated the issue intensely, and in June 1870, a draft entitled "On the Infallibility of the Roman Pontiff" was presented to the bishops for discussion. In a particularly dramatic moment, the Dominican theologian Cardinal Guidi, Archbishop of Bologna, criticized the title of the draft, insisting that the pope was not infallible, but rather the pope's teaching was. He warned against the dangers of rashly proclaiming infallibility because although his solemn *teachings* are considered true, the person of the pope is certainly not impeccable. The ultramontanists protested Guidi's argument, and even Bl. Pius IX admonished the cardinal for his comments. In the end, Guidi's understanding proved to be in line with Catholic teaching, and the final draft of the definition of papal infallibility made the distinction between infallible teaching and the assurance of moral integrity of the pope. It read, under the title "On the Infallible Teaching Authority of the Roman Pontiff":

> We teach and define as a divinely revealed dogma that when the Roman Pontiff speaks *ex cathedra*, that is, when, in the exercise of his office as shepherd and teacher of all Christians, in virtue of his supreme apostolic authority, he defines a doctrine concerning faith and morals to be held by the whole Church, he possesses, by the divine assistance promised to him in blessed Peter, that infallibility which the divine Redeemer willed his Church to enjoy in defining doctrine concerning faith or morals. Therefore, such definitions of the Roman Pontiff are of themselves, and not by the consent of the Church, irreformable (*Constitutio prima de Ecclesia* [First Dogmatic Constitution on the Church of Christ], 1870, 4.9).

This definition, approved by Bl. Pius IX, set specific parameters for infallible papal teachings. Therefore, without the necessary conditions for infallibility, encyclicals, letters, and homilies are simply ranked as ordinary teachings of the pope. Although these papal writings still enjoy very high authority of opinion, they are not to be considered infallible teachings of the Catholic Church on their own authority.

On July 19, 1870, the Franco-Prussian War broke out and the First Vatican Council was disbanded. It never reassembled but was never officially closed. In a certain sense, Vatican II, almost one hundred years later, would bring Vatican I to a close. Clarity on certain theological issues had been reached, and with the authority of an ecumenical council, Bl. Pius IX hoped to set about healing the divisions in the Church. No sooner had the council disbanded than the pope found himself victim of more political turmoil. In response to the Franco-Prussian War, the French garrison in Rome was withdrawn, and within a month, the defenseless city was taken by King Vittorio Emmanuelle. The Papal States finally fell, and the papacy, which had governed Rome for a millennium and a half, lost the city. The council had defined the pope's moral and religious authority just as his temporal power was finally stripped away.

THE ROMAN QUESTION

Pope Bl. Pius IX never accepted the "Law of Guarantees" declaring himself a "prisoner of the Vatican."

During the Franco-Prussian War, Germany sought to dominate northern Europe. Italian revolutionaries took advantage of France's wartime weakness, and King Vittorio Emmanuelle resumed the Italian political revolution and modernization called the *Risorgimento*. On September 19, 1870, he took Rome, and Bl. Pius IX, driven from his palace in the Quirinale, took refuge in the Vatican.

In November 1870, Italy passed the "Law of Guarantees" to regulate the new relations between Church and state. (A similar offer had been rejected by Bl. Pius IX before the conquest of Rome.) The law provided that the pope would retain all of the honors and immunities of a sovereign. It gave the pontiff use of the Vatican, the Lateran, and Castel Gandolfo, the papal residence in the hills southwest of Rome, and allotted him three and a half million lire each year as compensation for his territorial losses. Significantly, the law also stated that the pope would appoint all the Italian bishops (the highest concentration of bishops in the world). Before this time, papal appointment of bishops was not an assumed or guaranteed privilege. Paradoxically, by losing control of the Papal States, the pope gained greater moral authority in administering the Church as a whole.

Bl. Pius IX refused to accept the "Law of Guarantees." Instead, he locked himself inside the Vatican palace, declaring himself a "prisoner of the Vatican." The popes' official status would remain that of a prisoner until 1929, when Italy, under Mussolini, agreed to an independent Vatican city-state and granted the pope possession of his palaces (not just "use" as the "Law of Guarantees" had stated), resolving this "Roman Question," as it came to be called.

In the meantime, the pope was at the mercy of the Italian state, and consequently, Church and state were at odds. The Italian government seized Church properties, and took responsibility for education away from religious orders. Monasteries were suppressed and religious orders abolished. Those who protested these measures were either thrown in prison or exiled from the country.

In 1868, Bl. Pius IX had issued the decree *Non expedit* which forbade Catholics from participating in the Italian political process, either by voting or running for office. Catholics, who comprised the vast majority of the Italian population, became second-class citizens in their own country. Somehow the Italians, who were used to living under foreign rule, learned to discretely keep a foot in both worlds, Church and state, without allowing the two to mix.

GERMAN UNIFICATION AND THE *KULTURKAMPF*

The Franco-Prussian War, which allowed Italy the opportunity to seize the Papal States, was the culmination of a long process of German unification under the leadership of the master Prussian diplomat Otto von Bismarck.

Bismarck became chancellor to the Hohenzollern king, Wilhelm I, in 1873. Wilhelm I assumed leadership in 1861 after his older brother Frederick Wilhelm IV stepped down due to failing mental stability. Unlike his romantic and idealistic brother, Wilhelm I was determined to strengthen the Prussian military and expand the country's influence throughout the continent. However, he lacked

Otto von Bismarck-Schönhausen, (1815-1898). As Prime Minister of Prussia from 1862 to 1890, he engineered the unification of the numerous states of Germany. He then served as the first Chancellor of the German Empire from 1871 to 1890. Following unification, Germany became one of the most powerful nations in Europe.

the necessary political skills, and so he turned to his chancellor to lead the country. Bismarck, nicknamed the "Iron Chancellor," began an extended program of militarization and diplomatic manipulation through which he created a unified German Empire.

Bismarck's plan for German unification was supported by the general and awakened sentiment of German nationalism. The chancellor believed that the sense of nationalism was strong enough in Germany to overcome the traditional North-South, Protestant-Catholic divisions, which had previously prevented the formation of a unified Germany. With this in mind, Bismarck drew Prussia into war with the surrounding countries in order to inspire the other German states to fight along side their fellow Prussian Germans. Bismarck went to war with Denmark in 1864, Austria in 1866, and finally France in 1870. With each conflict, more German states joined Prussia. Finally, on January 18, 1871, after the conclusion of the Franco-Prussian War, Bismarck met with the heads of twenty-five German states at Versailles where Wilhelm I was proclaimed emperor of a new, unified German Empire. Having defeated both Austria and France, the new German Empire now the dominant force on the continent.

Despite success in unifying Germany, Bismarck and Protestant Prussia still saw the Catholic Church as an obstacle to the advancement of the new Empire. German Catholics opposed Bismarck's militaristic and nationalistic regime, forming the Center Party in 1870, which allied itself with liberal critics of Bismarck. In 1872, Germany passed the "Falk Laws" (alternately known as the "May Laws" as they were passed in May 1873) in an effort to dismantle Catholic unity within Germany. These laws, named after the "minister of cults," Dr. Falk, subjected Catholic schools and seminaries to state control, prohibited religious orders from teaching, and expelled the Jesuit order from Germany. (Eventually every religious order would be expelled from Germany.) Furthermore, any priest or bishop who did not acknowledge state supremacy over the Church in Germany would be fined or imprisoned. These laws ushered in Bismarck's new internal policy, the *Kulturkampf* (culture struggle), whose aim was to rid Germany of Catholicism.

By 1876, there were no longer any bishops in Prussia, and more than a thousand priests were either exiled or imprisoned, leaving Catholics without access to the Sacraments. Bismarck even tried to create divisions between Catholics themselves, offering exemptions to those who cooperated with the newly established laws and by supporting those Catholics who rejected the decrees of the recent Vatican Council. Nonetheless, German Catholics would not comply with the Chancellor's policies. They published Catholic journals and joined the Center Party, which grew in strength in opposition to Bismarck. German bishops who had been driven from the country continued to serve their dioceses while in exile. Bl. Pius IX voiced opposition to Bismarck's policies, stating that no Catholic in Germany was obliged to obey any of the Falk Laws.

Bismarck eventually realized that his anti-Catholic program was not working, and, as the new Socialist Party gained strength in Germany, he knew he would need Catholic support to preserve the empire. The death of Bl. Pius IX in 1878 provided Bismarck with an opportunity to abandon his *Kulturkampf* without the humiliation of giving in to papal pressure. On the day of Pope Leo XIII's election, Bismarck wrote the new pope a letter of apology. Bismarck ended his anti-Catholic policies, and shifted his support to the Catholic Center Party, which opposed the rising tide of socialism in Germany.

THE THIRD REPUBLIC OF FRANCE

During the Franco-Prussian War, Emperor Napoleon III was captured at Sedan in the East of France. When news of his capture reached Paris, liberals overthrew the government and set up the "Third Republic."

The emergence of the Third Republic worsened relations between the Church and state in France. During the early years of the Third Republic, France was divided between conservative and liberal interests. The cities were greatly influenced by extreme liberal reforms, whereas rural areas were more sympathetic to moderate and conservative policies. Two internal crises would soon move France further to the left than ever before.

In 1889, conservative factions, led by General Boulanger, attempted to overthrow the French Republic. The Boulanger Crisis, as it became called, came out of an extremely popular movement, which probably could have been successful had the general not fled the country, eventually committing suicide. A second anti-republican crisis known as the Dreyfus Affair erupted in 1899. Alfred Dreyfus, a Jewish army captain, was accused of spying for the Germans, inspiring a wave of anti-German and anti-Semitic antagonism among the French. Conservatives used these popular sentiments to mount a nationalistic campaign against the government. Dreyfus was eventually declared innocent, and republican forces put down the opposition.

Because of these two events, the republican government passed strong measures to suppress conservative factions. The Church, which was always seen as an ally to the right, also fell victim to these reactive measures, especially since some Catholic papers had opposed the retrial of Dreyfus. In 1905, a series of laws formally separated Church and state, abrogating the model of Church-state relations established by the 1801 Concordat. All religious communities were banned in France, and not a single religious—priest, brother, or nun—was permitted to practice his or her vocation in France. Salaries were withheld from priests, and Church officials were banned from the boards of charitable originations. Nuns were also barred from working in hospitals. Soldiers could not join Catholic organizations, and officers could be dismissed for being loyal Catholics.

The trial of Alfred Dreyfus. The Dreyfus trial opened on December 19, 1894, at Cherche-Midi and lasted four days. He was found guilty of treason and sentenced to life in prison on Devil's Island. False documents were created to justify the guilty sentence. On January 13, 1898, the writer Émile Zola exposed the scandal of the false conviction to the public in an open letter to the President, titled J'accuse! (I Accuse!) in the literary newspaper L'Aurore (The Dawn). Dreyfus was pardoned in 1899, readmitted into the army, and made a knight in the Legion of Honor. The political scandal divided France for decades.

THE UNIFICATION OF ITALY, 1859-1870

Piedmont's role in uniting Italy was in response to the actions of Garibaldi. In 1860, Garibaldi led an expedition of republican "Red Shirts" (also known as Garibaldi's Thousand) through the Kingdom of the Two Sicilies. He defeated the Neapolitan army in a series of battles and proclaimed himself ruler of the Two Sicilies. Piedmont, in response, sent a force to annex the Papal States. Garibaldi was persuaded to transfer his conquered territorties to the Piedmontese king. The unified kingdom of Italy was proclaimed in 1861. The remaining territories of Venetia and the Patrimony of St. Peter were annexed by 1870.

Giuseppe Garibaldi in 1866.

MISSIONS TO AFRICA

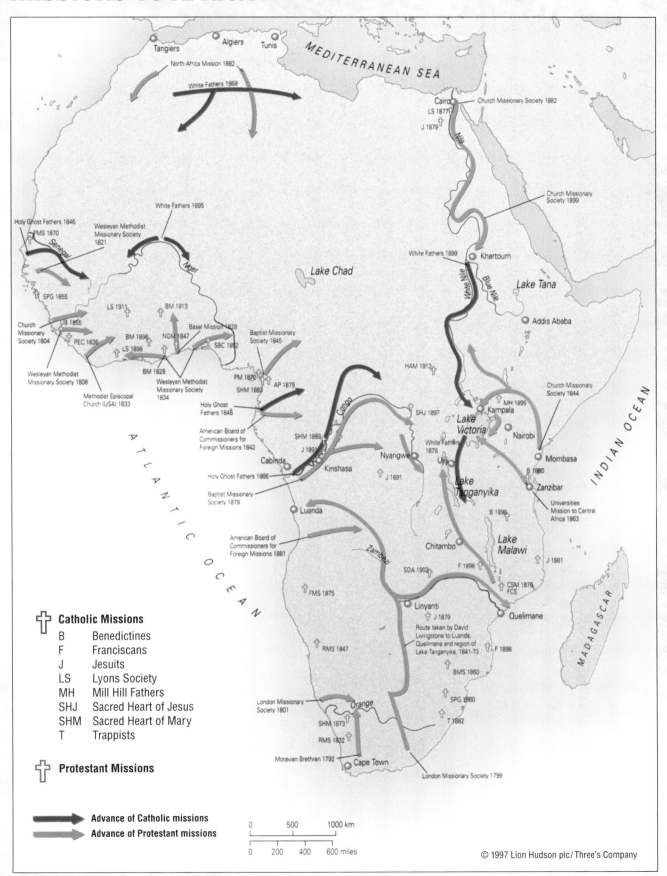

MEDITERRANEAN SEA

Tangiers
Algiers
Tunis

North Africa Mission 1882

White Fathers 1868

Cairo
Church Missionary Society 1882
LS 1877
J 1879

Church Missionary Society 1899

White Fathers 1895

Holy Ghost Fathers 1846
PMS 1870
Senegal

Wesleyan Methodist Missionary Society 1821

Niger

Lake Chad

White Fathers 1899
Khartoum

White Nile
Blue Nile

Lake Tana

SPG 1855

LS 1911
BM 1913

Church Missionary Society 1804
UB 1855
PEC 1836
BM 1896
LS 1898
NGM 1847
BM 1828
Basel Mission 1828

SBC 1852
Baptist Missionary Society 1845

Addis Ababa

Wesleyan Methodist Missionary Society 1808

Wesleyan Methodist Missionary Society 1834

PM 1870
SHM 1883
AP 1879

Methodist Episcopal Church (USA) 1833

Holy Ghost Fathers 1848

American Board of Commissioners for Foreign Missions 1842

HAM 1913

SHJ 1897

Church Missionary Society 1844

MH 1895
Kampala

Lake Victoria
Nairobi

SHM 1883
J 1891
Congo
Cabinda
Kinshasa

Nyangwe
White Fathers 1878
Uji

Mombasa
B 1880
Zanzibar

Holy Ghost Fathers 1866

J 1891

Baptist Missionary Society 1879

Lake Tanganyika

Universities Mission to Central Africa 1863

Luanda

American Board of Commissioners for Foreign Missions 1881

B 1898

Lake Malawi

Chitambo

J 1881

Zambezi

SDA 1903
F 1898

CSM 1876
FCS

FMS 1875

Linyanti
J 1879

Quelimane

Route taken by David Livingstone to Luanda, Quelimane and region of Lake Tanganyika, 1841-73

F 1898

RMS 1847

BMS 1860

London Missionary Society 1801
Orange

SPG 1860

T 1882

SHM 1873

RMS 1832

Moravian Brethren 1792
Cape Town

London Missionary Society 1799

ATLANTIC OCEAN

INDIAN OCEAN

MADAGASCAR

Catholic Missions

B	Benedictines
F	Franciscans
J	Jesuits
LS	Lyons Society
MH	Mill Hill Fathers
SHJ	Sacred Heart of Jesus
SHM	Sacred Heart of Mary
T	Trappists

Protestant Missions

Advance of Catholic missions
Advance of Protestant missions

0   500   1000 km

0   200   400   600 miles

© 1997 Lion Hudson plc/Three's Company

A political cartoon illustrates the extent of British expansion in the nineteenth century.

PART V
Imperialism

During the second half of the nineteenth century, as industrialization spread to the European continent, there was a growing need for new markets, greater supplies of raw materials, and new areas to invest surplus capital. At the same time, the process of nationalization created new nations, which, both out of economic necessity and nationalistic pride, began to expand their interests throughout the world, establishing colonies in Asia and Africa.

This effort for colonial expansion on the part of European nations, called Imperialism, was as much a cultural phenomenon as it was an economic necessity. During the nineteenth century, Europeans began to have an increasingly exalted view of their civilization. By this time, Europeans enjoyed a higher standard of living in terms of transportation, housing, food, and more sanitary conditions. They traveled freely on new railroads, crossed oceans on huge steam-powered liners, spoke on telephones, lit their streets with electricity, and sped from one side of the city to the other on networks of mechanized streetcars. Nineteenth century European philosophy, which was derived from one hundred fifty years of Enlightenment thinking, seemed progressive and insightful. Many believed that these material and intellectual advancements signified the superiority of Western civilization over the world, a sentiment typified by the British writer Rudyard Kipling, who famously called the civilizing of Asia and Africa the "white man's burden."

VICTORIAN ENGLAND

No nation exemplified the airs of imperialist Europe more explicitly than Great Britain. Called Victorian England, after Queen Victoria who ruled from 1837 until 1901, Great Britain was the most powerful, wealthy, and technologically advanced country on the planet, and the values of the age reflected this new wealth. Victorians believed in democracy, patriotism, individualism, progress, and the acquisition of wealth. Proud of her accomplishments, Britain saw herself as the pinnacle of civilization as she strove to spread the many positive values of British culture with the rest of the world.

Victorian spirit should not be understood too cynically, for along with the pomp and haughtiness of the age came an earnest morality, respect for the family, and a high regard for individual philanthropy. Victorians had a sense of social responsibility, which helped temper the harsh world of early industrialized capitalism. Democratic reforms during the Victorian era increased representation among the working classes and introduced social legislation that provided for health care and better factory working conditions. Nonetheless, it was pride in these just reforms and full confidence in their value for everyone that encouraged Britain to bring her culture and political system into Asia and Africa.

The Secret of England's Greatness by Thomas J. Barker, 1861. Queen Victoria presents a Bible to an African leader in the audience chamber of Windsor Castle. This painting symbolizes the widely held opinion that Victorian England's prosperity and power were in part a result of bringing Christianity to her colonies.

A sketch by Henry Morton Stanley (1841-1904) depicts his arrival to the village of Manyema (Kenya, East Africa). The journeys of Livingstone and Stanley opened Africa to Christian missions. Stanley was instructed in 1869 by the owner of his newspaper to "Find Livingstone!" Stanley traveled to Zanzibar and outfitted an expedition with the best equipment and 2,000 porters. He located Livingstone on November 10, 1871 near Lake Tanganyika (present-day Tanzania), and greeted him by saying "Dr. Livingstone, I presume?"

THE OPENING OF AFRICA

David Livingstone (1813-1873) was a Scottish missionary and explorer of the Victorian era. In 1852-56, he explored the African interior, discovering Victoria Falls (which he named after his monarch, Queen Victoria). Livingstone was one of the first Westerners to cross the African continent.

In the 1870s, the work of the Scottish doctor and missionary David Livingstone and the subsequent stories by the native Welshman and *New York Herald* reporter Henry Stanley helped draw attention to the wonders of the African continent. From the beginning, however, despite the motives of the explorers, these explorations were attached to political ends. Stanley's explorations of the Congo River were financed by King Leopold of Belgium, and as a result, Belgium created the Congo Free State in 1871. Britain and France quickly saw the potential for African colonization and, fearing competition from other European nations, entered the race to control the interior of Africa. Within twenty years, the entire African continent was divided among European nations.

Although the coast of Africa had been part of the European trade network since the fifteenth century, prior to 1845, virtually all the expeditions into the African interior resulted in failure due to the outbreaks of malaria, yellow fever, typhus, and dysentery. Disease seemed to protect the African interior with an impenetrable barrier. However, the introduction of Quinine (a drug made from bark used to treat malaria) and the discovery of the causes of yellow fever eventually protected Europeans as they traveled deeper into the African interior.

As had been the case with the explorations of the sixteenth century, Imperial expansion into Africa also brought about a great missionary revival. This time, both Catholics and Protestants flooded the newly-opened African interior. Protestant missionaries traveled with European traders and often had native tribes learn western cultural habits. On the other hand, Catholic missionaries in Africa continued to learn local languages and assimilate African ways of life and so better adapt the Faith to cultural subtleties. Unfortunately, because of this assimilation, many European nations saw the Catholic presence in Africa as a threat to colonization. Although Britain was generally tolerant of both Catholic and Protestant missionaries, King Leopold of Belgium forbade Catholic missionaries from entering the Congo, and the Portuguese colonies of Angola and Mozambique had relatively little Christian presence. At first, France welcomed Catholic missionaries and worked with them in the administration of their colonial possessions. However, after the establishment of the Third Republic in 1871, the French government's support for the Catholic missions dwindled.

As they had done in the past, Catholic missionaries worked at putting into place self-sufficient Catholic communities in Africa with native clergy and an African ecclesiastical hierarchy. The acquisition of native clergy would occur slowly at first, and large numbers of priests would not be ordained until well into the twentieth century. The first native African bishop since the Muslim expansion into North Africa was Laurean Cardinal Rugambwa, who was appointed in 1953. The African clergy founded schools to help maintain and develop the Church in Africa. As a result, most African Catholics owed their conversions to black catechists who had been trained to preach the gospel, and this effort produced a huge increase of African Catholics. In southern Nigeria, for example, the Catholic community grew from five thousand in 1900 to seventy-four thousand by 1912. The success of these early missionary efforts is reflected today in the strong and vigorous Catholic communities that are still thriving and growing in Africa.

MISSIONARY APOSTOLATE IN THE FAR EAST

Missionary efforts in the Far East would prove more difficult than in Africa. In China, apart from admitting a small number of Christian missionaries and European traders in the sixteenth century, for three thousand years the country remained isolated from the rest of the world. During the early part of the nineteenth century, China seemed interested in preserving this isolation, but Great Britain, determined to tap into the huge Chinese market, found ways to introduce the highly addictive drug opium into the country. The Chinese attempted to block the importation of opium, and between 1839 and 1841, China fought two wars with Britain over the sale of the drug. Britain won the Opium Wars, and in the Treaty of Nanking (1842), Britain obtained long-term access to the port city of Hong Kong—the first step towards open trade throughout all of the coastal Chinese ports. Soon, every European nation established "Spheres of Influence" in that country, i.e., regions in which the colonizers traded freely and administered under their own laws.

Before the opening of China, missionaries were subject to severe persecutions, and many were exiled and even killed. After the European nations established their Spheres of Influence, the Chinese government restored properties seized from Christians and protected churches from violence. Nevertheless, missionaries were still seen as representative of Western expansion, and popular violence against them continued. Two examples of these violent persecutions took place in 1866 when two bishops and seven priests were decapitated, and in 1870, when twenty-two

Christians were executed, including the French consul, the chancellor, an interpreter, his wife, and ten sisters of St. Vincent de Paul. Persecution and general rejection of the Western missionaries never ceased, nor did the overall precarious situation of the Church in China improve in the twentieth century.

In Japan, since 1640, after the Tokugawa Shogunate drove the last Europeans from the Japanese mainland, Japan had been closed to foreigners. In 1853 an American warship, commanded by Commodore Matthew Perry, forced a trade agreement with the Tokugawa leadership that reopened Japan to the West. In 1868 the Tokugawa were overthrown, and the new imperial house of Meiji took power. The new emperor began a rapid and remarkable policy of modernization in an effort to compete with Western powers and prevent future Western domination of their country. In just thirty years, Japan underwent an incredible period of change during which it adapted aspects of its business, legal system, and military to that of the United States, France, and Great Britain. Japan's extraordinary modernization was evident by 1901 when it defeated Russia in the Russo-Japanese War.

Japanese missionary activity resumed with the new access into Japan after 1853. At first, French missionaries, arriving in 1859, resided in open ports for the service of foreigners. In March 1865, in Nagasaki, fifteen Japanese Christians discreetly approached the French missionaries. They were careful not to disclose their full identity until they questioned the missionaries about three unique aspects of Catholicism. Some of the Japanese who were converted by the original Jesuit missionaries in the seventeenth century, had passed the Faith down from generation to generation, and looked to see if the new missionaries believed in loyalty to the authority of the Roman pontiff, the veneration of the Blessed Virgin, and celibacy of the clergy. When the fifteen were convinced that the French missionaries shared their same beliefs, over fifty thousand Japanese Christians came forth to support the missionaries. Unfortunately, the sudden appearance of the Japanese Christians drew the attention of the authorities, and persecution resumed. In July 1867, 40,000 faithful were exiled to various provinces. However, the restoration of the emperor in 1868 established a policy of toleration for Christians, and in 1873, persecution ceased and the exiles were allowed to return to their homes.

PART VI

Leo XIII (1878-1903): The Church Confronts a Changing World

Bl. Pius IX died on February 7, 1878, after thirty-two years as pope, the second-longest reign ever. (St. Peter, the first pope, reigned for about thirty-five years.) During his pontificate, the world and the Church's situation had changed dramatically. The new pope would not inherit the Papal States, and he would have to minister to a Church suffering persecution and marginalization in many European countries. At the same time, thanks to the First Vatican Council and changes in Italy, the pope would enjoy a position of greater moral authority, universally recognized as the focal point of unity in the Catholic world and the one responsible for the appointment of bishops throughout the world.

At the conclave, the cardinals chose the relatively unknown Bishop of Perugia, Gioacchino Pecci, who took the name Leo XIII. The choice of Leo XIII was surprising not only because he came from the small and obscure see of Perugia, but also because Gioacchino Pecci had been somewhat unsuccessful in his career in the papal service (he was removed as nuncio from Belgium after

mishandling a delicate political situation). In addition, Pecci was made Camerlengo (the person who oversees economic affairs and the convocation of the conclave for the papal election) just a few months before Bl. Pius' death. Usually due to age, the Camerlengo is not elected pope, and this appointment by the ailing pontiff may have signified Bl. Pius' desire to prevent Pecci from becoming pope.

There were a number of reasons why Pecci was elected. He had the reputation of being more traditional, and his opinions had helped form the content of Bl. Pius IX's *Syllabus of Errors.* Yet Pecci was also a successful and popular diocesan bishop who had published a series of pastoral letters that spoke positively about the possibilities of a modern society and the advances of science. Indeed, the successor of Bl. Pius IX would have the task of addressing a changing and hostile Europe, tackling the many new schools of thought that were shaping the future of the Western world. The election of Leo XIII placed a strong pastoral leader in the chair of St. Peter, a firm defender of the Faith who could mend rifts and speak positively about the con-temporary world. During his twenty-five year pontificate, Leo XIII served as a teacher, issuing eighty-seven encyclicals, addressing almost every major issue of the day.

THE BIRTH OF SECULAR HUMANISM

The nineteenth century saw the beginning of a new humanistic and philosophical mind-set devoid of any spiritual or religious component. This new humanism, called Secular Humanism, became perhaps the most comprehensive and influential general ideology since the Enlightenment. Growing nationalism, blind faith in the "progress" of civilization, and exaltation of man as a replacement for God, all gave rise to notions of the human person divested of any relationship with the Divine. Secular humanism better describes a general sentiment and spirit of thought more than a unified school. What binds these thinkers is their increasingly materialistic understanding of the human person. As philosophy drifted even further from notions of God and religion, many began to argue that the world does not reflect the eternal wisdom and law of God and, therefore, standards for governing what is right and wrong do not apply, or, at best, they are relative. Instead of God, man became the subject of study, and his motives and desires were believed to be quantifiable and calculable. This premise, which influenced nearly every discipline from science to politics, posed major challenges to the Church. The encyclicals of Leo XIII responded to these erroneous ideas with explanations that presented the human person, society, and politics from a Christian perspective.

CHARLES DARWIN AND THE SURVIVAL OF THE FITTEST

From 1831 to 1836, the British naturalist Charles Darwin sailed around the world, studying the wide variety of species of plants and animals found in the many corners of the globe. Besides surveying species in South America, Australia, and Asia, Darwin recorded observations about the abundant rare species found on the Galapagos Islands in the Pacific Ocean. As Darwin compared the many species, he believed he found similarities that led him to startling conclusions.

Darwin observed how some species, such as those living on the Galapagos Islands, seem to resemble species in other lands in every way except for a few peculiar characteristics — such as a lizard that swims or a bird which cannot fly. Darwin concluded that this was the result of the species' gradual adaptation to their specific environment. Over time, he argued, two animals living in two different places would develop into two entirely different species by way of accidental mutations, which better equip each organism to survive in its specific environs. Darwin called this process "natural selection" since nature seemed to determine which members of a species were better equipped for survival. Darwin theorized that, over the course of thousands — if not millions — of years, the process of natural selection causes various species to "evolve" from a single species. This theory of evolution proposed that every living thing originated from a distant source: man from apes, birds from dinosaurs, frogs from fish, and the like.

Charles Robert Darwin (1809-1882) was a British naturalist who achieved lasting fame as originator of the theory of evolution through natural selection. He wrote his theories after a five year voyage on the ship H.M.S. Beagle.

Besides creating an entirely new field of scientific research, Darwin's theories greatly influenced nineteenth and twentieth century social thought. Although Darwin was never concerned with the social and religious implications of his theories, others took his theories and applied them to many other branches of thought such as anthropology, philosophy, and economics. Natural selection, for instance, weeded out the weak, the poor, and the lower classes who were not strong enough to survive in harsh social environments. Wealthy industrialists believed their success reflected their "natural selection" in the continuation of the human species. (The full title of Darwin's best-known work is *On the Origin of Species by Means of Natural Selection, or the Preservation of Favoured Races in the Struggle for Life.*) No matter how unjust society became, they claimed that the future of humanity is determined by the "survival of the fittest," and economic or racial superiority leads to the advance and perfection of the human species.

KARL MARX AND THE POLITICS OF ATHEISM

Karl Marx (1818-1883) was born in Alsace (on the border between France and Germany) into a particularly violent and volatile world. He spent much of his life working as a writer and journalist in Germany and France where he witnessed firsthand both political and economic revolution. He saw the massive social problems brought about by industrialization, including the emergence of a large urban working class, the widening gap between the wealthy and the poor, and the miserable situations experienced by workers marginalized by *laissez-faire* economics. In response to these, Marx wrote articles that criticized capitalism, liberal democracy, and religious beliefs and practices referred to as the "the opiate of the masses." Instead of these systems, he proposed a social-political structure called communism, which, he argued, would inevitably emerge as the dominant force in the world.

More than a political system, communism was envisioned by Marx as a necessary historical development, the culmination of human history. Marx posited that throughout history the majority of people have suffered in society due to wealth and property being controlled by a few ruling elite. But history also shows, he said, that these elite have been continuously overthrown through violent rebellion and replaced by those citizens lower down the social ladder. He said the French Revolution, which succeeded feudal power with rule by the *bourgeoisie*, perfectly illustrated this historical process.

For Marx, history was approaching a new era because the working class (proletariat), who represented the lowest and most numerous members of society, were the next social class poised for rebellion. Instead of simply seizing control of wealth and property and taking the place of the ruling elite, Marx argued that this exploited class would establish, through revolution, a new socio-economic system in which social classes no longer existed. In theory, this system (called communism) offered a Utopian vision: the proletariat held all wealth and property in common, creating a society based on absolute equality in which the government provided everyone with whatever they needed.

Marx believed history and society were based primarily on material motives and not on transcendental forces. (He called religion "the opiate of the masses" since it made the lower classes content with their rotten state.) Based on his scientific examination of the laws of economics, Marx argued that the proletariat would rise up in a last, bloody, worldwide revolution, finally overthrowing the owners of capital and destroying the principle of private property. Although Marx's theories found fertile ground among those members of society who had been hurt and left behind by the proponents of *laissez-faire* economics, the communist regimes in reality have violated human dignity more than any other political system and has utterly failed in its attempt of promoting the rights and welfare of the workers and common people. Most communist countries began to take on more mercantilist or capitalist systems by the end of the twentieth century. By the dawn of the third millennium, only five countries could be described as communist, including the largest in population: China.

SIGMUND FREUD AND PSYCHOANALYSIS

Sigmund Freud (1856-1939) began his career as an assistant to the German psychologist Joseph Breuer, who conducted a series of experiments in the 1880s geared at determining underlying motives of human behavior through psychological evaluation. These experiments were designed to observe the causes and effects of complex behavioral abnormalities. These studies and observations eventually led Freud to develop his celebrated psychoanalysis, which served as a psychological method aimed at emotional healing and stability through a deeper and more accurate psychological assessment.

As part of his psychoanalysis, Freud developed a systematic understanding of the human self that was broken down into three basic faculties: the conscious mind (that which is present in the mind at any moment), the preconscious (that which can be remembered), and the subconscious (those thoughts and memories that are unavailable to the conscious mind). Freud called these three faculties, respectively, the ego, the superego, and the id.

For Freud, the id (subconscious mind) contains desires and wishes determined by basic instincts, such as hunger, sleep, and sexual appetite. Since the ego (conscious mind) perceives the outside world, the ego searches for what will satisfy the desires of the id. As the ego learns how to satisfy the id, it stores this information in the superego (preconscious mind, or memory). In this way, all three faculties work together to satisfy the instinctual needs of the human person.

Freud argued that although everyone is driven to satisfy desires for sensual pleasure, the subject is inhibited in this quest by social conventions and obstacles introduced by society. Whether it be through physical danger or social taboo, the ego is prohibited from completely satisfying the id. The superego therefore, remembering these restrictions, generates feelings such as pride, shame, or guilt in order to restrain the ego from placating the id.

Freud's model of the human person challenges both the Judeo-Christian notion of natural law and man's rational nature composed of body and spirit. Rather then attributing behavior to freely made good or bad choices, Freud argued that instincts awaken human desire, which conventional morality represses and restricts. For Freud, human happiness can be achieved when the id can be free of all restrictions. Freud's psychological description of human consciousness reduces the person to nothing more than a glorified animal whose all encompassing objective is sexual contentment. Freud's notion of man certainly does not even remotely include his capacity to act for spiritual motives.

The Encyclicals of Leo XIII

Leo XIII was the first pope in over a millennium and a half not to exercise temporal power. Being divested of temporal authority gave this new pope the capacity to focus on the pastoral needs of the Church and formulate Catholic teaching applicable to the needs of the times. He put out a staggering eighty-seven papal encyclicals, which reflected a papacy free of the distractions of temporal rule and focused on the moral leadership of the Church..

Leo XIII's encyclicals touched on the many burning issues affecting society as well as the spiritual welfare of the person. His writings include various and sundry themes such as doctrinal formation, freedom, scripture, and the Rosary.

Inscrutabili Dei (April 21, 1878)

Leo XIII issued his first encyclical just two months after becoming pope, and it set the tone for his later teachings. *Inscrutabili Dei* (On the Evils of Society) stated briefly all the accumulated problems affecting contemporary society. Evils have oppressed the human race "on every side," he argues. Among these he lists

> the widespread subversion of the primary truths on which all…human society is based; the obstinacy of mind that will not brook any authority however lawful;…the contempt of law which molds characters and is the shield of righteousness;…the insatiable craving for things perishable;…the reckless mismanagement, waste, and misappropriation of the public funds; the shamelessness of those who, full of treachery, make semblance of being champions of country, of freedom, and every kind of right. (*Inscrutabili Dei*, no. 2)

In this passage, *Inscrutabili Dei* summarizes over a hundred years of offences perpetrated by the revolutionary regimes whose excesses had plunged society into its present sorry state. The pope contends that these evils are a result of the setting aside of "the holy and venerable authority of the Church" (*Inscrutabili Dei*, no. 3). To support his argument, Pope Leo XIII quotes St. Paul who warned in his letter to the Colossians: "Beware lest any man cheat you by philosophy or vain deceit, according to the tradition of men, according to the elements of the world and not according to Christ (Col 2:8)" (*Inscrutabili Dei*, no. 13).

Inscrutabili Dei is an effective introduction to both Leo XIII's papacy and his extensive teachings. As if drawing a line in the sand, Leo identifies the problems of the age, illustrates their opposition to the Church, and argues that fidelity to the Christian message expressed through the Catholic

Pope Leo XIII, born Vincenzo Gioacchino Raffaele Luigi Pecci (1810-1903), succeeded Blessed Pius IX on February 20, 1878 and reigned until his death. Leo XIII worked to encourage understanding between the Church and the modern world. He firmly re-asserted the study of Scholastic philosophy, especially St. Thomas Aquinas, in his encyclical *Æterni Patris* (1880).

Church is the only hope for restoring and curing society. "[T]he hopes of Italy and of the whole world lie in the power…wherewith the authority of the apostolic see is endowed," he writes. "We recognize that nothing should be nearer Our heart than how to preserve safe and sound the dignity of the Roman see, and to strengthen ever more and more the union of the members with the head, of the children with their father" (*Inscrutabili Dei*, no. 11).

Picking up where Bl. Pius IX left off, Leo XIII strongly emphasized the important role of papal authority in preserving the future of the Church. The encyclical also shows that Leo XIII understood papal *teaching* as a central aspect of the church's mission. He illustrated in later encyclicals that the church guidance and mission will never be compromised by any kind of political regime governing a nation.

In the closing paragraphs of *Inscrutabili Dei*, the pope offers a hopeful solution to overcoming contemporary difficulties, stating that a healthy society is possible as long as "each member will gradually grow accustomed to the love of religion and piety, to the abhorrence of false and harmful teaching, to the pursuit of virtue, to obedience to elders, and to the restraint of the insatiable seeking after self-interest alone, which so spoils and weakens the character of men" (*Inscrutabili Dei*, no. 15).

Immortale Dei (November 1, 1885)

Leo XIII's encyclical *Immortale Dei* (On the Christian Constitution of States) exemplifies the pope's careful efforts to show understanding for liberal political movements while clearly transmitting the Church's doctrine on the dynamics and role of civil society. Leo XIII begins the encyclical by restating the Church's belief that God is the root and source of all political authority and that both civil and divine authority have a duty and responsibility to God. "For, men living together in society," he argues, "are under the power of God no less than individuals are, and society, no less than individuals, owes gratitude to God who gave it being and maintains it and whose ever bounteous goodness enriches it with countless blessings" (*Immortale Dei*, no. 6). Because civil authority is ultimately an expression of God's plan, Pope Leo warns against those who may incite revolution against civil government by quoting St. Paul's Letter to the Romans:

> "He that resisteth the power resisteth the ordinance of God, and they that resist, purchase to themselves damnation" (Rom 13:2). To cast aside obedience, and by popular violence to incite to revolt, is therefore treason, not against man only, but against God. (*Immortale Dei*, no. 5)

The pope was careful not to isolate the many liberal groups that sprang up against what was felt to be an unjust leadership of the old regime. He pointed out the problem which arises when one of the two authorities, civil and divine, have the same source of authority, but one of these misuses that authority although they have the same divine source. "Two powers," he states, "would be commanding contrary things, and it would be a dereliction of duty to disobey either of the two" (*Immortale Dei*, no. 13). In seeking a resolution to this potential conflict, the pope offers requirements for just civil rulers:

> In political affairs, and all matters civil, the laws aim at securing the common good, and are not framed according to the delusive caprices and opinions of the mass of the people, but by truth and by justice; the ruling powers are invested with a sacredness more than human, and are withheld from deviating from the path of duty, and from overstepping the bounds of rightful authority. (*Immortale Dei*, no. 18)

But in *Immortale Dei*, Leo XIII never offered an explicit instance when revolution would be justified, instead maintaining throughout that "the terrible upheavals of the last century were wildly conceived and…that [the] new conception of law…was at variance on many points with not only the Christian, but even the natural law" (*Immortale Dei*, no. 23).

Nonetheless, Leo XIII did not seek to separate the Church from legitimate political change and modernization. He devotes the closing section of his encyclical to insisting that the Church "most gladly welcomes whatever improvements the age brings forth" (*Immortale Dei*, no. 23). Neither does he endorse any specific form of government, such as a monarchy with the union of throne and altar. These were welcoming words to political progressives and provided some resolution to the ideological struggle between the Church and the modern world. Finally, the pope closes with an invitation to Catholics to participate in the new democratic societies that recently emerged:

> Catholics have just reasons for taking part in the conduct of public affairs…For in so doing they…seek to turn [democratic society]…to the genuine and true public good, and…to infuse…into all the veins of the State the healthy sap and blood of Christian wisdom and virtue. (*Immortale Dei*, no. 45)

Rerum novarum (May 15, 1891)

Among the eighty-seven encyclicals written by Leo XIII, none was so widely received, praised, and influential as *Rerum novarum* (On Capital and Labor), his encyclical on social justice. This encyclical is perhaps Leo XIII's most unique work since it outlines for the first time the principles of Catholic Social Teaching that would remain in force throughout the late nineteenth and twentieth centuries.

A large part of this encyclical is dedicated to a refutation of the principles of socialism which proposes a society that holds all property in common to be administered by the state. Leo XIII condemned socialism as an attack on human freedom and dignity, arguing that the worker would be the first to suffer from such a regime. "Remunerative labor," the pope says, is "the impelling reason and motive of . . . work [to obtain property]" (*Rerum novarum*, 5). Acquisition of private is an intrinsic right of every human being who is called by God to use the material resources for his own benefit and welfare. The worker gains private property as the fruit of his labor "Man not only should possess the fruits of the earth," the pope writes, "but also the very soil, inasmuch as from the produce of the earth he has to lay by provision for the future" (*Rerum novarum*, 7).

Leo XIII also argues that the loss of private ownership would cause harm to the human family. "That right to property," he says, "must in like wise belong to a man in his capacity of head of a family…The contention, then, that the civil government should at its opinion intrude into and exercise intimate control over the family and the household is a great and pernicious error" (*Rerum novarum*, 13-14).

Although he clarifies the evils of socialism, Pope Leo did not praise the capitalist economy of the Industrial Age, which he said had laid upon the poor "a yoke little better than that of slavery" (*Rerum novarum*, 3). Pope Leo referred instead to the Gospel. "If Christian precepts prevail," he argues, "the respective classes will not only be untied in the bonds of friendship, but also in those of brotherly love" (*Rerum novarum*, 25). Pope Leo saw Christianity, with its foundation in fraternal love, as the only solution to the problems of modern society. Only when there is recognition of our common Father, who is God, can a just society be formed, since justice is perfected by charity. The pope went on to rebuke the wealthy who by their unjust and uncharitable exploitation of the working classes ignore the words of Christ: "'It is more blessed to give than to receive' (Acts 20:35)" (*Rerum novarum*, 22).

Leo XIII also addressed the erroneous belief that the wealthy and working classes were intended by nature to live in mutual conflict. The pope maintained that this view was directly contrary to the truth, and that it was "ordained by nature that these two classes should dwell in harmony and agreement, so as to maintain the balance of the body politic" (*Rerum novarum*, 19). The employer provides the capital required for producing the goods and services and the employee provides the labor to turn the capital into the goods and services. One cannot exist without the other.

Both classes, however, have duties to the other that must be followed. The worker, for example, must fully and faithfully "perform the work which has been freely and equitably agreed upon" and "never to resort to violence in defending their own cause, nor to engage in riot or disorder" (*Rerum novarum*, 20). On the other hand, the employer is bound "not to look upon their work people as their bondsmen" and "never to tax his work people beyond their strength, or employ them in work unsuited to their sex and age" (*Rerum novarum*, 20). Additionally, although the employer and employee are free to bargain as to wages, the employer always has a duty to pay his workers a just wage sufficient "to support a frugal and well behaved wage-earner" (*Rerum novarum*, 45).

Rerum novarum was a double-edged sword. Leo XIII rejected both socialism and *laissez-faire* capitalism, which opposed human dignity and personal freedom. Instead, the pope maintained that all men have the right to property and a just wage. Christianity, Leo XIII declared, is the only known institution that can positively promote the dignity of the human person and effectively cultivate the richness of the human spirit. He reminded readers that "civil society was renovated in every part by Christian institutions; that in the strength of that renewal the human race was lifted up to better things.... And if human society is to be healed now, in no other way can it be healed save by a return to Christian life and Christian institutions" (*Rerum novarum*, 27).

CONCLUSION

In every period of history, the Church works to transmit the wealth of her wisdom. During this age of political, economic, and social change, together with persecution and suppression, the Church emerged once again as a strong moral force. It can be argued that the papacy, especially in the person of Leo XIII, not only plays the role of promoting unity in the Catholic Church, but also more and more becomes a champion of human rights and a defender of human dignity. As of the end of the nineteenth century, the pope not only serves as Holy Father for the Church, but as a common father for all humanity.

"And if human society is to be healed now, in no other way can it be healed save by a return to Christian life and Christian institutions."

—Pope Leo XIII, *Rerum novarum*, 27

SUPPLEMENTARY READING

Karl Marx, *Communinst Manifesto,* from Chapter One

In the condition of the proletariat, those of old society at large are already virtually swamped. The proletarian is without property; his relation to his wife and children has no longer anything in common with the *bourgeois* family relations; modern industry labour, modern subjection to capital, the same in England as in France, in America as in Germany, has stripped him of every trace of national character. Law, morality, religion, are to him so many bourgeois prejudices, behind which lurk in ambush just as many bourgeois interests.

All the preceding classes that got the upper hand sought to fortify their already acquired status by subjecting society at large to their conditions of appropriation. The proletarians cannot become masters of the productive forces of society, except by abolishing their own previous mode of appropriation, and thereby also every other previous mode of appropriation. They have nothing of their own to secure and to fortify; their mission is to destroy all previous securities for, and insurances of, individual property.

All previous historical movements were movements of minorities, or in the interest of minorities. The proletarian movement is the self-conscious, independent movement of the immense majority, in the interest of the immense majority. The proletariat, the lowest stratum of our present society, cannot stir, cannot raise itself up, without the whole superincumbent strata of official society being sprung into the air.

Rudyard Kipling, "The White Man's Burden," February 1899

Take up the White Man's burden—
Send forth the best ye breed—
Go send your sons to exile
To serve your captives' need;
To wait in heavy harness,
On fluttered folk and wild—
Your new-caught, sullen peoples,
Half devil and half child.

Take up the White Man's burden—
In patience to abide,
To veil the threat of terror
And check the show of pride;
By open speech and simple,
An hundred times made plain,
To seek another's profit
And work another's gain.

Take up the White Man's burden—
And reap his old reward:
The blame of those ye better,
The hate of those ye guard—
The cry of hosts ye humour
(Ah slowly!) toward the light:—
"Why brought ye us from bondage,
Our loved Egyptian night?"

Take up the White Man's burden—
Have done with childish days—
The lightly proffered laurel,
The easy, ungrudged praise.
Comes now, to search your manhood
Through all the thankless years,
Cold-edged with dear-bought wisdom,
The judgment of your peers!

John Paul II, *Centesimus annus*, 4, "Characteristics of *Rerum novarum*"

Towards the end of the last century the Church found herself facing an historical process which had already been taking place for some time, but which was by then reaching a critical point. The determining factor in this process was a combination of radical changes which had taken place in the political, economic and social fields, and in the areas of science and technology, to say nothing of the wide influence of the prevailing ideologies. In the sphere of politics, the result of these changes was a *new conception of society and of the State*, and consequently *of authority* itself. A traditional society was passing away and another was beginning to be formed—one which brought the hope of new freedoms but also the threat of new forms of injustice and servitude.

In the sphere of economics, in which scientific discoveries and their practical application come together, new structures for the production of consumer goods had progressively taken shape. A new form of *property* had appeared—capital; and a *new form of labour*—labour for wages, characterized by high rates of production which lacked due regard for sex, age or family situation, and were determined solely by efficiency, with a view to increasing profits.

In this way labour became a commodity to be freely bought and sold on the market, its price determined by the law of supply and demand, without taking into account the bare minimum required for the support of the individual and his family. Moreover, the worker was not even sure of being able to sell "his own commodity," continually threatened as he was by unemployment, which, in the absence of any kind of social security, meant the spectre of death by starvation.

The result of this transformation was a society "divided into two classes, separated by a deep chasm" (Leo XIII, Encyclical Letter *Rerum novarum: loc. cit.*, 132). This situation was linked to the marked change taking place in the political order already mentioned. Thus the prevailing political theory of the time sought to promote total economic freedom by appropriate laws, or, conversely, by a deliberate lack of any intervention. At the same time, another conception of property and economic life was beginning to appear in an organized and often violent form, one which implied a new political and social structure.

At the height of this clash, when people finally began to realize fully the very grave injustice of social realities in many places and the danger of a revolution fanned by ideals which were then called "socialist," Pope Leo XIII intervened with a document which dealt in a systematic way with the "condition of the workers."...Indeed, what is the origin of all the evils to which *Rerum novarum* wished to respond, if not a kind of freedom which, in the area of economic and social activity, cuts itself off from the truth about man?

VOCABULARY

CARBORNARI
Literally "charcoal burners," this Italian secret police society led a successful revolution against the King of Naples, the Bourbon monarch Ferdinand I.

COMMUNISM
As envisioned by Karl Marx, more than a political system, this was a necessary historical development, the culmination of human history. The exploited proletariat would establish, through revolution, a new social-economic system in which social classes no longer existed. In theory, this system offered a Utopian vision: the proletariat held all wealth and property in common, securing a society based on absolute equality in which the government provided everything that everyone needed.

CONCERT OF EUROPE
Alliance established by Metternich which sought to dismantle the reforms brought about by Napoleon and crush any liberal revolution. This arrangement left Austria, and Metternich, as the main arbiter of European affairs beginning in 1815.

HOLY ALLIANCE
In 1815, Czar Alexander I of Russia proposed the creation of this alliance (including Russia, Prussia, and Austria) which promised to uphold Christian principles of charity and peace. Despite Alexander's pious intentions, the Holy Alliance did not outline a program effective enough to ensure peace and was not taken seriously by its members.

IMPERIALISM
The process by which nations, both out of economic necessity and nationalistic pride, began to expand their interests throughout the world, establishing colonies in Asia and Africa.

INDUSTRIALIZATION
The rapid transformation from an agricultural to an industrial economy which altered the way people lived and dramatically changed how countries did business toward production of goods through mechanization.

KULTURKAMPF
Bismarck's policy of ridding Germany of Catholicism. It subjected Catholic schools and seminaries to state control, forbade religious orders to teach, and banned every religious order in Germany. Furthermore, any priest or bishop who did not acknowledge state supremacy over the Church in Germany was fined or imprisoned.

LAISSEZ-FAIRE CAPITALISM
Theory that state regulation of the economy, as found in mercantilism, only deterred the development of a healthy economy. A free market, on the other hand, would create a robust economic order wherein self-interest and voluntary charity would provide for all the needs of society.

LIBERALISM
Put generally, this ideology approved of everything that was modern, enlightened, efficient, and reasonable. Based on the principles of natural law, liberals saw monarchies as unjust, out-of-date, and not properly representative of the people.

MONROE DOCTRINE
American President James Monroe's isolationist announcement in 1823 that the Western Hemisphere was closed to further European colonization and that any attempt by European states to intervene in the affairs of Latin America would be considered an act of war against the United States.

VOCABULARY Continued

NATURAL SELECTION

According to Darwin's theory of the origin of the species, two animals living in two different places develop into two entirely different species by way of accidental mutations which better equip an organism to survive in a specific location. Others used this theory to interpret social phenomena. Natural selection, they said, weeded out the weak, the poor, and the lower classes who were not strong enough to survive in harsh social environments.

PAPAL INFALLIBILITY

The dogma that the pope cannot make an error, when speaking *ex cathedra* (when in the exercise of his office as shepherd and teacher of all Catholics) and defining a doctrine concerning Faith and morals to be held by the whole Church.

SECULAR HUMANISM

Nineteenth-century intellectual movement in which thinkers described an increasingly mechanical understanding of the human person. As philosophy drifted even further from notions of God and religion, many began to argue that the world is essentially amoral and that the guidelines for governing what is right and wrong no longer apply.

ULTRAMONTANISM

Literally "over the mountains." Catholics who looked to the pope for support and leadership, emphasizing his centrality and authority more than ever before.

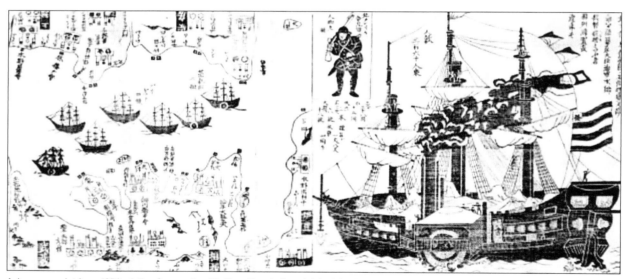

A Japanese print from 1854 relating Commodore Matthew Perry's first visit in July of 1853. Aboard a black-hulled steam frigate, Perry anchored near Edo (modern Tokyo) and was met by representatives of the Tokugawa Shogunate who told him to proceed to Nagasaki, the only Japanese port open to foreigners at that time. Perry refused to leave and demanded permission to present a letter from President Millard Fillmore, and threatened force if he was denied. Japanese military forces were no match for Perry's modern weaponry. The Japanese government had to accept Perry's demands which led to the Convention of Kanagawa in 1854 opening Japan to western trade. The "black ships" became a symbol to the Japanese of the threat of Western colonialism.

STUDY QUESTIONS

1. What diplomat dominated the affairs at the Congress of Vienna?

2. What two Enlightenment thinkers helped lay out the principles that developed into Liberalism?

3. Why was the Holy Alliance widely rejected among European powers?

4. What alliance established by Metternich dominated the European political sphere for fifteen years?

5. Why was the Monroe Doctrine respected by the European powers?

6. How were the Greeks eventually able to win their independence?

7. How did the Prussians seek to eliminate Catholic influence in the southern German States? How did Pope Pius VIII respond to this policy?

8. Lamennais, Lacordaire, and Montalembert started what French paper?

9. What positions helped the nativist Know-Nothing Party gain popularity?

10. What economic developments preceded the Industrial Revolution?

11. What changes did industrialization bring to family life?

12. According to Adam Smith, why should governments stay out of economics?

13. What event caused Bl. *Pio Nono* to grow suspicious of liberal reform?

14. What two Marian titles best express the Church Fathers' belief that Mary was immaculately conceived?

15. What miraculous event reinforced Bl. Pius IX's proclamation of the Immaculate Conception?

16. What did *Quanta cura* and the *Syllabus of Errors* address?

17. What event forced the disbanding of the First Vatican Council?

18. What was the Roman Question?

19. How did Bismarck successfully unite the German States?

20. What two events worsened the situation of the Church in France during the Third Republic?

21. Why was English society called "Victorian" at the end of the nineteenth century?

22. What drug helped open Africa to further exploration?

23. What three teachings did Japanese Christians use to verify the orthodoxy of French missionaries?

24. On what island chain did Charles Darwin conduct many of the observations that led to the formulation of his theory of natural selection?

25. Karl Marx believed that history and society was primarily driven by what?

26. According to Freud, the human self is divided into what three parts?

27. Leo XIII was the first pope in over a millennium and a half to lack what papal power upon his election?

28. According to Leo XIII's encyclical *Inscrutabili Dei*, what will help a healthy society emerge?

29. According to Leo XIII's encyclical *Immortale Dei*, who is the root and source of all political authority?

30. Leo XIII's *Rerum novarum* particularly condemns what nineteenth century political system and ideology?

PRACTICAL EXERCISES

1. Through a comparison of Pius VII and Leo XIII, explain how the events of the nineteenth century changed the role of the pope both in the world and in the Church. What specific events led to the shift?

2. What effects did industrialization and imperialism have on European and non-European countries? How did this change the role the Church played in Europe, Asia, Africa, and the Americas?

3. What problems did the three exemplary secular humanist thinkers pose to the Church? How have their ideas affected today's society?

An eyewitness illustration of the stifling congestion in 1869 London. Gustave Doré, a Frenchman, visited London in the spring of 1869 and made extensive sketches of the city for what would be a book titled *London: A Pilgrimage* compiled with journalist and friend Blanchard Jerrold who wrote for the *Daily News*, the paper founded by Charles Dickens.

FROM THE CATECHISM

1882 Certain societies, such as the family and the state, correspond more directly to the nature of man; they are necessary to him. To promote the participation of the greatest number in the life of a society, the creation of voluntary associations and institutions must be encouraged "on both national and international levels, which relate to economic and social goals, to cultural and recreational activities, to sport, to various professions, and to political affairs" (John XXIII, *MM* 60). This "*socialization*" also expresses the natural tendency for human beings to associate with one another for the sake of attaining objectives that exceed individual capacities. It develops the qualities of the person, especially the sense of initiative and responsibility, and helps guarantee his rights (cf. *GS* 25 § 2; *CA* 12).

1883 Socialization also presents dangers. Excessive intervention by the state can threaten personal freedom and initiative. The teaching of the Church has elaborated the principle of *subsidiarity*, according to which "a community of a higher order should not interfere in the internal life of a community of a lower order, depriving the latter of its functions, but rather should support it in case of need and help to coordinate its activity with the activities of the rest of society, always with a view to the common good" (*CA* 48 § 4; cf. Pius XI, *Quadragesimo anno* I, 184-186).

1897 "Human society can be neither well-ordered nor prosperous unless it has some people invested with legitimate authority to preserve its institutions and to devote themselves as far as is necessary to work and care for the good of all" (John XXIII, *PT* 46).

By "authority" one means the quality by virtue of which persons or institutions make laws and give orders to men and expect obedience from them.

2424 A theory that makes profit the exclusive norm and ultimate end of economic activity is morally unacceptable. The disordered desire for money cannot but produce perverse effects. It is one of the causes of the many conflicts which disturb the social order (cf. *GS* 63 § 3; *LE* 7; 20; *CA* 35).

A system that "subordinates the basic rights of individuals and of groups to the collective organization of production" is contrary to human dignity (*GS* 65 § 2). Every practice that reduces persons to nothing more than a means of profit enslaves man, leads to idolizing money, and contributes to the spread of atheism. "You cannot serve God and mammon" (Mt 6: 24, Lk 16: 13).

2425 The Church has rejected the totalitarian and atheistic ideologies associated in modern times with "communism" or "socialism." She has likewise refused to accept, in the practice of "capitalism," individualism and the absolute primacy of the law of the marketplace over human labor (cf. *CA* 10; 13; 44). Regulating the economy solely by centralized planning perverts the basis of social bonds; regulating it solely by the law of the marketplace fails social justice, for "there are many human needs which cannot be satisfied by the market" (*CA* 34). Reasonable regulation of the marketplace and economic initiatives, in keeping with a just hierarchy of values and a view to the common good, is to be commended.

2443 God blesses those who come to the aid of the poor and rebukes those who turn away from them: "Give to him who begs from you, do not refuse him who would borrow from you"; "you received without pay, give without pay" (Mt 5: 42, 10: 8). It is by what they have done for the poor that Jesus Christ will recognize his chosen ones (cf. Mt 25: 31-36). When "the poor have the good news preached to them," it is the sign of Christ's presence (Mt 11: 5, Lk 4: 18).

FROM THE CATECHISM Continued

2449 Beginning with the Old Testament, all kinds of juridical measures (the jubilee year of forgiveness of debts, prohibition of loans at interest and the keeping of collateral, the obligation to tithe, the daily payment of the day-laborer, the right to glean vines and fields) answer the exhortation of *Deuteronomy*: "For the poor will never cease out of the land; therefore I command you, 'You shall open wide your hand to your brother, to the needy and to the poor in the land'" (Dt 15:11). Jesus makes these words his own: "The poor you always have with you, but you do not always have me" (Jn 12:8). In so doing he does not soften the vehemence of former oracles against "buying the poor for silver and the needy for a pair of sandals...," but invites us to recognize his own presence in the poor who are his brethren (Am 8:6; cf. Mt 25:40):

> When her mother reproached her for caring for the poor and the sick at home, St. Rose of Lima said to her: "When we serve the poor and the sick, we serve Jesus. We must not fail to help our neighbors, because in them we serve Jesus." (P. Hansen, *Vita mirabilis* [Louvain, 1668])

The Basilica at Lourdes, France. This immense concrete church was built above the grotto in 1958 to accommodate the ever increasing number of pilgrims. It replaced the original basilica built in 1876. The basilica seats 20,000. The pilgrimage season lasts from April through October, with the main pilgrimage day being August 15, the Marian Feast of the Assumption. Four to six million pilgrims visit the shrine each year. It is estimated that more than 200 million pilgrims have come to Lourdes since 1860.

The Church Gives Witness In Wars And Revolutions

*The twentieth century was the bloodiest in history.
Two World Wars left the world desperate for spiritual healing.
Through words and action, the popes of the twentieth century
became the world's moral conscience.*

CHAPTER 19

The Church Gives Witness In Wars And Revolutions

It is only when hatred and injustice are sanctioned and organized by the ideologies based on them, rather than on the truth about man, that they take possession of entire nations and drive them to act....May the memory of those terrible events guide the actions of everyone, particularly the leaders of nations in our own time, when other forms of injustice are fueling new hatreds and when new ideologies which exalt violence are appearing on the horizon.

— Pope John Paul II, *Centesimus Annus, 1991*, no. 17

The twentieth century was the bloodiest in history with an estimated 188 million people killed due to war and revolt (White, *Historical Atlas of the Twentieth Century*, 2001, users.erols. com/mwhite28/20centry.htm [May 20, 2005]). It witnessed two world wars that claimed 70,000,000 lives; countless other wars, smaller but hardly less deadly; the rise and fall of vicious totalitarian systems—Fascism, Nazism, Communism—and the emergence of organized terrorism; genocidal acts ranging from the Nazi slaughter of millions of Jews to the killing fields of a vicious Communist regime in Cambodia (1.65 million); the development of nuclear weapons and their use by the United States against two Japanese cities (120,000) in World War II, and their threatened use, as a deterrent, by a growing number of nuclear-armed nations; repeated acts of religious persecution, especially directed at the Catholic Church; legalized abortion and euthanasia on a vast scale (46 million worldwide each year); and the casual destruction of human embryos and fetuses—human life at its earliest stages—in the name of scientific research, sex-selection, or eugenics. By the century's end, biotechnology was being abused by human cloning and other procedures. On a global scale, serious observers warned of a possible "clash of civilizations" involving the West and militant Islam or a resurgent China.

The twentieth century also witnessed astonishing progress. Among the advances were the widespread elimination of hunger and familiar diseases in many—though certainly not all—parts of the world; the spread of literacy; real progress in human rights, including those of women and

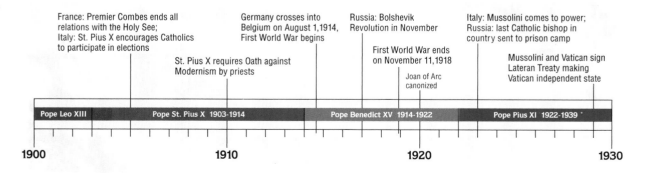

France: Premier Combes ends all relations with the Holy See;
Italy: St. Pius X encourages Catholics to participate in elections

St. Pius X requires Oath against Modernism by priests

Germany crosses into Belgium on August 1,1914, First World War begins

Russia: Bolshevik Revolution in November

First World War ends on November 11,1918

Joan of Arc canonized

Italy: Mussolini comes to power; Russia: last Catholic bishop in country sent to prison camp

Mussolini and Vatican sign Lateran Treaty making Vatican independent state

Pope Leo XIII

Pope St. Pius X 1903-1914

Pope Benedict XV 1914-1922

Pope Pius XI 1922-1939

1900   1910   1920   1930

World War I photograph. A young girl holds her doll in the streets of war-shattered Rheims, France in 1917.

World War II photograph. Young victims of the Nazi persecution in Poland 1940.

minorities; decolonization and the emergence of many new, independent nations; the replacement of repressive regimes by democratic governments in a number of places; astonishing technological progress in communications, media, transportation, and other fields; and tentative steps toward creation of an international order sustained by appropriate supranational economic and political institutions.

In the religious and spiritual realms, the conflicts and calamities of the twentieth century helped spur the rise of secularism and a growing crisis of faith, particularly in some Western nations. Atheism and agnosticism became dominant modes of thought among intellectuals in universities and the media, while consumerism spread among the masses of people. Throughout the century, but especially beginning in the 1960s, there was widespread rejection of traditional values manifested in growing acceptance of practices such as the use of pornography, violence in the media, contraception, abortion, cohabitation, and divorce.

Even so, many people experienced a significant rebirth of religious faith and fervor. For Catholics, much of this was associated with the program of renewal encouraged by the Second Vatican Council (1962-1965) and with the pontificate of Pope John Paul II, who was pope from 1978 to 2005. Christianity experienced explosive growth in much of Asia and Africa. Even in the materialistic West, many Catholics and other Christians made a stronger commitment to traditional faith and values, and to the living out of their religious convictions.

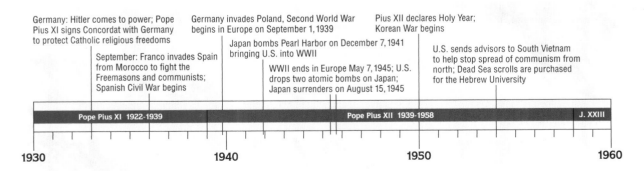

Germany: Hitler comes to power; Pope Pius XI signs Concordat with Germany to protect Catholic religious freedoms

September: Franco invades Spain from Morocco to fight the Freemasons and communists; Spanish Civil War begins

Germany invades Poland, Second World War begins in Europe on September 1, 1939

Japan bombs Pearl Harbor on December 7, 1941 bringing U.S. into WWII

WWII ends in Europe May 7, 1945; U.S. drops two atomic bombs on Japan; Japan surrenders on August 15, 1945

Pius XII declares Holy Year; Korean War begins

U.S. sends advisors to South Vietnam to help stop spread of communism from north; Dead Sea scrolls are purchased for the Hebrew University

Pope Pius XI 1922-1939   Pope Pius XII 1939-1958   J. XXIII

1930   1940   1950   1960

Pope St. Pius X is considered one of the greatest of all popes. He issued decrees encouraging frequent, even daily, reception of communion by the laity. He relaxed the rules for reception of communion by the sick, and allowed children to receive First Holy Communion at an earlier age, arguing that the Body and Blood of Christ should be available to children at the earliest age of reason. He made known his hope that the Catholic laity would form action groups and play a greater role in the apostolic life of the Church. His encyclicals condemning Modernism and promoting the teaching of Christian doctrine are noteworthy. In 1917 a new compilation of the Code of Canon Law was completed as well. He encouraged the Confraternity of Christian Doctrine (CCD) in every parish worldwide to educate everyone in the Faith.

PART I

Pope St. Pius X (1903-1914)

The first pope elected in the twentieth century was St. Pius X. St. Pius X was born Giuseppe Sarto at Riese, Upper Venice, on June 2, 1835. His father was a postman, and his mother a seamstress. A man of simple origins, after discovering his vocation, Giuseppe Sarto wished only for a simple life of servitude as a country priest. After studying at the seminary in Padua, he was ordained on September 18, 1858, and for the next nine years served as a rural parish priest. Sarto's intellectual gifts and exceptional spiritual depth were recognized by his superiors, and in 1875 he was asked to be chancellor of the Diocese of Treviso and spiritual director of its seminary.

In Treviso, Sarto worked tirelessly, taking on more jobs than was required of the priest. He restored the church, provided for the enlargement and maintenance of the hospital by his own means, and devoted himself to ministering to the poor and those who were suffering from cholera, which was especially widespread at the time. As rector of the seminary, Sarto was dedicated to teaching the Faith. He became well known as an excellent instructor of adults and worked to make it possible for students in public schools to receive religious instruction.

In 1884, Pope Leo XIII appointed him Bishop of Mantua, and nine years later Pope Leo named him Patriarch of Venice and a cardinal. In both places, he showed himself to be a hard-working, pastoral bishop devoted to his priests and people.

THE PONTIFICATE OF ST. PIUS X

At the conclave after Pope Leo's death, because the Austrian Emperor Franz Joseph intervened to veto the selection of another candidate, the cardinals chose Cardinal Sarto as the next pope on August 4, 1903. Taking the name Pius X, the new pope adopted the motto "To Restore All Things in Christ" (Eph 1:10), and his pontificate was indeed dedicated to a renewal of the Church in the ways of Christ. St. Pius X set the tone of his pontificate by formally ending the custom by which the Holy Roman Emperor could intervene in papal elections. It was but the first step the new pope took to further the independence of the Church from civil intervention.

Conflict with governments in several European countries was a central feature of St. Pius X's pontificate. In France, the government of Premier Emile Combes moved to end all relations with the Holy See, canceling a concordat and, at the end of 1905, transferring ownership of Church property to state-created lay associations. St. Pius X insisted that French Catholics refuse to cooperate with the law, but he could do little to prevent its enforcement. The Church suffered enormous financial losses as the state ceased to provide financial assistance to parishes and churches. As a result, the Church in France became dependent solely on the generosity of the faithful, a situation that, in the end, helped preserve the Church's independence from civil authority.

Pope St. Pius X similarly protested a "separation" law in Portugal, and defended the rights of Catholics in Ireland and Poland. In Italy, St. Pius took cautious steps to improve Church-state relations, and in 1905 authorized the bishops to withdraw the ban on Catholic participation in elections. By encouraging the participation of Catholics in the Italian political process, the pope prepared the way for eventual settlement of the Church-state conflict in that country.

St. Pius X also did much to strengthen Catholic life and religious practice. One of his earliest official acts was to launch the updating and systematic compilation of the law of the Church. The result — the Code of Canon Law of 1917 — was published after his death, but most of the work was done in his pontificate. He reorganized the Roman Curia and, in encyclicals in 1905 and 1906, encouraged Catholic Action, an organization that was to become a key instrument of lay apostolate.

Pope St. Pius X also took important steps in the area of liturgy and worship. New norms were published for liturgical music centering on encouragement of Gregorian Chant. The revision of the Divine Office was begun. He fostered religious education, and in a 1905 encyclical, strongly encouraged the program of the Confraternity of Christian Doctrine in every parish to help with the education of the young in the Faith.

St. Pius X is probably best known, however, as the "Pope of the Eucharist." He issued decrees encouraging frequent, even daily, reception of communion. The pope said that in receiving the Eucharist, "union with Christ is strengthened, the spiritual life more abundantly sustained, the soul more richly endowed with virtues, and the pledge of everlasting happiness more securely bestowed." (*Sacra Tridentina* [On Frequent and Daily Reception of Holy Communion], 1905, no. 6). St. Pius X relaxed the rules for reception of communion by the sick, and allowed children to receive First Holy Communion at an earlier age, arguing that the Body and Blood of Christ should be available to children at the earliest age of reason (about 7 years old).

CHRISTIAN MODERNISTS

The movement known as Modernism originated in the late nineteenth century. Some Catholic intellectuals, out of a desire to address contemporary currents of thought, embraced trends in psychology, science, and philosophy and tried to adapt Christian thought to them.

Never very numerous, the Modernists were found in only a few countries, principally France. Lack of any clear organization makes it hard to describe the movement precisely, but certain characteristics stand out. Considering religion to be a matter of psychological experience rather than objective truth, Modernism was fundamentally relativistic. Taking its lead from popular ideas about biological evolution, it regarded all Church doctrines and structures as always subject to change. It rejected the thought of St. Thomas Aquinas and Scholastic philosophy at the very time the Church was promoting a revival of Thomism. It viewed the Bible, including the New Testament, as a record of its human authors' religious experience rather than a divinely inspired source of truth. All traditional truths were questioned.

When World War I broke out, Pope St. Pius X was devastated and died only days after the hostilities had begun.

Pope St. Pius X called Modernism a "compendium of all heresies" and addressed the problem early in his pontificate. On July 3, 1907, the Vatican's doctrinal agency, the Holy Office, issued a decree called *Lamentabili* summing up the errors of Modernists in sixty-five propositions. The decree condemned modernist ideas such as revelation was "nothing other than the consciousness acquired by man of his relation to God" and Christ did not claim to be the messiah, found a Church, nor teach "a defined body of doctrine applicable to all times and all men." The sixty-fifth condemned proposition was the capstone of the rest: "Present day Catholicism cannot be reconciled with true science, unless it be transformed into a kind of nondogmatic Christianity, that is, into a broad and liberal Protestantism."

The Holy Office's decree was followed on September 8 by the encyclical *Pascendi Dominici gregis* (Pastoring the Lord's Flock), which criticized Modernist thinking in detail. The fundamental criticism was this:

> First of all they lay down the general principle that in a living religion everything is subject to change, and must change, and in this way they pass to what may be said to be, among the chief of their doctrines, that of Evolution. To the laws of evolution everything is subject—dogma, Church, worship, the Books we revere as sacred, even faith itself, and the penalty of disobedience is death. (*Pascendi Dominici gregis*, no. 26)

The ongoing growth in understanding of doctrine is an important principle of Catholic life. However, development of doctrine is vastly different from evolutionary change—change from one thing into something else. Pope St. Pius X criticized and condemned the idea that evolutionary change could take place in the revealed doctrines of Faith, that principles of Faith and doctrine that were true for one time were no longer true for another. This contradicts reason and the nature of truth.

In 1909 a Vatican priest, Umberto Benigni, organized an unofficial group of censors whose purpose was to combat Modernist tendencies within the Church. The roughly fifty members were known as the *Sodalitium Pianum* (Sodality of Pius). They were influential in Catholic journalism, but used overzealous methods that often hindered the Church's fight against Modernism. Although the society received some support from the Vatican hierarchy, it was dissolved by St. Pius X's successor, Benedict XV, in 1921.

Modernism was, and is, a genuine and serious problem, and Pope St. Pius X succeeded in eradicating outright declarations of its teachings. On September 1, 1910, St. Pius X issued a mandate requiring all priests to take a new Oath against Modernism. The Oath worked, but only to some extent; Modernist thinking went underground. Modernism was to resurface around the time of the Second Vatican Council when many of its proponents tried to reintroduce its relativistic principles. This would only produce confusion and dissent, but in the end it was the Holy Spirit guiding the Church through the decrees of Vatican II.

St. Pius X worked to keep the European powers from engaging in war until his death on August 20, 1914, just as World War I was getting underway. It is said he died of a broken heart because of this war. A man of great personal holiness, he was beatified by Pope Pius XII on June 3, 1951, and canonized by the same pope on May 29, 1954.

PART II
War, Revolution, and Persecution

With the outbreak of World War I, Europe—and soon much of the rest of the world—entered into prolonged period of instability, violence, and cataclysmic change. For the Church, the new era also brought persecution. The task of confronting this new era fell to Pope Benedict XV, a tiny, but spirited man known to be a progressive and elected as an alternative to the more conservative style of his predecessor. The election of Benedict XV made it clear that the new pope would emphasize his role as a promoter of peace given the horror of World War I. Furthermore, the Church needed an artful diplomat who possessed the same foresight exemplified by the saint and founder of monasticism whose name Benedict XV took.

POPE BENEDICT XV (1914-1922)

Born into an old family in Genoa on November 21, 1854, Giacomo della Chiesa received a doctorate in civil law at the University of Genoa in 1875, studied in Rome, and was ordained a priest in December 1878. He continued his studies at the Vatican's training academy for the papal diplomatic corps. From 1883 to 1887 he was an assistant to the Holy See's nuncio to Spain, Archbishop Mariano Rampolla, and when Leo XIII named Rampolla Secretary of State, della Chiesa returned to Rome to serve as his secretary. Della Chiesa was named Undersecretary of State in 1901, and he continued in that position under Pope St. Pius X. The Pope appointed him Archbishop of Bologna in 1907 and named him a cardinal in May 1914, just a few months before the conclave. Three months later, when the cardinals gathered to elect a successor to St. Pius X, the ominous international scene caused them to turn to an experienced diplomat, Cardinal della Chiesa.

Although some expected the war to be a short affair, World War I dragged on four long years. "A disaster has visited the world," wrote Cardinal Desire Mercier of invaded, occupied Belgium on Christmas 1914. No one understood that better than Benedict XV.

As pope, Benedict XV, a compassionate and sensitive priest, protested the barbarity of the war, but took great care to maintain strict impartiality, a policy that brought criticism from both sides. Benedict hoped that by

After the war, Benedict XV devoted himself to international reconciliation. France resumed diplomatic relations with the Holy See, warmed by the pope's canonization of Joan of Arc in 1920. Even Britain sent a chargé d'affaires to the Vatican in 1915, the first in 300 years.

remaining impartial, the Vatican could better serve the peace process. He outlined a seven-point peace program that he sent to the warring nations in August of 1917, but despite its basis for a just and stable settlement, the peace plan was ignored. Meanwhile, the pope acted vigorously to assist war victims. He sought humane treatment for the wounded and prisoners-of-war and carried on a large-scale charitable program without regard for nationality or religion.

After the war, Pope Benedict hoped to be a party to the peace talks in Versailles, but the Italian government vetoed the idea. The pope's exclusion from the peace process marked an important transition in the role of the pope in the modern world. For over a century, the papacy had retreated from direct involvement in the political scene, and was now forbidden any official political capacity. The pope began to serve a new purpose in the world, issuing many encyclicals that addressed specific moral and ethical problems, and offered the Church's wisdom and understanding to the world. In this capacity, the popes of the twentieth century began to act as the world's moral conscience, witnessing history and guiding it through their words and actions. The unfortunate reality was, however, that political leaders rarely took the words of the pope very seriously.

The first meeting of the League of Nations Assembly in Geneva, Switzerland in 1920. The League of Nations was an international organization founded after the First World War at the Paris Peace Conference in 1919. The League's goals included disarmament; preventing war through collective security; settling disputes between countries through negotiation and diplomacy; and improving global welfare. Because it had no real enforcement powers it failed to prevent a second World War. The United Nations replaced it after World War II and inherited a number of agencies and organizations founded by the League.

In the encyclical *Pacem, Dei munus pulcherrimum* (On Peace and Christian Reconciliation) issued on May 23, 1920, Pope Benedict XV urged international reconciliation. He warned against the vengeful tone of the Treaty of Versailles and its harsh treatment of postwar Germany. Nonetheless, Benedict welcomed the peace and was generally supportive of the new League of Nations.

Benedict XV's pontificate had many positive achievements. The new Code of Canon Law begun by St. Pius X was published on June 28, 1917. Steps were taken to improve relations with Italy, including further encouragement of Catholic participation in Italian political life. Diplomatic relations with France were restored. The number of diplomats accredited to the Holy See nearly doubled. Hoping for eventual reunion between Rome and the separated Eastern churches, he established the Congregation for the Oriental Church and the Pontifical Oriental Institute (1917).

GROWTH OF THE MISSIONS

Benedict XV died of influenza on January 22, 1922, but not before one of the important events of the pontificate: the publication of an apostolic letter on missionary work, *Maximum illud*, in November 1919.

The Church had been "missionary" from her earliest days, when Jesus' followers went out from Jerusalem to preach the Gospel, first in the Holy Land and then throughout the Mediterranean basin and beyond. The early centuries were centuries of evangelization.

In time, however, distance, lack of communication and transport, and the rise of Islam slowed the spread of Christianity. Although the Christendom of the Middle Ages was a remarkable achievement, it was not mission-oriented. Columbus' first voyage in 1492 suddenly opened a vast new field for evangelization. Through the efforts of zealous missionaries—especially Jesuits, Franciscans, and Dominicans—the Church spread throughout the Americas, and in a few places—

the Philippines, India, to a lesser extent China and Japan—in the Far East. The nineteenth century, the heyday of European colonialism, brought a new burst of Christian missionary activity, and the Church experienced rapid growth in new parts of the world, particularly Africa.

Understanding that for the Faith to grow strong and flourish, it was imperative that it not be perceived simply as a "European" phenomenon, Church authorities began to encourage a native clergy and native hierarchy. Pope Benedict's apostolic letter encouraged this development, urging respect for native cultures and the avoidance of nationalistic attitudes on the part of missionaries.

In China, there were 500,000 baptized Catholics and three hundred sixty-nine Chinese priests by 1890. By 1922, the number of Chinese Catholics grew to nearly two million, and the number of native clergy had grown significantly. In Japan, the Church experienced slow but steady expansion. The first native bishop was consecrated in 1927, and by the time of World War II, Catholics numbered a little over 120,000 in that island country. There also were significant numbers of Catholics in India, Vietnam, Indonesia, Taiwan, and other Asian countries, to say nothing of the overwhelmingly Catholic Philippines.

The most notable new expansion of Catholicism that began in the nineteenth century and continued in the twentieth was in Africa. Muslim resistance stymied missionary work in the north, but in the sub-Saharan region, the Church made notable progress in countries like Nigeria; Uganda

TODAY'S AFRICAN CHURCH

The end of the twentieth century witnessed an amazing growth of Catholicism in Africa. The Second Vatican Council and decolonization reshaped the Church's presence on the continent, especially in the use of vernacular and incorporation of African culture into the liturgy. In a 1995 visit to the continent, Pope John Paul II stressed that he considered Africa one of the most important areas in the world for the Church. Catholics currently constitute fourteen percent of the population, but the growth rate of new converts is increasing at a rapid pace.

In 1994, Pope John Paul II led a synod in Rome with the bishops of the African Church. As the pope stated, this was truly an historic moment and a "providential event of grace"—it was the first Synod concerned solely with the continent of Africa in the history of the Church. The Synod met from April 10 to May 8, producing sixty-four concise propositions covering many concerns of the African Church. Some of the most important concerns of the African Church were evangelization, inculturation, dialogue, justice and peace, and the means of social communication. With these propositions in mind, John Paul II wrote the apostolic exhortation *Ecclesia in Africa,* made public during his 1995 visit to the African continent.

While Africa is undoubtedly faced with many problems, there remains great hope that much can be done to better the conditions there. "The 'winds of change' are blowing strongly in many parts of Africa, and people are demanding ever more insistently the recognition and promotion of human rights and freedoms. In this regard I note with satisfaction that the Church in Africa, faithful to its vocation, stands resolutely on the side of the oppressed and of voiceless and marginalized peoples" (*Ecclesia in Africa,* no. 44).

Images of Pope John Paul II in Africa, 1995.

(one hundred fifty thousand Catholics by the time of World War I); the Belgian Congo (Zaire), where Catholics were over thirty-five percent of the population by mid-century; Rwanda and Burundi; Kenya; Malawi; Tanzania; Zambia; and Angola. The number of African bishops, priests, and sisters also rose dramatically. At a time when European Catholics faced increasing discrimination, persecution, and loss of the faithful, the Church in Africa would strengthen the hope of Catholics throughout the world as thousands of new believers flocked to the Faith and began to offer new life to Christ's Church.

THE RISE OF SOVIET COMMUNISM

It is on this account that one convulsion following upon another has marked the passage of the centuries, down to the revolution of our own days. This modern revolution, it may be said, has actually broken out or threatens everywhere, and it exceeds in amplitude and violence anything yet experienced in the preceding persecutions launched against the Church. Entire peoples find themselves in danger of falling back into a barbarism worse than that which oppressed the greater part of the world at the coming of the Redeemer.(Pius XI, *Divini Redemptoris* [On Atheistic Communism], 1937, no. 2)

Among the calamities spawned by World War I, none had more serious implications for the future than the rise of Communism in Russia. Soviet Communism was to become the driving force behind an international program of subversion, revolution, conquest, oppression, and religious and political persecution that cost millions of lives and threatened the peace and stability of the world for seven decades.

Soviet-style Communism had its roots in the theories of Karl Marx (1818-1883), who in 1848 with Friedrich Engels (1820-1895), set out their key ideas in the *Communist Manifesto*. During World War I, popular unrest and mutinies in the Russian military forced Czar Nicholas II to abdicate in March 1917. A brief period of rule by a liberal government was followed by the Bolshevik Revolution of November 1917, which brought Communists to power under the leadership of Vladimir Lenin (1870-1924). Upon seizing power, the country's new masters set about cruelly suppressing political opposition and managed to establish tight socialist control over the country, including the brutal execution of the czar and his family. Out of this bloodshed and violence, the Soviet Union emerged. Around the same time, (October 1917) the Blessed Virgin Mary appeared to three peasant children at Fatima, Portugal. Offering a message of hope in the face of this political calamity in the East, Mary spoke of these events and urged prayer for the conversion of Russia, which she promised would eventually occur.

Skilled in propaganda, the Communists in the 1920s and 1930s convinced many Western intellectuals that the Soviet Union was a workers' paradise and a model for the world. However, the harsh reality of life in the Soviet Union was vastly different from the propagandists' idealized picture, and under Lenin's successor, Joseph Stalin (1879-1953), brutality and totalitarian oppression only grew worse. During Stalin's dictatorship, nearly fifty million supposed opponents of the regime were either executed or sent to the vast system of Siberian prison camps and penal colonies called the *gulag*.

Religious persecution was a major element of the Communist program. Both Catholic and Orthodox churches were destroyed or desecrated and put to other uses including dance halls, stables, museums of atheism, chicken coops, and public baths. The Russian Orthodox Church was seen as nationalistic as well as religious and was therefore allowed to exist; however, its priests and bishops made many compromises with the communist regime. Soviet authorities set out to eradicate the Catholic Church in Russia. Before 1917 there were 54,000 churches in Russia, 300 of which were Catholic; by 1939, there were fewer than 100 churches, only two of which were

BEFORE AND AFTER THE FIRST WORLD WAR, 1914-1923

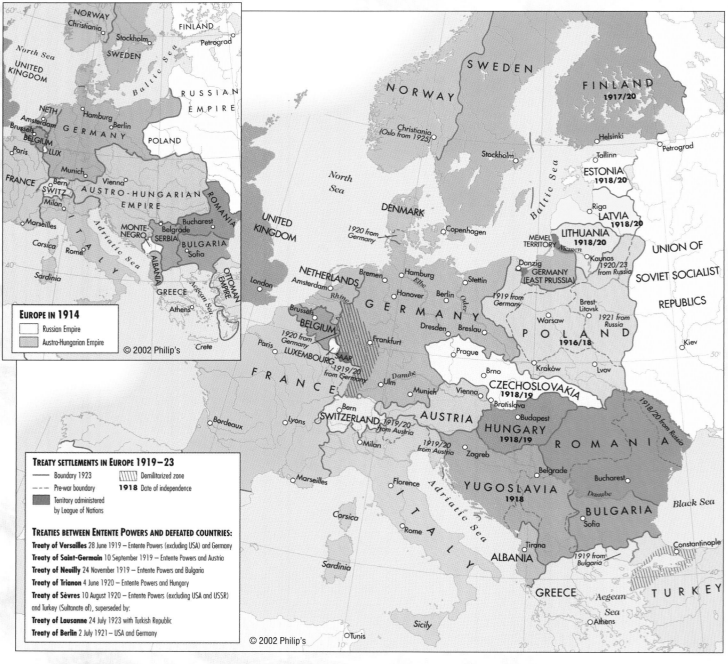

EUROPE IN 1914

☐ Russian Empire
▨ Austro-Hungarian Empire

© 2002 Philip's

TREATY SETTLEMENTS IN EUROPE 1919–23

— Boundary 1923
--- Pre-war boundary
▨ Territory administered by League of Nations
▨ Demilitarized zone
1918 Date of independence

TREATIES BETWEEN ENTENTE POWERS AND DEFEATED COUNTRIES:

Treaty of Versailles 28 June 1919 – Entente Powers (excluding USA) and Germany

Treaty of Saint-Germain 10 September 1919 – Entente Powers and Austria

Treaty of Neuilly 24 November 1919 – Entente Powers and Bulgaria

Treaty of Trianon 4 June 1920 – Entente Powers and Hungary

Treaty of Sèvres 10 August 1920 – Entente Powers (excluding USA and USSR) and Turkey (Sultanate of), superseded by:

Treaty of Lausanne 24 July 1923 with Turkish Republic

Treaty of Berlin 2 July 1921 – USA and Germany

© 2002 Philip's

The First World War changed the map of Europe and the Middle East forever. Centuries-old empires were destroyed and new national states were created.

The First World War finally broke up the Ottoman Empire but left much of the Middle East in limbo. Most of the region was assigned to British or French control.

The skeleton of Rheims, France in 1917 after massive bombings.

THE RISE OF NAZI GERMANY, 1933-1939

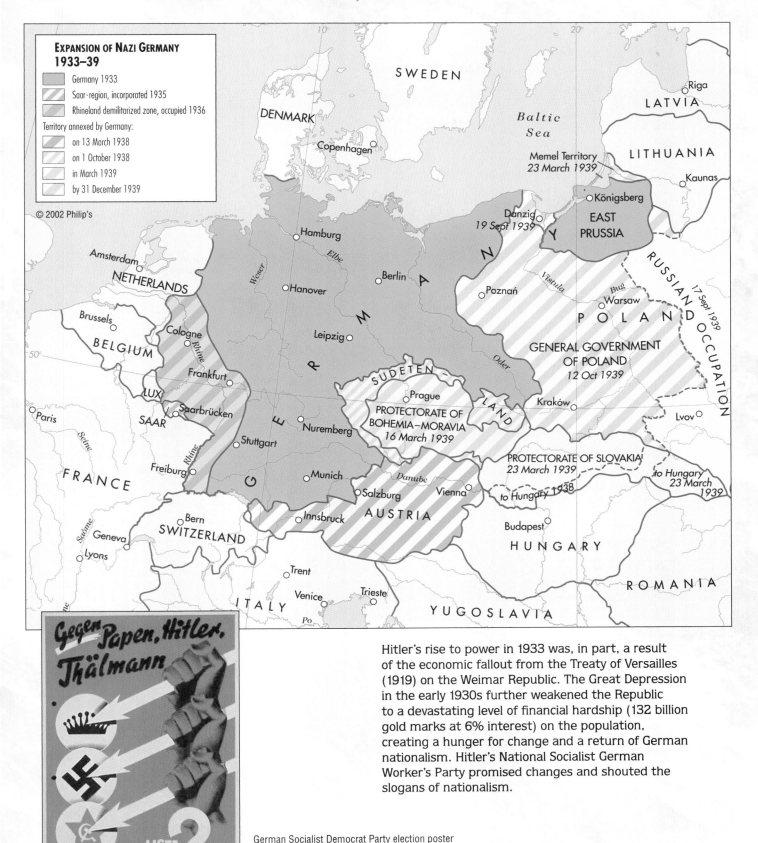

EXPANSION OF NAZI GERMANY 1933–39

- Germany 1933
- Saar-region, incorporated 1935
- Rhineland demilitarized zone, occupied 1936

Territory annexed by Germany:
- on 13 March 1938
- on 1 October 1938
- in March 1939
- by 31 December 1939

© 2002 Philip's

Hitler's rise to power in 1933 was, in part, a result of the economic fallout from the Treaty of Versailles (1919) on the Weimar Republic. The Great Depression in the early 1930s further weakened the Republic to a devastating level of financial hardship (132 billion gold marks at 6% interest) on the population, creating a hunger for change and a return of German nationalism. Hitler's National Socialist German Worker's Party promised changes and shouted the slogans of nationalism.

German Socialist Democrat Party election poster from 1932. "Against Papen, Hitler, Thälmann." The poster illustrates crushing their three ideological enemies: Monarchism, Nazism and Communism.

OUR LADY OF FATIMA

After making failed pleas for peace to the warring nations, Pope Benedict XV appealed directly to Mary. On May 5, 1917, he wrote a pastoral letter urging all Christians to ask Mary to bring peace to the world.

> To Mary, then, who is the Mother of Mercy and omnipotent by grace, let loving and devout appeal go up from every corner of the earth-from noble temples and tiniest chapels, from royal palaces and mansions of the rich as from the poorest hut-from blood-drenched plains and seas. Let it bear to Her the anguished cry of mothers and wives, the wailing of innocent ones, the sighs of every generous heart: that Her most tender and benign solicitude may be moved and the peace we ask for be obtained for our agitated world.

Mary's response came only one week later. On May 13, she appeared to three children in the small village of Fatima, Portugal. The three children, Bl. Jacinta, Bl. Francisco, and Lucia (ages 7, 9, and 10, respectively) had been visited by an angel the previous year in preparation for Mary's visit. In Lucia's own words, they saw "a lady, clothed in white, brighter than the sun, radiating a light more clear and intense than a crystal cup filled with sparkling water, lit by burning sunlight." The lady told them she had come from Heaven and that she would appear to them in the same place on the 13th of every month for the next 6 months. She asked them to say the rosary, offer themselves to God, and bear suffering as an act of reparation for the conversion of sinners.

Over the next few months, the children received a visit from the Blessed Virgin on the 13th of every month. During the July visit, she promised that in October she would tell them who she was and perform a miracle for all to see and believe. The children were also shown a vision of hell, and were told how God wished to save souls from eternal damnation through devotion to her Immaculate Heart. She also warned of another great war, the persecutions of the

Church and the Holy Father, and asked for prayers for the conversion of Russia.

On October 13, 1917, despite a terrible storm, speculation of a public miracle attracted tens of thousands of pilgrims to Fatima. With many onlookers present, Mary again appeared to the children, finally telling them who she was: "the Lady of the Rosary." Then, more than 70,000 people witnessed a true miracle. The grey clouds suddenly parted, and, according to a journalist from an atheist newspaper who was there:

> One could see the immense multitude turn towards the sun, which appeared free from clouds and at its zenith. It looked like a plaque of dull silver and it was possible to look at it without the least discomfort. It might have been an eclipse which was taking place. But at that moment a great shout went up and one could hear the spectators nearest at hand shouting: "A miracle! A miracle!" Before the astonished eyes of the crowd, whose aspect was Biblical as they stood bareheaded, eagerly searching the sky, the sun trembled, made sudden incredible movements outside all cosmic laws—the sun "danced" according to the typical expression of the people.

Bl. Jacinta and Bl. Francisco were beatified by John Paul II in 2000. Lucia passed away in 2005 at the age of 97.

Catholic. In 1923 the last Catholic bishop in Russia, John Cieplak, was sentenced to ten years in a prison camp. Eventually, only one Catholic priest was permitted to minister in the country, and he was stationed at the French embassy in Moscow and restricted to serving the diplomatic community. By 1959, according to a study by the U.S. House of Representatives' Judiciary Committee, some two and a half million Catholics in the Soviet Union had lost their lives, and millions more had been imprisoned or deported.

The Church opposed Communism from the start. In 1891, Pope Leo XIII wrote his landmark encyclical *Rerum novarum*, which presented a Christian alternative to socialist and Marxist theories of economic and social life. *Rerum novarum* prophetically warned against socialism, arguing that despite its apparent protection of the poor man, "the working man himself would be among the first to suffer" from a socialist regime. Instead, Leo XIII urged the protection of individual dignity and emphasized mutual responsibility between workers and employers.

Pope Pius XI's encyclical *Divini Redemptoris*, published in 1937, was a powerful critique of Communism. Soviet Communism, the pope warned, "aims at upsetting the social order and at undermining the very foundations of Christian civilization." Pius XI's assessment would become more and more haunting as the abuses of the Soviet regime were fully discovered and documented. Unfortunately, it would take fifty more years for the Soviet Union to crumble and for Communism to fall in Eastern Europe.

POPE PIUS XI (1922-1939)

The end of the First World War, "the war to end all wars," in no way brought an end to violence and difficulty. Benedict XV lived to see the rise of Communism in Russia. After the pope's death, the Church would suffer further persecution, not only in Russia, but in Mexico and Spain as well. Indeed, when Pius XI, a strong-minded and determined pope, was elected to the head of the Church, he did not foresee the end of war. He would reign during an era of crisis marked by global economic collapse, the spread of totalitarianism, and increasing international conflict. Nazism, an ideology and a political movement fundamentally opposed to Christianity, came to power in Germany and threatened the peace of Europe and the world.

The future Pope Pius XI, Achille Ratti, was born May 31, 1857, near Milan. His father was a factory manager. Following ordination in 1879, Ratti pursued graduate studies in Rome and taught at the seminary in Padua. An excellent scholar, he worked from 1888 to 1911 at the Ambrosian Library in Milan. In 1911 he joined the staff of the Vatican Library as pro-prefect, and in 1914 became its prefect

As soon as he became pope, Pius XI worked to resolve the relationship between the Vatican and the Kingdom of Italy. The Lateran Treaty with Mussolini was signed on February 11, 1929.

(director). In 1918, Pope Benedict XV sent Ratti to Poland on a diplomatic mission and later appointed him Nuncio to that country. While stationed in Warsaw, Ratti showed exemplary courage and dedication to his ministry when he refused to leave the city in the face of a threatened Bolshevik attack in August 1920. The following year, Pope Benedict named him Archbishop of Milan and a cardinal. Following Benedict's death, Ratti was elected pope on February 6, 1922, and he took the name Pius XI.

One of the first problems to confront Pius XI was the "Roman Question," that is, the difficulties that continued to arise over the relationship between the Vatican and the Italian government. Since the seizure of the Papal States in the nineteenth century, the popes declared themselves "prisoners of the Vatican," protesting their loss of the traditional lands ruled by the pope. In 1922, a Fascist government came to power under Benito Mussolini, and for the sake of national unity, Mussolini sought to improve relations with the pope. In 1929, they signed the Lateran Treaty, which recognized Vatican City as an independent state and reimbursed the Vatican for the loss of territory. Mussolini accepted Roman Catholicism as the established church of Italy and allowed religious instruction in the schools. In return, the Holy See recognized Italy's sovereignty with Rome as its capital. Despite the Lateran Treaty, the papacy and the Church were in growing conflict with the Fascists. In 1931, Pope Pius XI would vigorously protest their attacks in the encyclical *Non Abbiamo Bisogno* (On Catholic Action in Italy).

THE ENCYCLICALS OF PIUS XI

Pius XI published many notable encyclicals on various topics. *Divini illius magistri* (On the Christian Education of Youth), written in 1929, spelled out the rights and duties of parents, the state, and the Church in education. The right of parents to guide their children's education, Pope Pius said, "has precedence over any right of civil society and of the state, and for this reason, no power on earth may infringe upon it."

In 1931, Pius' encyclical *Quadragesimo anno* (The Fortieth Year: i.e., since the publication of Leo XIII's *Rerum novarum*) further expanded the Church's social teaching. This encyclical appeared at the height of the Great Depression, a global economic crisis that produced widespread unemployment and heightened social tensions in many countries, and presented a comprehensive vision of the economic structuring of a just society. Pius XI made a powerful case against totalitarianism, and particularly noteworthy was the statement of the principle of subsidiarity:

> A community of a higher order should not interfere in the internal life of a community of a lower order, depriving the latter of its functions, but rather should support it in case of need and help to coordinate its activity with the activities of the rest of society, always with a view of the common good.

Subsidiarity proved to be a valuable principle in an era of totalitarian governments and over-centralized state authority.

Pope Pius' encyclical on Christian Matrimony, *Casti connubii* (1930), reaffirmed Christian teaching on Matrimony and family life and restated the Church's condemnation of contraception. Declaring that some, "openly departing from the uninterrupted Christian tradition...recently have judged it possible solemnly to declare another doctrine regarding this question," Pope Pius said:

> [A]ny use whatsoever of matrimony exercised in such a way that the act is deliberately frustrated in its natural power to generate life is an offence against the law of God and of nature, and those who indulge in such are branded with the guilt of a grave sin.

Although the Church's views on morality and social ethics were becoming increasingly countercultural, Pius XI was not a pope of the past. On the contrary, Pius XI moved to bring the Church into the budding information age, and he embraced the new potentials of radio and the cinema. In 1931, Pius XI inaugurated Vatican Radio, which, operating by short wave throughout the world, was to become an international agency airing four hundred hours of programming weekly in thirty-seven languages. The role of Vatican Radio would only become more significant as Eastern Europe fell to Communist regimes, and information was increasingly censored in those countries. Throughout the Cold War era, Vatican Radio would act as both an ear to the outside world and passive form of resistance for those oppressed by totalitarian states.

In 1936, Pius XI published *Vigilanti Cura*, an encyclical on motion pictures. While noting the potentially dangerous and manipulative aspects of the cinema, the pope urged motion pictures to realize the great good they were capable of, and, like all great art, "to champion the cause of justice, to give new life to the claims of virtue, and to contribute positively to the genesis of a just social order in the world."

Pope Pius also championed Catholic Action, making it the subject of his first encyclical, *Ubi arcano Dei consilio*, in 1922. Catholic Action was for many years the Church's principal form of organized lay apostolate. The idea that lay people should play an active role in the mission of the Church is present also in documents of Pope Leo XIII and Pope St. Pius X, but Pius XI took up the cause vigorously and became known as "the Pope of Catholic Action."

With encouragement from popes and bishops, the Catholic Action movement spread rapidly in Europe, the United States, and other places. Canon (later Cardinal) Joseph Cardijn of Belgium (1882-1967), founder of the Young Christian Workers and other groups for the formation of the laity, helped tremendously with the growth of Catholic Action. On October 2, 1928, St. Josemaría Escrivá was inspired by a charism that would give lay people a greater awareness of their call to holiness and evangelization in the midst of the world. With this special grace, he formed Opus Dei, whose members would model themselves after the very first Christians. These new developments in the understanding of the lay vocation and the laity's role in the world would form part of the Church's teaching at the Second Vatican Council (1962-1965).

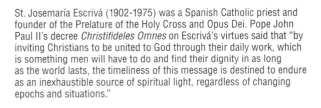

St. Josemaría Escrivá (1902-1975) was a Spanish Catholic priest and founder of the Prelature of the Holy Cross and Opus Dei. Pope John Paul II's decree *Christifideles Omnes* on Escrivá's virtues said that "by inviting Christians to be united to God through their daily work, which is something men will have to do and find their dignity in as long as the world lasts, the timeliness of this message is destined to endure as an inexhaustible source of spiritual light, regardless of changing epochs and situations."

THE CHURCH AND THE RISE OF NAZISM

One of the most critical challenges facing Pope Pius XI was the rise of Adolf Hitler (1889-1945) to power and the National Socialist (Nazi) party in Germany.

Deeply resenting the terms of the peace settlement after World War I, Germany was in political and economic turmoil when Hitler came to power in 1933. Working to consolidate power at home and win influence and favor abroad, one of the dictator's first acts was to seek a new concordat with the Church. On July 20, 1933, Germany and the Vatican signed an agreement.

The principal negotiator of the Concordat with Germany was Pius XI's Secretary of State, Cardinal Eugenio Pacelli, the future Pope Pius XII. Pacelli was especially concerned with the independence of the Church in Germany, and recognizing the potential radicalism of Hitler's regime, he wished to preserve religious freedom for German Catholics. The Concordat provided that the German clergy be subject to canon law and gained special privileges for Catholic schools and organizations. In exchange, the Vatican agreed to encourage the German clergy to temper their political resistance to Hitler. Although the Concordat did allow the Church to stay independent in Hitler's Germany, and therefore conduct many efforts to save those persecuted by the Nazi regime, the Concordat led to the self-disbanding of the once powerful Catholic Center Party, which may have helped with early resistance against the Nazi dictator. The members were urged to join the Nazi party.

Pius XI had no illusions about the intentions of the Nazi leader, but hoped, he said, to "safeguard the freedom of the Church" in Hitler's Germany. Despite the agreement, Hitler and the Nazis violated the concordat from the start. As systematic oppression began, the pope sent thirty-four separate notes of protest to the German government between 1933 and 1936. Hitler did not heed his policies.

Nazism was a blend of nationalist totalitarianism, racism aimed especially at Jews, neo-paganism, and the moral nihilism of the nineteenth-century German philosopher Friedrich Nietzsche (1844-1900). It maintained that superior individuals—"supermen"—had a right to ignore conventional morality and live by their own rules. Some German Catholics opposed the Nazi regime from the beginning and others turned against it as time passed; still others supported the government and served willingly in the military, believing this to be their patriotic duty.

Left: Eugenio Pacelli, Apostolic Nuncio to the German Weimar Republic, in 1929 leaving the Presidential Palace in Berlin. *Right:* The signing of the Concordat with Germany (The *Reichskonkordat*) on July 20, 1933. Left to right: German Vice-Chancellor Franz von Papen, representing Germany, Giuseppe Pizzardo, Cardinal Pacelli, Alfredo Cardinal Ottaviani, German ambassador Rudolf Buttmann. Today, the Concordat is still valid in Germany. Article 1 of the Concordat protects the right to freedom of religion. Article 31 protects Catholic organizations and religious practice. Article 21 allows for the Catholic religion to be taught in schools.

On March 14, 1937, Pope Pius XII published the encyclical *Mit Brennender Sorge* (With Burning Worry), a powerful indictment of Nazism and the Nazi regime. At his direction, the encyclical was read from the pulpit of every Catholic Church in Germany. Charging the regime with repeated violations of the concordat and an open attack on the Church, the pope said:

> None but superficial minds could stumble into concepts of a national God, of a national religion; or attempt to lock within the frontiers of a single people, within the narrow limits of a single race, God, the Creator of the universe, King and Legislator of all nations before whose immensity they are "as a drop of a bucket" (Isaiah xl, 15). (no. 11)

Infuriated by the pope's criticism, the Nazis launched a campaign of propaganda against the Church. The Concordat could no longer hide the animosity between Nazis and Catholics. The conflict was now in the open, and there would be no turning back.

PERSECUTION IN MEXICO AND SPAIN

During the pontificate of Pius XI, persecution of Catholics was not limited to the Soviet Union and Germany. Traditionally Catholic Mexico and Spain had broken into civil war, and Pius XI was forced to confront, as he described in his 1937 encyclical on Communism, *Divini Redemptoris*, the "indiscriminate slaughter" of bishops, priests, and men and women religious, as well as thousands of lay people.

Francisco Franco (1892-1975) was ruler of Spain from 1939 until his death in 1975.

The situation in Spain had been deteriorating for years, as forces of the "left" and the "right" competed for power. After King Alfonso XIII was forced to leave the country, a republic was proclaimed in 1931. The government disestablished the Church, secularized education, and sanctioned the burning of churches. In 1936, a leftist government of Socialists, Anarchists, and Communists called the Popular Front came to power in an election. Many feared that a revolution by the radical left was now imminent.

In July that year, Spanish army units in Morocco rebelled, and soon Spain was engulfed in a civil war. As Spain divided, European powers backed each side, mimicking the alliances they would soon build during World War II. The Nationalist forces, led by General Francisco Franco, had military support from Italy and Germany, while the Republicans were aided by the Soviet Union and leftist "international brigades."

For years before the civil war, leftists and Freemasons had waged attacks on the Church. Churches were sometimes sacked and burned, and clerics were assassinated. The civil war brought a reign of terror on a much larger scale. Between July 18 and July 31, 1936, fifty priests were killed in Madrid and a third of the city's one hundred fifty churches were sacked or burned. In August, more than two thousand priests and religious were killed in the Republican zone of the country.

The killings declined as Franco's government gained greater control of the country, but they continued sporadically until the war's end. In all, 6,832 priests and religious and thirteen bishops were martyred from 1936 to 1939. One out of seven Spanish diocesan priests and one out of five male members of religious orders were killed. There is no telling how many lay people lost their lives because of their Catholic Faith. Some executions occurred after hasty trials by "people's courts"; other victims were simply lynched. Pope Pius XI called this bloodbath "the natural fruit of a system which lacks all inner restraint."

An allegorical mural in a Madrid museum depicts the victorious Nationalist General Franco as a crusader.

One million people died in the brutal struggle from which the Nationalists emerged victorious in 1939. Franco's authoritarian regime suppressed opposition and executed opponents, but it maintained stability, ended much of the violence against the Catholic Church, and kept Spain out of World War II.

Events in Mexico followed a similar pattern. Mexico had been a Catholic country since colonial times, but revolutionaries, Freemasons, and various political "reformers" frequently turned on the Church after the coming of independence in the nineteenth century. A revolution in 1917 made Mexico the world's first officially socialist, anti-religious, constitutional revolutionary republic. The Church could not own property, and any privileges it previously held were removed. Anti-Christian sentiments were so high that the governor of the Tabasco province, a particularly brutal persecutor of religion, named his children Lenin, Lucifer, and Satan.

Violence was common in Mexico, particularly under the regime of Plutarco Calles (1924-1928), and persecution eventually led to an armed rebellion by Catholics called *Cristeros*. The rebellion was quickly put down, and a well-known martyr of the rebellion, Bl. Miguel Pro, S.J., was executed by a firing squad on November 23, 1927. Just before his death, he cried out "Viva Cristo Rey!"—Long Live Christ the King. Bl. Miguel Pro was beatified by Pope John Paul II in 1988, and in 2000 the same pope declared several of the *Cristeros* saints. His feast day is celebrated on November 23.

Bl. Miguel Pro held his arms out in the sign of the cross just before the shots were fired at his execution.

During the years after the rebellion, the government killed 250,000-300,000 people, most of them Catholics. Between late 1931 and early 1936, 480 churches, schools, orphanages, and hospitals were closed or used for other functions such as movie theaters, garages, and shops.

Beginning around 1940, there was a gradual easing of persecution in Mexico as authorities relaxed their enforcement of anticlerical laws. However, more than half a century still had to pass before the religious rights of the Church and the Mexican people were restored.

PART III
The Pontificate of Pope Pius XII
(1939-1958)

Through mutual greed for territory and power, Nazi Germany and the Soviet Union cooperated to invade Poland on September 1, 1939. World War II had begun. The conflict was to claim 55,000,000 lives before it ended six years later and would result in more sweeping political and social changes than even World War I had wrought.

Pope Pius XI died on February 10, 1939. As the conclave that elected Pope Benedict XV had done, so this time, too, the cardinals turned to a seasoned diplomat—Cardinal Eugenio Pacelli, the Vatican secretary of state.

THE POPE AND THE WORLD CRISIS

Eugenio Pacelli, a lawyer's son, was born in Rome on March 2, 1876. He studied for the priesthood in Rome and was ordained in April 1899. Two years later he entered the service of the Holy See and from 1904 to 1916 worked on the project that resulted in the 1917 Code of Canon Law. He also taught international law at the training academy for Vatican diplomats.

In April 1917, Pope Benedict XV named Pacelli an archbishop and appointed him Nuncio to Bavaria. Two years later he was named Nuncio to the new German republic, remaining in that post until 1929. When he returned to Rome, Pacelli was named a cardinal and became Secretary of State under Pope Pius XI. In the 1930s he traveled to a number of countries, and in 1936 visited the United States and conferred with President Franklin D. Roosevelt. Many saw Pacelli as an obvious choice for the next pope. Even Pius XI said that the reason he sent Pacelli all over the world was "so that he may get to know the world and the world may get to know him" (quoted in Duffy, *Saints and Sinners: A History of the Popes*, 2002, p. 346). Pacelli was elected on March 2, 1939, and took the name Pius XII.

When Pius XII was elected pope, all-out war in Europe was already thought inevitable. Nonetheless, Pope Pius XII worked strenuously to promote peace and try to prevent World War II. Once war broke out, he continued to appeal for peace. Unlike Benedict XV's untiring efforts to promote peace during World War I, Pius XII knew that World War II was a different kind of war and that the Vatican could not be satisfied with simply acting as a voice of peace. The Holy See remained officially neutral, but the pope privately offered to serve as a channel for communication between anti-Hitler elements in

Germany and the Allies. Through his diplomacy, he won for the city of Rome status as an "open city," exempt from military attacks. Repeatedly he appealed for peace, especially in a series of Christmas radio addresses from 1939 to 1942. Pius XII laid out a five-point peace plan of his own, and through the Pontifical Aid Commission, he directed a large-scale program of assistance to war victims and prisoners-of-war.

In 1943, after the fall of Mussolini's government and the occupation of Rome by German troops, church institutions throughout the city, acting at the pope's direction, sheltered thousands of Jewish and non-Jewish refugees. Many also took refuge at the papal summer residence at Castel Gandolfo, and others were sheltered in Vatican "safe houses" throughout the city of Rome. Hundreds of thousands of Jews' lives were saved through the efforts of Pope Pius and other Vatican officials working under the shelter of neutrality. After the war, Pope Pius XII won the praise of many prominent Jews and Jewish groups for his assistance during Nazi occupation. Remarkably, the Chief Rabbi of Rome, Israel Zolli, largely through the example of selfless risk and extraordinary charity exhibited by Vatican agents during the war, became a Catholic, taking as his baptismal name Eugene out of gratitude to Pius XII (Eugenio Pacelli).

In later years, Pope Pius XII was accused of not speaking out against the Nazi persecution of Jews. Complaints first surfaced in 1963 in a play by a German Protestant, Rolf Hochhuth. Pope Pius was indeed cautious in his public statements for fear of reprisals against the Church and the Jews. He knew when the Dutch bishops publicly denounced Nazism, the Nazis responded with a vicious crackdown against Jews. Pius XII did not want to give the Nazis an excuse to come down on the Church throughout Europe and compromise the Church's underground aid and resistance.

The pope's position was clear. As early as October 1939, in the encyclical *Summi Pontificatus*, Pius spoke of the natural unity of the human race and the respect due all persons of all races. He condemned racism in his Christmas messages, and prayed for "the hundreds of thousands of innocent people put to death or doomed to slow extinction, sometimes merely because of their race or descent" (quoted in Duffy, *Saints and Sinners: A History of the Popes*, 2002, p. 349). In 1944, Hitler was so upset with the effective resistance of the Vatican that the Nazi SS prepared a plan for assassinating Pius XII because of "the papal protest in favor of the Jews," but it was not carried out because the war ended too soon. Politically powerless against the Nazi machine and isolated on the neutral "island" of Vatican City, Pius XII sought to help the world through hands-on, practical methods. Waiting for the Allies to settle the war, the pope tried to save as many lives as possible. For this, historian Rabbi David G. Dalin joined Jews throughout the world, calling Pius XII "a righteous gentile."

St. Maximilian Kolbe

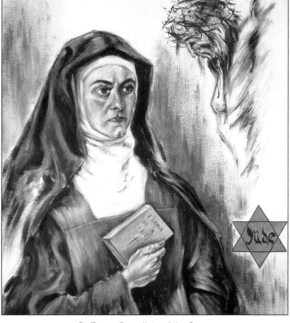

St. Teresa Benedicta of the Cross

TWO SAINTS OF THE NAZI PERSECUTION

Although the policy of Jewish genocide by the Nazis was a devastation, Jews were not the only ones who suffered under Nazi policies. Gypsies also were targets of genocide. Three million Polish Catholics died at the Auschwitz prison camp, including twenty percent (2600) of Poland's priests. Throughout these persecutions, many Catholics sacrificed themselves for their Faith and fellow man, and many were martyred by the Nazis. Among these, two figures typify the carnage and the heroism of this era: St. Maximilian Kolbe and St. Teresa Benedicta of the Cross, whose name by birth was Edith Stein.

Maximilian Kolbe (1894-1941), priest and martyr, was a Polish Conventual Franciscan. Devoted to the Blessed Virgin, he founded a group called the Militia of Mary Immaculate, edited its magazine, and established an international center of Marian devotion. After the fall of Poland, he was arrested by the Nazis, released, and then re-arrested in 1941 for assisting Jews and members of the Polish underground. Sent to Auschwitz, he was treated brutally because he was a priest. When ten of his fellow prisoners were marked out for execution in reprisal for a prison escape, Father Kolbe voluntarily took the place of one of them, who was a married man. He died on August 14, 1941, and Pope John Paul II canonized him in 1982. His feast day is celebrated on August 14.

Edith Stein (1891-1942) was born into a Jewish family and at an early age declared herself an atheist. A brilliant student, she studied philosophy under the renowned philosopher Edmund Husserl and became identified with the philosophical school called phenomenology. During her studies, and after beginning her career as a teacher and writer, she was led towards the Catholic Faith. After reading the autobiography of Saint Teresa of Avila, she was moved to convert, and was baptized on January 1, 1922. In 1934 she joined the Carmelites in Cologne, taking the religious name Teresa Benedicta of the Cross. As the Nazi campaign against Jews intensified, she was smuggled to the Netherlands in 1938. In 1942 she was arrested as part of the Nazi reaction to the Dutch bishops' condemnation of Nazism and sent to Auschwitz, where she was killed in the gas chamber on August 9, 1942. Pope John Paul canonized her in 1998. Her feast day is celebrated on August 9.

THE TEACHING OF PIUS XII

Along with being active in world affairs, Pope Pius XII produced a significant body of teaching, much of it is contained in a series of important encyclicals that helped set the stage for the Second Vatican Council.

Mystici corporis Christi (The Mystical Body of Christ) in 1943 draws on the teaching of St. Paul to present the Church as a communion whose members play complementary roles in continuing the mission of Christ. This encyclical makes clear both the Church's hierarchical structure, involving specific offices and authority, and her "charismatic" dimension whereby God gives individuals gifts to be used in the service of all. All the members of the Church are united to Christ, the head of the Church, in a relationship analogous to the connection of the organs of a physical body to the head.

Divino afflante Spiritu (Inspired by the Holy Spirit) in 1943 gave encouragement to Biblical studies. Scholars were told to respect the literal sense of Scripture while making use of historical-critical methods in order to understand the literary forms used by the inspired human authors and the historical circumstances in which they wrote.

Mediator Dei (Mediator of God) in 1947 endorsed the movement for liturgical renewal. Liturgical changes approved during the pontificate of Pius XII included the revision of the Holy Week rites, the reduction of the Eucharistic fast, and permission for afternoon and evening Masses.

Humani generis (The Human Race) in 1950 warned against emerging theological errors of the day contrary to the Christian tradition. In the various positions condemned by Pope Pius XII one can see a resurgence of Modernist thinking condemned four decades earlier by Pope St. Pius X.

Pope Pius declared 1950 a Holy Year and capped the observance by infallibly declaring the Assumption of Mary to be a dogma of Faith. The apostolic constitution *Munificentissimus Deus* (The Most Bountiful God) of Pope Pius XII (November 1, 1950) declared:

> …we pronounce, declare, and define it to be a divinely revealed dogma: that the Immaculate Mother of God, the ever Virgin Mary, having completed the course of her earthly life, was assumed body and soul into heavenly glory.

The definition of the Assumption is important not only as a contribution to teaching about the Blessed Virgin but for rejecting the idea of body-soul dualism.

Pope Pius XII appointed fifty-six cardinals, increased the number of dioceses in the world from 1696 to 2048, and established national hierarchies in China, Burma, and a number of African countries. By the time of his death in 1958, he had named more than two hundred of the two hundred sixty-five bishops of the United States and had created twenty-seven new U.S. dioceses. In 1946 he canonized the first U.S. citizen to be recognized as a saint, the Italian-born St. Frances Xavier Cabrini (1850-1917), who was famous for her work among immigrants.

Like Pius IX and Leo XIII, Pius XII was devoted to the Blessed Virgin Mary. In 1950, he declared a Holy Year, bringing millions of pilgrims to Rome. He closed the Holy Year in Fatima, Portugal, one of the great Marian shrines of the Catholic world.

Assumption of the Virgin by Juan Martin Cabezalero

PIUS XII AND THE JEWS

It is not uncommon today to hear people criticize Pope Pius XII's alleged indifference towards the Nazi persecution of the Jews during World War II. Some go even further, saying that Pius XII should be held personally responsible for deaths of thousands of Jews. Such allegations, however, have no basis in fact, and are the result of revisionist historians who ignore the fact that Pius XII saved hundreds of thousands of lives during the war. The impetus to slander the Vatican's role in World War II stems from a play called *The Deputy,* which appeared in 1963, almost twenty years after the war. This play portrayed Pius XII as a weak leader, too afraid to speak out publicly against the Nazis. Despite the fact that even the author of this play admitted that Pius XII actively supported the Jews during the war, it was to become the first of many works slandering the name of Pius XII, with the result that many today are ignorant of Pius XII's heroic actions.

Even before he was elected Pope Pius XII, Eugenio Pacelli had been a vociferous critic of the Nazis. In a 1935 speech he said that Nazis were "in reality only miserable plagiarists who dress up old errors with new tinsel," and in 1943 the Fascist press in Italy prejoratively called the Vatican paper "a mouthpiece of the Jews" and Pius XII the "chief rabbi of Rome." Pius XII seems to be blamed for saying too little but doing too much to save persecuted peoples. In fact, as had been learned from an incident in Holland, many actually under persecution did not want tough speeches from the Vatican thus resulting in reprisals, but rather they needed help in hiding and escaping persecution. As one Jewish couple who escaped the Nazis put it, "None of us wanted the pope to take an open stand. We were all fugitives, and fugitives do not wish to be pointed at."

The pope worked tirelessly to hide thousands of Jews throughout Rome. According to one account, "The pope sent out the order that religious buildings were to give refuge to Jews, even at the price of great personal sacrifice on the part of their occupants." Former Israeli diplomat Rabbi Pinchas Lapide wrote that "in Rome we saw a list of 155 convents and monasteries . . . which sheltered throughout the German occupation some 5,000 Jews in Rome. No less than 3,000 Jews found refuge at one time at the Pope's summer residence at Castel Gandolfo." In June 1944, the pope sent a message to Admiral Miklos Horthy, ruler of Hungary, and managed to stop the scheduled deportation of 800,000 Jews from that country.

In all, Pius helped save the lives of an estimated 860,000 individuals, a fact that did not go unappreciated by Jewish leaders at the time. Israel Zolli, who was the Chief Rabbi of Rome during the war, said "What the Vatican did will be indelibly and eternally engraved in our hearts. . . . Priests and even high prelates did things that will forever be an honor to Catholicism." After the war Zolli converted to Catholicism, and in honor of Pope Pius XII, took "Eugenio"—the pope's given name—as his baptismal name. Even during the war, Pius XII's work did not go unnoticed. In 1944 the Chief Rabbi of Jerusalem, Isaac Herzog, sent a message to the pope saying "The people of Israel will never forget what His Holiness and his illustrious delegates . . . are doing for us unfortunate brothers and sisters in the most tragic hour of our history."

PIUS XII AND THE JEWS Continued

Quotes from some other contemporary Jews may better illumine the good work of Pope Pius XII:

> Many Jews were persuaded to convert after the war, as a sign of gratitude, to that institution which had saved their lives. (Rabbi Barry Dov Schwartz, *Conservative Judaism*, Summer 1964)

> We share the grief of the world over the death of His Holiness Pius XII. . . . During the ten years of Nazi terror, when our people passed through the horrors of martyrdom, the Pope raised his voice to condemn the persecutors and to commiserate with their victims. (Golda Meir, Minister of Foreign Affairs and future Prime Minister of Israel, *Eulogy on behalf of the Nation of Israel to the United Nations*, 1958)

> With special gratitude we remember all he has done for the persecuted Jews during one of the darkest periods in their entire history. (Nahum Goldmann, President of the World Jewish Congress, *Letter of Condolence on Pope Pius' Death*, 1958)

> More than anyone else, we have had the opportunity to appreciate the great kindness, filled with compassion and magnanimity, that the Pope displayed during the terrible years of persecution and terror. (Elio Toaff, Chief Rabbi of Rome, following Rabbi Zolli's conversion, quoted in *Frankfurter Allgemeine Zeitung*, March 4, 1963)

> Only the Catholic Church protested against the Hitlerian onslaught on liberty. Up till then I had not been interested in the Church, but today I feel a great admiration for the Church, which alone has had the courage to struggle for spiritual truth and moral liberty. (Albert Einstein, quoted in *American Jewish Yearbook 1944-1945*, 251)

Yad VaShem Hall of Remembrance in Jerusalem

Mao Tse-Tung (1893-1976) declared the formation of the People's Republic of China at Tiananmen Square on October 1, 1949. Mao developed his own version of communism based on the theories of Hegel and Marx. The ideology of Maoism has influenced many communists around the world, including third world revolutionary movements such as Cambodia's Khmer Rouge, Peru's Shining Path, the revolutionary movement in Nepal, and the Revolutionary Communist Party in the United States.

THE CHURCH AND THE COMMUNIST EMPIRE

Military victory in World War II and the postwar settlement among the allies left the Soviet Union the master of Eastern Europe. The Soviets supported Communist puppet governments and stationed troops throughout the region. An Iron Curtain, as British Prime Minister Winston Churchill called it, descended across Europe, dividing the democratic West from the Communist East.

With significant American economic aid and military support, Western Europe enjoyed a dramatic recovery. Christian Democratic parties under Catholic leadership led the way in political rebirth. The major European statesmen of these years included Catholics Konrad Adenauer in Germany, Alcide De Gasperi in Italy, and Robert Schuman in France. Peace and reconciliation were fostered among former enemies, and the first steps were taken toward the economic and political unification of Europe.

In Eastern Europe, the Communists ruled with an iron fist. Persecution of religion, especially the Catholic Church, was a central part of their program. As early as 1942, for instance, the Communist party in Czechoslovakia had told party members to "undermine the authority of the Vatican by all means" and "break down unity among the clergy." After the war, Church leaders like Cardinal Bl. Aloysius Stepinac in Yugoslavia (beatified by Pope John Paul II in 1998), Cardinal Joseph Mindszenty in Hungary, Cardinal Joseph Beran in Czechoslovakia, Cardinal Stefan Wyszynski in Poland, and many other bishops, priests, religious, and lay people were tried and imprisoned. Many were tortured and martyred for their faith.

Pope Pius XII worked to rally Catholics against the threat of Communist takeover in the West. Looking to crucial elections in Italy, the Vatican's Holy Office in 1949 warned that Catholics who joined or supported Communist parties would be excommunicated.

"Communism is materialistic and anti-Christian," it said, and Communist leaders are "enemies of God, of the true religion, and of the Church of Christ." Although Communism would not spread to any other European countries, the Iron Curtain divided Europe for another 40 years.

International Communism was on the march outside Europe. The number of Catholics and other Christians in China was comparatively small, but the Church there had been making progress for several decades. That changed dramatically when the Communists under Mao Tse-tung took over mainland China in 1949. Foreign missionaries were expelled; many priests, religious, and lay people were imprisoned and forced to do slave labor; religious schools and institutions were closed; and Catholic movements were banned for alleged "counterrevolutionary activities."

The Communists concentrated on separating Chinese Catholics from the Holy See and creating a state-controlled national church. For this purpose, a Chinese Catholic Patriotic Association was established, and the government began choosing puppet bishops. Despite this state-sponsored nationalistic church, loyal bishops, priests, religious, and laity maintained an underground Church in communion with Rome. In response to the Chinese puppet church, Pope Pius XII underlined the universal nature of the Catholic Church and rejected the idea of national churches in his 1954 encyclical *Ad Sinarum gentem* (To the Chinese People).

CONCLUSION

Pius XII died on October 9, 1958. By that point in the twentieth century, the Catholic Church had weathered two world wars, numerous revolutions, and social turmoil, and had emerged as a strong, united community of Faith. However, it had serious external enemies. Secular humanism of two kinds posed a powerful threat to all religion—Marxist humanism, which dominated the Soviet Union, Eastern Europe, and China, and the materialistic, hedonistic secular humanism of the consumer societies of the West. Responding to these challenges would occupy the Church in the decades ahead.

OPENING PARAGRAPH OF POPE BENEDICT XV'S PEACE PROPOSAL, AUGUST 1, 1917

TO THE HEADS OF THE BELLIGERENT PEOPLES:

From the beginning of Our Pontificate, amidst the horrors of the terrible war unleashed upon Europe, We have kept before Our attention three things above all: to preserve complete impartiality in relation to all the belligerents, as is appropriate to him who is the common father and who loves all his children with equal affection; to endeavor constantly to do all the most possible good, without personal exceptions and without national or religious distinctions, a duty which the universal law of charity, as well as the supreme spiritual charge entrusted to Us by Christ, dictates to Us; finally, as Our peacemaking mission equally demands, to leave nothing undone within Our power, which could assist in hastening the end of this calamity, by trying to lead the peoples and their heads to more moderate frames of mind and to the calm deliberations of peace, of a "just and lasting" peace.

SUPPLEMENTARY READING

Pope Pius XI, *Quadragesimo anno,* May 15, 1931

1. Accordingly, when directing Our special attention to the changes which the capitalist economic system has undergone since Leo's time, We have in mind the good not only of those who dwell in regions given over to "capital" and industry, but of all mankind.

2. In the first place, it is obvious that not only is wealth concentrated in our times but an immense power and despotic economic dictatorship is consolidated in the hands of a few, who often are not owners but only the trustees and managing directors of invested funds which they administer according to their own arbitrary will and pleasure.

3. This dictatorship is being most forcibly exercised by those who, since they hold the money and completely control it, control credit also and rule the lending of money. Hence they regulate the flow, so to speak, of the life-blood whereby the entire economic system lives, and have so firmly in their grasp the soul, as it were, of economic life that no one can breathe against their will.

4. This concentration of power and might, the characteristic mark, as it were, of contemporary economic life, is the fruit that the unlimited freedom of struggle among competitors has of its own nature produced, and which lets only the strongest survive; and this is often the same as saying, those who fight the most violently, those who give least heed to their conscience.

5. This accumulation of might and of power generates in turn three kinds of conflict. First, there is the struggle for economic supremacy itself; then there is the bitter fight to gain supremacy over the State in order to use in economic struggles its resources and authority; finally there is conflict between States themselves, not only because countries employ their power and shape their policies to promote every economic advantage of their citizens, but also because they seek to decide political controversies that arise among nations through the use of their economic supremacy and strength.

Pope Pius XII, *Mystici corporis Christi,* June 29, 1943

3. From the outset it should be noted that the society established by the Redeemer of the human race resembles its divine Founder, who was persecuted, calumniated and tortured by those very men whom He had undertaken to save. We do not deny, rather from a heart filled with gratitude to God We admit, that even in our turbulent times there are many who, though outside the fold of Jesus Christ, look to the Church as the only haven of salvation; but We are also aware that the Church of God not only is despised and hated maliciously by those who shut their eyes to the light of Christian wisdom and miserably return to the teachings, customs and practices of ancient paganism, but is ignored and neglected, and even at times looked upon as irksome by many Christians who are allured by specious error or caught in the meshes of the world's corruption. In obedience, therefore, Venerable Brethren, to the voice of Our conscience and in compliance with the wishes of many, We will set forth before the eyes of all and extol the beauty, the praises, and the glory of Mother Church to whom, after God, we owe everything.

Pope John Paul II, *On the Fiftieth Anniversary of the Second World War in Europe*, June 11, 1995

A Humane Society Is Not Built on Violence

7. The Second World War was the direct result of this process of degeneration: But were the necessary lessons learned in the following decades? Sadly, the end of the war did not lead to the disappearance of the policies and ideologies which were its cause or contributed to its outbreak. Under another guise, totalitarian regimes continued and indeed spread, especially in Eastern Europe. After that May 8, in Europe and elsewhere, a number of concentration camps remained open, while many people continued to be imprisoned in contempt of every elementary human right. It was not understood that a society worthy of the person is not built by destroying the person, by repression and by discrimination. This lesson of the Second World War has not yet been learned completely and in all quarters. And yet it remains and must stand as a warning for the next millennium.

In particular, in the years preceding the Second World War, the cult of the nation, pushed even to the point of becoming a new kind of idolatry, brought about in those six terrible years an enormous catastrophe.

A railroad car used during the Holocaust stands symbolically at the Yad VaShem Memorial in Jerusalem.

VOCABULARY

CATHOLIC ACTION

An organization encouraged by Popes St. Pius X and Pius XI that was to become a key instrument of the lay apostolate.

CHRISTIAN MODERNISM

Originated in the late nineteenth century, some Catholic intellectuals, out of a desire to address contemporary currents of thought, embraced trends in psychology, science, and philosophy and tried to adapt Christian thought to them.

CODE OF CANON LAW OF 1917

Updated and systematic compilation of the law of the Church launched by St. Pius X and finished after his death.

CRISTEROS

This Catholic group led an armed rebellion under the regime of Plutarco Calles in Mexico. They sought to resist anti-Catholic persecution but were quickly put down. Several of the fighters are martyrs and saints.

GULAG

A vast system of Siberian prison camps and penal colonies set up during Stalin's dictatorship in which many thousands of opponents of the regime served long sentences or were executed.

NAZISM

A blend of nationalist totalitarianism, racism aimed especially at Jews, neo-paganism, and the moral nihilism of the nineteenth century German philosopher Friedrich Nietzsche, this political party, headed by Adolf Hitler, seized power in 1933 and initiated policies that sought to strengthen and unify Germany in order to bring about an expansive New World Order based on Nazi ideals.

OATH AGAINST MODERNISM

In an encyclical issued on September 1, 1910, St. Pius X required all Catholic priests to uphold Catholic teaching against modern heresies. Because of the Oath, much Modernist thinking in the Church went underground.

VATICAN RADIO

Inaugurated in 1931 by Pius XI, Vatican Radio was to become an international agency airing four hundred hours of programming weekly in thirty-seven languages. The role of Vatican Radio would only become more significant as Eastern Europe fell to communist regimes, and information was increasingly censored. Throughout the Cold War era, Vatican Radio would act as both an ear to the outside world and passive form of resistance for those oppressed by totalitarian states.

Pope John Paul II places a prayer for the people of the Covenant in the Wailing Wall of the Temple in Jerusalem during his pilgrimage there in 2000.

God of our fathers,
you chose Abraham and his descendants
to bring your Name to the Nations:
we are deeply saddened
by the behaviour of those
who in the course of history
have caused these children of yours to suffer,
and asking your forgiveness
we wish to commit ourselves
to genuine brotherhood
with the people of the Covenant.

STUDY QUESTIONS

1. Who was the first pope elected in the twentieth century?

2. What was the motto of St. Pius X?

3. At the beginning of his pontificate, St. Pius X launched the updating and systematic compilation of what Church document?

4. Why is St. Pius X known as the "Pope of the Eucharist"?

5. How did Modernists view religion?

6. Why did St. Pius X refer to Modernism as a "compendium of all heresies"?

7. What did the election of Giacomo della Chiesa as Pope Benedict XV imply?

8. What regions of the world saw a tremendous growth in Catholicism during the early decades of the twentieth century?

9. What dominating political regime rose to power after World War I?

10. What happened in Fatima?

11. Why did Russia need so many prayers?

12. Which pope inaugurated Vatican Radio?

13. Who founded the Young Christian Workers?

14. Who founded Opus Dei?

15. What was decided by the 1933 Concordat between Germany and the Vatican?

16. How did civil war in Spain affect Spanish Catholics?

17. Who were the *Cristeros* of Mexico?

18. Whose name did the chief rabbi of Rome take when he was baptized a Catholic after World War II?

19. How many Catholics died in Auschwitz?

20. Who was St. Maximilian Kolbe?

21. Who was Edith Stein?

22. Which were Pius XII's major encyclical works?

23. In what year did Pius XII define the Assumption of Mary a matter of dogma?

24. What was the Chinese Catholic Patriotic Association?

PRACTICAL EXERCISES

1. St. Pius X called Modernism a "compendium of all heresies." Choose any two heresies you have studied and compare them to Modernism. How does Modernism contain some of the principles of the heresy? How does Modernism reflect an alteration of earlier heresies?

2. The two major ideologies of the twentieth century, Communism and Fascism, represent two opposite ends of the political spectrum, and yet, their attitudes towards religion and the Church are comparable. Based on what you have read in previous chapters about the birth of these ideologies and the

Enlightenment principles which underlie their ideas, explain why both have such a negative understanding of the role of God and religion in the world.

3. Pius XII is often accused of being "silent" in the face of the Nazi atrocities during World War II. How did the silence of the Vatican enable the Church to aid those suffering under the Nazi regime? How would a more vocal and public stance against Nazism have affected the role the Church played during the war? How would this have been beneficial? How would it have been detrimental?

FROM THE CATECHISM

407 The doctrine of original sin, closely connected with that of redemption by Christ, provides lucid discernment of man's situation and activity in the world. By our first parents' sin, the devil has acquired a certain domination over man, even though man remains free. Original sin entails "captivity under the power of him who thenceforth had the power of death, that is, the devil" (Council of Trent (1546): DS 1511; cf. Heb 2:14). Ignorance of the fact that man has a wounded nature inclined to evil gives rise to serious errors in the areas of education, politics, social action (cf. John Paul II, *CA* 25), and morals.

412 *But why did God not prevent the first man from sinning?* St. Leo the Great responds, "Christ's inexpressible grace gave us blessings better than those the demon's envy had taken away" (St. Leo the Great, Sermo 73, 4: PL 54, 396). And St. Thomas Aquinas wrote, "There is nothing to prevent human nature's being raised up to something greater, even after sin; God permits evil in order to draw forth some greater good. Thus St. Paul says, 'Where sin increased, grace abounded all the more'; and the Exultet sings, 'O happy fault,…which gained for us so great a Redeemer!'" (St. Thomas Aquinas, *STh* III, 1, 3, *ad* 3; cf. Rom 5:20)

852 *Missionary paths.* The Holy Spirit is the protagonist, "the principal agent of the whole of the Church's mission" (John Paul II, *RMiss* 21). It is he who leads the Church on her missionary paths. "This mission continues and, in the course of history, unfolds the mission of Christ, who was sent to evangelize the poor; so the Church, urged on by the Spirit of Christ, must walk the road Christ himself walked, a way of poverty and obedience, of service and self-sacrifice even to death, a death from which he emerged victorious by his resurrection" (*AG* 5). So it is that "the blood of martyrs is the seed of Christians" (Tertullian, *Apol.* 50, 13: PL 1, 603).

2107 "If because of the circumstances of a particular people special civil recognition is given to one religious community in the constitutional organization of a state, the right of all citizens and religious communities to religious freedom must be recognized and respected as well" (*DH* 6 § 3).

2199 The fourth commandment is addressed expressly to children in their relationship to their father and mother, because this relationship is the most universal. It likewise concerns the ties of kinship between members of the extended family. It requires honor, affection, and gratitude toward elders and ancestors. Finally, it extends to the duties of pupils to teachers, employees to employers, subordinates to leaders, citizens to their country, and to those who administer or govern it.

This commandment includes and presupposes the duties of parents, instructors, teachers, leaders, magistrates, those who govern, all who exercise authority over others or over a community of persons.

2314 "Every act of war directed to the indiscriminate destruction of whole cities or vast areas with their inhabitants is a crime against God and man, which merits firm and unequivocal condemnation" (*GS* 80 § 3). A danger of modern warfare is that it provides the opportunity to those who possess modern scientific weapons—especially atomic, biological, or chemical weapons—to commit such crimes.

2437 On the international level, inequality of resources and economic capability is such that it creates a real "gap" between nations (cf. *SRS* 14). On the one side there are those nations possessing and developing the means of growth and, on the other, those accumulating debts.

Vatican II And The Church In The Modern World

By mid-century, an anti-authoritarian spirit of rebellion would revolutionize and secularize society. The Church faced unexpected controversies associated with the interpretation of the Second Vatican Council.

CHAPTER 20

Vatican II And The Church In The Modern World

Different philosophical systems have lured people into believing that they are their own absolute master, able to decide their own destiny and future in complete autonomy, trusting only in themselves and their own powers. But this can never be the grandeur of the human being, who can find fulfillment only in choosing to enter the truth, to make a home under the shade of Wisdom and dwell there. Only within this horizon of truth will people understand their freedom and its fullness and their call to know and love God as the supreme realization of their true self.

— John Paul II, *Fides et ratio*, 1998, no. 107

Midpoint in the twentieth century, the Catholic Church was united in doctrine, worship, and loyalty to the pope and bishops. The Catholic population was growing rapidly in many places, especially the Third World. Priestly and religious vocations flourished, and lay movements were strong and enthusiastic. Overall, the Church seemed strong despite frequently confused and troubled times the world had been experiencing.

At the same time, the Church faced different challenges. Living under the threat of nuclear extinction in the Cold War, Catholics along with everyone else wrestled with the moral dilemmas of nuclear deterrence and modern warfare. Totalitarian regimes in the Soviet Union, Eastern Europe, and China persecuted religion, and the "Church of Silence," as the Church in China became known, produced many martyrs. The gap between rich and poor nations broadened, and demands for recognition of human rights, especially within the women's and civil rights movements, placed new pressures on old patterns of behavior both within and without the Church.

In the twentieth century, increasingly secular attitudes towards Matrimony and sexuality changed the way the family and society understood itself. The practice of birth control by means of contraception was spreading, spurred by new oral contraceptives and the sexual permissiveness they encouraged, and by propaganda about a largely fictitious "population explosion." Abortion

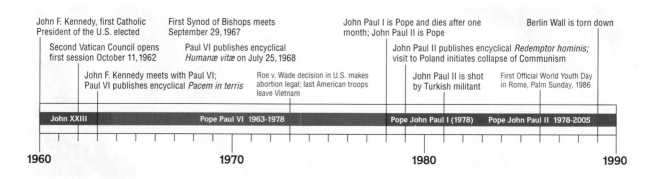

John F. Kennedy, first Catholic President of the U.S. elected

First Synod of Bishops meets September 29, 1967

John Paul I is Pope and dies after one month; John Paul II is Pope

Berlin Wall is torn down

Second Vatican Council opens first session October 11, 1962

Paul VI publishes encyclical *Humanæ vitæ* on July 25, 1968

John Paul II publishes encyclical *Redemptor hominis;* visit to Poland initiates collapse of Communism

John F. Kennedy meets with Paul VI; Paul VI publishes encyclical *Pacem in terris*

Roe v. Wade decision in U.S. makes abortion legal; last American troops leave Vietnam

John Paul II is shot by Turkish militant

First Official World Youth Day in Rome, Palm Sunday, 1986

John XXIII | Pope Paul VI 1963-1978 | Pope John Paul I (1978)   Pope John Paul II 1978-2005

1960   1970   1980   1990

already was legal in some places, and efforts were underway to bring about its legalization elsewhere. Marriage also came under assault from the growing acceptance of divorce.

Few people at mid-century anticipated how great an upheaval in ideas, values, and behavior lay ahead. In wider society, the sixties brought an anti-authoritarian spirit of rebellion, especially among the youth, and social movements would revolutionize the way life was lived in contemporary society. For the Church, much of the upheaval is associated with the Second Vatican Council, with controversy over how the Council's decisions should be interpreted and carried out, and with the dissent and defections from the clergy and religious life during and after the council. Vatican II itself did not encourage or cause these things, but the winds of change it occasioned unleashed contributed to bringing them about.

PART I

Blessed John XXIII and the Council

After the death of Pius XII, the Church looked for an alternative to the long papacy of the great pope. Within the College of Cardinals, ideas over the future direction of the Church differed. The College eventually compromised by electing someone whom they thought would simply serve as a caretaker pope, a pastoral figure who would make few changes. The cardinals turned to the seventy-six-year-old Patriarch of Venice, Cardinal Angelo Roncalli. The choice of the elderly cardinal made it clear that the College desired a shorter pontificate. Roncalli, by choosing the name John XXIII, which implicitly clarified a discrepancy in papal succession that stretched back to the time of the Western Schism, immediately showed the world that he was not going to slip away quietly. This pope would instead begin turning the wheels of reform that would lead the Church into the third millennium.

THE CARETAKER POPE

Angelo Giuseppe Roncalli was born on November 25, 1881, into a family of peasant farmers in Sotto il Monte, an Italian village near the town of Bergamo. He studied for the priesthood at the Bergamo diocesan seminaries and the St. Apollinare Institute in Rome and was ordained in 1904. From 1904 to 1914 he was secretary to the Bishop of Bergamo and taught Church history at one of

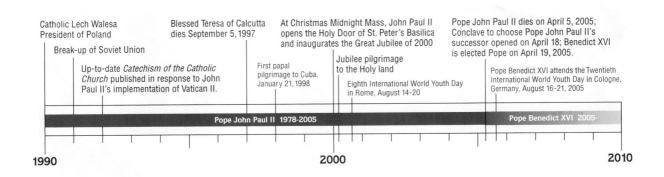

Catholic Lech Walesa President of Poland

Break-up of Soviet Union

Up-to-date *Catechism of the Catholic Church* published in response to John Paul II's implementation of Vatican II.

Blessed Teresa of Calcutta dies September 5, 1997

First papal pilgrimage to Cuba, January 21, 1998

At Christmas Midnight Mass, John Paul II opens the Holy Door of St. Peter's Basilica and inaugurates the Great Jubilee of 2000

Jubilee pilgrimage to the Holy land

Eighth International World Youth Day in Rome, August 14-20

Pope John Paul II dies on April 5, 2005; Conclave to choose Pope John Paul II's successor opened on April 18; Benedict XVI is elected Pope on April 19, 2005.

Pope Benedict XVI attends the Twentieth International World Youth Day in Cologne, Germany, August 16-21, 2005

Pope John Paul II 1978-2005

Pope Benedict XVI 2005-

1990   2000   2010

the local seminaries. In World War I, Father Roncalli was drafted into the Italian army and served as a hospital orderly and chaplain.

After the war, Pope Benedict XV named Roncalli Italian president of the Society for the Propagation of the Faith, an organization that supported missionary work. He wrote studies on the history of the Bergamo diocese and on St. Charles Borromeo (1538-1584), the Archbishop of Milan who was a leader of the Catholic Counter-Reformation. While researching at the Ambrosian Library in Milan, he met Achille Ratti, and after Ratti became Pope Pius XI, he named Roncalli an archbishop and appointed him apostolic visitor to Bulgaria and, in 1934, apostolic delegate to Turkey and Greece. Much of Roncalli's experience as an archbishop would highlight his ecumenical understanding of the universal Church and his strong background in Church history, especially of the Counter-Reformation period.

During his time as a delegate in the East, Archbishop Roncalli developed good relations with the Orthodox Church, and during World War II, he worked to assist Jews and other refugees. In December 1944, Pius XII named him apostolic nuncio to France where Roncalli had to deal with a number of difficult problems. He negotiated with the new government over the appointment of bishops and aid to church-sponsored schools; he worked out arrangements for seminarians who had served in the German army and were now prisoners of war to continue their theological studies; he dealt with the problem of bishops who had collaborated with the unpopular French Vichy government during the German occupation. In 1952, he was appointed the Holy See's representative at UNESCO (the United Nations Educational, Scientific, and Cultural Organization).

In June 1953, Pope Pius XII named Roncalli a cardinal and Patriarch of Venice, just as Pope St. Pius X had been five decades earlier. In Venice, he became a popular figure known for pastoral zeal and an informal style. At seventy-six, Roncalli was seen as a popular choice for pope, a well-loved man of the people who could offer a smooth transition between Pius XII and Roncalli's own successor.

Following his election as pope, one of Bl. John XXIII's first acts was to abolish the rule dating back to the sixteenth century which set the number of cardinals at seventy. Thereafter he took steps to increase the size of the College of Cardinals and make it a more international body. It was a bold and progressive move, but it was only the start for the seventy-six-year-old historian pope.

On January 25, 1959, Pope Bl. John XXIII announced to the world three projects for his pontificate: a diocesan synod for Rome, the drafting of a new Code of Canon Law, and an ecumenical council—the first such gathering of the world's bishops since Vatican Council I (1869-1870) and only the twenty-first ecumenical council in the Church's history. Preparatory commissions and secretariats for the council were established in June 1960, and a commission responsible for revising the Code of Canon Law was appointed in March 1962.

Bl. John XXIII was a man of faith and piety whose friendly manner won him fame as "Good Pope John." He cracked jokes and visited prisoners and hospital patients. He took ground breaking ecumenical steps, including establishing a Vatican office for Christian unity, sending envoys to Istanbul (Constantinople) to greet the Orthodox Ecumenical Patriarch, exchanging greetings with the Russian

Bl. Pope John XXIII signing his encyclical *Pacem in terris* (Peace on Earth) that captured the world's attention during a time of extremely dangerous tensions between the world's two superpowers.

Pope Blessed John XXIII, "Good Pope John." born Angelo Giuseppe Roncalli (1881-1963), reigned as pope from October 28, 1958, until his death in 1963. Bl. John XXIII was a man of traditional faith and piety whose friendly manner won him fame as "Good Pope John."

Orthodox Patriarch, receiving the Anglican Archbishop of Canterbury in audience, and sending official observers to a congress of the World Council of Churches. He also reached out to Jews, changing the Good Friday liturgy to avoid giving them offense, and famously greeted a group of Jewish visitors with the words of Genesis 45:4, "I am your brother, Joseph."

Bl. John XXIII published several notable encyclicals. *Ad Petri cathedram* (To the Chair of Peter), written in 1959, discussed the unity of the Church. *Mater et magistra* (Mother and Teacher), 1961, developed Catholic social teaching and stressed the duty of developed nations to provide assistance to underdeveloped ones.

Above all, it was *Pacem in terris* (Peace on Earth), published in April 1963 that captured the world's attention. The encyclical appeared less than six months after the U.S.-Soviet confrontation over Soviet missiles in Cuba had brought the two superpowers to the brink of war. During the incident, Pope Bl. John worked publicly and behind the scenes to relieve tensions and preserve peace. Now, in his encyclical, he made a powerful appeal for world peace and an international order with effective political structures committed to the common good.

Although he excommunicated Fidel Castro (Communist Cuba) on January 3, 1962, Pope Bl. John XXIII also encouraged peaceful coexistence with Communist governments, not only on the part of Western nations, but also on the part of the Church. His gesture in receiving in audience the son-in-law of Soviet Premier Nikita Khrushchev was widely noted and generally praised. This champion of peace died of stomach cancer on June 3, 1963, after the first session of his most lasting legacy, the Second Vatican Council. Pope John Paul II beatified him on September 3, 2000.

THE SECOND VATICAN COUNCIL

Why did Pope Bl. John XXIII convene Vatican Council II? Although he certainly had a number of purposes in mind, one stood out especially.

In the apostolic constitution *Humanæ salutis* (For the Salvation of Men) of December 25, 1961, formally convoking the Council, he spoke of a "twofold spectacle"—the secular world in "a grave state of spiritual poverty" and the Church, "so vibrant with vitality." He continued:

> We...have felt immediately the urgency of the duty to call our sons together, to give the Church the possibility to contribute more efficaciously to the solution of the problems of the modern age. For this reason...we considered that the times now were right to offer to the Catholic Church and to the world the gift of a new Ecumenical Council.

The Church, Pope Bl. John declared, was strong in faith and enjoyed an "awe-inspiring unity." Through an ecumenical council, it hoped to update herself in order to meet the urgent spiritual needs of the world.

The Second Vatican Council took place in four sessions: October 11–December 8, 1962; September 29–December 4, 1963; September 14–November 21, 1964; and September 14–December 8, 1965. General congregations were held in St. Peter's Basilica. About 2860 of the world's bishops attended some or all of the Council; 274 bishops did not attend because of age, health, or some other reason (including the refusal of Communist governments in some places to permit them to go). Representatives of other Christian churches and religious bodies also attended, along with selected clergy, religious, and lay people.

Extensively covered by secular and religious media, the council was one of the major media events of the 1960s. It became the focus of an enormous amount of speculation, hope, anxiety, pressure, and debate. Vatican II is widely considered to have been the most important event in the Church's life of the twentieth century.

Pope Paul VI opened the second session of the Second Vatican Council on September 29, 1963. Pope Paul's opening address stressed the pastoral nature of the Council, and set out four purposes: to more fully define the nature of the Church and the role of the bishops; to renew the Church; to restore unity among all Christians; and to start a dialog with the contemporary world.

In a hope-filled speech at the opening session of the Council, October 11, 1962, Pope Bl. John denounced "prophets of gloom who are always forecasting disaster, as though the end of the world were at hand." On the contrary, he insisted, a "new order of human relations" was emerging under the inspiration of God's providence; and the Council would allow the Church to make her proper contribution.

Less than eight months later Pope Bl. John died. On June 21, 1963, the cardinals elected Cardinal Giovanni Battista Montini of Milan as his successor. He took the name Paul VI, and immediately announced that the Council would continue.

The substantive work of the Second Vatican Council is embodied in sixteen documents. There are four "constitutions" (on the Church, on Divine Revelation, on Liturgy, and on the Church in the Modern World), nine "decrees" (on the pastoral office of bishops, on missionary activity, on ecumenism, on the Eastern Catholic Churches, on the ministry and life of priests, on priestly formation, on the appropriate renewal of religious life, on the apostolate of the laity, and on the instruments of social communication or media), and three "declarations" (on religious freedom, on the Church and non-Christian religions, and on Christian education).

The four constitutions are the central documents of Vatican II and provide the theological basis and vision for the rest.

THE DOGMATIC CONSTITUTION ON THE CHURCH

Lumen gentium (Light of Nations) uses scriptural images like Body of Christ and People of God to present the Church as a *communio*. The Church, it says, is a hierarchically structured community of faith whose members possess a fundamental equality in dignity and rights while having different but complementary roles in her mission. The constitution sets out collegiality, according to which the bishops, in union with and under the pope, share in teaching and governing the Church. Chapter V, "The Call to Holiness," teaches that all members of the Church, including lay people, are called to be saints. Chapter VIII, "Our Lady," contains the Council's principal treatment of the Blessed Virgin Mary.

THE DOGMATIC CONSTITUTION ON DIVINE REVELATION

Dei verbum (The Word of God) joins sacred tradition in Sacred Scripture as God's divinely inspired word with approval of the responsible use of contemporary scholarly methods for understanding its historical context and literary forms. Scripture and Tradition are not two independent sources of Revelation but are intimately and inextricably linked: "Sacred Tradition and Sacred Scripture make up a single sacred deposit of the Word of God, which is entrusted to the Church." It also stresses that the "authentic interpretation" of God's word "has been entrusted to the living teaching office of the Church alone."

THE CONSTITUTION ON THE SACRED LITURGY

Sacrosanctum concilium (The Sacred Council) recognized the liturgy as "the summit toward which the activity of the Church is directed, at the same time it is the font from which all her power flows." In a key passage, it called for "full, conscious, and active participation" by all members of the Church, especially in the Eucharistic liturgy. It opened the door to expanded use of vernacular languages and to liturgical adaptations suited to the needs of particular groups, provided these had the approval of Church authority, and called for other steps to foster "active participation."

THE PASTORAL CONSTITUTION ON THE CHURCH IN THE MODERN WORLD

Gaudium et spes (Joy and Hope) was the Council's most direct response to Pope Bl. John's desire that the Church be more directly at the service of the world. Its famous opening words declare: "The joys and the hopes, the griefs and the anxieties of the men of this age, especially those who are poor or in any way afflicted, these are the joys and hopes, the griefs and anxieties of the followers of Christ." Topics treated include the dignity of the human person in light of Christ, the causes of contemporary atheism, the nature of the common good, social justice and economic life, marriage and the family, the evangelization of culture, work, private property, politics, war and peace, and the sanctity of human life.

The official document declaring the Second Vatican Council completed was read at the closing ceremonies on December 8, 1965. Pope Paul VI summed up the Council thusly:

> It was the largest in the number of Fathers who came to the seat of Peter from every part of the world.... It was the richest because of the questions which for four sessions have been discussed carefully and profoundly. And finally it was the most opportune, because above all it sought to meet pastoral needs, bearing in mind the needs of the present day, and ... has made a great effort to reach not only Christians still separated from the Holy See but also the whole human family.

PART II

Pope Paul VI and the Postconciliar Years

Pope Paul VI became the first pope to visit all five* continents, earning him the nickname "the Pilgrim Pope." He was also the last pope to be crowned. Paul VI donated his Papal Tiara to the Basilica of the National Shrine of the Immaculate Conception in Washington, D.C.

* The Vatican considers North and South America as one continent.

The pope who saw Vatican II to its successful conclusion, Paul VI, also conscientiously directed its implementation. Despite his best efforts, however—and to his increasing sorrow—the optimism of the Council years was soon was replaced by some confusion, misinterpretations, and dissent.

Giovanni Battista Montini was born September 26, 1897, near the city of Brescia. His father was a lawyer, editor, and member of parliament. The studious young man prepared for the priesthood at the diocesan seminary, was ordained in 1920, and pursued graduate work in Rome. In 1922 he joined the Vatican Secretariat of State where, except for serving briefly in Warsaw in 1923, he was to remain for the next thirty-two years. He was active as a chaplain to Catholic students and taught at the training academy for Vatican diplomats.

Monsignor Montini held key posts in these years. In 1937 he became assistant to Cardinal Eugenio Pacelli, the Secretary of State, whose close collaborator he remained after Cardinal Pacelli was elected Pope Pius XII in 1939. In 1944, he was named head of the section of the Secretariat of State responsible for internal Church affairs, and in 1952 he became Pro-Secretary of State, or the second in charge of the department.

Pope Pius XII appointed Montini to be Archbishop of the huge Archdiocese of Milan in 1954. There he worked to resolve social tensions and win over industrial workers alienated from the Church; he also took a number of ecumenical initiatives. Pope Bl. John XXIII named him a cardinal in 1958, and he had an active role in preparations for the ecumenical council.

During the Council years, Pope Paul VI found time for dramatic trips. In 1964 he traveled to the Holy Land and to Bombay, India, for a Eucharistic congress. The next year he visited New York and the United Nations, where on October 4, 1965, he made a memorable plea for peace: "No more war! War never again!" Other journeys included a pilgrimage to the Marian shrine at Fatima, Portugal, in 1967, and trips to Bogotá in 1968, Uganda in 1969, and Australia and the Philippines in 1970, where he was the target of an assassination attempt. These journeys made him the most-traveled pope before John Paul II.

Pope Paul met with world leaders like Soviet President Nikolai Podgorny in 1967 and Yugoslavian President Tito in 1971. The encounters reflected a sometimes-controversial new Vatican policy called *Ostpolitik,* which sought improved relations with the Communist regimes of Eastern Europe.

Paul VI was strongly committed to Christian unity and pursued this cause through

During his trip to Jerusalem in January 1964, Paul VI met with the Patriarch of Constantinople, Athenagoras I.

meetings with the leaders of other churches and religious bodies. During his trip to Jerusalem in January 1964, he met with the Ecumenical Patriarch Athenagoras I, and on December 7, 1965, the pope and the patriarch issued a joint statement withdrawing the mutual excommunications that had formalized the Catholic-Orthodox split in the year 1054. He met with two Archbishops of Canterbury (Ramsey in 1966, Coggan in 1977) and again with Patriarch Athenagoras in Constantinople (1967). International bilateral commissions were established for Catholic dialogue with Anglicans, Lutherans, and others.

Pope Paul VI moved vigorously to carry out the decisions of Vatican Council II. New commissions and other structures were established and detailed documents were issued spelling out steps to take in the reform of the liturgy, the restoration of the permanent diaconate, and other areas. He approved the New Order of the Mass (that is, the new rite of the Eucharistic liturgy in the Western Church) and published a reformed liturgical calendar.

In addition, Paul VI reorganized the Curia and continued its internationalization, along with the internationalization of the College of Cardinals. He revised the rules for papal elections, decreeing that cardinals were no longer eligible to vote upon turning eighty.

Among his many canonizations were those of St. Elizabeth Seton, foundress of the Sisters of Charity in the United States and the first native-born American to be declared a saint (1975), and St. John Neumann, the fourth Bishop of Philadelphia (1977).

In line with a recommendation of the Council, Pope Paul established the Synod of Bishops as a permanent body expressing the collaborative relationship between the pope and the bishops central to collegiality. At general assemblies of the synod, held every few years, two hundred or more bishops—some chosen by national bishops' conferences, some appointed by the pope, and some attending *ex officio*—discuss a topic or topics designated by the pope and made recommendations for an eventual papal document. The first synod assembly was held September 29 to

October 29, 1967. Among topics considered since then have been evangelization, religious education, marriage and the family, and the roles of bishops, priests, religious, and lay people. In addition, special synod assemblies and regional assemblies were held from time to time.

Pope Paul VI published a number of important encyclicals and other documents. *Ecclesiam Suam* (His Church) in 1964 endorsed the continuing renewal of the Church and the practice of dialogue. *Mysterium Fidei* (The Mystery of Faith) in 1965 reaffirmed Catholic Faith regarding the Eucharist. *Populorum progressio* (The Progress of Peoples) in 1967 called on developed nations to take "concrete action" to correct imbalances of wealth between themselves and poor countries. In connection with a "Year of Faith" observed in 1968, the pope issued the *Credo of the People of God*, restating central beliefs of the Church. The apostolic exhortation *Evangelii nuntiandi* (On Evangelization in the Modern World) was published in 1975 in response to the bishops' synod on evangelization the year before; it underlined the central place of evangelization in the Church's mission and the duty of all Catholics to participate in this work.

HUMANÆ VITÆ

The document of Pope Paul VI that had the greatest impact was his encyclical *Humanæ vitæ* (On Human Life), published July 25, 1968, in which he reaffirmed that the use of artificial contraception is intrinsically wrong. In *Humanæ vitæ*, the pope wrote that "the Church, nevertheless, in urging men to the observance of the precepts of the natural law, which it interprets by its constant doctrine, teaches that each and every marital act must of necessity retain its intrinsic relationship to the procreation of human life" (no. 11).

It had been long expected that the pope would speak out definitively on this subject. In 1964 he had announced that Pope Bl. John XXIII several years earlier set up the Papal Commission for the Study of Problems of the Family, Population, and Birth Rate with bishops, theologians, and specialists in several fields as members. Paul VI continued and expanded this body, which came to be popularly called the "Birth Control Commission."

Pressure for approval of artificial contraception came from revisionist theories of some moral theologians, anxiety about the supposed "population explosion," the growing use of oral contraceptives, and the fever for change then existing among a good number of Catholics. Already the sexual revolution of the 1960s had tried to reject the traditional morality in favor of permissiveness: why not the Catholic Church? Thus, the stage was set for Paul VI's encyclical declaring that there could and would be no change in Catholic doctrine on this matter. He taught:

> This particular doctrine, often expounded by the magisterium of the Church, is based on the inseparable connection, established by God, which man on his own initiative may not break, between the unitive significance and the procreative significance which are both inherent to the marriage act. (HV 12)

Prophetically, the pope warned of an even broader breakdown of morality if this teaching were rejected.

Even before the encyclical appeared, dissenting theologians in Western Europe and North America organized to oppose it, and they received much favorable attention from the secular media. Many national bishops' conferences issued statements in support of *Humanæ vitæ*, but some strained to leave the door open to dissent. The pope was shocked by the hostile reaction to the encyclical, and those who accepted the Church's teachings could not find a way to stop this angry backlash.

A CULTURE OF DISSENT AND DEFECTION

Along with dissent from *Humanæ vitæ*, other factors made for troubled conditions in the Church beginning in the late 1960s. While some dissent and defections from the priesthood and religious life were increasing, and controversies over the interpretation of Vatican II were now becoming increasingly common.

The French Catholic philosopher Jacques Maritain offered a telling analysis of what was happening. His comments were particularly significant because Maritain, an exponent of Christian humanism, had a strong intellectual influence on Pope Paul VI, and through him on the Council.

In his book called *The Peasant of the Garonne*, Maritain spoke of what he called "kneeling before the world"—a phenomenon he saw spreading from some clergy to Catholics generally. According to Maritain, this "kneeling" meant uncritical acceptance of secular standards and values as the norm for the Church. This was just the reverse of what Pope Bl. John XXIII had hoped for from the ecumenical council—to make the spiritual and moral riches of the Church more accessible to a secular world desperately in need of them; it marked a throwback to a central element of the Modernist heresy condemned six decades earlier by Pope St. Pius X.

Twenty years after Maritain, Joseph Cardinal Ratzinger (the future Pope Benedict XVI) made a similar point in a booklength interview called *The Ratzinger Report*. This distinguished German theologian, who had played an important part at Vatican II, served as Prefect of the Vatican Congregation for the Doctrine of the Faith under Pope John Paul II until the conclave of 2005. In the years since the council, he said, "dissension...seems to have passed over from self-criticism to self-destruction." Especially destructive, he added, was the tendency to turn away from what the council actually taught, in favor of a so-called spirit of Vatican II—in reality, a "pernicious anti-spirit." ("How many old heresies have surfaced again in recent years that have been presented as something new!" he exclaimed.)

Reflecting on the turmoil of these years, Pope Paul VI said in a homily on June 29, 1972, that "the smoke of Satan" seemed to have entered the Church (Homily, June 29, 1972). Worn out by the long struggle to establish order and defend orthodoxy, he died on the Feast of the Transfiguration, August 6, 1978.

Jacques Maritain with his mentor Pope Paul VI.

Jacques Maritain (1882-1973), a French Catholic philosopher, converted to Catholicism in 1906. He authored more than sixty books and helped revive the works of St. Thomas Aquinas. Pope Paul VI, a long time friend and mentor, dedicated his "Message to Men of Thought and of Science" to Maritain at the close of Vatican II. From 1945 to 1948, Maritain was the French ambassador to the Vatican. He returned to Princeton University where he ultimately became a Professor Emeritus in 1956. From 1961, Maritain lived with the Little Brothers of Jesus in Toulouse, France. He became a Little Brother in 1970. His papers are held by the University of Notre Dame which established The Jacques Maritain Center in 1957.

PART III

The Restoration of Confidence and Hope

Pope John Paul I is seated on the *sedia gestatoria*, the portable papal throne which was carried on the shoulders of twelve footmen. This allowed the pope to be seen above the heads of the crowd. The *sedia* has since been replaced by the white "pope-mobile."

In the conclave that followed the death of Pope Paul VI, the cardinals chose the Patriarch of Venice, Cardinal Albino Luciani, as pope on August 26, 1978. He took two names—John Paul—to signify continuity with his immediate predecessors.

Born October 17, 1912, John Paul I had been a bishop since 1958 and had been Patriarch of Venice since 1969. His friendly manner won him the nickname "the smiling pope." Barely a month after his election, on September 28, 1978 the world was shocked to learn that he had died of a heart attack.

POPE JOHN PAUL II: THE EARLY YEARS

Dismayed at having to choose another pope so soon, the cardinals now turned to the first non-Italian in more than 450 years. (Pope Adrian VI, 1522-1523, was Dutch.) On October 16, 1978, Cardinal Karol Wojtyla of Krakow was elected the two hundred sixty-third successor of St. Peter as Vicar of Christ and head of the Church. He took the name John Paul II.

"Open wide the doors for Christ," he exhorted the crowd in St. Peter's Square—and the Church and the world—following his election. "To his saving power open the boundaries of states, economic and political systems, the vast fields of culture, civilization, and development." Here was the program the Polish pope made his own in the years that followed, becoming one of the most admired figures on the world scene and one of the most outstanding popes of modern times.

Karol Wojtyla was born May 18, 1920, in the Polish industrial town of Wadowice, the second son of a Polish army lieutenant also named Karol and Emilia Kaczorowska Wojtyla. His mother died in 1929. His older brother, Edmund, a physician, died in 1932. After attending school in Wadowice, he moved to Krakow with his father in 1938 and attended the Jagiellonian University in Krakow, where he studied philosophy and took part in an experimental theater group.

World War II erupted on September 1, 1939. Poland was rapidly overrun, and the German occupiers closed the university. Young Wojtyla worked in a stone quarry and later in a chemical factory, while also participating in underground theater as a cultural protest against the occupation. His father died in 1941.

In October 1942 the young man entered an underground seminary sponsored by Cardinal Adam Sapieha of Krakow. After his ordination on November 1, 1946, he traveled to Rome to study at the Pontifical University of St. Thomas Aquinas, the Dominican institution popularly known as the Angelicum. There he wrote a thesis on the sixteenth century Spanish Carmelite mystic, poet, and theologian St. John of the Cross.

Returning to Poland—by now ruled by a Communist regime backed by the Red Army—Father Wojtyla did pastoral work, served as a university chaplain, and pursued advanced studies in philosophy and theology. In 1954 he became a professor in the Krakow major seminary and at the Catholic University of Lublin. He wrote philosophical and theological works, poetry, and plays. His book *Love and Responsibility* appeared in 1960. Other books included *The Acting Person, Foundations of Renewal,* and *A Sign of Contradiction.*

Father Wojtyla took his first kayaking trip in September 1953 with a group of students far into the Polish countryside. The Communist regime did not permit priests to go out with groups of young people, so these trips were always risky. Mass was celebrated using an overturned kayak as an altar, with two paddles lashed together to form a cross. The kayaking trips were an annual tradition cherished by Wojtyla until August 1978.

Wojtyla was on a kayaking trip with students when, on July 4, 1958, he learned that Pope Pius XII had appointed him an auxiliary bishop to the apostolic administrator of Krakow. On January 13, 1964, Pope Paul VI named him Archbishop of Krakow—the first time in thirteen years that Poland's Communist rulers had allowed the appointment of a residential archbishop.

An active participant in the Second Vatican Council, Archbishop Wojtyla participated in drafting the Pastoral Constitution on the Church in the Modern World and the Declaration on Religious Freedom. Pope Paul VI named him a cardinal in June 1967. In that year, too, he was chosen to attend the first assembly of the world Synod of Bishops, but he chose to stay home as a gesture of solidarity with Cardinal Stefan Wyszynski of Warsaw, Primate of the Church in Poland, whom the authorities refused to allow out of the country. Thereafter he took part in the assemblies of the Synod of Bishops from 1969 until his election as pope. He also traveled widely, visiting Western Europe, North America, Australia, and the Philippines. In 1976 Pope Paul VI granted Wojtyla the special honor of preaching the annual Lenten retreat for himself and the Roman Curia, just two years before the Pole surprised the world at the October conclave of 1978.

THE RISE OF PERPETUAL EUCHARISTIC ADORATION

Devotion to the Real Presence of Christ in the Holy Eucharist experienced a phenomenal growth during the latter part of the twentieth century. Perpetual Adoration societies, Holy Hours, daily Exposition of and Benediction with the Eucharist in churches and chapels, and Nocturnal Adoration societies have once again become more common in countries throughout the world. These practices rest on timeless Catholic doctrine regarding the Real Presence of Christ in the Eucharist. The understanding of the doctrine of Eucharist has undergone a wonderful development over many centuries, and this can only be called the work of the Holy Spirit.

The Apostles and Evangelists all held a strong belief in the Real, physical Presence of Christ in the Eucharist. At the end of the first century, St. Ignatius of Antioch warned Christians about the Gnostics, who denied the Real Presence. The early hermits often would reserve the Eucharist in their cells. Although the primary purpose of such reservation was to allow these hermits to have access to Communion, they were vividly aware of the Real Presence and treated it with deep reverence. As early as the First Council of Nicea (A.D. 325), the Eucharist was reserved in churches of monasteries and convents.

Over the centuries that followed the Early Church, a deeper grasp of every aspect of the mystery of the Eucharist took place. One important example of this development is the growing realization of Christ's grace-filled presence in the Eucharist outside of the Mass itself. "It is on this doctrinal basis that the worship of adoring the Eucharist was founded and gradually developed as something distinct from the Sacrifice of the Mass. . . . This practice of adoration, in fact, is based on strong and solid reasons. . . . When, therefore, the Church bids us adore Christ

hidden behind the Eucharistic veils and pray to Him for the spiritual and temporal favors of which we ever stand in need, she manifests living faith in her divine Spouse who is present beneath these veils, she professes her gratitude to Him and she enjoys the intimacy of His friendship." (Pope Pius XII, *Mediator Dei,* no. 131)

The worship of the Eucharist outside of the Mass is of inestimable value for the life of the Church. This worship is strictly linked to the celebration of the Eucharistic Sacrifice. The presence of Christ under the sacred species reserved after Mass—a presence which lasts as long as the species of bread and of wine remain—derives from the celebration of the sacrifice and is directed towards communion, both sacramental and spiritual. It is the responsibility of Pastors to encourage, also by personal witness, the practice of Eucharistic adoration and exposition of the Blessed Sacrament in particular, as well as prayer of adoration before Christ present under the Eucharistic species. (*Ecclesia de Eucharistia,* John Paul II)

"Man's situation in the modern world seems indeed to be far removed from the objective demands of the moral order, from the requirements of justice, and even more of social love."— *Redemptor hominis,* no. 16

POPE JOHN PAUL II AND THE CONTEMPORARY WORLD

John Paul II spelled out the program of his pontificate in surprising detail in his first encyclical, *Redemptor hominis* (The Redeemer of Man), published March 4, 1979.

In it, John Paul II emphasized the irreducible dignity and rights of every human being, and a "Christian anthropology" based on the insight that, as Vatican II taught, the dignity and destiny of the human person can only be truly understood in the light of Christ. In this context, the encyclical discussed many issues in the contemporary Church as well as in the world, with constant reference to the teaching of the ecumenical council. In a key passage the pope wrote:

> If therefore our time, the time of our generation, the time that is approaching the end of the second millennium of the Christian era, shows itself a time of great progress, it is also seen as a time of threat in many forms for man. The Church must speak of this threat to all people of good will and must always carry on a dialogue with them about it. Man's situation in the modern world seems indeed to be far removed from the objective demands of the moral order, from the requirements of justice, and even more of social love. (RH 16)

The solution, he said, lay in "the priority of ethics over technology, in the primacy of the person over things, and in the superiority of spirit over matter."

Redemptor hominis made it clear that John Paul believed that God had called him to lead the Church into the third millennium of the Christian era by continuing her renewal according to the prescriptions of Vatican II. These themes—human dignity and rights, the challenge of the third millennium, and renewal of the Church as prescribed by the Council—would remain central to his pontificate. Underlining his conviction that God had chosen him to shepherd the Church into a new era, he proclaimed the year 2000 a Jubilee Year to launch the third millennium, and marked it by an outpouring of events, documents, and papal travels.

John Paul II saw two fundamental threats to Christianity in the contemporary world: the secular humanism of Marxist Communism, embodied especially in the Soviet Union and the puppet states of the Soviet empire, and the secular humanism of the consumer society present in the United States and Western Europe, which gave rise to a "culture of death." He set out to combat both forms of secular humanism with all the spiritual and intellectual weapons at his disposal.

In fact, the process leading to the collapse of Communism, the breakup of the Soviet Empire and the Soviet Union, and the end of the cold war began with the pope's spectacular first visit to his Polish homeland June 2-10, 1979. Despite the disapproval of the Communist authorities, huge crowds turned out to greet him and join him in Masses and religious rallies. In the years that followed, John Paul returned to Poland several times and gave important moral backing to the Solidarity labor movement that served as a rallying point for nonviolent popular resistance to the regime.

In his ninth encyclical, *Centesimus annus* (The Hundredth Year: i.e., since Pope Leo XIII's encyclical *Rerum novarum*), published May 1, 1991, he gave his analysis of the factors that produced the fall of Communism. After identifying "the violation of the rights of workers" and "the inefficiency of the economic system" as causes, he wrote:

> But the true cause of the new developments was the spiritual void brought about by atheism, which deprived the younger generations of a sense of direction and in many cases led them, in the irrepressible search for personal identity and for the meaning of life, to rediscover the religious roots of their national cultures, and to rediscover the person of Christ.... Marxism had promised to uproot the need for God from the human

heart, but the results have shown that it is not possible to succeed in this without throwing the heart into turmoil.

Modestly, he said nothing about his own role in these momentous events.

In some ways, Western consumerism—based on materialism and hedonism (the belief that pleasure is the chief good in life) and leading to a culture of death—proved a tougher adversary. At a United Nations (UN) population conference in Cairo, Egypt, in 1994, Pope John Paul opposed the UN Population Fund head-on, and for the most part successfully, over its support of abortion and population control. He spelled out his stand on the sanctity of human life from conception to natural death many times and especially in the encyclical *Evangelium vitæ* (The Gospel of Life), which appeared in 1995. Marriage and family life continued to arise as frequent themes of his teaching.

As affluent, secularized Europe moved toward unprecedented economic and political unity under the aegis of the European Union, the pope and Cardinal Ratzinger waged a dogged struggle against what he called "the loss of Europe's Christian memory." Despite his efforts, drafters of the new European constitution refused to include a reference to Europe's Christian roots. Meanwhile religious practice and new vocations to the priesthood and religious life were declining sharply. In many places in Europe, John Paul said in 2003, "it is easier to be identified as an agnostic than a believer."

Elected pope at the relatively young age of fifty-eight, John Paul II was not only an intellectual with a profound spiritual life but a man of notable physical vigor and stamina, fond of hiking during vacations and seemingly indefatigable during his many foreign trips. As pope he made more than one hundred pastoral visits outside Italy covering well over 750,000 miles.

On May 13, 1981, he was felled by an assassin's bullet in St. Peter's Square. It remains a mystery as to who or what was behind this shooting carried out by a Turkish terrorist named Mehmet Ali Agca. John Paul resumed his vigorous schedule after a long, difficult recuperation, but in the years that followed, he was slowed by broken bones, surgery, and Parkinson's disease.

JOHN PAUL II AND THE CHURCH

Upon becoming pope, John Paul II faced difficult situations throughout the Church, especially Western Europe and North America. Dissent and defections had weakened Catholic life. Resistance to papal and episcopal authority was entrenched. What could John Paul—or anyone—do to change things for the better? He set out at once to address that question.

One thing he could do was write and teach. He wrote fourteen encyclicals and countless other documents on topics from economics to the spiritual life. John Paul's writings make up probably the largest body of teaching by any pope. While taking bold and original stands on many current issues, he firmly upheld traditional positions on matters like contraception, abortion, divorce, the celibacy of priests in the Western Church, and the impossibility of women's ordination.

His major documents include *Laborem exercens* (On Human Work), 1981; *Sollicitudo rei socialis* (On Social Concerns), 1987; *Veritatis splendor* (The Splendor of Truth), a treatise on moral principles published in 1993; *Fides et ratio* (Faith and Reason), on the relationship of religion and philosophy, published in 1998; and *Ecclesia de Eucharistia* (The Church of the Eucharist), 2003, on the Sacrament of the Eucharist. He also found time to write books, including the best-selling *Crossing the Threshold of Hope,* which was published in 1994.

Beginning in 1981, Pope John Paul's principal collaborator in dealing with issues of faith and dissent was Joseph Cardinal Ratzinger—the future Pope Benedict XVI—Prefect of the Congregation for the Doctrine of the Faith. Under his direction and acting with the authority of the pope, the Vatican

JOHN PAUL II AND HIS ASSASSIN

One the afternoon of May 13, 1981, Pope John Paul II was struck by three bullets while being driven in a slow-moving convertible through St. Peter's Square, where 20,000 people had gathered to see the pontiff. The pope later recalled that, immediately after his assassination attempt, he had a "strange feeling of confidence" he would live. Some see his survival as a miraculous event; his would-be assassin, an international terrorist wanted for murder in his native Turkey, was no amateur, and he had fired from point-blank range. The bullet that entered the pope missed his main abdominal artery by a mere fraction of an inch. According to the pope himself, "one hand fired, and another [Mary's] guided the bullet." The pope later publicly forgave his would-be assassin for his actions soon after the event.

Almost as remarkable was the meeting on December 27, 1983, between the pope and his would-be assassin, Mehmet Ali Agca. Photographs of this meeting show the two seated in the corner of Agca's cell. In this encounter, Agca explained to the pope his fears that Our Lady of Fatima was going to have her revenge on him for his assassination attempt. (The pope was shot on May 13, the anniversary of the apparition of Our Lady of Fatima, and Mary is venerated by many Muslims.) Agca believed that "the Goddess of Fatima" saved the pope and was now going to kill him. John Paul patiently listened to Agca's concerns, and finally explained to him that Mary was the Mother of God and loved all people, and that he should not be afraid.

Fifteen years after the shooting, Pope John Paul II met with the mother of Mehmet Ali Agca. Aided by the personal intervention of the pope, Agca was eventually pardoned for his crime and, in 2000, was extradited to Turkey, where he remains imprisoned for other crimes.

The remarkable meeting of Pope John Paul II and Mehmet Ali Agca in 1983. They spoke quietly in Italian for twenty minutes.

Mehmet Ali Agca asked Turkish authorities permission to attend the funeral of Pope John Paul II. The request was denied.

doctrinal office issued important statements on liberation theology, the ordination of women, homosexuality and homosexual unions, the duties of Catholic politicians and citizens, the unique role of Christ in salvation and the Catholic Church, and some other issues.

John Paul II brought to completion and in 1983 published the new Code of Canon Law for the Western Church, a project begun by Pope Bl. John XXIII in 1959. The new compilation of Church law had been thoroughly revised in light of Vatican II. Its innovations included giving far more attention than ever before to the duties and rights of lay people, with a whole section devoted to the members of the Church in general and the laity in particular. A first-ever Oriental Code of Canon Law for the Eastern Churches was published in 1990.

Pope John Paul II's principal collaborator in dealing with issues of faith and dissent was Cardinal Joseph Ratzinger, the future Pope Benedict XVI.

Responding to a suggestion at an extraordinary assembly of the Synod of Bishops, which he convoked in 1985 to examine the implementation of the Vatican II, Pope John Paul commissioned the first new universal catechism of Catholic doctrine since the sixteenth century. The *Catechism of the Catholic Church,* an up-to-date statement of Faith incorporating the teaching of Vatican II, appeared in 1992. Since then it has had a central role in efforts to establish uniform, solid, and reliable content for Catholic religious education.

John Paul II traveled frequently. His pastoral visits were more than simply occasions for outdoor Masses and colorful ceremonies that drew huge crowds. They were a key means by which he asserted the authority of the Bishop of Rome as universal pastor of the Church, in order to foster unity and bolster Catholics' Faith.

Seeking to draw the bishops more closely into the affairs of the universal Church in line with the doctrine of collegiality, John Paul II convoked numerous ordinary assemblies of the Synod of Bishops, as well as special synod assemblies. Among themes addressed were family life, priestly formation, and the situation of the Church region by region on the eve of the third millennium. The 1987 synod assembly, on the vocation and mission of the laity, led to the apostolic exhortation *Christifideles laici* (The Lay Members of Christ's Faithful People), published in 1988. It repeated and expanded the teaching of Vatican II on the dignity and rights of the laity and their call to apostolate and holiness.

In his 1995 encyclical *Ut unum sint* (That They May Be One), Pope John Paul expressed his openness to new initiatives in the search for Christian unity. While seeking warmer relations with Anglicans and Protestants, he concentrated especially on efforts at reunion with the Orthodox, calling Orthodoxy and Catholicism the twin "lungs" of the Church. He also opened diplomatic relations between the Holy See and Israel, denounced anti-Semitism, and encouraged unprecedented Catholic-Jewish rapport, while at the same time seeking dialogue with Islam and other world religions. He strove to close the gap between Faith and science and fostered what he called a "purification of memory" by apologizing for Catholics' historical failings in relation to events from the Crusades to the sixteenth century treatment of Galileo. Along with a willingness to innovate, John Paul II had strong traditional devotions, especially to the Blessed Virgin. In October 2002, he surprised many people by adding to the Rosary five new Luminous mysteries based on Jesus' public life.

Despite his age and declining health, as the new millennium got underway Pope John Paul continued to travel and to launch initiatives. Among the latter was the proclaiming of a 2004-2005 Year of the Eucharist for the entire Church. The public witness of his perseverance in the face of personal suffering was an inspiration to countless persons. Finally, on April 2, 2005, worn out by the debilitating effects of Parkinson's disease, he died in his apartment in the Apostolic Palace. He was 84.

A remarkable worldwide outpouring of grief and expressions of admiration greeted the news of death of a man universally recognized as one of the towering figures of modern times. American president George W. Bush called him "one of history's great moral leaders and a hero for the ages." Hundreds of world leaders—heads of state from Afghanistan to Zimbabwe—attended John Paul II's funeral on April 8, as did religious leaders such as the Orthodox Patriarch Bartholomew I of Constantinople, Anglican Archbishop Rowan Williams of Canterbury, heads of numerous Protestant bodies, and many representatives of Jewish, Muslim, Buddhist, Sikh, and Hindu groups.

While millions throughout the world watched on television, a crowd of an estimated 300,000 filled St. Peter's Square and the streets around the Vatican for the funeral Mass. Presiding and preaching the homily was Pope John Paul II's longtime collaborator, Joseph Cardinal Ratzinger. Recalling the title of the late Pope's next-to-last book, *Rise, Let Us Be On Our Way!,* he said:

> "Rise, let us be on our way!" with these words he roused us from a lethargic faith, from the sleep of the disciples of both yesterday and today. "Rise, let us be our way!" he continues to say to us even today. The Holy Father was a priest to the last, for he offered his life to God for his flock and for the entire human family, in a daily self-oblation for the service of the Church....Thanks to his being profoundly rooted in Christ, he was able to bear a burden which transcends merely human abilities: that of being the shepherd of Christ's flock, his universal Church.

The conclave to choose Pope John Paul II's successor opened on April 18 with one hundred fifteen of the eligible cardinal-electors taking part. On the second day, Tuesday, April 19, and fourth ballot, white smoke billowed from the chimney of the Sistine Chapel, signaling the election of a new pope. At 6:48 P. M., preceded by the cross, Pope Benedict XVI—the former Cardinal Ratzinger—stepped onto the balcony of St. Peter's, greeted the crowd, and gave his blessing *Urbi et orbi* (To the City and the World) as the 265th pontiff of the Catholic Church. He invited the faithful in Rome and throughout the world, "Let us move forward in the joy of the Risen Lord." A new pontificate had begun.

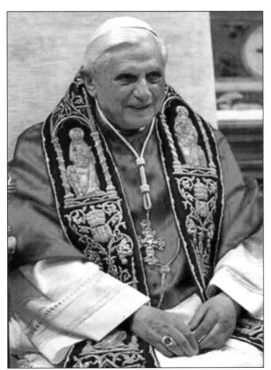

During the wake and funeral for the late Pope John Paul II, the crowds cried out, Santo subito! (A saint immediately!). Just eleven days into his pontificate, Pope Benedict XVI heeded their call, waiving the usual five-year waiting period and formally opening the cause for the beatification of John Paul II.

His Holiness Pope Benedict XVI (born in 1927 as Joseph Alois Ratzinger in Bavaria, Germany) is the 265th reigning pope. He was elected on April 19, 2005. He celebrated his Papal Inauguration Mass on April 24, 2005 and was enthroned in the Basilica di San Giovanni in Laterano on May 7, 2005.

One of the most influential academic theologians since the 1960s, Benedict XVI served as Archbishop of Munich, Prefect of the Congregation for the Doctrine of the Faith, and Dean of the College of Cardinals. He was a trusted friend and ally to Pope John Paul II.

CONCLUSION

Many of John Paul II's pastoral visits were made to local churches in Africa, Asia, and other parts of the developing world. He recognized that during the latter years of the twentieth century Catholicism and Christianity as a whole grew faster and displayed more vitality in countries of the Southern Hemisphere than anywhere else in the world.

Turn-of-the-century projections indicated that the number of Catholics in Europe was likely to decline between 2000 and 2025 (from 286 million to 276 million) and increase only slightly in the United States and Canada (from 71 million to 81 million). However, in Latin America the Catholic population would rise from 461 million to 606 million, in Africa from 120 million to 228 million, and in Asia from 110 million to 160 million. Already there were twice as many Catholics in metropolitan Manila as in the whole of the Netherlands. Sensitive to the southward shift in the Church's center of population gravity, the pope sought to respond to the growing opportunity—and need—it represented.

Despite this growth, however, the Church faced serious challenges as the twenty-first century began. Four stand out: the question of Islam, the new evangelization, the continuing crisis of dissent, and the culture of death.

Catholicism and Islam have had a frequently troubled relationship over the centuries. At times they have lived together peacefully, but often they have been in conflict, beginning in the seventh and eighth centuries with the Muslim conquest of the Middle East, North Africa, and much of Spain, and continuing through the Crusades and the repeated invasions of Europe by the Ottoman Turks. Lately militant Islam has made fresh attacks on Christians in a number of Asian and African countries. The challenge for the Church is to find a peaceful *modus vivendi* with Islam and avoid being drawn into the "clash of civilizations" about which students of history and international relations warn.

Pope John Paul called often for a "new evangelization" in formerly Christian regions—notably Western Europe—where faith and religious practice have declined in the face of affluence, pleasure-seeking, and the secularist mentality arising from the rationalism of eighteenth-century Enlightenment philosophy and the scientism of the nineteenth century. Only Christianity, he noted, has convincing, satisfying answers to perennial questions about life's meaning—"Who am I? Where have I come from and where am I going? Why is there evil? What is there after this life?" This human need for meaning provides the starting-point for renewal of faith.

Although conditions in the Church stabilized and improved under John Paul II, the crisis of dissent that began in the 1960s persisted, especially in Western Europe and North America. Neo-Modernism made deep inroads. The result in a number of countries was a catechetical collapse leading to ignorance of the Catholic tradition among many Catholics. Programs for implementing the *Catechism of the Catholic Church* have begun to address these problems within the context of the New Evangelization.

A deeply disturbing aspect of secularism in the twentieth century was the rise of the culture of death—a worldview and value system expressed in things like contraception, population control, and abortion. Moreover, other forces of evil were presented as progress: euthanasia, the acceptance of homosexual acts, human cloning, the destruction of nascent human life for the sake of scientific experimentation, embryonic stem-cell research, and the threat of large-scale warfare by nuclear, chemical, or other means. The Church supports genuine human rights and the progress of scientific knowledge at the service of human needs. However, it is necessary to distinguish true rights and legitimate advances from policies and practices based on utilitarian "ends-justify-the-means" reasoning.

Pope John Paul II said the essence of faith is not "a magic formula" but a Person—Jesus Christ.

In the face of these and other challenges now present or yet to come, however, the Church continues her pilgrimage through history with serenity and hope. In his apostolic letter *Novo millennio ineunte* (At the Beginning of the New Millennium), published January 6, 2001, as a kind of inaugural greeting to a new era, Pope John Paul II said the essence of faith is not "a magic formula" but a Person—Jesus Christ. "It is not therefore a matter of inventing a new 'program,'" added this highly innovative Pope.

> The program already exists: it is the plan found in the Gospel and in the living Tradition, it is the same as ever. Ultimately, it has its center in Christ himself...

SUPPLEMENTARY READING

Pope Bl. John XXIII, *Pacem in terris*, I-III

We must devote our attention first of all to that order which should prevail among men.

Any well-regulated and productive association of men in society demands the acceptance of one fundamental principle: that each individual man is truly a person. His is a nature, that is, endowed with intelligence and free will. As such he has rights and duties, which together flow as a direct consequence from his nature. These rights and duties are universal and inviolable, and therefore altogether inalienable.

When, furthermore, we consider man's personal dignity from the standpoint of divine revelation, inevitably our estimate of it is incomparably increased. Men have been ransomed by the blood of Jesus Christ. Grace has made them sons and friends of God, and heirs to eternal glory.

Vatican II, *Dei verbum*, November 18, 1965

Hearing the word of God with reverence and proclaiming it with faith, the sacred synod takes its direction from these words of St. John: "We announce to you the eternal life which dwelt with the Father and was made visible to us. What we have seen and heard we announce to you, so that you may have fellowship with us and our common fellowship be with the Father and His Son Jesus Christ" (1 John 1:2-3). Therefore, following in the footsteps of the Council of Trent and of the First Vatican Council, this present council wishes to set forth authentic doctrine on divine revelation and how it is handed on, so that by hearing the message of salvation the whole world may believe, by believing it may hope, and by hoping it may love.

Vatican II, *Apostolicam actuositatem*, November 18, 1965

The Church was founded for the purpose of spreading the kingdom of Christ throughout the earth for the glory of God the Father, to enable all men to share in His saving redemption, and that through them the whole world might enter into a relationship with Christ. All activity of the Mystical Body directed to the attainment of this goal is called the apostolate, which the Church carries on in various ways through all her members. For the Christian vocation by its very nature is also a vocation to the apostolate. No part of the structure of a living body is merely passive but has a share in the functions as well as life of the body: so, too, in the body of Christ, which is the Church, "the whole body...in keeping with the proper activity of each part, derives its increase from its own internal development" (Eph. 4: 16).

Indeed, the organic union in this body and the structure of the members are so compact that the member who fails to make his proper contribution to the development of the Church must be said to be useful neither to the Church nor to himself.

In the Church there is a diversity of ministry but a oneness of mission. Christ conferred on the Apostles and their successors the duty of teaching, sanctifying, and ruling in His name and power. But the laity likewise share in the priestly, prophetic, and royal office of Christ and therefore have their own share in the mission of the whole people of God in the Church and in the world.

They exercise the apostolate in fact by their activity directed to the evangelization and sanctification of men and to the penetrating and perfecting of the temporal order through the spirit of the Gospel. In this way, their temporal activity openly bears witness to Christ and promotes the salvation of men. Since the laity, in accordance with their state of life, live in the midst of the world and its concerns, they are called by God to exercise their apostolate in the world like leaven, with the ardor of the spirit of Christ.

John Paul II, Redemptor hominis, 7.1-7.2

While the ways on which the Council of this century has set the Church going, ways indicated by the late Paul VI in his first Encyclical, will continue to be for a long time the ways that all of us must follow, we can at the same time rightly ask at this new stage: How, in what manner should we continue? What should we do, in order that this new advent of the Church connected with the approaching end of the second millennium may bring us closer to Him whom Sacred Scripture calls "Everlasting Father," *Pater Futuri saeculi*? This is the fundamental question that the new pope must put to himself on

accepting in a spirit of obedience in faith the call corresponding to the command that Christ gave Peter several times: "Feed my lambs," meaning: Be the shepherd of my sheepfold and again: "And when you have turned again, strengthen your brethren." To this question dear brothers, sons and daughters, a fundamental and essential response must be given. Our response must be: Our spirit is set in one direction, the only direction for our intellect, will and heart is towards Christ our Redeemer, towards Christ, the Redeemer of man. We wish to look toward him—because there is salvation in no one else but him, the Son of God—repeating what Peter said: "Lord, to whom shall we go? You have the words of eternal life."

Pope John Paul II received Lech Walesa, leader of the anti-Communist Solidarity movement in Poland, at the Vatican in January 1981. John Paul's support of the Solidarity movement was a considerable force behind the collapse of Soviet domination in Poland.

VOCABULARY

CARETAKER POPE
Refers to an aged pope whom the College of Cardinals elects to serve as a pastoral figure who would make few changes. John XXXIII was elected as a caretaker pope but proved to be anything but.

CHURCH OF SILENCE
Refers to the Church under the communist Chinese totalitarian regime which produced many martyrs.

DOCTRINE OF COLLEGIALITY
Set out by the Dogmatic Constitution of the Church published by the Second Vatican Council, this states that bishops, in union with and under the pope, share in teaching and governing the Church.

HEDONISM
The erroneous belief that pleasure is the chief good in life.

NEW EVANGELIZATION
Called by Pope John Paul II, he hoped to reintroduce the Faith into formerly Christian regions—notably Western Europe—where religious practice had declined in the face of affluence, pleasure-seeking, and the secularistic mentality arising from the rationalism of eighteenth-century Enlightenment philosophy and the scientism of the nineteenth century.

OSTPOLITIK
Sometimes controversial Vatican policy which sought improved relations with the Communist regimes of Eastern Europe.

"John Paul's entire daily routine . . . was punctuated by prayer, not simply when he was in the chapel for Mass or the recitation of the Liturgy of the Hours (to which he attached great importance), but constantly—in between meetings, en route to audiences, in a car, in a helicopter, even on the roof. Paul VI had installed a solarium atop the Apostolic Palace, to which John Paul II added a set of modern stations of the cross. He prayed the stations every Friday during the year and every day during Lent. . . .Whatever the issue, he was, from the beginning, a man who made 'all his major decisions . . . on his knees before the Blessed Sacrament.' "—from *Witness To Hope* by George Weigel.

STUDY QUESTIONS

1. What are Bl. John XXIII's nicknames? Why does each apply?

2. What were the three most progressive and long-lasting changes made by Bl. John XXIII?

3. How were Bl. John XXIII's relations with the Jews?

4. What reasons did Bl. John XXIII give for calling the Second Vatican Council?

5. How long did Vatican II last? Where was it held?

6. What is *Lumen gentium*? Why was it significant?

7. What is *Dei verbum*? What Catholic teaching did it emphasize?

8. What does the document *Sacrosanctum concilium* discuss?

9. To what was the document *Gaudium et spes* written in response?

10. What pope was elected during Vatican II and saw it through to the end?

11. How did Paul VI help improve relations with the Eastern Orthodox Church?

12. What steps did Paul VI take to implement the teachings of Vatican II?

13. What was so significant about *Humanæ vitæ*?

14. What did the French Catholic philosopher Jacques Maritain say about the Catholic clergy in the twentieth century?

15. Who was "the smiling pope"?

16. At the time of John Paul II's election, how long had it been since a non-Italian was pope?

17. With what powerful words did John Paul II open his pontificate?

18. What did John Paul II's first encyclical, *Redemptor hominis,* emphasize as being the plan for his pontificate?

19. What two forms of secular humanism did John Paul II see as the biggest threat to Christianity in the modern world?

20. To what was John Paul II referring when he spoke of "the loss of Europe's Christian memory"?

21. Who was John Paul II's "right-hand man" on matters of faith and dissent?

22. What did John Paul II call the other "lung" of the Church?

PRACTICAL EXERCISES

1. Why did Bl. John XXIII call the Second Vatican Council? How did this council differ from others in the Church's history?

2. The 1960s and 1970s were a time of worldwide social change. Drawing from your knowledge of Church history, describe how those changes may have affected the Church had the Second Vatican Council not occurred.

3. How did John Paul II change the way the world saw the papacy? Choose a pope from the Church's history that you believe was similar to John Paul II. In what ways were their papacies similar? How did they differ in their understanding of the papacy? What do their similarities and differences say about the role of the Church in the world?

FROM THE CATECHISM

2127 Agnosticism assumes a number of forms. In certain cases the agnostic refrains from denying God; instead he postulates the existence of a transcendent being which is incapable of revealing itself, and about which nothing can be said. In other cases, the agnostic makes no judgment about God's existence, declaring it impossible to prove, or even to affirm or deny.

2128 Agnosticism can sometimes include a certain search for God, but it can equally express indifferentism, a flight from the ultimate question of existence, and a sluggish moral conscience. Agnosticism is all too often equivalent to practical atheism.

2304 Respect for and development of human life require peace. Peace is not merely the absence of war, and it is not limited to maintaining a balance of powers between adversaries. Peace cannot be attained on earth without safeguarding the goods of persons, free communication among men, respect for the dignity of persons and peoples, and the assiduous practice of fraternity. Peace is "the tranquillity of order" (St. Augustine, *De civ. Dei*, 19, 13, 1: PL 41, 640). Peace is the work of justice and the effect of charity (cf. Is 32:17; cf. *GS* 78 §§ 1-2).

2316 The *production and the sale of arms* affect the common good of nations and of the international community. Hence public authorities have the right and duty to regulate them. The short-term pursuit of private or collective interests cannot legitimate undertakings that promote violence and conflict among nations and compromise the international juridical order.

2364 The married couple forms "the intimate partnership of life and love established by the Creator and governed by his laws; it is rooted in the conjugal covenant, that is, in their irrevocable personal consent" (*GS* 48 § 1). Both give themselves definitively and totally to one another. They are no longer two; from now on they form one flesh. The covenant they freely contracted imposes on the spouses the obligation to preserve it as unique and indissoluble (cf. CIC, can. 1056). "What therefore God has joined together, let not man put asunder" (Mk 10:9; cf. Mt 19:1-12; 1 Cor 7:10-11).

2373 Sacred Scripture and the Church's traditional practice see in *large families* a sign of God's blessing and the parents' generosity (cf. *GS* 50 § 2).

2378 A child is not something owed to one, but is a gift. The "supreme gift of marriage" is a human person. A child may not be considered a piece of property, an idea to which an alleged "right to a child" would lead. In this area, only the child possesses genuine rights: the right "to be the fruit of the specific act of the conjugal love of his parents," and "the right to be respected as a person from the moment of his conception" (CDF, *Donum vitæ* II, 8).

In Krakow, Poland, one million faithful dressed in white prayed for the recovery of Pope John Paul II after the assassination attempt.

CHAPTER 27

The Church In The United States

Secularist hostility to religion and traditional morality is still central to the American culture war. American Catholics still need to define what it means to be both Catholic and American.

CHAPTER 21

The Church In The United States

[W]e are not able to give approval to those views which, in their collective sense, are called by some "Americanism."...For it would give rise to the suspicion that there are among you some who conceive and would have the Church in America to be different from what it is in the rest of the world.

— Pope Leo XIII, *Testem benevolentiæ*, January 22, 1899

Pope Leo XIII's apostolic letter in 1899 containing the words above also contained warm praise for the Church in the United States, but it pulled no punches in condemning "Americanism." Those who received Pope Leo's *Testem benevolentiæ* (Expression of Good Will) at the time, such as the prominent American churchmen James Cardinal Gibbons of Baltimore and Archbishop John Ireland of St. Paul, insisted they held no such views as those condemned by the pope. Nevertheless, his condemnation raises an important debate within the Catholic Church in America about which historians still argue.

Were the ideas described by Pope Leo XIII under the heading Americanism—about themes like passive and active virtues, the best form of the religious life, and the correct approach to evangelization—a real factor in American Catholicism at the turn of the twentieth century? The immediate cause of the Pope's concern appears to have been the French edition of a biography of Father Isaac Hecker, founder of the American religious community the Paulists, and, in particular, the introduction written by a French priest. If so, was Americanism a genuine threat or, as one critic claimed, a "phantom heresy"?

These questions about a particular episode are no closer to being resolved today than they were in the time of Leo XIII, Cardinal Gibbons, and Archbishop Ireland. Meanwhile, the underlying, central issue was, and remains, this: How far can the integration of Catholics and Catholicism into American secular culture go without weakening the Catholic Faith and Catholic religious identity?

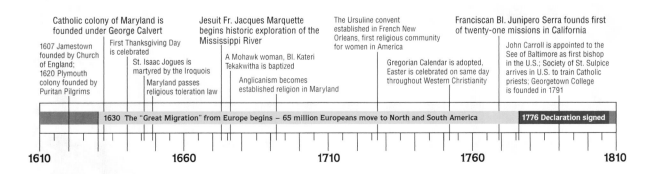

Catholic colony of Maryland is founded under George Calvert

Jesuit Fr. Jacques Marquette begins historic exploration of the Mississippi River

The Ursuline convent established in French New Orleans, first religious community for women in America

Franciscan Bl. Junipero Serra founds first of twenty-one missions in California

1607 Jamestown founded by Church of England; 1620 Plymouth colony founded by Puritan Pilgrims

First Thanksgiving Day is celebrated

St. Isaac Jogues is martyred by the Iroquois

Maryland passes religious toleration law

A Mohawk woman, Bl. Kateri Tekakwitha is baptized

Anglicanism becomes established religion in Maryland

Gregorian Calendar is adopted, Easter is celebrated on same day throughout Western Christianity

John Carroll is appointed to the See of Baltimore as first bishop in the U.S.; Society of St. Sulpice arrives in U.S. to train Catholic priests; Georgetown College is founded in 1791

1630 The "Great Migration" from Europe begins – 65 million Europeans move to North and South America

1776 Declaration signed

1610   1660   1710   1760   1810

This question has been central to Catholicism in the United States for two centuries. It is central to the experience of being Catholic in America today.

American Catholics have been richly blessed. Today they make up one of the best-educated and most affluent groups in the country. Catholic dioceses, parishes, schools, and other institutions and programs present a remarkable picture of institutional development. Catholics in the United States are far more regular in the practice of their religion than Catholics in many other Western countries. Still, the need to hammer out an identity both fully American and authentically Catholic not only persists but is growing more urgent.

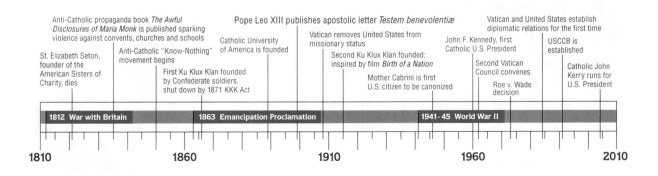

St. Elizabeth Seton, founder of the American Sisters of Charity, dies

Anti-Catholic propaganda book *The Awful Disclosures of Maria Monk* is published sparking violence against convents, churches and schools

Anti-Catholic "Know-Nothing" movement begins

First Ku Klux Klan founded by Confederate soldiers, shut down by 1871 KKK Act

Catholic University of America is founded

Pope Leo XIII publishes apostolic letter *Testem benevolentiæ*

Vatican removes United States from missionary status

Second Ku Klux Klan founded; inspired by film *Birth of a Nation*

Mother Cabrini is first U.S. citizen to be canonized

John F. Kennedy, first Catholic U.S. President

Second Vatican Council convenes

Roe v. Wade decision

Vatican and United States establish diplomatic relations for the first time

USCCB is established

Catholic John Kerry runs for U.S. President

1812 War with Britain

1863 Emancipation Proclamation

1941-45 World War II

1810   1860   1910   1960   2010

PART I
The Colonial Era

Before the founding of the United States, "Catholic identity" was not an issue. The Spanish and French explorers, conquerors, and colonizers who came to the New World starting in the sixteenth century were Catholics. Accompanying them were priests—Jesuits, Dominicans, Franciscans—who provided them with pastoral care and worked to convert the native peoples to Christianity.

These missionaries preached the gospel with great courage and dedication. Outstanding figures included the Franciscan Juan Padilla, Servant of God, martyred by Indians in Kansas around 1540, and six French Jesuit priests and two lay assistants, known as the North American Martyrs, who were killed by the Iroquois between 1642 and 1649 in parts of what are now northern New York and Ontario. These latter were canonized by Pope Pius XI in 1930.

Called "The Lily of the Mohawks."
Bl. Kateri Tekakwitha (1656-1680) was the daughter of a Mohawk warrior and a Christian Algonquin woman. Bl. Tekakwitha was converted in 1676 and received instruction from Fr. Jacques de Lamberville, a Jesuit. At her baptism, she took the name "Kateri," a Mohawk pronunciation of "Catherine." This image of Bl. Kateri Tekakwitha painted after her death by Fr. Claude Chauchetiere, a missionary priest at Sault Saint-Louis where she spent her final years. He was inspired to paint the portrait after having a radiant vision of Bl. Kateri. It hangs at the Saint Francis Xavier Mission at Kahnawake, Quebec.

Probably the best known of these heroic martyrs was the Jesuit priest St. Isaac Jogues who died in 1646. An account of his final days calls the opportunity to convert the Indians "the bond of his captivity," explaining: "He would have escaped a hundred times if providence had not checked him, by offering him…the means of opening the gates of paradise to some poor soul" (quoted in "The Jesuit Relations: The Sufferings and Martyrdom of Isaac Jogues, S.J." *Readings in Church History*, ed. Barry, 1985, pp. 812-813). Others like the Spanish Franciscan priest Bl. Junipero Serra devoted their lives to the spiritual and temporal advancement of the native peoples. Starting in 1769, Father Serra founded nine of the twenty-one Franciscan missions in present-day California and was president of the missions until his death in 1784. He was beatified by Pope John Paul II in 1988; his feast day is celebrated on July 1.

Thanks to the zeal of such missionaries, many Indians did become Christians—for example, Bl. Kateri Tekakwitha, a young Mohawk woman who was baptized in 1676 and died four years later at the age of twenty-four; she was beatified in 1980; her feast day is celebrated on July 14.

The early presence of Catholicism in parts of what is now the United States has left its mark on many parts of the country. Founded by the Spanish in 1565, the city of St. Augustine in Florida was the first permanent settlement in the United States and the site of the first parish, established the same year. The French Jesuit Jacques Marquette accompanied Louis Joliet on his historic exploratory voyage down the Mississippi River in 1673. Other missionaries also played important roles in opening up and developing the Southeast and Southwest.

By contrast, in the English colonies on the Eastern seaboard, Catholics were generally excluded by penal law. The exceptions to this exclusion were Quaker Pennsylvania and, especially, Maryland, which was granted to George Calvert (Lord Baltimore) in 1632 and settled by Catholics and Protestants in 1634. Two Jesuits, Andrew White and John Altham, accompanied the first settlers and, besides serving the settlers' spiritual needs, began to evangelize the Indians.

In 1649 Maryland's General Assembly adopted an unprecedented act of religious toleration providing that, for the sake of "quiet and peaceable government" and "mutual love and unity among the inhabitants," no Christian in Maryland was to be "troubled, molested, or discountenanced" for his or her faith or forced to practice another religion. Except for a four-year interval of Puritan control, religious toleration remained the rule until 1688, when Maryland was made a crown colony. In 1692 Anglicanism became the established religion in the English colony.

PART II

Catholicism and the Birth of a Nation

For abolishing the free system of English laws in a neighboring province, establishing therein an arbitrary government, and enlarging its boundaries so as to render it at once an example and fit instrument for introducing the same absolute rule in these colonies.
— A reason for colonialist revolt as listed in the Declaration of Independence

In 1774 the British Parliament adopted the Quebec Act, which extended political and legal concessions to the French Colonists of Quebec and also granted them religious freedom. This act of Parliament, the latest to enrage the colonists, was eventually listed in the *Declaration of Independence* as one of the many misdeeds of King George III that gave just reason for revolt. Americans viewed the Quebec Act of 1774 as another of the "Intolerable Acts" passed by Parliament over her colonies in North America. Roman Catholic colonists generally sided against the British. One of the wealthiest persons in the colonies, Charles Carroll of Carrollton, spent his entire fortune on the American cause for independence. He served in the Continental Congress and was among those who signed the *Declaration of Independence.* Such signators were automatically branded as traitors by the British government, subject (if captured) to execution and the confiscation of all their properties. Maryland and Pennsylvania Catholics also served in the Continental Army.

THE REVOLUTIONARY YEARS (1775-1783)

Catholics, few though they were, played a considerable role in the new country's emergence. Charles Carroll of Maryland was among the signers of the *Declaration of Independence,* and he and his cousin, Father John Carroll, accompanied an official delegation sent to Canada by the Continental Congress to secure Canadian neutrality in the Revolution. In the war itself, as many as fifty percent of George Washington's troops had Irish surnames, although certainly some number of these men were not Catholics. Catholic officers from abroad, like the French Lafayette and the Polish Pulaski and Kosciusko, served with Washington. John Barry, an Irish Catholic and commander of the first ship commissioned by Congress, is regarded as the "Father of

Commodore John Barry, USN, (1745-1803), an Irish Catholic, was commander of the first ship commissioned by Congress after the Revolutionary War, the frigate *United States.* The U.S. Navy has named four destroyers in honor of him. He is the "Father of the American Navy."

the American Navy." Catholic France provided crucial military and naval support, and Catholic Spain helped with money and neutrality. Two Catholics—Daniel Carroll of Maryland and Thomas FitzSimmons of Philadelphia—were signers of the U.S. Constitution.

In a letter to Catholics after the war, Washington spoke of their "patriotic part" in the Revolution and of the "important assistance" received from a nation—France—"in which the Roman Catholic faith is professed." The First Amendment to the U.S. Constitution rejected the idea of an established national church and guaranteed the right of free exercise of religion.

THE POST-REVOLUTIONARY PERIOD

At the close of the Revolution there were about 25,000 Catholics, mostly in Maryland and Pennsylvania, out of a total population of four million. They were served by twenty-four priests. Father Carroll was named "Superior of the Mission in the Thirteen United States" on June 9, 1784. In 1789 Baltimore was designated the first diocese of the new country, and Father Carroll was named its bishop after a vote by the priests. (This was the first and only time a bishop was appointed by vote.). At its founding, the territory of the Diocese of Baltimore covered all thirteen states.

Soon a number of Catholic institutions were founded in the United States. Georgetown University, the oldest Catholic institution of higher learning in the United States, dates its origin to 1789. The first seminary, St. Mary's in Baltimore, was established in 1791. The first Catholic women's school was founded by Visitation nuns in Washington, D.C., in 1799. In 1808 the Diocese of Baltimore became an archdiocese with Bishop Carroll as its archbishop, and four new dioceses were created: Boston; New York; Philadelphia; and Bardstown, Kentucky (now the Archdiocese of Louisville). Then, and for the century that followed, the United States was considered a missionary territory, and the Church was supervised closely by the Holy See.

Bishop St. John Neumann and St. Elizabeth Ann Seton were pioneers in the parochial school movement.

The first half of the nineteenth century saw a number of outstanding figures in American Catholicism. St. Elizabeth Ann Seton (1774-1821), a convert from Episcopalianism and widowed mother of five, began the Sisters of Charity in the United States and was canonized in 1975. Her feast day is celebrated on January 4. The French-born St. Rose Philippine Duchesne (1769-1852) established the first U.S. convent of the Religious of the Sacred Heart in Missouri in 1818 and was canonized in 1988. Her feast day is celebrated on November 18. Bishop St. John Neumann (1811-1860), a native of Bohemia, was the fourth Bishop of Philadelphia and was canonized in 1977. His feast day is celebrated on January 5. Mother Seton and Bishop Neumann were pioneers in the parochial school movement, which was to become one of the outstanding features of the Church in the United States. Fr. Michael J. McGivney founded the Knights of Columbus in 1882. The Knights are Catholic men who work to make their communities better places while enhancing their faith.

THE CARROLL FAMILY AND THE FOUNDING OF THE UNITED STATES

John Carroll was probably the most influential Catholic figure in the establishment of the Church in America. Appointed the first bishop in this country, he faced the difficult task of finding a place for the Faith in a new political order, a task most agree he handled with great skill. In addition to his own contributions during the American Revolution, other members of the Carroll family played prominent roles: his brother Daniel was one of two Catholic signers of the 1787 Constitution, and his cousin Charles Carroll, a signer of the Declaration of Independence.

Born in 1735, John received his education from the Jesuits at Bohemia Manor in Maryland. Because there were no schools for the training of seminarians in the colonies during this time, he went to St. Omer's College in French Flanders to continue his education. He entered the Society of Jesus in 1753, and after studying in Liege was ordained in 1769. After the suppression of the Jesuit order in Europe, he returned to America in 1774, only one year before the onset of the Revolutionary War.

In 1776 a committee composed of Benjamin Franklin, Samuel Chase, and Charles Carroll of Carrollton was elected by the Continental Congress to be sent to Canada to ask for their neutrality during the war. By a special resolution, John Carroll was asked to accompany this committee to "assist them in such matters as they shall think useful." He accepted this task, and spent the winter in Canada. While there he developed a close friendship with Benjamin Franklin, earning his admiration and respect.

Archbishop John Carroll painted by the most famous portrait artist of the American Revolution period, Gilbert Stuart.

Partly due to the recommendation of Benjamin Franklin, on June 9, 1784 the papal nuncio established Father Carroll as the Superior of the Mission in the Thirteen United States. He became the first bishop of Baltimore in 1790, his diocese covering the whole of the United States. As bishop he dealt with all the major issues of his time, including the controversy over lay trustees. Under his watch the U.S. Catholic population grew from 25,000 to 200,000. The influence of John Carroll over his fellow Americans cannot be overstated. For example, the four states that adopted constitutions allowing Catholics complete equality with other citizens (Pennsylvania, Delaware, Virginia, and Maryland) were all located nearest to Father (later Archbishop) John Carroll's area of ministry.

PART III
A Church of Immigrants

Massive Catholic immigration from Europe to the United States began early in the nineteenth century and continued well into the twentieth century. The newcomers were attracted by the promise of work, land, and religious and political freedom. Of the nearly three million Catholic migrants who came between 1830 and 1870, most came from Ireland, Germany, and France. The 1880s saw more than one million additional Catholic immigrants, with Catholics from Eastern and Southern Europe—Poles, Slovaks, Ukrainians, Italians, and others—joining the influx. These immigrants quickly fanned out from the East to many other parts of the expanding nation, so much so that new cities like Chicago, Milwaukee, and St. Louis became important Catholic population centers.

Due to immigration and higher birth rates, the growth of American Catholicism was remarkably rapid. Church leaders made heroic efforts to provide personnel and parishes, schools, convents, and other institutions to keep up with the expansion. By 1840, there were fifteen American dioceses and 663,000 American Catholics served by 500 priests, many of them foreign-born. The Catholic Church was the largest religious body in the country by about the 1860s.

LAY TRUSTEEISM

The closing years of the eighteenth and early decades of the nineteenth centuries witnessed bitter controversies over a system of church governance called lay trusteeism.

Partly to conform to American civil law, partly out of enthusiasm for democracy, and partly in imitation of the congregational system in American Protestantism, laymen became the owners of parish property, administered parish affairs, and in some places began hiring their own pastors in defiance of the bishop. Conflict over lay trusteeism was particularly heated in Philadelphia, but there also were problems in New York, Baltimore, Buffalo, New Orleans, and Charleston.

In Charleston, South Carolina, Irish-born Bishop John England dealt with the situation by adopting a diocesan constitution that allowed laymen to participate in the governance of the diocese through annual diocesan conventions. The system worked well until Bishop England's death in 1842. Elsewhere bishops took stern steps to stamp out the trustee movement. The conflict continued for years, and attitudes forged in this struggle negatively influenced clergy-laity relations. The controversy was definitively ended with the promulgation of the Code of Canon Law of 1917, placing all parishes and properties incontestably under the control of the bishop.

THE RISE OF ANTI-CATHOLICISM

Although the United States government is committed by its Constitution to religious toleration, starting in the 1830s Catholic immigration and rapid Catholic population growth were greeted by the rise of anti-Catholic Nativism.

Aiding the popularity of this anti-Catholic sentiment, *The Awful Disclosures of Maria Monk*, a book full of lurid tales of convent life, was published in 1835, and it became a best-seller second only to the Bible in American religious publishing history. Purporting to be the work of an ex-nun, it was written by Protestant ministers. The book helped fuel anti-Catholic violence throughout the United States. The year before it was published, an Ursuline convent in Charlestown, Massachusetts was attacked and burned by a mob. In 1844, thirteen people were killed, and two churches and a school

President Grover Cleveland joined the celebration dedicating the Statue of Liberty in New York Harbor on October 28, 1886.
Built on a colossal scale, the statue has become one of the most potent symbols of human freedom and is an icon to immigrants
coming to America. "Liberty Enlightening the World," was a gift from the people of France to the people of the United States.
Conceived by the French sculptor Frédéric de Bartholdi, it celebrated a century of friendship between the two Republics.

IN THIS TEMPLE
AS IN THE HEARTS OF THE PEOPLE
FOR WHOM HE SAVED THE UNION
THE MEMORY OF ABRAHAM LINCOLN
IS ENSHRINED FOREVER

The Lincoln Memorial in Washington D.C.– By 1860, there were 4.5 million slaves in the United States. Two major milestones marked slavery's final abolition during the war years: the Emancipation Proclamation and the Thirteenth Amendment to the Constitution. President Abraham Lincoln issued the Emancipation Proclamation on January 1, 1863, declaring that "all persons held as slaves . . . are and henceforward shall be free." Of the over four million slaves emancipated in 1863, an estimated one hundred thousand were Catholics.

were burned in Nativist riots in Philadelphia. The 1850s brought the Know-Nothing movement (so named because members were instructed to say they knew nothing about its activities), which sought to exclude foreigners and Catholics from public office. Abraham Lincoln remarked to a friend that if the Know-Nothings got power, the *Declaration of Independence* would have to be rewritten to read, "All men are created equal except negroes, foreigners, and Catholics."

The Know-Nothings were a significant political force until about 1860. Catholic political strength also grew during these years, especially in urban areas of the East and Midwest where the Irish proved skillful at political organization. However, anti-Catholicism remained a factor in American life throughout the rest of the century and much of the century that followed. Other noteworthy anti-Catholic groups included the virulently hostile American Protective Association, founded in 1887, and the Ku Klux Klan, which was also anti-black and anti-Jewish. In a famous incident in 1884, a Republican campaign speaker's attack on the Democrats as the party of "Rum, Romanism, and Rebellion" (in other words — anti-prohibitionism, Catholicism, and the old Confederacy) tipped the election in favor of the Democratic presidential candidate, Grover Cleveland.

SLAVERY AND THE CIVIL WAR

Although Pope Gregory XVI had condemned the slave trade in 1839, Catholic leadership in the United States, preoccupied with the problems of an immigrant community, had little to say about the issue. In fact, many Catholics, especially in the South, supported the legal institution of slavery. None of the Boston abolitionists was Catholic, and many abolitionists were actively hostile to the Church. Significantly, one of the characters in *Uncle Tom's Cabin,* the enormously popular and influential anti-slavery novel by Harriet Beecher Stowe, is a Catholic slave owner. The author's family had been openly and unapologetically anti-Catholic for years.

Large numbers of Catholics fought on both sides in the Civil War. More than twenty Union generals and eleven Confederate generals were Catholics. Forty Catholic chaplains served the Union forces and twenty-eight served the soldiers of the Confederacy. Hundreds of Catholic religious women also ministered to the wounded and sick. In Boston, the Pennsylvania coal region, and New York, however, Irish Catholics resisted the military draft, and draft riots in New York claimed 105 lives.

Of the four million slaves emancipated in 1863, an estimated 100,000 were Catholics, about 60,000 of those in New Orleans. In 1866 the Second Plenary Council of Baltimore adopted measures for their pastoral care, but unfortunately, like most other public and private schools and other institutions in the United States, Catholic parishes and schools in both the North and the South remained largely segregated by race until the middle years of the next century.

Elizabeth "Mumbet" Freeman. In states where slaves were considered persons before the law, they sued for, and sometimes won, their freedom in the courts. Elizabeth Freeman achieved freedom after petitioning the State of Massachusetts in 1781. "Anytime while I was a slave," she said, "if one minute's freedom had been offered to me, and I had been told I must die at the end of that minute, I would have taken it — just to stand one minute . . . on God's airth a free woman. I would."

— Massachusetts Historical Society, Boston

PART IV
Growth and Conflict

American Catholicism continued its remarkable expansion after the Civil War, with dioceses, parishes, educational institutions at all levels, hospitals, and other organizations and programs multiplying rapidly.

From 1829 to 1849, the bishops had addressed the needs of the growing Catholic community in a series of decision-making assemblies called provincial councils. (At the time, the country had only one ecclesiastical "province"—the Archdiocese of Baltimore—under which were the other dioceses). The provincial councils were followed in 1852, 1866, and 1884 by plenary councils, also held in Baltimore, which legislated for the needs of the expanding Church. The Third Plenary Council, the best known of these gatherings, took steps that led to the writing of the famous Baltimore Catechism, the normative text for Catholic religious education in the United States for some seventy-five years, and the founding of the Catholic University of America in Washington, D.C.

The major figures in American Catholicism in these decades included two who came to represent the opposing sides of the debate then taking shape over Catholic cultural assimilation: Isaac Hecker and Orestes Brownson.

Isaac T. Hecker (1819-1888) was a convert to Catholicism who first became a Redemptorist priest, then founded a new religious community, the Missionary Priests of St. Paul the Apostle (Paulists), committed to the conversion of Protestant America. In order to evangelize effectively, Hecker argued, the Church in the United States had to be fully and unreservedly American. Speaking to the bishops at the plenary council of 1866, he said:

> Here, thanks to the American Constitution, the Church is free to do her divine work. Here, she finds a civilization in harmony with her divine teachings. Here, Christianity is promised a reception from an intelligent and free people, that will give forth a development of unprecedented glory.

Apparently it was the French edition of a biography of Father Hecker by one of his Paulist disciples, and especially its introduction by a French priest, that prompted Pope Leo XIII to condemn "Americanism" in his apostolic letter *Testem benevolentiæ*.

Orestes Brownson converted to Catholicism in 1844. As a Catholic, he was politically conservative and repudiated his earlier ideas of socialism and utopianism. His 1857 memoir is titled *The Convert*.

Orestes Brownson (1803-1876), the leading Catholic intellectual of his day, had been part of the New England philosophical and religious movement called Transcendentalism before becoming a Catholic in 1844, the same year as his friend Hecker. A writer and social critic, he was editor of a periodical called *Brownson's Quarterly Review*.

Brownson at first shared Hecker's views about the need to "Americanize" Catholicism, but the Civil War shook his faith in American democracy, and as he grew older, he became increasingly skeptical that the secular culture of the United States could provide a congenial environment for the Church. Brownson, one historian remarked, "wanted to be fully Catholic, and he wanted to

President Teddy Roosevelt said to James Cardinal Gibbons, "Taking your life as a whole I think you now occupy the position of being the most respected and venerated and useful citizen of our country." In 1869, then Bishop Gibbons went to Rome as the youngest prelate at the First Vatican Council. As Archbishop he succeeded to the see of Baltimore in 1877, and was made a Cardinal in 1886. In his long episcopacy, he played an important role in improving Church-State relations, integrated great waves of immigrants into American society, defended the poor, preached morality, coped with the turbulence of World War I, and championed the rights of labor.

remain fully American, and it was becoming more and more difficult to be both" (quoted in O'Brien, *Public Catholicism,* 1989, p. 60).

The two leading figures in the hierarchy in this era—Cardinal Gibbons of Baltimore (1834-1921) and Archbishop Ireland of St. Paul (1838-1918)—were "Americanizers" who favored the full and rapid integration of Catholicism and Catholics into the surrounding culture. Speaking in France in 1892, Ireland declared his ardent patriotism as a Catholic American:

> By word and act we prove that we are patriots of patriots. Our hearts always beat with love for the republic. Our tongues are always eloquent in celebrating her praises. Our hands are always uplifted to bless her banners and her soldiers.

Others were not so sure rapid Americanization was a good idea. German Catholics in particular favored a slower approach that would allow immigrants to retain their own language and their German Catholic culture; they sought the appointment of German bishops in proportion to the number of Germans in the Catholic population and backed the establishment of German parishes. The argument came to a head over "Cahenslyism." This was a movement taking its name from Peter Paul Cahensly, a German layman who became alarmed about the spiritual state of the immigrants and petitioned Pope Leo XIII on their behalf.

Although it was often said that Pope Leo's *Testem benevolentiæ* spoke of problems that were non-existent in American Catholicism, conflicts and controversies like these undoubtedly provided at least part of the background for the pope's rejection of Americanism. Among the central tenets of this error, he said, was this:

> in order to more easily attract those who differ from her, the Church should shape her teachings more in accord with the spirit of the age and relax some of her ancient severity and make some concessions to new opinions. Many think that these concessions should be made... in regard to doctrines which belong to the deposit of the faith.

The pope, of course, thought this would not be a good idea. The Americanizers also insisted they wanted nothing of the sort.

THE LABOR MOVEMENT
AND THE SPANISH-AMERICAN WAR

Another difficult issue for the Church in these years concerned the emergence of the organized labor movement, a development marked by conflict and occasional violence. Catholic leaders like Cardinal Gibbons were anxious for the Church to remain on good terms with organized labor, lest Catholic workingmen be alienated and lost to the Church.

Thus Gibbons campaigned hard to keep the Vatican from forbidding Catholic membership in an early group called the Knights of Labor, which some people regarded as a forbidden secret society. The Cardinal's successful efforts are thought to have been one contribution to the thinking that led to Pope Leo XIII's encyclical *Rerum novarum* (1891), the landmark statement of Catholic social doctrine.

Cardinal Gibbons and Archbishop Ireland also worked behind the scenes to head off the Spanish-American war, with Ireland acting as a channel for the Holy See to communicate with the American government in hopes of preventing the United States and a European Catholic nation from going to war. When war came, nevertheless, they and American Catholics generally supported it.

Other milestones that marked the maturing of American Catholicism included the establishment of an Apostolic Delegation in the United States in 1893 and the Vatican's action formally removing the Church in the U.S. from missionary status in 1908. However, diplomatic relations between the Holy See and the United States were not established until 1984 due to anti-Catholic sentiment, and even then required congressional action to reverse a ban first enacted in 1867.

PART V

The Twentieth Century

By the year 1900, Catholics in the United States numbered 12,000,000 out of a total population of 76,000,000. They lived in eighty-two dioceses and were served by 12,000 priests and many thousands of religious men and women who staffed a large and growing network of Catholic schools and other institutions. Catholic immigration remained high. One notable figure of this era was the Italian-born St Frances Xavier Cabrini (1850-1917). Mother Cabrini founded the Missionary Sisters of the Sacred Heart, who worked among Italian immigrants in Chicago and other cities. She became an American citizen in 1909 and, in 1946, became the first U.S. citizen to be canonized. Her feast day is celebrated on November 13.

THE GREAT WAR AND YEARS OF DEPRESSION

During World War I, American Catholics in large numbers once again fought for their country. During the war, the bishops took the important step of establishing a new organization—the National Catholic War Council—to coordinate programs for military personnel. After the war, despite opposition from bishops concerned about possible interference in diocesan affairs and initial reservations on the Vatican's part, the hierarchy continued the organization, now renamed the National Catholic Welfare Conference. The NCWC was the bishops' vehicle for cooperative national-level action in social action, education and youth work, communications, and other fields.

Irish Catholic Al Smith (1873-1944) was Governor of New York and a U.S. presidential candidate in 1928.

Founder of the Catholic Worker Movement in 1933, Dorothy Day (1897-1980) was a social activist for the homeless and impoverished.

In the early 1950s, Bishop Fulton Sheen (1895-1979) became the first significant television preacher. Sheen's program *Life Is Worth Living* was highly regarded and received an Emmy award. Sheen remained on television until 1968. His programs can still be seen on EWTN.

In 1919 the bishops published their famous Program of Social Reconstruction, a postwar plan for the nation that advocated economic and social measures well ahead of their time. The document was largely the work of Msgr. John A. Ryan (1869-1945), a priest who served for years on the NCWC staff; he came to be known as "Monsignor New Dealer" for his support of President Franklin D. Roosevelt's Depression-era policies.

During the 1920s and 1930s, many Catholic organizations and movements were established to reflect the Catholic Action movement championed by Pope Pius XI to encourage lay involvement in social and political activity. The Liturgical Movement for renewal of the liturgy also became an important presence among American Catholics during these years.

In 1928 the Democratic Party nominated former New York governor Al Smith as its candidate for president. It was the first time a Catholic had run for the nation's highest office. There was little chance of any Democrat being elected president that year, but Smith's candidacy occasioned a resurgence of anti-Catholicism, and he lost badly.

With the Great Depression and the New Deal in the 1930s, Catholics swung more strongly than ever behind the Democrats. There also was another Catholic response to the economic and social crisis — the Catholic Worker movement, founded by Dorothy Day and Peter Maurin. The Catholic Worker movement was a sometimes controversial group committed to a radical brand of Catholicism that advocated social justice, aid to the poor, and pacifism. Although never large in numbers, the Catholic Worker movement helped shape the attitudes of many Catholic intellectuals and activists.

WORLD WAR II AND AFTER

When the United States entered World War II in 1941, many American Catholics again responded with patriotic fervor, though some Italians and Germans refused to fight their old-countrymen. With the return of peace, fervent anti-Communism, intensified by the Soviet-backed Communist takeover in Eastern Europe and the persecution of the Catholic Church there, soon put Catholics at the forefront of the national mobilization during the Cold War. Catholics also served in large numbers in the Korean War (1950-1953), fought by the U.S. and its allies under United Nations auspices to repel Communist aggression from Communist Red China and North Korea.

Meanwhile the Church in the United States was experiencing profound changes because of postwar socio-economic developments. Catholics flocked to college with the assistance of the GI Bill, a government program that paid military veterans' education costs. More education and increased prosperity fostered Catholics' upward mobility and accelerated their entry into the social mainstream. A vast movement of population—out of old inner-city ethnic neighborhoods, often focused on parish churches, into booming new suburbs—led Catholics to mix and mingle more freely than ever before with people of diverse religious and ethnic backgrounds.

In these years, too, churchmen like Francis Cardinal Spellman, the powerful Archbishop of New York; the convert and author turned Trappist monk, Thomas Merton; television preacher Bishop Fulton Sheen; and Church-state theologian John Courtney Murray, S.J., became national figures. Catholic personalities and Catholic themes were featured in popular films and other media. Catholic numbers continued to grow rapidly, and Catholic schools at all levels expanded dramatically. Catholicism was on its way to becoming a dominant force in shaping American culture. A rise in anti-Catholicism was one predictable result, reflected in the book *American Freedom and Catholic Power* (1949) by writer Paul Blanshard.

Against this background, the election in 1960 of Massachusetts Senator John F. Kennedy as the first Catholic President of the United States was a watershed event—a definitive defeat for anti-Catholicism. On the other hand, it came at a price. During the campaign, Kennedy gave a famous speech to Protestant ministers in Houston, Texas, assuring them that, if elected, he would not let his religion influence his performance in office. In doing so, he established a pattern—certainly not an integrated, Catholic approach—that many Catholic politicians would adopt in the decades that followed.

In July 1963, Pope Paul VI met with President John F. Kennedy, the first Catholic president of the United States. The audience was originally to have been with Pope John XXIII, but he died before the meeting. Kennedy would be assassinated only months later on November 22. This photo captures what could have been: "the most powerful man in the world" and "the parish priest of the world" working together.

VATICAN II AND THE AMERICAN CHURCH

American Catholics were generally enthusiastic about the Second Vatican Council (1962-1965), and implementation of its decisions seemed to go well at first. Responding to a Vatican II mandate, the bishops organized themselves as an episcopal conference—the National Conference of Catholic Bishops—replacing the old, more loosely structured NCWC. They also created a sister organization, the United States Catholic Conference, to collaborate with priests, religious, and laity in number of fields. (The NCCB and USCC were combined in 1991 into a single structure, the United States Conference of Catholic Bishops.)

Problems soon arose. New candidates for the priesthood and religious life began to drop sharply, and there was a continuing stream of defections. Enrollment in Catholic elementary and secondary schools plummeted. Though some remained staunchly faithful, many Catholic colleges and universities distanced themselves from the Church. Pope Paul VI's 1968 encyclical *Humanæ vitæ,* reaffirming the Church's condemnation of artificial birth control, met with organized dissent. Unauthorized liturgical experiments became commonplace. Mirroring the anti-authoritarian mood of the 1960s and growing opposition to the Vietnam War, authority in the Church came under attack. According to opinion polls, many Catholics rejected the doctrinal and moral teaching of the Church on numerous issues.

Perhaps the most damaging and disheartening development in the American Catholic Church was the disclosure of rampant sexual abuse of minors among some American clergy. During the early years of the twenty-first century, it was discovered that some priests had been sexually abusing minors, most cases going as far back as the 1960s and 1970s; many churchmen had hushed the abuse to avoid scandal. Decades of suppression of these clerical sins only contributed to the humiliation when these incidents were revealed in the media. Because of abuse, American dioceses paid settlements totaling hundreds of millions of dollars, even to the point of bankruptcy. Still, these financial penalties were insignificant compared to the Church's overall loss of moral credibility and public esteem in the United States.

CONCLUSION: PRESENT AND FUTURE

Recent events have reopened the debate about whether American culture at its roots is or is not compatible with Catholic beliefs and values. Some hold that founding documents like the *Declaration of Independence* and the Constitution are grounded in the natural law tradition largely shaped by Catholic thinkers such as St. Thomas Aquinas; as a result, they say, American values offer a congenial setting for Catholicism. Others maintain that the founding documents are grounded in the rationalism of the eighteenth century Enlightenment: moral relativism, religious indifferentism, individualism, and the ethic of "choice" visible in today's American culture.

Whichever may be the case, the religious and secularist worldviews have both been part of the American experience from the time of the nation's founding. In recent decades the conflict between religion and secularism has become an ongoing "culture war"—a struggle over values and beliefs that shape American institutions and policies.

As the twenty-first century began, the Catholic Church in the United States faced a host of challenges bearing in one way or another upon the question of Catholic identity: What does it mean to be an American Catholic? Catholics not only are part of America's culture war but also engaged in their own intramural, ideological struggles over the future of the Church. Moreover, although American Catholics are more numerous today than ever, only about one out of three regularly attends Sunday Mass, and many reject Church teachings on important matters of belief and practice. Although the number of priests and religious has fallen in the past forty years, new

NORTH AMERICAN CHURCHES AS OF 1995

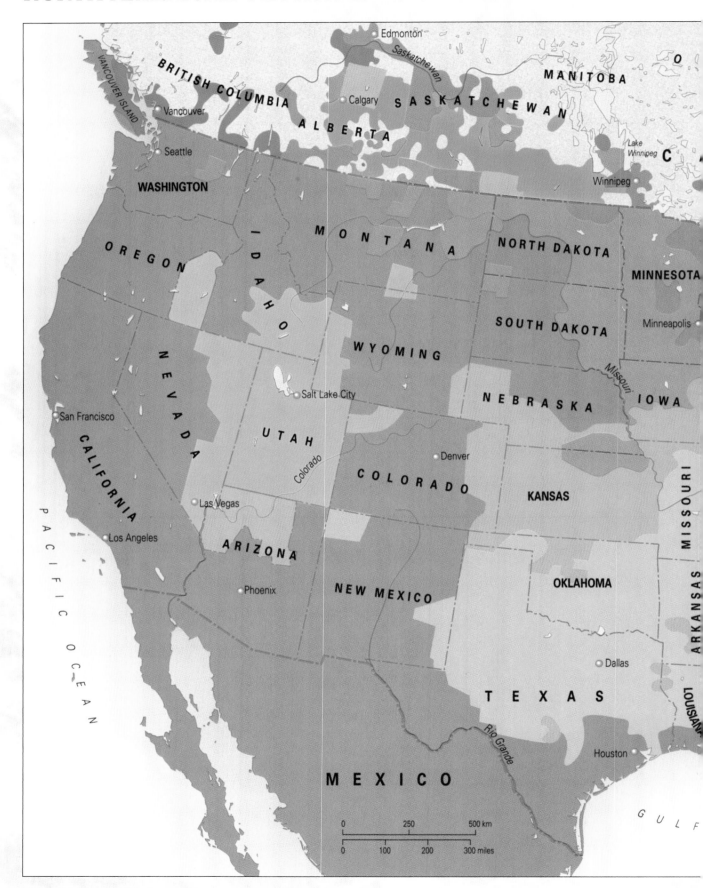

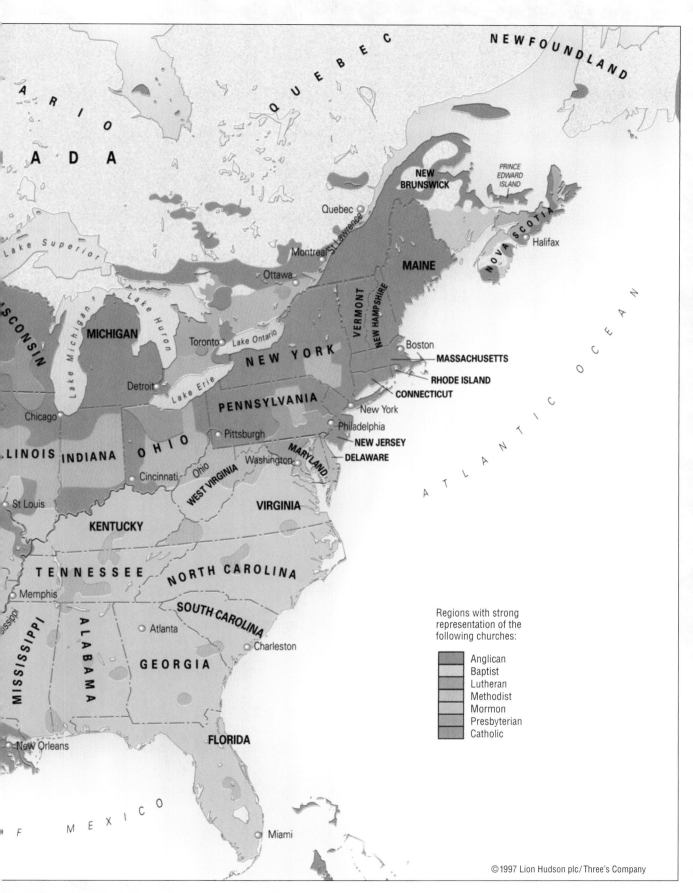

Regions with strong
representation of the
following churches:

Anglican
Baptist
Lutheran
Methodist
Mormon
Presbyterian
Catholic

©1997 Lion Hudson plc/ Three's Company

THE MISSION OF THE CHURCH IN AMERICA TODAY: THE NEW EVANGELIZATION

Excerpts from *Ecclesia in America* (post Synodal), Pope John Paul II

The Importance of Catechesis

The new evangelization in which the whole continent is engaged means that faith cannot be taken for granted, but must be explicitly proposed in all its breadth and richness. This is the principal objective of catechesis, which, by its very nature, is an essential aspect of the new evangelization. "Catechesis is a process of formation in faith, hope and charity; it shapes the mind and touches the heart, leading the person to embrace Christ fully and completely. It introduces the believer more fully into the experience of the Christian life, which involves the liturgical celebration of the mystery of the Redemption and the Christian service of others."

It is to be hoped that both documents will be employed "in the preparation and the evaluation of all parochial and diocesan programs of catechesis, bearing in mind that the religious situation of young people and adults calls for a catechesis which is more kerygmatic and more organic in its presentation of the contents of the faith."

Evangelizing Centers of Education

Education can play an outstanding role in promoting the inculturation of the Gospel.

The content of the education they impart should make constant reference to Jesus Christ and his message as the Church presents it in her dogmatic and moral teaching. Only in this way will they train truly Christian leaders in the different spheres of human activity, and in society, especially in politics, economics, science, art and philosophical reflection.

Pastoral work in Catholic universities will therefore be given special attention: it must encourage a commitment to the apostolate on the part of the students themselves, so that they can become the evangelizers of the university world.

Something similar must also be said about Catholic schools, particularly with regard to secondary education: "A special effort should be made to strengthen the Catholic identity of schools, whose specific character is based on an educational vision having its origin in the person of Christ and its roots in the teachings of the Gospel. Catholic schools must seek not only to impart a quality education from the technical and professional standpoint, but also and above all provide for the integral formation of the human person.

"The influence of these educational centers should extend to all sectors of society, without distinction or exclusion. It is essential that every possible effort be made to ensure that Catholic schools, despite financial difficulties, continue to provide 'a Catholic education to the poor and the marginalized in society.' It will never be possible to free the needy from their poverty unless they are first freed from the impoverishment arising from the lack of adequate education."

vocations to the priesthood and religious life are showing much promise that is expressed in serious spirituality and vibrant pastoral zeal. A number of dioceses and religious orders throughout the United States are showing hope in the form of a small resurgence of priestly vocations.

There are other positive signs. Steps are being taken toward the possible beatification and canonization of a significant number of American Catholics; by one recent count, more than thirty men and women are now going forward. These include familiar figures like Bishop Sheen, Father McGivney, and Dorothy Day, as well others less well known. New groups and Catholic movements such as Neocatechumenal Way, Opus Dei, and Regnum Christi are actively encouraging Catholics to deepen their faith and commitment in line with Vatican II's universal call to holiness and participate in the new evangelization that Pope John Paul II often called for. Even the U.S. Supreme Court's disastrous 1973 *Roe v. Wade* decision legalizing abortion has produced positive reaction, mobilizing thousands of Catholics in defense of human life. The continued infusion of Catholic immigrants from Mexico and Latin America, the Philippines, and other countries has the potential of introducing fresh vitality into American Catholicism. In addition, a new generation of bishops seems determined to provide vigorous leadership.

The old, religiously based anti-Catholicism seems largely to have been replaced by ecumenical goodwill. However, secularist hostility to religion and traditional morality is still central to the American culture war. Significantly, the third Catholic to run for president as a major party candidate—Massachusetts Senator John F. Kerry, who sought the office in 2004—was criticized by some bishops and many fellow Catholics for rejecting Church teaching on abortion and other moral issues. Catholics were twenty-seven percent of the electorate; continuing a trend of recent decades, the Catholic vote—at one time overwhelmingly Democratic—split, with fifty-two percent going to the Republican, President George W. Bush, and forty-seven percent to his Democratic opponent, John F. Kerry. Among Catholics who attend Mass weekly, the results were fifty-six percent for Bush and forty-four percent for Kerry.

The United States is the scene of a profound conflict between Americans who support religiously based values and secularized Americans who advocate a relativistic morality of individual "choice." Catholics can be found on both sides of this divide. In these new, and in some ways more difficult, circumstances, many American Catholics still face the old need to decide what it means to be both Catholic *and* American.

With the election of Pope Benedict XVI, the joyful optimism of his predecessor, John Paul II, is very much alive and well. Although the tensions between advocates of natural law, Judeo-Christian-based morality and proponents of moral relativism strongly persist, Pope Benedict's many references to the power of holiness and the charity of Christ will be the ultimate solution to these tensions. In a spirit of hope, at World Youth Day in Cologne during the summer of 2005, the Holy Father alluded to a spiritual "nuclear fission" which will extend Christ's kingdom of love, peace, truth, and justice as long as there are individuals who, like the early Christians, aspire to be great saints and evangelizers in their workplaces and in their families.

The history of the Church has demonstrated throughout the centuries that the witness of holiness will push the kingdom of God forward in the United States. Modern-day saints living and working for Christ in the world will show what it means to be a Catholic and an American.

The Basilica of the National Shrine of the Assumption of the Blessed Virgin Mary in Baltimore, Maryland is considered the motherchurch of the United States.

THE PASSION OF THE CHRIST

In 2004, actor/director Mel Gibson released an extraordinary and daring film portraying the last twelve hours of the life of Jesus Christ. Gibson based the movie on the four Gospels and the diaries of Bl. Anne Catherine Emmerich (1774-1824). The desire to produce this film was intensely personal, due to events in his own life that ultimately led him to embrace the Catholic Faith. In a 2004 interview, he stated: "About thirteen years ago I came to a difficult point in my life, and meditating on Christ's sufferings—on his Passion— got me through it. . . . And when I did that, through reading, and studying, and meditating, and praying, I began to see in my own mind what he really went through. . . . The story—the way I envisioned the suffering of Christ—got inside me and started to grow, and it reached a point where I just had to tell it, to get it out."

The production cost, totaling twenty-five million dollars, was covered by Gibson himself. Even after the movie was filmed, it was not certain that a company would be found to distribute the film. The movie was filmed in three so-called "dead languages": Hebrew, Latin, and Aramaic, with English subtitles, something which had never been done before. Most of the film industry was afraid to touch the movie, stating it was too violent, too religious, and, according to some, anti-Semitic. Gibson did not give up so easily. Despite considerable opposition and with the help of Evangelical and Catholic churches across the country, he worked hard to gather support for the film.

The movie was finally released on Ash Wednesday 2004. Many critics initially thought it was artistically brilliant but would be a flop, that in an age of religious apathy nobody would want to see an old story told in dead languages; they could not have been more wrong. The movie went on to become one of the highest-grossing films of all time, both in the United States and around the world. The incredible power of the movie moved many to tears of repentance and has brought Christ's message of love to millions.

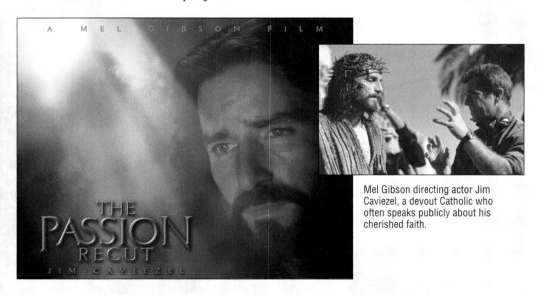

Mel Gibson directing actor Jim Caviezel, a devout Catholic who often speaks publicly about his cherished faith.

SUPPLEMENTARY READING

St. Isaac Jogues, from a letter written to a friend before returning to America, 1846

To maintain, and see what can be done for the instruction of these tribes, it is here deemed expedient to send them some father. I have reason to think I shall be sent, since I have some knowledge of the language and country. You see what need I have of the powerful aid of prayers while amidst these savages. I will have to remain among them, almost without liberty to pray, without Mass, without Sacraments, and be responsible for every accident among the Iroquois, French, Algonquins, and others. But what shall I say? My hope is in God, who needs not us to accomplish his designs. We must endeavor to be faithful to Him and not spoil His work by our shortcomings....

My heart tells me that if I have the happiness of being employed in this mission, *"Ibo et non redibo"* (I shall go and shall not return); but I shall be happy if our Lord will complete the sacrifice where He has begun it, and make the little blood I have shed in that land the earnest of what I would give from every vein of my body and my heart.

In a word, this people is "a bloody spouse" to me (Exodus 4: 25). May our good Master, who has purchased them in His blood, open to them the door of His Gospel, as well as to the four allied nations near them.

Adieu, dear Father. Pray Him to unite me inseparably to Him.

Leo XIII, from *Testem benevolentiæ*

To Our Beloved Son, James Cardinal Gibbons, Cardinal Priest of the Title Sancta Maria, Beyond the Tiber, Archbishop of Baltimore:

LEO XIII, Pope-Beloved Son, Health and Apostolic Blessing: We send to you by this letter a renewed expression of that good will which we have not failed during the course of our pontificate to manifest frequently to you and to your colleagues in the episcopate and to the whole American people, availing ourselves of every opportunity offered us by the progress of your church or whatever you have done for safeguarding and promoting Catholic interests. Moreover, we have often considered and admired the noble gifts of your nation which enable the American people to be alive to every good work which promotes the good of humanity and the splendor of civilization. Although this letter is not intended, as preceding ones, to repeat the words of praise so often spoken, but rather to call attention to some things to be avoided and corrected...

...We, therefore, on account of our apostolic office, having to guard the integrity of the faith and the security of the faithful, are desirous of writing to you more at length concerning this whole matter.

The underlying principle of these new opinions is that, in order to more easily attract those who differ from her, the Church should shape her teachings more in accord with the spirit of the age and relax some of her ancient severity and make some concessions to new opinions. Many think that these concessions should be made not only in regard to ways of living, but even in regard to doctrines which belong to the deposit of the faith. They contend that it would be opportune, in order to gain those who differ from us, to omit certain points of her teaching which are of lesser importance, and to tone down the meaning which the Church has always attached to them. It does not need many words, beloved son, to prove the falsity of these ideas if the nature and origin of the doctrine which the Church proposes are recalled to mind. The Vatican Council says concerning this point:

> For the doctrine of faith which God has revealed has not been proposed, like a philosophical invention to be perfected by human ingenuity, but has been delivered as a divine deposit to the Spouse of Christ to be faithfully kept and infallibly declared. Hence that meaning of the sacred dogmas is perpetually to be retained which our Holy Mother, the Church, has once declared, nor is that meaning ever to be departed from under the pretense or pretext of a deeper comprehension of them. (*Constitutio de Fide Catholica*, ch. iv)

John Paul II, Homily, August 15, 1993

When the Founding Fathers of this great nation enshrined certain unalienable rights in the Constitution - and something similar exists in many countries and in many International Declarations — they did so because they recognized the existence of a "law"—a series of rights and duties engraved by the Creator on each person's heart and conscience.

In much of contemporary thinking, any reference to a "law" guaranteed by the Creator is absent. There remains only each individual's choice of this or that objective as convenient or useful in a given set of circumstances. No longer is anything considered *intrinsically* "good" and "universally binding." Rights are affirmed but, because they are without any reference to an objective truth, they are deprived of any solid basis (cf. Congregation for the Doctrine of the Faith, *Threats to Human Life*, I, iii). Vast sectors of society are confused about what is right and what is wrong, and are at the mercy of those with the power to "create" opinion and impose it on others.

The family especially is under attack. And *the sacred character of human life denied.* Naturally the weakest members of society are the most at risk: *the unborn,* children, the sick, the handicapped, the old, the poor and unemployed, the immigrant and refugee, *the South of the world!*

Charles Carroll (1737-1832) a lawyer and politician from Maryland, was a delegate to the Continental Congress and later became a United States Senator. He was the only Catholic signer of the *Declaration of Independence.* His signature appears in the third column under John Hancock's name with the other Maryland delegates, Samuel Chase, William Paca, and Thomas Stone. Charles Carroll was cousin to Archbishop John Carroll and Daniel Carroll, a member of the Constitutional Convention and one of only two Catholic signers of the U.S. Constitution.

VOCABULARY

AMERICANISM

Condemned by Pope Leo XIII, this movement sought a way to adapt the Catholic Faith within American principles and modern ideas. It questioned themes like passive and active virtues, the best form of religious life, and the correct approach to evangelization.

LAY TRUSTEEISM

Partly to conform to American civil law, partly out of enthusiasm for democracy, and partly in imitation of the congregational system in American Protestantism, laymen became the owners of parish property, administered parish affairs, and in some places began hiring their own pastors in defiance of the bishop.

NATIONAL CATHOLIC WELFARE CONFERENCE

The NCWC was the bishops' vehicle in the early- and mid-twentieth century for cooperative national-level action in social action, education and youth work, communications, and other fields.

NATIONAL CONFERENCE OF CATHOLIC BISHOPS

(NCCB) Responding to a Vatican II mandate, the bishops organized themselves as an episcopal conference replacing the old, more loosely structured NCWC.

QUEBEC ACT

Passed in 1774 by the British Parliament, it extended political and legal concessions to the inhabitants of Quebec and granted them religious freedom.

UNITED STATES CATHOLIC CONFERENCE

(USCC) A sister organization to the NCCB created to collaborate with priests, religious, and laity in a number of fields.

UNITED STATES CONFERENCE OF CATHOLIC BISHOPS

(USCCB) Single structure that replaced the NCCB and USCC in 1991.

John Trumbull's famous painting depicts the signing of the *Declaration of Independence,* the event which is celebrated in the U.S. every July 4th. The independence of the American colonies was recognized by Great Britain on September 3, 1783, by the Treaty of Paris.

1. Who was St. Isaac Jogues?

2. What was the first Catholic parish in the New World?

3. What was the Quebec Act of 1774?

4. Name two Catholics who signed the Constitution.

5. What city was the seat of the first diocese in the United States?

6. What university is the oldest Catholic institution of higher learning in the United States?

7. Who is considered the founder of the American Navy?

8. How did lay trusteeism become a problem in America?

9. What book was written by some Protestant ministers to defame the Church?

10. Who were the Know-Nothings?

11. Why was the Democratic Party of the 1880s called the party of "Rum, Romanism and Rebellion"?

12. Who founded the Paulists?

13. Orestes Brownson edited what periodical?

14. What was particular about the German Catholics' experience in nineteenth-century America?

15. What Catholic leader worked to preserve good relations between the Church and labor unions?

16. Who founded the Missionary Sisters of the Sacred Heart?

17. Why was the NCWC organized?

18. What organization did the NCWC eventually become?

19. Who was the first major party Catholic to run for President of the U.S.?

20. Who founded the Catholic Worker Movement?

21. Who was the first Catholic President?

22. What papal encyclical was widely ignored by American Catholics?

23. What Catholic presidential candidate did not win a majority of the Catholic vote?

PRACTICAL EXERCISES

1. At the founding of America, the drafters of the Constitution secured toleration for all religions in the United States. In Europe, on the other hand, the revolutions of the eighteenth and nineteenth centuries brought about fierce anti-Catholic persecution. What factors in Europe made the same toleration difficult to attain? What was different about the situation in America that allowed for Catholic toleration?

2. Throughout the history of the Church, from Constantine and Charlemagne to Louis XIV and Vittorio Emmanuelle, various nations have tried to assert their own national identities onto the Church in their countries. Using the history of the Church in the United States as a reference, explain why "Gallicanism" has been so prevalent in the Church throughout the ages.

FROM THE CATECHISM

834 Particular Churches are fully catholic through their communion with one of them, the Church of Rome "which presides in charity" (St. Ignatius of Antioch, *Ad Rom.* 1, 1: *Apostolic Fathers,* II/2, 192; cf. *LG* 13). "For with this church, by reason of its pre-eminence, the whole Church, that is the faithful everywhere, must necessarily be in accord" (St. Irenaeus, *Adv. haeres.* 3, 3, 2: PG 7/1, 849; cf. Vatican Council I: DS 3057). Indeed, "from the incarnate Word's descent to us, all Christian churches everywhere have held and hold the great Church that is here [at Rome] to be their only basis and foundation since, according to the Savior's promise, the gates of hell have never prevailed against her" (St. Maximus the Confessor, *Opuscula theo.:* PG 91: 137-140).

882 The *Pope,* Bishop of Rome and Peter's successor, "is the perpetual and visible source and foundation of the unity both of the bishops and of the whole company of the faithful" (*LG* 23). "For the Roman Pontiff, by reason of his office as Vicar of Christ, and as pastor of the entire Church has full, supreme, and universal power over the whole Church, a power which he can always exercise unhindered" (*LG* 22; cf. *CD* 2, 9).

1905 In keeping with the social nature of man, the good of each individual is necessarily related to the common good, which in turn can be defined only in reference to the human person:

> Do not live entirely isolated, having retreated into yourselves, as if you were already justified, but gather instead to seek the common good together (*Ep. Barnabae,* 4, 10: PG 2, 734).

1913 "Participation" is the voluntary and generous engagement of a person in social interchange. It is necessary that all participate, each according to his position and role, in promoting the common good. This obligation is inherent in the dignity of the human person.

2104 "All men are bound to seek the truth, especially in what concerns God and his Church, and to embrace it and hold on to it as they come to know it" (*DH* 1 § 2). This duty derives from "the very dignity of the human person" (*DH* 2 § 1). It does not contradict a "sincere respect" for different religions which frequently "reflect a ray of that truth which enlightens all men," (*NA* 2 § 2) nor the requirement of charity, which urges Christians "to treat with love, prudence and patience those who are in error or ignorance with regard to the faith" (*DH* 14 § 4).

2188 In respecting religious liberty and the common good of all, Christians should seek recognition of Sundays and the Church's holy days as legal holidays. They have to give everyone a public example of prayer, respect, and joy and defend their traditions as a precious contribution to the spiritual life of society. If a country's legislation or other reasons require work on Sunday, the day should nevertheless be lived as the day of our deliverance which lets us share in this "festal gathering," this "assembly of the firstborn who are enrolled in heaven" (Heb 12: 22-23).

2241 The more prosperous nations are obliged, to the extent they are able, to welcome the *foreigner* in search of the security and the means of livelihood which he cannot find in his country of origin. Public authorities should see to it that the natural right is respected that places a guest under the protection of those who receive him.

Political authorities, for the sake of the common good for which they are responsible, may make the exercise of the right to immigrate subject to various juridical conditions, especially with regard to the immigrants' duties toward their country of adoption. Immigrants are obliged to respect with gratitude the material and spiritual heritage of the country that receives them, to obey its laws, and to assist in carrying civic burdens.

FROM THE CATECHISM Continued

2244 Every institution is inspired, at least implicitly, by a vision of man and his destiny, from which it derives the point of reference for its judgment, its hierarchy of values, its line of conduct. Most societies have formed their institutions in the recognition of a certain preeminence of man over things. Only the divinely revealed religion has clearly recognized man's origin and destiny in God, the Creator and Redeemer. The Church invites political authorities to measure their judgments and decisions against this inspired truth about God and man:

Societies not recognizing this vision or rejecting it in the name of their independence from God are brought to seek their criteria and goal in themselves or to borrow them from some ideology. Since they do not admit that one can defend an objective criterion of good and evil, they arrogate to themselves an explicit or implicit totalitarian power over man and his destiny, as history shows (cf. *CA* 45; 46).

2246 It is a part of the Church's mission "to pass moral judgments even in matters related to politics, whenever the fundamental rights of man or the salvation of souls requires it. The means, the only means, she may use are those which are in accord with the Gospel and the welfare of all men according to the diversity of times and circumstances" (*GS* 76 § 5).

The French Jesuit Jacques Marquette and Louis Joliet on their historic exploratory voyage down the Mississippi River in 1673. Father Jacques Marquette, S.J. (1637-1675) and Louis Joliet, a French Canadian explorer, were the first Europeans to see and map the Mississippi River. They departed from Mackinac, Michigan with two canoes and five other explorers of French-Indian ancestry. They followed Lake Michigan to the Bay of Green Bay and up the Fox River. From there, they portaged to the Wisconsin River entering the Mississippi River near Prairie du Chien, Wisconsin. The Joliet-Marquette expedition traveled to within 435 miles of the Gulf of Mexico, but turned back at the mouth of the Arkansas River fearing contact with the Spanish. They returned to Lake Michigan by way of the Illinois River. After a visit to the mission of St. Francis Xavier in Green Bay, Fr. Marquette returned to the Illinois River in 1674 to found a mission on the shore of Lake Michigan. The mission would later grow into the city of Chicago.

DOCTORS OF THE CHURCH

Proclaimed by Pope Boniface VIII, September 20, 1295

1. St. Ambrose
2. St. Jerome
3. St. Augustine of Hippo
4. St. Gregory the Great

Proclaimed by Pope St. Pius V, April 11, 1567

5. St. Thomas Aquinas

Proclaimed by Pope St. Pius V, 1568

6. St. Athanasius
7. St. Basil the Great
8. St. Gregory of Nazianzus
9. St. John Chrysostom

Proclaimed by Pope Sixtus V, March 14, 1588

10. St. Bonaventure

Proclaimed by Pope Clement XI, February 3, 1720

11. St. Anselm of Canterbury

Proclaimed by Pope Innocent XIII, April 25, 1722

12. St. Isidore of Seville

Proclaimed by Pope Benedict XIII, February 10, 1729

13. St. Peter Chrysologus

Proclaimed by Pope Benedict XIV, October 15, 1754

14. St. Leo the Great

Proclaimed by Pope Leo XII, September 27, 1828

15. St. Peter Damian

Proclaimed by Pope Bl. Pius VIII, August 20, 1830

16. St. Bernard of Clairvaux

Proclaimed by Pope Bl. Pius IX, May 13, 1851

17. St. Hilary of Poitiers

Proclaimed by Pope Bl. Pius IX, July 7, 1871

18. St. Alphonsus Liguori

Proclaimed by Pope Bl. Pius IX, November 16, 1871

19. St. Francis de Sales

Proclaimed by Pope Leo XIII, July 28, 1882

20. St. Cyril of Alexandria
21. St. Cyril of Jerusalem

Proclaimed by Pope Leo XIII, August 19, 1890

22. St. John of Damascus

Proclaimed by Pope Leo XIII, November 13, 1899

23. St. Bede the Venerable

Proclaimed by Pope Benedict XV, October 5, 1920

24. St. Ephraem of Syria

Proclaimed by Pope Pius XI, May 21, 1925

25. St. Peter Canisius

Proclaimed by Pope Pius XI, August 24, 1926

26. St. John of the Cross

Proclaimed by Pope Pius XI, September 17, 1931

27. St. Robert Bellarmine

Proclaimed by Pope Pius XI, December 16, 1931

28. St. Albert the Great

Proclaimed by Pope Pius XII, January 16, 1946

29. St. Anthony of Padua

Proclaimed by Pope Bl. John XXIII, March 19, 1959

30. St. Lawrence of Brindisi

Proclaimed by Pope Paul VI, September 27, 1970

31. St. Teresa of Avila

Proclaimed by Pope Paul VI, October 4, 1970

32. St. Catherine of Siena

Proclaimed by Pope John Paul II, October 19, 1997

33. St. Thérèse of Lisieux

St. Jerome was proclaimed a Doctor of the Church
by Pope Boniface VIII on September 20, 1295.

THE POPES

1. St. Peter

265. Benedict XVI

FIRST CENTURY
St. Peter (A.D. 33-67)
St. Linus (67-76)
St. Anacletus (76-88)
St. Clement I (88-97)
St. Evaristus (97-105)

SECOND CENTURY
St. Alexander I (105-115)
St. Sixtus I (115-125)
St. Telesphorus (125-136)
St. Hyginus (136-140)
St. Pius I (140-155)
St. Anicetus (155-166)
St. Soter (166-175)
St. Eleutherius (175-189)
St. Victor I (189-199)
St. Zephyrinus (199-217)

THIRD CENTURY
St. Callistus I (217-222)
St. Hippolytus (217-235)
St. Urban I (222-230)
St. Pontian (230-235)
St. Anterus (235-236)
St. Fabian (236-250)
St. Cornelius (251-253)
Novatianus (251)
St. Lucius I (253-254)
St. Stephen I (254-257)
St. Sixtus II (257-258)
St. Dionysius (259-268)
St. Felix I (269-274)
St. Eutychian (275-283)
St. Caius (283-296)
St. Marcellinus (296-304)

FOURTH CENTURY
St. Marcellus I (308-309)
St. Eusebius (309-310)
St. Miltiades (311-314)
St. Sylvester I (314-335)
St. Marcus (336)
St. Julius I (337-352)
Liberius (352-366)
Felix II (353-365)
St. Damasus I (366-384)
Ursinus (366-367)
St. Siricius (384-399)
St. Anastasius I (399-401)

FIFTH CENTURY
St. Innocent I (401-417)
St. Zozimus (417-418)
St. Boniface I (418-422)
Eulalius (418-419)

St. Celestine I (422-432)
St. Sixtus III (432-440)
St. Leo I (440-461)
St. Hilary (461-468)
St. Simplicius (468-483)
St. Felix III (II) (483-492)
St. Gelasius I (492-496)
Anastasius II (496-498)
St. Symmachus (498-514)
Laurentius (498-505)

SIXTH CENTURY
St. Hormisdas (514-523)
St. John I (523-526)
St. Felix IV (III) (526-530)
Boniface II (530-532)
Dioscurus (530)
John II (533-535)
St. Agapitus I (535-536)
St. Silverius (536-537)
Vigilius (537-555)
Pelagius I (556-561)
John III (561-574)
Benedict I (575-579)
Pelagius II (579-590)
St. Gregory I (590-604)

SEVENTH CENTURY
Sabinian (604-606)
Boniface III (607)
St. Boniface IV (608-615)
St. Deusdedit (615-618)
    or Adoedatus I
Boniface V (619-625)
Honorius I (625-638)
Severinus (640)
John IV (640-642)
Theodore I (642-649)
St. Martin I (649-655)
St. Eugene I (654-657)
St. Vitalian (657-672)
Adeodatus II (672-676)
Donus (676-678)
St. Agatho (678-681)
St. Leo II (682-683)
St. Benedict II (684-685)
John V (685-686)
Conon (686-687)
Theodore II (687)
Paschal I (687-692)
St. Sergius I (687-701)

EIGHTH CENTURY
John VI (701-705)
John VII (705-707)

Sisinnius (708)
Constantine (708-715)
St. Gregory II (715-731)
St. Gregory III (731-471)
St. Zachary (741-752)
Stephen II (752)
St. Paul I (757-767)
Constantine (767)
Philip (767)
Stephen III (768-772)
Adrian I (772-795)
St. Leo III (795-816)

NINTH CENTURY
Stephen IV (816-817)
St. Paschal I (817-824)
Eugene II (824-827)
Valentine (827)
Gregory IV (827-844)
John VIII (844)
Sergius II (844-847)
St. Leo IV (847-855)
Benedict III (855-858)
Anastasius III (855)
St. Nicholas I (858-867)
Adrian II (867-872)
John VIII (872-882)
Marinus I (882-884)
St. Adrian III (884-885)
Stephen V (VI) (885-891)
Formosus (891-896)
Boniface VI (896)
Stephen VI (VII) (896-897)
Romanus (897)
Theodore II (897)
John IX (898-900)

TENTH CENTURY
Benedict IV (900-903)
Leo V (903)
Christopher (903-904)
Sergius III (904-911)
Anastasius III (911-913)
Landus (913-914)
John X (914-928)
Leo VI (928)
Stephen VII (928-931)
John XI (931-935)
Leo VII (936-939)
Stephen VIII (IX) (939-942)
Marinus II (942-946)
Agapetus II (946-955)
John XII (955-964)
Leo VIII (963-965)
Benedict V (964-966)

John XIII (965-972)
Benedict VI (973-974)
Benedict VII (974-983)
John XIV (983-984)
Boniface VII (984-985)
John XV (985-996)
Gregory V (996-999)
Sylvester II (999-1003)

ELEVENTH CENTURY
John XVII (1003)
John XVIII (1004-1009)
Sergius IV (1009-1012)
Benedict VIII (1012-1024)
Gregory VI (1012)
John XIX (1024-1032)
Benedict IX (1032-1044)
Sylvester III (1045)
Gregory VI (1045-1046)
    (John Gratian Pierleoni)
Clement II (1046-1047)
    (Suitgar, Count of
    Morsleben)
Damasus II (1048)
    (Count Poppo)
St. Leo IX (1049-1054)
    (Bruno, Count of Toul)
Victor II (1055-1057)
    (Gebhard, Count of
    Hirschberg)
Stephen IX (X) (1057-1058)
    (Frederick of Lorraine)
Nicholas II (1059-1061)
    (Gerhard of Burgundy)
Alexander II (1061-1073)
    (Anselmo da Baggio)
Honorius II (1061-1064)
St. Gregory VII (1073-1085)
    (Hildebrand of Soana)
Clement III (1080-1100)
Bl. Victor III (1086-1087)
    (Desiderius, Prince of
    Beneventum)
Bl. Urban II (1088-1099)
    (Odo of Chatillon)
Paschal II (1099-1118)
    (Ranieri da Bieda)
Theodoric (1100-1102)
Albert (1102)
Sylvester IV (1105)

TWELFTH CENTURY
Gelasius II (1118-1119)
    (John Coniolo)
Gregory VIII (1118-1121)

Italicized = Anti-popes

Callistus II (1119-1124)
(Guido, Count of Burgundy)

Honorius II (1124-1130)
(Lamberto dei Fagnani)

Celestine II (1124)

Innocent II (1130-1143)
(Gregorio Papareschi)

Anacletus II (1130-1138)
(Cardinal Pierleone)

Victor IV (1138)

Celestine II (1143-1144)
(Guido di Castello)

Lucius II (1144-1145)
(Gherardo Caccianemici)

Bl. Eugene III (1145-1153)
(Bernardo Paganelli)

Anastasius IV (1153-1154)
(Corrado della Subarra)

Adrian IV (1154-1159)
(Nicholas Breakspear)

Alexander III (1159-1181)
(Orlando Bandinelli)

Victor IV (1159-1164)

Paschal III (1164-1168)

Calixtus III (1168-7118)

Innocent III (1179-1180)
(Lando da Sessa)

Lucius III (1181-1185)
(Ubaldo Allucingoli)

Urban III (1185-1187)
(Uberto Crivelli)

Gregory VIII (1187)
(Alberto del Morra)

Clement III (1187-1191)
(Paolo Scolari)

Celestine III (1191-1198)
(Giacinto Boboni-Orsini)

Innocent III (1198-1216)
(Lotario de Conti di Segni)

THIRTEENTH CENTURY

Honorius III (1216-1227)
(Cencio Savelli)

Gregory IX (1227-1241)
(Ugolino di Segni)

Celestine IV (1241)
(Goffredo Castiglione)

Innocent IV (1243-1254)
(Sinibaldo de Fieschi)

Alexander IV (1254-1261)
(Rinaldo di Segni)

Urban IV (1261-1264)
(Jacques Pantaléon)

Clement IV (1265-1268)
(Guy le Gros Foulques)

Bl. Gregory X (1271-1276)
(Tebaldo Visconti)

Bl. Innocent V (1276)
(Pierre de Champagni)

Adrian V (1276)
(Ottobono Fieschi)

John XXI (1276-1277)
(Pietro Rebuli-Giuliani)

Nicholas III (1277-1280)
(Giovanni Gaetano Orsini)

Martin IV (1281-1285)
(Simon Mompitie)

Honorius IV (1285-1287)
(Giacomo Savelli)

Nicholas IV (1288-1292)
(Girolamo Masci)

St. Celestine V (1294)
(Pietro Angelari da
Murrone)

Boniface VIII (1294-1303)
(Benedetto Gaetani)

FOURTEENTH CENTURY

Bl. Benedict XI (1303-1304)
(Nicolò Boccasini)

Clement V (1305-1314)
(Raimond Bertrand de Got)

John XXII (1316-1334)
(Jacques Dueze)

Nicholas V (1328-1330)
(Pietro di Corbara)

Benedict XII (1334-1342)
(Jacques Fournier)

Clement VI (1342-1352)
(Pierre Roger de Beaufort)

Innocent VI (1352-1362)
(Étienne Aubert)

Bl. Urban V (1362-1370)
(Guillaume de Grimord)

Gregory XI (1370-1378)
(Pierre Roger de
Beaufort, the Younger)

Urban VI (1378-1389)
(Bartolomeo Prignano)

Clement VII (1378-1394)
(Robert of Geneva)

Boniface IX (1389-1404)
(Pietro Tomacelli)

Benedict XIII (1394-1423)
(Pedro de Luna)

FIFTEENTH CENTURY

Innocent VII (1404-1406)
(Cosmato de Migliorati)

Gregory XII (1406-1415)
(Angelo Correr)

Alexander V (1409-1410)
(Petros Philargi)

John XXIII (1410-1415)
(Baldassare Cossa)

Martin V (1417-1431)
(Ottone Colonna)

Clement VIII (1423-1429)

Benedict XIV (1424)

Eugene IV (1431-1447)
(Gabriele Condulmer)

Felix V (1439-1449)
(Amadeus of Savoy)

Nicholas V (1447-1455)
(Tommaso Parentucelli)

Callistus III (1455-1458)
(Alonso Borgia)

Pius II (1458-1464)
(Aeneas Silvio de
Piccolomini)

Paul II (1464-1471)
(Pietro Barbo)

Sixtus IV (1471-1484)
(Francesco della Rovere)

Innocent VIII (1484-1492)
(Giovanni Battista Cibo)

Alexander VI (1492-1503)
(Rodrigo Lanzol y Borgia)

SIXTEENTH CENTURY

Pius III (1503)
(Francesco Todoeschini-
Piccolomini)

Julius II (1503-1513)
(Giuliano della Rovere)

Leo X (1513-1521)
(Giovanni de Medici)

Adrian VI (1522-1523)
(Adrian Florensz)

Clement VII (1523-1534)
(Giulio de Medici)

Paul III (1534-1549)
(Alessandro Farnese)

Julius III (1550-1555)
(Giovanni Maria Ciocchi
del Monte)

Marcellus II (1555)
(Marcello Cervini)

Paul IV (1555-1559)
(Gian Pietro Caraffa)

Pius IV (1559-1565)
(Giovanni Angelo de Medici)

St. Pius V (1566-1572)
(Antonio Michele Ghislieri)

Gregory XIII (1572-1585)
(Ugo Buoncompagni)

Sixtus V (1585-1590)
(Felice Peretti)

Urban VII (1590)
(Giambattista Castagna)

Gregory XIV (1590-1591)
(Nicolò Sfondrati)

Innocent IX (1591)
(Gian Antonio Facchinetti)

Clement VIII (1592-1605)
(Ippolito Aldobrandini)

SEVENTEENTH CENTURY

Leo XI (1605)
(Alessandro de Medici-
Ottaiano)

Paul V (1605-1621)
(Camillo Borghese)

Gregory XV (1621-1623)
(Alessandro Ludovisi)

Urban VIII (1623-1644)
(Maffeo Barberini)

Innocent X (1644-1655)
(Giambattista Pamfili)

Alexander VII (1655-1667)
(Fabio Chigi)

Clement IX (1667-1669)
(Giulio Rospigliosi)

Clement X (1670-1676)
(Emilio Altieri)

Bl. Innocent XI (1676-1689)
(Benedetto Odescalchi)

Alexander VIII (1689-1691)
(Pietro Ottoboni)

Innocent XII (1691-1700)
(Antonio Pignatelli)

EIGHTEENTH CENTURY

Clement XI (1700-1721)
(Gian Francesco Albani)

Innocent XIII (1721-1724)
(Michelangelo dei Conti)

Benedict XIII (1724-1730)
(Pietro Francesco Orsini)

Clement XII (1730-1740)
(Lorenzo Corsini)

Benedict XIV (1740-1758)
(Prospero Lambertini)

Clement XIII (1758-1769)
(Carlo Rezzonico)

Clement XIV (1769-1774)
(Lorenzo Ganganelli)

Pius VI (1775-1799)
(Gianangelo Braschi)

NINETEENTH CENTURY

Pius VII (1800-1823)
(Barnaba Chiaramonti)

Leo XII (1823-1829)
(Annibale della Genga)

Pius VIII (1829-1830)
(Francesco Saverio
Gastiglioni)

Gregory XVI (1831-1846)
(Bartolomeo Alberto
Cappellari)

Bl. Pius IX (1846-1878)
(Giovanni Mastai-Ferretti)

Leo XIII (1878-1903)
(Gioacchino Pecci)

TWENTIETH CENTURY

St. Pius X (1903-1914)
(Giuseppe Sarto)

Benedict XV (1914-1922)
(Giacomo della Chiesa)

Pius XI (1922-1939)
(Achille Ratti)

Pius XII (1939-1958)
(Eugenio Pacelli)

Bl. John XXIII (1958-1963)
(Angelo Roncalli)

Paul VI (1963-1978)
(Giovanni Battista Montini)

John Paul I (1978)
(Albino Luciani)

John Paul II (1978-2005)
(Karol Jozef Wojtyla)

TWENTY-FIRST CENTURY

Benedict XVI (2005-   )
(Joseph Alois Ratzinger)

ART AND PHOTO CREDITS

Cover
Montage–*St. Peter's Basilica*, Rome; Pictorial Library of Bible Lands; Todd Bolen, photographer and *St. Peter*, Pierre Etienne Monnot, San Giovanni in Laterano, Rome

Introduction
iii Montage (see cover source)
iv *Christ in Majesty with Alpha and Omega;* Wall painting from the Catacomb of Commodilla, south of Rome, Italy; *The Oxford Illustrated History of Christianity,* John McManners, Editor, 1990
xi *John Paul II,* Rafael Casal; Manila, Philippines; Midwest Theological Forum Archives
xii *John Paul II in the Valdostan forest,* from *In the Mountains with John Paul II,* Grzegorz Galazka, photographer; published by Midwest Theological Forum (2002)

Background
1 *Statue of Jupiter;* Prado Museum, Madrid, Spain; Archivo Oronoz
2 (top) *Alexander the Great in the Temple of Jerusalem,* Sebastiano Conca; Prado Museum, Madrid, Spain; Archivo Oronoz
2 (bottom) *Bust of Alexander the Great;* Museum of Archaeology, Seville, Spain; Archivo Oronoz
3 *Plato and Aristotle,* detail from *The School of Athens,* Raphael; Stanza della Segnatura, Palazzi Pontifici, Vatican
4 Page from *Commentary on the Logic of Aristotle,* St. Thomas Aquinas; Library of the Congress of the Deputies, Madrid, Spain; Archivo Oronoz
5 *Statue of Romulus and Remus,* Rome, Italy; Pictorial Library of Bible Lands; Todd Bolen, photographer
6 *Bust of Augustus Caesar;* National Museum of Art, Badajoz, Merida, Spain; Archivo Oronoz
7 *The Coliseum at Night,* Rome, Italy; Pictorial Library of Bible Lands; Todd Bolen, photographer
8 *Marcus Atilius Regulus Departs Rome;* Palazzo Madama (Senate House), Rome, Italy; Archivo Oronoz
9 (top) *Bust of Marcus Licinius Crassus;* AG Archives
9 (bottom) *Pompeii Amphitheater,* Pompeii, Italy; Pictorial Library of Bible Lands; Todd Bolen, photographer
10 Frieze from the *Altar of Peace: Procession of Senators;* Museum of the Ara Pacis, Rome, Italy; Archivo Oronoz
11 *Roman Road* (Syria); Archivo Oronoz
12 *Aeneas' Flight from Troy,* Federico Barrocci; Galleria Borghese, Rome, Italy
14 *The Jupiter Temple;* Baalbek, Lebanon; AG Archives
14 Coin: *Heliopolis,* Philip I Augusta, A.D. 244-249; CoinArchives.com
16 *Boudoir of a Roman Matron,* Juan Jimenez Martin; Congress of the Deputies, Madrid, Spain; Archivo Oronoz
17 Page from *The Sarajevo Haggadah* (1350); Private Collection, Madrid, Spain; Archivo Oronoz
19 (left) *Reconstruction of the Library of Alexandria;* from *Cosmos* by Carl Sagan, wikipedia.com
19 (right) *Book of Daniel,* Papyrus fragment PT16,9r; Papyrus Collection of the University of Cologne, Germany
20 Pages from the *Beatus Apocalypses* (10th Century); Gerona Cathedral Library, Gerona, Spain; Archivo Oronoz
21 (left) *Arch of Titus at Night,* Rome, Italy; Pictorial Library of Bible Lands; Todd Bolen, photographer
21 (right) *Arch of Titus* (detail) Temple Treasures, Rome, Italy; Pictorial Library of Bible Lands; Todd Bolen, photographer
23 *Bronze Bust of Ptolemy Philadelphus;* National Archaeological Museum of Naples, Italy; Archivo Oronoz
24 *The Roman Forum,* Rome, Italy; Hans Johansson, photographer
26 *Map of Ancient Rome;* Nordisk familjebok (Swedish Encyclopedia, 1876), public domain

Chapter 1
27 *Christ Handing the Keys to St. Peter* (detail), Pietro Perugino; Sistine Chapel, Vatican
29 *Christ Blessing,* Fernando Gallego; Prado Museum, Madrid, Spain; Archivo Oronoz
30 *Jesus Among the Doctors* (center panel), Frans Francken; Antwerp Cathedral, Antwerp, Belgium
31 (bottom) *Jordan River entering the Sea of Galilee;* Pictorial Library of Bible Lands; Todd Bolen, photographer
32 *Jesus Blessing the City,* Lombardo Simonet; Malaga Museum of Art, Malaga, Spain; Archivo Oronoz
33 Folio 27r, *The Book of Kells;* Trinity College, Dublin, Ireland; Archivo Oronoz
35 *Pentecost,* Francisco Zurbaran; Cádiz Museum, Cádiz, Spain; Archivo Oronoz
36 (top right) *The Plain of Sharon;* Pictorial Library of Bible Lands; Todd Bolen, photographer
36 (center right) *First Century Pavement in Antipatris;* Pictorial Library of Bible Lands; Todd Bolen, photographer
36 (bottom right) *Roman Aqueduct in Caesarea;* Pictorial Library of Bible Lands; Todd Bolen, photographer
37 *Christ and the Eucharist;* Midwest Theological Forum Archives
38 *Christ Handing the Keys to St. Peter,* Master of the Legend of the Holy Prior; Wallraf-Richartz Museum, Cologne, Germany
41 *Calling of the First Apostles,* Domenico Ghirlandaio; Sistine Chapel, Vatican
42 *Martyrdom of St. Stephen;* Church of St. Stephen, Seville, Spain; Archivo Oronoz
45 *The Conversion of St. Paul,* Bartolome Murillo; Prado Museum, Madrid, Spain; Archivo Oronoz
47 *St. Paul,* Antonio del Castillo; Cordoba Museum of Fine Arts, Cordoba, Spain; Archivo Oronoz
49 (right) *St. Paul in Ephesus,* Eustache le Sueur; Louvre, Paris
50 *Sts. Peter and Paul with a Supplicant;* Barcelona Museum of Art, Barcelona, Spain; Archivo Oronoz
51 (top left) *Martrydom of St. Peter,* Jose de Ribera; San Fernando Academy, Madrid, Spain; Archivo Oronoz
51 (bottom right) *Martyrdom of St. Andrew,* Peter Paul Rubens; Prado Museum, Madrid, Spain; Archivo Oronoz
52 (top left) *St. James the Greater,* Alonso Cano; Louvre, Paris, France
52 (center right) *Martyrdom of St. Bartholomew,* Francisco Camilo; Prado Museum, Madrid, Spain; Archivo Oronoz
53 (top left) *Incredulity of St. Thomas,* Alonso Sanchez Coello; Segovia Cathedral, Segovia, Spain; Archivo Oronoz
53 (bottom right) *St. Judas Thaddeus,* Juan de Valdés Leal; El Greco House and Museum, Toledo, Spain; Archivo Oronoz
55 *Christ Taking Leave of the Apostles,* Duccio; Museo dell'Opera del Duomo, Siena, Italy
56 *The Situation of the Ship on the Fifteenth Morning"* (detail), painting by H. Smartly, engraved by H. Adlard; from James Smith, *The Voyage and Shipwreck of St. Paul.* (1880)

ART AND PHOTO CREDITS

Chapter 2

59 *Martyrdom of St. Andrew*, Bartolome Murillo; Prado Museum, Madrid, Spain; Archivo Oronoz
60 *Adoration of the Saints and Angels*, Jacinto Gomez; Prado Museum, Madrid, Spain; Archivo Oronoz
61 *Pentecost*; Barcelona Museum of Art-Catalonia, Barcelona, Spain; Archivo Oronoz
62 *St. Paul*, Pedro Serra; Museum of Fine Arts, Bilbao, Spain; Archivo Oronoz
63 *Sacrament of Baptism*; Cathedral of San Salvador, Asturias, Spain; Archivo Oronoz
64 *St. Augustine*, Francisco Zurbaran; Private Collection, Madrid, Spain; Archivo Oronoz
66 (top left) *Mass of St. Gregory*; National Museum of Archaeology, Madrid, Spain; Archivo Oronoz
66 (bottom) *Domitilla Catacombs*; Basilica of St. Nereus, Rome, Italy; Archivo Oronoz
67 *Catacombs of St. Agnes*, Rome, Italy; Archivo Oronoz
69 *St. Peter's Grotto*, Antioch on the Orontes; AG Archives
70 *Tombstone in the Catacomb of St. Domitilla*; The Oxford Illustrated History of Christianity, John McManners, Editor, 1990
71 (top) *Pope Benedict XVI*; Midwest Theological Forum Archives
71 (bottom) *St. Peter Is Walking on the Water*, Luis Borrassa; Sant Pere, Terrassa, Barcelona, Spain
72 *Pope Paul VI presiding at a synod of bishops*; Vatican; Archivo Oronoz
73 *Council of Trent*, attributed to Titian; Louvre, Paris; Archivo Oronoz
74 *Bible Canon*; Léon Cathedral Library, Léon, France; Archivo Oronoz
75 *Liberation of Slaves*, illustration from The Alba Bible; Duke of Alba Collection, Madrid, Spain; Archivo Oronoz
77 *St. Thomas Aquinas*, Francisco Zurburan; Private Collection, Madrid, Spain; Archivo Oronoz
78 *The Holy Family*, Bartolome Murillo; Bakewell, England; Archivo Oronoz
79 *St. Cecilia*, Stefano Maderno; Santa Cecilia, Trastevere, Rome
80 *St. Monica and St. Augustine*, Ary Scheffer; Louvre, Paris, France
81 *St. John Chrysostom*; mosiac in Hagia Sophia, Istanbul, Turkey
83 *The Crucifixion of Christ*; Collection of Count Camporrey, Madrid, Spain; Archivo Oronoz
85 Folio 201, *Apologeticum*, Tertullian; Balliol College Library, Manuscript 79, Oxford, England
86 *Second Vatican Council*; St. Peter's Basilica, Vatican; Archivo Oronoz
87 *Martyrdom of St. Stephen*, Juan de Juanes; Prado Museum, Madrid, Spain; Archivo Oronoz
88 *The Martyrdom of St. Catherine*, Lucas Cranach the Elder; Collection of the Reforme Church, Budapest, Hungary

Chapter 3

93 *Martyrdom of St. Agnes*, Vicente Masip; Prado Museum, Madrid, Spain; Archivo Oronoz
95 *Last Prayers of the Christian Martyrs*, Jean-Léon Gérôme; Walters Art Museum, Baltimore, Maryland
96 *Nero and Seneca*, Gonzalez Edua Barron; Cordoba City Council, Cordoba, Spain; Archivo Oronoz
97 *The Burning of Rome*, Hubert Robert; Museum of Fine Arts, Havre, France; Archivo Oronoz
98 (top) *Emperor Caligula*; Athens National Museum, Athens, Greece; Pictorial Library of Bible Lands; Todd Bolen, photographer
98 (bottom) *Death in the Amphitheater*, mosaic; Leptis Magna Villa, North Africa
99 *The Christian Martyrs*, Gustave Doré; Private Collection
100 *Death in the Amphitheater*, mosaic; Leptis Magna Villa, North Africa
101 *Trajan's Column*, Rome, Italy; Archivo Oronoz
102 *Martyrdom of St. Ignatius*; AG Archives
103 *Coliseum's Door of Death*, Rome, Italy; Pictorial Library of Bible Lands; Todd Bolen, photographer
104 Coin: *Emperor Hadrian*, Roman sestertius, struck ca. A.D. 132-135; CoinArchives.com
104 *The Hadrian Arch*, Athens Greece; Pictorial Library of Bible Lands; Todd Bolen, photographer
105 (top inset) *St. Polycarp*; AG Archives
105 (bottom) *Excavations of Ancient Smyrna*, Izmir, Turkey; Pictorial Library of Bible Lands; Todd Bolen, photographer
106 (top) Page from *Meditations*, Marcus Aurelius; Congress of the Deputies, Madrid, Spain; Archivo Oronoz
106 (right) *Emperor Marcus Aurelius*; Istanbul Museum, Istanbul, Turkey; Pictorial Library of Bible Lands; Todd Bolen, photographer
107 *Rosia Montana Gold Mine*; Apuseni Mountains, Romania
108 *St. Perpetua*, mosaic; Archiepiscopal Chapel, Ravenna, Italy
109 *Emperor Septimus Severus*; Thessalonica Museum, Thessalonica, Greece; Pictorial Library of Bible Lands; Todd Bolen, photographer
110 *Decius Certificate of Sacrifice*; The Oxford Illustrated History of Christianity, John McManners, Editor, 1990
111 *Bust of Emperor Decius*; AG Archives
112 *Pope St. Sixtus Ordains St. Lawrence*, Fra Angelico; Cappella Niccolina, Palazzi Pontifici, Vatican
113 *Martyrdom of St. Lawrence*, Titian; Royal Monastery of St. Lawrence of Escorial, Madrid, Spain; Archivo Oronoz
114 *Diocletian and Maximian*; Vatican Library, Vatican; Archivo Oronoz
115 *Emperor Diocletian*; Istanbul Museum of Archaeology, Istanbul, Turkey; Archivo Oronoz
116 (top) *The Tetrarchy*; St. Mark's Basilica, Venice, Italy; Archivo Oronoz
116 (bottom) Coin: *Emperor Constantius I*, Gold aureus, Antioch mint, struck ca. A.D. 293-295; forumancientcoins.com
117 (top) Coin: *Emperor Diocletian*, Siscis mint, struck ca. 295, CoinArchives.com
118 *St. Agnes*, Fray Juan Rizzi; Prado Museum, Madrid, Spain; Archivo Oronoz
119 *The Battle at Pons Milvius* (detail), Raphael; Stanza di Constantino, Palazzi Pontifici, Vatican
120 (top) *Constantine Entering Rome*, Mico Spadar Gargiulo; Prado Museum, Madrid, Spain; Archivo Oronoz
120 (bottom) *The Baptism of Constantine*, Giovan Francesco Penni; Stanza di Constantino, Palazzi Pontifici, Vatican
121 left) *Constantine and Helena*; Archivo Oronoz
121 (right) Section of the *Titulus Crucis*; Santa Croce in Gerusalemme, Rome, Italy.
122 *Arch of Constantine*, Rome, Italy; Pictorial Library of Bible Lands; Todd Bolen, photographer
123 *Head of Constantine*; The Metropolitan Museum of Art, New York, N.Y.
124 (top inset) *Circus Maximus*, Jean-Léon Gérôme; Art Institute, Chicago, Illinois
124 (bottom) *Map of Central Rome in the Time of Diocletian*; Madrid National Library, Madrid, Spain; Archivo Oronoz
126 *Sts. Catherine and Agnes*, Alonso Sanchez Coello; Royal Monastery of St. Lawrence of Escorial, Madrid, Spain; Archivo Oronoz

ART AND PHOTO CREDITS

Chapter 4

127 *The Triumph of St. Augustine*, Claudio Coello; Prado Museum, Madrid, Spain; Archivo Oronoz
129 *Plato and Hippocrates;* Laurentian Library, Florence, Italy ; Archivo Oronoz
130 *Plato;* AG Archives
131 *The Holy Trinity*, Jose de Ribera; Prado Museum, Madrid, Spain; Archivo Oronoz
132 *Medicine Wheel;* Sedona, Arizona, AG Archives
133 (top) *Egyptian Coptic Symbol;* Archivo Oronoz
133 (bottom) *Gnostic Gem in Jasper;* Museum of Archaeology, Perusa, Italy; Archivo Oronoz
134 *St. Paul,* El Greco; Museum of Santa Cruz, Toledo, Spain; Archivo Oronoz
136 (top) *St. John on Patmos*, Hieronymus Bosch; Staatliche Museum, Berlin, Germany
136 (bottom) *Crucifixion*, Andrea del Castagno; National Gallery, London, England
137 *First Vatican Council;* Renaissance Museum, Rome, Italy; Archivo Oronoz
139 *St. Augustine*, Guercino; St. Peter in Vincoli, Rome, Italy
141 (right) *St. Athanasius* (detail), Alonso Sanchez Coello; Royal Monastery of St. Lawrence of Escorial, Madrid, Spain; Archivo Oronoz
142 *St. Ambrose*, Luca de Robbia, Florence, Italy; Archivo Oronoz
144 *St. Jerome*, Student of Marinus van Reymerswaele; Prado Museum, Madrid, Spain; Archivo Oronoz
145 *Pope St. Damasus*, mosaic; Patriarchal Basilica of Saint Paul Outside the Walls, Rome, Italy
146 *St. Jerome, St. Paula and St. Eustochium*, Francisco Zurbaran; National Gallery of Art, Washington D.C.
147 *St. John Chrysostom;* Vatican Museum, Vatican; Archivo Oronoz
149 *St. Cyril of Alexandria*, Osorio Meneses; Museum of Fine Arts, Seville, Spain; Archivo Oronoz
151 *St. Athanasius*, Master of St. Ildefon; Museum of Culture, Valladolid, Spain; Archivo Oronoz
152 *Council of Nicea;* Church of San Martino, Rome, Italy; Archivo Oronoz
153 Coin: *Emperor Constantius II*, Nicomedia mint, struck ca. A.D. 335-361; CoinArchives.com
155 *St. Basil* (detail), Alonso Sanchez Coello; Royal Monastery of St. Lawrence of Escorial, Madrid, Spain; Archivo Oronoz
157 *Emperor Theodosius Exiling Nestorius*, fresco; 16th Century Church, Cyprus
159 *Pope St. Leo I*, mosaic; Patriarchal Basilica of Saint Paul Outside the Walls, Rome, Italy
161 *Triumph of St. Augustine;* AG Archives
162 *St. Augustine Meditating on the Trinity*, Guercino; Prado Museum, Madrid, Spain; Archivo Oronoz
163 *Ordination of St. Augustine*, Jaime Huguet; Catalonia Museum of Art, Barcelona, Spain; Archivo Oronoz
164 *St Augustine Reading the Epistle of St Paul*, Benozzo Gozzoli; Apsidal Chapel, Sant'Agostino, San Gimignano, Italy
165 *Roman Coin with Christogram;* AG Archives
166 *Constantine;* Capitoline Museum, Rome, Italy; Pictorial Library of Bible Lands; Todd Bolen, photographer
167 *The Winged Victory of Samothrace;* Louvre, Paris, France
168 *Second Vatican Council;* St. Peter's Basilica, Vatican; Archivo Oronoz
169 *Emperor Theodosius I,* (detail) silver plate, fourth century; Royal Academy of History, Madrid, Spain
173 *St. Jerome*, Pedro Berruguete; Convent of St. Thomas, Avila, Spain; Archivo Oronoz
174 *St. Augustine*, Pedro Berruguete; Convent of St. Thomas, Avila, Spain; Archivo Oronoz; Archivo Oronoz
176 Opening text from *City of God* manuscript created ca. 1470, St. Augustine; Spencer Collection Ms. 30, New York Public Library, New York

Chapter 5

177 *St. Paul the Hermit and St. Anthony*, David Teniers the Younger; Prado Museum, Madrid, Spain; Archivo Oronoz
178 *St. Augustine Meditates on the Holy Trinity*, School of Rubens; Prado Museum, Madrid, Spain; Archivo Oronoz
180 *Battle Between Romans and Barbarians*, Angelo Falcone; Prado Museum, Madrid, Spain; Archivo Oronoz
181 *The Baptism of Clovis*, Master of Saint Gilles; National Gallery of Art, Washington D.C.
182 *German Barbarian Chief*, Vermorcken; Private Collection, Paris, France; Archivo Oronoz
183 *Attila and His Hordes Overrun Italy*, Delacroix; Bibliothèque, Palais Bourbon, Paris, France
185 *The Meeting Between Leo the Great and Attila*, Raphael; Stanza di Eliodoro, Palazzi Pontifici, Vatican
186 *Attila the Hun;* Private Collection, Paris, France; Archivo Oronoz
187 *The Ghent Altarpiece: The Holy Hermits*, Jan van Eyck; Cathedral of St Bavo, Ghent, Belgium
188 *St. Paul the Hermit and St. Anthony*, Alonso Sanchez Coello; Royal Monastery of St. Lawrence of Escorial, Madrid, Spain; Archivo Oronoz
189 (top right) *Cistercian Monks*, Francisco Zurbaran; Sanchez Muniain Collection, Madrid; Archivo Oronoz
189 (bottom left) *Scribe in a Scriptorium*, El Sabio Alfonso; Royal Monastery of St. Lawrence of Escorial, Madrid, Spain; Archivo Oronoz
190 Illustrated Manuscript, *Missal;* Archivo Oronoz
191 *St. Benedict Blessing Bread*, Fray Juan Rizzi; Prado Museum, Madrid, Spain; Archivo Oronoz
192 (left) Abbey of Monte Cassino (1944), wikipedia.com; (right) Abbey of Monte Cassino (2005)
195 *St. Gregory the Great*, Francisco de Goya; Romantic Museum, Madrid, Spain; Archivo Oronoz
196 *Gregorian Chant;* Midwest Theological Forum Archives
198 (left) *Pilgrims Going to Mecca*, Léon Belly; Private Collection
198 (right) *Three Worshipers Praying in a Corner of a Mosque*, Jean-Léon Gérôme; Private Collection
199 *Ishmael and His father Abraham Pray After Building the Ka'aba;* from *Prophets in the Quran: An Introduction to the Quran and Muslim Exegesis*, by Brandon Wheeler; Continuum, 2002
200 *Ma'ili manuscript* from first century AH; Tareq Rajab Museum, Kuwait
201 *Holy Mosque Center with Pilgrims Circling the Ka'aba*, Mecca, Saudi Arabia; AG Archives
203 *The Prayer at the Tomb*, Ludwig Deutsch; Private Collection
204 *Dome of the Rock*, Jerusalem; Pictorial Library of Bible Lands; Todd Bolen, photographer
205 *Prophet Muhammad Returns from His Night Journey and Ascension;* from *Prophets in the Quran: An Introduction to the Quran and Muslim Exegesis*, by Brandon Wheeler; Continuum, 2002
206 *Public Prayer in the Mosque of Amr, Cairo*, Jean-Léon Gérôme; Private Collection
207 *St. Benedict at Supper*, Fray Juan Rizzi; Prado Museum; Archivo Oronoz
209 *Scene from the Life of St. Jerome*, Juan Espinal; Museum of Fine Arts, Seville, Spain; Archivo Oronoz
210 *St. Paul the Hermit*, Jose de Ribera; Prado Museum, Madrid, Spain; Archivo Oronoz
211 *Jesus Speaks Immediately After His Birth;* from *Prophets in the Quran: An Introduction to the Quran and Muslim Exegesis*, by Brandon Wheeler; Continuum, 2002
212 *St. Gregory the Great*, Carlo Saraceni; National Gallery of Art (Antica), Rome, Italy

ART AND PHOTO CREDITS

Chapter 6

213 *Conversion of Reccard*, Jose Marti Monso; Madrid Senate Museum, Madrid, Spain; Archivo Oronoz
216 *St. Benedict Blessing St. Maurus*, Juan Correa de Vivar; Prado Museum, Madrid, Spain; Archivo Oronoz
217 *Clovis*, Private Collection, Paris, France; Archivo Oronoz
218 *St. James Inspired with the Holy Spirit*, Pedro Bocanegra; Abadia del Sacromonte, Granada, Spain; Archivo Oronoz
219 *Council of Toledo*, Jose Marti Monso; Madrid Senate Museum, Madrid, Spain; Archivo Oronoz
222 *St. Patrick*, Holy Card (detail); AG Archives
224 *St. Columba*, Icon; AG Archives
225 (left) *St. Patrick's Church*, (right) *St. Patrick's Statue in the churchyard*, Hill of Tara, Ireland; AG Archives
227 *St. Gregory*, Matthias Stom; Öffentliche Kunstsammlung, Basle, Switzerland
228 *St. Augustine of Canterbury*, Icon; AG Archives
230 (left) *St. Bede*, Bartolome Roman; Prado Museum, Madrid, Spain; Archivo Oronoz
230 (right) *Ecclesiastical History of the English People* (front cover A.D. 731), St. Bede; Robert Cotton Library, British Museum, London, England
232 *Pagan god Thor*; AG Archives
233 *St. Boniface*; AG Archives
234 *The Battle of Poitiers*, Charles de Steuben; Palace Art Collection, Versailles, France
237 *Sts. Cyril and Methodius*, Icon; AG Archives
238 *Glagolithic Alphabet*; AG Archives
239 *Interior of the Church of San Clemente*, Rome, Sir Lawrence Alma-Tadema; Fries Museum, Leeuwarden, Netherlands
240 *The Expulsion of St Adalbert*, Fifteenth century Altarpiece; Hungarian National Gallery, Budapest, Hungary
241 *Otto III Enthroned*, from the Gospel Book of Otto III, folio 23v-24r; Bavarian State Library, Munich
243 *Vladimir and Rogneda*, Anton Losenko; The Russian Museum, St. Petersburg, Russia
244 (top) *Baptism of King Boris*, Skyllitzes; Madrid National Library, Madrid, Spain; Archivo Oronoz
244 (bottom) *Pope St. Nicholas I*, mosaic; Patriarchal Basilica of Saint Paul Outside the Walls, Rome, Italy
245 *St. Benedict and His Monks at Supper*, fresco; Abbey of Monteoliveto Maggiore, Siena, Italy

Chapter 7

251 *Christ the Redeemer*, mosaic from Hagia Sophia, Istanbul, Turkey
254 *Fatih Sultan Mehmed Bridge* over the Bosporous Strait seen from over Rumelihisari; AG Archives
255 *Emperor Justinian I*, mosaic; Church of San Vitale, Ravenna, Italy
256 *Barberini Ivory*; Louvre, Paris, France; Archivo Oronoz
257 *Hagia Sophia*, Istanbul, Turkey; Pictorial Library of Bible Lands; Todd Bolen, photographer
258 Satellite image of *Bosporous Strait*; NASA Landsat image (2000)
259 *St. Catherine's Monastery*, Mount Sinai, Egypt; Pictorial Library of Bible Lands; Todd Bolen, photographer
260 *Battle of Nineveh*, Piero de Francesca; Church of San Francisco, Arezzo, Italy; Archivo Oronoz
262 *Our Lady of Vladimir*, Icon; Tretyakov Gallery, Moscow, Russia
263 *The Transfiguration*, Icon, Theophanes the Greek; Tretyakov Gallery, Moscow, Russia
264 Coin: *Emperor Leo III*, Constantinople mint, struck ca. A.D. 720-725; CoinArchives.com
265 *St. John of Damascus*, Greek Icon; from Skete of St. John, Hellenistic Ministry of Culture
266 Coin: *Empress Irene*, Constantinople mint, struck ca. 797-802; CoinArchives.com
267 *Writing an Icon of the Mother of God* (four images); Stephen J. Chojnicki, photographer
268 *The Triumph of Orthodoxy*, Icon; British Museum, London, England
270 *Charlemagne's Throne*; Palace Chapel, Aachen Cathedral, Aachen, Germany
271 *Emperor Charlemagne*, Albrecht Dürer; German Natonal Museum, Nuremburg, Germany
272 *Coronation of Charlemagne*; from the *Annals of Lorsch* (794-803), Richbod, Bishop of Trives, National Library, Vienna, Austria
273 *Charlemagne Receives Alcuin*, Victor Schnetz; Louvre, Paris, France
274 *Charlemagne's Crown*; Kunsthistorisches Museum, Vienna, Austria
276 *Hagia Sophia*, artist's concept of Justinian's Church; AG Archives
277 *Eastern Orthodox Liturgy* (3 images); AG Archives
279 *Hagia Sophia* interior, Istanbul, Turkey
280 (left) *Hagia Sophia* interior; Pictorial Library of Bible Lands; Todd Bolen, photographer
280 (right) *Pope Stephen X (IX)*, mosaic; Patriarchal Basilica of Saint Paul Outside the Walls, Rome, Italy
281 *Pope John Paul II* (2 images-2001); *Pope Paul VI and Patriarch Athenagoras* (1964); AG Archives
282 *Hagia Sophia* mosaic, Istanbul, Turkey

Chapter 8

287 *Virgin of the Caves*, Francisco Zurbaran; Museum of Fine Arts, Seville, Spain; Archivo Oronoz
292 *Paying Tribute to Alfonso II of Aragon*; Archives of Corona, Aragon, Barcelona, Spain; Archivo Oronoz
293 *Viking Navy*, Rafael Monleon; Naval Museum of Madrid, Spain; Archivo Oronoz
294 *Round Tower and High Cross*; Monasterboice Monastery, County Louth, Ireland
295 *St. Bruno and Pope Urban II*, Francisco Zurbaran; Museum of Fine Arts, Seville, Spain; Archivo Oronoz
297 (left) *Abbey of Cluny*; Cluny Museum, France
297 (right) *Bell Tower*, Cluny Abbey, France; Archivo Oronoz
299 *Cistercian Abbey of Zwetti*, Austria; Archivo Oronoz
301 *Otto I the Great*; Madrid National Library, Madrid, Spain; Archivo Oronoz
302 *St. Dunstan of Canterbury*; AG Archives
302 *Ruins of Glastonbury Abbey*; AG Archives
304 (top) *William I the Conqueror*; Private Collection, Paris, France; Archivo Oronoz
304 (bottom) *The Bayeaux Tapestry*, (section); Reading Museum, Reading, England
305 *Pope Gregory VII*; Salerno Cathedral, Salerno, Italy; Archivo Oronoz
307 *Dictatus Papæ*, Pope St. Gregory; Vatican Library, Vatican
308 *Henry IV and Pope Gregory VII*, Pietro Aldi; Pitigliano Cathedral, Pitigliano, Italy; Archivo Oronoz
309 *Henry II, King of England*; AG Archives

ART AND PHOTO CREDITS

310 *Assassination of Thomas Becket*, Ferdinan Raysky; British Museum, London, England; Archivo Oronoz
311 *Frederick I Enters Milan*, Villani; Vatican Library, Vatican; Archivo Oronoz
312 (top) *Pope Innocent III*, fresco, Maestro Conxulu; Church of Sacro Speco, Subiaco, Italy; Archivo Oronoz
312 (bottom) *Frederick II Enters Jerusalem*; Vatican Library, Vatican; Archivo Oronoz
313 *St. Bernard*; Convent of San Clemente, Toledo, Spain; Archivo Oronoz
314 *St. Bernard and St. Roberto*; Convent of Santa Ana, Valladolid, Spain; Archivo Oronoz
315 *St. Bruno Renounces the Bishop's Miter*, Vicente Carducho; Prado Museum, Madrid, Spain; Archivo Oronoz
316 *Carthusian Monks*, Francisco Zurbaran; Seville Cathedral, Seville, Spain; Archivo Oronoz
318 *St. Bernard*, Ju Carreño de Miranda; Colegiata de la Asuncion, Pastrana, Guadalajara, Spain; Archivo Oronoz
319 *Cluny Monastery*, 1088-1130; Cluny Museum, Cluny, France; Archivo Oronoz
321 *Developing Righteousness, Love and Justice*, Illuminated manuscript 27210, folio 15; British Museum, London, England; Archivo Oronoz
322 *Navy Armada of William I the Conqueror*, Rafael Monleon; Naval Museum of Madrid, Spain; Archivo Oronoz

Chapter 9

323 *The Battle Between King Richard I and Saladin*, Philip James de Loutherbourg; New Walk Museum, Leicester, England
326 *Kublai Khan Orders the Execution of Two Christians*, 14th century French Manuscript; British Library, London, England
327 *Pope Urban II Preaching the First Crusade at Clermont*, from *Livres des Passages d'Outremer*, 15th century French Manuscript
328 *Pope Urban II Arriving at Clermont*, 14th century French Manuscript; National Library, Paris, France
329 *Crusader Assault on a Muslim Castle*; Madrid National Library, Madrid, Spain; Archivo Oronoz
330 *St. Bernard of Clairvaux*, Alonso Sanchez Coello; Royal Monastery of St. Lawrence of Escorial, Madrid, Spain; Archivo Oronoz
331 *The Taking of Jerusalem by the Crusaders*, Emile Signol; Salles des Croisades, Palace of Versailles, France
332 *Godfrey IV of Bouillon*; Private Collection, Paris, France; Archivo Oronoz
333 (top left) *Richard the Lionheart Statue*, London, England; AG Archives
333 (top right) *Saladin Statue*, Damascus, Syria; AG Archives
333 (bottom) *King Richard the Lionheart and Saladin in a Joust*, Luttrell, British Museum, London, England; Archivo Oronoz
334 (bottom left) *Krak des Chevaliers*, Syria; wikipedia.com
334 (bottom right) *Twelfth Century Crusader*; British Museum, London, England; Archivo Oronoz
336 *The Taking of Constantinople by the Crusaders*, Delacroix; Louvre, Paris, France; Archivo Oronoz
337 *St. Francis: Test of Fire Before the Sultan*, Domenico Ghirlandaio, fresco; Santa Trinità, Florence, Italy
338 *Costumes of the Knights Templar*; Private Collection, Madrid, Spain; Archivo Oronoz
339 *St. Bernard of Clairvaux*; Museum of Mallorca, Palma de Mallorca, Spain; Archivo Oronoz
340 (left) *Jacques de Molay, Grand Master of the Knights Templar*, Chevadonet; Archivo Oronoz
340 (right) *Burning of Jacques de Molay and Geoffrey de Charnay*, 14th century French Manuscript; British Library, London, England
341 *Hospitalers Prepare to Defend Rhodes*, 15th century Manuscript; National Library, Paris, France
342 *Pope Gregory IX Approving the Decretals*, Raphael; Stanza della Segnatura, Palazzi Pontifici, Vatican
343 *St. Dominic in Prayer*, El Greco; Private Collection, Madrid, Spain
344 *St. Dominic de Guzman and the Albigensians*, Pedro Berruguete; Prado Museum, Madrid, Spain; Archivo Oronoz
346 *Burning of the Heretics (Auto-da-fé)*, Pedro Berruguete; Prado Museum, Madrid, Spain; Archivo Oronoz
347 *Battle of Las Navas de Tolosa*, Fco de Paula van Halen; Madrid Senate, Madrid, Spain; Archivo Oronoz
348 *Inquisition of Faith in the Madrid City Plaza*, Francisco Rizzi; Prado Museum, Madrid, Spain; Archivo Oronoz
349 *King Louis IX Prays before the Battle of Damietta*, Gustave Doré, from *Illustrations of the Crusades*; Dover Publications
350 *The Return from the Crusades*, Carl Friedrich Lessing; Rheimisches Landesmuseum, Bonn, Germany
351 *Discovery of the Holy Lance at Antioch*, from William of Tyre's *History of Deeds Done Beyond the Sea*; British Library, London, England

Chapter 10

355 *A Course on Aristotle at the University of Bologna*; Staatliche Museum, Berlin, Germany; Archivo Oronoz
357 *The Apotheosis of St. Thomas Aquinas*, Francisco Zurbaran; Museum of Fine Arts, Seville, Spain; Archivo Oronoz
359 (left) *College of Sorbonne*, University of Paris, Latin Quarter; photo of illustration by Fr. Richard J. Blinn, S.J.
359 (center) *University of Paris*; wikipedia.com
360 *Professor at the University of Paris*; National Library, Paris, France; Archivo Oronoz
362 *University in the Middle Ages*; National Library, Paris, France; Archivo Oronoz
363 *Books of Sentences* IV, MS 61, folio 149v, 13th century, Peter Lombard; Columbia University Rare Book Library, New York
364 *St. Thomas Aquinas*, Pedro Berruguete; Convent of St. Thomas, Avila, Spain; Archivo Oronoz
365 (top left) *The Triumph of St. Thomas Aquinas* (detail of Averroes), Andrea Bonaiuto; Church of Santa Maria Novella, Florence, Italy; Archivo Oronoz
365 (bottom right) *Aristotle with a Bust of Homer*, Rembrandt; Metropolitan Museum of Art, New York
366 *Bl. John Duns Scotus Memorial*; Duns Public Park, Duns, Scotland
367 (left) *The Temptation of St. Thomas Aquinas*, Diego Velazquez; Orihuela Cathedral, Alicante, Spain; Archivo Oronoz
367 (right) *Principles*, Sig II 3569, folio 1, St. Thomas Aquinas; Palace Real Library, Madrid, Spain; Archivo Oronoz
369 *St. Francis of Assisi*, Francisco Zurbaran; Museum of Fine Arts, Lyon, France; Archivo Oronoz
370 *St. Francis Talks to Brother Wolf*; Friends of Saint Francis of Assisi
371 *St. Francis Preaching to the Birds*, Cimabue; Basilica of San Francisco, Assisi, Italy; Archivo Oronoz
372 (top right) *St. Francis Receiving the Stigmata*, El Greco; Private Collection, Madrid, Spain; Archivo Oronoz
372 (bottom left) *St. Bonaventure*, Francisco Zurbaran; Church of San Francisco, Madrid, Spain; Archivo Oronoz
373 *The Meeting of St. Francis and St. Dominic*, Benozzo Gozzoli; Museum of Montefalco, Umbria, Italy ; Archivo Oronoz
374 *The Apparition of St. Francis*, Gil de Mena; National Museum of Culture, Valladolid, Spain; Archivo Oronoz
375 *The Virgin Gives the Rosary to St. Dominic de Guzman*, Sebastian Gomez; Museum of Fine Arts, Seville, Spain; Archivo Oronoz
376 *St. Dominic de Guzman*, Francisco Zurbaran; Duke of Alba Collection, Madrid, Spain; Archivo Oronoz
378 *Cathedral of Notre Dame*, Paris, France; wikipedia.com
379 *Chartres Cathedral*, Chartres, France; Archivo Oronoz
380 (left) *Santa Capilla*, Paris, France; Archivo Oronoz
380 (right) *Church of San Miguel*, Estella, Spain; Archivo Oronoz
381 *Allegory of the Divine Comedy*, Domenico Michelino; Cathedral of Santa Maria Fiori, Florence, Italy; Archivo Oronoz
382 (left) *The Inferno*, Canto 31, *The Giant Antaeus Lowering Dante and Virgil*, Gustave Doré; Private Collection

ART AND PHOTO CREDITS

ART AND PHOTO CREDITS

Chapter 13

463 *King Henry the VIII*, Hans Holbein; Barberini Palace, Rome, Italy; Archivo Oronoz
465 *An indulgence sold by Johann Tetzel in 1517;* wikipedia.com, public domain
467 *Martin Luther*, Lucas Cranach the Elder; Museo Poldi Pezzoli, Milan, Italy
468 *Martin Luther Nailing His Ninety-Five Theses to the Wittenburg Church Door*, Hugo Vogel; Archiv Für Kunst und Geschichte, Berlin, Germany
469 *Woodcut of an early Gutenburg Press*, from *Trades and Occupations;* Dover Publications
470 (top left) *Johann Eck;* AG Archives, public domain
470 (bottom right) *Martin Luther Burning the Papal Bull*, The Lutheran Church, Missouri Synod
471 *The Wartburg Castle*, Thuringia, Germany; wikipedia.com
472 (top left) *Frederick the Wise of Saxony*, Lucas Cranach the Elder; Uffizi Gallery, Florence, Italy; Archivo Oronoz
472 (bottom right) *Martin Luther Bible* (1534); Bade Institute of Biblical Archaeology, Pacific School of Religion, Berkeley, California
473 *Apostle St James the Less*, El Greco; Museo de El Greco, Toledo, Spain
474 *Prince Philip I of Hesse*, wikipedia.com
476 *John Calvin*, Museum of History, Geneva, Switzerland; Archivo Oronoz
478 *Ulrich Zwingli Statue*, Zürich, Switzerland; wikipedia.com
479 *Henry VIII and Anne Boleyn Deer Shooting in Windsor*, William Powell Frith; Private Collection
480 *Letter from King Henry VIII and Peers to Pope Clement* (1530); Vatican Museum, Vatican
481 *Thomas Cranmer*, Gerlach Flicke; National Portrait Gallery, London, England
482 *Martyrdom of the Carthusian Monks in England*, Juan Sanchez Cotan; Granada, Spain; Archivo Oronoz
483 *Thomas Cromwell*, anonymous, after Holbein; National Portrait Gallery, London, England
484 *King Henry VIII, King Edward VI and the Pope*, Unknown Artist; National Portrait Gallery, London, England
485 *Mary I Tudor*, Anthonis Mor; Prado Museum, Spain; Archivo Oronoz
486 *Elizabeth I at Her Coronation*, Unkown Artist; National Portrait Gallery, London, England
489 *Emperor Charles V*, Titian; Prado, Museum; Archivo Oronoz
490 *Pope Paul III*, Titian; Toledo Cathedral, Toledo, Spain; Archivo Oronoz
492 *Council of Trent*, Titian; Louvre, Paris, France; Archivo Oronoz
493 *Trento, Italy;* wikipedia.com
495 Title page to Council of Trent Canons, *Canones et decreta*, Paulus Manutius, publisher, Aldine Press, Rome (1564); Harold B. Lee Library, Brigham Young University, Provo, Utah
496 *Battle of Lepanto*, Luca Cambiaso; Royal Monastery of St. Lawrence of Escorial, Madrid, Spain; Archivo Oronoz
497 (left) *Original Plan for the Battle of Lepanto;* Spanish National Archives, Simancas, Valladolid, Spain; Archivo Oronoz
497 (right) *Pope St. Pius V* (detail from *The Adoration of Christ*), Miguel Parrasio; Prado Museum, Madrid, Spain; Archivo Oronoz
498 *St. Peter Canistus*, Icon; AG Archives
499 *St. Charles Borromeo Helping Plague Victims of Milan*, Mariano Salvad Maella; Bank of Spain Art Collection, Madrid, Spain; Archivo Oronoz
500 *The Vision of St. Teresa of Avila*, Domingo Chavarito; Museum of Fine Arts, Granada, Spain; Archivo Oronoz
502 *Pope Paul III Receives St. Ignatius and Confirms the Society of Jesus*, Juan Valdes Leal; Museum of Fine Arts, Seville, Spain; Archivo Oronoz
504 Handwritten page from *Life, the Autobiography of St. Teresa of Avila;* Royal Monastery of St. Lawrence of Escorial, Madrid, Spain; Archivo Oronoz
506 *St. Ignatius of Loyola in the Cave of Manresa*, Juan Leal Valdes; Museum of Fine Arts, Seville, Spain; Archivo Oronoz
508 *All Saints Church in Wittenberg*, Germany; AG Archives

Chapter 14

509 *St. Batholomew's Day Massacre*, Francois Dubois; Museum of Fine Arts, Lauzanne, Switzerland; Archivo Oronoz
511 *El Escorial*, Madrid, Spain; wikipedia.com
512 *Philip II*, Sofonisba Anguissola; Prado Museum, Madrid, Spain; Archivo Oronoz
513 *William I, Prince of Orange*, Anthonis Mor; Gemäldegalerie, Kassel, Germany
514 *Fernando Álvarez de Toledo, Duke of Alba*, Titian; Duke of Alba Collection, Madrid, Spain; Archivo Oronoz
515 *The Spanish Fury*, Hendrick Leys; Royal Museums of Fine Arts of Belgium, Brussels, Belgium; Archivo Oronoz
516 *William I, Prince of Orange*, Adriaen Thomas Key; Rijksmuseum, Amsterdam, Holland
518 *Assassination of William of Orange*, R de Hoge; National Library, Madrid, Spain; Archivo Oronoz
520 (left) *Mary Stuart* (as widow), Serrur; Palace Museum, Versailles, France; Archivo Oronoz
520 (center) *Gaspard de Coligny*, Francois Clouet; Conde Museum, Chantilly, France; Archivo Oronoz
520 (right) *Catherine de Medici*, School of Clouet; National Library, Paris, France; Archivo Oronoz
521 *The Murder of Admiral Coligny*, 17th century; Bildarchiv Preußischer Kulturbesitz (bpk), Berlin, Germany
522 *Triumphant Entrance of Henry IV into Paris*, Peter Paul Rubens; Uffizi Gallery, Florence, Italy; Archivo Oronoz
523 (left) *Richelieu on the Sea Wall at the Siege of La Rochelle*, Henri-Paul Motte; wikipedia.com
523 (right) *Entrance to the Port of La Rochelle*, France; Archivo Oronoz
524 *Triple Portrait of Richelieu*, Philippe de Champaigne; National Gallery, London, England
525 *Mary Stuart*, Duke of Alba Collection; Madrid, Spain; Archivo Oronoz
526 *St. Edmund Campion;* British Library, London, England; wikipedia.com, public domain
527 (top left) *The Execution of Mary Stuart*, Dutch Origin; Scottish National Portrait Gallery
527 (top right) *The Tomb of Mary Stuart;* Westminster Abbey, London, England
528 (top) *The Invincible Armada in Battle*, Juan de la Corte; Banco Bilbao Vizcaya-Azca, Madrid, Spain; Archivo Oronoz
528 (bottom) *The Invincible*, J. Gartner de la Peña; Museum of Fine Arts, Malaga, Spain; Archivo Oronoz
529 *The Armada Portrait of Queen Elizabeth I*, George Cower; Woburn Abbey, Bedfordshire, England
530 *St. John Ogilvie;* Mitchell Library, Glasgow, Scotland
537 *The Swearing of the Oath of Ratification of the Treaty of Münster*, Gerard ter Borch; National Gallery, London, England; Archivo Oronoz
539 *Defeat of the Spanish Armada, August 8, 1588*, Philippe-Jacques de Loutherbourg; National Maritime Museum, Greenwich, England
541 *Henry IV at the Battle of San Martin*, Peter Paul Rubens; Archivo Oronoz

ART AND PHOTO CREDITS

Chapter 15

543 *Columbus Lands on the Americas*, Tolin Dioscoro Puebla; Private Collection, Cadiz, Spain; Archivo Oronoz
544 *Bartholomew Dias Rounds the Cape of Good Hope*; wikipedia.com, public domain
545 *Map of the Americas-1540*, Sebastian Munster; National Library of Maps, Madrid, Spain; Archivo Oronoz
546 *Henry the Navigator*, Nuno Goncalves; Museum of Antique Art, Lisbon, Portugal; Archivo Oronoz
547 *Naval Vessels From the Age of Discovery*; Museum of Americas, Madrid, Spain; Archivo Oronoz
549 *Navigation Instruments of Columbus*; Museum of Christopher Columbus, Las Palmas, Canary Islands, Spain; Archivo Oronoz
550 *Columbus Departing La Rabida*, Anton Cabral Bejarano; La Rabida Monastery, Huelva, Spain; Archivo Oronoz
551 *The Ships of Magellan*, Gerardus Mercator; Archivo Oronoz
552 *The Landing of Columbus*, Albert Bierstadt; Public Collection
553 *Indian Buffalo Hunt*, Charles Craig; Private Collection
556 *Missionary Catechism of Fray Pedro de Gante*; National Library, Madrid, Spain; Archivo Oronoz
557 *St. Francis Xavier*, Juan Valdes Leal; Church de la Compañia de Jesus, Granada, Spain; Archivo Oronoz
558 *Map of the City of Goa*, Georg Braun; National Library, Madrid, Spain; Archivo Oronoz
559 *St. Francis Xavier*, Elias Salaverra; Javier Castillo Church, Navarra, Spain; Archivo Oronoz
560 *Map of China, Japan, India, Indonesia and Phillipines-16th century*, Juan Martinez; National Library, Madrid, Spain; Archivo Oronoz
562 *Matteo Ricci*; wikipedia.com, public domain
564 *Cortes Sinks His Ships*; Museum of Americas, Madrid, Spain; Archivo Oronoz
565 *Consecration of the Temple of Tenochtitian*; Museum of La Ciudad, Mexico; Archivo Oronoz
566 (top) *La Noche Triste* (The Night of Sorrow); Museum of Americas, Madrid, Spain; Archivo Oronoz
566 *The Ransom Room*, Caxamarca, Peru; wikipedia.com
567 (top) *Francisco Pizarro*, Daniel Vazquez Diaz; Instituto de Cooperación Iberoame, Madrid, Spain; Archivo Oronoz
567 (bottom) *Fray Bartolome de las Casas*; Biblioteca Colombina, Seville, Spain; Archivo Oronoz
568 *Triptych of the Our Lady of Guadalupe*, Vila Senen; Museum of Americas, Madrid, Spain; Archivo Oronoz
569 *Our Lady of Guadalupe* (3 images); wikipedia.com
570 *St. Juan Diego*; AG Archives
571 (left) *Mission San José Aguayo*, San Antonio, Texas; Archivo Oronoz
571 (right) *Map of Missions in Mexico*; Naval Museum, Madrid, Spain; Archivo Oronoz
572 *The Slave Trade-18th century*; Archivo Oronoz
573 (top) *Map of North America-1653*, J. Jansonio; Servicio Geografico Ejercito (Military Survey), Madrid, Spain; Archivo Oronoz
573 (lower inset) *Iroquois Chief*; The Colonial Williamsburg Foundation
575 *Indian Encampment, Late Afternoon*, Albert Bierstadt; Public Collection

Chapter 16

579 *Science and Art*, Adriaen Van Stalbent; Prado Museum, Madrid, Spain; Archivo Oronoz
583 *Louis XIV*, Hyacinthe Rigaud; Louvre, Paris, France; Archivo Oronoz
584 *The Crossing of the Rhine by the Army of Louis XIV, 1672*, Joseph Parrocel; Louvre, Paris, France
585 *Molière at Breakfast with Louis XIV*, Jean-Auguste-Dominique Ingres; Museo de la Comedia Francesa, Paris, France; Archivo Oronoz
586 (left) *Cornelius Jansen*; wikipedia.com, public domain
586 (right) *Ex Voto*, Philippe de Champaigne; Louvre, Paris, France
587 *Bust of Louis XIV*, Gian Lorenzo Bernini; Musée National de Versailles, Versailles, France
588 *Charles I, King of England*, Sir Anthony Van Dyck; National Gallery, London, England; Archivo Oronoz
589 *Oliver Cromwell*, Robert Walker; National Portrait Gallery, London, England; Archivo Oronoz
591 *Londonderry Plantation Plan-1622*, Thomas Raven; Movanagher Village Project, Historical Archaeology of the Ulster Plantation
592 *King William III*, after Sir Peter Lely; National Portrait Gallery, London, England
594 *René Descartes*, Jan Baptist Weenix; Museo Central, Utrecht, Holland; Archivo Oronoz
595 *Heliocentric System of the Universe*, Nicolas Copernicus; Private Collection; Archivo Oronoz
596 (left) Diagram from *On The Revolutions of the Heavenly Bodies*, Nicolas Copernicus; High Altitude Observatory website
596 (right) Engraving from Tycho's *Astronomiae instaurata mechanica*, published in Wansbeck in 1598; High Altitude Observatory website
597 *The Trial of Galileo*, Cristiano Banti; High Altitude Observatory website
598 *Sir Isaac Newton*, possibly after Enoch Seeman; National Portrait Gallery, London, England; Archivo Oronoz
599 *Initiation of Mozart into the Lodge of Freemasons*, Freimaurer; Kunsthistorisches Museum, Vienna, Austria; Archivo Oronoz
600 (top) *Denis Diderot*, Louis-Michel van Loo; Louvre, Paris, France; Archivo Oronoz
600 (bottom) Cover of the *Encyclopédie*; wikipedia.com, public domain
601 (top) *Bust of Voltaire*, Marie-Anne Collot; Hermitage, St Petersburg, Russia
601 (bottom) *Elmens de la philosophie de Neuton*, Voltaire; A Amsterdam: Chez Etienne Ledet & Compagnie, 1738
602 *Jean-Jacques Rousseau*, Quintin Latour; Museum of Art, Geneva, Switzerland; Archivo Oronoz
603 *Dinner Table with Frederick II and Voltaire at the Palace Sanssouci*, Adolfo Menzel; Galeria Moderna, Berlin, Germany; Archivo Oronoz
604 *Frederick II the Great*, Anna Therbusch; Palace Museum, Versailles, France; Archivo Oronoz
606 *Empress Maria Theresa*; AG Archives
607 *King Charles III*, Anton Raphael Mengs; Prado Museum, Madrid, Spain
611 *Cromwell at Dunbar*, Andrew Carrick Gow; Tate Gallery, London, England
612 *Gunpowder Plot Conspirators*; wikipedia.com, public domain
614 *The Army of Louis XIV in Front of Tournai in 1667*, Adam Frans van der Meulen; Musées Royaux des Beaux-Arts, Brussels, Belgium

Chapter 17

615 *Battle of the Bastille*, Jean-Pierre Louis Laurent Houel; Musée Carnavalet, Paris, France; Archivo Oronoz
617 *Petite Hameau*; Palace of Versailles, Versailles, France; wikipedia.com
619 *Louis XVI*, Antonio Franc Callet; Prado Museum, Madrid, Spain; Archivo Oronoz
620 *Emmanuel Joseph Sieyès*, Jacques-Louis David; Fogg Art Museum, Harvard University, Cambridge, Massachusetts
621 *The Tennis Court Oath*, Jacques-Louis David; Musée National du Chateau, Versailles, France
622 *Prise de la Bastille* (Storming the Bastille), Jean-Pierre Louis Laurent Houel; National Library, Paris, France
623 *The Declaration of the Rights of Man and Citizen*; Musée Carnavalet, Paris, France; Archivo Oronoz

ART AND PHOTO CREDITS

624 *Assault on Versailles*, Fery de Guyon; National Library, Paris France; Archivo Oronoz
627 (top) *Jean-Paul Marat*; Musèe Carnavalet, Paris, France; Archivo Oronoz
627 (bottom) *Decree Abolishing the Monarchy*; Private Collection, Paris, France; Archivo Oronoz
628 *French Revolution Calendar*; Private Collection, Paris, France; Archivo Oronoz
629 *French Revolution-September 10, 1792*; wikipedia.com, public domain
631 (top) *Feast of the Supreme Being*, De Machy; Musèe Carnavalet, Paris, France
631 (bottom) *Maximilien Robespierre*; Private Collection, Paris, France; Archivo Oronoz
632 *Procession of the Goddess of Reason*; National Library, Paris, France
633 *Bonaparte au Pont d'Arcole*, Antoine-Jean Gros; Hermitage Museum, St. Petersburg, Russia
634 (top) *Napoleon and His General Staff in Egypt*, Jean-Léon Gérôme; Private Collection
634 (inset) *Rosetta Stone*; British Museum, London, England
635 *Pope Pius VII*, Jacques-Louis David; Louvre, Paris, France
636 *Charles Maurice de Talleyrand*, Francois Gerard; Palace Museum, Versailles, France; Archivo Oronoz
637 *Napoleon Crossing the Great St. Bernard Pass*, Jacques-Louis David; Kunsthistorisches Museum, Vienna, Austria
639 *Napoleon Crowning Himself Emperor Before the Pope*, Jacques-Louis David; Louvre, Paris, France; Archivo Oronoz
641 *The Meeting of Pope Paul VII and Napoleon*; Fontainebleau Palace Museum, Fontainebleau, France; Archivo Oronoz
643 *Napoleon I on His Imperial Throne*, Jean Auguste Dominque Ingres; Musèe de L'Armee, Paris, France
644 *Self-Portrait*, Jacques-Louis David; Louvre, Paris, France
646 *Marie Antoinette on the Way to the Guillotine*, Jacques-Louis David; Louvre, Paris, France

Chapter 18

649 *The Strike*, Robert Koehler; Archivo Oronoz
652 *John Locke*; wikipedia.com, public domain
653 *Napoleon Bonaparte on the Island of Elba*, Paul Delaroche; Los Invalidos, Paris, France; Archivo Oronoz
654 (top) *Klemens Lothar Wenzel von Metternich* (Clement von Metternich), Thomas Lawrence; The Hermitage, St. Petersburg, Russia
654 (bottom) *James Monroe*, Gilbert Stuart; Metropolitan Museum of Art, New York
655 *Equestrian Portrait of Alexander I*, Franz Kruger; The Hermitage, St. Petersburg, Russia
656 *Francois-Rene de Chateaubriand*, Anne-Louis Girodet de Roussy-Trioson; Musée d'Histoire et du Pays Malouin, Saint-Malo, France
658 *Textile Factory-19th century*; Archivo Oronoz
659 *Child Laborer*, Newberry, South Carolina, 1908; wikipedia.com
660 *Coalbrookdale at Night*, Philip James de Loutherbourg; Science Museum, London, England
661 *Arthur Wellesley, 1st Duke of Wellington with Sir Robert Peel*, Franz Xavier Winterhalter; Private Collection
662 *Revolution in the Streets of Paris-1848*; National Library, Paris, France; Archivo Oronoz
664 *Emperor Napoleon III*, Franz Xavier Winterhalter; Napoleon Museum, Rome, Italy
665 *Pope Pius IX*, Antonio Soubelt; Palace Real, Madrid, Spain; Archivo Oronoz
667 *John Henry Newman*; The Oxford Illustrated History of Christianity, John McManners, Editor, 1990
668 (center) *The Immaculate Conception*, Bartolome Murillo; Prado Museum, Madrid, Spain; Archivo Oronoz
668 (inset) *St. Bernadette*, 19 years old, studio photograph at Tarbes, 1863; catholicpilgrims.com
669 *St. Bernadette at the Grotto in Lourdes-1862*; catholicpilgrims.com
670 *First Vatican Council*; Museo Renacimiento, Rome, Italy; Archivo Oronoz
671 Title page of *El Syllabus*, Bl. Pius IX; wikipedia.com
673 *Pope Bl. Pius IX*; wikipedia.com
674 *Otto Bismarck*; Archivo Oronoz
675 *The Trial of Alfred Dreyfus*; Private Collection, Paris, France; Archivo Oronoz
676 *Giuseppe Garibaldi-1866*; wikipedia.com
678 *Cartoon portraying British Imperialism*; wikipedia.com, public domain
679 *The Bible: The Secret of England's Greatness*, Thomas Jones Barker; National Portrait Gallery, London, England
680 (top) *Arriving at Manyema*, sketched by Henry Morton Stanley; The Oxford Illustrated History of Christianity, John McManners, Editor, 1990
680 (bottom) *David Livingstone*; David Livingstone Centre, Blantyre, Scotland
683 *Pope Leo XIII*, Franz von Lenbach; Wallraf-Richartz Museum, Cologne, Germany
684 (top) *Charles Darwin*; Private Collection, London, England; Archivo Oronoz
684 (bottom) *Karl Marx-1861*; public domain
685 *Sigmund Freud*; Archivo Oronoz
687 *Pope Leo XIII*; Archivo Oronoz
690 *Pope Leo XIII*; wikipedia.com
694 *Perry's Fleet Anchored Near Edo*, Japanese print-1854; wikipedia.com, public domain
696 *Ludgate Hill, a Block in the Street*, from *London, a Pilgrimage*, Gustave Doré and Blanchard Jerrold; Dover Publications
698 *The Basilica at Lourdes*, France; Archivo Oronoz

Chapter 19

699 *Adolf Hitler Giving a Speech*; Archivo Oronoz
701 (left) *Young girl playing with a doll beside rifles and a soldier's bag* (Rheims The Marne, France 1917); French Army World War I Photographs; Gallica, bibliothèque numérique de la Bibliothèque nationale de France
701 (right) *Poland, 1940*, from *Witness to Hope: The Life of Karol Wojtyla, Pope John Paul II* (2002); film by Judith Hallet, produced by Catherine Wyler
702 *Pope Pius X*; Vatican Embassy, Madrid, Spain; Archivo Oronoz
704 *Pope Pius X*; wikipedia.com
706 (top) *Benedict XV*; wikipedia.com
706 (bottom) *First meeting of League of Nations Assembly in Geneva-1920*; wikipedia.com
707 *Missionaries in Africa*; Archivo Oronoz
708 Images (3) from *Witness to Hope: The Life of Karol Wojtyla, Pope John Paul II* (2002); film by Judith Hallet, produced by Catherine Wyler
710 (bottom) *City of Reims, France, 1917 after massive bombing*; French Army World War I Photographs; Gallica, bibliothèque numérique de la Bibliothèque nationale de France
711 (bottom) *Election Poster, 1932, German Socialist Democrat Party*; wikipedia.com

ART AND PHOTO CREDITS

712   *Bl. Jacinta, Bl. Francisco, and Lucia Fatima*; public domain
713   *Pope Pius XI*; Vatican Embassy, Madrid, Spain; Archivo Oronoz
715   *St. Josemaría Escrivá*, Luis Mosquera; Opus Dei Prelature, Madrid, Spain; Archivo Oronoz
716   (left) *Eugenio Pacelli Leaving the Presidential Palace in Berlin-1929*; wikipedia.com
716   (right) *Cardinal Pacelli Signing the 1933 Concordat with Germany*; wikipedia.com
717   *Francisco Franco*, Genaro Lahuerta; Bank of Spain Art Collection, Madrid, Spain; Archivo Oronoz
718   (top) *Allegory of Franco the Crusader*, Meruvia Arturo Reque; Archives of Military History, Madrid, Spain; Archivo Oronoz
718   (bottom) *The Martyrdom of Blessed Miguel Pro, S.J.*, photograph; puffin.creighton.edu/jesuit/pro/index.html
719   *Pope Pius XII*; Midwest Theological Forum Archives
720   *Adolf Hitler at the Harvest Festival in Buckeberg, Germany, 1938*; Archivo Oronoz
721   (left) *St. Maximilian Kolbe*, Lorenzo Olaverri; Maximilian Kolbe Collection, Madrid, Spain; Archivo Oronoz
721   (right) *St. Teresa Benedicta (Edith Stein)*, Lorenzo Olaverri; Maximilian Kolbe Collection, Madrid, Spain; Archivo Oronoz
722   *Pope Pius XII*; Midwest Theological Forum Archives
723   *Assumption of the Virgin*, Juan Martin Cabezalero; Prado Museum, Madrid, Spain
725   *Yad VaShem Hall of Remembrance*; Pictorial Library of Bible Lands; Todd Bolen, photographer
726   *Mao Tse-Tung Declares the Formation of The People's Republic of China-1949*; wikipedia.com
729   *Holocaust Railroad Car*, Yad VaShem Memorial; Pictorial Library of Bible Lands; Todd Bolen, photographer
730   (left) *Pope John Paul II at the Wailing Wall*; from *Witness to Hope: The Life of Karol Wojtyla, Pope John Paul II* (2002);
      film by Judith Hallet, produced by Catherine Wyler
730   (right) *Prayer placed by Pope John Paul II at the Wailing Wall*; from *Witness to Hope: The Life of Karol Wojtyla, Pope John Paul II* (2002);
      film by Judith Hallet, produced by Catherine Wyler

Chapter 20

733   *Second Vatican Council*; St. Peter's Basilica, Vatican; Archivo Oronoz
736   *Pope John XXIII Signing Pacem in Terris*; wikipedia.com
737   *Pope John XXIII*; Venice, Italy; Archivo Oronoz
739   *Pope Paul VI Opening the Second Vatican Council*; St. Peter's Basilica, Vatican; Archivo Oronoz
741   *Pope Paul VI Celebrating Mass*; Archivo Oronoz
742   *Pope Paul VI and Patriarch Athenagoras I*; Archivo Oronoz
744   *Jacques Maritain and Pope Paul VI*; The Maritain Photo Gallery; innerexplorations.com
745   *Pope John Paul I*; from *Chronicle of the Popes*, published by Thames and Hudsen (197)
746   *Fr. Karol Wojtyla on a kayaking retreat in Poland*; from *Witness to Hope: The Life of Karol Wojtyla, Pope John Paul II* (2002);
      film by Judith Hallet, produced by Catherine Wyler
747   *Pope John Paul II Celebrating the Eucharist*; Dominican Sisters of Saint Cecilia Congregation; www.nashvilledominican.org
748   *Pope John Paul II*; Midwest Theological Forum Archives
751   (left) *Pope John Paul II Visits with Mehmet Ali Agca in Prison-1983*; wikipedia.com
751   (right) *Mehmet Ali Agca*; Web News Archives
752   *Pope John Paul II Meets with Cardinal Ratzinger*; L'Osservatore Romano, Vatican City, wikipedia.com
753   *Pope Benedict XVI*; L'Osservatore Romano, Vatican City, wikipedia.com
755   *Crucifixion*, Nicolas Tournier; Louvre, Paris, France
757   *John Paul II Meets with Lech Walesa*; wikipedia.com, public domain
758   *Pope John Paul II at Prayer*; Archivo Oronoz
760   *Millions Gather in Krakow to Pray for Pope John Paul II*; from *Witness to Hope: The Life of Karol Wojtyla, Pope John Paul II* (2002);
      film by Judith Hallet, produced by Catherine Wyler

Chapter 21

761   *St. Paul of the Cross Church*, Park Ridge, Illinois; Julie Koenig, Photographer
763   *St. Mary of the Angels Church*, Chicago, Illinois; Julie Koenig, Photographer
764   *Bl. Kateri Tekakwitha*, Fr. Claude Chauchetiere; Saint Francis Xavier Mission, Kahnawake, Quebec
765   *Commodore John Barry*, USN, Gilbert Stuart; White House, Washington D.C.
766   (left) *Bishop St. John Neumann*; wikipedia.com, public domain
766   (right) *St. Elizabeth Seton Saying the Rosary*; Mother Seton School, Emmitsburg, Maryland website
767   *Archbishop John Carroll*, Gilbert Stuart; Georgetown University, Washington, D.C.
769   *Unveiling the Statue of Liberty*, Edward Moran; Public Collection
770   *A Family Visits the Lincoln Memorial in Washington, D.C.*; Archivo Oronoz
771   *Elizabeth "Mumbet" Freeman*, Susan Anne Livingston Ridley Sedgwick, 1811; Massachusetts Historical Society, Boston, Massachusetts
772   *Orestes Augustus Brownson*, George Peter Alexander Healy; National Portrait Gallery, Smithsonian Institution, Washington, D.C.
773   (left) *James Cardinal Gibbons and Teddy Roosevelt*; Maryland Historical Society, Baltimore, Maryland
773   (right) *James Cardinal Gibbons*; Antiquity Project, ironorchid.com
775   (top) *Al Smith, 1928*; wikipedia.com
775   (center) *Dorothy Day, 1933*, Vivian Cherry photographer
775   (bottom) *Bishop Fulton Sheen*, from his TV show *Life is Worth Living*; *How Sweet It Was*, published by Bonanza Books, New York (1966)
776   *President John F. Kennedy Meets with Pope Paul VI, 1963*; from *The Cultural Atlas of the World: Christian Church*, published by
      Stonehenge Press (1987)
780   *Pope John Paul II*; from *Witness to Hope: The Life of Karol Wojtyla, Pope John Paul II* (2002);
      film by Judith Hallet, produced by Catherine Wyler
781   *The Basilica of the National Shrine of the Assumption of the Blessed Virgin Mary* in Baltimore, Maryland; wikipedia.cpm
782   (left) *Promotion poster for The Passion*; Icon Productions; (right) *Production scene from The Passion*; Icon Productions
784   *Charles Carroll of Carrollton*, Chester Harding; National Portrait Gallery, Washington, D.C.
785   *Signing the Declaration of Independence*, John Trumbull; Yale University Art Gallery, New Haven, Connecticut
788   *Jacques Marquette and Louis Joliet Exploring the Mississippi River*; Library of Congress, Washington, D.C.

789   *St Jerome in His Study*, Domenico Ghirlandaio; Ognissanti, Florence
790   (left) *St. Peter*, mosaic; Patriarchal Basilica of Saint Paul Outside the Walls, Rome, Italy; (right) *Pope Benedict XVI*; MTF Archives

INDEX

INDEX

INDEX

INDEX

INDEX

INDEX

INDEX

INDEX

INDEX

Muret, Battle of (1312), 345
Music, 378
  Gregorian Chant, 194, 196, 704
  in Eastern Churches, 277
  in Middle Ages, 378
  notation of, 196
Muslim philosophy, 358, 364-365
Muslims, 256, 264, 289
Mystery
  of the existence of evil, 648
Mystical Betrothal, 212
Myth(ology), 25, 461

N

Naples, 366
  University of, 367
Napoleon Bonaparte
  chosen as First Consul, 636
  claims "Donation of Pepin" (establishing the Papal
    States) can be rescinded by him, 641
  Concordat of (1801), 636
    Pope Pius VII, the Vatican and, 638
    restoration of Catholicism in France, 638
  Congress of Vienna (1814), 644
  defeat (1814), 642
  emperor of France (1804-1814), 341
  his escape from Elba (1815), 652
  march into Rome against Pope Pius VII, 640
  new French Empire to emerge out of chaos, 636
  Organic Articles limit papal authority over French
    churches, 638
  Pius VII imprisoned in France for seven years, 641
  self-coronation as Emperor of France, 638
Nation(s)
  justice and solidarity among, 732
  teach all, 250, 578
  undertakings that compromise peace among, 542
Nationalism, Emergence of (nineteenth century), 651
  German Unification
    Kulturkampf (struggle of culture), 674
      Falk Laws, 674
        Pope Bl. Pius IX's rejection of, 674
      purpose of, 674
  Industrialization
    Capitalism, Marxism, Nationalism,
      Imperialism, 651
    produces new ideologies and philosophies, 651
    social consequences of, 659
  Liberalization of Government, 651
Natural Law Theory, 598
Naturalism, 82
Nature
  created nature
    to be in harmony with, 461
  human and divine nature of Christ, 148, 150, 158,
    160, 175, 257
    consubstantialis, 152
    Hypostatic Union, 158
  human nature
    as the foundation of authority, 462
    rights and duties pertaining to, 542
    sin and human nature inclined to evil, 162, 732
    societies corresponding to, 697
    ultimate disposition of, 732
Navarre Bible, 55
Nazareth, 30
Nazism, 134
Necessity
  help must be given to those in need, 697
Needy
  and help to be given to, 697
  charity towards, 698
Neighbor
  to consider one's neighbor as another self, 542
Neoplatonism, 130, 150, 163, 173, 365-366
Nepotism, 316, 319
  meaning of, 292
Nero, 13, 95-97, 99, 102-103, 120

Nestorianism. See Heresy(ies)
Nestorius, 150, 157-158, 161
Neumann, Bishop St. John, 766
  pioneer in parochial school movement, 766
New Age movement, 54, 132
  and gnosticism, 132
Newman, Ven. John Henry Cardinal, 667
  and "Oxford Movement," 667
  conversion to Catholicism, 667
Nicæa, 265, 332
Nicene Creed, 39, 128-129, 152-154, 156, 158, 163,
  172, 279
Nicene-Constantinopolitan Creed, 154, 158, 278
  text of, 154
Nicephorus, 266
Nicholas I, St., 237, 244, 278-279, 289-290
Normans, 282, 303, 308
  conquest of England (1066), 303
North Africa, 34
  fall to Muslims, 204
North American Martyrs, 764
  killed by the Iroquois (1642-1649), 764
  martyrdom of St. John de Brébeuf, St. Isaac
    Jogues, and Companions, 573, 764
Northumberland, 273
Northumbria, 228
Norway, 293
  conversion of, 235
Novgorod, 263
Nyssa, 155

O

Oak of Thor (Wata), 232-233, 247
Oath-taking
  refusal to take an oath for trivial matters, 648
Obedience, 76
  duty of, 421
Obligation
  of lay people participating in the apostolate, 578
  to sanctify Sundays and Holy Days, 70
Octavian. See Augustus, Caesar
Odo, St., 295
Odoacer (Odovacar), 179
Ogilvie, St. John, 530
Olaf III, 235
Olaf, St., 236
Olaf Tryggvason, 236
Old Testament, 17
  juridical measures in, 698
Olga, St., 242
Opus Dei, 715
  founded by St. Josemaría Escrivá (1928), 715
Order, social or public, 697
Origen, 64, 73, 111-112, 130, 134, 148, 150, 155,
  176, 286
Origin of the Church
  beginning of the Church, 58
Original sin, 61
  consequences of original sin
    difficulty in knowing God, 648
    in man's history, 25
    introduction of evil, 648
    reason why God permitted, 732
Orthodox Church(es), 277
  unity of the Catholic Church, 507, 578
Orthodox(y), 128-129
  meaning of, 130
Ostia, 11
Ostrogoths, 179, 182, 256
Otto I (the Great), 240-241, 300
Otto II, 241, 300
Otto III, 240, 242, 301
Otto of Lagery. See Urban II
Ottoman Turks, 166
  and fall of Constantinople (1453), 253, 336
Ottoman Empire. See Holy Roman Empire
Our Lady of Fatima, 709, 712
  miracle of the Sun, 712

persecutions of the Church and Holy Father, 712
  Pope Benedict XV Appeals to Mary for World
    Peace, 712
  pray for Conversion of Russia, 712
  warnings of another Great War, 712
Our Lady of Guadalupe, 568
  appearance to St. Juan Diego, 568
  recent investigation of the image, 569
Our Lady of Lourdes, 668-669
  appearances to St. Bernadette, 668-669
  "I am the Immaculate Conception," 668-669
Oxford, University of, 360, 362

P

Pachomian Rule, 147
Pachomius, St., 147, 188
Paganism, 242
  Roman pagan culture and early Christianity, 84
  under Julian the Apostate, 167
Pagans, 25, 73
Palestine, 2-3, 17-18, 20-21, 48, 51-52, 95, 106, 111, 121,
  146, 253-254, 326, 332, 338
  map of (in the time of Christ), 31
Palladius, 222
Pallium, definition of, 228, 247
Pamiers, 346
Pantheism, 82
Papacy. See Supreme Pontiff
Papal States, 217, 284, 288, 312, 429, 447, 451, 512, 634,
  641, 662, 664, 672-673, 682, 714
  establishment of, 269-270
  Law of Guarantees (1870), 673
    independent Vatican State (1929), 673
    Pope possesses the Vatican, the Lateran, Castel
      Gandolfo, another papal residence, 673
    Pope retains honors and immunities of a
      sovereign, 673
Papias, 82
Parable(s)
  of the poor man Lazarus, 391
Paris, 289, 340
  University of, 358-359, 360, 362, 364, 376, 398, 418,
    476, 559
Parthia, 101
Parthians, 53
Participation in social life, 697
  necessity and role of authorities in society, 697
Passover, 30, 32
Pastoral
  discernment is needed to sustain and support
    popular piety, 461
  duty of the Magisterium, 58, 322
Patmos, 52
Patriarchs of the Jewish people, 26
Patrick, St., 222-223, 225
  supplementary reading, Confessions, 246
Patros, 51
Paul, Apostle, 4, 40, 43, 47, 50, 54-55, 129, 134-135, 218
  and slavery, 16, 75-76
  and St. Stephen's martyrdom, 44
  conversion of, 44-45
  epistles of, 47
  martyrdom in Rome, 51
  travels of (map), 48-49
Paul of Thebes, St., 187
Paul VI, 739, 741
  dissent and defections from the priesthood and
    the religious life, 744
  encyclical, Humanæ vitæ (Human Life), 1968, 743
  establishes the Synod of Bishops, 742
  fears of the spreading of Modernist heresy, 744
  Jacques Maritain develops "Christian
    Humanism", 744
  met with Ecumenical Patriarch (1965), 742
  New Order of the Mass, 742
  Ostpolitik, 742
  reforming liturgical calendar, 742
  revising papal election rules, 742

INDEX

said "the smoke of Satan has entered the Church" (1972), 744
supplementary reading, Joint Declaration, December 7, 1965, 283
Paula, St., 146
Paulinus of Antioch, St., 146
Pax Romana (Roman Peace), 10, 21, 23
Peace, 30
Pelagianism. *See* Heresy(ies)
Pelagius II, 194
Pelagius, 161
Penance and Reconciliation, 70, 224, 226, 313, 328, 467-468, 478, 483, 491, 494, 586
effect of, 491
practice of frequent confession, 224, 226
reconciliation of all Christians in the unity of Christ's Church, 421
Pentateuch, 18
Pentecost, 28, 34-35, 56
People of God, 37, 39
belonging to, 507, 578
definition of, 56
diversity of peoples and cultures, 507
Jews, non-Christians and, 26
the Church as, 25
universality of, 249
Pepin the Short, 231, 269-271
Perfection
Christ as the way of, 614
Perpetua, St., 76, 80, 108-109
Perpetual Eucharistic Adoration, 747
Adoration societies, Holy Hours in churches and chapels, 747
Exposition and Benediction, 747
Persecution, 63, 66, 103
of Jews in Roman Empire, 108
of the Church, 44, 60-61, 67, 73, 79
Ad metalla, 107, 124
in Spain. *See* Spain
of the early Church, 95
of the Irish. *See* Ireland
Roman Persecution, 94-95, 98
under Decius, 109-112
under Diocletian, 114-115, 118-119, 151, 160
under Domitian, 99-100
under Hadrian, 104
under Marcus Aurelius, 106-107
under Nero, 96-97, 99
under Serevus, 108-109
under Trajan, 101-102
under Valerian, 112, 114
Plantation System and creation of Northern Ireland, 592
Persia, 3, 34, 52-53, 112, 114, 134, 159, 167, 256, 260
Person(s)
and religious freedom, 462
and social justice, 421
and the common good, 462
dignity of, 78, 80, 295, 430, 462, 542, 740, 760
rights and duties of, 92, 462
transcendent nature of the human, 353, 422
Perugia, 270
Peter Damian, St., 300, 305
Peter II, 342, 345
Peter Lombard, 363-364
Peter the Hermit, 330
Peter, St., Apostle, 34, 39-40, 46, 52, 54, 148, 270
at Council of Jerusalem, 50
faith in Christ, 578
first pope, 71
head of Apostles, 41
martyrdom in Rome, 51, 99
rock on whom the Church is built, 28
Petrarch
"Father of Humanism", 432
"poet laureate", 432
supplementary reading, Letter to his brother about the Plague, 417

Pharisees, 18, 20, 23, 50, 52
behavior of, 25
Philip II, 312, 330, 333
Philip II, 511
Philip IV "the Fair", 340
Philip of Macedon, 3
Philip, Apostle, 40, 53
Philippi, 48
Philomelium, 105
Philosophy, 106, 363-366
as servant of theology, 365
Stoicism, 15
Photius, 278-279
Phrygia, 136
Picts, 224, 227
Pierre de Castelnau, 343
Pietas, 13, 23
Pius V, St., 495
Pius X, St., 704
and the liturgy, 704
called, "Pope of the Eucharist", 704
Code of Canon Law (1917), 704
condemnation of Modernism, 704
Confraternity of Christian Doctrine, 704
encyclical, *Pascendi Dominici gregis* (Pastoring the Lord's Flock), 705
First Communion reception at an earlier age, 704
motto, "To Restore All Things in Christ", 703
Pius XI, 710
Catholic Action Lay Apostolate, 704, 714-715, 775
Concordat with Germany (1933), 716
encyclical, *Divini redemptoris*, 713
encyclical, *Mit Brennender Sorge* (With Burning Anxiety), condemns Nazism and Nazi Regime, 717
Lateran Treaty Recognizes independence of Vatican City State, 714
supplementary reading, *Quadragesimo anno*, 728
Vatican Radio inaugurated (1931), 714
Pius XII
Assumption of Mary declared a dogma, 722
conversion of Chief Rabbi of Rome after WWII, 720
diplomacy makes Rome an "open city", 720
encyclical, *Ad Sinarum gentem* (To the Chinese People), 727
encyclical, *Summi pontificatus*, 720
his encyclicals help shape the Second Vatican Council, 722
Holy Year (1950), 722
Jews during WWII and, 720, 724
Pontifical Aid Commission, 720
sheltered thousands of Jews and non-Jews in Rome, 720, 724
supplementary reading, *Mystici corporis Christi*, 722, 728
Plato, 3-4, 130, 156, 173, 364-365, 389, 431, 433, 443
Platonic Forms, 389
Pleasure(s)
spiritual, 392
Pliny the Younger, 101
Poetry, 381-382
Poland, 240, 313
conversion of, 240-241
Political authority/community
community and the Church, 353, 422
distinction between the service of God and the service of, 508
prayer for political authorities, 421
Polo, Marco, 337
Polycarp, St., 82, 102, 105, 109
Pompeii, 9
Pontifex Maximus, definition of, 23
Pontius Pilate, 55
Pope. *See* Supreme Pontiff.
Poverty, 30
concern, care, and love for the poor, 697
detachment from riches as a lifestyle, 391
in spirit, 391

Power
military force, 354
of human nature, 421
of the state, 353, 422, 542
Power of God
manifestations of God's power, 392
Prague, 240
Prayer, 187
in the Holy Spirit, 175
of the Church
first community of Jerusalem, 697
intentions of supplications and intercessions for ecumenism, 421
ecumenical sense of, 508
Priest/priesthood, 72
in the early Church, 72
meaning of "Presbyter", 90
ministry of the priest
cooperation of the laity in exercising, 578
participation in the priesthood of Christ through Baptism, 64
Primacy
of the Roman Church, 250, 507
Pro, Bl. Miguel, 718
Cristeros rebellion in Mexico, 718
Procreation
children as an end of marriage, 78
within marriage is good and blessed, 78
Profession
of the evangelical counsels, 212
of the one Faith as the bond of Church unity, 420
Protestant Reformation, 72, 82
and the sale of indulgences, 465
some causes of, 464
Protestantism, 525
"First Covenant" in Scotland, 525
Church of England, 526
Elizabeth I executes Mary Queen of Scots, 527
Mary Queen of Scots a threat to Elizabeth I, 525
Presbyterianism in Scotland, 525
war in Ireland
English murder, starve and suppress the Irish, 529
Providence
and evil, 648
Divine, 348
Prudentius, 118
Prussia, 240, 341
Ptolemy Philadelphus, 19
Punic Wars, 8, 23
Punishment
Ad metalla, 107, 124
capital, 272, 343, 604
divine, 20
during the Inquisition, 346
Purgatory, 65
Purification
Gospel and its power of, 214-215, 578
Purity, 79
Pyrenees, 217

Q

Questions
response to man's principal questions, 461-462
Quietism, 587

R

Race, 337, 717, 771
human, 80, 97, 283, 343, 686, 690, 720
idolatry of, 126
Ramadan, 209
Raphael Sanzio, 442
his teachers, 442
Rationalism, 82
Ravenna, 270, 358
Raymond of Toulouse, 331
Raymond VI, 345

INDEX

INDEX

Secular Humanism, 683
  characteristics of, 683
Selfishness
  charity as a way to overcome, 542
Seljuk Turks, 325-326, 332
Seneca, Lucius Annæus, 96, 430
Sense(s)
  good popular, 461-462
  moral, 614
  of Faith, 58, 322
  religious, 461-462
Septuagint. *See* Sacred Scripture
Seraphia, St., 79
Serenus Granianus, 104
Sergius I, 159-160
Sergius I, 231
Serra, Bl. Junipero
  founded nine of the twenty-one California Missions
    (Franciscan), 764
Service
  rendered to civil authority and to God, 508
Servites, 164
Seton, St. Elizabeth Ann, 742
  first native-born American to be canonized
    (1975), 742
  foundress of Sisters of Charity, 742
  pioneer in parochial school movement, 766
Severinus, 160
Severus, Alexander, 109
Severus, Septimus, 101, 108
Seville, 219
Sexuality
  equal dignity of man and woman, 92
Shahada, meaning of, 202, 209
Sheen, Bishop Fulton J., 775-776
  television evangelization by, 775-776
Shepherds of the Church
  laity offers help to, 578
Sicily, 8-9, 23
Sign of the Cross. *See* Cross
Silverius, St., 260
Simeon, 30
Simeon of Durham, 294
Simon de Montfort, 345
Simon Magus, 54, 135
Simon of Cyrene, St., 136
Simon the Zealot, St., Apostle, 40
Simony, 290, 304, 306, 309, 316, 319
  meaning of, 292
Simplicity, 62, 246, 270, 454
  of the birth of Jesus, 30
  of the Church, 30
  of the Cistercians, 319
Sin(s)
  against Faith, 614
  and Baptism, 64
  forgiveness of, 46
    in Baptism, 63
  interpretations of sin
    schisms, heresies, apostasies, 286, 420-421
    threats to Church unity and communion, 507
  original. *See* Original sin
  St. Augustine on, 162
Sinner(s)
  all men "were made sinners", 25
  and the Crusades, 330
  called by Christ to repent, 45
Sinope, 133
Sixtus II, St., 112, 114
Slaughter of the Innocents, 30
Slavery, 80
  and Christianity, 16, 75-76
  chattel, 23
  in Roman Empire, 15-16, 75
  of sin, 732
Slavonic, 237-238
Slavorum Apostoli, 247

Slavs, 256, 289, 300, 331, 341
  conversion of, 237-244, 313
Smith, Al
  first Catholic nominated for President (1928), 775
  resurgence of anti-Catholicism arose, 775
Smyrna, 102, 105, 109
Socialization, 697
Society
  and Christians, 60-61, 62
  authorities
    obedience to and respect for, 462
  duties of citizens, 422
    building up society, 462
    giving due honor to, 421
    refusing to obey the directives of civil authorities
      contrary to conscience, 508
    taking an active part in public life, 462
  duties of society
    right to religious freedom, 542
  participation in social life, 697
  political community and the Church, 353, 422
  relations between societies and the state, 697
  social
    doctrine of the Church, 176
  society of law, 542
  vision of man in, 353, 422
Society of St. Vincent de Paul, 656
Sodality
  Marian, 625
  of Pius (*Sodalitium Pianum*), 705
Solidarity
  and John Paul II, 749
  among nations, 732
Solomon, King, 18
Sophronius, 159
Soul
  body and, 39, 60
  natural law written in our hearts, 614
  salvation of, 176
Spain, 8, 10, 23, 48, 51, 99, 114, 182, 204-205, 216, 219,
    256, 347, 364, 381, 383
  conversion of, 216, 218-219
  Muslim invasion of (711), 219
  persecution of the Church in, 717
    a republic declared (1931), disestablishes the
      Church, secularizes education, 717
    leftists (socialists, anarchists, communists) seize
      government (1936), 717
Spartacus, 9
St. Thomas Christians, 558
Stanislaus, St., 362
State, political
  and personal freedom, 697
  and the early Church, 77, 111, 122, 168-169
  caesaropapism, 165, 171
  idolatry in reference to, 126
  in the Middle Ages, 342
  society of law, 542
Stefnir Thorgilsson, 236
Stein, Edith. *See* Teresa Benedicta of the Cross, St.
Stephen II, 269
Stephen IV, 290
Stephen the Younger, St., 265
Stephen VI, 290
Stephen X, 280, 300, 305
Stephen, St. (deacon martyr), 42-44
Stephen, St. (King of Hungary), 241, 242
Stigmata, 372, 389
  definition of, 372, 389
Stoicism, 15, 23, 106
Submission, man's
  refusal to submit to the Supreme Pontiff (schism),
    176, 421
Subsidiarity, 697, 714
Substance (nature, essence)
  the Son, *consubstantialis* with the Father, 175
Summa Theologiæ, 364, 388

Supernatural
  Faith as a supernatural virtue, 578
Superstition, 180
Supreme Pontiff, 39, 71, 90, 276, 282
  [*See* individual name for specific pope]
  and the Roman Empire, 165
  infallibility of, 58, 160, 322
  offices, power, and authority of, 311
    Dictatus papæ, 306-307
    historical evidence for, 71
  role of Supreme Pontiff in ecumenical councils, 137
  titles of
    bishop of Rome, 71
    Servus servorum Dei, 194, 209
    Vicar of Christ, 71, 90, 311, 319
    Vicar of St. Peter, 311
Sweden, 235
  conversion of, 235
Switzerland, 12, 182
  conversion of, 224
Syllabus of Errors, 670
  Pope Bl. Pius IX's Encyclical, 670
  what it condemned, 670
Sylvester I, St., 152
Sylvester II, 301
Symbols of faith, 70
Synod
  definition of, 90
Synod of Rome (382), 74
Synod(s). *See* Councils, Local
Syria, 10, 108, 146, 148, 204, 253, 326
Syrian Orthodox Church, 158

T

Tacitus
  supplementary reading, *The Annals*, 22
Tacitus, Cornelius, 13, 22, 97, 100, 430
Tancred, 331
Tara, Hill of, 225
Tartars, 341
Tekakwitha, Bl. Kateri, 764
Temple (in Jerusalem), 18, 30
  destruction of (70), 20, 62
  and the Dome of the Rock, 205
Temptation
  idolatry as a constant temptation of faith, 126
Ten Commandments, 32
Teresa Benedicta of the Cross, St., (Edith Stein), 721
Teresa of Avila, St., 139
  The Way of Perfection, Foundations, 502
Tertullian, 15, 64, 66, 70, 76, 78, 82, 84, 89, 92, 100,
    133-134, 136, 732
  supplementary reading, To His Wife, 89
Teutonic Knights, 338, 341
Thagaste, 161, 163
Thames River, 228
The Genius of Christianity (1802), 657
Theban Legion, 76
Theodelinda, 195
Theodora (empress wife of Justinian I), 257, 260
Theodora (empress wife of Theophilus), 268
Theodore I, 160
Theodoret, 167
Theodoric, 179, 182
Theodosius I (the Great), 142, 168, 253
Theodosius II, 157-158, 169, 180, 184, 253
Theology
  and St. Paul, 47
  role of, 365
Theophanes the Greek, 263
Theophilus, 261, 266, 268
Thérèse of Lisieux, St., 139
Thessalonica, 142, 237

INDEX